# American Casebook Series
# Hornbook Series and Basic Legal Texts
# Black Letter Series and Nutshell Series

of

## WEST PUBLISHING COMPANY
P.O. Box 64526
St. Paul, Minnesota 55164–0526

---

### Accounting

FARIS' ACCOUNTING AND LAW IN A NUT-SHELL, 377 pages, 1984. Softcover. (Text)

FIFLIS, KRIPKE AND FOSTER'S TEACHING MATERIALS ON ACCOUNTING FOR BUSINESS LAWYERS, Third Edition, 838 pages, 1984. (Casebook)

SIEGEL AND SIEGEL'S ACCOUNTING AND FINANCIAL DISCLOSURE: A GUIDE TO BASIC CONCEPTS, 259 pages, 1983. Softcover. (Text)

### Administrative Law

BONFIELD AND ASIMOW'S STATE AND FEDERAL ADMINISTRATIVE LAW, 826 pages, 1989. Teacher's Manual available. (Casebook)

GELLHORN AND LEVIN'S ADMINISTRATIVE LAW AND PROCESS IN A NUTSHELL, Third Edition, approximately 420 pages, 1990. Softcover. (Text)

MASHAW AND MERRILL'S CASES AND MATERIALS ON ADMINISTRATIVE LAW—THE AMERICAN PUBLIC LAW SYSTEM, Second Edition, 976 pages, 1985. (Casebook) 1989 Supplement.

ROBINSON, GELLHORN AND BRUFF'S THE ADMINISTRATIVE PROCESS, Third Edition, 978 pages, 1986. (Casebook)

### Admiralty

HEALY AND SHARPE'S CASES AND MATERIALS ON ADMIRALTY, Second Edition, 876 pages, 1986. (Casebook)

MARAIST'S ADMIRALTY IN A NUTSHELL, Second Edition, 379 pages, 1988. Softcover. (Text)

SCHOENBAUM'S HORNBOOK ON ADMIRALTY AND MARITIME LAW, Student Edition, 692 pages, 1987 with 1989 pocket part. (Text)

### Agency—Partnership

FESSLER'S ALTERNATIVES TO INCORPORATION FOR PERSONS IN QUEST OF PROFIT, Second Edition, 326 pages, 1986. Softcover. Teacher's Manual available. (Casebook)

HENN'S CASES AND MATERIALS ON AGENCY, PARTNERSHIP AND OTHER UNINCORPORATED BUSINESS ENTERPRISES, Second Edition, 733 pages, 1985. Teacher's Manual available. (Casebook)

REUSCHLEIN AND GREGORY'S HORNBOOK ON THE LAW OF AGENCY AND PARTNERSHIP, Second Edition, 683 pages, 1990. (Text)

SELECTED CORPORATION AND PARTNERSHIP STATUTES, RULES AND FORMS. Softcover. 727 pages, 1989.

STEFFEN AND KERR'S CASES ON AGENCY-PARTNERSHIP, Fourth Edition, 859 pages, 1980. (Casebook)

STEFFEN'S AGENCY-PARTNERSHIP IN A NUTSHELL, 364 pages, 1977. Softcover. (Text)

### Agricultural Law

MEYER, PEDERSEN, THORSON AND DAVIDSON'S AGRICULTURAL LAW: CASES AND MATERIALS, 931 pages, 1985. Teacher's Manual available. (Casebook)

### Alternative Dispute Resolution

KANOWITZ' CASES AND MATERIALS ON ALTERNATIVE DISPUTE RESOLUTION, 1024 pages,

**Alternative Dispute Resolution**—Cont'd
1986. Teacher's Manual available. (Casebook) 1990 Supplement.

RISKIN AND WESTBROOK'S DISPUTE RESOLUTION AND LAWYERS, 468 pages, 1987. Teacher's Manual available. (Casebook)

RISKIN AND WESTBROOK'S DISPUTE RESOLUTION AND LAWYERS, Abridged Edition, 223 pages, 1987. Softcover. Teacher's Manual available. (Casebook)

**American Indian Law**

CANBY'S AMERICAN INDIAN LAW IN A NUTSHELL, Second Edition, 336 pages, 1988. Softcover. (Text)

GETCHES AND WILKINSON'S CASES AND MATERIALS ON FEDERAL INDIAN LAW, Second Edition, 880 pages, 1986. (Casebook)

**Antitrust**—see also Regulated Industries, Trade Regulation

FOX AND SULLIVAN'S CASES AND MATERIALS ON ANTITRUST, 935 pages, 1989. Teacher's Manual available. (Casebook)

GELLHORN'S ANTITRUST LAW AND ECONOMICS IN A NUTSHELL, Third Edition, 472 pages, 1986. Softcover. (Text)

HOVENKAMP'S BLACK LETTER ON ANTITRUST, 323 pages, 1986. Softcover. (Review)

HOVENKAMP'S HORNBOOK ON ECONOMICS AND FEDERAL ANTITRUST LAW, Student Edition, 414 pages, 1985. (Text)

OPPENHEIM, WESTON AND MCCARTHY'S CASES AND COMMENTS ON FEDERAL ANTITRUST LAWS, Fourth Edition, 1168 pages, 1981. (Casebook) 1985 Supplement.

POSNER AND EASTERBROOK'S CASES AND ECONOMIC NOTES ON ANTITRUST, Second Edition, 1077 pages, 1981. (Casebook) 1984–85 Supplement.

SULLIVAN'S HORNBOOK OF THE LAW OF ANTITRUST, 886 pages, 1977. (Text)

**Appellate Advocacy**—see Trial and Appellate Advocacy

**Architecture and Engineering Law**

SWEET'S LEGAL ASPECTS OF ARCHITECTURE, ENGINEERING AND THE CONSTRUCTION PROCESS, Fourth Edition, 889 pages, 1989. Teacher's Manual available. (Casebook)

**Art Law**

DUBOFF'S ART LAW IN A NUTSHELL, 335 pages, 1984. Softcover. (Text)

**Banking Law**

LOVETT'S BANKING AND FINANCIAL INSTITUTIONS LAW IN A NUTSHELL, Second Edition, 464 pages, 1988. Softcover. (Text)

SYMONS AND WHITE'S TEACHING MATERIALS ON BANKING LAW, Second Edition, 993 pages, 1984. Teacher's Manual available. (Casebook) 1987 Supplement.

**Business Planning**—see also Corporate Finance

PAINTER'S PROBLEMS AND MATERIALS IN BUSINESS PLANNING, Second Edition, 1008 pages, 1984. (Casebook) 1990 Supplement.

Statutory Supplement. *See Selected Corporation and Partnership*

SELECTED CORPORATION AND PARTNERSHIP STATUTES, RULES AND FORMS. 727 pages, 1989. Softcover.

**Civil Procedure**—see also Federal Jurisdiction and Procedure

AMERICAN BAR ASSOCIATION SECTION OF LITIGATION—READINGS ON ADVERSARIAL JUSTICE: THE AMERICAN APPROACH TO ADJUDICATION, 217 pages, 1988. Softcover. (Coursebook)

CLERMONT'S BLACK LETTER ON CIVIL PROCEDURE, Second Edition, 332 pages, 1988. Softcover. (Review)

COUND, FRIEDENTHAL, MILLER AND SEXTON'S CASES AND MATERIALS ON CIVIL PROCEDURE, Fifth Edition, 1284 pages, 1989. Teacher's Manual available. (Casebook)

COUND, FRIEDENTHAL, MILLER AND SEXTON'S CIVIL PROCEDURE SUPPLEMENT. Approximately 450 pages, 1990. Softcover. (Casebook Supplement)

FEDERAL RULES OF CIVIL PROCEDURE—EDUCATIONAL EDITION. Softcover. Approximately 635 pages, 1990.

FRIEDENTHAL, KANE AND MILLER'S HORNBOOK ON CIVIL PROCEDURE, 876 pages, 1985. (Text)

KANE AND LEVINE'S CIVIL PROCEDURE IN CALIFORNIA: STATE AND FEDERAL 498 pages, 1989. Softcover. (Casebook Supplement)

### Civil Procedure—Cont'd

KANE'S CIVIL PROCEDURE IN A NUTSHELL, Second Edition, 306 pages, 1986. Softcover. (Text)

KOFFLER AND REPPY'S HORNBOOK ON COMMON LAW PLEADING, 663 pages, 1969. (Text)

MARCUS, REDISH AND SHERMAN'S CIVIL PROCEDURE: A MODERN APPROACH, 1027 pages, 1989. Teacher's Manual available. (Casebook)

MARCUS AND SHERMAN'S COMPLEX LITIGATION—CASES AND MATERIALS ON ADVANCED CIVIL PROCEDURE, 846 pages, 1985. Teacher's Manual available. (Casebook) 1989 Supplement.

PARK'S COMPUTER-AIDED EXERCISES ON CIVIL PROCEDURE, Second Edition, 167 pages, 1983. Softcover. (Coursebook)

SIEGEL'S HORNBOOK ON NEW YORK PRACTICE, 1011 pages, 1978, with 1987 pocket part. (Text)

### Commercial Law

BAILEY AND HAGEDORN'S SECURED TRANSACTIONS IN A NUTSHELL, Third Edition, 390 pages, 1988. Softcover. (Text)

EPSTEIN, MARTIN, HENNING AND NICKLES' BASIC UNIFORM COMMERCIAL CODE TEACHING MATERIALS, Third Edition, 704 pages, 1988. Teacher's Manual available. (Casebook)

HENSON'S HORNBOOK ON SECURED TRANSACTIONS UNDER THE U.C.C., Second Edition, 504 pages, 1979, with 1979 pocket part. (Text)

MURRAY'S COMMERCIAL LAW, PROBLEMS AND MATERIALS, 366 pages, 1975. Teacher's Manual available. Softcover. (Coursebook)

NICKLES' BLACK LETTER ON COMMERCIAL PAPER, 450 pages, 1988. Softcover. (Review)

NICKLES, MATHESON AND DOLAN'S MATERIALS FOR UNDERSTANDING CREDIT AND PAYMENT SYSTEMS, 923 pages, 1987. Teacher's Manual available. (Casebook)

NORDSTROM, MURRAY AND CLOVIS' PROBLEMS AND MATERIALS ON SALES, 515 pages, 1982. (Casebook)

NORDSTROM, MURRAY AND CLOVIS' PROBLEMS AND MATERIALS ON SECURED TRANSACTIONS, 594 pages, 1987. (Casebook)

RUBIN AND COOTER'S THE PAYMENT SYSTEM: CASES, MATERIALS AND ISSUES, 885 pages, 1989. (Casebook)

SELECTED COMMERCIAL STATUTES. Softcover. Approximately 1650 pages, 1990.

SPEIDEL'S BLACK LETTER ON SALES AND SALES FINANCING, 363 pages, 1984. Softcover. (Review)

SPEIDEL, SUMMERS AND WHITE'S COMMERCIAL LAW: TEACHING MATERIALS, Fourth Edition, 1448 pages, 1987. Teacher's Manual available. (Casebook)

SPEIDEL, SUMMERS AND WHITE'S COMMERCIAL PAPER: TEACHING MATERIALS, Fourth Edition, 578 pages, 1987. Reprint from Speidel et al., Commercial Law, Fourth Edition. Teacher's Manual available. (Casebook)

SPEIDEL, SUMMERS AND WHITE'S SALES: TEACHING MATERIALS, Fourth Edition, 804 pages, 1987. Reprint from Speidel et al., Commercial Law, Fourth Edition. Teacher's Manual available. (Casebook)

SPEIDEL, SUMMERS AND WHITE'S SECURED TRANSACTIONS: TEACHING MATERIALS, Fourth Edition, 485 pages, 1987. Reprint from Speidel et al., Commercial Law, Fourth Edition. Teacher's Manual available. (Casebook)

STOCKTON'S SALES IN A NUTSHELL, Second Edition, 370 pages, 1981. Softcover. (Text)

STONE'S UNIFORM COMMERCIAL CODE IN A NUTSHELL, Third Edition, 580 pages, 1989. Softcover. (Text)

WEBER AND SPEIDEL'S COMMERCIAL PAPER IN A NUTSHELL, Third Edition, 404 pages, 1982. Softcover. (Text)

WHITE AND SUMMERS' HORNBOOK ON THE UNIFORM COMMERCIAL CODE, Third Edition, Student Edition, 1386 pages, 1988. (Text)

### Community Property

MENNELL AND BOYKOFF'S COMMUNITY PROPERTY IN A NUTSHELL, Second Edition, 432 pages, 1988. Softcover. (Text)

VERRALL AND BIRD'S CASES AND MATERIALS

**Community Property—Cont'd**

ON CALIFORNIA COMMUNITY PROPERTY, Fifth Edition, 604 pages, 1988. (Casebook)

**Comparative Law**

BARTON, GIBBS, LI AND MERRYMAN'S LAW IN RADICALLY DIFFERENT CULTURES, 960 pages, 1983. (Casebook)

GLENDON, GORDON AND OSAKWE'S COMPARATIVE LEGAL TRADITIONS: TEXT, MATERIALS AND CASES ON THE CIVIL LAW, COMMON LAW AND SOCIALIST LAW TRADITIONS, 1091 pages, 1985. (Casebook)

GLENDON, GORDON AND OSAKWE'S COMPARATIVE LEGAL TRADITIONS IN A NUTSHELL. 402 pages, 1982. Softcover. (Text)

LANGBEIN'S COMPARATIVE CRIMINAL PROCEDURE: GERMANY, 172 pages, 1977. Softcover. (Casebook)

**Computers and Law**

MAGGS AND SPROWL'S COMPUTER APPLICATIONS IN THE LAW, 316 pages, 1987. (Coursebook)

MASON'S USING COMPUTERS IN THE LAW: AN INTRODUCTION AND PRACTICAL GUIDE, Second Edition, 288 pages, 1988. Softcover. (Coursebook)

**Conflict of Laws**

CRAMTON, CURRIE AND KAY'S CASES–COMMENTS–QUESTIONS ON CONFLICT OF LAWS, Fourth Edition, 876 pages, 1987. (Casebook)

HAY'S BLACK LETTER ON CONFLICT OF LAWS, 330 pages, 1989. Softcover. (Review)

SCOLES AND HAY'S HORNBOOK ON CONFLICT OF LAWS, Student Edition, 1085 pages, 1982, with 1988–89 pocket part. (Text)

SEIGEL'S CONFLICTS IN A NUTSHELL, 470 pages, 1982. Softcover. (Text)

**Constitutional Law—Civil Rights**—see also Foreign Relations and National Security Law

ABERNATHY'S CASES AND MATERIALS ON CIVIL RIGHTS, 660 pages, 1980. (Casebook)

BARRON AND DIENES' BLACK LETTER ON CONSTITUTIONAL LAW, Second Edition, 310 pages, 1987. Softcover. (Review)

BARRON AND DIENES' CONSTITUTIONAL LAW IN A NUTSHELL, 389 pages, 1986. Softcover. (Text)

ENGDAHL'S CONSTITUTIONAL FEDERALISM IN A NUTSHELL, Second Edition, 411 pages, 1987. Softcover. (Text)

FARBER AND SHERRY'S HISTORY OF THE AMERICAN CONSTITUTION, 458 pages, 1990. Softcover. Teacher's Manual available. (Text)

GARVEY AND ALEINIKOFF'S MODERN CONSTITUTIONAL THEORY: A READER, 494 pages, 1989. Softcover. (Reader)

LOCKHART, KAMISAR, CHOPER AND SHIFFRIN'S CONSTITUTIONAL LAW: CASES–COMMENTS–QUESTIONS, Sixth Edition, 1601 pages, 1986. (Casebook) 1990 Supplement.

LOCKHART, KAMISAR, CHOPER AND SHIFFRIN'S THE AMERICAN CONSTITUTION: CASES AND MATERIALS, Sixth Edition, 1260 pages, 1986. Abridged version of Lockhart, et al., Constitutional Law: Cases–Comments–Questions, Sixth Edition. (Casebook) 1990 Supplement.

LOCKHART, KAMISAR, CHOPER AND SHIFFRIN'S CONSTITUTIONAL RIGHTS AND LIBERTIES: CASES AND MATERIALS, Sixth Edition, 1266 pages, 1986. Reprint from Lockhart, et al., Constitutional Law: Cases–Comments–Questions, Sixth Edition. (Casebook) 1990 Supplement.

MARKS AND COOPER'S STATE CONSTITUTIONAL LAW IN A NUTSHELL, 329 pages, 1988. Softcover. (Text)

NOWAK, ROTUNDA AND YOUNG'S HORNBOOK ON CONSTITUTIONAL LAW, Third Edition, 1191 pages, 1986 with 1988 pocket part. (Text)

ROTUNDA'S MODERN CONSTITUTIONAL LAW: CASES AND NOTES, Third Edition, 1085 pages, 1989. (Casebook) 1990 Supplement.

VIEIRA'S CONSTITUTIONAL CIVIL RIGHTS IN A NUTSHELL, Second Edition, 322 pages, 1990. Softcover. (Text)

WILLIAMS' CONSTITUTIONAL ANALYSIS IN A NUTSHELL, 388 pages, 1979. Softcover. (Text)

**Consumer Law**—see also Commercial Law

EPSTEIN AND NICKLES' CONSUMER LAW IN A NUTSHELL, Second Edition, 418 pages,

## Consumer Law—Cont'd

1981. Softcover. (Text)

SELECTED COMMERCIAL STATUTES. Softcover. Approximately 1650 pages, 1990.

SPANOGLE AND ROHNER'S CASES AND MATERIALS ON CONSUMER LAW, 693 pages, 1979. Teacher's Manual available. (Casebook) 1982 Supplement.

## Contracts

CALAMARI AND PERILLO'S BLACK LETTER ON CONTRACTS, Second Edition, approximately 450 pages, 1990. Softcover. (Review)

CALAMARI AND PERILLO'S HORNBOOK ON CONTRACTS, Third Edition, 1049 pages, 1987. (Text)

CALAMARI, PERILLO AND BENDER'S CASES AND PROBLEMS ON CONTRACTS, Second Edition, 905 pages, 1989. Teacher's Manual Available. (Casebook)

CORBIN'S TEXT ON CONTRACTS, One Volume Student Edition, 1224 pages, 1952. (Text)

FESSLER AND LOISEAUX'S CASES AND MATERIALS ON CONTRACTS—MORALITY, ECONOMICS AND THE MARKET PLACE, 837 pages, 1982. Teacher's Manual available. (Casebook)

FRIEDMAN'S CONTRACT REMEDIES IN A NUTSHELL, 323 pages, 1981. Softcover. (Text)

FULLER AND EISENBERG'S CASES ON BASIC CONTRACT LAW, Fifth Edition, approximately 1100 pages, 1990. (Casebook)

HAMILTON, RAU AND WEINTRAUB'S CASES AND MATERIALS ON CONTRACTS, 830 pages, 1984. (Casebook)

JACKSON AND BOLLINGER'S CASES ON CONTRACT LAW IN MODERN SOCIETY, Second Edition, 1329 pages, 1980. Teacher's Manual available. (Casebook)

KEYES' GOVERNMENT CONTRACTS IN A NUTSHELL, Second Edition, approximately 530 pages, 1990. Softcover. (Text)

SCHABER AND ROHWER'S CONTRACTS IN A NUTSHELL, Third Edition, approximately 438 pages, 1990. Softcover. (Text)

SUMMERS AND HILLMAN'S CONTRACT AND RELATED OBLIGATION: THEORY, DOCTRINE AND PRACTICE, 1074 pages, 1987. Teacher's Manual available. (Casebook)

## Copyright—see Patent and Copyright Law

## Corporate Finance

HAMILTON'S CASES AND MATERIALS ON CORPORATION FINANCE, Second Edition, 1221 pages, 1989. (Casebook)

## Corporations

HAMILTON'S BLACK LETTER ON CORPORATIONS, Second Edition, 513 pages, 1986. Softcover. (Review)

HAMILTON'S CASES AND MATERIALS ON CORPORATIONS—INCLUDING PARTNERSHIPS AND LIMITED PARTNERSHIPS, Fourth Edition, approximately 1250 pages, 1990. (Casebook) 1990 Statutory Supplement.

HAMILTON'S THE LAW OF CORPORATIONS IN A NUTSHELL, Second Edition, 515 pages, 1987. Softcover. (Text)

HENN'S TEACHING MATERIALS ON THE LAW OF CORPORATIONS, Second Edition, 1204 pages, 1986. Teacher's Manual available. (Casebook)

Statutory Supplement. *See Selected Corporation and Partnership*

HENN AND ALEXANDER'S HORNBOOK ON LAWS OF CORPORATIONS, Third Edition, Student Edition, 1371 pages, 1983, with 1986 pocket part. (Text)

SELECTED CORPORATION AND PARTNERSHIP STATUTES, RULES AND FORMS. Softcover. 727 pages, 1989.

SOLOMON, SCHWARTZ AND BAUMAN'S MATERIALS AND PROBLEMS ON CORPORATIONS: LAW AND POLICY, Second Edition, 1391 pages, 1988. Teacher's Manual available. (Casebook) 1990 Supplement.

Statutory Supplement. *See Selected Corporation and Partnership*

## Corrections

KRANTZ' CASES AND MATERIALS ON THE LAW OF CORRECTIONS AND PRISONERS' RIGHTS, Third Edition, 855 pages, 1986. (Casebook) 1988 Supplement.

KRANTZ' THE LAW OF CORRECTIONS AND PRISONERS' RIGHTS IN A NUTSHELL, Third Edition, 407 pages, 1988. Softcover. (Text)

ROBBINS' CASES AND MATERIALS ON POST-CONVICTION REMEDIES, 506 pages, 1982. (Casebook)

**Creditors' Rights**

BANKRUPTCY CODE, RULES AND OFFICIAL FORMS, LAW SCHOOL EDITION. Approximately 875 pages, 1990. Softcover.

EPSTEIN'S DEBTOR-CREDITOR RELATIONS IN A NUTSHELL, Third Edition, 383 pages, 1986. Softcover. (Text)

EPSTEIN, LANDERS AND NICKLES' CASES AND MATERIALS ON DEBTORS AND CREDITORS, Third Edition, 1059 pages, 1987. Teacher's Manual available. (Casebook)

LoPUCKI'S PLAYER'S MANUAL FOR THE DEBTOR-CREDITOR GAME, 123 pages, 1985. Softcover. (Coursebook)

NICKLES AND EPSTEIN'S BLACK LETTER ON CREDITORS' RIGHTS AND BANKRUPTCY, 576 pages, 1989. (Review)

RIESENFELD'S CASES AND MATERIALS ON CREDITORS' REMEDIES AND DEBTORS' PROTECTION, Fourth Edition, 914 pages, 1987. (Casebook) 1990 Supplement.

WHITE'S CASES AND MATERIALS ON BANKRUPTCY AND CREDITORS' RIGHTS, 812 pages, 1985. Teacher's Manual available. (Casebook) 1987 Supplement.

**Criminal Law and Criminal Procedure**—see also Corrections, Juvenile Justice

ABRAMS' FEDERAL CRIMINAL LAW AND ITS ENFORCEMENT, 866 pages, 1986. (Casebook) 1988 Supplement.

AMERICAN CRIMINAL JUSTICE PROCESS: SELECTED RULES, STATUTES AND GUIDELINES. 723 pages, 1989. Softcover.

CARLSON'S ADJUDICATION OF CRIMINAL JUSTICE: PROBLEMS AND REFERENCES, 130 pages, 1986. Softcover. (Casebook)

DIX AND SHARLOT'S CASES AND MATERIALS ON CRIMINAL LAW, Third Edition, 846 pages, 1987. (Casebook)

GRANO'S PROBLEMS IN CRIMINAL PROCEDURE, Second Edition, 176 pages, 1981. Teacher's Manual available. Softcover. (Coursebook)

HEYMANN AND KENETY'S THE MURDER TRIAL OF WILBUR JACKSON: A HOMICIDE IN THE FAMILY, Second Edition, 347 pages, 1985. (Coursebook)

ISRAEL, KAMISAR AND LaFAVE'S CRIMINAL

PROCEDURE AND THE CONSTITUTION: LEADING SUPREME COURT CASES AND INTRODUCTORY TEXT. Approximately 725 pages, 1990 Edition. Softcover. (Casebook)

ISRAEL AND LaFAVE'S CRIMINAL PROCEDURE—CONSTITUTIONAL LIMITATIONS IN A NUTSHELL, Fourth Edition, 461 pages, 1988. Softcover. (Text)

JOHNSON'S CASES, MATERIALS AND TEXT ON CRIMINAL LAW, Fourth Edition, approximately 790 pages, 1990. Teacher's Manual available. (Casebook)

JOHNSON'S CASES AND MATERIALS ON CRIMINAL PROCEDURE, 859 pages, 1988. (Casebook) 1990 Supplement.

KAMISAR, LaFAVE AND ISRAEL'S MODERN CRIMINAL PROCEDURE: CASES, COMMENTS AND QUESTIONS, Seventh Edition, 1593 pages, 1990. (Casebook) 1990 Supplement.

KAMISAR, LaFAVE AND ISRAEL'S BASIC CRIMINAL PROCEDURE: CASES, COMMENTS AND QUESTIONS, Seventh Edition, 792 pages, 1990. Softcover reprint from Kamisar, et al., Modern Criminal Procedure: Cases, Comments and Questions, Seventh Edition. (Casebook) 1990 Supplement.

LaFAVE'S MODERN CRIMINAL LAW: CASES, COMMENTS AND QUESTIONS, Second Edition, 903 pages, 1988. (Casebook)

LaFAVE AND ISRAEL'S HORNBOOK ON CRIMINAL PROCEDURE, Student Edition, 1142 pages, 1985, with 1989 pocket part. (Text)

LaFAVE AND SCOTT'S HORNBOOK ON CRIMINAL LAW, Second Edition, 918 pages, 1986. (Text)

LANGBEIN'S COMPARATIVE CRIMINAL PROCEDURE: GERMANY, 172 pages, 1977. Softcover. (Casebook)

LOEWY'S CRIMINAL LAW IN A NUTSHELL, Second Edition, 321 pages, 1987. Softcover. (Text)

LOW'S BLACK LETTER ON CRIMINAL LAW, Revised First Edition, approximately 430 pages, 1990. Softcover. (Review)

SALTZBURG'S CASES AND COMMENTARY ON AMERICAN CRIMINAL PROCEDURE, Third Edition, 1302 pages, 1988. Teacher's Manual available. (Casebook) 1990 Supplement.

**Criminal Law and Criminal Procedure—Cont'd**

UVILLER'S THE PROCESSES OF CRIMINAL JUSTICE: INVESTIGATION AND ADJUDICATION, Second Edition, 1384 pages, 1979. (Casebook) 1979 Statutory Supplement. 1986 Update.

VORENBERG'S CASES ON CRIMINAL LAW AND PROCEDURE, Second Edition, 1088 pages, 1981. Teacher's Manual available. (Casebook) 1990 Supplement.

**Decedents' Estates**—see Trusts and Estates

**Domestic Relations**

CLARK'S HORNBOOK ON DOMESTIC RELATIONS, Second Edition, Student Edition, 1050 pages, 1988. (Text)

CLARK AND GLOWINSKY'S CASES AND PROBLEMS ON DOMESTIC RELATIONS, Fourth Edition. Approximately 1125 pages, 1990. Teacher's Manual available. (Casebook)

KRAUSE'S BLACK LETTER ON FAMILY LAW, 314 pages, 1988. Softcover. (Review)

KRAUSE'S CASES, COMMENTS AND QUESTIONS ON FAMILY LAW, Third Edition, 1433 pages, 1990. (Casebook)

KRAUSE'S FAMILY LAW IN A NUTSHELL, Second Edition, 444 pages, 1986. Softcover. (Text)

KRAUSKOPF'S CASES ON PROPERTY DIVISION AT MARRIAGE DISSOLUTION, 250 pages, 1984. Softcover. (Casebook)

**Economics, Law and**—see also Antitrust, Regulated Industries

GOETZ' CASES AND MATERIALS ON LAW AND ECONOMICS, 547 pages, 1984. (Casebook)

MALLOY'S LAW AND ECONOMICS: A COMPARATIVE APPROACH TO THEORY AND PRACTICE, Approximately 152 pages, 1990. Softcover. (Text)

**Education Law**

ALEXANDER AND ALEXANDER'S THE LAW OF SCHOOLS, STUDENTS AND TEACHERS IN A NUTSHELL, 409 pages, 1984. Softcover. (Text)

**Employment Discrimination**—see also Women and the Law

ESTREICHER AND HARPER'S CASES AND MATERIALS ON THE LAW GOVERNING THE EMPLOYMENT RELATIONSHIP, 962 pages, 1990. Teacher's Manual available. (Casebook) Statutory Supplement.

JONES, MURPHY AND BELTON'S CASES AND MATERIALS ON DISCRIMINATION IN EMPLOYMENT, (The Labor Law Group). Fifth Edition, 1116 pages, 1987. (Casebook) 1990 Supplement.

PLAYER'S FEDERAL LAW OF EMPLOYMENT DISCRIMINATION IN A NUTSHELL, Second Edition, 402 pages, 1981. Softcover. (Text)

PLAYER'S HORNBOOK ON EMPLOYMENT DISCRIMINATION LAW, Student Edition, 708 pages, 1988. (Text)

PLAYER, SHOBEN AND LIEBERWITZ' CASES AND MATERIALS ON EMPLOYMENT DISCRIMINATION LAW, Approximately 810 pages, 1990. (Casebook)

**Energy and Natural Resources Law**—see also Oil and Gas

LAITOS' CASES AND MATERIALS ON NATURAL RESOURCES LAW, 938 pages, 1985. Teacher's Manual available. (Casebook)

SELECTED ENVIRONMENTAL LAW STATUTES—EDUCATIONAL EDITION. Softcover. Approximately 1040 pages, 1990.

**Environmental Law**—see also Energy and Natural Resources Law; Sea, Law of

BONINE AND McGARITY'S THE LAW OF ENVIRONMENTAL PROTECTION: CASES—LEGISLATION—POLICIES, 1076 pages, 1984. Teacher's Manual available. (Casebook)

FINDLEY AND FARBER'S CASES AND MATERIALS ON ENVIRONMENTAL LAW, Second Edition, 813 pages, 1985. (Casebook) 1988 Supplement.

FINDLEY AND FARBER'S ENVIRONMENTAL LAW IN A NUTSHELL, Second Edition, 367 pages, 1988. Softcover. (Text)

RODGERS' HORNBOOK ON ENVIRONMENTAL LAW, 956 pages, 1977, with 1984 pocket part. (Text)

SELECTED ENVIRONMENTAL LAW STATUTES—EDUCATIONAL EDITION. Softcover. Approximately 1040 pages, 1990.

**Equity**—see Remedies

**Estate Planning**—see also Trusts and Estates; Taxation—Estate and Gift

LYNN'S AN INTRODUCTION TO ESTATE PLANNING IN A NUTSHELL, Third Edition, 370 pages, 1983. Softcover. (Text)

**Evidence**

BROUN AND BLAKEY'S BLACK LETTER ON EVIDENCE, 269 pages, 1984. Softcover. (Review)

BROUN, MEISENHOLDER, STRONG AND MOSTELLER'S PROBLEMS IN EVIDENCE, Third Edition, 238 pages, 1988. Teacher's Manual available. Softcover. (Coursebook)

CLEARY, STRONG, BROUN AND MOSTELLER'S CASES AND MATERIALS ON EVIDENCE, Fourth Edition, 1060 pages, 1988. (Casebook)

FEDERAL RULES OF EVIDENCE FOR UNITED STATES COURTS AND MAGISTRATES. Softcover. Approximately 380 pages, 1990.

GRAHAM'S FEDERAL RULES OF EVIDENCE IN A NUTSHELL, Second Edition, 473 pages, 1987. Softcover. (Text)

LEMPERT AND SALTZBURG'S A MODERN APPROACH TO EVIDENCE: TEXT, PROBLEMS, TRANSCRIPTS AND CASES, Second Edition, 1232 pages, 1983. Teacher's Manual available. (Casebook)

LILLY'S AN INTRODUCTION TO THE LAW OF EVIDENCE, Second Edition, 585 pages, 1987. (Text)

McCORMICK, SUTTON AND WELLBORN'S CASES AND MATERIALS ON EVIDENCE, Sixth Edition, 1067 pages, 1987. (Casebook)

McCORMICK'S HORNBOOK ON EVIDENCE, Third Edition, Student Edition, 1156 pages, 1984, with 1987 pocket part. (Text)

ROTHSTEIN'S EVIDENCE IN A NUTSHELL: STATE AND FEDERAL RULES, Second Edition, 514 pages, 1981. Softcover. (Text)

**Federal Jurisdiction and Procedure**

CURRIE'S CASES AND MATERIALS ON FEDERAL COURTS, Fourth Edition, approximately 1125 pages, 1990. (Casebook)

CURRIE'S FEDERAL JURISDICTION IN A NUTSHELL, Third Edition, approximately 260 pages, 1990. Softcover. (Text)

FEDERAL RULES OF CIVIL PROCEDURE—EDUCATIONAL EDITION. Softcover. Approxi-

mately 635 pages, 1990.

REDISH'S BLACK LETTER ON FEDERAL JURISDICTION, 219 pages, 1985. Softcover. (Review)

REDISH'S CASES, COMMENTS AND QUESTIONS ON FEDERAL COURTS, Second Edition, 1122 pages, 1989. (Casebook) 1990 Supplement.

VETRI AND MERRILL'S FEDERAL COURTS PROBLEMS AND MATERIALS, Second Edition, 232 pages, 1984. Softcover. (Coursebook)

WRIGHT'S HORNBOOK ON FEDERAL COURTS, Fourth Edition, Student Edition, 870 pages, 1983. (Text)

**Foreign Relations and National Security Law**

FRANCK AND GLENNON'S FOREIGN RELATIONS AND NATIONAL SECURITY LAW, 941 pages, 1987. (Casebook)

**Future Interests**—see Trusts and Estates

**Health Law**—see Medicine, Law and

**Human Rights**—see International Law

**Immigration Law**

ALEINIKOFF AND MARTIN'S IMMIGRATION PROCESS AND POLICY, Second Edition, approximately 1100 pages, October, 1990 (Casebook)

Statutory Supplement. *See Immigration and Nationality Laws*

IMMIGRATION AND NATIONALITY LAWS OF THE UNITED STATES: SELECTED STATUTES, REGULATIONS AND FORMS. Softcover. Approximately 400 pages, 1990.

WEISSBRODT'S IMMIGRATION LAW AND PROCEDURE IN A NUTSHELL, Second Edition, 438 pages, 1989, Softcover. (Text)

**Indian Law**—see American Indian Law

**Insurance Law**

DEVINE AND TERRY'S PROBLEMS IN INSURANCE LAW, 240 pages, 1989. Softcover. Teacher's Manual available. (Course book)

DOBBYN'S INSURANCE LAW IN A NUTSHELL, Second Edition, 316 pages, 1989. Softcover. (Text)

KEETON'S CASES ON BASIC INSURANCE LAW,

**Insurance Law—Cont'd**

Second Edition, 1086 pages, 1977. Teacher's Manual available. (Casebook)

KEETON'S COMPUTER-AIDED AND WORKBOOK EXERCISES ON INSURANCE LAW, 255 pages, 1990. Softcover. (Coursebook)

KEETON AND WIDISS' INSURANCE LAW, Student Edition, 1359 pages, 1988. (Text)

WIDISS AND KEETON'S COURSE SUPPLEMENT TO KEETON AND WIDISS' INSURANCE LAW, 502 pages, 1988. Softcover. (Casebook)

WIDISS' INSURANCE: MATERIALS ON FUNDAMENTAL PRINCIPLES, LEGAL DOCTRINES AND REGULATORY ACTS, 1186 pages, 1989. (Casebook)

YORK AND WHELAN'S CASES, MATERIALS AND PROBLEMS ON GENERAL PRACTICE INSURANCE LAW, Second Edition, 787 pages, 1988. Teacher's Manual available. (Casebook)

**International Law**—see also Sea, Law of

BUERGENTHAL'S INTERNATIONAL HUMAN RIGHTS IN A NUTSHELL, 283 pages, 1988. Softcover. (Text)

BUERGENTHAL AND MAIER'S PUBLIC INTERNATIONAL LAW IN A NUTSHELL, Second Edition, 275 pages, 1990. Softcover. (Text)

FOLSOM, GORDON AND SPANOGLE'S INTERNATIONAL BUSINESS TRANSACTIONS—A PROBLEM-ORIENTED COURSEBOOK, 1160 pages, 1986. Teacher's Manual available. (Casebook) 1989 Documents Supplement.

FOLSOM, GORDON AND SPANOGLE'S INTERNATIONAL BUSINESS TRANSACTIONS IN A NUTSHELL, Third Edition, 509 pages, 1988. Softcover. (Text)

HENKIN, PUGH, SCHACHTER AND SMIT'S CASES AND MATERIALS ON INTERNATIONAL LAW, Second Edition, 1517 pages, 1987. (Casebook) Documents Supplement.

JACKSON AND DAVEY'S CASES, MATERIALS AND TEXT ON LEGAL PROBLEMS OF INTERNATIONAL ECONOMIC RELATIONS, Second Edition, 1269 pages, 1986. (Casebook) 1989 Documents Supplement.

KIRGIS' INTERNATIONAL ORGANIZATIONS IN THEIR LEGAL SETTING, 1016 pages, 1977. Teacher's Manual available. (Casebook) 1981 Supplement.

WESTON, FALK AND D'AMATO'S INTERNATIONAL LAW AND WORLD ORDER—A PROBLEM-ORIENTED COURSEBOOK, Second Edition, approximately 1305 pages, 1990. Teacher's Manual available. (Casebook) Documents Supplement.

**Interviewing and Counseling**

BINDER AND PRICE'S LEGAL INTERVIEWING AND COUNSELING, 232 pages, 1977. Teacher's Manual available. Softcover. (Coursebook)

BINDER, BERGMAN AND PRICE'S LAWYERS AS COUNSELORS: A CLIENT CENTERED APPROACH, Approximately 400 pages, October, 1990 Pub. Softcover. (Coursebook)

SHAFFER AND ELKINS' LEGAL INTERVIEWING AND COUNSELING IN A NUTSHELL, Second Edition, 487 pages, 1987. Softcover. (Text)

**Introduction to Law**—see Legal Method and Legal System

**Introduction to Law Study**

HEGLAND'S INTRODUCTION TO THE STUDY AND PRACTICE OF LAW IN A NUTSHELL, 418 pages, 1983. Softcover. (Text)

KINYON'S INTRODUCTION TO LAW STUDY AND LAW EXAMINATIONS IN A NUTSHELL, 389 pages, 1971. Softcover. (Text)

**Judicial Process**—see Legal Method and Legal System

**Jurisprudence**

CHRISTIE'S JURISPRUDENCE—TEXT AND READINGS ON THE PHILOSOPHY OF LAW, 1056 pages, 1973. (Casebook)

**Juvenile Justice**

FOX'S CASES AND MATERIALS ON MODERN JUVENILE JUSTICE, Second Edition, 960 pages, 1981. (Casebook)

FOX'S JUVENILE COURTS IN A NUTSHELL, Third Edition, 291 pages, 1984. Softcover. (Text)

**Labor and Employment Law**—see also Employment Discrimination, Social Legislation

FINKIN, GOLDMAN AND SUMMERS' LEGAL PROTECTION OF INDIVIDUAL EMPLOYEES, (The La-

**Labor and Employment Law**—Cont'd

bor Law Group). 1164 pages, 1989. (Casebook)

GORMAN'S BASIC TEXT ON LABOR LAW—UNIONIZATION AND COLLECTIVE BARGAINING, 914 pages, 1976. (Text)

LESLIE'S LABOR LAW IN A NUTSHELL, Second Edition, 397 pages, 1986. Softcover. (Text)

NOLAN'S LABOR ARBITRATION LAW AND PRACTICE IN A NUTSHELL, 358 pages, 1979. Softcover. (Text)

OBERER, HANSLOWE, ANDERSEN AND HEINSZ' CASES AND MATERIALS ON LABOR LAW—COLLECTIVE BARGAINING IN A FREE SOCIETY, Third Edition, 1163 pages, 1986. (Casebook) Statutory Supplement.

RABIN, SILVERSTEIN AND SCHATZKI'S LABOR AND EMPLOYMENT LAW: PROBLEMS, CASES AND MATERIALS IN THE LAW OF WORK, (The Labor Law Group). 1014 pages, 1988. Teacher's Manual available. (Casebook) 1988 Statutory Supplement.

**Land Finance—Property Security**—see Real Estate Transactions

**Land Use**

CALLIES AND FREILICH'S CASES AND MATERIALS ON LAND USE, 1233 pages, 1986. (Casebook) 1988 Supplement.

HAGMAN AND JUERGENSMEYER'S HORNBOOK ON URBAN PLANNING AND LAND DEVELOPMENT CONTROL LAW, Second Edition, Student Edition, 680 pages, 1986. (Text)

WRIGHT AND GITELMAN'S CASES AND MATERIALS ON LAND USE, Third Edition, 1300 pages, 1982. Teacher's Manual available. (Casebook) 1987 Supplement.

WRIGHT AND WRIGHT'S LAND USE IN A NUTSHELL, Second Edition, 356 pages, 1985. Softcover. (Text)

**Legal History**—see also Legal Method and Legal System

PRESSER AND ZAINALDIN'S CASES AND MATERIALS ON LAW AND JURISPRUDENCE IN AMERICAN HISTORY, Second Edition, 1092 pages, 1989. Teacher's Manual available. (Casebook)

**Legal Method and Legal System**—see also Legal Research, Legal Writing

ALDISERT'S READINGS, MATERIALS AND CASES IN THE JUDICIAL PROCESS, 948 pages, 1976. (Casebook)

BERCH AND BERCH'S INTRODUCTION TO LEGAL METHOD AND PROCESS, 550 pages, 1985. Teacher's Manual available. (Casebook)

BODENHEIMER, OAKLEY AND LOVE'S READINGS AND CASES ON AN INTRODUCTION TO THE ANGLO-AMERICAN LEGAL SYSTEM, Second Edition, 166 pages, 1988. Softcover. (Casebook)

DAVIES AND LAWRY'S INSTITUTIONS AND METHODS OF THE LAW—INTRODUCTORY TEACHING MATERIALS, 547 pages, 1982. Teacher's Manual available. (Casebook)

DVORKIN, HIMMELSTEIN AND LESNICK'S BECOMING A LAWYER: A HUMANISTIC PERSPECTIVE ON LEGAL EDUCATION AND PROFESSIONALISM, 211 pages, 1981. Softcover. (Text)

KEETON'S JUDGING, 842 pages, 1990. Softcover. (Coursebook)

KELSO AND KELSO'S STUDYING LAW: AN INTRODUCTION, 587 pages, 1984. (Coursebook)

KEMPIN'S HISTORICAL INTRODUCTION TO ANGLO-AMERICAN LAW IN A NUTSHELL, Third Edition, approximately 302 pages, 1990. Softcover. (Text)

REYNOLDS' JUDICIAL PROCESS IN A NUTSHELL, 292 pages, 1980. Softcover. (Text)

**Legal Research**

COHEN'S LEGAL RESEARCH IN A NUTSHELL, Fourth Edition, 452 pages, 1985. Softcover. (Text)

COHEN, BERRING AND OLSON'S HOW TO FIND THE LAW, Ninth Edition, 716 pages, 1989. (Text)

COHEN, BERRING AND OLSON'S FINDING THE LAW, 570 pages, 1989. Softcover reprint from Cohen, Berring and Olson's How to Find the Law, Ninth Edition. (Coursebook)

Legal Research Exercises, 3rd Ed., for use with Cohen, Berring and Olson, 229 pages, 1989. Teacher's Manual available.

ROMBAUER'S LEGAL PROBLEM SOLVING—

## Legal Research—Cont'd

ANALYSIS, RESEARCH AND WRITING, Fourth Edition, 424 pages, 1983. Teacher's Manual with problems available. (Coursebook)

STATSKY'S LEGAL RESEARCH AND WRITING, Third Edition, 257 pages, 1986. Softcover. (Coursebook)

TEPLY'S LEGAL RESEARCH AND CITATION, Third Edition, 472 pages, 1989. Softcover. (Coursebook)

Student Library Exercises, 3rd ed., 391 pages, 1989. Answer Key available.

## Legal Writing

CHILD'S DRAFTING LEGAL DOCUMENTS: MATERIALS AND PROBLEMS, 286 pages, 1988. Softcover. Teacher's Manual available. (Coursebook)

DICKERSON'S MATERIALS ON LEGAL DRAFTING, 425 pages, 1981. Teacher's Manual available. (Coursebook)

FELSENFELD AND SIEGEL'S WRITING CONTRACTS IN PLAIN ENGLISH, 290 pages, 1981. Softcover. (Text)

GOPEN'S WRITING FROM A LEGAL PERSPECTIVE, 225 pages, 1981. (Text)

MELLINKOFF'S LEGAL WRITING—SENSE AND NONSENSE, 242 pages, 1982. Softcover. Teacher's Manual available. (Text)

PRATT'S LEGAL WRITING: A SYSTEMATIC APPROACH, 422 pages, 1989. Teacher's Manual available. (Coursebook)

RAY AND RAMSFIELD'S LEGAL WRITING: GETTING IT RIGHT AND GETTING IT WRITTEN, 250 pages, 1987. Softcover. (Text)

SQUIRES AND ROMBAUER'S LEGAL WRITING IN A NUTSHELL, 294 pages, 1982. Softcover. (Text)

STATSKY AND WERNET'S CASE ANALYSIS AND FUNDAMENTALS OF LEGAL WRITING, Third Edition, 424 pages, 1989. Teacher's Manual available. (Text)

TEPLY'S LEGAL WRITING, ANALYSIS AND ORAL ARGUMENT, 576 pages, 1990. Softcover. Teacher's Manual available. (Coursebook)

WEIHOFEN'S LEGAL WRITING STYLE, Second Edition, 332 pages, 1980. (Text)

## Legislation

DAVIES' LEGISLATIVE LAW AND PROCESS IN A NUTSHELL, Second Edition, 346 pages, 1986. Softcover. (Text)

ESKRIDGE AND FRICKEY'S CASES AND MATERIALS ON LEGISLATION: STATUTES AND THE CREATION OF PUBLIC POLICY, 937 pages, 1988. Teacher's Manual available. (Casebook) 1990 Supplement.

NUTTING AND DICKERSON'S CASES AND MATERIALS ON LEGISLATION, Fifth Edition, 744 pages, 1978. (Casebook)

STATSKY'S LEGISLATIVE ANALYSIS AND DRAFTING, Second Edition, 217 pages, 1984. Teacher's Manual available. (Text)

## Local Government

FRUG'S CASES AND MATERIALS ON LOCAL GOVERNMENT LAW, 1005 pages, 1988. (Casebook)

MCCARTHY'S LOCAL GOVERNMENT LAW IN A NUTSHELL, Third Edition, approximately 400 pages, 1990. Softcover. (Text)

REYNOLDS' HORNBOOK ON LOCAL GOVERNMENT LAW, 860 pages, 1982, with 1990 pocket part. (Text)

VALENTE'S CASES AND MATERIALS ON LOCAL GOVERNMENT LAW, Third Edition, 1010 pages, 1987. Teacher's Manual available. (Casebook) 1989 Supplement.

## Mass Communication Law

GILLMOR, BARRON, SIMON AND TERRY'S CASES AND COMMENT ON MASS COMMUNICATION LAW, Fifth Edition, 947 pages, 1990. (Casebook)

GINSBURG'S REGULATION OF BROADCASTING: LAW AND POLICY TOWARDS RADIO, TELEVISION AND CABLE COMMUNICATIONS, 741 pages, 1979 (Casebook) 1983 Supplement.

ZUCKMAN, GAYNES, CARTER AND DEE'S MASS COMMUNICATIONS LAW IN A NUTSHELL, Third Edition, 538 pages, 1988. Softcover. (Text)

## Medicine, Law and

FURROW, JOHNSON, JOST AND SCHWARTZ' HEALTH LAW: CASES, MATERIALS AND PROBLEMS, 1005 pages, 1987. Teacher's Manual available. (Casebook) 1989 Supplement.

HALL AND ELLMAN'S HEALTH CARE LAW AND

**Medicine, Law and**—Cont'd

ETHICS IN A NUTSHELL, 401 pages, 1990. Softcover (Text)

KING'S THE LAW OF MEDICAL MALPRACTICE IN A NUTSHELL, Second Edition, 342 pages, 1986. Softcover. (Text)

SHAPIRO AND SPECE'S CASES, MATERIALS AND PROBLEMS ON BIOETHICS AND LAW, 892 pages, 1981. (Casebook)

SHARPE, BOUMIL, FISCINA AND HEAD'S CASES AND MATERIALS ON MEDICAL LIABILITY, Approximately 500 pages, September, 1990 Pub. (Casebook)

**Military Law**

SHANOR AND TERRELL'S MILITARY LAW IN A NUTSHELL, 378 pages, 1980. Softcover. (Text)

**Mortgages**—see Real Estate Transactions

**Natural Resources Law**—see Energy and Natural Resources Law, Environmental Law

**Negotiation**

GIFFORD'S LEGAL NEGOTIATION: THEORY AND APPLICATIONS, 225 pages, 1989. Softcover. (Text)

WILLIAMS' LEGAL NEGOTIATION AND SETTLEMENT, 207 pages, 1983. Softcover. Teacher's Manual available. (Coursebook)

**Office Practice**—see also Computers and Law, Interviewing and Counseling, Negotiation

HEGLAND'S TRIAL AND PRACTICE SKILLS IN A NUTSHELL, 346 pages, 1978. Softcover (Text)

STRONG AND CLARK'S LAW OFFICE MANAGEMENT, 424 pages, 1974. (Casebook)

**Oil and Gas**—see also Energy and Natural Resources Law

HEMINGWAY'S HORNBOOK ON OIL AND GAS, Second Edition, Student Edition, 543 pages, 1983, with 1989 pocket part. (Text)

KUNTZ, LOWE, ANDERSON AND SMITH'S CASES AND MATERIALS ON OIL AND GAS LAW, 857 pages, 1986. Teacher's Manual available. (Casebook) Forms Manual. Revised.

LOWE'S OIL AND GAS LAW IN A NUTSHELL,

Second Edition, 465 pages, 1988. Softcover. (Text)

**Partnership**—see Agency—Partnership

**Patent and Copyright Law**

CHOATE, FRANCIS AND COLLINS' CASES AND MATERIALS ON PATENT LAW, INCLUDING TRADE SECRETS, COPYRIGHTS, TRADEMARKS, Third Edition, 1009 pages, 1987. (Casebook)

MILLER AND DAVIS' INTELLECTUAL PROPERTY—PATENTS, TRADEMARKS AND COPYRIGHT IN A NUTSHELL, Second Edition, approximately 440 pages, 1990. Softcover. (Text)

NIMMER'S CASES AND MATERIALS ON COPYRIGHT AND OTHER ASPECTS OF ENTERTAINMENT LITIGATION ILLUSTRATED—INCLUDING UNFAIR COMPETITION, DEFAMATION AND PRIVACY, Third Edition, 1025 pages, 1985. (Casebook) 1989 Supplement.

**Products Liability**

FISCHER AND POWERS' CASES AND MATERIALS ON PRODUCTS LIABILITY, 685 pages, 1988. Teacher's Manual available. (Casebook)

NOEL AND PHILLIPS' CASES ON PRODUCTS LIABILITY, Second Edition, 821 pages, 1982. (Casebook)

PHILLIPS' PRODUCTS LIABILITY IN A NUTSHELL, Third Edition, 307 pages, 1988. Softcover. (Text)

**Professional Responsibility**

ARONSON, DEVINE AND FISCH'S PROBLEMS, CASES AND MATERIALS IN PROFESSIONAL RESPONSIBILITY, 745 pages, 1985. Teacher's Manual available. (Casebook)

ARONSON AND WECKSTEIN'S PROFESSIONAL RESPONSIBILITY IN A NUTSHELL, 399 pages, 1980. Softcover. (Text)

MELLINKOFF'S THE CONSCIENCE OF A LAWYER, 304 pages, 1973. (Text)

PIRSIG AND KIRWIN'S CASES AND MATERIALS ON PROFESSIONAL RESPONSIBILITY, Fourth Edition, 603 pages, 1984. Teacher's Manual available. (Casebook)

ROTUNDA'S BLACK LETTER ON PROFESSIONAL RESPONSIBILITY, Second Edition, 414 pages, 1988. Softcover. (Review)

SCHWARTZ AND WYDICK'S PROBLEMS IN LE-

**Professional Responsibility**—Cont'd

GAL ETHICS, Second Edition, 341 pages, 1988. (Coursebook)

SELECTED STATUTES, RULES AND STANDARDS ON THE LEGAL PROFESSION. Softcover. Approximately 600 pages, 1990.

SMITH AND MALLEN'S PREVENTING LEGAL MALPRACTICE, 264 pages, 1989. Reprint from Mallen and Smith's Legal Malpractice, Third Edition. (Text)

SUTTON AND DZIENKOWSKI'S CASES AND MATERIALS ON THE PROFESSIONAL RESPONSIBILITY FOR LAWYERS, 839 pages, 1989. Teacher's Manual available. (Casebook)

WOLFRAM'S HORNBOOK ON MODERN LEGAL ETHICS, Student Edition, 1120 pages, 1986. (Text)

**Property**—see also Real Estate Transactions, Land Use, Trusts and Estates

BERNHARDT'S BLACK LETTER ON PROPERTY, 318 pages, 1983. Softcover. (Review)

BERNHARDT'S REAL PROPERTY IN A NUTSHELL, Second Edition, 448 pages, 1981. Softcover. (Text)

BOYER'S SURVEY OF THE LAW OF PROPERTY, Third Edition, 766 pages, 1981. (Text)

BROWDER, CUNNINGHAM, NELSON, STOEBUCK AND WHITMAN'S CASES ON BASIC PROPERTY LAW, Fifth Edition, 1386 pages, 1989. Teacher's Manual available. (Casebook)

BRUCE, ELY AND BOSTICK'S CASES AND MATERIALS ON MODERN PROPERTY LAW, Second Edition, 953 pages, 1989. Teacher's Manual available. (Casebook)

BURKE'S PERSONAL PROPERTY IN A NUTSHELL, 322 pages, 1983. Softcover. (Text)

CUNNINGHAM, STOEBUCK AND WHITMAN'S HORNBOOK ON THE LAW OF PROPERTY, Student Edition, 916 pages, 1984, with 1987 pocket part. (Text)

DONAHUE, KAUPER AND MARTIN'S CASES ON PROPERTY, Second Edition, 1362 pages, 1983. Teacher's Manual available. (Casebook)

HILL'S LANDLORD AND TENANT LAW IN A NUTSHELL, Second Edition, 311 pages, 1986. Softcover. (Text)

KURTZ AND HOVENKAMP'S CASES AND

MATERIALS ON AMERICAN PROPERTY LAW, 1296 pages, 1987. Teacher's Manual available. (Casebook) 1988 Supplement.

MOYNIHAN'S INTRODUCTION TO REAL PROPERTY, Second Edition, 239 pages, 1988. (Text)

**Psychiatry, Law and**

REISNER AND SLOBOGIN'S LAW AND THE MENTAL HEALTH SYSTEM, CIVIL AND CRIMINAL ASPECTS, Second Edition, approximately 1127 pages, 1990. (Casebook)

**Real Estate Transactions**

BRUCE'S REAL ESTATE FINANCE IN A NUTSHELL, Second Edition, 262 pages, 1985. Softcover. (Text)

MAXWELL, RIESENFELD, HETLAND AND WARREN'S CASES ON CALIFORNIA SECURITY TRANSACTIONS IN LAND, Third Edition, 728 pages, 1984. (Casebook)

NELSON AND WHITMAN'S BLACK LETTER ON LAND TRANSACTIONS AND FINANCE, Second Edition, 466 pages, 1988. Softcover. (Review)

NELSON AND WHITMAN'S CASES ON REAL ESTATE TRANSFER, FINANCE AND DEVELOPMENT, Third Edition, 1184 pages, 1987. (Casebook)

NELSON AND WHITMAN'S HORNBOOK ON REAL ESTATE FINANCE LAW, Second Edition, 941 pages, 1985 with 1989 pocket part. (Text)

**Regulated Industries**—see also Mass Communication Law, Banking Law

GELLHORN AND PIERCE'S REGULATED INDUSTRIES IN A NUTSHELL, Second Edition, 389 pages, 1987. Softcover. (Text)

MORGAN, HARRISON AND VERKUIL'S CASES AND MATERIALS ON ECONOMIC REGULATION OF BUSINESS, Second Edition, 666 pages, 1985. (Casebook)

**Remedies**

DOBBS' HORNBOOK ON REMEDIES, 1067 pages, 1973. (Text)

DOBBS' PROBLEMS IN REMEDIES. 137 pages, 1974. Teacher's Manual available. Softcover. (Coursebook)

DOBBYN'S INJUNCTIONS IN A NUTSHELL, 264 pages, 1974. Softcover. (Text)

## Remedies—Cont'd

FRIEDMAN'S CONTRACT REMEDIES IN A NUT-SHELL, 323 pages, 1981. Softcover. (Text)

LEAVELL, LOVE AND NELSON'S CASES AND MATERIALS ON EQUITABLE REMEDIES, RESTITUTION AND DAMAGES, Fourth Edition, 1111 pages, 1986. Teacher's Manual available. (Casebook)

McCORMICK'S HORNBOOK ON DAMAGES, 811 pages, 1935. (Text)

O'CONNELL'S REMEDIES IN A NUTSHELL, Second Edition, 320 pages, 1985. Softcover. (Text)

SCHOENBROD, MACBETH, LEVINE AND JUNG'S CASES AND MATERIALS ON REMEDIES: PUBLIC AND PRIVATE, Approximately 807 pages, 1990. Teacher's Manual available. (Casebook)

YORK, BAUMAN AND RENDLEMAN'S CASES AND MATERIALS ON REMEDIES, Fourth Edition, 1029 pages, 1985. Teacher's Manual available. (Casebook)

## Sea, Law of

SOHN AND GUSTAFSON'S THE LAW OF THE SEA IN A NUTSHELL, 264 pages, 1984. Softcover. (Text)

## Securities Regulation

HAZEN'S HORNBOOK ON THE LAW OF SECURITIES REGULATION, Second Edition, Student Edition, approximately 1000 pages, 1990. (Text)

RATNER'S MATERIALS ON SECURITIES REGULATION, Third Edition, 1000 pages, 1986. Teacher's Manual available. (Casebook) 1989 Supplement.

  Statutory Supplement. *See Selected Securities Regulation*

RATNER'S SECURITIES REGULATION IN A NUTSHELL, Third Edition, 316 pages, 1988. Softcover. (Text)

SELECTED STATUTES, REGULATIONS, RULES, DOCUMENTS AND FORMS ON SECURITIES REGULATION. Softcover. 1272 pages, 1990.

## Social Legislation

HOOD, HARDY AND LEWIS' WORKERS' COMPENSATION AND EMPLOYEE PROTECTION LAWS IN A NUTSHELL, Second Edition, 361 pages, 1990. Softcover. (Text)

LAFRANCE'S WELFARE LAW: STRUCTURE AND ENTITLEMENT IN A NUTSHELL, 455 pages, 1979. Softcover. (Text)

MALONE, PLANT AND LITTLE'S CASES ON WORKERS' COMPENSATION AND EMPLOYMENT RIGHTS, Second Edition, 951 pages, 1980. Teacher's Manual available. (Casebook)

## Sports Law

SCHUBERT, SMITH AND TRENTADUE'S SPORTS LAW, 395 pages, 1986. (Text)

## Tax Practice and Procedure

GARBIS, STRUNTZ AND RUBIN'S CASES AND MATERIALS ON TAX PROCEDURE AND TAX FRAUD, Second Edition, 687 pages, 1987. (Casebook)

MORGAN'S TAX PROCEDURE AND TAX FRAUD IN A NUTSHELL, Approximately 382 pages, 1990. Softcover. (Text)

## Taxation—Corporate

KAHN AND GANN'S CORPORATE TAXATION, Third Edition, 980 pages, 1989. Teacher's Manual available. (Casebook)

WEIDENBRUCH AND BURKE'S FEDERAL INCOME TAXATION OF CORPORATIONS AND STOCKHOLDERS IN A NUTSHELL, Third Edition, 309 pages, 1989. Softcover. (Text)

## Taxation—Estate & Gift—see also Estate Planning, Trusts and Estates

McNULTY'S FEDERAL ESTATE AND GIFT TAXATION IN A NUTSHELL, Fourth Edition, 496 pages, 1989. Softcover. (Text)

PENNELL'S CASES AND MATERIALS ON INCOME TAXATION OF TRUSTS, ESTATES, GRANTORS AND BENEFICIARIES, 460 pages, 1987. Teacher's Manual available. (Casebook)

## Taxation—Individual

DODGE'S THE LOGIC OF TAX, 343 pages, 1989. Softcover. (Text)

GUNN AND WARD'S CASES, TEXT AND PROBLEMS ON FEDERAL INCOME TAXATION, Second Edition, 835 pages, 1988. Teacher's Manual available. (Casebook) 1990 Supplement.

HUDSON AND LIND'S BLACK LETTER ON FEDERAL INCOME TAXATION, Third Edition, approximately 390 pages, 1990. Softcover. (Review)

### Taxation—Individual—Cont'd

KRAGEN AND MCNULTY'S CASES AND MATERIALS ON FEDERAL INCOME TAXATION—INDIVIDUALS, CORPORATIONS, PARTNERSHIPS, Fourth Edition, 1287 pages, 1985. (Casebook)

MCNULTY'S FEDERAL INCOME TAXATION OF INDIVIDUALS IN A NUTSHELL, Fourth Edition, 503 pages, 1988. Softcover. (Text)

POSIN'S HORNBOOK ON FEDERAL INCOME TAXATION, Student Edition, 491 pages, 1983, with 1989 pocket part. (Text)

ROSE AND CHOMMIE'S HORNBOOK ON FEDERAL INCOME TAXATION, Third Edition, 923 pages, 1988, with 1989 pocket part. (Text)

SELECTED FEDERAL TAXATION STATUTES AND REGULATIONS. Softcover. Approximately 1650 pages, 1991.

SOLOMON AND HESCH'S PROBLEMS, CASES AND MATERIALS ON FEDERAL INCOME TAXATION OF INDIVIDUALS, 1068 pages, 1987. Teacher's Manual available. (Casebook)

### Taxation—International

DOERNBERG'S INTERNATIONAL TAXATION IN A NUTSHELL, 325 pages, 1989. Softcover. (Text)

KAPLAN'S FEDERAL TAXATION OF INTERNATIONAL TRANSACTIONS: PRINCIPLES, PLANNING AND POLICY, 635 pages, 1988. (Casebook)

### Taxation—Partnership

BERGER AND WIEDENBECK'S CASES AND MATERIALS ON PARTNERSHIP TAXATION, 788 pages, 1989. Teacher's Manual available. (Casebook)

### Taxation—State & Local

GELFAND AND SALSICH'S STATE AND LOCAL TAXATION AND FINANCE IN A NUTSHELL, 309 pages, 1986. Softcover. (Text)

HELLERSTEIN AND HELLERSTEIN'S CASES AND MATERIALS ON STATE AND LOCAL TAXATION, Fifth Edition, 1071 pages, 1988. (Casebook)

### Torts—see also Products Liability

CHRISTIE AND MEEKS' CASES AND MATERIALS ON THE LAW OF TORTS, Second Edition, 1264 pages, 1990. (Casebook)

DOBBS' TORTS AND COMPENSATION—PERSONAL ACCOUNTABILITY AND SOCIAL RESPONSIBILITY FOR INJURY, 955 pages, 1985. Teacher's Manual available. (Casebook) 1990 Supplement.

KEETON, KEETON, SARGENTICH AND STEINER'S CASES AND MATERIALS ON TORT AND ACCIDENT LAW, Second Edition, 1318 pages, 1989. (Casebook)

KIONKA'S BLACK LETTER ON TORTS, 339 pages, 1988. Softcover. (Review)

KIONKA'S TORTS IN A NUTSHELL: INJURIES TO PERSONS AND PROPERTY, 434 pages, 1977. Softcover. (Text)

MALONE'S TORTS IN A NUTSHELL: INJURIES TO FAMILY, SOCIAL AND TRADE RELATIONS, 358 pages, 1979. Softcover. (Text)

PROSSER AND KEETON'S HORNBOOK ON TORTS, Fifth Edition, Student Edition, 1286 pages, 1984 with 1988 pocket part. (Text)

ROBERTSON, POWERS AND ANDERSON'S CASES AND MATERIALS ON TORTS, 932 pages, 1989. Teacher's Manual available. (Casebook)

### Trade Regulation—see also Antitrust, Regulated Industries

MCMANIS' UNFAIR TRADE PRACTICES IN A NUTSHELL, Second Edition, 464 pages, 1988. Softcover. (Text)

OPPENHEIM, WESTON, MAGGS AND SCHECHTER'S CASES AND MATERIALS ON UNFAIR TRADE PRACTICES AND CONSUMER PROTECTION, Fourth Edition, 1038 pages, 1983. Teacher's Manual available. (Casebook) 1986 Supplement.

SCHECHTER'S BLACK LETTER ON UNFAIR TRADE PRACTICES, 272 pages, 1986. Softcover. (Review)

### Trial and Appellate Advocacy—see also Civil Procedure

APPELLATE ADVOCACY, HANDBOOK OF, Second Edition, 182 pages, 1986. Softcover. (Text)

BERGMAN'S TRIAL ADVOCACY IN A NUTSHELL, Second Edition, 354 pages, 1989. Softcover. (Text)

BINDER AND BERGMAN'S FACT INVESTIGATION: FROM HYPOTHESIS TO PROOF, 354 pages, 1984. Teacher's Manual available. (Coursebook)

**Trial and Appellate Advocacy**—Cont'd

CARLSON AND IMWINKELRIED'S DYNAMICS OF TRIAL PRACTICE: PROBLEMS AND MATERIALS, 414 pages, 1989. Teacher's Manual available. (Coursebook)

GOLDBERG'S THE FIRST TRIAL (WHERE DO I SIT? WHAT DO I SAY?) IN A NUTSHELL, 396 pages, 1982. Softcover. (Text)

HAYDOCK, HERR, AND STEMPEL'S FUNDAMENTALS OF PRE-TRIAL LITIGATION, 768 pages, 1985. Softcover. Teacher's Manual available. (Coursebook)

HEGLAND'S TRIAL AND PRACTICE SKILLS IN A NUTSHELL, 346 pages, 1978. Softcover. (Text)

HORNSTEIN'S APPELLATE ADVOCACY IN A NUTSHELL, 325 pages, 1984. Softcover. (Text)

JEANS' HANDBOOK ON TRIAL ADVOCACY, Student Edition, 473 pages, 1975. Softcover. (Text)

LISNEK AND KAUFMAN'S DEPOSITIONS: PROCEDURE, STRATEGY AND TECHNIQUE, Law School and CLE Edition. 250 pages, 1990. Softcover. (Text)

MARTINEAU'S CASES AND MATERIALS ON APPELLATE PRACTICE AND PROCEDURE, 565 pages, 1987. (Casebook)

NOLAN'S CASES AND MATERIALS ON TRIAL PRACTICE, 518 pages, 1981. (Casebook)

SONSTENG AND HAYDOCK'S TRIAL: THEORIES, TACTICS, TECHNIQUE, Approximately 650 pages, 1990. Softcover. (Text)

SONSTENG, HAYDOCK AND BOYD'S THE TRIALBOOK: A TOTAL SYSTEM FOR PREPARATION AND PRESENTATION OF A CASE, 404 pages, 1984. Softcover. (Coursebook)

WHARTON, HAYDOCK AND SONSTENG'S CALIFORNIA CIVIL TRIALBOOK, Law School and CLE Edition. Approximately 300 pages, 1990. Softcover. (Text)

**Trusts and Estates**

ATKINSON'S HORNBOOK ON WILLS, Second Edition, 975 pages, 1953. (Text)

AVERILL'S UNIFORM PROBATE CODE IN A NUTSHELL, Second Edition, 454 pages, 1987. Softcover. (Text)

BOGERT'S HORNBOOK ON TRUSTS, Sixth Edition, Student Edition, 794 pages, 1987. (Text)

CLARK, LUSKY AND MURPHY'S CASES AND MATERIALS ON GRATUITOUS TRANSFERS, Third Edition, 970 pages, 1985. (Casebook)

DODGE'S WILLS, TRUSTS AND ESTATE PLANNING—LAW AND TAXATION, CASES AND MATERIALS, 665 pages, 1988. (Casebook)

KURTZ' PROBLEMS, CASES AND OTHER MATERIALS ON FAMILY ESTATE PLANNING, 853 pages, 1983. Teacher's Manual available. (Casebook)

McGOVERN'S CASES AND MATERIALS ON WILLS, TRUSTS AND FUTURE INTERESTS: AN INTRODUCTION TO ESTATE PLANNING, 750 pages, 1983. (Casebook)

McGOVERN, KURTZ AND REIN'S HORNBOOK ON WILLS, TRUSTS AND ESTATES—INCLUDING TAXATION AND FUTURE INTERESTS, 996 pages, 1988. (Text)

MENNELL'S WILLS AND TRUSTS IN A NUTSHELL, 392 pages, 1979. Softcover. (Text)

SIMES' HORNBOOK ON FUTURE INTERESTS, Second Edition, 355 pages, 1966. (Text)

TURANO AND RADIGAN'S HORNBOOK ON NEW YORK ESTATE ADMINISTRATION, 676 pages, 1986. (Text)

UNIFORM PROBATE CODE, OFFICIAL TEXT WITH COMMENTS. 615 pages, 1989. Softcover.

WAGGONER'S FUTURE INTERESTS IN A NUTSHELL, 361 pages, 1981. Softcover. (Text)

WATERBURY'S MATERIALS ON TRUSTS AND ESTATES, 1039 pages, 1986. Teacher's Manual available. (Casebook)

**Water Law**—see also Energy and Natural Resources Law, Environmental Law

GETCHES' WATER LAW IN A NUTSHELL, Second Edition, approximately 441 pages, 1990. Softcover. (Text)

SAX AND ABRAMS' LEGAL CONTROL OF WATER RESOURCES: CASES AND MATERIALS, 941 pages, 1986. (Casebook)

TRELEASE AND GOULD'S CASES AND MATERIALS ON WATER LAW, Fourth Edition, 816 pages, 1986. (Casebook)

# CRIMINAL PROCEDURE AND THE CONSTITUTION

## LEADING SUPREME COURT CASES AND INTRODUCTORY TEXT

## 1990 EDITION

By

**Jerold H. Israel**
*Alene and Allan F. Smith*
*Professor of Law, University of Michigan*

**Yale Kamisar**
*Henry K. Ransom Professor of Law,*
*University of Michigan*

**Wayne R. LaFave**
*David C. Baum Professor of Law,*
*University of Illinois*

**AMERICAN CASEBOOK SERIES** ®

**WEST PUBLISHING CO.**
ST. PAUL, MINN., 1990

American Casebook Series, the key number appearing on the front cover and the WP symbol are registered trademarks of West Publishing Co. Registered in U.S. Patent and Trademark Office.

**Library of Congress Cataloging-in-Publication Data**

Israel, Jerold H., 1934–
    Criminal procedure and the Constitution: leading Supreme Court cases and introductory text / by Jerold H. Israel, Yale Kamisar, and Wayne R. LaFave. — 1990 ed.
       p.     cm. — (American casebook series)
    ISBN 0–314–76477–1
    1. Criminal procedure—United States—Cases. I. Kamisar, Yale. II. LaFave, Wayne R. III. Title. IV. Series.
KF9618.I85  1990
345.73'05—cc20
[347.3055]                                90–41930
                                          CIP

**ISBN** 0–314–76477–1

∞

# Preface

This collection of leading Supreme Court cases is designed for those instructors who want to cover a wide range of criminal procedure topics but have available only a limited amount of time. In the main, the cases in this book were selected because of their substantial contemporary significance; they reflect the Supreme Court's current position on issues of major importance regarding the operation of our federal and state criminal justice systems. But we have also included some venerable cases that contribute significantly to an understanding of current trends and developments.

These materials differ in important ways from our two other sets of teaching materials in this field, *Modern Criminal Procedure (Modern)* and *Basic Criminal Procedure (Basic)*. Both *Modern* and *Basic* also include a goodly number of lower court cases, many of which focus on state law developments, and contain many authors' Notes and Questions and extracts from books, reports, articles, model codes, and proposed standards. By contrast, the present book is limited to the Supreme Court decisions themselves.

We have, of course, relied on and profited by the rich literature in this field in the course of preparing the introductory comments that appear at the outset of each chapter and at the beginning of most sections of each chapter. But this introductory text does not explore any particular issue in depth. Nor is it contentious, as are many of the law review articles extracted in our other books. The brief introductory comments, rather, are designed only to place the selected cases that follow in general historical and doctrinal perspective.

Although the topics covered in *Basic* are treated in considerable depth, the scope of that book is quite limited. *Basic*'s major emphasis is on police practices, e.g., arrest, search and seizure, police interrogation and confessions, and pre-trial identification procedures; no attention is given to the more formal phases of the criminal process. The present volume, on the other hand, not only gives issues involving the police considerable attention but covers a number of other aspects of the criminal process, e.g., criminal discovery, double jeopardy, fair trial/free press, plea bargaining, and the trial. Our "big book," *Modern*, also covers a wide range of topics, but because it explores these topics in much greater depth it is about twice the size of this book. (There is, of course, no law prohibiting an instructor from dipping into *Modern* in order to enrich class discussion of one or more of the issues raised by the materials in this book.)

As is apparent from these comparisons, we envision this collection of leading cases as being used in a course of a distinctly different character than the various possibilities we contemplated with respect to either *Modern* or *Basic*. This book is especially suited to a survey course having as its purpose a critical examination of how the United States Supreme Court has grappled with a range of basic and highly controversial issues that arise at various stages of the criminal process—issues as diverse as when the police should be permitted to "search" or "seize" without prior judicial approval or traditional "probable cause," how far a secret government agent may go in "encouraging" a person to commit a crime or "tricking" him into making an incriminating statement, when a defense lawyer's performance is so "ineffective" as to vitiate a conviction, when a prosecutor must disclose information in his files, and when a defendant must endure a second trial for the same or a related offense.

In *Modern* and *Basic*, our hope and expectation has been that a student working with those materials descry not only the forest (or in the case of *Basic*, at least a good-sized grove), but also the trees. Here, by contrast, the emphasis is decidedly sylvan.

It is possible, of course, to produce a thin volume of teaching materials by collecting snippets of many opinions. This approach has been emphatically rejected. The modest size of this volume has been attained, rather, by the judicious selection of leading cases. Those cases that have been selected are set forth at considerable length.

Moreover, because the use of these materials will mark many students' first real exposure to the U.S. Supreme Court as an institution, we have resisted the temptation to delete, or even to summarize, concurring and dissenting opinions. Instead, we have taken pains to set forth the views of *all* members of the Court at considerable length in such cases as *Leon, Mapp* and *Miranda*.

In the main, we have followed a chronological approach in ordering the cases which appear in this book. Following the introductory materials, which include an overview of the criminal justice system and a general consideration of due process, the criminal justice system is examined from arrest and search and "on the street" questioning all the way through to the decision on guilt and imposition of sentence.

We have occasionally departed from the chronological scheme when it seemed appropriate to do so. For example, the right to counsel, "the most pervasive right" of an accused, is first considered in advance of the confession and lineup chapters so that the Court's reliance on the right to counsel in those contexts may be better understood. (Other aspects of the right to counsel, such as the necessary character and quality of representation at trial and in preparing for trial, are considered later in the book.) So too, post conviction review is considered in the context of the review of particular claims (e.g., lawyer error) rather than in a separate chapter on habeas corpus.

The cases in this book have been edited with the above-stated purposes in mind. We have tried hard—indeed, it would not be an exaggeration to say that we have made heroic efforts—to keep these materials lean and manageable. We have also tried to ensure that within the confines of particular cases the student's attention is focused upon the broader themes and issues.

Case citations and footnotes have been eliminated from the judicial opinions without so specifying. When three asterisks appear, this designates omission of a portion of the opinion deemed inessential to an understanding and appraisal of the issues and holding in that case.

Numbered footnotes are from the original material) are ours. We would call particular attention to th' which contain summaries of Supreme Court decisor cases presented in this book. These footnotes ofter later dealt with a problem alluded to in the comment in the principal case later came to have related issue.

To make our sentence structure as short and direct as po҆ have not used the phrases "he or she" or "his or her." Where we the masculine or feminine pronoun alone, consistent with the traai rules of construction in legal texts, the pronoun should be read to encompa҆ both male and female actors unless the context clearly indicates otherwise.

This volume contains all significant divisions handed down during the 1989–90 Supreme Court term. Citations are to the United States Reports, unless the case had not yet appeared in those reports. In that event, we have referred to the Supreme Court Reporter.

Experience has taught us that there will undoubtedly be some typographical errors in a publication of this length. We would appreciate your calling such errors to our attention, so they can be corrected in the next printing. We would, of course, also appreciate hearing from readers who have criticisms or suggestions regarding the substantive content of the volume.

JEROLD H. ISRAEL
YALE KAMISAR
WAYNE R. LaFAVE

August, 1990

*

# Summary of Contents

# Table of Contents

\*

# Table of Cases

The principal cases are in bold type. Cases cited or discussed in the text are roman type. References are to pages.

xxxiii

# CRIMINAL PROCEDURE
# AND THE CONSTITUTION

\*

# Chapter 1

# AN OVERVIEW OF THE CRIMINAL JUSTICE PROCESS

## SECTION 1.  INTRODUCTION

*The Limits of an Overview.*  This book presents a collection of leading Supreme Court decisions in the field of "constitutional criminal procedure"— that is, decisions dealing with the application of the United States Constitution to what is commonly described as the "criminal justice process."  The criminal justice process consists of that series of procedures through which this country's criminal laws (those laws defining criminal acts and providing for the punishment of offenders) are enforced.  In this chapter, we will present a brief introduction to the most important of those procedures and to the persons responsible for their administration.  Our overview is designed to provide some general background information that should assist in your reading of the collected cases.  In particular, it hopefully will give you some sense of the place of the individual procedure discussed in a particular case as that procedure relates to the overall process.

An overview of a process as complex as the criminal justice process necessarily requires a certain degree of overgeneralization.  There is no single set of criminal justice procedures uniformly used throughout the United States.  Each of the 50 states and the federal government has enacted its own criminal code applicable within the general reach of its laws.[1]  Just as there is diversity among

---

1.  The criminal laws of a state are limited in application to offenses that occurred in their entirety or in part within that state. The federal criminal law, in contrast, has a territorial reach that extends throughout the United States and its territories. However, the federal government, unlike the state governments, cannot declare an action to be criminal simply because it is contrary to the public welfare. The federal government's regulatory authority in the criminal field, as in other fields, is limited to those subjects as to which the federal constitution grants Congress legislative authority, such as interstate and foreign commerce, and the maintenance of national services (e.g., the postal service and the armed forces).

Viewed by reference to their relationship to particular areas of federal authority, federal crimes tend to fall into three categories.

First, there are those crimes that interfere with the performance of basic functions of the federal government (e.g., espionage or bribery of federal officials). A second, closely related group of federal offenses seeks to protect certain private facilities in which the federal government has a special interest as a result of its close regulation or financial involvement (e.g., robbery of federally insured banks). A third category of federal offenses are those based upon Congress' specific regulatory powers, such as its authority over interstate commerce. These include crimes involving the use of the interstate communications facilities, actions of state officials that violate rights guaranteed under the Fourteenth Amendment, and even prostitution when the participants move in interstate commerce.

For those criminal activities relating to unique federal governmental functions (e.g.,

1

those 51 jurisdictions in their definition of crime, there is diversity as well in the processes they use to enforce their criminal laws. Each jurisdiction's procedures must comply with the federal constitution, but those constitutional limitations, as will be seen, allow the individual jurisdictions considerable leeway in shaping many elements of their criminal justice process.

While the diversity among the jurisdictions must be kept in mind, there is sufficient similarity in the basic structure of the process among the different jurisdictions—provided in part by the common heritage of the English common law—to make helpful a description of the process that largely ignores state-by-state variations. Our overview seeks to provide such a description, concentrating on the sequence of procedures commonly applied in most of the 51 jurisdictions. It notes only a few of the many variations, concentrating on those variations that are fundamental and are followed in a substantial group of jurisdictions.

To assist you in following the overview, it should be helpful at the outset if you would carefully examine the chart at page 32. Note that the chart follows the flow of the criminal justice process through a horizontal line which starts at the point of the commission of the crime and continues through to the sentencing of the convicted offender. The thickness of this horizontal line gradually narrows to indicate the decreasing number of cases involved at each succeeding stage of the process. The various lines pointing upward or downward indicate cases leaving the process. The process has a "sieve effect," constantly sifting cases out of the criminal justice system before they complete all of the stages in the process.[2] You also will note that the horizontal line eventually divides into

coining money), federal criminal statutes are the primary (and sometimes exclusive) source of prosecution. For most types of criminal activity, however, even where both federal and state laws apply (as in gambling and narcotics), the vast majority of all prosecutions are brought under state law. Thus, overall, over 95% of all prosecutions for felony offenses are brought under state law, and most of the major industrial states individually have more felony prosecutions each year than does the whole federal government. When consideration is given as well to misdemeanor prosecutions, which outnumber felony prosecutions by a ratio of roughly 9 or 10 to 1, the federal criminal justice process accounts for less than 1% of all criminal prosecutions.

2. Thus, there is a progressive reduction in the volume of cases as one moves from the beginning to the end of the process. More persons are investigated than are arrested, more arrested than charged, more charged than tried, and more tried than convicted. Consider, for example, the following model which approximates the distribution found in several urban communities. Start with 5,000 possible felonies that come to the attention of the police either through citizen complaint or officer observations. Because many of these reported offenses cannot be solved, the police investigation of those crimes is likely to result in the arrest of no more than 1,500 persons. Out of this group of arrestees, approximately 400 will be juveniles, who will be transferred to the juvenile process. After the police and prosecutor have reviewed the case against the

remaining 1100 arrestees, about 350 will be released without any charges being pressed. In an additional 150 cases, the charges will immediately be reduced to misdemeanors. Thus, of 1,500 felony arrestees, only 600 actually will have felony charges filed against them. The 600 felony charges will then be screened at preliminary hearings or grand jury proceedings, and will be subject to challenge by defense motions of various sorts. These procedures are likely to result in the dismissal of roughly 50 cases. Still another 50 cases may be dismissed by the prosecutor as a result of his review of the case once it reaches the trial court. Of the 500 felony cases that are left, approximately 400 will be resolved by guilty pleas. Perhaps half of those pleas will be to misdemeanor charges, and the others will be to the felony charged or to a lesser felony. There remain roughly 100 felony cases that will go to trial. Approximately 70 of the trials will result in convictions, although not necessarily for felonies. In the end, approximately 250 of the original group of arrestees will be convicted on a felony charge (including felonies lesser than that originally charged) and 350 will be convicted of misdemeanors. As many as 300 of the 600 convicted persons will receive a sentence that includes some incarceration, but for most of the 300, incarceration will be limited to a short jail term, typically combined with probation. Approximately 125 of those convicted (all for felonies) will be sentenced to prison terms.

three major prongs. The first division occurs quite early in the process and notes the beginning of the separate treatment of juveniles through the juvenile justice process. The decisions in this book do not deal with that process, which traditionally is separated in goals and procedures from the criminal justice process. Farther along in the flow of the criminal process itself, the horizontal line again divides as felonies and misdemeanors are separated.[3] We will concentrate in our overview primarily on the processing of felony cases since felonies are more serious crimes and require more complex procedures than misdemeanors. Along the way (primarily in footnotes), we will note most of the key distinctions in the processing of misdemeanors.[4] Most of the leading decisions included in this volume deal with felonies.

*Ongoing Procedures.* Both the chart on page 32 and our overview present the various procedures in the process in the chronological order in which they commonly occur. By and large, each procedure constitutes a separate stage in the criminal justice process that follows upon the completion of a prior procedure. There are certain procedures, however, that tend to be ongoing. The investigatory process, for example, starts at an early stage but may continue on through to the time of trial. Similarly, the prosecutor's decision to charge is subject to an ongoing opportunity for review at various points throughout the process. The judge's review of the evidence before the jury is another step that is ongoing as it may be repeated at various points during the trial. Generally, we will discuss these ongoing procedures only at the point at which they first arise and will not consider them again at later points at which they may be repeated. Our discussion of the investigatory process will be split, however, to consider separately pre-arrest and post-arrest investigations, since investigatory procedures may be somewhat different at these two stages of the process.

*Functions of the Process.* Although the interrelationship of the different procedures is suggested by the chronological development of the process, it might be helpful in this connection also to identify several basic functions that will be achieved during the course of the process. Those functions are: (1) determining whether a crime has been committed, (2) detecting the possible offender, (3) apprehending that person, (4) providing for a review of the evidence by the prosecutor to determine whether the case against the alleged offender merits prosecution, (5) providing for a review of the prosecutor's decision by an independent agency, such as a magistrate or grand jury, (6) providing for a determina-

---

**3.** American jurisdictions commonly use either of two different standards in distinguishing between felonies and misdemeanors. Some classify as felonies all crimes punishable by a maximum term of imprisonment of more than one year; crimes punishable by imprisonment for one year or less are then misdemeanors. Other jurisdictions look to the location of the possible imprisonment: if the crime is punishable by incarceration in a penitentiary, it is a felony; if punishable only by a jail term, it is a misdemeanor. As a matter of practice, both dividing lines frequently produce the same result since state correction codes commonly provide for imprisonment in the penitentiary if a sentence exceeds one year and for imprisonment in jail if the sentence is for one year or less.

**4.** Our discussion of the processing of misdemeanors excludes the ordinary traffic violation. In many jurisdictions, all but the most serious traffic violations (e.g., driving while intoxicated) have been decriminalized. Indeed, even in those jurisdictions in which all traffic violations are technically misdemeanors, the less serious traffic offenses often are governed by somewhat different procedures than misdemeanors generally. On the other hand, our discussion does encompass city ordinance violations in those jurisdictions in which ordinances largely duplicate in substance and penalty state misdemeanor provisions governing such offenses as assault, petty theft, etc. Such ordinances commonly are used as a basis for prosecution in lieu of the state misdemeanor provisions (often because the fines collected for ordinance violations go to the city). In jurisdictions of this type, the procedure applied to ordinance violations is basically the same as that applied to misdemeanors punishable by state law.

tion by a jury or judge as to the alleged offender's guilt, and (7) setting the punishment where the alleged offender has been found guilty. Almost every one of the procedures discussed in the next section will contribute to the performance of at least one of these functions. In some instances, the procedure will serve more than one function, and in most instances, performance of the function will be dependent upon the effectiveness of more than one procedure. Variations in the process will often be explained by a jurisdiction's choice between alternative procedures aimed at achieving the same basic function.

## SECTION 2.  THE PROCESSING OF A FELONY CASE—THE STEPS IN THE PROCESS

1. *Commission of the Crime.*  Note that the flow line in our chart has its greatest thickness at the first stage, the commission of crime, and then narrows sharply at the next stage, the investigation of crime.  Many crimes are never reported to the police, and thus there are far fewer crimes investigated than committed.[5]  Where a possible crime comes to the attention of the police, that usually occurs, as the chart indicates, after the crime has been completed.  In a limited number of situations, however, police may initiate an investigation of a crime even before it is completed.  Thus, in the investigation of crimes between willing participants—so called "victimless crimes," such as gambling or narcotics distribution—police often use undercover agents and other investigative techniques aimed more at trapping potential offenders as they move into the criminal activity than the investigation of completed crimes.

2. *Pre-arrest Investigation.*  Once the police became aware of the possible commission of a crime, they then must determine (1) whether the crime actually was committed and (2) if it was committed, whether there is sufficient information pointing to the guilt of a particular person to justify arresting that person.  Pre-arrest investigation is aimed primarily at making these determinations.  The degree of investigation needed will, of course, vary with the circumstances.  Where a police officer observes a crime being committed in his presence, that officer usually can make an arrest "on the spot."  In such a situation, the pre-arrest investigation will have consisted of no more than the officer's initial observation.  Where the officer observes suspicious activity, but is uncertain as to exactly what has occurred, he may stop the suspect on the street and briefly question him before deciding whether to make an arrest.  In this type of case, the pre-arrest investigation will have consisted of the officer's observations, some interrogation (i.e., questioning), and possibly a frisk (i.e., a "pat-down") to ensure that the suspect is not carrying a weapon.

Where the officer does not observe the commission of the crime, the pre-arrest investigation often is more complex.  Initially, the officer will obtain a statement from the person who reports the crime and from any bystanders.[6]

**5.**  A typical breakdown of reported crimes would be 60% property offenses (e.g., theft, burglary), 10% assaults of various types, 10% offenses relating to alcohol and drugs, and the remaining 20% distributed among a variety of crimes, with less than 5% involving the most serious violent crimes (robbery, rape, and murder).  Because some crimes are far less likely to be reported than others, the mix of crimes actually committed is somewhat different.  Crimes between willing participants, for example, are rarely reported unless observed by the officer.  On the other side, thefts of

motor vehicles are almost always reported as such a report is needed to collect insurance.

**6.**  For those offenses not likely to be observed by the police officer or to involve an offender known to the victim, there tends to be a much lower likelihood of a successful investigation that results in a "clearance," even as measured simply by an arrest (i.e., without regard to whether there eventually is a conviction).  Thus, burglary, a crime that typically falls in this category, commonly has a clearance rate within the range of 10–20%

Any physical evidence left at the scene of the crime may be removed and examined, sometimes by the police laboratory. Potential suspects may be visited at their homes or stopped on the street and questioned. Here too, where the crime being investigated involved violence, the officer may frisk the suspect to ensure that he is not carrying a weapon. If a suspect makes a statement, it may be verified through interviews with other persons, such as employers or friends. If the officer has reason to believe that evidence of the crime can be found in a particular location (e.g., a car or a home), a search of that location may be conducted. This usually will be done pursuant to a "search warrant" (a court order authorizing the search) where the place searched is a home, but it will be done without a warrant when the place searched is a car. In unusual cases, the police may place a suspect under surveillance or utilize the services of an undercover agent to obtain information from the unwitting suspect. In other cases, a wiretap or other form of electronic surveillance will be instituted pursuant to a court order. In still others, the prosecutor may be asked to obtain a court order requiring a suspect to produce for examination certain documents or records.[7]

Among the various pre-arrest investigatory procedures discussed above, the most common procedures are the personal observation by the officer, the questioning of witnesses, and the questioning of the suspect. Even in serious felony cases, procedures such as the search of the suspect's home, wiretapping, surveillance, and scientific examination of evidence are used in only a small percentage of investigations.

3. *The Arrest.* The term "arrest" has various definitions, and discussions of arrest practices often are confused because of the failure of the discussants to agree on the meaning of that term. For the purpose of this overview, we will use a common statutory definition of "arrest"—the taking of a person into custody for the purpose of charging him with a crime. This ordinarily involves the officer's exercise of physical control over the suspect for the purpose of first transporting him to a police facility and then requesting that felony charges be filed against him.[8] To make an arrest the officer must have reasonable grounds ("probable cause") to believe that a crime was committed and that the person to be arrested was the offender.

Where there is no immediate need to arrest a suspect, an officer may first seek a court order, commonly called an arrest warrant, which authorizes the officer to make the arrest. The arrest warrant is issued by a magistrate upon a finding of probable cause and offers the advantage of prior judicial approval of the arrest. In the vast majority of felony cases, however, the officer will act without a warrant and will make the arrest as soon as he is convinced that he has sufficient grounds to lawfully do so. The arrest made without a court order commonly is described as a "warrantless" arrest.

---

(as opposed to over 60% for aggravated assault).

7. In a small percentage of cases, the pre-arrest investigation will be conducted primarily by the prosecuting attorney rather than the police. The prosecuting attorney's primary means of investigation is the grand jury. While the most noted function of the grand jury is to review the sufficiency of the evidence supporting a criminal charge (see step 11), the grand jury also has authority to obtain information concerning possible criminal activities. The grand jury investigation,

which operates through the use of the subpoena (a court order issued on behalf of the grand jury), is described in Chapter 8.

8. In the case of a misdemeanor, the arrested person may not be transported to the police facility, but instead may simply be released on the street after the officer has given him a citation (similar to a traffic ticket). The citation will direct the individual to appear in court on a certain day to answer charges specified in the citation. His failure to do so will result in a court order directing his arrest (a "bench warrant").

Typically, contemporaneously with the arrest, the officer will search the arrestee and remove any weapons, contraband, or evidence of the crime found on his person. If the person is arrested in a car or was carrying packages, the passenger compartment of the car and those packages readily opened may be searched for the same purposes.

After being taken into custody, the arrestee will be transported to a police precinct station, a centrally located jail, or some similar police facility. If the officer should determine, however, that the arrestee is young enough to be a juvenile under state law, he will take the arrestee directly to a juvenile facility. The description of the process from this point on assumes that the arrestee is not a juvenile.

4. *Booking.* Once the arrestee arrives at the police facility, he will be "booked." Booking is the clerical process by which an administrative record is made of the arrest. The arrestee's name, time of arrival, and the offense involved are listed on the police "blotter" or "log" as an official record of the arrest. As part of the booking process, the arrestee ordinarily will be photographed and his fingerprints will be taken.

While at the police facility, the arrestee typically will be given the right to make a telephone call and will be informed of the charge on which he has been booked. He then will be placed in a "holding" unit, usually a cell in the station or a nearby jail, where he will await his presentation before a magistrate. Ordinarily, the arrestee will be searched before being placed in this facility, and that search will be more thorough than the search conducted by the officer contemporaneously with the arrest. This second search is designed primarily to make an inventory of the individual's personal belongings and to prevent the introduction of contraband into the holding unit.

5. *Post-arrest Investigation.* Whether there will be significant post-arrest investigation will vary with the fact situation. In some cases, such as where the arrestee has been caught "red-handed," there will be little post-arrest investigation. In other situations, the post-arrest investigation will involve many of the same kinds of investigative activities as could have been performed before the arrest, such as witness interviews, search of the suspect's home, viewing the scene of the crime, etc. Where the officer has sufficient grounds to justify an arrest without the evidence that might be obtained through such investigative techniques, he may use those techniques at his convenience, either before or after the arrest.

Post-arrest investigation does offer one investigative source that ordinarily is not available prior to the arrest—the person of the arrestee (who is now in custody). Thus the arrestee may be placed in a lineup where he can be viewed by witnesses, or he may be required to provide handwriting or voice samples. The arrestee also may be interrogated after having been warned of his rights. Although we do not have precise data on the extent of these post-arrest procedures, the best available estimates indicate that they are not utilized for the vast majority of arrestees.

6. *The Decision to Charge.* Sometime between the booking of the arrestee and his presentation before a magistrate (see step 9), there will be a review of the decision to press charges, first by the police and then by the prosecutor.[9] The review procedure varies considerably from jurisdiction to jurisdiction, both as to

---

**9.** In those cases where the arrest is made pursuant to an arrest warrant, the available evidence often will be reviewed prior to obtaining the warrant and a subsequent review of the decision to charge will be unnecessary. We assume from this point on that the arrest in the case we are following was made without a warrant.

the participants involved and the standards they apply. Ordinarily, it starts with an arrest report that will be filled out by the arresting officer. The officer's report will contain a narrative account of the crime and the circumstances of the arrest. It commonly will include a brief description of all evidence then available (e.g., witnesses, seized contraband). A higher ranking officer, such as a "desk sergeant" or precinct duty officer, then will review the report to decide whether the case should be approved for prosecution. In many instances, this officer may reduce a recommended felony charge to a misdemeanor charge or direct that the arrestee be released. The arrestee's release may be ordered because the evidence is insufficient to support a criminal charge or because the police department has a policy against pressing charges under the special circumstances of the case (e.g., an intrafamily assault). When the arrestee is released because the available evidence is insufficient, there may be a follow-up investigation and the individual may later be rearrested.

Assuming that the higher ranking officer has approved the charge, the next step in the review process is the presentation of the case to the prosecutor's office. In some jurisdictions, the review of the case by a prosecuting attorney commonly does not occur until sometime after the arrestee's initial appearance before a magistrate (see step 9). In such jurisdictions, the complaint (see step 7) will be prepared and filed by the police without the prior approval of the prosecutor. In most jurisdictions, however, the prosecutor will review the case before the arrestee's initial appearance, and a complaint will be filed only upon review (and approval) of the prosecutor. The information considered by the prosecuting attorney in reviewing the proposed charge will vary according to local practice. In some communities, the prosecutor's review ordinarily is limited to the police report. In others, the prosecuting attorney also will interview the arresting officer, the victim, or some other eyewitness.[10]

The prosecuting attorney must decide whether the arrestee should be charged and, if so, whether the charge should be that recommended by the police. Of course, the prosecutor must consider the strength of the evidence. If it is not sufficient to support the proposed charge, then the arrestee must be released or, if the evidence does support a lesser charge, the charge must be reduced. The prosecutor also may consider various other factors, besides the weight of the evidence, in determining whether to proceed. Thus, consideration will be given to the amount of harm caused by the crime, the victim's attitude (and willingness to testify), the criminal record of the arrestee, and the adequacy of any alternative remedies that may be utilized without invoking the criminal process. Such factors are weighed because the prosecutor has responsibilities beyond avoiding the prosecution of the innocent. Even though the individual clearly is guilty and that guilt can be proven, the prosecuting attorney may decide that the prosecution recommended by the police would not serve the ends of justice or would be inappropriate considering limited prosecutorial resources.[11]

10. Though we can hardly characterize any particular pre-charge screening program as typical of most jurisdictions, a fairly common pattern is found as to the end result of the overall governmental screening conducted throughout the process (that is the combination of pre-charge police and prosecutor screening and post-charge prosecutorial screening, carried on up to the point of trial). Quite commonly, the cases against a substantial percentage of all felony arrestees (e.g., 30–50%) will be dropped as a result of such screening. Thus, far more felony arrests do not reach the point of conviction because of police and prosecutor screening than because of the combination of all other screens, i.e., the rejection of charges by independent screening agencies (the grand jury or the magistrate), successful pretrial legal challenges, or acquittals at trial.

11. Many prosecutors have developed pre-charge "diversion programs" that provide a formal structure for the prosecutor's refusal to charge notwithstanding sufficient evidence. Under these programs, certain types of

7. *Filing the Complaint.* Assuming the prosecutor decides to proceed, the next step is the formal initiation of criminal prosecution through the filing of a "charging" document before a court. A charging document accuses the arrestee of committing a crime, and its filing officially makes him a "defendant" in a criminal case. The most common titles for the charging documents used in the criminal law are the "complaint," the "information" and the "indictment." Although they differ in other respects, each of these documents is similar in its basic statement of the charge.

In most felony cases, the initial charging document is the complaint, which will be filed with the magistrates court prior to the arrested person's initial appearance (see step 9).[12] At later stages in the process, an indictment or information will replace the complaint as the charging document.[13] The complaint ordinarily will set forth facts alleging that the accused, at a particular time and place, committed specified acts that constitute a violation of a particular criminal statute. The complaint must be signed by a "complainant," a person who swears under oath that he believes the facts alleged in the complaint to be true. Ordinarily, the complainant will be either the victim of the crime or the investigating officer. The prosecuting attorney, in the course of reviewing the decision to charge, will make certain that the complaint is properly prepared. Once the complaint is completed and approved, it is filed with the local magistrates court, before which the arrestee will soon be presented.

8. *Magistrate Review of the Complaint.* Although the complaint is filed with the magistrates court, that court does not have authority to hold a trial in a felony case. Its function is only to handle several preliminary tasks before transferring the felony case to a trial court of general jurisdiction. The first of these tasks is to determine whether there is a sufficient legal basis to support the arrest under which the defendant is being held in custody. The magistrate is, in effect, reviewing the judgment of the police and prosecutor that the accused could properly be arrested and charged with the offense alleged in the complaint. This determination, usually made before the defendant's first appearance, is an *ex parte* determination (that is, a determination made on the presentation of the prosecution alone, without the participation of the defense). The magistrate's decision ordinarily is based on facts presented in either the complaint itself, a supporting affidavit, or a brief oral statement given by the victim or arresting officer. To sustain the arrest, the magistrate need only find that the officer had probable cause to believe that the arrestee committed the crime charged. However, if the magistrate finds that the facts alleged do not establish probable cause, he must dismiss the complaint and the arrestee must be released.

9. *The First Appearance.* After the complaint has been filed and affirmatively reviewed, the defendant is taken from the holding facility and presented before the magistrate. This first appearance of the defendant in court is the next major step in the criminal justice process. It usually is described simply as

charges (usually misdemeanors) will not be prosecuted if the arrestee agrees to comply with specified "rehabilitative conditions" (e.g., making restitution to the victim, maintaining regular employment, etc.). Other prosecutors prefer not to tie the decision to charge to such conditions. They will bring charges and then seek to have the rehabilitative conditions imposed as conditions of probation following conviction.

12. The magistrates court is described at page 27 infra.

13. In misdemeanor cases which are tried before the magistrate, the complaint ordinarily is the only charging instrument used in the case. The substitution of an indictment or information for the complaint only occurs when a case is taken before the general trial court, as in a felony case (see step 12).

the "first appearance," but some jurisdictions refer to it as the "initial present-ment" or the "arraignment on the complaint (or arrest warrant)." [14]

All jurisdictions have a requirement that an arrested person be presented before the magistrate without unnecessary delay. In most communities, the time consumed in booking, transportation, police and prosecutor review of the decision to charge, preparation of the complaint, and performing other prelimi-nary matters will delay the first appearance for several hours. Indeed, in many places, unless the individual is arrested in the early morning hours, his case will not be ready for presentation to the magistrate until after the courts have closed for that day. If the community does not have a "night court," the arrested person will have to spend the night in jail before being presented the next morning. Moreover, if arrested on a Friday afternoon, he may spend three nights in jail, awaiting a first appearance on Monday morning, unless the magistrates court has a special weekend session.[15]

The first appearance itself often is quite brief. Initially, the magistrate will make certain that the person before him is, in fact, the person whose name is stated in the complaint as the defendant. The magistrate then will inform the defendant of the charge set forth in the complaint. The magistrate also will inform the defendant of various rights that he has under the law. The scope of this advice varies from state to state. Ordinarily, the magistrate will at least inform the defendant of his right to remain silent and warn him that anything he says in court or to the police may be used against him at trial.

The defendant also will be told that he has a right to be assisted by counsel and that counsel will be appointed at the expense of the state if he is indigent (i.e., he cannot afford to hire an attorney).[16] Although the timing varies, most jurisdictions at least initiate the appointment process at the first appearance. The magistrate will determine if the defendant is financially eligible and desires the assistance of appointed counsel. The magistrate then will either make the appointment himself or notify the judge in charge of making such appointments. In many communities, lawyers employed by the office of the public defender will automatically represent almost all indigent defendants. They often begin that representation shortly after the indigent is arrested and thus are present when he appears before the magistrate. In those jurisdictions where the appointed counsel is selected from the "private bar" (i.e., those lawyers who are self-employed), the appointment process often is not completed until after the first appearance. The appointed lawyer will be available to the defendant, however, before the next stage in the process, the preliminary hearing on the complaint (see step 10).

Perhaps the most important function performed by the magistrate at the first appearance is the "setting of bail",—that is, the determination of those conditions that the defendant will have to meet to gain his release from custody pending his trial. The term "bail" referred originally to cash or other property that a defendant had to deposit with the court to obtain his release from custody. The property served as a guarantee that the defendant would appear at trial. If

---

**14.** This is to be distinguished from the later "arraignment" at the trial court stage (see step 13), where the defendant must enter a plea to the felony charge.

**15.** For misdemeanors, the arrestee may be able to obtain his release on "stationhouse" bail, i.e., by posting cash as a security deposit with the police and promising to appear be-fore the magistrate on a specific date.

**16.** Appointed counsel will not necessarily be provided in misdemeanor cases, as jurisdic-tions are not constitutionally required to ap-point counsel to assist indigent defendants where conviction for a misdemeanor does not result in incarceration (see Chapter 5).

he failed to do so (i.e., "skipped bail"), his property would be forfeited to the state. The most common form of bail gradually became the secured bond (the "bailbond") purchased from a professional bondsman, rather than the cash deposit. Today, however, bail also can take several other forms, as described in the introduction to Chapter Nine. In many situations, no posting of cash or a bailbond will be required. The individual will be released upon his own recognizance (i.e., a personal promise to appear) or a condition that he comply with certain requirements (e.g., stay in the community). Under special circumstances, the law of the particular jurisdiction may even allow the magistrate to simply refuse to set bail because of the likelihood of the accused's flight or danger to the community if released. Although bail setting practices vary widely, in a fairly typical jurisdiction, roughly 10–20% of all felony defendants will not gain their pretrial release either because the magistrate found the circumstances to justify a refusal to set bail or because the defendant was unable to post a bailbond or meet other conditions required by the magistrate.

Other aspects of the first appearance are likely to depend upon whether the defendant is charged with a felony or misdemeanor. In the felony case, the magistrate will advise the defendant of the next step in the process, the preliminary hearing, and will set a date for that hearing unless the defendant desires to waive it. If the defendant is charged with a misdemeanor, he will not be entitled to a preliminary hearing (or a subsequent grand jury review). The misdemeanor charge is triable to the magistrate,[17] and the magistrate therefore can proceed with a misdemeanor case in the same fashion as would a general trial court receiving a felony case. For the misdemeanor, the first appearance becomes an arraignment on the complaint, equivalent to the arraignment on the information or indictment in a felony case (see step 12).

10. *Preliminary Hearing.* The next step in the processing of a felony case often is the preliminary hearing. The preliminary hearing is one of three independent "screening" processes that may be available in a felony case. Each involves a review of the prosecution's evidence to safeguard against unwarranted prosecutions. They are described as "screening" procedures because they operate like a sieve to "screenout" those prosecutions that lack substantial evidentiary support. The first of these screens is the magistrate's ex parte review of the arrest, described previously in step 8. The second screening is the preliminary hearing, which also is conducted by the magistrate, and the third is the grand jury's review of the evidence (see step 11). The availability of the preliminary hearing and of grand jury review varies from state to state. Only about twenty states regularly provide grand jury review. Many more states regularly provide a preliminary hearing. Almost all states provide one or the other and some utilize both.

The magistrate's task at the preliminary hearing is to determine whether there is sufficient evidence supporting the charge. The standard for testing the sufficiency of the evidence is one of probable cause, considerably less than the burden the prosecution must bear in establishing guilt at trial. If probable cause is found, the case is "boundover" (i.e., sent forward) either to the grand jury or directly to the trial court, depending on whether the state also requires grand jury review. If the evidence is found insufficient, the charges are dismissed and the defendant is released from jail or from any bail restrictions.

---

**17.** In some jurisdictions, the magistrate's trial jurisdiction does not extend to all misdemeanors, but only those punishable by no more than a certain term of imprisonment. See p. 27 infra. For the sake of brevity, our discussion will assume a dividing line between the trial authority of the magistrates court and the general trial court that coincides with the division between misdemeanors and felonies.

The magistrate can also reduce the charge where the evidence is found sufficient only to support a lesser charge. If the charge is reduced to a misdemeanor, it will then be set for later trial before the magistrates court itself.

Unlike the magistrate's initial screening of the complaint prior to the first appearance, the preliminary hearing is an "adversary proceeding"—that is, both sides are represented. The defendant is there with counsel and is entitled to challenge the prosecution's evidence and introduce his own evidence. As a result, the preliminary hearing sometimes resembles a mini-trial. (It is at the preliminary hearing, not the trial, that television's Perry Mason wins all of his cases). The prosecutor ordinarily will rely on live witnesses, rather than affidavits, in presenting the state's evidence. Those witnesses are then subject to cross-examination by the defense counsel, and the defense may also introduce its own witnesses.

11. *Grand Jury Review.* The function of the grand jury, like that of the preliminary hearing, is to screen out those cases in which there is insufficient evidence to continue the prosecution. The standard of proof applied by the grand jury is very much like the probable cause standard applied at the preliminary hearing, but the two screening procedures are quite different in other respects. The grand jury is composed of a group of private citizens (from 16 to 23 in the federal system), who are selected to review cases for a term of one to several months. Unlike the magistrate at the preliminary hearing, which is a public proceeding, the grand jury hears evidence in secret. Moreover, the evidence it hears is only that presented by the prosecutor. The defendant is not present and the defense has no opportunity to present evidence or cross-examine the prosecution's witnesses. After the grand jury has heard the prosecutor's evidence, it receives from the prosecutor a proposed "indictment." The indictment is the document which will replace the complaint at the trial level as the formal charging document in the case (see step 12). The grand jury votes on the proposed indictment, with the majority prevailing. If the majority concludes that there is sufficient evidence for the prosecution to proceed, the indictment is approved by the grand jury as a "true bill." If the grand jury majority concludes that the prosecution should not proceed, then the complaint must be dismissed and the defendant released from jail or from any bail restrictions.

12. *Filing of the Indictment or Information.* Assuming that the case has survived the screening of the preliminary hearing or the grand jury (or both, in some jurisdictions), it is now ready for presentation before the trial court. The next step is the filing of a new charging document with that court. If the case was reviewed and approved by the grand jury, that document will be the indictment noted previously. In states where grand jury review is not required and the case moves directly from the preliminary hearing to the trial court, the charging document is signed by the prosecutor alone. It is then referred to as an "information." The information or indictment will be similar in substance to the complaint. It will set forth the time, date, and place of the alleged criminal act as well as the nature of the act. This charging document will not be signed by the complainant, but by the prosecutor (information) or the prosecutor and the grand jury foreman (indictment). Ordinarily the offense alleged will be the same as that alleged in the complaint, but sometimes the precise charge will have been changed as a result of evidence brought out at the preliminary hearing or the grand jury review.

13. *Arraignment on the Information or Indictment.* Shortly after the information or indictment is filed with the trial court, the defendant is "arraigned" before that court. The arraignment is a brief process designed to serve

two purposes: (1) to inform the defendant of the specific charge against him, and (2) to permit him to answer that charge by pleading not guilty, guilty, or *nolo contendere* (no-contest). At the arraignment the court will first read the information or indictment to the defendant and then ask him how he pleads. The defendant, ordinarily attended by his counsel, will then enter his plea. If defendant pleads not guilty, the case is set for trial. If the defendant pleads guilty or no-contest, the case is then set for sentence. The no-contest plea largely has the impact of a guilty plea, but does not require the defendant to admit his guilt.

Although the trial is, in many respects, the capstone of the criminal justice system, most of the cases reaching the trial court will be disposed of by a guilty plea rather than a trial. Many of those guilty pleas are a product of a negotiated agreement between prosecutor and defense under which the defendant receives some concession in exchange for his guilty plea. This process of negotiation is commonly called "plea-bargaining" and the resulting guilty pleas are commonly described as "negotiated pleas." Plea bargaining varies in both form and availability from one community to another. Some prosecutors' offices rarely will offer concessions for a guilty plea; others do so regularly. As discussed in Chapter 14, the exchange for the plea may be a reduction of the charge, the dismissal of possible additional charges, a recommendation as to sentence, or a specific sentence approved by the trial court.

14. *Pre-trial Procedures.* Assuming that the defendant pleads not guilty at the arraignment, there are a series of procedures that may then be utilized prior to the scheduled trial. Perhaps the most significant of these is the process by which each side will learn about the evidence to be presented by the other side (a process commonly described as "discovery"). Another major pretrial procedure is the defendant's presentation of various legal challenges to the prosecution. Most of these challenges are based on alleged violations of state law or the federal constitution. One such challenge may be the claimed denial of a speedy trial through delay in bringing the case to trial. Another pretrial challenge may not seek to bar the entire prosecution, but to bar certain evidence (e.g., a confession) that the prosecution intends to use but the defense believes to be inadmissible. Often, without such evidence, the prosecution's case may be too weak to proceed. The pretrial challenges are presented to the trial judge and are decided after a hearing before that judge.

15. *The Trial.* The trial is a fact-finding process aimed at determining whether the defendant is guilty or innocent of the offense charged. It is an adversary proceeding in which each side produces its evidence and argument. A neutral fact-finder then determines the facts and reaches a conclusion as to guilt or innocence based upon an application of the substantive criminal law to those facts. The defendant is entitled to have a jury sit as that neutral fact-finder, although he ordinarily can waive his right to a jury and have the trial judge sit as the finder of fact. In most states, juries in felony cases are composed of twelve persons.[18]

At the trial, each side has the opportunity to make an opening statement (explaining its case) and a closing statement (reviewing the strength of the evidence it has presented), to present its own witnesses and to cross-examine the

---

**18.** The situation in misdemeanor cases may differ. In some jurisdictions, the defendant does not have a right to a jury trial in minor misdemeanor cases. This is particularly true in those states that utilize magistrate courts that are not of record and provide a trial de novo before a general trial court (see page 27 infra). In those jurisdictions providing for jury trials in magistrates courts, the juries usually are composed of six persons rather than twelve.

opposing witnesses. The evidence introduced at trial must meet legal standards designed in large part to assist the jury in making an accurate factual determination. In particular, hearsay evidence—statements made out of court and introduced to establish the truth of the contents of the statement—may be used only under limited circumstances. A very important exception to the general bar against hearsay allows the prosecution to use incriminating statements made by the defendant, including those given to the police. The defendant may testify at trial, but he also has the right not to do so, with no negative inference to be drawn from the exercise of that right.

After the jury has heard the evidence, the judge will explain to the jury the substantive law governing the crimes charged. The judge also will explain the jury's duty to assess the facts in accordance with the legal standard that permits it to find the defendant guilty only if the prosecution has established that guilt beyond a reasonable doubt. The jury will reach its conclusions through its private deliberations. In most jurisdictions, the jury's final decision of guilty or not-guilty (the jury's "verdict") must be agreed upon by all of the jurors.

A jury that cannot reach a unanimous verdict is known as a "hung jury." Where the jury "hangs," it is dismissed and the case ordinarily is retried before a new jury. In the vast majority of trials, however, the jury will reach a verdict of either guilty or not-guilty. If the jury finds the defendant not-guilty (i.e., "acquits" the defendant), the charges against the defendant are dismissed and he can never again be prosecuted on the same charges. If, on the other hand, the defendant is found guilty, he will then move to the next stage of the criminal justice process, the imposition of sentence. In most jurisdictions at least two thirds of the felony defendants who go to trial will be convicted on at least one of the charges brought against them. The rate of conviction at trial typically is even higher in misdemeanor cases.

16. *Sentencing.* Once guilt is determined, either through a trial or the entry of a guilty plea, the trial judge is obligated to impose a sentence in accordance with the statute under which defendant was convicted. State law often will allow the judge a choice between imposing a sentence of probation or imprisonment. If probation is used, the court must select appropriate standards of conduct (probation "conditions") which the defendant must adhere to while on probation. For some offenses imprisonment will be required, and for others the judge will chose imprisonment over probation. Here, if the jurisdiction uses what is described "indeterminate sentencing," the judge ordinarily will have considerable discretion in setting the sentence within a wide range allowed by law. The judge sets a maximum and minimum sentence and the parole board determines the actual length of the sentence within those limits. In some jurisdictions, specific guidelines direct the judge's discretion in setting maximum and minimum sentences. Where the state uses what is described as presumptive-determinative sentencing, the judge is given less discretion. The judge sets a single fixed term of imprisonment which must fall within a narrow range set by the legislature for the particular crime, with the judge directed to look to specified aggravating or mitigating circumstances to either add to or deduct from the middle of the range set by the legislature.[19]

The procedure followed in imposing felony sentences will vary from state to state, but certain basic features are quite common. Ordinarily, felony sentenc-

---

**19.** In misdemeanor cases, the magistrate ordinarily is given discretion to impose a flat sentence of imprisonment not to exceed a specified maximum of a certain number of days or months in jail. The judge is likely to impose that sentence immediately upon a finding of guilt, although the defense will be given an opportunity to present any information it views as relevant to sentencing.

ing will not be undertaken immediately upon a finding of guilt, but will be delayed for a week or more to permit the collection of information relevant to determining the proper sentence. That information ordinarily will be brought together in a presentence report prepared by a probation officer. The prosecution and the defense also may call to the court's attention any information that it views as relevant to sentencing. There will not be a trial-type hearing, however. Witnesses will not be called, and the judge may consider information that would not be admissible at trial.[20]

17. *Appeals.* Following the imposition of sentence, defendant may appeal his conviction.[21] In most jurisdictions, defendant is given an automatic right to have his conviction reviewed by an appellate court. The function of the appellate court is to provide a higher court review of the legal rulings made by the trial court. If the appellate court finds no substantial legal error in the trial court proceedings, the conviction will be affirmed. For most types of error (but not for certain constitutional violations), the appellate court may find that, though the trial court erred, the error was so unlikely to have affected the outcome of the case that the error may be deemed "harmless" (i.e., not substantial). If the appellate court finds a substantial legal error was committed, the conviction will be reversed. Subsequent proceedings will then depend upon the basis for the reversal. If the appellate court relied on a ground establishing a total lack of authority to convict (e.g., no crime was committed), a new trial will not be permitted. On the other hand, if the reversal was based on an error that could be avoided in a new trial (e.g., an improper restriction of cross-examination), a new trial will be permitted.

18. *Collateral Challenges to the Conviction.* If the defendant's appeal is unsuccessful, there may be a remaining avenue for challenging his conviction. In order to ensure full consideration of possible fundamental defects in the process, the federal government and many states have provided systems for a collateral challenge to a conviction. The challenge is viewed as "collateral" because it does not flow out of the direct appellate process. Collateral challenges take many forms. The most common (and most famous) is the writ of habeas corpus, a directive of the court (to the jailer) to bring the prisoner forward so it can consider the legality of his continued detention. Collateral challenges may present only the most basic legal errors (e.g., certain constitutional defects).[22] To ensure enforcement of federal constitutional limitations on state procedure, Congress has provided since shortly after the Civil War a federal writ of habeas corpus through which state prisoners may seek relief in the federal courts.

19. *Administering the Sentence.* The sentence imposed by the trial court ordinarily must be administered (assuming that the defendant's conviction is not reversed on appeal or collateral attack). If the defendant is placed on probation, he will be subject to certain conditions that must be enforced. If sentenced to imprisonment, his incarceration must be managed, and if subsequently released on parole, supervision of that status is required. Although some commentators view the administration of the sentence as part of the criminal justice process, we have not treated it as such. Sentence administration commonly is governed by a separate body of laws and is primarily the responsibility of a separate group

**20.** The procedure for the death penalty is quite different, as discussed in Chapter 20.

**21.** As to the prosecution's more limited right of appeal, see page 29 infra and Chapter 19, § 3.

**22.** All states also have separate postconviction procedures for presenting newly discovered evidence, but relief will not be provided unless it is quite clear that, if the new evidence had been presented at trial, defendant would have been acquitted.

of officials working in the field of corrections (primarily probation officers, prison officials, and parole officers).

It should be noted, however, that there are instances in which the police, prosecutors, and courts may be involved in the administration of corrections. A probationer or parolee who violates a condition of probation or parole is subject to arrest and the subsequent initiation of a proceeding to revoke his probation or parole. Ordinarily, these matters are left to the discretion of the probation or parole officer, but the police or prosecutor may also be involved, particularly where the action that violates probation or parole is itself a crime. The probation revocation hearing itself is commonly conducted by the trial court. Parole revocation, in contrast, ordinarily is decided by the parole board, but the board's decision to revoke may then be challenged in the courts. So too, incarceration practices may be challenged in the courts on the ground that they violate state law or the constitutional prohibition against cruel and unusual punishment. Not surprisingly, there are many leading Supreme Court decisions dealing with various aspects of sentence administration, but because our concern is with the criminal justice process itself, we have not included any of those decisions in this volume.

## SECTION 3. THE PARTICIPANTS IN THE ADMINISTRATION OF THE PROCESS

Throughout the Supreme Court opinions reprinted in this volume you will find references of a generic nature to "police," "prosecutors," "defense counsel" and "judges." These are the groups primarily responsible for the administration of the criminal justice process, and many of the Supreme Court opinions in this volume will be dealing with the question of whether to impose certain obligations or restrictions on persons in these positions. In this section, we will briefly introduce some of the more significant aspects of the institutional settings within which these persons perform their respective roles. As will be seen, there are certain institutional factors that extend across the board to all persons occupying the particular position, but there is also variety in the institutional settings which can lead one to distinguish between different types of police, prosecutors, defense counsel, and judges.[23]

## POLICE AGENCIES

*Fragmentation.* The police agencies constitute the largest of the four major groups involved in the administration of the criminal justice system. They also have the greatest volume of work, the most diverse range of functions, and the most complex organizational structure. The key element of that structure is the fragmentation of police authority among a large number of separate units of government. Over 15,000 different governmental agencies in the United States can be classified as "police" agencies in that (1) they have been given primary responsibility for the enforcement of one or more criminal statutes, and (2) at least some of their employees have been given the special enforcement authority (e.g., special arrest powers) that distinguishes the police officer from the private citizen. Most of these 15,000 governmental agencies are units of local govern-

---

**23.** Of course, there is even more variety within each group because of differences among individuals. Since there is considerable discretion involved in the exercise of each of these roles, the values of the particular individual will also contribute significantly to the shaping of the individual's performance in his or her position.

ment (counties, cities, townships), but close to a thousand are part of a state government and about fifty are part of the federal government.

Most of the agencies at the state and federal levels are "specialized" police agencies; they have authority to enforce only a limited group of criminal laws (as in the case of state conservation officers) or to deal with offenses committed within a special geographic enclave (as in the case of the National Park Rangers). However, the vast majority of all police agencies, including almost all of those that are part of local governments, are "general" police agencies. Such agencies have authority to enforce the total range of criminal laws throughout the geographical limits of their particular unit of government.

At the federal level, the primary general police agency is the Federal Bureau of Investigation.[24] At the state level, the key general agency is the state police (in those jurisdictions in which the responsibility of the state police extends beyond traffic control). But by far the most significant general agencies are those found at the local level. In 1986, there were roughly 12,000 such agencies, employing roughly 475,000 sworn officers (roughly 2.1 per 100,000 inhabitants).

At the county level, the primary local police agency is the sheriff's department. While sheriff's departments in some states are limited to administering the county jail and serving process, most states grant those departments full law enforcement responsibilities. To avoid overlap, sheriff's deputies commonly concentrate their efforts in those communities that lack their own police departments (usually villages and sometimes townships). Far out-numbering the sheriff's department are the local police agencies found at the city and township level. Over 90% of all municipalities with a population of 2,500 or more have their own police force. As might be expected, most of those police agencies have small staffs. Close to two-thirds have less than 20 sworn officers, and over one-third employ less than 5 officers. Standing in sharp contrast to the typical small municipal department are the roughly 100 local departments employing more than 300 sworn officers, with the largest, the New York City police department, having over 25,000 officers.

The fragmentation of police agencies means that in any particular community more than one agency will have the authority to enforce at least some criminal laws. Indeed, in any single metropolitan area, several dozen different police agencies are likely to be actively exercising law enforcement authority. In the tri-county area of metropolitan Detroit, for example, over 125 police agencies are separately engaged in the investigation of crime. Initially, over a dozen federal agencies have agents assigned to the area. The state adds several agencies, including the state police. Each of the three counties contributes its sheriff's department. Finally, over 100 cities and townships provide their own police departments.

The wide distribution of police authority in the United States stands in sharp contrast to the national police force found in many countries. In this

---

**24.** Although considered a general agency because its enforcement responsibilities extend to almost all major areas of federal criminal law, the F.B.I. is quite unlike any local or state general police agency. With over 8,500 agents, it is larger than any other police agency except for the police departments of New York and Chicago. It insists upon educational prerequisites for its agents (generally a law degree or a bachelor's degree with expertise in accounting or other specialized field) that go beyond those found in any local or state agency. The mix of the crimes it investigates is substantially different from those found in any other jurisdiction, with a much smaller portion of typical "street crimes" and a much higher portion of white collar offenses. Finally, and most significantly, the F.B.I. does not bear the general peacekeeping, traffic control, and social service functions that occupy so much of the effort of general police agencies at the state and local levels.

country, such a centralized police force would be viewed with deep suspicion, for fear that it could be misused by any leader seeking an authoritarian regime. Just as our political philosophy looks to federalism as a means of protecting individual liberty, it also looks to the decentralization of police authority as a safeguard against the subversion of democracy. Quite obviously, however, the dangers thought to inhere in a centralized police force could be avoided without the extreme diffusion of police authority that we have in this country. That aspect of the fragmentation of police authority reflects the additional goal of maintaining local community control over the administration of the criminal law. Each community may exercise its own influence in the shaping of the police agency predominantly responsible for law enforcement in that community.

Although it has its benefits, the fragmentation of police agencies also has its law enforcement costs. The proliferation of agencies can result in considerable duplication of effort, a rivalry between departments that is not always healthy, and even spillover tactics by which an agency in one community tends to shift certain policing problems to agencies in neighboring communities. As criminal enterprises often extend beyond community borders, an effective law enforcement response requires a degree of coordination among different agencies that extensive fragmentation often makes difficult to arrange. Fragmentation necessarily also produces less uniformity and more inequality in police enforcement. This is particularly true for those aspects of police administration in which discretion plays a large role (e.g., the treatment of intrafamily assaults), but it also arises where the law itself is ambiguous and therefore subject to varying interpretation by different departments. Attempts to impose minimal standards of police administration (as in many of the Supreme Court rulings presented in this book) also face obstacles due to fragmentation, as there is no single executive authority in the police world that can assume responsibility for implementing those standards.

Perhaps the most significant cost of fragmentation stems from the large number of police agencies thought to be too small to be fully effective in the investigation of crime. Departments without at least 50 sworn officers generally are too small to create the specialized units that may be more effective in dealing with particular types of crimes (e.g., tactical patrol units, vice squads, robbery investigative teams) or to make use of sophisticated criminal investigative techniques drawing on the use of laboratories and computers. Proponents of small departments maintain, however, that those departments have a closer relationship to the community that more than offsets such disadvantages, as the most critical factor in criminal investigation will often be the cooperation of victims, witnesses, and other citizens who have relevant information. They also note that small departments can turn to the state police for assistance on such matters as laboratory analysis of physical evidence, and can develop joint investigative task forces with neighboring communities to deal with offenses such as narcotics distribution.[25]

*Multiple Functions.* Although we refer to the police as "law enforcement" officers, the enforcement of the criminal law (i.e., the investigation of crime and the apprehension of criminals) is only one of several tasks allocated to a local

---

**25.** Another obstacle faced by small departments—and one not readily remedied by efforts at coordination and cooperation—is the high employee turnover rate. Whereas the rate of voluntary resignations is quite low for larger departments (particularly after officers have gone beyond the probationary stage and their retirement benefits are building), the rate of annual voluntary resignation in departments of 25 officers or less can readily be as high as 25%. Police departments almost invariably recruit at the lowest rank and promote from within the system, and smaller departments simply offer less room for promotion (as well as, in many cases, less competitive salaries).

police department.  The professional roles of that department also include the providing of basic social services, the maintenance of order, and the prevention of crime.

In the area of social services, a primary police responsibility is to help people who need emergency assistance, whether that is providing emergency first aid, assisting a person stuck in an elevator, comforting lost children, or rescuing a cat stuck in a tree.  Typically, over 50% of the telephone calls to the police requesting assistance will involve such social service functions, as compared to the less than 20% relating to the reported commission of a crime.  Among the local department's order maintenance functions are traffic control, crowd control, resolving domestic and streetcorner disputes, and moving panhandlers or prostitutes from the streets.  While the officers here often are responding to activities that constitute minor crimes, the focus of order maintenance is on reaching a solution that preserves the public peace rather than the enforcement of the law.  The appropriate order-maintenance solution may be the making of an arrest, but it quite often will be some less formal action (e.g., merely getting the illegal panhandler to move on).  Finally, even in the area of crime control, the prevention of crime exists alongside the investigation of completed crime.  Indeed, the prevention of crime involves the most time consuming of police activities—the patrol of the community—which ideally provides a police presence that will deter would be criminals and provide assurance to shopkeepers and residents.

The varied responsibilities of the police tend to restrict, in several ways, police effectiveness in investigating serious crime.  First and foremost, the limited resources available to the police must be spread over a broad range of activities, many of which are only remotely related to investigation of felonies and the apprehension of felons.  The traditional image of police work—the image conveyed over the years in countless television dramas, comic strips, and newspaper articles—is that of the officer who outwits, outshoots, and outwrestles a dangerous criminal in the course of investigating a serious crime.  In fact, even in a major metropolitan area (where the rate of serious crime is likely to be highest), roughly half of the officers in the local department probably will not have made a felony arrest during the past year, and the total annual rate of weapon discharges per hundred officers (excluding the shooting range) is likely to have been in the range of 2 to 6.  With their multiple functions, patrol officers, who represent the vast bulk of the sworn force, are likely to have spent less than 20% of their time on activities directly related to investigating felonies.  As a result, although patrol officers are responsible for the first line of investigation, which will largely determine whether the criminal will be identified,[26] many are involved in felony investigations so infrequently as to be relatively inexperienced.  Indeed, even the detectives (who represent only a small portion of the total force), while assigned basically to the investigation of crime, spend a substantial portion of their time on other matters, such as simply closing out files on cases that obviously cannot be solved or arranging for the presentation of evidence at trial in cases that have been solved.

The diversity of police responsibilities also has a bearing on the police department's law enforcement capacity by pushing the department to adopt a broader perspective in the selection of officers.  The qualities needed in criminal investigation are not necessarily the same qualities required to perform other

---

**26.** The two most important determinations of whether a crime will be solved are (1) whether the police are able to arrive on the scene so promptly as to arrest the felon con-temporaneously with the crime, and (2) whether the victim or other witnesses furnish the investigating patrol officer with sufficient information to identify the offender.

police functions. It often is difficult, for example, to find people who will act effectively and courageously in apprehending a felon, yet have the ability to endure the long periods of monotony involved in routine patrol. Similarly, the social service functions may require officers inclined toward a generally informal and flexible approach that would pose for them difficulties in adhering to the formalistic legal requirements typically imposed in the area of criminal investigation.[27]

The diverse responsibilities of the local police agency may also detract from the agency's law enforcement function by pushing the department in other directions when formulating policies for activities that serve multiple functions. A prime example is in the area of patrol, where commentators have identified three departmental patrol styles that guide officers in their choices among patrol tasks and in their handling of similar incidents. Arguably, from the viewpoint of law enforcement alone, the most effective patrol style is that of an aggressive, proactive patrol. The approach here is to make all traffic stops legally permissible (meanwhile gaining the opportunity to check the driver for outstanding warrants and to observe the interior of the car), to make all permissible arrests for minor crimes (allowing for the incidental search of the person), to stop and interrogate persons behaving suspiciously, and to employ intensive patrolling in high crime areas (so as to facilitate an immediate response to alarms or calls reporting serious crime). Such tactics, by maximizing interventions and observations, increase the likelihood that the police will interrupt serious crimes in progress, which remains the very best method of solving offenses such as burglary and robbery. Another style of patrol (sometimes described as the "watchman" style) puts greater emphasis on the maintenance of order. Here the police focus primarily on responding to disturbances and potential disturbances, utilizing informal, non-arrest sanctions where the offenses are minor. A third patrol style, operating in the most direct conflict with aggressive patrolling, is a service oriented patrol. Here high priority is given to citizen requests for assistance and police are advised against unnecessarily utilizing their authority in non-threatening citizen interactions. Under this style of patrol, police are less likely to be in a position where they will come across a crime in progress, although some contend that that weakness is more than offset by the building of solid community support that produces more leads from citizens.

*Autonomy.* Three aspects of police autonomy also have a bearing upon the institutional setting in which police operate. First, there is the independence of the police from the political forces in the community and from the community in general. Second, there is the independence of the individual officer within the department, the leeway that he or she is offered under departmental policy in taking law enforcement actions. Finally, there is the independence of the police agency from the prosecutor, who will be using the agency's product in bringing prosecution. This aspect of police autonomy is discussed in the next section in connection with our description of the setting within which prosecutors operate.

A major problem that plagued law enforcement for many decades was the political dominance of local police. In large cities, in particular, political

---

**27.** The two major developments in police recruiting over the last few decades may both be seen as looking especially to the non-investigative aspects of police functions. Initially, there was a focus on raising educational levels, employing a higher percentage of recruits with some college education, although studies indicate that college educated officers, at least at the patrolman level, are not gener-ally more effective except in reducing the number of citizen complaints. Second, starting in the 1960's, in recognition of the diverse roles of police and special sensitivity of policing minority neighborhoods, there has been a greater emphasis on having a more pluralistic police force, with greater numbers of females and minorities.

machines controlled the filling of police positions, high and low, and thus made the police departments primarily responsible to the needs of the politicians in gaining reelection. During the early and middle 1900's, a strong reform movement instituted various measures designed to free the police from the role of politics. A primary component of that reform was the placing of police employment under civil service, thereby both guaranteeing officer tenure and ensuring that tests and other standardized measures would be used in both selecting recruits and making promotions. While civil service did not apply to the very top positions, so sheriffs were still elected and the local department chiefs were still appointed by elected officials, professional qualifications tended to be given greater emphasis in the selection process even at that level. Indeed, in some communities, special commissions or administrative boards were created to stand as a buffer between the appointed chiefs and the elected officials. The basic reform model also stressed the professionalization of the police department. The emphasis was on efficiency, objectivity, and integrity, achieved through a tight quasi-military structure, higher recruitment standards, a statutorily prescribed minimum period of preservice training (typically mandating at least 200 hours of classroom training and some period of field training), and taking full advantage of new technology.

During the 1960's and 1970's, there was widespread reexamination of what the earlier reforms had produced with respect to the accountability of police departments to civil authority. That reexamination was the product of concerns arising out of several professional and social developments; those included a sharp rise in crime, the demands imposed on police in dealing with racial tensions, riots, and demonstrations, the problems connected with the enforcement of drug laws (including police corruption), and the increased influence of police unions in the shaping of police policies. Subjected to unprecedented public scrutiny and debate were such police practices as the use of deadly force, the stopping, questioning, and frisking of "suspicious" persons, the surveillance of "radical" groups, and the use of informants and undercover agents. Police departments were criticized as having grown too distant from local government and local needs, as the critics rhetorically posed the question: "Who will police the police"? The increased influence of the courts, as illustrated by the cases reprinted in this volume, arguably reflected the judiciary's response to that criticism. Other responses came from the police departments themselves and from elected officials in local government. Efforts were made to expand the influence of elected officials on major issues of police administration (with those officials at least offering "advice," and sometimes legislating, on such issues as the use of chokeholds in making arrests and the proper police response to incidents of domestic violence), to make more effective use of internal police disciplinary procedures in dealing with citizen complaints, and to gain the input of community representatives through such structures as Civilian Review Boards and community liaison officers.

Today, many local departments, responding to community concerns, have adopted administrative guidelines governing the officer's use of various aspects of police authority. Notwithstanding such guidelines and extensive reporting requirements for certain actions (e.g., weapons discharges), the individual officer, particularly on patrol, remains largely autonomous. Police departments do not impose highly routinized protocols such as those applied to other public employees (e.g., bus drivers). The incidents faced by the police are viewed as too varied to be governed by a series of set procedures. Police officers, the departments note, must be given sufficient flexibility to shape their response to the incident. They must be allowed the freedom to fashion a quick, sometimes intuitive response, as well as to develop the distinct style (in light of individual strengths) that makes the particular officer most effective. In sum, police work is viewed as a craft, not readily subjected to bureaucratic controls.[28]

# PROSECUTORS

Although the British common law tradition was one of private prosecution (i.e., the complainant hired private counsel to press the prosecution), Americans had established an office of public prosecutor even before the Revolution. In most of the colonies, public prosecution was originally superimposed upon a system of private prosecution, but private prosecution was eventually seen as impracticable, too often subject to abuse, and inconsistent with the view that crimes were "acts against the state" and not simply wrongs inflicted upon an individual victim. As the office of public prosecutor grew in status and prosecutors became elected officials (a product of the Jacksonian reform movement), the public prosecutor was gradually given a virtual monopoly over criminal prosecutions, with extensive discretion/over both the filing and selection of criminal charges.

*Fragmentation.* As in the case of police power, the authority of the public prosecutor has not been centralized, but divided among a group of officials. Initially, there is the division between state officials responsible for prosecutions under state laws (the vast majority of all prosecutions), and federal officials responsible for prosecutions under federal laws. The Attorney General of the United States is the chief federal prosecutor, but federal prosecutorial authority has long been delegated to the various United States Attorneys, who are ultimately responsible to the Attorney General. There are 94 United States Attorneys, one for each federal judicial district, and their offices range in size from one or two assistants to over 50 in the large urban districts. They receive further assistance from the Criminal Division in the Department of Justice, and that Division itself initiates prosecutions in several fields (e.g., organized crime, public corruption), operating in part through special strike forces.

Ordinarily, the official with primary responsibility for prosecutions under state law is the local prosecuting attorney (also called the "district attorney," "county attorney," or "state's attorney"). The local prosecutor is selected either from a single county or from a group of counties that are combined to form a prosecutorial district in a sparsely populated area. The local prosecutor has the primary responsibility for bringing prosecutions for all violations of state law committed within his county or district. In many states, the local prosecutor's prosecutions are subject, at least theoretically, to the superceding authority of the state attorney general. Some states allow the attorney general on his own initiative to replace the prosecuting attorney in any pending prosecution, while certain other states permit the attorney general to intervene in a pending prosecution only upon direction of the governor. In practice, such intervention or replacement is rare. In still other states, the attorney general's office may initiate prosecution itself. Most often, attorneys general use their power to initiate prosecutions with respect only to a limited class of offenses, such as tax fraud and criminal antitrust violations, where local prosecutors are likely to lack

---

**28.** Indeed, there are those who question whether such controls could readily be imposed even if police departments were more willing to adopt them. There tends to be a strong subculture among police officers that emphasizes mutual support and resistance to outside influence. When this is combined with the obvious difficulty of supervising persons in the field, the end result is that departmental regulations, where simply adopted in response to political forces or community pressures and lacking support of the rank and file, are likely to have only a limited impact upon the street behavior of police.

sufficient expertise. In a few states, there are no locally selected prosecutors and the attorney general is responsible for all prosecutions under state law.[29]

The fragmentation of prosecutorial authority is designed, as with the fragmentation of police authority, to ensure local community responsiveness, a matter of extreme importance for an office expected to exercise considerable discretion. Prosecutors are elected officials and thought therefore to take into consideration the values of the community in their decisions as to whether or not to charge, in their selection of charges, in their offering of plea concessions to defendants, and in their recommendations on sentence.[30] The other side of the coin, however, is a loss of consistency in the statewide application of the criminal law. Different prosecutors in different counties can follow quite different policies on such matters as the decision to charge, the use of diversion programs, plea bargaining, and the discretionary employment of various pretrial and trial procedures. To achieve closer communications among local prosecutors, state prosecuting attorneys associations and some state attorneys general have established special programs designed to keep local prosecutors informed of the various policies being followed across the state.[31] While such efforts have helped to lessen the differences in the policies followed by the various prosecutors, those policies still remain far from uniform—particularly with respect to plea negotiation.

Another problem presented by the fragmentation of prosecuting authority is that many offices are too small to be efficient. Again, state attorneys general and prosecuting attorney associations have sought to offset this deficiency by providing various support services to the smaller offices, such as legal research assistance, office management programs, and shared use of computer facilities. Also, almost a third of the states have moved to a district selection system, which permits them to create multiple county districts large enough to support a full-time prosecutor with part-time assistants in each county. These reforms have been only partially successful, however, and the inefficiency of the smaller offices remains a major difficulty in most states.

*Local Prosecutors: The Urban and Large Suburban Office.* Prosecuting attorneys in metropolitan districts not uncommonly have a larger legal staff than even the largest of the private law firms in the community. Los Angeles County, for example, has over 600 assistant prosecutors. Notwithstanding their size, these offices commonly have extraordinarily heavy caseloads per prosecutor. Assistants handling felony cases may receive as many as 150 cases per year and assistants responsible for misdemeanors may receive several times that number of cases. To assist the local prosecutor in handling that caseload, some counties have relieved the prosecutor's office of most of its civil responsibilities, or have provided a separate staff for civil cases. Prosecutors in metropolitan areas are also provided with various support services, including special investiga-

---

**29.** The prosecuting attorney and the attorney general ordinarily are the only officials with authority to prosecute violations of state law. Public attorneys at other levels of government, such as a city or township attorney, cannot enforce state provisions. Those attorneys may, however, bring prosecutions to enforce local ordinances, and such ordinances frequently duplicate state misdemeanors both in substance and authorized punishments. See note 4 supra.

**30.** In the federal system, the U.S. Attorneys, while not elected, are appointees of the

president currently in office. When a president of a different political party takes office, tradition dictates that the U.S. Attorney resign.

**31.** United States Attorneys are directed by an extensive set of guidelines issued by the Attorney General, and for the exercise of certain types of authority, must receive approval from the Attorney General or an Assistant Attorney General.

tors, librarians, record control clerks, and where the office is large enough to support an automated case tracking system, computer programers and systems analysts. Large offices may also support a substantial diversion program staffed by a director and several counselors. All of these procedures help, but the caseload remains too heavy to take every felony charge through each stage in the process. Some cases must be disposed of by dismissals or by negotiated pleas of guilty.

Large offices also face serious obstacles in seeking to achieve consistency in the exercise of discretion by assistants. Some seek to maintain consistency by assigning experienced assistants to major areas of discretionary decisionmaking (e.g., charging and plea negotiation) and relying upon those deputies to provide direction to the prosecutors under their supervision. Other offices utilize detailed guidelines and require assistants to justify their decision in writing by reference to those guidelines. Spot checks and statistical analysis are also utilized to ensure that all prosecutors are adhering basically to the same policies. Even with such controls, however, individual prosecutors retain considerable flexibility, particularly in evaluating the factual elements of the case.

*Local Prosecutors: The Rural and Small Suburban Office.* The public image of the prosecutor's office has been shaped largely by the big city office, but this single image largely ignores the tremendous variety in the setting and size of local prosecutor's offices. There are over 2,500 such offices in the United States, and a substantial majority represent districts with populations under 60,000. In contrast to large urban or suburban offices, many prosecutors in these districts operate without even one full time assistant. Indeed, less than 20% of all local prosecutor's offices have four or more assistants. In districts with an especially small population, the prosecutor is likely to be a part-time official, maintaining a private practice in addition to his public office.

The problems faced in small offices tend to be quite different from those presented in the larger offices. The criminal caseload in small districts often is fairly light, particularly as to felonies. Solo prosecutors may process no more than two felonies per month. The difficulties presented in handling such caseloads stem from the presence of other responsibilities and limited flexibility in assignments. In most small districts, the prosecutor's responsibility is not limited to criminal prosecution. The prosecutor also handles juvenile cases and often has extensive civil responsibilities. Where prosecutors are part-time employees, there is also the draw of private practice. Moreover, while resources may be adequate to handle the typical case, there is not likely to be available the extra manpower needed for the time consuming complicated fraud or homicide case that will produce a lengthy trial. The limited range of felonies typically presented also makes it likely that the assistants will not have the expertise needed to deal with the exceptional case. Very often the answer here will be to turn to the state attorney general's office for special assistance.

Small prosecutor offices have no need for a complicated bureaucratic structure to ensure consistency. The assistants, if any, work closely with the prosecutor and should fully understand his prosecutorial policies. Dealings with defense counsel, who are likely to be known socially as well as professionally, require no formal guidelines. There is neither the resources nor the need for highly structured internal programs governing matters such as diversion, which tend instead to be handled informally.

*Local Prosecutors: Selection.* Whether the offices are large or small, a major problem in prosecutor's offices is the high rate of turnover. As elected officials, local prosecutors know that their tenure is always subject to the whims of the electorate. While the incumbent usually has a very good chance of being reelected, elections for this post often attract a fair degree of voter attention due to the centrality of the crime issue. In part because of their limited job security, most local prosecutors do not view their office as a career position. Many see it as a stepping stone to higher political office and others view it as an opportunity to make a reputation and gain contacts that will later be helpful in private practice. Thus, studies of prosecutor career patterns report that 50% of the prosecutors in a particular state are likely to be serving their first term and close to 50% may have a current interest in seeking another government position. Of course, there are exceptions to the general pattern. In almost every state, one can find local prosecutors who have remained in office for twenty to thirty years, rejecting numerous opportunities to become judges or enter private practices.

In most offices, the assistant prosecutors also have a fairly short tenure. Estimates of the annual turnover rate throughout the country range as high as 25–33%. Like the prosecuting attorney, the assistants generally do not view themselves as occupying a career position. In some jurisdictions, the process of their selection is so highly political that assistants are likely to lose their positions, or at least be demoted from supervisory positions, if the prosecutor hiring them is succeeded in office by a candidate from another party. Prosecutors in most larger counties, however, tend to hire on a nonpartisan, merit-oriented basis (as do United States Attorneys). While the assistants in such offices are not protected by civil service, they do have substantial job security. Nevertheless, their turnover rate also tends to be substantial. The assistants commonly are hired at an early stage in their legal careers, often immediately upon their graduation from law school. They stay for a few years, gaining considerable practical experience at a relatively low pay. They then leave to enter various fields of private practice (including criminal defense work) where their experience in litigation will be most valuable. Various prosecutor's offices, in an effort to produce more career professionals, have sought to establish salaries for higher ranked, experienced assistants at a level only slightly below that of a trial judge.

*Local Prosecutors: Prosecutor/Police Relations.* Another problem facing prosecutors' offices is the limited means available for imposing the policies of the office (which often are derived from the desire to avoid legal difficulties) upon the police. The local prosecutor is commonly characterized as the "chief law enforcement officer" of the local district, but this does not mean that the prosecutor has the authority to simply order the police to engage or not engage in certain investigative practices as he so directs. Police departments usually do follow the legal advice of the prosecutor but they do so because the interaction of police and prosecutor make cooperation necessary, not because they are legally required to do so. The local prosecutor and the local police are separate agencies, often receiving their funding from separate sources. Unlike the federal system, where the U.S. Attorney and F.B.I. are both subject to the supervisory power of the Attorney General, the local police and local prosecutor are not subject to the higher authority of a single executive. Short of threatening to withdraw his power to prosecute, the prosecutor must rely on his power of persuasion to gain any changes in police practices thought to be desirable.

A complete breakdown in prosecutor/police relations is rare, but various studies have found more tensions and conflict than one might initially expect, considering the shared interest of prosecutor and police in law enforcement. The lack of smoother prosecutor/police relations may often be a product of inadequate communication, but it also is attributable to the different vantage points from which police and prosecutor view the same event. Unlike the prosecutor, police see crime as it is committed in the streets rather than as reported in a law office. They are more likely to be influenced in their appraisal of a case by the extent of the victim's suffering, by the accused's subsequent reaction to his criminal behavior, and by the officer's own peril in making the arrest. Although both prosecutor and police officer are interested in effective law enforcement, their immediate goals and interests also tend to differ. The police are concerned primarily with their responsibility for keeping the streets safe, while the prosecutor is focusing upon his role as the legal representative of the state, the need to keep the court process moving, and his participation in the courtroom "work group" of prosecutor, defense counsel, and judge.

# DEFENSE COUNSEL

*Counsel for the Indigent.* In most jurisdictions, 60–70% of all felony defendants are "indigent" in the sense that they lack the funds to hire defense counsel. The percentage of misdemeanor defendants who are indigent usually is somewhat lower, but it can easily fall in the range of 30–50%. As will be seen in Chapter Five, indigent felony defendants are constitutionally entitled to defense representation paid for by the state. Indigent misdemeanor defendants have a similar right only when sentenced to incarceration, but many jurisdictions provide free representation for all indigent misdemeanor defendants charged with a misdemeanor or ordinance violation that carries a potential sentence of imprisonment.

A majority of local judicial districts provide counsel for the indigent defendant through an assigned counsel system; the court makes individual appointments of private practitioners who receive compensation from the state for the work done in the particular case, usually at a rate somewhat lower than that which would be earned in private practice. In the more heavily populated districts, however, a public defender agency is likely to be the primary provider of counsel for the indigent. Only one-third of all counties have defender agencies, but those counties contain over 60% of the nation's population. In most of these districts, defender agencies are the almost exclusive provider of representation for the indigent, with private counsel being assigned only to avoid potential conflicts in cases of jointly charged codefendants. In other districts, a "mixed system" is used, with the defender agency and appointed counsel each representing a substantial portion of the indigents (although the defender agency usually has the larger group).

In many respects, local defender agencies or local branches of statewide defender agencies present a mirror image of a local prosecutor's office. Individual offices range in size from a single part-time defender to a staff of more than 200 lawyers. A majority of all local public defender offices employ 3 or fewer lawyers. Larger offices are likely to include such support personnel as investigators and paralegals. However, lawyers in these offices are also likely to have very heavy caseloads (e.g., close to 200 cases per year for a deputy handling felonies, and nearly 500 for the misdemeanor deputy). While most offices assign each client to a single lawyer, some use a horizontal assignment system similar to that found in prosecutor's offices. Separate deputies may handle the first appearance, preliminary hearing, pretrial motions, and the trial.

As with local prosecutor's offices, defender offices tend to hire young and relatively inexperienced attorneys and have a high employee turnover. Large offices, in particular, face a substantial problem of "burnout." Young lawyers enter the office filled with idealism and enthusiasm but frequently leave it disillusioned and cynical. Faced with a heavy caseload, judges who sometimes force them to take a backseat in scheduling to private practitioners, clients who sometimes misuse them and often suspect their motives (or at least view them as second-rate attorneys), and cases requiring infrequent use of their trial skills, deputy defenders often are ready to give up on defense work after only a few years (turning instead to a private civil practice or to the prosecutor's office). Thus, a nationwide survey found that only about one-third of the deputies had more than four years service with their agency.

*Retained Counsel.* The representation of criminal defendants able to afford counsel comes largely from a small segment of the private bar. A good many general practitioners, particularly in smaller communities, will handle a few criminal cases each year. Corporate practitioners from some of the largest firms will occasionally find themselves involved in a narrow segment of the criminal caseload—the white collar crime cases often tried in federal courts. A small cadre of the most highly publicized and highly skilled trial lawyers are available primarily to defendants able to pay large fees (although such lawyers not infrequently will take on other cases with special appeal). For the general run of criminal defendants who can retain counsel (most of whom are just barely above the line of indigency), at least in medium and large cities, the private bar makes available primarily a small group of attorneys who specialize in handling a high volume of criminal cases.[32]

Why do a substantial majority of all lawyers either never take a criminal case or do so only on rare occasions? These lawyers commonly view criminal defense work as one of the least desirable fields of specialization. Compensation tends to be lower than that for practitioners in other fields, and collection of the fee is often a difficult task (leading many defense lawyers to insist upon an "up-front" payment). Perhaps even more important, the working conditions are decidedly unappealing, at least to the typical member of the private bar. The defense counsel must expect to spend most of his time in police stations, jails, and the crowded (and often hectic) misdemeanor courts. His clients generally will be people who have committed acts which he views as questionable at best. He must be reconciled to the fact that, no matter how great his ability, he will "lose" most of his cases (in the sense that his clients will be convicted). Finally, as compared to lawyers in other fields, the defense specialist is likely to rank low in public esteem and in reputation among fellow-lawyers. Of course, many very good lawyers do make criminal law their specialty, but most lawyers with other options prefer those alternatives.

# THE JUDICIARY

All of the opinions contained in this volume are opinions of the Supreme Court of the United States. Through the reading of those opinions, you will surely gain an understanding of the institutional setting in which that court operates. Our discussion here is limited to the lower courts. These are the

**32.** These specialists tend to come from two groups—the young lawyers who also are relying upon court appointments (in jurisdictions without public defenders) to provide a steady monetary base in the building of their practices, and the so-called "courthouse regulars" (usually having offices in a "down on the heels" district located close to the courthouse, and commonly described as the "bar" of that district, as in Detroit's "Clinton Street Bar"). The latter group of more experienced lawyers usually rely on a private clientele developed through direct solicitation of unrepresented defendants awaiting court appearances and through contacts with bail bondsmen and others who might recommend them to prospective clients.

magistrates and trial judges who are given front line responsibility for administering most of the standards set forth in those Supreme Court rulings and the state appellate courts whose rulings are being reviewed by the Supreme Court.

*Magistrates Courts.* The courts of first instance in the administration of the criminal justice process ordinarily are the courts of "limited jurisdiction"—that is, courts lacking authority to try the most serious criminal cases, but given more limited functions. These courts are known in different states as "magistrates courts," "justice of the peace courts," "municipal courts," "district courts," "police courts," and "recorder's courts." [33] We will refer to them as magistrates courts because the judges of these courts are commonly described in judicial opinions as magistrates. The magistrates courts traditionally have trial jurisdiction only over some or all misdemeanors. Where their jurisdiction does not extend to all misdemeanors, the dividing line is usually determined by the maximum punishment for the offense (e.g., the magistrates court will have trial jurisdiction over misdemeanors punishable by 90 days imprisonment or less). In addition to their trial jurisdiction, magistrates courts play an important role in the processing of felonies (and any misdemeanors that are beyond their trial authority). Cases involving those offenses are brought before the magistrates court for preliminary processing before being sent to the courts of "general" jurisdiction where they can be tried. The preliminary matters that may be handled by the magistrate include: (i) the issuance of search and arrest warrants; (ii) the first appearance of the arrested person before a court; (iii) the setting of bail; (iv) the appointment of counsel for indigent defendants; and (v) the preliminary hearing for felony cases.

The structure and staffing of magistrates courts differ considerably from state to state. Perhaps the greatest variation is found in the drawing of the judicial districts served by the magistrates courts. Some states have divided the state into uniform districts with the same type of magistrates court for each district. Others have districts that coincide with different political subdivisions (city, township, village, etc.). In these states, there may be several different types of magistrates courts, each with different limits on its trial jurisdiction, different qualifications required for its judges, and even different procedures for review of its decisions.

Almost all states permit judges in at least some magistrates courts to serve as part-time jurists. Where those judges are lawyers, state law commonly restricts their private practice to avoid a conflict of interest with their judicial duties. In approximately 40 states, judges in at least some magistrates courts need not be lawyers. Typically, a state will require that judges of magistrates courts in metropolitan areas be lawyers and serve full-time, while judges in rural magistrate courts may be nonlawyers and may serve part-time. Magistrates courts with lay judges commonly are treated as courts "not of record." Misdemeanor convictions in such courts are subject to retrial before a general trial court (a trial *de novo*) rather than simply the normal appellate review on the record of the earlier trial. This trial *de novo* procedure is made available out of concern that a person convicted of a misdemeanor be entitled to a more formal and thorough trial than typically is provided in courts not of record. Magistrates who are not lawyers sometimes follow the traditional rules governing

**33.** In the federal system, there is not a separate magistrates court, but basically the same functions as performed by magistrates courts are delegated by the District Court to United States Magistrates (court officers appointed by the district judges). Several states similarly do not have separate magistrates courts, but assign to a division of the general trial court the functions of those courts.

trials only in a rather loose fashion, but many defendants, though convicted, view that as sufficient and do not seek a trial *de novo*.

Over the years, national and local commissions examining the judicial system have repeatedly cited the importance of the magistrates courts to the administration of justice (for most people, these are the only courts in which they will ever appear) and the need for improvement in the structure and administration of those courts. Magistrates courts in the rural areas, staffed by non-lawyer judges, have been criticized for their lack of legal competency and the lack of dignity and decorum in their courtrooms. Lay judges, it has been argued, too often ignore the law and reflect a local bias rather than the "good common sense" that is allegedly their strong point. Complaints as to the lack of dignity and decorum have also been leveled at the magistrates courts in metropolitan areas, where a form of "assembly line justice" too frequently prevails. In those courts, it is reported, judges tend to place greater emphasis on the speedy disposition of cases than on ensuring that the correct result is attained in each and every case. With their crowded facilities, lack of adequate staffing, and routinized procedures, big city magistrates courts create an atmosphere, critics contend, that is more appropriate for a supermarket than a court of justice.

State legislatures have sought to respond to such criticism in various ways. Lay judges have been required to participate in training programs, and even to pass examinations testing their legal knowledge. Magistrates courts have been required to extend their hours so that defendants arrested on weekends may be promptly presented. Various measures have been adopted to provide some relief from the pressure of the tremendously heavy caseloads typically borne by the urban courts. Traffic cases have either been removed from the court's jurisdiction or largely assigned to court personnel other than the judges. To reduce the civil docket, more cases have been brought within the range of the small claims division of the court. Decriminalization of public drunkenness (which otherwise might constitute as much as 15–20 percent of the misdemeanor docket) has also helped to reduce the court's docket. Even with such reforms, however, the caseload per judge, including misdemeanors, minor civil cases, and preliminary proceedings in felony cases, can easily reach 2,000 cases a year in a busy urban court.

*Trial Courts of General Jurisdiction.* The courts that try felony cases (and any misdemeanors beyond the magistrates court's trial jurisdiction) are commonly described as the trial courts of "general" (i.e., not limited) jurisdiction. In the federal system, that general trial court is the United States District Court. In the state system, that court is commonly called the "superior court," "circuit court," or "district court." In addition to its felony trial jurisdiction, this court will also provide the first level of appellate review for misdemeanors tried in the magistrates court.

Although the general trial court is responsible for both criminal and civil cases, the criminal portion of its docket is sufficiently significant so that even those trial judges who had no previous experience with the criminal field as practicing lawyers quickly gain considerable familiarity with the criminal process. Criminal cases commonly constitute anywhere from 15–40% of the general trial court's docket, with the lower figure applicable primarily where that docket includes juvenile and probate cases in addition to the traditional civil cases. Moreover, when caseloads are weighted according to the time spent on the particular type of case, the significance of the criminal caseload increases at least twofold. Although, as we have seen, only a small percentage of felony cases actually go to trial, that rate is still much higher than the trial rate in civil cases. Thus, even where criminal cases constitute no more than 25% of the court's total docket, those cases can readily provide over 50% of all jury trials.

*Appellate Courts.* In approximately two-thirds of the states, there are two levels of appellate courts: first, an intermediate court of appeals, and then the highest state court (commonly called that state's supreme court). In the remainder of the states, there is a single appellate court, the state supreme court. In the federal system, appeals are taken initially to the federal intermediate appellate court, the United States Court of Appeals, and then to the Supreme Court of the United States.

A convicted felony defendant ordinarily will have an automatic right to have his conviction reviewed by the first level appellate court. This means that defendant will have an automatic appeal to the intermediate court where the state has two levels of review or to the state supreme court where it has only one. Any further appellate review generally lies in the discretion of the higher appellate court. Thus, a defendant whose conviction is affirmed by the state intermediate appellate court can only obtain review from the state supreme court if he can convince that court that issues posed by his case are of sufficient general importance to merit its attention.

The state supreme court will be the court of last resort in state criminal cases unless a federal constitutional issue is presented. Where such an issue is posed, the defendant can seek further review of that issue from the Supreme Court of the United States. The Supreme Court's appellate jurisdiction is largely discretionary, and the defendant seeks such review through a "petition for certiorari." The Supreme Court also has discretionary appellate jurisdiction over federal criminal cases coming from the United States Court of Appeals, but here its reviewing authority is total; that is, it can review any issue posed in the case, not simply those involving the interpretation of the federal constitution. The Supreme Court annually grants review in only a small number (typically, about 175) of the several thousand cases, civil and criminal, in which petitions for certiorari are filed.[34]

Most criminal cases reviewed by an appellate court come to that court after a conviction at the trial level. The defendant can appeal a conviction, but the prosecution cannot appeal an acquittal. Indeed, the prosecution's initial right of appeal is limited to certain rulings issued before trial that either result in the dismissal of charges or hold inadmissible evidence that the prosecution deems critical to its case. Where the defendant appeals following a conviction and that appeal is successful (i.e., the conviction is reversed), the prosecution can then seek the discretionary review of any higher appellate court in the state system. If the conviction was reversed by the state court on the basis of a federal constitutional ruling, the prosecution can then seek review by the Supreme Court through a petition for certiorari.

Those state appellate courts to which the defendant has an automatic right to review generally spend a considerable portion of their efforts on criminal cases. For such a court, often more than half of its docket consists of criminal appeals. In anywhere from 80 to 90% of those cases, the defendant's claim is likely to be rejected and the conviction affirmed. Where the appellate court has discretion as to which cases it will review, the proportion of criminal cases heard will be much lower, but the percentage of reversals is likely to be higher. This is

**34.** Whereas the Supreme Court decision on the merits of any appeal is determined by a majority vote (5 out of 9, where all Justices are sitting), certiorari will be granted where at least 4 Justices desire to review the case.

because discretionary review permits the appellate court to screen out the many cases in which the convicted defendant does not have a strong claim, but appeals nonetheless because there is nothing to lose by seeking appellate review. In some states, as many as 90% of the felony defendants who were both convicted after a trial and sentenced to imprisonment will exercise their right to automatic review by the first level appellate court.

*Selection.* At least since the Jacksonian era, what constitutes the best method for selecting judges has been a matter of considerable controversy and division among the states. Basically five different procedures are used in this country to select judges: (1) partisan elections (i.e., candidates running as nominees of political parties); (2) nonpartisan elections (i.e., all candidates running as independents); (3) appointment by the chief executive, with the consent of the legislature; (4) election by the legislature; and (5) the Missouri Plan, a system that includes the selection of a panel of several nominees by an independent commission, appointment of one of those nominees by the chief executive, a probationary period of judicial service, and the subsequent retention or rejection of the appointed judge in an election in which the judge runs unopposed.[35]

The division among the states in choosing one selection system over another has rested in part upon a disagreement as to what qualities are most needed in judges. In particular, there is a disagreement as to the significance of the candidate's political philosophy, including both the candidate's basic value judgments and his or her view of the rule of the judiciary. Some contend that, assuming there exists the qualities that are a prerequisite for any public office (e.g., integrity), judicial philosophy is the most critical factor. Judges are said to have broad discretion in shaping the law and it is therefore important that they reflect the value judgments and perspectives of the communities that they serve. This may require, it is argued, that the judicial selection process take into consideration, to some extent, such factors as gender, race, ethnic and socio-economic background, and previous experiences that might assist one in understanding all elements of a diverse society.

A contrary view acknowledges that at the level of the Supreme Court, and perhaps the highest state appellate courts, the judge's basic value judgments play an important role in judicial lawmaking (although it may be argued that even here, legal methodology significantly restricts the judge's discretion). The judge's value system is viewed as far less significant, however, in selecting judges of other courts. Here, the legal issues presented to the judge are said to be controlled largely by prior decisions of higher courts, except for unusual cases.

---

**35.** The characterization of a state's system as fitting into one category or another is likely to be quite rough. Initially, some states do not adhere to the basic elements of any single selection system, but have what may best be described as a hybrid system. Thus, a state may initially use a nonpartisan election, but then, borrowing from the Missouri Plan, have the judge run for reelection unopposed, in what is described as a "retention election." Secondly, even though a jurisdiction adheres to the basic elements of one of the five systems, it is likely to have adopted significant variations within that structure. Perhaps the single most significant variant within any one structure will be the length of the judicial term for which the judge is selected. Federal judges and the judges of a few states are given the security (and independence) of lifetime tenure or tenure up to a mandatory retirement age. The remaining states use terms varying from four years to sixteen years. Another problem presented in categorizing jurisdictions is the use of different methods to select judges at different levels of the judicial hierarchy. Gubernatorial appointment, legislative election, and the Missouri Plan are all too time consuming for the high-level officials responsible for the selection to apply those methods of selection to magistrates. Accordingly, jurisdictions that otherwise use those methods commonly select magistrates through a local election or appointment by a lower-level official (e.g., the city council in the case of a municipal court).

The critical qualities are those that enable judges to apply that law and to make fair and accurate factfinding determinations. These qualities, sometimes described as "professional qualifications," are said to include an ability to carefully analyze statutes and high court rulings, a capacity to carefully evaluate facts, and an understanding of human nature.

Of course, desirable professional qualifications and a desired political philosophy are not mutually exclusive criteria. The division arises over which should be given the greater emphasis in the selection of judges. Supporters of the first view often prefer the popular election of judges both because it provides community control over the initial selection process [36] and because it keeps the judge attuned to community values by requiring that he or she run for reelection every several years. Proponents of executive appointment with legislative approval (as in the federal system), or the less common legislative election system, also tend to emphasize the judge's philosophy, but argue that judges representative of the populace and possessing adequate professional qualifications are more likely to be produced by those systems than the rarely illuminating election campaign. Supporters of the Missouri Plan tend to give greater weight to professional qualifications, although some prefer that selection system primarily because it eliminates considerations of partisan politics.

**36.** In practice, however, the elective system commonly produces a substantial number of judges who are selected initially by appointment. When a vacancy occurs during a judicial term, usually due to the sitting judge's death or retirement, it is the governor who appoints an interim successor. While that person must stand for election in the next regularly scheduled election, he or she will be listed on the ballot as the incumbent, which will greatly aid in gaining election. Surveys of sitting judges in several elective jurisdictions found that more than half of those judges were initially selected by the governor to fill a vacancy, and that incumbents have a reelection record of better than 95%.

# A general view of The Criminal Justice System

This chart seeks to present a simple yet comprehensive view of the movement of cases through the criminal justice system. Procedures in individual jurisdictions may vary from the pattern shown here. The differing weights of line indicate the relative volumes of cases disposed of at various points in the system, but this is only suggestive since no nationwide data of this sort exists.

Source: Adapted from *The challenge of crime in a free society*, President's Commission on Law Enforcement and Administration of Justice, 1967.

[E5933]

# Chapter 2

# THE NATURE AND SCOPE OF FOURTEENTH AMENDMENT DUE PROCESS; THE APPLICABILITY OF THE BILL OF RIGHTS TO THE STATES

## SECTION 1. THE "FUNDAMENTAL RIGHTS" (OR "ORDERED LIBERTY") AND "INCORPORATION" THEORIES

The first eight amendments were enacted as limitations solely upon the federal government. But some argued that the Fourteenth Amendment had "totally incorporated" all the provisions of the Bill of Rights, i.e., made them fully applicable to the states. As it had done earlier (see *Twining v. New Jersey*, 211 U.S. 78 (1908)), in *Palko v. Connecticut* and *Adamson v. California*, the two cases set forth in this section, the Court emphatically rejected the "total incorporation" view of the history of the Fourteenth Amendment—a view which has never commanded a majority.

Instead, the Court in *Palko* and *Adamson* (as well as other cases) adopted what has been called the "fundamental rights" or "ordered liberty" interpretation of the Fourteenth Amendment's due process clause, an approach that prevailed until the early 1960's. This approach finds no necessary relationship between the content of the Fourteenth Amendment and the guarantees of the Bill of Rights. It regards the due process clause as simply incorporating all principles of justice "implicit in the concept of ordered liberty" or "so rooted in the traditions and conscience of our people as to be ranked as fundamental." As applied to criminal procedure, this approach requires, but requires only, that the state afford a defendant "that fundamental fairness essential to the very concept of justice." If the presence of a specific Bill of Rights guarantee is not decisive under this approach, neither is its absence. A particular practice may violate "fundamental fairness" even though it is not specifically prohibited by the Bill of Rights. Under this approach, the Due Process Clause of the Fourteenth Amendment, as Justice Frankfurter emphasized in his *Adamson* concurring opinion, "has an independent potency."

The cases applying the "fundamental rights" approach recognized the possibility that some of the personal rights safeguarded by the first eight Amendments against federal action may also be protections against state action, because a denial of them would be a denial of due process.  Thus, the Court held in *Powell v. Alabama* (1932) (discussed in Chapter Five) that, under the circumstances of the case, defendants charged with and convicted of capital offenses were denied Fourteenth Amendment Due Process when a state did not afford them the effective assistance of counsel.  "The logically critical thing, however," pointed out Justice Harlan years later (dissenting in *Duncan v. Louisiana,* set forth in the next section), "was not that the rights had been found in the Bill of Rights but that they were deemed [to] be fundamental."

If *Powell v. Alabama* did not hold that the right to counsel was fully "incorporated into" or implicit in Fourteenth Amendment Due Process, neither did *Palko* hold that the prohibition against double jeopardy was completely "out" of the Fourteenth Amendment.  As *Palko* illustrates, the Court often had to pass on state procedures transgressing the "outer edges," rather than the basic concept, of a particular Bill of Rights guarantee.  It seems most doubtful that in sustaining such challenged procedures the Court was authorizing the states to abolish completely—or to avoid the "hardcore" of—e.g., the protection against double jeopardy, or the privilege against self-incrimination, or the right to trial by jury in criminal cases.

Rather the Court probably meant that the state rule in question did not violate the Fourteenth Amendment because the specific provision of the Bill of Rights invoked by the defendant did not apply to the states *to the full extent* it applied to the federal government.  To hold that a particular Bill of Rights guarantee is not *totally* "incorporated," i.e., not binding on the states *in its entirety,* is not to say it is completely "out" of the Fourteenth Amendment.

The total incorporation position received its strongest support in the *Adamson* dissents, especially Justice Black's memorable dissent.  But the *Adamson* case also produced the most powerful rejection of the total incorporation theory—and perhaps the most famous articulation of the "ordered liberty"-"fundamental fairness" approach—concurring Justice Frankfurter's response to the *Adamson* dissenters.

## PALKO v. CONNECTICUT

302 U.S. 319, 58 S.Ct. 149, 82 L.Ed. 288 (1937).

JUSTICE CARDOZO delivered the opinion of the Court.  *  *  *

Appellant was indicted for the crime of murder in the first degree.  A jury found him guilty of murder in the second degree, and he was sentenced to confinement in the state prison for life.  Thereafter the State of Connecticut [appealed, pursuant to a state statute permitting appeals "upon all questions of law arising on the trial of criminal cases, [with] the permission of the presiding judge"].  [T]he Supreme Court of Errors reversed [finding] error of law to the prejudice of the state [in excluding certain evidence and] in the instructions to the jury as to the difference between first and second degree murder.

*  *  *  Before a jury was impaneled [defendant unsuccessfully objected] that the effect of the new trial was to place him twice in jeopardy for the same offense, and in so doing to violate the Fourteenth Amendment.  [The] jury returned a verdict of murder in the first degree, and the court sentenced the defendant to the punishment of death.  The Supreme Court of Errors affirmed.

[The] argument for appellant is that whatever is forbidden by the Fifth Amendment is forbidden by the Fourteenth also.  [To] retry a defendant, though under one indictment and only one, subjects him, it is said, to double jeopardy in violation of the Fifth Amendment, if the prosecution is one on behalf of the

United States. From this the consequence is said to follow that there is a denial of life or liberty without due process of law.

[Appellant's] thesis is even broader. Whatever would be a violation of the original bill of rights (Amendments 1 to 8) if done by the federal government is now equally unlawful by force of the Fourteenth Amendment if done by a state. There is no such general rule.

The Fifth Amendment provides, among other things, that no person shall be held to answer for a capital or otherwise infamous crime unless on presentment or indictment of a grand jury. This court has held that, in prosecutions by a state, presentment or indictment by a grand jury may give way to informations at the instance of a public officer. *Hurtado v. California*, 110 U.S. 516 (1884). The Fifth Amendment provides also that no person shall be compelled in any criminal case to be a witness against himself. This court has said that, in prosecutions by a state, the exemption will fail if the state elects to end it. *Twining v. New Jersey*, 211 U.S. 78 (1908). The Sixth Amendment calls for a jury trial in criminal cases and the Seventh for a jury trial in civil cases at common law where the value in controversy shall exceed $20. This court has ruled that consistently with those amendments trial by jury may be modified by a state or abolished altogether. * * *

On the other hand, the due process clause of the Fourteenth Amendment may make it unlawful for a state to abridge by its statutes the freedom of speech which the First Amendment safeguards against encroachment by the Congress; or the like freedom of the press; or the free exercise of religion; or the right of peaceable assembly. [In] these and other situations immunities that are valid as against the federal government by force of the specific pledges of particular amendments have been found to be implicit in the concept of ordered liberty and thus through the Fourteenth Amendment, become valid as against the states.

The line of division may seem to be wavering and broken if there is a hasty catalogue of the cases on the one side and the other. Reflection and analysis will induce a different view. There emerges the perception of a rationalizing principle which gives to discrete instances a proper order and coherence. The right to trial by jury and the immunity from prosecution except as the result of an indictment may have value and importance. Even so, they are not of the very essence of a scheme of ordered liberty. To abolish them is not to violate a "principle of justice so rooted in the traditions and conscience of our people as to be ranked as fundamental." Few would be so narrow or provincial as to maintain that a fair and enlightened system of justice would be impossible without them. What is true of jury trials and indictments is true also, as the cases show, of the immunity from compulsory self-incrimination. This too might be lost, and justice still be done. Indeed, today as in the past there are students of our penal system who look upon the immunity as a mischief rather than a benefit, and who would limit its scope, or destroy it altogether. No doubt there would remain the need to give protection against torture, physical or mental. Justice, however, would not perish if the accused were subject to a duty to respond to orderly inquiry. The exclusion of these immunities and privileges from the privileges and immunities protected against the action of the States has not been arbitrary or casual. It has been dictated by a study and appreciation of the meaning, the essential implications, of liberty itself.

We reach a different plane of social and moral values when we pass to the privileges and immunities that have been taken over from the earlier articles of the Federal Bill of Rights and brought within the Fourteenth Amendment by a process of absorption. These in their origin were effective against the federal government alone. If the Fourteenth Amendment has absorbed them, the process of absorption has had its source in the belief that neither liberty nor justice would exist if they were sacrificed. *Twining.* This is true, for illustration, of freedom of thought and speech. Of that freedom one may say that it is the matrix, the indispensable condition, of nearly every other form of freedom. * * * Fundamental too in the concept of due process, and so in that of liberty, is the thought that condemnation shall be rendered only after trial. The hearing, moreover, must be a real one, not a sham or a pretense. For that reason, ignorant defendants in a capital case were held to have been condemned unlawfully when in truth, though not in form, they were refused the aid of counsel. *Powell v. Alabama* [discussed in Ch. 5.] The decision did not turn upon the fact that the benefit of counsel would have been guaranteed to the defendants by the provisions of the Sixth Amendment if they had been prosecuted in a federal court. The decision turned upon the fact that in the particular situation laid before us in the evidence the benefit of counsel was essential to the substance of a hearing.

Our survey of the cases serves, we think, to justify the statement that the dividing line between them, if not unfaltering throughout its course, has been true for the most part to a unifying principle. On which side of the line the case made out by the appellant has appropriate location must be the next inquiry and the final one. Is that kind of double jeopardy to which the statute has subjected him a hardship so acute and shocking that our polity will not endure it? Does it violate those "fundamental principles of liberty and justice which lie at the base of all our civil and political institutions"? The answer surely must be "no." What the answer would have to be if the state were permitted after a trial free from error to try the accused over again or to bring another case against him, we have no occasion to consider. We deal with the statute before us and no other. The state is not attempting to wear the accused out by a multitude of cases with accumulated trials. It asks no more than this, that the case against him shall go on until there shall be a trial free from the corrosion of substantial legal error. [This] is not cruelty at all, nor even vexation in any immoderate degree. If the trial had been infected with error adverse to the accused, there might have been review at his instance, and as often as necessary to purge the vicious taint. A reciprocal privilege, subject at all times to the discretion of the presiding judge [has] now been granted to the state. There is here no seismic innovation. The edifice of justice stands, its symmetry, to many, greater than before. * * *

The judgment is affirmed.[a]

JUSTICE BUTLER dissents.

## ADAMSON v. CALIFORNIA

332 U.S. 46, 67 S.Ct. 1672, 91 L.Ed. 1903 (1947).

JUSTICE REED delivered the opinion of the Court.

The appellant, Adamson, a citizen of the United States, was convicted without recommendation for mercy, by a jury [of] murder in the first degree [and sentenced to death]. The provisions of California law which were challenged in the state proceedings as invalid under the Fourteenth Amendment * * * permit the failure of a defendant to explain or to deny evidence against him to be commented upon by court and by counsel and to be considered by court and

---

**a.** *Palko* was later overruled in *Benton v. Maryland*, 395 U.S. 784 (1969), which found that "the double jeopardy prohibition of the Fifth Amendment represents a fundamental ideal in our constitutional heritage, and that it should apply to the States through the Fourteenth Amendment."

jury. The defendant did not testify. [T]he trial court gave its instructions and the District Attorney argued the case in accordance with the [California] provisions just referred to * * *.

We shall assume, but without any intention thereby of ruling upon the issue, that state permission by law to the court, counsel and jury to comment upon and consider the failure of defendant "to explain or to deny by his testimony any evidence or facts in the case against him" would infringe defendant's privilege against self-incrimination under the Fifth Amendment if this were a trial in a court of the United States under a similar law. Such an assumption does not determine appellant's rights under the Fourteenth Amendment. It is settled law that the clause of the Fifth Amendment, protecting a person against being compelled to be a witness against himself, is not made effective by the Fourteenth Amendment as a protection against state action on the ground that freedom from testimonial compulsion is a right of national citizenship, or because it is a personal privilege or immunity secured by the Federal Constitution as one of the rights of man that are listed in the Bill of Rights. * * *

Appellant secondly contends [that] the privilege against self-incrimination [to] its full scope under the Fifth Amendment, inheres in the right to a fair trial. A right to a fair trial is a right admittedly protected by the due process clause of the Fourteenth Amendment. [The] due process clause of the Fourteenth Amendment, however, does not draw all the rights of the federal Bill of Rights under its protection. That contention was made and rejected in *Palko* [which] held that such provisions of the Bill of Rights as were "implicit in the concept of ordered liberty," became secure from state interference by the clause. But it held nothing more. * * *

Generally, comment on the failure of an accused to testify is forbidden in American jurisdictions. This arises from state constitutional or statutory provisions similar in character to the federal provisions. California, however, is one of a few states that permit limited comment upon a defendant's failure to testify. That permission is narrow. The California law authorizes comment by court and counsel upon the "failure of the defendant to explain or to deny by his testimony any evidence or facts in the case against him. This does not involve any presumption, rebuttable or irrebuttable, either of guilt or of the truth of any fact, that is offered in evidence. It allows inferences to be drawn from proven facts. Because of this clause, the court can direct the jury's attention to whatever evidence there may be that a defendant could deny and the prosecution can argue as to inferences that may be drawn from the accused's failure to testify. * * * However sound may be the legislative conclusion that an accused should not be compelled in any criminal case to be a witness against himself, we see no reason why comment should not be made upon his silence. It seems quite natural that when a defendant has opportunity to deny or explain facts and determines not to do so, the prosecution should bring out the strength of the evidence by commenting upon defendant's failure to explain or deny it. * * *

Appellant sets out the circumstances of this case, however, to show coercion and unfairness in permitting comment. [His] argument here is that he could not take the stand to deny the evidence against him because he would be subjected to a cross-examination as to former crimes to impeach his veracity and the evidence so produced might well bring about his conviction. * * *

It is true that if comment were forbidden, an accused in this situation could remain silent and avoid evidence of former crimes and comment upon his failure to testify. We are of the view, however, that a state may control such a situation in accordance with its own ideas of the most efficient administration of criminal justice. The purpose of due process is not to protect an accused against a proper conviction but against an unfair conviction. When evidence is before a jury that threatens conviction, it does not seem unfair to require him to choose between leaving the adverse evidence unexplained and subjecting himself to impeachment through disclosure of former crimes. Indeed, this is a dilemma with which any defendant may be faced. If facts, adverse to the defendant, are proven by the prosecution, there may be no way to explain them favorably to the accused except by a witness who may be vulnerable to impeachment on cross-examination. The defendant must then decide whether or not to use such a witness. The fact that the witness may also be the defendant makes the choice more difficult but a denial of due process does not emerge from the circumstances.

\* \* \*

Affirmed.

JUSTICE FRANKFURTER (concurring).

\* \* \* Only a technical rule of law would exclude from consideration that which is relevant, as a matter of fair reasoning, to the solution of a problem. Sensible and just-minded men, in important affairs of life, deem it significant that a man remains silent when confronted with serious and responsible evidence against himself which it is within his power to contradict. The notion that to allow jurors to do that which sensible and rightminded men do every day violates the "immutable principles of justice" as conceived by a civilized society is to trivialize the importance of "due process."

[For] historical reasons a limited immunity from the common duty to testify was written into the Federal Bill of Rights, and I am prepared to agree that, as part of that immunity, comment on the failure of an accused to take the witness stand is forbidden in federal prosecutions. It is so, of course, by explicit act of Congress. But to suggest that such a limitation can be drawn out of "due process" in its protection of ultimate decency in a civilized society is to suggest that the Due Process Clause fastened fetters of unreason upon the States.

\* \* \*

Between the incorporation of the Fourteenth Amendment into the Constitution and the beginning of the present membership of the Court—a period of 70 years—the scope of that Amendment was passed upon by 43 judges. Of all these judges only one, who may respectfully be called an eccentric exception, ever indicated the belief that the Fourteenth Amendment was a shorthand summary of the first eight Amendments theretofore limiting only the Federal Government, and that due process incorporated those eight Amendments as restrictions upon the powers of the States. [To] suggest that it is inconsistent with a truly free society to begin prosecutions without an indictment, to try petty civil cases without the paraphernalia of a common law jury, to take into consideration that one who has full opportunity to make a defense remains silent is, in de Tocqueville's phrase, to confound the familiar with the necessary.

The short answer to the suggestion that the [Due Process Clause] of the Fourteenth Amendment \* \* \* was a way of saying that every State must thereafter initiate prosecutions through indictment by a grand jury, must have a trial by a jury of 12 in criminal cases, and must have trial by such a jury in common law suits where the amount in controversy exceeds $20, is that it is a strange way of saying it. It would be extraordinarily strange for a Constitution to convey such specific commands in such a roundabout and inexplicit way.
\* \* \* Those reading the English language with the meaning which it ordinarily conveys, those conversant with the political and legal history of the concept

of due process, those sensitive to the relations of the States to the central government as well as the relation of some of the provisions of the Bill of Rights to the process of justice, would hardly recognize the Fourteenth Amendment as a cover for the various explicit provisions of the first eight Amendments. Some of these are enduring reflections of experience with human nature, while some express the restricted views of Eighteenth–Century England regarding the best methods for the ascertainment of facts. The notion that the Fourteenth Amendment was a covert way of imposing upon the States all the rules which it seemed important to Eighteenth Century statesmen to write into the Federal Amendments, was rejected by judges who were themselves witnesses of the process by which the Fourteenth Amendment became part of the Constitution. Arguments that may now be adduced to prove that the first eight Amendments were concealed within the historic phrasing of the Fourteenth Amendment were not unknown at the time of its adoption. A surer estimate of their bearing was possible for judges at the time than distorting distance is likely to vouchsafe. Any evidence of design or purpose not contemporaneously known could hardly have influenced those who ratified the Amendment. [A]t the time of the ratification of the Fourteenth Amendment the constitutions of nearly half of the ratifying States did not have the rigorous requirements of the Fifth Amendment for instituting criminal proceedings through a grand jury. It could hardly have occurred to these States that by ratifying the Amendment they uprooted their established methods for prosecuting crime and fastened upon themselves a new prosecutorial system.

Indeed, the suggestion that the Fourteenth Amendment incorporates the first eight Amendments as such is not unambiguously urged. [There] is suggested merely a selective incorporation of the first eight Amendments into the Fourteenth Amendment. Some are in and some are out, but we are left in the dark as to which are in and which are out. Nor are we given the calculus for determining which go in and which stay out. If the basis of selection is merely that those provisions of the first eight Amendments are incorporated which commend themselves to individual justices as indispensable to the dignity and happiness of a free man, we are thrown back to a merely subjective test. The protection against unreasonable search and seizure might have primacy for one judge, while trial by a jury of 12 for every claim above $20 might appear to another as an ultimate need in a free society. In the history of thought "natural law" has a much longer and much better founded meaning and justification than such subjective selection of the first eight Amendments for incorporation into the Fourteenth. If all that is meant is that due process contains within itself certain minimal standards which are "of the very essence of a scheme of ordered liberty," *Palko v. Connecticut,* putting upon this Court the duty of applying these standards from time to time, then we have merely arrived at the insight which our predecessors long ago expressed.

* * * The [Fourteenth] Amendment neither comprehends the specific provisions by which the founders deemed it appropriate to restrict the federal government nor is it confined to them. The Due Process Clause of the Fourteenth Amendment has an independent potency, precisely as does the Due Process Clause of the Fifth Amendment in relation to the Federal Government. It ought not to require argument to reject the notion that due process of law meant one thing in the Fifth Amendment and another in the Fourteenth. The Fifth Amendment specifically prohibits prosecution of an "infamous crime" except upon indictment; it forbids double jeopardy; it bars compelling a person to be a witness against himself in any criminal case; it precludes deprivation of "life, liberty, or property, without due process of law." Are Madison and his

contemporaries in the framing of the Bill of Rights to be charged with writing into it a meaningless clause? * * *

A construction which gives to due process no independent function but turns it into a summary of the specific provisions of the Bill of Rights * * * would deprive the States of opportunity for reforms in legal process designed for extending the area of freedom. It would assume that no other abuses would reveal themselves in the course of time than those which had become manifest in 1791. Such a view not only disregards the historic meaning of "due process." It leads inevitably to a warped construction of specific provisions of the Bill of Rights to bring within their scope conduct clearly condemned by due process but not easily fitting into the pigeonholes of the specific provisions.

* * * Judicial review of [the Due Process Clause] of the Fourteenth Amendment inescapably imposes upon this Court an exercise of judgment upon the whole course of the proceedings in order to ascertain whether they offend those canons of decency and fairness which express the notions of justice of English-speaking peoples even toward those charged with the most heinous offenses. These standards of justice are not authoritatively formuled anywhere as though they were prescriptions in a pharmacopoeia. But neither does the application of the Due Process Clause imply that judges are wholly at large. The judicial judgment in applying the Due Process Clause must move within the limits of accepted notions of justice and is not to be based upon the idiosyncracies of a merely personal judgment. The fact that judges among themselves may differ whether in a particular case a trial offends accepted notions of justice is not disproof that general rather than idiosyncratic standards are applied. An important safeguard against such merely individual judgment is an alert deference to the judgment of the State court under review.

JUSTICE BLACK, dissenting.

* * * In my judgment [the Fourteenth Amendment's] history conclusively demonstrates that the language of the first section of the Fourteenth Amendment, taken as a whole, was thought by those responsible for its submission to the people, and by those who opposed its submission, sufficiently explicit to guarantee that thereafter no state could deprive its citizens of the privileges and protections of the Bill of Rights. Whether this Court ever will, or whether it now should, in the light of past decisions, give full effect to what the Amendment was intended to accomplish is not necessarily essential to a decision here. However that may be, our prior decisions, including *Twining*, do not prevent our carrying out that purpose, at least to the extent of making applicable to the states, not a mere part, as the Court has, but the full protection of the Fifth Amendment's provision against compelling evidence from an accused to convict him of crime. And I further contend that the "natural law" formula which the Court uses to reach its conclusion in this case should be abandoned as an incongruous excrescence on our Constitution. I believe that formula to be itself a violation of our Constitution, in that it subtly conveys to courts, at the expense of legislatures, ultimate power over public policies in fields where no specific provision of the Constitution limits legislative power. And my belief seems to be in accord with the views expressed by this Court, at least for the first two decades after the Fourteenth Amendment was adopted. * * *

I cannot consider the Bill of Rights to be an outworn 18th Century "strait jacket" as the *Twining* opinion did. Its provisions may be thought outdated abstractions by some. And it is true that they were designed to meet ancient evils. But they are the same kind of human evils that have emerged from century to century wherever excessive power is sought by the few at the expense of the many. In my judgment the people of no nation can lose their liberty so long as a Bill of Rights like ours survives and its basic purposes are conscientiously interpreted, enforced and respected so as to afford continuous protection against old, as well as new, devices and practices which might thwart those purposes. I fear to see the consequences of the Court's practice of substituting its own concepts of decency and fundamental justice for the language of the Bill of Rights as its point of departure in interpreting and enforcing that Bill of Rights. If the choice must be between the selective process of the *Palko* decision applying some of the Bill of Rights to the States, or the *Twining* rule applying none of them, I would choose the *Palko* selective process. But rather than accept either of these choices, I would follow what I believe was the original purpose of the Fourteenth Amendment—to extend to all the people of the nation the complete protection of the Bill of Rights. To hold that this Court can determine what, if any, provisions of the Bill of Rights will be enforced, and if so to what degree, is to frustrate the great design of a written Constitution.

Conceding the possibility that this Court is now wise enough to improve on the Bill of Rights by substituting natural law concepts for the Bill of Rights, I think the possibility is entirely too speculative to agree to take that course. I would therefore hold in this case that the full protection of the Fifth Amendment's proscription against compelled testimony must be afforded by California. This I would do because of reliance upon the original purpose of the Fourteenth Amendment.

It is an illusory apprehension that literal application of some or all of the provisions of the Bill of Rights to the States would unwisely increase the sum total of the powers of this Court to invalidate state legislation. The Federal Government has not been harmfully burdened by the requirement that enforcement of federal laws affecting civil liberty conform literally to the Bill of Rights. Who would advocate its repeal? It must be conceded, of course, that the natural-law-due-process formula, which the Court today reaffirms, has been interpreted to limit substantially this Court's power to prevent state violations of the individual civil liberties guaranteed by the Bill of Rights. But this formula also has been used in the past and can be used in the future, to license this Court, in considering regulatory legislation, to roam at large in the broad expanses of policy and morals and to trespass, all too freely, on the legislative domain of the States as well as the Federal Government.

Since *Marbury v. Madison* was decided, the practice has been firmly established for better or worse, that courts can strike down legislative enactments which violate the Constitution. This process, of course, involves interpretation, and since words can have many meanings, interpretation obviously may result in contraction or extension of the original purpose of a constitutional provision thereby affecting policy. But to pass upon the constitutionality of statutes by looking to the particular standards enumerated in the Bill of Rights and other parts of the Constitution is one thing; to invalidate statutes because of application of "natural law" deemed to be above and undefined by the Constitution is another. "In the one instance, courts proceeding within clearly marked constitutional boundaries seek to execute policies written into the Constitution; in the other they roam at will in the limitless area of their own beliefs as to reasonableness and actually select policies, a responsibility which the Constitution entrusts to the legislative representatives of the people." *Federal Power Commission v. Natural Gas Pipeline Co.*, 315 U.S. 575 (1942).[a]

---

**a.** In *Rochin v. California,* 342 U.S. 165 (1952), the famous "stomach-pumping" case,     Justice Black also criticized what he called the majority's use of a due process test that "em-

JUSTICE DOUGLAS joins in this opinion. * * *

JUSTICE MURPHY, with whom JUSTICE RUTLEDGE concurs, dissenting.

While in substantial agreement with the views of Mr. Justice Black, I have one reservation and one addition to make.

I agree that the specific guarantees of the Bill of Rights should be carried over intact into the first section of the Fourteenth Amendment. But I am not prepared to say that the latter is entirely and necessarily limited by the Bill of Rights. Occasions may arise where a proceeding falls so far short of conforming to fundamental standards of procedure as to warrant constitutional condemnation in terms of a lack of due process despite the absence of a specific provision in the Bill of Rights.

That point, however, need not be pursued here inasmuch as the Fifth Amendment is explicit in its provision that no person shall be compelled in any criminal case to be a witness against himself. That provision, as Mr. Justice Black demonstrates, is a constituent part of the Fourteenth Amendment.

* * *

Much can be said pro and con as to the desirability of allowing comment on the failure of the accused to testify. But policy arguments are to no avail in the face of a clear constitutional command.[b]

* * *

powers this Court to nullify any state law if its application 'shocks the conscience,' offends 'a sense of justice' or runs counter to the 'decencies of civilized conduct.' "

Rochin was suspected of selling narcotics. When the police burst into his room, he swallowed two capsules. He was then handcuffed and taken to a hospital where, at the direction of the police, "a doctor forced an emetic solution through a tube into Rochin's stomach against his will." This "stomach pumping" produced vomiting—and two capsules that proved to contain morphine. The Court, per Frankfurter, J., ruled that the morphine should have been excluded from evidence because the methods used by the police to obtain it violated Fourteenth Amendment Due Process:

"This is conduct that shocks the conscience. * * * [T]his course of proceeding by agents of government to obtain evidence is bound to offend even hardened sensibilities. They are methods too close to the rack and the screw to permit of constitutional differentiation."

Concurring Justice Black criticized the "nebulous" and "accordion-like" quality of the majority's approach and maintained that "faithful adherence to the specific guarantees in the Bill of Rights ensures a more permanent protection of individual liberty." In a separate concurring opinion, Justice Douglas also criticized the majority's approach: "[W]e cannot in fairness free the state courts from [the specific restraints of the Fifth Amendment privilege against self-incrimination] and yet excoriate them for flouting the 'decencies of civilized conduct' when they admit the evidence. This is to make the rule turn not on the Constitution but on the idiosyncrasies of the judges who sit here."

The "conduct that shocks the conscience" test did not prevent the admission of the evidence in *Irvine v. California*, 347 U.S. 128 (1954), despite the fact that "few police measures have come to [the Court's] attention that more flagrantly, deliberately, and persistently violated the fundamental principle declared by the Fourth Amendment." In *Irvine* the police had surreptitiously entered the home of a suspected bookmaker, installed a concealed microphone in a bedroom, and listened to the conversations of the occupants for over a month.

Because of the "aggravating" and "repulsive" police misconduct in *Irvine*, dissenting Justice Frankfurter insisted that *Rochin* was controlling. But Justice Jackson, who announced the judgment of the Court and wrote the principal opinion, responded: "However obnoxious are the facts in the case before us, they do not involve coercion, violence or brutality to the person [as did *Rochin*], but rather a trespass to property, plus eavesdropping."

According to some commentators, the demonstrated incapacity of the *Rochin* test to deal with the problem of egregious police misconduct was a major reason the Court overruled *Wolf v. Colorado*, 338 U.S. 25 (1949), and held in *Mapp v. Ohio*, 367 U.S. 643 (1961), that the federal exclusionary rule in search and seizure cases was binding on the states via the Due Process Clause of the Fourteenth Amendment. See generally Ch. 3.

b. The position taken in *Twining* and *Adamson*—that the Fifth Amendment privilege against self-incrimination was not incorporated in the Fourteenth—was rejected in

## SECTION 2. THE MODERN APPROACH: THE SHIFT TO "SELECTIVE INCORPORATION"

Although the Court has remained unwilling to accept the total incorporationists' reading of the Fourteenth Amendment, in the 1960's it "selectively" "incorporated" or "absorbed" more and more of the specific provisions of the Bill of Rights into the Fourteenth Amendment. "Selective incorporation" combines aspects of both the "fundamental rights" and "total incorporation" approaches. It accepts the basic premise of the fundamental rights proponents that the Fourteenth Amendment encompasses only rights that are "of the very essence of the scheme of ordered liberty." It also recognizes that not all rights enumerated in the Bill of Rights are necessarily fundamental and that other rights may be fundamental even though not found in the first eight Amendments. But the "selective incorporation" approach rejects the fundamental rights interpretation insofar as that view emphasizes the "totality of the circumstances" in the particular case.

In determining whether an enumerated right is "fundamental," therefore, the selective incorporation doctrine requires that the Court look at the total right guaranteed by the particular Bill of Rights provision, not merely at a single aspect of that right nor the application of that aspect in the case before it. If a particular guarantee is determined to be "fundamental," that provision is incorporated into the Fourteenth Amendment and applied to the states *to the same extent* that it applies to the federal government—or, as critics of this approach expressed it, applied "jot-for-jot and case-for-case" (Harlan, J., joined by Stewart, J., concurring in *Duncan v. Louisiana,* infra); "bag and baggage, however securely or insecurely affixed they may be by law and precedent to federal proceedings" (Fortas, J., concurring in *Duncan* ).

Although strongly criticized as an artificial compromise between the fundamental rights and total incorporation approaches, and lacking even the "internal consistency" of the total incorporation view of the Fourteenth Amendment (Harlan, J., dissenting in *Duncan* ), selective incorporation gained the ascendancy in the 1960's. The adoption of this position was accompanied by a movement towards a broader view of the nature of "fundamental procedural rights."

As Justice White pointed out for the Court in *Duncan,* the question asked was no longer whether the procedural safeguard at issue was "of the very essence of a scheme of ordered liberty" or required by "the 'immutable principles of justice' as conceived by a civilized society" or whether "a civilized system could be imagined" without it. Instead, the Court inquired whether the procedural safeguard in question was "fundamental to the American scheme of justice" or "necessary" or "fundamental" "in the context of the criminal process maintained by the American states."

By the time *Duncan* reached the Court the following Bill of Rights guarantees had been "selectively incorporated" (and thus held enforceable against the states according to the same standards that protect these rights against federal encroachment):

> the freedom from unreasonable searches and seizures and the right to
> have excluded from criminal trials any evidence obtained in violation

---

*Malloy v. Hogan* (1964), discussed in Ch. 6, § 3. *Griffin v. California,* 380 U.S. 609 (1965), then applied *Malloy* to overrule the specific holdings of *Twining* and *Adamson,* which had permitted comment on a state defendant's failure to take the stand.

thereof, *Mapp v. Ohio*, (1961) (set forth in Ch. 3) and *Ker v. California*, 374 U.S. 23 (1963);

the prohibition against cruel and unusual punishment, *Robinson v. California*, 370 U.S. 660 (1962);

the right to the assistance of counsel, *Gideon v. Wainwright*, (1963) (set forth in Ch. 5);

the privilege against compelled self-incrimination, *Malloy v. Hogan*, 378 U.S. 1 (1964);

the right to confront opposing witnesses, *Pointer v. Texas*, 380 U.S. 400 (1965);

the right to a speedy trial, *Klopfer v. North Carolina*, 386 U.S. 213 (1967); and

the right to compulsory process for obtaining witnesses, *Washington v. Texas*, 388 U.S. 14 (1967).[a]

These developments did not escape Justice Black. Concurring in *Duncan*, he reaffirmed his belief in the "total incorporation" theory, but expressed his willingness to support the "selective incorporation" doctrine "as an alternative": "[I]t keeps judges from roaming at will in their own notions of what policies outside the Bill of Rights are desirable and what are not. And, most importantly for me, the selective incorporation process has the virtue of having already worked to make most of the Bill of Rights protections applicable to the States."

## DUNCAN v. LOUISIANA

391 U.S. 145, 88 S.Ct. 1444, 20 L.Ed.2d 491 (1968).

JUSTICE WHITE delivered the opinion of the Court.

[Appellant] was convicted of simple battery [which under Louisiana law] is a misdemeanor, punishable by two years' imprisonment and a $300 fine. Appellant sought trial by jury, but because the Louisiana Constitution grants jury trials only in cases in which capital punishment or imprisonment at hard labor may be imposed, the trial judge denied the request. Appellant was convicted and sentenced to serve 60 days in the parish prison and pay a fine of $150.

* * * Because we believe that trial by jury in criminal cases is fundamental to the American scheme of justice, we hold that the Fourteenth Amendment guarantees a right of jury trial in all criminal cases which—were they to be tried in a federal court—would come within the Sixth Amendment's guarantee.[14]

a. In addition, *Duncan*, infra, held the right to jury trial applicable to the states and, a year later, *Benton v. Maryland*, 395 U.S. 784 (1969) made the prohibition against double jeopardy binding on the states. The only guarantees addressed specifically to criminal procedure not held applicable to the states are the Eighth Amendment prohibition against excessive bail and the Fifth Amendment requirement of prosecution of infamous crimes by grand jury indictment. The Supreme Court has not yet ruled directly on the bail clause, but the Court's characterization of that clause is *Schilb v. Kuebel*, 404 U.S. 357 (1971), suggests that it would qualify for protection under the Fourteenth Amendment Due Process Clause, too, if the issue were squarely presented. Still on the books, however, is *Hurtado v. California*, 110 U.S. 516 (1884),

declining to apply to the states the indictment by grand jury requirement. That decision continues to be followed as valid precedent and appears unlikely to be overruled. See Ch. 11.

14. In one sense recent cases applying provisions of the first eight amendments to the States represent a new approach to the "incorporation" debate. Earlier the Court can be seen as having asked, when inquiring into whether some particular procedural safeguard was required of a State, if a civilized system could be imagined that would not accord the particular protection. [The] recent cases, on the other hand, have proceeded upon the valid assumption that state criminal processes are not imaginary and theoretical schemes but actual systems bearing virtually every charac-

Since we consider the appeal before us to be such a case, we hold that the Constitution was violated when appellant's demand for jury trial was refused.

[B]y the time our Constitution was written, jury trial in criminal cases had been in existence in England for several centuries and carried impressive credentials traced by many to Magna Carta. Its preservation and proper operation as a protection against arbitrary rule were among the major objectives of the revolutionary settlement which was expressed in the Declaration and Bill of Rights of 1689. * * *

Jury trial came to America with English colonists, and received strong support from them. Royal interference with the jury trial was deeply resented. Among the resolutions adopted by the First Congress of the American Colonies (the Stamp Act Congress) on October 19, 1765—resolutions deemed by their authors to state "the most essential rights and liberties of the colonists"—was the declaration: "That trial by jury is the inherent and invaluable right of every British subject in these colonies."

[The] constitutions adopted by the original States guaranteed jury trial. Also, the constitution of every State entering the Union thereafter in one form or another protected the right to jury trial in criminal cases. * * *

Jury trial continues to receive strong support. The laws of every State guarantee a right to jury trial in serious criminal cases; no State has dispensed with it; nor are there significant movements underway to do so. * * *

We are aware of prior cases in this Court in which the prevailing opinion contains statements contrary to our holding today that the right to jury trial in serious criminal cases is a fundamental right and hence must be recognized by the States as part of their obligation to extend due process of law to all persons within their jurisdiction. Louisiana relies especially on *Maxwell v. Dow; Palko;* and *Snyder v. Massachusetts,* 291 U.S. 97 (1934). None of these cases, however, dealt with a State which had purported to dispense entirely with a jury trial in serious criminal cases. * * *

The guarantees of jury trial in the Federal and State Constitutions reflect a profound judgment about the way in which law should be enforced and justice administered. A right to jury trial is granted to criminal defendants in order to

teristic of the common-law system that has been developing contemporaneously in England and in this country. The question thus is whether given this kind of system a particular procedure is fundamental—whether, that is, a procedure is necessary to an Anglo–American regime of ordered liberty. [Of] immediate relevance for this case are the Court's holdings that the States must comply with certain provisions of the Sixth Amendment, specifically that the States may not refuse a speedy trial, confrontation of witnesses, and the assistance, at state expense if necessary, of counsel. Of each of these determinations that a constitutional provision originally written to bind the Federal Government should bind the States as well it might be said that the limitation in question is not necessarily fundamental to fairness in every criminal system that might be imagined but is fundamental in the context of the criminal processes maintained by the American States.

When the inquiry is approached in this way the question whether the States can impose criminal punishment without granting a jury trial appears quite different from the way it appeared in the older cases opining that States might abolish jury trial. See, e.g., *Maxwell v. Dow,* 176 U.S. 581 (1900). A criminal process which was fair and equitable but used no juries is easy to imagine. It would make use of alternative guarantees and protections which would serve the purposes that the jury serves in the English and American systems. Yet no American State has undertaken to construct such a system. Instead, every American State, including Louisiana, uses the jury extensively, and imposes very serious punishments only after a trial at which the defendant has a right to a jury's verdict. In every State, including Louisiana, the structure and style of the criminal process—the supporting framework and the subsidiary procedures—are of the sort that naturally complement jury trial, and have developed in connection with and in reliance upon jury trial.

prevent oppression by the Government. Those who wrote our constitutions knew from history and experience that it was necessary to protect against unfounded criminal charges brought to eliminate enemies and against judges too responsive to the voice of higher authority. The framers of the constitutions strove to create an independent judiciary but insisted upon further protection against arbitrary action. Providing an accused with the right to be tried by a jury of his peers gave him an inestimable safeguard against the corrupt or overzealous prosecutor and against the compliant, biased, or eccentric judge. If the defendant preferred the commonsense judgment of a jury to the more tutored but perhaps less sympathetic reaction of the single judge, he was to have it. Beyond this, the jury trial provisions in the Federal and State Constitutions reflect a fundamental decision about the exercise of official power—a reluctance to entrust plenary powers over the life and liberty of the citizen to one judge or to a group of judges. Fear of unchecked power, so typical of our State and Federal Governments in other respects, found expression in the criminal law in this insistence upon community participation in the determination of guilt or innocence. The deep commitment of the Nation to the right of jury trial in serious criminal cases as a defense against arbitrary law enforcement qualifies for protection under the Due Process Clause of the Fourteenth Amendment, and must therefore be respected by the States.

Of course jury trial has "its weaknesses and the potential for misuse." We are aware of the long debate, especially in this century, among those who write about the administration of justice, as to the wisdom of permitting untrained laymen to determine the facts in civil and criminal proceedings. Although the debate has been intense, with powerful voices on either side, most of the controversy has centered on the jury in civil cases. Indeed, some of the severest critics of civil juries acknowledge that the arguments for criminal juries are much stronger. In addition, at the heart of the dispute have been express or implicit assertions that juries are incapable of adequately understanding evidence or determining issues of fact, and that they are unpredictable, quixotic, and little better than a roll of dice. Yet, the most recent and exhaustive study of the jury in criminal cases concluded that juries do understand the evidence and come to sound conclusions in most of the cases presented to them and that when juries differ with the result at which the judge would have arrived, it is usually because they are serving some of the very purposes for which they were created and for which they are now employed.

The State of Louisiana urges that holding that the Fourteenth Amendment assures a right to jury trial will cast doubt on the integrity of every trial conducted without a jury. Plainly, this is not the import of our holding.

\* \* \*

We would not assert [that] every criminal trial—or any particular trial—held before a judge alone is unfair or that a defendant may never be as fairly treated by a judge as he would be by a jury. Thus we hold no constitutional doubts about the practices, common in both federal and state courts, of accepting waivers of jury trial and prosecuting petty crimes without extending a right to jury trial. However, the fact is that in most places more trials for serious crimes are to juries than to a court alone; a great many defendants prefer the judgment of a jury to that of a court. Even where defendants are satisfied with bench trials, the right to a jury trial very likely serves its intended purpose of making judicial or prosecutorial unfairness less likely.

Louisiana's final contention is that even if it must grant jury trials in serious criminal cases, the conviction before us is valid and constitutional because here the petitioner was tried for simple battery and was sentenced to only 60 days in the parish prison. We are not persuaded. It is doubtless true that there is a category of petty crimes or offenses which is not subject to the Sixth Amendment jury trial provision and should not be subject to the Fourteenth Amendment jury trial requirement here applied to the States. [But] the penalty authorized for a particular crime is of major relevance in determining whether it is serious or not and may in itself, if severe enough, subject the trial to the mandates of the Sixth Amendment. [In] the case before us the Legislature of Louisiana has made simple battery a criminal offense punishable by imprisonment for two years and a fine. The question, then is whether a crime carrying such a penalty is an offense which Louisiana may insist on trying without a jury. * * *

In determining whether the length of the authorized prison term or the seriousness of other punishment is enough in itself to require a jury trial, we are counseled [by precedent] to refer to objective criteria, chiefly the existing laws and practices in the Nation. In the federal system, petty offenses are defined as those punishable by no more than six months in prison and a $500 fine. In 49 of the 50 States crimes subject to trial without a jury, which occasionally include simple battery, are punishable by no more than one year in jail. Moreover, in the late 18th century in America crimes triable without a jury were for the most part punishable by no more than a six-month prison term * * *. We need not, however, settle in this case the exact location of the line between petty offenses and serious crimes. It is sufficient for our purposes to hold that a crime punishable by two years in prison is, based on past and contemporary standards in this country, a serious crime and not a petty offense. Consequently, appellant was entitled to a jury trial and it was error to deny it. * * *

JUSTICE BLACK, with whom JUSTICE DOUGLAS joins, concurring.

* * * I said in *Adamson* that while I would "extend to all the people of the nation the complete protection of the Bill of Rights," that "[i]f the choice must be between the selective process of the *Palko* decision applying some of the Bill of Rights to the States, or the *Twining* rule applying none of them, I would choose the *Palko* selective process." And I am very happy to support this selective process through which our Court has since the *Adamson* case held most of the specific Bill of Rights' protections applicable to the States to the same extent they are applicable to the Federal Government. * * *

All of these holdings making Bill of Rights' provisions applicable as such to the States mark, of course, a departure from the *Twining* doctrine holding that none of those provisions were enforceable as such against the States. The dissent in this case, however, makes a spirited and forceful defense of that now discredited doctrine.

[In] addition to the adoption of Professor Fairman's "history," the dissent states that "the great words of the four clauses of the first section of the Fourteenth Amendment would have an exceedingly peculiar way to say that 'The rights heretofore guaranteed against federal intrusion by the first eight amendments are henceforth guaranteed against State intrusion as well.'" In response to this I can say only that the words "No State shall make or enforce any law which shall abridge the privileges or immunities of citizens of the United States" seems to me an eminently reasonable way of expressing the idea that henceforth the Bill of Rights shall apply to the States.[1] What more

---

1. My view has been and is that the Fourteenth Amendment, *as a whole*, makes the Bill of Rights applicable to the States. This would certainly include the language of the Privileges and Immunities Clause, as well as the Due Process Clause.

precious "privilege" of American citizenship could there be than that privilege to claim the protections of our great Bill of Rights? * * *

While I do not wish at this time to discuss at length my disagreement with Brother Harlan's forthright and frank restatement of the now discredited *Twining* doctrine, I do want to point out what appears to me to be the basic difference between us. His view, as was indeed the view of *Twining*, is that "due process is an evolving concept" and therefore that it entails a "gradual process of judicial inclusion and exclusion" to ascertain those "immutable principles [of] free government which no member of the Union may disregard." Thus the Due Process Clause is treated as prescribing no specific and clearly ascertainable constitutional command that judges must obey in interpreting the Constitution, but rather as leaving judges free to decide at any particular time whether a particular rule or judicial formulation embodies an "immutable principl[e] of free government" or is "implicit in the concept of ordered liberty," or whether certain conduct "shocks the judge's conscience" or runs counter to some other similar, undefined and undefinable standard.[a] Thus due process, according to my Brother Harlan, is to be a phrase with no permanent meaning, but one which is found to shift from time to time in accordance with judges' predilections and understandings of what is best for the country. If due process means this, the Fourteenth Amendment, in my opinion, might as well have been written that "no person shall be deprived of life, liberty or property except by laws that the judges of the United States Supreme Court shall find to be consistent with the immutable principles of free government." It is impossible for me to believe that such unconfined power is given to judges in our Constitution that is a written one in order to limit governmental power.

Another tenet of the *Twining* doctrine as restated by my Brother Harlan is that "due process of law requires only fundamental fairness." But the "fundamental fairness" test is one on a par with that of shocking the conscience of the Court. Each of such tests depends entirely on the particular judge's idea of ethics and morals instead of requiring him to depend on the boundaries fixed by the written words of the Constitution. Nothing in the history of the phrase "due process of law" suggests that constitutional controls are to depend on any particular judge's sense of values. * * *

Finally I want to add that I am not bothered by the argument that applying the Bill of Rights to the States "according to the same standards that protect those rights against federal encroachment," interferes with our concept of federalism in that it may prevent States from trying novel social and economic experiments. I have never believed that under the guise of federalism the States should be able to experiment with the protections afforded our citizens through the Bill of Rights. [It] seems to me totally inconsistent to advocate on the one hand, the power of this Court to strike down any state law or practice which it finds "unreasonable" or "unfair," and on the other hand urge that the States be given maximum power to develop their own laws and procedures. Yet the due process approach of my Brothers Harlan and Fortas (see other concurring opinion) does just that since in effect it restricts the States to practices which a majority of this Court is willing to approve on a case-by-case basis. No one is more concerned than I that the States be allowed to use the full scope of their powers as their citizens see fit. And that is why I have continually fought against the expansion of this Court's authority over the States through the use of

---

**a.** Although Justice Black cites no case at this point, this appears to be a reference to the famous "stomach-pumping" case of *Rochin v. California,* discussed in *Adamson* supra at note a.

a broad, general interpretation of due process that permits judges to strike down state laws they do not like.

In closing I want to emphasize that I believe as strongly as ever that the Fourteenth Amendment was intended to make the Bill of Rights applicable to the States. I have been willing to support the selective incorporation doctrine, however, as an alternative, although perhaps less historically supportable than complete incorporation. The selective incorporation process, if used properly, does limit the Supreme Court in the Fourteenth Amendment field to specific Bill of Rights' protections only and keeps judges from roaming at will in their own notions of what policies outside the Bill of Rights are desirable and what are not. And, most importantly for me, the selective incorporation process has the virtue of having already worked to make most of the Bill of Rights' protections applicable to the States.

JUSTICE FORTAS, concurring * * *

[A]lthough I agree with the decision of the Court, I cannot agree [that] the tail must go with the hide: that when we hold, influenced by the Sixth Amendment, that "due process" requires that the States accord the right of jury trial for all but petty offenses, we automatically import all of the ancillary rules which have been or may hereafter be developed incidental to the right to jury trial in the federal courts. I see no reason whatever, for example, to assume that our decision today should require us to impose federal requirements such as unanimous verdicts or a jury of 12 upon the States. We may well conclude that these and other features of federal jury practice are by no means fundamental—that they are not essential to due process of law—and that they are not obligatory on the States.

I would make these points clear today. Neither logic nor history nor the intent of the draftsmen of the Fourteenth Amendment can possibly be said to require that the Sixth Amendment or its jury trial provision be applied to the States together with the total gloss that this Court's decisions have supplied. The draftsmen of the Fourteenth Amendment intended what they said, not more or less: that no State shall deprive any person of life, liberty, or property without due process of law. It is ultimately the duty of this Court to interpret, to ascribe specific meaning to this phrase. There is no reason whatever for us to conclude that, in so doing, we are bound slavishly to follow not only the Sixth Amendment but all of its bag and baggage, however securely or insecurely affixed they may be by law and precedent to federal proceedings. To take this course, in my judgment, would be not only unnecessary but mischievous because it would inflict a serious blow upon the principle of federalism. The Due Process Clause commands us to apply its great standard to state court proceedings to assure basic fairness. It does not command us rigidly and arbitrarily to impose the exact pattern of federal proceedings upon the 50 States. On the contrary, the Constitution's command, in my view, is that in our insistence upon state observance of due process, we should, so far as possible, allow the greatest latitude for state differences. It requires, within the limits of the lofty basic standards that it prescribes for the States as well as the Federal Government, maximum opportunity for diversity and minimal imposition of uniformity of method and detail upon the States. Our Constitution sets up a federal union, not a monolith.

This Court has heretofore held that various provisions of the Bill of Rights such as the freedom of speech and religion guarantees of the First Amendment, the prohibition of unreasonable searches and seizures in the Fourth Amendment, the privilege against self-incrimination of the Fifth Amendment, and the right to counsel and to confrontation under the Sixth Amendment "are all to be enforced against the States under the Fourteenth Amendment according to the same standards that protect those rights against federal encroachment." I need not quarrel with the specific conclusion in those specific instances. But unless one adheres slavishly to the incorporation theory, body and substance, the same conclusion need not be superimposed upon the jury trial right. I respectfully but urgently suggest that it should not be. Jury trial is more than a principle of justice applicable to individual cases. It is a system of administration of the business of the State. * * * We should be ready to welcome state variations which do not impair—indeed, which may advance—the theory and purpose of trial by jury.

JUSTICE HARLAN, whom JUSTICE STEWART joins, dissenting.

Every American jurisdiction provides for trial by jury in criminal cases. The question before us is not whether jury trial is an ancient institution, which it is; nor whether it plays a significant role in the administration of criminal justice, which it does; nor whether it will endure, which it shall. The question in this case is whether the State of Louisiana, which provides trial by jury for all felonies, is prohibited by the Constitution from trying charges of simple battery to the court alone. In my view, the answer to that question, mandated alike by our constitutional history and by the longer history of trial by jury, is clearly "no." * * *

The Court's approach to this case is an uneasy and illogical compromise among the views of various Justices on how the Due Process Clause should be interpreted. The Court does not say that those who framed the Fourteenth Amendment intended to make the Sixth Amendment applicable to the States. And the Court concedes that it finds nothing unfair about the procedure by which the present appellant was tried. Nevertheless, the Court reverses his conviction: it holds, for some reason not apparent to me, that the Due Process Clause incorporates the particular clause of the Sixth Amendment that requires trial by jury in federal criminal cases—including, as I read its opinion, the sometimes trivial accompanying baggage of judicial interpretation in federal contexts. * * *

A few members of the Court have taken the position that the intention of those who drafted the first section of the Fourteenth Amendment was simply, and exclusively, to make the provisions of the first eight amendments applicable to state action. This view has never been accepted by this Court. In my view [the] first section of the Fourteenth Amendment was meant neither to incorporate, nor to be limited to, the specific guarantees of the first eight amendments. The overwhelming historical evidence marshalled by Professor Fairman demonstrates, to me conclusively, that the Congressmen and state legislators who wrote, debated, and ratified the Fourteenth Amendment did not think they were "incorporating" the Bill of Rights and the very breadth and generality of the Amendment's provisions suggests that its authors did not suppose that the Nation would always be limited to mid–19th century conceptions of "liberty" and "due process of law" but that the increasing experience and evolving conscience of the American people would add new "intermediate premises." In short, neither history, nor sense, supports using the Fourteenth Amendment to put the States in a constitutional straitjacket with respect to their own development in the administration of criminal or civil law.

Although I therefore fundamentally disagree with the total incorporation view of the Fourteenth Amendment, it seems to me that such a position does at least have the virtue, lacking in the Court's selective incorporation approach, of internal consistency: we look to the Bill of Rights, word for word, clause for clause, precedent for precedent because, it is said, the men who wrote the Amendment wanted it that way. For those who do not accept this "history," a different source of "intermediate premises" must be found. The Bill of Rights is not necessarily irrelevant to the search for guidance in interpreting the Fourteenth Amendment, but the reason for and the nature of its relevance must be articulated.

Apart from the approach taken by the absolute incorporationists, I can see only one method of analysis that has any internal logic. That is to start with the words "liberty" and "due process of law" and attempt to define them in a way that accords with American traditions and our system of government. This approach, involving a much more discriminating process of adjudication than does "incorporation," is, albeit difficult, the one that was followed throughout the Nineteenth and most of the present century. It entails a "gradual process of judicial inclusion and exclusion," seeking, with due recognition of constitutional tolerance for state experimentation and disparity, to ascertain those "immutable principles of justice which inhere in the very idea of free government which no member of the Union may disregard." * * *

The relationship of the Bill of Rights to this "gradual process" seems to me to be twofold. In the first place it has long been clear that the Due Process Clause imposes some restrictions on state action that parallel Bill of Rights restrictions on federal action. Second, and more important than this accidental overlap, is the fact that the Bill of Rights is evidence, at various points, of the content Americans find in the term "liberty" and of American standards of fundamental fairness.

[In *Gideon v. Wainwright* (1963), set forth in Ch. 5, and other cases], the right guaranteed against the States by the Fourteenth Amendment was one that had also been guaranteed against the Federal Government by one of the first eight amendments. The logically critical thing, however, was not that the rights had been found in the Bill of Rights, but that they were deemed, in the context of American legal history, to be fundamental. * * *

Today's Court still remains unwilling to accept the total incorporationists' view of the history of the Fourteenth Amendment. This, if accepted, would afford a cogent reason for applying the Sixth Amendment to the States. The Court is also, apparently, unwilling to face the task of determining whether denial of trial by jury in the situation before us, or in other situations, is fundamentally unfair. Consequently, the Court has compromised on the ease of the incorporationist position, without its internal logic. It has simply assumed that the question before us is whether the Jury Trial Clause of the Sixth Amendment should be incorporated into the Fourteenth, jot-for-jot and case-for-case, or ignored. Then the Court merely declares that the clause in question is "in" rather than "out."

The Court has justified neither its starting place nor its conclusion. If the problem is to discover and articulate the rules of fundamental fairness in criminal proceedings, there is no reason to assume that the whole body of rules developed in this Court constituting Sixth Amendment jury trial must be regarded as a unit. The requirement of trial by jury in federal criminal cases has given rise to numerous subsidiary questions respecting the exact scope and content of the right. It surely cannot be that every answer the Court has given, or will give, to such a question is attributable to the Founders; or even that every rule announced carries equal conviction of this Court; still less can it be that every such subprinciple is equally fundamental to ordered liberty.[18]

Examples abound. I should suppose it obviously fundamental to fairness that a "jury" means an "impartial jury." I should think it equally obvious that the rule, imposed long ago in the federal courts, that "jury" means "jury of exactly twelve," is not fundamental to anything: there is no significance except to mystics in the number 12. Again, trial by jury has been held to require a unanimous verdict of jurors in the federal courts, although unanimity has not been found essential to liberty in Britain, where the requirement has been abandoned. * * *

Even if I could agree that the question before us is whether Sixth Amendment jury trial is totally "in" or totally "out," I can find in the Court's opinion no real reasons for concluding that it should be "in." The basis for differentiating among clauses in the Bill of Rights cannot be that only some clauses are in the Bill of Rights, or that only some are old and much praised, or that only some have played an important role in the development of federal law. These things are true of all. The Court says that some clauses are more "fundamental" than others, but it turns out to be using this word in a sense that would have astonished Mr. Justice Cardozo and which, in addition, is of no help. The word does not mean "analytically critical to procedural fairness" for no real analysis of the role of the jury in making procedures fair is even attempted. Instead, the word turns out to mean "old," "much praised," and "found in the Bill of Rights." The definition of "fundamental" thus turns out to be circular.

Since, as I see it, the Court has not even come to grips with the issues in this case, it is necessary to start from the beginning. When a criminal defendant contends that his state conviction lacked "due process of law," the question before this Court, in my view, is whether he was denied any element of fundamental procedural fairness. Believing, as I do, that due process is an evolving concept and that old principles are subject to re-evaluation in light of later experience, I think it appropriate to deal on its merits with the question whether Louisiana denied appellant due process of law when it tried him for simple assault without a jury. * * *

The argument that jury trial is not a requisite of due process is quite simple. The central proposition of *Palko,* a proposition to which I would adhere, is that "due process of law" requires only that criminal trials be fundamentally fair. [A]part from the theory that it was historically intended as a mere shorthand for the Bill of Rights, I do not see what else "due process of law" can intelligibly be thought to mean. If due process of law requires only fundamental fairness, then the inquiry in each case must be whether a state trial process was a fair one. The Court has held, properly I think, that in an adversary process it is a requisite of fairness, for which there is no adequate substitute, that a criminal defendant be afforded a right to counsel and to cross-examine opposing witnesses. But it simply has not been demonstrated, nor, I think, can it be demonstrated, that trial by jury is the only fair means of resolving issues of fact.

---

18. The same illogical way of dealing with a Fourteenth Amendment problem was employed in *Malloy v. Hogan* [discussed in Ch. 5, § 3], which held that the Due Process Clause guaranteed the protection of the Self-Incrimination Clause of the Fifth Amendment against state action. I disagreed at that time both with the way the question was framed and with the result the Court reached. I consider myself bound by the Court's holding in *Malloy* with respect to self-incrimination. I do not think that *Malloy* held, nor would I consider myself bound by a holding, that every question arising under the Due Process Clause shall be settled by an arbitrary decision whether a clause in the Bill of Rights is "in" or "out."

The jury is of course not without virtues. It affords ordinary citizens a valuable opportunity to participate in a process of government, an experience fostering, one hopes, a respect for law. It eases the burden on judges by enabling them to share a part of their sometimes awesome responsibility. A jury may, at times, afford a higher justice by refusing to enforce harsh laws (although it necessarily does so haphazardly, raising the questions whether arbitrary enforcement of harsh laws is better than total enforcement, and whether the jury system is to be defended on the ground that jurors sometimes disobey their oaths). And the jury may, or may not, contribute desirably to the willingness of the general public to accept criminal judgments as just.

It can hardly be gainsaid, however, that the principal original virtue of the jury trial—the limitations a jury imposes on a tyrannous judiciary—has largely disappeared. We no longer live in a medieval or colonial society. Judges enforce laws enacted by democratic decision, not by regal fiat. They are elected by the people or appointed by the people's elected officials, and are responsible not to a distant monarch alone but to reviewing courts, including this one.

The jury system can also be said to have some inherent defects, which are multiplied by the emergence of the criminal law from the relative simplicity that existed when the jury system was devised. It is a cumbersome process, not only imposing great cost in time and money on both the State and the jurors themselves, but also contributing to delay in the machinery of justice. Untrained jurors are presumably less adept at reaching accurate conclusions of fact than judges, particularly if the issues are many or complex. And it is argued by some that trial by jury, far from increasing public respect for law, impairs it: the average man, it is said, reacts favorably neither to the notion that matters he knows to be complex are being decided by other average men, nor to the way the jury system distorts the process of adjudication.

That trial by jury is not the only fair way of adjudicating criminal guilt is well attested by the fact that it is not the prevailing way, either in England or in this country. * * *

In the United States, where it has not been as generally assumed that jury waiver is permissible, the statistics are only slightly less revealing. Two experts have estimated that, of all prosecutions for crimes triable to a jury, 75% are settled by guilty plea and 40% of the remainder are tried to the court. In one State, Maryland, which has always provided for waiver, the rate of court trial appears in some years to have reached 90%. The Court recognizes the force of these statistics in stating, "We would not assert, however, that every criminal trial—or any particular trial—held before a judge alone is unfair or that a defendant may never be as fairly treated by a judge as he would be by a jury." I agree. I therefore see no reason why this Court should reverse the conviction of appellant, absent any suggestion that his particular trial was in fact unfair, or compel the State of Louisiana to afford jury trial in an as yet unbounded category of cases that can, without unfairness, be tried to a court.

Indeed, even if I were persuaded that trial by jury is a fundamental right in some criminal cases, I could see nothing fundamental in the rule, not yet formulated by the Court, that places the prosecution of appellant for simple battery within the category of "jury crimes" rather than "petty crimes."

[The] point is not that many offenses that English-speaking communities have, at one time or another, regarded as triable without a jury are more serious, and carry more serious penalties, than the one involved here. The point is rather that until today few people would have thought the exact location of the line mattered very much. There is no obvious reason why a jury trial is a requisite of fundamental fairness when the charge is robbery, and not a requisite of fairness when the same defendant, for the same actions, is charged with assault and petit theft. The reason for the historic exception for relatively minor crimes is the obvious one: the burden of jury trial was thought to outweigh its marginal advantages. Exactly why the States should not be allowed to make continuing adjustments, based on the state of their criminal dockets and the difficulty of summoning jurors, simply escapes me.

In sum, there is a wide range of views on the desirability of trial by jury, and on the ways to make it most effective when it is used; there is also considerable variation from State to State in local conditions such as the size of the criminal caseload, the ease or difficulty of summoning jurors, and other trial conditions bearing on fairness. We have before us, therefore, an almost perfect example of a situation in which the celebrated dictum of Mr. Justice Brandeis should be invoked. It is, he said, "one of the happy incidents of the federal system that a single courageous state may, if its citizens choose, serve as a laboratory * * *." *New State Ice Co. v. Liebmann*, 285 U.S. 262 (1932) (dissenting opinion). This Court, other courts, and the political process are available to correct any experiments in criminal procedure that prove fundamentally unfair to defendants. That is not what is being done today: instead, and quite without reason, the Court has chosen to impose upon every State one means of trying criminal cases; it is a good means, but it is not the only fair means, and it is not demonstrably better than the alternatives States might devise. * * *[b]

**b.** Post–*Duncan* jury trial cases arguably seemed to confirm Justice Harlan's warning that "selective incorporation" might lead to *dilution in federal cases* of Bill of Rights "specifics." In *Williams v. Florida*, 399 U.S. 78 (1970), the Court reconsidered the scope of the right to jury trial, concluded that the fact "that [the] jury at common law was composed of precisely 12 is an historical accident, unnecessary to effect the purposes of the jury system," and concluded that the Sixth Amendment permitted six-person juries in state *or federal* non-capital felony cases. Concurring in the result, Justice Harlan charged that "before today it would have been unthinkable to suggest that the Sixth Amendment's right to a trial by jury is satisfied by a jury of six, or less, as is left open, [or] by less than a unanimous verdict, a question also reserved in today's decision."

The issues left open in *Duncan*—whether the jury could be less than 6 and whether a verdict could be less than unanimous—were decided in cases discussed in Chapter 15, § 1. One of those cases, *Apodaca v. Oregon*, 406 U.S. 404 (1972), produced a result inconsistent with *Duncan*'s selective incorporation analysis although a clear majority favored that analysis. In *Apodaca*, eight members of the Court—all but newly appointed Justice Powell—adhered to the *Duncan* approach that each element of the Sixth Amendment Jury Trial Clause applies to the states to the same extent it applies to the federal government, but these eight Justices split 4–4 over whether the Sixth Amendment *did require* unanimity in federal criminal cases. The deadlock was broken by Justice Powell, but broken *in two different directions*. He read the Sixth Amendment to require unanimity *in federal cases*, but concluded that *this feature* of the Jury Trial Clause is not "so fundamental to the essentials of jury trial" as to require unanimity in state cases as a matter of Fourteenth Amendment Due Process. Justice Powell reached these positions by adopting a Harlan-type approach to Fourteenth Amendment Due Process: "Although it is perhaps late in the day for an expression of my views, I [believe] that, at least in defining the elements of the right to jury trial, there is no sound basis for interpreting the Fourteenth Amendment to require blind adherence by the States to all details of the federal Sixth Amendment standards." Thus, *Apodaca* produced an 8–1 majority reaffirming the view that the Jury Trial Clause is to be enforced against the states to the same extent it applies to the federal government, a 5–4 majority that would hold that the Sixth Amendment does require a unanimous verdict in federal criminal trials, and a 5–4 majority that upheld a less than unanimous verdict (10–2) in a state case.

# Chapter 3

# ARREST, SEARCH AND SEIZURE

## SECTION 1.  THE EXCLUSIONARY RULE

The Fourth Amendment to the United States Constitution reads: "The right of the people to be secure in their persons, houses, papers, and effects, against unreasonable searches and seizures, shall not be violated, and no Warrants shall issue, but upon probable cause, supported by Oath or affirmation, and particularly describing the place to be searched, and the persons or things to be seized." The Amendment says nothing about how it is to be enforced, a matter which has been the subject of vigorous debate for a good many years.  Most of this debate has focused upon the wisdom of and constitutional necessity for the so-called exclusionary rule, whereunder evidence obtained in violation of the Fourth Amendment is ordinarily inadmissible in a criminal trial.  This exclusionary rule has existed in the federal criminal justice system for nearly 75 years, but has been mandated at the state level not nearly as long.  In the first two cases in this section, *Wolf v. Colorado* and *Mapp v. Ohio,* we see the Court first rejecting and then accepting the notion that this exclusionary rule is constitutionally required in the state courts.

*Mapp* by no means ended the argument, though in more recent years much of the debate has centered upon the proper scope of the exclusionary rule.  If, as the Supreme Court often indicated, a primary purpose of the rule is deterrence of the police, then precisely when is exclusion appropriate in the sense that it will likely have such a deterrent effect?  The Court's answer to this question in *United States v. Leon,* the final case in this section, produced the so-called "good faith" exception to the exclusionary rule in state and federal courts.

## WOLF v. COLORADO
### 338 U.S. 25, 69 S.Ct. 1359, 93 L.Ed. 1782 (1949).

JUSTICE FRANKFURTER delivered the opinion of the Court.

The precise question for consideration is this: Does a conviction by a State court for a State offense deny the "due process of law" required by the Fourteenth Amendment, solely because evidence that was admitted at the trial was obtained under circumstances which would have rendered it inadmissible in a prosecution for violation of a federal law in a court of the United States because there deemed to be an infraction of the Fourth Amendment?  *  *  *

The security of one's privacy against arbitrary intrusion by the police— which is at the core of the Fourth Amendment—is basic to a free society.  It is therefore implicit in "the concept of ordered liberty" and as such enforceable against the States through the Due Process Clause. * * *

Accordingly, we have no hesitation in saying that were a State affirmatively to sanction such police incursion into privacy it would run counter to the guaranty of the Fourteenth Amendment. But the ways of enforcing such a basic right raise questions of a different order. How such arbitrary conduct should be checked, what remedies against it should be afforded, the means by which the right should be made effective, are all questions that are not to be so dogmatically answered as to preclude the varying solutions which spring from an allowable range of judgment on issues not susceptible of quantitative solution.

In *Weeks v. United States,* 232 U.S. 383 (1914), this Court held that in a federal prosecution the Fourth Amendment barred the use of evidence secured through an illegal search and seizure. This ruling * * * was not derived from the explicit requirements of the Fourth Amendment; it was not based on legislation expressing Congressional policy in the enforcement of the Constitution. The decision was a matter of judicial implication. Since then it has been frequently applied and we stoutly adhere to it. But the immediate question is whether the basic right to protection against arbitrary intrusion by the police demands the exclusion of logically relevant evidence obtained by an unreasonable search and seizure because, in a federal prosecution for a federal crime, it would be excluded. As a matter of inherent reason, one would suppose this to be an issue as to which men with complete devotion to the protection of the right of privacy might give different answers. When we find that in fact most of the English-speaking world does not regard as vital to such protection the exclusion of evidence thus obtained, we must hesitate to treat this remedy as an essential ingredient of the right. The contrariety of views of the States is particularly impressive in view of the careful reconsideration which they have given the problem in the light of the *Weeks* decision.

* * * As of today 30 States reject the *Weeks* doctrine, 17 States are in agreement with it. * * * Of 10 jurisdictions within the United Kingdom and the British Commonwealth of Nations which have passed on the question, none has held evidence obtained by illegal search and seizure inadmissible. * * *

The jurisdictions which have rejected the *Weeks* doctrine have not left the right to privacy without other means of protection. Indeed, the exclusion of evidence is a remedy which directly serves only to protect those upon whose person or premises something incriminating has been found. We cannot, therefore, regard it as a departure from basic standards to remand such persons, together with those who emerge scatheless from a search, to the remedies of private action and such protection as the internal discipline of the police, under the eyes of an alert public opinion, may afford. Granting that in practice the exclusion of evidence may be an effective way of deterring unreasonable searches, it is not for this Court to condemn as falling below the minimal standards assured by the Due Process Clause a State's reliance upon other methods which, if consistently enforced, would be equally effective. * * * There are, moreover, reasons for excluding evidence unreasonably obtained by the federal police which are less compelling in the case of police under State or local authority. The public opinion of a community can far more effectively be exerted against oppressive conduct on the part of police directly responsible to the community itself than can local opinion, sporadically aroused, be brought to bear upon remote authority pervasively exerted throughout the country.

We hold, therefore, that in a prosecution in a State court for a State crime the Fourteenth Amendment does not forbid the admission of evidence obtained by an unreasonable search and seizure. * * *

JUSTICE BLACK, concurring.

* * * I agree with what appears to be a plain implication of the Court's opinion that the federal exclusionary rule is not a command of the Fourth Amendment but is a judicially created rule of evidence which Congress might negate. * * *

JUSTICE MURPHY, with whom JUSTICE RUTLEDGE joins, dissenting.

[T]here is but one alternative to the rule of exclusion. That is no sanction at all.

* * * Little need be said concerning the possibilities of criminal prosecution. Self-scrutiny is a lofty ideal, but its exaltation reaches new heights if we expect a District Attorney to prosecute himself or his associates for well-meaning violations of the search and seizure clause during a raid the District Attorney or his associates have ordered. But there is an appealing ring in another alternative. A trespass action for damages is a venerable means of securing reparation for unauthorized invasion of the home. Why not put the old writ to a new use? When the Court cites cases permitting the action, the remedy seems complete.

But what an illusory remedy this is, if by "remedy" we mean a positive deterrent to police and prosecutors tempted to violate the Fourth Amendment. The appealing ring softens when we recall that in a trespass action the measure of damages is simply the extent of the injury to physical property. If the officer searches with care, he can avoid all but nominal damages—a penny, or a dollar. Are punitive damages possible? Perhaps. But a few states permit none, whatever the circumstances. In those that do, the plaintiff must show the real ill will or malice of the defendant, and surely it is not unreasonable to assume that one in honest pursuit of crime bears no malice toward the search victim. If that burden is carried, recovery may yet be defeated by the rule that there must be physical damages before punitive damages may be awarded. In addition, some states limit punitive damages to the actual expenses of litigation. * * * Even assuming the ill will of the officer, his reasonable grounds for belief that the home he searched harbored evidence of crime is admissible in mitigation of punitive damages. * * * The bad reputation of the plaintiff is likewise admissible. * * * If the evidence seized was actually used at a trial, that fact has been held a complete justification of the search, and a defense against the trespass action. * * * And even if the plaintiff hurdles all these obstacles, and gains a substantial verdict, the individual officer's finances may well make the judgment useless—for the municipality, of course, is not liable without its consent. Is it surprising that there is so little in the books concerning trespass actions for violation of the search and seizure clause? * * *

JUSTICE DOUGLAS, dissenting.

* * * I agree with Justice Murphy that * * * in absence of [an exclusionary] rule of evidence the Amendment would have no effective sanction. * * *

# MAPP v. OHIO

367 U.S. 643, 81 S.Ct. 1684, 6 L.Ed.2d 1081 (1961).

JUSTICE CLARK delivered the opinion of the Court.  *  *  *

On May 23, 1957, three Cleveland police officers arrived at appellant's residence in that city pursuant to information that "a person [was] hiding out in the home who was wanted for questioning in connection with a recent bombing, and that there was a large amount of policy paraphernalia being hidden in the home." Miss Mapp and her daughter by a former marriage lived on the top floor of the two-family dwelling. Upon their arrival at that house, the officers knocked on the door and demanded entrance but appellant, after telephoning her attorney, refused to admit them without a search warrant.  *  *  *

The officers again sought entrance some three hours later when four or more additional officers arrived on the scene. When Miss Mapp did not come to the door immediately, at least one of the several doors to the house was forcibly opened and the policemen gained admittance. Meanwhile Miss Mapp's attorney arrived, but the officers, having secured their own entry, and continuing in their defiance of the law, would permit him neither to see Miss Mapp nor to enter the house. [When the officers broke into the hall, Miss Mapp] demanded to see the search warrant. A paper, claimed to be a warrant, was held up by one of the officers. She grabbed the "warrant" and placed it in her bosom. A struggle ensued in which the officers recovered the piece of paper and as a result of which they handcuffed appellant because she had been "belligerent" in resisting their official rescue of the "warrant" from her person.  *  *  *  Appellant, in hand-cuffs, was then forcibly taken upstairs to her bedroom where the officers searched a dresser, a chest of drawers, a closet and some suitcases.  *  *  *  The search spread to the rest of the second floor  *  *  *. The basement of the building and a trunk found therein were also searched. The obscene materials for possession of which she was ultimately convicted were discovered in the course of that widespread search.

At the trial no search warrant was produced by the prosecution, nor was the failure to produce one explained or accounted for. At best [as the Ohio Supreme Court, which affirmed the conviction, expressed it], "there is, in the record, considerable doubt as to whether there ever was any warrant for the search of defendant's home."  *  *  *

The State says that even if the search were made without authority, or otherwise unreasonably, it is not prevented from using the unconstitutionally seized evidence at trial, citing *Wolf v. Colorado,*  *  *  *. On this appeal,  *  *  * it is urged once again that we review that holding.  *  *  *

The Court in *Wolf* first stated that "[t]he contrariety of views of the States" on the adoption of the exclusionary rule of *Weeks* was "particularly impressive"  *  *  *. While in 1949, prior to the *Wolf* case, almost two-thirds of the States were opposed to the use of the exclusionary rule, now, despite the *Wolf* case, more than half of those since passing upon it, by their own legislative or judicial decision, have wholly or partly adopted or adhered to the *Weeks* rule.  *  *  * Significantly, among those now following the rule is California which, according to its highest court, was "compelled to reach that conclusion because other remedies have completely failed to secure compliance with the constitutional provisions  *  *  *." In connection with this California case, we note that the second basis elaborated in *Wolf* in support of its failure to enforce the exclusionary doctrine against the States was that "other means of protection" have been afforded "the right to privacy." The experience of California that such other remedies have been worthless and futile is buttressed by the experience of other States.

Likewise, time has set its face against what *Wolf* called the "weighty testimony" of *People v. Defore,* 1926, 242 N.Y. 13, 150 N.E. 585. There Justice (then Judge) Cardozo, rejecting adoption of the *Weeks* exclusionary rule in New York, had said that "[t]he Federal rule as it stands is either too strict or too lax." However the force of that reasoning has been largely vitiated by later decisions of this Court. These include the recent discarding of the "silver platter" doctrine, *Elkins v. United States;* [a] the relaxation of the formerly strict requirements as to standing to challenge the use of evidence thus seized, * * * and finally, the formulation of a method to prevent state use of evidence unconstitutionally seized by federal agents, *Rea v. United States.* [b] * * *

It, therefore, plainly appears that the factual considerations supporting the failure of the *Wolf* Court to include the *Weeks* exclusionary rule when it recognized the enforceability of the right to privacy against the States in 1949, while not basically relevant to the constitutional consideration, could not, in any analysis, now be deemed controlling.

* * * Today we once again examine *Wolf's* constitutional documentation of the right to privacy free from unreasonable state intrusion, and, after its dozen years on our books, are led by it to close the only courtroom door remaining open to evidence secured by official lawlessness in flagrant abuse of that basic right, reserved to all persons as a specific guarantee against that very same unlawful conduct. We hold that all evidence obtained by searches and seizures in violation of the Constitution is, by that same authority, inadmissible in a state court.[c]

**a.** 364 U.S. 206 (1960). Under the "silver platter" doctrine, evidence of a federal crime seized by state police in the course of an illegal search while investigating a state crime could be turned over to federal authorities and used in a federal prosecution so long as federal agents had not participated in the illegal search but had simply received the evidence on a "silver platter." In rejecting the doctrine, the Court pointed out that the determination in *Wolf* that Fourteenth Amendment Due Process prohibited illegal searches and seizures by state officers, marked the "removal of the doctrinal underpinning" for the admissibility of state-seized evidence in federal prosecutions.

**b.** 350 U.S. 214 (1956), where the Court held that a federal law enforcement agent who seized evidence on the basis of an invalid search warrant should be enjoined from turning over such evidence to state authorities for use in a state prosecution and from giving testimony concerning the evidence: "The District Court is not asked to enjoin state officials nor in any way to interfere with state agencies in enforcement of state law. * * * The only relief asked is against a federal agent, who obtained the property as a result of the abuse of process issued by a United States Commissioner. * * * In this posture we have then a case that raises not a constitutional question but one concerning our

supervisory powers over federal law enforcement agencies."

**c.** Although an illegal arrest or other unreasonable seizure of the person is itself a violation of the Fourth and Fourteenth Amendments, the *Mapp* exclusionary sanction comes into play only when the police have obtained evidence as a result of the unconstitutional seizure. Such is the case when, for example, the police make an illegal arrest and then conduct a fruitful search which is "incident to" that arrest and thus dependent upon the lawfulness of the arrest for its legality. Such may also be the case when the connection between the illegality and the evidence is less apparent, and even when the evidence is verbal, such as a confession obtained from a defendant some time after his illegal arrest. As explained in *Wong Sun v. United States,* 371 U.S. 471 (1963), not "all evidence is 'fruit of the poisonous tree' simply because it would not have come to light but for the illegal actions of the police. Rather, the more apt question in such a case is 'whether, granting establishment of the primary illegality [the evidence] has been come at by exploitation of that illegality or instead by means sufficiently distinguishable to be purged of the primary taint.'" In making that judgment, the "temporal proximity of the arrest and the confession, the presence of intervening circumstances and, particularly, the purpose and

Since the Fourth Amendment's right of privacy has been declared enforceable against the States through the Due Process Clause of the Fourteenth, it is enforceable against them by the same sanction of exclusion as is used against the Federal Government. Were it otherwise then just as without the *Weeks* rule the assurance against unreasonable federal searches and seizures would be "a form of words," valueless and undeserving of mention in a perpetual charter of inestimable human liberties, so too, without that rule the freedom from state invasions of privacy would be so ephemeral and so neatly severed from its conceptual nexus with the freedom from all brutish means of coercing evidence as not to merit this Court's high regard as a freedom "implicit in 'the concept of ordered liberty.'"

* * * [I]n extending the substantive protections of due process to all constitutionally unreasonable searches—state or federal—it was logically and constitutionally necessary that the exclusion doctrine—an essential part of the right to privacy—be also insisted upon as an essential ingredient of the right newly recognized by the *Wolf* case. In short, the admission of the new constitutional right by *Wolf* could not consistently tolerate denial of its most important constitutional privilege, namely, the exclusion of the evidence which an accused had been forced to give by reason of the unlawful seizure. To hold otherwise is to grant the right but in reality to withhold its privilege and enjoyment. Only last year the Court itself recognized that the purpose of the exclusionary rule "is to deter—to compel respect for the constitutional guaranty in the only effectively available way—by removing the incentive to disregard it."

Indeed, we are aware of no restraint, similar to that rejected today, conditioning the enforcement of any other basic constitutional right. The right to privacy, no less important than any other right carefully and particularly reserved to the people, would stand in marked contrast to all other rights declared as "basic to a free society." * * * [N]othing could be more certain than that when a coerced confession is involved, "the relevant rules of evidence" are overridden without regard to "the incidence of such conduct by the police," slight or frequent. Why should not the same rule apply to what is tantamount to coerced testimony by way of unconstitutional seizure of goods, papers, effects, documents, etc.? We find that, as to the Federal Government the Fourth and Fifth Amendments and, as to the States, the freedom from unconscionable invasions of privacy and the freedom from convictions based upon coerced confessions do enjoy an "intimate relation" in their perpetuation of "principles of humanity and civil liberty * * *." They express "supplementing phases of the same constitutional purpose—to maintain inviolate large areas of personal

---

flagrancy of the official misconduct, are all relevant. The voluntariness of the statement is a threshold requirement." *Brown v. Illinois,* 422 U.S. 590 (1975).

In *United States v. Crews,* 445 U.S. 463 (1980), the Court held that an illegally arrested defendant "is not himself a suppressible 'fruit' and the illegality of his detention cannot deprive the Government of the opportunity to prove his guilt through the introduction of evidence wholly untainted by the police misconduct." Moreover, it is no defense to a state or federal criminal prosecution that the defendant was illegally arrested or forcibly brought within the jurisdiction of the court. The trial of such a defendant violates neither Fifth nor Fourteenth Amendment due process.

As explained in *Frisbie v. Collins,* 342 U.S. 519 (1952), this rule rests "on the sound basis that due process of law is satisfied when one present in court is convicted of crime after having been fairly apprized of the charges against him and after a fair trial in accordance with constitutional procedural safeguards. There is nothing in the Constitution that requires a court to permit a guilty person rightfully convicted to escape justice because he was brought to trial against his will." The Court added that even if the conduct in obtaining defendant's presence violated the federal kidnapping statute the result would be the same, for Congress had not included a bar to prosecution as an available sanction under that law.

privacy." The philosophy of each Amendment and of each freedom is complementary to, although not dependent upon, that of the other in its sphere of influence—the very least that together they assure in either sphere is that no man is to be convicted on unconstitutional evidence.

Moreover, our holding * * * is not only the logical dictate of prior cases, but it also makes very good sense. There is no war between the Constitution and common sense. Presently, a federal prosecutor may make no use of evidence illegally seized, but a State's attorney across the street may, although he supposedly is operating under the enforceable prohibitions of the same Amendment. Thus the State, by admitting evidence unlawfully seized, serves to encourage disobedience to the Federal Constitution which it is bound to uphold.
* * *

There are those who say, as did Justice (then Judge) Cardozo, that under our constitutional exclusionary doctrine "[t]he criminal is to go free because the constable has blundered." *People v. Defore.* In some cases this will undoubtedly be the result. But, as was said in *Elkins,* "there is another consideration—the imperative of judicial integrity." The criminal goes free, if he must, but it is the law that sets him free. Nothing can destroy a government more quickly than its failure to observe its own laws, or worse, its disregard of the charter of its own existence. As Mr. Justice Brandeis, dissenting, said in *Olmstead v. United States,* 277 U.S. 438 (1928): "Our government is the potent, the omnipresent teacher. For good or for ill, it teaches the whole people by its example. * * * If the government becomes a lawbreaker, it breeds contempt for law; it invites every man to become a law unto himself; it invites anarchy." Nor can it lightly be assumed that, as a practical matter, adoption of the exclusionary rule fetters law enforcement. Only last year this Court expressly considered that contention and found that "pragmatic evidence of a sort" to the contrary was not wanting. * * *. The Court noted that:

> "The federal courts themselves have operated under the exclusionary rule of *Weeks* for almost half a century; yet it has not been suggested either that the Federal Bureau of Investigation has thereby been rendered ineffective, or that the administration of criminal justice in the federal courts has thereby been disrupted. Moreover, the experience of the states is impressive * * *. The movement toward the rule of exclusion has been halting but seemingly inexorable."

The ignoble shortcut to conviction left open to the State tends to destroy the entire system of constitutional restraints on which the liberties of the people rest. Having once recognized that the right to privacy embodied in the Fourth Amendment is enforceable against the States, and that the right to be secure against rude invasions of privacy by state officers is, therefore, constitutional in origin, we can no longer permit that right to remain an empty promise. Because it is enforceable in the same manner and to like effect as other basic rights secured by the Due Process Clause, we can no longer permit it to be revocable at the whim of any police officer who, in the name of law enforcement itself, chooses to suspend its enjoyment. Our decision, founded on reason and truth, gives to the individual no more than that which the Constitution guarantees him, to the police officer no less than that to which honest law enforcement is entitled, and, to the courts, that judicial integrity so necessary in the true administration of justice. * * *

Reversed and remanded.

JUSTICE BLACK, concurring. ＊ ＊ ＊

I am still not persuaded that the Fourth Amendment, standing alone, would be enough to bar the introduction into evidence against an accused of papers and effects seized from him in violation of its commands. For the Fourth Amendment does not itself contain any provision expressly precluding the use of such evidence, and I am extremely doubtful that such a provision could properly be inferred from nothing more than the basic command against unreasonable searches and seizures. Reflection on the problem, however, in the light of cases coming before the Court since *Wolf,* has led me to conclude that when the Fourth Amendment's ban against unreasonable searches and seizures is considered together with the Fifth Amendment's ban against compelled self-incrimination, a constitutional basis emerges which not only justifies but actually requires the exclusionary rule. ＊ ＊ ＊

JUSTICE DOUGLAS, concurring.

＊ ＊ ＊ I believe that this is an appropriate case in which to put an end to the asymmetry which *Wolf* imported into the law. ＊ ＊ ＊

Memorandum of JUSTICE STEWART.

＊ ＊ ＊ I express no view as to the merits of the constitutional issue which the Court today decides. ＊ ＊ ＊

JUSTICE HARLAN, whom JUSTICE FRANKFURTER and JUSTICE WHITTAKER join, dissenting.

＊ ＊ ＊ I would not impose upon the States this federal exclusionary remedy. The reasons given by the majority for now suddenly turning its back on *Wolf* seem to me notably unconvincing.

First, it is said that "the factual grounds upon which *Wolf* was based" have since changed, in that more States now follow the *Weeks* exclusionary rule than was so at the time *Wolf* was decided. While that is true, a recent survey indicates that at present one half of the States still adhere to the common-law non-exclusionary rule, and one, Maryland, retains the rule as to felonies. ＊ ＊ ＊ But in any case surely all this is beside the point, as the majority itself indeed seems to recognize. Our concern here, as it was in *Wolf,* is not with the desirability of that rule but only with the question whether the States are Constitutionally free to follow it or not as they may themselves determine, and the relevance of the disparity of views among the States on this point lies simply in the fact that the judgment involved is a debatable one. Moreover, the very fact on which the majority relies, instead of lending support to what is now being done, points away from the need of replacing voluntary state action with federal compulsion.

The preservation of a proper balance between state and federal responsibility in the administration of criminal justice demands patience on the part of those who might like to see things move faster among the States in this respect. Problems of criminal law enforcement vary widely from State to State. One State, in considering the totality of its legal picture, may conclude that the need for embracing the *Weeks* rule is pressing because other remedies are unavailable or inadequate to secure compliance with the substantive Constitutional principle involved. Another, though equally solicitous of Constitutional rights, may choose to pursue one purpose at a time, allowing all evidence relevant to guilt to be brought into a criminal trial, and dealing with Constitutional infractions by other means. Still another may consider the exclusionary rule too rough and ready a remedy, in that it reaches only unconstitutional intrusions which eventuate in criminal prosecution of the victims. Further, a State after experi-

menting with the *Weeks* rule for a time may, because of unsatisfactory experience with it, decide to revert to a non-exclusionary rule.  And so on.  *  *  *
For us the question remains, as it has always been, one of state power, not one of
passing judgment on the wisdom of one state course or another.  In my view this
Court should continue to forbear from fettering the States with an adamant rule
which may embarrass them in coping with their own peculiar problems in
criminal law enforcement.  *  *  *

*  *  *  Our role in promulgating the *Weeks* rule and its extensions  *  *  *
was quite a different one than it is here.  There, in implementing the Fourth
Amendment, we occupied the position of a tribunal having the ultimate responsibility for developing the standards and procedures of judicial administration
within the judicial system over which it presides.  Here we review State
procedures whose measure is to be taken not against the specific substantive
commands of the Fourth Amendment but under the flexible contours of the Due
Process Clause.  I do not believe that the Fourteenth Amendment empowers this
Court to mould state remedies effectuating the right to freedom from "arbitrary
intrusion by the police" to suit its own notions of how things should be done
*  *  *.

Finally, it is said that the overruling of *Wolf* is supported by the established
doctrine that the admission in evidence of an involuntary confession renders a
state conviction constitutionally invalid.  Since such a confession may often be
entirely reliable, and therefore of the greatest relevance to the issue of the trial,
the argument continues, this doctrine is ample warrant in precedent that the
way evidence was obtained and not just its relevance, is constitutionally significant to the fairness of a trial.  I believe this analogy is not a true one.  The
"coerced confession" rule is certainly not a rule that any illegally obtained
statements may not be used in evidence.  I would suppose that a statement
which is procured during a period of illegal detention is, as much as unlawfully
seized evidence, illegally obtained, but this Court has consistently refused to
reverse state convictions resting on the use of such statements.  *  *  *

The point, then, must be that in requiring exclusion of an involuntary
statement of an accused, we are concerned not with an appropriate remedy for
what the police have done, but with something which is regarded as going to the
heart of our concepts of fairness in judicial procedure.  The operative assumption of our procedural system is that "ours is the accusatorial as opposed to the
inquisitorial system.  *  *  *."  *  *  *  The pressures brought to bear against
an accused leading to a confession, unlike an unconstitutional violation of
privacy, do not, apart from the use of the confession at trial, necessarily involve
independent Constitutional violations.  What is crucial is that the trial defense
to which an accused is entitled should not be rendered an empty formality by
reason of statements wrung from him, for then "a prisoner  *  *  * [has been]
made the deluded instrument of his own conviction."  That this is a *procedural
right,* and that its violation occurs at the time his improperly obtained statement
is admitted at trial, is manifest.  *  *  *

This, and not the disciplining of the police, as with illegally seized evidence,
is surely the true basis for excluding a statement of the accused which was
unconstitutionally obtained.  In sum, I think the coerced confession analogy
works strongly *against* what the Court does today.  *  *  *

# UNITED STATES v. LEON

468 U.S. 897, 104 S.Ct. 3405, 82 L.Ed.2d 677 (1984).

Justice White delivered the opinion of the Court.  * * *

This case presents the question whether the Fourth Amendment exclusionary rule should be modified so as not to bar the use in the prosecution's case-in-chief of evidence obtained by officers acting in reasonable reliance on a search warrant issued by a detached and neutral magistrate but ultimately found to be unsupported by probable cause.  * * *

The Fourth Amendment contains no provision expressly precluding the use of evidence obtained in violation of its commands, and an examination of its origin and purposes makes clear that the use of fruits of a past unlawful search or seizure "work[s] no new Fourth Amendment wrong." The wrong condemned by the Amendment is "fully accomplished" by the unlawful search or seizure itself, and the exclusionary rule is neither intended nor able to "cure the invasion of the defendant's rights which he has already suffered." The rule thus operates as "a judicially created remedy designed to safeguard Fourth Amendment rights generally through its deterrent effect, rather than a personal constitutional right of the person aggrieved."

Whether the exclusionary sanction is appropriately imposed in a particular case, our decisions make clear, is "an issue separate from the question whether the Fourth Amendment rights of the party seeking to invoke the rule were violated by police conduct." Only the former question is currently before us,[a] and it must be resolved by weighing the costs and benefits of preventing the use in the prosecution's case-in-chief of inherently trustworthy tangible evidence obtained in reliance on a search warrant issued by a detached and neutral magistrate that ultimately is found to be defective.

The substantial social costs exacted by the exclusionary rule for the vindication of Fourth Amendment rights have long been a source of concern. "Our cases have consistently recognized that unbending application of the exclusionary sanction to enforce ideals of governmental rectitude would impede unacceptably the truth-finding functions of judge and jury." An objectionable collateral consequence of this interference with the criminal justice system's truth-finding function is that some guilty defendants may go free or receive reduced sentences as a result of favorable plea bargains.[6] Particularly when law enforcement

---

**a.** A large quantity of drugs were suppressed on the ground the warrant had not issued on probable cause, in that the affidavit reported only the allegations of an untested informant and limited corroboration by police surveillance of events themselves "as consistent with innocence as * * * with guilt." The Court earlier noted that whether this warrant would pass muster under the intervening and less demanding test of *Illinois v. Gates*, § 3 infra, "has not been briefed or argued," and thus chose "to take the case as it comes to us."

**6.** Researchers have only recently begun to study extensively the effects of the exclusionary rule on the disposition of felony arrests. One study suggests that the rule results in the non-prosecution or nonconviction of between 0.6% and 2.35% of individuals arrested for felonies. Davies, *A Hard Look at What We Know (and Still Need to Learn) About the "Costs" of the Exclusionary Rule: The NIJ Study and Other Studies of "Lost" Arrests*, 1983 A.B.F.Res.J. 611, 621. The estimates are higher for particular crimes the prosecution of which depends heavily on physical evidence. Thus, the cumulative loss due to nonprosecution or nonconviction of individuals arrested on felony drug charges is probably in the range of 2.8% to 7.1%. Davies' analysis of California data suggests that screening by police and prosecutors results in the release because of illegal searches or seizures of as many as 1.4% of all felony arrestees, id., at 650, that 0.9% of felony arrestees are released because of illegal searches or seizures at the preliminary hearing or after trial, id., at 653, and that roughly 0.5% of all felony arrestees benefit from reversals on appeal because of illegal searches. * * *

officers have acted in objective good faith or their transgressions have been minor, the magnitude of the benefit conferred on such guilty defendants offends basic concepts of the criminal justice system. Indiscriminate application of the exclusionary rule, therefore, may well "generat[e] disrespect for the law and the administration of justice." Accordingly, "[a]s with any remedial device, the application of the rule has been restricted to those areas where its remedial objectives are thought most efficaciously served."

Close attention to those remedial objectives has characterized our recent decisions concerning the scope of the Fourth Amendment exclusionary rule. The Court has, to be sure, not seriously questioned, "in the absence of a more efficacious sanction, the continued application of the rule to suppress evidence from the [prosecution's] case where a Fourth Amendment violation has been substantial and deliberate * * *." Nevertheless, the balancing approach that has evolved in various contexts—including criminal trials—"forcefully suggest[s] that the exclusionary rule be more generally modified to permit the introduction of evidence obtained in the reasonable good-faith belief that a search or seizure was in accord with the Fourth Amendment." * * *

Only [when a warrant is grounded upon an affidavit knowingly or recklessly false] has the Court set forth a rationale for suppressing evidence obtained pursuant to a search warrant;[b] in the other areas, it has simply excluded such evidence without considering whether Fourth Amendment interests will be advanced. To the extent that proponents of exclusion rely on its behavioral effects on judges and magistrates in these areas, their reliance is misplaced. First, the exclusionary rule is designed to deter police misconduct rather than to punish the errors of judges and magistrates. Second, there exists no evidence suggesting that judges and magistrates are inclined to ignore or subvert the Fourth Amendment or that lawlessness among these actors requires application of the extreme sanction of exclusion.[14]

✓Third, and most important, we discern no basis, and are offered none, for believing that exclusion of evidence seized pursuant to a warrant will have a significant deterrent effect on the issuing judge or magistrate. Many of the factors that indicate that the exclusionary rule cannot provide an effective "special" or "general" deterrent for individual offending law enforcement officers apply as well to judges or magistrates. And, to the extent that the rule is thought to operate as a "systemic" deterrent on a wider audience, it clearly can have no such effect on individuals empowered to issue warrants. Judges and magistrates are not adjuncts to the law enforcement team; as neutral judicial officers, they have no stake in the outcome of particular criminal prosecutions. The threat of exclusion thus cannot be expected significantly to deter them. Imposition of the exclusionary sanction is not necessary meaningfully to inform judicial officers of their errors, and we cannot conclude that admitting evidence

Many of these researchers have concluded that the impact of the exclusionary rule is insubstantial, but the small percentages with which they deal mask a large absolute number of felons who are released because the cases against them were based in part on illegal searches or seizures. * * * Because we find that the rule can have no substantial deterrent effect in the sorts of situations under consideration in this case, we conclude that it cannot pay its way in those situations.

**b.** The reference is to *Franks v. Delaware,* 438 U.S. 154 (1978), where the Court declared

"it would be an unthinkable imposition upon [the magistrate's] authority if a warrant affidavit, revealed after the fact to contain a deliberately or recklessly false statement, were to stand beyond impeachment."

**14.** Although there are assertions that some magistrates become rubber stamps for the police and others may be unable effectively to screen police conduct, we are not convinced that this is a problem of major proportions.

obtained pursuant to a warrant while at the same time declaring that the warrant was somehow defective will in any way reduce judicial officers' professional incentives to comply with the Fourth Amendment, encourage them to repeat their mistakes, or lead to the granting of all colorable warrant requests.[18]

If exclusion of evidence obtained pursuant to a subsequently invalidated warrant is to have any deterrent effect, therefor, it must alter the behavior of individual law enforcement officers or the policies of their departments. One could argue that applying the exclusionary rule in cases where the police failed to demonstrate probable cause in the warrant application deters future inadequate presentations or "magistrate shopping" and thus promotes the ends of the Fourth Amendment. Suppressing evidence obtained pursuant to a technically defective warrant supported by probable cause also might encourage officers to scrutinize more closely the form of the warrant and to point out suspected judicial errors. We find such arguments speculative and conclude that suppression of evidence obtained pursuant to a warrant should be ordered only on a case-by-case basis and only in those unusual cases in which exclusion will further the purposes of the exclusionary rule.[19]

We have frequently questioned whether the exclusionary rule can have any deterrent effect when the offending officers acted in the objectively reasonable belief that their conduct did not violate the Fourth Amendment. "No empirical researcher, proponent or opponent of the rule, has yet been able to establish with any assurance whether the rule has a deterrent effect * * *." But even assuming that the rule effectively deters some police misconduct and provides incentives for the law enforcement profession as a whole to conduct itself in accord with the Fourth Amendment, it cannot be expected, and should not be applied, to deter objectively reasonable law enforcement activity. * * *[20]

**18.** Limiting the application of the exclusionary sanction may well increase the care with which magistrates scrutinize warrant applications. We doubt that magistrates are more desirous of avoiding the exclusion of evidence obtained pursuant to warrants they have issued than of avoiding invasions of privacy.

Federal magistrates, moreover, are subject to the direct supervision of district courts. They may be removed for "incompetency, misconduct, neglect of duty, or physical or mental disability." 28 U.S.C. § 631(i). If a magistrate serves merely as a "rubber stamp" for the police or is unable to exercise mature judgment, closer supervision or removal provides a more effective remedy than the exclusionary rule.

**19.** Our discussion of the deterrent effect of excluding evidence obtained in reasonable reliance on a subsequently invalidated warrant assumes, of course, that the officers properly executed the warrant and searched only those places and for those objects that it was reasonable to believe were covered by the warrant. * * *

**20.** We emphasize that the standard of reasonableness we adopt is an objective one. Many objections to a good-faith exception assume that the exception will turn on the subjective good faith of individual officers.

"Grounding the modification in objective reasonableness, however, retains the value of the exclusionary rule as an incentive for the law enforcement profession as a whole to conduct themselves in accord with the Fourth Amendment." The objective standard we adopt, moreover, requires officers to have a reasonable knowledge of what the law prohibits. As Professor Jerold Israel has observed:

"The key to the [exclusionary] rule's effectiveness as a deterrent lies, I believe, in the impetus it has provided to police training programs that make officers aware of the limits imposed by the fourth amendment and emphasize the need to operate within those limits. [An objective good-faith exception] * * * is not likely to result in the elimination of such programs, which are now viewed as an important aspect of police professionalism. Neither is it likely to alter the tenor of those programs; the possibility that illegally obtained evidence may be admitted in borderline cases is unlikely to encourage police instructors to pay less attention to fourth amendment limitations. Finally, [it] * * * should not encourage officers to pay less attention to what they are taught, as the requirement that the officer act in 'good faith' is inconsistent with closing one's mind to the possibility of illegality."

This is particularly true, we believe, when an officer acting with objective good faith has obtained a search warrant from a judge or magistrate and acted within its scope. In most such cases, there is no police illegality and thus nothing to deter. It is the magistrate's responsibility to determine whether the officer's allegations establish probable cause and, if so, to issue a warrant comporting in form with the requirements of the Fourth Amendment. In the ordinary case, an officer cannot be expected to question the magistrate's proba-ble-cause determination or his judgment that the form of the warrant is technically sufficient. "[O]nce the warrant issues, there is literally nothing more the policeman can do in seeking to comply with the law." Penalizing the officer for the magistrate's error, rather than his own, cannot logically contrib-ute to the deterrence of Fourth Amendment violations.[22]

We conclude that the marginal or nonexistent benefits produced by sup-pressing evidence obtained in objectively reasonable reliance on a subsequently invalidated search warrant cannot justify the substantial costs of exclusion. We do not suggest, however, that exclusion is always inappropriate in cases where an officer has obtained a warrant and abided by its terms. [T]he officer's reliance on the magistrate's probable-cause determination and on the technical sufficiency of the warrant he issues must be objectively reasonable,[23] and it is clear that in some circumstances the officer [24] will have no reasonable grounds for believing that the warrant was properly issued.

Suppression therefore remains an appropriate remedy if the magistrate or judge in issuing a warrant was misled by information in an affidavit that the affiant knew was false or would have known was false except for his reckless disregard of the truth. The exception we recognize today will also not apply in cases where the issuing magistrate wholly abandoned his judicial role in the manner condemned in *Lo–Ji Sales, Inc. v. New York*, 442 U.S. 319 (1979);[c] in such circumstances, no reasonably well-trained officer should rely on the war-rant. Nor would an officer manifest objective good faith in relying on a warrant based on an affidavit "so lacking in indicia of probable cause as to render official belief in its existence entirely unreasonable." Finally, depending on the circum-stances of the particular case, a warrant may be so facially deficient—i.e., in

**22.** * * * Our cases establish that the question whether the use of illegally obtained evidence in judicial proceedings represents ju-dicial participation in a Fourth Amendment violation and offends the integrity of the courts "is essentially the same as the inquiry into whether exclusion would serve a deter-rent purpose." * * * Absent unusual cir-cumstances, when a Fourth Amendment viola-tion has occurred because the police have reasonably relied on a warrant issued by a detached and neutral magistrate but ultimate-ly found to be defective, "the integrity of the courts is not implicated."

**23.** [O]ur good-faith inquiry is confined to the objectively ascertainable question whether a reasonably well-trained officer would have known that the search was illegal despite the magistrate's authorization. In making this determination, all of the circumstances—in-cluding whether the warrant application had previously been rejected by a different magis-trate—may be considered.

**24.** References to "officer" throughout this opinion should not be read too narrowly. It is necessary to consider the objective reasonable-ness, not only of the officers who eventually executed a warrant, but also of the officers who originally obtained it or who provided information material to the probable-cause de-termination. Nothing in our opinion sug-gests, for example, that an officer could obtain a warrant on the basis of a "bare bones" affidavit and then rely on colleagues who are ignorant of the circumstances under which the warrant was obtained to conduct the search.

**c.** There the magistrate was held not to have "manifest[ed] that neutrality and detach-ment demanded of a judicial officer when pre-sented with a warrant application," where he went to the scene and made judgments there about what should be seized as obscene, as he "allowed himself to become a member, if not the leader of the search party which was essentially a police operation."

failing to particularize the place to be searched or the things to be seized—that the executing officers cannot reasonably presume it to be valid.[d]

    * * * The good-faith exception for searches conducted pursuant to warrants is not intended to signal our unwillingness strictly to enforce the requirements of the Fourth Amendment, and we do not believe that it will have this effect. As we have already suggested, the good-faith exception, turning as it does on objective reasonableness, should not be difficult to apply in practice. When officers have acted pursuant to a warrant, the prosecution should ordinarily be able to establish objective good faith without a substantial expenditure of judicial time.

    Nor are we persuaded that application of a good-faith exception to searches conducted pursuant to warrants will preclude review of the constitutionality of the search or seizure, deny needed guidance from the courts, or freeze Fourth Amendment law in its present state.[25] There is no need for courts to adopt the inflexible practice of always deciding whether the officers' conduct manifested objective good faith before turning to the question whether the Fourth Amendment has been violated. * * *

    If the resolution of a particular Fourth Amendment question is necessary to guide future action by law enforcement officers and magistrates, nothing will prevent reviewing courts from deciding that question before turning to the good-faith issue.[26] Indeed, it frequently will be difficult to determine whether the officers acted reasonably without resolving the Fourth Amendment issue. Even if the Fourth Amendment question is not one of broad import, reviewing courts could decide in particular cases that magistrates under their supervision need to be informed of their errors and so evaluate the officers' good faith only after finding a violation. In other circumstances, those courts could reject suppression motions posing no important Fourth Amendment questions by turning immediately to a consideration of the officers' good faith. We have no reason to believe that our Fourth Amendment jurisprudence would suffer by allowing

---

    **d.** Compare the companion case of *Massachusetts v. Sheppard*, 468 U.S. 981 (1984), where a detective prepared an affidavit for a search warrant to search for various specified items of evidence of a homicide but, because it was Sunday, could only find a warrant form for controlled substances. He presented his affidavit and that form to a judge at his home and pointed out the problem to him, and the judge, unable to locate a more suitable form, told the detective that he would make the necessary changes to make it a proper warrant. He made some changes, but failed to change that part of the warrant which authorized a search only for controlled substances and related paraphernalia. The detective took the two documents and he and other officers then executed the warrant, seizing evidence of the homicide. That evidence was suppressed in the state court because the warrant failed to particularly describe the items to be seized, as required by the Fourth Amendment. The Supreme Court, per White, J., held this situation fell within *Leon* because "there was an objectively reasonable basis for the officers' mistaken belief" that "the warrant authorized the search that they conducted." As for defendant's objection that the detective knew when he went to the judge

that the warrant was defective, the Court stated: "Whatever an officer may be required to do when he executes a warrant without knowing beforehand what items are to be seized, we refuse to rule that an officer is required to disbelieve a judge who has just advised him, by word and by action, that the warrant he possesses authorizes him to conduct the search he has requested."

    **25.** The argument that defendants will lose their incentive to litigate meritorious Fourth Amendment claims as a result of the good-faith exception we adopt today is unpersuasive. Although the exception might discourage presentation of insubstantial suppression motions, the magnitude of the benefit conferred on defendants by a successful motion makes it unlikely that litigation of colorable claims will be substantially diminished.

    **26.** It has been suggested, in fact, that "the recognition of a 'penumbral zone,' within which an inadvertent mistake would not call for exclusion, * * * will make it less tempting for judges to bend fourth amendment standards to avoid releasing a possibly dangerous criminal because of a minor and unintentional miscalculation by the police."

reviewing courts to exercise an informed discretion in making this choice.
*  *  *

In the absence of an allegation that the magistrate abandoned his detached and neutral role, suppression is appropriate only if the officers were dishonest or reckless in preparing their affidavit or could not have harbored an objectively reasonable belief in the existence of probable cause. Only respondent Leon has contended that no reasonably well-trained police officer could have believed that there existed probable cause to search his house; significantly, the other respondents advance no comparable argument. Officer Rombach's application for a warrant clearly was supported by much more than a "bare bones" affidavit. The affidavit related the results of an extensive investigation and, as the opinions of the divided panel of the Court of Appeals make clear, provided evidence sufficient to create disagreement among thoughtful and competent judges as to the existence of probable cause. Under these circumstances, the officers' reliance on the magistrate's determination of probable cause was objectively reasonable, and application of the extreme sanction of exclusion is inappropriate.[e]

Accordingly, the judgment of the Court of Appeals is reversed.

JUSTICE BLACKMUN, concurring.

[A]ny empirical judgment about the effect of the exclusionary rule in a particular class of cases necessarily is a provisional one. *  *  * If it should emerge from experience that, contrary to our expectations, the good faith exception to the exclusionary rule results in a material change in police compliance with the Fourth Amendment, we shall have to reconsider what we have undertaken here. The logic of a decision that rests on untested predictions about police conduct demands no less. *  *  *

JUSTICE BRENNAN, with whom JUSTICE MARSHALL joins, dissenting. *  *  *

[The majority's reading of the Fourth Amendment] appears plausible, because, as critics of the exclusionary rule never tire of repeating, the Fourth Amendment makes no express provision for the exclusion of evidence secured in violation of its commands. A short answer to this claim, of course, is that many of the Constitution's most vital imperatives are stated in general terms and the task of giving meaning to these precepts is therefore left to subsequent judicial

---

**e.** Prior to *Leon,* the Supreme Court had often applied the exclusionary rule even when the police acted in reliance upon a subsequently invalidated statute conferring authority to search. But when confronted with such a situation once again in *Illinois v. Krull,* 107 S.Ct. 1160 (1987), the Court, 5–4, ruled otherwise. Blackmun, J., reasoned for the majority: "The approach used in *Leon* is equally applicable to the present case. The application of the exclusionary rule to suppress evidence obtained by an officer acting in objectively reasonable reliance on a statute would have as little deterrent effect on the officer's actions as would the exclusion of evidence when an officer acts in objectively reasonable reliance on a warrant. Unless a statute is clearly unconstitutional, an officer cannot be expected to question the judgment of the legislature that passed the law." The Court in *Krull* further reasoned that there was no "evidence to suggest that legislators 'are inclined to ignore or subvert the Fourth Amendment'"

or "to indicate that applying the exclusionary rule to evidence seized pursuant to the statute prior to the declaration of its invalidity will act as a significant additional deterrent" of legislators.

O'Connor, J., for the dissenters, emphasized: (1) "The distinction drawn between the legislator and the judicial officer is sound" because "a legislature's unreasonable authorization of searches may affect thousands or millions" and thus "poses a greater threat to liberty." (2) "[L]egislators by virtue of their political role are more often subjected to the political pressures that may threaten Fourth Amendment values than are judicial officers." (3) "Providing legislatures a grace period during which the police may freely perform unreasonable searches in order to convict those who might have otherwise escaped creates a positive incentive to promulgate unconstitutional laws."

decision-making in the context of concrete cases. The nature of our Constitution, as Chief Justice Marshall long ago explained, "requires that only its great outlines should be marked, its important objects designated, and the minor ingredients which compose those objects be deduced from the nature of the objects themselves."

A more direct answer may be supplied by recognizing that the Amendment, like other provisions of the Bill of Rights, restrains the power of the government as a whole; it does not specify only a particular agency and exempt all others. The judiciary is responsible, no less than the executive, for ensuring that constitutional rights are respected.

When that fact is kept in mind, the role of the courts and their possible involvement in the concerns of the Fourth Amendment comes into sharper focus. Because seizures are executed principally to secure evidence, and because such evidence generally has utility in our legal system only in the context of a trial supervised by a judge, it is apparent that the admission of illegally obtained evidence implicates the same constitutional concerns as the initial seizure of that evidence. Indeed, by admitting unlawfully seized evidence, the judiciary becomes a part of what is in fact a single governmental action prohibited by the terms of the Amendment. Once that connection between the evidence-gathering role of the police and the evidence-admitting function of the courts is acknowledged, the plausibility of the Court's interpretation becomes more suspect. Certainly nothing in the language or history of the Fourth Amendment suggests that a recognition of this evidentiary link between the police and the courts was meant to be foreclosed. It is difficult to give any meaning at all to the limitations imposed by the Amendment if they are read to proscribe only certain conduct by the police but to allow other agents of the same government to take advantage of evidence secured by the police in violation of its requirements. The Amendment therefore must be read to condemn not only the initial unconstitutional invasion of privacy—which is done, after all, for the purpose of securing evidence—but also the subsequent use of any evidence so obtained. * * *

Such a conception of the rights secured by the Fourth Amendment was unquestionably the original basis of what has come to be called the exclusionary rule when it was first formulated in *Weeks v. United States.* * * *

[T]he question whether the exclusion of evidence would deter future police misconduct was never considered a relevant concern in the early cases * * *. In those formative decisions, the Court plainly understood that the exclusion of illegally obtained evidence was compelled not by judicially fashioned remedial purposes, but rather by a direct constitutional command. * * *

* * * Indeed, no other explanation suffices to account for the Court's holding in *Mapp,* since the only possible predicate for the Court's conclusion that the States were bound by the Fourteenth Amendment to honor the *Weeks* doctrine is that the exclusionary rule was "part and parcel of the Fourth Amendment's limitation upon [governmental] encroachment of individual privacy."

Despite this clear pronouncement, however, the Court * * * has gradually pressed the deterrence rationale for the rule back to center stage. The various arguments advanced by the Court in this campaign have only strengthened my conviction that the deterrence theory is both misguided and unworkable. First, the Court has frequently bewailed the "cost" of excluding reliable evidence. In large part, this criticism rests upon a refusal to acknowledge the function of the Fourth Amendment itself. If nothing else, the Amendment plainly operates to disable the government from gathering information and securing evidence in certain ways. In practical terms, of course, this restriction of official power means that some incriminating evidence inevitably will go undetected if the government obeys these constitutional restraints. It is the loss of that evidence that is the "price" our society pays for enjoying the freedom and privacy safeguarded by the Fourth Amendment. Thus, some criminals will go free *not,* in Justice (then Judge) Cardozo's misleading epigram, "because the constable has blundered," but rather because official compliance with Fourth Amendment requirements makes it more difficult to catch criminals. Understood in this way, the Amendment directly contemplates that some reliable and incriminating evidence will be lost to the government; therefore, it is not the exclusionary rule, but the Amendment itself that has imposed this cost.

In addition, the Court's decisions over the past decade have made plain that the entire enterprise of attempting to assess the benefits and costs of the exclusionary rule in various contexts is a virtually impossible task for the judiciary to perform honestly or accurately. Although the Court's language in those cases suggests that some specific empirical basis may support its analyses, the reality is that the Court's opinions represent inherently unstable compounds of intuition, hunches, and occasional pieces of partial and often inconclusive data. * * * To the extent empirical data is available regarding the general costs and benefits of the exclusionary rule, it has shown, on the one hand, as the Court acknowledges today, that the costs are not as substantial as critics have asserted in the past, and, on the other hand, that while the exclusionary rule may well have certain deterrent effects, it is extremely difficult to determine with any degree of precision whether the incidence of unlawful conduct by police is now lower than it was prior to *Mapp.* The Court has sought to turn this uncertainty to its advantage by casting the burden of proof upon proponents of the rule. "Obviously," however, "the assignment of the burden of proof on an issue where evidence does not exist and cannot be obtained is outcome determinative. [The] assignment of the burden is merely a way of announcing a predetermined conclusion."

By remaining within its redoubt of empiricism and by basing the rule solely on the deterrence rationale, the Court has robbed the rule of legitimacy. A doctrine that is explained as if it were an empirical proposition but for which there is only limited empirical support is both inherently unstable and an easy mark for critics. The extent of this Court's fidelity to Fourth Amendment requirements, however, should not turn on such statistical uncertainties. * * *

Even if I were to accept the Court's general approach to the exclusionary rule, I could not agree with today's result. * * *

At the outset, the Court suggests that society has been asked to pay a high price—in terms either of setting guilty persons free or of impeding the proper functioning of trials—as a result of excluding relevant physical evidence in cases where the police, in conducting searches and seizing evidence, have made only an "objectively reasonable" mistake concerning the constitutionality of their actions. But what evidence is there to support such a claim?

Significantly, the Court points to none, and, indeed, as the Court acknowledges, recent studies have demonstrated that the "costs" of the exclusionary rule—calculated in terms of dropped prosecutions and lost convictions—are quite low. Contrary to the claims of the rule's critics that exclusion leads to "the release of countless guilty criminals," these studies have demonstrated that federal and state prosecutors very rarely drop cases because of potential search and seizure problems. For example, a 1979 study prepared at the request of

Congress by the General Accounting Office reported that only 0.4% of all cases actually declined for prosecution by federal prosecutors were declined primarily because of illegal search problems.  If the GAO data are restated as a percentage of *all* arrests, the study shows that only 0.2% of all felony arrests are declined for prosecution because of potential exclusionary rule problems.[11]  Of course, these data describe only the costs attributable to the exclusion of evidence in all cases; the costs due to the exclusion of evidence in the narrower category of cases where police have made objectively reasonable mistakes must necessarily be even smaller.  The Court, however, ignores this distinction and mistakenly weighs the aggregated costs of exclusion in *all* cases, irrespective of the circumstances that led to exclusion, against the potential benefits associated with only those cases in which evidence is excluded because police reasonably but mistakenly believe that their conduct does not violate the Fourth Amendment.  When such faulty scales are used, it is little wonder that the balance tips in favor of restricting the application of the rule.

What then supports the Court's insistence that this evidence be admitted?  Apparently, the Court's only answer is that even though the costs of exclusion are not very substantial, the potential deterrent effect in these circumstances is so marginal that exclusion cannot be justified.  The key to the Court's conclusion in this respect is its belief that the prospective deterrent effect of the exclusionary rule operates only in those situations in which police officers, when deciding whether to go forward with some particular search, have reason to know that their planned conduct will violate the requirements of the Fourth Amendment.

*  *  * But what the Court overlooks is that the deterrence rationale for the rule is not designed to be, nor should it be thought of as, a form of "punishment" of individual police officers for their failures to obey the restraints imposed by the Fourth Amendment.  Instead, the chief deterrent function of the rule is its tendency to promote institutional compliance with Fourth Amendment requirements on the part of law enforcement agencies generally.  Thus, as the Court has previously recognized, "over the long term, [the] demonstration [provided by the exclusionary rule] that our society attaches serious consequences to violation of constitutional rights is thought to encourage those who formulate law enforcement policies, and the officers who implement them, to incorporate Fourth Amendment ideals into their value system."  It is only through such an institu-

---

11.  In a series of recent studies, researchers have attempted to quantify the actual costs of the rule.  A recent National Institute of Justice study based on data for the four year period 1976–1979 gathered by the California Bureau of Criminal Statistics showed that 4.8% of all cases that were declined for prosecution by California prosecutors were rejected because of illegally seized evidence.  However, if these data are calculated as a percentage of all arrests that were declined for prosecution, they show that only 0.8% of all arrests were rejected for prosecution because of illegally seized evidence.

In another measure of the rule's impact—the number of prosecutions that are dismissed or result in acquittals in cases where evidence has been excluded—the available data again show that the Court's past assessment of the rule's costs has generally been exaggerated.  For example, a study based on data from 9 mid-sized counties in Illinois, Michigan and Pennsylvania reveals that motions to suppress physical evidence were filed in approximately 5% of the 7,500 cases studied, but that such motions were successful in only 0.7% of all these cases.  The study also shows that only 0.6% of all cases resulted in acquittals because evidence had been excluded.  In the GAO study, suppression motions were filed in 10.5% of all federal criminal cases surveyed, but of the motions filed, approximately 80–90% were denied.  Evidence was actually excluded in only 1.3% of the cases studied, and only 0.7% of all cases resulted in acquittals or dismissals after evidence was excluded.  And in another study based on data from cases during 1978 and 1979 in San Diego and Jacksonville, it was shown that only 1% of all cases resulting in nonconviction were caused by illegal searches.

tion-wide mechanism that information concerning Fourth Amendment standards can be effectively communicated to rank and file officers.[13]

If the overall educational effect of the exclusionary rule is considered, application of the rule to even those situations in which individual police officers have acted on the basis of a reasonable but mistaken belief that their conduct was authorized can still be expected to have a considerable long-term deterrent effect. If evidence is consistently excluded in these circumstances, police departments will surely be prompted to instruct their officers to devote greater care and attention to providing sufficient information to establish probable cause when applying for a warrant, and to review with some attention the form of the warrant that they have been issued, rather than automatically assuming that whatever document the magistrate has signed will necessarily comport with Fourth Amendment requirements.

After today's decision, however, that institutional incentive will be lost. Indeed, the Court's "reasonable mistake" exception to the exclusionary rule will tend to put a premium on police ignorance of the law. Armed with the assurance provided by today's decision that evidence will always be admissible whenever an officer has "reasonably" relied upon a warrant, police departments will be encouraged to train officers that if a warrant has simply been signed, it is reasonable, without more, to rely on it. Since in close cases there will no longer be any incentive to err on the side of constitutional behavior, police would have every reason to adopt a "let's-wait-until-its-decided" approach in situations in which there is a question about a warrant's validity or the basis for its issuance.[14]

Although the Court brushes these concerns aside, a host of grave consequences can be expected to result from its decision to carve this new exception out of the exclusionary rule. A chief consequence of today's decision will be to convey a clear and unambiguous message to magistrates that their decisions to issue warrants are now insulated from subsequent judicial review. Creation of this new exception for good faith reliance upon a warrant implicitly tells magistrates that they need not take much care in reviewing warrant applications, since their mistakes will from now on have virtually no consequence: If their decision to issue a warrant was correct, the evidence will be admitted; if their decision was incorrect but the police relied in good faith on the warrant, the evidence will also be admitted. Inevitably, the care and attention devoted to such an inconsequential chore will dwindle. Although the Court is correct to note that magistrates do not share the same stake in the outcome of a criminal case as the police, they nevertheless need to appreciate that their role is of some moment in order to continue performing the important task of carefully reviewing warrant applications. Today's decision effectively removes that incentive.

Moreover, the good faith exception will encourage police to provide only the bare minimum of information in future warrant applications. The police will now know that if they can secure a warrant, so long as the circumstances of its

---

**13.** * * * A former United States Attorney and now Attorney General of Maryland, Stephen Sachs, has described the impact of the rule on police practices in similar terms: "I have watched the rule deter, routinely, throughout my years as a prosecutor * * *. [P]olice-prosecutor consultation is customary in all our cases when Fourth Amendment concerns arise * * *. In at least three Maryland jurisdictions, for example, prosecutors are on twenty-four hour call to field search and seizure questions presented by police officers."

**14.** The authors of a recent study of the warrant process in seven cities concluded that application of a good faith exception where an officer relies upon a warrant "would further encourage police officers to seek out the less inquisitive magistrates and to rely on boilerplate formulae, thereby lessening the value of search warrants overall. * * *

issuance are not "entirely unreasonable," all police conduct pursuant to that warrant will be protected from further judicial review. The clear incentive that operated in the past to establish probable cause adequately because reviewing courts would examine the magistrate's judgment carefully, has now been so completely vitiated that the police need only show that it was not "entirely unreasonable" under the circumstances of a particular case for them to believe that the warrant they were issued was valid. The long-run effect unquestionably will be to undermine the integrity of the warrant process. * * *

JUSTICE STEVENS, * * * dissenting * * *.

* * * It is probable, though admittedly not certain, that the Court of Appeals would now conclude that the warrant in *Leon* satisfied the Fourth Amendment if it were given the opportunity to reconsider the issue in the light of *Gates.* Adherence to our normal practice following the announcement of a new rule would therefore postpone, and probably obviate, the need for the promulgation of the broad new rule the Court announces today.

[W]hen the Court goes beyond what is necessary to decide the case before it, it can only encourage the perception that it is pursuing its own notions of wise social policy, rather than adhering to its judicial role. I do not believe the Court should reach out to decide what is undoubtedly a profound question concerning the administration of criminal justice before assuring itself that this question is actually and of necessity presented by the concrete facts before the Court. * * *

# SECTION 2. PROTECTED AREAS AND INTERESTS

If certain police activity is neither a "search" nor a "seizure" in the Fourth Amendment sense, then quite obviously the protections of the Amendment are inapplicable. Deciding just what constitutes a "search" has been especially troublesome. In the leading case (and the first case in this section) of *Katz v. United States,* holding electronic eavesdropping is governed by the Fourth Amendment, the Court decided a search could occur without a physical intrusion into a constitutionally protected area. By requiring instead an infringement upon a justified expectation of privacy, *Katz* unquestionably broadened the scope of the Fourth Amendment. But the Court has since taken a rather narrow view of what privacy expectations are in fact "justified," as is illustrated by the next two cases, *California v. Greenwood* and *Florida v. Riley,* dealing, respectively, with examination of garbage and aerial surveillance. The fourth case in this section, *United States v. Karo,* involving use of an electronic tracking device, concerns the Fourth Amendment's application to sense-enhancing devices. The meaning of *Katz* is also explored in *United States v. White,* concerning the troublesome question of whether it is a search or seizure for an undercover agent secretly to record or transmit the conversations he has with others.

Those objecting to police search activity have sometimes relied upon constitutional protections in addition to those in the Fourth Amendment. The claim that the Fifth Amendment privilege against self-incrimination bars a search for or seizure of private papers was rejected in *Andresen v. Maryland,* 427 U.S. 463 (1976). Distinguishing the situation discussed in Chapter Eight (§ 2), the Court in *Andresen* concluded that "although the Fifth Amendment may protect an individual from complying with a subpoena for the production of his personal records in his possession because the very act of production may constitute a compulsory authentication of incriminating information, a seizure of the same materials by law enforcement officers differs in a crucial respect—the individual against whom the search is directed is not required to aid in the discovery, production, or authentication of incriminating evidence." The claim that the First Amendment freedom of the press is violated by the search of the office of a newsgathering organization is considered in *Zurcher v. Stanford Daily*, the final case in this section.

## KATZ v. UNITED STATES
389 U.S. 347, 88 S.Ct. 507, 19 L.Ed.2d 576 (1967).

JUSTICE STEWART delivered the opinion of the Court.

The petitioner was convicted [of] transmitting wagering information by telephone from Los Angeles to Miami and Boston in violation of a federal statute. At trial the Government was permitted, over the petitioner's objection, to introduce evidence of the petitioner's end of telephone conversations, overheard by FBI agents who had attached an electronic listening and recording device to the outside of the public telephone booth from which he had placed his calls. In affirming his conviction, the Court of Appeals rejected the contention that the recordings had been obtained in violation of the Fourth Amendment, because "[t]here was no physical entrance into the area occupied by [the petitioner]." We granted certiorari in order to consider the constitutional questions thus presented.

The petitioner has phrased those questions as follows:

"A. Whether a public telephone booth is a constitutionally protected area so that evidence obtained by attaching an electronic listening recording device to the top of such a booth is obtained in violation of the right to privacy of the user of the booth.

"B. Whether physical penetration of a constitutionally protected area is necessary before a search and seizure can be said to be violative of the Fourth Amendment to the United States Constitution."

We decline to adopt this formulation of the issues. In the first place the correct solution of Fourth Amendment problems is not necessarily promoted by incantation of the phrase "constitutionally protected area." Secondly, the Fourth Amendment cannot be translated into a general constitutional "right to privacy." That Amendment protects individual privacy against certain kinds of governmental intrusion, but its protections go further, and often have nothing to do with privacy at all. Other provisions of the Constitution protect personal privacy from other forms of governmental invasion. But the protection of a person's *general* right to privacy—his right to be let alone by other people—is, like the protection of his property and of his very life, left largely to the law of the individual States.

Because of the misleading way the issues have been formulated, the parties have attached great significance to the characterization of the telephone booth from which the petitioner placed his calls. The petitioner has strenuously argued that the booth was a "constitutionally protected area." The Government has maintained with equal vigor that it was not. But this effort to decide whether or not a given "area," viewed in the abstract, is "constitutionally protected" deflects attention from the problem presented by this case. For the Fourth Amendment protects people, not places. What a person knowingly exposes to the public, even in his own home or office, is not a subject of Fourth Amendment protection. * * * But what he seeks to preserve as private, even in an area accessible to the public, may be constitutionally protected. * * *

The Government stresses the fact that the telephone booth from which the petitioner made his calls was constructed partly of glass, so that he was as visible after he entered it as he would have been if he had remained outside. But what he sought to exclude when he entered the booth was not the intruding eye—it was the uninvited ear. He did not shed his right to do so simply because he made his calls from a place where he might be seen. No less than an individual in a business office, in a friend's apartment, or in a taxicab, a person in a telephone booth may rely upon the protection of the Fourth Amendment. One who occupies it, shuts the door behind him, and pays the toll that permits him to place a call, is surely entitled to assume that the words he utters into the mouthpiece will not be broadcast to the world. To read the Constitution more narrowly is to ignore the vital role that the public telephone has come to play in private communication.

The Government contends, however, that the activities of its agents in this case should not be tested by Fourth Amendment requirements, for the surveillance technique they employed involved no physical penetration of the telephone booth from which the petitioner placed his calls.

\* \* \* [A]lthough a closely divided Court supposed in *Olmstead* [*v. United States,* 277 U.S. 438 (1928),] that surveillance without any trespass and without the seizure of any material object fell outside the ambit of the Constitution, we have since departed from the narrow view on which that decision rested. Indeed, we have expressly held that the Fourth Amendment governs not only the seizure of tangible items, but extends as well to the recording of oral statements overheard without any "technical trespass under \* \* \* local property law." Once this much is acknowledged, and once it is recognized that the Fourth Amendment protects people—and not simply "areas"—against unreasonable searches and seizures it becomes clear that the reach of that Amendment cannot turn upon the presence or absence of a physical intrusion into any given enclosure.

We conclude that the underpinnings of *Olmstead* have been so eroded by our subsequent decisions that the "trespass" doctrine there enunciated can no longer be regarded as controlling. The Government's activities in electronically listening to and recording the petitioner's words violated the privacy upon which he justifiably relied while using the telephone booth and thus constituted a "search and seizure" within the meaning of the Fourth Amendment.[a] The fact that the

---

a. More precisely, it could be said that if the government's activities have violated *anyone's* justified expectation of privacy, then that activity constitutes a Fourth Amendment search. However, it has long been established that a defendant in a criminal case who is seeking the suppression of evidence on Fourth Amendment grounds may invoke the violation of his own rights but not the rights of third parties; this concept has traditionally been referred to as "standing." In more recent years the *Katz* analysis has been utilized on that issue: a defendant has standing only if the government violated the privacy on which *he* (as opposed to some other person) justifiably relied. Illustrative is *Rakas v. Illinois,* 439 U.S. 128 (1978), holding that passengers in a car who did not challenge the stopping of the vehicle in which they were riding but only the subsequent search under the seat and in the glove compartment lacked standing to challenge that search; because they asserted no property or possessory interest in the automobile searched or in the property seized, they had not shown they had a legitimate expectation of privacy in the places searched.

Indeed, the Court in *Rakas* suggested that separate treatment of standing was no longer necessary. The Court saw no "useful analytical purpose" in considering the defendant's victim-status as a matter "apart from the merits of the defendant's Fourth Amendment claim." The appropriate question, the Court noted, is whether the "disputed search infringed an interest of the defendant which the Fourth Amendment was designed to protect." This was more direct, it reasoned, than asking whether the defendant's alleged standing is based on his own rights or those of a third party. The Court acknowledged, however, that looking directly at the merits would not alter the results in past cases or make the issue any easier to resolve. Perhaps because electronic device employed to achieve that end did not happen to penetrate the wall of the booth can have no constitutional significance.

The question remaining for decision, then, is whether the search and seizure conducted in this case complied with constitutional standards. In that regard, the Government's position is that its agents acted in an entirely defensible manner: They did not begin their electronic surveillance until investigation of the petitioner's activities had established a strong probability that he was using the telephone in question to transmit gambling information to persons in other States, in violation of federal law. Moreover, the surveillance was limited, both in scope and in duration to the specific purpose of establishing the contents of the petitioner's unlawful telephonic communications. The agents confined their surveillance to the brief periods during which he used the telephone booth, and they took great care to overhear only the conversations of the petitioner himself.

Accepting this account of the Government's actions as accurate, it is clear that this surveillance was so narrowly circumscribed that a duly authorized magistrate, properly notified of the need for such investigation, specifically informed of the basis on which it was to proceed, and clearly apprised of the precise intrusion it would entail, could constitutionally have authorized, with appropriate safeguards, the very limited search and seizure that the Government asserts in fact took place.  *  *  * b

The Government * * * urges the creation of a new exception to cover this case. It argues that surveillance of a telephone booth should be exempted from the usual requirement of advance authorization by a magistrate upon a showing of probable cause. We cannot agree. Omission of such authorization "bypasses the safeguards provided by an objective predetermination of probable cause, and substitutes instead the far less reliable procedure of an after-the-event justification for the * * * search, too likely to be subtly influenced by the familiar shortcomings of hindsight judgment." And bypassing a neutral predetermination of the *scope* of a search leaves individuals secure from Fourth Amendment violations "only in the discretion of the police."

the Court foresaw some confusion between the question asked in determining whether there was a search (did the police intrude upon *anyone's* justified expectation of privacy) and the question traditionally labeled as one of standing (did the police intrude upon *this defendant's* expectation of privacy), the Court's subsequent opinions have not totally discarded the practice of referring to the latter issue as one of standing.

**b.** The Court went on to distinguish the present situation from the kind of electronic surveillance possible under a New York statute which was invalidated in *Berger v. New York,* 388 U.S. 41 (1967), as a "blanket grant of permission to eavesdrop * * * without adequate supervision or protective procedures." That statute, the Court explained in *Berger,* (1) permitted a court order to issue merely on reasonable grounds to believe that evidence of crime may be obtained, without specifying what crime has been or is being committed and without describing what conversations are to be overheard, thus failing to "particularly [describe] the place to be searched, and the person or things to be seized," as required by the Fourth Amendment; (2) permitted installation and operation of surveillance equipment for 60 days, "the equivalent of a series of intrusions, searches and seizures pursuant to a single showing of probable cause"; (3) permitted renewal of the order on the basis of the original grounds on which the initial order was issued, deemed "insufficient without a showing of present probable cause for continuance of the eavesdrop"; (4) placed no termination on the eavesdrop once the conversation sought is seized, as "this is left entirely to the discretion of the officer"; and (5) did not provide for a return on the warrant, "thereby leaving full discretion in the officer as to the use of seized conversations of innocent as well as guilty parties."

Nonconsensual electronic surveillance is authorized in limited circumstances by Title III of the Omnibus Crime Control and Safe Streets Act of 1968, 18 U.S.C.A. §§ 2510–2520. Although the Supreme Court has never passed upon the Act, it has been consistently upheld by the lower courts. Consequently, the focus of litigation in recent years has been upon whether particular wiretapping and electronic eavesdropping activities conform to the requirements of the Act.

These considerations do not vanish when the search in question is transferred from the setting of a home, an office, or a hotel room, to that of a telephone booth. Wherever a man may be, he is entitled to know that he will remain free from unreasonable searches and seizures. The government agents here ignored "the procedure of antecedent justification * * * that is central to the Fourth Amendment," procedure that we hold to be a constitutional precondition of the kind of electronic surveillance involved in this case. * * *

Judgment reversed.[c]

JUSTICE HARLAN, concurring.

* * * As the Court's opinion states, "The Fourth Amendment protects people, not places." The question, however, is what protection it affords to those people. Generally, as here, the answer to that question requires reference to a "place." My understanding of the rule that has emerged from prior decisions is that there is a twofold requirement, first that a person have exhibited an actual (subjective) expectation of privacy and, second, that the expectation be one that society is prepared to recognize as "reasonable." Thus a man's home is, for most purposes, a place where he expects privacy, but objects, activities, or statements that he exposes to the "plain view" of outsiders are not "protected" because no intention to keep them to himself has been exhibited. On the other hand, conversations in the open would not be protected against being overheard, for the expectation of privacy under the circumstances would be unreasonable. * * *

The critical fact in this case is that "[o]ne who occupies it, [a telephone booth] shuts the door behind him, and pays the toll that permits him to place a call, is surely entitled to assume" that his conversation is not being intercepted. The point is not that the booth is "accessible to the public" at other times, but that it is a temporarily private place whose momentary occupants' expectations of freedom from intrusion are recognized as reasonable. * * *

JUSTICE BLACK, dissenting.

* * * Tapping telephone wires, of course, was an unknown possibility at the time the Fourth Amendment was adopted. But eavesdropping (and wiretapping is nothing more than eavesdropping by telephone) was "an ancient practice which at common law was condemned as a nuisance. In those days the eavesdropper listened by naked ear under the eaves of houses or their windows, or beyond their walls seeking out private discourse." There can be no doubt that the Framers were aware of this practice, and if they had desired to outlaw or restrict the use of evidence obtained by eavesdropping, I believe that they would have used the appropriate language to do so in the Fourth Amendment. They certainly would not have left such a task to the ingenuity of language-stretching judges. * * *

* * * By clever word juggling the Court finds it plausible to argue that language aimed specifically at searches and seizures of things that can be searched and seized may, to protect privacy, be applied to eavesdropped evidence of conversations that can neither be searched nor seized. Few things happen to an individual that do not affect his privacy in one way or another. Thus, by arbitrarily substituting the Court's language, designed to protect privacy, for the Constitution's language, designed to protect against unreasonable searches and seizures, the Court has made the Fourth Amendment its vehicle for holding all

**c.** The concurring opinions of Justice Douglas and Justice White are omitted. Justice Marshall did not participate.

laws violative of the Constitution which offend the Court's broadest concept of privacy. * * *

The Fourth Amendment protects privacy only to the extent that it prohibits unreasonable searches and seizures of "persons, houses, papers and effects." No general right is created by the Amendment so as to give this Court the unlimited power to hold unconstitutional everything which affects privacy. Certainly the Framers, well acquainted as they were with the excesses of governmental power, did not intend to grant this Court such omnipotent lawmaking authority as that. The history of governments proves that it is dangerous to freedom to repose such powers in courts. * * *

## CALIFORNIA v. GREENWOOD

486 U.S. 35, 108 S.Ct. 1625, 100 L.Ed.2d 30 (1988).

JUSTICE WHITE delivered the opinion of the Court. * * *

In early 1984, Investigator Jenny Stracner of the Laguna Beach Police Department received information indicating that respondent Greenwood might be engaged in narcotics trafficking. * * *

On April 6, 1984, Stracner asked the neighborhood's regular trash collector to pick up the plastic garbage bags that Greenwood had left on the curb in front of his house and to turn the bags over to her without mixing their contents with garbage from other houses. The trash collector cleaned his truck bin of other refuse, collected the garbage bags from the street in front of Greenwood's house, and turned the bags over to Stracner. The officer searched through the rubbish and found items indicative of narcotics use. She recited the information that she had gleaned from the trash search in an affidavit in support of a warrant to search Greenwood's home.

Police officers encountered both respondents at the house later that day when they arrived to execute the warrant. The police discovered quantities of cocaine and hashish during their search of the house. Respondents were arrested on felony narcotics charges. They subsequently posted bail.

The police continued to receive reports of many late-night visitors to the Greenwood house. On May 4, Investigator Robert Rahaeuser obtained Greenwood's garbage from the regular trash collector in the same manner as had Stracner. The garbage again contained evidence of narcotics use.

Rahaeuser secured another search warrant for Greenwood's home based on the information from the second trash search. The police found more narcotics and evidence of narcotics trafficking when they executed the warrant. Greenwood was again arrested.

The Superior Court dismissed the charges against respondents on the authority of *People v. Krivda,* 486 P.2d 1262 (Cal.1971), which held that warrantless trash searches violate the Fourth Amendment and the California Constitution. The court found that the police would not have had probable cause to search the Greenwood home without the evidence obtained from the trash searches.

The Court of Appeal affirmed. * * *

The California Supreme Court denied the State's petition for review of the Court of Appeal's decision. We granted certiorari, and now reverse.

The warrantless search and seizure of the garbage bags left at the curb outside the Greenwood house would violate the Fourth Amendment only if respondents manifested a subjective expectation of privacy in their garbage that society accepts as objectively reasonable. Respondents do not disagree with this standard.

They assert, however, that they had, and exhibited, an expectation of privacy with respect to the trash that was searched by the police: The trash, which was placed on the street for collection at a fixed time, was contained in opaque plastic bags, which the garbage collector was expected to pick up, mingle with the trash of others, and deposit at the garbage dump. The trash was only temporarily on the street, and there was little likelihood that it would be inspected by anyone.

It may well be that respondents did not expect that the contents of their garbage bags would become known to the police or other members of the public. An expectation of privacy does not give rise to Fourth Amendment protection, however, unless society is prepared to accept that expectation as objectively reasonable.

Here, we conclude that respondents exposed their garbage to the public sufficiently to defeat their claim to Fourth Amendment protection. It is common knowledge that plastic garbage bags left on or at the side of a public street are readily accessible to animals, children, scavengers, snoops,[4] and other members of the public. Moreover, respondents placed their refuse at the curb for the express purpose of conveying it to a third party, the trash collector, who might himself have sorted through respondents' trash or permitted others, such as the police, to do so. Accordingly, having deposited their garbage "in an area particularly suited for public inspection and, in a manner of speaking, public consumption, for the express purpose of having strangers take it," respondents could have had no reasonable expectation of privacy in the inculpatory items that they discarded.

Furthermore, as we have held, the police cannot reasonably be expected to avert their eyes from evidence of criminal activity that could have been observed by any member of the public. Hence, "[w]hat a person knowingly exposes to the public, even in his own home or office, is not a subject of Fourth Amendment protection." *Katz v. United States.* We held in *Smith v. Maryland,* 442 U.S. 735 (1979), for example, that the police did not violate the Fourth Amendment by causing a pen register to be installed at the telephone company's offices to record the telephone numbers dialed by a criminal suspect. An individual has no legitimate expectation of privacy in the numbers dialed on his telephone, we reasoned, because he voluntarily conveys those numbers to the telephone company when he uses the telephone. Again, we observed that "a person has no legitimate expectation of privacy in information he voluntarily turns over to third parties." * * *

Our conclusion that society would not accept as reasonable respondents' claim to an expectation of privacy in trash left for collection in an area accessible to the public is reinforced by the unanimous rejection of similar claims by the Federal Courts of Appeals. In addition, of those state appellate courts that have considered the issue, the vast majority have held that the police may conduct warrantless searches and seizures of garbage discarded in public areas.

---

**4.** Even the refuse of prominent Americans has not been invulnerable. In 1975, for example, a reporter for a weekly tabloid seized five bags of garbage from the sidewalk outside the home of Secretary of State Henry Kissinger. Washington Post, July 9, 1975, p. A1, col. 8. A newspaper editorial criticizing this journalistic "trashpicking" observed that "[e]vidently . . . 'everybody does it.'" Washington Post, July 10, 1975, p. A18, col. 1. We of course do not, as the dissent implies, "bas[e] [our] conclusion" that individuals have no reasonable expectation of privacy in their garbage on this "sole incident."

* * *[a]

JUSTICE BRENNAN, with whom JUSTICE MARSHALL joins, dissenting. * * *

The Framers of the Fourth Amendment understood that "unreasonable searches" of "paper[s] and effects"—no less than "unreasonable searches" of "person[s] and houses"—infringe privacy. * * * In short, so long as a package is "closed against inspection," the Fourth Amendment protects its contents, "wherever they may be," and the police must obtain a warrant to search it just "as is required when papers are subjected to search in one's own household." * * *

Our precedent, therefore, leaves no room to doubt that had respondents been carrying their personal effects in opaque, sealed plastic bags—identical to the ones they placed on the curb—their privacy would have been protected from warrantless police intrusion. * * *

Respondents deserve no less protection just because Greenwood used the bags to discard rather than to transport his personal effects. Their contents are not inherently any less private, and Greenwood's decision to discard them, at least in the manner in which he did, does not diminish his expectation of privacy.[2]

A trash bag, like any of the above-mentioned containers, "is a common repository for one's personal effects" and, even more than many of them, is "therefore * * * inevitably associated with the expectation of privacy." * * * A single bag of trash testifies eloquently to the eating, reading, and recreational habits of the person who produced it. A search of trash, like a search of the bedroom, can relate intimate details about sexual practices, health, and personal hygiene. Like rifling through desk drawers or intercepting phone calls, rummaging through trash can divulge the target's financial and professional status, political affiliations and inclinations, private thoughts, personal relationships, and romantic interests. It cannot be doubted that a sealed trash bag harbors telling evidence of the "intimate activity associated with the 'sanctity of a man's home and the privacies of life,'" which the Fourth Amendment is designed to protect.

The Court properly rejects the State's attempt to distinguish trash searches from other searches on the theory that trash is abandoned and therefore not entitled to an expectation of privacy. As the author of the Court's opinion observed last Term, a defendant's "property interest [in trash] does not settle the matter for Fourth Amendment purposes, for the reach of the Fourth Amendment is not determined by state property law." In evaluating the reasonableness of Greenwood's expectation that his sealed trash bags would not be invaded, the Court has held that we must look to "understandings that are recognized and permitted by society." Most of us, I believe, would be incensed to discover a meddler—whether a neighbor, a reporter, or a detective—scrutinizing our sealed trash containers to discover some detail of our personal lives. That was, quite naturally, the reaction to the sole incident on which the Court bases its

---

**a** Justice Kennedy took no part in the consideration or decision of this case.

**2.** Both to support its position that society recognizes no reasonable privacy interest in sealed, opaque trash bags and to refute the prediction that "society will be shocked to learn" of that conclusion, the Court relies heavily upon a collection of lower court cases finding no Fourth Amendment bar to trash searches. But the authority that leads the Court to be "distinctively unimpressed" with our position, is itself impressively undistinguished. Of 11 Federal Court of Appeals cases cited by the Court, at least two are factually or legally distinguishable, and seven rely entirely or almost entirely on an abandonment theory that the Court has discredited. A reading of the Court's collection of state-court cases reveals an equally unimpressive pattern.

conclusion that "snoops" and the like defeat the expectation of privacy in trash. When a tabloid reporter examined then-Secretary of State Henry Kissinger's trash and published his findings, Kissinger was "really revolted" by the intrusion and his wife suffered "grave anguish." N.Y. Times, July 9, 1975, p. A1, col. 8. The public response roundly condemning the reporter demonstrates that society not only recognized those reactions as reasonable, but shared them as well. Commentators variously characterized his conduct as "a disgusting invasion of personal privacy," Flieger, Investigative Trash, U.S. News & World Report, July 28, 1975, p. 72 (editor's page); "indefensible * * * as civilized behavior," Washington Post, July 10, 1975, p. A18, col. 1 (editorial); and contrary to "the way decent people behave in relation to each other," ibid. * * *

That is not to deny that isolated intrusions into opaque, sealed trash containers occur. When, acting on their own, "animals, children, scavengers, snoops, [or] other members of the general public," *actually* rummage through a bag of trash and expose its contents to plain view, "police cannot reasonably be expected to avert their eyes from evidence of criminal activity that could have been observed by any member of the public."

Had Greenwood flaunted his intimate activity by strewing his trash all over the curb for all to see, or had some nongovernmental intruder invaded his privacy and done the same, I could accept the Court's conclusion that an expectation of privacy would have been unreasonable. Similarly, had police searching the city dump run across incriminating evidence that, despite commingling with the trash of others, still retained its identity as Greenwood's, we would have a different case. But all that Greenwood "exposed * * * to the public" were the exteriors of several opaque, sealed containers. * * *

The mere *possibility* that unwelcome meddlers *might* open and rummage through the containers does not negate the expectation of privacy in its contents any more than the possibility of a burglary negates an expectation of privacy in the home; or the possibility of a private intrusion negates an expectation of privacy in an unopened package; or the possibility that an operator will listen in on a telephone conversation negates an expectation of privacy in the words spoken on the telephone. "What a person * * * seeks to preserve as private, *even in an area accessible to the public,* may be constitutionally protected." *Katz.* We have therefore repeatedly rejected attempts to justify a State's invasion of privacy on the ground that the privacy is not absolute. See *Chapman v. United States,* 365 U.S. 610 (1961) (search of a house invaded tenant's Fourth Amendment rights even though landlord had authority to enter house for some purposes); *Stoner v. California,* 376 U.S. 483 (1964) (implicit consent to janitorial personnel to enter motel room does not amount to consent to police search of room); *O'Connor v. Oretega,* 480 U.S. ___ (1987) (a government employee has a reasonable expectation of privacy in his office, even though "it is the nature of government offices that others—such as fellow employees, supervisors, consensual visitors, and the general public—may have frequent access to an individual's office"). * * *

Nor is it dispositive that "respondents placed their refuse at the curb for the express purpose of conveying it to a third party, * * * who might himself have sorted through respondents' trash or permitted others, such as police, to do so." In the first place, Greenwood can hardly be faulted for leaving trash on his curb when a county ordinance commanded him to do so and prohibited him from disposing of it in any other way. * * * More importantly, even the voluntary relinquishment of possession or control over an effect does not necessarily amount to a relinquishment of a privacy expectation in it. Were it otherwise, a letter or package would lose all Fourth Amendment protection when placed in a mail box or other depository with the "express purpose" of entrusting it to the postal officer or a private carrier; those bailees are just as likely as trash collectors (and certainly have greater incentive) to "sor[t] through" the personal effects entrusted to them, "or permi[t] others, such as police to do so." Yet, it has been clear for at least 110 years that the possibility of such an intrusion does not justify a warrantless search by police in the first instance. * * *

## FLORIDA v. RILEY
—— U.S. ——, 109 S.Ct. 693, 102 L.Ed.2d 835 (1989).

JUSTICE WHITE announced the judgment of the Court and delivered an opinion, in which THE CHIEF JUSTICE, JUSTICE SCALIA and JUSTICE KENNEDY join.

On certification to it by a lower state court, the Florida Supreme Court addressed the following question: "Whether surveillance of the interior of a partially covered greenhouse in a residential backyard from the vantage point of a helicopter located 400 feet above the greenhouse constitutes a 'search' for which a warrant is required under the Fourth Amendment and Article I, Section 12 of the Florida Constitution." The court answered the question in the affirmative, and we granted the State's petition for certiorari challenging that conclusion. * * *

We agree with the State's submission that our decision in *California v. Ciraolo*, 476 U.S. 207, 106 S.Ct. 1809, 90 L.Ed.2d 210 (1986), controls this case. There, acting on a tip, the police inspected the back yard of a particular house while flying in a fixed-wing aircraft at 1,000 feet. With the naked-eye the officers saw what they concluded was marijuana growing in the yard. A search warrant was obtained on the strength of this airborne inspection, and marijuana plants were found. The trial court refused to suppress this evidence, but a state appellate court held that the inspection violated the Fourth and Fourteenth Amendments of the United States Constitution and that the warrant was therefore invalid. We in turn reversed, holding that the inspection was not a search subject to the Fourth Amendment. We recognized that the yard was within the curtilage of the house, that a fence shielded the yard from observation from the street and that the occupant had a subjective expectation of privacy. We held, however, that such an expectation was not reasonable and not one "that society is prepared to honor." * * * "In an age where private and commercial flight in the public airways is routine, it is unreasonable for respondent to expect that his marijuana plants were constitutionally protected from being observed with the naked eye from an altitude of 1,000 feet. The Fourth Amendment simply does not require the police traveling in the public airways at this altitude to obtain a warrant in order to observe what is visible to the naked eye."

We arrive at the same conclusion in the present case. * * *

Nor on the facts before us, does it make a difference for Fourth Amendment purposes that the helicopter was flying at 400 feet when the officer saw what was growing in the greenhouse through the partially open roof and sides of the structure. We would have a different case if flying at that altitude had been contrary to law or regulation. But helicopters are not bound by the lower limits of the navigable airspace allowed to other aircraft. Any member of the public could legally have been flying over Riley's property in a helicopter at the altitude of 400 feet and could have observed Riley's greenhouse. The police officer did no more. This is not to say that an inspection of the curtilage of a house from an aircraft will always pass muster under the Fourth Amendment simply because the plane is within the navigable airspace specified by law. But it is of obvious importance that the helicopter in this case was *not* violating the law, and there is nothing in the record or before us to suggest that helicopters flying at 400 feet are sufficiently rare in this country to lend substance to respondent's claim that he reasonably anticipated that his greenhouse would not be subject to observation from that altitude. Neither is there any intimation here that the helicopter interfered with respondent's normal use of the greenhouse or of other parts of the curtilage. As far as this record reveals, no intimate details connected with the use of the home or curtilage were observed, and there was no undue noise, no wind, dust, or threat of injury. In these circumstances, there was no violation of the Fourth Amendment. * * *

JUSTICE O'CONNOR, concurring in the judgment. * * *

In determining whether Riley had a reasonable expectation of privacy from aerial observation, the relevant inquiry after *Ciraolo* is not whether the helicopter was where it had a right to be under FAA regulations. Rather, consistent with *Katz*, we must ask whether the helicopter was in the public airways at an altitude at which members of the public travel with sufficient regularity that Riley's expectation of privacy from aerial observation was not "one that society is prepared to recognize as 'reasonable.'" * * *

Because there is reason to believe that there is considerable public use of airspace at altitudes of 400 feet and above, and because Riley introduced no evidence to the contrary before the Florida courts, I conclude that Riley's expectation that his curtilage was protected from naked-eye aerial observation from that altitude was not a reasonable one. However, public use of altitudes lower than that—particularly public observations from helicopters circling over the curtilage of a home—may be sufficiently rare that police surveillance from such altitudes would violate reasonable expectations of privacy, despite compliance with FAA air safety regulations.

JUSTICE BRENNAN, with whom JUSTICE MARSHALL and JUSTICE STEVENS, join, dissenting.

* * * Under the plurality's exceedingly grudging Fourth Amendment theory, the expectation of privacy is defeated if a single member of the public could conceivably position herself to see into the area in question without doing anything illegal. It is defeated whatever the difficulty a person would have in so positioning herself, and however infrequently anyone would in fact do so. In taking this view the plurality ignores the very essence of *Katz*. * * *

It is a curious notion that the reach of the Fourth Amendment can be so largely defined by administrative regulations issued for purposes of flight safety. It is more curious still that the plurality relies to such an extent on the legality of the officer's act, when we have consistently refused to equate police violation of the law with infringement of the Fourth Amendment.[3] But the plurality's willingness to end its inquiry when it finds that the officer was in a position he had a right to be in is misguided for an even more fundamental reason. Finding determinative the fact that the officer was where he had a right to be is, at bottom, an attempt to analogize surveillance from a helicopter to surveillance by

---

3. In *Oliver v. United States*, 466 U.S. 170, 104 S.Ct. 1735, 80 L.Ed.2d 214 (1984), for example, we held that police officers who trespassed upon posted and fenced private land did not violate the Fourth Amendment, despite the fact that their action was subject to criminal sanctions. We noted that the interests vindicated by the Fourth Amendment were not identical with those served by the common law of trespass.

a police officer standing on a public road and viewing evidence of crime through an open window or a gap in a fence.  In such a situation, the occupant of the home may be said to lack any reasonable expectation of privacy in what can be seen from that road—even if, in fact, people rarely pass that way.

The police officer positioned 400 feet above Riley's backyard was not, however, standing on a public road.  The vantage point he enjoyed was not one any citizen could readily share.  His ability to see over Riley's fence depended on his use of a very expensive and sophisticated piece of machinery to which few ordinary citizens have access.  In such circumstances it makes no more sense to rely on the legality of the officer's position in the skies than it would to judge the constitutionality of the wiretap in *Katz* by the legality of the officer's position outside the telephone booth.  The simply inquiry whether the police officer had the legal right to be in the position from which he made his observations cannot suffice, for we cannot assume that Riley's curtilage was so open to the observations of passersby in the skies that he retained little privacy or personal security to be lost to police surveillance.  The question before us must be not whether the police were where they had a right to be, but whether public observation of Riley's curtilage was so commonplace that Riley's expectation of privacy in his backyard could not be considered reasonable.  * * *

What separates me from Justice O'Connor is essentially an empirical matter concerning the extent of public use of the airspace at that altitude, together with the question of how to resolve that issue.  I do not think the constitutional claims should fail simply because "there is reason to believe" that there is "considerable" public flying this close to earth or because Riley "introduced no evidence to the contrary before the Florida courts."  * * * I think we could take judicial notice that, while there may be an occasional privately owned helicopter that flies over populated areas at an altitude of 400 feet, such flights are a rarity and are almost entirely limited to approaching or leaving airports or to reporting traffic congestion near major roadways.  And, as the concurring opinion agrees, the extent of police surveillance traffic cannot serve as a bootstrap to demonstrate public use of the airspace.

If, however, we are to resolve the issue by considering whether the appropriate party carried its burden of proof, I again think that Riley must prevail.  Because the State has greater access to information concerning customary flight patterns and because the coercive power of the State ought not be brought to bear in cases in which it is unclear whether the prosecution is a product of an unconstitutional, warrantless search, the burden of proof properly rests with the State and not with the individual defendant.  The State quite clearly has not carried this burden.  * * *

JUSTICE BLACKMUN, dissenting.

[B]ecause I believe that private helicopters rarely fly over curtilages at an altitude of 400 feet, I would impose upon the prosecution the burden or proving contrary facts necessary to show that Riley lacked a reasonable expectation of privacy.  Indeed, I would establish this burden of proof for any helicopter surveillance case in which the flight occurred below 1000 feet—in other words, for any aerial surveillance case not governed by the Court's decision in *California v. Ciraolo.*

In this case, the prosecution did not meet this burden of proof, as Justice Brennan notes.  This failure should compel a finding that a Fourth Amendment search occurred.  But because our prior cases gave the parties little guidance on the burden of proof issue, I would remand this case to allow the prosecution an opportunity to meet this burden.  * * *

## UNITED STATES v. KARO

468 U.S. 705, 104 S.Ct. 3296, 82 L.Ed.2d 530 (1984).

JUSTICE WHITE delivered the opinion of the Court.

In *United States v. Knotts*, 460 U.S. 276 (1983), we held that the warrantless monitoring of an electronic tracking device ("beeper")[1] inside a container of chemicals did not violate the Fourth Amendment when it revealed no information that could not have been obtained through visual surveillance. In this case, we are called upon to address two questions left unresolved in *Knotts:* (1) whether installation of a beeper in a container of chemicals with the consent of the original owner constitutes a search or seizure within the meaning of the Fourth Amendment when the container is delivered to a buyer having no knowledge of the presence of the beeper, and (2) whether monitoring of a beeper falls within the ambit of the Fourth Amendment when it reveals information that could not have been obtained through visual surveillance.

In August 1980 Agent Rottinger of the Drug Enforcement Administration (DEA) learned that respondents James Karo, Richard Horton, and William Harley had ordered 50 gallons of ether from government informant Carl Muehlenweg of Graphic Photo Design in Albuquerque, New Mexico. Muehlenweg told Rottinger that the ether was to be used to extract cocaine from clothing that had been imported into the United States. The Government obtained a court order authorizing the installation and monitoring of a beeper in one of the cans of ether. * * *

At about 6:00 p.m. on February 6, * * * two vehicles were under both physical and electronic surveillance. When the vehicles arrived at a house in Taos rented by Horton, Harley, and Michael Steele, the agents did not maintain tight surveillance for fear of detection. When the vehicles left the Taos residence, agents determined using the beeper monitor that the beeper can was still inside the house. Again on February 7, the beeper revealed that the ether can was still on the premises. * * * On February 8, the agents applied for and obtained a warrant to search the Taos residence based in part on information derived through use of the beeper. The warrant was executed on February 10, 1981, and Horton, Harley, Steele, and Evan Roth were arrested, and cocaine and laboratory equipment were seized.

* * * The District Court granted respondents' pre-trial motion to suppress the evidence seized from the Taos residence on the grounds that the initial warrant to install the beeper was invalid and that the Taos seizure was the tainted fruit of an unauthorized installation and monitoring of that beeper. The United States appealed but did not challenge the invalidation of the initial warrant. The Court of Appeals affirmed, holding that a warrant was required to install the beeper in one of the 10 cans of ether and to monitor it in private dwellings and storage lockers. The warrant for the search in Taos and the resulting seizure were tainted by the prior illegal conduct of the Government. * * *

Because the judgment below in favor of Karo rested in major part on the conclusion that the installation violated his Fourth Amendment rights and that any information obtained from monitoring the beeper was tainted by the initial illegality, we must deal with the legality of the warrantless installation. It is clear that the actual placement of the beeper into the can violated no one's

1. "A beeper is a radio transmitter, usually battery operated, which emits periodic signals that can be picked up by a radio receiver."

Fourth Amendment rights. The can into which the beeper was placed belonged at the time to the DEA, and by no stretch of the imagination could it be said that respondents then had any legitimate expectation of privacy in it. The ether and the original 10 cans, on the other hand, belonged to, and were in the possession of, Muehlenweg, who had given his consent to any invasion of those items that occurred. Thus, even if there had been no substitution of cans and the agents had placed the beeper into one of the original 10 cans, Muehlenweg's consent was sufficient to validate the placement of the beeper in the can.

* * * The mere transfer to Karo of a can containing an unmonitored beeper infringed no privacy interest. It conveyed no information that Karo wished to keep private, for it conveyed no information at all. To be sure, it created a *potential* for an invasion of privacy, but we have never held that potential, as opposed to actual, invasions of privacy constitute searches for purposes of the Fourth Amendment. * * *

We likewise do not believe that the transfer of the container constituted a seizure. A "seizure" of property occurs when "there is some meaningful interference with an individual's possessory interests in that property." Although the can may have contained an unknown and unwanted foreign object, it cannot be said that anyone's possessory interest was interfered with in a meaningful way. At most, there was a technical trespass on the space occupied by the beeper. The existence of a physical trespass is only marginally relevant to the question of whether the Fourth Amendment has been violated, however, for an actual trespass is neither necessary nor sufficient to establish a constitutional violation. * * *

In *United States v. Knotts,* law enforcement officials, with the consent of the seller, installed a beeper in a five-gallon can of chloroform and monitored the beeper after delivery of the can to the buyer in Minneapolis, Minnesota. Although there was partial visual surveillance as the automobile containing the can moved along the public highways, the beeper enabled the officers to locate the can in the area of a cabin near Shell Lake, Wisconsin, and it was this information that provided the basis for the issuance of a search warrant. As the case came to us, the installation of the beeper was not challenged; only the monitoring was at issue. The Court held that since the movements of the automobile and the arrival of the can containing the beeper in the area of the cabin could have been observed by the naked eye, no Fourth Amendment violation was committed by monitoring the beeper during the trip to the cabin. In *Knotts,* the record did not show that the beeper was monitored while the can containing it was inside the cabin, and we therefore had no occasion to consider whether a constitutional violation would have occurred had the fact been otherwise.

Here, there is no gainsaying that the beeper was used to locate the ether in a specific house in Taos, New Mexico, and that that information was in turn used to secure a warrant for the search of the house. * * *

At the risk of belaboring the obvious, private residences are places in which the individual normally expects privacy free of governmental intrusion not authorized by a warrant, and that expectation is plainly one that society is prepared to recognize as justifiable. Our cases have not deviated from this basic Fourth Amendment principle. Searches and seizures inside a home without a warrant are presumptively unreasonable absent exigent circumstances. In this case, had a DEA agent thought it useful to enter the Taos residence to verify that the ether was actually in the house and had he done so surreptitiously and without a warrant, there is little doubt that he would have engaged in an unreasonable search within the meaning of the Fourth Amendment. For purposes of the Amendment, the result is the same where, without a warrant, the Government surreptitiously employs an electronic device to obtain information that it could not have obtained by observation from outside the curtilage of the house. The beeper tells the agent that a particular article is actually located at a particular time in the private residence and is in the possession of the person or persons whose residence is being surveilled.[a] Even if visual surveillance has revealed that the article to which the beeper is attached has entered the house, the later monitoring not only verifies the officers' observations but also establishes that the article remains on the premises. Here, for example, the beeper was monitored for a significant period after the arrival of the ether in Taos and before the application for a warrant to search. * * *

We cannot accept the Government's contention that it should be completely free from the constraints of the Fourth Amendment to determine by means of an electronic device, without a warrant and without probable cause or reasonable suspicion, whether a particular article—or a person, for that matter—is in an individual's home at a particular time. Indiscriminate monitoring of property that has been withdrawn from public view would present far too serious a threat to privacy interests in the home to escape entirely some sort of Fourth Amendment oversight.

We also reject the Government's contention that it should be able to monitor beepers in private residences without a warrant if there is the requisite justification in the facts for believing that a crime is being or will be committed and that monitoring the beeper wherever it goes is likely to produce evidence of criminal activity. Warrantless searches are presumptively unreasonable, though the Court has recognized a few limited exceptions to this general rule. * * *

If agents are required to obtain warrants prior to monitoring a beeper when it has been withdrawn from public view, the Government argues, for all practical purposes they will be forced to obtain warrants in every case in which they seek to use a beeper, because they have no way of knowing in advance whether the beeper will be transmitting its signals from inside private premises. The argument that a warrant requirement would oblige the Government to obtain warrants in a large number of cases is hardly a compelling argument against the requirement. It is worthy of note that, in any event, this is not a particularly attractive case in which to argue that it is impractical to obtain a warrant, since a warrant was in fact obtained in this case, seemingly on probable cause.

**a.** Compare *United States v. Place*, 462 U.S. 696 (1983), dealing with a temporary seizure of luggage at an airport so that it could be brought into contact with a drug detection dog. The majority declared "that a person possesses a privacy interest in the contents of personal luggage that is protected by the Fourth Amendment. A 'canine sniff' by a well-trained narcotics detection dog, however, does not require opening the luggage. It does not expose noncontraband items that otherwise would remain hidden from public view, as does, for example, an officer's rummaging through the contents of the luggage. Thus, the manner in which information is obtained through this investigative technique is much less intrusive than a typical search. Moreover, the sniff discloses only the presence or absence of narcotics, a contraband item. Thus, despite the fact that the sniff tells the authorities something about the contents of the luggage, the information obtained is limited. This limited disclosure also ensures that the owner of the property is not subjected to the embarrassment and inconvenience entailed in less discriminate and more intrusive investigative methods.

"In these respects, the canine sniff is *sui generis*. We are aware of no other investigative procedure that is so limited both in the manner in which the information is obtained and in the content of the information revealed by the procedure. Therefore, we conclude that the particular course of investigation that the agents intended to pursue here—exposure of respondent's luggage, which was located in a public place, to a trained canine—did not constitute a 'search' within the meaning of the Fourth Amendment."

We are also unpersuaded by the argument that a warrant should not be required because of the difficulty in satisfying the particularity requirement of the Fourth Amendment. The Government contends that it would be impossible to describe the "place" to be searched, because the location of the place is precisely what is sought to be discovered through the search. However true that may be, it will still be possible to describe the object into which the beeper is to be placed, the circumstances that led agents to wish to install the beeper, and the length of time for which beeper surveillance is requested. In our view, this information will suffice to permit issuance of a warrant authorizing beeper installation and surveillance.

In sum, we discern no reason for deviating from the general rule that a search of a house should be conducted pursuant to a warrant.[5]

[But] it is clear that the warrant affidavit, after striking the facts about monitoring the beeper while it was in the Taos residence, contained sufficient untainted information to furnish probable cause for the issuance of the search warrant. The evidence seized in the house should not have been suppressed with respect to any of the respondents. * * *

JUSTICE O'CONNOR, with whom JUSTICE REHNQUIST joins, concurring in part and concurring in the judgment. * * *

[A] privacy interest in the location of a closed container that enters a home with the homeowner's permission cannot be inferred mechanically by reference to the more general privacy interests in the home itself. The homeowner's privacy interests are often narrower than those of the owner of the container. A defendant should be allowed to challenge evidence obtained by monitoring a beeper installed in a closed container only if (1) the beeper was monitored when visual tracking of the container was not possible, so that the defendant had a reasonable expectation that the container's movements would remain private, and (2) the defendant had an interest in the container itself sufficient to empower him to give effective consent to a search of the container. A person's right not to have a container tracked by means of a beeper depends both on his power to prevent visual observation of the container and on his power to control its location, a power that can usually be inferred from a privacy interest in the container itself. One who lacks either power has no legitimate expectation of privacy in the movements of the container. * * *

JUSTICE STEVENS, with whom JUSTICE BRENNAN and JUSTICE MARSHALL join, concurring in part and dissenting in part. * * *

The attachment of the beeper, in my judgment, constituted a "seizure." The owner of property, of course, has a right to exclude from it all the world, including the Government, and a concomitant right to use it exclusively for his own purposes. When the Government attaches an electronic monitoring device to that property, it infringes that exclusionary right; in a fundamental sense it has converted the property to its own use. Surely such an invasion is an "interference" with possessory rights; the right to exclude, which attached as soon as the can respondents purchased was delivered, had been infringed.[2] That

---

**5.** The United States insists that if beeper monitoring is deemed a search, a showing of reasonable suspicion rather than probable cause should suffice for its execution. That issue, however, is not before us. The initial warrant was not invalidated for want of probable cause, which plainly existed, but for misleading statements in the affidavit. The Government did not appeal the invalidation of the warrant and as the case has turned out, the Government prevails without a warrant authorizing installation. It will be time enough to resolve the probable cause-reasonable suspicion issue in a case that requires it.

**2.** It makes no difference in this case that when the beeper was initially attached, the can had not yet been delivered to respondents.

interference is also "meaningful"; the character of the property is profoundly different when infected with an electronic bug than when it is entirely germ free. * * *

The Court recognizes that concealment of personal property from public view gives rise to Fourth Amendment protection when it writes: "Indiscriminate monitoring of property that has been withdrawn from public view would present far too serious a threat to privacy interests in the home to escape entirely some sort of Fourth Amendment oversight." This protection is not limited to times when the beeper was in a home. The beeper also revealed when the can of ether had been moved. When a person drives down a public thoroughfare in a car with a can of ether concealed in the trunk, he is not exposing to public view the fact that he is in possession of a can of ether; the can is still "withdrawn from public view" and hence its location is entitled to constitutional protection. * * *

# UNITED STATES v. WHITE

401 U.S. 745, 91 S.Ct. 1122, 28 L.Ed.2d 453 (1971).

[On numerous occasions a government informer, carrying a concealed radio transmitter, engaged defendant in conversations which were electronically overheard by federal narcotics agents. The conversations in a restaurant, defendant's home and in the informer's car were overheard by the use of radio equipment. A number of conversations in the informer's home were not only electronically overheard by an agent stationed outside the house but by another agent who, with the informer's consent, concealed himself in the latter's kitchen closet. At no time did the agents obtain a warrant or court order. The informer was not produced at the trial, but the testimony of the "eavesdropping" agents was admitted and led to defendant's conviction of narcotics violations. The Court of Appeals Circuit read *Katz* as prohibiting testimony about the electronically overheard statements.]

JUSTICE WHITE announced the judgment of the Court and an opinion in which THE CHIEF JUSTICE, JUSTICE STEWART, and JUSTICE BLACKMUN join. * * *

*Hoffa v. United States,* 385 U.S. 293 (1966), which was left undisturbed by *Katz,* held that however strongly a defendant may trust an apparent colleague, his expectations in this respect are not protected by the Fourth Amendment when it turns out that the colleague is a government agent regularly communicating with the authorities. In these circumstances, "no interest legitimately protected by the Fourth Amendment is involved," for that amendment affords no protection to "a wrongdoer's misplaced belief that a person to whom he voluntarily confides his wrongdoing will not reveal it." * * *

Concededly a police agent who conceals his police connections may write down for official use his conversations with a defendant and testify concerning them, without a warrant authorizing his encounters with the defendant and without otherwise violating the latter's Fourth Amendment rights. For constitutional purposes, no different result is required if the agent instead of immediately reporting and transcribing his conversations with defendant, either (1) simultaneously records them with electronic equipment which he is carrying on his person, (2) or carries radio equipment which simultaneously transmits the conversations either to recording equipment located elsewhere or to other agents

Once the delivery had been effected, the container was respondents' property from which they had the right to exclude all the world. It was at that point that the infringement of this constitutionally protected interest began.

monitoring the transmitting frequency. If the conduct and revelations of an agent operating without electronic equipment do not invade the defendant's constitutionally justifiable expectations of privacy, neither does a simultaneous recording of the same conversations made by the agent or by others from transmissions received from the agent to whom the defendant is talking and whose trustworthiness the defendant necessarily risks.

Our problem is not what the privacy expectations of particular defendants in particular situations may be or the extent to which they may in fact have relied on the discretion of their companions. Very probably, individual defendants neither know nor suspect that their colleagues have gone or will go to the police or are carrying recorders or transmitters. Otherwise, conversation would cease and our problem with these encounters would be nonexistent or far different from those now before us. Our problem, in terms of the principles announced in *Katz*, is what expectations of privacy are constitutionally "justifiable"—what expectations the Fourth Amendment will protect in the absence of a warrant. * * * If the law gives no protection to the wrongdoer whose trusted accomplice is or becomes a police agent, neither should it protect him when that same agent has recorded or transmitted the conversations which are later offered in evidence to prove the State's case.

Inescapably, one contemplating illegal activities must realize and risk that his companions may be reporting to the police. If he sufficiently doubts their trustworthiness, the association will very probably end or never materialize. But if he has no doubts, or allays them, or risks what doubt he has, the risk is his. In terms of what his course will be, what he will or will not do or say, we are unpersuaded that he would distinguish between probable informers on the one hand and probable informers with transmitters on the other. Given the possibility or probability that one of his colleagues is cooperating with the police, it is only speculation to assert that the defendant's utterances would be substantially different or his sense of security any less if he also thought it possible that the suspected colleague is wired for sound. At least there is no persuasive evidence that the difference in this respect between the electronically equipped and the unequipped agent is substantial enough to require discrete constitutional recognition, particularly under the Fourth Amendment which is ruled by fluid concepts of "reasonableness."

Nor should we be too ready to erect constitutional barriers to relevant and probative evidence which is also accurate and reliable. An electronic recording will many times produce a more reliable rendition of what a defendant has said than will the unaided memory of a police agent. It may also be that with the recording in existence it is less likely that the informant will change his mind, less chance that threat or injury will suppress unfavorable evidence and less chance that cross-examination will confound the testimony. Considerations like these obviously do not favor the defendant, but we are not prepared to hold that a defendant who has no constitutional right to exclude the informer's unaided testimony nevertheless has a Fourth Amendment privilege against a more accurate version of the events in question.

It is thus untenable to consider the activities and reports of the police agent himself, though acting without a warrant, to be a "reasonable" investigative effort and lawful under the Fourth Amendment but to view the same agent with a recorder or transmitter as conducting an "unreasonable" and unconstitutional search and seizure. * * *

No different result should obtain where, as in the instant case, the informer disappears and is unavailable at trial; for the issue of whether specified events on a certain day violate the Fourth Amendment should not be determined by what later happens to the informer. His unavailability at trial and proffering the testimony of other agents may raise evidentiary problems or pose issues of prosecutorial misconduct with respect to the informer's disappearance, but they do not appear critical to deciding whether prior events invaded the defendant's Fourth Amendment rights.

The Court of Appeals was in error for another reason. In *Desist v. United States,* 394 U.S. 244 (1969), we held that our decision in *Katz v. United States* applied only to those electronic surveillances that occurred subsequent to the date of that decision. Here the events in question took place in late 1965 and early 1966, long prior to *Katz.* * * *

The judgment of the Court of Appeals is reversed.

JUSTICE BLACK * * * concurs in the judgment of the Court for the reasons set forth in his dissent in *Katz v. United States.*

JUSTICE BRENNAN, concurring in the result.

I agree that *Desist* requires reversal of the judgment of the Court of Appeals. * * * [I]t is my view that current Fourth Amendment jurisprudence interposes a warrant requirement not only in cases of third-party electronic monitoring (the situation in this case) but also in cases of electronic recording by a government agent of a face-to-face conversation with a criminal suspect. * * *

JUSTICE DOUGLAS, dissenting.

* * * Monitoring, if prevalent, certainly kills free discourse and spontaneous utterances. Free discourse—a First Amendment value—may be frivolous or serious, humble or defiant, reactionary or revolutionary, profane or in good taste; but it is not free if there is surveillance. Free discourse liberates the spirit, though it may produce only froth. The individual must keep some facts concerning his thoughts within a small zone of people. At the same time he must be free to pour out his woes or inspirations or dreams to others. He remains the sole judge as to what must be said and what must remain unspoken. This is the essence of the idea of privacy implicit in the First and Fifth Amendments as well as in the Fourth. * * *

JUSTICE HARLAN, dissenting.

* * * Since it is the task of the law to form and project, as well as mirror and reflect, we should not, as judges, merely recite the expectations and risks without examining the desirability of saddling them upon society. The critical question, therefore, is whether under our system of government, as reflected in the Constitution, we should impose on our citizens the risks of the electronic listener or observer without at least the protection of a warrant requirement.

This question must, in my view, be answered by assessing the nature of a particular practice and the likely extent of its impact on the individual's sense of security balanced against the utility of the conduct as a technique of law enforcement. For those more extensive intrusions that significantly jeopardize the sense of security which is the paramount concern of Fourth Amendment liberties, I am of the view that more than self-restraint by law enforcement officials is required and at the least warrants should be necessary.

The impact of the practice of third-party bugging, must, I think, be considered such as to undermine that confidence and sense of security in dealing with one another that is characteristic of individual relationships between citizens in a free society. * * * The argument of the plurality opinion, to the effect that it is irrelevant whether secrets are revealed by the mere tattletale or the transistor, ignores the differences occasioned by third-party monitoring and recording which insures full and accurate disclosure of all that is said, free of the possibility of error and oversight that inheres in human reporting.

Authority is hardly required to support the proposition that words would be measured a good deal more carefully and communication inhibited if one suspected his conversations were being transmitted and transcribed. Were third-party bugging a prevalent practice, it might well smother that spontaneity—reflected in frivolous, impetuous, sacrilegious, and defiant discourse—that liberates daily life. Much offhand exchange is easily forgotten and one may count on the obscurity of his remarks, protected by the very fact of a limited audience, and the likelihood that the listener will either overlook or forget what is said, as well as the listener's inability to reformulate a conversation without having to contend with a documented record. All these values are sacrificed by a rule of law that permits official monitoring of private discourse limited only by the need to locate a willing assistant.

\* \* \* The interest [the plurality] fails to protect is the expectation of the ordinary citizen, who has never engaged in illegal conduct in his life, that he may carry on his private discourse freely, openly, and spontaneously without measuring his every word against the connotations it might carry when instantaneously heard by others unknown to him and unfamiliar with his situation or analyzed in a cold, formal record played days, months, or years after the conversation. Interposition of a warrant requirement is designed not to shield "wrongdoers," but to secure a measure of privacy and a sense of personal security throughout our society. \* \* \*

JUSTICE MARSHALL, dissenting.

I am convinced that the correct view of the Fourth Amendment in the area of electronic surveillance is one that brings the safeguards of the warrant requirement to bear on the investigatory activity involved in this case. In this regard I agree with the dissents of Justice Douglas and Justice Harlan.

## ZURCHER v. STANFORD DAILY

436 U.S. 547, 98 S.Ct. 1970, 56 L.Ed.2d 525 (1978).

JUSTICE WHITE delivered the opinion of the Court.

[Nine policemen were injured by demonstrators at Stanford University Hospital. Two days later the Stanford Daily carried articles and photos devoted to the demonstration and attack; the photos by a staff member indicated he had been located where he could have photographed the assailants. A warrant was obtained to search the Daily's offices for negatives, film and pictures relevant to identification of the assailants. Executing officers searched photo labs, filing cabinets and desks, but found no evidence. The Daily later brought a civil action in district court, where declaratory relief was granted. That court held (i) that the Fourth Amendment forbade the issuance of a warrant to search for materials in the possession of one not suspected of crime except upon a showing of probable cause a subpoena *duces tecum* would be impracticable; and (ii) that the First Amendment bars search of newspaper offices except upon a clear showing that important materials would otherwise be destroyed or removed and that a restraining order would be futile.]

It is an understatement to say that there is no direct authority in this or any other federal court for the District Court's sweeping revision of the Fourth Amendment. Under existing law, valid warrants may be issued to search *any* property, whether or not occupied by a third party, at which there is probable cause to believe that fruits, instrumentalities, or evidence of a crime will be found. Nothing on the face of the Amendment suggests that a third-party search warrant should not normally issue. * * *

Against this background, it is untenable to conclude that property may not be searched unless its occupant is reasonably suspected of crime and is subject to arrest. * * * The Fourth Amendment has itself struck the balance between privacy and public need, and there is no occasion or justification for a court to revise the Amendment and strike a new balance by denying the search warrant in the circumstances present here and by insisting that the investigation proceed by subpoena *duces tecum,* whether on the theory that the latter is a less intrusive alternative, or otherwise. * * *

In any event, the reasons presented by the District Court and adopted by the Court of Appeals for arriving at its remarkable conclusion do not withstand analysis. First, as we have said, it is apparent that whether the third-party occupant is suspect or not, the State's interest in enforcing the criminal law and recovering the evidence remains the same; and it is the seeming innocence of the property owner that the District Court relied on to foreclose the warrant to search. But as respondents themselves now concede, if the third party knows that contraband or other illegal materials are on his property, he is sufficiently culpable to justify the issuance of a search warrant. Similarly, if his ethical stance is the determining factor, it seems to us that whether or not he knows that the sought-after articles are secreted on his property and whether or not he knows that the articles are in fact the fruits, instrumentalities, or evidence of crime, he will be so informed when the search warrant is served, and it is doubtful that he should then be permitted to object to the search, to withhold, if it is there, the evidence of crime reasonably believed to be possessed by him or secreted on his property, and to forbid the search and insist that the officers serve him with a subpoena *duces tecum.*

Second, we are unpersuaded that the District Court's new rule denying search warrants against third parties and insisting on subpoenas would substantially further privacy interests without seriously undermining law enforcement efforts. As the District Court understands it, denying third-party search warrants would not have substantial adverse effects on criminal investigations because the nonsuspect third party, once served with a subpoena, will preserve the evidence and ultimately, lawfully respond. The difficulty with this assumption is that search warrants are often employed early in an investigation, perhaps before the identity of any likely criminal and certainly before all the perpetrators are or could be known. The seemingly blameless third party in possession of the fruits or evidence may not be innocent at all; and if he is, he may nevertheless be so related to or so sympathetic with the culpable that he cannot be relied upon to retain and preserve the articles that may implicate his friends, or at least not to notify those who would be damaged by the evidence that the authorities are aware of its location. In any event, it is likely that the real culprits will have access to the property, and the delay involved in employing the subpoena *duces tecum,* offering as it does the opportunity to litigate its validity, could easily result in the disappearance of the evidence, whatever the good faith of the third party. * * *[8]

8. It is also far from clear, even apart from the dangers of destruction and removal, whether the use of the subpoena *duces tecum* under circumstances where there is probable cause to believe that a crime has been committed and that the materials sought constitute evidence of its commission will result in the production of evidence with sufficient regularity to satisfy the public interest in law enforcement. Unlike the individual whose

We are also not convinced that the net gain to privacy interests by the District Court's new rule would be worth the candle.[9] In the normal course of events, search warrants are more difficult to obtain than subpoenas, since the latter do not involve the judiciary and do not require proof of probable cause. Where, in the real world, subpoenas would suffice, it can be expected that they will be employed by the rational prosecutor. On the other hand, when choice is available under local law and the prosecutor chooses to use the search warrant, it is unlikely that he has needlessly selected the more difficult course. His choice is more likely to be based on the solid belief, arrived at through experience but difficult, if not impossible, to sustain a specific case, that the warranted search is necessary to secure and to avoid the destruction of evidence.

[The Framers] did not forbid warrants where the press was involved, did not require special showings that subpoenas would be impractical, and did not insist that the owner of the place to be searched, if connected with the press, must be shown to be implicated in the offense being investigated. Further, the prior cases do no more than insist that the courts apply the warrant requirements with particular exactitude when First Amendment interests would be endangered by the search. As we see it, no more than this is required where the warrant requested is for the seizure of criminal evidence reasonably believed to be on the premises occupied by a newspaper. Properly administered, the preconditions for a warrant—probable cause, specificity with respect to the place to be searched and the things to be seized, and overall reasonableness—should afford sufficient protection against the harms that are assertedly threatened by warrants for searching newspaper offices.

There is no reason to believe, for example, that magistrates cannot guard against searches of the type, scope, and intrusiveness that would actually interfere with the timely publication of a newspaper. Nor, if the requirements of specificity and reasonableness are properly applied, policed, and observed, will there be any occasion or opportunity for officers to rummage at large in newspaper files or to intrude into or to deter normal editorial and publication decisions. The warrant issued in this case authorized nothing of this sort. Nor are we convinced, * * * that confidential sources will disappear and that the press will suppress news because of fears of warranted searches. Whatever incremental effect there may be in this regard if search warrants, as well as subpoenas, are permissible in proper circumstances, it does not make a constitutional difference in our judgment.

The fact is that respondents and *amici* have pointed to only a very few instances in the entire United States since 1971 involving the issuance of warrants for searching newspaper premises. This reality hardly suggests abuse;

privacy is invaded by a search, the recipient of a subpoena may assert the Fifth Amendment privilege against self-incrimination in response to a summons to produce evidence or give testimony. This privilege is not restricted to suspects. We have construed it broadly as covering any individual who might be incriminated by the evidence in connection with which the privilege is asserted. The burden of overcoming an assertion of the Fifth Amendment privilege, even if prompted by a desire not to cooperate rather than any real fear of self-incrimination, is one which prosecutors would rarely be able to meet in the early stages of an investigation despite the fact they did not regard the witness as a suspect. Even

time spent litigating such matters could seriously impede criminal investigations.

**9.** We reject totally the reasoning of the District Court that additional protections are required to assure that the Fourth Amendment rights of third parties are not violated because of the unavailability of the exclusionary rule as a deterrent to improper searches of premises in the control of nonsuspects. * * * It is probably seldom that police during the investigatory stage when most searches occur will be so convinced that no potential defendant will have standing to exclude evidence on Fourth Amendment grounds that they will feel free to ignore constitutional restraints. * * *

and if abuse occurs, there will be time enough to deal with it. Furthermore, the press is not only an important, critical, and valuable asset to society, but it is not easily intimidated—nor should it be. * * *

JUSTICE BRENNAN took no part in the consideration or decision of this case.

JUSTICE POWELL, concurring.

* * * Even aside from the difficulties involved in deciding on a case-by-case basis whether a subpoena can serve as an adequate substitute,[1] I agree with the Court that there is no constitutional basis for such a reading. * * *

JUSTICE STEWART, with whom JUSTICE MARSHALL joins, dissenting.

* * * It seems to me self-evident that police searches of newspaper offices burden the freedom of the press. The most immediate and obvious First Amendment injury caused by such a visitation by the police is physical disruption of the operation of the newspaper. Policemen occupying a newsroom and searching it thoroughly for what may be an extended period of time will inevitably interrupt its normal operations, and thus impair or even temporarily prevent the processes of newsgathering, writing, editing, and publishing. By contrast, a subpoena would afford the newspaper itself an opportunity to locate whatever material might be requested and produce it.

But there is another and more serious burden on a free press imposed by an unannounced police search of a newspaper office: the possibility of disclosure of information received from confidential sources, or of the identity of the sources themselves. Protection of those sources is necessary to ensure that the press can fulfill its constitutionally designated function of informing the public, because important information can often be obtained only by an assurance that the source will not be revealed. * * *

Today the Court does not question the existence of this constitutional protection, but says only that it is not "convinced . . . that confidential sources will disappear and that the press will suppress news because of fears of warranted searches." This facile conclusion seems to me to ignore common experience. It requires no blind leap of faith to understand that a person who gives information to a journalist only on condition that his identity will not be revealed will be less likely to give that information if he knows that, despite the journalist's assurance his identity may in fact be disclosed. And it cannot be denied that confidential information may be exposed to the eyes of police officers who execute a search warrant by rummaging through the files, cabinets, desks and wastebaskets of a newsroom. Since the indisputable effect of such searches will thus be to prevent a newsman from being able to promise confidentiality to his potential sources, it seems obvious to me that a journalist's access to information, and thus the public's will thereby be impaired.

A search warrant allows police officers to ransack the files of a newspaper, reading each and every document until they have found the one named in the warrant,[7] while a subpoena would permit the newspaper itself to produce only

1. For example, respondent had announced a policy of destroying any photographs that might aid prosecution of protestors. While this policy probably reflected the deep feelings of the Vietnam era, and one may assume that under normal circumstances few, if any, press entities would adopt a policy so hostile to law enforcement, respondent's policy at least illustrates the possibility of such hostility. Use of a subpoena, as proposed by the dissent would be of no utility in face of a policy of destroying

evidence. And unless the policy were publicly announced, it probably would be difficult to show the impracticality of a subpoena as opposed to a search warrant.

7. The Court says that "if the requirements of specificity and reasonableness are properly applied, policed, and observed" there will be no opportunity for the police to "rummage at large in newspaper files." But in order to find a particular document, no matter

the specific documents requested. A search, unlike a subpoena, will therefore lead to the needless exposure of confidential information completely unrelated to the purpose of the investigation. The knowledge that police officers can make an unannounced raid on a newsroom is thus bound to have a deterrent effect on the availability of confidential news sources. The end result, wholly inimical to the First Amendment, will be a diminishing flow of potentially important information to the public. \* \* \*

JUSTICE STEVENS, dissenting.

\* \* \* [Before 1967] warrants were used to search for contraband, weapons and plunder, but not for "mere evidence." The practical effect of the rule prohibiting the issuance of warrants to search for mere evidence was to narrowly limit not only the category of objects, but also the category of persons and the character of the privacy interests that might be affected by an unannounced police search.

Just as the witnesses who participate in an investigation or a trial far outnumber the defendants, the persons who possess evidence that may help to identify an offender, or explain an aspect of a criminal transaction, far outnumber those who have custody of weapons or plunder. Countless law abiding citizens—doctors, lawyers, merchants, customers, bystanders—may have documents in their possession that relate to an ongoing criminal investigation. The consequences of subjecting this large category of persons to unannounced police searches are extremely serious. The *ex parte* warrant procedure enables the prosecutor to obtain access to privileged documents that could not be examined if advance notice gave the custodian an opportunity to object. The search for the documents described in a warrant may involve the inspection of files containing other private matter. The dramatic character of a sudden search may cause an entirely unjustified injury to the reputation of the persons searched. \* \* \*

A showing of probable cause that was adequate to justify the issuance of a warrant to search for stolen goods in the 18th century does not automatically satisfy the new dimensions of the Fourth Amendment [whereunder a warrant may issue for "mere evidence"]. The only conceivable justification for an unannounced search of an innocent citizen is the fear that, if notice were given, he would conceal or destroy the object of the search. Probable cause to believe that the custodian is a criminal, or that he holds a criminal's weapons, spoils, or the like, justifies that fear, and therefore such a showing complies with the Clause. But if nothing said under oath in the warrant application demonstrates the need for an unannounced search by force, the probable cause requirement is not satisfied. In the absence of some other showing of reasonableness, the ensuing search violates the Fourth Amendment. \* \* \*

# SECTION 3. PROBABLE CAUSE

Because the warrant clause of the Fourth Amendment provides that "no Warrants shall issue, but upon probable cause," it is apparent that a valid arrest warrant or search warrant may issue only upon a showing of probable cause to the issuing authority. In the many instances in which police may arrest and search without first obtaining a warrant, their conduct is governed by the other half of the Amendment, which declares the right of the people to be secure "against unreasonable searches and seizures." But such an arrest or search is

how specifically it is identified in the warrant, the police will have to search every place where it might be—including, presumably, every file in the office—and to examine each document they find to see if it is the correct one. I thus fail to see how the Fourth Amendment would provide an effective limit to these searches.

unreasonable unless based upon probable cause; as stated in *Wong Sun v. United States*, 371 U.S. 471 (1963), were the requirements less stringent than when a warrant is obtained, then "a principal incentive now existing for the procurement of * * * warrants would be destroyed."

When the police arrest or search without a warrant, they initially make the probable cause decision themselves. But upon a motion to suppress evidence found in the arrest or search (or, sometimes, pursuant to efforts to justify continued custody of the arrestee) there will occur a subsequent judicial determination of the probable cause issue. When the police arrest or search with a warrant, the probable cause determination is made by a magistrate in the first instance. But his decision is not final; subject to the *Leon* "good faith" limitation, the defendant on a motion to suppress may still seek exclusion of evidence on the ground that the warrant was not in fact issued upon probable cause.

The two cases in this section, *Spinelli v. United States* and *Illinois v. Gates*, reflect how the Supreme Court's approach to the probable cause issue has changed in recent years as the Court shifted to a less structured "totality of the circumstances" test.

## SPINELLI v. UNITED STATES
393 U.S. 410, 89 S.Ct. 584, 21 L.Ed.2d 637 (1969).

JUSTICE HARLAN delivered the opinion of the Court.

William Spinelli was convicted * * * of traveling to St. Louis, Missouri, from a nearby Illinois suburb with the intention of conducting gambling activities proscribed by Missouri law. At every appropriate stage in the proceedings in the lower courts, the petitioner challenged the constitutionality of the warrant which authorized the FBI search that uncovered the evidence necessary for his conviction. * * * Believing it desirable that the principles of [*Aguilar v. Texas*, 378 U.S. 108 (1964)] should be further explicated, we granted certiorari * * *.

In *Aguilar*, a search warrant had issued upon an affidavit of police officers who swore only that they had "received reliable information from a credible person and do believe" that narcotics were being illegally stored on the described premises. While recognizing that the constitutional requirement of probable cause can be satisfied by hearsay information, this Court held the affidavit inadequate for two reasons. First, the application failed to set forth any of the "underlying circumstances" necessary to enable the magistrate independently to judge of the validity of the informant's conclusion that the narcotics were where he said they were. Second, the affiant-officers did not attempt to support their claim that their informant was "'credible' or his information 'reliable.'" The Government is, however, quite right in saying that the FBI affidavit in the present case is more ample than that in *Aguilar*. Not only does it contain a report from an anonymous informant, but it also contains a report of an independent FBI investigation which is said to corroborate the informant's tip. We are, then, required to delineate the manner in which *Aguilar's* two-pronged test should be applied in these circumstances.

In essence, the affidavit * * * contained the following allegations:

1. The FBI had kept track of Spinelli's movements on five days during the month of August 1965. On four of these occasions, Spinelli was seen crossing one of two bridges leading from Illinois into St. Louis, Missouri, between 11 a.m. and 12:15 p.m. On four of the five days, Spinelli was also

seen parking his car in a lot used by residents of an apartment house at 1108 Indian Circle Drive in St. Louis, between 3:30 p.m. and 4:45 p.m. On one day, Spinelli was followed further and seen to enter a particular apartment in the building.

2. An FBI check with the telephone company revealed that this apartment contained two telephones listed under the name of Grace P. Hagen, and carrying the numbers WYdown 4–0029 and WYdown 4–0136.

3. The application stated that "William Spinelli is known to this affiant and to federal law enforcement agents and local law enforcement agents as a bookmaker, an associate of bookmakers, a gambler, and an associate of gamblers."

4. Finally, it was stated that the FBI "has been informed by a confidential reliable informant that William Spinelli is operating a handbook and accepting wagers and disseminating wagering information by means of the telephones which have been assigned the numbers WYdown 4–0029 and WYdown 4–0136."

There can be no question that the last item mentioned, detailing the informant's tip, has a fundamental place in this warrant application. Without it, probable cause could not be established. The first two items reflect only innocent-seeming activity and data. Spinelli's travels to and from the apartment building and his entry into a particular apartment on one occasion could hardly be taken as bespeaking gambling activity; and there is surely nothing unusual about an apartment containing two separate telephones. Many a householder indulges himself in this petty luxury. Finally, the allegation that Spinelli was "known" to the affiant and to other federal and local law enforcement officers as a gambler and an associate of gamblers is but a bald and unilluminating assertion of suspicion that is entitled to no weight in appraising the magistrate's decision. *Nathanson v. United States*, 290 U.S. 41 (1933).

So much indeed the Government does not deny. Rather, following the reasoning of the Court of Appeals, the Government claims that the informant's tip gives a suspicious color to the FBI's reports detailing Spinelli's innocent-seeming conduct and that, conversely, the FBI's surveillance corroborates the informant's tip, thereby entitling it to more weight. * * * We believe, however, that the "totality of circumstances" approach taken by the Court of Appeals paints with too broad a brush. Where, as here, the informer's tip is a necessary element in a finding of probable cause, its proper weight must be determined by a more precise analysis.

The informer's report must first be measured against *Aguilar's* standards so that its probative value can be assessed. If the tip is found inadequate under *Aguilar*, the other allegations which corroborate the information contained in the hearsay report should then be considered. At this stage as well, however, the standards enunciated in *Aguilar* must inform the magistrate's decision. He must ask: Can it fairly be said that the tip, even when certain parts of it have been corroborated by independent sources, is as trustworthy as a tip which would pass *Aguilar's* tests without independent corroboration? * * *

Applying these principles to the present case, we first consider the weight to be given the informer's tip when it is considered apart from the rest of the affidavit. It is clear that a Commissioner could not credit it without abdicating his constitutional function. Though the affiant swore that his confidant was "reliable," he offered the magistrate no reason in support of this conclusion. Perhaps even more important is the fact that *Aguilar's* other test has not been satisfied. The tip does not contain a sufficient statement of the underlying circumstances from which the informer concluded that Spinelli was running a bookmaking operation. We are not told how the FBI's source received his information—it is not alleged that the informant personally observed Spinelli at work or that he had ever placed a bet with him. Moreover, if the informant came by the information indirectly, he did not explain why his sources were reliable. In the absence of a statement detailing the manner in which the information was gathered, it is especially important that the tip describe the accused's criminal activity in sufficient detail so that the magistrate may know that he is relying on something more substantial than a casual rumor circulating in the underworld or an accusation based merely on an individual's general reputation.

The detail provided by the informant in *Draper v. United States*, 358 U.S. 307 (1959), provides a suitable benchmark. While Hereford, the FBI's informer in that case, did not state the way in which he had obtained his information, he reported that Draper had gone to Chicago the day before by train and that he would return to Denver by train with three ounces of heroin on one of two specified mornings. Moreover, Hereford went on to describe, with minute particularity, the clothes that Draper would be wearing upon his arrival at the Denver station. A magistrate, when confronted with such detail, could reasonably infer that the informant had gained his information in a reliable way. Such an inference cannot be made in the present case. Here, the only facts supplied were that Spinelli was using two specified telephones and that these phones were being used in gambling operations. This meager report could easily have been obtained from an off-hand remark heard at a neighborhood bar.

Nor do we believe that the patent doubts *Aguilar* raises as to the report's reliability are adequately resolved by a consideration of the allegations detailing the FBI's independent investigative efforts. At most, these allegations indicated that Spinelli could have used the telephones specified by the informant for some purpose. This cannot by itself be said to support both the inference that the informer was generally trustworthy and that he had made his charge against Spinelli on the basis of information obtained in a reliable way. Once again, *Draper* provides a relevant comparison. Independent police work in that case corroborated much more than one small detail that had been provided by the informant. There, the police, upon greeting the inbound Denver train on the second morning specified by informer Hereford, saw a man whose dress corresponded precisely to Hereford's detailed description. It was then apparent that the informant had not been fabricating his report out of whole cloth; since the report was of the sort which in common experience may be recognized as having been obtained in a reliable way, it was perfectly clear that probable cause had been established.

We conclude, then, that in the present case the informant's tip—even when corroborated to the extent indicated—was not sufficient to provide the basis for a finding of probable cause. ＊ ＊ ＊ The judgment of the Court of Appeals is reversed ＊ ＊ ＊.

Justice White, concurring.

＊ ＊ ＊ The tension between *Draper* and the *Nathanson–Aguilar* line of cases is evident from the course followed by the majority opinion. ＊ ＊ ＊ Since [the informant's] specific information about Spinelli using two phones with particular numbers had been verified, did not his allegation about gambling thereby become sufficiently more believable if the *Draper* principle is to be given any scope at all? I would think so, particularly since the information from the informant which was verified was not neutral, irrelevant information but was material to proving the gambling allegation: two phones with different numbers in an apartment used away from home indicates a business use in an operation, like bookmaking, where multiple phones are needed. The *Draper* approach would reasonably justify the issuance of a warrant in this case, particularly since the police had some awareness of Spinelli's past activities. The majority, however, while seemingly embracing *Draper*, confines that case to its own facts. Pending full scale reconsideration of that case, on the one hand, or of the *Nathanson–Aguilar* cases on the other, I join the opinion of the Court and the judgment of reversal especially since a vote to affirm would produce an equally divided Court.[a]

## ILLINOIS v. GATES

462 U.S. 213, 103 S.Ct. 2317, 76 L.Ed.2d 527 (1983).

JUSTICE REHNQUIST delivered the opinion of the Court.

\* \* \* A chronological statement of events usefully introduces the issues at stake. Bloomingdale, Ill., is a suburb of Chicago located in DuPage County. On May 3, 1978, the Bloomingdale Police Department received by mail an anonymous handwritten letter which read as follows:

> "This letter is to inform you that you have a couple in your town who strictly make their living on selling drugs. They are Sue and Lance Gates, they live on Greenway, off Bloomingdale Rd. in the condominiums. Most of their buys are done in Florida. Sue his wife drives their car to Florida, where she leaves it to be loaded up with drugs, then Lance flys down and drives it back. Sue flys back after she drops the car off in Florida. May 3 she is driving down there again and Lance will be flying down in a few days to drive it back. At the time Lance drives the car back he has the trunk loaded with over $100,000.00 in drugs. Presently they have over $100,000.00 worth of drugs in their basement.
>
> They brag about the fact they never have to work, and make their entire living on pushers.
>
> I guarantee if you watch them carefully you will make a big catch. They are friends with some big drugs dealers, who visit their house often.
>
> Lance & Susan Gates
>
> Greenway
>
> in Condominiums"

The letter was referred by the Chief of Police of the Bloomingdale Police Department to Detective Mader, who decided to pursue the tip. Mader learned, from the office of the Illinois Secretary of State, that an Illinois driver's license had been issued to one Lance Gates, residing at a stated address in Bloomingdale. He contacted a confidential informant, whose examination of certain financial records revealed a more recent address for the Gates, and he also learned from a police officer assigned to O'Hare Airport that "L. Gates" had made a reservation on Eastern Airlines flight 245 to West Palm Beach, Fla., scheduled to depart from Chicago on May 5 at 4:15 p.m.

Mader then made arrangements with an agent of the Drug Enforcement Administration for surveillance of the May 5 Eastern Airlines flight. The agent

---

**a.** The separate dissents of Black, Fortas, and Stewart, JJ., are omitted. Marshall, J., did not participate.

later reported to Mader that Gates had boarded the flight, and that federal agents in Florida had observed him arrive in West Palm Beach and take a taxi to the nearby Holiday Inn. They also reported that Gates went to a room registered to one Susan Gates and that, at 7:00 a.m. the next morning, Gates and an unidentified woman left the motel in a Mercury bearing Illinois license plates and drove northbound on an interstate frequently used by travelers to the Chicago area. In addition, the DEA agent informed Mader that the license plate number on the Mercury registered to a Hornet station wagon owned by Gates. The agent also advised Mader that the driving time between West Palm Beach and Bloomingdale was approximately 22 to 24 hours.

Mader signed an affidavit setting forth the foregoing facts, and submitted it to a judge of the Circuit Court of DuPage County, together with a copy of the anonymous letter. The judge of that court thereupon issued a search warrant for the Gates' residence and for their automobile. The judge, in deciding to issue the warrant, could have determined that the *modus operandi* of the Gates had been substantially corroborated. As the anonymous letter predicted, Lance Gates had flown from Chicago to West Palm Beach late in the afternoon of May 5th, had checked into a hotel room registered in the name of his wife, and, at 7:00 a.m. the following morning, had headed north, accompanied by an unidentified woman, out of West Palm Beach on an interstate highway used by travelers from South Florida to Chicago in an automobile bearing a license plate issued to him.

At 5:15 a.m. on May 7th, only 36 hours after he had flown out of Chicago, Lance Gates, and his wife, returned to their home in Bloomingdale, driving the car in which they had left West Palm Beach some 22 hours earlier. The Bloomingdale police were awaiting them, searched the trunk of the Mercury, and uncovered approximately 350 pounds of marijuana. A search of the Gates' home revealed marijuana, weapons, and other contraband. The Illinois Circuit Court ordered suppression of all these items, on the ground that the affidavit submitted to the Circuit Judge failed to support the necessary determination of probable cause to believe that the Gates' automobile and home contained the contraband in question. This decision was affirmed in turn by the Illinois Appellate Court and by a divided vote of the Supreme Court of Illinois.

The Illinois Supreme Court concluded—and we are inclined to agree—that, standing alone, the anonymous letter sent to the Bloomingdale Police Department would not provide the basis for a magistrate's determination that there was probable cause to believe contraband would be found in the Gates' car and home. The letter provides virtually nothing from which one might conclude that its author is either honest or his information reliable; likewise, the letter gives absolutely no indication of the basis for the writer's predictions regarding the Gates' criminal activities. Something more was required, then, before a magistrate could conclude that there was probable cause to believe that contraband would be found in the Gates' home and car.

The Illinois Supreme Court also properly recognized that Detective Mader's affidavit might be capable of supplementing the anonymous letter with information sufficient to permit a determination of probable cause. In holding that the affidavit in fact did not contain sufficient additional information to sustain a determination of probable cause, the Illinois court applied a "two-pronged test," derived from our decision in *Spinelli v. United States*. The Illinois Supreme Court, like some others, apparently understood *Spinelli* as requiring that the anonymous letter satisfy each of two independent requirements before it could be relied on. According to this view, the letter, as supplemented by Mader's affidavit, first had to adequately reveal the "basis of knowledge" of the letter writer—the particular means by which he came by the information given in his report. Second, it had to provide facts sufficiently establishing either the "veracity" of the affiant's informant, or, alternatively, the "reliability" of the informant's report in this particular case.

The Illinois court, alluding to an elaborate set of legal rules that have developed among various lower courts to enforce the "two-pronged test," [4] found that the test had not been satisfied. First, the "veracity" prong was not satisfied because, "there was simply no basis [for] * * * conclud[ing] that the anonymous person [who wrote the letter to the Bloomingdale Police Department] was credible." The court indicated that corroboration by police of details contained in the letter might never satisfy the "veracity" prong, and in any event, could not do so if, as in the present case, only "innocent" details are corroborated. In addition, the letter gave no indication of the basis of its writer's knowledge of the Gates' activities. The Illinois court understood *Spinelli* as permitting the detail contained in a tip to be used to infer that the informant had a reliable basis for his statements, but it thought that the anonymous letter failed to provide sufficient detail to permit such an inference. Thus, it concluded that no showing of probable cause had been made.

We agree with the Illinois Supreme Court that an informant's "veracity," "reliability" and "basis of knowledge" are all highly relevant in determining the value of his report. We do not agree, however, that these elements should be understood as entirely separate and independent requirements to be rigidly exacted in every case, which the opinion of the Supreme Court of Illinois would imply. Rather, as detailed below, they should be understood simply as closely intertwined issues that may usefully illuminate the common sense, practical question whether there is "probable cause" to believe that contraband or evidence is located in a particular place.

This totality of the circumstances approach is far more consistent with our prior treatment of probable cause than is any rigid demand that specific "tests" be satisfied by every informant's tip. Perhaps the central teaching of our decisions bearing on the probable cause standard is that it is a "practical, nontechnical conception." "In dealing with probable cause, * * * as the very name implies, we deal with probabilities. These are not technical; they are the factual and practical considerations of everyday life on which reasonable and prudent men, not legal technicians, act." Our observation regarding "particularized suspicion," is also applicable to the probable cause standard:

> The process does not deal with hard certainties, but with probabilities. Long before the law of probabilities was articulated as such, practical people formulated certain common-sense conclusions about human behavior; jurors as factfinders are permitted to do the same—and so are law enforcement officers. Finally, the evidence thus collected must be seen and weighed not in terms of library analysis by scholars, but as understood by those versed in the field of law enforcement.

**4.** In summary, these rules posit that the "veracity" prong of the *Spinelli* test has two "spurs"—the informant's "credibility" and the "reliability" of his information. Various interpretations are advanced for the meaning of the "reliability" spur of the "veracity" prong. Both the "basis of knowledge" prong and the "veracity" prong are treated as entirely separate requirements, which must be independently satisfied in every case in order to sustain a determination of probable cause. Some ancillary doctrines are relied on to satisfy certain of the foregoing requirements. For example, the "self-verifying detail" of a tip may satisfy the "basis of knowledge" requirement, although not the "credibility" spur of the "veracity" prong. Conversely, corroboration would seem not capable of supporting the "basis of knowledge" prong, but only the "veracity" prong. * * *

As these comments illustrate, probable cause is a fluid concept—turning on the assessment of probabilities in particular factual contexts—not readily, or even usefully, reduced to a neat set of legal rules. Informants' tips doubtless come in many shapes and sizes from many different types of persons. * * * Rigid legal rules are ill-suited to an area of such diversity. "One simple rule will not cover every situation." [7]

Moreover, the "two-pronged test" directs analysis into two largely independent channels—the informant's "veracity" or "reliability" and his "basis of knowledge." There are persuasive arguments against according these two elements such independent status. Instead, they are better understood as relevant considerations in the totality of circumstances analysis that traditionally has guided probable cause determinations: a deficiency in one may be compensated for, in determining the overall reliability of a tip, by a strong showing as to the other, or by some other indicia of reliability.

If, for example, a particular informant is known for the unusual reliability of his predictions of certain types of criminal activities in a locality, his failure, in a particular case, to thoroughly set forth the basis of his knowledge surely should not serve as an absolute bar to a finding of probable cause based on his tip. Likewise, if an unquestionably honest citizen comes forward with a report of criminal activity—which if fabricated would subject him to criminal liability— we have found rigorous scrutiny of the basis of his knowledge unnecessary. Conversely, even if we entertain some doubt as to an informant's motives, his explicit and detailed description of alleged wrongdoing, along with a statement that the event was observed firsthand, entitles his tip to greater weight than might otherwise be the case. Unlike a totality of circumstances analysis, which permits a balanced assessment of the relative weights of all the various indicia of reliability (and unreliability) attending an informant's tip, the "two-pronged test" has encouraged an excessively technical dissection of informants' tips, with

---

**7.** The diversity of informants' tips, as well as the usefulness of the totality of the circumstances approach to probable cause, is reflected in our prior decisions on the subject. In *Jones v. United States*, 362 U.S. 257 (1960), we held that probable cause to search petitioners' apartment was established by an affidavit based principally on an informant's tip. The unnamed informant claimed to have purchased narcotics from petitioners at their apartment; the affiant stated that he had been given correct information from the informant on a prior occasion. This, and the fact that petitioners had admitted to police officers on another occasion that they were narcotics users, sufficed to support the magistrate's determination of probable cause.

Likewise, in *Rugendorf v. United States*, 376 U.S. 528 (1964), the Court upheld a magistrate's determination that there was probable cause to believe that certain stolen property would be found in petitioner's apartment. The affidavit submitted to the magistrate stated that certain furs had been stolen, and that a confidential informant, who previously had furnished confidential information, said that he saw the furs in petitioner's home. Moreover, another confidential informant, also claimed to be reliable, stated that one Schweihs had stolen the furs. Police reports indicated that petitioner had been seen in

Schweihs' company and a third informant stated that petitioner was a fence for Schweihs.

Finally, in *Ker v. California*, 374 U.S. 23 (1963), we held that information within the knowledge of officers who searched the Ker's apartment provided them with probable cause to believe drugs would be found there. The officers were aware that one Murphy had previously sold marijuana to a police officer; the transaction had occurred in an isolated area, to which Murphy had led the police. The night after this transaction, police observed Ker and Murphy meet in the same location. Murphy approached Ker's car, and, although police could see nothing change hands, Murphy's *modus operandi* was identical to what it had been the night before. Moreover, when police followed Ker from the scene of the meeting with Murphy he managed to lose them after performing an abrupt U-turn. Finally, the police had a statement from an informant who had provided reliable information previously, that Ker was engaged in selling marijuana, and that his source was Murphy. We concluded that "To say that this coincidence of information was sufficient to support a reasonable belief of the officers that Ker was illegally in possession of marijuana is to indulge in understatement."

undue attention being focused on isolated issues that cannot sensibly be divorced from the other facts presented to the magistrate. * * *

We also have recognized that affidavits "are normally drafted by non-lawyers in the midst and haste of a criminal investigation. Technical requirements of elaborate specificity once exacted under common law pleading have no proper place in this area." Likewise, search and arrest warrants long have been issued by persons who are neither lawyers nor judges, and who certainly do not remain abreast of each judicial refinement of the nature of "probable cause." The rigorous inquiry into the *Spinelli* prongs and the complex superstructure of evidentiary and analytical rules that some have seen implicit in our *Spinelli* decision, cannot be reconciled with the fact that many warrants are—quite properly—issued on the basis of nontechnical, common-sense judgments of lay-men applying a standard less demanding than those used in more formal legal proceedings. Likewise, given the informal, often hurried context in which it must be applied, the "built-in subtleties" of the "two-pronged test" are particu-larly unlikely to assist magistrates in determining probable cause.

Similarly, we have repeatedly said that after-the-fact scrutiny by courts of the sufficiency of an affidavit should not take the form of *de novo* review. A magistrate's "determination of probable cause should be paid great deference by reviewing courts." "A grudging or negative attitude by reviewing courts toward warrants" is inconsistent with the Fourth Amendment's strong preference for searches conducted pursuant to a warrant "court should not invalidate * * * warrant[s] by interpreting affidavit[s] in a hypertechnical, rather than a com-mon-sense, manner."

If the affidavits submitted by police officers are subjected to the type of scrutiny some courts have deemed appropriate, police might well resort to warrantless searches, with the hope of relying on consent or some other excep-tion to the warrant clause that might develop at the time of the search. In addition, the possession of a warrant by officers conducting an arrest or search greatly reduces the perception of unlawful or intrusive police conduct, by assuring "the individual whose property is searched or seized of the lawful authority of the executing officer, his need to search, and the limits of his power to search." Reflecting this preference for the warrant process, the traditional standard for review of an issuing magistrate's probable cause determination has been that so long as the magistrate had a "substantial basis for * * * conclud[ing]" that a search would uncover evidence of wrongdoing, the Fourth Amendment requires no more. We think reaffirmation of this standard better serves the purpose of encouraging recourse to the warrant procedure and is more consistent with our traditional deference to the probable cause determinations of magistrates than is the "two-pronged test."

Finally, the direction taken by decisions following *Spinelli* poorly serves "the most basic function of any government": "to provide for the security of the individual and of his property. The strictures that inevitably accompany the "two-pronged test" cannot avoid seriously impeding the task of law enforcement. If, as the Illinois Supreme Court apparently thought, that test must be rigorously applied in every case, [anonymous tips would be] of greatly diminished value in police work. Ordinary citizens, like ordinary witnesses, generally do not provide extensive recitations of the basis of their everyday observations. Likewise, as the Illinois Supreme Court observed in this case, the veracity of persons supply-ing anonymous tips is by hypothesis largely unknown, and unknowable. As a result, anonymous tips seldom could survive a rigorous application of either of the *Spinelli* prongs. Yet, such tips, particularly when supplemented by independent police investigation, frequently contribute to the solution of otherwise "perfect crimes." While a conscientious assessment of the basis for crediting such tips is required by the Fourth Amendment, a standard that leaves virtually no place for anonymous citizen informants is not.

For all these reasons, we conclude that it is wiser to abandon the "two-pronged test" established by our decisions in *Aguilar* and *Spinelli*.[11] In its place we reaffirm the totality of the circumstances analysis that traditionally has informed probable cause determinations. The task of the issuing magistrate is simply to make a practical, common-sense decision whether, given all the circumstances set forth in the affidavit before him, including the "veracity" and "basis of knowledge" of persons supplying hearsay information, there is a fair probability that contraband or evidence of a crime will be found in a particular place. And the duty of a reviewing court is simply to ensure that the magistrate had a "substantial basis for * * * conclud[ing]" that probable cause existed. We are convinced that this flexible, easily applied standard will better achieve the accommodation of public and private interests that the Fourth Amendment requires than does the approach that has developed from *Aguilar* and *Spinelli*.

Our earlier cases illustrate the limits beyond which a magistrate may not venture in issuing a warrant. A sworn statement of an affiant that "he has cause to suspect and does believe that" liquor illegally brought into the United States is located on certain premises will not do. *Nathanson v. United States*. An affidavit must provide the magistrate with a substantial basis for determining the existence of probable cause, and the wholly conclusory statement at issue in *Nathanson* failed to meet this requirement. An officer's statement that "affiants have received reliable information from a credible person and believe" that heroin is stored in a home, is likewise inadequate. *Aguilar v. Texas*. As in *Nathanson*, this is a mere conclusory statement that gives the magistrate virtually no basis at all for making a judgment regarding probable cause. Sufficient information must be presented to the magistrate to allow that official to determine probable cause; his action cannot be a mere ratification of the bare conclusions of others. In order to ensure that such an abdication of the magistrate's duty does not occur, courts must continue to conscientiously review the sufficiency of affidavits on which warrants are issued. But when we move beyond the "bare bones" affidavits present in cases such as *Nathanson* and *Aguilar*, this area simply does not lend itself to a prescribed set of rules, like that which had developed from *Spinelli*. Instead, the flexible, common-sense standard articulated in *Jones* [and other cases] better served the purposes of the Fourth Amendment's probable cause requirement.

Justice Brennan's dissent suggests in several places that the approach we take today somehow downgrades the role of the neutral magistrate, because *Aguilar* and *Spinelli* "preserve the role of magistrates as independent arbiters of probable cause * * *." Quite the contrary, we believe, is the case. Nothing in our opinion in any way lessens the authority of the magistrate to draw such reasonable inferences as he will from the material supplied to him by applicants for a warrant; indeed, he is freer than under the regime of *Aguilar* and *Spinelli* to draw such inferences, or to refuse to draw them if he is so minded.

**11.** * * * Whether the allegations submitted to the magistrate in *Spinelli* would, under the view we now take, have supported a finding of probable cause, we think it would not be profitable to decide. There are so many variables in the probable cause equation that one determination will seldom be a useful "precedent" for another. Suffice it to say that while we in no way abandon *Spinelli's* concern for the trustworthiness of informers and for the principle that it is the magistrate who must ultimately make a finding of probable cause, we reject the rigid categorization suggested by some of its language.

The real gist of Justice Brennan's criticism seems to be a second argument, somewhat at odds with the first, that magistrates should be restricted in their authority to make probable cause determinations by the standards laid down in *Aguilar* and *Spinelli* and that such findings "should not be authorized unless there is some assurance that the information on which they are based has been obtained in a reliable way by an honest or credible person." However, under our opinion magistrates remain perfectly free to exact such assurances as they deem necessary, as well as those required by this opinion, in making probable cause determinations. Justice Brennan would apparently prefer that magistrates be restricted in their findings of probable cause by the development of an elaborate body of case law dealing with the "veracity" prong of the *Spinelli* test, which in turn is broken down into two "spurs"—the informant's "credibility" and the "reliability" of his information, together with the "basis of knowledge" prong of the *Spinelli* test. That such a labyrinthine body of judicial refinement bears any relationship to familiar definitions of probable cause is hard to imagine. * * *

Justice Brennan's dissent also suggests that "words such as 'practical,' 'nontechnical,' and 'common sense,' as used in the Court's opinion, are but code words for an overly permissive attitude towards police practices in derogation of the rights secured by the Fourth Amendment." * * * "Fidelity" to the commands of the Constitution suggests balanced judgment rather than exhortation. The highest "fidelity" is achieved neither by the judge who instinctively goes furthest in upholding even the most bizarre claim of individual constitutional rights, any more than it is achieved by a judge who instinctively goes furthest in accepting the most restrictive claims of governmental authorities. The task of this Court, as of other courts, is to "hold the balance true," and we think we have done that in this case.

Our decisions applying the totality of circumstances analysis outlined above have consistently recognized the value of corroboration of details of an informant's tip by independent police work.

Our decision in *Draper v. United States,* however, is the classic case on the value of corroborative efforts of police officials. There, an informant named Hereford reported that Draper would arrive in Denver on a train from Chicago on one of two days, and that he would be carrying a quantity of heroin. The informant also supplied a fairly detailed physical description of Draper, and predicted that he would be wearing a light colored raincoat, brown slacks and black shoes, and would be walking "real fast." Hereford gave no indication of the basis for his information.[12]

On one of the stated dates police officers observed a man matching this description exit a train arriving from Chicago; his attire and luggage matched Hereford's report and he was walking rapidly. We explained in *Draper* that, by this point in his investigation, the arresting officer "had personally verified every facet of the information given him by Hereford except whether petitioner had accomplished his mission and had the three ounces of heroin on his person or in his bag. And surely with every other bit of Hereford's information being thus personally verified, [the officer] had 'reasonable grounds' to believe that the

---

**12.** The tip in *Draper* might well not have survived the rigid application of the "two-pronged test" that developed following *Spinelli.* The only reference to Hereford's reliability was that he had "been engaged as a 'special employee' of the Bureau of Narcotics at Denver for about six months, and from time to time gave information to [the police] for small sums of money, and that [the officer] had always found the information given by Hereford to be accurate and reliable." Likewise, the tip gave no indication of how Hereford came by his information. At most, the detailed and accurate predictions in the tip indicated that, however Hereford obtained his information, it was reliable.

remaining unverified bit of Hereford's information—that Draper would have the heroin with him—was likewise true."

The showing of probable cause in the present case was fully as compelling as that in *Draper*. Even standing alone, the facts obtained through the independent investigation of Mader and the DEA at least suggested that the Gates were involved in drug trafficking. In addition to being a popular vacation site, Florida is well-known as a source of narcotics and other illegal drugs. Lance Gates' flight to Palm Beach, his brief, overnight stay in a motel, and apparent immediate return north to Chicago in the family car, conveniently awaiting him in West Palm Beach, is as suggestive of a prearranged drug run, as it is of an ordinary vacation trip.

In addition, the magistrate could rely on the anonymous letter, which had been corroborated in major part by Mader's efforts—just as had occurred in *Draper*.[13] The Supreme Court of Illinois reasoned that *Draper* involved an informant who had given reliable information on previous occasions, while the honesty and reliability of the anonymous informant in this case were unknown to the Bloomingdale police. While this distinction might be an apt one at the time the police department received the anonymous letter, it became far less significant after Mader's independent investigative work occurred. The corroboration of the letter's predictions that the Gates' car would be in Florida, that Lance Gates would fly to Florida in the next day or so, and that he would drive the car north toward Bloomingdale all indicated, albeit not with certainty, that the informant's other assertions also were true. "Because an informant is right about some things, he is more probably right about other facts," *Spinelli*, supra (White, J., concurring)—including the claim regarding the Gates' illegal activity. This may well not be the type of "reliability" or "veracity" necessary to satisfy some view of the "veracity prong" of *Spinelli*, but we think it suffices for the practical, common-sense judgment called for in making a probable cause determination. It is enough, for purposes of assessing probable cause, that "corroboration through other sources of information reduced the chances of a reckless or prevaricating tale," thus providing "a substantial basis for crediting the hearsay."

Finally, the anonymous letter contained a range of details relating not just to easily obtained facts and conditions existing at the time of the tip, but to future actions of third parties ordinarily not easily predicted. The letter writer's accurate information as to the travel plans of each of the Gates was of a character likely obtained only from the Gates themselves, or from someone

---

**13.** The Illinois Supreme Court thought that the verification of details contained in the anonymous letter in this case amounted only to "the corroboration of innocent activity," and that this was insufficient to support a finding of probable cause. We are inclined to agree, however, with the observation of Justice Moran in his dissenting opinion that "In this case, just as in *Draper*, seemingly innocent activity became suspicious in the light of the initial tip." And it bears noting that *all* of the corroborating detail established in *Draper*, supra, was of entirely innocent activity—a fact later pointed out by the Court in both *Jones v. United States*, and *Ker v. California*.

This is perfectly reasonable. As discussed previously, probable cause requires only a probability or substantial chance of criminal activity, not an actual showing of such activity. By hypothesis, therefore, innocent behavior frequently will provide the basis for a showing of probable cause; to require otherwise would be to *sub silentio* impose a drastically more rigorous definition of probable cause than the security of our citizens demands. We think the Illinois court attempted a too rigid classification of the types of conduct that may be relied upon in seeking to demonstrate probable cause. In making a determination of probable cause the relevant inquiry is not whether particular conduct is "innocent" or "guilty," but the degree of suspicion that attaches to particular types of non-criminal acts.

familiar with their not entirely ordinary travel plans. If the informant had access to accurate information of this type a magistrate could properly conclude that it was not unlikely that he also had access to reliable information of the Gates' alleged illegal activities.[14] Of course, the Gates' travel plans might have been learned from a talkative neighbor or travel agent; under the "two-pronged test" developed from *Spinelli*, the character of the details in the anonymous letter might well not permit a sufficiently clear inference regarding the letter writer's "basis of knowledge." But, as discussed previously, probable cause does not demand the certainty we associate with formal trials. It is enough that there was a fair probability that the writer of the anonymous letter had obtained his entire story either from the Gates or someone they trusted. And corroboration of major portions of the letter's predictions provides just this probability. It is apparent, therefore, that the judge issuing the warrant had a "substantial basis for * * * conclud[ing]" that probable cause to search the Gates' home and car existed. The judgment of the Supreme Court of Illinois therefore must be reversed.

JUSTICE WHITE, concurring in the judgment.[a]

* * * Although I agree that the warrant should be upheld, I reach this conclusion in accordance with the *Aguilar–Spinelli* framework.

For present purposes, the *Aguilar–Spinelli* rules can be summed up as follows. First, an affidavit based on an informer's tip, standing alone, cannot provide probable cause for issuance of a warrant unless the tip includes information that apprises the magistrate of the informant's basis for concluding that the contraband is where he claims it is (the "basis of knowledge" prong), *and* the affiant informs the magistrate of his basis for believing that the informant is credible (the "veracity" prong).[20] Second, if a tip fails under either or both of the

---

**14.** The dissent seizes on one inaccuracy in the anonymous informant's letter—its statement that Sue Gates would fly from Florida to Illinois, when in fact she drove—and argues that the probative value of the entire tip was undermined by this allegedly "material mistake." We have never required that informants used by the police be infallible, and can see no reason to impose such a requirement in this case. Probable cause, particularly when police have obtained a warrant, simply does not require the perfection the dissent finds necessary.

Likewise, there is no force to the dissent's argument that the Gates' action in leaving their home unguarded undercut the informant's claim that drugs were hidden there. Indeed, the line-by-line scrutiny that the dissent applies to the anonymous letter is akin to that we find inappropriate in reviewing magistrate's decisions. The dissent apparently attributes to the magistrate who issued the warrant in this case the rather implausible notion that persons dealing in drugs always stay at home, apparently out of fear that to leave might risk intrusion by criminals. If accurate, one could not help sympathizing with the self-imposed isolation of people so situated. In reality, however, it is scarcely likely that the magistrate ever thought that the anonymous tip "kept one spouse" at home, much less that he relied on the theory advanced by the dissent. The letter simply says that Sue

would fly from Florida to Illinois, without indicating whether the Gates' made the bitter choice of leaving the drugs in their house, or those in their car, unguarded. The magistrate's determination that there might be drugs or evidence of criminal activity in the Gates' home was well-supported by the less speculative theory, noted in text, that if the informant could predict with considerable accuracy the somewhat unusual travel plans of the Gates, he probably also had a reliable basis for his statements that the Gates' kept a large quantity of drugs in their home and frequently were visited by other drug traffickers there.

**a.** In an omitted portion of his opinion, Justice White argued for adoption of a "good-faith" exception to the exclusionary rule.

**20.** The "veracity" prong is satisfied by a recitation in the affidavit that the informant previously supplied accurate information to the police, or by proof that the informant gave his information against his penal interest, see *United States v. Harris*, 403 U.S. 573 (1971) (plurality opinion). [Editor's Note: In *Harris*, the informant said that he had purchased illicit whiskey from defendant for two years, most recently within the past two weeks, and had often seen defendant get the whiskey for him and others from a certain building. The plurality opinion concluded that because "people do not lightly admit a crime and place two prongs, probable cause may yet be established by independent police investigatory work that corroborates the tip to such an extent that it supports "both the inference that the informer was generally trustworthy and that he made his charge on the basis of information obtained in a reliable way." In instances where the officers rely on corroboration, the ultimate question is whether the corroborated tip "is as trustworthy as a tip which would pass *Aguilar's* tests without independent corroboration."

In the present case, it is undisputed that the anonymous tip, by itself, did not furnish probable cause. The question is whether those portions of the affidavit describing the results of the police investigation of the respondents, when considered in light of the tip, "would permit the suspicions engendered by the informant's report to ripen into a judgment that a crime was probably being committed." * * *

In my view, the lower court's characterization of the Gates' activity here as totally "innocent" is dubious. In fact, the behavior was quite suspicious. I agree with the Court that Lance Gates' flight to Palm Beach, an area known to be a source of narcotics, the brief overnight stay in a motel, and apparent immediate return North, suggest a pattern that trained law-enforcement officers have recognized as indicative of illicit drug-dealing activity.

Even, however, had the corroboration related only to completely innocuous activities, this fact alone would not preclude the issuance of a valid warrant. The critical issue is not whether the activities observed by the police are innocent or suspicious. Instead, the proper focus should be on whether the actions of the suspects, whatever their nature, give rise to an inference that the informant is credible and that he obtained his information in a reliable manner.

Thus, in *Draper v. United States* an informant stated on Sept. 7 that Draper would be carrying narcotics when he arrived by train in Denver on the morning of Sept. 8 or Sept. 9. The informant also provided the police with a detailed physical description of the clothes Draper would be wearing when he alighted from the train. The police observed Draper leaving a train on the morning of Sept. 9, and he was wearing the precise clothing described by the informant. The Court held that the police had probable cause to arrest Draper at this point, even though the police had seen nothing more than the totally innocent act of a man getting off a train carrying a briefcase. As we later explained in *Spinelli*, the important point was that the corroboration showed both that the informant was credible, i.e. that he "had not been fabricating his report out of whole cloth," and that he had an adequate basis of knowledge for his allegations, "since the report was of the sort which in common experience may be recognized as having been obtained in a reliable way." The fact that the informer was able to predict, two days in advance, the exact clothing Draper would be wearing dispelled the possibility that his tip was just based on rumor or "an off-hand remark heard at

critical evidence in the hands of the police in the form of their own admissions," such admissions "carry their own indicia of credibility—sufficient at least to support finding of probable cause to search" when, as here, the basis of knowledge is also indicated (as almost inevitably will be the case when there is such an admission). The four dissenters objected that "the effect of adopting such a rule would be to encourage the Government to prefer as informants participants in criminal enterprises rather than ordinary citizens, a goal the Government specifically eschews in its brief in this case upon the explicit premise that such

persons are often less reliable than those who obey the law."] The "basis of knowledge" prong is satisfied by a statement from the informant that he personally observed the criminal activity, or, if he came by the information indirectly, by a satisfactory explanation of why his sources were reliable, or, in the absence of a statement detailing the manner in which the information was gathered, by a description of the accused's criminal activity in sufficient detail that the magistrate may infer that the informant is relying on something more substantial than casual rumor or an individual's general reputation.

a neighborhood bar." Probably Draper had planned in advance to wear these specific clothes so that an accomplice could identify him. A clear inference could therefore be drawn that the informant was either involved in the criminal scheme himself or that he otherwise had access to reliable, inside information.[22]

As in *Draper*, the police investigation in the present case satisfactorily demonstrated that the informant's tip was as trustworthy as one that would alone satisfy the *Aguilar* tests. The tip predicted that Sue Gates would drive to Florida, that Lance Gates would fly there a few days after May 3, and that Lance would then drive the car back. After the police corroborated these facts, the magistrate could reasonably have inferred, as he apparently did, that the informant, who had specific knowledge of these unusual travel plans, did not make up his story and that he obtained his information in a reliable way. It is theoretically possible, as respondents insist, that the tip could have been supplied by a "vindictive travel agent" and that the Gates' activities, although unusual, might not have been unlawful. But *Aguilar* and *Spinelli*, like our other cases, do not require that certain guilt be established before a warrant may properly be issued. "[O]nly the probability, and not a prima facie showing, of criminal activity is the standard of probable cause." I therefore conclude that the judgment of the Illinois Supreme Court invalidating the warrant must be reversed.

The Court agrees that the warrant was valid, but, in the process of reaching this conclusion, it overrules the *Aguilar–Spinelli* tests and replaces them with a "totality of the circumstances" standard. As shown above, it is not at all necessary to overrule *Aguilar–Spinelli* in order to reverse the judgment below. Therefore, because I am inclined to believe that, when applied properly, the *Aguilar–Spinelli* rules play an appropriate role in probable cause determinations, and because the Court's holding may foretell an evisceration of the probable cause standard, I do not join the Court's holding.

The Court reasons that the "veracity" and "basis of knowledge" tests are not independent, and that a deficiency as to one can be compensated for by a strong showing as to the other. Thus, a finding of probable cause may be based on a tip from an informant "known for the unusual reliability of his predictions" or from "an unquestionably honest citizen," even if the report fails thoroughly to set forth the basis upon which the information was obtained. If this is so, then it must follow *a fortiori* that "the affidavit of an officer, known by the magistrate

---

**22.** Thus, as interpreted in *Spinelli*, the Court in *Draper* held that there was probable cause because "the kind of information related by the informant [was] not generally sent ahead of a person's arrival in a city except to those who are intimately connected with making careful arrangements for meeting him." *Spinelli* (White, J., concurring). As I said in *Spinelli*, the conclusion that *Draper* itself was based on this fact is far from inescapable. Prior to *Spinelli*, *Draper* was susceptible to the interpretation that it stood for the proposition that "the existence of the tenth and critical fact is made sufficiently probable to justify the issuance of a warrant by verifying nine other facts coming from the same source." *Spinelli* (White, J., concurring). But it now seems clear that the Court in *Spinelli* rejected this reading of *Draper*.

Justice Brennan erroneously interprets my *Spinelli* concurrence as espousing the view that "corroboration of certain details in a tip may be sufficient to satisfy the veracity, but not the basis of knowledge, prong of *Aguilar*." I did not say that corroboration could *never* satisfy the basis of knowledge prong. My concern was, and still is, that the prong might be deemed satisfied on the basis of corroboration of information that does not in any way suggest that the informant had an adequate basis of knowledge for his report. If, however, as in *Draper*, the police corroborate information from which it can be inferred that the informant's tip was grounded on inside information, this corroboration is sufficient to satisfy the basis of knowledge prong. *Spinelli* (White, J., concurring). The rules would indeed be strange if, as Justice Brennan suggests, the basis of knowledge prong could be satisfied by detail in the tip alone, but not by independent police work.

to be honest and experienced, stating that [contraband] is located in a certain building" must be acceptable. It would be "quixotic" if a similar statement from an honest informant, but not one from an honest officer, could furnish probable cause. But we have repeatedly held that the unsupported assertion or belief of an officer does not satisfy the probable cause requirement. Thus, this portion of today's holding can be read as implicitly rejecting the teachings of these prior holdings.

The Court may not intend so drastic a result. Indeed, the Court expressly reaffirms the validity of cases such as *Nathanson* that have held that, no matter how reliable the affiant-officer may be, a warrant should not be issued unless the affidavit discloses supporting facts and circumstances. The Court limits these cases to situations involving affidavits containing only "bare conclusions" and holds that, if an affidavit contains anything more, it should be left to the issuing magistrate to decide, based solely on "practical[ity]" and "common-sense," whether there is a fair probability that contraband will be found in a particular place.

Thus, as I read the majority opinion, it appears that the question whether the probable cause standard is to be diluted is left to the common-sense judgments of issuing magistrates. I am reluctant to approve any standard that does not expressly require, as a prerequisite to issuance of a warrant, some showing of facts from which an inference may be drawn that the informant is credible and that his information was obtained in a reliable way. The Court is correctly concerned with the fact that some lower courts have been applying *Aguilar–Spinelli* in an unduly rigid manner. I believe, however, that with clarification of the rule of corroborating information, the lower courts are fully able to properly interpret *Aguilar–Spinelli* and avoid such unduly-rigid applications. I may be wrong; it ultimately may prove to be the case that the only profitable instruction we can provide to magistrates is to rely on common sense. But the question whether a particular anonymous tip provides the basis for issuance of a warrant will often be a difficult one, and I would at least attempt to provide more precise guidance by clarifying *Aguilar–Spinelli* and the relationship of those cases with *Draper* before totally abdicating our responsibility in this area. Hence, I do not join the Court's opinion rejecting the *Aguilar–Spinelli* rules.

JUSTICE BRENNAN, with whom JUSTICE MARSHALL joins, dissenting.

Although I join Justice Stevens' dissenting opinion and agree with him that the warrant is invalid even under the Court's newly announced "totality of the circumstances" test, I write separately to dissent from the Court's unjustified and ill-advised rejection of the two-prong test for evaluating the validity of a warrant based on hearsay announced in *Aguilar v. Texas*, and refined in *Spinelli v. United States*.

* * * In *Spinelli*, the Court reviewed a search warrant based on an affidavit that was "more ample" than the one in *Aguilar*. The affidavit in *Spinelli* contained not only a tip from an informant, but also a report of an independent police investigation that allegedly corroborated the informant's tip. Under these circumstances, the Court stated that it was "required to delineate the manner in which *Aguilar's* two-pronged test should be applied * * *."

The Court held that the *Aguilar* test should be applied to the tip, and approved two additional ways of satisfying that test. First, the Court suggested that if the tip contained sufficient detail describing the accused's criminal activity it might satisfy *Aguilar's* basis of knowledge prong. Such detail might assure the magistrate that he is "relying on something more substantial than a casual rumor circulating in the underworld or an accusation based merely on an individual's general reputation." Although the tip in the case before it did not meet this standard, "[t]he detail provided by the informant in *Draper v. United States* provide[d] a suitable benchmark" because "[a] magistrate, when confronted with such detail, could reasonably infer that the informant had gained his information in a reliable way."

Second, the Court stated that police corroboration of the details of a tip could provide a basis for satisfying *Aguilar.* The Court's opinion is not a model of clarity on this issue since it appears to suggest that corroboration can satisfy both the basis of knowledge and veracity prongs of *Aguilar.* Justice White's concurring opinion, however, points the way to a proper reading of the Court's opinion. After reviewing the Court's decision in *Draper v. United States,* Justice White concluded that "[t]he thrust of *Draper* is not that the verified facts have independent significance with respect to proof of [another unverified fact]." In his view, "[t]he argument instead relates to the reliability of the source: because an informant is right about some things, he is more probably right about other facts, usually the critical, unverified facts." Justice White then pointed out that prior cases had rejected "the notion that the past reliability of an officer is sufficient reason for believing his current assertions." Justice White went on to state:

> "Nor would it suffice, I suppose, if a reliable informant states there is gambling equipment in Apartment 607 and then proceeds to describe in detail Apartment 201, a description which is verified before applying for the warrant. He was right about 201, but that hardly makes him more believable about the equipment in 607. But what if he states that there are narcotics locked in a safe in Apartment 300, which is described in detail, and the apartment manager verifies everything but the contents of the safe? I doubt that the report about the narcotics is made appreciably more believable by the verification. The informant could still have gotten his information concerning the safe from others about whom nothing is known or could have inferred the presence of narcotics from circumstances which a magistrate would find unacceptable."

I find this reasoning persuasive. Properly understood, therefore, *Spinelli* stands for the proposition that corroboration of certain details in a tip may be sufficient to satisfy the veracity, but not the basis of knowledge, prong of *Aguilar.* As noted, *Spinelli* also suggests that in some limited circumstances considerable detail in an informant's tip may be adequate to satisfy the basis of knowledge prong of *Aguilar.* * * *

In rejecting the *Aguilar–Spinelli* standards, the Court * * * relies on * * * the "practical, nontechnical" nature of probable cause.

[O]ne can concede that probable cause is a "practical, nontechnical" concept without betraying the values that *Aguilar* and *Spinelli* reflect. As noted, *Aguilar* and *Spinelli* require the police to provide magistrates with certain crucial information. They also provide structure for magistrates' probable cause inquiries. In so doing, *Aguilar* and *Spinelli* preserve the role of magistrates as independent arbiters of probable cause, insure greater accuracy in probable cause determinations, and advance the substantive value of precluding findings of probable cause, and attendant intrusions, based on anything less than information from an honest or credible person who has acquired his information in a reliable way. Neither the standards nor their effects are inconsistent with a "practical, nontechnical" conception of probable cause. Once a magistrate has determined that he has information before him that he can reasonably say has been obtained in a reliable way by a credible person, he has ample room to use his common sense and to apply a practical, nontechnical conception of probable cause. * * *

The Court also insists that the *Aguilar–Spinelli* standards must be abandoned because they are inconsistent with the fact that non-lawyers frequently serve as magistrates. To the contrary, the standards help to structure probable cause inquiries and, properly interpreted, may actually help a non-lawyer magistrate in making a probable cause determination. * * *

At the heart of the Court's decision to abandon *Aguilar* and *Spinelli* appears to be its belief that "the direction taken by decisions following *Spinelli* poorly serves 'the most basic function of any government: to provide for the security of the individual and of his property.'" This conclusion rests on the judgment that *Aguilar* and *Spinelli* "seriously imped[e] the task of law enforcement," and render anonymous tips valueless in police work. Surely, the Court overstates its case. But of particular concern to all Americans must be that the Court gives virtually no consideration to the value of insuring that findings of probable cause are based on information that a magistrate can reasonably say has been obtained in a reliable way by an honest or credible person. * * *

The Court's complete failure to provide any persuasive reason for rejecting *Aguilar* and *Spinelli* doubtlessly reflects impatience with what it perceives to be "overly technical" rules governing searches and seizures under the Fourth Amendment. Words such as "practical," "nontechnical," and "commonsense," as used in the Court's opinion, are but code words for an overly permissive attitude towards police practices in derogation of the rights secured by the Fourth Amendment. Everyone shares the Court's concern over the horrors of drug trafficking, but under our Constitution only measures consistent with the Fourth Amendment may be employed by government to cure this evil. We must be ever mindful of Justice Stewart's admonition that "[i]n times of unrest, whether caused by crime or racial conflict or fear of internal subversion, this basic law and the values that it represents may appear unrealistic or 'extravagant' to some. But the values were those of the authors of our fundamental constitutional concepts." * * *

Rights secured by the Fourth Amendment are particularly difficult to protect because their "advocates are usually criminals." But the rules "we fashion [are] for the innocent and guilty alike." By replacing *Aguilar* and *Spinelli* with a test that provides no assurance that magistrates, rather than the police, or informants, will make determinations of probable cause; imposes no structure on magistrates' probable cause inquiries; and invites the possibility that intrusions may be justified on less than reliable information from an honest or credible person, today's decision threatens to "obliterate one of the most fundamental distinctions between our form of government, where officers are under the law, and the police-state where they are the law."

JUSTICE STEVENS, with whom JUSTICE BRENNAN joins, dissenting.

* * * The informant had indicated that "Sue drives their car to Florida *where she leaves it to be loaded up with drugs * * *. Sue flies back after she drops the car off in Florida.*" (emphasis added). Yet Detective Mader's affidavit reported that she "left the West Palm Beach area driving the Mercury northbound."

The discrepancy between the informant's predictions and the facts known to Detective Mader is significant for three reasons. First, it cast doubt on the informant's hypothesis that the Gates already had "over $100,000 worth of drugs in their basement." The informant had predicted an itinerary that always kept one spouse in Bloomingdale, suggesting that the Gates did not want to leave their home unguarded because something valuable was hidden within. That inference obviously could not be drawn when it was known that the pair was actually together over a thousand miles from home.

Second, the discrepancy made the Gates' conduct seem substantially less unusual than the informant had predicted it would be. It would have been odd if, as predicted, Sue had driven down to Florida on Wednesday, left the car, and flown right back to Illinois. But the mere facts that Sue was in West Palm Beach with the car,[1] that she was joined by her husband at the Holiday Inn on Friday,[2] and that the couple drove north together the next morning [3] are neither unusual nor probative of criminal activity.

Third, the fact that the anonymous letter contained a material mistake undermines the reasonableness of relying on it as a basis for making a forcible entry into a private home.

Of course, the activities in this case did not stop when the magistrate issued the warrant. The Gates drove all night to Bloomingdale, the officers searched the car and found 400 pounds of marijuana, and then they searched the house. However, none of these subsequent events may be considered in evaluating the warrant, and the search of the house was legal only if the warrant was valid. I cannot accept the Court's casual conclusion that, *before the Gates arrived in Bloomingdale*, there was probable cause to justify a valid entry and search of a private home. No one knows who the informant in this case was, or what motivated him or her to write the note. Given that the note's predictions were faulty in one significant respect, and were corroborated by nothing except ordinary innocent activity, I must surmise that the Court's evaluation of the warrant's validity has been colored by subsequent events. * * *

# SECTION 4. WARRANTLESS ARREST AND SEARCH OF PERSONS

The Supreme Court has long expressed a strong preference for the use of arrest warrants and search warrants. As the Court has indicated in a host of cases, resort to the warrant process is preferred because it "interposes an orderly procedure" involving "judicial impartiality" whereby "a neutral and detached magistrate" can make "informed and deliberate determinations" on the issue of probable cause. To leave such decisions to the police would allow "hurried actions" by those "engaged in the often competitive enterprise of ferreting out crime." Yet, as the cases in this section and the two following—dealing, respectively, with search of premises and search of vehicles—clearly demon-

---

**1.** The anonymous note suggested that she was going down on Wednesday, but for all the officers knew she had been in Florida for a month.

**2.** Lance does not appear to have behaved suspiciously in flying down to Florida. He made a reservation in his own name and gave an accurate home phone number to the airlines. And Detective Mader's affidavit does not report that he did any of the other things drug couriers are notorious for doing, such as paying for the ticket in cash, dressing casually, looking pale and nervous, improperly filling out baggage tags, carrying American Tourister luggage, not carrying any luggage, or changing airlines en route.

**3.** Detective Mader's affidavit hinted darkly that the couple had set out upon "that interstate highway commonly used by travelers to the Chicago area." But the same highway is also commonly used by travelers to Disney World, Sea World, and Ringling Brothers and Barnum and Bailey Circus World. It is also the road to Cocoa Beach, Cape Canaveral, and Washington, D.C. I would venture that each year dozens of perfectly innocent people fly to Florida, meet a waiting spouse, and drive off together in the family car.

strate, there are a great many exceptions to the warrant requirement. When the Court approves warrantless activity, it is typically because of a view that the police (1) were acting in exigent circumstances, (2) were intruding upon lesser Fourth Amendment interests, or (3) were otherwise not involved in activity as to which before-the-fact judicial scrutiny would be useful.

The first case in this section, *United States v. Watson*, explains why it is that no warrant is required to make an arrest. The next case, *United States v. Robinson*, addresses warrantless search of the person incident to arrest. The final case in this section, *Tennessee v. Garner*, teaches that sometimes an arrest will be "unreasonable" in a Fourth Amendment sense because of the amount of force used in making it.

## UNITED STATES v. WATSON
### 423 U.S. 411, 96 S.Ct. 820, 46 L.Ed.2d 598 (1976).

JUSTICE WHITE delivered the opinion of the Court.

[Reliable informant Khoury told a federal postal inspector that Watson had supplied him with a stolen credit card and had agreed to furnish additional cards at their next meeting, scheduled for a few days later. At that meeting, which occurred in a restaurant, Khoury signaled the inspector that Watson had the cards, at which point the inspector arrested Watson without a warrant, as he was authorized to do under 18 U.S.C. § 3061 and applicable postal regulations. The court of appeals held the arrest unconstitutional because the inspector had failed to secure an arrest warrant although he concededly had time to do so, and this was a significant factor in the court's additional holding that Watson's consent to a search of his car was not voluntary.]

* * * Section 3061 represents a judgment by Congress that it is not unreasonable under the Fourth Amendment for postal inspectors to arrest without a warrant provided they have probable cause to do so. This was not an isolated or quixotic judgment of the legislative branch. Other federal law enforcement officers have been expressly authorized by statute for many years to make felony arrests on probable cause but without a warrant. * * *

Because there is a "strong presumption of constitutionality due to an Act of Congress, especially when it turns on what is 'reasonable,' * * * [o]bviously the Court should be reluctant to decide that a search thus authorized by Congress was unreasonable and that the Act was therefore unconstitutional." Moreover, there is nothing in the Court's prior cases indicating that under the Fourth Amendment a warrant is required to make a valid arrest for a felony. Indeed, the relevant prior decisions are uniformly to the contrary. * * *

* * * Just last Term, while recognizing that maximum protection of individual rights could be assured by requiring a magistrate's review of the factual justification prior to any arrest, we stated that "such a requirement would constitute an intolerable handicap for legitimate law enforcement" and noted that the Court "has never invalidated an arrest supported by probable cause solely because the officers failed to secure a warrant." *Gerstein v. Pugh*, 420 U.S. 103 (1975).[a]

a. The Supreme Court in *Gerstein* went on to say:

"Under this practical compromise, a policeman's on-the-scene assessment of probable cause provides legal justification for arresting a person suspected of crime, and for a brief period of detention to take the administrative steps incident to arrest. Once the suspect is in custody, however, the reasons that justify dispensing with the magistrate's neutral judgment evaporate. There no longer is any danger that the suspect will escape or commit further crimes while the police submit their evidence to a magistrate. And, while the

The cases construing the Fourth Amendment thus reflect the ancient common-law rule that a peace officer was permitted to arrest without a warrant for a misdemeanor or felony committed in his presence as well as for a felony not committed in his presence if there was reasonable grounds for making the arrest. This has also been the prevailing rule under state constitutions and statutes.
*   *   *

Because the common-law rule authorizing arrests without warrant generally prevailed in the States, it is important for present purposes to note that in 1792 Congress invested United States Marshals and their deputies with "the same powers in executing the laws of the United States, as sheriffs and their deputies in their several states have by law, in executing the laws of their respective states." The Second Congress thus saw no inconsistency between the Fourth Amendment and giving United States Marshals the same power as local peace officers to arrest for a felony without a warrant. *   *   *

The balance struck by the common law in generally authorizing felony arrests on probable cause, but without a warrant, has survived substantially intact. It appears in almost all of the States in the form of express statutory authorization. *   *   *

This is the rule Congress has long directed its principal law enforcement officers to follow. Congress has plainly decided against conditioning warrantless arrest power on proof of exigent circumstances. Law enforcement officers may find it wise to seek arrest warrants where practicable to do so, and their judgments about probable cause may be more readily accepted where backed by a warrant issued by a magistrate. But we decline to transform this judicial preference into a constitutional rule when the judgment of the Nation and Congress has for so long been to authorize warrantless public arrests on probable cause rather than to encumber criminal prosecutions with endless litigation with respect to the existence of exigent circumstances, whether it was practicable to get a warrant, whether the suspect was about to flee, and the like. *   *   *

Reversed.

JUSTICE STEVENS took no part in the consideration or decision of this case.

JUSTICE POWELL, concurring.

*   *   * On its face, our decision today creates a certain anomaly. There is no more basic constitutional rule in the Fourth Amendment area than that which makes a warrantless search unreasonable except in a few "jealously and carefully drawn" exceptional circumstances. *   *   * In short, the course of judicial development of the Fourth Amendment with respect to searches has remained true to the principles so well expressed by Mr. Justice Jackson:

> "Any assumption that evidence sufficient to support a magistrate's disinterested determination to issue a search warrant will justify the officers in making a search without a warrant would reduce the Amendment to a nullity and leave the people's homes secure only in the discretion of police officers. *   *   * When the right of privacy must reasonably yield to the

State's reasons for taking summary action subside, the suspect's need for a neutral determination of probable cause increases significantly. The consequences of prolonged detention may be more serious than the interference occasioned by arrest. Pretrial confinement may imperil the suspect's job, interrupt his source of income, and impair his family relationships. Even pretrial release may be accompanied by burdensome conditions that effect a significant restraint of liberty. When the stakes are this high, the detached judgment of a neutral magistrate is essential if the Fourth Amendment is to furnish meaningful protection from unfounded interference with liberty. Accordingly, we hold that the Fourth Amendment requires a judicial determination of probable cause as a prerequisite to extended restraint of liberty following arrest."

right of search is, as a rule, to be decided by a judicial officer, not by a policeman or Government enforcement agent."

Since the Fourth Amendment speaks equally to both searches and seizures, and since an arrest, the taking hold of one's person, is quintessentially a seizure, it would seem that the constitutional provision should impose the same limitations upon arrests that it does upon searches. Indeed, as an abstract matter an argument can be made that the restrictions upon arrest perhaps should be greater. A search may cause only annoyance and temporary inconvenience to the law-abiding citizen, assuming more serious dimension only when it turns up evidence of criminality. An arrest, however, is a serious personal intrusion regardless of whether the person seized is guilty or innocent. Although an arrestee cannot be held for a significant period without some neutral determination that there are grounds to do so, no decision that he should go free can come quickly enough to erase the invasion of his privacy that already will have occurred. Logic therefore would seem to dictate that arrests be subject to the warrant requirement at least to the same extent as searches.

But logic sometimes must defer to history and experience. The Court's opinion emphasizes the historical sanction accorded warrantless felony arrests.

\* \* \*

The historical momentum for acceptance of warrantless arrests, already strong at the adoption of the Fourth Amendment, has gained strength during the ensuing two centuries. \* \* \* Given the revolutionary implications of such a holding, a declaration at this late date that warrantless felony arrests are constitutionally infirm would have to rest upon reasons more substantial than a desire to harmonize the rules for arrest with those governing searches.

Moreover, a constitutional rule permitting felony arrests only with a warrant or in exigent circumstances could severely hamper effective law enforcement. Good police practice often requires postponing an arrest, even after probable cause has been established, in order to place the suspect under surveillance or otherwise develop further evidence necessary to prove guilt to a jury. Under the holding of the Court of Appeals such additional investigative work could imperil the entire prosecution. Should the officers fail to obtain a warrant initially, and later be required by unforeseen circumstances to arrest immediately with no chance to procure a last-minute warrant, they would risk a court decision that the subsequent exigency did not excuse their failure to get a warrant in the interim since they first developed probable cause. If the officers attempted to meet such a contingency by procuring a warrant as soon as they had probable cause and then merely held it during their subsequent investigation, they would risk a court decision that the warrant had grown stale by the time it was used.[5] Law enforcement personnel caught in this squeeze could ensure validity of their arrests only by obtaining a warrant and arresting as soon as probable cause existed, thereby foreclosing the possibility of gathering vital additional evidence from the suspect's continued actions. \* \* \*[6]

---

5. The probable cause to support issuance of an arrest warrant normally would not grow stale as easily as that which supports a warrant to search a particular place for particular objects. This is true because once there is probable cause to believe that someone is a felon the passage of time often will bring new supporting evidence. But in some cases the original grounds supporting the warrant could be disproved by subsequent investigation that at the same time turns up wholly new evidence supporting probable cause on a different theory. In those cases the warrant could be stale because based upon discredited information.

6. Justice Stewart's opinion concurring in the result is omitted.

JUSTICE MARSHALL, with whom JUSTICE BRENNAN joins, dissenting. * * *

The signal of the reliable informant that Watson was in possession of stolen credit cards gave the postal inspectors probable cause to make the arrest. This probable cause was separate and distinct from the probable cause relating to the offense six days earlier, and provided an adequate independent basis for the arrest. Whether or not a warrant ordinarily is required prior to making an arrest, no warrant is required when exigent circumstances are present. When law enforcement officers have probable cause to believe that an offense is taking place in their presence and that the suspect is at that moment in possession of the evidence, exigent circumstances exist. Delay could cause the escape of the suspect or the destruction of the evidence. Accordingly, Watson's warrantless arrest was valid under the recognized exigent circumstances exception to the warrant requirement, and the Court has no occasion to consider whether a warrant would otherwise be necessary. * * *

Since, for reasons it leaves unexpressed, the Court does not take this traditional course, I am constrained to express my views on the issues it unnecessarily decides. The Court reaches its conclusion that a warrant is not necessary for a police officer to make an arrest in a public place, so long as he has probable cause to believe a felony has been committed, on the basis of its views of precedent and history. As my Brother Powell correctly observes, the precedent is spurious. None of the cases cited by the Court squarely confronted the issue decided today. * * *

The Court next turns to history. It relies on the English common-law rule of arrest and the many state and federal statutes following it. There are two serious flaws in this approach. First, as a matter of factual analysis, the substance of the ancient common-law rule provides no support for the far-reaching modern rule that the Court fashions on its model. Second, as a matter of doctrine, the longstanding existence of a Government practice does not immunize the practice from scrutiny under the mandate of our Constitution.

* * * Only the most serious crimes were felonies at common law, and many crimes now classified as felonies under federal or state law were treated as misdemeanors. * * * To make an arrest for any of these crimes at common law, the police officer was required to obtain a warrant, unless the crime was committed in his presence. Since many of these same crimes are commonly classified as felonies today however, under the Court's holding a warrant is no longer needed to make such arrests, a result in contravention of the common law.

* * * As a matter of substance, the balance struck by the common law in accommodating the public need for the most certain and immediate arrest of criminal suspects with the requirement of magisterial oversight to protect against mistaken insults to privacy decreed that only in the most serious of cases could the warrant be dispensed with. This balance is not recognized when the common-law rule is unthinkingly transposed to our present classifications of criminal offenses. Indeed, the only clear lesson of history is contrary to the one the Court draws: the common law considered the arrest warrant far more important than today's decision leaves it.

I do not mean by this that a modern warrant requirement should apply only to arrests precisely analogous to common-law misdemeanors, and be inapplicable to analogues of common-law felonies. Rather, the point is simply that the Court's unblinking literalism cannot replace analysis of the constitutional interests involved. * * *

Lastly, the Court relies on the numerous state and federal statutes codifying the common-law rule. But this, too, is no substitute for reasoned analysis.

\* \* \*

The Court has typically engaged in a two-part analysis in deciding whether the presumption favoring a warrant should be given effect in situations where a warrant has not previously been clearly required. Utilizing that approach we must now consider (1) whether the privacy of our citizens will be better protected by ordinarily requiring a warrant to be issued before they may be arrested; and (2) whether a warrant requirement would unduly burden legitimate governmental interests.

The first question is easily answered. Of course the privacy of our citizens will be better protected by a warrant requirement. We have recognized that "the Fourth Amendment protects people, not places." Indeed, the privacy guaranteed by the Fourth Amendment is quintessentially personal. Thus a warrant is required in search situations not because of some high regard for property, but because of our regard for the individual, and *his* interest in his possessions and person. \* \* \*

The Government's assertion that a warrant requirement would impose an intolerable burden stems, in large part, from the specious supposition that procurement of an arrest warrant would be necessary as soon as probable cause ripens. There is no requirement that a search warrant be obtained the moment police have probable cause to search. The rule is only that present probable cause be shown and a warrant obtained before a search is undertaken. The same rule should obtain for arrest warrants, where it may even make more sense. Certainly, there is less need for prompt procurement of a warrant in the arrest situation. Unlike probable cause to search, probable cause to arrest, once formed will continue to exist for the indefinite future, at least if no intervening exculpatory facts come to light.

This sensible approach obviates most of the difficulties that have been suggested with an arrest warrant rule. Police would not have to cut their investigation short the moment they obtain probable cause to arrest, nor would undercover agents be forced suddenly to terminate their work and forfeit their covers. Moreover, if in the course of the continued police investigation exigent circumstances develop that demand an immediate arrest, the arrest may be made without fear of unconstitutionality, so long as the exigency was unanticipated and not used to avoid the arrest warrant requirement. Likewise, if in the course of the continued investigation police uncover evidence tying the suspect to another crime, they may immediately arrest him for that crime if exigency demands it, and still be in full conformity with the warrant rule. This is why the arrest in this case was not improper.[15] Other than where police attempt to evade the warrant requirement, the rule would invalidate an arrest only in the obvious situation: where police, with probable cause but without exigent circumstances, set out to arrest a suspect. Such an arrest must be void, even if exigency develops in the course of the arrest that would ordinarily validate it; otherwise the warrant requirement would be reduced to a toothless prescription.

\* \* \*

It is suggested, however, that even if application of this rule does not require police to secure a warrant as soon as they obtain probable cause, the confused

---

**15.** Although the postal inspectors here anticipated the occurrence of the second crime, they could not have obtained a warrant for Watson's arrest for that crime until probable cause formed, just moments before the arrest. A warrant based on anticipated facts is premature and void.

officer would nonetheless be prone to do so. If so, police "would risk a court decision that the warrant had grown stale by the time it was used." (Powell, J., concurring). This fear is groundless. First, as suggested above, the requirement that police procure a warrant before an arrest is made is rather simple of application. Thus, there is no need for the police to find themselves in this "squeeze." Second, the "squeeze" is nonexistent. Just as it is virtually impossible for probable cause for an arrest to grow stale between the time of formation and the time a warrant is procured, it is virtually impossible for probable cause to become stale between procurement and arrest. Delay by law enforcement officers in executing an arrest warrant does not ordinarily affect the legality of the arrest. * * *

## UNITED STATES v. ROBINSON

414 U.S. 218, 94 S.Ct. 467, 38 L.Ed.2d 427 (1973).

JUSTICE REHNQUIST delivered the opinion of the Court.

Respondent Robinson was convicted in United States District Court for the District of Columbia of the possession and facilitation of concealment of heroin. * * * [T]he Court of Appeals *en banc* reversed the judgment of conviction, holding that the heroin introduced in evidence against respondent had been obtained as a result of a search which violated the Fourth Amendment to the United States Constitution.

On April 23, 1968, at approximately 11 o'clock p.m., Officer Richard Jenks, a 15–year veteran of the District of Columbia Metropolitan Police Department, observed the respondent driving a 1965 Cadillac near the intersection of 8th and C Streets, Southeast, in the District of Columbia. Jenks, as a result of previous investigation following a check of respondent's operator's permit four days earlier, determined there was reason to believe that respondent was operating a motor vehicle after the revocation of his operator's permit. This is an offense defined by statute in the District of Columbia which carries a mandatory minimum jail term, a mandatory minimum fine, or both.

Jenks signaled respondent to stop the automobile, which respondent did, and all three of the occupants emerged from the car. At that point Jenks informed respondent that he was under arrest for "operating after revocation and obtaining a permit by misrepresentation." It was assumed by the majority of the Court of Appeals, and is conceded by the respondent here, that Jenks had probable cause to arrest respondent, and that he effected a full custody arrest.

In accordance with procedures prescribed in Police Department instructions,[2] Jenks then began to search respondent. He explained at a subsequent hearing that he was "face to face" with the respondent, and "placed [his] hands on [the respondent], my right hand to his left breast like this (demonstrating) and proceeded to pat him down thus (with the right hand)." During this

2. The government introduced testimony at the evidentiary hearing upon the original remand by the Court of Appeals as to certain standard operating procedures of the Metropolitan Police Department. Sergeant Dennis C. Donaldson, a Training Division Instructor, testified that when a police officer makes "a full custody arrest" which he defined as where an officer "would arrest a subject and subsequently transport him to a police facility for booking," the officer is trained to make a full "field type search" * * *. Sergeant Donaldson testified that officers are instructed to examine the "contents of all of the pockets" of the arrestee in the course of the field search. * * * Those regulations also provide that in the case of some traffic offenses, including the crime of operating a motor vehicle after revocation of an operator's permit, the officer shall make a summary arrest of the violator and take the violator, in custody, to the stationhouse for booking. D.C. Metropolitan Police Department General Order No. 3, series 1959 (April 24, 1959). Such operating procedures are not, of course, determinative of the constitutional issues presented by this case.

patdown, Jenks felt an object in the left breast pocket of the heavy coat respondent was wearing, but testified that he "couldn't tell what it was" and also that he "couldn't actually tell the size of it." Jenks then reached into the pocket and pulled out the object, which turned out to be a "crumpled up cigarette package." Jenks testified that at this point he still did not know what was in the package:

> "As I felt the package I could feel objects in the package but I couldn't tell what they were. * * * I knew they weren't cigarettes."

The officer then opened the cigarette pack and found 14 gelatin capsules of white powder which he thought to be, and which later analysis proved to be, heroin. Jenks then continued his search of respondent to completion, feeling around his waist and trouser legs, and examining the remaining pockets. The heroin seized from the respondent was admitted into evidence at the trial which resulted in his conviction in the District Court. * * *

It is well settled that a search incident to a lawful arrest is a traditional exception to the warrant requirement of the Fourth Amendment. This general exception has historically been formulated into two distinct propositions. The first is that a search may be made of the *person* of the arrestee by virtue of the lawful arrest. The second is that a search may be made of the area within the control of the arrestee.

Examination of this Court's decisions in the area show that these two propositions have been treated quite differently. The validity of the search of a person incident to a lawful arrest has been regarded as settled from its first enunciation, and has remained virtually unchallenged until the present case. The validity of the second proposition, while likewise conceded in principle, has been subject to differing interpretations as to the extent of the area which may be searched. * * *

Throughout the series of cases in which the Court has addressed the second proposition relating to a search incident to a lawful arrest—the permissible area beyond the person of the arrestee which such a search may cover—no doubt has been expressed as to the unqualified authority of the arresting authority to search the person of the arrestee. * * *

Thus the broadly stated rule, and the reasons for it, have been repeatedly affirmed in the decisions of this Court since *Weeks v. United States* nearly 60 years ago. Since the statements in the cases speak not simply in terms of an exception to the warrant requirement, but in terms of an affirmative authority to search, they clearly imply that such searches also meet the Fourth Amendment's requirement of reasonableness. * * *

Virtually all of the statements of this Court affirming the existence of an unqualified authority to search incident to a lawful arrest are dicta. We would not therefore be foreclosed by principles of *stare decisis* from further examination into history and practice in order to see whether the sort of qualifications imposed by the Court of Appeals in this case were in fact intended by the Framers of the Fourth Amendment or recognized in cases decided prior to *Weeks.* Unfortunately such authorities as exist are sparse. * * *

While these earlier authorities are sketchy, they tend to support the broad statement of the authority to search incident to arrest found in the successive decisions of this Court, rather than the restrictive one which was applied by the Court of Appeals in this case. * * *

The justification or reason for the authority to search incident to a lawful arrest rests quite as much on the need to disarm the suspect in order to take him into custody as it does on the need to preserve evidence on his person for later use at trial. The standards traditionally governing a search incident to lawful arrest are not, therefore, commuted to the stricter *Terry* standards [a] by the absence of probable fruits or further evidence of the particular crime for which the arrest is made.

Nor are we inclined, on the basis of what seems to us to be a rather speculative judgment, to qualify the breadth of the general authority to search incident to a lawful custodial arrest on an assumption that persons arrested for the offense of driving while their license has been revoked are less likely to be possessed of dangerous weapons than are those arrested for other crimes.[5] It is scarcely open to doubt that the danger to an officer is far greater in the case of the extended exposure which follows the taking of a suspect into custody and transporting him to the police station than in the case of the relatively fleeting contact resulting from the typical *Terry*-type stop. This is an adequate basis for treating all custodial arrests alike for purposes of search justification.

But quite apart from these distinctions, our more fundamental disagreement with the Court of Appeals arises from its suggestion that there must be litigated in each case the issue of whether or not there was present one of the reasons supporting the authority for a search of the person incident to a lawful arrest. We do not think the long line of authorities of this Court dating back to *Weeks*, nor what we can glean from the history of practice in this country and in England, requires such a case by case adjudication. A police officer's determination as to how and where to search the person of a suspect whom he has arrested is necessarily a quick *ad hoc* judgment which the Fourth Amendment does not require to be broken down in each instance into an analysis of each step in the search. The authority to search the person incident to a lawful custodial arrest, while based upon the need to disarm and to discover evidence, does not depend on what a court may later decide was the probability in a particular arrest situation that weapons or evidence would in fact be found upon the person of the suspect. A custodial arrest of a suspect based on probable cause is a reasonable intrusion under the Fourth Amendment; that intrusion being lawful, a search incident to the arrest requires no additional justification. It is the fact of the lawful arrest which establishes the authority to search, and we hold that in the case of a lawful custodial arrest a full search of the person is not only an exception to the warrant requirement of the Fourth Amendment, but is also a "reasonable" search under that Amendment.[b]

**a.** The reference is to *Terry v. Ohio*, § 7 infra, relied upon here by the Court of Appeals, where the Supreme Court held that on reasonable suspicion (that is, individualized suspicion short of the probable cause needed for arrest) the police may stop a person for investigation. The Court also held that incident to such a stop the police may take limited steps for their own protection: a full incident-to-arrest type search of the person is not permitted, but upon reasonable suspicion that the person is "armed and dangerous" the officer may pat him down and then reach into pockets upon feeling an object which might be a weapon.

**5.** Such an assumption appears at least questionable in light of the available statistical data concerning assaults on police officers who are in the course of making arrests. The danger to the police officer flows from the fact

of the arrest, and its attendant proximity, stress and uncertainty, and not from the grounds for arrest. One study concludes that approximately 30% of the shootings of police officers occur when the officer approaches a person seated in a car. Bristow, *Police Officer Shootings—A Tactical Evaluation*, 54 J.Crim. L.C. & P.S. 93 (1963). The Government in its brief notes that the Uniform Crime Reports, prepared by the Federal Bureau of Investigation, indicate that a significant percentage of police officers murders occur when the officers are making traffic stops. Those reports indicate that during January–March, 1973, 35 police officers were murdered; 11 of those officers were killed while engaged in traffic stops.

**b.** Compare the situation where there is a warrantless search of a person without any contemporaneous arrest, confronted by the

The search of respondent's person conducted by Officer Jenks in this case and the seizure from him of the heroin, were permissible under established Fourth Amendment law. * * * Since it is the fact of custodial arrest which gives rise to the authority to search, it is of no moment that Jenks did not indicate any subjective fear of the respondent or that he did not himself suspect that respondent was armed.[7] Having in the course of a lawful search come upon the crumpled package of cigarettes, he was entitled to inspect it; and when his inspection revealed the heroin capsules, he was entitled to seize them as "fruits, instrumentalities, or contraband" probative of criminal conduct. The judgment of the Court of Appeals holding otherwise is reversed.[c]

Court in the pre-*Robinson* case of *Cupp v. Murphy*, 412 U.S. 291 (1973). The Court, per Stewart, J., held that where Murphy voluntarily appeared at the station for questioning concerning the strangulation of his wife, at which time the police noticed what appeared to be blood on his finger, and the police had probable cause to arrest him but did not formally place him under arrest, the warrantless taking of scrapings from his fingernails "was constitutionally permissible." Noting that Murphy was aware of the police suspicion and tried to wipe his fingers clean, the Court concluded that the rationale underlying the search-incident-to-arrest doctrine "justified the police in subjecting him to the very limited search necessary to preserve the highly evanescent evidence they found under his fingernails." But, because a person not under formal arrest "might well be less hostile to the police and less likely to take conspicuous, immediate steps to destroy incriminating evidence on his person," the Court emphasized it was *not* holding "that a full * * * search would have been justified in this case without a formal arrest and without a warrant." Marshall, J., concurring, noted that the police could not have preserved the evidence by "close surveillance" and that detaining Murphy while a warrant was sought "would have been as much a seizure as detaining him while his fingernails were scraped." Douglas, J., dissenting, argued: "There was time to get a warrant; Murphy could have been detained while one was sought; and that detention would have preserved the perishable evidence the police sought."

Murphy was not arrested until over a month later, and thus the case is unlike those in which the arrest followed the search by a matter of minutes. The prevailing view is that a search "incident" to arrest may actually come before the formal making of an arrest if the police had grounds to arrest at the time the search was made. As stated in *Rawlings v. Kentucky*, 448 U.S. 98 (1980): "Where the formal arrest followed quickly on the heels of the challenged search of petitioner's person, we do not believe it particularly important that the search preceded the arrest rather than vice versa."

**7.** The United States concedes that "in searching respondent, [Officer Jenks] was not motivated by a feeling of imminent danger

and was not specifically looking for weapons." Brief for the United States. Officer Jenks testified, "I just searched him [Robinson]. I didn't think about what I was looking for. I just searched him." Officer Jenks also testified that upon removing the cigarette package from the respondent's custody, he was still unsure what was in the package, but that he knew it was not cigarettes.

**c.** Consider also *Illinois v. Lafayette*, 462 U.S. 640 (1983), concerning the basis for search upon the arrestee's arrival at the place of detention:

"The governmental interests underlying a stationhouse search of the arrestee's person and possessions may in some circumstances be even greater than those supporting a search immediately following arrest. Consequently, the scope of a stationhouse search will often vary from that made at the time of arrest. Police conduct that would be impractical or unreasonable—or embarrassingly intrusive—on the street can more readily—and privately—be performed at the station. For example, the interests supporting a search incident to arrest would hardly justify disrobing an arrestee on the street, but the practical necessities of routine jail administration may even justify taking a prisoner's clothes before confining him, although that step would be rare. * * *.

"At the stationhouse, it is entirely proper for police to remove and list or inventory property found on the person or in the possession of an arrested person who is to be jailed. A range of governmental interests support an inventory process. It is not unheard of for persons employed in police activities to steal property taken from arrested persons; similarly, arrested persons have been known to make false claims regarding what was taken from their possession at the stationhouse. A standardized procedure for making a list or inventory as soon as reasonable after reaching the stationhouse not only deters false claims but also inhibits theft or careless handling of articles taken from the arrested person. Arrested persons have also been known to injure themselves—or others—with belts, knives, drugs or other items on their person while being detained. Dangerous instrumentalities—such as razor blades, bombs, or weapons—can be concealed in innocent-looking ar-

Reversed.

JUSTICE MARSHALL, with whom JUSTICE DOUGLAS and JUSTICE BRENNAN join, dissenting.

Certain fundamental principles have characterized this Court's Fourth Amendment jurisprudence over the years. Perhaps the most basic of these was expressed by Justice Butler, speaking for a unanimous Court in *Go–Bart Co. v. United States,* 282 U.S. 344 (1931): "There is no formula for the determination of reasonableness. Each case is to be decided on its own facts and circumstances."

\* \* \*

The majority's attempt to avoid case-by-case adjudication of Fourth Amendment issues is not only misguided as a matter of principle, but is also doomed to fail as a matter of practical application. As the majority itself is well aware, the powers granted the police in this case are strong ones, subject to potential abuse. Although, in this particular case, Officer Jenks was required by Police Department regulation to make an in-custody arrest rather than to issue a citation, in most jurisdictions and for most traffic offenses the determination of whether to issue a citation or effect a full arrest is discretionary with the officer. There is always the possibility that a police officer, lacking probable cause to obtain a search warrant, will use a traffic arrest as a pretext to conduct a search. I suggest this possibility not to impugn the integrity of our police, but merely to point out that case-by-case adjudication will always be necessary to determine whether a full arrest was effected for purely legitimate reasons or, rather, as a pretext for searching the arrestee.

The majority states that "A police officer's determination as to how and where to search the person of a suspect whom he has arrested is necessarily a quick *ad hoc* judgment which the Fourth Amendment does not require to be broken down in each instance into an analysis of each step in the search." No precedent is cited for this broad assertion—not surprisingly, since there is none. Indeed, we only recently rejected such "a rigid all-or-nothing model of justification and regulation under the Amendment, [for] it obscures the utility of limitations upon the scope, as well as the initiation, of police action as a means of constitutional regulation. This Court has held in the past that a search which is reasonable at its inception may violate the Fourth Amendment by virtue of its intolerable intensity and scope." *Terry v. Ohio.* As we there concluded, "in determining whether the seizure and search were 'unreasonable' our inquiry is a dual one—whether the officer's action was justified at its inception, and whether it was reasonably related in scope to the circumstances which justified the interference in the first place."

As I view the matter, the search in this case divides into three distinct phases: the patdown of respondent's coat pocket; the removal of the unknown object from the pocket; and the opening of the crumpled up cigarette package.

No question is raised here concerning the lawfulness of the patdown of respondent's coat pocket. The Court of Appeals unanimously affirmed the right of a police officer to conduct a limited frisk for weapons when making an in-

ticles taken from the arrestee's possession. The bare recital of these mundane realities justifies reasonable measures by police to limit these risks—either while the items are in the police possession or at the time they are returned to the arrestee upon his release. Examining all the items removed from the arrestee's person or possession and listing or inventorying them is an entirely reasonable administrative procedure. It is immaterial whether the police actually fear any particular package or container; the need to protect against such risks arises independent of a particular officer's subjective concerns. Finally, inspection of an arrestee's personal property may assist the police in ascertaining or verifying his identity."

custody arrest, regardless of the nature of the crime for which the arrest was made.  As it said,

> "it would seem clearly unreasonable to expect a police officer to place a suspect in his squad car for transportation to the station house without first taking reasonable measures to insure that the suspect is unarmed.  We therefore conclude that whenever a police officer, acting within the bounds of his authority, makes an in-custody arrest, he may also conduct a limited *frisk* of the suspect's outer clothing in order to remove any weapons the suspect may have in his possession."

With respect to the removal of the unknown object from the coat pocket, * * * Officer Jenks had no reason to believe and did not in fact believe that the object in respondent's coat pocket was a weapon.  He admitted later that the object did not feel like a gun.  * * *

Since the removal of the object from the pocket cannot be justified as part of a limited *Terry* weapons frisk, the question arises whether it is reasonable for a police officer, when effecting an in-custody arrest of a traffic offender, to make a fuller search of the person than is permitted pursuant to *Terry*.  * * *

The Government does not now contend that the search of respondent's pocket can be justified by any need to find and seize evidence in order to prevent its concealment or destruction, for as the Court of Appeals found, there are no evidence or fruits of the offense with which respondent was charged.  The only rationale for a search in this case, then, is the removal of weapons which the arrestee might use to harm the officer and attempt an escape.  This rationale, of course, is identical to the rationale of the search permitted in *Terry*.  * * *

Since the underlying rationale of a *Terry* search and the search of a traffic violator are identical, the Court of Appeals held that the scope of the searches must be the same.  * * *

The problem with this approach, however, is that it ignores several significant differences between the context in which a search incident to arrest for a traffic violation is made, and the situation presented in *Terry*.  Some of these differences would appear to suggest permitting a more thorough search in this case than was permitted in *Terry*; other differences suggest a narrower, more limited right to search than was there recognized.

The most obvious difference between the two contexts relates to whether the officer has cause to believe that the individual he is dealing with possesses weapons which might be used against him.  *Terry* did not permit an officer to conduct a weapons frisk of anyone he lawfully stopped on the street, but rather, only where "he has reason to believe that he is dealing with an armed and dangerous individual.  * * *" While the policeman who arrests a suspected rapist or robber may well have reason to believe he is dealing with an armed and dangerous person, certainly this does not hold true with equal force with respect to persons arrested for motor vehicle violations of the sort involved in this case.

Nor was there any particular reason in this case to believe that respondent was dangerous.  He had not attempted to evade arrest, but had quickly complied with the police both in bringing his car to a stop after being signalled to do so and in producing the documents Officer Jenks requested.  In fact, Jenks admitted that he searched respondent face-to-face rather than in spread-eagle fashion because he had no reason to believe respondent would be violent.

While this difference between the situation presented in *Terry* and the context presented in this case would tend to suggest a lesser authority to search here than was permitted in *Terry*, other distinctions between the two contexts suggest just the opposite. As the Court of Appeals noted, a crucial feature distinguishing the in-custody arrest from the *Terry* context "is not the greater likelihood that a person taken into custody is armed, but rather the increased likelihood of danger to the officer *if* in fact the person is armed." A *Terry* stop involves a momentary encounter between officer and suspect, while an in-custody arrest places the two in close proximity for a much longer period of time. If the individual happens to have a weapon on his person, he will certainly have much more opportunity to use it against the officer in the in-custody situation. The prolonged proximity also makes it more likely that the individual will be able to extricate any small hidden weapon which might go undetected in a weapons frisk, such as a safety pin or razor blade. In addition, a suspect taken into custody may feel more threatened by the serious restraint on his liberty than a person who is simply stopped by an officer for questioning, and may therefore be more likely to resort to force.

Thus, in some senses there is less need for a weapons search in the in-custody traffic arrest situation than in a *Terry* context, while in other ways, there is a greater need. Balancing these competing considerations in order to determine what is a reasonable warrantless search in the traffic arrest context is a difficult process, one for which there may be no easy analytical guideposts. We are dealing in factors not easily quantified and, therefore, not easily weighed one against the other. And the competing interests we are protecting—the individual's interest in remaining free from unnecessarily intrusive invasions of privacy and society's interest that police officers not take unnecessary risks in the performance of their duties—are each deserving of our most serious attention and do not themselves tip the balance in any particular direction. * * *

The majority relies on statistics indicating that a significant percentage of police officer murders occur when the officers are making traffic stops. But these statistics only confirm what we recognized in *Terry*—that "American criminals have a long tradition of armed violence, and every year in this country many law enforcement officers are killed in the line of duty, and thousands more are wounded." As the very next sentence in *Terry* recognized, however, "Virtually all of these deaths and a substantial portion of the injuries are inflicted with guns and knives." The statistics relied on by the Government in this case support this observation. Virtually all of the killings are caused by guns and knives, the very type of weapons which will not go undetected in a properly conducted weapons frisk.[5] * * *

The majority opinion fails to recognize that the search conducted by Officer Jenks did not merely involve a search of respondent's person. It also included a separate search of effects found on his person. And even were we to assume, *arguendo,* that it was reasonable for Jenks to remove the object he felt in respondent's pocket, clearly there was no justification consistent with the Fourth Amendment which would authorize his opening the package and looking inside.

To begin with, after Jenks had the cigarette package in his hands, there is no indication that he had reason to believe or did in fact believe that the package contained a weapon. More importantly, even if the crumpled up cigarette package had in fact contained some sort of small weapon, it would have been impossible for respondent to have used it once the package was in the officer's

**5.** The Uniform Crime Reports prepared by the Federal Bureau of Investigation which are relied on by the majority, see n. 5, indicate that 112 police officers were killed nationwide in 1972. Of these, 108 were killed by firearms. Two of the remaining four were killed with knives, and the last two cases involved a bomb and an automobile.

hands. Opening the package therefore did not further the protective purpose of the search. * * *

The Government argues that it is difficult to see what constitutionally protected "expectation of privacy" a prisoner has in the interior of a cigarette pack. One wonders if the result in this case would have been the same were respondent a businessman who was lawfully taken into custody for driving without a license and whose wallet was taken from him by the police. Would it be reasonable for the police officer, because of the possibility that a razor blade was hidden somewhere in the wallet, to open it, remove all the contents, and examine each item carefully? Or suppose a lawyer lawfully arrested for a traffic offense is found to have a sealed envelope on his person. Would it be permissible for the arresting officer to tear open the envelope in order to make sure that it did not contain a clandestine weapon—perhaps a pin or a razor blade? Would it not be more consonant with the purpose of the Fourth Amendment and the legitimate needs of the police to require the officer, if he has any question whatsoever about what the wallet or letter contains, to hold onto it until the arrestee is brought to the precinct station?

I, for one, cannot characterize any of these intrusions into the privacy of an individual's papers and effects as being negligible incidents to the more serious intrusion into the individual's privacy stemming from the arrest itself. Nor can any principled distinction be drawn between the hypothetical searches I have posed and the search of the cigarette package in this case. The only reasoned distinction is between warrantless searches which serve legitimate protective and evidentiary functions and those that do not.[d]

## TENNESSEE v. GARNER

471 U.S. 1, 105 S.Ct. 1694, 85 L.Ed.2d 1 (1985).

JUSTICE WHITE delivered the opinion of the Court.

* * * At about 10:45 p.m. on October 3, 1974, Memphis Police Officers Elton Hymon and Leslie Wright were dispatched to answer a "prowler inside call." Upon arriving at the scene they saw a woman standing on her porch and gesturing toward the adjacent house. She told them she had heard glass breaking and that "they" or "someone" was breaking in next door. While Wright radioed the dispatcher to say that they were on the scene, Hymon went behind the house. He heard a door slam and saw someone run across the back yard. The fleeing suspect, who was appellee-respondent's decedent, Edward

---

d. In the companion case of *Gustafson v. Florida*, 414 U.S. 260 (1973), petitioner was arrested for failure to have an operator's license after the car he was driving was observed weaving across the center line several times, and was then searched, resulting in the discovery of a cigarette box within which the arresting officer found marijuana cigarettes. Petitioner contended his case was different from *Robinson* in that (a) he had experienced no previous encounters with the officer; (b) the offense for which he was arrested was "benign or trivial in nature," carrying with it no mandatory minimum sentence; and (c) there were no police regulations which required the officer to take petitioner into custody or which required full scale body searches upon arrest in the field. The Court, per Rehnquist, J., did "not find these differences deter-

minative of the constitutional issue," and thus upheld the search on the basis of *Robinson*.

Marshall, Douglas, and Brennan, JJ., dissented for the reasons stated in *Robinson*. Stewart, J., concurring, noted "that a persuasive claim might have been made in this case that the custodial arrest of the petitioner for a minor traffic offense violated his rights under the Fourth and Fourteenth Amendments," but since petitioner had "fully conceded the constitutional validity of his custodial arrest," the search of his person should be accepted as incidental to that arrest. Powell, J., concurring in both cases, emphasized that for him the "essential premise" of both decisions was "that an individual lawfully subjected to a custodial arrest retains no significant Fourth Amendment interest in the privacy of his person."

Garner, stopped at a 6–feet-high chain link fence at the edge of the yard.  With the aid of a flashlight, Hymon was able to see Garner's face and hands.  He saw no sign of a weapon, and, though not certain, was "reasonably sure" and "figured" that Garner was unarmed.  He thought Garner was 17 or 18 years old and about 5'5" or 5'7" tall.  While Garner was crouched at the base of the fence, Hymon called out "police, halt" and took a few steps toward him.  Garner then began to climb over the fence.  Convinced that if Garner made it over the fence he would elude capture, Hymon shot him.  The bullet hit Garner in the back of the head.  Garner was taken by ambulance to a hospital, where he died on the operating table.  Ten dollars and a purse taken from the house were found on his body.

In using deadly force to prevent the escape, Hymon was acting under the authority of a Tennessee statute and pursuant to Police Department policy.  The statute provides that "[i]f, after notice of the intention to arrest the defendant, he either flee or forcibly resist, the officer may use all the necessary means to effect the arrest."  The Department policy was slightly more restrictive than the statute, but still allowed the use of deadly force in cases of burglary.  * * *

Garner's father then brought this action in the Federal District Court for the Western District of Tennessee, seeking damages under 42 U.S.C. § 1983 for asserted violations of Garner's constitutional rights.  * * * The District Court * * * found that the statute, and Hymon's actions, were constitutional.  * * * The Court of Appeals reversed and remanded.  * * *[7]  The State of Tennessee, which had intervened to defend the statute, appealed to this Court.

Whenever an officer restrains the freedom of a person to walk away, he has seized that person.  While it is not always clear just when minimal police interference becomes a seizure, there can be no question that apprehension by the use of deadly force is a seizure subject to the reasonableness requirement of the Fourth Amendment.

A police officer may arrest a person if he has probable cause to believe that person committed a crime.  Petitioners and appellant argue that if this requirement is satisfied the Fourth Amendment has nothing to say about *how* that seizure is made.  This submission ignores the many cases in which this Court, by balancing the extent of the intrusion against the need for it, has examined the reasonableness of the manner in which a search or seizure is conducted.  * * * Because one of the factors is the extent of the intrusion, it is plain that reasonableness depends on not only when a seizure is made, but also how it is carried out.  * * *

The same balancing process applied in the cases cited above demonstrates that, notwithstanding probable cause to seize a suspect, an officer may not always do so by killing him.  The intrusiveness of a seizure by means of deadly force is unmatched.  The suspect's fundamental interest in his own life need not be elaborated upon.  The use of deadly force also frustrates the interest of the

---

**7.**  The Court of Appeals concluded that the rule set out in the Model Penal Code "accurately states Fourth Amendment limitations on the use of deadly force against fleeing felons."  The relevant portion of the Model Penal Code provides:

"The use of deadly force is not justifiable * * * unless (i) the arrest is for a felony; and (ii) the person effecting the arrest is authorized to act as a peace officer or is assisting a person whom he believes to be authorized to act as a peace officer; and (iii)

the actor believes that the force employed creates no substantial risk of injury to innocent persons; and (iv) the actor believes that (1) the crime for which the arrest is made involved conduct including the use or threatened use of deadly force; or (2) there is a substantial risk that the person to be arrested will cause death or serious bodily harm if his apprehension is delayed."  American Law Institute, Model Penal Code § 3.07(2)(b) (Proposed Official Draft 1962).  * * *

individual, and of society, in judicial determination of guilt and punishment. Against these interests are ranged governmental interests in effective law enforcement. It is argued that overall violence will be reduced by encouraging the peaceful submission of suspects who know that they may be shot if they flee. Effectiveness in making arrests requires the resort to deadly force, or at least the meaningful threat thereof. "Being able to arrest such individuals is a condition precedent to the state's entire system of law enforcement."

Without in any way disparaging the importance of these goals, we are not convinced that the use of deadly force is a sufficiently productive means of accomplishing them to justify the killing of nonviolent suspects. The use of deadly force is a self-defeating way of apprehending a suspect and so setting the criminal justice mechanism in motion. If successful, it guarantees that that mechanism will not be set in motion. And while the meaningful threat of deadly force might be thought to lead to the arrest of more live suspects by discouraging escape attempts, the presently available evidence does not support this thesis. The fact is that a majority of police departments in this country have forbidden the use of deadly force against nonviolent suspects. If those charged with the enforcement of the criminal law have abjured the use of deadly force in arresting nondangerous felons, there is a substantial basis for doubting that the use of such force is an essential attribute of the arrest power in all felony cases. Petitioners and appellant have not persuaded us that shooting nondangerous fleeing suspects is so vital as to outweigh the suspect's interest in his own life.

The use of deadly force to prevent the escape of all felony suspects, whatever the circumstances, is constitutionally unreasonable. It is not better that all felony suspects die than that they escape. Where the suspect poses no immediate threat to the officer and no threat to others, the harm resulting from failing to apprehend him does not justify the use of deadly force to do so. It is no doubt unfortunate when a suspect who is in sight escapes, but the fact that the police arrive a little late or are a little slower afoot does not always justify killing the suspect. A police officer may not seize an unarmed, nondangerous suspect by shooting him dead. The Tennessee statute is unconstitutional insofar as it authorizes the use of deadly force against such fleeing suspects.

It is not, however, unconstitutional on its face. Where the officer has probable cause to believe that the suspect poses a threat of serious physical harm, either to the officer or to others, it is not constitutionally unreasonable to prevent escape by using deadly force. Thus, if the suspect threatens the officer with a weapon or there is probable cause to believe that he has committed a crime involving the infliction or threatened infliction of serious physical harm, deadly force may be used if necessary to prevent escape, and if, where feasible, some warning has been given. As applied in such circumstances, the Tennessee statute would pass constitutional muster.

It is insisted that the Fourth Amendment must be construed in light of the common-law rule, which allowed the use of whatever force was necessary to effect the arrest of a fleeing felon, though not a misdemeanant. * * *

The State and city argue that because this was the prevailing rule at the time of the adoption of the Fourth Amendment and for some time thereafter, and is still in force in some States, use of deadly force against a fleeing felon must be "reasonable." It is true that this Court has often looked to the common law in evaluating the reasonableness, for Fourth Amendment purposes, of police activity. On the other hand, it "has not simply frozen into constitutional law those law enforcement practices that existed at the time of the Fourth Amendment's passage." Because of sweeping change in the legal and technological context, reliance on the common-law rule in this case would be a mistaken literalism that ignores the purposes of a historical inquiry.

It has been pointed out many times that the common-law rule is best understood in light of the fact that it arose at a time when virtually all felonies were punishable by death. * * * Courts have also justified the common-law rule by emphasizing the relative dangerousness of felons.

Neither of these justifications makes sense today. Almost all crimes formerly punishable by death no longer are or can be. And while in earlier times "the gulf between the felonies and the minor offences was broad and deep," today the distinction is minor and often arbitrary. Many crimes classified as misdemeanors, or nonexistent, at common law are now felonies. These changes have undermined the concept, which was questionable to begin with, that use of deadly force against a fleeing felon is merely a speedier execution of someone who has already forfeited his life. They have also made the assumption that a "felon" is more dangerous than a misdemeanant untenable. Indeed, numerous misdemeanors involve conduct more dangerous than many felonies.

There is an additional reason why the common-law rule cannot be directly translated to the present day. The common-law rule developed at a time when weapons were rudimentary. Deadly force could be inflicted almost solely in a hand-to-hand struggle during which, necessarily, the safety of the arresting officer was at risk. Handguns were not carried by police officers until the latter half of the last century. Only then did it become possible to use deadly force from a distance as a means of apprehension. As a practical matter, the use of deadly force under the standard articulation of the common-law rule has an altogether different meaning—and harsher consequences—now than in past centuries.

One other aspect of the common-law rule bears emphasis. It forbids the use of deadly force to apprehend a misdemeanant, condemning such action as disproportionately severe.

In short, though the common law pedigree of Tennessee's rule is pure on its face, changes in the legal and technological context mean the rule is distorted almost beyond recognition when literally applied.

In evaluating the reasonableness of police procedures under the Fourth Amendment, we have also looked to prevailing rules in individual jurisdictions. The rules in the States are varied. Some 19 States have codified the common-law rule, though in two of these the courts have significantly limited the statute. Four States, though without a relevant statute, apparently retain the common-law rule. Two States have adopted the Model Penal Code's provision [§ 3.07(2) (b)] verbatim. Eighteen others allow, in slightly varying language, the use of deadly force only if the suspect has committed a felony involving the use or threat of physical or deadly force, or is escaping with a deadly weapon, or is likely to endanger life or inflict serious physical injury if not arrested. Louisiana and Vermont, though without statutes or case law on point, do forbid the use of deadly force to prevent any but violent felonies. The remaining States either have no relevant statute or case-law, or have positions that are unclear.

It cannot be said that there is a constant or overwhelming trend away from the common-law rule. In recent years, some States have reviewed their laws and expressly rejected abandonment of the common-law rule. Nonetheless, the long-term movement has been away from the rule that deadly force may be used against any fleeing felon, and that remains the rule in less than half the States.

This trend is more evident and impressive when viewed in light of the policies adopted by the police departments themselves. Overwhelmingly, these are more restrictive than the common-law rule. * * * Overall, only 7.5% of departmental and municipal policies explicitly permit the use of deadly force against any felon; 86.8% explicitly do not. In light of the rules adopted by those who must actually administer them, the older and fading common-law view is a dubious indicium of the constitutionality of the Tennessee statute now before us.

Actual departmental policies are important for an additional reason. We would hesitate to declare a police practice of long standing "unreasonable" if doing so would severely hamper effective law enforcement. But the indications are to the contrary. There has been no suggestion that crime has worsened in any way in jurisdictions that have adopted, by legislation or departmental policy, rules similar to that announced today. * * *

Nor do we agree with petitioners and appellant that the rule we have adopted requires the police to make impossible, split-second evaluations of unknowable facts. We do not deny the practical difficulties of attempting to assess the suspect's dangerousness. However, similarly difficult judgments must be made by the police in equally uncertain circumstances. Nor is there any indication that in States that allow the use of deadly force only against dangerous suspects, the standard has been difficult to apply or has led to a rash of litigation involving inappropriate second-guessing of police officers' split-second decisions. Moreover, the highly technical felony/misdemeanor distinction is equally, if not more, difficult to apply in the field. An officer is in no position to know, for example, the precise value of property stolen, or whether the crime was a first or second offense. Finally, as noted above, this claim must be viewed with suspicion in light of the similar self-imposed limitations of so many police departments.

* * * Officer Hymon could not reasonably have believed that Garner— young, slight, and unarmed—posed any threat. Indeed, Hymon never attempted to justify his actions on any basis other than the need to prevent an escape. * * *

The dissent argues that the shooting was justified by the fact that Officer Hymon had probable cause to believe that Garner had committed a nighttime burglary. While we agree that burglary is a serious crime, we cannot agree that it is so dangerous as automatically to justify the use of deadly force. The FBI classifies burglary as a "property" rather than a "violent" crime. Although the armed burglar would present a different situation, the fact that an unarmed suspect has broken into a dwelling at night does not automatically mean he is physically dangerous. This case demonstrates as much. In fact, the available statistics demonstrate that burglaries only rarely involve physical violence. During the 10–year period from 1973–1982, only 3.8% of all burglaries involved violent crime.[23]

---

**23.** The dissent points out that three-fifths of all rapes in the home, three-fifths of all home robberies, and about a third of home assaults are committed by burglars. These figures mean only that if one knows that a suspect committed a rape in the home, there is a good chance that the suspect is also a burglar. That has nothing to do with the question here, which is whether the fact that someone has committed a burglary indicates that he has committed, or might commit, a violent crime.

The dissent also points out that this 3.8% adds up to 2.8 million violent crimes over a 10–year period, as if to imply that today's holding will let loose 2.8 million violent burglars. The relevant universe is, of course, far smaller. At issue is only that tiny fraction of cases where violence has taken place and an officer who has no other means of apprehending the suspect is unaware of its occurrence.

* * * The judgment of the Court of Appeals is affirmed * * *.

JUSTICE O'CONNOR, with whom THE CHIEF JUSTICE and JUSTICE REHNQUIST join, dissenting. * * *

Because burglary is a serious and dangerous felony, the public interest in the prevention and detection of the crime is of compelling importance. Where a police officer has probable cause to arrest a suspected burglar, the use of deadly force as a last resort might well be the only means of apprehending the suspect. With respect to a particular burglary, subsequent investigation simply cannot represent a substitute for immediate apprehension of the criminal suspect at the scene. Indeed, the Captain of the Memphis Police Department testified that in his city, if apprehension is not immediate, it is likely that the suspect will not be caught. Although some law enforcement agencies may choose to assume the risk that a criminal will remain at large, the Tennessee statute reflects a legislative determination that the use of deadly force in prescribed circumstances will serve generally to protect the public. Such statutes assist the police in apprehending suspected perpetrators of serious crimes and provide notice that a lawful police order to stop and submit to arrest may not be ignored with impunity. * * *

Against the strong public interests justifying the conduct at issue here must be weighed the individual interests implicated in the use of deadly force by police officers. The majority declares that "[t]he suspect's fundamental interest in his own life need not be elaborated upon." This blithe assertion hardly provides an adequate substitute for the majority's failure to acknowledge the distinctive manner in which the suspect's interest in his life is even exposed to risk. For purposes of this case, we must recall that the police officer, in the course of investigating a nighttime burglary, had reasonable cause to arrest the suspect and ordered him to halt. The officer's use of force resulted because the suspected burglar refused to heed this command and the officer reasonably believed that there was no means short of firing his weapon to apprehend the suspect. Without questioning the importance of a person's interest in his life, I do not think this interest encompasses a right to flee unimpeded from the scene of a burglary. * * *

A proper balancing of the interests involved suggests that use of deadly force as a last resort to apprehend a criminal suspect fleeing from the scene of a nighttime burglary is not unreasonable within the meaning of the Fourth Amendment. * * *

The Court's silence on critical factors in the decision to use deadly force simply invites second-guessing of difficult police decisions that must be made quickly in the most trying of circumstances. Police are given no guidance for determining which objects, among an array of potentially lethal weapons ranging from guns to knives to baseball bats to rope, will justify the use of deadly force. The Court also declines to outline the additional factors necessary to provide "probable cause" for believing that a suspect "poses a significant threat of death or serious physical injury," when the officer has probable cause to arrest and the suspect refuses to obey an order to halt. But even if it were appropriate in this case to limit the use of deadly force to that ambiguous class of suspects, I believe the class should include nighttime residential burglars who resist arrest by attempting to flee the scene of the crime. We can expect an escalating volume of litigation as the lower courts struggle to determine if a police officer's split-second decision to shoot was justified by the danger posed by a particular object and other facts related to the crime. Thus, the majority opinion portends a burgeoning area of Fourth Amendment doctrine concerning

the circumstances in which police officers can reasonably employ deadly force.
*  *  *

# SECTION 5. WARRANTLESS SEIZURE AND SEARCH OF PREMISES

The cases in this section reflect the basic notion that in the hierarchy of Fourth Amendment values, the privacy and sanctity of the home rank very high. Thus *Payton v. New York,* in contrast to the *Watson* case in the last section, holds that a warrant usually is required for an in-premises arrest. *Chimel v. California* permits only a limited search of the premises incident to an arrest therein, and *Vale v. Louisiana* holds that a warrant is ordinarily necessary to conduct an in-premises search on probable cause.

## PAYTON v. NEW YORK
### 445 U.S. 573, 100 S.Ct. 1371, 63 L.Ed.2d 639 (1980).

Justice Stevens delivered the opinion of the Court.  *  *  *

On January 14, 1970, after two days of intensive investigation, New York detectives had assembled evidence sufficient to establish probable cause to believe that Theodore Payton had murdered the manager of a gas station two days earlier. At about 7:30 a.m. on January 15, six officers went to Payton's apartment in the Bronx, intending to arrest him. They had not obtained a warrant. Although light and music emanated from the apartment, there was no response to their knock on the metal door. They summoned emergency assistance and, about 30 minutes later, used crowbars to break open the door and enter the apartment. No one was there. In plain view, however, was a 30-caliber shell casing that was seized and later admitted into evidence at Payton's murder trial.  *  *  *

On March 14, 1974, Obie Riddick was arrested for the commission of two armed robberies that had occurred in 1971. He had been identified by the victims in June of 1973 and in January 1974 the police had learned his address. They did not obtain a warrant for his arrest. At about noon on March 14, a detective, accompanied by three other officers, knocked on the door of the Queens house where Riddick was living. When his young son opened the door, they could see Riddick sitting in bed covered by a sheet. They entered the house and placed him under arrest. Before permitting him to dress, they opened a chest of drawers two feet from the bed in search of weapons and found narcotics and related paraphernalia. Riddick was subsequently indicted on narcotics charges.  *  *  *

The New York Court of Appeals, in a single opinion, affirmed the convictions of both Payton and Riddick.  *  *  *

Before addressing the narrow question presented by these appeals, we put to one side other related problems that are *not* presented today. Although it is arguable that the warrantless entry to effect Payton's arrest might have been justified by exigent circumstances, none of the New York courts relied on any such justification. The Court of Appeals majority treated both *Payton's* and *Riddick's* cases as involving routine arrests in which there was ample time to obtain a warrant, and we will do the same. Accordingly, we have no occasion to consider the sort of emergency or dangerous situation, described in our cases as "exigent circumstances," that would justify a warrantless entry into a home for the purpose of either arrest or search.

Nor do these cases raise any question concerning the authority of the police, without either a search or arrest warrant, to enter a third party's home to arrest a suspect. The police broke into Payton's apartment intending to arrest Payton and they arrested Riddick in his own dwelling. We also note that in neither case is it argued that the police lacked probable cause to believe that the suspect was at home when they entered. Finally, in both cases we are dealing with entries into homes made without the consent of any occupant. In *Payton*, the police used crowbars to break down the door and in *Riddick*, although his three-year-old son answered the door, the police entered before Riddick had an opportunity either to object or to consent. * * *

It is a "basic principle of Fourth Amendment law" that searches and seizures inside a home without a warrant are presumptively unreasonable. Yet it is also well-settled that objects such as weapons or contraband found in a public place may be seized by the police without a warrant. The seizure of property in plain view involves no invasion of privacy and is presumptively reasonable, assuming that there is probable cause to associate the property with criminal activity. * * *

As the late Judge Leventhal recognized, this distinction has equal force when the seizure of a person is involved. Writing on the constitutional issue now before us for the United States Court of Appeals for the District of Columbia Circuit sitting en banc, *Dorman v. United States*, 435 F.2d 385 (D.C.Cir.1970), Judge Leventhal first noted the settled rule that warrantless arrests in public places are valid. He immediately recognized, however, that

"[a] greater burden is placed [   ] on officials who enter a home or dwelling without consent. Freedom from intrusion into the home or dwelling is the archetype of the privacy protection secured by the Fourth Amendment."

His analysis of this question then focused on the long-settled premise that, absent exigent circumstances, a warrantless entry to search for weapons or contraband is unconstitutional even when a felony has been committed and there is probable cause to believe that incriminating evidence will be found within. He reasoned that the constitutional protection afforded to the individual's interest in the privacy of his own home is equally applicable to a warrantless entry for the purpose of arresting a resident of the house; for it is inherent in such an entry that a search for the suspect may be required before he can be apprehended. Judge Leventhal concluded that an entry to arrest and an entry to search for and to seize property implicate the same interest in preserving the privacy and the sanctity of the home, and justify the same level of constitutional protection. * * * We find this reasoning to be persuasive and in accord with this Court's Fourth Amendment decisions.

The majority of the New York Court of Appeals, however, suggested that there is a substantial difference in the relative intrusiveness of an entry to search for property and an entry to search for a person. It is true that the area that may legally be searched is broader when executing a search warrant than when executing an arrest warrant in the home. This difference may be more theoretical than real, however, because the police may need to check the entire premises for safety reasons, and sometimes they ignore the restrictions on searches incident to arrest.

But the critical point is that any differences in the intrusiveness of entries to search and entries to arrest are merely ones of degree rather than kind. The two intrusions share this fundamental characteristic: the breach of the entrance to an individual's home. * * * In terms that apply equally to seizures of property and to seizures of persons, the Fourth Amendment has drawn a firm line at the entrance to the house. Absent exigent circumstances, that threshold may not reasonably be crossed without a warrant. * * *[a]

The parties have argued at some length about the practical consequences of a warrant requirement as a precondition to a felony arrest in the home. In the absence of any evidence that effective law enforcement has suffered in those States that already have such a requirement, we are inclined to view such arguments with skepticism. More fundamentally, however, such arguments of policy must give way to a constitutional command that we consider to be unequivocal.

Finally, we note the State's suggestion that only a search warrant based on probable cause to believe the suspect is at home at a given time can adequately protect the privacy interests at stake, and since such a warrant requirement is manifestly impractical, there need be no warrant of any kind. We find this ingenious argument unpersuasive. It is true that an arrest warrant requirement may afford less protection than a search warrant requirement, but it will suffice to interpose the magistrate's determination of probable cause between the zealous officer and the citizen. If there is sufficient evidence of a citizen's participation in a felony to persuade a judicial officer that his arrest is justified, it is constitutionally reasonable to require him to open his doors to the officers of the law. Thus, for Fourth Amendment purposes, an arrest warrant founded on probable cause implicitly carries with it the limited authority to enter a dwelling in which the suspect lives [b] when there is reason to believe the suspect is within.

**a.** At this point, Stevens, J., observed that New York argued that "the reasons supporting the *Watson* holding require a similar result here. In *Watson* the Court relied on (a) the well-settled common-law rule that a warrantless arrest in a public place is valid if the arresting officer had probable cause to believe the suspect is a felon; (b) the clear consensus among the States adhering to that well-settled common-law rule; and (c) the expression of the judgment of Congress that such an arrest is 'reasonable.' We consider each of these reasons as it applies to a warrantless entry into a home for the purpose of making a routine felony arrest."

In an extended analysis, the *Payton* majority concluded (a) that "the relevant common law does not provide the same guidance that was present in *Watson*," as there is "no direct authority supporting forcible entries into a home to make a routine arrest and the weight of the scholarly opinion is somewhat to the contrary"; (b) that presently 24 states permit such warrantless entries, 15 prohibit them, and 11 have taken no position, with "a significant decline during the last decade in the number of States permitting warrantless entries for arrest"; and (c) that "no congressional determination that warrantless entries into the home are 'reasonable' has been called to our attention." While the majority then concluded from this that "neither history nor this Nation's experience" lent support to the New York position, the *Payton* dissenters read essentially the same data as supporting their position.

**b.** In *Steagald v. United States,* 451 U.S. 204 (1981), police entered Steagald's home in

an effort to find one Lyons, for whom they had an arrest warrant; they did not find Lyons but did find drugs in plain view, resulting in Steagald's prosecution and conviction. In reversing the conviction, the Court, per Marshall, J., reasoned that "whether the arrest warrant issued in this case adequately safeguarded the interests protected by the Fourth Amendment depends upon what the warrant authorized the agents to do. To be sure, the warrant embodied a judicial finding that there was probable cause to believe that Ricky Lyons had committed a felony, and the warrant therefore authorized the officers to seize Lyons. However, the agents sought to do more than use the warrant to arrest Lyons in a public place or in his home; instead, they relied on the warrant as legal authority to enter the home of a third person based on their belief that Ricky Lyons might be a guest there. Regardless of how reasonable this belief might have been, it was never subjected to the detached scrutiny of a judicial officer. Thus, while the warrant in this case may have protected Lyons from an unreasonable seizure, it did absolutely nothing to protect petitioner's privacy interest in being free from an unreasonable invasion and search of his home. Instead, petitioner's only protection from an illegal entry and search was the agent's personal determination of probable cause. In the absence of exigent circumstances, we have consistently held that such judicially untested determinations are not reliable enough to justify an entry into a person's home to arrest him without a warrant, or a search of a home for objects in the absence of a search warrant. We see no reason to depart from this settled

Because no arrest warrant was obtained in either of these cases, the judgments must be reversed * * *.[c]

JUSTICE WHITE, with whom THE CHIEF JUSTICE and JUSTICE REHNQUIST join, dissenting. * * *

Today's decision ignores the carefully crafted restrictions on the common-law power of arrest entry and thereby overestimates the dangers inherent in that practice. At common law, absent exigent circumstances, entries to arrest could be made only for felony. Even in cases of felony, the officers were required to announce their presence, demand admission, and be refused entry before they were entitled to break doors. Further, it seems generally accepted that entries could be made only during daylight hours. And, in my view, the officer entering to arrest must have reasonable grounds to believe, not only that the arrestee has committed a crime, but also that the person suspected is present in the house at the time of the entry.[13]

These four restrictions on home arrests—felony, knock and announce, daytime, and stringent probable cause—constitute powerful and complementary protections for the privacy interests associated with the home. The felony requirement guards against abusive or arbitrary enforcement and ensures that invasions of the home occur only in case of the most serious crimes. The knock and announce and daytime requirement protect individuals against the fear, humiliation and embarrassment of being aroused from the beds in states of partial or complete undress. And these requirements allow the arrestee to surrender at his front door, thereby maintaining his dignity and preventing the officers from entering other rooms of the dwelling. The stringent probable cause requirement would help ensure against the possibility that the police would enter when the suspect was not home, and, in searching for him, frighten members of the family or ransack parts of the house, seizing items in plain view. In short, these requirements, taken together, permit an individual suspected of a serious crime to surrender at the front door of his dwelling and thereby avoid most of the humiliation and indignity that the Court seems to believe necessarily accompany a house arrest entry. Such a front door arrest, in my view, is no more intrusive on personal privacy than the public warrantless arrests which we found to pass constitutional muster in *Watson*.[14]

All of these limitations on warrantless arrest entries are satisfied on the facts of the present cases. The arrests here were for serious felonies—murder and armed robbery—and both occurred during daylight hours. The authorizing statutes required that the police announce their business and demand entry; neither Payton nor Riddick makes any contention that these statutory requirements were not fulfilled. And it is not argued that the police had no probable cause to believe that both Payton and Riddick were in their dwellings at the time of the entries. Today's decision, therefore, sweeps away any possibility that warrantless home entries might be permitted in some limited situations other

course when the search of a home is for a person rather than an object."

**c.** Justice Blackmun's concurring opinion is omitted.

**13.** I do not necessarily disagree with the Court's discussion of the quantum of probable cause necessary to make a valid home arrest. The Court indicates that only an arrest warrant, and not a search warrant, is required. To obtain the warrant, therefore, the officers need only show probable cause that a crime has been committed and that the suspect committed it. However, under today's decision, the officers apparently need an extra increment of probable cause when executing the arrest warrant, namely grounds to believe that the suspect is within the dwelling.

**14.** If the suspect flees or hides, of course, the intrusiveness of the entry will be somewhat greater; but the policeman's hands should not be tied merely because of the possibility that the suspect will fail to cooperate with legitimate actions by law enforcement personnel.

than those in which exigent circumstances are present. The Court substitutes, in one sweeping decision, a rigid constitutional rule in place of the common-law approach, evolved over hundreds of years, which achieved a flexible accommodation between the demands of personal privacy and the legitimate needs of law enforcement.

A rule permitting warrantless arrest entries would not pose a danger that officers would use their entry power as a pretext to justify an otherwise invalid warrantless search. A search pursuant to a warrantless arrest entry will rarely, if ever, be as complete as one under authority of a search warrant. If the suspect surrenders at the door, the officers may not enter other rooms. Of course, the suspect may flee or hide, or may not be at home, but the officers cannot anticipate the first two of these possibilities and the last is unlikely given the requirement of probable cause to believe that the suspect is at home. Even when officers are justified in searching other rooms, they may seize only items within the arrestee's position [sic] or immediate control or items in plain view discovered during the course of a search reasonably directed at discovering a hiding suspect. Hence a warrantless home entry is likely to uncover far less evidence than a search conducted under authority of a search warrant. Furthermore, an arrest entry will inevitably tip off the suspects and likely result in destruction or removal of evidence not uncovered during the arrest. I therefore cannot believe that the police would take the risk of losing valuable evidence through a pretextual arrest entry rather than applying to a magistrate for a search warrant.

While exaggerating the invasion of personal privacy involved in home arrests, the Court fails to account for the danger that its rule will "severely hamper effective law enforcement." The policeman on his beat must now make subtle discriminations that perplex even judges in their chambers. As Justice Powell noted, concurring in *United States v. Watson*, police will sometimes delay making an arrest, even after probable cause is established, in order to be sure that they have enough evidence to convict. Then, if they suddenly have to arrest, they run the risk that the subsequent exigency will not excuse their prior failure to obtain a warrant. This problem cannot effectively be cured by obtaining a warrant as soon as probable cause is established because of the chance that the warrant will go stale before the arrest is made.

Further, police officers will often face the difficult task of deciding whether the circumstances are sufficiently exigent to justify their entry to arrest without a warrant. This is a decision that must be made quickly in the most trying of circumstances. If the officers mistakenly decide that the circumstances are exigent, the arrest will be invalid and any evidence seized incident to the arrest or in plain view will be excluded at trial. On the other hand, if the officers mistakenly determine that exigent circumstances are lacking, they may refrain from making the arrest, thus creating the possibility that a dangerous criminal will escape into the community. The police could reduce the likelihood of escape by staking out all possible exits until the circumstances become clearly exigent or a warrant is obtained. But the costs of such a stakeout seem excessive in an era of rising crime and scarce police resources.

The uncertainty inherent in the exigent circumstances determination burdens the judicial system as well. In the case of searches, exigent circumstances are sufficiently unusual that this Court has determined that the benefits of a warrant outweigh the burdens imposed, including the burdens on the judicial system. In contrast, arrests recurringly involve exigent circumstances, and this Court has heretofore held that a warrant can be dispensed with without undue sacrifice in Fourth Amendment values. The situation should be no different with respect to arrests in the home. Under today's decision, whenever the police have made a warrantless home arrest there will be the possibility of "endless litigation with respect to the existence of exigent circumstances, whether it was practicable to get a warrant, whether the suspect was about to flee, and the like."

\* \* \* It would be far preferable to adopt a clear and simple rule: after knocking and announcing their presence, police may enter the home to make a daytime arrest without a warrant when there is probable cause to believe that the person to be arrested committed a felony and is present in the house.

\* \* \*

# CHIMEL v. CALIFORNIA

395 U.S. 752, 89 S.Ct. 2034, 23 L.Ed.2d 685 (1969).

JUSTICE STEWART delivered the opinion of the Court. \* \* \*

The relevant facts are essentially undisputed. Late in the afternoon of September 13, 1965, three police officers arrived at the Santa Ana, California, home of the petitioner with a warrant authorizing his arrest for the burglary of a coin shop. The officers knocked on the door, identified themselves to the petitioner's wife, and asked if they might come inside. She ushered them into the house, where they waited 10 or 15 minutes until the petitioner returned home from work. When the petitioner entered the house, one of the officers handed him the arrest warrant and asked for permission to "look around." The petitioner objected, but was advised that "on the basis of the lawful arrest," the officers would nonetheless conduct a search. No search warrant had been issued.

Accompanied by the petitioner's wife, the officers then looked through the entire three-bedroom house, including the attic, the garage, and a small workshop. In some rooms the search was relatively cursory. In the master bedroom and sewing room, however the officers directed the petitioner's wife to open drawers and "to physically move contents of the drawers from side to side so that [they] might view any items that would have come from [the] burglary." After completing the search, they seized numerous items—primarily coins, but also several medals, tokens, and a few other objects. The entire search took between 45 minutes and an hour.

At the petitioner's subsequent state trial on two charges of burglary, the items taken from his house were admitted into evidence against him, over his objection that they had been unconstitutionally seized. He was convicted, and the judgments \* \* \* affirmed \* \* \*.

Without deciding the question, we proceed on the hypothesis that the California courts were correct in holding that the arrest of the petitioner was valid under the Constitution. This brings us directly to the question whether the warrantless search of the petitioner's entire house can be constitutionally justified as incident to that arrest. The decisions of this Court bearing upon that question have been far from consistent, as even the most cursory review makes evident.[a]

---

a. In an omitted portion of the opinion, the Court described how dictum on search incident to arrest broadened from search of the "person," *Weeks v. United States,* 232 U.S. 383 (1914), to search for what is "upon his person or in his control," *Carroll v. United States,* 267 U.S. 132 (1925), to search of "persons lawfully arrested" and "the place where the arrest is made," *Agnello v. United States,* 269 U.S. 20 (1925). Then, in *Marron v. United States,* 275 U.S. 192 (1927), concerning seizure of evidence at a place where illegal liquor sales were

In 1950 * * * came *United States v. Rabinowitz*, 339 U.S. 56 (1950), the decision upon which California primarily relies in the case now before us. In *Rabinowitz*, federal authorities had been informed that the defendant was dealing in stamps bearing forged overprints. On the basis of that information they secured a warrant for his arrest, which they executed at his one-room business office. At the time of the arrest, the officers "searched the desk, safe, and file cabinets in the office for about an hour and a half," and seized 573 stamps with forged overprints. The stamps were admitted into evidence at the defendant's trial, and this Court affirmed his conviction, rejecting the contention that the warrantless search had been unlawful. The Court held that the search in its entirety fell within the principle giving law enforcement authorities "[t]he right 'to search the place where the arrest is made in order to find and seize things connected with the crime * * *.'" * * * The test, said the Court, "is not whether it is reasonable to procure a search warrant, but whether the search was reasonable."

*Rabinowitz* has come to stand for the proposition, inter alia, that a warrantless search "incident to a lawful arrest" may generally extend to the area that is considered to be in the "possession" or under the "control" of the person arrested. And it was on the basis of that proposition that the California courts upheld the search of the petitioner's entire house in this case. That doctrine, however, at least in the broad sense in which it was applied by the California courts in this case, can withstand neither historical nor rational analysis.

Even limited to its own facts, the *Rabinowitz* decision was, as we have seen, hardly founded on an unimpeachable line of authority. * * *

Nor is the rationale by which the State seeks here to sustain the search of the petitioner's house supported by a reasoned view of the background and purpose of the Fourth Amendment. Mr. Justice Frankfurter wisely pointed out in his *Rabinowitz* dissent that the Amendment's proscription of "unreasonable searches and seizures" must be read in light of "the history that gave rise to the words"—a history of "abuses so deeply felt by the Colonies as to be one of the potent causes of the Revolution * * *." The Amendment was in large part a reaction to the general warrants and warrantless searches that had so alienated the colonists and had helped speed the movement for independence. In the scheme of the Amendment, therefore, the requirement that "no Warrants shall issue, but upon probable cause," plays a crucial part. * * * Even in the *Agnello* case the Court relied upon the rule that "[b]elief, however well founded, that an article sought is concealed in a dwelling house furnishes no justification for a search of that place without a warrant. And such searches are held unlawful notwithstanding facts unquestionably showing probable cause." Clearly, the general requirement that a search warrant be obtained is not lightly to be dispensed with, and "the burden is on those seeking [an] exemption [from the requirement] to show the need for it * * *."

occurring, the Court held that because the police had made an arrest on the premises they "had a right without a warrant contemporaneously to search the place in order to find and seize the things used to carry on the criminal enterprise." But in *Go–Bart Importing Co. v. United States*, 282 U.S. 344 (1931), *Marron* was limited to where the items seized "were visible and accessible and in the offender's immediate custody" and there "was no threat of force or general search or rummaging of the place." This limitation was reiter-

ated in *United States v. Lefkowitz*, 285 U.S. 452 (1932), which, like *Go–Bart*, held unlawful a search of a desk despite the fact the search had accompanied a lawful arrest, but was abandoned in *Harris v. United States*, 331 U.S. 145 (1947), upholding the search of a four-room apartment as "incident to arrest." But *Harris* was not followed in *Trupiano v. United States*, 334 U.S. 699 (1948), declaring that "law enforcement agents must secure and use search warrants wherever reasonably practicable."

* * * When an arrest is made, it is reasonable for the arresting officer to search the person arrested in order to remove any weapons that the latter might seek to use in order to resist arrest or effect his escape. Otherwise, the officer's safety might well be endangered, and the arrest itself frustrated. In addition, it is entirely reasonable for the arresting officer to search for and seize any evidence on the arrestee's person in order to prevent its concealment or destruction. And the area into which an arrestee might reach in order to grab a weapon or evidentiary items must, of course, be governed by a like rule. A gun on a table or in a drawer in front of one who is arrested can be as dangerous to the arresting officer as one concealed in the clothing of the person arrested. There is ample justification, therefore, for a search of the arrestee's person and the area "within his immediate control"—construing that phrase to mean the area from within which he might gain possession of a weapon or destructible evidence.

There is no comparable justification, however, for routinely searching rooms other than that in which an arrest occurs—or, for that matter, for searching through all the desk drawers or other closed or concealed areas in that room itself.[b] Such searches, in the absence of well-recognized exceptions, may be made only under the authority of a search warrant. The "adherence to judicial processes" mandated by the Fourth Amendment requires no less. * * *

It is argued in the present case that it is "reasonable" to search a man's house when he is arrested in it. But that argument is founded on little more than a subjective view regarding the acceptability of certain sorts of police conduct, and not on considerations relevant to Fourth Amendment interests. Under such an unconfined analysis, Fourth Amendment protection in this area would approach the evaporation point. It is not easy to explain why, for instance, it is less subjectively "reasonable" to search a man's house when he is arrested on his front lawn—or just down the street—than it is when he happens to be in the house at the time of arrest. * * *

It would be possible, of course, to draw a line between *Rabinowitz* and *Harris* on the one hand, and this case on the other. For *Rabinowitz* involved a single room, and *Harris* a four-room apartment, while in the case before us an entire house was searched. But such a distinction would be highly artificial. The rationale that allowed the searches and seizures in *Rabinowitz* and *Harris* would allow the searches and seizures in this case. No consideration relevant to the Fourth Amendment suggests any point of rational limitation, once the search is allowed to go beyond the area from which the person arrested might obtain weapons or evidentiary items. The only reasoned distinction is one

**b.** But the Court later held 7–2, in *Maryland v. Buie,* ___ U.S. ___ (1990), that police lawfully inside premises for the purpose of making an arrest may make a "protective sweep" for their own protection:

"We agree with the State, as did the court below, that a warrant was not required. We also hold that as an incident to the arrest the officers could, as a precautionary matter and without probable cause or reasonable suspicion, look in closets and other spaces immediately adjoining the place of arrest from which an attack could be immediately launched. Beyond that, however, we hold that there must be articulable facts which, taken together with the rational inferences from those facts, would warrant a reasonable prudent officer in believing that the area to be swept harbors an individual posing a danger to those on the arrest scene. * * *

"We should emphasize that such a protective sweep, aimed at protecting the arresting officers, if justified by the circumstances, is nevertheless not a full search of the premises, but may extend only to a cursory inspection of those spaces where a person may be found. The sweep lasts no longer than is necessary to dispel the reasonable suspicion of danger and in any event no longer than it takes to complete the arrest and depart the premises."

between a search of the person arrested and the area within his reach on the one hand, and more extensive searches on the other.[12]

The petitioner correctly points out that one result of decisions such as *Rabinowitz* and *Harris* is to give law enforcement officials the opportunity to engage in searches not justified by probable cause, by the simple expedient of arranging to arrest suspects at home rather than elsewhere. We do not suggest that the petitioner is necessarily correct in his assertion that such a strategy was utilized here, but the fact remains that had he been arrested earlier in the day, at his place of employment rather than at home, no search of his house could have been made without a search warrant. In any event, even apart from the possibility of such police tactics, the general point so forcefully made by Judge Learned Hand remains:

> "After arresting a man in his house, to rummage at will among his papers in search of whatever will convict him, appears to us to be indistinguishable from what might be done under a general warrant; indeed, the warrant would give more protection, for presumably it must be issued by a magistrate. True, by hypothesis the power would not exist, if the supposed offender were not found on the premises; but it is small consolation to know that one's papers are safe only so long as one is not at home."

*Rabinowitz* and *Harris* have been the subject of critical commentary for many years, and have been relied upon less and less in our own decisions. It is time, for the reasons we have stated, to hold that on their own facts, and insofar as the principles they stand for are inconsistent with those that we have endorsed today, they are no longer to be followed.

Application of sound Fourth Amendment principles to the facts of this case produces a clear result. The search here went far beyond the petitioner's person and the area from within which he might have obtained either a weapon or something that could have been used as evidence against him. There was no constitutional justification, in the absence of a search warrant, for extending the search beyond that area. The scope of the search was, therefore, "unreasonable" under the Fourth and Fourteenth Amendments, and the petitioner's conviction cannot stand.

Reversed.

JUSTICE HARLAN, concurring.

* * * The only thing that has given me pause in voting to overrule *Harris* and *Rabinowitz* is that as a result of *Mapp v. Ohio*, every change in Fourth Amendment law must now be obeyed by state officials facing widely different

---

12. It is argued in dissent that so long as there is probable cause to search the place where an arrest occurs, a search of that place would be permitted even though no search warrant has been obtained. This position seems to be based principally on two premises: first, that once an arrest has been made, the additional invasion of privacy stemming from the accompanying search is "relatively minor"; and second, that the victim of the search may "shortly thereafter" obtain a judicial determination of whether the search was justified by probable cause. With respect to the second premise, one may initially question whether all of the States in fact provide the speedy suppression procedures the dissent assumes. More fundamentally, however, we cannot accept the view that Fourth Amendment interests are vindicated so long as "the rights of the criminal" are "protect[ed] * * * against introduction of evidence seized without probable cause." The Amendment is designed to prevent, not simply to redress, unlawful police action. In any event, we cannot join in characterizing the invasion of privacy that results from a top-to-bottom search of a man's house as "minor." And we can see no reason why, simply because some interference with an individual's privacy and freedom of movement has lawfully taken place, further intrusions should automatically be allowed despite the absence of a warrant that the Fourth Amendment would otherwise require.

problems of local law enforcement. We simply do not know the extent to which cities and towns across the Nation are prepared to administer the greatly expanded warrant system which will be required by today's decision; nor can we say with assurance that in each and every local situation, the warrant requirement plays an essential role in the protection of those fundamental liberties protected against state infringement by the Fourteenth Amendment. * * *

JUSTICE WHITE, with whom JUSTICE BLACK joins, dissenting.

* * * The Court has always held, and does not today deny, that when there is probable cause to search and it is "impracticable" for one reason or another to get a search warrant, then a warrantless search may be reasonable. This is the case whether an arrest was made at the time of the search or not. * * *

This case provides a good illustration of my point that it is unreasonable to require police to leave the scene of an arrest in order to obtain a search warrant when they already have probable cause to search and there is a clear danger that the items for which they may reasonably search will be removed before they return with a warrant. Petitioner was arrested in his home after an arrest whose validity will be explored below, but which I will now assume was valid. There was doubtless probable cause not only to arrest petitioner, but to search his house. He had obliquely admitted both to a neighbor, and to the owner of the burglarized store, that he had committed the burglary. In light of this, and the fact that the neighbor had seen other admittedly stolen property in petitioner's house, there was surely probable cause on which a warrant could have issued to search the house for the stolen coins. Moreover, had the police simply arrested petitioner, taken him off to the station house, and later returned with a warrant,[5] it seems very likely that petitioner's wife, who in view of petitioner's generally garrulous nature must have known of the robbery, would have removed the coins. For the police to search the house while the evidence they had probable cause to search out and seize was still there cannot be considered unreasonable.

This line of analysis, supported by the precedents of this Court, hinges on two assumptions. One is that the arrest of petitioner without a valid warrant[7] was constitutional as the majority assumes; the other is that the police were not required to obtain a search warrant in advance, even though they knew that the effect of the arrest might well be to alert petitioner's wife that the coins had better be removed soon. * * * It must very often be the case that by the time probable cause to arrest a man is accumulated, the man is aware of police interest in him or for other good reasons is on the verge of flight. Moreover, it will likely be very difficult to determine the probability of his flight. Given this situation, it may be best in all cases simply to allow the arrest if there is probable cause, especially since that issue can be determined very shortly after the arrest. * * *

**5.** There were three officers at the scene of the arrest, one from the city where the coin burglary had occurred, and two from the city where the arrest was made. Assuming that one policeman from each city would be needed to bring the petitioner in and obtain a search warrant, one policeman could have been left to guard the house. However, if he not only could have remained in the house against petitioner's wife's will, but followed her about to assure that no evidence was being tampered with, the invasion of her privacy would be almost as great as that accompanying an actual search. Moreover, had the wife summoned an accomplice, one officer could not have watched them both.

**7.** An arrest warrant was in fact issued, but it was issued on an inadequate supporting affidavit and was therefore invalid, so that the case must be considered as though no warrant had issued.

If circumstances so often require the warrantless arrest that the law generally permits it, the typical situation will find the arresting officers lawfully on the premises without arrest or search warrant. * * * [W]here as here the existence of probable cause is independently established and would justify a warrant for a broader search for evidence, I would follow past cases and permit such a search to be carried out without a warrant, since the fact of arrest supplies an exigent circumstance justifying police action before the evidence can be removed, and also alerts the suspect to the fact of the search so that he can immediately seek judicial determination of probable cause in an adversary proceeding, and appropriate redress. * * *

## VALE v. LOUISIANA

399 U.S. 30, 90 S.Ct. 1969, 26 L.Ed.2d 409 (1970).

JUSTICE STEWART delivered the opinion of the Court.

* * * The evidence adduced at the pretrial hearing on a motion to suppress showed that on April 24, 1967, officers possessing two warrants for Vale's arrest and having information that he was residing at a specified address proceeded there in an unmarked car and set up a surveillance of the house. The evidence of what then took place was summarized by the Louisiana Supreme Court as follows:

"After approximately 15 minutes the officers observed a green 1958 Chevrolet drive up and sound the horn and after backing into a parking place, again blew the horn. At this juncture Donald Vale, who was well known to Officer Brady having arrested him twice in the previous month, was seen coming out of the house and walk up to the passenger side of the Chevrolet where he had a close brief conversation with the driver; and after looking up and down the street returned inside of the house. Within a few minutes he reappeared on the porch, and again cautiously looked up and down the street before proceeding to the passenger side of the Chevrolet, leaning through the window. From this the officers were convinced a narcotics sale had taken place. They returned to their car and immediately drove toward Donald Vale, and as they reached within approximately three cars lengths from the accused, (Donald Vale) he looked up and, obviously recognizing the officers, turned around, walking quickly toward the house. At the same time the driver of the Chevrolet started to make his get away when the car was blocked by the police vehicle. The three officers promptly alighted from the car, whereupon Officers Soule and Laumann called to Donald Vale to stop as he reached the front steps of the house, telling him he was under arrest. Officer Brady at the same time, seeing the driver of the Chevrolet, Arizzio Saucier, whom the officers knew to be a narcotic addict, place something hurriedly in his mouth, immediately placed him under arrest and joined his co-officers. Because of the transaction they had just observed they, informed Donald Vale they were going to search the house, and thereupon advised him of his constitutional rights. After they all entered the front room, Officer Laumann made a cursory inspection of the house to ascertain if anyone else was present and within about three minutes Mrs. Vale and James Vale, mother and brother of Donald Vale, returned home carrying groceries and were informed of the arrest and impending search."

The search of a rear bedroom revealed a quantity of narcotics.

The Louisiana Supreme Court held that the search of the house did not violate the Fourth Amendment because it occurred "in the immediate vicinity of the arrest" of Donald Vale and was "substantially contemporaneous therewith * * *." We cannot agree. * * *

A search may be incident to an arrest " 'only if it is substantially contemporaneous with the arrest and is confined to the *immediate* vicinity of the arrest.' " If a search of a house is to be upheld as incident to an arrest, that arrest must take place *inside* the house, not somewhere outside—whether two blocks away, twenty feet away, or on the sidewalk near the front steps. "Belief, however well founded, that an article sought is concealed in a dwelling house furnishes no justification for a search of that place without a warrant." That basic rule "has never been questioned in this Court."

The Louisiana Supreme Court thought the search independently supportable because it involved narcotics, which are easily removed, hidden, or destroyed. It would be unreasonable, the Louisiana court concluded, "to require the officers under the facts of the case to first secure a search warrant before searching the premises, as time is of the essence inasmuch as the officers never know whether there is anyone on the premises to be searched who could very easily destroy the evidence." Such a rationale could not apply to the present case, since by their own account the arresting officers satisfied themselves that no one else was in the house when they first entered the premises. But entirely apart from that point, our past decisions make clear that only in "a few specifically established and well-delineated" situations, may a warrantless search of a dwelling withstand constitutional scrutiny, even though the authorities have probable cause to conduct it. The burden rests on the State to show the existence of such an exceptional situation. And the record before us discloses none.

There is no suggestion that anyone consented to the search. The officers were not responding to an emergency. The goods ultimately seized were not in the process of destruction. Nor were they about to be removed from the jurisdiction.

The officers were able to procure two warrants for Vale's arrest. They also had information that he was residing at the address where they found him. There is thus no reason, so far as anything before us appears, to suppose that it was impracticable for them to obtain a search warrant as well. We decline to hold that an arrest on the street can provide its own "exigent circumstance" so as to justify a warrantless search of the arrestee's house. * * *

Reversed and remanded.

JUSTICE BLACKMUN took no part in the consideration or decision of this case.

JUSTICE BLACK, with whom THE CHIEF JUSTICE joins, dissenting.

* * * The police placed both Vale and Saucier under arrest. At this point the police had probable cause to believe that Vale was engaged in a narcotics transfer, and that a supply of narcotics would be found in the house, to which Vale had returned after his first conversation, from which he had emerged furtively bearing what the police could readily deduce was a supply of narcotics, and toward which he hurried after seeing the police. But the police did not know then who else might be in the house. Vale's arrest took place near the house, and anyone observing from inside would surely have been alerted to destroy the stocks of contraband which the police believed Vale had left there. The police had already seen Saucier, the narcotics addict, apparently swallow what Vale had given him. Believing that some evidence had already been destroyed and that other evidence might well be, the police were faced with the choice of risking the immediate destruction of evidence or entering the house and conducting a search. I cannot say that their decision to search was

unreasonable.  Delay in order to obtain a warrant would have given an accomplice just the time he needed.

That the arresting officers did, in fact, believe that others might be in the house is attested to by their actions upon entering the door left open by Vale. The police at once checked the small house to determine if anyone else was present.  Just as they discovered the house was empty, however, Vale's mother and brother arrived.  Now what had been a suspicion became a certainty: Vale's relatives were in possession and knew of his arrest.  To have abandoned the search at this point, and left the house with Vale, would not have been the action of reasonable police officers.  *  *  *[a]

Moreover, the circumstances here were sufficiently exceptional to justify a search, even if the search was not strictly "incidental" to an arrest.  The Court recognizes that searches to prevent the destruction or removal of evidence have long been held reasonable by this Court.  Whether the "exceptional circumstances" justifying such a search exist or not is a question that may be, as it is here, quite distinct from whether or not the search was incident to a valid arrest.

**a.** This, of course, raises the question of whether the police could have remained within the premises with Vale's brother and mother while a search warrant was obtained.  The Supreme Court has not addressed this precise point, but considered a related matter in *Segura v. United States,* 468 U.S. 796 (1984). The police, upon confirming that they had in fact observed a drug sale by Colon and Segura, went to their apartment building.  Segura was arrested in the lobby, and when Colon answered a knock on the door she was also arrested.  Police made a warrantless entry of the apartment and remained there until a search warrant was issued, which occurred some 19 hours later because of "administrative delay."  The Court held "that where officers, having probable cause, enter premises, and with probable cause, arrest the occupants who have legitimate possessory interests in its contents and take them into custody and, for no more than the period here involved, secure the premises from within to preserve the status quo while others, in good faith, are in the process of obtaining a warrant, they do not violate the Fourth Amendment's proscription against unreasonable seizures."  This holding was explicated in a portion of an opinion by The Chief Justice in which only O'Connor, J., joined:

"In this case, the agents entered and secured the apartment from within.  Arguably, the wiser course would have been to depart immediately and secure the premises from the outside by a 'stakeout' once the security check revealed that no one other than those taken into custody were in the apartment.  But the method actually employed does not require a different result under the Fourth Amendment, insofar as the *seizure* is concerned.  As the Court of Appeals held, absent exigent circumstances, the entry may have constituted an illegal *search,* or interference with petitioners' privacy interests, requiring suppression of all evidence observed during the entry.  Se-

curing of the premises from within, however, was no more an interference with the petitioners' possessory interests in the contents of the apartment than a perimeter 'stakeout.'  In other words, the initial entry—legal or not—does not affect the reasonableness of the seizure.  Under either method—entry and securing from within or a perimeter stakeout—agents control the apartment pending arrival of the warrant; both an internal securing and a perimeter stakeout interfere to the same extent with the possessory interests of the owners.  *  *  *

"Of course, a seizure reasonable at its inception because based upon probable cause may become unreasonable as a result of its duration or for other reasons.  Here, because of the delay in securing the warrant, the occupation of the apartment continued throughout the night and into the next day.  Such delay in securing a warrant in a large metropolitan center unfortunately is not uncommon; this is not, in itself, evidence of bad faith.  *  *  *

"  *  *  * Here, of course, Segura and Colon, whose possessory interests were interfered with by the occupation, were under arrest and in the custody of the police throughout the entire period the agents occupied the apartment.  The actual interference with their possessory interests in the apartment and its contents was, thus, virtually nonexistent.  We are not prepared to say under these limited circumstances that the seizure was unreasonable under the Fourth Amendment."

The four dissenters, per Stevens, J., argued that the occupation was an unreasonable search, infringing upon a reasonable expectation of privacy, and an unreasonable seizure, involving exercise of "complete dominion and control over the apartment and its contents"; and that the Fourth Amendment protects possessory interests in a residence even when the occupants are in custody.

It is thus unnecessary to determine whether the search was valid as incident to the arrest  *  *  *.

The Court, however, finds the search here unreasonable. First, the Court suggests that the contraband was not "in the process of destruction." None of the cases cited by the Court supports the proposition that "exceptional circumstances" exist only when the process of destruction has already begun. On the contrary we implied that those circumstances did exist when "evidence or contraband was *threatened* with removal or destruction."

Second, the Court seems to argue that the search was unreasonable because the police officers had time to obtain a warrant. I agree that the opportunity to obtain a warrant is one of the factors to be weighed in determining reasonableness. But the record conclusively shows that there was no such opportunity here. As I noted above, once the officers had observed Vale's conduct in front of the house they had probable cause to believe that a felony had been committed and that immediate action was necessary. At no time after the events in front of Mrs. Vale's house would it have been prudent for the officers to leave the house in order to secure a warrant.

The Court asserts, however, that because the police obtained two warrants for Vale's arrest there is "no reason  *  *  * to suppose that it was impracticable for them to obtain a search warrant as well." The difficulty is that the two arrest warrants on which the Court seems to rely so heavily were not issued because of any present misconduct of Vale's; they were issued because the bond had been increased for an earlier narcotics charge then pending against Vale. When the police came to arrest Vale, they knew only that his bond had been increased. There is nothing in the record to indicate that, absent the increased bond, there would have been probable cause for an arrest, much less a search. Probable cause for the search arose for the first time when the police observed the activity of Vale and Saucier in and around the house.  *  *  *

# SECTION 6.   WARRANTLESS SEIZURE AND SEARCH OF VEHICLES AND EFFECTS

Three of the cases in this section clearly illustrate that motor vehicles receive substantially less Fourth Amendment protection than premises. *California v. Carney* (in contradistinction to *Vale*) permits probable cause searches of vehicles without a warrant; *New York v. Belton* (in contradistinction to *Chimel*) allows a broad search of vehicles incident to arrest of an occupant; and *Colorado v. Bertine* authorizes a warrantless inventory of lawfully seized vehicles.

Personal effects, such as luggage, rank somewhere between premises and vehicles in the Fourth Amendment hierarchy of values. The second case in this section, *United States v. Ross,* explores why this is so and addresses the eventuating issue of what rules should control when personal effects are located inside a vehicle.

## CALIFORNIA v. CARNEY
### 471 U.S. 386, 105 S.Ct. 2066, 85 L.Ed.2d 406 (1985).

CHIEF JUSTICE BURGER delivered the opinion of the Court.  *  *  *

On May 31, 1979, Drug Enforcement Agency Agent Robert Williams watched respondent, Charles Carney, approach a youth in downtown San Diego. The youth accompanied Carney to a Dodge Mini Motor Home parked in a nearby lot. Carney and the youth closed the window shades in the motor home, including one across the front window. Agent Williams had previously received uncorroborated information that the same motor home was used by another person who was exchanging marihuana for sex. Williams, with assistance from other agents, kept the motor home under surveillance for the entire one and one-quarter hours that Carney and the youth remained inside. When the youth left the motor home, the agents followed and stopped him. The youth told the agents that he had received marijuana in return for allowing Carney sexual contacts.

At the officers' request, the youth returned to the motor home and knocked on its door; Carney stepped out. The agents identified themselves as law enforcement officers. Without a warrant or consent, one agent entered the motor home and observed marihuana, plastic bags, and a scale of the kind used in weighing drugs on a table. Agent Williams took Carney into custody and took possession of the motor home. A subsequent search of the motor home at the police station revealed additional marihuana in the cupboards and refrigerator.

Respondent was charged with possession of marihuana for sale. At a preliminary hearing, he moved to suppress the evidence discovered in the motor home. The Magistrate denied the motion, [but later the state supreme court reversed the conviction, holding the search was unreasonable because no warrant was obtained.]

* * * There are, of course, exceptions to the general rule that a warrant must be secured before a search is undertaken; one is the so-called "automobile exception" at issue in this case. This exception to the warrant requirement was first set forth by the Court 60 years ago in *Carroll v. United States*, 267 U.S. 132 (1925). There, the Court recognized that the privacy interests in an automobile are constitutionally protected; however, it held that the ready mobility of the automobile justifies a lesser degree of protection of those interests. The Court rested this exception on a long-recognized distinction between stationary structures and vehicles:

"[T]he guaranty of freedom from unreasonable searches and seizures by the Fourth Amendment has been construed, practically since the beginning of Government, as recognizing a necessary difference between a search of a store, dwelling house or other structure in respect of which a proper official warrant readily may be obtained, and a search of a ship, motor boat, wagon or automobile, for contraband goods, where it is not practicable to secure a warrant because the vehicle can be *quickly moved* out of the locality or jurisdiction in which the warrant must be sought."

The capacity to be "quickly moved" was clearly the basis of the holding in *Carroll*, and our cases have consistently recognized ready mobility as one of the principal bases of the automobile exception. * * *

However, although ready mobility alone was perhaps the original justification for the vehicle exception, our later cases have made clear that ready mobility is not the only basis for the exception. The reasons for the vehicle exception, we have said, are twofold. "Besides the element of mobility, less rigorous warrant requirements govern because the expectation of privacy with respect to one's automobile is significantly less than that relating to one's home or office."

Even in cases where an automobile was not immediately mobile, the lesser expectation of privacy resulting from its use as a readily mobile vehicle justified application of the vehicular exception. In some cases, the configuration of the vehicle contributed to the lower expectations of privacy; for example, we held that, because the passenger compartment of a standard automobile is relatively open to plain view, there are lesser expectations of privacy. But even when enclosed "repository" areas have been involved, we have concluded that the lesser expectations of privacy warrant application of the exception. We have applied the exception in the context of a locked car trunk, a sealed package in a car trunk, a closed compartment under the dashboard, the interior of a vehicle's upholstery, or sealed packages inside a covered pickup truck.

These reduced expectations of privacy derive not from the fact that the area to be searched is in plain view, but from the pervasive regulation of vehicles capable of traveling on the public highways. As we explained in [an earlier] case:

> "Automobiles, unlike homes, are subjected to pervasive and continuing governmental regulation and controls, including periodic inspection and licensing requirements. As an everyday occurrence, police stop and examine vehicles when license plates or inspection stickers have expired, or if other violations, such as exhaust fumes or excessive noise, are noted, or if headlights or other safety equipment are not in proper working order."

The public is fully aware that it is accorded less privacy in its automobiles because of this compelling governmental need for regulation. Historically, "individuals always [have] been on notice that movable vessels may be stopped and searched on facts giving rise to probable cause that the vehicle contains contraband, without the protection afforded by a magistrate's prior evaluation of those facts." In short, the pervasive schemes of regulation, which necessarily lead to reduced expectations of privacy, and the exigencies attendant to ready mobility justify searches without prior recourse to the authority of a magistrate so long as the overriding standard of probable cause is met.

When a vehicle is being used on the highways, or if it is readily capable of such use and is found stationary in a place not regularly used for residential purposes—temporary or otherwise—the two justifications for the vehicle exception come into play. First, the vehicle is obviously readily mobile by the turn of a switch key, if not actually moving. Second, there is a reduced expectation of privacy stemming from its use as a licensed motor vehicle subject to a range of police regulation inapplicable to a fixed dwelling. At least in these circumstances, the overriding societal interests in effective law enforcement justify an immediate search before the vehicle and its occupants become unavailable.

While it is true that respondent's vehicle possessed some, if not many of the attributes of a home, it is equally clear that the vehicle falls clearly within the scope of the exception laid down in *Carroll* and applied in succeeding cases. Like the automobile in *Carroll*, respondent's motor home was readily mobile. Absent the prompt search and seizure, it could readily have been moved beyond the reach of the police. Furthermore, the vehicle was licensed to "operate on public streets; [was] serviced in public places; * * * and [was] subject to extensive regulation and inspection." And the vehicle was so situated that an objective observer would conclude that it was being used not as a residence, but as a vehicle.

Respondent urges us to distinguish his vehicle from other vehicles within the exception because it was *capable of functioning as a home*. In our increasingly mobile society, many vehicles used for transportation can be and are being used not only for transportation but for shelter, i.e., as a "home" or "residence." To distinguish between respondent's motor home and an ordinary sedan for purposes of the vehicle exception would require that we apply the exception depending upon the size of the vehicle and the quality of its appointments.

Moreover, to fail to apply the exception to vehicles such as a motor home ignores the fact that a motor home lends itself easily to use as an instrument of illicit drug traffic and other illegal activity. * * *

Our application of the vehicle exception has never turned on the other uses to which a vehicle might be put. The exception has historically turned on the ready mobility of the vehicle, and on the presence of the vehicle in a setting that objectively indicates that the vehicle is being used for transportation.[3] These two requirements for application of the exception ensure that law enforcement officials are not unnecessarily hamstrung in their efforts to detect and prosecute criminal activity, and that the legitimate privacy interests of the public are protected. Applying the vehicle exception in these circumstances allows the essential purposes served by the exception to be fulfilled, while assuring that the exception will acknowledge legitimate privacy interests. * * *

This search was not unreasonable; it was plainly one that the magistrate could authorize if presented with these facts. * * *

The judgment of the California Supreme Court is reversed * * *.

JUSTICE STEVENS, with whom JUSTICE BRENNAN and JUSTICE MARSHALL join, dissenting. * * *

In this case, the motor home was parked in an off-the-street lot only a few blocks from the courthouse in downtown San Diego where dozens of magistrates were available to entertain a warrant application. The officers clearly had the element of surprise with them, and with curtains covering the windshield, the motor home offered no indication of any imminent departure. The officers plainly had probable cause to arrest the petitioner and search the motor home, and on this record, it is inexplicable why they eschewed the safe harbor of a warrant.

In the absence of any evidence of exigency in the circumstances of this case, the Court relies on the inherent mobility of the motor home to create a conclusive presumption of exigency. This Court, however, has squarely held that mobility of the place to be searched is not a sufficient justification for abandoning the warrant requirement. In *United States v. Chadwick*, 433 U.S. 1 (1977), the Court held that a warrantless search of a footlocker violated the Fourth Amendment even though there was ample probable cause to believe it contained contraband. The Government had argued that the rationale of the automobile exception applied to movable containers in general, and that the warrant requirement should be limited to searches of homes and other "core" areas of privacy. We categorically rejected the Government's argument observing that there are greater privacy interests associated with containers than with automobiles, and that there are less practical problems associated with the temporary detention of a container than with the detention of an automobile.

* * * It is perfectly obvious that the citizen has a much greater expectation of privacy concerning the interior of a mobile home than of a piece of luggage such as a footlocker. If "inherent mobility" does not justify warrantless searches of containers, it cannot rationally provide a sufficient justification for the search of a person's dwelling place.

3. We need not pass on the application of the vehicle exception to a motor home that is situated in a way or place that objectively indicates that it is being used as a residence. Among the factors that might be relevant in determining whether a warrant would be required in such a circumstance is its location, whether the vehicle is readily mobile or instead, for instance, elevated on blocks, whether the vehicle is licensed, whether it is connected to utilities, and whether it has convenient access to a public road.

Unlike a brick bungalow or a frame Victorian, a motor home seldom serves as a permanent lifetime abode. The motor home in this case, however, was designed to accommodate a breadth of ordinary everyday living. Photographs in the record indicate that its height, length and beam provided substantial living space inside: stuffed chairs surround a table; cupboards provide room for storage of personal effects; bunk-beds provide sleeping space; and a refrigerator provides ample space for food and beverages. Moreover, curtains and large opaque walls inhibit viewing the activities inside from the exterior of the vehicle. The interior configuration of the motor home establishes that the vehicle's size, shape, and mode of construction should have indicated to the officers that it was a vehicle containing mobile living quarters.

The State contends that officers in the field will have an impossible task determining whether or not other vehicles contain mobile living quarters. It is not necessary for the Court to resolve every unanswered question in this area in a single case, but common English usage suggests that we already distinguish between a "motor home" which is "equipped as a self-contained traveling home," a "camper" which is only equipped for "casual travel and camping," and an automobile which is "designed for passenger transportation." Surely the exteriors of these vehicles contain clues about their different functions which could alert officers in the field to the necessity of a warrant.   *   *   *

In my opinion, searches of places that regularly accommodate a wide range of private human activity are fundamentally different from searches of automobiles which primarily serve a public transportation function. Although it may not be a castle, a motor home is usually the functional equivalent of a hotel room, a vacation and retirement home, or a hunting and fishing cabin. These places may be as spartan as a humble cottage when compared to the most majestic mansion, but the highest and most legitimate expectations of privacy associated with these temporary abodes should command the respect of this Court. In my opinion, a warrantless search of living quarters in a motor home is "presumptively unreasonable absent exigent circumstances."

I respectfully dissent.

## UNITED STATES v. ROSS

456 U.S. 798, 102 S.Ct. 2157, 72 L.Ed.2d 572 (1982).

JUSTICE STEVENS delivered the opinion of the Court.

[On the basis of information from an informant that Ross had just made a narcotics sale and had more drugs in the trunk of his car, police stopped the vehicle and, after arresting Ross, located a closed paper bag in the trunk which upon examination was found to contain heroin. At the station, after a more thorough search of the car, a zippered leather pouch was also found in the trunk, and it was opened and $3,200 in cash was discovered therein. Ross moved to suppress the heroin and money, but the motion was denied and he was convicted of possession of heroin with intent to distribute. A panel of the court of appeals held that the police had probable cause to search the car and that no search warrant was needed, but then concluded that a warrantless search may not extend to a container in the car when the owner has a reasonable expectation of privacy in its contents, which was deemed to be the case as to the pouch but not as to the paper bag. On rehearing en banc, the court rejected the conclusion that a distinction of constitutional significance existed between the two containers and held the police should not have opened either of them without a warrant.]

* * * [S]ince its earliest days Congress had recognized the impracticability of securing a warrant in cases involving the transportation of contraband goods. It is this impracticability, viewed in historical perspective, that provided the basis for the *Carroll* decision. Given the nature of an automobile in transit, the Court recognized that an immediate intrusion is necessary if police officers are to secure the illicit substance. In this class of cases, the Court held that a warrantless search of an automobile is not unreasonable. * * *

The rationale justifying a warrantless search of an automobile that is believed to be transporting contraband arguably applies with equal force to any movable container that is believed to be carrying an illicit substance. That argument, however, was squarely rejected in *United States v. Chadwick*, 433 U.S. 1 (1977).

*Chadwick* involved the warrantless search of a 200-pound footlocker secured with two padlocks. Federal railroad officials in San Diego became suspicious when they noticed that a brown footlocker loaded onto a train bound for Boston was unusually heavy and leaking talcum powder, a substance often used to mask the odor of marijuana. Narcotics agents met the train in Boston and a trained police dog signaled the presence of a controlled substance inside the footlocker. The agents did not seize the footlocker, however, at this time; they waited until respondent Chadwick arrived and the footlocker was placed in the trunk of Chadwick's automobile. Before the engine was started, the officers arrested Chadwick and his two companions. The agents then removed the footlocker to a secured place, opened it without a warrant, and discovered a large quantity of marijuana. * * *

The Court in *Chadwick* specifically rejected the argument that the warrantless search was "reasonable" because a footlocker has some of the mobile characteristics that support warrantless searches of automobiles. The Court recognized that "a person's expectations of privacy in personal luggage are substantially greater than in an automobile," and noted that the practical problems associated with the temporary detention of a piece of luggage during the period of time necessary to obtain a warrant are significantly less than those associated with the detention of an automobile. In ruling that the warrantless search of the footlocker was unjustified, the Court reaffirmed the general principle that closed packages and containers may not be searched without a warrant. In sum, the Court in *Chadwick* declined to extend the rationale of the "automobile exception" to permit a warrantless search of any movable container found in a public place.[16]

The facts in *Arkansas v. Sanders*, 442 U.S. 753 (1979), were similar to those in *Chadwick*. In *Sanders*, a Little Rock police officer received information from a reliable informant that Sanders would arrive at the local airport on a specified flight that afternoon carrying a green suitcase containing marijuana. The officer went to the airport. Sanders arrived on schedule and retrieved a green suitcase from the airline baggage service. Sanders gave the suitcase to a waiting companion who placed it in the trunk of a taxi. Sanders and his companion drove off in the cab; police officers followed and stopped the taxi several blocks from the airport. The officers opened the trunk, seized the suitcase, and

---

**16.** The Court concluded that there is a significant difference between the seizure of a sealed package and a subsequent search of its contents; the search of the container in that case was "a far greater intrusion into Fourth Amendment values than the impoundment of the footlocker." A temporary seizure of a package or piece of luggage often may be accomplished without as significant an intrusion upon the individual—and without as great a burden on the police—as in the case of the seizure of an automobile.

searched it on the scene without a warrant. As predicted, the suitcase contained marijuana.

The Arkansas Supreme Court ruled that the warrantless search of the suitcase was impermissible under the Fourth Amendment, and this Court affirmed. As in *Chadwick,* the mere fact that the suitcase had been placed in the trunk of the vehicle did not render the automobile exception of *Carroll* applicable; the police had probable cause to seize the suitcase before it was placed in the trunk of the cab and did not have probable cause to search the taxi itself. Since the suitcase had been placed in the trunk, no danger existed that its contents could have been secreted elsewhere in the vehicle. \* \* \*

The Court in *Sanders* did not, however, rest its decision solely on the authority of *Chadwick.* In rejecting the State's argument that the warrantless search of the suitcase was justified on the ground that it had been taken from an automobile lawfully stopped on the street, the Court broadly suggested that a warrantless search of a container found in an automobile could never be sustained as part of a warrantless search of the automobile itself.[19] The Court did not suggest that it mattered whether probable cause existed to search the entire vehicle. It is clear, however, that in neither *Chadwick* nor *Sanders* did the police have probable cause to search the vehicle or anything within it except the footlocker in the former case and the green suitcase in the latter.

\* \* \* Unlike *Chadwick* and *Sanders,* in this case police officers had probable cause to search respondent's entire vehicle. [T]he parties have squarely addressed the question whether, in the course of a legitimate warrantless search of an automobile, police are entitled to open containers found within the vehicle. We now address that question. Its answer is determined by the scope of the search that is authorized by the exception to the warrant requirement set forth in *Carroll.*

In *Carroll* itself, the whiskey that the prohibition agents seized was not in plain view. It was discovered only after an officer opened the rumble seat and tore open the upholstery of the lazyback. The Court did not find the scope of the search unreasonable. Having stopped Carroll and Kiro on a public road and subjected them to the indignity of a vehicle search—which the Court found to be a reasonable intrusion on their privacy because it was based on probable cause that their vehicle was transporting contraband—prohibition agents were entitled to tear open a portion of the roadster itself. The scope of the search was no greater than a magistrate could have authorized by issuing a warrant based on the probable cause that justified the search. Since such a warrant could have authorized the agents to open the rear portion of the roadster and to rip the upholstery in their search for concealed whiskey, the search was constitutionally permissible.

In *Chambers v. Maroney,* 399 U.S. 42 (1970), the police found weapons and stolen property "concealed in a compartment under the dashboard." No suggestion was made that the scope of the search was impermissible. It would be illogical to assume that the outcome of *Chambers*—or the outcome of *Carroll*

---

**19.** The Court stated that "the extent to which the Fourth Amendment applies to containers and other parcels depends not at all upon whether they are seized from an automobile." This general rule was limited only by the observation that "[n]ot all containers and packages found by police during the course of a search will deserve the full protection of the Fourth Amendment. Thus, some containers (for example a kit of burglar tools or a gun case) by their very nature cannot support any reasonable expectation of privacy because their contents can be inferred from their outward appearance. Similarly, in some cases the contents of a package will be open to 'plain view,' thereby obviating the need for a warrant."

itself—would have been different if the police had found the secreted contraband enclosed within a secondary container and had opened that container without a warrant. If it was reasonable for prohibition agents to rip open the upholstery in *Carroll*, it certainly would have been reasonable for them to look into a burlap sack stashed inside; if it was reasonable to open the concealed compartment in *Chambers*, it would have been equally reasonable to open a paper bag crumpled within it. A contrary rule could produce absurd results inconsistent with the decision in *Carroll* itself.

In its application of *Carroll*, this Court in fact has sustained warrantless searches of containers found during a lawful search of an automobile. * * * In these cases it was not contended that police officers needed a warrant to open * * * packages. These decisions nevertheless "have much weight, as they show that this point neither occurred to the bar or the bench." The fact that no such argument was even made illuminates the profession's understanding of the scope of the search permitted under *Carroll*. Indeed, prior to the decisions in *Chadwick* and *Sanders,* courts routinely had held that containers and packages found during a legitimate warrantless search of an automobile also could be searched without a warrant.

As we have stated, the decision in *Carroll* was based on the Court's appraisal of practical considerations viewed in the perspective of history. It is therefore significant that the practical consequences of the *Carroll* decision would be largely nullified if the permissible scope of a warrantless search of an automobile did not include containers and packages found inside the vehicle. Contraband goods rarely are strewn across the trunk or floor of a car; since by their very nature such goods must be withheld from public view, they rarely can be placed in an automobile unless they are enclosed within some form of container. The Court in *Carroll* held that "contraband goods *concealed* and illegally transported in an automobile or other vehicle may be searched for without a warrant." As we [later] noted, the decision in *Carroll* "merely relaxed the requirements for a warrant on grounds of impracticability." It neither broadened nor limited the scope of a lawful search based on probable cause.

A lawful search of fixed premises generally extends to the entire area in which the object of the search may be found and is not limited by the possibility that separate acts of entry or opening may be required to complete the search. Thus, a warrant that authorizes an officer to search a home for illegal weapons also provides authority to open closets, chests, drawers, and containers in which the weapon might be found. A warrant to open a footlocker to search for marijuana would also authorize the opening of packages found inside. A warrant to search a vehicle would support a search of every part of the vehicle that might contain the object of the search. When a legitimate search is under way, and when its purpose and its limits have been precisely defined, nice distinctions between closets, drawers, and containers, in the case of a home, or between glove compartments, upholstered seats, trunks, and wrapped packages, in the case of a vehicle, must give way to the interest in the prompt and efficient completion of the task at hand.[28]

28. The practical considerations that justify a warrantless search of an automobile continue to apply until the entire search of the automobile and its contents has been completed. Arguably, the entire vehicle itself (including its upholstery) could be searched without a warrant, with all wrapped articles and containers found during that search then taken to a magistrate. But prohibiting police from opening immediately a container in which the object of the search is most likely to be found and instead forcing them first to comb the entire vehicle would actually exacerbate the intrusion on privacy interests. Moreover, until the container itself was opened the police could never be certain that the contraband was not secreted in a yet undiscovered portion of the vehicle; thus in every case in which a

This rule applies equally to all containers, as indeed we believe it must. [A] constitutional distinction between "worthy" and "unworthy" containers would be improper. Even though such a distinction perhaps could evolve in a series of cases in which paper bags, locked trunks, lunch buckets, and orange crates were placed on one side of the line or the other, the central purpose of the Fourth Amendment forecloses such a distinction. For just as the most frail cottage in the kingdom is absolutely entitled to the same guarantees of privacy as the most majestic mansion, so also may a traveler who carries a toothbrush and a few articles of clothing in a paper bag or knotted scarf claim an equal right to conceal his possessions from official inspection as the sophisticated executive with the locked attaché case.

[A]n individual's expectation of privacy in a vehicle and its contents may not survive if probable cause is given to believe that the vehicle is transporting contraband. Certainly the privacy interests in a car's trunk or glove compartment may be no less than those in a movable container. An individual undoubtedly has a significant interest that the upholstery of his automobile will not be ripped or a hidden compartment within it opened. These interests must yield to the authority of a search, however, which—in light of *Carroll*—does not itself require the prior approval of a magistrate. The scope of a warrantless search based on probable cause is no narrower—and no broader—than the scope of a search authorized by a warrant supported by probable cause. Only the prior approval of the magistrate is waived; the search otherwise is as the magistrate could authorize.

The scope of a warrantless search of an automobile thus is not defined by the nature of the container in which the contraband is secreted. Rather, it is defined by the object of the search and the places in which there is probable cause to believe that it may be found. Just as probable cause to believe that a stolen lawnmower may be found in a garage will not support a warrant to search an upstairs bedroom, probable cause to believe that undocumented aliens are being transported in a van will not justify a warrantless search of a suitcase. Probable cause to believe that a container placed in the trunk of a taxi contains contraband or evidence does not justify a search of the entire cab.

\* \* \* We hold that the scope of the warrantless search authorized by [the automobile] exception is no broader and no narrower than a magistrate could legitimately authorize by warrant. If probable cause justifies the search of a lawfully stopped vehicle, it justifies the search of every part of the vehicle and its contents that may conceal the object of the search. \* \* \*

JUSTICE BLACKMUN, concurring.

My dissents in prior cases have indicated my continuing dissatisfaction and discomfort with the Court's vacillation in what is rightly described as "this troubled area."

I adhere to the views expressed in those dissents. \* \* \* In order to have an authoritative ruling, I join the Court's opinion and judgment.[a]

JUSTICE MARSHALL, with whom JUSTICE BRENNAN joins, dissenting.

\* \* \*

Our cases do recognize a narrow exception to the warrant requirement for certain automobile searches. Throughout our decisions, two major considera-

container was found, the vehicle would need to be secured while a warrant was obtained. Such a requirement would be directly inconsistent with the rationale supporting the decisions in *Carroll* and *Chambers*.

**a.** Justice Powell's concurring opinion and Justice White's dissenting opinion (in which he noted agreement with "much of Justice Marshall's dissent") are omitted.

tions have been advanced to justify the automobile exception to the warrant requirement. We have upheld only those searches that are actually justified by those considerations.

First, these searches have been justified on the basis of the exigency of the mobility of the automobile. This "mobility" rationale is something of a misnomer, since the police ordinarily can remove the car's occupants and secure the vehicle on the spot. However, the inherent mobility of the vehicle often creates situations in which the police's only alternative to an immediate search may be to release the automobile from their possession.[2] This alternative creates an unacceptably high risk of losing the contents of the vehicle, and is a principal basis for the Court's automobile exception to the warrant requirement.

In many cases, however, the police will, prior to searching the car, have cause to arrest the occupants and bring them to the station for booking. In this situation, the police can ordinarily seize the automobile and bring it to the station. Because the vehicle is now in the exclusive control of the authorities, any subsequent search cannot be justified by the mobility of the car. Rather, an immediate warrantless search of the vehicle is permitted because of the second major justification for the automobile exception: the diminished expectation of privacy in an automobile.

* * * By focusing on the defendant's reasonable expectation of privacy, this Court has refused to require a warrant in situations where the process of obtaining such a warrant would be more intrusive than the actual search itself. A defendant may consider the seizure of the car a greater intrusion than an immediate search. Therefore, even where police *can* bring both the defendants and the automobile to the station safely and can house the car while they seek a warrant, the police are permitted to decide whether instead to conduct an immediate search of the car. In effect, the warrantless search is permissible because a warrant requirement would not provide significant protection of the defendant's Fourth Amendment interests.

The majority's rule is flatly inconsistent with these established Fourth Amendment principles * * *.

The practical mobility problem—deciding what to do with both the car and the occupants if an immediate search is not conducted—is simply not present in the case of movable containers, which can easily be seized and brought to the magistrate. The lesser expectation of privacy rationale also has little force. A container, as opposed to the car itself, does not reflect diminished privacy interests. Moreover, the practical corollary that this Court has recognized—that depriving occupants of the use of a car may be a greater intrusion than an immediate search—is of doubtful relevance here, since the owner of a container will rarely suffer significant inconvenience by being deprived of its use while a warrant is being obtained. * * *

Here, because appellant Ross had placed the evidence in question in a closed paper bag, the container could be seized, but not searched, without a warrant. No practical exigencies required the warrantless searches on the street or at the station: Ross had been arrested and was in custody when both searches occurred, and the police succeeded in transporting the bag to the station without inadvertently spilling its contents. * * *

---

**2.** The fact that the police are able initially to remove the occupants from the car does not remove the justification for an immediate search. If police could not conduct an immediate search of a stopped automobile, they would often be left with the difficult task of deciding what to do with the occupants while a warrant is obtained. In the case of a parked automobile, by contrast, if the automobile is unoccupied, this problem is not presented.

[T]he Court's argument that allowing warrantless searches of certain integral compartments of the car in *Carroll* and *Chambers*, while protecting movable containers within the car, would be "illogical" and "absurd," ignores the reason why this Court has allowed warrantless searches of automobile compartments. Surely an integral compartment within a car is just as mobile, and presents the same practical problems of safekeeping, as the car itself. This cannot be said of movable containers located within the car. The fact that there may be a high expectation of privacy in both containers and compartments is irrelevant, since the privacy rationale is not, and cannot be, the justification for the warrantless search of compartments.

The Court's second argument, which focuses on the practical advantages to police of the *Carroll* doctrine, fares no better. The practical considerations which concerned the *Carroll* Court involved the difficulty of immobilizing a vehicle while a warrant must be obtained. The Court had no occasion to address whether *containers* present the same practical difficulties as the car itself or integral compartments of the car. They do not. *Carroll* hardly suggested, as the Court implies, that a warrantless search is justified simply because it assists police in obtaining more evidence.

Although it can find no support for its rule in this Court's precedents or in the traditional justifications for the automobile exception, the majority offers another justification. In a footnote [28], the majority suggests that "practical considerations" militate against securing containers found during an automobile search and taking them to the magistrate. * * *

This explanation is unpersuasive. As this Court explained in *Sanders* and as the majority today implicitly concedes, the burden to police departments of seizing a package or personal luggage simply does not compare to the burden of seizing and safeguarding automobiles. Other aspects of the Court's explanation are also implausible. The search will not always require a "combing" of the entire vehicle, since police may be looking for a particular item and may discover it promptly. If, instead, they are looking more generally for evidence of a crime, the immediate opening of the container will not protect the defendant's privacy; whether or not it contains contraband, the police will continue to search for new evidence. Finally, the defendant, not the police, should be afforded the choice whether he prefers the immediate opening of his suitcase or other container to the delay incident to seeking a warrant. The more reasonable presumption, if a presumption is to replace the defendant's consent, is surely that the immediate search of a closed container will be a greater invasion of the defendant's privacy interests than a mere temporary seizure of the container.

Finally, the majority's new rule is theoretically unsound and will create anomalous and unwarranted results. These consequences are readily apparent from the Court's attempt to reconcile its new rule with the holdings of *Chadwick* and *Sanders*. The Court suggests that probable cause to search only a container does not justify a warrantless search of an automobile in which it is placed, absent reason to believe that the contents could be secreted elsewhere in the vehicle. This, the majority asserts, is an indication that the new rule is carefully limited to its justification, and is not inconsistent with *Chadwick* and *Sanders*. But why is such a container more private, less difficult for police to seize and store, or in any other relevant respect more properly subject to the warrant requirement, than a container that police discover in a probable cause search of an entire automobile? [10] This rule plainly has peculiar and unwork-

---

**10.** In a footnote, the Court appears to suggest a more pragmatic rationale for distin-  guishing *Chadwick* and *Sanders*—that no practical problems comparable to those engenable consequences: the Government "must show that the investigating officer knew enough but not too much, that he had sufficient knowledge to establish probable cause but insufficient knowledge to know exactly where the contraband was located."

Alternatively, the majority may be suggesting that *Chadwick* and *Sanders* may be explained because the connection of the container to the vehicle was incidental in these two cases. That is, because police had preexisting probable cause to seize and search the containers, they were not entitled to wait until the item was placed in a vehicle to take advantage of the automobile exception. I wholeheartedly agree that police cannot employ a pretext to escape Fourth Amendment prohibitions and cannot rely on an exigency that they could easily have avoided. This interpretation, however, might well be an exception that swallows up the majority's rule. In neither *Chadwick* nor *Sanders* did the Court suggest that the delay of the police was a pretext for taking advantage of the automobile exception. For all that appears, the Government may have had legitimate reasons for not searching as soon as they had probable cause. In any event, asking police to rely on such an uncertain line in distinguishing between legitimate and illegitimate searches for containers in automobiles hardly indicates that the majority's approach has brought clarification to this area of the law.[11]

## NEW YORK v. BELTON

453 U.S. 454, 101 S.Ct. 2860, 69 L.Ed.2d 768 (1981).

JUSTICE STEWART delivered the opinion of the Court. * * *

On April 9, 1978, Trooper Douglas Nicot, a New York State policeman driving an unmarked car on the New York Thruway, was passed by another automobile travelling at an excessive rate of speed. Nicot gave chase, overtook the speeding vehicle, and ordered its driver to pull it over to the side of the road and stop. There were four men in the car, one of whom was Roger Belton, the respondent in this case. The policeman asked to see the driver's license and automobile registration, and discovered that none of the men owned the vehicle or was related to its owner. Meanwhile, the policeman had smelled burnt marihuana and had seen on the floor of the car an envelope marked "Supergold" that he associated with marihuana. He therefore directed the men to get out of the car, and placed them under arrest for the unlawful possession of marihuana. He patted down each of the men and "split them up into four separate areas of the Thruway at this time so they would not be in physical touching area of each other." He then picked up the envelope marked "Supergold" and found that it contained marihuana. After giving the arrestees the warnings required by

dered by a general search of a vehicle would arise if the official suspicion is confined to a particular piece of luggage. This suggestion is illogical. A general search might disclose only a single item worth searching; conversely, pre-existing suspicion might attach to a number of items later placed in a car. Surely the protection of the warrant requirement cannot depend on a numerical count of the items subject to search.

11. Unless one of these alternative explanations is adopted, the Court's attempt to distinguish the holdings in *Chadwick* and *Sanders* is not only unpersuasive but appears to contradict the Court's own theory. The Court

suggests that in each case, the connection of the container to the vehicle was simply coincidental, and notes that the police did not have probable cause to search the entire vehicle. But the police assuredly did have probable cause to search the vehicle *for the container*. The Court states that the scope of the permitted warrantless search is determined only by what a magistrate could authorize. Once police found that container, according to the Court's own rule, they should have been entitled to search at least the container without a warrant. There was probable cause to search and the car was mobile in each case.

*Miranda v. Arizona*, the state policeman searched each one of them. He then searched the passenger compartment of the car. On the back seat he found a black leather jacket belonging to Belton. He unzipped one of the pockets of the jacket and discovered cocaine. Placing the jacket in his automobile, he drove the four arrestees to a nearby police station.

Belton was subsequently indicted for criminal possession of a controlled substance. In the trial court he moved that the cocaine the troooper had seized from the jacket pocket be suppressed. The court denied the motion. Belton then pleaded guilty to a lesser included offense, but preserved his claim that the cocaine had been seized in violation of the Fourth and Fourteenth Amendments. The Appellate Division of the New York Supreme Court upheld the constitutionality of the search and seizure, reasoning that "[o]nce defendant was validly arrested for possession of marihuana, the officer was justified in searching the immediate area for other contraband."

The New York Court of Appeals reversed, holding that "[a] warrantless search of the zippered pockets of an unaccessible jacket may not be upheld as a search incident to a lawful arrest where there is no longer any danger that the arrestee or a confederate might gain access to the article." * * *

It is a first principle of Fourth Amendment jurisprudence that the police may not conduct a search unless they first convince a neutral magistrate that there is probable cause to do so. This Court has recognized, however, that "the exigencies of the situation" may sometimes make exemption from the warrant requirement "imperative." Specifically, the Court held in *Chimel v. California* that a lawful custodial arrest creates a situation which justifies the contemporaneous search without a warrant of the person arrested and of the immediately surrounding area. Such searches have long been considered valid because of the need "to remove any weapons that [the arrestee] might seek to use in order to resist arrest or effect his escape" and the need to prevent the concealment or destruction of evidence.

The Court's opinion in *Chimel* emphasized the principle that, "The scope of [a] search must be 'strictly tied to and justified by' the circumstances which rendered its initiation permissible." Thus while the Court in *Chimel* found "ample justification" for a search of "the area from within which [an arrestee] might gain possession of a weapon or destructible evidence," the Court found "no comparable justification * * * for routinely searching any room other than that in which an arrest occurs—or, for that matter, for searching through all the desk drawers or other closed or concealed areas in that room itself."

Although the principle that limits a search incident to a lawful custodial arrest may be stated clearly enough, courts have discovered the principle difficult to apply in specific cases. Yet, as one commentator has pointed out, the protection of the Fourth and Fourteenth Amendments "can only be realized if the police are acting under a set of rules which, in most instances, makes it possible to reach a correct determination beforehand as to whether an invasion of privacy is justified in the interest of law enforcement." This is because

"Fourth Amendment doctrine, given force and effect by the exclusionary rule, is primarily intended to regulate the police in their day-to-day activities and thus ought to be expressed in terms that are readily applicable by the police in the context of the law enforcement activities in which they are necessarily engaged. A highly sophisticated set of rules, qualified by all sorts of ifs, ands, and buts and requiring the drawing of subtle nuances and hairline distinctions, may be the sort of heady stuff upon which the facile minds of lawyers and judges eagerly feed, but they may be 'literally impossible of application by the officer in the field.' "

In short, "A single, familiar standard is essential to guide police officers, who have only limited time and expertise to reflect on and balance the social and individual interests involved in the specific circumstances they confront."

\* \* \*

But no straightforward rule has emerged from the litigated cases respecting the question involved here—the question of the proper scope of a search of the interior of an automobile incident to a lawful custodial arrest of its occupants. The difficulty courts have had is reflected in the conflicting views of the New York judges who dealt with the problem in the present case, and is confirmed by a look at even a small sample drawn from the narrow class of cases in which courts have decided whether, in the course of a search incident to the lawful custodial arrest of the occupants of an automobile, police may search inside the automobile after the arrestees are no longer in it. \* \* \*

When a person cannot know how a court will apply a settled principle to a recurring factual situation, that person cannot know the scope of his constitutional protection, nor can a policeman know the scope of his authority. While the *Chimel* case established that a search incident to an arrest may not stray beyond the area within the immediate control of the arrestee, courts have found no workable definition of "the area within the immediate control of the arrestee" when that area arguably includes the interior of an automobile and the arrestee is its recent occupant. Our reading of the cases suggests the generalization that articles inside the relatively narrow compass of the passenger compartment of an automobile are in fact generally, even if not inevitably, within "the area into which an arrestee might reach in order to grab a weapon or evidentiary item." In order to establish the workable rule this category of cases requires, we read *Chimel*'s definition of the limits of the area that may be searched in light of that generalization. Accordingly, we hold that when a policeman has made a lawful custodial arrest of the occupant of an automobile, he may, as a contemporaneous incident of that arrest, search the passenger compartment of that automobile.[3]

It follows from this conclusion that the police may also examine the contents of any containers found within the passenger compartment, for if the passenger compartment is within reach of the arrestee, so also will containers in it be within his reach.[4] Such a container may, of course, be searched whether it is open or closed, since the justification for the search is not that the arrestee has no privacy interest in the container, but that the lawful custodial arrest justifies the infringement of any privacy interest the arrestee may have. Thus, while the Court in *Chimel* held that the police could not search all the drawers in an arrestee's house simply because the police had arrested him at home, the Court noted that drawers within an arrestee's reach could be searched because of the danger their contents might pose to the police.

---

**3.** Our holding today does not more than determine the meaning of *Chimel*'s principles in this particular and problematic content. It in no way alters the fundamental principles established in the *Chimel* case regarding the basic scope of searches incident to lawful custodial arrests.

**4.** "Container" here denotes any object capable of holding another object. It thus in-

cludes closed or open glove compartments, consoles, or other receptacles located anywhere within the passenger compartment, as well as luggage, boxes, bags, clothing, and the like. Our holding encompasses only the interior of the passenger compartment of an automobile and does not encompass the trunk.

It is true, of course, that these containers will sometimes be such that they could hold neither a weapon nor evidence of the criminal conduct for which the suspect was arrested. However, in *United States v. Robinson,* the Court rejected the argument that such a container—there a "crumpled up cigarette package"— located during a search of Robinson incident to his arrest could not be searched: "The authority to search the person incident to a lawful custodial arrest, while based upon the need to disarm and to discover evidence, does not depend on what a court may later decide was the probability in a particular arrest situation that weapons or evidence would in fact be found upon the person of the suspect. A custodial arrest of a suspect based on probable cause is a reasonable intrusion under the Fourth Amendment; that intrusion being lawful, a search incident to the arrest requires no additional justification." * * *[5]

It is not questioned that the respondent was the subject of a lawful custodial arrest on a charge of possessing marihuana. The search of the respondent's jacket followed immediately upon that arrest. The jacket was located inside the passenger compartment of the car in which the respondent had been a passenger just before he was arrested. The jacket was thus within the area which we have concluded was "within the arrestee's immediate control" within the meaning of the *Chimel* case. The search of the jacket, therefore, was a search incident to a lawful custodial arrest, and it did not violate the Fourth and Fourteenth Amendments. Accordingly, the judgment is reversed.[a]

JUSTICE STEVENS, concurring in the judgment.

For the reasons stated in my dissenting opinion in *Robbins v. California,* 453 U.S. 420 (1981), I agree [that] this judgment should be reversed. [That opinion follows.—ed.]

The Court's careful and repeated use of the term "lawful custodial arrest" seems to imply that a significant distinction between custodial arrests and ordinary arrests exists. I am familiar with the distinction between a "stop" and an "arrest," but I am not familiar with any difference between custodial arrests and any other kind of arrest. It is, of course, true that persons apprehended for traffic violations are frequently not required to accompany the arresting officer to the police station before they are permitted to leave on their own recognizance or by using their driver's licenses as a form of bond. It is also possible that state law or local regulations may in some cases forbid police officers from taking persons into custody for violation of minor traffic laws. As a matter of constitutional law, however, any person lawfully arrested for the pettiest misdemeanor may be temporarily placed in custody.[11] Indeed, as the Court has repeatedly

---

**5.** It seems to have been the theory of the Court of Appeals that the search and seizure in the present case could not have been incident to the respondent's arrest, because Trooper Nicot, by the very act of searching the respondent's jacket and seizing the contents of its pocket, had gained "exclusive control" of them. But under this fallacious theory no search or seizure incident to a lawful custodial arrest would ever be valid; by seizing an article even on the arrestee's person, an officer may be said to have reduced that article to his "exclusive control."

**a.** Justice Rehnquist's concurring opinion is omitted.

**11.** Justice Stewart apparently believes that the Fourth and Fourteenth Amendments might provide some impediment to police tak-

ing a defendant into custody for violation of a "minor traffic offense." See *Gustafson v. Florida* (Stewart, J. concurring). Although I agree that a police officer's authority to restrain an individual's liberty should be limited in the context of stops for routine traffic violations, the Court has not directly considered the question whether "there are constitutional limits upon the use of 'custodial arrests' as the means for invoking the criminal process when relatively minor offenses are involved." To the extent that the Court has considered the scope of an officer's authority in making routine traffic stops, the Court has not imposed constitutional restrictions on that authority. Thus the Court may be assuming that its new rule will be limited by a constitutional restriction that does not exist.

held, every arrest is a seizure of the person within the meaning of the Fourth Amendment. The rule of constitutional law the Court fashions today therefore potentially applies to every arrest of every occupant of an automobile.[12]

After the vehicle in which respondent was riding was stopped, the officer smelled marihuana and thereby acquired probable cause to believe that the vehicle contained contraband. A thorough search of the car was therefore reasonable. But if there were no reason to believe that anything more than a traffic violation had occurred, I should think it palpably unreasonable to require the driver of a car to open his briefcase or his luggage for inspection by the officer. The driver so compelled, however, could make no constitutional objection to a decision by the officer to take the driver into custody and thereby obtain justification for a search of the entire interior of the vehicle. Indeed, under the Court's new rule, the arresting officer may find reason to follow that procedure whenever he sees an interesting looking briefcase or package in a vehicle that has been stopped for a traffic violation. That decision by a police officer will therefore provide the constitutional predicate for broader vehicle searches than any neutral magistrate could authorize by issuing a warrant.

* * *

JUSTICE BRENNAN, with whom JUSTICE MARSHALL joins, dissenting. * * *

By approving the constitutionality of the warrantless search in this case, the Court carves out a dangerous precedent that is not justified by the concerns underlying *Chimel*. Disregarding the principle "that the scope of a warrantless search must be commensurate with the rationale that excepts the search from the warrant requirement," the Court for the first time grants police officers authority to conduct a warrantless "area" search under circumstances where there is no chance that the arrestee "might gain possession of a weapon or destructible evidence." Under the approach taken today, the result would presumably be the same even if Officer Nicot had handcuffed Belton and his companions in the patrol car before placing them under arrest, and even if his search had extended to locked luggage or other inaccessible containers located in the back seat of the car. * * *

The Court seeks to justify its departure from the principles underlying *Chimel* by proclaiming the need for a new bright line rule to guide the officer in the field. * * * [H]owever, "the mere fact that law enforcement may be made more efficient can never by itself justify disregard of the Fourth Amendment." Moreover, the Court's attempt to forge a "bright line" rule fails on its own terms. * * * The Court's new approach leaves open too many questions and, more important, it provides the police and the courts with too few tools with which to find the answers.

Thus, although the Court concludes that a warrantless search of a car may take place even though the suspect was arrested outside the car, it does not indicate how long after the suspect's arrest that search may validly be conducted. Would a warrantless search incident to arrest be valid if conducted five

12. After today, the driver of a vehicle stopped for a minor traffic violation must look to state law for protection from unreasonable searches. Such protection may come from two sources. Statutory law may provide some protection. Legislatures in some states permit officers to take traffic violators into custody only for certain violations. In some states, however, the police officer has the discretion to make a "custodial arrest" for violation of any motor vehicle law. Additionally, the failure to produce a satisfactory bond will often justify "detention and custodial arrest." Given the incomplete protection afforded by statutory law, drivers in many States will have to persuade state supreme courts to interpret their state constitution's equivalent to the Fourth Amendment to prohibit the unreasonable searches permitted by the Court here.

minutes after the suspect left his car?  Thirty minutes?  Three hours?  Does it matter whether the suspect is standing in close proximity to the car when the search is conducted?  Does it matter whether the police formed probable cause to arrest before or after the suspect left his car?  And *why* is the rule announced today necessarily limited to searches of cars?  What if a suspect is seen walking out of a house where the police, peering in from outside, had formed probable cause to believe a crime was being committed?  Could the police then arrest that suspect and enter the house to conduct a search incident to arrest?  Even assuming today's rule is limited to searches of the "interior" of cars—an assumption not demanded by logic—what is meant by "interior"?  Does it include locked glove compartments, the interior of door panels, or the area under the floorboards?  Are special rules necessary for station wagons and hatchbacks, where the luggage compartment may be reached through the interior, or taxicabs, where a glass panel might separate the driver's compartment from the rest of the car?  Are the only containers that may be searched those that are large enough to be "capable of holding another object"?  Or does the new rule apply to any container, even if it "could hold neither a weapon nor evidence of the criminal conduct for which the suspect was arrested"?

The Court does not give the police any "bright line" answers to these questions.  More important, because the Court's new rule abandons the justifications underlying *Chimel, it offers no guidance to the police officer seeking to work out these answers for himself.*  *  *  *

The standard announced in *Chimel* is not nearly as difficult to apply as the Court suggests.  To the contrary, I continue to believe that *Chimel* provides a sound, workable rule for determining the constitutionality of a warrantless search incident to arrest.  Under *Chimel,* searches incident to arrest may be conducted without a warrant only if limited to the person of the arrestee, or to the area within the arrestee's "immediate control."  While it may be difficult in some cases to measure the exact scope of the arrestee's immediate control, relevant factors would surely include the relative number of police officers and arrestees, the manner of restraint placed on the arrestee, and the ability of the arrestee to gain access to a particular area or container.[5]  Certainly there will be some close cases, but when in doubt the police can always turn to the rationale underlying *Chimel*—the need to prevent the arrestee from reaching weapons or contraband—before exercising their judgment.  A rule based on that rationale should provide more guidance than the rule announced by the Court today.  Moreover, unlike the Court's rule, it would be faithful to the Fourth Amendment.

JUSTICE WHITE, with whom JUSTICE MARSHALL joins, dissenting.

*  *  * The Court now holds that as incident to the arrest of the driver or any other person in an automobile, the interior of the car and any container found therein, whether locked or not, may not only be seized but also searched even absent probable cause to believe that contraband or evidence of crime will

---

**5.** The Court sets up a straw man when it claims that under the "exclusive control" approach taken by the Court of Appeals, "no search or seizure incident to a lawful custodial arrest would ever be valid; by seizing an article even on the arrestee's person, an officer may be said to have reduced that article to his 'exclusive control.'"

If a police officer could obtain exclusive control of an article by simply holding it in his hand, I would certainly agree with the Court.  But as we recognized in *United States v. Chadwick,* exclusive control means more than that.  It means sufficient control such that there is no significant risk that the arrestee or his confederates "might gain possession of a weapon or destructible evidence." *Chimel v. California.*  The issue of exclusive control presents a question of fact to be decided under the circumstances of each case, just as the New York Court of Appeals has decided it here.

be found.  As to luggage, briefcases or other containers, this seems to me an extreme extension of *Chimel* and one to which I cannot subscribe.  * * *

## COLORADO v. BERTINE

479 U.S. 367, 107 S.Ct. 738, 93 L.Ed.2d 739 (1987).

CHIEF JUSTICE REHNQUIST delivered the opinion of the Court.

[A Boulder, Colorado, police officer arrested respondent for driving his van while under the influence of alcohol.  After respondent was taken into custody and before a tow truck arrived to take the van to an impoundment lot, another officer, acting in accordance with local police procedures, inventoried the van's contents, opening a closed backpack in which he found various containers holding controlled substances, cocaine paraphernalia, and a large amount of cash.  Prior to his trial on charges including drug offenses, the state trial court granted respondent's motion to suppress the evidence found during the inventory search.  Although the court determined that the search did not violate respondent's rights under the Fourth Amendment of the Federal Constitution, it held that the search violated the Colorado Constitution.  The Colorado Supreme Court affirmed, but premised its ruling on the Federal Constitution.]

We granted certiorari to consider the important and recurring question of federal law decided by the Colorado Supreme Court.  As that court recognized, inventory searches are now a well-defined exception to the warrant requirement of the Fourth Amendment.  The policies behind the warrant requirement are not implicated in an inventory search, nor is the related concept of probable cause:

> "The standard of probable cause is peculiarly related to criminal investigations, not routine, noncriminal procedures * * *.  The probable-cause approach is unhelpful when analysis centers upon the reasonableness of routine administrative caretaking functions, particularly when no claim is made that the protective procedures are a subterfuge for criminal investigations."

For these reasons, the Colorado Supreme Court's reliance on *Arkansas v. Sanders, supra,* and *United States v. Chadwick, supra,* was incorrect.  Both of these cases concerned searches solely for the purpose of investigating criminal conduct, with the validity of the searches therefore dependent on the application of the probable cause and warrant requirements of the Fourth Amendment.

By contrast, an inventory search may be "reasonable" under the Fourth Amendment even though it is not conducted pursuant to warrant based upon probable cause.  In [*South Dakota v.*] *Opperman* [428 U.S. 364 (1976),] this Court assessed the reasonableness of an inventory search of the glove compartment in an abandoned automobile impounded by the police.  We found that inventory procedures serve to protect an owner's property while it is in the custody of the police, to insure against claims of lost, stolen, or vandalized property, and to guard the police from danger.  In light of these strong governmental interests and the diminished expectation of privacy in an automobile, we upheld the search.  In reaching this decision, we observed that our cases accorded deference to police caretaking procedures designed to secure and protect vehicles and their contents within police custody.

In our more recent decision, [*Illinois v.*] *Lafayette* [462 U.S. 640 (1983),] a police officer conducted an inventory search of the contents of a shoulder bag in the possession of an individual being taken into custody.  In deciding whether this search was reasonable, we recognized that the search served legitimate governmental interests similar to those identified in *Opperman*. We determined that those interests outweighed the individual's Fourth Amendment interests and upheld the search.

In the present case, as in *Opperman* and *Lafayette,* there was no showing that the police, who were following standardized procedures, acted in bad faith or for the sole purpose of investigation. In addition, the governmental interests justifying the inventory searches in *Opperman* and *Lafayette* are nearly the same as those which obtain here. In each case, the police were potentially responsible for the property taken into their custody. By securing the property, the police protected the property from unauthorized interference. Knowledge of the precise nature of the property helped guard against claims of theft, vandalism, or negligence. Such knowledge also helped to avert any danger to police or others that may have been posed by the property.[5]

The Supreme Court of Colorado opined that *Lafayette* was not controlling here because there was no danger of introducing contraband or weapons into a jail facility. Our opinion in *Lafayette,* however, did not suggest that the stationhouse setting of the inventory search was critical to our holding in that case. Both in the present case and in *Lafayette,* the common governmental interests described above were served by the inventory searches.

The Supreme Court of Colorado also expressed the view that the search in this case was unreasonable because Bertine's van was towed to a secure, lighted facility and because Bertine himself could have been offered the opportunity to make other arrangements for the safekeeping of his property. But the security of the storage facility does not completely eliminate the need for inventorying; the police may still wish to protect themselves or the owners of the lot against false claims of theft or dangerous instrumentalities. And while giving Bertine an opportunity to make alternate arrangements would undoubtedly have been possible, we said in *Lafayette:*

> "[t]he real question is not what 'could have been achieved,' but whether the Fourth Amendment *requires* such steps * * * The reasonableness of any particular governmental activity does not necessarily or invariably turn on the existence of alternative 'less intrusive' means."

We conclude that here, as in *Lafayette,* reasonable police regulations relating to inventory procedures administered in good faith satisfy the Fourth Amendment, even though courts might as a matter of hindsight be able to devise equally reasonable rules requiring a different procedure.[6]

The Supreme Court of Colorado also thought it necessary to require that police, before inventorying a container, weigh the strength of the individual's privacy interest in the container against the possibility that the container might serve as a repository for dangerous or valuable items. We think that such a requirement is contrary to our decisions in *Opperman* and *Lafayette:*

**5.** In arguing that the latter two interests are not implicated here, the dissent overlooks the testimony of the back-up officer who conducted the inventory of Bertine's van. According to the officer, the vehicle inventory procedures of the Boulder Police Department are designed for the "[p]rotection of the police department" in the event that an individual later claims that "there was something of value taken from within the vehicle." The officer added that inventories are also conducted in order to check "[f]or any dangerous items such as explosives [or] weapons." The officer testified that he had found such items in vehicles.

**6.** We emphasize that, in this case, the trial court found that the police department's procedures mandated the opening of closed containers and the listing of their contents. Our decisions have always adhered to the requirement that inventories be conducted according to standardized criteria.

"Even if less intrusive means existed of protecting some particular types of property, it would be unreasonable to expect police officers in the everyday course of business to make fine and subtle distinctions in deciding which containers or items may be searched and which must be sealed as a unit." *Lafayette,* supra. * * *

Bertine finally argues that the inventory search of his van was unconstitutional because departmental regulations gave the police officers discretion to choose between impounding his van and parking and locking it in a public parking place. The Supreme Court of Colorado did not rely on this argument in reaching its conclusion, and we reject it. Nothing in *Opperman* or *Lafayette* prohibits the exercise of police discretion so long as that discretion is exercised according to standard criteria and on the basis of something other than suspicion of evidence of criminal activity. Here, the discretion afforded the Boulder police was exercised in light of standardized criteria, related to the feasibility and appropriateness of parking and locking a vehicle rather than impounding it. There was no showing that the police chose to impound Bertine's van in order to investigate suspected criminal activity. * * * The judgment of the Supreme Court of Colorado is therefore reversed.

JUSTICE BLACKMUN, with whom JUSTICE POWELL and JUSTICE O'CONNOR join, concurring.

* * * I join the Court's opinion, but write separately to underscore the importance of having such inventories conducted only pursuant to standardized police procedures * * * that mandate the opening of such containers in every impounded vehicle. * * * [a]

JUSTICE MARSHALL, with whom JUSTICE BRENNAN joins, dissenting.

* * * [T]he record indicates that *no* standardized criteria limit a Boulder police officer's discretion. According to a departmental directive, after placing a driver under arrest, an officer has three options for disposing of the vehicle. First, he can allow a third party to take custody. Second, the officer or the driver (depending on the nature of the arrest) may take the car to the nearest public parking facility, lock it, and take the keys. Finally, the officer can do what was done in this case: impound the vehicle, and search and inventory its contents, including closed containers.

Under the first option, the police have no occasion to search the automobile. Under the "park and lock" option, "[c]losed containers that give no indication of

---

**a.** In *Florida v. Wells,* ___ U.S. ___ (1990), where all members of the Court agreed that the inventory of a locked suitcase found in an impounded vehicle was unlawful under *Bertine* because "the Florida Highway Patrol had no policy whatever with respect to the opening of closed containers encountered during an inventory search," five members of the Court went on to say that the state court erred in saying *Bertine* requires a policy either mandating or barring inventory of all containers: "A police officer may be allowed sufficient latitude to determine whether a particular container should or should not be opened in light of the nature of the search and characteristics of the container itself. Thus, while policies of opening all containers or opening no containers are unquestionably permissible, it would be equally permissible, for example, to allow the opening of closed con-

tainers whose contents officers determine they are unable to ascertain from examining the containers' exteriors."

Brennan and Marshall, JJ., concurring, disagreed with that assertion, which they characterized as "pure dictum given the disposition of the case." Blackmun, J. concurring, agreed that the Fourth Amendment did not impose an "all or nothing" requirement, so that a state "probably could adopt a policy which requires the opening of all containers that are not locked, or a policy which requires the opening of all containers over or under a certain size," but objected it was "an entirely different matter * * * to say, as this majority does, that an individual policeman may be afforded discretion in conducting an inventory search." Stevens, J., concurring separately, agreed with Blackmun.

containing either valuables or a weapon *may not be opened and the contents searched* (i.e., inventoried)." (emphasis added). Only if the police choose the third option are they entitled to search closed containers in the vehicle. Where the vehicle is not itself evidence of a crime, as in this case, the police apparently have totally unbridled discretion as to which procedure to use. Consistent with this conclusion, Officer Reichenbach testified that such decisions were left to the discretion of the officer on the scene.

Once a Boulder police officer has made this initial completely discretionary decision to impound a vehicle, he is given little guidance as to which areas to search and what sort of items to inventory. The arresting officer, Officer Toporek, testified at the suppression hearing as to what items would be inventoried: "That would I think be very individualistic as far as what an officer may or may not go into. I think whatever arouses his suspicious [*sic*] as far as what may be contained in any type of article in the car." * * *

Inventory searches are not subject to the warrant requirement because they are conducted by the government as part of "community caretaking" function, "totally divorced from the detection, investigation, or acquisition of evidence relating to the violation of a criminal statute." Standardized procedures are necessary to ensure that this narrow exception is not improperly used to justify, after the fact, a warrantless investigative foray. Accordingly, to invalidate a search that is conducted without established procedures, it is not necessary to establish that the police actually acted in bad faith, or that the inventory was in fact a "pretext." By allowing the police unfettered discretion, Boulder's discretionary scheme is unreasonable because of the " 'grave danger' of abuse of discretion."

In *South Dakota v. Opperman*, and *Illinois v. Lafayette*, both of which involved inventories conducted pursuant to standardized procedures, we balanced the individual's expectation of privacy against the government's interests to determine whether the search was reasonable. Even if the search in this case did constitute a legitimate inventory, it would nonetheless be unreasonable under this analysis. * * *

Not only are the government's interests weaker here than in *Opperman* and *Lafayette*, but respondent's privacy interest is greater. In upholding the search in *Opperman*, the Court emphasized the fact that the defendant had a diminished expectation of privacy in his automobile, due to "pervasive and continuing governmental regulation and controls, including periodic inspection and licensing requirements" and "the obviously public nature of automobile travel." Similarly, in *Lafayette*, the Court emphasized the fact that the defendant was in custody at the time the inventory took place.

Here the Court completely ignores respondent's expectation of privacy in his backpack. Whatever his expectation of privacy in his automobile generally, our prior decisions clearly establish that he retained a reasonable expectation of privacy in the backpack and its contents. See *Arkansas v. Sanders* ("[L]uggage is a common repository for one's personal effects, and therefore is inevitably associated with the expectation of privacy"); *United States v. Chadwick*, ("[A] person's expectations of privacy in personal luggage are substantially greater than in an automobile"). Indeed, the Boulder police officer who conducted the inventory acknowledged that backpacks commonly serve as repositories for personal effects. Thus, even if the governmental interests in this case were the same as those in *Opperman*, they would nonetheless be outweighed by respondent's comparatively greater expectation of privacy in his luggage. * * *

# SECTION 7. LESSER INTRUSIONS:
## STOP AND FRISK

Under the monolithic approach to the Fourth Amendment which once obtained, the assumption was that every form of activity which constituted either a search or a seizure had to be grounded in the same quantum of evidence suggested by the Amendment's "probable cause" requirement. But this changed when the Supreme Court recognized in *Camara v. Municipal Court*, 387 U.S. 523 (1967), that at least some Fourth Amendment activity should be judged under a balancing test, that is, by "balancing the need to search against the invasion which the search entails." Doubtless the most significant application of this new balancing test came a year later when, in *Terry v. Ohio*, the first case in this section, the Court applied it to the common police practice of detaining suspicious persons briefly on the street for purposes of investigation.

If there is to be a discrete form of police activity, typically called stop-and-frisk, which is subject to a lesser evidentiary standard, then it is necessary to distinguish such activity from full-fledged arrests requiring probable cause on the one hand and no-seizure police encounters requiring no justification whatsoever on the other. The problems attendant the drawing of such lines are seen in *Florida v. Royer*. The final case, *United States v. Place*, indicates one way in which the *Terry* rule has been expanded: by extension of the authority to seize on reasonable suspicion to personal effects such as luggage.

## TERRY v. OHIO
### 392 U.S. 1, 88 S.Ct. 1868, 20 L.Ed.2d 889 (1968).

CHIEF JUSTICE WARREN delivered the opinion of the court.

[Officer McFadden, a Cleveland plainclothes detective, became suspicious of two men standing on a street corner in the downtown area at about 2:30 in the afternoon. One of the suspects walked up the street, peered into a store, walked on, started back, looked into the same store, and then joined and conferred with his companion. The other suspect repeated this ritual, and between them the two men went through this performance about a dozen times. They also talked with a third man, and then followed him up the street about ten minutes after his departure. The officer, thinking that the suspects were "casing" a stickup and might be armed, followed and confronted the three men as they were again conversing. He identified himself and asked the suspects for their names. The men only mumbled something, and the officer spun Terry around and patted his breast pocket. He felt a pistol, which he removed. A frisk of Terry's companion also uncovered a pistol; a frisk of the third man did not disclose that he was armed, and he was not searched further. Terry was charged with carrying a concealed weapon, and he moved to suppress the weapon as evidence. The motion was denied by the trial judge, who upheld the officer's actions on a stop-and-frisk theory. The Ohio court of appeals affirmed, and the state supreme court dismissed Terry's appeal.]

* * * The question is whether in all the circumstances of this on-the-street encounter, [Terry's] right to personal security was violated by an unreasonable search and seizure.

We would be less than candid if we did not acknowledge that this question thrusts to the fore difficult and troublesome issues regarding a sensitive area of police activity—issues which have never before been squarely presented to this Court. * * *

On the one hand, it is frequently argued that in dealing with the rapidly unfolding and often dangerous situations on city streets the police are in need of an escalating set of flexible responses, graduated in relation to the amount of information they possess. For this purpose it is urged that distinctions should be made between a "stop" and an "arrest" (or a "seizure" of a person), and between a "frisk" and a "search." Thus, it is argued, the police should be allowed to "stop" a person and detain him briefly for questioning upon suspicion that he may be connected with criminal activity. Upon suspicion that the person may be armed, the police should have the power to "frisk" him for weapons. If the "stop" and the "frisk" give rise to probable cause to believe that the suspect has committed a crime, then the police should be empowered to make a formal "arrest," and a full incident "search" of the person. This scheme is justified in part upon the notion that a "stop" and a "frisk" amount to a mere "minor inconvenience and petty indignity," which can properly be imposed upon the citizen in the interest of effective law enforcement on the basis of a police officer's suspicion.

On the other side the argument is made that the authority of the police must be strictly circumscribed by the law of arrest and search as it has developed to date in the traditional jurisprudence of the Fourth Amendment. It is contended with some force that there is not—and cannot be—a variety of police activity which does not depend solely upon the voluntary cooperation of the citizen and yet which stops short of an arrest based upon probable cause to make such an arrest. The heart of the Fourth Amendment, the argument runs, is a severe requirement of specific justification for any intrusion upon protected personal security, coupled with a highly developed system of judicial controls to enforce upon the agents of the State the commands of the Constitution. \* \* \*

\* \* \* The State has characterized the issue here as "the right of a police officer \* \* \* to make an on-the-street stop, interrogate and pat down for weapons (known in the street vernacular as 'stop and frisk')." But this is only partly accurate. For the issue is not the abstract propriety of the police conduct, but the admissibility against petitioner of the evidence uncovered by the search and seizure. \* \* \* [I]n our system evidentiary rulings provide the context in which the judicial process of inclusion and exclusion approves some conduct as comporting with constitutional guarantees and disapproves other actions by state agents. A ruling admitting evidence in a criminal trial, we recognize, has the necessary effect of legitimizing the conduct which produced the evidence, while an application of the exclusionary rule withholds the constitutional imprimatur.

The exclusionary rule has its limitations, however, as a tool of judicial control. It cannot properly be invoked to exclude the products of legitimate police investigative techniques on the ground that much conduct which is closely similar involves unwarranted intrusions upon constitutional protections. Moreover, in some contexts the rule is ineffective as a deterrent. Street encounters between citizens and police officers are incredibly rich in diversity. They range from wholly friendly exchanges of pleasantries or mutually useful information to hostile confrontations of armed men involving arrests, or injuries, or loss of life. Moreover, hostile confrontations are not all of a piece. Some of them begin in a friendly enough manner, only to take a different turn upon the injection of some unexpected element into the conversation. Encounters are initiated by the police for a wide variety of purposes, some of which are wholly unrelated to a desire to prosecute for crime. Doubtless some police "field interrogation" conduct violates the Fourth Amendment. But a stern refusal by this Court to condone such activity does not necessarily render it responsive to the exclusionary rule. Regardless of how effective the rule may be where obtaining convictions is an important objective of the police, it is powerless to deter invasions of constitutionally guaranteed rights where the police either have no interest in prosecuting or are willing to forego successful prosecution in the interest of serving some other goal.

Proper adjudication of cases in which the exclusionary rule is invoked demands a constant awareness of these limitations. The wholesale harassment by certain elements of the police community, of which minority groups, particularly Negroes, frequently complain, will not be stopped by the exclusion of any evidence from any criminal trial. Yet a rigid and unthinking application of the exclusionary rule, in futile protest against practices which it can never be used effectively to control, may exact a high toll in human injury and frustration of efforts to prevent crime. No judicial opinion can comprehend the protean variety of the street encounter, and we can only judge the facts of the case before us. * * *

[W]e turn our attention to the quite narrow question posed by the facts before us: whether it is always unreasonable for a policeman to seize a person and subject him to a limited search for weapons unless there is probable cause for an arrest.

* * * It is quite plain that the Fourth Amendment governs "seizures" of the person which do not eventuate in a trip to the station house and prosecution for crime—"arrests" in traditional terminology. It must be recognized that whenever a police officer accosts an individual and restrains his freedom to walk away, he has "seized" that person. And it is nothing less than sheer torture of the English language to suggest that a careful exploration of the outer surfaces of a person's clothing all over his or her body in an attempt to find weapons is not a "search." Moreover, it is simply fantastic to urge that such a procedure performed in public by a policeman while the citizen stands helpless, perhaps facing a wall with his hands raised, is a "petty indignity." [13] It is a serious intrusion upon the sanctity of the person, which may inflict great indignity and arouse strong resentment, and it is not to be undertaken lightly.

* * * We therefore reject the notions that the Fourth Amendment does not come into play at all as a limitation upon police conduct if the officers stop short of something called a "technical arrest" or a "full-blown search."

In this case there can be no question, then, that Officer McFadden "seized" petitioner and subjected him to a "search" when he took hold of him and patted down the outer surfaces of his clothing. We must decide whether at that point it was reasonable for Officer McFadden to have interfered with petitioner's personal security as he did. [16] And in determining whether the seizure and search were

**13.** Consider the following apt description:

"[T]he officer must feel with sensitive fingers every portion of the prisoner's body. A thorough search must be made of the prisoner's arms and armpits, waistline and back, the groin and area about the testicles, and entire surface of the legs down to the feet." Priar & Martin, *Searching and Disarming Criminals*, 45 J.Crim.L.C. & P.S. 481 (1954).

**16.** We thus decide nothing today concerning the constitutional propriety of an investigative "seizure" upon less than probable cause for purposes of "detention" and/or interrogation. Obviously, not all personal intercourse between policemen and citizens involves "seizures" of persons. Only when the officer, by means of physical force or show of authority, has in some way restrained the liberty of a citizen may we conclude that a "seizure" has occurred. We cannot tell with any certainty upon this record whether any such "seizure" took place here prior to Officer McFadden's initiation of physical contact for purposes of searching Terry for weapons, and we thus may assume that up to that point no intrusion upon constitutionally protected rights had occurred.

"unreasonable" our inquiry is a dual one—whether the officer's action was justified at its inception, and whether it was reasonably related in scope to the circumstances which justified the interference in the first place.

If this case involved police conduct subject to the Warrant Clause of the Fourth Amendment, we would have to ascertain whether "probable cause" existed to justify the search and seizure which took place. However, that is not the case. We do not retreat from our holdings that the police must, whenever practicable, obtain advance judicial approval of searches and seizures through the warrant procedure, * * * or that in most instances failure to comply with the warrant requirement can only be excused by exigent circumstances. * * * But we deal here with an entire rubric of police conduct—necessarily swift action predicated upon the on-the-spot observations of the officer on the beat—which historically has not been, and as a practical matter could not be, subjected to the warrant procedure. Instead, the conduct involved in this case must be tested by the Fourth Amendment's general proscription against unreasonable searches and seizures.

Nonetheless, the notions which underlie both the warrant procedure and the requirement of probable cause remain fully relevant in this context. In order to assess the reasonableness of Officer McFadden's conduct as a general proposition, it is necessary "first to focus upon the governmental interest which allegedly justifies official intrusion upon the constitutionally protected interests of the private citizen," for there is "no ready test for determining reasonableness other than by balancing the need to search [or seize] against the invasion which the search [or seizure] entails." And in justifying the particular intrusion the police officer must be able to point to specific and articulable facts which, taken together with rational inferences from those facts, reasonably warrant that intrusion. The scheme of the Fourth Amendment becomes meaningful only when it is assured that at some point the conduct of those charged with enforcing the laws can be subjected to the more detached, neutral scrutiny of a judge who must evaluate the reasonableness of a particular search or seizure in light of the particular circumstances. And in making that assessment it is imperative that the facts be judged against an objective standard: would the facts available to the officer at the moment of the seizure or the search "warrant a man of reasonable caution in the belief" that the action taken was appropriate? * * * Anything less would invite intrusions upon constitutionally guaranteed rights based on nothing more substantial than inarticulate hunches, a result this Court has consistently refused to sanction. * * *

Applying these principles to this case, we consider first the nature and extent of the governmental interests involved. One general interest is of course that of effective crime prevention and detection; it is this interest which underlies the recognition that a police officer may in appropriate circumstances and in an appropriate manner approach a person for purposes of investigating possibly criminal behavior even though there is no probable cause to make an arrest. It was this legitimate investigative function Officer McFadden was discharging when he decided to approach petitioner and his companions. He had observed Terry, Chilton, and Katz go through a series of acts, each of them perhaps innocent in itself, but which taken together warranted further investigation. There is nothing unusual in two men standing together on a street corner, perhaps waiting for someone. Nor is there anything suspicious about people in such circumstances strolling up and down the street, singly or in pairs. Store windows, moreover, are made to be looked in. But the story is quite different where, as here, two men hover about a street corner for an extended period of time, at the end of which it becomes apparent that they are not waiting for anyone or anything; where these men pace alternately along an identical route, pausing to stare in the same store window roughly 24 times; where each completion of this route is followed immediately by a conference between the two men on the corner; where they are joined in one of these conferences by a third man who leaves swiftly; and where the two men finally follow the third and rejoin him a couple of blocks away. It would have been poor police work indeed for an officer of 30 years' experience in the detection of thievery from stores in this same neighborhood to have failed to investigate this behavior further.[a]

The crux of this case, however, is not the propriety of Officer McFadden's taking steps to investigate petitioner's suspicious behavior, but rather, whether there was justification for McFadden's invasion of Terry's personal security by searching him for weapons in the course of that investigation. We are now concerned with more than the governmental interest in investigating crime; in addition, there is the more immediate interest of the police officer in taking steps to assure himself that the person with whom he is dealing is not armed with a weapon that could unexpectedly and fatally be used against him. Certainly it would be unreasonable to require that police officers take unnecessary risks in the performance of their duties. American criminals have a long tradition of armed violence, and every year in this country many law enforcement officers are killed in the line of duty, and thousands more are wounded. Virtually all of these deaths and a substantial portion of the injuries are inflicted with guns and knives.

In view of these facts, we cannot blind ourselves to the need for law enforcement officers to protect themselves and other prospective victims of violence in situations where they may lack probable cause for an arrest. When an officer is justified in believing that the individual whose suspicious behavior

---

**a.** This does not mean that a *Terry* stop is never permissible upon suspicion of *past* criminal activity. In *United States v. Hensley*, 469 U.S. 221 (1985), rejecting the lower court's position that *Terry* is limited to ongoing criminal activity, the Court explained:

"The factors in the balance may be somewhat different when a stop to investigate past criminal activity is involved rather than a stop to investigate ongoing criminal conduct. This is because the governmental interest and the nature of the intrusions involved in the two situations may differ. As we noted in *Terry*, one general interest present in the context of ongoing or imminent criminal activity is 'that of effective crime prevention and detection.' A stop to investigate an already completed crime does not necessarily promote the interest of crime prevention as directly as a stop to investigate suspected ongoing criminal activity. Similarly, the exigent circumstances which require a police officer to step in before a crime is committed or completed are not necessarily as pressing long afterwards. Public safety may be less threatened by a suspect in a past crime who now appears to be going about his lawful business than it is by a suspect who is currently in the process of violating the law. Finally, officers making a stop to investigate past crimes may have a wider range of opportunity to choose the time and circumstances of the stop.

"Despite these differences, where police have been unable to locate a person suspected of involvement in a past crime, the ability to briefly stop that person, ask questions, or check identification in the absence of probable cause promotes the strong government interest in solving crimes and bringing offenders to justice. Restraining police action until after probable cause is obtained would not only hinder the investigation, but might also enable the suspect to flee in the interim and to remain at large. Particularly in the context of felonies or crimes involving a threat to public safety, it is in the public interest that the crime be solved and the suspect detained as promptly as possible. The law enforcement interests at stake in these circumstances outweigh the individual's interest to be free of a stop and detention that is no more extensive than permissible in the investigation of imminent or ongoing crimes.

"We need not and do not decide today whether *Terry* stops to investigate all past crimes, however serious, are permitted. It is enough to say that, if police have a reasonable suspicion, grounded in specific and articulable facts, that a person they encounter was involved in or is wanted in connection with a completed felony, then a *Terry* stop may be made to investigate that suspicion."

he is investigating at close range is armed and presently dangerous to the officer or to others, it would appear to be clearly unreasonable to deny the officer the power to take necessary measures to determine whether the person is in fact carrying a weapon and to neutralize the threat of physical harm. ⁎ ⁎ ⁎

Petitioner ⁎ ⁎ ⁎ does not say that an officer is always unjustified in searching a suspect to discover weapons. Rather, he says it is unreasonable for the policeman to take that step until such time as the situation evolves to a point where there is probable cause to make an arrest. ⁎ ⁎ ⁎

There are two weaknesses in this line of reasoning however. First, it fails to take account of traditional limitations upon the scope of searches, and thus recognizes no distinction in purpose, character, and extent between a search incident to an arrest and a limited search for weapons. The former, although justified in part by the acknowledged necessity to protect the arresting officer from assault with a concealed weapon, is also justified on other grounds, and can therefore involve a relatively extensive exploration of the person. A search for weapons in the absence of probable cause to arrest, however, must, like any other search, be strictly circumscribed by the exigencies which justify its initiation. Thus it must be limited to that which is necessary for the discovery of weapons which might be used to harm the officer or others nearby, and may realistically be characterized as something less than a "full" search, even though it remains a serious intrusion.

A second, and related, objection to petitioner's argument is that it assumes that the law of arrest has already worked out the balance between the particular interests involved here—the neutralization of danger to the policeman in the investigative circumstance and the sanctity of the individual. But this is not so. An arrest is a wholly different kind of intrusion upon individual freedom from a limited search for weapons, and the interests each is designed to serve are likewise quite different. An arrest is the initial stage of a criminal prosecution. It is intended to vindicate society's interest in having its laws obeyed, and it is inevitably accompanied by future interference with the individual's freedom of movement, whether or not trial or conviction ultimately follows. The protective search for weapons, on the other hand, constitutes a brief, though far from inconsiderable intrusion upon the sanctity of the person. It does not follow that because an officer may lawfully arrest a person only when he is apprised of facts sufficient to warrant a belief that the person has committed or is committing a crime, the officer is equally unjustified, absent that kind of evidence, in making any intrusions short of an arrest. Moreover, a perfectly reasonable apprehension of danger may arise long before the officer is possessed of adequate information to justify taking a person into custody for the purpose of prosecuting him for a crime. ⁎ ⁎ ⁎

Our evaluation of the proper balance that has to be struck in this type of case leads us to conclude that there must be a narrowly drawn authority to permit a reasonable search for weapons for the protection of the police officer, where he has reason to believe that he is dealing with an armed and dangerous individual, regardless of whether he has probable cause to arrest the individual for a crime. The officer need not be absolutely certain that the individual is armed; the issue is whether a reasonably prudent man in the circumstances would be warranted in the belief that his safety or that of others was in danger. ⁎ ⁎ ⁎ And in determining whether the officer acted reasonably in such circumstances, due weight must be given, not to his inchoate and unparticularized suspicion or "hunch", but to the specific reasonable inferences which he is entitled to draw from the facts in light of his experience.

We must now examine the conduct of Officer McFadden in this case to determine whether his search and seizure of petitioner were reasonable, both at their inception and as conducted. He had observed Terry, together with Chilton and another man, acting in a manner he took to be preface to a "stick-up." We think on the facts and circumstances Officer McFadden detailed before the trial judge a reasonably prudent man would have been warranted in believing petitioner was armed and thus presented a threat to the officer's safety while he was investigating his suspicious behavior. The actions of Terry and Chilton were consistent with McFadden's hypothesis that these men were contemplating a daylight robbery—which, it is reasonable to assume, would be likely to involve the use of weapons—and nothing in their conduct from the time he first noticed them until the time he confronted them and identified himself as a police officer gave him sufficient reason to negate that hypothesis. Although the trio had departed the original scene, there was nothing to indicate abandonment of an intent to commit a robbery at some point. Thus, when Officer McFadden approached the three men gathered before the display window at Zucker's store he had observed enough to make it quite reasonable to fear that they were armed; and nothing in their response to his hailing them, identifying himself as a police officer, and asking their names served to dispel that reasonable belief. We cannot say his decision at that point to seize Terry and pat his clothing for weapons was the product of a volatile or inventive imagination, or was undertaken simply as an act of harassment; the record evidences the tempered act of a policeman who in the course of an investigation had to make a quick decision as to how to protect himself and others from possible danger, and took limited steps to do so.

The manner in which the seizure and search were conducted is, of course, as vital a part of the inquiry as whether they were warranted at all. The Fourth Amendment proceeds as much by limitations upon the scope of governmental action as by imposing preconditions upon its initiation. The entire deterrent purpose of the rule excluding evidence seized in violation of the Fourth Amendment rests on the assumption that "limitations upon the fruit to be gathered tend to limit the quest itself." * * * Thus, evidence may not be introduced if it was discovered by means of a seizure and search which were not reasonably related in scope to the justification for their initiation.

[A protective search for weapons,] unlike a search without a warrant incident to a lawful arrest, is not justified by any need to prevent the disappearance or destruction of evidence of crime. The sole justification of the search in the present situation is the protection of the police officer and others nearby, and it must therefore be confined in scope to an intrusion reasonably designed to discover guns, knives, clubs, or other hidden instruments for the assault of the police officer.

The scope of the search in this case presents no serious problem in light of these standards. Officer McFadden patted down the outer clothing of petitioner and his two companions. He did not place his hands in their pockets or under the outer surface of their garments until he had felt weapons, and then he merely reached for and removed the guns. He never did invade Katz's person beyond the outer surfaces of his clothes, since he discovered nothing in his pat down which might have been a weapon. Officer McFadden confined his search strictly to what was minimally necessary to learn whether the men were armed and to disarm them once he discovered the weapons. He did not conduct a general exploratory search for whatever evidence of criminal activity he might find.

We conclude that the revolver seized from Terry was properly admitted in evidence against him. At the time he seized petitioner and searched him for weapons, Officer McFadden had reasonable grounds to believe that petitioner was armed and dangerous, and it was necessary for the protection of himself and others to take swift measures to discover the true facts and neutralize the threat of harm if it materialized. The policeman carefully restricted his search to what was appropriate to the discovery of the particular items which he sought. Each case of this sort will, of course, have to be decided on its own facts. We merely hold today that where a police officer observes unusual conduct which leads him reasonably to conclude in light of his experience that criminal activity may be afoot and that the persons with whom he is dealing may be armed and presently dangerous; where in the course of investigating this behavior he identifies himself as a policeman and makes reasonable inquiries; and where nothing in the initial stages of the encounter serves to dispel his reasonable fear for his own or others' safety, he is entitled for the protection of himself and others in the area to conduct a carefully limited search of the outer clothing of such persons [b] in an attempt to discover weapons which might be used to assault him. Such a search is a reasonable search under the Fourth Amendment, and any weapons

---

**b.** *Michigan v. Long,* 463 U.S. 1032 (1983), extended the self-protective search principle of *Terry* to search of a vehicle. Two deputies saw a car swerve into a ditch and stopped to investigate. Long, the only occupant of the car, met the deputies at the rear of the car, supplied his driver's license upon demand, and started back toward the open door when asked for his vehicle registration. The officers saw a large hunting knife on the floorboard, so Long was frisked and one officer then entered the vehicle and found an open pouch of marijuana under an armrest. The Court concluded "that the search of the passenger compartment of an automobile, limited to those areas in which a weapon may be placed or hidden, is permissible if the police officer possesses a reasonable belief based on 'specific and articulable facts which, taken together with the rational inferences from those facts, reasonably warrant' the officers in believing that the suspect is dangerous and the suspect may gain immediate control of weapons." In explaining why this was such a case, the Court stated:

"The Michigan Supreme Court appeared to believe that it was not reasonable for the officers to fear that Long could injure them, because he was effectively under their control during the investigative stop and could not get access to any weapons that might have been located in the automobile. This reasoning is mistaken in several respects. During any investigative detention, the suspect is 'in the control' of the officers in the sense that he 'may be briefly detained against his will * * *.' Just as a *Terry* suspect on the street may, despite being under the brief control of a police officer, reach into his clothing and retrieve a weapon, so might a *Terry* suspect in Long's position break away from police control and retrieve a weapon from his automobile. In addition, if the suspect is not placed under

arrest, he will be permitted to reenter his automobile, and he will then have access to any weapons inside. Or, as here, the suspect may be permitted to reenter the vehicle before the *Terry* investigation is over, and again, may have access to weapons. In any event, we stress that a *Terry* investigation, such as the one that occurred here, involves a police investigation 'at close range,' when the officer remains particularly vulnerable in part *because* a full custodial arrest has not been effected, and the officer must make a 'quick decision as to how to protect himself and others from possible danger * * *.' In such circumstances, we have not required that officers adopt alternative means to ensure their safety in order to avoid the intrusion involved in a *Terry* encounter."

Brennan and Marshall, JJ., dissenting, objected: "Putting aside the fact that the search at issue here involved a far more serious intrusion than that 'involved in a *Terry* encounter,' and as such might suggest the need for resort to 'alternate means,' the Court's reasoning is perverse. The Court's argument in essence is that the *absence* of probable cause to arrest compels the conclusion that a broad search, traditionally associated in scope with a search incident to arrest, must be permitted based on reasonable suspicion. But *United States v. Robinson* stated: 'It is scarcely open to doubt that the danger to an officer is far greater in the case of the extended exposure which follows the taking of a suspect into custody and transporting him to the police station than in the case of the relatively fleeting contact resulting from the typical *Terry*-type stop.' In light of *Robinson*'s observation, today's holding leaves in grave doubt the question of whether the Court's assessment of the relative dangers posed by given confrontations is based on any principled standard."

seized may properly be introduced in evidence against the person from whom they were taken.

Affirmed.

JUSTICE HARLAN, concurring.

* * * The holding has * * * two logical corollaries that I do not think the Court has fully expressed.

In the first place, if the frisk is justified in order to protect the officer during an encounter with a citizen, the officer must first have constitutional grounds to insist on an encounter, to make a *forcible* stop. Any person, including a policeman, is at liberty to avoid a person he considers dangerous. If and when a policeman has a right instead to disarm such a person for his own protection, he must first have a right not to avoid him but to be in his presence. That right must be more than the liberty (again, possessed by every citizen) to address questions to other persons, for ordinarily the person addressed has an equal right to ignore his interrogator and walk away; he certainly need not submit to a frisk for the questioner's protection. I would make it perfectly clear that the right to frisk in this case depends upon the reasonableness of a forcible stop to investigate a suspected crime.

Where such a stop is reasonable, however, the right to frisk must be immediate and automatic if the reason for the stop is, as here, an articulable suspicion of a crime of violence. Just as a full search incident to a lawful arrest requires no additional justification, a limited frisk incident to a lawful stop must often be rapid and routine. There is no reason why an officer, rightfully but forcibly confronting a person suspected of a serious crime, should have to ask one question and take the risk that the answer might be a bullet. * * *

JUSTICE WHITE, concurring.

* * * I think an additional word is in order concerning the matter of interrogation during an investigative stop. There is nothing in the Constitution which prevents a policeman from addressing questions to anyone on the streets. Absent special circumstances, the person approached may not be detained or frisked but may refuse to cooperate and go on his way. However, given the proper circumstances, such as those in this case, it seems to me the person may be briefly detained against his will while pertinent questions are directed to him. Of course, the person stopped is not obliged to answer, answers may not be compelled, and refusal to answer furnishes no basis for an arrest, although it may alert the officer to the need for continued observation. * * *

JUSTICE DOUGLAS, dissenting.

* * * Had a warrant been sought, a magistrate would, therefore, have been unauthorized to issue one, for he can act only if there is a showing of "probable cause." We hold today that the police have greater authority to make a "seizure" and conduct a "search" than a judge has to authorize such action. We have said precisely the opposite over and over again. * * *

The infringement on personal liberty of any "seizure" of a person can only be "reasonable" under the Fourth Amendment if we require the police to possess "probable cause" before they seize him. Only that line draws a meaningful distinction between an officer's mere inkling and the presence of facts within the officer's personal knowledge which would convince a reasonable man that the person seized has committed, is committing, or is about to commit a particular crime. * * *

## FLORIDA v. ROYER

460 U.S. 491, 103 S.Ct. 1319, 75 L.Ed.2d 229 (1983).

JUSTICE WHITE announced the judgment of the Court and delivered an opinion, in which JUSTICE MARSHALL, JUSTICE POWELL, and JUSTICE STEVENS joined.

[After purchasing a one-way airline ticket to New York City at Miami International Airport under an assumed name and checking his two suitcases bearing identification tags with the same assumed name, respondent went to the concourse leading to the airline boarding area, where he was approached by two detectives, who previously had observed him and believed that his characteristics fit the so-called "drug courier profile." Upon request, but without oral consent, respondent produced his airline ticket and driver's license, which carried his correct name. When the detectives asked about the discrepancy in names, respondent explained that a friend had made the ticket reservation in the assumed name. The detectives then informed respondent that they were narcotics investigators and that they had reason to suspect him of transporting narcotics, and, without returning his airline ticket or driver's license, asked him to accompany them to a small room adjacent to the concourse. Without respondent's consent, one of the detectives retrieved respondent's luggage from the airline and brought it to the room. While he did not respond to the detectives' request that he consent to a search of the luggage, respondent produced a key and unlocked one of the suitcases in which marihuana was found. When respondent said he did not know the combination to the lock on the second suitcase but did not object to its being opened, the officers pried it open and found more marihuana. Respondent was then told he was under arrest. Following the Florida trial court's denial of his pretrial motion to suppress the evidence obtained in the search of the suitcases, respondent was convicted of felony possession of marihuana. The Florida District Court of Appeal reversed, holding that respondent had been involuntarily confined within the small room without probable cause, that at the time his consent to search was obtained, the involuntary detention had exceeded the limited restraint permitted by *Terry v. Ohio*, and that such consent was therefore invalid because tainted by the unlawful confinement.]

Some preliminary observations are in order. First, it is unquestioned that without a warrant to search Royer's luggage and in the absence of probable cause and exigent circumstances, the validity of the search depended on Royer's purported consent. Neither is it disputed that where the validity of a search rests on consent, the State has the burden of proving that the necessary consent was obtained and that it was freely and voluntarily given, a burden that is not satisfied by showing a mere submission to a claim of lawful authority.

Second, law enforcement officers do not violate the Fourth Amendment by merely approaching an individual on the street or in another public place, by asking him if he is willing to answer some questions, by putting questions to him if the person is willing to listen, or by offering in evidence in a criminal prosecution his voluntary answers to such questions. Nor would the fact that the officer identifies himself as a police officer, without more, convert the encounter into a seizure requiring some level of objective justification. The person approached, however, need not answer any question put to him; indeed, he may decline to listen to the questions at all and may go on his way. He may not be detained even momentarily without reasonable, objective grounds for doing so; and his refusal to listen or answer does not, without more, furnish those grounds.  If there is no detention—no seizure within the meaning of the Fourth Amendment—then no constitutional rights have been infringed.

Third, it is also clear that not all seizures of the person must be justified by probable cause to arrest for a crime.  *  *  *  *  *  *  *  *  *  *  *  Terry created a limited exception to this general rule: certain seizures are justifiable under the Fourth Amendment if there is articulable suspicion that a person has committed or is about to commit a crime.  *  *  *  Royer does not suggest, nor do we, that a similar rationale would not warrant temporary detention for questioning on less than probable cause where the public interest involved is the suppression of illegal transactions in drugs or of any other serious crime.  *  *  *

Fourth, Terry and its progeny nevertheless created only limited exceptions to the general rule that seizures of the person require probable cause to arrest. Detentions may be "investigative" yet violative of the Fourth Amendment absent probable cause.  In the name of investigating a person who is no more than suspected of criminal activity, the police may not carry out a full search of the person or of his automobile or other effects.  Nor may the police seek to verify their suspicions by means that approach the conditions of arrest.  *Dunaway v. New York*, [442 U.S. 200 (1979)], made this clear.  There, the suspect was taken to the police station from his home and, without being formally arrested, interrogated for an hour.  The resulting incriminating statements were held inadmissible: reasonable suspicion of crime is insufficient to justify custodial interrogation even though the interrogation is investigative.[a]

The Fourth Amendment's prohibition against unreasonable searches and seizures has always been interpreted to prevent a search that is not limited to the particularly described "place to be searched, and the persons or things to be seized," even if the search is made pursuant to a warrant and based upon

---

**a.**  This is not to suggest that all at-the-station investigation must be on full probable cause.  In *Davis v. Mississippi*, 394 U.S. 721 (1969), petitioner and 24 other black youths were detained for questioning and fingerprinting in connection with a rape for which the only leads were a general description given by the victim and a set of fingerprints around the window through which the assailant entered. Petitioner's prints were found to match those at the scene of the crime, and this evidence was admitted at his trial.  The Court, per Brennan, J., held that the prints should have been excluded as the fruits of a seizure of petitioner in violation of the Fourth Amendment, but intimated that a detention for such a purpose might sometimes be permissible on evidence insufficient for arrest:

"Detentions for the sole purpose of obtaining fingerprints are no less subject to the constraints of the Fourth Amendment.  It is arguable, however, that because of the unique nature of the fingerprinting process, such detentions might, under narrowly defined circumstances, be found to comply with the Fourth Amendment even though there is no probable cause in the traditional sense.  Detention for fingerprinting may constitute a much less serious intrusion upon personal security than other types of police searches and detentions.  Fingerprinting involves none of the probing into an individual's private life and thoughts which marks an interrogation or

search.  Nor can fingerprint detention be employed repeatedly to harass any individual, since the police need only one set of each person's prints.  Furthermore, fingerprinting is an inherently more reliable and effective crime-solving tool than eyewitness identifications or confessions and is not subject to such abuses as the improper line-up and the 'third degree.'  Finally, because there is no danger of destruction of fingerprints, the limited detention need not come unexpectedly or at an inconvenient time.  For this same reason, the general requirement that the authorization of a judicial officer be obtained in advance of detention would seem not to admit of any exception in the fingerprinting context.

"We have no occasion in this case, however, to determine whether the requirements of the Fourth Amendment could be met by narrowly circumscribed procedures for obtaining, during the course of a criminal investigation, the fingerprints of individuals for whom there is no probable cause to arrest.  For it is clear that no attempt was made here to employ procedures which might comply with the requirements of the Fourth Amendment: the detention at police headquarters of petitioner and the other young Negroes was not authorized by a judicial officer; petitioner was unnecessarily required to undergo two fingerprinting sessions; and petitioner was not merely fingerprinted during the December 3 detention but also subjected to interrogation."

probable cause. The Amendment's protection is not diluted in those situations where it has been determined that legitimate law enforcement interests justify a warrantless search: the search must be limited in scope to that which is justified by the particular purposes served by the exception. * * * The reasonableness requirement of the Fourth Amendment requires no less when the police action is a seizure permitted on less than probable cause because of legitimate law enforcement interests. The scope of the detention must be carefully tailored to its underlying justification.

The predicate permitting seizures on suspicion short of probable cause is that law enforcement interests warrant a limited intrusion on the personal security of the suspect. The scope of the intrusion permitted will vary to some extent with the particular facts and circumstances of each case. This much, however, is clear: an investigative detention must be temporary and last no longer than is necessary to effectuate the purpose of the stop. Similarly, the investigative methods employed should be the least intrusive means reasonably available to verify or dispel the officer's suspicion in a short period of time.[b] It is the State's burden to demonstrate that the seizure it seeks to justify on the basis of a reasonable suspicion was sufficiently limited in scope and duration to satisfy the conditions of an investigative seizure.

Fifth, statements given during a period of illegal detention are inadmissible even though voluntarily given if they are the product of the illegal detention and not the result of an independent act of free will. * * *

Sixth, if the events in this case amounted to no more than a permissible police encounter in a public place or a justifiable *Terry*-type detention, Royer's consent, if voluntary, would have been effective to legalize the search of his two suitcases. * * *

The State proffers three reasons for holding that when Royer consented to the search of his luggage, he was not being illegally detained. First, it is submitted that the entire encounter was consensual and hence Royer was not being held against his will at all. We find this submission untenable. Asking for and examining Royer's ticket and his driver's license were no doubt permissible in themselves, but when the officers identified themselves as narcotics agents, told Royer that he was suspected of transporting narcotics, and asked him to accompany them to the police room, while retaining his ticket and driver's license and without indicating in any way that he was free to depart, Royer was effectively seized for the purposes of the Fourth Amendment. These circumstances surely amount to a show of official authority such that "a reasonable person would have believed that he was not free to leave."

Second, the State submits that if Royer was seized, there existed reasonable, articulable suspicion to justify a temporary detention and that the limits of a *Terry*-type stop were never exceeded. We agree with the State that when the

---

**b.** But in *United States v. Sharpe,* 470 U.S. 675 (1985), the Court cautioned:

"In assessing whether a detention is too long in duration to be justified as an investigative stop, we consider it appropriate to examine whether the police diligently pursued a means of investigation that was likely to confirm or dispel their suspicions quickly, during which time it was necessary to detain the defendant. A court making this assessment should take care to consider whether the police are acting in a swiftly developing situation, and in such cases the court should not indulge in unrealistic second-guessing. A creative judge engaged in *post hoc* evaluation of police conduct can almost always imagine some alternative means by which the objectives of the police might have been accomplished. But '[t]he fact that the protection of the public might, in the abstract, have been accomplished by "less intrusive" means does not, in itself, render the search unreasonable.' The question is not simply whether some other alternative was available, but whether the police acted unreasonably in failing to recognize or to pursue it."

officers discovered that Royer was traveling under an assumed name, this fact, and the facts already known to the officers—paying cash for a one-way ticket, the mode of checking the two bags, and Royer's appearance and conduct in general—were adequate grounds for suspecting Royer of carrying drugs and for temporarily detaining him and his luggage while they attempted to verify or dispel their suspicions in a manner that did not exceed the limits of an investigative detention. We also agree that had Royer voluntarily consented to the search of his luggage while he was justifiably being detained on reasonable suspicion, the products of the search would be admissible against him. We have concluded, however, that at the time Royer produced the key to his suitcase, the detention to which he was then subjected was a more serious intrusion on his personal liberty than is allowable on mere suspicion of criminal activity.

By the time Royer was informed that the officers wished to examine his luggage, he had identified himself when approached by the officers and had attempted to explain the discrepancy between the name shown on his identification and the name under which he had purchased his ticket and identified his luggage. The officers were not satisfied, for they informed him they were narcotics agents and had reason to believe that he was carrying illegal drugs. They requested him to accompany them to the police room. Royer went with them. He found himself in a small room—a large closet—equipped with a desk and two chairs. He was alone with two police officers who again told him that they thought he was carrying narcotics. He also found that the officers, without his consent, had retrieved his checked luggage from the airline. What had begun as a consensual inquiry in a public place had escalated into an investigatory procedure in a police interrogation room, where the police, unsatisfied with previous explanations, sought to confirm their suspicions. The officers had Royer's ticket, they had his identification, and they had seized his luggage. Royer was never informed that he was free to board his plane if he so chose, and he reasonably believed that he was being detained. At least as of that moment, any consensual aspects of the encounter had evaporated, and we cannot fault the Florida District Court of Appeal for concluding that *Terry v. Ohio* and the cases following it did not justify the restraint to which Royer was then subjected. As a practical matter, Royer was under arrest. Consistent with this conclusion, the State conceded in the Florida courts that Royer would not have been free to leave the interrogation room had he asked to do so. Furthermore, the State's brief in this Court interprets the testimony of the officers at the suppression hearing as indicating that had Royer refused to consent to a search of his luggage, the officers would have held the luggage and sought a warrant to authorize the search.

We also think that the officers' conduct was more intrusive than necessary to effectuate an investigative detention otherwise authorized by the *Terry* line of cases. First, by returning his ticket and driver's license, and informing him that he was free to go if he so desired, the officers might have obviated any claim that the encounter was anything but a consensual matter from start to finish. Second, there are undoubtedly reasons of safety and security that would justify moving a suspect from one location to another during an investigatory detention, such as from an airport concourse to a more private area. There is no indication in this case that such reasons prompted the officers to transfer the site of the encounter from the concourse to the interrogation room. It appears, rather, that the primary interest of the officers was not in having an extended conversation with Royer but in the contents of his luggage, a matter which the officers did not pursue orally with Royer until after the encounter was relocated to the police room. The record does not reflect any facts which would support a finding that the legitimate law enforcement purposes which justified the detention in the first instance were furthered by removing Royer to the police room prior to the officer's attempt to gain his consent to a search of his luggage. As we have noted, had Royer consented to a search on the spot, the search could have been conducted with Royer present in the area where the bags were retrieved by Detective Johnson and any evidence recovered would have been admissible against him. If the search proved negative, Royer would have been free to go much earlier and with less likelihood of missing his flight, which in itself can be a very serious matter in a variety of circumstances.

Third, the State has not touched on the question whether it would have been feasible to investigate the contents of Royer's bags in a more expeditious way. The courts are not strangers to the use of trained dogs to detect the presence of controlled substances in luggage. There is no indication here that this means was not feasible and available. If it had been used, Royer and his luggage could have been momentarily detained while this investigative procedure was carried out. Indeed, it may be that no detention at all would have been necessary. A negative result would have freed Royer in short order; a positive result would have resulted in his justifiable arrest on probable cause.

We do not suggest that there is a litmus-paper test for distinguishing a consensual encounter from a seizure or for determining when a seizure exceeds the bounds of an investigative stop. Even in the discrete category of airport encounters, there will be endless variations in the facts and circumstances, so much variation that it is unlikely that the courts can reduce to a sentence or a paragraph a rule that will provide unarguable answers to the question whether there has been an unreasonable search or seizure in violation of the Fourth Amendment. Nevertheless, we must render judgment, and we think that the Florida District Court of Appeal cannot be faulted in concluding that the limits of a *Terry*-stop had been exceeded.

The State's third and final argument is that Royer was not being illegally held when he gave his consent because there was probable cause to arrest him at that time. Detective Johnson testified at the suppression hearing and the Florida District Court of Appeal held that there was no probable cause to arrest until Royer's bags were opened, but the fact that the officers did not believe there was probable cause and proceeded on a consensual or *Terry*-stop rationale would not foreclose the State from justifying Royer's custody by proving probable cause and hence removing any barrier to relying on Royer's consent to search. We agree with the Florida District Court of Appeal, however, that probable cause to arrest Royer did not exist at the time he consented to the search of his luggage. The facts are that a nervous young man with two American Tourister bags paid cash for an airline ticket to a "target city". These facts led to inquiry, which in turn revealed that the ticket had been bought under an assumed name. The proffered explanation did not satisfy the officers. We cannot agree with the State, if this is its position, that every nervous young man paying cash for a ticket to New York City under an assumed name and carrying two heavy American Tourister bags may be arrested and held to answer for a serious felony charge.

Because we affirm the Florida District Court of Appeal's conclusion that Royer was being illegally detained when he consented to the search of his luggage, we agree that the consent was tainted by the illegality and was ineffective to justify the search. The judgment of the Florida District Court of Appeal is accordingly affirmed.[c]

JUSTICE BRENNAN, concurring in the result. *  *  *

To the extent that the plurality endorses the legality of the officers' initial stop of Royer, it was wholly unnecessary to reach that question. For even assuming the legality of the initial stop, the plurality correctly holds, and I agree, that the officers' subsequent actions clearly exceeded the permissible bounds of a *Terry* "investigative" stop. *  *  *

The scope of a *Terry*-type "investigative" stop and any attendant search must be extremely limited or the *Terry* exception would "swallow the general rule that Fourth Amendment seizures [and searches] are 'reasonable' only if based on probable cause." In my view, any suggestion that the *Terry* reasonable-suspicion standard justifies anything but the briefest of detentions or the most limited of searches finds no support in the *Terry* line of cases.[*]

In any event, I dissent from the plurality's view that the initial stop of Royer was legal. For plainly Royer was "seized" for purposes of the Fourth Amendment when the officers asked him to produce his driver's license and airline ticket. *  *  * By identifying themselves and asking for Royer's airline ticket and driver's license the officers, as a practical matter, engaged in a "show of authority" and "restrained [Royer's] liberty." It is simply wrong to suggest that a traveler feels free to walk away when he has been approached by individuals who have identified themselves as police officers and asked for, and received, his airline ticket and driver's license. *  *  *

JUSTICE BLACKMUN, dissenting.

*  *  * In my view, the police conduct in this case was minimally intrusive. Given the strength of society's interest in overcoming the extraordinary obstacles to the detection of drug traffickers, such conduct should not be subjected to a requirement of probable cause. Because the Court holds otherwise, I dissent. *  *  *

At the suppression hearing in this case, Royer agreed that he was not formally arrested until after his suitcases were opened. In my view, it cannot fairly be said that, prior to the formal arrest, the functional equivalent of an arrest had taken place. The encounter had far more in common with automobile stops justifiable on reasonable suspicion, than with the detention deemed the functional equivalent of a formal arrest in *Dunaway v. New York*. In *Dunaway*, the suspect was taken from his neighbor's home and involuntarily transported to the police station in a squad car. At the precinct house, he was placed in an interrogation room and subjected to extended custodial interrogation. Here, Royer was not taken from a private residence, where reasonable expectations of privacy perhaps are at their greatest. Instead, he was approached in a major international airport where, due in part to extensive antihijacking surveillance and equipment, reasonable privacy expectations are of significantly lesser magnitude, certainly no greater than the reasonable privacy expectations of travelers in automobiles. *  *  *

c. Justice Powell's concurring opinion (in which he noted that he "join[ed] the plurality opinion") is omitted.

* I interpret the plurality's requirement that the investigative methods employed pursuant to a *Terry* stop be "the least intrusive means reasonably available to verify or dispel the officer's suspicion in a short period of time," to mean that the availability of a less intrusive means may make an otherwise reasonable stop unreasonable. I do not interpret it to mean that the absence of a less intrusive means can make an otherwise unreasonable stop reasonable. *  *  *

What followed was within the scope of the lesser intrusions approved on less than probable cause in our prior cases, and was far removed from the circumstances of *Dunaway.*  \* \* \* Like Justice Rehnquist, I do not understand the plurality to dispute that Royer consented to go to the police room. Because the detention up to this point was not unlawful, the voluntariness of Royer's consent is to be judged on the totality of the circumstances.

Justice Rehnquist, with whom The Chief Justice and Justice O'Connor join, dissenting. \* \* \*

The point at which I part company with the plurality's opinion is in the assessment of the reasonableness of the officers' conduct following their initial conversation with Royer. The plurality focuses on the transfer of the place of the interview from the main concourse of the airport to the room off the concourse and observes that Royer "found himself in a small room—a large closet—equipped with a desk and two chairs. He was alone with two police officers who again told him that they thought he was carrying narcotics. He also found that the officers, without his consent, had retrieved his checked luggage from the airlines."

Obviously, this quoted language is intended to convey stern disapproval of the described conduct of the officers. To my mind, it merits no such disapproval and was eminently reasonable. Would it have been preferable for the officers to have detained Royer for further questioning, as they concededly had a right to do, without paying any attention to the fact that his luggage had already been checked on the flight to New York, and might be put aboard the flight even though Royer himself was not on the plane? Would it have been more "reasonable" to interrogate Royer about the contents of his suitcases, and to seek his permission to open the suitcases when they were retrieved, in the busy main concourse of the Miami Airport, rather than to find a room off the concourse where the confrontation would surely be less embarrassing to Royer? If the room had been large and spacious, rather than small, if it had possessed three chairs rather than two, would the officers' conduct have been made reasonable by these facts?

The plurality's answers to these questions, to the extent that it attempts any, are scarcely satisfying. It commences with the observation that "the officers' conduct was more intrusive than necessary to effectuate an investigative detention otherwise authorized by the *Terry* line of cases." \* \* \*

All of this to my mind adds up to little more than saying that if my aunt were a man, she would be my uncle. The officers might have taken different steps than they did to investigate Royer, but the same may be said of virtually every investigative encounter that has more than one step to it. The question we must decide is what was *unreasonable* about the steps which *these officers* took with respect to *this* suspect in the Miami Airport on this particular day. \* \* \*

But since even the plurality concedes that there was articulable suspicion warranting an investigatory detention, the fact that the inquiry had become an "investigatory procedure in a police interrogation room" would seem to have little bearing on the proper disposition of a claim that the officers violated the Fourth Amendment. \* \* \*

The reasonableness of the officers' activity in this case did not depend on Royer's consent to the investigation. Nevertheless, the presence of consent further justifies the action taken. The plurality does not seem to dispute that

Royer consented to go to the room in the first instance. Certainly that conclusion is warranted by the totality of the circumstances. * * *

[I]f Royer was legally approached in the first instance and consented to accompany the detectives to the room, it does not follow that his consent went up in smoke and he was "arrested" upon entering the room. As we made clear in *Mendenhall*, logical analysis would focus on whether the environment in the room rendered the subsequent consent to a search of the luggage involuntary.

* * *

## UNITED STATES v. PLACE
462 U.S. 696, 103 S.Ct. 2637, 77 L.Ed.2d 110 (1983).

JUSTICE O'CONNOR delivered the opinion of the Court.

Respondent Raymond J. Place's behavior aroused the suspicions of law enforcement officers as he waited in line at the Miami International Airport to purchase a ticket to New York's La Guardia Airport. As Place proceeded to the gate for his flight, the agents approached him and requested his airline ticket and some identification. Place complied with the request and consented to a search of the two suitcases he had checked. Because his flight was about to depart, however, the agents decided not to search the luggage.

Prompted by Place's parting remark that he had recognized that they were police, the agents inspected the address tags on the checked luggage and noted discrepancies in the two street addresses. Further investigation revealed that neither address existed and that the telephone number Place had given the airline belonged to a third address on the same street. On the basis of their encounter with Place and this information, the Miami agents called Drug Enforcement Administration (DEA) authorities in New York to relay their information about Place.

Two DEA agents waited for Place at the arrival gate at La Guardia Airport in New York. There again, his behavior aroused the suspicion of the agents. After he had claimed his two bags and called a limousine, the agents decided to approach him. They identified themselves as federal narcotics agents, to which Place responded that he knew they were "cops" and had spotted them as soon as he had deplaned. One of the agents informed Place that, based on their own observations and information obtained from the Miami authorities, they believed that he might be carrying narcotics. After identifying the bags as belonging to him, Place stated that a number of police at the Miami Airport had surrounded him and searched his baggage. The agents responded that their information was to the contrary. The agents requested and received identification from Place—a New Jersey driver's license, on which the agents later ran a computer check that disclosed no offenses, and his airline ticket receipt. When Place refused to consent to a search of his luggage, one of the agents told him that they were going to take the luggage to a federal judge to try to obtain a search warrant and that Place was free to accompany them. Place declined, but obtained from one of the agents telephone numbers at which the agents could be reached.

The agents then took the bags to Kennedy Airport, where they subjected the bags to a "sniff test" by a trained narcotics detection dog. The dog reacted positively to the smaller of the two bags but ambiguously to the larger bag. Approximately 90 minutes had elapsed since the seizure of respondent's luggage. Because it was late on a Friday afternoon, the agents retained the luggage until Monday morning, when they secured a search warrant from a Magistrate for the smaller bag.   Upon opening that bag, the agents discovered 1,125 grams of cocaine.

Place was indicted for possession of cocaine with intent to distribute in violation of 21 U.S.C. § 841(a)(1).   In the District Court, Place moved to suppress the contents of the luggage seized from him at La Guardia Airport, claiming that the warrantless seizure of the luggage violated his Fourth Amendment rights. The District Court denied the motion.   *   *   *

On appeal of the conviction, the United States Court of Appeals for the Second Circuit reversed.   *   *   *

In this case, the Government asks us to recognize the reasonableness under the Fourth Amendment of warrantless seizures of personal luggage from the custody of the owner on the basis of less than probable cause, for the purpose of pursuing a limited course of investigation, short of opening the luggage, that would quickly confirm or dispel the authorities' suspicion.   Specifically, we are asked to apply the principles of *Terry v. Ohio* to permit such seizures on the basis of reasonable, articulable suspicion, premised on objective facts, that the luggage contains contraband or evidence of a crime.   In our view, such application is appropriate.   *   *   *

The exception to the probable-cause requirement for limited seizures of the person recognized in *Terry* and its progeny rests on a balancing of the competing interests to determine the reasonableness of the type of seizure involved within the meaning of "the Fourth Amendment's general proscription against unreasonable searches and seizures."   *   *   *

We examine first the governmental interest offered as a justification for a brief seizure of luggage from the suspect's custody for the purpose of pursuing a limited course of investigation.   The Government contends that, where the authorities possess specific and articulable facts warranting a reasonable belief that a traveler's luggage contains narcotics, the governmental interest in seizing the luggage briefly to pursue further investigation is substantial.   We agree.   *   *   *

Respondent suggests that, absent some special law enforcement interest such as officer safety, a generalized interest in law enforcement cannot justify an intrusion on an individual's Fourth Amendment interests in the absence of probable cause.   Our prior cases, however, do not support this proposition.   In *Terry*, we described the governmental interests supporting the initial seizure of the person as "effective crime prevention and detection; it is this interest which underlies the recognition that a police officer may in appropriate circumstances and in an appropriate manner approach a person for purposes of investigating possibly criminal behavior even though there is no probable cause to make an arrest."   *   *   *

Against this strong governmental interest, we must weigh the nature and extent of the intrusion upon the individual's Fourth Amendment rights when the police briefly detain luggage for limited investigative purposes.   On this point, respondent Place urges that the rationale for a *Terry* stop of the person is wholly inapplicable to investigative detentions of personalty.   Specifically, the *Terry* exception to the probable-cause requirement is premised on the notion that a *Terry*-type stop of the person is substantially less intrusive of a person's liberty interests than a formal arrest.   In the property context, however, Place urges, there are no degrees of intrusion.   Once the owner's property is seized, the dispossession is absolute.

We disagree.   The intrusion on possessory interests occasioned by a seizure of one's personal effects can vary both in its nature and extent.   The seizure may be made after the owner has relinquished control of the property to a third party or, as here, from the immediate custody and control of the owner. Moreover, the police may confine their investigation to an on-the-spot inquiry—for example, immediate exposure of the luggage to a trained narcotics detection dog—or transport the property to another location. Given the fact that seizures of property can vary in intrusiveness, some brief detentions of personal effects may be so minimally intrusive of Fourth Amendment interests that strong countervailing governmental interests will justify a seizure based only on specific articulable facts that the property contains contraband or evidence of a crime.

In sum, we conclude that when an officer's observations lead him reasonably to believe that a traveler is carrying luggage that contains narcotics, the principles of *Terry* and its progeny would permit the officer to detain the luggage briefly to investigate the circumstances that aroused his suspicion, provided that the investigative detention is properly limited in scope. * * *

* * * We therefore examine whether the agents' conduct in this case was such as to place the seizure within the general rule requiring probable cause for a seizure or within *Terry*'s exception to that rule.

At the outset, we must reject the Government's suggestion that the point at which probable cause for seizure of luggage from the person's presence becomes necessary is more distant than in the case of a *Terry* stop of the person himself. The premise of the Government's argument is that seizures of property are generally less intrusive than seizures of the person. While true in some circumstances, that premise is faulty on the facts we address in this case. The precise type of detention we confront here is seizure of personal luggage from the immediate possession of the suspect for the purpose of arranging exposure to a narcotics detection dog. Particularly in the case of detention of luggage within the traveler's immediate possession, the police conduct intrudes on both the suspect's possessory interest in his luggage as well as his liberty interest in proceeding with his itinerary. The person whose luggage is detained is technically still free to continue his travels or carry out other personal activities pending release of the luggage. Moreover, he is not subjected to the coercive atmosphere of a custodial confinement or to the public indignity of being personally detained. Nevertheless, such a seizure can effectively restrain the person since he is subjected to the possible disruption of his travel plans in order to remain with his luggage or to arrange for its return.[8] Therefore, when the police seize luggage from the suspect's custody, we think the limitations applicable to investigative detentions of the person should define the permissible scope of an investigative detention of the person's luggage on less than probable cause. Under this standard, it is clear that the police conduct here exceeded the permissible limits of a *Terry*-type investigative stop.

The length of the detention of respondent's luggage alone precludes the conclusion that the seizure was reasonable in the absence of probable cause. Although we have recognized the reasonableness of seizures longer than the momentary ones involved in *Terry*, the brevity of the invasion of the individual's Fourth Amendment interests is an important factor in determining whether the seizure is so minimally intrusive as to be justifiable on reasonable suspicion. Moreover, in assessing the effect of the length of the detention, we take into account whether the police diligently pursue their investigation. We note that

8. "At least when the authorities do not make it absolutely clear how they plan to reunite the suspect and his possessions at some future time and place, seizure of the object is tantamount to seizure of the person. This is because that person must either remain on the scene or else seemingly surrender his effects permanently to the police."

here the New York agents knew the time of Place's scheduled arrival at La Guardia, had ample time to arrange for their additional investigation at that location, and thereby could have minimized the intrusion on respondent's Fourth Amendment interests. Thus, although we decline to adopt any outside time limitation for a permissible *Terry* stop,[10] we have never approved a seizure of the person for the prolonged 90–minute period involved here and cannot do so on the facts presented by this case.

Although the 90–minute detention of respondent's luggage is sufficient to render the seizure unreasonable, the violation was exacerbated by the failure of the agents to accurately inform respondent of the place to which they were transporting his luggage, of the length of time he might be dispossessed, and of what arrangements would be made for return of the luggage if the investigation dispelled the suspicion. In short, we hold that the detention of respondent's luggage in this case went beyond the narrow authority possessed by police to detain briefly luggage reasonably suspected to contain narcotics. * * *

JUSTICE BRENNAN, with whom JUSTICE MARSHALL joins, concurring in the result. * * *

In this case, the officers' seizure of respondent and their later independent seizure of his luggage implicated separate Fourth Amendment interests. First, respondent had a protected interest in maintaining his personal security and privacy. *Terry* allows this interest to be overcome, and authorizes a limited intrusion, if the officers have reason to suspect that criminal activity is afoot. Second, respondent had a protected interest in retaining possession of his personal effects. While *Terry* may authorize seizures of personal effects incident to a lawful seizure of the person, nothing in the *Terry* line of cases authorizes the police to seize personal property, such as luggage, independent of the seizure of the person. Such seizures significantly expand the scope of a *Terry* stop and may not be effected on less than probable cause. Obviously, they also significantly expand the scope of the intrusion. * * *

In my view, as soon as the officers seized respondent's luggage, independent of their seizure of him, they exceeded the scope of a permissible *Terry* stop and violated respondent's Fourth Amendment rights. In addition, the officers' seizure of respondent's luggage violated the established rule that seizures of personal effects must be based on probable cause. Their actions, therefore, should not be upheld. * * *

JUSTICE BLACKMUN, with whom JUSTICE MARSHALL joins, concurring in the judgment. * * *

In providing guidance to other courts, we often include in our opinions material that, technically, constitutes dictum. I cannot fault the Court's desire to set guidelines for *Terry* seizures of luggage based on reasonable suspicion. I am concerned, however, with what appears to me to be an emerging tendency on the part of the Court to convert the *Terry* decision into a general statement that the Fourth Amendment requires only that any seizure be reasonable.[1] * * *

---

10. Cf. ALI, Model Code of Pre–Arraignment Procedure § 110.2(1) (1975) (recommending a maximum of 20 minutes for a *Terry* stop). We understand the desirability of providing law enforcement authorities with a clear rule to guide their conduct. Nevertheless, we question the wisdom of a rigid time limitation. Such a limit would undermine the equally important need to allow authorities to graduate their responses to the demands of any particular situation.

1. The Court states that the applicability of the *Terry* exception "rests on a balancing of the competing interests to determine the reasonableness of the type of seizure involved within the meaning of 'the Fourth Amendment's general proscription against unreasonable searches and seizures.' " quoting *Terry*.

# SECTION 8.  LESSER INTRUSIONS: INSPECTIONS AND REGULATORY SEARCHES

The Supreme Court and the lower courts have upheld a rather broad range of administrative inspections and so-called regulatory searches even when conducted without a warrant and without the traditional quantum of probable cause.  These decisions manifest further application of the *Camara* balancing test, previously considered as utilized in *Terry* to assay the discrete police practice of stop-and-frisk.  But *Camara* itself was an administrative inspection type of case, involving inspection of dwellings for housing code violations, and thus it is not surprising that this balancing process has since been utilized in various other administrative inspection or regulatory search contexts.

One difficult question presented in such cases is that of what *kind* of departure from the traditional probable cause requirement is permissible.  One kind of departure, which we have already confronted in *Terry* and which is also sometimes used in the present context as well, is to require individualized suspicion (typically referred to as reasonable suspicion) less compelling than is needed for the usual law enforcement search.  Illustrative are *O'Connor v. Ortega*, 107 S.Ct. 1492 (1987), authorizing search of a government employee's workplace for work-related reasons on reasonable suspicion;  and *New Jersey v. T.L.O.*, 469 U.S. 325 (1985), upholding search of a public school student on reasonable suspicion of a violation of school rules.  Another kind of departure is to require no individualized suspicion whatsoever, but instead to require that the inspections or searches be conducted pursuant to some neutral criteria which guard against arbitrary selection of those subjected to such procedures.  Illustrative are court decisions upholding airport security checks, driver's license check roadblocks, and, as in the immediately following Supreme Court decision, sobriety checkpoints.

## MICHIGAN DEPARTMENT OF STATE POLICE v. SITZ
___ U.S. ___, 110 S.Ct. 2481, ___ L.Ed.2d ___ (1990).

CHIEF JUSTICE REHNQUIST delivered the opinion of the Court. * * *

Under the guidelines [for a sobriety checkpoint pilot program established by the Department], checkpoints would be set up at selected sites along state roads. All vehicles passing through a checkpoint would be stopped and their drivers briefly examined for signs of intoxication.  In cases where a checkpoint officer detected signs of intoxication, the motorist would be directed to a location out of the traffic flow where an officer would check the motorist's driver's license and car registration and, if warranted, conduct further sobriety tests.  Should the field tests and the officer's observations suggest that the driver was intoxicated, an arrest would be made.  All other drivers would be permitted to resume their journey immediately.

The first—and to date the only—sobriety checkpoint operated under the program was conducted in Saginaw County with the assistance of the Saginaw

As the context of the quotation from *Terry* makes clear, however, this balancing to determine reasonableness occurs only under the exceptional circumstances that justify the *Terry* exception:

"But we deal here with an entire rubric of police conduct—necessarily swift action predicated upon the on-the-spot observa-tions of the officer on the beat—which historically has not been, and as a practical matter could not be, subjected to the warrant procedure.  Instead, the conduct involved in this case must be tested by the Fourth Amendment's general proscription against unreasonable searches and seizures."

County Sheriff's Department. During the hour-and-fifteen-minute duration of the checkpoint's operation, 126 vehicles passed through the checkpoint. The average delay for each vehicle was approximately 25 seconds. Two drivers were detained for field sobriety testing, and one of the two was arrested for driving under the influence of alcohol. A third driver who drove through without stopping was pulled over by an officer in an observation vehicle and arrested for driving under the influence.

On the day before the operation of the Saginaw County checkpoint, respondents filed a complaint in the Circuit Court of Wayne County seeking declaratory and injunctive relief from potential subjection to the checkpoints. Each of the respondents "is a licensed driver in the State of Michigan . . . who regularly travels throughout the State in his automobile." During pretrial proceedings, petitioners agreed to delay further implementation of the checkpoint program pending the outcome of this litigation.

After the trial, * * * the court ruled that the Michigan program violated the Fourth Amendment * * *. On appeal, the Michigan Court of Appeals affirmed * * *.

To decide this case the trial court performed a balancing test derived from our opinion in *Brown v. Texas,* 443 U.S. 47 (1979). * * *

As characterized by the Court of Appeals, the trial court's findings with respect to the balancing factors were that the State has "a grave and legitimate" interest in curbing drunken driving; that sobriety checkpoint programs are generally "ineffective" and, therefore, do not significantly further that interest; and that the checkpoints' "subjective intrusion" on individual liberties is substantial. * * *

In this Court respondents seek to defend the judgment in their favor by insisting that the balancing test derived from *Brown v. Texas,* was not the proper method of analysis. Respondents maintain that the analysis must proceed from a basis of probable cause or reasonable suspicion and rely for support on language from our decision last Term in *Treasury Employees v. Von Raab,* 489 U.S. ___ (1989). We said in *Von Raab:*

"Where a Fourth Amendment intrusion serves special governmental needs, beyond the normal need for law enforcement, it is necessary to balance the individual's privacy expectations against the Government's interests to determine whether it is impractical to require a warrant or some level of individualized suspicion in the particular context."

Respondents argue that there must be a showing of some special governmental need "beyond the normal need" for criminal law enforcement before a balancing analysis is appropriate, and that petitioners have demonstrated no such special need.

But it is perfectly plain from a reading of *Von Raab,* which cited and discussed with approval our earlier decision in *United States v. Martinez–Fuerte,* 428 U.S. 543 (1976), that it was in no way designed to repudiate our prior cases dealing with police stops of motorists on public highways. *Martinez–Fuerte,* which utilized a balancing analysis in approving highway checkpoints for detecting illegal aliens, and *Brown v. Texas,* are the relevant authorities here.

Petitioners concede, correctly in our view, that a Fourth Amendment "seizure" occurs when a vehicle is stopped at a checkpoint. * * * The question thus becomes whether such seizures are "reasonable" under the Fourth Amendment.

It is important to recognize what our inquiry is *not* about. No allegations are before us of unreasonable treatment of any person after an actual detention at a particular checkpoint. See *Martinez–Fuerte*, ("claim that a particular exercise of discretion in locating or operating a checkpoint is unreasonable is subject to post-stop judicial review"). As pursued in the lower courts, the instant action challenges only the use of sobriety checkpoints generally. We address only the initial stop of each motorist passing through a checkpoint and the associated preliminary questioning and observation by checkpoint officers. Detention of particular motorists for more extensive field sobriety testing may require satisfaction of an individualized suspicion standard.

No one can seriously dispute the magnitude of the drunken driving problem or the States' interest in eradicating it. Media reports of alcohol-related death and mutilation on the Nation's roads are legion. The anecdotal is confirmed by the statistical. "Drunk drivers cause an annual death toll of over 25,000 and in the same time span cause nearly one million personal injuries and more than five billion dollars in property damage." * * *

Conversely, the weight bearing on the other scale—the measure of the intrusion on motorists stopped briefly at sobriety checkpoints—is slight. We reached a similar conclusion as to the intrusion on motorists subjected to a brief stop at a highway checkpoint for detecting illegal aliens. See *Martinez–Fuerte*. We see virtually no difference between the levels of intrusion on law-abiding motorists from the brief stops necessary to the effectuation of these two types of checkpoints, which to the average motorist would seem identical save for the nature of the questions the checkpoint officers might ask. The trial court and the Court of Appeals, thus, accurately gauged the "objective" intrusion, measured by the duration of the seizure and the intensity of the investigation, as minimal.

With respect to what it perceived to be the "subjective" intrusion on motorists, however, the Court of Appeals found such intrusion substantial. The court first affirmed the trial court's finding that the guidelines governing checkpoint operation minimize the discretion of the officers on the scene. But the court also agreed with the trial court's conclusion that the checkpoints have the potential to generate fear and surprise in motorists. This was so because the record failed to demonstrate that approaching motorists would be aware of their option to make U-turns or turnoffs to avoid the checkpoints. On that basis, the court deemed the subjective intrusion from the checkpoints unreasonable.

We believe the Michigan courts misread our cases concerning the degree of "subjective intrusion" and the potential for generating fear and surprise. The "fear and surprise" to be considered are not the natural fear of one who has been drinking over the prospect of being stopped at a sobriety checkpoint but, rather, the fear and surprise engendered in law abiding motorists by the nature of the stop. This was made clear in *Martinez–Fuerte*. Comparing checkpoint stops to roving patrol stops considered in prior cases, we said,

"we view checkpoint stops in a different light because the subjective intrusion—the generating of concern or even fright on the part of lawful travelers—is appreciably less in the case of a checkpoint stop. In [*United States v.* ] *Ortiz*, [422 U.S. 891 (1975),] we noted:

" '[T]he circumstances surrounding a checkpoint stop and search are far less intrusive than those attending a roving-patrol stop. Roving patrols often operate at night on seldom-traveled roads, and their approach may frighten motorists. At traffic checkpoints the motorist can see that other vehicles are being stopped, he can see visible signs of the officers' authority, and he is much less likely to be frightened or annoyed by the intrusion.' "

Here, checkpoints are selected pursuant to the guidelines, and uniformed police officers stop every approaching vehicle. The intrusion resulting from the brief stop at the sobriety checkpoint is for constitutional purposes indistinguishable from the checkpoint stops we upheld in *Martinez-Fuerte.*

The Court of Appeals went on to consider as part of the balancing analysis the "effectiveness" of the proposed checkpoint program. Based on extensive testimony in the trial record, the court concluded that the checkpoint program failed the "effectiveness" part of the test, and that this failure materially discounted petitioners' strong interest in implementing the program. We think the Court of Appeals was wrong on this point as well.

The actual language from *Brown v. Texas,* upon which the Michigan courts based their evaluation of "effectiveness," describes the balancing factor as "the degree to which the seizure advances the public interest." This passage from *Brown* was not meant to transfer from politically accountable officials to the courts the decision as to which among reasonable alternative law enforcement techniques should be employed to deal with a serious public danger. Experts in police science might disagree over which of several methods of apprehending drunken drivers is preferrable as an ideal. But for purposes of Fourth Amendment analysis, the choice among such reasonable alternatives remains with the governmental officials who have a unique understanding of, and a responsibility for, limited public resources, including a finite number of police officers. *Brown*'s rather general reference to "the degree to which the seizure advances the public interest" was derived, as the opinion makes clear, from the line of cases culminating in *Martinez–Fuerte.* Neither *Martinez–Fuerte* nor *Delaware v. Prouse,* 440 U.S. 648 (1979), however, the two cases cited by the Court of Appeals as providing the basis for its "effectiveness" review, supports the searching examination of "effectiveness" undertaken by the Michigan court.

In *Delaware v. Prouse,* we disapproved random stops made by Delaware Highway Patrol officers in an effort to apprehend unlicensed drivers and unsafe vehicles. We observed that *no* empirical evidence indicated that such stops would be an effective means of promoting roadway safety and said that "[i]t seems common sense that the percentage of all drivers on the road who are driving without a license is very small and that the number of licensed drivers who will be stopped in order to find one unlicensed operator will be large indeed." We observed that the random stops involved the "kind of standardless and unconstrained discretion [which] is the evil the Court has discerned when in previous cases it has insisted that the discretion of the official in the field be circumscribed, at least to some extent." We went on to state that our holding did not "cast doubt on the permissibility of roadside truck weigh-stations and inspection checkpoints, at which some vehicles may be subjected to further detention for safety and regulatory inspection than are others."

Unlike *Prouse,* this case involves neither a complete absence of empirical data nor a challenge to random highway stops. During the operation of the Saginaw County checkpoint, the detention of each of the 126 vehicles that entered the checkpoint resulted in the arrest of two drunken drivers. Stated as a percentage, approximately 1.5 percent of the drivers passing through the checkpoint were arrested for alcohol impairment. In addition, an expert witness testified at the trial that experience in other States demonstrated that, on the whole, sobriety checkpoints resulted in drunken driving arrests of around 1 percent of all motorists stopped. By way of comparison, the record from one of the consolidated cases in *Martinez–Fuerte*, showed that in the associated check-point, illegal aliens were found in only 0.12 percent of the vehicles passing through the checkpoint.  The ratio of illegal aliens detected to vehicles stopped (considering that on occasion two or more illegal aliens were found in a single vehicle) was approximately 0.5 percent.  We concluded that this "record . . . provides a rather complete picture of the effectiveness of the San Clemente checkpoint", and we sustained its constitutionality.  We see no justification for a different conclusion here.

In sum, the balance of the State's interest in preventing drunken driving, the extent to which this system can reasonably be said to advance that interest, and the degree of intrusion upon individual motorists who are briefly stopped, weighs in favor of the state program.  We therefore hold that it is consistent with the Fourth Amendment.  The judgment of the Michigan Court of Appeals is accordingly reversed, and the cause is remanded for further proceedings not inconsistent with this opinion.[a]

JUSTICE STEVENS, with whom JUSTICE BRENNAN and JUSTICE MARSHALL join as to Parts I and II, dissenting.  *  *  *

I

There is a critical difference between a seizure that is preceded by fair notice and one that is effected by surprise.  That is one reason why a border search, or indeed any search at a permanent and fixed checkpoint, is much less intrusive than a random stop.  A motorist with advance notice of the location of a permanent checkpoint has an opportunity to avoid the search entirely, or at least to prepare for, and limit, the intrusion on her privacy.

No such opportunity is available in the case of a random stop or a temporary checkpoint, which both depend for their effectiveness on the element of surprise.  A driver who discovers an unexpected checkpoint on a familiar local road will be startled and distressed.  She may infer, correctly, that the checkpoint is not simply "business as usual," and may likewise infer, again correctly, that the police have made a discretionary decision to focus their law enforcement efforts upon her and others who pass the chosen point.

This element of surprise is the most obvious distinction between the sobriety checkpoints permitted by today's majority and the interior border checkpoints approved by this Court in *Martinez–Fuerte*.  The distinction casts immediate doubt upon the majority's argument, for *Martinez–Fuerte* is the only case in which we have upheld suspicionless seizures of motorists.  But the difference between notice and surprise is only one of the important reasons for distinguishing between permanent and mobile checkpoints.  With respect to the former, there is no room for discretion in either the timing or the location of the stop—it is a permanent part of the landscape.  In the latter case, however, although the checkpoint is most frequently employed during the hours of darkness on week-ends (because that is when drivers with alcohol in their blood are most apt to be found on the road), the police have extremely broad discretion in determining the exact timing and placement of the roadblock.

There is also a significant difference between the kind of discretion that the officer exercises after the stop is made.  A check for a driver's license, or for identification papers at an immigration checkpoint, is far more easily standard-ized than is a search for evidence of intoxication.  A Michigan officer who questions a motorist at a sobriety checkpoint has virtually unlimited discretion

---

**a.** Justice Blackmun's concurring opinion is omitted, as is a separate dissenting opinion     by Justice Brennan, joined by Justice Marshall.

to detain the driver on the basis of the slightest suspicion. A ruddy complexion, an unbuttoned shirt, bloodshot eyes or a speech impediment may suffice to prolong the detention. Any driver who had just consumed a glass of beer, or even a sip of wine, would almost certainly have the burden of demonstrating to the officer that her driving ability was not impaired.

Finally, it is significant that many of the stops at permanent checkpoints occur during daylight hours, whereas the sobriety checkpoints are almost invariably operated at night. A seizure followed by interrogation and even a cursory search at night is surely more offensive than a daytime stop that is almost as routine as going through a toll gate. Thus we thought it important to point out that the random stops at issue in *Ortiz* frequently occurred at night.

These fears are not, as the Court would have it, solely the lot of the guilty. To be law abiding is not necessarily to be spotless, and even the most virtuous can be unlucky. Unwanted attention from the local police need not be less discomforting simply because one's secrets are not the stuff of criminal prosecutions. Moreover, those who have found—by reason of prejudice or misfortune— that encounters with the police may become adversarial or unpleasant without good cause will have grounds for worrying at any stop designed to elicit signs of suspicious behavior. Being stopped by the police is distressing even when it should not be terrifying, and what begins mildly may by happenstance turn severe.

For all these reasons, I do not believe that this case is analogous to *Martinez–Fuerte*. In my opinion, the sobriety checkpoints are instead similar to—and in some respects more intrusive than—the random investigative stops that the Court held unconstitutional in [*United States v.*] *Brignoni–Ponce* [, 422 U.S. 873 (1975),] and *Prouse*. In the latter case the Court explained:

> "We cannot agree that stopping or detaining a vehicle on an ordinary city street is less intrusive than a roving-patrol stop on a major highway and that it bears greater resemblance to a permissible stop and secondary detention at a checkpoint near the border. In this regard, we note that *Brignoni–Ponce* was not limited to roving-patrol stops on limited-access roads, but applied to any roving-patrol stop by Border Patrol agents on any type of roadway on less than reasonable suspicion. We cannot assume that the physical and psychological intrusion visited upon the occupants of a vehicle by a random stop to check documents is of any less moment than that occasioned by a stop by border agents on roving patrol. Both of these stops generally entail law enforcement officers signaling a moving automobile to pull over to the side of the roadway, by means of a possibly unsettling show of authority. Both interfere with freedom of movement, are inconvenient, and consume time. Both may create substantial anxiety."

We accordingly held that the State must produce evidence comparing the challenged seizure to other means of law enforcement, so as to show that the seizure

> "is a sufficiently productive mechanism to justify the intrusion upon Fourth Amendment interests which such stops entail. On the record before us, that question must be answered in the negative. Given the alternative mechanisms available, both those in use and those that might be adopted, we are unconvinced that the incremental contribution to highway safety of the random spot check justifies the practice under the Fourth Amendment."

## II

* * *

The Court's analysis of [the degree to which the sobriety checkpoint seizures advance the public interest] resembles a business decision that measures profits by counting gross receipts and ignoring expenses. The evidence in this case indicates that sobriety checkpoints result in the arrest of a fraction of one percent of the drivers who are stopped, but there is absolutely no evidence that this figure represents an increase over the number of arrests that would have been made by using the same law enforcement resources in conventional patrols. Thus, although the *gross* number of arrests is more than zero, there is a complete failure of proof on the question whether the wholesale seizures have produced any *net* advance in the public interest in arresting intoxicated drivers.

Indeed, the position adopted today by the Court is not one endorsed by any of the law enforcement authorities to whom the Court purports to defer. The Michigan police do not rely, as the Court does, on the *arrest rate* at sobriety checkpoints to justify the stops made there. Colonel Hough, the commander of the Michigan State Police and a leading proponent of the checkpoints, admitted at trial that the arrest rate at the checkpoints was "very low." Instead, Colonel Hough and the State have maintained that the mere *threat* of such arrests is sufficient to deter drunk driving and so to reduce the accident rate. * * * There is, obviously, nothing wrong with a law enforcement technique that reduces crime by pure deterrence without punishing anybody; on the contrary, such an approach is highly commendable. One cannot, however, prove its efficacy by counting the arrests that were made. One must instead measure the number of crimes that were avoided. Perhaps because the record is wanting, the Court simply ignores this point.

The Court's sparse analysis of this issue differs markedly from Justice Powell's opinion for the Court in *Martinez–Fuerte*. He did not merely count the 17,000 arrests made at the San Clemente checkpoint in 1973; he also carefully explained why those arrests represented a net benefit to the law enforcement interest at stake.[15] Common sense, moreover, suggests that immigration checkpoints are more necessary than sobriety checkpoints: there is no reason why smuggling illegal aliens should impair a motorist's driving ability, but if intoxication did not noticeably affect driving ability it would not be unlawful. Drunk driving, unlike smuggling, may thus be detected absent any checkpoints. A program that produces thousands of otherwise impossible arrests is not a relevant precedent for a program that produces only a handful of arrests which

---

**15.** "Our previous cases have recognized that maintenance of a traffic-checking program in the interior is necessary because the flow of illegal aliens cannot be controlled effectively at the border. We note here only the substantiality of the public interest in the practice of routine stops for inquiry at permanent checkpoints, a practice which the Government identifies as the most important of the traffic-checking operations. These checkpoints are located on important highways; in their absence such highways would offer illegal aliens a quick and safe route into the interior. Routine checkpoint inquiries apprehend many smugglers and illegal aliens who succumb to the lure of such highways. And the prospect of such inquiries forces others onto less efficient roads that are less heavily traveled, slowing their movement and making them more vulnerable to detection by roving patrols.

"A requirement that stops on major routes inland always be based on reasonable suspicion would be impractical because the flow of traffic tends to be too heavy to allow the particularized study of a given car that would enable it to be identified as a possible carrier of illegal aliens. In particular, such a requirement would largely eliminate any deterrent to the conduct of well-disguised smuggling operations, even though smugglers are known to use these highways regularly."

would be more easily obtained without resort to suspicionless seizures of hundreds of innocent citizens.

### III

[M]y objections to random seizures or temporary checkpoints do not apply to a host of other investigatory procedures that do not depend upon surprise and are unquestionably permissible. These procedures have been used to address other threats to human life no less pressing than the threat posed by drunken drivers. It is, for example, common practice to require every prospective airline passenger, or every visitor to a public building, to pass through a metal detector that will reveal the presence of a firearm or an explosive. Permanent, nondiscretionary checkpoints could be used to control serious dangers at other publicly operated facilities. Because concealed weapons obviously represent one such substantial threat to public safety, I would suppose that all subway passengers could be required to pass through metal detectors, so long as the detectors were permanent and every passenger was subjected to the same search. Likewise, I would suppose that a State could condition access to its toll roads upon not only paying the toll but also taking a uniformly administered breathalizer test. That requirement might well keep all drunken drivers off the highways that serve the fastest and most dangerous traffic. This procedure would not be subject to the constitutional objections that control this case: the checkpoints would be permanently fixed, the stopping procedure would apply to all users of the toll road in precisely the same way, and police officers would not be free to make arbitrary choices about which neighborhoods should be targeted or about which individuals should be more thoroughly searched. * * *

## SECTION 9. CONSENT SEARCHES

So-called consent searches are frequently relied upon by police as a means of investigating suspected criminal conduct. Sometimes probable cause is present but the police feel either that they do not have time to get a warrant or that they would simply like to avoid that time-consuming process, but more often an effort is made to obtain consent where probable cause is lacking and no warrant could be obtained. The exact meaning of "consent" in this context, the question explored in *Schneckloth v. Bustamonte*, is thus a matter of some importance.

In *Schneckloth*, by way of showing that the protections of the Fourth Amendment "are of a wholly different order" than various other constitutional rights, the Court noted that a person's privacy may sometimes be lawfully invaded by virtue of consent obtained by police from a third party. The Supreme Court has experienced some difficulty over the years in identifying just what it takes to give a certain third party this power. The Court's current approach is reflected in *Illinois v. Rodriguez*.

### SCHNECKLOTH v. BUSTAMONTE
412 U.S. 218, 93 S.Ct. 2041, 36 L.Ed.2d 854 (1973).

JUSTICE STEWART delivered the opinion of the Court. * * *

[While on routine patrol at 2:40 a.m., a police officer stopped an automobile when he observed that one headlight and its license plate light were burned out. Six men were in the vehicle. When the driver could not produce a driver's license, the officer asked if any of the other five had any evidence of identification. Only Alcala produced a license, and he explained that the car was his brother's. The officer asked Alcala if he could search the car. Alcala replied, "Sure, go ahead," and actually helped in the search of the car, by opening the trunk and glove compartment.  Three checks that had previously been stolen from a car wash were found wadded up under the left rear seat.  The checks in question were admitted in evidence at Bustamonte's trial.  He was convicted, and the California Court of Appeal affirmed the conviction.  Thereafter, the respondent sought a writ of habeas corpus in a federal district court.  It was denied.  On appeal, the Court of Appeals for the Ninth Circuit set aside the District Court's order.]

The precise question in this case is what must the state prove to demonstrate that a consent was "voluntarily" given.  *  *  *

The most extensive judicial exposition of the meaning of "voluntariness" has been developed in those cases in which the Court has had to determine the "voluntariness" of a defendant's confession for purposes of the Fourteenth Amendment.  *  *  * It is to that body of case law to which we turn for initial guidance on the meaning of "voluntariness" in the present context.  *  *  *

The significant fact about all of these decisions is that none of them turned on the presence or absence of a single controlling criterion; each reflected a careful scrutiny of all the surrounding circumstances.  In none of them did the Court rule that the Due Process Clause required the prosecution to prove as part of its initial burden that the defendant knew he had a right to refuse to answer the questions that were put.  While the state of the accused's mind, and the failure of the police to advise the accused of his rights, were certainly factors to be evaluated in assessing the "voluntariness" of an accused's responses, they were not in and of themselves determinative.

Similar considerations lead us to agree with the courts of California that the question whether a consent to a search was in fact "voluntary" or was the product of duress or coercion, express or implied, is a question of fact to be determined from the totality of all the circumstances.  While knowledge of the right to refuse consent is one factor to be taken into account, the government need not establish such knowledge as the *sine qua non* of an effective consent.  As with police questioning, two competing concerns must be accommodated in determining the meaning of a "voluntary" consent—the legitimate need for such searches and the equally important requirement of assuring the absence of coercion.

In situations where the police have some evidence of illicit activity, but lack probable cause to arrest or search, a search authorized by a valid consent may be the only means of obtaining important and reliable evidence.  In the present case for example, while the police had reason to stop the car for traffic violations, the State does not contend that there was probable cause to search the vehicle or that the search was incident to a valid arrest of any of the occupants.  Yet, the search yielded tangible evidence that served as a basis for a prosecution, and provided some assurance that others, wholly innocent of the crime, were not mistakenly brought to trial.  And in those cases where there is probable cause to arrest or search, but where the police lack a warrant, a consent search may still be valuable.  If the search is conducted and proves fruitless, that in itself may convince the police that an arrest with its possible stigma and embarrassment is unnecessary, or that a far more extensive search pursuant to a warrant is not justified.  In short a search pursuant to consent may result in considerably less inconvenience for the subject of the search, and, properly conducted, is a constitutionally permissible and wholly legitimate aspect of effective police activity.

But the Fourth and Fourteenth Amendments require that a consent not be coerced, by explicit or implicit means, by implied threat or covert force.  For, no matter how subtly the coercion were applied, the resulting "consent" would be no more than a pretext for the unjustified police intrusion against which the Fourth Amendment is directed. * * *

The problem of reconciling the recognized legitimacy of consent searches with the requirement that they be free from any aspect of official coercion cannot be resolved by an infallible touchstone. To approve such searches without the most careful scrutiny would sanction the possibility of official coercion; to place artificial restrictions upon such searches would jeopardize their basic validity. Just as was true with confessions, the requirement of a "voluntary" consent reflects a fair accommodation of the constitutional requirements involved. In examining all the surrounding circumstances to determine if in fact the consent to search was coerced, account must be taken of subtly coercive police questions, as well as the possibly vulnerable subjective state of the person who consents. Those searches that are the product of police coercion can thus be filtered out without undermining the continuing validity of consent searches. In sum, there is no reason for us to depart in the area of consent searches, from the traditional definition of "voluntariness."

The approach of the Court of Appeals for the Ninth Circuit finds no support in any of our decisions that have attempted to define the meaning of "voluntariness." Its ruling, that the State must affirmatively prove that the subject of the search knew that he had a right to refuse consent, would, in practice, create serious doubt whether consent searches could continue to be conducted. There might be rare cases where it could be proved from the record that a person in fact affirmatively knew of his right to refuse—such as a case where he announced to the police that if he didn't sign the consent form, "you [police] are going to get a search warrant;" or a case where by prior experience and training a person had clearly and convincingly demonstrated such knowledge. But more commonly where there was no evidence of any coercion, explicit or implicit, the prosecution would nevertheless be unable to demonstrate that the subject of the search in fact had known of his right to refuse consent.

The very object of the inquiry—the nature of a person's subjective understanding—underlines the difficulty of the prosecution's burden under the rule applied by the Court of Appeals in this case. Any defendant who was the subject of a search authorized solely by his consent could effectively frustrate the introduction into evidence of the fruits of that search by simply failing to testify that he in fact knew he could refuse to consent. And the near impossibility of meeting this prosecutorial burden suggests why this Court has never accepted any such litmus-paper test of voluntariness. * * *

One alternative that would go far towards proving that the subject of a search did know he had a right to refuse consent would be to advise him of that right before eliciting his consent. That, however, is a suggestion that has been almost universally repudiated by both federal and state courts, and, we think, rightly so. For it would be thoroughly impractical to impose on the normal consent search the detailed requirements of an effective warning. Consent searches are part of the standard investigatory techniques of law enforcement agencies. They normally occur on the highway, or in a person's home or office, and under informal and unstructured conditions. The circumstances that prompt the initial request to search may develop quickly or be a logical extension of investigative police questioning. The police may seek to investigate further suspicious circumstances or to follow up leads developed in questioning persons at the scene of a crime. These situations are a far cry from the structured atmosphere of a trial where, assisted by counsel if he chooses, a defendant is informed of his trial rights. And, while surely a closer question, these situations are still immeasurably far removed from "custodial interrogation" where, in *Miranda v. Arizona* [Ch. 6, § 3] we found that the Constitution required certain now familiar warnings as a prerequisite to police interrogation.

\* \* \*

It is said, however, that a "consent" is a "waiver" of a person's rights under the Fourth and Fourteenth Amendments. The argument is that by allowing the police to conduct a search, a person "waives" whatever right he had to prevent the police from searching. It is argued that under the doctrine of *Johnson v. Zerbst*, 304 U.S. 458 (1938), to establish such a "waiver" the state must demonstrate "an intentional relinquishment or abandonment of a known right or privilege." \* \* \*

Almost without exception the requirement of a knowing and intelligent waiver has been applied only to those rights which the Constitution guarantees to a criminal defendant in order to preserve a fair trial. Hence, and hardly surprisingly in view of the facts of *Johnson* itself, the standard of a knowing and intelligent waiver has most often been applied to test the validity of a waiver of counsel, either at trial, or upon a guilty plea. And the Court has also applied the *Johnson* criteria to assess the effectiveness of a waiver of other trial rights such as the right to confrontation, to a jury trial, and to a speedy trial, and the right to be free from twice being placed in jeopardy. Guilty pleas have been carefully scrutinized to determine whether the accused knew and understood all the rights to which he would be entitled at trial, and that he had intentionally chosen to forgo them. And the Court has evaluated the knowing and intelligent nature of the waiver of trial rights in trial-type situations, such as the waiver of the privilege against compulsory self-incrimination before an administrative agency or a congressional committee, or the waiver of counsel in a juvenile proceeding.

The guarantees afforded a criminal defendant at trial also protect him at certain stages before the actual trial, and any alleged waiver must meet the strict standard of an intentional relinquishment of a "known" right. But the "trial" guarantees that have been applied to the "pretrial" stage of the criminal process are similarly designed to protect the fairness of the trial itself. \* \* \*[a]

The standards of *Johnson* were, therefore, found to be a necessary prequisite to a finding of a valid waiver.[29] \* \* \*

A strict standard of waiver has been applied to those rights guaranteed to a criminal defendant to insure that he will be accorded the greatest possible opportunity to utilize every facet of the constitutional model of a fair criminal trial. Any trial conducted in derogation of that model leaves open the possibility that the trial reached an unfair result precisely because all the protections

---

**a.** At this point, the Court noted that "the standard of a knowing and intelligent waiver" applies to waiver of counsel at a lineup under *United States v. Wade*, [Ch. 7, § 1], and *Gilbert v. California*, [Ch. 7, § 1] because counsel is provided to protect the right of cross-examination at trial; and that the same standard applies to waiver of counsel at custodial interrogation under *Miranda v. Arizona* because counsel is provided to ensure that the safeguards concerning the giving of testimony at trial do not "become empty formalities."

**29.** As we have already noted, *Miranda* itself involved interrogation of a suspect de-

tained in custody and did not concern the investigatory procedures of the police in general on-the-scene questioning. By the same token, the present case does not require a determination of the proper standard to be applied in assessing the validity of a search authorized solely by an alleged consent that is obtained from a person after he has been placed in custody. We do note, however, that other courts have been particularly sensitive to the heightened possibilities for coercion when the "consent" to a search was given by a person in custody.

specified in the Constitution were not provided. A prime example is the right to counsel. For without that right, a wholly innocent accused faces the real and substantial danger that simply because of his lack of legal expertise he may be convicted. * * *

The protections of the Fourth Amendment are of a wholly different order, and have nothing whatever to do with promoting the fair ascertainment of truth at a criminal trial. Rather, as Mr. Justice Frankfurter's opinion for the Court put it in *Wolf v. Colorado* [Ch. 3, § 1] the Fourth Amendment protects the "security of one's privacy against arbitrary intrusion by the police. * * *"
* * *

Nor can it even be said that a search, as opposed to an eventual trial, is somehow "unfair" if a person consents to a search. While the Fourth and Fourteenth Amendments limit the circumstances under which the police can conduct a search, there is nothing constitutionally suspect in a person voluntarily allowing a search. The actual conduct of the search may be precisely the same as if the police had obtained a warrant. And, unlike those constitutional guarantees that protect a defendant at trial, it cannot be said every reasonable presumption ought to be indulged against voluntary relinquishment. We have only recently stated: "[I]t is no part of the policy underlying the Fourth and Fourteenth Amendments to discourage citizens from aiding to the utmost of their ability in the apprehension of criminals." Rather the community has a real interest in encouraging consent, for the resulting search may yield necessary evidence for the solution and prosecution of crime, evidence that may insure that a wholly innocent person is not wrongly charged with a criminal offense.

Those cases that have dealt with the application of the *Johnson v. Zerbst* rule make clear that it would be next to impossible to apply to a consent search the standard of "an intentional relinquishment or abandonment of a known right or privilege." To be true to *Johnson* and its progeny, there must be examination into the knowing and understanding nature of the waiver, an examination that was designed for a trial judge in the structured atmosphere of a courtroom. * * * It would be unrealistic to expect that in the informal, unstructured context of a consent search, a policeman, upon pain of tainting the evidence obtained, could make the detailed type of examination demanded by *Johnson*. And, if for this reason a diluted form of "waiver" were found acceptable, that would itself be ample recognition of the fact that there is no universal standard that must be applied in every situation where a person forgoes a constitutional right.[33]

Similarly, a "waiver" approach to consent searches would be thoroughly inconsistent with our decisions that have approved "third party consents." [I]t is inconceivable that the Constitution could countenance the waiver of a defendant's right to counsel by a third party, or that a waiver could be found because a trial judge reasonably though mistakenly believed a defendant had waived his right to plead not guilty. * * *

**33.** It seems clear that even a limited view of the demands of "an intentional relinquishment or abandonment of a known right or privilege" standard would inevitably lead to a requirement of detailed warnings before any consent search—a requirement all but universally rejected to date. As the Court stated in *Miranda* with respect to the privilege against compulsory self-incrimination: "[W]e will not pause to inquire in individual cases whether the defendant was aware of his rights without a warning being given. Assessments of the knowledge the defendant possessed, based on information as to his age, education, intelligence, or prior contact with authorities, can never be more than speculation; a warning is a clearcut fact."

Much of what has already been said disposes of the argument that the Court's decision in the *Miranda* case requires the conclusion that knowledge of a right to refuse is an indispensable element of a valid consent. The considerations that informed the Court's holding in *Miranda* are simply inapplicable in the present case. In *Miranda* the Court found that the techniques of police questioning and the nature of custodial surroundings produce an inherently coercive situation. The Court concluded that "[u]nless adequate protective devices are employed to dispel the compulsion inherent in custodial surroundings, no statement obtained from the defendant can truly be the product of his free choice." And at another point the Court noted that "without proper safeguards the process of in-custody interrogation of persons suspected or accused of crime contains inherently compelling pressures which work to undermine the individual's will to resist and to compel him to speak where he would not otherwise do so freely."

In this case there is no evidence of any inherently coercive tactics—either from the nature of the police questioning or the environment in which it took place. Indeed, since consent searches will normally occur on a person's own familiar territory, the spectre of incommunicado police interrogation in some remote station house is simply inapposite. There is no reason to believe, under circumstances such as are present here, that the response to a policeman's question is presumptively coerced; and there is, therefore, no reason to reject the traditional test for determining the voluntariness of a person's response. *Miranda,* of course, did not reach investigative questioning of a person not in custody, which is most directly analogous to the situation of a consent search, and it assuredly did not indicate that such questioning ought to be deemed inherently coercive.

It is also argued that the failure to require the Government to establish knowledge as a prerequisite to a valid consent, will relegate the Fourth Amendment to the special province of "the sophisticated, the knowledgeable, and the privileged." We cannot agree. The traditional definition of voluntariness we accept today has always taken into account evidence of minimal schooling, low intelligence, and the lack of any effective warnings to a person of his rights; and the voluntariness of any statement taken under those conditions has been carefully scrutinized to determine whether it was in fact voluntarily given.

Our decision today is a narrow one. We hold only that when the subject of a search is not in custody and the State attempts to justify a search on the basis of his consent, the Fourth and Fourteenth Amendments require that it demonstrate that the consent was in fact voluntarily given, and not the result of duress or coercion, express or implied. Voluntariness is a question of fact to be determined from all the circumstances, and while the subject's knowledge of a right to refuse is a factor to be taken into account, the prosecution is not required to demonstrate such knowledge as a prerequisite to establishing a voluntary consent.[b]

b. Powell, J., joined by the Chief Justice and Rehnquist, J., concurred on the ground "that federal collateral review of a state prisoner's Fourth Amendment claims—claims which rarely bear on innocence—should be confined solely to the question of whether the petitioner was provided a fair opportunity to raise and have adjudicated the question in state courts." Blackmun, J., concurred to express substantial agreement with the Powell opinion. Douglas, J., dissenting, would have remanded for a determination of whether Alcala knew he had the right to refuse. Brennan, J., dissenting, declared: "It wholly escapes me how our citizens can meaningfully be said to have waived something as precious as a constitutional guarantee without ever being aware of its existence."

JUSTICE MARSHALL, dissenting.

\* \* \* The Court assumes that the issue in this case is, what are the standards by which courts are to determine that consent is voluntarily given? It then imports into the law of search and seizure standards developed to decide entirely different questions about coerced confessions.

The Fifth Amendment, in terms, provides that no person "shall be compelled in any criminal case to be a witness against himself." Nor is the interest protected by the Due Process Clause of the Fourteenth Amendment any different. The inquiry in a case where a confession is challenged as having been elicited in an unconstitutional manner is, therefore, whether the behavior of the police amounted to compulsion of the defendant. \* \* \*

In contrast, this case deals not with "coercion," but with "consent," a subtly different concept to which different standards have been applied in the past. Freedom from coercion is a substantive right, guaranteed by the Fifth and Fourteenth Amendments. Consent, however, is a mechanism by which substantive requirements, otherwise applicable, are avoided. \* \* \* Thus, consent searches are permitted not because such an exception to the requirements of probable cause and warrant is essential to proper law enforcement, but because we permit our citizens to choose whether or not they wish to exercise their constitutional rights. Our prior decisions simply do not support the view that a meaningful choice has been made solely because no coercion was brought to bear on the subject. \* \* \*

If consent to search means that a person has chosen to forego his right to exclude the police from the place they seek to search, it follows that his consent cannot be considered a meaningful choice unless he knew that he could in fact exclude the police. \* \* \* I would therefore hold, at a minimum, that the prosecution may not rely on a purported consent to search if the subject of the search did not know that he could refuse to give consent. Where the police claim authority to search yet in fact lack such authority, the subject does not know that he may permissibly refuse them entry, and it is this lack of knowledge that invalidates the consent. \* \* \*

The burden on the prosecutor would disappear, of course, if the police, at the time they requested consent to search, also told the subject that he had a right to refuse consent and thus his decision to refuse would be respected. The Court's assertions to the contrary notwithstanding, there is nothing impractical about this method of satisfying the prosecution's burden of proof. \* \* \*

The Court contends that if an officer paused to inform the subject of his rights, the informality of the exchange would be destroyed. I doubt that a simple statement by an officer of an individual's right to refuse consent would do much to alter the informality of the exchange, except to alert the subject to a fact that he surely is entitled to know. It is not without significance that for many years the agents of the Federal Bureau of Investigation have routinely informed subjects of their right to refuse consent, when they request consent to search. The reported cases in which the police have informed subject of their right to refuse consent show, also, that the information can be given without disrupting the casual flow of events. What evidence there is, then, rather strongly suggests that nothing disastrous would happen if the police, before requesting consent, informed the subject that he had a right to refuse consent and that his refusal would be respected.[12]

---

12. The Court's suggestion that it would be "unrealistic" to require the officers to make "the detailed type of examination" involved    when a court considers whether a defendant has waived a trial right, deserves little comment. The question before us relates to the

I must conclude, with some reluctance, that when the Court speaks of practicality, what it really is talking of is the continued ability of the police to capitalize on the ignorance of citizens so as to accomplish by subterfuge what they could not achieve by relying only on the knowing relinquishment of constitutional rights. Of course it would be "practical" for the police to ignore the commands of the Fourth Amendment, if by practicality we mean that more criminals will be apprehended, even though the constitutional rights of innocent people also go by the boards. But such a practical advantage is achieved only at the cost of permitting the police to disregard the limitations that the Constitution places on their behavior, a cost that a constitutional democracy cannot long absorb. * * *

## ILLINOIS v. RODRIGUEZ

___ U.S. ___, 110 S.Ct. ___, ___ L.Ed.2d ___ (1990).

JUSTICE SCALIA delivered the opinion of the Court. * * *

On July 26, 1985, police were summoned to the residence of Dorothy Jackson on South Wolcott in Chicago. They were met by Ms. Jackson's daughter, Gail Fischer, who showed signs of a severe beating. She told the officers that she had been assaulted by respondent Edward Rodriguez earlier that day in an apartment on South California. Fischer stated that Rodriguez was then asleep in the apartment, and she consented to travel there with the police in order to unlock the door with her key so that the officers could enter and arrest him. During this conversation, Fischer several times referred to the apartment on South California as "our" apartment, and said that she had clothes and furniture there. It is unclear whether she indicated that she currently lived at the apartment, or only that she used to live there.

The police officers drove to the apartment on South California, accompanied by Fischer. They did not obtain an arrest warrant for Rodriguez, nor did they seek a search warrant for the apartment. At the apartment, Fischer unlocked the door with her key and gave the officers permission to enter. They moved through the door into the living room, where they observed in plain view drug paraphernalia and containers filled with white powder that they believed (correctly, as later analysis showed) to be cocaine. They proceeded to the bedroom, where they found Rodriguez asleep and discovered additional containers of white powder in two open attaché cases. The officers arrested Rodriguez and seized the drugs and related paraphernalia.

Rodriguez was charged with possession of a controlled substance with intent to deliver. He moved to suppress all evidence seized at the time of his arrest, claiming that Fischer had vacated the apartment several weeks earlier and had no authority to consent to the entry. The Cook County Circuit Court granted the motion, holding that at the time she consented to the entry Fischer did not have common authority over the apartment. The Court concluded that Fischer was not a "usual resident" but rather an "infrequent visitor" at the apartment on South California, based upon its findings that Fischer's name was not on the lease, that she did not contribute to the rent, that she was not allowed to invite others to the apartment on her own, that she did not have access to the apartment when respondent was away, and that she had moved some of her

inquiry to be made in court when the prosecution seeks to establish that consent was given. I therefore do not address the Court's strained argument that one may waive constitutional rights without making a knowing and inten- tional choice so long as the rights do not relate to the fairness of a criminal trial. I would suggest, however, that that argument is fundamentally inconsistent with the law of unconstitutional conditions.

possessions from the apartment. The Circuit Court also rejected the State's contention that, even if Fischer did not possess common authority over the premises, there was no Fourth Amendment violation if the police *reasonably believed* at the time of their entry that Fischer possessed the authority to consent. * * *

The Fourth Amendment generally prohibits the warrantless entry of a person's home, whether to make an arrest or to search for specific objects. The prohibition does not apply, however, to situations in which voluntary consent has been obtained, either from the individual whose property is searched, or from a third party who possesses common authority over the premises, see *United States v. Matlock,* [415 U.S. 164 (1974)]. The State of Illinois contends that that exception applies in the present case.

As we stated in *Matlock,* "[c]ommon authority" rests "on mutual use of the property by persons generally having joint access or control for most purposes. . . ." The burden of establishing that common authority rests upon the State. On the basis of this record, it is clear that burden was not sustained. The evidence showed that although Fischer, with her two small children, had lived with Rodriguez beginning in December 1984, she had moved out on July 1, 1985, almost a month before the search at issue here, and had gone to live with her mother. She took her and her children's clothing with her, though leaving behind some furniture and household effects. During the period after July 1 she sometimes spent the night at Rodriguez's apartment, but never invited her friends there, and never went there herself when he was not home. Her name was not on the lease nor did she contribute to the rent. She had a key to the apartment, which she said at trial she had taken without Rodriguez's knowledge (though she testified at the preliminary hearing that Rodriguez had given her the key). On these facts the State has not established that, with respect to the South California apartment, Fischer had "joint access or control for most purposes." To the contrary, the Appellate Court's determination of no common authority over the apartment was obviously correct.

[R]espondent asserts that permitting a reasonable belief of common authority to validate an entry would cause a defendant's Fourth Amendment rights to be "vicariously waived." We disagree.

We have been unyielding in our insistence that a defendant's waiver of his trial rights cannot be given effect unless it is "knowing" and "intelligent." We would assuredly not permit, therefore, evidence seized in violation of the Fourth Amendment to be introduced on the basis of a trial court's mere "reasonable belief"—derived from statements by unauthorized persons—that the defendant has waived his objection. But one must make a distinction between, on the one hand, trial rights that *derive* from the violation of constitutional guarantees and, on the other hand, the nature of those constitutional guarantees themselves. * * *

What Rodriguez is assured by the trial right of the exclusionary rule, where it applies, is that no evidence seized in violation of the Fourth Amendment will be introduced at his trial unless he consents. What he is assured by the Fourth Amendment itself, however, is not that no government search of his house will occur unless he consents; but that no such search will occur that is "unreasonable." There are various elements, of course, that can make a search of a person's house "reasonable"—one of which is the consent of the person or his cotenant. The essence of respondent's argument is that we should impose upon this element a requirement that we have not imposed upon other elements that regularly compel government officers to exercise judgment regarding the facts: namely, the requirement that their judgment be not only responsible but correct.

[I]n order to satisfy the "reasonableness" requirement of the Fourth Amendment, what is generally demanded of the many factual determinations that must regularly be made by agents of the government—whether the magistrate issuing a warrant, the police officer executing a warrant, or the police officer conducting a search or seizure under one of the exceptions to the warrant requirement—is not that they always be correct, but that they always be reasonable. As we put it in *Brinegar v. United States,* 338 U.S. 160, 176 (1949):

> "Because many situations which confront officers in the course of executing their duties are more or less ambiguous, room must be allowed for some mistakes on their part. But the mistakes must be those of reasonable men, acting on facts leading sensibly to their conclusions of probability."

We see no reason to depart from this general rule with respect to facts bearing upon the authority to consent to a search. Whether the basis for such authority exists is the sort of recurring factual question to which law enforcement officials must be expected to apply their judgment; and all the Fourth Amendment requires is that they answer it reasonably. The Constitution is no more violated when officers enter without a warrant because they reasonably (though erroneously) believe that the person who has consented to their entry is a resident of the premises, than it is violated when they enter without a warrant because they reasonably (though erroneously) believed they are in pursuit of a violent felon who is about to escape.

*Stoner v. California,* 376 U.S. 483 (1964) is in our view not to the contrary. There, in holding that police had improperly entered the defendant's hotel room based on the consent of a hotel clerk, we stated that "the rights protected by the Fourth Amendment are not to be eroded . . . by unrealistic doctrines of 'apparent authority.' " It is ambiguous, of course, whether the word "unrealistic" is descriptive or limiting—that is, whether we were condemning as unrealistic all reliance upon apparent authority, or whether we were condemning only such reliance upon apparent authority as is unrealistic. Similarly ambiguous is the opinion's earlier statement that "there [is no] substance to the claim that the search was reasonable because police, relying upon the night clerk's expressions of consent, had a reasonable basis for the belief that the clerk had authority to consent to the search." Was there no substance to it because it failed as a matter of law, or because the facts could not possibly support it? At one point the opinion does seem to speak clearly:

> "It is important to bear in mind that it was the petitioner's constitutional right which was at stake here, and not the night clerk's nor the hotel's. It was a right, therefore, which only the petitioner could waive by word or deed, either directly or through an agent."

But as we have discussed, what is at issue when a claim of apparent consent is raised is not whether the right to be free of searches has been *waived,* but whether the right to be free of *unreasonable* searches has been *violated.* Even if one does not think the *Stoner* opinion had this subtlety in mind, the supposed clarity of its foregoing statement is immediately compromised, as follows:

> "It is true that the night clerk clearly and unambiguously consented to the search. But there is nothing in the record to indicate that *the police had any basis whatsoever to believe that* the night clerk had been authorized by the petitioner to permit the police to search the petitioner's room."

The italicized language should have been deleted, of course, if the statement two sentences earlier meant that an appearance of authority could never validate a search. In the last analysis, one must admit that the rationale of *Stoner* was ambiguous—and perhaps deliberately so. It is at least a reasonable reading of the case, and perhaps a preferable one, that the police could not rely upon the obtained consent because they knew it came from a hotel clerk, knew that the room was rented and exclusively occupied by the defendant, and could not reasonably have believed that the former had general access to or control over the latter. * * *

As *Stoner* demonstrates, what we hold today does not suggest that law enforcement officers may always accept a person's invitation to enter premises. Even when the invitation is accompanied by an explicit assertion that the person lives there, the surrounding circumstances could conceivably be such that a reasonable person would doubt its truth and not act upon it without further inquiry. As with other factual determinations bearing upon search and seizure, determination of consent to enter must "be judged against an objective standard: would the facts available to the officer at the moment . . . 'warrant a man of reasonable caution in the belief'" that the consenting party had authority over the premises? If not, then warrantless entry without further inquiry is unlawful unless authority actually exists. But if so, the search is valid.

In the present case, the Appellate Court found it unnecessary to determine whether the officers reasonably believed that Fischer had the authority to consent, because it ruled as a matter of law that a reasonable belief could not validate the entry. Since we find that ruling to be in error, we remand for consideration of that question. The judgment of the Illinois Appellate Court is reversed and remanded for further proceedings not inconsistent with this opinion.

JUSTICE MARSHALL, with whom JUSTICE BRENNAN and JUSTICE STEVENS join, dissenting. * * *

Unlike searches conducted pursuant to the recognized exceptions to the warrant requirement, third-party consent searches are not based on an exigency and therefore serve no compelling social goal. Police officers, when faced with the choice of relying on consent by a third party or securing a warrant, should secure a warrant, and must therefore accept the risk of error should they instead choose to rely on consent. * * *

Acknowledging that the third party in this case lacked authority to consent, the majority seeks to rely on cases suggesting that reasonable but mistaken factual judgments by police will not invalidate otherwise reasonable searches. The majority reads these cases as establishing a "general rule" that "what is generally demanded of the many factual determinations that must regularly be made by agents of the government—whether the magistrate issuing a warrant, the police officer executing a warrant, or the police officer conducting a search or seizure under one of the exceptions to the warrant requirement—is not that they always be correct, but that they always be reasonable."

The majority's assertion, however, is premised on the erroneous assumption that third-party consent searches are generally reasonable. The cases the majority cites thus provide no support for its holding. In *Brinegar v. United States,* for example, the Court confirmed the unremarkable proposition that police need only probable cause, not absolute certainty, to justify the arrest of a suspect on a highway. As *Brinegar* makes clear, the possibility of factual error is built into the probable cause standard, and such a standard, by its very definition, will in some cases result in the arrest of a suspect who has not actually committed a crime. Because probable cause defines the reasonableness of searches and seizures outside of the home, a search is reasonable under the Fourth Amendment whenever that standard is met, notwithstanding the possibility of "mistakes" on the part of police. In contrast, our cases have already struck the balance against warrantless home intrusions in the absence of an exigency. Because reasonable factual errors by law enforcement officers will not validate unreasonable searches, the reasonableness of the officer's mistaken belief that the third party had authority to consent is irrelevant. * * *

# Chapter 4

# POLICE "ENCOURAGEMENT" AND THE DEFENSE OF ENTRAPMENT

"Our national integrity has been on a downhill slide for seven years; we really don't need the FBI to grease the skids with Operation ABSCAM.[a] Where no crime has been contemplated, the FBI has, through entrapment, induced to crime men who were previously involved in no wrongdoing. Aren't there enough naturally encouraging crimes to keep the FBI busy? Must they spend astronomical sums creating crime?"

— Letter to the Editor, Newsweek, Mar. 1, 1980, p. 5

"House Speaker Thomas P. (Tip) O'Neill may have thundered that '[Operation ABSCAM] was a setup, a goddam setup,' but a crook is a crook is a crook. Whether set up or not, honest people do not take bribes."

— Letter to the Editor, Newsweek, Mar. 1, 1980, p. 5.

As illustrated by the two letters set forth above, the use of undercover police officers or other secret government agents to detect crime or to tempt people into committing crime evokes widely varying responses. Moreover, the label "entrapment" is often affixed to police conduct that is not "entrapment" at all, as the courts have defined that term, but "encouragement"—a police technique whereby an officer or law enforcement agent acts as a willing victim, intends by his action to encourage the suspect (a "target") to commit a crime, communicates this encouragement to the suspect, and thereby influences the commission of a crime.

---

**a.** "Abscam" is an acronym combining the first two letters of Abdul Enterprises, a fictitious Middle Eastern corporation, and "scam," a slang term for swindle or confidence game. Abscam began as a standard "sting" operation, i.e., an FBI undercover scheme to recover stolen securities and paintings. In 1978, the operation shifted to political corruption in the New Jersey area. A year later, it had turned its attention to the "Asylum Scenario"; unsuspecting "middlemen" (private persons unaware that they were part of a government undercover operation) passed the word to various Congressmen, or to their aides and acquaintances, that wealthy Arabs were willing to bribe members of Congress in order to ensure that they would introduce private immigration bills on the Arabs' behalf if and when necessary. In early 1980, shortly before shutting down, the operation shifted to political corruption in Philadelphia.

As a result of Abscam, a U.S. Senator, six U.S. Representatives and a number of other public officials and lawyers were convicted of various corrupt acts. Although many of the defendants (and many critics of the operation both in and out of Congress) charged that the FBI's methods constituted entrapment and/or violated the due process rights of the individuals caught in the operation, not a single Abscam defendant prevailed in the courts. See, e.g., *United States v. Kelly*, 707 F.2d 1460 (D.C. Cir.1983), which discusses one phase of the Abscam operation at considerable length.

Such tactics are commonly used to detect "vice crimes" (e.g., prostitution, illicit liquor sales, narcotics and gambling offenses) and, perhaps most spectacularly, to uncover the bribery of public officials. For these offenses are committed privately with a willing victim who will not complain, making normal detection exceedingly difficult.

"Encouragement" as such is not an improper law enforcement technique, but when extended too far—"when the criminal design originates with the officials of the government, and they implant in the mind of an innocent person the disposition to commit the alleged offense and induce its commission in order that they may prosecute" [b] —the government's tactics do constitute "entrapment."

There are currently two major approaches to the defense of entrapment: the majority view, usually called the "subjective approach," and the "objective approach" or "hypothetical person" approach.

Under the "subjective approach," as explained in Justice Rehnquist's opinion for the Court in *United States v. Russell*, infra, "the entrapment defense prohibits law enforcement officers from instigating criminal acts by persons 'otherwise innocent in order to lure them to its commission and to punish them.' " This approach "focus[es] on the intent or predisposition of the defendant to commit the crime" rather than on the government's conduct. Under this approach, to determine whether entrapment has occurred, "a line must be drawn between the trap for the unwary innocent and the trap for the unwary criminal."

The emphasis of the "objective" approach is not on the defendant's propensity to commit the offense, but on the inducements used by the government agents. This approach is based on the premise that an affirmative duty resides in the courts to control police excesses in inducing criminal behavior, and that this duty should not be limited to instances in which the defendant is otherwise "innocent."

Under this approach, as concurring Justice Stewart put it in *United States v. Russell,* the entrapment defense is designed "to prohibit unlawful governmental activity in instigating crime. * * * If that is so, then whether the particular defendant was 'predisposed' or 'otherwise innocent' is irrelevant; and the important question becomes whether the Government's conduct in inducing the crime was beyond judicial toleration."

Although defendants, such as the one in *Russell,* who are forced to concede that the jury could have found them "predisposed" to commit the offense, must urge the court to adopt the objective approach, neither the objective nor the subjective approach is uniformly more favorable to defendants. As explained in the commentary to the American Law Institute's Model Penal Code (which favors the "objective approach"):

"Under the [subjective approach], if A, an informer, makes overreaching appeals to compassion and friendship and thus moves D to sell narcotics, D has no defense if he is predisposed to narcotics peddling. Under the [objective approach] a defense would be established because the police conduct, not D's predisposition, determines the issue. Under the [subjective approach], A's mere offer to purchase narcotics from D may give rise to the defense provided D is not predisposed to sell. A contrary result is reached

b. *Sorrells v. United States,* 287 U.S. 435 (1932), quoted with approval in *Sherman v. United States,* 356 U.S. 369 (1958) (articulat- ing the majority view of entrapment, often called the "subjective" test).

under the [objective approach]. A mere offer to buy hardly creates a serious risk of offending by the innocent."

## UNITED STATES v. RUSSELL

411 U.S. 423, 93 S.Ct. 1637, 36 L.Ed.2d 366 (1973).

JUSTICE REHNQUIST delivered the opinion of the Court.

Respondent Richard Russell was charged in three counts of a five-count indictment returned against him and codefendants John and Patrick Connolly. After a jury trial in the District Court, in which his sole defense was entrapment, respondent was convicted on all three counts of having unlawfully manufactured and processed methamphetamine ("speed") and of having unlawfully sold and delivered that drug * * *. On appeal, the United States Court of Appeals for the Ninth Circuit [reversed] the conviction solely for the reason that an undercover agent supplied an essential chemical for manufacturing the methamphetamine which formed the basis of respondent's conviction. * * *

There is little dispute concerning the essential facts in this case. On December 7, 1969, Joe Shapiro, an undercover agent for the Federal Bureau of Narcotics and Dangerous Drugs, went to respondent's home [where] he met with respondent and his two codefendants, John and Patrick Connolly. Shapiro's assignment was to locate a laboratory where it was believed that methamphetamine was being manufactured illicitly. He told the respondent and the Connollys that he represented an organization [that] was interested in controlling the manufacture and distribution of methamphetamine. He then made an offer to supply the defendants with the chemical phenyl–2–propanone, an essential ingredient in the manufacture of methamphetamine, in return for one-half of the drug produced. This offer was made on the condition that Agent Shapiro be shown a sample of the drug which they were making and the laboratory where it was being produced.

During the conversation, Patrick Connolly revealed that he had been making the drug since May 1969 and since then had produced three pounds of it. John Connolly gave the agent a bag containing a quality of methamphetamine that he represented as being from "the last batch that we made." Shortly thereafter, Shapiro and Patrick Connolly left respondent's house to view the laboratory which was located in the Connolly house on Whidbey Island. At the house, Shapiro observed an empty bottle bearing the chemical label phenyl–2–propanone.

By prearrangement, Shapiro returned to the Connolly house on December 9, 1969, to supply 100 grams of propanone and observe the manufacturing process. When he arrived he observed Patrick Connolly and the respondent cutting up pieces of aluminum foil and placing them in a large flask. There was testimony that some of the foil pieces accidentally fell on the floor and were picked up by the respondent and Shapiro and put into the flask. Thereafter, Patrick Connolly added all of the necessary chemicals, including the propanone brought by Shapiro, to make two batches of methamphetamine. The manufacturing process having been completed the following morning, Shapiro was given one-half of the drug and respondent kept the remainder. Shapiro offered to buy, and the respondent agreed to sell, part of the remainder for $60.

About a month later, Shapiro returned to the Connolly house and met with Patrick Connolly to ask if he was still interested in their "business arrangement." Connolly replied that he was interested but that he had recently obtained two additional bottles of phenyl–2–propanone and would not be finished with them for a couple of days. He provided some additional methamphetamine to Shapiro at that time. Three days later Shapiro returned to the Connolly house with a search warrant and, among other items, seized an empty 500–gram bottle of propanone and a 100–gram bottle, not the one he had provided, that was partially filled with the chemical.

There was testimony at the trial of respondent and Patrick Connolly that phenyl–2–propanone was generally difficult to obtain. At the request of the Bureau of Narcotics and Dangerous Drugs, some chemical supply firms had voluntarily ceased selling the chemical.

At the close of the evidence, and after receiving the District Judge's standard entrapment instruction,[4] the jury found the respondent guilty on all counts charged. On appeal, the respondent conceded that the jury could have found him predisposed to commit the offenses, but argued that on the facts presented there was entrapment as a matter of law. The Court of Appeals agreed, although it did not find the District Court had misconstrued or misapplied the traditional standards governing the entrapment defense. Rather, the court in effect expanded the traditional notion of entrapment, which focuses on the predisposition of the defendant, to mandate dismissal of a criminal prosecution whenever the court determines that there has been "an intolerable degree of governmental participation in the criminal enterprise." In this case the court decided that the conduct of the agent in supplying a scarce ingredient essential for the manufacture of a controlled substance established that defense.

This new defense was held to rest on either of two alternative theories. One theory is based on two lower court decisions which have found entrapment, regardless of predisposition, whenever the government supplies contraband to the defendants. The second theory, a non-entrapment rationale, is based on a recent Ninth Circuit decision that reversed a conviction because a government investigator was so enmeshed in the criminal activity that the prosecution of the defendants was held to be repugnant to the American criminal justice system. The court below held that these two rationales constitute the same defense, and that only the label distinguishes them. In any event, it held that "[b]oth theories are premised on fundamental concepts of due process and evince the reluctance of the judiciary to countenance 'overzealous law enforcement.'"

This Court first recognized and applied the entrapment defense in *Sorrells v. United States,* 287 US 435 (1932). In *Sorrells,* a federal prohibition agent visited the defendant while posing as a tourist and engaged him in conversation about their common war experiences. After gaining the defendant's confidence, the agent asked for some liquor, was twice refused, but upon asking a third time the defendant finally capitulated, and was subsequently prosecuted for violating the National Prohibition Act.

Mr. Chief Justice Hughes, speaking for the Court, held that as a matter of statutory construction the defense of entrapment should have been available to the defendant. Under the theory propounded by the Chief Justice, the entrapment defense prohibits law enforcement officers from instigating a criminal act by persons "otherwise innocent in order to lure them to its commission and to punish them." Thus, the thrust of the entrapment defense was held to focus on

---

4. The District Judge stated the governing law on entrapment as follows: "Where a person already has the willingness and the readiness to break the law, the mere fact that the government agent provides what appears to be a favorable opportunity is not entrapment." He then instructed the jury to acquit respondent if it had a "reasonable doubt whether the defendant had the previous intent or purpose to commit the offense * * * and did so only because he was induced or persuaded by some officer or agent of the government." No exception was taken by respondent to this instruction.

the intent or predisposition of the defendant to commit the crime. "[I]f the defendant seeks acquittal by reason of entrapment he cannot complain of an appropriate and searching inquiry into his own conduct and predisposition as bearing upon that issue."

Mr. Justice Roberts concurred but was of the view "that courts must be closed to the trial of a crime instigated by the government's own agents." The difference in the view of the majority and the concurring opinions is that in the former the inquiry focuses on the predisposition of the defendant, whereas in the latter the inquiry focuses on whether the government "instigated the crime."

In *Sherman v. United States* (1958) the Court again considered the theory underlying the entrapment defense and expressly reaffirmed the view expressed by the *Sorrells* majority. In *Sherman* the defendant was convicted of selling narcotics to a Government informer. As in *Sorrells*, it appears that the Government agent gained the confidence of the defendant and, despite initial reluctance, the defendant finally acceded to the repeated importunings of the agent to commit the criminal act. On the basis of *Sorrells*, this Court reversed the affirmance of the defendant's conviction.

In affirming the theory underlying *Sorrells*, Mr. Chief Justice Warren for the Court, held that "[t]o determine whether entrapment has been established, a line must be drawn between the trap for the unwary innocent and the trap for the unwary criminal." Mr. Justice Frankfurter stated in an opinion concurring in the result that he believed Mr. Justice Roberts had the better view in *Sorrells* and would have framed the question to be asked in an entrapment defense in terms of "whether the police conduct revealed in the particular case falls below standards [for] the proper use of governmental power."

In the instant case, respondent asks us to reconsider the theory of the entrapment defense as it is set forth in the majority opinions in *Sorrells* and *Sherman*. His principal contention is that the defense should rest on constitutional grounds. He argues that the level of Shapiro's involvement in the manufacture of the methamphetamine was so high that a criminal prosecution for the drug's manufacture violates the fundamental principles of due process. The respondent contends that the same factors that led this Court to apply the exclusionary rule to illegal searches and seizures [and] confessions should be considered here. But he would have the Court go further in deterring undesirable official conduct by requiring that any prosecution be barred absolutely because of the police involvement in criminal activity. The analogy is imperfect in any event, for the principal reason behind the adoption of the exclusionary rule was the Government's "failure to observe its own laws." [Here, however, the government's conduct] violated no independent constitutional right of the respondent. Nor did Shapiro violate any federal statute or rule or commit any crime in infiltrating the respondent's drug enterprise.

Respondent would overcome this basic weakness in his analogy to the exclusionary rule cases by having the Court adopt a rigid constitutional rule that would preclude any prosecution when it is shown that the criminal conduct would not have been possible had not an undercover agent "supplied an indispensable means to the commission of the crime that could not have been obtained otherwise, through legal or illegal channels." Even if we were to surmount the difficulties attending the notion that due process of law can be embodied in fixed rules, and those attending respondent's particular formulation, the rule he proposes would not appear to be of significant benefit to him. For, on the record presented, it appears that he cannot fit within the terms of the very rule he proposes.

The record discloses that although the propanone was difficult to obtain, it was by no means impossible. The defendants admitted making the drug both before and after those batches made with the propanone supplied by Shapiro. [Thus,] the facts in the record amply demonstrate that the propanone used in the illicit manufacture of methamphetamine not only *could* have been obtained without the intervention of Shapiro but was in fact obtained by these defendants.

While we may some day be presented with a situation in which the conduct of law enforcement agents is so outrageous that due process principles would absolutely bar the government from invoking judicial processes to obtain a conviction, the instant case is distinctly not of that breed. Shapiro's contribution of propanone to the criminal enterprise already in process was scarcely objectionable. The chemical is by itself a harmless substance and its possession is legal. While the Government may have been seeking to make it more difficult for drug rings, such as that of which respondent was a member, to obtain the chemical, the evidence described above shows that it nonetheless was obtainable. The law enforcement conduct here stops far short of violating that "fundamental fairness, shocking to the universal sense of justice," mandated by the Due Process Clause of the Fifth Amendment.

The illicit manufacture of drugs is not a sporadic, isolated criminal incident, but a continuing, though illegal, business enterprise. In order to obtain convictions for illegally manufacturing drugs, the gathering of evidence of past unlawful conduct frequently proves to be an all but impossible task. Thus in drug-related offenses law enforcement personnel have turned to one of the only practicable means of detection: the infiltration of drug rings and a limited participation in their unlawful present practices. Such infiltration is a recognized and permissible means of investigation; if that be so, then the supply of some item of value that the drug ring requires must, as a general rule, also be permissible. For an agent will not be taken into the confidence of the illegal entrepreneurs unless he has something of value to offer them. Law enforcement tactics such as this can hardly be said to violate "fundamental fairness" or "shocking to the universal sense of justice."

Respondent also urges, as an alternative to his constitutional argument, that we broaden the nonconstitutional defense of entrapment in order to sustain the judgment of the Court of Appeals. This Court's opinions in *Sorrells* and *Sherman* held that the principal element in the defense of entrapment was the defendant's predisposition to commit the crime. Respondent conceded in the Court of Appeals, as well he might, "that he may have harbored a predisposition to commit the charged offenses." Yet he argues that the jury's refusal to find entrapment under the charge submitted to it by the trial court should be overturned and the views of Justices Roberts and Frankfurter, in *Sorrells* and *Sherman,* respectively, which make the essential element of the defense turn on the type and degree of governmental conduct, be adopted as the law.

We decline to overrule these cases. [Since] the defense is not of a constitutional dimension, Congress may address itself to the question and adopt any substantive definition of the defense that it may find desirable.

Critics of the rule laid down in *Sorrells* and *Sherman* have suggested that its basis in the implied intent of Congress is largely fictitious, and have pointed to what they conceive to be the anomalous difference between the treatment of a defendant who is solicited by a private individual and one who is entrapped by a government agent. Questions have been likewise raised as to whether "predisposition" can be factually established with the requisite degree of certainty. Arguments such as these, while not devoid of appeal, have been twice previously made to this Court, and twice rejected by it, first in *Sorrells* and then in *Sherman*.

We believe that at least equally cogent criticism has been made of the concurring views in these cases. Commenting in *Sherman* on Mr. Justice Roberts' position in *Sorrells* that "although the defendant could claim that the Government had induced him to commit the crime, the Government could not reply by showing that the defendant's criminal conduct was due to his own readiness and not to the persuasion of government agents," Mr. Chief Justice Warren quoted the observation of Judge Learned Hand in an earlier stage of that proceeding:

" 'Indeed, it would seem probable that, if there were no reply [to the claim of inducement], it would be impossible ever to secure convictions of any offences which consist of transactions that are carried on in secret.' "

Nor does it seem particularly desirable for the law to grant complete immunity from prosecution to one who himself planned to commit a crime, and then committed it, simply because government undercover agents subjected him to inducements which might have seduced a hypothetical individual who was not so predisposed.

[Several lower federal court decisions] have undoubtedly gone beyond this Court's opinions in *Sorrells* and *Sherman* in order to bar prosecutions because of what they thought to be, for want of a better term, "overzealous law enforcement." But the defense of entrapment enunciated in those opinions was not intended to give the federal judiciary a "chancellor's foot" veto over law enforcement practices of which it did not approve. The execution of the federal laws under our Constitution is confided primarily to the Executive Branch of the Government, subject to applicable constitutional and statutory limitations and to judicially fashioned rules to enforce those limitations. We think that the decision of the Court of Appeals in this case quite unnecessarily introduces an unmanageably subjective standard which is contrary to the holdings of this Court in *Sorrells* and *Sherman*.

[In light of *Sorrells* and *Sherman*, respondent's concession] that the jury finding as to predisposition was supported by the evidence [is] therefore, fatal to his claim of entrapment. He was an active participant in an illegal drug manufacturing enterprise which began before the Government agent appeared on the scene, and continued after the Government agent had left the scene. He was, in the words of *Sherman*, not an "unwary innocent" but an "unwary criminal." The Court of Appeals was wrong, we believe, when it sought to broaden the principle laid down in *Sorrells* and *Sherman*. Its judgment is therefore Reversed.

JUSTICE STEWART, with whom JUSTICE BRENNAN and JUSTICE MARSHALL join, dissenting. * * *

In *Sorrells* and *Sherman* the Court took what might be called a "subjective" approach to the defense of entrapment. In that view, the defense is predicated on an unexpressed intent of Congress to exclude from its criminal statutes the prosecution and conviction of persons, "otherwise innocent," who have been lured to the commission of the prohibited act through the Government's instigation. The key phrase in this formulation is "otherwise innocent," for the entrapment defense is available under this approach only to those who would not have committed the crime but for the Government's inducements. Thus, the subjective approach focuses on the conduct and propensities of the particular defendant in each individual case: if he is "otherwise innocent," he may avail himself of the defense; but if he had the "predisposition" to commit the crime, or if the "criminal design" originated with him, then—regardless of the nature and extent of the Government's participation—there has been no entrapment. And, in the absence of a conclusive showing one way or the other, the question of the defendant's "predisposition" to the crime is a question of fact for the jury. The Court today adheres to this approach.

The concurring opinion of Mr. Justice Roberts, joined by Justices Brandeis and Stone, in the *Sorrells* case, and that of Mr. Justice Frankfurter, joined by Justices Douglas, Harlan, and Brennan, in the *Sherman* case, took a different view of the entrapment defense. In their concept, the defense is not grounded on some unexpressed intent of Congress to exclude from punishment under its statutes those otherwise innocent persons tempted into crime by the Government, but rather on the belief that "the methods employed on behalf of the Government to bring about conviction cannot be countenanced." Thus, the focus of this approach is not on the propensities and predisposition of a specific defendant, but on "whether the police conduct revealed in the particular case falls below standards, to which common feelings respond, for the proper use of governmental power." Phrased another way, the question is whether—regardless of the predisposition to crime of the particular defendant involved—the governmental agents have acted in such a way as is likely to instigate or create a criminal offense. Under this approach, the determination of the lawfulness of the Government's conduct must be made—as it is on all questions involving the legality of law enforcement methods—by the trial judge, not the jury.

In my view, this objective approach to entrapment * * * is the only one truly consistent with the underlying rationale of the defense.[1] Indeed, the very basis of the entrapment defense itself demands adherence to an approach that focuses on the conduct of the governmental agents, rather than on whether the defendant was "predisposed" or "otherwise innocent." I find it impossible to believe that the purpose of the defense is to effectuate some unexpressed congressional intent to exclude from its criminal statutes persons who committed a prohibited act, but would not have done so except for the Government's inducements. * * *

Furthermore, to say that such a defendant is "otherwise innocent" or not "predisposed" to commit the crime is misleading, at best. The very fact that he has committed an act that Congress has determined to be illegal demonstrates conclusively that he is not innocent of the offense. He may not have originated the precise plan or the precise details, but he was "predisposed" in the sense that he has proved to be quite capable of committing the crime. That he was induced, provoked, or tempted to do so by government agents does not make him any more innocent or any less predisposed than he would be if he had been induced, provoked, or tempted by a private person—which, of course, would not entitle him to cry "entrapment." Since the only difference between these situations is the identity of the temptor, it follows that the significant focus must be on the conduct of the government agents, and not on the predisposition of the defendant.

The purpose of the entrapment defense, then, cannot be to protect persons who are "otherwise innocent." Rather, it must be to prohibit unlawful governmental activity in instigating crime. [If] that is so, then whether the particular defendant was "predisposed" or "otherwise innocent" is irrelevant; and the

1. Both the Proposed New Federal Criminal Code (1971), Final Report of the National Commission on Reform of Federal Criminal Laws § 702, and the American Law Institute's Model Penal Code § 2.13 (Proposed Official Draft, 1962), adopt this objective approach.

important question becomes whether the Government's conduct in inducing the crime was beyond judicial toleration.

Moreover, a test that makes the entrapment defense depend on whether the defendant had the requisite predisposition permits the introduction into evidence of all kinds of hearsay, suspicion, and rumor—all of which would be inadmissible in any other context—in order to prove the defendant's predisposition. It allows the prosecution, in offering such proof, to rely on the defendant's bad reputation or past criminal activities, including even rumored activities of which the prosecution may have insufficient evidence to obtain an indictment, and to present the agent's suspicions as to why they chose to tempt this defendant. This sort of evidence is not only unreliable, as the hearsay rule recognizes; but it is also highly prejudicial, especially if the matter is submitted to the jury, for, despite instructions to the contrary, the jury may well consider such evidence as probative not simply of the defendant's predisposition, but of his guilt of the offense with which he stands charged.

More fundamentally, focusing on the defendant's innocence or predisposition has the direct effect of making what is permissible or impermissible police conduct depend upon the past record and propensities of the particular defendant involved. Stated another way, this subjective test means that the Government is permitted to entrap a person with a criminal record or bad reputation, and then to prosecute him for the manufactured crime, confident that his record or reputation itself will be enough to show that he was predisposed to commit the offense anyway. * * * In my view, a person's alleged "predisposition" to crime should not expose him to government participation in the criminal transaction that would be otherwise unlawful.

This does not mean, of course, that the Government's use of undercover activity, strategy, or deception is necessarily unlawful. Indeed, many crimes, especially so-called victimless crimes, could not otherwise be detected. Thus, government agents may engage in conduct that is likely, when objectively considered, to afford a person ready and willing to commit the crime an opportunity to do so.

But when the agents' involvement in criminal activities goes beyond the mere offering of such an opportunity, and when their conduct is of a kind that could induce or instigate the commission of a crime by one not ready and willing to commit it, then—regardless of the character or propensities of the particular person induced—I think entrapment has occurred. For in that situation, the Government has engaged in the impermissible manufacturing of crime, and the federal courts should bar the prosecution in order to preserve the institutional integrity of the system of federal criminal justice.

In the case before us, I think that the District Court erred in submitting the issue of entrapment to the jury, with instructions to acquit only if it had a reasonable doubt as to the respondent's predisposition to committing the crime. Since, under the objective test of entrapment, predisposition is irrelevant and the issue is to be decided by the trial judge, the Court of Appeals, I believe, would have been justified in reversing the conviction on this basis alone. But since the appellate court did not remand for consideration of the issue by the District Judge under an objective standard, but rather found entrapment as a matter of law and directed that the indictment be dismissed, we must reach the merits of the respondent's entrapment defense.

Since, in my view, it does not matter whether the respondent was predisposed to commit the offense of which he was convicted, the focus must be, rather, on the conduct of the undercover government agent. What the agent did here was to meet with a group of suspected producers of methamphetamine, including the respondent; to request the drug; to offer to supply the chemical phenyl–2–propanone in exchange for one-half of the methamphetamine to be manufactured therewith; and, when that offer was accepted, to provide the needed chemical ingredient, and to purchase some of the drug from the respondent.

\* \* \*

Although the Court of Appeals found that the phenyl–2–propanone could not have been obtained without the agent's intervention—that "there could not have been the manufacture, delivery, or sale of the illicit drug had it not been for the Government's supply of one of the essential ingredients"—the Court today rejects this finding as contradicted by the facts revealed at trial. The record, as the Court states, discloses that one of the respondent's accomplices, though not the respondent himself, had obtained phenyl–2–propanone from independent sources both before and after receiving the agent's supply, and had used it in the production of methamphetamine. This demonstrates, it is said, that the chemical was obtainable other than through the government agent; and hence the agent's furnishing it for the production of the methamphetamine involved in this prosecution did no more than afford an opportunity for its production to one ready and willing to produce it. Thus, the argument seems to be, there was no entrapment here, any more than there would have been if the agent had furnished common table salt, had that been necessary to the drug's production.

It cannot be doubted that if phenyl–2–propanone had been wholly unobtainable from other sources, the agent's undercover offer to supply it to the respondent in return for part of the illicit methamphetamine produced therewith—an offer initiated and carried out by the agent for the purpose of prosecuting the respondent for producing methamphetamine—would be precisely the type of governmental conduct that constitutes entrapment under any definition. For the agent's conduct in that situation would make possible the commission of an otherwise totally impossible crime, and, I should suppose, would thus be a textbook example of instigating the commission of a criminal offense in order to prosecute someone for committing it.[a]

**a.** Consider, however, *Hampton v. United States,* 425 U.S. 484 (1976), where, unlike *Russell,* the material provided by the undercover agents was contraband (heroin). The district court refused to charge the jury that if it found, as petitioner claimed, that the heroin he sold to government agents (posing as narcotics buyers) had been supplied to him by a government informant he must be acquitted regardless of his predisposition to commit the offense charged. On appeal, petitioner conceded he was "predisposed." A majority of the Court rejected petitioner's contention, but there was no opinion of the Court. Justice Rehnquist, who announced the judgment of the Court in an opinion joined by Burger, C.J., and White, J., observed:

"In urging that this [is the case of outrageous police conduct reserved in *Russell* ], petitioner misapprehends [the relevant language quoted] in *Russell.* Admittedly petitioner's case is different from Russell's but the difference is one of degree, not of kind. In *Russell* the ingredient supplied by the government agent was a legal drug which the defendants demonstrably could have obtained from other sources besides the Government. Here the

drug which the government informant allegedly supplied [was] both illegal and constituted the *corpus delicti* for the sale of which the petitioner was convicted. The Government obviously played a more significant role in enabling petitioner to see contraband in this case than it did in *Russell.*

"But in each case the government agents were acting in concert with the defendant, and in each case either the jury found or the defendant conceded that he was predisposed to commit the crime for which he was convicted. The remedy of the criminal defendant with respect to the act of government agents, which, far from being resisted, are encouraged by him, lies solely in the defense of entrapment. But, as noted, petitioner's conceded predisposition rendered this defense unavailable to him."

Concurring Justice Powell, joined by Blackmun, J., agreed that "this case is controlled completely by *Russell,*" but was unwilling to join the plurality in concluding that, no matter what the circumstances, neither due process principles nor our supervisory power could support a bar to conviction in any case

But assuming in this case that the phenyl–2–propanone was obtainable through independent sources, the fact remains that that used for the particular batch of methamphetamine involved in all three counts of the indictment with which the respondent was charged—i.e., that produced on December 10, 1969— was supplied by the Government. This essential ingredient was indisputably difficult to obtain, and yet what was used in committing the offenses of which the respondent was convicted was offered to the respondent by the Government agent, on the agent's own initiative, and was readily supplied to the respondent in needed amounts.

[In] this case, the chemical ingredient was available only to licensed persons, and the Government itself had requested suppliers not to sell that ingredient even to people with a license. Yet the Government agent readily offered, and supplied, that ingredient to an unlicensed person and asked him to make a certain illegal drug with it. The Government then prosecuted that person for making the drug produced *with the very ingredient* which its agent had so helpfully supplied. This strikes me as the very pattern of conduct that should be held to constitute entrapment as a matter of law.

It is the Government's duty to prevent crime, not to promote it. Here, the Government's agent asked that the illegal drug be produced for him, solved his quarry's practical problems with the assurance that he could provide the one essential ingredient that was difficult to obtain, furnished that element as he had promised, and bought the finished product from the respondent—all so that the respondent could be prosecuted for producing and selling the very drug for which the agent had asked and for which he had provided the necessary component. Under the objective approach that I would follow, this respondent was entrapped, regardless of his predisposition or "innocence." * * * [b]

where the Government is able to prove disposition."

Justice Brennan, joined by Stewart and Marshall, JJ., dissented, urging that conviction be "barred as a matter of law where the subject of the criminal charge is the sale of contraband provided to the defendant by a Government agent." The dissenters reiterated support for the "objective" approach to entrapment, but considered reversal compelled even "for those who follow the 'subjective' approach." Continued the dissent:

"Two facts sufficiently distinguish the case from *Russell*. First, the chemical supplied in that case was not contraband. * * * Second, [Russell] 'was an active participant in an illegal drug manufacturing enterprise which began before the Government agent appeared on the scene, and continued after the Government agent had left * * *.' [But] the two sales for which petitioner was convicted were allegedly instigated by Government agents and completed by the Government's purchase.

"[Where] the Government's agent deliberately sets up the accused by supplying him with contraband and then bringing him to another agent as a potential purchaser, the Government's role has passed the point of toleration. The Government is doing nothing less than buying contraband from itself through an intermediary and jailing the intermediary."

**b.** In a separate dissent, Justice Douglas, joined by Brennan, J., maintained that "[f]ederal agents play a debased role when they become the instigators of the crime, or partners in its commission, or the creative brain behind the illegal scheme. That is what the federal agent did here when he furnished the accused with one of the chemical ingredients needed to manufacture the unlawful drug."

# Chapter 5

## THE RIGHT TO COUNSEL, TRANSCRIPTS AND OTHER AIDS; POVERTY, EQUALITY AND THE ADVERSARY SYSTEM [a]

### SECTION 1.  THE RIGHT TO APPOINTED COUNSEL [b]

When the Court, per Sutherland, J., spoke eloquently of the importance of the right to counsel and the essential relationship between "the right to be heard" and "the right to be heard by counsel" in the landmark case of *Powell v. Alabama*, 287 U.S. 45 (1932), which has been called the first "modern" procedural due process case, it was talking about a person's right to be heard by counsel "employed by and appearing for him."  Although Justice Black's analysis for the Court thirty years later in *Gideon v. Wainwright* appears to ignore this fact, *Powell* dealt primarily not with the right to appointed counsel, but the historically separate right of the individual to employ her own counsel.

The *Powell* opinion spelled out at some length why the defendants were not afforded "a fair opportunity to secure counsel of [their] own choice" and why, under the circumstances, this constituted a denial of due process.  The *Powell* Court went on to say however, and it did this only in the last few pages of a lengthy opinion, that "assuming the inability, even if opportunity had been given, to employ counsel," the failure of the trial court "to make an effective appointment of counsel was likewise a denial of due process."  Continued the Court, using very measured language:

> "Whether this would be so in other criminal prosecutions, or under other circumstances, we need not determine.  All that is necessary now to decide, as we do decide, is that in a capital case, where the defendant is unable to employ counsel, and is incapable adequately of making his own

**a.**  The right to counsel is treated in Chapter 17 as well as in this chapter.  Because the right to appointed counsel and the *Griffin–Douglas* "equality" principle provide important background for the confessions cases (Ch. 6) and the lineup cases (Ch. 7), these aspects of the right to counsel are treated at this point.  Because it seemed more appropriate to take up other aspects of the right to counsel, such as the right to "effective" assistance of counsel, in the context of the role of counsel, these aspects of the right are treated in Chapter 17.

**b.**  *Douglas v. California* also deals with the right to appointed counsel—on the first appeal, granted by the state as a matter of right—but because it is based primarily on the Equal Protection Clause it is set forth in the next section.

defense because of ignorance, feeblemindedness, illiteracy, or the like, it is the duty of the court, whether requested or not, to assign counsel for him as a necessary requisite of due process of law; and that duty is not discharged by an assignment at such a time or under such circumstances as to preclude the giving of effective aid in the preparation and trial of the case."

Despite the *Powell* Court's carefully limited statement about the right to appointed counsel in state criminal cases, when the Court held, six years later, in *Johnson v. Zerbst*, 304 U.S. 458 (1938), that the Sixth Amendment required *federal* courts to provide indigent defendants with appointed counsel in all serious criminal cases (at least all felony cases), many thought the same rule would soon be applied to state prosecutions. For Justice Black, who wrote the opinion for the *Johnson* Court, painted with a broad brush, giving the impression that the Court was prepared to say that the right to counsel, appointed or retained, was a "fundamental" right made obligatory upon the states by the Fourteenth Amendment.

Thus, Justice Black called the right to counsel "one of the safeguards * * * deemed necessary to insure fundamental human rights of life and liberty" and the Sixth Amendment "a constant admonition that if the constitutional safeguards it provides be lost, justice will not 'still be done.'" Relying heavily on *Powell*'s discussion of the general need for, and importance of, the right to counsel, *Johnson* concluded that the Sixth Amendment embodies "the obvious truth that the average defendant does not have the professional legal skill to protect himself when brought before a tribunal" and that the Amendment "withholds from federal courts, in all criminal proceedings, the power and authority to deprive an accused of his life or liberty unless he has or waives the assistance of counsel."

However, in *Betts v. Brady*, the first case set forth in this section, the Court refused to read *Powell* broadly or to apply *Johnson* to the states via the Fourteenth Amendment's due process clause. Instead, the Court formulated a "prejudice" or "special circumstances" rule: an indigent defendant in a noncapital case [c] had to show specifically that he had been "prejudiced" by the absence of a lawyer or that "special circumstances" (e.g., the defendant's lack of education or intelligence or the gravity and complexity of the offense charged) rendered criminal proceedings without the assistance of defense counsel "fundamentally unfair." [d]

One of the troubles with the *Betts v. Brady* doctrine was that its application was inherently speculative and problematic. A record produced by a layperson defending himself often makes the person *look* overwhelmingly guilty and the case *look* exceedingly simple. Such a record does not reflect what defenses or mitigating circumstances a trained advocate would have seen or what lines of inquiry she would have pursued. This point was made very forcefully by Justice Black (joined by Douglas and Murphy, JJ.), dissenting in *Betts*. Twenty-one years later, Justice Black wrote the opinion for the Court in *Gideon v. Wainwright*, overruling *Betts*.

**c.** Soon after *Betts*, the Court indicated that an indigent person had a "flat" or unqualified right to appointed counsel when (but only when) charged with a crime punishable by death.

**d.** When the Court reviewed Betts' case, he had appellate counsel, but his lawyer was confident—too confident—that the Court would apply the full measure of the Sixth Amendment right to counsel to the states. Thus, he did not make any analysis of the trial and present any specific examples of how Betts was, or might have been, prejudiced by the absence of counsel. Commentators, upon review of the *Betts* record, have maintained that a number of such examples could have been shown.

The opinion in *Gideon,* the second case set forth in this section, might have been written differently. It might, to use concurring Justice Harlan's phrase, have accorded *Betts* "a more respectful burial." For example, Justice Black might have pointed out that in the two decades since *Betts* the assumption that a lawyerless defendant would usually be able to defend himself had fared poorly as the Court repeatedly found "special circumstances" requiring the services of counsel and constantly expanded the concept of "special circumstances." [e] Justice Black might also have noted that the assumption that a "special circumstances" test was more consistent with the "obligations of federalism" than an "absolute rule" had collapsed in the face of the proliferation of federal habeas corpus cases produced by the *Betts* rule and the resulting friction between state and federal courts.

But Justice Black made no attempt to show that developments in the two decades since *Betts* militated in favor of its demise. Perhaps he was reluctant to admit even the *original validity* of a decision that exemplified the evils (to him) of the "fundamental rights" interpretation of Fourteenth Amendment Due Process.[f] Perhaps he was determined to vindicate his own dissenting opinion in *Betts.*

Although *Gideon* was one of the most popular cases ever decided by the Supreme Court, it came fairly late in the day. Indeed, it is quite surprising that the Court did not establish the constitutional right to appointed counsel in all serious criminal cases until *two years after* it imposed the Fourth Amendment exclusionary rule on state courts as a matter of due process.

It is helpful to view criminal procedural due process as containing two major values or objectives. The first and the more obvious one is insuring the reliability of the guilt-determining process. The second and more elusive one is insuring respect for the dignity or liberty of the individual without regard to the reliability of the criminal process. The exclusionary rule (Ch. 3, § 1) implements the second goal; the right to counsel (sometimes called "the most pervasive right" of the accused or "the master key" to all rights) effectuates the first—and the most basic goal. Yet the Court moved ahead on the search and seizure front before it overruled the *Betts* rule.

Moreover, a major criticism of *Weeks* and *Mapp* (Ch. 3, § 1) was that because they addressed problems beyond the direct control of the courts these cases could not accomplish their goal—deterring illegal searches and seizures. But this criticism was not applicable to enlargement of the indigent defendant's right to counsel. For the *Betts–Gideon* line of cases dealt with the right to appointed counsel at arraignment, trial and sentencing, matters within the immediate and continuing control of the courts. Assuming arguendo that police officers and sheriffs are insensitive to acquittals and reversals, trial judges and prosecutors are not—and they would be entrusted with the task of carrying out the requirements of an enlarged right to appointed counsel.

Note, too, that when the Court in *Mapp* imposed the exclusionary rule on the states in 1961, the states were evenly split on the question. But when the

---

**e.** In *Chewning v. Cunningham,* 368 U.S. 443 (1962), the last of the *Betts* rule cases, the Court not only found "special circumstances" requiring the services of counsel, as it had in every case after 1950, but indicated that these circumstances would be made out whenever issues existed that "may well be considered by an *imaginative lawyer*" (emphasis added) without regard to "whether *any would have*

merit" (emphasis added). As concurring Justice Harlan protested on that occasion, "the bare possibility that any of these improbable claims could have been asserted does not amount [to] 'exceptional circumstances'" as the *Betts* rule had long been understood.

**f.** See also, Black, J., dissenting in *Adamson v. California,* Ch. 2, § 1.

Court in *Gideon* reconsidered the *Betts* doctrine in 1963, some thirty-seven states—about a three to one margin—provided counsel for all indigent felony defendants regardless of special circumstances. Moreover, as Mr. Gideon's lawyers pointed out to the Supreme Court, of the thirteen states whose laws or rules did not require the appointment of counsel in all felony cases, eight usually did so as a matter of practice. Only five southern states made no regular provision for counsel in noncapital cases.

Of course, three years after *Gideon,* when the Court applied the right to assigned counsel to the proceedings in the police station (see *Miranda,* Ch. 6, § 3), *no* state had chosen to go nearly that far on its own and, unlike *Gideon* (when twenty-two states asked the Court to overrule *Betts* ), no state urged the Court to go that far. That is one reason (but hardly the only reason) that *Miranda* had a much colder reception than *Gideon.*

How early in the criminal process the right to counsel should "begin" was not the only question left open by *Gideon.* Another was: At what stage in the criminal process does the right to counsel "end"? The first appeal as of right? Discretionary review in the state supreme court? Discretionary review in the U.S. Supreme Court? (See the next section, infra.) Still another question left open by *Gideon* was: What *kinds* of criminal cases are covered by *Gideon* ?

Some thought *Gideon* should be limited to felony cases. Others thought it should include any crime *punishable* by a term of imprisonment. Still others thought a line should be drawn, as it had been in cases dealing with the right to jury, between serious misdemeanors and "petty offenses" (those punishable by six months imprisonment or less). As demonstrated by the last two cases in this section, *Argersinger v. Hamlin* and *Scott v. Illinois,* the Court adopted none of the aforementioned approaches.

## BETTS v. BRADY

316 U.S. 455, 62 S.Ct. 1252, 86 L.Ed. 1595 (1942).

Justice Roberts delivered the opinion of the Court.

Petitioner, an indigent, was indicted for robbery. His request for counsel was denied because local practice permitted appointment only in rape and murder prosecutions. Petitioner then pled not guilty and elected to be tried without a jury. At the trial he chose not to take the stand. He was convicted and sentenced to eight years imprisonment.

[The] due process clause of the Fourteenth Amendment does not incorporate, as such, the specific guarantees found in the Sixth Amendment although a denial by a state of rights or privileges specifically embodied in that and others of the first eight amendments may, in certain circumstances, or in connection with other elements, operate, in a given case, to deprive a litigant of due process of law in violation of the Fourteenth. [Due process] formulates a concept less rigid and more fluid than those envisaged in other specific and particular provisions of the Bill of Rights. Its application is less a matter of rule. Asserted denial is to be tested by an appraisal of the totality of facts in a given case.

[Petitioner] says the rule to be deduced from our former decisions is that, in every case, whatever the circumstances, one charged with crime, who is unable to obtain counsel, must be furnished counsel by the state. Expressions in the opinions of this court lend color to the argument, but, as the petitioner admits, none of our decisions squarely adjudicates the question now presented.

In *Powell v. Alabama,* 287 U.S. 45 (1932), ignorant and friendless negro youths, strangers in the community, without friends or means to obtain counsel, were hurried to trial for a capital offense without effective appointment of counsel [and] without adequate opportunity to consult even the counsel casually appointed to represent them. This occurred in a State whose statute law required the appointment of counsel for indigent defendants prosecuted for the offense charged. Thus the trial was conducted in disregard of every principle of fairness and in disregard of that which was declared by the law of the State a requisite of a fair trial. This court [stated] further that "under the circumstances [the] necessity of counsel was so vital and imperative that the failure of the trial court to make an effective appointment of counsel was likewise a denial of due process," but added: "whether this would be so in other criminal prosecutions, or under other circumstances, we need not determine. All that it is necessary now to decide, as we do decide, is that in a capital case, where the defendant is unable to employ counsel, and is incapable adequately of making his own defense because of ignorance, feeble-mindedness, illiteracy, or the like, it is the duty of the court, whether requested or not, to assign counsel for him as a necessary requisite of due process of law * * *"

* * * We have construed the [Sixth Amendment] to require appointment of counsel in all [federal] cases where a defendant is unable to procure the services of an attorney, and where the right has not been intentionally and competently waived. [*Johnson v. Zerbst*, 304 U.S. 458 (1938)]. Though [the] amendment lays down no rule for the conduct of the states, the question recurs whether the constraint laid by the amendment upon the national courts expresses a rule so fundamental and essential to a fair trial, and so, to due process of law, that it is made obligatory upon the states by the Fourteenth Amendment. Relevant data on the subject are afforded by constitutional and statutory provisions subsisting in the colonies and the states prior to the inclusion of the Bill of Rights in the national Constitution, and in the constitutional, legislative, and judicial history of the states to the present date.

[I]n the great majority of the states, it has been the considered judgment of the people, their representatives and their courts that appointment of counsel is not a fundamental right, essential to a fair trial. On the contrary, the matter has generally been deemed one of legislative policy. In the light of this evidence we are unable to say that the concept of due process incorporated in the Fourteenth Amendment obligates the states, whatever may be their own views, to furnish counsel in every such case. Every court has power, if it deems proper, to appoint counsel where that course seems to be required in the interest of fairness.

The practice of the courts of Maryland gives point to the principle that the states should not be straight-jacketed in this respect, by a construction of the Fourteenth Amendment. Judge Bond's opinion states, and counsel at the bar confirmed the fact, that in Maryland the usual practice is for the defendant to waive a trial by jury. This the petitioner did in the present case. Such trials, as Judge Bond remarks, are much more informal than jury trials and it is obvious that the judge can much better control the course of the trial and is in a better position to see impartial justice done than when the formalities of a jury trial are involved.

In this case there was no question of the commission of a robbery. The State's case consisted of evidence identifying the petitioner as the perpetrator. The defense was an alibi. Petitioner called and examined witnesses to prove that he was at another place at the time of the commission of the offense. The simple issue was the veracity of the testimony for the State and that for the defendant. As Judge Bond says, the accused was not helpless, but was a man forty-three years old, of ordinary intelligence and ability to take care of his own interests on the trial of that narrow issue. He had once before been in a criminal court, pleaded guilty to larceny and served a sentence and was not wholly unfamiliar with criminal procedure. It is quite clear that in Maryland, if the situation had been otherwise and it had appeared that the petitioner was, for any reason, at a serious disadvantage by reason of the lack of counsel, a refusal to appoint would have resulted in the reversal of a judgment of conviction.

[To] deduce from the due process clause a rule binding upon the states in this matter would be to impose upon them, as Judge Bond points out, a requirement without distinction between criminal charges of different magnitude or in respect of courts of varying jurisdiction. As he says: "Charges of small crimes tried before justices of the peace and capital charges tried in the higher courts would equally require the appointment of counsel. Presumably it would be argued that trials in the Traffic Court would require it." * * *

As we have said, the Fourteenth Amendment prohibits the conviction and incarceration of one whose trial is offensive to the common and fundamental ideas of fairness and right, and while want of counsel in a particular case may result in a conviction lacking in such fundamental fairness, we cannot say that the amendment embodies an inexorable command that no trial for any offense, or in any court, can be fairly conducted and justice accorded a defendant who is not represented by counsel.

The judgment is affirmed.

Justice Black, dissenting, with whom Justice Douglas and Justice Murphy concur.

To hold that the petitioner had a constitutional right to counsel in this case does not require us to say that "no trial for any offense, or in any court, can be fairly conducted and justice accorded a defendant who is not represented by counsel." This case can be determined by resolution of a narrower question: whether in view of the nature of the offense and the circumstances of his trial and conviction, this petitioner was denied the procedural protection which is his right under the federal constitution. I think he was.

The petitioner [was] a farm hand, out of a job and on relief. [The] court below found that [he] had "at least an ordinary amount of intelligence." It is clear from his examination of witnesses that he was a man of little education.

If this case had come to us from a federal court, it is clear we should have to reverse it, because the Sixth Amendment makes the right to counsel in criminal cases inviolable by the federal government. I believe that the Fourteenth Amendment made the sixth applicable to the states. But this view [has] never been accepted by a majority of this Court and is not accepted today. * * * I believe, however, that under the prevailing view of due process, as reflected in the opinion just announced, a view which gives this Court such vast supervisory powers that I am not prepared to accept it without grave doubts, the judgment below should be reversed.

[The] right to counsel in a criminal proceeding is "fundamental." *Powell v. Alabama.* [A] practice cannot be reconciled with "common and fundamental ideas of fairness and right" which subjects innocent men to increased dangers of conviction merely because of their poverty. Whether a man is innocent cannot be determined from a trial in which as here, denial of counsel has made it impossible to conclude, with any satisfactory degree of certainty, that the defendant's case was adequately presented. * * *

Denial to the poor of the request for counsel in proceedings based on charges of serious crime has long been regarded as shocking to the "universal sense of justice" throughout this country.  In 1854, for example, the Supreme Court of Indiana said: "It is not to be thought of, in a civilized community, for a moment, that any citizen put in jeopardy of life or liberty should be debarred of counsel because he was too poor to employ such aid.  No Court could be respected, or respect itself, to sit and hear such a trial.  The defence of the poor, in such cases, is a duty resting somewhere, which will be at once conceded as essential to the accused, to the Court, and to the public."  And most of the other states have shown their agreement by constitutional provisions, statutes, or established practice judicially approved which assure that no man shall be deprived of counsel merely because of his poverty.  Any other practice seems to me to defeat the promise of our democratic society to provide equal justice under the law.

## GIDEON v. WAINWRIGHT

372 U.S. 335, 83 S.Ct. 792, 9 L.Ed.2d 799 (1963).

JUSTICE BLACK delivered the opinion of the Court.

Petitioner was charged in a Florida state court with having broken and entered a poolroom with intent to commit a misdemeanor.  This offense is a felony under Florida law.  Appearing in court without funds and without a lawyer, petitioner asked the court to appoint counsel for him, whereupon the following colloquy took place:

"The Court: Mr. Gideon, I am sorry, but I cannot appoint Counsel to represent you in this case.  Under the laws of the State of Florida, the only time the Court can appoint Counsel to represent a Defendant is when that person is charged with a capital offense.  * * *

"The Defendant: The United States Supreme Court says I am entitled to be represented by Counsel."

Put to trial before a jury, Gideon conducted his defense about as well as could be expected from a layman.  He made an opening statement to the jury, cross-examined the State's witnesses, presented witnesses in his own defense, declined to testify himself, and made a short argument "emphasizing his innocence to the charge contained in the Information filed in this case."  The jury returned a verdict of guilty, and petitioner was sentenced to serve five years in the state prison.  Later, petitioner [unsuccessfully attacked his conviction and sentence in the state supreme court on the ground that the trial court's refusal to appoint counsel for him violated his constitutional rights].  Since 1942, when *Betts v. Brady* was decided by a divided Court, the problem of a defendant's federal constitutional right to counsel in a state court has been a continuing source of controversy and litigation in both state and federal courts.  To give this problem another review here, we granted certiorari [and] appointed counsel to represent [petitioner].

We accept *Betts* 's assumption, based as it was on our prior cases, that a provision of the Bill of Rights which is "fundamental and essential to a fair trial" is made obligatory upon the States by the Fourteenth Amendment.  We think the Court in *Betts* was wrong, however, in concluding that the Sixth Amendment's guarantee of counsel is not one of these fundamental rights.  Ten years before *Betts,* this Court, after full consideration of all the historical data examined in *Betts,* had unequivocally declared that "the right to the aid of counsel is of this fundamental character."  *Powell.*  While the Court at the close of its *Powell* opinion did by its language, as this Court frequently does, limit its holding to the particular facts and circumstances of that case, its conclusions about the fundamental nature of the right to counsel are unmistakable. [The] fact is that in deciding as it did—that "appointment of counsel is not a fundamental right, essential to a fair trial"—the [*Betts* Court] made an abrupt break with its own well-considered precedents. In returning to these old precedents, sounder we believe than the new, we but restore constitutional principles established to achieve a fair system of justice. Not only these precedents but also reason and reflection require us to recognize that in our adversary system of criminal justice, any person haled into court, who is too poor to hire a lawyer, cannot be assured a fair trial unless counsel is provided for him. This seems to us to be an obvious truth. Governments, both state and federal, quite properly spend vast sums of money to establish machinery to try defendants accused of crime. Lawyers to prosecute are everywhere deemed essential to protect the public's interest in an orderly society. Similarly, there are few defendants charged with crime, few indeed, who fail to hire the best lawyers they can get to prepare and present their defenses. That government hires lawyers to prosecute and defendants who have the money hire lawyers to defend are the strongest indications of the widespread belief that lawyers in criminal courts are necessities, not luxuries. The right of one charged with crime to counsel may not be deemed fundamental and essential to fair trials in some countries, but it is in ours. From the very beginning, our state and national constitutions and laws have laid great emphasis on procedural and substantive safeguards designed to assure fair trials before impartial tribunals in which every defendant stands equal before the law. This noble ideal cannot be realized if the poor man charged with crime has to face his accusers without a lawyer to assist him.

\* \* \*

The Court in *Betts* departed from the sound wisdom upon which the Court's holding in *Powell* rested. Florida, supported by two other States, has asked that *Betts v. Brady* be left intact. Twenty-two States, as friends of the Court, argue that *Betts* was "an anachronism when handed down" and that it should now be overruled. We agree. \* \* \* Reversed.[a]

JUSTICE CLARK, concurring in the result. \* \* \*

[T]he Constitution makes no distinction between capital and noncapital cases. The Fourteenth Amendment requires due process of law for the deprival of "liberty" just as for deprival of "life," and there cannot constitutionally be a difference in the quality of the process based merely upon a supposed difference in the sanction involved. How can the Fourteenth Amendment tolerate a procedure which it condemns in capital cases on the ground that deprival of liberty may be less onerous than deprival of life—a value judgment not universally accepted—or that only the latter deprival is irrevocable? \* \* \*

JUSTICE HARLAN, concurring.

I agree that *Betts* should be overruled, but consider it entitled to a more respectful burial than has been accorded, at least on the part of those of us who were not on the Court when that case was decided.

I cannot subscribe to the view that *Betts* represented "an abrupt break with its own well-considered precedents." [In *Powell* ] this Court declared that under the particular facts there presented—"the ignorance and illiteracy of the defendants, their youth, the circumstances of public hostility [and] above all that they stood in deadly peril of their lives"—the state court had a duty to assign counsel

a. Gideon was retried, this time with appointed counsel, and acquitted. See Lewis, *Gideon's Trumpet* 223–38 (1964).

for the trial as a necessary requisite of due process of law. It is evident that these limiting facts were not added to the opinion as an afterthought; they were repeatedly emphasized [and] were clearly regarded as important to the result.

Thus when this Court, a decade later, decided *Betts,* it did no more than to admit of the possible existence of special circumstances in noncapital as well as capital trials, while at the same time to insist that such circumstances be shown in order to establish a denial of due process. The right to appointed counsel had been recognized as being considerably broader in federal prosecutions, see *Johnson v. Zerbst,* but to have imposed these requirements on the States would indeed have been "an abrupt break" with the almost immediate past. The declaration that the right to appointed counsel in state prosecutions, as established in *Powell,* was not limited to capital cases was in truth not a departure from, but an extension of, existing precedent.

The principles declared in *Powell* and in *Betts,* however, had a troubled journey throughout the years that have followed first the one case and then the other. Even by the time of the *Betts* decision, dictum in at least one of the Court's opinions had indicated that there was an absolute right to the services of counsel in the trial of state capital cases. * * *

In noncapital cases, the "special circumstances" rule has continued to exist in form while its substance has been substantially and steadily eroded. In the first decade after *Betts,* there were cases in which the Court found special circumstances to be lacking, but usually by a sharply divided vote. However, no such decision has been cited to us, and I have found none, [after] 1950. At the same time, there have been not a few cases in which special circumstances were found in little or nothing more than the "complexity" of the legal questions presented, although those questions were often of only routine difficulty. The Court has come to recognize, in other words, that the mere existence of a serious criminal charge constituted in itself special circumstances requiring the services of counsel at trial. In truth the *Betts* rule is no longer a reality.

This evolution, however, appears not to have been fully recognized by many state courts, in this instance charged with the front-line responsibility for the enforcement of constitutional rights. To continue a rule which is honored by this Court only with lip service is not a healthy thing and in the long run will do disservice to the federal system.

The special circumstances rule has been formally abandoned in capital cases, and the time has now come when it should be similarly abandoned in noncapital cases, at least as to offenses which, as the one involved here, carry the possibility of a substantial prison sentence. (Whether the rule should extend to *all* criminal cases need not now be decided.)

* * * In what is done today I do not understand the Court to depart from the principles laid down in *Palko* [or] to embrace the concept that the Fourteenth Amendment "incorporates" the Sixth Amendment as such. On these premises I join in the judgment of the Court.

## ARGERSINGER v. HAMLIN

407 U.S. 25, 92 S.Ct. 2006, 32 L.Ed.2d 530 (1972).

JUSTICE DOUGLAS delivered the opinion of the Court.

Petitioner, an indigent, was charged in Florida with carrying a concealed weapon, an offense punishable by imprisonment up to six months, a $1,000 fine, or both. The trial was to a judge, and petitioner was unrepresented by counsel. [He was convicted and sentenced to 90 days in jail. The Florida Supreme Court

affirmed.   Following the line marked out in the jury trial cases, the state court]
held that the right to court-appointed counsel extends only to trials "for nonpetty offenses punishable by more than six months imprisonment."  *  *  *

While there is historical support for limiting the [right] to trial by jury [to]
"serious criminal cases," there is no such support for a similar limitation on the
right to assistance of counsel.  [Thus,] we reject [the] premise that since prosecutions for crimes punishable by imprisonment for less than six months may be
tried without a jury, they may always be tried without a lawyer.  [The]
requirement of counsel may well be necessary for a fair trial even in a petty
offense prosecution.  We are by no means convinced that legal and constitutional questions involved in a case that actually leads to imprisonment even for a
brief period are any less complex than when a person can be sent off for six
months or more.  *  *  *

Beyond the problem of trials and appeals is that of the guilty plea, a
problem which looms large in misdemeanor as well as in felony cases.  Counsel
is needed so that the accused may know precisely what he is doing, so that he is
fully aware of the prospect of going to jail or prison, and so that he is treated
fairly by the prosecution.

In addition, the volume of misdemeanor cases, far greater in number than
felony prosecutions, may create an obsession for speedy dispositions, regardless
of the fairness of the result.  *  *  *

We must conclude, therefore, that the problems associated with misdemean-
or and petty offenses often require the presence of counsel to insure the accused
a fair trial.  [In his concurring opinion,] Mr. Justice Powell suggests that these
problems are raised even in situations where there is no prospect of imprisonment.  We need not consider the requirements of the Sixth Amendment as
regards the right to counsel where loss of liberty is not involved, however, for
here, petitioner was in fact sentenced to jail  *  *  *.

Under the rule we announce today, every judge will know when the trial of
a misdemeanor starts that no imprisonment may be imposed, even though local
law permits it, unless the accused is represented by counsel.  He will have a
measure of the seriousness and gravity of the offense and therefore know when
to name a lawyer to represent the accused before the trial starts.[a]

JUSTICE POWELL, with whom JUSTICE REHNQUIST joins, concurring with the
result.  *  *  *

I am unable to agree with the Supreme Court of Florida that an indigent
defendant, charged with a petty offense, may in every case be afforded a fair
trial without the assistance of counsel.  Nor can I agree with [the Court's] new
rule of due process [that] "absent a [valid] waiver, no person may be imprisoned
[unless] he was represented by counsel at his trial."  It seems to me that the line
should not be drawn with such rigidity.

There is a middle course, between the extremes of Florida's six-month rule
and the Court's rule, which comports with the requirements of the Fourteenth
Amendment.  I would adhere to the principle of due process that requires
fundamental fairness in criminal trials, a principle which I believe encompasses
the right to counsel in petty cases whenever the assistance of counsel is
necessary to assure a fair trial.

Due process, perhaps the most fundamental concept in our law, embodies
principles of fairness rather than immutable line-drawing as to every aspect of a

a.  Burger, C.J. concurred in the result.      JJ. joined the Court's opinion and, added a
Brennan, J., joined by Douglas and Stewart,     brief concurring opinion.

criminal trial. While counsel is often essential to a fair trial, this is by no means a universal fact. Some petty offense cases are complex; others are exceedingly simple. [The] government often does not hire lawyers to prosecute petty offenses; instead the arresting police officer presents the case. Nor does every defendant who can afford to do so hire lawyers to defend petty charges. Where the possibility of a jail sentence is remote and the probable fine seems small, or where the evidence of guilt is overwhelming, the costs of assistance of counsel may exceed the benefits. It is anomalous that the Court's opinion today will extend the right of appointed counsel to indigent defendants in cases where the right to counsel would rarely be exercised by nonindigent defendants.

Indeed, one of the effects of this ruling will be to favor defendants classified as indigents over those not so classified yet who are in low income groups where engaging counsel in a minor petty offense case would be a luxury the family could not afford. The line between indigency and assumed capacity to pay for counsel is necessarily somewhat arbitrary, drawn differently from State to State and often resulting in serious inequities to accused persons. The Court's new rule will accent the disadvantage of being barely self-sufficient economically.

\* \* \*

The rule adopted today [is] limited to petty offense cases in which the sentence is some imprisonment. The thrust of the Court's position indicates, however, that when the decision must be made, the rule will be extended to all petty offense cases except perhaps the most minor traffic violations. If the Court rejects on constitutional grounds, as it has today, the exercise of any judicial discretion as to need for counsel if a jail sentence is imposed, one must assume a similar rejection of discretion in other petty offense cases. It would be illogical—and without discernible support in the Constitution—to hold that no discretion may ever be exercised where a nominal jail sentence is contemplated and at the same time endorse the legitimacy of discretion in 'non-jail' petty offense cases which may result in far more serious consequences than a few hours or days of incarceration. \* \* \*

[The] Court's opinion foreshadows the adoption of a broad prophylactic rule applicable to all petty offenses [whether or not the defendant is actually incarcerated]. No one can foresee the consequences of such a drastic enlargement of the constitutional right to free counsel. But even today's decision could have a seriously adverse impact upon the day to day functioning of the criminal justice system. \* \* \*

I would hold that the right to counsel in petty offense cases is not absolute but is one to be determined by the trial courts exercising a judicial discretion on a case-by-case basis. \* \* \*

[T]hree general factors should be weighed. First, the court should consider the complexity of the offense charged. For example, charges of traffic law infractions would rarely present complex legal or factual questions, but charges that contain difficult intent elements or which raise collateral legal questions, such as search and seizure problems, would usually be too complex for an unassisted layman. If the offense were one where the State is represented by counsel and where most defendants who can afford to do so obtain counsel, there would be a strong indication that the indigent also needs the assistance of counsel.

Second, the court should consider the probable sentence that will follow if a conviction is obtained. The more serious the likely consequences, the greater is the probability that a lawyer should be appointed. [I]mprisonment is not the only serious consequence the court should consider.

Third, the court should consider the individual factors peculiar to each case. These, of course, would be the most difficult to anticipate. One relevant factor would be the competency of the individual defendant to present his own case. The attitude of the community toward a particular defendant or particular incident would be another consideration. But there might be other reasons why a defendant would have a peculiar need for a lawyer which would compel the appointment of counsel in a case where the court would normally think this unnecessary. * * *

Such a rule is similar in certain respects to the special circumstances rule applied to felony cases in *Betts,* which this Court overruled in *Gideon.* One of the reasons for seeking a more definitive standard in felony cases was the failure of many state courts to live up to their responsibilities in determining on a case-by-case basis whether counsel should be appointed. But this Court should not assume that the past insensitivity of some state courts to the rights of defendants will continue. Certainly if the Court follows the course of reading rigid rules into the Constitution, so that the state courts will be unable to exercise judicial discretion within the limits of fundamental fairness, there is little reason to think that insensitivity will abate.

* * * We are all strongly drawn to the ideal of extending the right to counsel, but I differ as to two fundamentals: (i) what the Constitution *requires,* and (ii) the effect upon the criminal justice system, especially in the smaller cities and the thousands of police, municipal and justice of the peace courts across the country.

## SCOTT v. ILLINOIS

440 U.S. 367, 99 S.Ct. 1158, 59 L.Ed.2d 383 (1979).

JUSTICE REHNQUIST delivered the opinion of the Court. * * *

[Petitioner, an indigent, was charged with shoplifting merchandise valued at less than $150, punishable by as much as a $500 fine, or one year in jail, or both. He was not provided counsel. After a bench trial he was convicted of the offense and fined $50. The Supreme Court of Illinois declined to "extend *Argersinger*" to a case where one is charged with an offense for which imprisonment upon conviction is authorized but not actually imposed.]

In *Argersinger* the Court rejected arguments that social cost or a lack of available lawyers militated against its holding, in some part because it thought these arguments were factually incorrect. But they were rejected in much larger part because of the Court's conclusion that incarceration was so severe a sanction that it should not be imposed as a result of a criminal trial unless an indigent defendant has been offered appointed counsel to assist in his defense, regardless of the cost to the States implicit in such a rule. * * *

Although the intentions of the *Argersinger* Court are not unmistakably clear from its opinion, we conclude today that *Argersinger* did indeed delimit the constitutional right to appointed counsel in state criminal proceedings. Even were the matter *res nova,* we believe that the central premise of *Argersinger*—that actual imprisonment is a penalty different in kind from fines or the mere threat of imprisonment—is eminently sound and warrants adoption of actual imprisonment as the line defining the constitutional right to appointment of counsel. *Argersinger* has proved reasonably workable, whereas any extension would create confusion and impose unpredictable, but necessarily substantial, costs on 50 quite diverse States. We therefore hold that the Sixth and Fourteenth Amendments * * * require only that no indigent criminal defendant be sentenced to a term of imprisonment unless the State has afforded him the right to assistance of appointed counsel in his defense. The judgment [below] is accordingly [affirmed.] [a]

JUSTICE BRENNAN, with whom JUSTICE MARSHALL and JUSTICE STEVENS join, dissenting. * * *

In my view petitioner could prevail in this case without extending the right to counsel beyond what was assumed to exist in *Argersinger*. Neither party in that case questioned the existence of the right to counsel in trials involving "non-petty" offenses punishable by more than six months in jail. The question the Court addressed was whether the right applied to some "petty" offenses to which the right to jury trial did not extend. The Court's reasoning in applying the right to counsel in the case before it—that the right to counsel is more fundamental to a fair proceeding than the right to jury trial and that the historical limitations on the jury trial right are irrelevant to the right to counsel—certainly cannot support a standard for the right to counsel that is more restrictive than the standard for granting a right to a jury trial. [Argersinger] thus established a "two-dimensional" test for the right to counsel: the right attaches to any "non-petty" offense punishable by more than six months in jail and in addition to any offense where actual incarceration is likely regardless of the maximum authorized penalty.

The offense of "theft" with which Scott was charged is certainly not a "petty" one. It is punishable by a sentence of up to one year in jail. Unlike many traffic or other "regulatory" offenses, it carries the moral stigma associated with common-law crimes traditionally recognized as indicative of moral depravity. The State indicated at oral argument that the services of a professional prosecutor were considered essential to the prosecution of this offense. Likewise, nonindigent defendants charged with this offense would be well advised to hire the "best lawyers they can get." Scott's right to the assistance of appointed counsel is thus plainly mandated by the logic of the Court's prior cases, including *Argersinger* itself.

* * * Not only is the "actual imprisonment" standard unprecedented as the exclusive test, but the problems inherent in its application demonstrate the superiority of an "authorized imprisonment" standard that would require the appointment of counsel for indigents accused of any offense for which imprisonment for any time is authorized. * * *

Perhaps the strongest refutation of respondent's alarmist prophecies that an authorized imprisonment standard would wreak havoc on the States is that the standard has not produced that result in the substantial number of States that already provide counsel in all cases where imprisonment is authorized—States that include a large majority of the country's population and a great diversity of urban and rural environments. Moreover, of those States that do not yet provide counsel in all cases where *any* imprisonment is authorized, many provide

**a.** Concurring Justice Powell noted that "the drawing of a line based on whether there is imprisonment (even for overnight) can have the practical effect of precluding provision of counsel in other types of cases in which conviction can have more serious consequences." He also thought that an "actual imprisonment" rule "tends to impair the proper functioning of the criminal justice system in that trial judges, in advance of hearing any evidence and before knowing anything about the case except the charge, all too often will be compelled to forego the legislatively granted option to impose a sentence of imprisonment upon conviction." Despite his "continuing reservations about the *Argersinger* rule," however, Justice Powell joined the opinion of the Court because "[i]t is important that this Court provide clear guidance to the hundreds of courts across the country that confront this problem daily." He hoped, however, "that in due time a majority will recognize that a more flexible rule is consistent with due process and will better serve the cause of justice."

counsel when periods of imprisonment longer than 30 days, 3 months, or 6 months are authorized. In fact, Scott would be entitled to appointed counsel under the current laws of at least 33 States.

It may well be that adoption by this Court of an authorized imprisonment standard would lead state and local governments to re-examine their criminal statutes. A state legislature or local government might determine that it no longer desired to authorize incarceration for certain minor offenses in light of the expense of meeting the requirements of the Constitution. In my view this re-examination is long overdue. In any event, the Courts actual imprisonment standard must inevitably lead the courts to make this re-examination, which plainly should more properly be a legislative responsibility.

The Court's opinion turns the reasoning of *Argersinger* on its head. It restricts the right to counsel, perhaps the most fundamental Sixth Amendment right, more narrowly than the admittedly less fundamental right to jury trial.

* * *[b]

# SECTION 2.  THE *GRIFFIN–DOUGLAS* "EQUALITY" PRINCIPLE

Many commentators believe that the Warren Court's "revolution" in criminal procedure got underway when it handed down *Mapp v. Ohio* (Ch. 3, § 1) in 1961. But arguably the revolution began five years earlier, with *Griffin v. Illinois,* 351 U.S. 12 (1956).

In holding that indigent defendants must be furnished trial transcripts at state expense if such transcripts were necessary to effectuate appellate review, *Griffin* departed from then traditional equal protection doctrine. It viewed the "equality" principle as not only prohibiting the creation of inequalities by a state but imposing an "affirmative duty" to eliminate at least some inequalities not of the state's own doing. Illinois had simply ignored private inequalities of wealth and offered trial transcripts to every appellant on "equal terms," i.e., at a price which amounted to the cost of preparing them. But this was not enough.

There was no opinion of the Court in *Griffin*. Justice Black announced the judgment in a forceful and oft-quoted four-Justice opinion. He called the denial of a transcript for those who need but are unable to pay for one "a misfit in a country dedicated to affording equal justice to all and special privileges to none in the administration of its criminal law." Continued Black: "There can be no equal justice where the kind of trial a man gets depends on the amount of money he has. Destitute defendants must be afforded as adequate appellate review as defendants who have money enough to buy transcripts."

---

**b.** In a separate dissent, Blackmun, J., maintained that the right to appointed counsel "extends at least as far as the right to jury trial" and thus that "an indigent defendant in a state criminal case must be afforded appointed counsel whenever [he] is prosecuted for a nonpetty criminal offense, that is, one punishable by more than six months' imprisonment *or* whenever the defendant is actually subjected to a term of imprisonment."

In *Baldasar v. Illinois,* 446 U.S. 222 (1980) (per curiam), a 5–4 majority held that an uncounselled misdemeanor theft conviction (valid under *Scott* because defendant had received only a fine and probation) could not be used to elevate a subsequent conviction for a similar offense to a felony. (The maximum punishment for misdemeanor theft was one year imprisonment, but a second conviction for the same offense could be treated as a felony with a prison term of one to three years—the sentence Baldasar actually received.)

Dissenting Justice Powell, joined by the Chief Justice and Justices White and Rehnquist, protested that the Court's holding "undermines the rationale of *Scott* and *Argersinger* and leaves no coherent rationale in its place. A constitutionally valid conviction is not constitutionally invalid if relied upon as the predicate for enhancing the sentence of a recidivist."

Dissenting Justice Harlan voiced sharp disagreement with Justice Black's approach. Harlan maintained that the Court's resolution of the equal protection claim in effect *required state discrimination*—in favor of indigents. It forced Illinois to give free to indigents "what it requires others to pay for."

But for *Douglas v. California*, the first case set forth in this section, *Griffin* and its early progeny,[a] could be narrowly interpreted as not affecting the right to counsel at all. Rather, the *Griffin* principle could be viewed as concerned merely with the *availability* of direct and collateral review, not the *quality* of such review. But for the *Douglas* case, *Griffin* could be read as requiring only that an indigent be allowed *access* to the courts, not that he be furnished with counsel as well. For the presence of counsel is not a *sine qua non* to access to the courts, as was the availability of the transcript in *Griffin* or the payment of filing fees in other cases applying *Griffin*.

Under this analysis, *Griffin* and the pre-*Gideon* doctrine of *Betts v. Brady* were reconcilable: The state need only provide a road, not guarantee that every person have equally as good a car to drive down it. After *Douglas*, however, the "access to the courts" interpretation of *Griffin* seemed untenable. For the *Douglas* Court considered denying counsel to an indigent appellant "a discrimination at least as invidious as that condemned in *Griffin*."

Although it was careful to note that it was "dealing only with the *first appeal* granted as a matter of right to [all]" (emphasis in the original), the *Douglas* opinion contains language suggesting that *whenever* an indigent is permitted access to the courts he is *entitled to counsel* as well—that the state must do more than simply place a defendant "on the road," it must see that he has some vehicle—counsel—to use in travelling that "road." Nor is that all. *Griffin* and *Douglas*, at least if read generously, also suggest that the government must furnish an indigent defendant with *any* and *every* legal tool or legal service that a wealthy defendant is able to purchase.

In short not a few people thought that the *Griffin–Douglas* "equality" principle—the view that the administration of criminal justice cannot turn on the amount of money a defendant has—had no "stopping point," at least no obvious one. But the Court found a stopping point in *Ross v. Moffitt*, the second case set forth in this section.

## DOUGLAS v. CALIFORNIA

372 U.S. 353, 83 S.Ct. 814, 9 L.Ed.2d 811 (1963).

JUSTICE DOUGLAS delivered the opinion of the Court.   *   *   *

[The] record shows that petitioners requested, and were denied, the assistance of counsel on appeal, even though it plainly appeared they were indigents. In denying petitioners' requests, the California District Court of Appeal stated that it had "gone through" the record and had come to the conclusion that "no good whatever could be served by appointment of counsel." [The court] was

**a.** In the decade and a half following *Griffin*, its underlying principle was broadly applied. *Mayer v. Chicago*, 404 U.S. 189 (1971) carried the *Griffin* principle further than the Court ever carried the *Gideon* principle by holding that an indigent appellant cannot be denied a record of sufficient completeness to permit proper consideration of his claims even though he was convicted of ordinary violations punishable by fine only. More generally, a number of cases seemed to read *Griffin* for the proposition that an indigent defendant must be furnished any valuable or useful "tool" or instrument available for a price to others. See, e.g., *Roberts v. LaVallee*, 389 U.S. 40 (1967) (indigent defendant entitled to free transcript of preliminary hearing for use at trial, even though both defendant and his lawyer attended preliminary hearing and no indication of use to which preliminary hearing transcript could be put—points stressed by dissenting Justice Harlan).

acting in accordance with a California rule of criminal procedure which provides that state appellate courts, upon the request of an indigent for counsel, may make "an independent investigation of the record and determine whether it would be of advantage to the defendant or helpful to the appellate court to have counsel appointed. [After] such investigation, appellate courts should appoint counsel if in their opinion it would be helpful to the defendant or the court, and should deny the appointment of counsel only if in their judgment such appointment would be of no value to either the defendant or the court." * * *

We agree, however, with Justice Traynor of the California Supreme Court, who said that the "[d]enial of counsel on appeal [to an indigent] would seem to be a discrimination at least as invidious as that condemned in [*Griffin*,*]" where] we held that a State may not grant appellate review in such a way as to discriminate against some convicted defendants on account of their poverty. [Whether the issue is a transcript on appeal or the assistance of counsel on appeal] the evil is the same: discrimination against the indigent. For there can be no equal justice where the kind of an appeal a man enjoys "depends on the amount of money he has." * * *

[Under California's] present practice the type of an appeal [one is afforded] hinges upon whether or not he can pay for the assistance of counsel. If he can the appellate court passes on the merits of his case only after having the full benefit of written briefs and oral argument by counsel. If he cannot the appellate court is forced to prejudge the merits before it can even determine whether counsel should be provided. At this stage in the proceedings only the barren record speaks for the indigent, and, unless the printed pages show that an injustice has been committed, he is forced to go without a champion on appeal. Any real chance he may have had of showing that his appeal has hidden merit is deprived him when the court decides on an *ex parte* examination of the record that the assistance of counsel is not required.

* * * We are dealing only with the first appeal, granted as a matter of right to rich and poor alike, from a criminal conviction. We need not now decide whether California would have to provide counsel for an indigent seeking [discretionary review or] whether counsel must be appointed for an indigent seeking review of an appellate affirmance of his conviction in this Court. [But] it is appropriate to observe that a State can, consistently with the Fourteenth Amendment, provide for differences so long as the result does not amount to a denial of due process or an "invidious discrimination." Absolute equality is not required; lines can be and are drawn and we often sustain them. [But] where the merits of the one and only appeal an indigent has as of right are decided without benefit of counsel, we think an unconstitutional line has been drawn between rich and poor.

When an indigent is forced to run this gantlet of a preliminary showing of merit, the right to appeal does not comport with fair procedure. [T]he discrimination is not between "possibly good and obviously bad cases," but between cases where the rich man can require the court to listen to argument of counsel before deciding on the merits, but a poor man cannot. There is lacking that equality demanded by the Fourteenth Amendment where the rich man, who appeals as of right, enjoys the benefit of counsel's examination into the record, research of the law, and marshalling of arguments on his behalf, while the indigent, already burdened by a preliminary determination that his case is without merit, is forced to shift for himself. The indigent, where the record is unclear or the errors are hidden, has only the right to a meaningless ritual, while the rich man has a meaningful appeal. * * *

Judgment of the District Court of Appeals vacated and case remanded.

JUSTICE CLARK, dissenting.

* * * We all know that the overwhelming percentage of *in forma pauperis* appeals are frivolous. Statistics of this Court show that over 96% of the petitions filed here are of this variety. [California's courts] after examining the record certified that [an] appointment [of counsel] would be neither advantageous to the petitioners nor helpful to the court. It, therefore, refused to go through the useless gesture of appointing an attorney. In my view neither the Equal Protection Clause nor the Due Process Clause requires more. I cannot understand why the Court says that this procedure afforded petitioners "a meaningless ritual." To appoint an attorney would not only have been utter extravagance and a waste of the State's funds but as surely "meaningless" to petitioners.

JUSTICE HARLAN, whom JUSTICE STEWART joins, dissenting.

[T]he Court appears to rely both on the Equal Protection Clause and on the guarantees of fair procedure inherent in the Due Process Clause of the Fourteenth Amendment, with obvious emphasis on "equal protection." In my view the Equal Protection Clause is not apposite, and its application to cases like the present one can lead only to mischievous results. This case should be judged solely under the Due Process Clause, and I do not believe that the California procedure violates that provision.

EQUAL PROTECTION

To approach the present problem in terms of the Equal Protection Clause is, I submit, but to substitute resounding phrases for analysis. I dissented from this approach in [*Griffin* ] and I am constrained to dissent from the implicit extension of the equal protection approach here—to a case in which the State denies no one an appeal, but seeks only to keep within reasonable bounds the instances in which appellate counsel will be assigned to indigents.

The States, of course, are prohibited by the Equal Protection Clause from discriminating between "rich" and "poor" *as such* in the formulation and application of their laws. But it is a far different thing to suggest that this provision prevents the State from adopting a law of general applicability that may affect the poor more harshly than it does the rich, or, on the other hand, from making some effort to redress economic imbalances while not eliminating them entirely.

Every financial exaction which the State imposes on a uniform basis is more easily satisfied by the well-to-do than by the indigent. Yet I take it that no one would dispute the constitutional power of the State to levy a uniform sales tax, to charge tuition at a state university, to fix rates for the purchase of water from a municipal corporation, to impose a standard fine for criminal violations, or to establish minimum bail for various categories of offenses. Nor could it be contended that the State may not classify as crimes acts which the poor are more likely to commit than are the rich. And surely, there would be no basis for attacking a state law which provided benefits for the needy simply because those benefits fell short of the goods or services that others could purchase for themselves.

Laws such as these do not deny equal protection to the less fortunate for one essential reason: the Equal Protection Clause does not impose on the States "an affirmative duty to lift the handicaps flowing from differences in economic circumstances." To so construe it would be to read into the Constitution a philosophy of leveling that would be foreign to many of our basic concepts of the proper relations between government and society. The State may have a moral obligation to eliminate the evils of poverty, but it is not required by the Equal Protection Clause to give to some whatever others can afford.

* * * [I]t should be noted that if the present problem may be viewed as one of equal protection, so may the question of the right to appointed counsel at trial, and the Court's analysis of that right in *Gideon* [is] wholly unnecessary. The short way to dispose of *Gideon,* in other words, would be simply to say that the State deprives the indigent of equal protection whenever it fails to furnish him with legal services, and perhaps with other services as well, equivalent to those that the affluent defendant can obtain.[a]

The real question in this case, I submit, and the only one that permits of satisfactory analysis, is whether or not the state rule, as applied in this case, is consistent with the requirements of fair procedure guaranteed by the Due Process Clause. Of course, in considering this question, it must not be lost sight of that the State's responsibility under the Due Process Clause is to provide justice for all. Refusal to furnish criminal indigents with some things that others can afford may fall short of constitutional standards of fairness. The problem before us is whether this is such a case.

## DUE PROCESS * * *

We have today held that in a case such as the one before us, there is an absolute right to the services of counsel at trial. *Gideon.* [But] the appellate procedures involved here stand on an entirely different constitutional footing. *First,* appellate review is in itself not required by the Fourteenth Amendment, *McKane v. Durston,* 153 U.S. 684 (1894); see *Griffin,* and thus the question presented is the narrow one whether the State's rules with respect to the appointment of counsel are so arbitrary or unreasonable, *in the context of the particular appellate procedure that it has established,* as to require their invalidation. *Second,* the kinds of questions that may arise on appeal are circumscribed by the record of the proceedings that led to the conviction; they do not encompass the large variety of tactical and strategic problems that must be resolved at the trial. *Third,* as California applies its rule, the indigent appellant receives the benefit of expert and conscientious legal appraisal of the merits of his case on the basis of the trial record, and whether or not he is assigned counsel, is guaranteed full consideration of his appeal. It would be painting with too broad a brush to conclude that under these circumstances an appeal is just like a trial.

What the Court finds constitutionally offensive in California's procedure bears a striking resemblance to the rules of this Court and many state courts of last resort on petitions for certiorari or for leave to appeal filed by indigent defendants *pro se.* Under the practice of this Court, only if it appears from the petition for certiorari that a case merits review is leave to proceed *in forma pauperis* granted, the case transferred to the Appellate Docket, and counsel appointed. Since our review is generally discretionary, and since we are often not even given the benefit of a record in the proceedings below, the disadvantages to the indigent petitioner might be regarded as more substantial than in California. But as conscientiously committed as this Court is to the great

a. One may ask, too, why the Court failed even to discuss the applicability of the *Griffin–Douglas* "equality" principle to the issue raised in *Scott v. Illinois* (§ 1 supra). Since it is plain that one charged with an offense *punishable* by incarceration may *retain* counsel for his defense, does not the "equality" principle—especially in light of its application in *Mayer v. Chicago,* note a supra—suggest that the "actual imprisonment" standard, even if it defensibly defines the Sixth Amendment right to appointed counsel, is unsatisfactory under the equal protection clause?

principle of "Equal Justice Under Law," it has never deemed itself constitutionally required to appoint counsel to assist in the preparation of each of the more than 1,000 *pro se* petitions for certiorari currently being filed each Term. We should know from our own experience that appellate courts generally go out of their way to give fair consideration to those who are unrepresented.

The Court distinguishes our review from the present case on the grounds that the California rule relates to "the first appeal, granted as a matter of right." [But] I fail to see the significance of this difference. Surely, it cannot be contended that the requirements of fair procedure are exhausted once an indigent has been given one appellate review. Nor can it well be suggested that having appointed counsel is more necessary to the fair administration of justice in an initial appeal taken as a matter of right, which the reviewing court on the full record has already determined to be frivolous, than in a petition asking a higher appellate court to exercise its discretion to consider what may be a substantial constitutional claim.

I cannot agree that the Constitution prohibits a State in seeking to redress economic imbalances at its bar of justice and to provide indigents with full review, from taking reasonable steps to guard against needless expense. This is all that California has done. * * *

## ROSS v. MOFFITT

417 U.S. 600, 94 S.Ct. 2437, 41 L.Ed.2d 341 (1974).

[Like many other states, the North Carolina appellate system is multitiered, providing for both an intermediate Court of Appeals and a Supreme Court. North Carolina authorizes appointment of counsel for a convicted defendant appealing to the intermediate court of appeals, but not for a defendant who seeks either discretionary review in the state supreme court or a writ of certiorari in the U.S. Supreme Court. In one case, the Mecklenburg County forgery conviction, respondent sought appointed counsel for discretionary review in the state supreme court. In another case, the Guilford County forgery conviction, respondent was represented by the public defender in the state supreme court, but sought court-appointed counsel to prepare a writ of certiorari to the U.S. Supreme Court. On federal habeas corpus, a unanimous panel of the U.S. Court of Appeals for the Fourth Circuit, per Haynsworth, C.J., held that the *Douglas* rationale required appointment of counsel in both instances.]

JUSTICE REHNQUIST delivered the opinion of the Court.

[In *Griffin,* the Court struck down] an Illinois rule allowing a convicted criminal defendant to present claims of trial error to the [state supreme court] only if he procured a transcript of the testimony adduced at his trial. No exception was made for the indigent defendant, and thus one who was unable to pay the cost of obtaining such a transcript was precluded from obtaining appellate review of asserted trial error * * *.

[*Griffin* and succeeding cases] stand for the proposition that a State cannot arbitrarily cut off appeal rights for indigents while leaving open avenues of appeal for more affluent persons. In *Douglas,* however, [the] Court departed somewhat from the limited doctrine of [these] cases and undertook an examination of whether an indigent's access to the appellate system was adequate. [The *Douglas* Court] concluded that a State does not fulfill its responsibility toward indigent defendants merely by waiving its own requirements that a convicted defendant procure a transcript or pay a fee in order to appeal, and held that the

State must go further and provide counsel for the indigent on his first appeal as of right. It is this decision we are asked to extend today. * * *

The precise rationale for the *Griffin* and *Douglas* lines of cases has never been explicitly stated, some support being derived from the Equal Protection Clause of the Fourteenth Amendment, and some from the Due Process Clause of that Amendment. Neither clause by itself provides an entirely satisfactory basis for the result reached, each depending on a different inquiry which emphasizes different factors. "Due process" emphasizes fairness between the State and the individual dealing with the State, regardless of how other individuals in the same situation may be treated. "Equal protection," on the other hand, emphasizes disparity in treatment by a State between classes of individuals whose situations are arguably indistinguishable. We will address these issues separately in the succeeding sections.

Recognition of the due process rationale in *Douglas* is found both in the Court's opinion and in the dissenting opinion of Mr. Justice Harlan. The Court in *Douglas* stated that "[w]hen an individual is forced to run this gantlet of a preliminary showing of merit, the right to appeal does not comport with fair procedure." Mr. Justice Harlan thought that the due process issue in *Douglas* was the only one worthy of extended consideration. * * *

We do not believe that the Due Process Clause requires North Carolina to provide respondent with counsel on his discretionary appeal to the State Supreme Court. At the trial stage of a criminal proceeding, the right of an indigent defendant to counsel [is] fundamental and binding upon the States by virtue of the Sixth and Fourteenth Amendments. But there are significant differences between the trial and appellate stages of a criminal proceeding. The purpose of the trial stage from the State's point of view is to convert a criminal defendant from a person presumed innocent to one found guilty beyond a reasonable doubt. To accomplish this purpose, the State employs a prosecuting attorney who presents evidence to the court, challenges any witnesses offered by the defendant, argues rulings of the court, and makes direct arguments to the court or jury seeking to persuade them of the defendant's guilt. Under these circumstances " * * * reason and reflection require us to recognize that in our adversary system of criminal justice, any person haled into court, who is too poor to hire a lawyer, cannot be assured a fair trial unless counsel is provided for him." *Gideon.*

By contrast, it is ordinarily the defendant, rather than the State, who initiates the appellate process, seeking not to fend off the efforts of the State's prosecutor but rather to overturn a finding of guilt made by a judge or jury below. The defendant needs an attorney on appeal not as a shield to protect him against being "haled into court" by the State and stripped of his presumption of innocence, but rather as a sword to upset the prior determination of guilt. This difference is significant for, while no one would agree that the State may simply dispense with the trial stage of proceedings without a criminal defendant's consent, it is clear that the State need not provide any appeal at all. *McKane v. Durston.* The fact that an appeal *has* been provided does not automatically mean that a State then acts unfairly by refusing to provide counsel to indigent defendants at every stage of the way. Unfairness results only if indigents are singled out by the State and denied meaningful access to that system because of their poverty. That question is more profitably considered under an equal protection analysis.

Language invoking equal protection notions is prominent both in *Douglas* and in other cases treating the rights of indigents on appeal. * * * Despite the tendency of all rights "to declare themselves absolute to their logical extreme," there are obviously limits beyond which the equal protection analysis may not be pressed without doing violence to principles recognized in other decisions of this Court. The Fourteenth Amendment "does not require absolute equality or precisely equal advantages," nor does it require the State to "equalize economic conditions." *Griffin* (Frankfurter, J., concurring). It does require [that] indigents have an adequate opportunity to present their claims fairly within the adversarial system. The State cannot adopt procedures which leave an indigent defendant "entirely cut off from any appeal at all," by virtue of his indigency, *Lane,* or extend to such indigent defendants merely a "meaningless ritual" while others in better economic circumstances have a "meaningful appeal." *Douglas.* The question is not one of absolutes, but one of degrees. In this case we do not believe that the Equal Protection Clause when interpreted in the context of these cases, requires North Carolina to provide free counsel for indigent defendants seeking to take discretionary appeals to the North Carolina Supreme Court, or to file petitions for certiorari in this Court.

[The] facts show that respondent, in connection with his Mecklenburg County conviction, received the benefit of counsel in examining the record of his trial and in preparing an appellate brief on his behalf for the state Court of Appeals. Thus, prior to his seeking discretionary review in the State Supreme Court, his claims "had once been presented by a lawyer and passed upon by an appellate court." *Douglas.* We do not believe that it can be said, therefore, that a defendant in respondent's circumstances is denied meaningful access to the North Carolina Supreme Court simply because the State does not appoint counsel to aid him in seeking review in that court. At that stage he will have, at the very least, a transcript or other record of trial proceedings, a brief on his behalf in the Court of Appeals setting forth his claims of error, and in many cases an opinion by the Court of Appeals disposing of his case. These materials, supplemented by whatever submission respondent may make *pro se,* would appear to provide the Supreme Court of North Carolina with an adequate basis on which to base its decision to grant or deny review.

We are fortified in this conclusion by our understanding of the function served by discretionary review in the North Carolina Supreme Court. The critical issue in that court, as we perceive it, is not whether there has been "a correct adjudication of guilt" in every individual case, but rather whether "the subject matter of the appeal has significant public interest," whether "the cause involves legal principles of major significance to the jurisprudence of the state," or whether the decision below is in probable conflict with a decision of the Supreme Court. The Supreme Court may deny certiorari even though it believes that the decision of the Court of Appeals was incorrect, since a decision which appears incorrect may nevertheless fail to satisfy any of the criteria discussed above. Once a defendant's claims of error are organized and presented in a lawyer-like fashion to the Court of Appeals, the justices of the Supreme Court of North Carolina who make the decision to grant or deny discretionary review should be able to ascertain whether his case satisfies the standards established by the legislature for such review.

This is not to say, of course, that a skilled lawyer, particularly one trained in the somewhat arcane art of preparing petitions for discretionary review, would not prove helpful to any litigant able to employ him. An indigent defendant seeking review in the Supreme Court of North Carolina is therefore somewhat handicapped in comparison with a wealthy defendant who has counsel assisting him in every conceivable manner at every stage in the proceeding. But both the opportunity to have counsel prepare an initial brief in the Court of Appeals and the nature of discretionary review in the Supreme Court of North Carolina make this relative handicap far less than the handicap borne by the indigent defendant denied counsel on his initial appeal as of right in *Douglas*. And the fact that a particular service might be of benefit to an indigent defendant does not mean that the service is constitutionally required. The duty of the State under our cases is not to duplicate the legal arsenal that may be privately retained by a criminal defendant in a continuing effort to reverse his conviction, but only to assure the indigent defendant an adequate opportunity to present his claims fairly in the context of the State's appellate process. We think respondent was given that opportunity under the existing North Carolina system.

Much of the discussion in the preceding section is equally relevant to the question of whether a State must provide counsel for a defendant seeking review of his conviction in this Court. North Carolina will have provided counsel for a convicted defendant's only appeal as of right, and the brief prepared by that counsel together with one and perhaps two North Carolina appellate opinions will be available to this Court in order that it may decide whether or not to grant certiorari. This Court's review, much like that of the Supreme Court of North Carolina, is discretionary and depends on numerous factors other than the perceived correctness of the judgment we are asked to review.

There is also a significant difference between the source of the right to seek discretionary review in the Supreme Court of North Carolina and the source of the right to seek discretionary review in this Court. The former is conferred by the statutes of the State of North Carolina, but the latter is granted by statutes enacted by Congress. Thus the argument relied upon in the *Griffin* and *Douglas* cases, that the State having once created a right of appeal must give all persons an equal opportunity to enjoy the right, is by its terms inapplicable. The right to seek certiorari in this Court is not granted by any State, and exists by virtue of federal statute with or without the consent of the State whose judgment is sought to be reviewed.

The suggestion that a State is responsible for providing counsel to one petitioning this Court simply because it initiated the prosecution which led to the judgment sought to be reviewed is unsupported by either reason or authority. It would be quite as logical under the rationale of *Douglas* and *Griffin*, and indeed perhaps more so, to require that the Federal Government or this Court furnish and compensate counsel for petitioners who seek certiorari here to review state judgments of conviction. Yet this Court has followed a consistent policy of denying applications for appointment of counsel by persons seeking to file jurisdictional statements or petitions for certiorari in this Court. In the light of these authorities, it would be odd, indeed, to read the Fourteenth Amendment to impose such a requirement on the States, and we decline to do so.

We do not mean by this opinion to in any way discourage those States which have, as a matter of legislative choice, made counsel available to convicted defendants at all stages of judicial review. Some States which might well choose to do so as a matter of legislative policy may conceivably find that other claims for public funds within or without the criminal justice system preclude the implementation of such a policy at the present time. [T]he Fourteenth Amendment leaves these choices to the State \* \* \*.[a]

---

**a.** A decade after *Ross v. Moffitt*, the Court broke its many years of silence on the issue of an indigent defendant's right to a psychiatrist and other expert assistance and held that, at least when an indigent defendant has made a preliminary showing that his sanity at the time of the offense is likely to be a significant factor at the trial, the state must provide the assistance of a psychiatrist for his defense. *Ake v. Oklahoma*, 470 U.S. 68 (1985).

JUSTICE DOUGLAS, with whom JUSTICE BRENNAN and JUSTICE MARSHALL concur, dissenting.

[In his opinion below] Chief Judge Haynsworth could find "no logical basis for differentiation between appeals of right and permissive review procedures in the context of the Constitution and the right to counsel." More familiar with the functioning of the North Carolina criminal justice system than are we, he concluded that "in the context of constitutional questions arising in criminal prosecutions, permissive review in the state's highest court may be predictably the most meaningful review the conviction will receive." The North Carolina Court of Appeals, for example, will be constrained in diverging from an earlier opinion of the State Supreme Court, even if subsequent developments have rendered the earlier Supreme Court decision suspect. "[T]he state's highest court remains the ultimate arbiter of the rights of its citizens."

Chief Judge Haynsworth also correctly observed that the indigent defendant proceeding without counsel is at a substantial disadvantage relative to wealthy defendants represented by counsel when he is forced to fend for himself in seeking discretionary review from the State Supreme Court or from this Court. It may well not be enough to allege error in the courts below in layman's terms; a more sophisticated approach may be demanded:

"An indigent defendant is as much in need of the assistance of a lawyer in preparing and filing a petition for certiorari as he is in the handling of an appeal as of right. In many appeals, an articulate defendant could file an effective brief by telling his story in simple language without legalisms, but the technical requirement for applications for writs of certiorari are hazards which one untrained in the law could hardly be expected to negotiate.

" 'Certiorari proceedings constitute a highly specialized aspect of appellate work. The factors which [a court] deems important in connection with deciding whether to grant certiorari are certainly not within the normal knowledge of an indigent appellant.' Boskey, *The Right to Counsel in Appellate Proceedings*, 45 Minn.L.Rev. 783, 797 (1961)."

\* \* \* The right to discretionary review is a substantial one, and one where a lawyer can be of significant assistance to an indigent defendant. It was correctly perceived below that the "same concepts of fairness and equality which require counsel in a first appeal of right, require counsel in other and subsequent discretionary appeals."

*Ake* confirms the tendency of the post-*Ross* cases to rely on due process rather than equal protection analysis in determining the constitutional rights of indigent criminal defendants. Thus the *Ake* Court reaffirmed the need for the state to take steps to assure that an indigent defendant had "a fair opportunity" or "an adequate opportunity" to present his defense. The Court also noted that in implementing the *Griffin* "equality" principle it had "focused on identifying the 'basic tools of an adequate defense or appeal' [and] required that such tools be provided to [those] who cannot afford to pay for them." See also *Evitts v. Lucey*, 469 U.S. 387, 403 (1985); *Bearden v. Georgia*, 461 U.S. 660, 665 (1983); *United States v. MacCollom*, 426 U.S. 317, 324 (1976).

# Chapter 6

# POLICE INTERROGATION AND CONFESSIONS

## SECTION 1. THE DUE PROCESS "VOLUNTARINESS" TEST FOR ADMITTING CONFESSIONS

Whatever the meaning of the elusive terms "involuntary" and "coerced" confessions in the 1950's and 1960's, for centuries the rule that a confession was admissible so long as it was "voluntary" was more or less an alternative statement of the rule that a confession was admissible so long as it was free of influences which made it "untrustworthy" or "probably untrue." Thus, Wigmore, the leading authority on evidence, reflected the law prevailing at the time when in 1940 he pointed out that a confession was not inadmissible because of "any *illegality* in the method of obtaining it" or "because of any connection with the *privilege against self-incrimination*." (The Court did not apply the privilege against compulsory self-incrimination to the proceedings in the police station and other "in-custody questioning" until its 1966 decision in *Miranda*.)

The "untrustworthiness" rationale, the view that the rules governing the admissibility of confessions were merely a system of safeguards against false confessions, could explain the exclusion of the confession in *Brown v. Mississippi*, 297 U.S. 278 (1936), the first Fourteenth Amendment Due Process confession case, where the deputy sheriff who had presided over the beatings of the defendants conceded that one had been whipped, "but not too much for a Negro." And the same rationale was also adequate to explain the exclusion of confessions in the cases that immediately followed the *Brown* case, such as *Chambers v. Florida*, 309 U.S. 227 (1940) and *Ward v. Texas*, 316 U.S. 547 (1942), for they too, involved actual or threatened physical violence. But as the crude practices of the early cases grew outmoded and cases involving more subtle pressures began to appear, it became more difficult to assume that the resulting confessions were untrustworthy.

The first case in this section, *Ashcraft v. Tennessee*, illustrates how the rationale for excluding confessions was changing. There was good reason to think that Ashcraft had indeed been involved in his wife's murder. Nevertheless, calling the extended police questioning to which Ashcraft had been subjected "inherently coercive," the Court ruled that the defendant's confession should not have been allowed into evidence. Under the circumstances, *Ashcraft* seems to reflect less concern with the reliability of the confession than disapproval of police methods which the Court considered to be dangerous and subject to abuse.

Although he joined Justice Jackson's dissent in *Ashcraft,* Justice Frankfurter soon became the leading exponent of the "police misconduct" or "police methods" rationale for barring the use of confessions. According to this rationale, in order to condemn, and deter, offensive or otherwise objectionable police interrogation methods, it was necessary to exclude confessions produced by such methods regardless of how trustworthy they might be.

Thus in *Watts v. Indiana,* the second case set forth in this section, and two companion cases, the Court reversed three convictions resting on coerced confessions without disputing the accuracy of Justice Jackson's observation (concurring in *Watts* and dissenting in the other cases) that "checked with external evidence [the confessions in each case] are inherently believable and were not shaken as to truth by anything that occurred at the trial." Justice Frankfurter, who wrote the principal opinion in *Watts,* commented: "In holding that the Due Process Clause *bars police procedure* which violates the basic notions of our accusatorial mode of prosecuting crime and vitiates a conviction based on the fruits of such procedure, we apply the Due Process Clause to its historic function of *assuring appropriate procedure* before liberty is curtailed or life is taken." (Emphasis added.)

Three years later, speaking for the Court in the famous "stomach-pumping" case of *Rochin v. California,* discussed in Chapter Two, Justice Frankfurter viewed the coerced confession cases as "only instances of the general requirement that states in their prosecution respect certain decencies of civilized conduct." Involuntary confessions, he pointed out, "are inadmissible under the Due Process Clause even though statements contained in them may be independently established as true" because they "offend the community's sense of fair play and decency."

Perhaps the most emphatic statement of the "police methods" rationale appears in *Rogers v. Richmond,* 365 U.S. 534 (1961), one of Justice Frankfurter's last opinions on confessions. After more conventional methods had failed to produce any incriminating statements, a police chief pretended to order petitioner's ailing wife brought down to headquarters for questioning. Petitioner promptly confessed to the murder for which he was later convicted. The trial judge found that the police chief's pretense had "no tendency to produce a confession that was not in accord with the truth" and in his charge to the jury he indicated that the admissibility of the confession should turn on its probable reliability. But the Court, speaking through Justice Frankfurter, disagreed:

> "[Convictions based on involuntary confessions must fall] not so much because such confessions are unlikely to be true but because the methods used to extract them offend an underlying principle in the enforcement of our criminal law; that ours is an accusatorial and not an inquisitional system. * * * Indeed, in many of the cases [reversing] state convictions involving the use of confessions obtained by impermissible methods, independent corroborating evidence left little doubt of the truth of what the defendant had confessed. * * * The attention of the trial judge should have been focused [on] whether the [police behavior] was such as to overbear petitioner's will to resist and bring about confessions not freely self determined—a question to be answered with complete disregard of whether or not petitioner in fact spoke the truth." [a]

a. At least in its advanced stage (the early 1960's), some commentators thought that the "due process" or "voluntariness" test had *three* underlying values or goals, barring the use of confessions (a) which were of doubtful reliability because of the police methods used to obtain them; (b) which were produced by offensive police methods even though the reliability of the confession was not in question; and (c) which were obtained from a person

Justice Jackson strongly resisted the expansion of the grounds for excluding confessions. *Ashcraft* is a great case only because Jackson's dissent made it so. No piece of writing better illustrates his famed powers of advocacy and extraordinary directness of approach. The crucial question, maintained Jackson, was not whether other suspects might have been overcome by the prolonged questioning, but whether *this particular defendant* had been. Jackson insisted that he had not; Ashcraft "was in possession of his own will and self-control at the time of confession." Ashcraft had decided to match wits with the police and after accusing another who in turn accused him "he knew he had lost the battle of wits." What was wrong with that? If the state is denied the right to apply any pressure to get someone to confess which is "inherently coercive," what pressure *could* it apply? And if it could not apply any "pressure," how could it be expected to get any suspect to confess?

Concurring in *Watts* and dissenting in the two companion cases, Justice Jackson again manifested his resistance to the expansion of the rights of suspects. He articulated concerns that many critics of the Warren Court's "revolution" in criminal procedure would repeat decades later. He underscored the "dilemma" facing a free society: To subject one without counsel to police interrogation "is a real peril to individual freedom," but bringing in a lawyer "means a real peril to solution of the crime."

Jackson voiced strong doubts that prohibiting the police from taking a suspect into custody and questioning him about an unwitnessed murder without advising him of his rights was "a necessary price to pay for the fairness which we know as 'due process of law.'" He recognized that the Bill of Rights, "even if construed as these provisions traditionally have been, * * * contain an aggregate of restrictions which seriously limit the power of society to solve such crimes as confront us in these cases," but he considered that "good reason for indulging in no unnecessary expansion of them."

A majority of the Court, however, was unpersuaded. As perhaps he knew, Jackson was swimming against the tide.

whose volitional power was seriously impaired (e.g., a drugged, extremely intoxicated or "insane" person), even though the confession was neither untrustworthy (because impressively corroborated) nor the product of any conscious police wrongdoing. However, in *Colorado v. Connelly*, 479 U.S. 157 (1986), upholding the confession of a mentally ill person (according to expert testimony, "God's voice" told defendant he had only two options: confess his murder or commit suicide), the Court, per Rehnquist, C.J., rejected the third value or goal:

"[All the 'involuntary' confession cases] have contained a substantial element of coercive police conduct. Absent police conduct causally related to the confession, there is simply no basis for concluding that any state action has deprived a criminal defendant of due process of law.

" * * * The flaw in respondent's argument is that it would expand our previous line of 'voluntariness' cases into a far-ranging requirement that courts must divine a defendant's motivation for speaking or acting as he did even though there be no claim that governmental conduct coerced his decision.

" * * * We think the Constitution rightly leaves [inquiries into the state of mind of one who has confessed quite apart from any state coercion] to be resolved by state laws governing the admission of evidence and erects no standard of its own in this area. A statement rendered by one in the condition of respondent might be proved to be quite unreliable, but this is a matter to be governed by the evidentiary laws of the forum and not by the Due Process Clause * * *."

## ASHCRAFT v. TENNESSEE

322 U.S. 143, 64 S.Ct. 921, 88 L.Ed. 1192 (1944).

JUSTICE BLACK delivered the opinion of the Court.  *  *  *

[Early in the evening of Saturday, June 14, nine days after Ashcraft's wife had been murdered,] the officers came to Ashcraft's home and "took him into custody."  In the words of the Tennessee Supreme Court,

> "They took him to an office or room on the northwest corner of the fifth floor of the Shelby County jail.  This office is equipped with all sorts of crime and detective devices such as a fingerprint outfit, cameras, high-powered lights, and such other devices as might be found in a homicide investigating office.  *  *  * It appears that the officers placed Ashcraft at a table in this room on the fifth floor of the county jail with a light over his head and began to quiz him.  They questioned him in relays until the following Monday morning, June 16, 1941, around nine-thirty or ten o'clock. It appears that Ashcraft from Saturday evening at seven o'clock until Monday morning at approximately nine-thirty never left this homicide room on the fifth floor."

Testimony of the officers shows that the reason they questioned Ashcraft "in relays" was that they became so tired they were compelled to rest.  But from 7:00 Saturday evening until 9:30 Monday morning Ashcraft had no rest.  One officer did say that he gave the suspect a single five minutes' respite, but except for this five minutes the procedure consisted of one continuous stream of questions.

As to what happened in the fifth-floor jail room during this thirty-six hour secret examination the testimony follows the usual pattern and is in hopeless conflict.  Ashcraft swears that the first thing said to him when he was taken into custody was, "Why in hell did you kill your wife?"; that during the course of the examination he was threatened and abused in various ways; and that as the hours passed his eyes became blinded by a powerful electric light, his body became weary, and the strain on his nerves became unbearable.  The officers, on the other hand, swear that throughout the questioning they were kind and considerate.  They say that they did not accuse Ashcraft of the murder until four hours after he was brought to the jail building, though they freely admit that from that time on their barrage of questions was constantly directed at him on the assumption that he was the murderer.  Together with other persons whom they brought in on Monday morning to witness the culmination of the thirty-six hour ordeal the officers declare that at that time Ashcraft was "cool," "calm," "collected," "normal;" that his vision was unimpaired and his eyes not bloodshot; and that he showed no outward signs of being tired or sleepy.

As to whether Ashcraft actually confessed there is a similar conflict of testimony.  Ashcraft maintains that although the officers incessantly attempted by various tactics of intimidation to entrap him into a confession, not once did he admit knowledge concerning or participation in the crime.  And he specifically denies the officers' statements that he accused Ware of the crime, insisting that in response to their questions he merely gave them the name of Ware as one of several men who occasionally had ridden with him to work.  The officers' version of what happened, however, is that about 11 P.M. on Sunday night, after twenty-eight hours' constant questioning, Ashcraft made a statement that Ware had overpowered him at his home and abducted the deceased, and was probably the killer.  About midnight the officers found Ware and took him into custody, and, according to their testimony, Ware made a self-incriminating statement as of early Monday morning, and at 5:40 A.M. signed by mark a written confession in which appeared the statement that Ashcraft had hired him to commit the murder. This alleged confession of Ware was read to Ashcraft about six o'clock Monday morning, whereupon Ashcraft is said substantially to have admitted its truth in a detailed statement taken down by a reporter. About 9:30 Monday morning a transcript of Ashcraft's purported statement was read to him. The State's position is that he affirmed its truth but refused to sign the transcript, saying that he first wanted to consult his lawyer. As to this latter 9:30 episode the officers' testimony is reinforced by testimony of the several persons whom they brought in to witness the end of the examination.

In reaching our conclusion as to the validity of Ashcraft's confession we do not resolve any of the disputed questions of fact relating to the details of what transpired within the confession chamber of the jail or whether Ashcraft actually did confess.[7] Such disputes, we may say, are an inescapable consequence of secret inquisitorial practices. And always evidence concerning the inner details of secret inquisitions [8] is weighted against an accused, particularly where, as here, he is charged with a brutal crime, or where, as in many other cases, his supposed offense bears relation to an unpopular economic, political, or religious cause.

Our conclusion is that if Ashcraft made a confession it was not voluntary but compelled. We reach this conclusion from facts which are not in dispute at all. * * *

We think a situation such as that here shown by uncontradicted evidence is so inherently coercive that its very existence is irreconcilable with the possession of mental freedom by a lone suspect against whom its full coercive force is brought to bear. It is inconceivable that any court of justice in the land, conducted as our courts are, open to the public, would permit prosecutors serving in relays to keep a defendant witness under continuous cross examination for thirty-six hours without rest or sleep in an effort to extract a "voluntary" confession. Nor can we, consistently with Constitutional due process of law, hold voluntary a confession where prosecutors do the same thing away from the restraining influences of a public trial in an open court room.

The Constitution of the United States stands as a bar against the conviction of any individual in an American court by means of a coerced confession. There have been, and are now, certain foreign nations with governments dedicated to an opposite policy: governments which convict individuals with testimony obtained by police organizations possessed of an unrestrained power to seize persons suspected of crimes against the state, hold them in secret custody, and wring from them confessions by physical or mental torture. So long as the Constitution remains the basic law of our Republic, America will not have that kind of government. * * *

JUSTICE JACKSON, with whom JUSTICE ROBERTS and JUSTICE FRANKFURTER join, dissenting. * * *

As we read the present decision the Court in effect [departs from] well-established principles. Instead, it: (1) substitutes for determination on conflict-

---

7. The use in evidence of a defendant's coerced confession cannot be justified on the ground that the defendant has denied he ever gave the confession.

8. State and federal courts, textbook writers, legal commentators, and governmental commissions consistently have applied the name of "inquisition" to prolonged examination of suspects conducted as was the examination of Ashcraft. * * *

ing evidence the question whether the confession was actually produced by coercion, a presumption that it was, on a new doctrine that examination in custody of this duration is "inherently coercive;" (2) it makes that presumption irrebuttable—i.e., a rule of law—because, while it goes back of the State decisions to find certain facts, it refuses to resolve conflicts in evidence to determine whether other of the State's proof is sufficient to overcome such presumption; and, in so doing, (3) it sets aside the findings by the courts of Tennessee that on all the facts this confession did not result from coercion, either giving those findings no weight or regarding them as immaterial. * * *

The burden of protecting society from most crimes against persons and property falls upon the state. Different states have different crime problems and some freedom to vary procedures according to their own ideas. Here, a state was forced by an unwitnessed and baffling murder to vindicate its law and protect its society. To nullify its conviction in this particular case upon a consideration of all the facts would be a delicate exercise of federal judicial power. But to go beyond this, as the Court does today, and divine in the due process clause of the Fourteenth Amendment an exclusion of confessions on an irrebuttable presumption that custody and examination are "inherently coercive" if of some unspecified duration within thirty-six hours, requires us to make more than a passing expression of our doubts and disagreements. * * *

This Court never yet has held that the Constitution denies a State the right to use a confession just because the confessor was questioned in custody where it did not also find other circumstances that deprived him of a "free choice to admit, to deny, or to refuse to answer." The Constitution requires that a conviction rest on a fair trial. Forced confessions are ruled out of a fair trial. They are ruled out because they have been wrung from a prisoner by measures which are offensive to concepts of fundamental fairness. Different courts have used different terms to express the test by which to judge the inadmissibility of a confession, such as "forced," "coerced," "involuntary," "extorted," "loss of freedom of will." But always where we have professed to speak with the voice of the due process clause, the test, in whatever words stated, has been applied to the particular confessor at the time of confession.

It is for this reason that American courts hold almost universally and very properly that a confession obtained during or shortly after the confessor has been subjected to brutality, torture, beating, starvation, or physical pain of any kind is prima facie "involuntary." The effect of threats alone may depend more on individual susceptibility to fear. But men are so constituted that many will risk the postponed consequences of yielding to a demand for a confession in order to be rid of present or imminent physical suffering. Actual or threatened violence have no place in eliciting truth and it is fair to assume that no officer of the law will resort to cruelty if truth is what he is seeking. We need not be too exacting about proof of the effects of such violence on the individual involved, for their effect on the human personality is invariably and seriously demoralizing.

When, however, we consider a confession obtained by questioning, even if persistent and prolonged, we are in a different field. Interrogation per se is not, while violence per se is, an outlaw. Questioning is an indispensable instrumentality of justice. It may be abused, of course, as cross-examination in court may be abused, but the principles by which we may adjudge when it passes constitutional limits are quite different from those that condemn police brutality, and are far more difficult to apply. And they call for a more responsible and cautious exercise of our office. For we may err on the side of hostility to violence without doing injury to legitimate prosecution of crime; we cannot read an undiscriminating hostility to mere interrogation into the Constitution without unduly fettering the States in protecting society from the criminal.

It probably is the normal instinct to deny and conceal any shameful or guilty act. Even a "voluntary confession" is not likely to be the product of the same motives with which one may volunteer information that does not incriminate or concern him. The term "voluntary" confession does not mean voluntary in the sense of a confession to a priest merely to rid one's soul of a sense of guilt. "Voluntary confessions" in criminal law are the product of calculations of a different order, and usually proceed from a belief that further denial is useless and perhaps prejudicial. To speak of any confessions of crime made after arrest as being "voluntary" or "uncoerced" is somewhat inaccurate, although traditional.

A confession is wholly and incontestably voluntary only if a guilty person gives himself up to the law and becomes his own accuser. The Court bases its decision on the premise that custody and examination of a prisoner for thirty-six hours is "inherently coercive." Of course it is. And so is custody and examination for one hour. Arrest itself is inherently coercive, and so is detention. When not justified, infliction of such indignities upon the person is actionable as a tort. Of course such acts put pressure upon the prisoner to answer questions, to answer them truthfully, and to confess if guilty.

But does the Constitution prohibit use of all confessions made after arrest because questioning, while one is deprived of freedom, is "inherently coercive?" The Court does not quite say so, but it is moving far and fast in that direction. The step it now takes is to hold this confession inadmissible because of the time taken in getting it.

The duration and intensity of an examination or inquisition always have been regarded as one of the relevant and important considerations in estimating its effect on the will of the individual involved. Thirty-six hours is a long stretch of questioning. That the inquiry was prolonged and persistent is a factor that in any calculation of its effect on Ashcraft would count heavily against the confession. But some men would withstand for days pressures that would destroy the will of another in hours. Always heretofore the ultimate question has been whether the confessor was in possession of his own will and self-control at the time of confession. For its bearing on this question the Court always has considered the confessor's strength or weakness, whether he was educated or illiterate, intelligent or moronic, well or ill, Negro or white. * * *

If the constitutional admissibility of a confession is no longer to be measured by the mental state of the individual confessor but by a general doctrine dependent on the clock, it should be capable of statement in definite terms. If thirty-six hours is more than is permissible, what about 24? or 12? or 6? or 1? All are "inherently coercive." Of course questions of law like this often turn on matters of degree. But are not the states entitled to know, if this Court is able to state, what the considerations are which make any particular degree decisive? How else may state courts apply our tests? * * *

Apart from Ashcraft's uncorroborated testimony, which the Tennessee courts refused to believe, there is much evidence in this record from persons whom they did believe and were justified in believing. This evidence shows that despite the "inherent coerciveness" of the circumstances of his examination, the confession when made was deliberate, free, and voluntary in the sense in which that term is used in criminal law. This Court could not, in our opinion, hold this confession an involuntary one except by substituting its presumption in place of analysis of the evidence and refusing to weigh the evidence even in rebuttal of its presumption. * * *

[Early Monday morning, a copy of Ware's confession, stating that Ashcraft had hired him to kill the latter's wife,] was given to Ashcraft, and he then admitted that he had hired Ware to kill his wife. He was given breakfast and then in response to questions made a statement which was taken down by the court reporter, Waldauer. It was transcribed, but Ashcraft declined to sign it, saying that he wanted his lawyer to see it before he signed it. No effort was made to compel him to sign the confession. However, two businessmen of Memphis, Mr. Castle, vice president of a bank, and Mr. Pidgeon, president of the Coca–Cola Bottling Company, were called in. Both testified that Ashcraft in their presence asserted that the transcript was correct but that he declined to sign it. The officers also called [Ashcraft's family physician to] the jail to make a physical examination of both Ashcraft and Ware. [In] the presence of this friendly doctor Ashcraft might have complained of his treatment and avowed his innocence. The doctor testified, however, that Ashcraft said he had been treated all right, that he made no complaint about his eyes, and that they were not bloodshot. The doctor made a physical examination, and says Ashcraft appeared normal. He further testified as to Ashcraft, "Well, sir, he said he had not been able to get along with his wife for some time [and] that he offered [Ware] a sum of money to make away with his wife." The doctor says that that statement was entirely voluntary. No matter what pressure had been put on Ashcraft before, the courts below could reasonably believe that he made this statement voluntarily to a man of whom he had no fear and who knew his family relations.

Ashcraft's story of torture could only be accepted by disbelieving such credible and unimpeached contradiction. Ashcraft testified that he was refused food, was not allowed to go to the lavatory, and was denied even a drink of water. Other testimony is that on Saturday night he was brought a sandwich and coffee about midnight; that he drank the coffee but refused the sandwich; that on Sunday morning he was given a breakfast and was fed again about noon a plate lunch consisting of meat and vegetables and coffee. Both Waldauer, the Reporter, and Dr. McQuiston testified that they saw breakfast served to Ashcraft the next morning, before the statement taken down by Waldauer. Ashcraft claims he was threatened and that a cigarette was slapped out of his mouth. This is all denied.

This Court rejects the testimony of the officers and disinterested witnesses in this case that the confession was voluntary not because it lacked probative value in itself nor because the witnesses were self-contradictory or were impeached. On the contrary, it is impugned only on grounds such as that such disputes "are an inescapable consequence of secret inquisitorial practices." We infer from this that since a prisoner's unsupported word often conflicts with that of the officers, the officer's testimony for constitutional purposes is always prima facie false. We know that police standards often leave much to be desired, but we are not ready to believe that the democratic process brings to office men generally less believable than the average of those accused of crime. * * *

This questioning is characterized as a "secret inquisition," invoking all of the horrendous historical associations of those words. Certainly the inquiry was participated in by a good many persons, and we do not see how it could have been much less "secret" unless the press should have been called in. Of course, any questioning may be characterized as an "inquisition," but the use of such characterizations is no substitute for the detached and judicial consideration that the court below gave to the case.

We conclude that even going behind the state court decisions into the facts, no independent judgment on the whole evidence that Ashcraft's confession was in fact coerced is possible. And against this background of facts the extreme character of the Court's ruling becomes apparent.

I am not sure whether the Court denies the State all right to arrest and question the husband of the slain woman. No investigation worthy of the name could fail to examine him. Of all persons he was most likely to know whether she had enemies or rivals. Would not the State have a constitutional right, whether he was accused or not, to arrest and detain him as a material witness? If it has the right to detain one as a witness, presumably it has the right to examine him.

Could the State not confront Ashcraft with his false statements and ask his explanation? He did not throw himself at any time on his rights, refuse to answer, and demand counsel, even according to his own testimony. The strategy of the officers evidently was to keep him talking, to give him plenty of rope and see if he would not hang himself. He does not claim to have made objection to this. Instead he relied on his wits. The time came when it dawned on him that his own story brought him under suspicion, and that he could not meet it. Must the officers stop at this point because he was coming to appreciate the uselessness of deception?

Then he became desperate and accused [Ware]. Certainly from this point the State was justified in holding and questioning him as a witness, for he claimed to know the killer. That accusation backfired and only turned up a witness against him. He had run out of expedients and inventions; he knew he had lost the battle of wits. After all honesty seemed to be the best, even if the last, policy. He confessed in detail.

At what point in all this investigation does the Court hold that the Constitution commands these officers to send Ashcraft on his way and give up the murder as insoluble? If the state is denied the right to apply any pressure to him which is "inherently coercive" it could hardly deprive him of his freedom at all. I, too, dislike to think of any man, under the disadvantages and indignities of detention being questioned about his personal life for thirty-six hours or for one hour. In fact, there is much in our whole system of penology that seems archaic and vindictive and badly managed. Every person in the community, no matter how inconvenient or embarrassing, no matter what retaliation it exposes him to, may be called upon to take the witness stand and tell all he knows about a crime—except the person who knows most about it. ＊ ＊ ＊

No conclusion that this confession was actually coerced can be reached on this record except by reliance upon the utterly uncorroborated statements of defendant Ashcraft. His testimony does not carry even ordinary guaranties of truthfulness, and the courts and jury were not bound to accept it. Perjury is a light offense compared to murder and they may well have believed that Ashcraft was ready to resort to a lesser crime to avoid conviction of a greater one. Furthermore, the very grounds on which this Court now upsets his conviction Ashcraft repudiated at the trial. He asserts that he was abused, but he does not testify as this Court holds that it had the effect of forcing an involuntary confession from him. On the contrary, he flatly insists that it had no such effect and that he never did confess at all.

Against Ashcraft's word the state courts and jury accepted the testimony of several apparently disinterested witnesses of high standing in their communities, in addition to that of the accused officers. One of the witnesses to Ashcraft's admission of guilt was his own family physician, two were disinterested business men of substance and standing, another was an experienced court reporter who had long held this position of considerable trust. Another was a member of the bar. Certainly, the state courts were not committing an offense against the Constitution of the United States in refusing to believe that this whole group of apparently reputable citizens entered into a conspiracy to swear a murder onto an innocent man, against whom not one of them is shown to have had a grievance or a grudge.

This is not the case of an ignorant and unrepresented defendant who has been the victim of prejudice. Ashcraft was a white man of good reputation, good position, and substantial property. For a week after this crime was discovered he was not detained, although his stories to the officers did not hang together, but was at large, free to consult his friends and counsel. There was no indecent haste, but on the contrary evident deliberation, in suspecting and accusing him.

\* \* \*

The use of the due process clause to disable the states in protection of society from crime is quite as dangerous and delicate a use of federal judicial power as to use it to disable them from social or economic experimentation.

## WATTS v. INDIANA
### 338 U.S. 49, 69 S.Ct. 1347, 93 L.Ed. 1801 (1949).

JUSTICE FRANKFURTER announced the judgment of the Court and a opinion in which JUSTICE MURPHY and JUSTICE RUTLEDGE join.

\* \* \* This case is here because the Supreme Court of Indiana rejected petitioner's claim that confessions elicited from him were procured under circumstances rendering their admission as evidence against him a denial of due process of law.[2]

In the application of so embracing a constitutional concept as "due process," it would be idle to expect at all times unanimity of views. Nevertheless, in all the cases that have come here during the last decade from the courts of the various States in which it was claimed that the admission of coerced confessions vitiated convictions for murder, there has been complete agreement that any conflict in testimony as to what actually led to a contested confession is not this Court's concern. Such conflict comes here authoritatively resolved by the State's adjudication. Therefore only those elements of the events and circumstances in which a confession was involved that are unquestioned in the State's version of what happened are relevant to the constitutional issue here. But if force has been applied, this Court does not leave to local determination whether or not the confession was voluntary. There is torture of mind as well as body; the will is as much affected by fear as by force. And there comes a point where this Court should not be ignorant as judges of what we know as men. \* \* \*

On November 12, 1947, a Wednesday, petitioner was arrested and held as the suspected perpetrator of an alleged criminal assault earlier in the day. Later the same day, in the vicinity of this occurrence, a woman was found dead under conditions suggesting murder in the course of an attempted criminal assault. Suspicion of murder quickly turned towards petitioner and the police began to question him. They took him from the county jail to State Police Headquarters, where he was questioned by officers in relays from about eleven

2. In the petitioner's statements there was acknowledgment of the possession of an incriminating gun, the existence of which the police independently established. But a co-erced confession is inadmissible under the Due Process Clause even though statements in it may be independently established as true.

thirty that night until sometime between 2:30 and 3 o'clock the following morning. The same procedure of persistent interrogation from about 5:30 in the afternoon until about 3 o'clock the following morning, by a relay of six to eight officers, was pursued on Thursday the 13th, Friday the 14th, Saturday the 15th, Monday the 17th. Sunday was a day of rest from interrogation. About 3 o'clock on Tuesday morning, November 18, the petitioner made an incriminating statement after continuous questioning since 6 o'clock of the preceding evening. The statement did not satisfy the prosecutor who had been called in and he then took petitioner in hand. Petitioner, questioned by an interrogator of twenty years' experience as lawyer, judge and prosecutor, yielded a more incriminating document.

Until his inculpatory statements were secured, the petitioner was a prisoner in the exclusive control of the prosecuting authorities. He was kept for the first two days in solitary confinement in a cell aptly enough called "the hole" in view of its physical conditions as described by the State's witnesses. Apart from the five night sessions, the police intermittently interrogated Watts during the day and on three days drove him around town, hours at a time, with a view to eliciting identifications and other disclosures. Although the law of Indiana required that petitioner be given a prompt preliminary hearing before a magistrate, with all the protection a hearing was intended to give him, the petitioner was not only given no hearing during the entire period of interrogation but was without friendly or professional aid and without advice as to his constitutional rights. Disregard of rudimentary needs of life—opportunities for sleep and a decent allowance of food—are also relevant, not as aggravating elements of petitioner's treatment, but as part of the total situation out of which his confessions came and which stamped their character.

A confession by which life becomes forfeit must be the expression of free choice. A statement to be voluntary of course need not be volunteered. But if it is the product of sustained pressure by the police it does not issue from a free choice. When a suspect speaks because he is overborne, it is immaterial whether he has been subjected to a physical or mental ordeal. Eventual yielding to questioning under such circumstances is plainly the product of the suction process of interrogation and therefore the reverse of voluntary. We would have to shut our minds to the plain significance of what here transpired to deny that this was a calculated endeavor to secure a confession through the pressure of unrelenting interrogation. The very relentlessness of such interrogation implies that it is better for the prisoner to answer than to persist in the refusal of disclosure which is his constitutional right. To turn the detention of an accused into a process of wrenching from him evidence which could not be extorted in open court with all its safeguards, is so grave an abuse of the power of arrest as to offend the procedural standards of due process.

This is so because it violates the underlying principle in our enforcement of the criminal law. Ours is the accusatorial as opposed to the inquisitorial system. Such has been the characteristic of Anglo–American criminal justice since it freed itself from practices borrowed by the Star Chamber from the Continent whereby an accused was interrogated in secret for hours on end. Under our system society carries the burden of proving its charge against the accused not out of his own mouth. It must establish its case, not by interrogation of the accused even under judicial safeguards, but by evidence independently secured through skillful investigation. [The] requirement of specific charges, their proof beyond a reasonable doubt, the protection of the accused from confessions extorted through whatever form of police pressures, the right to a prompt hearing before a magistrate, the right to assistance of counsel, to be supplied by government when circumstances make it necessary, the duty to advise an accused of his constitutional rights—these are all characteristics of the accusatorial system and manifestations of its demands.    Protracted, systematic and uncontrolled subjection of an accused to interrogation by the police for the purpose of eliciting disclosures or confessions is subversive of the accusatorial system.    It is the inquisitorial system without its safeguards.    For while under that system the accused is subjected to judicial interrogation, he is protected by the disinterestedness of the judge in the presence of counsel.

In holding that the Due Process Clause bars police procedure which violates the basic notions of our accusatorial mode of prosecuting crime and vitiates a conviction based on the fruits of such procedure, we apply the Due Process Clause to its historic function of assuring appropriate procedure before liberty is curtailed or life is taken.    We are deeply mindful of the anguishing problems which the incidence of crime presents to the States.    But the history of the criminal law proves overwhelmingly that brutal methods of law enforcement are essentially self-defeating, whatever may be their effect in a particular case.    Law triumphs when the natural impulses aroused by a shocking crime yield to the safeguards which our civilization has evolved for an administration of criminal justice at once rational and effective.   *   *   * Reversed.

JUSTICE DOUGLAS, concurring   *   *   *

It would be naive to think that [petitioner] was subject to anything less than the inquisition.    The man was held until he broke.    Then and only then was he arraigned and given the protection which the law provides all accused.    Detention without arraignment is a time-honored method for keeping an accused under the exclusive control of the police.    They can then operate at their leisure.    The accused is wholly at their mercy.    He is without the aid of counsel or friends; and he is denied the protection of the magistrate.    We should unequivocally condemn the procedure and stand ready to outlaw [any] confession obtained during the period of unlawful detention.    The procedure breeds coerced confessions.    It is the root of the evil.    It is the procedure without which the inquisition could not flourish in the country.[a]

JUSTICE JACKSON, concurring in the result in [ *Watts v. Indiana* ] and dissenting in [two companion cases, *Harris v. South Carolina* and *Turner v. Pennsylvania*, where the Court also reversed convictions resting on coerced confessions].

These three cases, from widely separated states, present essentially the same problem.    Its recurrence suggests that it has roots in some condition fundamental and general to our criminal system.

In each case police were confronted with one or more brutal murders which the authorities were under the highest duty to solve.    Each of these murders was unwitnessed, and the only positive knowledge on which a solution could be based was possessed by the killer.    In each there was reasonable ground to *suspect* an individual but not enough legal evidence to *charge* him with guilt.    In each the police attempted to meet the situation by taking the suspect into custody and interrogating him.    This extended over varying periods.    In each, confessions were made and received in evidence at the trial.    Checked with external evidence, they are inherently believable, and were not shaken as to truth by

a.   Justice Black's opinion concurring in
the judgment of the Court is omitted.

anything that occurred at the trial. Each confessor was convicted by a jury and state courts affirmed. This Court sets all three convictions aside.

The seriousness of the Court's judgment is that no one suggests that any course held promise of solution of these murders other than to take the suspect into custody for questioning. The alternative was to close the books on the crime and forget it, with the suspect at large. This is a grave choice for a society in which two-thirds of the murders already are closed out as insoluble.

A concurring opinion, however, goes to the very limit and seems to declare for outlawing any confession, however freely given, if obtained during a period of custody between arrest and arraignment—which, in practice, means all of them.

Others would strike down these confessions because of conditions which they say make them "involuntary." In this, on only a printed record, they pit their judgment against that of the trial judge and the jury. Both, with the great advantage of hearing and seeing the confessor and also the officers whose conduct and bearing toward him is in question, have found that the confessions were voluntary. In addition, the majority overrule in each case one or more state appellate courts, which have the same limited opportunity to know the truth that we do.

Amid much that is irrelevant or trivial one serious situation seems to me to stand out in these cases. The suspect neither had nor was advised of his right to get counsel. This presents a real dilemma in a free society. To subject one without counsel to questioning which may and is intended to convict him, is a real peril to individual freedom. To bring in a lawyer means a real peril to solution of the crime because, under our adversary system, he deems that his sole duty is to protect his client—guilty or innocent—and that in such a capacity he owes no duty whatever to help society solve its crime problem. Under this conception of criminal procedure, any lawyer worth his salt will tell the suspect in no uncertain terms to make no statement to police under any circumstances.

If the State may arrest on suspicion and interrogate without counsel, there is no denying the fact that it largely negates the benefits of the constitutional guaranty of the right to assistance of counsel. Any lawyer who has ever been called into a case after his client has "told all" and turned any evidence he has over to the Government, knows how helpless he is to protect his client against the facts thus disclosed.

I suppose the view one takes will turn on what one thinks should be the right of an accused person against the State. Is it his right to have the judgment on the facts? Or is it his right to have a judgment based on only such evidence as he cannot conceal from the authorities, who cannot compel him to testify in court and also cannot question him before? Our system comes close to the latter by any interpretation, for the defendant is shielded by such safeguards as no system of law except the Anglo–American concedes to him.

Of course, no confession that has been obtained by any form of physical violence to the person is reliable and hence no conviction should rest upon one obtained in that manner. Such treatment not only breaks the will to conceal or lie, but may even break the will to stand by the truth. Nor is it questioned that the same result can sometimes be achieved by threats, promises, or inducements, which torture the mind but put no scar on the body. If the opinion of Mr. Justice Frankfurter in *Watts* were based solely on the State's admissions as to the treatment of Watts, I should not disagree. But if ultimate quest in a criminal trial is the truth and if the circumstances indicate no violence or threats of it, should society be deprived of the suspect's help in solving a crime merely because he was confined and questioned when uncounseled?

We must not overlook that in these, as in some previous cases, once a confession is obtained it supplies ways of verifying its trustworthiness. In these cases before us the verification is sufficient to leave me in no doubt that the admissions of guilt were genuine and truthful. Such corroboration consists in one case of finding a weapon where the accused has said he hid it, and in others that conditions which could only have been known to one who was implicated correspond with his story. It is possible, but it is rare, that a confession, if repudiated on the trial, standing alone will convict unless there is external proof of its verity.

In all such cases, along with other conditions criticized, the continuity and duration of the questioning is invoked and it is called an "inquiry," "inquest" or "inquisition," depending mainly on the emotional state of the writer. But as in some of the cases here, if interrogation is permissible at all, there are sound reasons for prolonging it—which the opinions here ignore. The suspect at first perhaps makes an effort to exculpate himself by alibis or other statements. These are verified, found false, and he is then confronted with his falsehood. Sometimes (though such cases do not reach us) verification proves them true or credible and the suspect is released. Sometimes, as here, more than one crime is involved. The duration of an interrogation may well depend on the temperament, shrewdness and cunning of the accused and the competence of the examiner. But assuming a right to examine at all, the right must include what is made reasonably necessary by the facts of the particular case.

If the right of interrogation be admitted, then it seems to me that we must leave it to trial judges and juries and state appellate courts to decide individual cases, unless they show some want of proper standards of decision. I find nothing to indicate that any of the courts below in these cases did not have a correct understanding of the Fourteenth Amendment, unless this Court thinks it means absolute prohibition of interrogation while in custody before arraignment.

I suppose no one would doubt that our Constitution and Bill of Rights, grounded in revolt against the arbitrary measures of George III and in the philosophy of the French Revolution, represent the maximum restrictions upon the power of organized society over the individual that are compatible with the maintenance of organized society itself. They were so intended and should be so interpreted. It cannot be denied that, even if construed as these provisions traditionally have been, they contain an aggregate of restrictions which seriously limit the power of society to solve such crimes as confront us in these cases. Those restrictions we should not for that reason cast aside, but that is good reason for indulging in no unnecessary expansion of them.

I doubt very much if they require us to hold that the State may not take into custody and question one suspected reasonably of an unwitnessed murder. If it does, the people of this country must discipline themselves to seeing their police stand by helplessly while those suspected of murder prowl about unmolested. Is it a necessary price to pay for the fairness which we know as "due process of law"? And if not a necessary one, should it be demanded by this Court? I do not know the ultimate answer to these questions; but, for the present, I should not increase the handicap on society.[b]

b. Vinson, C.J., and Reed and Burton, JJ. dissented, "on the record before us and in view of the consideration given to the evidence by the state courts".

## SECTION 2. *MASSIAH* AND *ESCOBEDO*: THE COURT GROWS DISENCHANTED WITH THE "VOLUNTARINESS" TEST AND TURNS TO THE RIGHT TO COUNSEL

As the rationales for the Court's coerced confession cases evolved, it became increasingly doubtful that terms such as "voluntariness," "coercion" and "breaking the will" were very helpful in deciding the admissibility of confessions. It appeared that such terms were not being used as tools of analysis, but as mere conclusions. When a court concluded that the police had resorted to unacceptable interrogation techniques, it called the resulting confession "involuntary." On the other hand, it seemed, when a court decided the methods the police had employed were permissible or tolerable, it called the resulting confession "voluntary." Moreover, such terms as "voluntariness," "coercion" and "overbearing the will" focused directly on neither of the two underlying reasons that led the courts to bar the use of confessions—the offensiveness of police interrogation methods or the risk that these methods had produced an untrue confession. Thus, as the Court, per O'Connor, J., recently noted in *Miller v. Fenton,* 474 U.S. 104 (1985), "[t]he voluntariness rubric has been variously condemned as 'useless,' 'perplexing,' and 'legal "doubletalk." ' "

Almost everything was relevant under the due process "totality of the circumstances"—"voluntariness" test, e.g., the suspect's age, intelligence, education and prior criminal record; whether he was advised of his rights, held incommunicado or given meals at regular intervals. But with a very few exceptions, e.g. the use or threatened use of physical violence, no single factor was decisive. Because there were so many variables in the voluntariness equation that one determination seldom served as a useful precedent for another, the test offered neither the police nor the courts much guidance. Trial courts were almost invited to give weight to their subjective preferences and appellate courts were discouraged from active review.

Understandably, some members of the Court looked for an alternative approach. In the 1959 *Crooker* case, discussed below, the four dissenters turned to the right to counsel. Five years later, as illustrated by the two cases in this section, *Massiah v. United States* and *Escobedo v. Illinois,* the right to counsel approach to confessions had gained ascendancy.

*Crooker v. California,* 357 U.S. 433 (1958), involved a petitioner who had attended one year of law school, during which time he studied criminal law, and who indicated that he was fully aware of his right to remain silent. On the basis of a challenged confession, he was convicted of the murder of his paramour and sentenced to death. A 5–4 majority rejected his argument that by persisting in interrogating him after denying his specific request to contact his lawyer the police had violated his due process right to legal representation and advice and that therefore the use of any confession obtained from him under these circumstances should be barred, even though "voluntarily" made under traditional standards. Such a rule, retorted the Court, per Clark, J., "would have [a] devastating effect on enforcement of criminal law, for it would effectively preclude police questioning—fair as well as unfair—until the accused was afforded opportunity to call his lawyer. Due process * * * demands no such rule." But four dissenting Justices, Douglas, J., joined by Warren, C.J., and Black and Brennan, JJ., maintained that "[t]he demands of our civilization, expressed in the Due Process Clause require that the accused who wants a counsel should have one at any time after the moment of arrest."

The following year, by virtue of *Spano v. New York,* 360 U.S. 315 (1959), it appeared that a majority of the Court may have arrived at the view that once a person is *formally charged* by indictment or information her constitutional right to counsel has "begun"—at least the right to the assistance of counsel she herself has retained. Four concurring Justices took this position in *Spano*: Justices Black, Douglas and Brennan, all of whom had dissented in *Crooker,* and newly appointed Justice Stewart, who had replaced Justice Burton. In two separate opinions, the concurring Justices emphasized that *Spano* was not a case where the police were questioning a suspect in the course of investigating an unsolved crime, but one where the person interrogated was already under indictment for murder when he surrendered to the authorities.

A majority of the *Spano* Court did not decide the case on the grounds suggested by the concurring Justices because it found the confession inadmissible under the traditional due process "voluntariness" test. But Chief Justice Warren, who wrote the majority opinion, had taken the position a year earlier in *Crooker* that the right to counsel should "begin" even earlier than at the point of indictment. Thus, counting heads, it appeared that by 1959 the views of the concurring Justices in *Spano* commanded a majority of the Court. Any doubts were dispelled by *Massiah v. United States,* the first case in this section.

When, a short five weeks after it had decided *Massiah,* the Court threw out the confession in *Escobedo v. Illinois,* the second case in this section, even though Escobedo had been interrogated *before* "judicial" or "adversary" proceedings had commenced against him, many members of the bench and bar grew alarmed. As they saw it, the "right to counsel" approach to the confession problem threatened the admissibility of even *"volunteered"* statements. They feared that the Court might be in the process of shaping a novel right not to confess except knowingly and with the tactical assistance of counsel.

Perhaps the enthusiastic public reaction to the *Gideon* decision a year earlier had led some members of the Court to believe that *Massiah* and *Escobedo* would also be well-received. But many members of the bench and bar, and the general public as well, soon left little doubt that they were much more enthusiastic about a lawyer for a defendant in the courtroom than they were about a lawyer for a suspect in the police station.

## MASSIAH v. UNITED STATES
### 377 U.S. 201, 84 S.Ct. 1199, 12 L.Ed.2d 246 (1964).

JUSTICE STEWART delivered the opinion of the Court. * * *

[After he had been indicted for conspiracy to possess narcotics aboard a United States vessel and other federal narcotics violations, Massiah retained a lawyer, pled not guilty, and was released on bail. Colson, a codefendant, also retained a lawyer, pled not guilty, and was released on bail. Colson then invited Massiah to discuss the pending case in Colson's car, parked on a city street. Unknown to Massiah, Colson had decided to cooperate with federal agents in their continuing investigation of the case. A radio transmitter was installed under the front seat of Colson's car, enabling a nearby federal agent (Murphy), who was equipped with a recording device, to overhear the Massiah–Colson conversation. As expected, Massiah made several damaging admissions. On the basis of these admissions, Massiah was convicted of several narcotics offenses.

The convictions were affirmed by the U.S. Court of Appeals for the Second Circuit.]

In *Spano v. New York,* this Court reversed a state criminal conviction because a confession had been wrongly admitted into evidence against the defendant at his trial. In that case the defendant had already been indicted for first-degree murder at the time he confessed. The Court held that the defendant's conviction could not stand under the Fourteenth Amendment. While the Court's opinion relied upon the totality of the circumstances under which the confession had been obtained, four concurring Justices pointed out that the Constitution required reversal of the conviction upon the sole and specific ground that the confession had been deliberately elicited by the police after the defendant had been indicted, and therefore at a time when he was clearly entitled to a lawyer's help. It was pointed out that under our system of justice the most elemental concepts of due process of law contemplate that an indictment be followed by a trial, "in an orderly courtroom, presided over by a judge, open to the public, and protected by all the procedural safeguards of the law." (Stewart, J., concurring). It was said that a Constitution which guarantees a defendant the aid of counsel at such a trial could surely vouchsafe no less to an indicted defendant under interrogation by the police in a completely extrajudicial proceeding. Anything less, it was said, might deny a defendant "effective representation by counsel at the only stage when legal aid and advice would help him." (Douglas, J., concurring).

[The view taken by the *Spano* concurring Justices] no more than reflects a constitutional principle established as long ago as *Powell v. Alabama,* where the Court noted that "during perhaps the most critical period of the proceedings, [that] is to say, from the time of their arraignment until the beginning of their trial, when consultation, thoroughgoing investigation and preparation [are] vitally important, the defendants [are] as much entitled to such aid [of counsel] during that period as at the trial itself." * * *

Here we deal not with a state court conviction, but with a federal case, where the specific guarantee of the Sixth Amendment directly applies. We hold that the petitioner was denied the basic protections of that guarantee when there was used against him at his trial evidence of his own incriminating words, which federal agents had deliberately elicited from him after he had been indicted and in the absence of his counsel. It is true that in the Spano case the defendant was interrogated in a police station, while here the damaging testimony was elicited from the defendant without his knowledge while he was free on bail. But, as Judge Hays pointed out in his dissent in the Court of Appeals, "if such a rule is to have any efficacy it must apply to indirect and surreptitious interrogations as well as those conducted in the jailhouse. In this case, Massiah was more seriously imposed upon * * * because he did not even know that he was under interrogation by a government agent."

The Solicitor General [has] strenuously contended that the federal law enforcement agents had the right, if not indeed the duty, to continue their investigation of the petitioner and his alleged criminal associates even though the petitioner had been indicted. [He] says that the quantity of narcotics involved was such as to suggest that the petitioner was part of a large and well-organized ring, and indeed that the continuing investigation confirmed this suspicion, since it resulted in criminal charges against many defendants. Under these circumstances the Solicitor General concludes that the government agents were completely "justified in making use of Colson's cooperation by having Colson continue his normal associations and by surveilling them."

* * * We do not question that in this case, as in many cases, it was entirely proper to continue an investigation of the suspected criminal activities of the defendant and his alleged confederates, even though the defendant had already been indicted. All that we hold is that the defendant's own incriminating statements, obtained by federal agents under the circumstances here disclosed, could not constitutionally be used by the prosecution as evidence against *him* at his trial. * * *

JUSTICE WHITE, with whom JUSTICE CLARK and JUSTICE HARLAN join, dissenting.

* * * [It is] a rather portentous occasion when a constitutional rule is established barring the use of evidence which is relevant, reliable and highly probative of the issue which the trial court has before it—whether the accused committed the act with which he is charged. Without the evidence, the quest for truth may be seriously impeded and in many cases the trial court, although aware of proof showing defendant's guilt, must nevertheless release him because the crucial evidence is deemed inadmissible. This result is entirely justified in some circumstances because exclusion serves other policies of overriding importance, as where evidence seized in an illegal search is excluded, not because of the quality of the proof, but to secure meaningful enforcement of the Fourth Amendment. But this only emphasizes that the soundest of reasons is necessary to warrant the exclusion of evidence otherwise admissible and the creation of another area of privileged testimony. With all due deference, I am not at all convinced that the additional barriers to the pursuit of truth which the Court today erects rest on anything like the solid foundations which decisions of this gravity should require.

The importance of the matter should not be underestimated, for today's rule promises to have wide application well beyond the facts of this case. The reason given for the result here—the admissions were obtained in the absence of counsel—would seem equally pertinent to statements obtained at any time after the right to counsel attaches, whether there has been an indictment or not; to admissions made prior to arraignment, at least where the defendant has counsel or asks for it; to the fruits of admissions improperly obtained under the new rule; to criminal proceedings in state courts; and to defendants long since convicted upon evidence including such admissions. The new rule will immediately do service in a great many cases.

Whatever the content or scope of the rule may prove to be, I am unable to see how this case presents an unconstitutional interference with Massiah's right to counsel. Massiah was not prevented from consulting with counsel as often as he wished. No meetings with counsel were disturbed or spied upon. Preparation for trial was in no way obstructed. It is only a sterile syllogism—an unsound one, besides—to say that because Massiah had a right to counsel's aid before and during the trial, his out-of-court conversations and admissions must be excluded if obtained without counsel's consent or presence. The right to counsel has never meant as much before and its extension in this case requires some further explanation, so far unarticulated by the Court.

Since the new rule would exclude all admissions made to the police, no matter how voluntary and reliable, the requirement of counsel's presence or approval would seem to rest upon the probability that counsel would foreclose any admissions at all. This is nothing more than a thinly disguised constitutional policy of minimizing or entirely prohibiting the use in evidence of voluntary out-of-court admissions and confessions made by the accused. Carried as far as blind logic may compel some to go, the notion that statements from the mouth of the defendant should not be used in evidence would have a severe and unfortunate impact upon the great bulk of criminal cases.

Viewed in this light, the Court's newly fashioned exclusionary principle goes far beyond the constitutional privilege against self-incrimination, which neither requires nor suggests the barring of voluntary pretrial admissions.

\* \* \* Whether as a matter of self-incrimination or of due process, the proscription is against compulsion—coerced incrimination. Under the prior law, announced in countless cases in this Court, the defendant's pretrial statements were admissible evidence if voluntarily made; inadmissible if not the product of his free will. Hardly any constitutional area has been more carefully patrolled by this Court, and until now the Court has expressly rejected the argument that admissions are to be deemed involuntary if made outside the presence of counsel.

The Court presents no facts, no objective evidence, no reasons to warrant scrapping the voluntary-involuntary test for admissibility in this area. Without such evidence I would retain it in its present form.

This case cannot be analogized to the American Bar Association's rule forbidding an attorney to talk to the opposing party litigant outside the presence of his counsel. Aside from the fact that the Association's canons are not of constitutional dimensions, the specific canon argued is inapposite because it deals with the conduct of lawyers and not with the conduct of investigators. Lawyers are forbidden to interview the opposing party because of the supposed imbalance of legal skill and acumen between the lawyer and the party litigant; the reason for the rule does not apply to nonlawyers and certainly not to Colson, Massiah's codefendant.

Applying the new exclusionary rule is peculiarly inappropriate in this case. At the time of the conversation in question, petitioner was not in custody but free on bail. He was not questioned in what anyone could call an atmosphere of official coercion. What he said was said to his partner in crime who had also been indicted. There was no suggestion or any possibility of coercion. What petitioner did not know was that Colson had decided to report the conversation to the police. Had there been no prior arrangements between Colson and the police, had Colson simply gone to the police after the conversation had occurred, his testimony relating Massiah's statements would be readily admissible at the trial, as would a recording which he might have made of the conversation. In such event, it would simply be said that Massiah risked talking to a friend who decided to disclose what he knew of Massiah's criminal activities. But if, as occurred here, Colson had been cooperating with the police prior to his meeting with Massiah, both his evidence and the recorded conversation are somehow transformed into inadmissible evidence despite the fact that the hazard to Massiah remains precisely the same—the defection of a confederate in crime.

\* \* \*

[The question presented] is this: when the police have arrested and released on bail one member of a criminal ring and another member, a confederate, is cooperating with the police, can the confederate be allowed to continue his association with the ring or must he somehow be withdrawn to avoid challenge to trial evidence on the ground that it was acquired after rather than before the arrest, after rather than before the indictment?

Defendants who are out on bail have been known to continue their illicit operations. That an attorney is advising them should not constitutionally immunize their statements made in furtherance of these operations and relevant to the question of their guilt at the pending prosecution. \* \* \* Undoubtedly, the evidence excluded in this case would not have been available but for the conduct of Colson in cooperation with Agent Murphy, but is it this kind of conduct which should be forbidden to those charged with law enforcement? It is one thing to establish safeguards against procedures fraught with the potentiality of coercion and to outlaw "easy but self-defeating ways in which brutality is substituted for brains as an instrument of crime detection." But here there was no substitution of brutality for brains, no inherent danger of police coercion justifying the prophylactic effect of another exclusionary rule. Massiah was not being interrogated in a police station, was not surrounded by numerous officers or questioned in relays, and was not forbidden access to others. Law enforcement may have the elements of a contest about it, but it is not a game. Massiah and those like him receive ample protection from the long line of precedents in this Court holding that confessions may not be introduced unless they are voluntary. In making these determinations the courts must consider the absence of counsel as one of several factors by which voluntariness is to be judged. This is a wiser rule than the automatic rule announced by the Court, which requires courts and juries to disregard voluntary admissions which they might well find to be the best possible evidence in discharging their responsibility for ascertaining truth.

## ESCOBEDO v. ILLINOIS
378 U.S. 478, 84 S.Ct. 1758, 12 L.Ed.2d 977 (1964).

JUSTICE GOLDBERG delivered the opinion of the Court.

[On the night of January 19, petitioner's brother-in-law was fatally shot. A few hours later petitioner was taken into custody for questioning, but he made no statement and was released the following afternoon pursuant to a writ of habeas corpus obtained by his retained counsel. On January 30, one DiGerlando, who was then in police custody and who was later indicted for the murder along with petitioner, stated that petitioner had fired the shots which killed his brother-in-law. That evening petitioner was again arrested and taken to police headquarters. En route to the police station he was told that DiGerlando had named him as the one who fired the fatal shots and that he might as well admit it, but petitioner replied (probably because his attorney had obtained his release from police custody only 11 days earlier or because he had consulted with his attorney in the meantime): "I am sorry but I would like to have advice from my lawyer."

[Shortly after petitioner reached police headquarters, his retained lawyer arrived and spent the next three or four hours trying unsuccessfully to speak to his client. He talked to every officer he could find, but was repeatedly told that he could not see his client and that he would have to get a writ of habeas corpus. In the meantime, petitioner repeatedly but unsuccessfully asked to speak to his lawyer. At one point, petitioner and his attorney came into each other's view for a few moments, but the attorney was quickly ushered away. Petitioner testified that he heard a detective tell his attorney that the latter could not see him until the police "were done."

[Instead of allowing petitioner to meet with his lawyer, the police arranged a confrontation between petitioner and DiGerlando. Petitioner denied that he had fired the fatal shots. He maintained that DiGerlando was lying and, in the presence of the police, told him: "I didn't shoot Manuel, you did it." In this way, petitioner admitted to some knowledge of the crime. After that, he made other statements further implicating himself in the murder plot. At this point, an assistant prosecutor arrived "to take" a statement. The statement, made in response to carefully framed questions, was admitted into evidence. Petitioner was convicted of murder. The Supreme Court of Illinois affirmed.]

The critical question in this case is whether, under the circumstances, the refusal by the police to honor petitioner's request to consult with his lawyer during the course of an interrogation constitutes a denial of "the Assistance of Counsel" in violation of the Sixth Amendment to the Constitution as "made obligatory upon the States by the Fourteenth Amendment," *Gideon,* and thereby renders inadmissible in a state criminal trial any incriminating statement elicited by the police during the interrogation. * * *

In *Massiah* this Court observed that "a Constitution which guarantees a defendant the aid of counsel [at] trial could surely vouchsafe no less to an indicted defendant under interrogation by the police in a completely extrajudicial proceeding. Anything less [might] deny a defendant 'effective representation by counsel at the only stage when legal aid and advice would help him.'"

The interrogation here was conducted before petitioner was formally indicted. But in the context of this case, that fact should make no difference. When petitioner requested, and was denied, an opportunity to consult with his lawyer, the investigation had ceased to be a general investigation of "an unsolved crime." Petitioner had become the accused, and the purpose of the interrogation was to "get him" to confess his guilt despite his constitutional right not to do so. At the time of his arrest and throughout the course of the interrogation, the police told petitioner that they had convincing evidence that he had fired the fatal shots. Without informing him of his absolute right to remain silent in the face of this accusation, the police urged him to make a statement.[5] * * *

Petitioner, a layman, was undoubtedly unaware that under Illinois law an admission of "mere" complicity in the murder plot was legally as damaging as an admission of firing of the fatal shots. The "guiding hand of counsel" was essential to advise petitioner of his rights in this delicate situation. This was the "stage when legal aid and advice" were most critical to petitioner. *Massiah.* * * * It would exalt form over substance to make the right to counsel, under these circumstances, depend on whether at the time of the interrogation, the authorities had secured a formal indictment. Petitioner had, for all practical purposes, already been charged with murder. * * *

In *Gideon* we held that every person accused of a crime, whether state or federal, is entitled to a lawyer at trial. The rule sought by the State here, however, would make the trial no more than an appeal from the interrogation; and the "right to use counsel at the formal trial [would be] a very hollow thing [if], for all practical purposes, the conviction is already assured by pretrial examination." *In re Groban,* 352 U.S. 330 (1957) (Black, J., dissenting). "One can imagine a cynical prosecutor saying: 'Let them have the most illustrious counsel, now. They can't escape the noose. There is nothing that counsel can do for them at the trial.'"

It is argued that if the right to counsel is afforded prior to indictment, the number of confessions obtained by the police will diminish significantly, because most confessions are obtained during the period between arrest and indictment, and "any lawyer worth his salt will tell the suspect in no uncertain terms to make no statement to police under any circumstances." This argument, of course, cuts two ways. The fact that many confessions are obtained during this

---

**5.** Although there is testimony in the record that petitioner and his lawyer had previously discussed what petitioner should do in the event of interrogation, there is no evidence that they discussed what petitioner should, or could, do in the face of a false accusation that he had fired the fatal bullets.

period points up its critical nature as a "stage when legal aid and advice" are surely needed. *Massiah.* The right to counsel would indeed be hollow if it began at a period when few confessions were obtained. There is necessarily a direct relationship between the importance of a stage to the police in their quest for a confession and the criticalness of that stage to the accused in his need for legal advice. Our Constitution, unlike some others, strikes the balance in favor of the right of the accused to be advised by his lawyer of his privilege against self-incrimination.

We have learned the lesson of history, ancient and modern, that a system of criminal law enforcement which comes to depend on the "confession" will, in the long run, be less reliable and more subject to abuses than a system which depends on extrinsic evidence independently secured through skillful investigation. * * *

We have also learned the companion lesson of history that no system of criminal justice can, or should, survive if it comes to depend for its continued effectiveness on the citizens' abdication through unawareness of their constitutional rights. No system worth preserving should have to *fear* that if an accused is permitted to consult with a lawyer, he will become aware of, and exercise, these rights. If the exercise of constitutional rights will thwart the effectiveness of a system of law enforcement, then there is something very wrong with that system.[14]

We hold, therefore, that where, as here, the investigation is no longer a general inquiry into an unsolved crime but has begun to focus on a particular suspect, the suspect has been taken into police custody, the police carry out a process of interrogations that lends itself to eliciting incriminating statements, the suspect has requested and been denied an opportunity to consult with his lawyer, and the police have not effectively warned him of his absolute constitutional right to remain silent, the accused has been denied "the Assistance of Counsel" in violation of the Sixth Amendment to the Constitution as "made obligatory upon the States by the Fourteenth Amendment," *Gideon,* and that no statement elicited by the police during the interrogation may be used against him at a criminal trial. * * *

Nothing we have said today affects the powers of the police to investigate "an unsolved crime" by gathering information from witnesses and by other "proper investigative efforts." We hold only that when the process shifts from investigatory to accusatory—when its focus is on the accused and its purpose is to elicit a confession—our adversary system begins to operate, and, under the circumstances here, the accused must be permitted to consult with his lawyer.

The judgment of the Illinois Supreme Court is reversed and the case remanded for proceedings not inconsistent with this opinion. * * *

JUSTICE HARLAN, dissenting.

* * * Like my Brother White, I think the rule announced today is most ill-conceived and that it seriously and unjustifiably fetters perfectly legitimate methods of criminal law enforcement.

JUSTICE STEWART, dissenting. * * *

*Massiah* is not in point here. * * * Putting to one side the fact that the case now before us is not a federal case, the vital fact remains that this case does

---

14. The accused may, of course, intelligently and knowingly waive his privilege against self-incrimination and his right to counsel either at a pretrial stage or at the trial. But no knowing and intelligent waiver of any constitutional right can be said to have occurred under the circumstances of this case.

not involve the deliberate interrogation of a defendant after the initiation of judicial proceedings against him. The Court disregards this basic difference between the present case and Massiah's, with the bland assertion that "that fact should make no difference."

It is "that fact," I submit, which makes all the difference. Under our system of criminal justice the institution of formal, meaningful judicial proceedings, by way of indictment, information, or arraignment, marks the point at which a criminal investigation has ended and adversary proceedings have commenced. It is at this point that the constitutional guarantees attach which pertain to a criminal trial. Among those guarantees are the right to a speedy trial, the right of confrontation, and the right to trial by jury. Another is the guarantee of the assistance of counsel.

The confession which the Court today holds inadmissible was a voluntary one. It was given during the course of a perfectly legitimate police investigation of an unsolved murder. The Court says that what happened during this investigation "affected" the trial. I had always supposed that the whole purpose of a police investigation of a murder was to "affect" the trial of the murderer, and that it would be only an incompetent, unsuccessful, or corrupt investigation which would not do so. The Court further says that the Illinois police officers did not advise the petitioner of his "constitutional rights" before he confessed to the murder. This Court has never held that the Constitution requires the police to give any "advice" under circumstances such as these.

Supported by no stronger authority than its own rhetoric, the Court today converts a routine police investigation of an unsolved murder into a distorted analogue of a judicial trial. It imports into this investigation constitutional concepts historically applicable only after the onset of formal prosecutorial proceedings. By doing so, I think the Court perverts those precious constitutional guarantees, and frustrates the vital interests of society in preserving the legitimate and proper function of honest and purposeful police investigation.

\*   \*   \*

JUSTICE WHITE, whom JUSTICE CLARK and JUSTICE STEWART join, dissenting.

In *Massiah* the Court held that as of the date of the indictment the prosecution is disentitled to secure admissions from the accused. The Court now moves that date back to the time when the prosecution begins to "focus" on the accused. Although the opinion purports to be limited to the facts of this case, it would be naive to think that the new constitutional right announced will depend upon whether the accused has retained his own counsel, or has asked to consult with counsel in the course of interrogation. At the very least the Court holds that once the accused becomes a suspect and, presumably, is arrested, any admission made to the police thereafter is inadmissible in evidence unless the accused has waived his right to counsel. The decision is thus another major step in the direction of the goal which the Court seemingly has in mind—to bar from evidence all admissions obtained from an individual suspected of crime, whether involuntarily made or not. It does of course put us one step "ahead" of the English judges who have had the good sense to leave the matter a discretionary one with the trial court. I reject this step and the invitation to go farther which the court has now issued.

By abandoning the voluntary-involuntary test for admissibility of confessions, the Court seems driven by the notion that it is uncivilized law enforcement to use an accused's own admissions against him at his trial. It attempts to find a home for this new and nebulous rule of due process by attaching it to the right to counsel guaranteed in the federal system by the Sixth Amendment and binding upon the States by virtue of the due process guarantee of the Fourteenth Amendment. The right to counsel now not only entitles the accused to counsel's advice and aid in preparing for trial but stands as an impenetrable barrier to any interrogation once the accused has become a suspect. From that very moment apparently his right to counsel attaches, a rule wholly unworkable and impossible to administer unless police cars are equipped with public defenders and undercover agents and police informants have defense counsel at their side. I would not abandon the Court's prior cases defining with some care and analysis the circumstances requiring the presence or aid of counsel and substitute the amorphous and wholly unworkable principle that counsel is constitutionally required whenever he would or could be helpful. [Under the Court's] new approach one might just as well argue that a potential defendant is constitutionally entitled to a lawyer before, not after, he commits a crime, since it is then that crucial incriminating evidence is put within the reach of the Government by the would-be accused. Until now there simply has been no right guaranteed by the Federal Constitution to be free from the use at trial of a voluntary admission made prior to indictment.

It is incongruous to assume that the provision for counsel in the Sixth Amendment was meant to amend or supersede the self-incrimination provision of the Fifth Amendment, which is now applicable to the States. That amendment addresses itself to the very issue of incriminating admissions of an accused and resolves it by proscribing only compelled statements. Neither the Framers, the constitutional language, a century of decisions of this Court nor Professor Wigmore provides an iota of support for the idea that an accused has an absolute constitutional right not to answer even in the absence of compulsion—the constitutional right not to incriminate himself by making voluntary disclosures.

\*   \*   \*

The Court chooses [to] rely on the virtues and morality of a system of criminal law enforcement which does not depend on the "confession." No such judgment is to be found in the Constitution. It might be appropriate for a legislature to provide that a suspect should not be consulted during a criminal investigation; that an accused should never be called before a grand jury to answer, even if he wants to, what may well be incriminating questions; and that no person, whether he be a suspect, guilty criminal or innocent bystander, should be put to the ordeal of responding to orderly noncompulsory inquiry by the State. But this is not the system our Constitution requires. The only "inquisitions" the Constitution forbids are those which compel incrimination. Escobedo's statements were not compelled and the Court does not hold that they were.

This new American judges' rule, which is to be applied in both federal and state courts, is perhaps thought to be a necessary safeguard against the possibility of extorted confessions. To this extent it reflects a deep-seated distrust of law enforcement officers everywhere, unsupported by relevant data or current material based upon our own experience. Obviously law enforcement officers can make mistakes and exceed their authority, as today's decision shows that even judges can do, but I have somewhat more faith than the Court evidently has in the ability and desire of prosecutors and of the power of the appellate courts to discern and correct such violations of the law.

The Court may be concerned with a narrower matter: the unknowing defendant who responds to police questioning because he mistakenly believes that he must and that his admissions will not be used against him. But this worry hardly calls for the broadside the Court has now fired. The failure to inform an accused that he need not answer and that his answers may be used against him is very relevant indeed to whether the disclosures are compelled. Cases in this Court, to say the least, have never placed a premium on ignorance of constitutional rights. If an accused is told he must answer and does not know better, it would be very doubtful that the resulting admissions could be used against him. When the accused has not been informed of his rights at all the Court characteristically and properly looks very closely at the surrounding circumstances. I would continue to do so. But in this case Danny Escobedo knew full well that he did not have to answer and knew full well that his lawyer had advised him not to answer.

I do not suggest for a moment that law enforcement will be destroyed by the rule announced today. The need for peace and order is too insistent for that. But it will be crippled and its task made a great deal more difficult, all in my opinion, for unsound, unstated reasons, which can find no home in any of the provisions of the Constitution.

## SECTION 3. *MIRANDA*: THE COURT BUILDS A CONFESSION DOCTRINE ON THE PRIVILEGE AGAINST COMPELLED SELF–INCRIMINATION

Recall that dissenting in the 1944 *Ashcraft* case, Justice Jackson agreed that the detention and questioning of a suspect for thirty-six hours is "inherently coercive," but quickly added: "[S]o is custody and examination for one hour. Arrest itself is inherently coercive and so is detention. * * * But does the Constitution prohibit use of all confessions made after arrest because questioning, while one is deprived of freedom, is 'inherently coercive'?" Both Jackson and Justice Black, who wrote the majority opinion in *Ashcraft*, knew that in 1944 the Court was not ready for an affirmative answer to Jackson's question. But by 1966 the Court had grown ready.

Yes, answered a 5–4 majority in *Miranda v. Arizona*, the Constitution does prohibit use of all confessions obtained by "in-custody questioning" unless "adequate protective devices" are used to dispel the coercion inherent in such questioning. The protective devices deemed necessary to neutralize the compulsion inherent in the interrogation environment (unless the government adopts other equally effective means, and what they may be remains unclear) are the now familiar "*Miranda* warnings."

The *Miranda* Court's reasoning, if not its result, surprised the late John J. Flynn, Miranda's lawyer in the U.S. Supreme Court. As Flynn later recalled, he and others working on the case had "agreed that the briefs should be written with the entire focus on the Sixth Amendment [right to counsel] because that is where the Court was headed after *Escobedo*," but "in the very first paragraph [of the *Miranda* opinion] Chief Justice Warren said [in effect], 'It is the Fifth Amendment [privilege against compulsory self-incrimination] that is at issue today.' That was Miranda's effective use of counsel."

Although not happy with the continued momentum of the Warren Court in favor of the rights of suspects, those alarmed by *Massiah* and *Escobedo* must have found some comfort in the *Miranda* Court's switch in emphasis from the right to counsel to the privilege against compelled self-incrimination. Recall that the *Escobedo* dissenters expressed a preference for a self-incrimination approach, rather than a right to counsel approach, because the self-incrimination clause proscribes only *compelled* statements. Of course, the four *Escobedo* dissenters (all of whom also dissented in *Miranda*) were not pleased with the way the *Miranda* majority defined "compulsion" within the meaning of the privilege.

Why, in the thirty years between *Brown v. Mississippi* (1936), the first Fourteenth Amendment Due Process case, and *Miranda,* had the Fifth Amendment's ban against compelling a person in any criminal case "to be a witness against himself" been so neglected in the confession cases? For one thing, this prohibition had not been deemed applicable to the states until 1964, and by that time a large body of law pertaining to "involuntary" or "coerced" confessions had developed. Moreover, and more important, the prevailing pre-*Miranda* view was that compulsion to testify meant *legal* compulsion.

Since a suspect is threatened neither with perjury for testifying falsely nor contempt for refusing to testify at all, it cannot be said, ran the argument, that a person undergoing police interrogation is being "compelled" to be "a witness against himself" within the meaning of the privilege—even though under such circumstances a person may assume or be led to believe that there *are* legal (or extralegal) sanctions for "refusing to cooperate." Since the police have no *legal right* to make a suspect answer (although, prior to *Miranda,* the police did not have to *tell* a person that), there was no legal obligation to answer, ran the argument, to which a privilege in the technical sense could apply.

Although the right to counsel had dominated the confessions scene in the years immediately preceding *Miranda,* there was some reason to think that, at long last, the self-incrimination clause might move to centerstage. In *Malloy v. Hogan,* 378 U.S. 1 (1964) (which did not involve a confession), the Court, per Brennan, J., performed what some called a "shotgun wedding" of the privilege against self-incrimination to the confession rule. *Malloy* not only held the self-incrimination clause applicable to the states, but declared that whenever a question arises in a state *or* federal court "whether a confession is incompetent because not voluntary, the issue is controlled by [the self-incrimination] portion of the Fifth Amendment."

Whether or not this view made good sense, it constituted very questionable recent history. In none of the dozens of state *or* federal confession cases decided in the 1930's, 40's or 50's had the self-incrimination clause been the basis for judgment (although it had occasionally been mentioned in an opinion). But how the *Malloy* opinion looked back was not as important as how it looked forward. The confession rules and the privilege against self-incrimination had become intertwined in *Malloy*—and they would be fused in *Miranda.*

## MIRANDA v. ARIZONA (No. 759) *

384 U.S. 436, 86 S.Ct. 1602, 16 L.Ed.2d 694 (1966).

CHIEF JUSTICE WARREN delivered the opinion of the Court.

The cases before us raise questions which go to the roots of American criminal jurisprudence: the restraints society must observe consistent with the Federal Constitution in prosecuting individuals for crime. More specifically, we deal with the admissibility of statements obtained from an individual who is subjected to custodial police interrogation and the necessity for procedures which assure that the individual is accorded his privilege under the Fifth Amendment to the Constitution not to be compelled to incriminate himself. * * *

* Together with No. 760, *Vignera v. New York* [and] No. 761, *Westover v. United States* [and] No. 584, *California v. Stewart* * * *.

We start here, as we did in *Escobedo* with the premise that our holding is not an innovation in our jurisprudence, but is an application of principles long recognized and applied in other settings. We have undertaken a thorough re-examination of the *Escobedo* decision and the principles it announced, and we reaffirm it. That case was but an explication of basic rights that are enshrined in our Constitution—that "No person * * * shall be compelled in any criminal case to be a witness against himself," and that "the accused [shall] have the Assistance of Counsel"—rights which were put in jeopardy in that case through official overbearing. * * *

Our holding will be spelled out with some specificity in the pages which follow but briefly stated it is this: the prosecution may not use statements, whether exculpatory or inculpatory, stemming from custodial interrogation of the defendant unless it demonstrates the use of procedural safeguards effective to secure the privilege against self-incrimination. By custodial interrogation, we mean questioning initiated by law enforcement officers after a person has been taken into custody or otherwise deprived of his freedom of action in any significant way.[4] As for the procedural safeguards to be employed, unless other fully effective means are devised to inform accused persons of their right of silence and to assure a continuous opportunity to exercise it, the following measures are required. Prior to any questioning, the person must be warned that he has a right to remain silent, that any statement he does make may be used as evidence against him, and that he has a right to the presence of an attorney, either retained or appointed. The defendant may waive effectuation of these rights, provided the waiver is made voluntarily, knowingly and intelligently. If, however, he indicates in any manner and at any stage of the process that he wishes to consult with an attorney before speaking there can be no questioning. Likewise, if the individual is alone and indicates in any manner that he does not wish to be interrogated, the police may not question him. The mere fact that he may have answered some questions or volunteered some statements on his own does not deprive him of the right to refrain from answering any further inquiries until he has consulted with an attorney and thereafter consents to be questioned.

The constitutional issue we decide in each of these cases is the admissibility of statements obtained from a defendant questioned while in custody and deprived of his freedom of action in any significant way. In each, the defendant was questioned by police officers, detectives, or a prosecuting attorney in a room in which he was cut off from the outside world. In none of these cases was the defendant given a full and effective warning of his rights at the outset of the interrogation process. In all the cases, the questioning elicited oral admissions, and in three of them, signed statements as well which were admitted at their trials. They all thus share silent features—incommunicado interrogation of individuals in a police-dominated atmosphere, resulting in self-incriminating statements without full warnings of constitutional rights. * * *

Again we stress that the modern practice of in-custody interrogation is psychologically rather than physically oriented. * * * Interrogation still takes place in privacy. Privacy results in secrecy and this in turn results in a gap in our knowledge as to what in fact goes on in the interrogation rooms. A valuable source of information about present police practices, however, may be found in various police manuals and texts which document procedures employed

4. This is what we meant in *Escobedo* when we spoke of an investigation which had focused on an accused.

with success in the past, and which recommend various other effective tactics. These texts are used by law enforcement agencies themselves as guides.[9] It should be noted that these texts professedly present the most enlightened and effective means presently used to obtain statements through custodial interrogation. By considering these texts and other data, it is possible to describe procedures observed and noted around the country. * * *

To highlight the isolation and unfamiliar surroundings, the manuals instruct the police to display an air of confidence in the suspect's guilt and from outward appearance to maintain only an interest in confirming certain details. The guilt of the subject is to be posited as a fact. The interrogator should direct his comments toward the reasons why the subject committed the act, rather than court failure by asking the subject whether he did it. Like other men, perhaps the subject has had a bad family life, had an unhappy childhood, had too much to drink, had an unrequited desire for women. The officers are instructed to minimize the moral seriousness of the offense, to cast blame on the victim or on society. These tactics are designed to put the subject in a psychological state where his story is but an elaboration of what the police purport to know already—that he is guilty. Explanations to the contrary are dismissed and discouraged.

The texts thus stress that the major qualities an interrogator should possess are patience and perseverance. * * *

[When other techniques] prove unavailing, the texts recommend they be alternated with a show of some hostility. One ploy often used has been termed the "friendly-unfriendly" or the "Mutt and Jeff" act:

"[In] this technique, two agents are employed. Mutt, the relentless investigator, who knows the subject is guilty and is not going to waste any time. He's sent a dozen men away for this crime and he's going to send the subject away for the full term. Jeff, on the other hand, is obviously a kindhearted man. He has a family himself. He has a brother who was involved in a little scrape like this. He disapproves of Mutt and his tactics and will arrange to get him off the case if the subject will cooperate. He can't hold Mutt off for very long. The subject would be wise to make a quick decision. The technique is applied by having both investigators present while Mutt acts out his role. Jeff may stand by quietly and demur at some of Mutt's tactics. When Jeff makes his plea for cooperation, Mutt is not present in the room."

The interrogators sometimes are instructed to induce a confession out of trickery. The technique here is quite effective in crimes which require identification or which run in series. In the identification situation, the interrogator may take a break in his questioning to place the subject among a group of men in a line-up. "The witness or complainant (previously coached, if necessary) studies the line-up and confidently points out the subject as the guilty party."

**9.** The methods described in Inbau and Reid, *Criminal Interrogation and Confessions* (1962), are a revision and enlargement of material presented in three prior editions of a predecessor text, *Lie Detection and Criminal Interrogation* (3d ed. 1953). The authors and their associates are officers of the Chicago Police Scientific Crime–Detection Laboratory and have had extensive experience in writing, lecturing and speaking to law enforcement authorities over a 20–year period. They say that the techniques portrayed in their manuals reflect their experiences and are the most effective psychological strategems to employ during interrogations. Similarly, the techniques described in O'Hara, *Fundamentals of Criminal Investigation* (1959), were gleaned from long service as observer, lecturer in police science, and work as a federal criminal investigator. All these texts have had rather extensive use among law enforcement agencies and among students of police science, with total sales and circulation of over 44,000.

Then the questioning resumes "as though there were now no doubt about the guilt of the subject." A variation on this technique is called the "reverse line-up":

> "The accused is placed in a line-up, but this time he is identified by several fictitious witnesses or victims who associated him with different offenses. It is expected that the subject will become desperate and confess to the offense under investigation in order to escape from the false accusations."

The manuals also contain instructions for police on how to handle the individual who refuses to discuss the matter entirely, or who asks for an attorney or relatives. The examiner is to concede him the right to remain silent. "This usually has a very undermining effect. First of all, he is disappointed in his expectation of an unfavorable reaction on the part of the interrogator. Secondly, a concession of this right to remain silent impresses the subject with the apparent fairness of his interrogator." After this psychological conditioning, however, the officer is told to point out the incriminating significance of the suspect's refusal to talk:

> "Joe, you have a right to remain silent. That's your privilege and I'm the last person in the world who'll try to take it away from you. If that's the way you want to leave this, O.K. But let me ask you this. Suppose you were in my shoes and I were in yours and you called me in to ask me about this and I told you, 'I don't want to answer any of your questions.' You'd think I had something to hide, and you'd probably be right in thinking that. That's exactly what I'll have to think about you, and so will everybody else. So let's sit here and talk this whole thing over."

Few will persist in their initial refusal to talk, it is said, if this monologue is employed correctly.

In the event that the subject wishes to speak to a relative or an attorney, the following advice is tendered:

> "[T]he interrogator should respond by suggesting that the subject first tell the truth to the interrogator himself rather than get anyone else involved in the matter. If the request is for an attorney, the interrogator may suggest that the subject save himself or his family the expense of any such professional service, particularly if he is innocent of the offense under investigation. The interrogator may also add, 'Joe, I'm only looking for the truth, and if you're telling the truth, that's it. You can handle this by yourself.'"

From these representative samples of interrogation techniques, the setting prescribed by the manuals and observed in practice becomes clear. In essence, it is this: To be alone with the subject is essential to prevent distraction and to deprive him of any outside support. The aura of confidence in his guilt undermines his will to resist. He merely confirms the preconceived story the police seek to have him describe. Patience and persistence, at times relentless questioning, are employed. To obtain a confession, the interrogator must "patiently maneuver himself or his quarry into a position from which the desired object may be obtained." When normal procedures fail to produce the needed result, the police may resort to deceptive stratagems such as giving false legal advice. It is important to keep the subject off balance, for example, by trading on his insecurity about himself or his surroundings. The police then persuade, trick, or cajole him out of exercising his constitutional rights.

Even without employing brutality, the "third degree" or the specific stratagems described above, the very fact of custodial interrogation exacts a heavy toll on individual liberty and trades on the weakness of individuals. * * *

In the cases before us today, given this background, we concern ourselves primarily with this interrogation atmosphere and the evils it can bring. In *Miranda v. Arizona,* the police arrested the defendant and took him to a special interrogation room where they secured a confession. In *Vignera v. New York,* the defendant made oral admissions to the police after interrogation in the afternoon, and then signed an inculpatory statement upon being questioned by an assistant district attorney later the same evening. In *Westover v. United States,* the defendant was handed over to the Federal Bureau of Investigation by local authorities after they had detained and interrogated him for a lengthy period, both at night and the following morning. After some two hours of questioning, the federal officers had obtained signed statements from the defendant. Lastly, in *California v. Stewart,* the local police held the defendant five days in the station and interrogated him on nine separate occasions before they secured his inculpatory statement.

In these cases, we might not find the defendants' statements to have been involuntary in traditional terms. Our concern for adequate safeguards to protect precious Fifth Amendment rights is, of course, not lessened in the slightest. In each of the cases, the defendant was thrust into an unfamiliar atmosphere and run through menacing police interrogation procedures. The potentiality for compulsion is forcefully apparent, for example, in *Miranda,* where the indigent Mexican defendant was a seriously disturbed individual with pronounced sexual fantasies, and in *Stewart,* in which the defendant was an indigent Los Angeles Negro who had dropped out of school in the sixth grade. To be sure, the records do not evince overt physical coercion or patented psychological ploys. The fact remains that in none of these cases did the officers undertake to afford appropriate safeguards at the outset of the interrogation to insure that the statements were truly the product of free choice.

It is obvious that such an interrogation environment is created for no purpose other than to subjugate the individual to the will of his examiner. This atmosphere carries its own badge of intimidation. To be sure, this is not physical intimidation, but it is equally destructive of human dignity. The current practice of incommunicado interrogation is at odds with one of our Nation's most cherished principles—that the individual may not be compelled to incriminate himself. Unless adequate protective devices are employed to dispel the compulsion inherent in custodial surroundings, no statement obtained from the defendant can truly be the product of his free choice.

From the foregoing, we can readily perceive an intimate connection between the privilege against self-incrimination and police custodial questioning. It is fitting to turn to history and precedent underlying the Self–Incrimination Clause to determine its applicability in this situation.

[W]e may view the historical development of the privilege as one which groped for the proper scope of governmental power over the citizen. As a "noble principle often transcends its origins," the privilege has come rightfully to be recognized in part as an individual's substantive right, a "right to a private enclave where he may lead a private life. That right is the hallmark of our democracy." We have recently noted that the privilege against self-incrimination—the essential mainstay of our adversary system—is founded on a complex of values. All these policies point to one overriding thought: the constitutional foundation underlying the privilege is the respect a government—state or federal—must accord to the dignity and integrity of its citizens. To maintain a "fair state-individual balance," to require the government "to shoulder the entire load," 8 Wigmore, *Evidence* (McNaughton rev., 1961), 317, to respect the inviolability of the human personality, our accusatory system of criminal justice demands that the government seeking to punish an individual produce the evidence against him by its own independent labors, rather than by the cruel, simple expedient of compelling it from his own mouth. In sum, the privilege is fulfilled only when the person is guaranteed the right "to remain silent unless he chooses to speak in the unfettered exercise of his own will." *Malloy v. Hogan.*

\* \* \* We are satisfied that all the principles embodied in the privilege apply to informal compulsion exerted by law-enforcement officers during in-custody questioning. An individual swept from familiar surroundings into police custody, surrounded by antagonistic forces, and subjected to the techniques of persuasion described above cannot be otherwise than under compulsion to speak. As a practical matter, the compulsion to speak in the isolated setting of the police station may well be greater than in courts or other official investigations, where there are often impartial observers to guard against intimidation or trickery. \* \* \*

Because of the adoption by Congress of Rule 5(a) of the Federal Rules of Criminal Procedure, and this Court's effectuation of that Rule in *McNabb* and *Mallory,* we have had little occasion in the past quarter century to reach the constitutional issues in dealing with federal interrogations. These supervisory rules, requiring production of an arrested person before a commissioner "without unnecessary delay" and excluding evidence obtained in default of that statutory obligation, were nonetheless responsive to the same considerations of Fifth Amendment policy that unavoidably face us now as to the States. In [the *McNabb* and *Mallory* cases] we recognized both the dangers of interrogation and the appropriateness of prophylaxis stemming from the very fact of interrogation itself.[32]

Our decision in *Malloy v. Hogan* necessitates an examination of the scope of the privilege in state cases as well. In *Malloy,* we squarely held the privilege applicable to the States, and held that the substantive standards underlying the privilege applied with full force to state court proceedings. [T]he reasoning in *Malloy* made clear what had already become apparent—that the substantive and procedural safeguards surrounding admissibility of confessions in state cases had become exceedingly exacting, reflecting all the policies embedded in the privilege. The voluntariness doctrine in the state cases, as *Malloy* indicates, encompasses all interrogation practices which are likely to exert such pressure upon an individual as to disable him from making a free and rational choice. The implications of this proposition were elaborated in our decision in *Escobedo,* decided one week after *Malloy* applied the privilege to the States. \* \* \*

[In *Escobedo* ], as in the cases today, we sought a protective device to dispel the compelling atmosphere of the interrogation. In *Escobedo,* however, the police did not relieve the defendant of the anxieties which they had created in the interrogation rooms. Rather, they denied his request for the assistance of counsel.[35] This heightened his dilemma, and made his later statements the product of this compulsion. \* \* \* The denial of the defendant's request for his attorney thus undermined his ability to exercise the privilege—to remain silent

**32.** Our decision today does not indicate in any manner, of course, that these rules can be disregarded. When federal officials arrest an individual, they must as always comply with the dictates of the congressional legislation and cases thereunder. \* \* \*

**35.** The police also prevented the attorney from consulting with his client. Independent

of any other constitutional proscription, this action constitutes a violation of the Sixth Amendment right to the assistance of counsel and excludes any statement obtained in its wake. See *People v. Donovan,* 193 N.E.2d 628 (N.Y.1963) (Fuld, J.).

if he chose or to speak without any intimidation, blatant or subtle. The presence of counsel, in all the cases before us today, would be the adequate protective device necessary to make the process of police interrogation conform to the dictates of the privilege. His presence would insure that statements made in the government-established atmosphere are not the product of compulsion.

It was in this manner that *Escobedo* explicated another facet of the pre-trial privilege, noted in many of the Court's prior decisions: the protection of rights at trial. That counsel is present when statements are taken from an individual during interrogation obviously enhances the integrity of the fact-finding processes in court. The presence of an attorney, and the warnings delivered to the individual, enable the defendant under otherwise compelling circumstances to tell his story without fear, effectively, and in a way that eliminates the evils in the interrogation process. Without the protections flowing from adequate warnings and the rights of counsel, "all the careful safeguards erected around the giving of testimony, whether by an accused or any other witness, would become empty formalities in a procedure where the most compelling possible evidence of guilt, a confession, would have already been obtained at the unsupervised pleasure of the police." *Mapp v. Ohio* (Harlan, J., dissenting).

Today, then, there can be no doubt that the Fifth Amendment privilege is available outside of criminal court proceedings and serves to protect persons in all settings in which their freedom of action is curtailed from being compelled to incriminate themselves. We have concluded that without proper safeguards the process of in-custody interrogation of persons suspected or accused of crime contains inherently compelling pressures which work to undermine the individual's will to resist and to compel him to speak where he would not otherwise do so freely. In order to combat these pressures and to permit a full opportunity to exercise the privilege against self-incrimination, the accused must be adequately and effectively apprised of his rights and the exercise of those rights must be fully honored.

It is impossible for us to foresee the potential alternatives for protecting the privilege which might be devised by Congress or the States in the exercise of their creative rule-making capacities. Therefore we cannot say that the Constitution necessarily requires adherence to any particular solution for the inherent compulsions of the interrogation process as it is presently conducted. Our decision in no way creates a constitutional straitjacket which will handicap sound efforts at reform, nor is it intended to have this effect. We encourage Congress and the States to continue their laudable search for increasingly effective ways of protecting the rights of the individual while promoting efficient enforcement of our criminal laws. However, unless we are shown other procedures which are at least as effective in apprising accused persons of their right of silence and in assuring a continuous opportunity to exercise it, the following safeguards must be observed.

At the outset, if a person in custody is to be subjected to interrogation, he must first be informed in clear and unequivocal terms that he has the right to remain silent. For those unaware of the privilege, the warning is needed simply to make them aware of it—the threshold requirement for an intelligent decision as to its exercise. More important, such a warning is an absolute prerequisite in overcoming the inherent pressures of the interrogation atmosphere. It is not just the subnormal or woefully ignorant who succumb to an interrogator's imprecations, whether implied or expressly stated, that the interrogation will continue until a confession is obtained or that silence in the face of accusation is itself damning and will bode ill when presented to a jury.[37] Further, the warning will show the individual that his interrogators are prepared to recognize his privilege should he choose to exercise it.

The Fifth Amendment privilege is so fundamental to our system of constitutional rule and the expedient of giving an adequate warning as to the availability of the privilege so simple, we will not pause to inquire in individual cases whether the defendant was aware of his rights without a warning being given. Assessments of the knowledge the defendant possessed, based on information as to his age, education, intelligence, or prior contact with authorities, can never be more than speculation;[38] a warning is a clearcut fact. More important, whatever the background of the person interrogated, a warning at the time of the interrogation is indispensable to overcome its pressures and to insure that the individual knows he is free to exercise the privilege at that point in time.

The warning of the right to remain silent must be accompanied by the explanation that anything said can and will be used against the individual in court. This warning is needed in order to make him aware not only of the privilege, but also of the consequences of forgoing it. It is only through an awareness of these consequences that there can be any assurance of real understanding and intelligent exercise of the privilege. Moreover, this warning may serve to make the individual more acutely aware that he is faced with a phase of the adversary system—that he is not in the presence of persons acting solely in his interest.

The circumstances surrounding in-custody interrogation can operate very quickly to overbear the will of one merely made aware of his privilege by his interrogators. Therefore, the right to have counsel present at the interrogation is indispensable to the protection of the Fifth Amendment privilege under the system we delineate today. Our aim is to assure that the individual's right to choose between silence and speech remains unfettered throughout the interrogation process. A once-stated warning, delivered by those who will conduct the interrogation, cannot itself suffice to that end among those who must require knowledge of their rights. A mere warning given by the interrogators is not alone sufficient to accomplish that end. Prosecutors themselves claim that the admonishment of the right to remain silent without more "will benefit only the recidivist and the professional." Brief for the National District Attorneys Association as *amicus curiae.* Even preliminary advice given to the accused by his own attorney can be swiftly overcome by the secret interrogation process. Thus, the need for counsel to protect the Fifth Amendment privilege comprehends not merely a right to consult with counsel prior to questioning but also to have counsel present during any questioning if the defendant so desires.

The presence of counsel at the interrogation may serve several significant subsidiary functions as well. If the accused decides to talk to his interrogators, the assistance of counsel can mitigate the dangers of untrustworthiness. With a lawyer present the likelihood that the police will practice coercion is reduced, and if coercion is nevertheless exercised the lawyer can testify to it in court. The presence of a lawyer can also help to guarantee that the accused gives a fully accurate statement to the police and that the statement is rightly reported by the prosecution at trial. See *Crooker v. California* (Douglas, J., dissenting).

---

**37.** ∗ ∗ ∗ In accord with this decision, it is impermissible to penalize an individual for exercising his Fifth Amendment privilege when he is under police custodial interrogation. The prosecution may not, therefore, use at trial the fact that he stood mute or claimed his privilege in the face of accusation. Cf. *Griffin v. California* [Ch. 5, § 2].

**38.** Cf. *Betts v. Brady* [Ch. 5, § 1], and the recurrent inquiry into special circumstances it necessitated. ∗ ∗ ∗

An individual need not make a preinterrogation request for a lawyer. While such request affirmatively secures his right to have one, his failure to ask for a lawyer does not constitute a waiver. No effective waiver of the right to counsel during interrogation can be recognized unless specifically made after the warnings we here delineate have been given. The accused who does not know his rights and therefore does not make a request may be the person who most needs counsel. * * *

Accordingly we hold that an individual held for interrogation must be clearly informed that he has the right to consult with a lawyer and to have the lawyer with him during interrogation under the system for protecting the privilege we delineate today. As with the warnings of the right to remain silent and that anything stated can be used in evidence against him, this warning is an absolute prerequisite to interrogation. No amount of circumstantial evidence that the person may have been aware of this right will suffice to stand in its stead. Only through such a warning is there ascertainable assurance that the accused was aware of this right.

If an individual indicates that he wishes the assistance of counsel before any interrogation occurs, the authorities cannot rationally ignore or deny his request on the basis that the individual does not have or cannot afford a retained attorney. The financial ability of the individual has no relationship to the scope of the rights involved here. The privilege against self-incrimination secured by the Constitution applies to all individuals. The need for counsel in order to protect the privilege exists for the indigent as well as the affluent. In fact, were we to limit these constitutional rights to those who can retain an attorney, our decisions today would be of little significance. The cases before us as well as the vast majority of confession cases with which we have dealt in the past involve those unable to retain counsel. While authorities are not required to relieve the accused of his poverty, they have the obligation not to take advantage of indigence in the administration of justice.[41] Denial of counsel to the indigent at the time of interrogation while allowing an attorney to those who can afford one would be no more supportable by reason or logic than the similar situation at trial and on appeal struck down in *Gideon* and *Douglas v. California.*

In order fully to apprise a person interrogated of the extent of his rights under this system then, it is necessary to warn him not only that he has the right to consult with an attorney, but also that if he is indigent a lawyer will be appointed to represent him. Without this additional warning, the admonition of the right to consult with counsel would often be understood as meaning only that he can consult with a lawyer if he has one or has the funds to obtain one. The warning of a right to counsel would be hollow if not couched in terms that would convey to the indigent—the person most often subjected to interrogation—the knowledge that he too has a right to have counsel present. As with the warnings of the right to remain silent and of the general right to counsel, only by effective and express explanation to the indigent of this right can there be assurance that he was truly in a position to exercise it.[43]

**41.** See Kamisar, *Equal Justice in the Gatehouses and Mansions of American Criminal Procedure*, in Criminal Justice in Our Time (1965), 64–81; * * * Report of the Attorney General's Committee on *Poverty and the Administration of Federal Criminal Justice* (1963), p. 9 * * *.

**43.** While a warning that the indigent may have counsel appointed need not be given to the person who is known to have an attorney or is known to have ample funds to secure one, the expedient of giving a warning is too simple and the rights involved too important to engage in *ex post facto* inquiries into financial ability when there is any doubt at all on that score.

Once warnings have been given, the subsequent procedure is clear. If the individual indicates in any manner, at any time prior to or during questioning, that he wishes to remain silent, the interrogation must cease.[44] At this point he has shown that he intends to exercise his Fifth Amendment privilege; any statement taken after the person invokes his privilege cannot be other than the product of compulsion, subtle or otherwise. Without the right to cut off questioning, the setting of in-custody interrogation operates on the individual to overcome free choice in producing a statement after the privilege has been once invoked. If the individual states that he wants an attorney, the interrogation must cease until an attorney is present. At that time, the individual must have an opportunity to confer with the attorney and to have him present during any subsequent questioning. If the individual cannot obtain an attorney and he indicates that he wants one before speaking to police, they must respect his decision to remain silent.

This does not mean, as some have suggested, that each police station must have a "station house lawyer" present at all times to advise prisoners. It does mean, however, that if police propose to interrogate a person they must make known to him that he is entitled to a lawyer and that if he cannot afford one, a lawyer will be provided for him prior to any interrogation. If authorities conclude that they will not provide counsel during a reasonable period of time in which investigation in the field is carried out, they may do so without violating the person's Fifth Amendment privilege so long as they do not question him during that time.

If the interrogation continues without the presence of an attorney and a statement is taken, a heavy burden rests on the Government to demonstrate that the defendant knowingly and intelligently waived his privilege against self-incrimination and his right to retained or appointed counsel. This Court has always set high standards of proof for the waiver of constitutional rights, *Johnson v. Zerbst,* and we reassert these standards as applied to in-custody interrogation. Since the State is responsible for establishing the isolated circumstances under which the interrogation takes place and has the only means of making available corroborated evidence of warnings given during incommunicado interrogation, the burden is rightly on its shoulders.

An express statement that the individual is willing to make a statement and does not want an attorney followed closely by a statement could constitute a waiver. But a valid waiver will not be presumed simply from the silence of the accused after warnings are given or simply from the fact that a confession was in fact eventually obtained. A statement we made in *Carnley v. Cochran,* 369 U.S. 506 (1962), is applicable here:

> "Presuming waiver from a silent record is impermissible. The record must show, or there must be an allegation and evidence which show, that an accused was offered counsel but intelligently and understandably rejected the offer. Anything less is not waiver."

* * * Moreover, where in-custody interrogation is involved, there is no room for the contention that the privilege is waived if the individual answers

---

**44.** If an individual indicates his desire to remain silent, but has an attorney present, there may be some circumstances in which further questioning would be permissible. In the absence of evidence of overbearing, state- ments then made in the presence of counsel might be free of the compelling influence of the interrogation process and might fairly be construed as a waiver of the privilege for purposes of these statements.

some questions or gives some information on his own prior to invoking his right to remain silent when interrogated.[45]

Whatever the testimony of the authorities as to waiver of rights by an accused, the fact of lengthy interrogation or incommunicado incarceration before a statement is made is strong evidence that the accused did not validly waive his rights. In these circumstances the fact that the individual eventually made a statement is consistent with the conclusion that the compelling influence of the interrogation finally forced him to do so. It is inconsistent with any notion of a voluntary relinquishment of the privilege. Moreover, any evidence that the accused was threatened, tricked, or cajoled into a waiver will, of course, show that the defendant did not voluntarily waive his privilege. The requirement of warnings and waiver of rights is a fundamental with respect to the Fifth Amendment privilege and not simply a preliminary ritual to existing methods of interrogation.

The warnings required and the waiver necessary in accordance with our opinion today are, in the absence of a fully effective equivalent, prerequisites to the admissibility of any statement made by a defendant. No distinction can be drawn between statements which are direct confessions and statements which amount to "admissions" of part or all of an offense. The privilege against self-incrimination protects the individual from being compelled to incriminate himself in any manner; it does not distinguish degrees of incrimination. Similarly, for precisely the same reason, no distinction may be drawn between inculpatory statements and statements alleged to be merely "exculpatory." If a statement made were in fact truly exculpatory it would, of course, never be used by the prosecution. In fact, statements merely intended to be exculpatory by the defendant are often used to impeach his testimony at trial or to demonstrate untruths in the statement given under interrogation and thus to prove guilt by implication. These statements are incriminating in any meaningful sense of the word and may not be used without the full warnings and effective waiver required for any other statement. In *Escobedo* itself, the defendant fully intended his accusation of another as the slayer to be exculpatory as to himself.

The principles announced today deal with the protection which must be given to the privilege against self-incrimination when the individual is first subjected to police interrogation while in custody at the station or otherwise deprived of his freedom of action in any significant way. It is at this point that our adversary system of criminal proceedings commences, distinguishing itself at the outset from the inquisitorial system recognized in some countries. Under the system of warnings we delineate today or under any other system which may be devised and found effective, the safeguards to be erected about the privilege must come into play at this point.

Our decision is not intended to hamper the traditional function of police officers in investigating crime. When an individual is in custody on probable cause, the police may, of course, seek out evidence in the field to be used at trial against him. Such investigation may include inquiry of persons not under restraint. General on-the-scene questioning as to facts surrounding a crime or other general questioning of citizens in the fact-finding process is not affected by

**45.** Although this Court held in *Rogers v. United States,* 340 U.S. 367 (1951), over strong dissent, that a witness before a grand jury may not in certain circumstances decide to answer some questions and then refuse to answer others that decision has no application to the interrogation situation we deal with today. No legislative or judicial fact-finding authority is involved here, nor is there a possibility that the individual might make self-serving statements of which he could make use at trial while refusing to answer incriminating statements.

our holding. It is an act of responsible citizenship for individuals to give whatever information they may have to aid in law enforcement. In such situations the compelling atmosphere inherent in the process of in-custody interrogation is not necessarily present.[46]

In dealing with statements obtained through interrogation, we do not purport to find all confessions inadmissible. Confessions remain a proper element in law enforcement. Any statement given freely and voluntarily without any compelling influences is, of course, admissible in evidence. The fundamental import of the privilege while an individual is in custody is not whether he is allowed to talk to the police without the benefit of warnings and counsel, but whether he can be interrogated. There is no requirement that police stop a person who enters a police station and states that he wishes to confess to a crime, or a person who calls the police to offer a confession or any other statement he desires to make. Volunteered statements of any kind are not barred by the Fifth Amendment and their admissibility is not affected by our holding today.

To summarize, we hold that when an individual is taken into custody or otherwise deprived of his freedom by the authorities in any significant way and is subjected to questioning, the privilege against self-incrimination is jeopardized. Procedural safeguards must be employed to protect the privilege, and unless other fully effective means are adopted to notify the person of his right of silence and to assure that the exercise of the right will be scrupulously honored, the following measures are required. He must be warned prior to any questioning that he has the right to remain silent, that anything he says can be used against him in a court of law, that he has the right to the presence of an attorney, and that if he cannot afford an attorney one will be appointed for him prior to any questioning if he so desires. Opportunity to exercise these rights must be afforded to him throughout the interrogation. After such warnings have been given, and such opportunity afforded him, the individual may knowingly and intelligently waive these rights and agree to answer questions or make a statement. But unless and until such warnings and waiver are demonstrated by the prosecution at trial, no evidence obtained as a result of interrogation can be used against him.  *  *  *

If the individual desires to exercise his privilege, he has the right to do so. This is not for the authorities to decide. An attorney may advise his client not to talk to police until he has had an opportunity to investigate the case, or he may wish to be present with his client during any police questioning. In doing so an attorney is merely exercising the good professional judgment he has been taught. This is not cause for considering the attorney a menace to law enforcement. He is merely carrying out what he is sworn to do under his oath—to protect to the extent of his ability the rights of his client. In fulfilling this responsibility the attorney plays a vital role in the administration of criminal justice under our Constitution.

In announcing these principles, we are not unmindful of the burdens which law enforcement officials must bear, often under trying circumstances. We also fully recognize the obligation of all citizens to aid in enforcing the criminal law.

---

**46.** The distinction and its significance has been aptly described in the opinion of a Scottish court:

"In former times such questioning, if undertaken, would be conducted by police officers visiting the house or place of business of the suspect and there questioning him, probably in the presence of a relation or friend. However convenient the modern practice may be, it must normally create a situation very unfavorable to the suspect." *Chalmers v. H.M. Advocate,* [1954] Sess.Cas. 66, 78 (J.C.).

This Court, while protecting individual rights, has always given ample latitude to law enforcement agencies in the legitimate exercise of their duties. The limits we have placed on the interrogation process should not constitute an undue interference with a proper system of law enforcement. As we have noted, our decision does not in any way preclude police from carrying out their traditional investigatory functions. Although confessions may play an important role in some convictions, the cases before us present graphic examples of the overstatement of the "need" for confessions. In each case authorities conducted interrogations ranging up to five days in duration despite the presence, through standard investigating practices, of considerable evidence against each defendant.[51] Further examples are chronicled in our prior cases.[52]

It is also urged that an unfettered right to detention for interrogation should be allowed because it will often redound to the benefit of the person questioned. When police inquiry determines that there is no reason to believe that the person has committed any crime, it is said, he will be released without need for further formal procedures. The person who has committed no offense, however, will be better able to clear himself after warnings, with counsel present than without. It can be assumed that in such circumstances a lawyer would advise his client to talk freely to police in order to clear himself.

Custodial interrogation, by contrast, does not necessarily afford the innocent an opportunity to clear themselves. A serious consequence of the present practice of the interrogation alleged to be beneficial for the innocent is that many arrests "for investigation" subject large numbers of innocent persons to detention and interrogation. In one of the cases before us, *California v. Stewart,* police held four persons, who were in the defendant's house at the time of the arrest, in jail for five days until defendant confessed. At that time they were finally released. Police stated that there was "no evidence to connect them with any crime." Available statistics on the extent of this practice where it is condoned indicate that these four are far from alone in being subjected to arrest, prolonged detention, and interrogation without the requisite probable cause.

\*   \*   \*

The experience in some other countries \*   \*   \* suggests that the danger to law enforcement in curbs on interrogation is overplayed. The English procedure since 1912 under the Judge's Rules is significant. As recently strengthened, the Rules require that a cautionary warning be given an accused by a police officer as soon as he has evidence that affords reasonable grounds for suspicion; they also require that any statement made be given by the accused without questioning by police.[57] The right of the individual to consult with an attorney during this period is expressly recognized. \*   \*   \*

**51.** Miranda, Vignera, and Westover were identified by eyewitnesses. Marked bills from the bank robbed were found in Westover's car. Articles stolen from the victim as well as from several other robbery victims were found in Stewart's home at the outset of the investigation.

**52.** Dealing as we do here with constitutional standards in relation to statements made, the existence of independent corroborating evidence produced at trial is, of course, irrelevant to our decisions. \*   \*   \*

**57.** [1964] Crim.L.Rev. 166–170. These Rules provide in part:

"II. As soon as a police officer has evidence which would afford reasonable grounds for suspecting that a person has committed an offence, he shall caution that person or cause him to be cautioned before putting to him any questions, or further questions, relating to that offence.

"The caution shall be in the following terms:

" 'You are not obliged to say anything unless you wish to do so but what you say may be put into writing and given in evidence.'

Because of the nature of the problem and because of its recurrent significance in numerous cases, we have to this point discussed the relationship of the Fifth Amendment privilege to police interrogation without specific concentration on the facts of the cases before us. We turn now to these facts to consider the application to these cases of the constitutional principles discussed above. In each instance, we have concluded that statements were obtained from the defendant under circumstances that did not meet constitutional standards for protection of the privilege.

No. 759. *Miranda v. Arizona.*

On March 13, 1963, petitioner, Ernesto Miranda, was arrested at his home and taken in custody to a Phoenix police station. He was there identified by the complaining witness. The police then took him to "Interrogation Room No. 2" of the detective bureau. There he was questioned by two police officers. The officers admitted at trial that Miranda was not advised that he had a right to have an attorney present. Two hours later, the officers emerged from the interrogation room with a written confession signed by Miranda. At the top of the statement was a typed paragraph stating that the confession was made voluntarily, without threats or promises of immunity and "with full knowledge of my legal rights, understanding any statement I make may be used against me." [67]

[Miranda] was found guilty of kidnapping and rape. [On] appeal, the Supreme Court of Arizona held that Miranda's constitutional rights were not violated in obtaining the confession and affirmed the conviction. In reaching its decision, the court emphasized heavily the fact that Miranda did not specifically request counsel.

We reverse. From the testimony of the officers and by the admission of respondent, it is clear that Miranda was not in any way apprised of his right to consult with an attorney and to have one present during the interrogation, nor

"When after being cautioned a person is being questioned, or elects to make a statement, a record shall be kept of the time and place at which any such questioning or statement began and ended and of the persons present.

\* \* \*

"(b) It is only in exceptional cases that questions relating to the offence should be put to the accused person after he has been charged or informed that he may be prosecuted.

\* \* \*

"IV. All written statements made after caution shall be taken in the following manner:

"(a) If a person says that he wants to make a statement he shall be told that it is intended to make a written record of what he says.

"He shall always be asked whether he wishes to write down himself what he wants to say; if he says that he cannot write or that he would like someone to write it for him, a police officer may offer to write the statement for him. \* \* \*

"(b) Any person writing his own statement shall be allowed to do so without any prompting as distinct from indicating to him what matters are material.

\* \* \*

"(d) Whenever a police officer writes the statement, he shall take down the exact words spoken by the person making the statement, without putting any questions other than such as may be needed to make the statement coherent, intelligible and relevant to the material matters: he shall not prompt him."

\* \* \*

[Ed. Note—*The Police and Criminal Evidence 1984* grants British police new powers. E.g., the police are permitted to detain a person without charge for questioning for 24 hours and under certain circumstances to detain a person arrested for a "serious arrestable offense" (e.g., treason, terrorism, murder and kidnapping) up to 36 hours when authorized by a police officer of at least superintendent rank. To counterbalance these additional police powers, the Act contains new safeguards. E.g., a person detained in custody has a right to have this fact notified to a friend or relative and a person detained for an offense other than a "serious arrestable offense" has an absolute right to consult a solicitor at any time.]

**67.** One of the officers testified that he read this paragraph to Miranda. Apparently, however, he did not do so until after Miranda had confessed orally.

was his right not to be compelled to incriminate himself effectively protected in any other manner. Without these warnings the statements were inadmissible. The mere fact that he signed a statement which contained a typed-in clause stating that he had "full knowledge" of his legal rights does not approach the knowing and intelligent waiver required to relinquish constitutional rights.

* * *

No. 760.  *Vignera v. New York.*

Petitioner, Michael Vignera, was picked up by New York police on October 14, 1960, in connection with the robbery three days earlier of a Brooklyn dress shop. They took him to the 17th Detective Squad headquarters in Manhattan. Sometime thereafter he was taken to the 66th Detective Squad. There a detective questioned Vignera with respect to the robbery. Vignera orally admitted the robbery to the detective. [T]he defense was precluded from making any showing that warnings had not been given. While at the 66th Detective Squad, Vignera was identified by the store owner and a saleslady as the man who robbed the dress shop. At about 3:00 p.m. he was formally arrested. The police then transported him to still another station, the 70th Precinct in Brooklyn, "for detention". At 11:00 p.m. Vignera was questioned by an assistant district attorney in the presence of a hearing reporter who transcribed the questions and Vignera's answers. This verbatim account of these proceedings contains no statement of any warnings given by the assistant district attorney. * * *

Vignera was [convicted of first degree robbery]. We reverse. The foregoing indicates that Vignera was not warned of any of his rights before the questioning by the detective and by the assistant district attorney. No other steps were taken to protect these rights. Thus he was not effectively apprised of his Fifth Amendment privilege or of his right to have counsel present and his statements are inadmissible.

No. 761.  *Westover v. United States.*

At approximately 9:45 p.m. on March 20, 1963, petitioner, Carl Calvin Westover, was arrested by local police in Kansas City as a suspect in two Kansas City robberies. A report was also received from the FBI that he was wanted on a felony charge in California. The local authorities took him to a police station and placed him in a line-up on the local charges, and at about 11:45 p.m. he was booked. Kansas City police interrogated Westover on the night of his arrest. He denied any knowledge of criminal activities. The next day local officers interrogated him again throughout the morning. Shortly before noon they informed the FBI that they were through interrogating Westover and that the FBI could proceed to interrogate him. There is nothing in the record to indicate that Westover was ever given any warning as to his rights by local police. At noon, three special agents of the FBI continued the interrogation in a private interview room of the Kansas City Police Department, this time with respect to the robbery of a savings and loan association and a bank in Sacramento, California. After two or two and one-half hours, Westover signed separate confessions to each of these two robberies which had been prepared by one of the agents during the interrogation. At trial one of the agents testified, and a paragraph on each of the statements states, that the agents advised Westover that he did not have to make a statement, that any statement he made could be used against him, and that he had the right to see an attorney.

Westover was tried by a jury in federal court and convicted of the California robberies. * * *

We reverse. On the facts of this case we cannot find that Westover knowingly and intelligently waived his right to remain silent and his right to consult with counsel prior to the time he made the statement. At the time the FBI agents began questioning Westover, he had been in custody for over 14 hours and had been interrogated at length during that period. The FBI interrogation began immediately upon the conclusion of the interrogation by Kansas City police and was conducted in local police headquarters. Although the two law enforcement authorities are legally distinct and the crimes for which they interrogated Westover were different, the impact on him was that of a continuous period of questioning. There is no evidence of any warning given prior to the FBI interrogation nor is there any evidence of an articulated waiver of rights after the FBI commenced their interrogation. The record simply shows that the defendant did in fact confess a short time after being turned over to the FBI following interrogation by local police. Despite the fact that the FBI agents gave warnings at the outset of their interview, from Westover's point of view the warnings came at the end of the interrogation process. In these circumstances an intelligent waiver of constitutional rights cannot be assumed.

We do not suggest that law enforcement authorities are precluded from questioning any individual who has been held for a period of time by other authorities and interrogated by them without appropriate warnings. A different case would be presented if an accused were taken into custody by the second authority, removed both in time and place from his original surroundings, and then adequately advised of his rights and given an opportunity to exercise them. But here the FBI interrogation was conducted immediately following the state interrogation in the same police station—in the same compelling surroundings. Thus, in obtaining a confession from Westover the federal authorities were the beneficiaries of the pressure applied by the local in-custody interrogation. In these circumstances the giving of warnings alone was not sufficient to protect the privilege.

No. 584. *California v. Stewart.*

In the course of investigating a series of purse-snatch robberies in which one of the victims had died of injuries inflicted by her assailant, respondent, Roy Allen Stewart, was pointed out to Los Angeles police as the endorser of dividend checks taken in one of the robberies. At about 7:15 p.m., January 31, 1963, police officers went to Stewart's house and arrested him. One of the officers asked Stewart if they could search the house, to which he replied, "Go ahead." The search turned up various items taken from the five robbery victims. At the time of Stewart's arrest, police also arrested Stewart's wife and three other persons who were visiting him. These four were jailed along with Stewart and were interrogated. Stewart was taken to the University Station of the Los Angeles Police Department where he was placed in a cell. During the next five days, police interrogated Stewart on nine different occasions. Except during the first interrogation session, when he was confronted with an accusing witness, Stewart was isolated with his interrogators.

During the ninth interrogation session, Stewart admitted that he had robbed the deceased and stated that he had not meant to hurt her. Police then brought Stewart before a magistrate for the first time. Since there was no evidence to connect them with any crime, the police then released the other four persons arrested with him.

Nothing in the record specifically indicates whether Stewart was or was not advised of his right to remain silent or his right to counsel. In a number of instances, however, the interrogating officers were asked to recount everything that was said during the interrogations. None indicated that Stewart was ever advised of his rights.

[The] jury found Stewart guilty of robbery and first degree murder and fixed the penalty as death. On appeal, the Supreme Court of California reversed. It held that under this Court's decision in *Escobedo*, Stewart should have been advised of his right to remain silent and of his right to counsel and that it would not presume in the face of a silent record that the police advised Stewart of his rights.

We affirm. In dealing with custodial interrogation, we will not presume that a defendant has been effectively apprised of his rights and that his privilege against self-incrimination has been adequately safe-guarded on a record that does not show that any warnings have been given or that any effective alternative has been employed. Nor can a knowing and intelligent waiver of these rights be assumed on a silent record. Furthermore, Stewart's steadfast denial of the alleged offenses through eight of the nine interrogations over a period of five days is subject to no other construction than that he was compelled by persistent interrogation to forgo his Fifth Amendment privilege.

Therefore, in accordance with the foregoing, [*Miranda*,[a] *Vignera*, and *Westover* are reversed and *Stewart* is affirmed].[b]

JUSTICE CLARK, dissenting in [*Miranda, Vignera,* and *Gilbert,* and concurring in the result in *Stewart.*]

[I cannot] agree with the Court's characterization of the present practices of police and investigatory agencies as to custodial interrogation. The materials referred to as "police manuals" are not shown by the record here to be the official manuals of any police department, much less in universal use in crime detection. Moreover, the examples of police brutality mentioned by the Court are rare exceptions to the thousands of cases that appear every year in the law reports. * * *

[The Court's] strict constitutional specific inserted at the nerve center of crime detection may well kill the patient. Since there is at this time a paucity of information and an almost total lack of empirical knowledge on the practical operation of requirements truly comparable to those announced by the majority, I would be more restrained lest we go too far too fast. * * *

Rather than employing the arbitrary Fifth Amendment rule which the Court lays down I would follow the more pliable dictates of Due Process Clauses of the Fifth and Fourteenth Amendments which we are accustomed to administering and which we know from our cases are effective instruments in protecting persons in police custody. In this way we would not be acting in the dark nor in one full sweep changing the traditional rules of custodial interrogation which this Court has for so long recognized as a justifiable and proper tool in balancing individual rights against the rights of society. It will be soon enough to go further when we are able to appraise with somewhat better accuracy the effect of such a holding. * * *

JUSTICE HARLAN, whom JUSTICE STEWART and JUSTICE WHITE join, dissenting. * * *

While the fine points of [the Court's new constitutional code of rules for confessions] are far less clear than the Court admits, the tenor is quite apparent.

---

**a.** On retrial, *Miranda* was again convicted of kidnapping and rape. The conviction was affirmed in *State v. Miranda*, 450 P.2d 364 (Ariz.1969).

**b.** A week later, the Court ruled that *Escobedo* and *Miranda* applied only to trials begun after the decisions were announced.

The new rules are not designed to guard against police brutality or other unmistakably banned forms of coercion. Those who use third-degree tactics and deny them in court are equally able and destined to lie as skillfully about warnings and waivers. Rather, the thrust of the new rules is to negate all pressures, to reinforce the nervous or ignorant suspect, and ultimately to discourage any confession at all. The aim in short is toward "voluntariness" in a utopian sense, or to view it from a different angle, voluntariness with a vengeance.

To incorporate this notion into the Constitution requires a strained reading of history and precedent and a disregard of the very pragmatic concerns that alone may on occasion justify such strains. I believe that reasoned examination will show that the Due Process Clauses provide an adequate tool for coping with confessions and that, even if the Fifth Amendment privilege against self-incrimination be invoked, its precedents taken as a whole do not sustain the present rules. Viewed as a choice based on pure policy, these new rules prove to be a highly debatable if not one-sided appraisal of the competing interests, imposed over wide-spread objection, at the very time when judicial restraint is most called for by the circumstances. * * *

[The] Court's asserted reliance on the Fifth Amendment [is] an approach which I frankly regard as a *trompe l'oeil.* The Court's opinion in my view reveals no adequate basis for extending the Fifth Amendment's privilege against self-incrimination to the police station. Far more important, it fails to show that the Court's new rules are well supported, let alone compelled, by Fifth Amendment precedents. Instead, the new rules actually derive from quotation and analogy drawn from precedents under the Sixth Amendment, which should properly have no bearing on police interrogation. * * *

Having decided that the Fifth Amendment privilege does apply in the police station, the Court reveals that the privilege imposes more exacting restrictions than does the Fourteenth Amendment's voluntariness test. It then emerges from a discussion of *Escobedo* that the Fifth Amendment requires for an admissible confession that it be given by one distinctly aware of his right not to speak and shielded from "the compelling atmosphere" of interrogation. From these key premises, the Court finally develops the safeguards of warning, counsel, and so forth. I do not believe these premises are sustained by precedents under the Fifth Amendment.[9]

The more important premise is that pressure on the suspect must be eliminated though it be only the subtle influence of the atmosphere and surroundings. The Fifth Amendment, however, has never been thought to forbid *all* pressure to incriminate one's self in the situations covered by it.
* * *

A closing word must be said about the Assistance of Counsel Clause of the Sixth Amendment, which is never expressly relied on by the Court but whose judicial precedents turn out to be linchpins of the confession rules announced today. * * *

The only attempt in this Court to carry the right to counsel into the station house occurred in *Escobedo,* the Court repeating several times that that stage was no less "critical" than trial itself. * * * This is hardly persuasive when we consider that a grand jury inquiry, the filing of a certiorari petition, and certainly the purchase of narcotics by an undercover agent from a prospective

**9.** I lay aside *Escobedo* itself; it contains no reasoning or even general conclusions addressed to the Fifth Amendment and indeed its citation in this regard seems surprising in view of *Escobedo's* primary reliance on the Sixth Amendment.

defendant may all be equally "critical" yet provision of counsel and advice on that score have never been thought compelled by the Constitution in such cases. The sound reason why this right is so freely extended for a criminal trial is the severe injustice risked by confronting an untrained defendant with a range of technical points of law, evidence, and tactics familiar to the prosecutor but not to himself. This danger shrinks markedly in the police station where indeed the lawyer in fulfilling his professional responsibilities of necessity may become an obstacle to truthfinding. See infra, n. 12.  *  *  *

The Court's new rules aim to offset [the] minor pressures and disadvantages intrinsic to any kind of police interrogation. The rules do not serve due process interests in preventing blatant coercion since, as I noted earlier, they do nothing to contain the policeman who is prepared to lie from the start. The rules work for reliability in confessions almost only in the Pickwickian sense that they can prevent some from being given at all.[12]  *  *  *

What the Court largely ignores is that its rules impair, if they will not eventually serve wholly to frustrate, an instrument of law enforcement that has long and quite reasonably been thought worth the price paid for it. There can be little doubt that the Court's new code would markedly decrease the number of confessions. To warn the suspect that he may remain silent and remind him that his confession may be used in court are minor obstructions. To require also an express waiver by the suspect and an end to questioning whenever he demurs must heavily handicap questioning. And to suggest or provide counsel for the suspect simply invites the end of the interrogation. See supra, n. 12.  *  *  *

While passing over the costs and risks of its experiment, the Court portrays the evils of normal police questioning in terms which I think are exaggerated. Albeit stringently confined by the due process standards interrogation is no doubt often inconvenient and unpleasant for the suspect. However, it is no less so for a man to be arrested and jailed, to have his house searched, or to stand trial in court, yet all this may properly happen to the most innocent given probable cause, a warrant, or an indictment. Society has always paid a stiff price for law and order, and peaceful interrogation is not one of the dark moments of the law.

This brief statement of the competing considerations seems to me ample proof that the Court's preference is highly debatable at best and therefore not to be read into the Constitution. However, it may make the analysis more graphic to consider the actual facts of one of the four cases reversed by the Court. *Miranda* serves best, being neither the hardest nor easiest of the four under the Court's standards.[15]

On March 3, 1963, an 18-year-old girl was kidnapped and forcibly raped near Phoenix, Arizona. Ten days later, on the morning of March 13, petitioner Miranda was arrested and taken to the police station. At this time Miranda was 23 years old, indigent, and educated to the extent of completing half the ninth grade. He had "an emotional illness" of the schizophrenic type, according to the

**12.** The Court's vision of a lawyer "mitigat[ing] the dangers of untrustworthiness" by witnessing coercion and assisting accuracy in the confession is largely a fancy; for if counsel arrives, there is rarely going to be a police station confession. *Watts v. Indiana* (separate opinion of Jackson, J.): "[A]ny lawyer worth his salt will tell the suspect in no uncertain terms to make no statement to police under any circumstances."

**15.** In *Westover*, a seasoned criminal was practically given the Court's full complement of warnings and did not heed them. The *Stewart* case, on the other hand, involves long detention and successive questioning. In *Vignera*, the facts are complicated and the record somewhat incomplete.

doctor who eventually examined him; the doctor's report also stated that Miranda was "alert and oriented as to time, place, and person", intelligent within normal limits, competent to stand trial, and sane within the legal definition.  At the police station, the victim picked Miranda out of a lineup, and two officers then took him into a separate room to interrogate him, starting about 11:30 a.m.  Though at first denying his guilt, within a short time Miranda gave a detailed oral confession and then wrote out in his own hand and signed a brief statement admitting and describing the crime.  All this was accomplished in two hours or less without any force, threats or promises and—I will assume this though the record is uncertain * * *—without any effective warnings at all.

Miranda's oral and written confessions are now held inadmissible under the Court's new rules.  One is entitled to feel astonished that the Constitution can be read to produce this result.  These confessions were obtained during brief, daytime questioning conducted by two officers and unmarked by any of the traditional indicia of coercion.  They assured a conviction for a brutal and unsettling crime, for which the police had and quite possibly could obtain little evidence other than the victim's identifications, evidence which is frequently unreliable.  There was, in sum, a legitimate purpose, no perceptible unfairness, and certainly little risk of injustice in the interrogation.  Yet the resulting confessions, and the responsible course of police practice they represent, are to be sacrificed to the Court's own finespun conception of fairness which I seriously doubt is shared by many thinking citizens in this country.  * * *

[It is] instructive to compare the attitude in this case of those responsible for law enforcement with the official views that existed when the Court undertook three major revisions of prosecutorial practice prior to this case, *Johnson v. Zerbst, Mapp,* and *Gideon.*  In *Johnson,* which established that appointed counsel must be offered the indigent in federal criminal trials, the Federal Government all but conceded the basic issue, which had in fact been recently fixed as Department of Justice policy.  In *Mapp,* which imposed the exclusionary rule on the States for Fourth Amendment violations, more than half of the States had themselves already adopted some such rule.  In *Gideon,* which extended *Johnson v. Zerbst* to the States, an *amicus* brief was filed by 22 States and Commonwealths urging that course; only two States beside the respondent came forward to protest.  By contrast, in this case new restrictions on police questioning have been opposed by the United States and in an *amicus* brief signed by 27 States and Commonwealths, not including the three other States who are parties.  No State in the country has urged this Court to impose the newly announced rules, nor has any State chosen to go nearly so far on its own.  * * *

The law of the foreign countries described by the Court * * * reflects a more moderate conception of the rights of the accused as against those of society when other data is considered.  Concededly, the English experience is most relevant.  In that country, a caution as to silence but not counsel has long been mandated by the "Judges' Rules," which also place other somewhat imprecise limits on police cross-examination of suspects.  However, in the court's discretion confessions can be and apparently quite frequently are admitted in evidence despite disregard of the Judges' Rules, so long as they are found voluntary under the common-law test.  Moreover, the check that exists on the use of pretrial statements is counter-balanced by the evident admissibility of fruits of an illegal confession and by the judge's often-used authority to comment adversely on the defendant's failure to testify.  * * *

[S]ome reference must be made to [the] ironic untimeliness [of these confession rules]. There is now in progress in this country a massive re-examination of criminal law enforcement procedures on a scale never before witnessed. Participants in this undertaking include a Special Committee of the American Bar Association, under the chairmanship of Chief Judge Lumbard of the Court of Appeals for the Second Circuit; a distinguished study group of the American Law Institute, headed by Professor Vorenberg of the Harvard Law School; and the President's Commission on Law Enforcement and Administration of Justice, under the leadership of the Attorney General of the United States. Studies are also being conducted by [other groups] equipped to do practical research.

* * *

It is no secret that concern has been expressed lest long-range and lasting reforms be frustrated by this Court's too rapid departure from existing constitutional standards. Despite the Court's disclaimer, the practical effect of the decision made today must inevitably be to handicap seriously sound efforts at reform, not least by removing options necessary to a just compromise of competing interests. [T]he legislative reforms when they came would have the vast advantage of empirical data and comprehensive study, they would allow experimentation and use of solutions not open to the courts, and they would restore the initiative in criminal law reform to those forums where it truly belongs. * * *

JUSTICE WHITE, with whom JUSTICE HARLAN and JUSTICE STEWART join, dissenting.

The proposition that the privilege against self-incrimination forbids in-custody interrogation without the warnings specified in the majority opinion and without a clear waiver of counsel has no significant support in the history of the privilege or in the language of the Fifth Amendment. As for the English authorities and the common-law history, the privilege, firmly established in the second half of the seventeenth century, was never applied except to prohibit compelled judicial interrogations. The rule excluding coerced confessions matured about 100 years later, "[b]ut there is nothing in the reports to suggest that the theory has its roots in the privilege against self-incrimination. And so far as the cases reveal, the privilege, as such, seems to have been given effect only in judicial proceedings, including the preliminary examinations by authorized magistrates." Morgan, *The Privilege Against Self-Incrimination*, 34 Minn.L.Rev. 1, 18 (1949). * * *

That the Court's holding today is neither compelled nor even strongly suggested by the language of the Fifth Amendment, is at odds with American and English legal history, and involves a departure from a long line of precedent does not prove either that the Court has exceeded its powers or that the Court is wrong or unwise in its present reinterpretation of the Fifth Amendment. It does, however, underscore the obvious—that the Court has not discovered or found the law in making today's decision, nor has it derived it from some irrefutable sources; what it has done is to make new law and new public policy in much the same way that it has in the course of interpreting other great clauses of the Constitution. This is what the Court historically has done. Indeed, it is what it must do and will continue to do until and unless there is some fundamental change in the constitutional distribution of governmental powers.

But if the Court is here and now to announce new and fundamental policy to govern certain aspects of our affairs, it is wholly legitimate to examine the mode of this or any other constitutional decision in this Court and to inquire into the advisability of its end product in terms of the long-range interest of the country.

At the very least the Court's text and reasoning should withstand analysis and be a fair exposition of the constitutional provision which its opinion interprets. Decisions like these cannot rest alone on syllogism, metaphysics or some ill-defined notions of natural justice, although each will perhaps play its part. * * *

[The Court] extrapolates a picture of what it conceives to be the norm from police investigatorial manuals, published in 1959 and 1962 or earlier, without any attempt to allow for adjustments in police practices that may have occurred in the wake of more recent decisions of state appellate tribunals or this Court. But even if the relentless application of the described procedures could lead to involuntary confessions, it most assuredly does not follow that each and every case will disclose this kind of interrogation or this kind of consequence.[2] Insofar as it appears from the Court's opinion, it has not examined a single transcript of any police interrogation, let alone the interrogation that took place in any one of these cases which it decides today. Judged by any of the standards for empirical investigation utilized in the social sciences the factual basis for the Court's premises is patently inadequate.

Although in the Court's view in-custody interrogation is inherently coercive, it says that the spontaneous product of the coercion of arrest and detention is still to be deemed voluntary. An accused, arrested on probable cause, may blurt out a confession which will be admissible despite the fact that he is alone and in custody, without any showing that he had any notion of his right to remain silent or of the consequences of his admission. Yet, under the Court's rule, if the police ask him a single question such as "Do you have anything to say?" or "Did you kill your wife?" his response, if there is one, has somehow been compelled, even if the accused has been clearly warned of his right to remain silent. Common sense informs us to the contrary. While one may say that the response was "involuntary" in the sense the question provoked or was the occasion for the response and thus the defendant was induced to speak out when he might have remained silent if not arrested and not questioned, it is patently unsound to say the response is compelled. * * *

If the rule announced today were truly based on a conclusion that all confessions resulting from custodial interrogation are coerced, then it would simply have no rational foundation. * * * Even if one were to postulate that the Court's concern is not that all confessions induced by police interrogation are coerced but rather that some such confessions are coerced and present judicial procedures are believed to be inadequate to identify the confessions that are coerced and those that are not, it would still not be essential to impose the rule that the Court has now fashioned. Transcripts or observers could be required, specific time limits, tailored to fit the cause, could be imposed, or other devices could be utilized to reduce the chances that otherwise indiscernible coercion will produce an inadmissible confession.

On the other hand, even if one assumed that there was an adequate factual basis for the conclusion that all confessions obtained during in-custody interroga-

---

2. In fact, the type of sustained interrogation described by the Court appears to be the exception rather than the rule. A survey of 399 cases in one city found that in almost half of the cases the interrogation lasted less than 30 minutes. Barrett, *Police Practices and the Law—From Arrest to Release or Charge*, 50 Calif.L.Rev. 11, 41–45 (1962). Questioning tends to be confused and sporadic and is usu- ally concentrated on confrontations with witnesses or new items of evidence, as these are obtained by officers conducting the investigation. See generally LaFave, *Arrest: The Decision to Take a Suspect into Custody* 386 (1965); ALI, *Model Pre–Arraignment Procedure Code*, Commentary § 5.01, at 170, n. 4 (Tent.Draft No. 1, 1966).

tion are the product of compulsion, the rule propounded by the Court would still be irrational, for, apparently, it is only if the accused is also warned of his right to counsel and waives both that right and the right against self-incrimination that the inherent compulsiveness of interrogation disappears.  But if the defendant may not answer without a warning a question such as "Where were you last night?" without having his answer be a compelled one, how can the court ever accept his negative answer to the question of whether he wants to consult his retained counsel or counsel whom the court will appoint?  And why if counsel is present and the accused nevertheless confesses, or counsel tells the accused to tell the truth, and that is what the accused does, is the situation any less coercive insofar as the accused is concerned?  The court apparently realizes its dilemma of foreclosing questioning without the necessary warnings but at the same time permitting the accused, sitting in the same chair in front of the same policemen, to waive his right to consult an attorney.  It expects, however, that not too many will waive the right; and if it is claimed that he has, the State faces a severe, if not impossible burden of proof.

All of this makes very little sense in terms of the compulsion which the Fifth Amendment proscribes.  That amendment deals with compelling the accused himself.  It is his free will that is involved.  Confessions and incriminating admissions, as such, are not forbidden evidence; only those which are compelled are banned.  I doubt that the Court observes these distinctions today. By considering any answers to any interrogation to be compelled regardless of the content and course of examination and by escalating the requirements to prove waiver, the Court not only prevents the use of compelled confessions but for all practical purposes forbids interrogation except in the presence of counsel. That is, instead of confining itself to protection of the right against compelled self-incrimination the Court has created a limited Fifth Amendment right to counsel—or, as the Court expresses it, a "right to counsel to protect the Fifth Amendment privilege * * *."  The focus then is not on the will of the accused but on the will of counsel and how much influence he can have on the accused. Obviously there is no warrant in the Fifth Amendment for thus installing counsel as the arbiter of the privilege.

In sum, for all the Court's expounding on the menacing atmosphere of police interrogation procedures it has failed to supply any foundation for the conclusions it draws or the measures it adopts.

Criticism of the Court's opinion, however, cannot stop at a demonstration that the factual and textual bases for the rule it propounds are, at best, less than compelling.  Equally relevant is an assessment of the rule's consequences measured against community values.  The Court's duty to assess the consequences of its action is not satisfied by the utterance of the truth that a value of our system of criminal justice is "to respect the inviolability of the human personality" and to require government to produce the evidence against the accused by its own independent labors.  More than the human dignity of the accused is involved; the human personality of others in the society must also be preserved.  Thus the values reflected by the privilege are not the sole desideratum; society's interest in the general security is of equal weight.

The obvious underpinning of the Court's decision is a deep-seated distrust of all confessions.  As the Court declares that the accused may not be interrogated without counsel present, absent a waiver of the right to counsel, and as the Court all but admonishes the lawyer to advise the accused to remain silent, the result adds up to a judicial judgment that evidence from the accused should not be used against him in any way, whether compelled or not.  This is the not so subtle overtone of the opinion—that it is inherently wrong for the police to gather evidence from the accused himself. And this is precisely the nub of this dissent. I see nothing wrong or immoral, and certainly nothing unconstitutional, with the police asking a suspect whom they have reasonable cause to arrest whether or not he killed his wife or with confronting him with the evidence on which the arrest was based, at least where he has been plainly advised that he may remain completely silent. * * * Particularly when corroborated, as where the police have confirmed the accused's disclosure of the hiding place of implements or fruits of the crime, such confessions have the highest reliability and significantly contribute to the certitude with which we may believe the accused is guilty. * * *

The rule announced today [is] a deliberate calculus to prevent interrogations, to reduce the incidence of confessions and pleas of guilty and to increase the number of trials. [Under] the present law, the prosecution fails to prove its case in about 30% of the criminal cases actually tried in the federal courts. But it is something else again to remove from the ordinary criminal case all those confessions which heretofore have been held to be free and voluntary acts of the accused and to thus establish a new constitutional barrier to the ascertainment of truth by the judicial process. There is, in my view, every reason to believe that a good many criminal defendants, who otherwise would have been convicted on what this Court has previously thought to be the most satisfactory kind of evidence, will now, under this new version of the Fifth Amendment, either not be tried at all or acquitted if the State's evidence, minus the confession, is put to the test of litigation.

I have no desire whatsoever to share the responsibility for any such impact on the present criminal process. * * *

There is another aspect to the effect of the Court's rule on the person whom the police have arrested on probable cause. The fact is that he may not be guilty at all and may be able to extricate himself quickly and simply if he were told the circumstances of his arrest and were asked to explain. This effort, and his release, must now await the hiring of a lawyer or his appointment by the court, consultation with counsel and then a session with the police or the prosecutor. Similarly, where probable cause exists to arrest several suspects as where the body of the victim is discovered in a house having several residents, it will often be true that a suspect may be cleared only through the results of interrogation of other suspects. Here too the release of the innocent may be delayed by the Court's rule.

Much of the trouble with the Court's new rule is that it will operate indiscriminately in all criminal cases, regardless of the severity of the crime or the circumstances involved. It applies to every defendant whether the professional criminal or one committing a crime of momentary passion who is not part and parcel of organized crime. It will slow down the investigation and the apprehension of confederates in those cases where time is of the essence, such as kidnapping, [those] involving the national security, [and] some organized crime situations. In the latter context the lawyer who arrives may also be the lawyer for the defendants' colleagues and can be relied upon to insure that no breach of the organization's security takes place even though the accused may feel that the best thing he can do is to cooperate.

At the same time, the Court's *per se* approach may not be justified on the ground that it provides a "bright line" permitting the authorities to judge in advance whether interrogation may safely be pursued without jeopardizing the admissibility of any information obtained as a consequence. Nor can it be claimed that judicial time and effort, assuming that is a relevant consideration, will be conserved because of the ease of application of the new rule. Today's decision leaves open such questions as whether the accused was in custody, whether his statements were spontaneous or the product of interrogation, whether the accused has effectively waived his rights, and whether nontestimonial evidence introduced at trial is the fruit of statements made during a prohibited interrogation, all of which are certain to prove productive of uncertainty during investigation and litigation during prosecution. For all these reasons, if further restrictions on police interrogation are desirable at this time, a more flexible approach makes much more sense than the Court's constitutional strait-jacket which forecloses more discriminating treatment by legislative or rule-making pronouncements. * * *

### Note: Can Congress "Repeal" Miranda?

Title II of the Crime Control Act of 1968, which purports to repeal *Miranda* in federal prosecutions, amends Chapter 223, title 18, United States Code, by adding the following new sections:

### "§ 3501. Admissibility of confessions

"(a) In any criminal prosecution brought by the United States or by the District of Columbia, a confession, as defined in subsection (e) hereof, shall be admissible in evidence if it is voluntarily given. Before such confession is received in evidence, the trial judge shall, out of the presence of the jury, determine any issue as to voluntariness. If the trial judge determines that the confession was voluntarily made it shall be admitted in evidence and the trial judge shall permit the jury to hear relevant evidence on the issue of voluntariness and shall instruct the jury to give such weight to the confession as the jury feels it deserves under all the circumstances.

"(b) The trial judge in determining the issue of voluntariness shall take into consideration all the circumstances surrounding the giving of the confession, including (1) the time elapsing between arrest and arraignment of the defendant making the confession, if it was made after arrest and before arraignment, (2) whether such defendant knew the nature of the offense with which he was charged or of which he was suspected at the time of making the confession, (3) whether or not such defendant was advised or knew that he was not required to make any statement and that any such statement could be used against him, (4) whether or not such defendant had been advised prior to questioning of his right to the assistance of counsel; and (5) whether or not such defendant was without the assistance of counsel when questioned and when giving such confession.

"The presence or absence of any of the above-mentioned factors to be taken into consideration by the judge need not be conclusive on the issue of voluntariness of the confession.

"(c) In any criminal prosecution by the United States or by the District of Columbia, a confession made or given by a person who is a defendant therein, while such person was under arrest or other detention in the custody of any law-enforcement officer or law-enforcement agency, shall not be inadmissible solely because of delay in bringing such person before a commissioner or other officer empowered to commit persons charged with offenses against the laws of the United States or of the District of Columbia if such confession is found by the trial judge to have been made voluntarily and if the weight to be given the confession is left to the jury and if such confession was made or given by such person within six hours immediately following his arrest or other detention: *Provided,* That the time limitation contained in this subsection shall not apply in any case in which the delay in bringing such person before such commissioner or other officer beyond such six-hour period is found by the trial judge to be reasonable considering the means of transportation and the distance to be traveled to the nearest available such commissioner or other officer.

"(d) Nothing contained in this section shall bar the admission in evidence of any confession made or given voluntarily by any person to any other person without interrogation by anyone, or at any time at which the person who made or gave such confession was not under arrest or other detention.

"(e) As used in this section, the term 'confession' means any confession of guilt of any criminal offense or any self-incriminating statement made or given orally or in writing."

Although § 3501 purports to overrule *Miranda,* to date it has not provoked the head-on collision that might have been predicted. The Attorney General in office when the statute was passed instructed his subordinates not to rely on it where it differed from *Miranda,* and, although a later Attorney General changed this as official policy, most U.S. Attorneys appear to have continued to adhere to the restrained position initially taken. According to a 1986 report to the Attorney General by Assistant Attorney General Stephen Markman, head of the Office of Legal Policy (the "Markman report"), at some point the Department of Justice "attempted to establish the validity of [§ 3501] in litigation for several years with inconclusive results," but then "terminated this litigative effort." However, the Markman report urges the Department of Justice "to persuade the Supreme Court to abrogate or overrule the decision in *Miranda*" and views "reliance on [the 1968 statute] designed to achieve that end" as "the most promising line of attack."

When § 3501 was first enacted, most commentators thought it was invalid. Even those who conceded that *Miranda* was subject to congressional revision, i.e., could be displaced by a statute that provides an adequate alternative to the now-familiar warnings, maintained that Title II still fell short because it did little more than "turn the clock back" to the "voluntariness" test espoused by the *Miranda* dissents.

But the case for upholding § 3501 has grown stronger with the passage of years. For the Supreme Court has repeatedly called the *Miranda* rules "not themselves rights protected by the Constitution" but only "procedural safeguards" or "prophylactic rules" designed to "provide practical reinforcement" for the privilege against compelled self-incrimination.

This language first appeared in *Michigan v. Tucker,* 417 U.S. 433 (1974). *Tucker* allowed the testimony of a prosecution witness whose identity had been discovered by questioning defendant in violation of *Miranda.* Although the case involved various factors that arguably limited its implications (e.g., the deviation between the warnings given and the *Miranda* requirements was not substantial and, although the defendant's trial took place after *Miranda,* the police questioning occurred before that case was decided), the *Tucker* Court, per Rehnquist, J., spoke in general terms of the difference between a *Miranda* violation and a constitutional violation:

"[T]he Court in *Miranda,* for the first time, expressly declared that the Self–Incrimination Clause was applicable to state interrogations at a police station, and that a defendant's statements might be excluded at trial despite their voluntary character under traditional principles.

"To supplement this new doctrine, and to help police officers conduct interrogations without facing a continued risk that valuable evidence would be lost, the [*Miranda* Court] established a set of specific guidelines, now commonly known as the *Miranda* rules. * * *

"The [*Miranda* Court] recognized that these procedural safeguards were not themselves rights protected by the Constitution but were instead measures to insure that the right against compulsory self-incrimination was protected. As [it] remarked: '[W]e cannot say that the Constitution necessarily requires adherence to any particular solution for the inherent compulsions of the interrogation process as it is presently conducted.' The suggested safeguards were not intended to 'create a constitutional straitjacket,' *Miranda*, but rather to provide practical reinforcement for the right against compulsory self-incrimination.[d]

"A comparison of the facts in this case with the historical circumstances underlying the privilege against compulsory self-incrimination strongly indicates that the police conduct here did not deprive [Tucker] of his privilege against self-incrimination as such, but rather failed to make available to him the full measure of procedural safeguards associated with that right since *Miranda*. Certainly no one could contend that the interrogation faced by [Tucker] bore any resemblance to the historical practices at which the right against compulsory self-incrimination was aimed. [H]is statements could hardly be termed involuntary as that term has been defined in the decisions of this Court. * * *

"Our determination that the interrogation in this case involved no compulsion sufficient to breach the right against compulsory self-incrimination does not mean there was not a disregard, albeit an inadvertent disregard, of the procedural rules later established in *Miranda*. The question for decision is how sweeping the judicially imposed consequences of this disregard shall be."

A decade later, first in *New York v. Quarles* (1984) [§ 4 infra], and then in *Oregon v. Elstad* (1985) [§ 4 infra], the Court reiterated *Tucker*'s way of looking at, and thinking about, *Miranda*. (Both cases are set forth in the next section.) In both *Quarles* and *Elstad* the Court underscored the distinction between incriminating statements that are *actually* "coerced" or "compelled" and those obtained *merely* in violation of *Miranda*'s "procedural safeguards" or "prophylactic rules."

Does the language in *Tucker, Quarles* and *Elstad* imply that the Court would now uphold the validity of § 3501, which purports to "overrule" *Miranda*? Since the Court has no "supervisory power" over *state* criminal justice, if the *Miranda*

---

**d.** But as Justice Douglas observed in his *Tucker* dissent, the Court, per Rehnquist, J., overlooked other language in the *Miranda* opinion. For example, in the same paragraph from *Miranda* quoted by Justice Rehnquist in *Tucker*, the *Miranda* Court added: "However, unless we are shown other procedures which are at least as effective in apprising accused persons of their right of silence and in assuring a continuous opportunity to exercise it, the following safeguards [the *Miranda* warnings] must be observed." Moreover, later in the opinion, the *Miranda* Court reiterated:

"The warnings required and the waiver necessary in accordance with our opinion today are, in the absence of a fully effective equivalent, prerequisites to the admissibility of any statements made by a defendant. * * * Procedural safeguards must be employed to protect the privilege, and unless other fully effective means are adopted to notify the person of his right of silence and to assure that the exercise of the right will be scrupulously honored, the following measures [the *Miranda* warnings] are required."

rules are not constitutional requirements (but only "second-class" prophylactic safeguards) and *Miranda* violations not constitutional violations (but only "second-class" wrongs), where did the Court get the authority to impose *Miranda* on the states in the first place?

# SECTION 4. APPLYING AND EXPLAINING
## *MIRANDA*

Because *Miranda* was the centerpiece of the Warren Court's "revolution in American criminal procedure" and the prime target of those who thought the courts were "soft" on criminals, almost everyone expected the so-called Burger Court to treat *Miranda* unkindly. And it did—at first. But it must also be said that the Burger Court interpreted *Miranda* fairly generously in some important respects.

The first blows the Burger Court dealt *Miranda* were the impeachment cases, *Harris v. New York*, 401 U.S. 222 (1971) and *Oregon v. Hass*, 420 U.S. 714 (1975). *Harris* held that statements preceded by defective warnings, and thus inadmissible to establish the prosecution's case-in-chief, could nevertheless be used to impeach the defendant's credibility if he chose to take the stand in his own defense.[a] The Court noted, but seemed unperturbed by the fact, that some language in the *Miranda* opinion could be read as barring the use of statements obtained in violation of *Miranda* for *any* purpose.

The Court went a step beyond *Harris* in the *Hass* case. In this case, after being advised of his rights, the defendant *asserted* them. Nevertheless, the police refused to honor the defendant's request for a lawyer and continued to question him. The Court ruled that here, too, the resulting incriminating statements could be used for impeachment purposes. Since many suspects make incriminating statements even after the receipt of complete *Miranda* warnings, *Harris* might have been explained—and contained—on the ground that permitting impeachment use of statements acquired without complete warnings would not greatly encourage the police to violate *Miranda*. But in light of the *Hass* ruling, when a suspect asserts his rights, the police arguably have very little to lose and everything to gain by continuing to question him.[b]

Although language in *Miranda* could be read as establishing a *per se* rule against any further questioning of one who has asserted his "right to silence" (as opposed to his *right to counsel*, discussed below), *Michigan v. Mosley*, 423 U.S. 96 (1975) held that under certain circumstances (and what they are is unclear), if they cease questioning on the spot, the police may "try again," and succeed at a later interrogation session. At the very least, it seems, the police must promptly

---

**a.** However, as the Court suggested in *Harris* and subsequently made clear in *Mincey v. Arizona*, 437 U.S. 385 (1978), "involuntary" or "coerced" statements, as opposed to those obtained only in violation of *Miranda,* cannot be used for impeachment purposes.

**b.** The Court subsequently held that a defendant's prior silence could be used to impeach him when he testified in his own defense, *Jenkins v. Anderson,* 447 U.S. 231 (1980), and that even a defendant's *post*arrest silence (so long as he was not given the *Miranda* warnings) could be used for impeachment purposes, *Fletcher v. Weir,* 455 U.S. 603 (1982). Both *Jenkins* and *Weir* distinguished *Doyle v. Ohio,* 426 U.S. 610 (1976), which deemed it a violation of due process to use a defendant's silence for impeachment purposes when the defendant remained silent *after* being given *Miranda* warnings.

But the Court balked at further expansion of the "impeachment exception" to the ban against illegally seized evidence in *James v. Illinois,* the next to the last case in this section. *James* refused to expand the class of impeachable witnesses from the defendant alone to *all* defense witnesses, maintaining such an expansion "would not promote the truthseeking function to the same extent as did creation of the original exception, and yet it would significantly undermine the deterrent effect of the general exclusionary rule."

terminate the original interrogation, resume questioning after the passage of a significant period of time, and give the suspect a fresh set of warnings at the outset of the second session. Whether *Mosley* requires more is a matter of dispute.

Perhaps the most frequently litigated *Miranda* question is what constitutes "custody" or "custodial interrogation"? In the first case in this section, *Berkemer v. McCarty*, the Court, per Marshall, J. one of *Miranda*'s strongest defenders, explains at considerable length why the "roadside questioning" of a motorist detained pursuant to a traffic stop is quite different from stationhouse interrogation and thus should not be deemed "custodial interrogation." The *McCarty* Court reached its conclusion without a dissent. More controversial are *Oregon v. Mathiason*, 429 U.S. 492 (1977) and *California v. Beheler*, 463 U.S. 1121 (1983), which demonstrate that if the suspect goes to the stationhouse on his own or "voluntarily" agrees to accompany the police to that site, even *police station* questioning designed to produce incriminating statements may not be "custodial interrogation." Both cases are discussed in *McCarty*.

Another frequently litigated question is what constitutes "interrogation" or "questioning" within the meaning of *Miranda*? This question is addressed by the next two cases in the section: *Rhode Island v. Innis* (1980) and *Illinois v. Perkins* (1990). Considering the alternatives (e.g., limiting "interrogation" to instances where the police directly address a suspect or to situations where the record establishes that the police *intended* to elicit a response), *Innis* gave the key term "interrogation" a fairly generous reading. *Perkins* holds that the coercive atmosphere calling for the *Miranda* warnings is not present when a suspect is *unaware* that he is speaking to a law enforcement officer (in this instance an undercover agent posing as a fellow-prisoner).

In *Edwards v. Arizona*, the fourth case in this section, the Court gladdened the hearts of *Miranda* supporters by reinvigorating the doctrine in an important respect. Sharply distinguishing *Mosley*, the *Edwards* Court held that when a suspect asserts his right to counsel (as opposed to his right to remain silent), the police *cannot* "try again."

But then, as discussed earlier, Justice Rehnquist's way of thinking about *Miranda*, which had first surfaced in *Michigan v. Tucker* [see Note on Congressional Overruling in § 3 supra], reappeared in *New York v. Quarles* and *Oregon v. Elstad*, the next two cases in this section. *Quarles* recognized a "public safety" exception to *Miranda*. *Elstad* held that a second confession, immediately preceded by the *Miranda* warnings, was admissible although an earlier statement from the defendant had been obtained in violation of *Miranda*. More generally, both cases viewed *Miranda* warnings as only second-class prophylactic safeguards and *Miranda* violations as only second-class wrongs.

Some of *Miranda*'s defenders found further cause for concern in *Moran v. Burbine*, the last case in this section. That case held that a confession preceded by an otherwise valid waiver of *Miranda* rights should not be excluded either because the police misled an inquiring attorney (asked by defendant's sister to represent him) or because the police failed to inform the defendant that an attorney was trying to reach him. But other commentators noted that the *Burbine* Court had viewed *Miranda* as a serious effort to strike a "proper balance" between, or to "reconcile," law enforcement needs and a suspect's rights and pointed out that this is the way many of *Miranda*'s defenders—not its critics—have talked about the case for the past twenty years.

### 1.  What constitutes "custody" or "custodial interrogation?"

## BERKEMER v. McCARTY

468 U.S. 420, 104 S.Ct. 3138, 82 L.Ed.2d 317 (1984).

JUSTICE MARSHALL delivered the opinion of the Court.

[After observing McCarty's car weaving in and out of a highway lane, Trooper Williams forced him to stop and asked him to get out of the car. Noticing that McCarty had difficulty standing, the officer concluded that he would be charged with a traffic offense and not allowed to leave the scene. But the officer did not tell McCarty this. When asked to perform a field sobriety test, commonly known as a "balancing test," McCarty could not do so without falling. The officer then asked McCarty whether he had been using intoxicants. McCarty replied that he had consumed two beers and smoked marijuana a short time before. Moreover, his speech was slurred. The officer then formally arrested McCarty and drove him to a county jail where questioning resumed and McCarty made more incriminating statements. At no point in this sequence of events did Williams or anyone else give McCarty the *Miranda* warnings. McCarty's statements were admitted into evidence and he was convicted of operating a motor vehicle while under the influence of alcohol and/or drugs, a first-degree misdemeanor under Ohio law.

[The Court rejected the argument that *Miranda* does not apply to misdemeanor traffic offenses and held that one subjected to custodial interrogation is entitled to the *Miranda* warnings "regardless of the nature or severity of the offense of which he is suspected or for which he was arrested." Thus, since "[t]here can be no question that respondent was 'in custody' at least as of the moment he was formally placed under arrest and instructed to get into the police car," and he was not informed of his rights at that juncture, his subsequent admissions should not have been used against him. The Court then addressed the question whether respondent had been in custody at an earlier point, i.e., "whether the roadside questioning of a motorist detained pursuant to a routine traffic stop should be considered 'custodial interrogation.'"]

* * * Fidelity to the doctrine announced in Miranda requires that it be enforced strictly, but only in those types of situations in which the concerns that powered the decision are implicated. Thus, we must decide whether a traffic stop exerts upon a detained person pressures that sufficiently impair his free exercise of his privilege against self-incrimination to require that he be warned of his constitutional rights.

Two features of an ordinary traffic stop mitigate the danger that a person questioned will be induced "to speak where he would not otherwise do so freely," *Miranda.* First, detention of a motorist pursuant to a traffic stop is presumptively temporary and brief. The vast majority of roadside detentions last only a few minutes. A motorist's expectations, when he sees a policeman's light flashing behind him, are that he will be obliged to spend a short period of time answering questions and waiting while the officer checks his license and registration, that he may then be given a citation, but that in the end he most likely will be allowed to continue on his way. In this respect, questioning incident to an ordinary traffic stop is quite different from stationhouse interrogation, which frequently is prolonged, and in which the detainee often is aware that questioning will continue until he provides his interrogators the answers they seek.

Second, circumstances associated with the typical traffic stop are not such that the motorist feels completely at the mercy of the police. To be sure, the aura of authority surrounding an armed, uniformed officer and the knowledge that the officer has some discretion in deciding whether to issue a citation, in combination, exert some pressure on the detainee to respond to questions. But other aspects of the situation substantially offset these forces. Perhaps most importantly, the typical traffic stop is public, at least to some degree. [This] exposure to public view both reduces the ability of an unscrupulous policeman to use illegitimate means to elicit self-incriminating statements and diminishes the motorist's fear that, if he does not cooperate, he will be subjected to abuse. The fact that the detained motorist typically is confronted by only one or at most two policemen further mutes his sense of vulnerability. In short, the atmosphere surrounding an ordinary traffic stop is substantially less "police dominated" than that surrounding the kinds of interrogation at issue in *Miranda* itself and in the subsequent cases in which we have applied *Miranda.*[a]

In both of these respects, the usual traffic stop is more analogous to a so-called "*Terry* stop" than to a formal arrest. Under the Fourth Amendment, we have held, a policeman who lacks probable cause but whose "observations lead him reasonably to suspect" that a particular person has committed, is committing, or is about to commit a crime, may detain that person briefly in order to "investigate the circumstances that provoke suspicion." * * * Typically, this means that the officer may ask the detainee a moderate number of questions to determine his identity and to try to obtain information confirming or dispelling the officer's suspicions. But the detainee is not obliged to respond. And, unless the detainee's answers provide the officer with probable cause to arrest him, he must then be released. The comparatively nonthreatening character of detentions of this sort explains the absence of any suggestion in our opinions that *Terry* stops are subject to the dictates of *Miranda*.

Respondent contends that to "exempt" traffic stops from the coverage of *Miranda* will open the way to widespread abuse. Policemen will simply delay formally arresting detained motorists, and will subject them to sustained and intimidating interrogation at the scene of their initial detention. * * *

We are confident that the state of affairs projected by respondent will not come to pass. It is settled that the safeguards prescribed by *Miranda* become applicable as soon as a suspect's freedom of action is curtailed to a "degree associated with formal arrest." *California v. Beheler,* 463 U.S. 1121 (1983) (per curiam). If a motorist who has been detained pursuant to a traffic stop thereafter is subjected to treatment that renders him "in custody" for practical purposes, he will be entitled to the full panoply of protections prescribed by *Miranda.* See *Oregon v. Mathiason,* 429 U.S. 492 (1977) (per curiam).[b] * * *

a. At this point the Court referred to *Orozco v. Texas,* 394 U.S. 324 (1969) (applying *Miranda* to a situation where defendant was questioned in his bedroom by four police officers at 4:00 a.m., circumstances that produced a "potentiality for compulsion" equivalent to police station interrogation) and *Mathis v. United States,* 391 U.S. 1 (1968) (applying *Miranda* to the questioning of defendant about his tax returns by an internal revenue agent when defendant was incarcerated in jail on another matter.)

b. *Mathiason* makes plain that *Miranda* warnings are not required "simply because the questioning takes place in the station house." *Mathiason,* a suspect in a burglary, agreed over the phone to meet with a police officer at a convenient time and place (the state patrol office, only two blocks from defen-

dant's apartment). Mathiason went to the patrol office on his own. When he arrived the officer told him he was not under arrest. The officer then said he wanted to talk to defendant about a burglary. When Mathiason confessed a few moments later he was not, held the Court, being subjected to "custodial interrogation."

There was some reason to think that *Mathiason* might be limited to situations where suspects go to the station house *unaccompanied* by police officers. But *Beheler* made it clear that *Mathiason* could not be read that narrowly. Some hours after the murder weapon (which defendant claimed others had hidden) was found in his backyard, Beheler, as the Court described it, "voluntarily agreed to accompany police to the station house, although the police specifically told

Turning to the case before us, we find nothing in the record that indicates that respondent should have been given *Miranda* warnings at any point prior to the time Trooper Williams placed him under arrest. At no point [during the short period of time between the stop and the formal arrest] was respondent informed that his detention would not be temporary. Although Trooper Williams apparently decided as soon as respondent stepped out of his car that respondent would be taken into custody and charged with a traffic offense, Williams never communicated his intention to respondent. A policeman's unarticulated plan has no bearing on the question whether a suspect was "in custody" at a particular time; the only relevant inquiry is how a reasonable man in the suspect's position would have understood his situation.[c] Nor do other aspects of the interaction of Williams and respondent support the contention that respondent was exposed to "custodial interrogation" at the scene of the stop. From aught that appears in the stipulation of facts, a single police officer asked respondent a modest number of questions and requested him to perform a simple balancing test at a location visible to passing motorists. Treatment of this sort cannot fairly be characterized as the functional equivalent of formal arrest.

We conclude, in short, that respondent was not taken into custody for the purposes of *Miranda* until Williams arrested him. Consequently, the statements respondent made prior to that point were admissible against him. * * *

## 2. What constitutes "interrogation" within the meaning of Miranda?

### RHODE ISLAND v. INNIS

446 U.S. 291, 100 S.Ct. 1682, 64 L.Ed.2d 297 (1980).

JUSTICE STEWART delivered the opinion of the Court.

[*Miranda*] held that, once a defendant in custody asks to speak with a lawyer, all interrogation must cease until a lawyer is present. The issue in this case is whether the respondent was "interrogated" in violation [of *Miranda*].

[At approximately 4:30 a.m., a patrolman arrested respondent, suspected of robbing a taxicab driver and murdering him with a shotgun blast to the back of the head. Respondent was unarmed. He was advised of his rights. Within minutes a sergeant (who advised respondent of his rights) and then a captain arrived at the scene of the arrest. The captain also gave respondent the *Miranda* warnings, whereupon respondent asked to speak with a lawyer. The captain then directed that respondent be placed in a police vehicle with a wire screen mesh between the front and rear seats and be driven to the police station. Three officers were assigned to accompany the arrestee. Although the record is somewhat unclear, it appears that Patrolman Williams was in the back seat with respondent and that Patrolmen Gleckman and McKenna were in front.]

[him] that he was not under arrest." At the station house, Beheler agreed to talk about the murder, but the police did not advise him of his *Miranda* rights. The incriminating statements made at the police station, ruled the Court, were not the product of "custodial interrogation."

**c.** Prior to *Berkemer v. McCarty,* it was unclear what test should apply in determining when questioning becomes "custodial": (a) the *subjective intention* of the questioning officer to take the suspect into custody; (b) the *subjective belief* of the suspect that he was in custody; or (c) whether *a reasonable person* in the suspect's situation would believe he was in custody. The objective standard adopted by the *McCarty* Court reflects the approach taken by most of the lower courts. They regarded this test as the most sensible and the most consistent with *Miranda's* underlying concerns. For it avoided reliance on self-serving statements by the police or the suspect, also avoided the need to determine the officer's state of mind, and freed the police of responsibility for the idiosyncracies of various suspects.

While enroute to the central station, Patrolman Gleckman initiated a conversation with Patrolman McKenna concerning the missing shotgun.[1] As Patrolman Gleckman later testified:

"A.   At this point, I was talking back and forth with Patrolman McKenna stating that I frequent this area while on patrol and [that because a school for handicapped children is located nearby,] there's a lot of handicapped children running around in this area, and God forbid one of them might find a weapon with shells and they might hurt themselves."

Patrolman McKenna apparently shared his fellow officer's concern:

"A.   I more or less concurred with him [Gleckman] that it was a safety factor and that we should, you know, continue to search for the weapon and try to find it."

* * *

[Respondent then interrupted the conversation, stating that he would show the officers where the gun was located.  The police vehicle then returned to the scene of the arrest where a search for the shotgun was in progress.  There, the captain again advised respondent of his rights.  He replied that he understood his rights, but "wanted to get the gun out of the way because of the kids in the area in the school."  He then led the police to a nearby field, where he pointed out the shotgun under some rocks.

[Respondent was convicted of murder.  The trial judge admitted the shotgun and testimony related to its discovery.  On appeal, the Rhode Island Supreme Court concluded that the police had "interrogated" respondent without a valid waiver of his right to counsel; the conversation in the police vehicle had constituted "subtle coercion" that was the equivalent of *Miranda* "interrogation."]

[Since the parties agree that respondent was fully informed of his *Miranda* rights, that he asserted his right to counsel, and that he was "in custody" while being driven to the police station, the issue is whether he was "interrogated" in violation of *Miranda*.]  In resolving this issue, we first define the term "interrogation" under *Miranda* before turning to a consideration of the facts of this case.

[Various references throughout the *Miranda* opinion] to "questioning" might suggest that the *Miranda* rules were to apply only to those police interrogation practices that involve express questioning of a defendant while in custody.

We do not, however, construe the *Miranda* opinion so narrowly.  The concern of the Court in *Miranda* was that the "interrogation environment" created by the interplay of interrogation and custody would "subjugate the individual to the will of his examiner" and thereby undermine the privilege against compulsory self-incrimination.  The police practices that evoked this concern included several that did not involve express questioning [such as] the so-called "reverse lineup" in which a defendant would be identified by coached witnesses as the perpetrator of a fictitious crime, [to induce] him to confess to the actual crime of which he was suspected in order to escape the false prosecution. * * * It is clear that these techniques of persuasion, no less than express questioning, were thought, in a custodial setting, to amount to interrogation.

This is not to say, however, that all statements obtained by the police after a person has been taken into custody are to be considered the product of interrogation. * * * It is clear [that the *Miranda* warnings] are required not where a suspect is simply taken into custody, but rather where a suspect in custody is

1.   Although there was conflicting testimony about the exact seating arrangements, it is clear that everyone in the vehicle heard the conversation.

subjected to interrogation. "Interrogation," as conceptualized [in *Miranda*], must reflect a measure of compulsion above and beyond that inherent in custody itself.[4]

We conclude that the *Miranda* safeguards come into play whenever a person in custody is subjected to either express questioning or its functional equivalent. That is to say, the term "interrogation" under *Miranda* refers not only to express questioning, but also to any words or actions on the part of the police (other than those normally attendant to arrest and custody) that the police should know are reasonably likely to elicit an incriminating response from the suspect. The latter portion of this definition focuses primarily upon the perceptions of the suspect, rather than the intent of the police. This focus reflects the fact that the *Miranda* safeguards were designed to vest a suspect in custody with an added measure of protection against coercive police practices, without regard to objective proof of the underlying intent of the police. A practice that the police should know is reasonably likely to evoke an incriminating response from a suspect thus amounts to interrogation.[7] But, since the police surely cannot be held accountable for the unforeseeable results of their words or actions, the definition of interrogation can extend only to words or actions on the part of police officers that they *should have known* were reasonably likely to elicit an incriminating response.[8]

Turning to the facts of the present case, we conclude that the respondent was not "interrogated" within the meaning of *Miranda*. It is undisputed that the first prong of the definition of "interrogation" was not satisfied, for the [Gleckman–McKenna conversation] included no express questioning of the respondent. Rather, that conversation was, at least in form, nothing more than a dialogue between the two officers to which no response from the respondent was invited.

Moreover, it cannot be fairly concluded that the respondent was subjected to the "functional equivalent" of questioning. It cannot be said, in short, that [the officers should have known that their conversation was reasonably likely to elicit an incriminating response from the respondent. There is nothing in the record to suggest that the officers were aware that the respondent was peculiarly susceptible to an appeal to his conscience concerning the safety of handicapped

**4.** There is language in the opinion of the Rhode Island Supreme Court in this case suggesting that the definition of "interrogation" under *Miranda* is informed by this Court's decision in *Brewer v. Williams,* [Sec. 5 infra, reaffirming and expansively interpreting the *Massiah* doctrine]. This suggestion is erroneous. Our decision in *Brewer* rested solely on the Sixth and Fourteenth Amendment right to counsel. That right, as we held in *Massiah,* prohibits law enforcement officers from "deliberately elicit[ing]" incriminating information from a defendant in the absence of counsel after a formal charge against the defendant has been filed. Custody in such a case is not controlling; indeed, the petitioner in *Massiah* was not in custody. By contrast, the right to counsel at issue in the present case is based not on the Sixth and Fourteenth Amendments, but rather on the Fifth and Fourteenth Amendments as interpreted in the *Miranda* opinion. The definitions of "interrogation" under the Fifth and Sixth Amendments, if indeed the term "interrogation" is

even apt in the Sixth Amendment context, are not necessarily interchangeable, since the policies underlying the two constitutional protections are quite distinct.

**7.** This is not to say that the intent of the police is irrelevant, for it may well have a bearing on whether the police should have known that their words or actions were reasonably likely to evoke an incriminating response. In particular, where a police practice is designed to elicit an incriminating response from the accused, it is unlikely that the practice will not also be one which the police should have known was reasonably likely to have that effect.

**8.** Any knowledge the police may have had concerning the unusual susceptibility of a defendant to a particular form of persuasion might be an important factor in determining whether the police should have known that their words or actions were reasonably likely to elicit an incriminating response from the suspect.

children [or that] the police knew that the respondent was unusually disoriented or upset at the time of his arrest.[9]

The case thus boils down to whether, in the context of a brief conversation, the officers should have known that the respondent would suddenly be moved to make a self-incriminating response. Given the fact that the entire conversation appears to have consisted of no more than a few off-hand remarks, we cannot say that the officers should have known that it was reasonably likely that Innis would so respond. This is not a case where the police carried on a lengthy harangue in the presence of the suspect. Nor does the record support the respondent's contention that, under the circumstances, the officers' comments were particularly "evocative." * * *

The Rhode Island Supreme Court erred, in short, in equating "subtle compulsion" with interrogation. That the officers' comments struck a responsive cord is readily apparent. Thus, it may be said, as the Rhode Island Supreme Court did say, that one respondent was subjected to "subtle compulsion." But that is not the end of the inquiry. It must also be established that a suspect's incriminating response was the product of words or actions on the part of the police that they should have known were reasonably likely to elicit an incriminating response.[10] This was not established in the present case. * * *[a]

CHIEF JUSTICE BURGER, concurring in the judgment. * * *

The meaning of *Miranda* has become reasonably clear and law enforcement practices have adjusted to its strictures; I would neither overrule *Miranda,* disparage it, nor extend it at this late date. I fear, however, that [the Court's opinion] may introduce new elements of uncertainty; under the Court's test, a police officer, in the brief time available, apparently must evaluate the suggesti-

---

**9.** The record in no way suggests that the officers' remarks were *designed* to elicit a response. It is significant that the trial judge, after hearing the officers' testimony, concluded that it was "entirely understandable that [the officers] would voice their concern [for the safety of the handicapped children] to each other."

**10.** By way of example, if the police had done no more than to drive past the site of the concealed weapon while taking the most direct route to the police station, and if the respondent, upon noticing for the first time the proximity of the school for handicapped children, had blurted out that he would show the officers where the gun was located, it could not seriously be argued that this "subtle compulsion" would have constituted "interrogation" within the meaning of the *Miranda* opinion.

**a.** Notwithstanding language in *Innis,* as *Arizona v. Mauro,* 107 S.Ct. 1931 (1987) illustrates, it is not inevitably "interrogation" within the meaning of *Miranda* for the police to allow a scenario to occur which they know may prompt the defendant to incriminate himself. In *Mauro,* a 5–4 majority, per Powell, J., held that it was not interrogation for the police to accede to the request of defendant's wife, also a suspect in the murder of their son, to speak with defendant (who had been given the *Miranda* warnings and had asserted his right to counsel) in the presence of a police officer, who placed a tape recorder in plain sight on a desk. Observed the Court:

"The tape recording of the conversation between Mauro and his wife shows that [the detective who attended their meeting] asked Mauro no questions about the crime or his conduct. Nor is it suggested [that the police decision] to allow Mauro's wife to see him was the kind of psychological ploy that properly could be treated as the functional equivalent of interrogation.

"* * * Mauro was not subjected to compelling influences, psychological ploys, or direct questioning. Thus, his volunteered statements cannot properly be considered the result of police interrogation.

"In deciding whether particular police conduct is interrogation, we must remember the purpose behind [*Miranda* ]: preventing government officials from using the coercive nature of confinement to extract confessions that would not be given in an unrestrained environment. The government actions in this case do not implicate this purpose in any way. Police departments need not adopt inflexible rules barring suspects from speaking with their spouses, nor must they ignore legitimate security concerns by allowing spouses to meet in private. In short, the officers in this case acted reasonably and lawfully by allowing Mrs. Mauro to speak with her husband."

bility and susceptibility of an accused. Few, if any, police officers are competent to make the kind of evaluation seemingly contemplated; even a psychiatrist asked to express an expert opinion on these aspects of a suspect in custody would very likely employ extensive questioning and observation to make the judgment now charged to police officers. * * *

JUSTICE MARSHALL, with whom JUSTICE BRENNAN joins, dissenting.

I am substantially in agreement with the Court's definition of "interrogation" within the meaning of *Miranda.* In my view, the *Miranda* safeguards apply whenever police conduct is intended or likely to produce a response from a suspect in custody. As I read the Court's opinion, its definition of "interrogation" for *Miranda* purposes is equivalent, for practical purposes, to my formulation, since it contemplates that "where a police practice is designed to elicit an incriminating response from the accused, it is unlikely that the practice will not also be one which the police should have known was reasonably likely to have that effect" [fn. 7]. Thus, the Court requires an objective inquiry into the likely effect of police conduct on a typical individual, taking into account any special susceptibility of the suspect to certain kinds of pressure of which the police know or have reason to know.

I am utterly at a loss, however, to understand how this objective standard as applied to the facts before us can rationally lead to the conclusion that there was no interrogation. * * *

One can scarcely imagine a stronger appeal to the conscience of a suspect— *any* suspect—than the assertion that if the weapon is not found an innocent person will be hurt or killed. And not just any innocent person, but an innocent child—a little girl—a helpless, handicapped little girl on her way to school. The notion that such an appeal could not be expected to have any effect unless the suspect were known to have some special interest in handicapped children verges on the ludicrous. As a matter of fact, the appeal to a suspect to confess for the sake of others, to "display some evidence of decency and honor," is a classic interrogation technique.

Gleckman's remarks would obviously have constituted interrogation if they had been explicitly directed to petitioner, and the result should not be different because they were nominally addressed to McKenna. This is not a case where police officers speaking among themselves are accidentally overheard by a suspect. These officers were "talking back and forth" in close quarters with the handcuffed suspect, traveling past the very place where they believed the weapon was located. They knew petitioner would hear and attend to their conversation, and they are chargeable with knowledge of and responsibility for the pressures to speak which they created.

I firmly believe that this case is simply an aberration, and that in future cases the Court will apply the standard adopted today in accordance with its plain meaning.

JUSTICE STEVENS, dissenting.

* * * In my view any statement that would normally be understood by the average listener as calling for a response is the functional equivalent of a direct question, whether or not it is punctuated by a question mark. The Court, however, takes a much narrower view. It holds that police conduct is not the "functional equivalent" of direct questioning unless the police should have known that what they were saying or doing was likely to elicit an incriminating response from the suspect. This holding represents a plain departure from the principles set forth in *Miranda.* * * *

From the suspect's point of view, the effectiveness of the warnings depends on whether it appears that the police are scrupulously honoring his rights. Apparent attempts to elicit information from a suspect after he has invoked his right to cut off questioning necessarily demean that right and tend to reinstate the imbalance between police and suspect that the *Miranda* warnings are designed to correct. Thus, if the rationale for requiring those warnings in the first place is to be respected, any police conduct or statements that would appear to a reasonable person in the suspect's position to call for a response must be considered "interrogation."

In short, in order to give full protection to a suspect's right to be free from any interrogation at all, the definition of "interrogation" must include any police statement or conduct that has the same purpose or effect as a direct question. Statements that appear to call for a response from the suspect, as well as those that are designed to do so, should be considered interrogation. By prohibiting only those relatively few statements or actions that a police officer should know are likely to elicit an incriminating response, the Court today accords a suspect considerably less protection. Indeed, since I suppose most suspects are unlikely to incriminate themselves even when questioned directly, this new definition will almost certainly exclude every statement that is not punctuated with a question mark from the concept of "interrogation."

The difference between the approach required by a faithful adherence to *Miranda* and the stinted test applied by the Court today can be illustrated by comparing three different ways in which Officer Gleckman could have communicated his fears about the possible dangers posed by the shotgun to handicapped children. He could have:

(1) directly asked Innis:

Will you please tell me where the shotgun is so we can protect handicapped schoolchildren from danger?

(2) announced to the other officers in the wagon:

If the man sitting in the back seat with me should decide to tell us where the gun is, we can protect handicapped children from danger.

or (3) stated to the other officers:

It would be too bad if a little handicapped girl would pick up the gun that this man left in the area and maybe kill herself.

In my opinion, all three of these statements should be considered interrogation because all three appear to be designed to elicit a response from anyone who in fact knew where the gun was located. Under the Court's test, on the other hand, the form of the statements would be critical. Statement # 3 would not be interrogation because in the Court's view there was no reason for Officer Gleckman to believe that Innis was susceptible to this type of an implied appeal; therefore, the statement would not be reasonably likely to elicit an incriminating response. Assuming that this is true, then it seems to me that the first two statements, which would be just as unlikely to elicit such a response, should also not be considered interrogation. But, because the first statement is clearly an express question, it *would* be considered interrogation under the Court's test. The second statement, although just as clearly a deliberate appeal to Innis to reveal the location of the gun, would presumably not be interrogation because (a) it was not in form a direct question and (b) it does not fit within the "reasonably likely to elicit an incriminating response" category that applies to indirect interrogation.

As this example illustrates, the Court's test creates an incentive for police to ignore a suspect's invocation of his rights in order to make continued attempts to extract information from him. If a suspect does not appear to be susceptible to a particular type of psychological pressure, the police are apparently free to exert that pressure on him despite his request for counsel, so long as they are careful not to punctuate their statements with question marks. And if, contrary to all reasonable expectations, the suspect makes an incriminating statement, that statement can be used against him at trial. The Court thus turns *Miranda's* unequivocal rule against any interrogation at all into a trap in which unwary suspects may be caught by police deception.

\* \* \* I think the Court is clearly wrong in holding, as a matter of law, that Officer Gleckman should not have realized that his statement was likely to elicit an incriminating response. The Court implicitly assumes that, at least in the absence of a lengthy harangue, a criminal suspect will not be likely to respond to indirect appeals to his humanitarian impulses.

[This assumption] is directly contrary to the teachings of police interrogation manuals, which recommend appealing to a suspect's sense of morality as a standard and often successful interrogation technique. Surely the practical experience embodied in such manuals should not be ignored in a case such as this in which the record is devoid of any evidence—one way or the other—as to the susceptibility of suspects in general or of Innis in particular.

Moreover, there is evidence in the record to support the view that Officer Gleckman's statement was intended to elicit a response from Innis. Officer Gleckman, who was not regularly assigned to the caged wagon, was directed by a police captain to ride with respondent to the police station. Although there is a dispute in the testimony, it appears that Gleckman may well have been riding in the back seat with Innis. The record does not explain why, notwithstanding the fact that respondent was handcuffed, unarmed, and had offered no resistance when arrested by an officer acting alone, the captain ordered Officer Gleckman to ride with respondent. It is not inconceivable that two professionally trained police officers concluded that a few well-chosen remarks might induce respondent to disclose the whereabouts of the shotgun.[18] This conclusion becomes even more plausible in light of the emotionally charged words chosen by Officer Gleckman ("God forbid" that a "little girl" should find the gun and hurt herself).

Under my view of the correct standard, the judgment of the Rhode Island Supreme Court should be affirmed because the statements made within Innis' hearing were as likely to elicit a response as a direct question. However, even if I were to agree with the Court's much narrower standard, I would disagree with its disposition of this particular case because the Rhode Island courts should be given an opportunity to apply the new standard to the facts of this case.

## ILLINOIS v. PERKINS
—— U.S. ——, 110 S.Ct. 2394, —— L.Ed.2d —— (1990).

JUSTICE KENNEDY delivered the opinion of the Court.

\* \* \* We hold [that] *Miranda* warnings are not required when the suspect is unaware that he is speaking to a law enforcement officer and gives a voluntary statement.

---

**18.** Although Officer Gleckman testified that the captain told him not to interrogate, intimidate or coerce respondent on the way back, this does not rule out the possibility that either or both of them thought an indirect psychological ploy would be permissible.

[When Charlton, who had been a fellow inmate of respondent Perkins in another prison, told police that Perkins had implicated himself in the Stephenson murder, the police placed Charlton and Parisi, an undercover agent, in the same cellblock with Perkins, who was incarcerated on charges unrelated to the Stephenson murder. Parisi and Charlton posed as escapees from a work release program who had been arrested in the course of a burglary. They were instructed to engage Perkins in casual conversation and to report anything he said about the Stephenson murder.

[The cellblock consisted of 12 separate cells that opened onto a common room. Perkins greeted Charlton, who introduced Parisi by his alias. Parisi suggested that the three of them escape. There was further conversation. After telling Charlton that he would be responsible for any killing that might occur during a prison break, Parisi asked Perkins if he had ever "done" anybody. Perkins replied that he had, and proceeded to describe the Stephenson murder in detail.

[The trial court suppressed the statements made to Parisi in the jail. The Appellate Court of Illinois affirmed, reading *Miranda* as prohibiting all undercover contacts with incarcerated suspects which are reasonably likely to elicit an incriminating response.]

In *Miranda* the Court held that the Fifth Amendment privilege against self-incrimination prohibits admitting statements given by a suspect during "custodial interrogation" without a prior warning. [The] warning mandated by *Miranda* was meant to preserve the privilege during "incommunicado interrogation of individuals in a police-dominated atmosphere." That atmosphere is said to generate "inherently compelling pressures which work to undermine the individual's will to resist and to compel him to speak where he would not otherwise do so freely." * * *

Conversations between suspects and undercover agents do not implicate the concerns underlying *Miranda*. The essential ingredients of a "police-dominated atmosphere" and compulsion are not present when an incarcerated person speaks freely to someone that he believes to be a fellow inmate. Coercion is determined from the perspective of the suspect. When a suspect considers himself in the company of cellmates and not officers, the coercive atmosphere is lacking. * * * There is no empirical basis for the assumption that a suspect speaking to those whom he assumes are not officers will feel compelled to speak by the fear of reprisal for remaining silent or in the hope of more lenient treatment should he confess.

It is the premise of *Miranda* that the danger of coercion results from the interaction of custody and official interrogation. We reject the argument that *Miranda* warnings are required whenever a suspect is in custody in a technical sense and converses with someone who happens to be a government agent. Questioning by captors, who appear to control the suspect's fate, may create mutually reinforcing pressures that the Court has assumed will weaken the suspect's will, but where a suspect does not know that he is conversing with a government agent, these pressures do not exist. The State Court here mistakenly assumed that because the suspect was in custody, no undercover questioning could take place. When the suspect has no reason to think that the listeners have official power over him, it should not be assumed that his words are motivated by the reaction he expects from his listeners. "[W]hen the agent carries neither badge nor gun and wears not 'police blue,' but the same prison gray" as the suspect, there is no "*interplay* between police interrogation and police custody." Kamisar, *Brewer v. Williams, Massiah and Miranda: What is "Interrogation"? When Does it Matter?*, 67 Geo.L.J. 1, 67, 63 (1978).  *  *  *

*Miranda* was not meant to protect suspects from boasting about their criminal activities in front of persons whom they believe to be their cellmates. This case is illustrative. Respondent had no reason to feel that undercover agent Parisi had any legal authority to force him to answer questions or that Parisi could affect respondent's future treatment. Respondent viewed the cellmate-agent as an equal and showed no hint of being intimidated by the atmosphere of the jail. In recounting the details of the Stephenson murder, respondent was motivated solely by the desire to impress his fellow inmates. He spoke at his own peril.

The tactic employed here to elicit a voluntary confession from a suspect does not violate the Self–Incrimination Clause. We held in *Hoffa v. United States*, 385 U.S. 293 (1966), that placing an undercover agent near a suspect in order to gather incriminating information was permissible under the Fifth Amendment. In *Hoffa*, while petitioner Hoffa was on trial, he met often with one Partin, who, unbeknownst to Hoffa, was cooperating with law enforcement officials. Partin reported to officials that Hoffa had divulged his attempts to bribe jury members. We approved using Hoffa's statements at his subsequent trial for jury tampering, on the rationale that "no claim ha[d] been or could [have been] made that [Hoffa's] incriminating statements were the product of any sort of coercion, legal or factual." [The] only difference between this case and *Hoffa* is that the suspect here was incarcerated, but detention, whether or not for the crime in question, does not warrant a presumption that the use of an undercover agent to speak with an incarcerated suspect makes any confession thus obtained involuntary.  *  *  *

This Court's Sixth Amendment decisions in *Massiah v. United States, United States v. Henry, and Maine v. Moulton* [all discussed in Section 5 of this Chapter], also do not avail respondent. We held in those cases that the government may not use an undercover agent to circumvent the Sixth Amendment right to counsel once a suspect has been charged with the crime. After charges have been filed, the Sixth Amendment prevents the government from interfering with the accused's right to counsel. In the instant case no charges had been filed on the subject of the interrogation, and our Sixth Amendment precedents are not applicable.

Respondent can seek no help from his argument that a bright-line rule for the application of *Miranda* is desirable. Law enforcement officers will have little difficulty putting into practice our holding that undercover agents need not give *Miranda* warnings to incarcerated suspects. The use of undercover agents is a recognized law enforcement technique, often employed in the prison context to detect violence against correctional officials or inmates, as well as for the purposes served here. The interests protected by *Miranda* are not implicated in these cases, and the warnings are not required to safeguard the constitutional rights of inmates who make voluntary statements to undercover agents.  *  *  *

JUSTICE BRENNAN, concurring in the judgment.

Although I do not subscribe to the majority's characterization of *Miranda* in its entirety, I do agree that when a suspect does not know that his questioner is a police agent, such questioning does not amount to "interrogation" in an "inherently coercive" environment so as to require application of *Miranda*. Since the only issue raised at this stage of the litigation is the applicability of *Miranda*, I concur in the judgment of the Court.

This is not to say that I believe the Constitution condones the method by which the police extracted the confession in this case. To the contrary, the deception and manipulation practiced on respondent raise a substantial claim that the confession was obtained in violation of the Due Process Clause. As we recently stated in *Miller v. Fenton*, 474 U.S. 104, 109–110 (1985):

"This Court has long held that certain interrogation techniques, either in isolation or as applied to the unique characteristics of a particular suspect, are so offensive to a civilized system of justice that they must be condemned under the Due Process Clause of the Fourteenth Amendment ＊ ＊ ＊."

That the right is derived from the Due Process Clause "is significant because it reflects the Court's consistently held view that the admissibility of a confession turns as much on whether the techniques for extracting the statements, as applied to this suspect, are compatible with a system that presumes innocence and assures that a conviction will not be secured by inquisitorial means as on whether the defendant's will was in fact overborne." *Miller.* ＊ ＊ ＊

The method used to elicit the confession in this case deserves close scrutiny. [As] Justice Marshall points out, the pressures of custody make a suspect more likely to confide in others and to engage in "jailhouse bravado." The State is in a unique position to exploit this vulnerability because it has virtually complete control over the suspect's environment. Thus, the State can ensure that a suspect is barraged with questions from an undercover agent until the suspect confesses. The testimony in this case suggests the State did just that.

The deliberate use of deception and manipulation by the police appears to be incompatible "with a system that presumes innocence and assures that a conviction will not be secured by inquisitorial means," *Miller*, and raises serious concerns that respondent's will was overborne. It is open to the lower court on remand to determine whether, under the totality of the circumstances, respondent's confession was elicited in a manner that violated the Due Process Clause.

＊ ＊ ＊

JUSTICE MARSHALL, dissenting.

The conditions that require the police to apprise a defendant of his constitutional rights—custodial interrogation conducted by an agent of the police—were present in this case. Because Lloyd Perkins received no *Miranda* warnings before he was subjected to custodial interrogation, his confession was not admissible.

The Court reaches the contrary conclusion by fashioning an exception to the *Miranda* rule that applies whenever "an undercover law enforcement officer posing as a fellow inmate ＊ ＊ ＊ ask[s] questions that may elicit an incriminating response" from an incarcerated suspect. This exception is inconsistent with the rationale supporting *Miranda* and allows police officers intentionally to take advantage of suspects unaware of their constitutional rights. I therefore dissent.

＊ ＊ ＊

While Perkins was confined, an undercover police officer, with the help of a police informant, questioned him about a serious crime. Although the Court does not dispute that Perkins was interrogated, it downplays the nature of the 35–minute questioning by disingenuously referring to it as a "conversatio[n]." The officer's narration of the "conversation" at Perkins' trial, however, reveals that it clearly was [an] interrogation. ＊ ＊ ＊

Because Perkins was interrogated by police while he was in custody, *Miranda* required that the officer inform him of his rights. In rejecting that conclusion, the Court finds that "conversations" between undercover agents and suspects are devoid of the coercion inherent in stationhouse interrogations conducted by law enforcement officials who openly represent the State. *Miranda* was not, however, concerned solely with police *coercion*. It dealt with *any* police tactics that may operate to compel a suspect in custody to make incriminating statements without full awareness of his constitutional rights. [Thus,] when a law enforcement agent structures a custodial interrogation so that a suspect feels compelled to reveal incriminating information, he must inform the suspect of his constitutional rights and give him an opportunity to decide whether or not to talk.

The compulsion proscribed by *Miranda* includes deception by the police. See *Miranda* at 453 (indicting police tactics "to induce a confession out of trickery," such as using fictitious witnesses or false accusations) * * *.

Custody works to the State's advantage in obtaining incriminating information. The psychological pressures inherent in confinement increase the suspect's anxiety, making him likely to seek relief by talking with others. Dix, *Undercover Investigations and Police Rulemaking*, 53 Texas L.Rev. 203, 230 (1975). The inmate is thus more susceptible to efforts by undercover agents to elicit information from him. Similarly, where the suspect is incarcerated, the constant threat of physical danger peculiar to the prison environment may make him demonstrate his toughness to other inmates by recounting or inventing past violent acts. "Because the suspect's ability to select people with whom he can confide is completely within their control, the police have a unique opportunity to exploit the suspect's vulnerability. In short, the police can insure that if the pressures of confinement lead the suspects to confide in anyone, it will be a police agent." W. White, *Police Trickery in Inducing Confessions*, 127 U.Pa.L.Rev. 581, 605 (1979). In this case, the police deceptively took advantage of Perkins' psychological vulnerability by including him in a sham escape plot, a situation in which he would feel compelled to demonstrate his willingness to shoot a prison guard by revealing his past involvement in a murder. ([The] agent stressed that a killing might be necessary in the escape and then asked Perkins if he had ever murdered someone).

Thus, the pressures unique to custody allow the police to use deceptive interrogation tactics to compel a suspect to make an incriminating statement. The compulsion is not eliminated by the suspect's ignorance of his interrogator's true identity. The Court therefore need not inquire past the bare facts of custody and interrogation to determine whether *Miranda* warnings are required.

[The] Court's holding today complicates a previously clear and straightforward doctrine. The Court opines that "[l]aw enforcement officers will have little difficulty putting into practice our holding that undercover agents need not give *Miranda* warnings to incarcerated suspects." Perhaps this prediction is true with respect to fact patterns virtually identical to the one before the Court today. But the outer boundaries of the exception created by the Court, are by no means clear. Would *Miranda* be violated, for instance, if an undercover police officer beat a confession out of a suspect, but the suspect thought the officer was another prisoner who wanted the information for his own purposes?

Even if *Miranda*, as interpreted by the Court, would not permit such obviously compelled confessions, the ramifications of today's opinion are still disturbing. The exception carved out of the *Miranda* doctrine today may well result in a proliferation of departmental policies to encourage police officers to conduct interrogations of confined suspects through undercover agents, thereby circumventing the need to administer *Miranda* warnings. Indeed, if *Miranda* now requires a police officer to issue warnings only in those situations in which the suspect might feel compelled "to speak by the fear of reprisal for remaining silent or in the hope of more lenient treatment should he confess," presumably it allows custodial interrogation by an undercover officer posing as a member of the clergy or a suspect's defense attorney. Although such abhorrent tricks would play on a suspect's need to confide in a trusted adviser, neither would cause the suspect to "think that the listeners have official power over him." The Court's adoption of the "undercover agent" exception to the *Miranda* rule thus is necessarily also the adoption of a substantial loophole in our jurisprudence protecting suspects' Fifth Amendment rights. \* \* \*

### 3. If a suspect asserts his rights, may the police "try again"? Does it matter which right the suspect asserts?

## EDWARDS v. ARIZONA
451 U.S. 477, 101 S.Ct. 1880, 68 L.Ed.2d 378 (1981).

JUSTICE WHITE delivered the opinion of the Court.

[Edwards was arrested for burglary, robbery and first-degree murder. At the police station, after waiving his *Miranda* rights, Edwards was told that another suspect had implicated him in the crimes. Edwards sought to "make a deal," but the interrogating officer said he lacked authority to negotiate a deal. Some time thereafter, Edwards said, "I want an attorney before making a deal." At that point questioning ceased and Edwards was taken to jail. The following morning two detectives paid Edwards a visit. When a guard informed Edwards that two detectives wanted to talk to him, he stated that he did not want to talk to anyone. But the guard told Edwards that "he had" to talk to the detectives and then took him to meet with them.

[After the detectives informed him of his *Miranda* rights, Edwards expressed a willingness to talk, but only after hearing the taped statement of the alleged accomplice who had implicated him. After listening to the tape, Edwards said he would make a statement so long as it was not tape recorded. After being informed that whether or not his statement was recorded, the detectives could still testify as to what he said, Edwards replied: "I'll tell you anything you want to know, but I don't want it on tape." He then incriminated himself. The state supreme court held that although Edwards had invoked his right to counsel the day before, he waived that right the following morning when he voluntarily made a statement after again being advised of his *Miranda* rights.]

[T]he Arizona Supreme Court applied an erroneous standard for determining waiver where the accused has specifically invoked his right to counsel. [W]aivers of counsel must not only be voluntary, but constitute a knowing and intelligent relinquishment or abandonment of a known right or privilege, a matter which depends in each case "upon the particular facts and circumstances surrounding that case, including the background, experience and conduct of the accused." *Johnson v. Zerbst.*

Considering the proceedings in the state courts in the light of this standard, we note [that] the trial court found [Edwards' waiver and confession] to have been "voluntary" without separately focusing on whether [he] had knowingly and intelligently relinquished his right to counsel. [The Arizona Supreme Court] stated that the issue of [the "voluntariness" of a confession] should be determined based on the totality of the circumstances as it related to whether an accused's action was "knowing and intelligent and whether his will was overborne." [It] then upheld the trial court's finding that the "waiver and confession was voluntarily and knowingly made."

\* \* \* [H]owever sound the conclusion of the state courts as to the voluntariness of Edwards' admissions may be, [they did not undertake] to focus on whether Edwards understood his right to counsel and intelligently and knowingly relinquished it. It is thus apparent that the decision below misunderstood the requirement for finding a valid waiver of the right to counsel, once invoked.

[A]lthough we have held that after initially being advised of his *Miranda* rights, the accused may himself validly waive his rights and respond to interrogation, see *North Carolina v. Butler,* 441 U.S. 369 (1979),[a] the Court has strongly indicated that additional safeguards are necessary when the accused asks for counsel; and we now hold that when an accused has invoked his right to have counsel present during custodial interrogation, a valid waiver of that right cannot be established by showing only that he responded to further police-initiated custodial interrogation even if he has been advised of his rights. We further hold that an accused, such as Edwards, having expressed his desire to deal with the police only through counsel, is not subject to further interrogation by the authorities until counsel has been made available to him unless the accused himself initiates further communication, exchanges, or conversations with the police.

*Miranda* itself indicated that the assertion of the right to counsel was a significant event and that once exercised by the accused, "the interrogation must cease until an attorney is present." Our later cases have not abandoned that view. In *Michigan v. Mosley,* 423 U.S. 96 (1975), [we] noted that *Miranda* had distinguished between the procedural safeguards triggered by a request to remain silent and a request for an attorney and had required that interrogation cease until an attorney was present only if the individual stated that he wanted counsel.[b]

**a.** The *Butler* Court pointed out that a waiver of *Miranda* rights may be recognized even though not "specifically made" after the warnings are given. Although "mere silence" in the face of the warnings is not enough, "the defendant's silence, coupled with an understanding of his rights and a course of conduct indicating waiver," may support a conclusion that a defendant has waived his rights. Not only may an "implied" waiver suffice, but as *Butler* also indicates, so may a "qualified" waiver. A suspect may refuse to sign a waiver form, but nonetheless indicate that he is willing to talk. Or he may object to any notetaking by an officer but agree to discuss the case or indicate that he will talk only if a tape recorder is turned off.

**b.** In *Mosley* the Court, per Stewart, rejected the argument that *Miranda* created "a *per se* proscription of indefinite duration upon any further questioning by any police officer on any subject, once the person in custody has indicated a desire to remain silent." Rather, "the admissibility of statements obtained after [a suspect] has decided to remain silent depends under *Miranda* on whether his right to cut off questioning was 'scrupulously honored.'"

After receiving the *Miranda* warnings, Mosley declined to discuss the robberies for which he was arrested. But two hours later, after again being advised of his *Miranda* rights by another officer, Mosley agreed to talk about an unrelated holdup murder. In holding his incriminating statements admissible, the Court emphasized:

"This is not a case [where] the police failed to honor a decision of a person in custody to cut off questioning, either by refusing to discontinue the interrogation upon request or by persisting in repeated efforts to wear down his resistance and make him change his mind. [Instead,] the police here immediately ceased the interrogation, resumed questioning only after the passage of a significant period of time and the provision of a fresh set of warnings, and restricted the second interrogation to a crime that had not been a subject of the earlier interrogation."

Concurring Justice White added that when the *Miranda* Court "wanted to create a *per se* rule against further interrogation after assertion of a right, it knew how to do so. The Court [said that] 'if the individual states that he wants an attorney, the interrogation must cease *until an attorney is present.*' However, when the individual indicates that *he* will decide unaided by counsel whether or not to assert his 'right to silence' the situation is different."

" * * * Had Edwards initiated the [several meetings with the police, nothing] would prohibit the police from merely listening to his voluntary, volunteered statements and using them against him at the trial. [Absent any custodial interrogation], there would have been no infringement of the right that Edwards invoked and there would be no occasion to determine whether there had been a valid waiver. *Rhode Island v. Innis* makes this sufficiently clear.

"But this is not what the facts of this case show. * * * We think it is clear [that at the second meeting] Edwards was subjected to custodial interrogation [within] the meaning of *Innis* and that this occurred at the instance of the authorities. His statement, made without having access to counsel, did not amount to a valid waiver and hence was inadmissible." c

CHIEF JUSTICE BURGER, concurring in the judgment.

I concur only in the judgment because I do not agree that either any constitutional standard or the holding of *Miranda*—as distinguished from its dicta—calls for a special rule as to how an accused in custody may waive the right to be free from interrogations. * * * For me, the inquiry in this setting is whether resumption of interrogation is a result of a voluntary waiver, and that inquiry should be resolved under the traditional standard established in *Johnson v. Zerbst.*

JUSTICE POWELL, with whom JUSTICE REHNQUIST joining, concurring in the result. * * *

I have thought it settled law [that] one accused of crime may waive *any* of the constitutional safeguards * * *. Whatever the right, the standard for waiver is whether the actor fully understands the right in question and voluntarily intends to relinquish it. * * *

In view of the emphasis placed on "initiation," I find the Court's opinion unclear. If read to create a new *per se* rule, requiring a threshold inquiry as to precisely who opened any conversation between an accused and state officials, I cannot agree. I would not superimpose a new element of proof on the established doctrine of waiver of counsel. * * *

c. What constitutes "initiating" further communication with the police? Consider *Oregon v. Bradshaw,* 462 U.S. 1039 (1983), where defendant asserted his right to counsel but a few moments later, either while still at the police station or enroute to the jail, asked the officer: "Well, what is going to happen to me now?" The officer responded: "You do not have to talk to me. * * * I don't want you talking to me unless you so desire * * *." Defendant said he understood and general conversation followed. A 5–4 majority held that the incriminating statements obtained as a result of the general conversation were admissible.

The plurality opinion, written by Justice Rehnquist, joined by Burger, C.J., and White and O'Connor, JJ. observed:

"There are some inquiries such as a request for a drink of water or a request to use a telephone that are so routine that they cannot be fairly said to represent a desire on the part of an accused to open up a more generalized discussion relating directly or indirectly to the investigation.

Such [statements] relating to routine incidents of the custodial relationship, will not generally 'initiate' a conversation in the sense in which that word was used in *Edwards*. [But Bradshaw's question] as to what was going to happen to him evinced a willingness and a desire for a generalized discussion about the investigation; it was not merely a necessary inquiry arising out of the incidents of the custodial relationship. It could reasonably have been interpreted by the officer as relating generally to the investigation."

Dissenting Justice Marshall, joined by Brennan, Blackmun and Stevens, JJ., "agree[d] with the plurality that in order to constitute 'initiation' under *Edwards,* an accused's inquiry must demonstrate a desire to discuss the subject matter of the criminal investigation," but was "baffled [at] the plurality's application of that standard to the facts of this case. * * * [It] is plain that [Bradshaw's] only 'desire' was to find out where the police were going to take him."

[O]nce warnings have been given and the right to counsel has been invoked, the relevant inquiry—whether the suspect now desires to talk to police without counsel—is a question of fact to be determined in light of all of the circumstances. Who "initiated" a conversation may be relevant to the question of waiver, but it is not the *sine qua non* to the inquiry. The ultimate question is whether there was a free and knowing waiver of counsel before interrogation commenced.

### 4. Questioning prompted by concern for "public safety."

## NEW YORK v. QUARLES

467 U.S. 649, 104 S.Ct. 2626, 81 L.Ed.2d 550 (1984).

JUSTICE REHNQUIST delivered the opinion of the Court.

[At approximately 12:30 a.m., police apprehended respondent in the rear of a supermarket. He matched the description of the man who had just raped a woman. The woman had told the police that the rapist had just entered the supermarket and that he was carrying a gun. Apparently upon seeing Officer Kraft enter the store, respondent turned and ran toward the rear. Officer Kraft pursued him with a drawn gun and, upon regaining sight of him, ordered him to stop and put his hands over his head. Although several other officers had arrived at the scene by then, Kraft was the first to reach respondent. He frisked him and discovered he was wearing an empty shoulder holster. After handcuffing him, the officer asked where the gun was. Respondent nodded in the direction of some empty cartons and responded, "the gun is over there." At that time, emphasized the New York Court of Appeals, respondent was surrounded by four officers whose guns had been returned to their holsters because, as one testified, the situation was under control.

[The gun was not visible, but Officer Kraft reached into one of the cartons and retrieved a loaded revolver. Respondent was then formally placed under arrest and advised of his *Miranda* rights. Respondent waived his rights. In response to questions, he then stated that he owned the revolver and had purchased it in Miami.

[In the subsequent prosecution of respondent for criminal possession of a weapon (the record does not reveal why the state failed to pursue the rape charge), the New York courts suppressed the statement "the gun is over there" as well as the gun itself because they had been obtained in violation of respondent's *Miranda* rights. Respondent's statements about his ownership of the gun and the place of purchase were also excluded as having been fatally tainted by the seizure of the gun and the prewarning response as to its location.]

\* \* \* We conclude that under the circumstances involved in this case, overriding considerations of public safety justify the officer's failure to provide *Miranda* warnings before he asked questions devoted to locating the abandoned weapon. \* \* \*

The Fifth Amendment itself does not prohibit all incriminating admissions; "[a]bsent some officially *coerced* self-accusation, the Fifth Amendment privilege is not violated by even the most damning admissions." *United States v. Washington*, 431 U.S. 181 (1977) (emphasis added).[a]

---

**a.** *Washington* held that a person appearing before a grand jury need not be warned that he is a target of the grand jury investigation. Defendant had been given *Miranda* warnings prior to any questioning. He re- plied that he understood these rights and was prepared to answer questions relating to the crime being investigated. He contended, however that his grand jury testimony should be suppressed on the ground that his privilege

The *Miranda* Court, however, presumed that interrogation in certain custodial circumstances is inherently coercive and held that statements made under those circumstances are inadmissible unless the suspect is specifically informed of his *Miranda* rights and freely decides to forgo those rights. The prophylactic *Miranda* warnings therefore are "not themselves rights protected by the Constitution but [are] instead measures to insure that the right against compulsory self-incrimination [is] protected." *Michigan v. Tucker.* * * *

In this case we have before us no claim that respondent's statements were actually compelled by police conduct which overcame his will to resist. Thus the only issue before us is whether Officer Kraft was justified in failing to make available to respondent the procedural safeguards associated with the privilege against compulsory self-incrimination since *Miranda.*

The New York Court of Appeals was undoubtedly correct in deciding that the facts of this case come within the ambit of the *Miranda* decision as we have subsequently interpreted it. [As] the New York Court of Appeals observed, [when the questioning at issue took place] there was nothing to suggest that any of the officers were any longer concerned for their own physical safety. The New York Court of Appeals' majority declined to express an opinion as to whether there might be an exception to the *Miranda* rule if the police had been acting to protect the public, because the lower courts in New York had made no factual determination that the police had acted with that motive.

We hold that on these facts there is a "public safety" exception to the requirement that *Miranda* warnings be given before a suspect's answers may be admitted into evidence, and that the availability of that exception does not depend upon the motivation of the individual officers involved. In a kaleidoscopic situation such as the one confronting these officers, where spontaneity rather than adherence to a police manual is necessarily the order of the day, the application of the exception which we recognize today should not be made to depend on *post hoc* findings at a suppression hearing concerning the subjective motivation of the arresting officer. Undoubtedly most police officers, if placed in Officer Kraft's position, would act out of a host of different, instinctive, and largely unverifiable motives—their own safety, the safety of others, and perhaps as well the desire to obtain incriminating evidence from the suspect.

Whatever the motivation of individual officers in such a situation, we do not believe that the doctrinal underpinnings of *Miranda* require that it be applied in all its rigor to a situation in which police officers ask questions reasonably prompted by a concern for the public safety.

[The] police in this case, in the very act of apprehending a suspect, were confronted with the immediate necessity of ascertaining the whereabouts of a gun which they had every reason to believe the suspect had just removed from his empty holster and discarded in the supermarket. So long as the gun was concealed somewhere in the supermarket, with its actual whereabouts unknown, it obviously posed more than one danger to the public safety: an accomplice might make use of it, a customer or employee might later come upon it.

In such a situation, if the police are required to recite the familiar *Miranda* warnings before asking the whereabouts of the gun, suspects in Quarles' position might well be deterred from responding. Procedural safeguards which deter a

against self-incrimination had been violated by the prosecutor's failure to advise him that he was a potential defendant. In rejecting this argument the Court noted that because a witness' target status "neither enlarges nor diminishes the constitutional protection against compelled self-incrimination, potential defendant warnings add nothing of value to protection of Fifth Amendment rights." See also note c to *Mandujano,* Ch. 8, § 2.

suspect from responding were deemed acceptable in *Miranda* in order to protect the Fifth Amendment privilege; when the primary social cost of those added protections is the possibility of fewer convictions, the *Miranda* majority was willing to bear that cost. Here, had *Miranda* warnings deterred Quarles from responding to Officer Kraft's question about the whereabouts of the gun, the cost would have been something more than merely the failure to obtain evidence useful in convicting Quarles. Officer Kraft needed an answer to his question not simply to make his case against Quarles but to insure that further danger to the public did not result from the concealment of the gun in a public area.

We conclude that the need for answers to questions in a situation posing a threat to the public safety outweighs the need for the prophylactic rule protecting the Fifth Amendment's privilege against self-incrimination. We decline to place officers such as Officer Kraft in the untenable position of having to consider, often in a matter of seconds, whether it best serves society for them to ask the necessary questions without the *Miranda* warnings and render whatever probative evidence they uncover inadmissible, or for them to give the warnings in order to preserve the admissibility of evidence they might uncover but possibly damage or destroy their ability to obtain that evidence and neutralize the volatile situation confronting them.[7]

\* \* \* [W]e recognize [the] importance of a workable rule "to guide police officers, who have only limited time and expertise to reflect on and balance the social and individual interests involved in the specific circumstances they confront." *Dunaway.* [But] we believe that the exception which we recognize today lessens the necessity of that on-the-scene balancing process. The exception will not be difficult for police officers to apply because in each case it will be circumscribed by the exigency which justifies it. We think police officers can and will distinguish almost instinctively between questions necessary to secure their own safety or the safety of the public and questions designed solely to elicit testimonial evidence from a suspect.

The facts of this case clearly demonstrate that distinction and an officer's ability to recognize it. Officer Kraft asked only the question necessary to locate the missing gun before advising respondent of his rights. It was only after securing the loaded revolver and giving the warnings that he continued with investigatory questions about the ownership and place of purchase of the gun. The exception which we recognize today, far from complicating the thought processes and the on-the-scene judgments of police officers, will simply free them to follow their legitimate instincts when confronting situations presenting a danger to the public safety.[8]

---

**7.** The dissent argues that a public safety exception to *Miranda* is unnecessary because in every case an officer can simply ask the necessary questions to protect himself or the public, and then the prosecution can decline to introduce any incriminating responses at a subsequent trial. But absent actual coercion by the officer, there is no constitutional imperative requiring the exclusion of the evidence that results from police inquiry of this kind; and we do not believe that the doctrinal underpinnings of *Miranda* require us to exclude the evidence, thus penalizing officers for asking the very questions which are the most crucial to their efforts to protect themselves and the public.

**8.** Although it involves police questions in part relating to the whereabouts of a gun, *Orozco v. Texas*, 394 U.S. 324 (1969) [where the police entered a sleeping defendant's room in the early hours of the morning and questioned him about a gun used in a murder several hours earlier] is in no sense inconsistent with our disposition of this case. [In *Orozco*,] the questions about the gun were clearly investigatory; they did not in any way relate to an objectively reasonable need to protect the police or the public from any immediate danger associated with the weapon. In short there was no exigency requiring immediate action by the officers beyond the normal need expeditiously to solve a serious crime.

We hold that the Court of Appeals in this case erred in excluding the statement, "the gun is over there," and the gun because of the officer's failure to read respondent his *Miranda* rights before attempting to locate the weapon. Accordingly we hold that it also erred in excluding the subsequent statements as illegal fruits of a *Miranda* violation.[9] * * *

JUSTICE O'CONNOR, concurring in part in the judgment and dissenting in part. * * *

In my view, a "public safety" exception unnecessarily blurs the edges of the clear line heretofore established and makes *Miranda's* requirements more difficult to understand. In some cases, police will benefit because a reviewing court will find that an exigency excused their failure to administer the required warnings. But in other cases, police will suffer because, though they thought an exigency excused their noncompliance, a reviewing court will view the "objective" circumstances differently and require exclusion of admissions thereby obtained. The end result will be a finespun new doctrine on public safety exigencies incident to custodial interrogation, complete with the hair-splitting distinctions that currently plague our Fourth Amendment jurisprudence. * * *

The justification the Court provides for upsetting the equilibrium that has finally been achieved—that police cannot and should not balance considerations of public safety against the individual's interest in avoiding compulsory testimonial self-incrimination—really misses the critical question to be decided. *Miranda* has never been read to prohibit the police from asking questions to secure the public safety. Rather, the critical question *Miranda* addresses is who shall bear the cost of securing the public safety when such questions are asked and answered: the defendant or the State. *Miranda,* for better or worse, found the resolution of that question implicit in the prohibition against compulsory self-incrimination and placed the burden on the State. When police ask custodial questions without administering the required warnings, *Miranda* quite clearly requires that the answers received be presumed compelled and that they be excluded from evidence at trial. * * *[c]

JUSTICE MARSHALL, with whom JUSTICE BRENNAN and JUSTICE STEVENS join, dissenting * * *.

*Innis* also involved the whereabouts of a missing weapon, but our holding in that case depended entirely on our conclusion that no police interrogation took place so as to require consideration of the applicability of the *Miranda* prophylactic.

**9.** Because we hold that there is no violation of *Miranda* in this case, we have no occasion to [decide whether] the gun is admissible either because it is nontestimonial or because the police would inevitably have discovered it absent their questioning.

[A year earlier, in *Nix v. Williams* (Williams II), 467 U.S. 431 (1984), the Court ruled that the "fruit of the poisonous tree" doctrine did not bar the use of evidence derived from a constitutional violation if such evidence would "ultimately" or "inevitably" have been discovered as a result of lawful police investigatory work without regard to that violation. The "fruits" doctrine, formulated initially in applying the Fourth Amendment exclusionary rule, bars the use of evidence derived from, and thus "tainted" by, a constitutional violation.]

**c.** Although Justice O'Connor would suppress Quarles' initial statement, "the gun is over there," she would not exclude the gun itself because "nothing in *Miranda* or the privilege [against compelled self-incrimination] itself requires exclusion of nontestimonial evidence derived from informal custodial interrogation." "Only the introduction of a defendant's own *testimony*," maintained Justice O'Connor, "is proscribed by the Fifth Amendment's mandate that no person 'shall be compelled in any criminal case to be a witness against himself.' That mandate does not protect an accused from being compelled to surrender *nontestimonial* evidence against himself."

For further discussion of the application (or nonapplication) of the "fruit of the poisonous tree" doctrine to *Miranda* violations, see *Oregon v. Elstad*, the next case set forth in this section.

The majority's entire analysis rests on the factual assumption that the public was at risk during Quarles' interrogation. This assumption is completely in conflict with the facts as found by New York's highest court. Before the interrogation began, Quarles had been "reduced to a condition of physical powerlessness." Contrary to the majority's speculations, Quarles was not believed to have, nor did he in fact have, an accomplice to come to his rescue. When the questioning began, the arresting officers were sufficiently confident of their safety to put away their guns.

[The] New York court's conclusion that neither Quarles nor his missing gun posed a threat to the public's safety is amply supported by the evidence presented at the suppression hearing. * * * Although the supermarket was open to the public, Quarles' arrest took place during the middle of the night when the store was apparently deserted except for the clerks at the checkout counter. The police could easily have cordoned off the store and searched for the missing gun. Had they done so, they would have found the gun forthwith. [As] the State acknowledged before the New York Court of Appeals: "After Officer Kraft had handcuffed and frisked the defendant in the supermarket, *he knew with a high degree of certainty that the defendant's gun was within the immediate vicinity of the encounter.* He undoubtedly would have searched for it in the carton a few feet away without the defendant having looked in that direction and saying that it was there." (Emphasis added.) * * *

This case is illustrative of the chaos the "public-safety" exception will unleash. The circumstances of Quarles' arrest have never been in dispute. [T]he New York Court of Appeals concluded that there was "no evidence in the record before us that there were exigent circumstances posing a risk to the public safety." Upon reviewing the same facts and hearing the same arguments, a majority of this Court has come to precisely the opposite conclusion * * *.

If after plenary review two appellate courts so fundamentally differ over the threat to public safety presented by the simple and uncontested facts of this case, one must seriously question how law enforcement officers will respond to the majority's new rule in the confusion and haste of the real world. * * * Not only will police officers have to decide whether the objective facts of an arrest justify an unconsented custodial interrogation; they will also have to remember to interrupt the interrogation and read the suspect his *Miranda* warnings once the focus of the inquiry shifts from protecting the public's safety to ascertaining the suspect's guilt. Disagreements of the scope of the "public-safety" exception and mistakes in its application are inevitable.[4] * * *

Though unfortunate, the difficulty of administering the "public-safety" exception is not the most profound flaw in the majority's decision. The majority has lost sight of the fact that *Miranda* and our earlier custodial-interrogation cases all implemented a constitutional privilege against self-incrimination. The rules established in these cases were designed to protect criminal defendants against prosecutions based on coerced self-incriminating statements. The majority today turns its back on these constitutional considerations, and invites the government to prosecute through the use of what necessarily are coerced statements.

**4.** One of the peculiarities of the majority's decision is its suggestion that police officers can "distinguish almost instinctively" questions tied to public safety and questions designed to elicit testimonial evidence. Obviously, these distinctions are extraordinarily difficult to draw. In many cases—like this one—custodial questioning may serve both purposes. It is therefore wishful thinking for the majority to suggest that the intuitions of police officers will render its decision self-executing.

The majority's error stems from a serious misunderstanding of *Miranda* and of the Fifth Amendment upon which that decision was based. The majority implies that *Miranda* consisted of no more than a judicial balancing act in which the benefits of "enlarged protection for the Fifth Amendment privilege" were weighed against "the cost to society in terms of fewer convictions of guilty suspects." Supposedly because the scales tipped in favor of the privilege against self-incrimination, the *Miranda* Court erected a prophylactic barrier around statements made during custodial interrogations. The majority now proposes to return to the scales of social utility to calculate whether *Miranda's* prophylactic rule remains cost-effective when threats to the public's safety are added to the balance.

[The] majority misreads *Miranda*. Though the *Miranda* dissent prophesized dire consequences, the *Miranda* Court refused to allow such concerns to weaken the protections of the Constitution * * *.

Whether society would be better off if the police warned suspects of their rights before beginning an interrogation or whether the advantages of giving such warnings would outweigh their costs did not inform the *Miranda* decision. On the contrary, the *Miranda* Court was concerned with the proscriptions of the Fifth Amendment, and, in particular, whether the Self–Incrimination Clause permits the government to prosecute individuals based on statements made in the course of custodial interrogations.

[In] fashioning its "public-safety" exception to *Miranda*, the majority makes no attempt to deal with the constitutional presumption established by that case. The majority does not argue that police questioning about issues of public safety is any less coercive than custodial interrogations into other matters. The majority's only contention is that police officers could more easily protect the public if *Miranda* did not apply to custodial interrogations concerning the public's safety. But *Miranda* was not a decision about public safety; it was a decision about coerced confessions. Without establishing that interrogations concerning the public's safety are less likely to be coercive than other interrogations, the majority cannot endorse the "public-safety" exception and remain faithful to the logic of *Miranda*.

[That] the application of the "public-safety" exception in this case entailed coercion is no happenstance. The majority's *ratio decidendi* is that interrogating suspects about matters of public safety *will* be coercive. In its cost-benefit analysis, the Court's strongest argument in favor of a public-safety exception to *Miranda* is that the police would be better able to protect the public's safety if they were not always required to give suspects their *Miranda* warnings. The crux of this argument is that, by deliberately withholding *Miranda* warnings, the police can get information out of suspects who would refuse to respond to police questioning were they advised of their constitutional rights. The "public-safety" exception is efficacious precisely because it permits police officers to coerce criminal defendants into making involuntary statements. * * *

[The] irony of the majority's decision is that the public's safety can be perfectly well protected without abridging the Fifth Amendment. If a bomb is about to explode or the public is otherwise imminently imperiled, the police are free to interrogate suspects without advising them of their constitutional rights. * * * If trickery is necessary to protect the public, then the police may trick a suspect into confessing. While the Fourteenth Amendment sets limits on such behavior, nothing in the Fifth Amendment or our decision in *Miranda* proscribes this sort of emergency questioning. All the Fifth Amendment forbids is the introduction of coerced statements at trial.

\* \* \* [The] policies underlying the Fifth Amendment's privilege against self-incrimination are not diminished simply because testimony is compelled to protect the public's safety. The majority should not be permitted to elude the Amendment's absolute prohibition simply by calculating special costs that arise when the public's safety is at issue. Indeed, were constitutional adjudication always conducted in such an *ad hoc* manner, the Bill of Rights would be a most unreliable protector of individual liberties.

### 5. Does an initial failure to inform a suspect of his rights bar subsequent admissions by the suspect after he has been fully advised of his rights?

## OREGON v. ELSTAD

470 U.S. 298, 105 S.Ct. 1285, 84 L.Ed.2d 222 (1985).

JUSTICE O'CONNOR delivered the opinion of the Court.

This case requires us to decide whether an initial failure of law enforcement officers to administer the warnings required by *Miranda*, without more, "taints" subsequent admissions made after a suspect has been fully advised of and has waived his *Miranda* rights. [Respondent was convicted of burglary.] The Oregon Court of Appeals reversed, holding that respondent's signed confession, although voluntary, was rendered inadmissible by a prior remark made in response to questioning without benefit of *Miranda* warnings. [We] reverse.

[When the Gross home was burglarized, a witness contacted the sheriff's office, implicating respondent Elstad, an 18–year–old neighbor and friend of the Grosses' teenage son. Officers Burke and McAllister went to Elstad's home, with a warrant for his arrest for the aforementioned burglary. Elstad's mother led the officers to his room. The officers asked Elstad to get dressed and to accompany them to the living room. Officer Burke sat down with Elstad in the living room and, without telling him that the police had a warrant for his arrest, stated that he "felt" Elstad was involved in the Gross burglary. Elstad replied, "Yes, I was there."

[Elstad was then transported to sheriff headquarters and, approximately an hour later, Officer McAllister, in the presence of Officer Burke, advised Elstad of his *Miranda* rights for the first time. Elstad agreed to talk to the police and made a statement detailing his involvement in the burglary. The statement was typed, reviewed by Elstad, read back to him for correction and signed by him.

[The trial judge excluded the incriminating remark Elstad made in his living room, but admitted the statement made at the sheriff's office. Following his conviction of burglary, Elstad appealed. The state conceded that Elstad had been in custody when he replied, "Yes, I was there," and thus that this statement was obtained in violation of *Miranda*, but maintained that any conceivable "taint" had been dissipated prior to Elstad's written confession by Officer McAllister's careful administration of the *Miranda* warnings. The Oregon Court of Appeals disagreed.

[In reversing Elstad's conviction, the Oregon court identified the crucial constitutional inquiry as whether there was "a sufficient break in the stream of events" between the inadmissible statement in respondent's living room and the written confession in the sheriff's office "to insulate the latter statement from the effect of what went before." It concluded that, because of the brief period separating the two incidents, the "cat was sufficiently out of the bag to exert a coercive impact on [respondent's later admissions."]

[The] Oregon court assumed and respondent here contends that a failure to administer *Miranda* warnings necessarily breeds the same consequences as police infringement of a constitutional right, so that evidence uncovered following an unwarned statement must be suppressed as "fruit of the poisonous tree." We believe this view misconstrues the nature of the protections afforded by *Miranda* warnings and therefore misreads the consequences of police failure to supply them.

[A]s we explained in *Quarles* and *Tucker,* a procedural *Miranda* violation differs in significant respects from violations of the Fourth Amendment, which have traditionally mandated a broad application of the "fruits" doctrine. The purpose of the Fourth Amendment exclusionary rule is to deter unreasonable searches, no matter how probative their fruits. * * *

The *Miranda* exclusionary rule, however, serves the Fifth Amendment and sweeps more broadly than the Fifth Amendment itself. It may be triggered even in the absence of a Fifth Amendment violation.[1] The Fifth Amendment prohibits use by the prosecution in its case in chief only of *compelled* testimony. Failure to administer *Miranda* warnings creates a presumption of compulsion. * * *

But the *Miranda* presumption, though irrebuttable for purposes of the prosecution's case in chief, does not require that the statements and their fruits be discarded as inherently tainted. * * *[a]

Where an unwarned statement is preserved for use in situations that fall outside the sweep of the *Miranda* presumption, "the primary criterion of admissibility [remains] the 'old' due process voluntariness test." Schulholfer, *Confessions and the Court,* 79 Mich.L.Rev. 865, 877 (1981).

[In] deciding "how sweeping the judicially imposed consequences" of a failure to administer *Miranda* warnings should be, the *Tucker* Court noted that neither the general goal of deterring improper police conduct nor the Fifth Amendment goal of assuring trustworthy evidence would be served by suppression of the witness' testimony. The unwarned confession must, of course, be suppressed, but the Court ruled that introduction of the third-party witness' testimony did not violate Tucker's Fifth Amendment rights.

We believe that this reasoning applies with equal force when the alleged "fruit" of a noncoercive *Miranda* violation is neither a witness nor an article of evidence but the accused's own voluntary testimony. As in *Tucker,* the absence of any coercion or improper tactics undercuts the twin rationales—trustworthi-

---

**1.** Justice Stevens expresses puzzlement at our statement that a simple failure to administer *Miranda* warnings is not in itself a violation of the Fifth Amendment. Yet the Court so held in *Quarles* and *Tucker.* The *Miranda* Court itself recognized this point when it disclaimed any intent to create a "constitutional straight-jacket" and invited Congress and the States to suggest "potential alternatives for protecting the privilege." A *Miranda* violation does not *constitute* coercion but rather affords a bright-line, legal presumption of coercion, requiring suppression of all unwarned statements. It has never been remotely suggested that any statement taken from Mr. Elstad without benefit of *Miranda* warnings would be admissible.

**a.** At this point, the Court discusses *Harris v. New York,* 401 U.S. 222 (1971) and *Michi-*

*gan v. Tucker,* 417 U.S. 433 (1974). *Harris* held that incriminating statements preceded by defective *Miranda* warnings, and thus inadmissible for the purposes of establishing the prosecution's case-in-chief, could nevertheless be used to impeach the defendant's credibility if he chose to take the stand in his own defense. *Tucker* declined to apply the "fruit of the poisonous tree" doctrine to the testimony of a witness whose identity had been discovered by questioning the defendant without giving him a complete set of *Miranda* warnings. Although the *Tucker* case involved various factors that arguably limited its implications, the *Tucker* Court, per Rehnquist, J., spoke in general terms of the difference between a *Miranda* violation and a constitutional violation. See the Note on Congressional Overruling in § 3 supra.

ness and deterrence—for a broader rule. Once warned, the suspect is free to exercise his own volition in deciding whether or not to make a statement to the authorities.

* * * If errors are made by law enforcement officers in administering the prophylactic *Miranda* procedures, they should not breed the same irremediable consequences as police infringement of the Fifth Amendment itself. It is an unwarranted extension of *Miranda* to hold that a simple failure to administer the warnings, unaccompanied by any actual coercion or other circumstances calculated to undermine the suspect's ability to exercise his free will so taints the investigatory process that a subsequent voluntary and informed waiver is ineffective for some indeterminate period. Though *Miranda* requires that the unwarned admission must be suppressed, the admissibility of any subsequent statement should turn in these circumstances solely on whether it is knowingly and voluntarily made. * * *

There is a vast difference between the direct consequences flowing from coercion of a confession by physical violence or other deliberate means calculated to break the suspect's will and the uncertain consequences of disclosure of a "guilty secret" freely given in response to an unwarned but noncoercive question, as in this case. Justice Brennan's contention that it is impossible to perceive any causal distinction between this case and one involving a confession that is coerced by torture is wholly unpersuasive.[3] Certainly, in respondent's case, the causal connection between any psychological disadvantage created by his admission and his ultimate decision to cooperate is speculative and attenuated at best. It is difficult to tell with certainty what motivates a suspect to speak. * * * We must conclude that, absent deliberately coercive or improper tactics in obtaining the initial statement, the mere fact that a suspect has made an unwarned admission does not warrant a presumption of compulsion. A subsequent administration of *Miranda* warnings to a suspect who has given a voluntary but unwarned statement ordinarily should suffice to remove the conditions that precluded admission of the earlier statement. In such circumstances, the finder of fact may reasonably conclude that the suspect made a rational and intelligent choice whether to waive or invoke his rights.

Though belated, the reading of respondent's rights was undeniably complete. [There] is no question that respondent knowingly and voluntarily waived his right to remain silent before he described his participation in the burglary. It is also beyond dispute that respondent's earlier remark was voluntary, within the meaning of the Fifth Amendment. Neither the environment nor the manner of either "interrogation" was coercive. The initial conversation took place at midday, in the living room area of respondent's own home, with his mother in the kitchen area, a few steps away. Although in retrospect the officers testified that respondent was then in custody, at the time he made his statement he had not been informed that he was under arrest. The arresting officers' testimony indicates that the brief stop in the living room before proceeding to the station

**3.** Most of the 50 cases cited by Justice Brennan in his discussion of consecutive confessions concern an initial unwarned statement obtained through overtly or inherently coercive methods which raise serious Fifth Amendment and Due Process concerns [discussing many cases].

Justice Brennan cannot seriously mean to equate such situations with the case at bar.

Likewise inapposite are the cases the dissent cites concerning suspects whose invocation of their rights to remain silent and to have counsel present were flatly ignored while police subjected them to continued interrogation. * * *

house was not to interrogate the suspect but to notify his mother of the reason for his arrest.

The state has conceded the issue of custody and thus we must assume that Burke breached *Miranda* procedures in failing to administer *Miranda* warnings before initiating the discussion in the living room. [But] the incident had none of the earmarks of coercion. Nor did the officers exploit the unwarned admission to pressure respondent into waiving his right to remain silent.

Respondent, however, has argued that he was unable to give a fully *informed* waiver of his rights because he was unaware that his prior statement could not be used against him. Respondent suggests that Deputy McAllister, to cure this deficiency, should have added an additional warning to those given him at the Sheriff's office. Such a requirement is neither practicable nor constitutionally necessary. In many cases, a breach of *Miranda* procedures may not be identified as such until long after full *Miranda* warnings are administered and a valid confession obtained. The standard *Miranda* warnings explicitly inform the suspect of his right to consult a lawyer before speaking. Police officers are ill equipped to pinch-hit for counsel, construing the murky and difficult questions of when "custody" begins or whether a given unwarned statement will ultimately be held admissible.

When police ask questions of a suspect in custody without administering the required warnings, *Miranda* dictates that the answers received be presumed compelled and that they be excluded from evidence at trial in the State's case in chief. The Court has carefully adhered to this principle, permitting a narrow exception only where pressing public safety concerns demanded. See *Quarles*. The Court today in no way retreats from the bright line rule of *Miranda*. [But] where the suspect's initial inculpatory statement, though technically in violation of *Miranda,* was voluntary, [the] relevant inquiry is whether, in fact, the second statement was also voluntarily made. As in any such inquiry, the finder of fact must examine the surrounding circumstances and the entire course of police conduct with respect to the suspect in evaluating the voluntariness of his statements. The fact that a suspect chooses to speak after being informed of his rights is, of course, highly probative. We find that the dictates of *Miranda* and the goals of the Fifth Amendment proscription against use of compelled testimony are fully satisfied in the circumstances of this case by barring use of the unwarned statement in the case in chief. No further purpose is served by imputing "taint" to subsequent statements obtained pursuant to a voluntary and knowing waiver. We hold today that a suspect who has once responded to unwarned yet uncoercive questioning is not thereby disabled from waiving his rights and confessing after he has been given the requisite *Miranda* warnings.

\* \* \*

JUSTICE BRENNAN, with whom JUSTICE MARSHALL joins, dissenting.

\* \* \* [Today's decision] delivers a potentially crippling blow to *Miranda* and the ability of courts to safeguard the rights of persons accused of crime. For at least with respect to successive confessions, the Court today appears to strip remedies for *Miranda* violations of the "fruit of the poisonous tree" doctrine prohibiting the use of evidence presumptively derived from official illegality.[2]

Two major premises undergird the Court's decision. The Court rejects as nothing more than "speculative" the long-recognized presumption that an ille-

---

**2.** The Court repeatedly casts its analysis in terms of the "fruits" of a *Miranda* violation, but its dicta nevertheless surely should not be read as necessarily foreclosing applica-tion of derivative-evidence rules where the *Miranda* violation produces evidence other than a subsequent confession by the accused. See n. 29, infra.

gally extracted confession causes the accused to confess again out of the mistaken belief that he already has sealed his fate, and it condemns as " 'extravagant' " the requirement that the prosecution affirmatively rebut the presumption before the subsequent confession may be admitted.  The Court instead adopts a new rule that, so long as the accused is given the usual *Miranda* warnings before further interrogation, the taint of a previous confession obtained in violation of *Miranda* "ordinarily" must be viewed as *automatically* dissipated.

In the alternative, the Court asserts that neither the Fifth Amendment itself nor the judicial policy of deterring illegal police conduct requires the suppression of the "fruits" of a confession obtained in violation of *Miranda,* reasoning that to do otherwise would interfere with "legitimate law enforcement activity."  As the Court surely understands, however, "[t]o forbid the direct use of methods [but] to put no curb on their full indirect use would only invite the very methods deemed 'inconsistent with ethical standards and destructive of personal liberty.' "  *Nardone.*  *  *  *

The threshold question is this:  What effect should an admission or confession of guilt obtained in violation of an accused's *Miranda* rights be presumed to have upon the voluntariness of subsequent confessions that are preceded by *Miranda* warnings?  *  *  *

This Court has had long experience with the problem of confessions obtained after an earlier confession has been illegally secured.  Subsequent confessions in these circumstances are not *per se* inadmissible, but the prosecution must demonstrate facts "sufficient to insulate the [subsequent] statement from the effect of all that went before."  *Clewis v. Texas,* 386 U.S. 707 (1967).  [The] question in each case is whether the accused's will was "overborne at the time he confessed," and the prosecution must demonstrate that the second confession "was an act independent of the [earlier] confession."  *Reck v. Pate,* 367 U.S. 433 (1961).

*  *  * Although we have thus rejected a *per se* rule forbidding the introduction of subsequent statements in these circumstances, we have emphasized that the psychological impact of admissions and confessions of criminal guilt nevertheless can have a decisive impact in undermining the voluntariness of a suspect's responses to continued police interrogation and must be accounted for in determining their admissibility.  *  *  *

Our precedents did not develop in a vacuum.  They reflect an understanding of the realities of police interrogation *  *  *.  Standard interrogation manuals advise that "[t]he securing of the first admission is the biggest stumbling block."  A. Aubry & R. Caputo, *Criminal Interrogation* 290 (3d ed. 1980).  If this first admission can be obtained, "there is every reason to expect that the first admission will lead to others and eventually to the full confession."  *  *  *

Interrogators describe the point of the first admission as the "breakthrough" and the "beachhead," R. Royal & S. Schutt, *The Gentle Art of Interviewing and Interrogation* 143 (1976), which once obtained will give them enormous "tactical advantages," F. Inbau & J. Reid, *Criminal Interrogation and Confessions* 82 (2d ed. 1967).  Thus "[t]he securing of incriminating admissions might well be considered as the beginning of the final stages in crumbling the defenses of the suspect," and the process of obtaining such admissions is described as "the spadework required to motivate the subject into making the full confession."  Aubry & Caputo, supra.

*  *  * Expert interrogators and experienced lower-court judges will be startled, to say the least, to learn that the connection between multiple confes-

sions is "speculative" and that a subsequent rendition of *Miranda* warnings "ordinarily" enables the accused in these circumstances to exercise his "free will" and to make "a rational and intelligent choice whether to waive or invoke his rights." * * *

* * * Where an accused believes that it is futile to resist because the authorities already have elicited an admission of guilt, the mere rendition of *Miranda* warnings does not convey the information most critical at that point to ensuring his informed and voluntary decision to speak again: that the earlier confession may not be admissible and thus that he need not speak out of any feeling that he already has sealed his fate. The Court therefore is flatly wrong in arguing, as it does repeatedly, that the mere provision of *Miranda* warnings prior to subsequent interrogation supplies the accused with "the relevant information" and ensures that a subsequent confession "ordinarily" will be the product of "a rational and intelligent choice" and "an act of free will."

The Court's new approach is therefore completely at odds with established dissipation analysis. A comparison of the Court's analysis with the factors most frequently relied on by lower courts in considering the admissibility of subsequent confessions demonstrates the practical and legal flaws of the new rule.

*Advice that earlier confession may be inadmissible.* The most effective means to ensure the voluntariness of an accused's subsequent confession is to advise the accused that his earlier admissions may not be admissible and therefore that he need not speak solely out of a belief that "the cat is out of the bag." Many courts have required such warnings in the absence of other dissipating factors, and this Court has not uncovered anything to suggest that this approach has not succeeded in the real world. The Court, however, believes that law enforcement authorities could never possibly understand "the murky and difficult question" of when *Miranda* warnings must be given, and therefore that they are "ill equipped" to make the decision whether supplementary warnings might be required.

This reasoning is unpersuasive for two reasons. First, the whole point of *Miranda* and its progeny has been to prescribe "bright line" rules for the authorities to follow. * * * Second, even where the authorities are not certain that an earlier confession has been illegally obtained, courts and commentators have recognized that a supplementary warning merely advising the accused that his earlier confession *may* be inadmissible can dispel his belief that he has nothing to lose by repetition.

*Proximity in time and place.* Courts have frequently concluded that a subsequent confession was so removed in time and place from the first that the accused most likely was able fully to exercise his independent judgment in deciding whether to speak again. As in the instant case, however, a second confession frequently follows immediately on the heels of the first and is obtained by the same officials in the same or similar coercive surroundings. In such situations, it is wholly unreasonable to assume that the mere rendition of *Miranda* warnings will safeguard the accused's freedom of action. * * *

*Intervening factors.* Some lower courts have found that because of intervening factors—such as consultation with a lawyer or family members, or an independent decision to speak—an accused's subsequent confession could not fairly be attributed to the earlier statement taken in violation of *Miranda*. On the other hand, where as here an accused has continuously been in custody and there is no legitimate suggestion of an intervening event sufficient to break the impact of the first confession, subsequent confessions are inadmissible. The Court reasons, however, that because "[a] suspect's confession *may* be traced [to] an intervening event," it "*must* [be] conclude[d]" that subsequent *Miranda* warnings presumptively enable the suspect to make "a rational and intelligent choice" whether to repeat his confession (emphasis added). [The] only proper inquiry is whether a meaningful intervening event *actually* occurred, not whether a court simply chooses to shut its eyes to human nature and the realities of custodial interrogation.

[The Court's] analysis is wholly at odds with established dissipation analysis. To begin with, the Court repeatedly suggests that a confession may be suppressed only if the police have used "improper tactics"; this obscure reasoning overlooks the fact that a violation of *Miranda* is obviously *itself* an "improper tactic," one frequently used precisely to undermine the voluntariness of subsequent confessions. The Court's negative implication that *Miranda* violations are *not* "improper tactics" is, to say the least, disquieting. Second, the Court reasons that the fact that the accused gave a subsequent confession is *itself* "highly probative" evidence that he was able to exercise his free will. This inaccurate premise follows from the Court's erroneous rejection of the "cat out of the bag" presumption in these circumstances and its inexplicable assertion that the previous extraction of a "guilty secret" neither constitutes compulsion nor compromises the voluntariness of later confessions. Finally, the foundation of the derivative-evidence doctrine has always been that, where the authorities have acted illegally, *they* must bear the "ultimate burden" of proving that their misconduct did not "taint" subsequently obtained evidence. That is precisely the point of the derivative-evidence presumption. By rejecting this presumption in *Miranda* cases, the Court today appears to adopt a "go ahead and try to prove it" posture toward citizens whose Fifth Amendment *Miranda* rights have been violated, an attitude that marks a sharp break from the Court's traditional approach to official lawlessness. * * *

In sum, today's opinion marks an evisceration of the established fruit of the poisonous tree doctrine, but its reasoning is sufficiently obscure and qualified as to leave state and federal courts with continued authority to combat obvious flouting by the authorities of the privilege against self-incrimination. I am confident that lower courts will exercise this authority responsibly, as they have for the most part prior to this Court's intervention.

Not content merely to ignore the practical realities of police interrogation and the likely effects of its abolition of the derivative-evidence presumption, the Court goes on to assert that nothing in the Fifth Amendment or the general judicial policy of deterring illegal police conduct "ordinarily" requires the suppression of evidence derived proximately from a confession obtained in violation of *Miranda*. The Court does not limit its analysis to successive confessions, but recurrently refers generally to the "fruits" of the illegal confession. Thus the potential impact of the Court's reasoning might extend far beyond the "cat out of the bag" context to include the discovery of physical evidence and other derivative fruits of *Miranda* violations as well.[29]

**29.** Notwithstanding the sweep of the Court's language, today's opinion surely ought not be read as also foreclosing application of the traditional derivative-evidence presumption to physical evidence obtained as a proximate result of a *Miranda* violation. The Court relies heavily on individual "volition" as an insulating factor in successive-confession cases. Although the Court's reliance on this factor is clearly misplaced, the factor is altogether missing in the context of inanimate evidence.

As they have in successive-confession cases, most courts considering the issue have recognized that physical evidence proximately derived from a *Miranda* violation is presumptively inadmissible. * * *

Twice in the last ten years, [first in *Tucker,* then in *Quarles,* the] Court has suggested that the *Miranda* safeguards are not themselves rights guaranteed by the Fifth Amendment. [The assertions in these cases] are erroneous. *Miranda's* requirement of warnings and an effective waiver was not merely an exercise of supervisory authority over interrogation practices. * * * *Miranda* clearly emphasized that warnings and an informed waiver are essential to the Fifth Amendment privilege itself. [The] Court in *Tucker* omitted to mention that in *Miranda,* after concluding that no "particular solution" is required, we went on to emphasize that "unless we are shown other procedures which are at least as effective in apprising accused persons of their right of silence and in assuring a continuous opportunity to exercise it, the [prescribed] safeguards must be observed." Thus "the use of [any] admissions obtained in the absence of the required warnings [is] a flat violation of the Self–Incrimination Clause of the Fifth Amendment * * *." *Orozco.*

The Court today finally recognizes these flaws in the logic of *Tucker* and *Quarles.* Although disastrous in so many other respects, today's opinion at least has the virtue of rejecting the inaccurate assertion in *Quarles* that confessions extracted in violation of *Miranda* are not presumptively coerced for Fifth Amendment purposes. Instead, the Court holds squarely that there is an "irrebuttable" presumption that such confessions are indeed coerced and are therefore inadmissible under the Fifth Amendment except in narrow circumstances.

Unfortunately, the Court takes away with one hand far more than what it has given with the other. Although the Court concedes, as it must, that a confession obtained in violation of *Miranda* is irrebuttably presumed to be coerced and that the Self–Incrimination Clause therefore prevents its use in the prosecution's case-in-chief, the Court goes on to hold that nothing in the Fifth Amendment prevents the introduction at trial of evidence proximately derived from the illegal confession. It contends, for example, that the Fifth Amendment prohibits introduction "only" of the "compelled testimony," and that this constitutional guarantee "is not concerned with nontestimonial evidence."

This narrow compass of the protection against compelled self-incrimination does not accord with our historic understanding of the Fifth Amendment. Although the Self–Incrimination Clause "protects an accused only from being compelled to testify against himself, or otherwise provide the State with evidence of a testimonial or communicative nature," *Schmerber,* it prohibits the use of such communications "against" the accused in any way. The Fifth Amendment therefore contains a self-executing rule commanding the exclusion of evidence derived from such communications. It bars "the use of compelled testimony, as well as evidence derived directly and indirectly therefrom," and "prohibits the prosecutorial authorities from using the compelled testimony in *any* respect." *Kastigar v. United States* (emphasis in original) [Ch. 8, § 2]. If a coerced statement leads to "sources of information which may supply other means of convicting" the accused, those sources must also be suppressed. *Counselman v. Hitchcock* [Ch. 8, § 2]. Under this constitutional exclusionary rule, the authorities are thus "prohibited from making any * * * use of compelled testimony *and its fruits* [in] connection with a criminal prosecution against" the accused. *Murphy v. Waterfront Comm'n* (emphasis added) [Ch. 8, § 2]. * * *

Even if I accepted the Court's conclusion that the Fifth Amendment does not command the suppression of evidence proximately derived from a *Miranda* violation, I would nevertheless dissent from the Court's refusal to recognize the importance of deterring *Miranda* violations in appropriate circumstances.

[The] Court today refuses to apply the derivative-evidence rule even to the extent necessary to deter objectively unreasonable failures by the authorities to honor a suspect's *Miranda* rights. Incredibly, faced with an obvious violation of *Miranda,* the Court asserts that it will not countenance suppression of a subsequent confession in such circumstances where the authorities have acted "legitimate[ly]" and have not used "improper tactics." One can only respond: whither went *Miranda?*

* * * How can the Court possibly expect the authorities to obey *Miranda* when they have every incentive now to interrogate suspects without warnings or an effective waiver, knowing that the fruits of such interrogations "ordinarily" will be admitted, that an admissible subsequent confession "ordinarily" can be obtained simply by reciting the *Miranda* warnings shortly after the first has been procured and asking the accused to repeat himself, and that unless the accused can demonstrate otherwise his confession will be viewed as an "act of free will" in response to "legitimate law enforcement activity"? By condoning such a result, the Court today encourages practices that threaten to reduce *Miranda* to a mere "form of words," and it is shocking that the Court nevertheless disingenuously purports that it "in no way retreats" from the *Miranda* safeguards. * * *

JUSTICE STEVENS dissenting.

* * * I find nothing objectionable in [the Court's] holding. Moreover, [because] the Court places so much emphasis on the special facts of this case, I am persuaded that the Court intends its holding to apply only to a narrow category of cases in which the initial questioning of the suspect was made in a totally uncoercive setting and in which the first confession obviously had no influence on the second. I nevertheless dissent because even such a narrowly confined exception is inconsistent with the Court's prior cases, because the attempt to identify its boundaries in future cases will breed confusion and uncertainty in the administration of criminal justice, and because it denigrates the importance of one of the core constitutional rights that protects every American citizen from the kind of tyranny that has flourished in other societies.

The desire to achieve a just result in this particular case has produced an opinion that is somewhat opaque and internally inconsistent. If I read it correctly, its conclusion rests on two untenable premises: (1) that the respondent's first confession was not the product of coercion; and (2) that no constitutional right was violated when respondent was questioned in a tranquil, domestic setting.

Even before the decision in *Miranda,* it had been recognized that police interrogation of a suspect who has been taken into custody is presumptively coercive. That presumption had its greatest force when the questioning occurred in a police station, when it was prolonged, and when there was evidence that the prisoner had suffered physical injury. * * *

[*Miranda* ] clarified the law in three important respects. First, it provided the prosecutor with a simple method of overcoming the presumption of coercion. If the police interrogation is preceded by the warning specified in that opinion, the usual presumption does not attach. Second, it provided an important protection to the accused by making the presumption of coercion irrebuttable if the prescribed warnings are not given. Third, the decision made it clear that a self-incriminatory statement made in response to custodial interrogation was always to be considered "compelled" within the meaning of the Fifth Amendment to the Federal Constitution if the interrogation had not been preceded by appropriate warnings. Thus the irrebuttable presumption of coercion that applies to such a self-incriminatory statement, like a finding of actual coercion, renders the resulting confession inadmissible as a matter of federal constitutional law.[9]

In my opinion, the Court's attempt to fashion a distinction between actual coercion "by physical violence or other deliberate means calculated to break the suspect's will" and irrebuttably presumed coercion cannot succeed. The presumption is only legitimate if it is assumed that there is always a coercive aspect to custodial interrogation that is not preceded by adequate advice of the constitutional right to remain silent. Although I would not support it, I could understand a rule that refused to apply the presumption unless the interrogation took place in an especially coercive setting—perhaps only in the police station itself—but if the presumption arises whenever the accused has been taken into custody or his freedom has been restrained in any significant way, it will surely be futile to try to develop subcategories of custodial interrogation. Indeed, a major purpose of treating the presumption of coercion as irrebuttable is to avoid the kind of fact-bound inquiry that today's decision will surely engender.

\* \* \* [S]urely the fact that an earlier confession was obtained by unlawful methods should add force to the presumption of coercion that attaches to subsequent custodial interrogation and should require the prosecutor to shoulder a heavier burden of rebuttal than in a routine case. Simple logic, as well as the interest in not providing an affirmative incentive to police misconduct, requires that result. I see no reason why the violation of a rule that is as well recognized and easily administered as the duty to give *Miranda* warnings should not also impose an additional burden on the prosecutor.[13] If we are faithful to the holding in *Miranda* itself, when we are considering the admissibility of evidence in the prosecutor's case-in-chief, we should not try to fashion a distinction between police misconduct that warrants a finding of actual coercion and police misconduct that establishes an irrebuttable presumption of coercion.

For me, the most disturbing aspect of the Court's opinion is its somewhat opaque characterization of the police misconduct in this case. The Court appears ambivalent on the question whether there was any constitutional violation.[14] This ambivalence is either disingenuous or completely lawless. This Court's power to require state courts to exclude probative self-incriminatory statements rests entirely on the premise that the use of such evidence violates the Federal Constitution.[15] The same constitutional analysis applies whether

**9.** \* \* \* Obviously, the Court's power to reverse Miranda's conviction rested entirely on the determination that a violation of the Federal Constitution had occurred.

The constitutional violation was established without any evidence that the police actually coerced Miranda in any way. The fact that Miranda had confessed while he was in custody and without having been adequately advised of his right to remain silent was sufficient to establish the constitutional violation. To phrase it another way, the absence of an adequate warning plus the fact of custody created an irrebuttable presumption of coercion. \* \* \*

**13.** In view of the Court's holding, it is not necessary to consider how that additional burden should be discharged in all cases. In general, however, I should think that before the second session of custodial interrogation begins, the prisoner should be advised that his

earlier statement is, or may be, inadmissible. I am not persuaded that the *Miranda* rule is so "murky" that the law-enforcement profession would be unable to identify the cases in which a supplementary warning would be appropriate. *Miranda* was written, in part, "to give concrete constitutional guidelines for law enforcement agencies and courts to follow." \* \* \* Nearly two decades after that disposition, it is undisputed that the *Miranda* rule—now so deeply embedded in our culture that most schoolchildren know not only the warnings, but also when they are required—has given that clarity. \* \* \*

**14.** \* \* \* Indeed, the Court's holding rests on its view that there were no "improper tactics in obtaining the initial statement."

**15.** At least that is my view. In response to this dissent, however, the Court has added a fn. 1, implying that whenever the Court commands exclusion of a presumptively co-the custodial interrogation is actually coercive or irrebuttably presumed to be coercive. If the Court does not accept that premise, it must regard the holding in the *Miranda* case itself, as well as all of the Federal jurisprudence that has evolved from that decision, as nothing more than an illegitimate exercise of raw judicial power.  *  *  *

### 6. May the "impeachment exception" to the exclusionary rule be expanded to permit the prosecution to impeach all *defense witnesses* with illegally seized evidence?

### JAMES v. ILLINOIS *
___ U.S. ___, 110 S.Ct. 648, 107 L.Ed.2d 676 (1990).

JUSTICE BRENNAN delivered the opinion of the Court.

[A day after a shooting occurred, which left one of a group of eight boys dead, the police took James, a suspect, into custody. He was found at his mother's beauty salon sitting under a hair dryer; when he emerged, his hair was black and curly. When the police questioned James about his prior hair color, he told them it had been reddish-brown, long, and combed straight back. When questioned later at the police station, James stated that he had his hair dyed black and curled at the beauty parlor in order to change his appearance. Because the police lacked probable cause for James' arrest, both statements regarding his hair were suppressed.

[At the trial, five eye witnesses testified that the person responsible for slaying the boy had long, "reddish" hair, worn in a slicked-back style and that they had seen James several weeks earlier, at which time he had the aforementioned hair color and style. James did not testify in his own defense. He called as a witness Jewel Henderson, a family friend. She testified that on the day of the shooting James' hair had been black. The state then was permitted to impeach Henderson's testimony by reporting James' prior admissions that he had reddish hair at the time of the shooting and had dyed and curled his hair the next day in order to change his appearance. James ultimately was convicted of murder.

[The Illinois Supreme Court affirmed the conviction, reasoning that, in order to deter "perjury by proxy," the impeachment exception ought to allow the state to impeach the testimony of defense witnesses other than the defendant himself.]

[T]he Illinois Supreme Court held that [the balancing approach this Court has used in earlier impeachment cases] justifies expanding the scope of the impeachment exception to permit prosecutors to use illegally obtained evidence to impeach the credibility of defense witnesses. We disagree. Expanding the class of impeachable witnesses from the defendant alone to all defense witnesses would create different incentives affecting the behavior of both defendants and law enforcement officers. As a result, this expansion would not promote the truthseeking function to the same extent as did creation of the original exception, and yet it would significantly undermine the deterrent effect of the general exclusionary rule. Hence, we believe that this proposed expansion would frustrate rather than further the purposes underlying the exclusionary rule.
*  *  *

erced confession, it is standing—not on a constitutional predicate—but merely on its own shoulders.

  * Although this case deals with the prosecutor's attempt to use evidence obtained in viola-
tion of the Fourth Amendment for impeachment purposes, it appears in the *Miranda* chapter, for it is clear that the reasoning of the Court applies as well to statements obtained in violation of *Miranda*.

The previously recognized exception penalizes defendants for committing perjury by allowing the prosecution to expose their perjury through impeachment using illegally obtained evidence. Thus defendants are discouraged in the first instance from "affirmatively resort[ing] to perjurious testimony." But the exception leaves defendants free to testify truthfully on their own behalf; they can offer probative and exculpatory evidence to the jury without opening the door to impeachment by carefully avoiding any statements that directly contradict the suppressed evidence. The exception thus generally discourages perjured testimony without discouraging truthful testimony.

In contrast, expanding the impeachment exception to encompass the testimony of all defense witnesses would not have the same beneficial effects. First, the mere threat of a subsequent criminal prosecution for perjury is far more likely to deter a witness from intentionally lying on a defendant's behalf than to deter a defendant, already facing conviction for the underlying offense, from lying on his own behalf. Hence the Illinois Supreme Court's underlying premise that a defendant frustrated by our previous impeachment exception can easily find a witness to engage in "perjury by proxy" is suspect.[4]

More significantly, expanding the impeachment exception to encompass the testimony of all defense witnesses likely would chill some defendants from presenting their best defense—and sometimes any defense at all—through the testimony of others. Whenever police obtained evidence illegally, defendants would have to assess prior to trial the likelihood that the evidence would be admitted to impeach the otherwise favorable testimony of any witness they call. Defendants might reasonably fear that one or more of their witnesses, in a position to offer truthful and favorable testimony, would also make some statement in sufficient tension with the tainted evidence to allow the prosecutor to introduce that evidence for impeachment. First, defendants sometimes need to call "reluctant" or "hostile" witnesses to provide reliable and probative exculpatory testimony, and such witnesses likely will not share the defendants' concern for avoiding statements that invite impeachment through contradictory evidence. Moreover, defendants often cannot trust even "friendly" witnesses to testify without subjecting themselves to impeachment, simply due to insufficient care or attentiveness. This concern is magnified in those occasional situations when defendants must call witnesses to testify despite having had only a limited opportunity to consult with or prepare them in advance. For these reasons, we have recognized in a variety of contexts that a party "cannot be absolutely certain that his witnesses will testify as expected." As a result, an expanded impeachment exception likely would chill some defendants from calling witnesses who would otherwise offer probative evidence.

This realization alters the balance of values underlying the current impeachment exception governing defendants' testimony. Our prior cases make clear that defendants ought not to be able to "pervert" the exclusion of illegally obtained evidence into a shield for perjury, but it seems no more appropriate for the State to brandish such evidence as a sword with which to dissuade defendants from presenting a meaningful defense through other witnesses. Given the potential chill created by expanding the impeachment exception, the conceded gains to the truthseeking process from discouraging or disclosing perjured testimony would be offset to some extent by the concomitant loss of probative

---

4. The dissent concedes, as it must, that "of course, false testimony can result from faulty recollection" as opposed to intentional lying. Even assuming that Henderson's testimony in this case (as opposed to the detective's contrary testimony) was indeed false, nothing in the record suggests that Henderson intentionally committed perjury rather than honestly provided her best (even if erroneous) perception and recollection of events.

witness testimony. Thus, the truthseeking rationale supporting the impeachment of defendants in *Walder* and its progeny does not apply to other witnesses with equal force.[a]

Moreover, the proposed expansion of the current impeachment exception would significantly weaken the exclusionary rule's deterrent effect on police misconduct. This Court has characterized as a mere "speculative possibility," *Harris v. New York*,[b] the likelihood that permitting prosecutors to impeach defendants with illegally obtained evidence would encourage police misconduct. Law enforcement officers will think it unlikely that the defendant will first decide to testify at trial and will also open the door inadvertently to admission of any illegally obtained evidence. Hence, the officers' incentive to acquire evidence through illegal means is quite weak.

In contrast, expanding the impeachment exception to *all* defense witnesses would significantly enhance the expected value to the prosecution of illegally obtained evidence. First, this expansion would vastly increase the number of occasions on which such evidence could be used. Defense witnesses easily outnumber testifying defendants, both because many defendants do not testify themselves and because many if not most defendants call multiple witnesses on their behalf. Moreover, due to the chilling effect identified above, illegally obtained evidence holds even greater value to the prosecution for each individual witness than for each defendant. The prosecutor's access to impeachment evidence would not just deter perjury; it would also deter defendants from calling witnesses in the first place, thereby keeping from the jury much probative exculpatory evidence. For both of these reasons, police officers and their superiors would recognize that obtaining evidence through illegal means stacks the deck heavily in the prosecution's favor. It is thus far more than a "speculative possibility" that police misconduct will be encouraged by permitting such use of illegally obtained evidence.

The United States argues that this result is constitutionally acceptable because excluding illegally obtained evidence solely from the prosecution's case in chief would still provide a quantum of deterrence sufficient to protect the privacy interests underlying the exclusionary rule. We disagree. Of course, a police officer might in certain situations believe that obtaining particular evidence through illegal means, resulting in its suppression from the case in chief, would prevent the prosecution from establishing a prima facie case to take to a jury. In such situations, the officer likely would be deterred from obtaining the evidence illegally for fear of jeopardizing the entire case. But much if not most of the time, police officers confront opportunities to obtain evidence illegally after they have already legally obtained (or know that they have other means of legally obtaining) sufficient evidence to sustain a prima facie case. In these situations, a rule requiring exclusion of illegally obtained evidence from only the government's case in chief would leave officers with little to lose and much to gain by overstepping constitutional limits on evidence gathering.[8] Narrowing

---

a. In *Walder v. United States*, 347 U.S. 62 (1954), defendant, charged with various legal narcotics transactions, asserted early on his direct examination that he had never possessed any narcotics or sold or given any narcotics to anyone in his life. The Court held that this assertion "opened the door," for purposes of attacking the defendant's credibility, to evidence of heroin seized from the defendant's home, in his presence, in an earlier, unrelated case.

b. *Harris* is discussed in the Introduction to this Section.

8. Indeed, the detectives who unlawfully detained James and elicited his incriminating statements already knew that there were several eyewitnesses to the shooting. Because the detectives likely believed that the exclusion of any statement they obtained from James probably would not have precluded the prosecution from making a prima facie case, an exclusionary rule applicable only to the

the exclusionary rule in this manner, therefore, would significantly undermine the rule's ability "to compel respect for the constitutional guaranty in the only effectively available way—by removing the incentive to disregard it." So long as we are committed to protecting the people from the disregard of their constitutional rights during the course of criminal investigations, inadmissibility of illegally obtained evidence must remain the rule, not the exception.

The cost to the truthseeking process of evidentiary exclusion invariably is perceived more tangibly in discrete prosecutions than is the protection of privacy values through deterrence of future police misconduct. When defining the precise scope of the exclusionary rule, however, we must focus on systemic effects of proposed exceptions to ensure that individual liberty from arbitrary or oppressive police conduct does not succumb to the inexorable pressure to introduce all incriminating evidence, no matter how obtained, in each and every criminal case. Our previous recognition of an impeachment exception limited to the testimony of defendants reflects a careful weighing of the competing values. Because expanding the exception to encompass the testimony of all defense witnesses would not further the truthseeking value with equal force but would appreciably undermine the deterrent effect of the exclusionary rule, we adhere to the line drawn in our previous cases. * * *[c]

JUSTICE KENNEDY, with whom THE CHIEF JUSTICE, JUSTICE O'CONNOR, and JUSTICE SCALIA join, dissenting.

To deprive the prosecution of probative evidence acquired in violation of the law may be a tolerable and necessary cost of the exclusionary rule. Implementation of the rule requires us to draw certain lines to effect its purpose of deterring unlawful conduct. But the line drawn by today's opinion grants the defense side in a criminal case broad immunity to introduce whatever false testimony it can produce from the mouth of a friendly witness. Unless petitioner's conviction is reversed, we are told, police would flout the Fourth Amendment, and as a result, the accused would be unable to offer any defense. This exaggerated view leads to a drastic remedy: The jury cannot learn that defense testimony is inconsistent with probative evidence of undoubted value. A more cautious course is available, one that retains Fourth Amendment protections and yet safeguards the truth-seeking function of the criminal trial. * * *

I agree with the majority that the resolution of this case depends on a balance of values that informs our exclusionary rule jurisprudence. We weigh the " 'likelihood [of] deterrence against the costs of withholding reliable information from the truth-seeking process.' " The majority adopts a sweeping rule that the testimony of witnesses other than the defendant may never be rebutted with excludable evidence. I cannot draw the line where the majority does.

The interest in protecting the truth-seeking function of the criminal trial is every bit as strong in this case as in our earlier cases that allowed rebuttal with evidence that was inadmissible as part of the prosecution's case in chief. Here a witness who knew the accused well took the stand to testify about the accused's personal appearance. The testimony could be expected to create real doubt in the mind of jurors concerning the eyewitness identifications by persons who did not know the accused. To deprive the jurors of knowledge that statements of the defendant himself revealed the witness' testimony to be false would result in a decision by triers of fact who were not just kept in the dark as to excluded evidence, but positively misled. The potential for harm to the truth-seeking process resulting from the majority's new rule in fact will be greater than if the

prosecution's case in chief likely would have provided little deterrent effect in this case.

c. Stevens, J., who joined the opinion of the Court, also wrote a separate opinion.

defendant himself had testified. It is natural for jurors to be skeptical of self-serving testimony by the defendant. Testimony by a witness said to be independent has the greater potential to deceive. And if a defense witness can present false testimony with impunity, the jurors may find the rest of the prosecution's case suspect, for ineffective and artificial cross-examination will be viewed as a real weakness in the State's case. Jurors will assume that if the prosecution had any proof the statement was false, it would make the proof known. The majority does more than deprive the prosecution of evidence. The State must also suffer the introduction of false testimony and appear to bolster the falsehood by its own silence.

The majority's fear that allowing the jury to know the whole truth will chill defendants from putting on any defense seems to me far too speculative to justify the rule here announced. No restriction on the defense results if rebuttal of testimony by witnesses other than the defendant is confined to the introduction of excludable evidence that is in direct contradiction of the testimony. If mere "tension with the tainted evidence" opened the door to introduction of *all* the evidence subject to suppression, then the majority's fears might be justified. But in this context rebuttal can and should be confined to situations where there is direct conflict, which is to say where, within reason, the witness' testimony and the excluded testimony cannot both be true.

Also missing from the majority's analysis is the almost certain knowledge that the testimony immunized from rebuttal is false. The majority's apparent assumption that defense witnesses protected by today's rule have only truth-telling in mind strikes me as far too sanguine to support acceptance of a rule that controls the hard reality of contested criminal trials. The majority expresses the common sense of the matter in saying that presentation of excluded evidence must sometimes be allowed because it "penalizes defendants for committing perjury."

In some cases, of course, false testimony can result from faulty recollection. But the majority's ironclad rule is one that applies regardless of the witness' motives, and may be misused as a license to perjure. Even if the witness testifies in good faith, the defendant and his lawyer, who offer the testimony, know the facts. Indeed, it is difficult here to imagine the defense attorney's reason for asking Henderson about petitioner's hair color if he did not expect her to cast doubt on the eyewitness identification of petitioner by giving a description of petitioner's hair color contrary to that contained in his own (suppressed) statement.

The suggestion that the threat of a perjury prosecution will provide sufficient deterrence to prevent false testimony is not realistic. A heightened proof requirement applies in Illinois and other States, making perjury convictions difficult to sustain. Where testimony presented on behalf of a friend or family member is involved, the threat that a future jury will convict the witness may be an idle one.

The damage to the truthseeking process caused by the majority's rule is certain to be great whether the testimony is perjured or merely false. In this case there can be little doubt of the falsity, since petitioner's description of his own hair was at issue. And as a general matter the alternative to rebuttal is endorsement of judicial proceedings conducted in reliance on information known to be untrue. Suppressed evidence is likely to consist of either voluntary statements by the defendant himself or physical evidence. Both have a high degree of reliability, and testimony in direct conflict to such evidence most often will represent an attempt to place falsehoods before the jury.

The suggestion that all this is so far beyond the control of the defendant that he will put on no defense is not supported. As to sympathetic witnesses, such as the family friend here, it should not be too hard to assure the witness does not volunteer testimony in contradiction of the facts. The defendant knows the content of the suppressed evidence. Even in cases where the time for consultation is limited, the defense attorney can take care not to elicit contradicting testimony. And in the case of truly neutral witnesses, or witnesses hostile to the accused, it is hard to see the danger that they will present false testimony for the benefit of the defense.

The majority's concerns may carry greater weight where contradicting testimony is elicited from a defense witness on cross-examination. In that situation there might be a concern that the prosecution would attempt to produce such testimony as the foundation to put excluded evidence before the jury. We have found that possibility insufficient to justify immunity for a defendant's own false testimony on cross-examination. *United States v. Havens*, 446 U.S. 620 (1980).[d] As to cross-examination of other witnesses, perhaps a different rule could be justified. Rather than wait for an appropriate case to consider this or similar measures, however, the majority opts for a wooden rule immunizing all defense testimony from rebuttal, without regard to knowledge that the testimony introduced at the behest of the defendant is false or perjured.

I also cannot agree that admission of excluded evidence on rebuttal would lead to the "disregard [of] constitutional rights" by law enforcement officers that the majority fears. This argument has been raised in our previous cases in this area of the law. To date we have rejected it. Now the spectre appears premised on an assumption that a single slip of the tongue by any defense witness will open the door to any suppressed evidence at the prosecutor's disposal. If this were so, the majority's concern that officers would be left with little to lose from conducting an illegal search would be understandable. And the argument might hold more force if, as the majority speculates, police confront the temptation to seize evidence illegally "much if not most of the time" after gathering sufficient evidence to present proof of guilt beyond a reasonable doubt in the case in chief. Again, however, I disagree with the predictions.

It is unrealistic to say that the decision to make an illegal search turns on a precise calculation of the possibilities of rebuttal at some future trial. There is no reason to believe a police officer, unschooled in the law, will assess whether evidence already in his possession would suffice to survive a motion for acquittal following the case in chief. The officer may or may not even know the identity of the ultimate defendant.[3] He certainly will not know anything about potential

---

**d.** On direct examination, the defendant in *Havens* denied being involved with his codefendant in the transportation of cocaine. On cross-examination, the defendant denied being involved in sewing a pocket (in which drugs were found) into his codefendant's clothing or having in his own suitcase cloth from which the swatch was cut to make the pocket. Defendant's testimony was impeached by admitting the illegally seized cloth. A 5–4 majority, per White, J., rejected the argument that illegally seized evidence could be used for impeachment only when it contradicts a defendant's direct testimony, "see[ing] no difference of constitutional magnitude between the defendant's direct statements on direct examination and his answers to questions put to him on cross-examination that are plainly within the scope of the defendant's direct examination."

**3.** In this case, contrary to the impression conveyed by the majority, n. 8, the arresting officers knew almost nothing of the state of a future prosecution case. The officers did know there were several eyewitnesses to the shooting. But these eyewitnesses had made no identification of any suspect. The officers did not know petitioner's real name or his true appearance, but had sought him out at the beauty parlor on an anonymous tip. They could not know what physical evidence, such as the murder weapon, they might find on petitioner, or might lose to the case in chief as a result of illegal conduct. The suggestion that the officers' calculated assessment of a defense witnesses, much less what the content of their testimony might be. What he will know for certain is that evidence from an illegal search or arrest (which may well be crucial to securing a conviction) will be lost to the case in chief. Our earlier assessments of the marginal deterrent effect are applicable here. "Assuming that the exclusionary rule has a deterrent effect on proscribed police conduct, sufficient deterrence flows when the evidence in question is made unavailable to the prosecution in its case in chief." *Harris.*

In this case, the defense witness, one Jewel Henderson, testified that petitioner's hair was black on the date of the offense. Her statement, perjured or not, should not have been offered to the jurors without giving them the opportunity to consider the unequivocal and contradicting description by the person whose own hair it was. I would allow the introduction of petitioner's statement that his hair was red on the day of the shootings. The result is consistent with our line of cases from *Walder* to *Havens*, and compelled by their reasoning.

The prosecution, it is true, did not limit itself to petitioner's description of his hair color. It went beyond this to introduce petitioner's statement that he went to the beauty shop to "change his appearance." The prosecutor used this statement to suggest that petitioner had a guilty mind and an intention to evade capture by disguise. This goes beyond what was necessary to rebut Henderson's testimony, and raises many of the concerns expressed in the majority opinion. Nonetheless, there was overwhelming evidence of petitioner's guilt in this case, including the testimony of five eyewitnesses. In view of these circumstances, I agree with the Illinois Supreme Court that any error as to the additional statements or the prosecutor's argument had no effect on petitioner's trial, and may be considered harmless.

Where the jury is misled by false testimony, otherwise subject to flat contradiction by evidence illegally seized, the protection of the exclusionary rule is " 'perverted into a license to use perjury by way of a defense, free from the risk of confrontation with prior inconsistent utterances.' " *Havens.* The perversion is the same where the perjury is by proxy.   *   *   *

**7. If a suspect does not request a lawyer but, unbeknownst to him, a relative or friend retains a lawyer for him, does the failure of the police to allow the lawyer to see the suspect or the failure to inform the suspect that an attorney is trying to reach him vitiate an otherwise valid waiver of Miranda rights?**

## MORAN v. BURBINE

475 U.S. 412, 106 S.Ct. 1135, 89 L.Ed.2d 410 (1986).

JUSTICE O'CONNOR delivered the opinion of the Court.

After being informed of his rights pursuant to *Miranda* and after executing a series of written waivers, respondent confessed to the murder of a young woman. At no point during the course of the interrogation, which occurred prior to arraignment, did he request an attorney. While he was in police custody, his sister attempted to retain a lawyer to represent him. The attorney telephoned the police station and received assurances that respondent would not be questioned further until the next day. In fact, the interrogation session that yielded the inculpatory statements began later that evening. The question

future trial allowed them to ignore the exclusionary rule finds no support in the record
and, in fact, is pure speculation.

presented is whether either the conduct of the police or respondent's ignorance of the attorney's efforts to reach him taints the validity of the waivers and therefore requires exclusion of the confessions.

On the morning of March 3, 1977, Mary Jo Hickey was found unconscious in a factory parking lot in Providence, Rhode Island. Suffering from injuries to her skull apparently inflicted by a metal pipe found at the scene, she was rushed to a nearby hospital. Three weeks later she died from her wounds.

Several months after her death, the Cranston, Rhode Island police arrested respondent and two others in connection with a local burglary. Shortly before the arrest, Detective Ferranti of the Cranston police force had learned from a confidential informant that the man responsible for Ms. Hickey's death lived at a certain address and went by the name of "Butch." Upon discovering that respondent lived at that address and was known by that name, Detective Ferranti informed respondent of his *Miranda* rights. When respondent refused to execute a written waiver, Detective Ferranti spoke separately with the two other suspects arrested on the breaking and entering charge and obtained statements further implicating respondent in Ms. Hickey's murder. At approximately 6:00 p.m., Detective Ferranti telephoned the police in Providence to convey the information he had uncovered. An hour later, three officers from that department arrived at the Cranston headquarters for the purpose of questioning respondent about the murder.

That same evening, at about 7:45 p.m., respondent's sister telephoned the Public Defender's Office to obtain legal assistance for her brother. Her sole concern was the breaking and entering charge, as she was unaware that respondent was then under suspicion for murder. She asked for Richard Casparian, who had been scheduled to meet with respondent earlier that afternoon to discuss another charge unrelated to either the break-in or the murder. As soon as the conversation ended, the attorney who took the call attempted to reach Mr. Casparian. When those efforts were unsuccessful, she telephoned Allegra Munson, another Assistant Public Defender, and told her about respondent's arrest and his sister's subsequent request that the office represent him.

At 8:15 p.m., Ms. Munson telephoned the Cranston police station and asked that her call be transferred to the detective division. In the words of the Supreme Court of Rhode Island, whose factual findings we treat as presumptively correct, 28 U.S.C. § 2254(d), the conversation proceeded as follows:

> "A male voice responded with the word 'Detectives.' Ms. Munson identified herself and asked if Brian Burbine was being held; the person responded affirmatively. Ms. Munson explained to the person that Burbine was represented by attorney Casparian who was not available; she further stated that she would act as Burbine's legal counsel in the event that the police intended to place him in a lineup or question him. The unidentified person told Ms. Munson that the police would not be questioning Burbine or putting him in a lineup and that they were through with him for the night. Ms. Munson was not informed that the Providence Police were at the Cranston police station or that Burbine was a suspect in Mary's murder."

At all relevant times, respondent was unaware of his sister's efforts to retain counsel and of the fact and contents of Ms. Munson's telephone conversation.

Less than an hour later, the police brought respondent to an interrogation room and conducted the first of a series of interviews concerning the murder. Prior to each session, respondent was informed of his *Miranda* rights, and on three separate occasions he signed a written form acknowledging that he understood his right to the presence of an attorney and explicitly indicating that he "[did] not want an attorney called or appointed for [him]" before he gave a statement. Uncontradicted evidence at the suppression hearing indicated that at least twice during the course of the evening, respondent was left in a room where he had access to a telephone, which he apparently declined to use. Eventually, respondent signed three written statements fully admitting to the murder.

Prior to trial, respondent moved to suppress the statements. The court denied the motion, finding that respondent had received the *Miranda* warnings and had "knowingly, intelligently, and voluntarily waived his privilege against self-incrimination [and] his right to counsel." Rejecting the contrary testimony of the police, the court found that Ms. Munson did telephone the detective bureau on the evening in question, but concluded that "there was no * * * conspiracy or collusion on the part of the Cranston Police Department to secrete this defendant from his attorney." In any event, the court held, the constitutional right to request the presence of an attorney belongs solely to the defendant and may not be asserted by his lawyer. Because the evidence was clear that respondent never asked for the services of an attorney, the telephone call had no relevance to the validity of the waiver or the admissibility of the statements.

The jury found respondent guilty of murder in the first degree, and he appealed to the Supreme Court of Rhode Island. A divided court rejected his contention that the Fifth and Fourteenth Amendments to the Constitution required the suppression of the inculpatory statements and affirmed the conviction. Failure to inform respondent of Ms. Munson's efforts to represent him, the court held, did not undermine the validity of the waivers. "It hardly seems conceivable that the additional information that an attorney whom he did not know had called the police station would have added significantly to the quantum of information necessary for the accused to make an informed decision as to waiver." Nor, the court concluded, did *Miranda* or any other decision of this Court independently require the police to honor Ms. Munson's request that interrogation not proceed in her absence. In reaching that conclusion, the court noted that because two different police departments were operating in the Cranston station house on the evening in question, the record supported the trial court's finding that there was no "conspiracy or collusion" to prevent Ms. Munson from seeing respondent. In any case, the court held, the right to the presence of counsel belongs solely to the accused and may not be asserted by "benign third parties, whether or not they happen to be attorneys."

[On federal habeas corpus, the U.S. Court of Appeals for the First Circuit] held that the police's conduct had fatally tainted respondent's "otherwise valid" waiver of his Fifth Amendment privilege against self incrimination and right to counsel. The court reasoned that by failing to inform respondent that an attorney had called and that she had been assured that no questioning would take place until the next day, the police had deprived respondent of information crucial to his ability to waive his rights knowingly and intelligently. The court also found that the record would support "no other explanation for the refusal to tell Burbine of Attorney Munson's call [than] deliberate or reckless irresponsibility." This kind of "blameworthy action by the police," the court concluded, together with respondent's ignorance of the telephone call, "vitiate[d] any claim that [the] waiver of counsel was knowing and voluntary."

We granted certiorari to decide whether a pre-arraignment confession preceded by an otherwise valid waiver must be suppressed either because the police misinformed an inquiring attorney about their plans concerning the suspect or because they failed to inform the suspect of the attorney's efforts to reach him. We now reverse.  *  *  *

Respondent does not dispute that the Providence police followed [the *Miranda* procedures] with precision. [Nor does he contest the state] courts' determination that he at no point requested the presence of a lawyer. He contends instead that the confessions must be suppressed because the police's failure to inform him of the attorney's telephone call deprived him of information essential to his ability to knowingly waive his Fifth Amendment rights. In the alternative, he suggests that to fully protect the Fifth Amendment values served by *Miranda,* we should extend that decision to condemn the conduct of the Providence police. We address each contention in turn.

Echoing the standard first articulated in *Johnson v. Zerbst, Miranda* holds that "[t]he defendant may waive effectuation" of the rights conveyed in the warnings "provided the waiver is made voluntarily, knowingly and intelligently." The inquiry has two distinct dimensions. First the relinquishment of the right must have been voluntary in the sense that it was the product of a free and deliberate choice rather than intimidation, coercion or deception. Second, the waiver must have been made with a full awareness both of the nature of the right being abandoned and the consequences of the decision to abandon it. Only if the "totality of the circumstances surrounding the interrogation" reveal both an uncoerced choice and the requisite level of comprehension may a court properly conclude that the *Miranda* rights have been waived.

Under this standard, we have no doubt that respondent validly waived his right to remain silent and to the presence of counsel. The voluntariness of the waiver is not at issue. [Nor] is there any question about respondent's comprehension of the full panoply of rights set out in the *Miranda* warnings and of the potential consequences of a decision to relinquish them. Nonetheless, the Court of Appeals believed that the "[d]eliberate or reckless" conduct of the police, in particular their failure to inform respondent of the telephone call, fatally undermined the validity of the otherwise proper waiver. We find this conclusion untenable as a matter of both logic and precedent.

Events occurring outside of the presence of the suspect and entirely unknown to him surely can have no bearing on the capacity to comprehend and knowingly relinquish a constitutional right. Under the analysis of the Court of Appeals, the same defendant, armed with the same information and confronted with precisely the same police conduct, would have knowingly waived his *Miranda* rights had a lawyer not telephoned the police station to inquire about his status. Nothing in any of our waiver decisions or in our understanding of the essential components of a valid waiver requires so incongruous a result. No doubt the additional information would have been useful to respondent; perhaps even it might have affected his decision to confess. But we have never read the Constitution to require that the police supply a suspect with a flow of information to help him calibrate his self interest in deciding whether to speak or stand by his rights.[a] Once it is determined that a suspect's decision not to rely on his rights was uncoerced, that he at all times knew he could stand mute and request a lawyer, and that he was aware of the state's intention to use his statements to

---

**a.** A year later, this language was quoted with approval in *Colorado v. Spring,* 479 U.S. 564 (1987), holding that the police need not advise a suspect of the crimes they wish to question him about even though the subject matter of the interrogation is likely to be quite different from what the suspect expects.

secure a conviction, the analysis is complete and the waiver is valid as a matter of law.[1] The Court of Appeals' conclusion to the contrary was in error.

Nor do we believe that the level of the police's culpability in failing to inform respondent of the telephone call has any bearing on the validity of the waiver. In light of the state-court findings that there was no "conspiracy or collusion" on the part of the police, we have serious doubts about whether the Court of Appeals was free to conclude that their conduct constituted "deliberate or reckless irresponsibility." But whether intentional or inadvertent, the state of mind of the police is irrelevant to the question of the intelligence and voluntariness of respondent's election to abandon his rights. Although highly inappropriate, even deliberate deception of an attorney could not possibly affect a suspect's decision to waive his *Miranda* rights unless he were at least aware of the incident. Compare *Escobedo* (excluding confession where police incorrectly told the *suspect* that his lawyer " 'didn't want to see' him"). Nor was the failure to inform respondent of the telephone call the kind of "trick[ery]" that can vitiate the validity of a waiver. *Miranda.* Granting that the "deliberate or reckless" withholding of information is objectionable as a matter of ethics, such conduct is only relevant to the constitutional validity of a waiver if it deprives a defendant of knowledge essential to his ability to understand the nature of his rights and the consequences of abandoning them. Because respondent's voluntary decision to speak was made with full awareness and comprehension of all the information *Miranda* requires the police to convey, the waivers were valid.

At oral argument respondent acknowledged that a constitutional rule requiring the police to inform a suspect of an attorney's efforts to reach him would represent a significant extension of our precedents. He contends, however, that the conduct of the Providence police was so inimical to the Fifth Amendment values *Miranda* seeks to protect that we should read that decision to condemn their behavior. Regardless of any issue of waiver, he urges, the Fifth Amendment requires the reversal of a conviction if the police are less than forthright in their dealings with an attorney or if they fail to tell a suspect of a lawyer's unilateral efforts to contact him. Because the proposed modification ignores the underlying purposes of the *Miranda* rules and because we think that the decision as written strikes the proper balance between society's legitimate law enforcement interests and the protection of the defendant's Fifth Amendment rights, we decline the invitation to further extend *Miranda's* reach.

At the outset, while we share respondent's distaste for the deliberate misleading of an officer of the court, reading *Miranda* to forbid police deception of an *attorney* "would cut [the decision] completely loose from its own explicitly stated rationale." As is now well established, "[the] *Miranda* warnings are 'not themselves rights protected by the Constitution but [are] instead measures to insure that the [suspect's] right against compulsory self-incrimination [is] protected.' " *Quarles.* Their objective is not to mold police conduct for its own sake. Nothing in the Constitution vests in us the authority to mandate a code of behavior for state officials wholly unconnected to any federal right or privilege. The purpose of the *Miranda* warnings instead is to dissipate the compulsion inherent in custodial interrogation and, in so doing, guard against abridgement

---

**1.** The dissent incorrectly reads our analysis of the components of a valid waiver to be inconsistent [with] *Edwards.* [But] the dissent never comes to grips with the crucial distinguishing feature of this case—that Burbine at no point requested the presence of counsel, as was his right under *Miranda* to do. [We re-

ject] the dissent's entirely undefended suggestion that the Fifth Amendment "right to counsel" requires anything more than that the police inform the suspect of his right to representation and honor his request that the interrogation cease until his attorney is present.

of the suspect's Fifth Amendment rights. Clearly, a rule that focuses on how the police treat an attorney—conduct that has no relevance at all to the degree of compulsion experienced by the defendant during interrogation—would ignore both *Miranda's* mission and its only source of legitimacy.

Nor are we prepared to adopt a rule requiring that the police inform a suspect of an attorney's efforts to reach him. While such a rule might add marginally to *Miranda's* goal of dispelling the compulsion inherent in custodial interrogation, overriding practical considerations counsel against its adoption. As we have stressed on numerous occasions, "[o]ne of the principal advantages" of *Miranda* is the ease and clarity of its application. *Berkemer v. McCarty.* We have little doubt that the approach urged by respondent and endorsed by the Court of Appeals would have the inevitable consequence of muddying *Miranda's* otherwise relatively clear waters. The legal questions it would spawn are legion: To what extent should the police be held accountable for knowing that the accused has counsel? Is it enough that someone in the station house knows, or must the interrogating officer himself know of counsel's efforts to contact the suspect? Do counsel's efforts to talk to the suspect concerning one criminal investigation trigger the obligation to inform the defendant before interrogation may proceed on a wholly separate matter? We are unwilling to modify *Miranda* in a manner that would so clearly undermine the decision's central "virtue of informing police and prosecutors with specificity [what] they may do in conducting [a] custodial interrogation, and of informing courts under what circumstances statements obtained during such interrogation are not admissible."

Moreover, problems of clarity to one side, reading *Miranda* to require the police in each instance to inform a suspect of an attorney's efforts to reach him would work a substantial and, we think, inappropriate shift in the subtle balance struck in that decision. Custodial interrogations implicate two competing concerns. On the one hand, "the need for police questioning as a tool for effective enforcement of criminal laws" cannot be doubted. Admissions of guilt [are] essential to society's compelling interest in finding, convicting and punishing those who violate the law. On the other hand, the Court has recognized that the interrogation process is "inherently coercive" and that, as a consequence, there exists a substantial risk that the police will inadvertently traverse the fine line between legitimate efforts to elicit admissions and constitutionally impermissible compulsion. *Miranda* attempted to reconcile these opposing concerns by giving the *defendant* the power to exert some control over the course of the interrogation. Declining to adopt the more extreme position that the actual presence of a lawyer was necessary to dispel the coercion inherent in custodial interrogation, the Court found that the suspect's Fifth Amendment rights could be adequately protected by less intrusive means. Police questioning, often an essential part of the investigatory process, could continue in its traditional form, the Court held, but only if the suspect clearly understood that, at any time, he could bring the proceeding to a halt or, short of that, call in an attorney to give advice and monitor the conduct of his interrogators.

The position urged by respondent would upset this carefully drawn approach in a manner that is both unnecessary for the protection of the Fifth Amendment privilege and injurious to legitimate law enforcement. Because, as *Miranda* holds, full comprehension of the rights to remain silent and request an attorney are sufficient to dispel whatever coercion is inherent in the interrogation process, a rule requiring the police to inform the suspect of an attorney's efforts to contact him would contribute to the protection of the Fifth Amendment privilege only incidentally, if at all. This minimal benefit, however, would come at a substantial cost to society's legitimate and substantial interest in securing admissions of guilt. Indeed, the very premise of the Court of Appeals was not that awareness of Ms. Munson's phone call would have dissipated the coercion of the interrogation room, but that it might have convinced respondent not to speak at all. Because neither the letter nor purposes of *Miranda* require this additional handicap on otherwise permissible investigatory efforts, we are unwilling to expand the *Miranda* rules to require the police to keep the suspect abreast of the status of his legal representation.

We acknowledge that a number of state courts have reached a contrary conclusion. We recognize also that our interpretation of the Federal Constitution, if given the dissent's expansive gloss, is at odds with the police recommendations embodied in the American Bar Association Standards of Criminal Justice. [§ 5–7.1.] Notwithstanding the dissent's protestations, however, our interpretive duties go well beyond deferring to the numerical preponderance of lower court decisions or to the subconstitutional recommendations of even so esteemed a body as the American Bar Association. Nothing we say today disables the States from adopting different requirements for the conduct of its employees and officials as a matter of state law. We hold only that the Court of Appeals erred in construing the Fifth Amendment to the Federal Constitution to require the exclusion of respondent's three confessions.

Respondent also contends that the Sixth Amendment requires exclusion of his three confessions. It is clear, of course, that, absent a valid waiver, the defendant has the right to the presence of an attorney during any interrogation occurring after the first formal charging proceeding, the point at which the Sixth Amendment right to counsel initially attaches. And we readily agree that once the right *has* attached, it follows that the police may not interfere with the efforts of a defendant's attorney to act as a " 'medium' between [the suspect] and the State" during the interrogation. The difficulty for respondent is that the interrogation sessions that yielded the inculpatory statements took place *before* the initiation of "adversary judicial proceedings." He contends, however, that this circumstance is not fatal to his Sixth Amendment claim. At least in some situations, he argues, the Sixth Amendment protects the integrity of the attorney-client relationship regardless of whether the prosecution has in fact commenced "by way of formal charge, preliminary hearing, indictment, information or arraignment." Placing principal reliance on a footnote in *Miranda* [n. 35] and on *Escobedo,* he maintains that [the] right to non-interference with an attorney's dealings with a [suspect] arises the moment that the relationship is formed, or, at the very least, once the defendant is placed in custodial interrogation.

We are not persuaded. At the outset, subsequent decisions foreclose any reliance on *Escobedo* and *Miranda* for the proposition that the Sixth Amendment right, in any of its manifestations, applies prior to the initiation of adversary judicial proceedings. Although *Escobedo* was originally decided as a Sixth Amendment case, "the Court in retrospect perceived that the 'prime purpose' of *Escobedo* was not to vindicate the constitutional right to counsel as such, but, like *Miranda,* 'to guarantee full effectuation of the privilege against self-incrimination. * * *' " *Kirby v. Illinois* [Ch. 7, § 2, holding that the right to counsel at pretrial identifications attaches "only at or after the time that adversary judicial proceedings have been initiated."] Clearly then, *Escobedo* provides no support for respondent's argument. Nor, of course, does *Miranda,* the holding of which rested exclusively on the Fifth Amendment. * * *

Questions of precedent to one side, we find respondent's understanding of the Sixth Amendment both practically and theoretically unsound. As a practical matter, it makes little sense to say that the Sixth Amendment right to counsel attaches at different times depending on the fortuity of whether the suspect or his family happens to have retained counsel prior to interrogation. More importantly, the suggestion that the existence of an attorney-client relationship itself triggers the protections of the Sixth Amendment misconceives the underlying purposes of the right to counsel. The Sixth Amendment's intended function is not to wrap a protective cloak around the attorney-client relationship for its own sake any more than it is to protect a suspect from the consequences of his own candor. [By] its very terms, [the Sixth Amendment] becomes applicable only when the government's role shifts from investigation to accusation. For it is only then that the assistance of one versed in the "intricacies [of] law" is needed to assure that the prosecution's case encounters "the crucible of meaningful adversarial testing." * * *

Respondent contends, however, that custodial interrogations require a different rule. Because confessions elicited during the course of police questioning often seal a suspect's fate, he argues, the need for an advocate—and the concomitant right to non-interference with the attorney-client relationship—is at its zenith, regardless of whether the state has initiated the first adversary judicial proceeding. We do not doubt that a lawyer's presence could be of value to the suspect; and we readily agree that if a suspect confesses, his attorney's case at trial will be that much more difficult. But [for] an interrogation, no more or less than for any other "critical" pre-trial event, the possibility that the encounter may have important consequences at trial, standing alone, is insufficient to trigger the Sixth Amendment right to counsel. * * *

Finally, respondent contends that the conduct of the police was so offensive as to deprive him of the fundamental fairness guaranteed by the Due Process Clause of the Fourteenth Amendment. Focusing primarily on the impropriety of conveying false information to an attorney, he invites us to declare that such behavior should be condemned as violative of canons fundamental to the " 'traditions and conscience of our people.' " *Rochin.* We do not question that on facts more egregious than those presented here police deception might rise to a level of a due process violation. Accordingly, Justice Stevens' apocalyptic suggestion that we have approved any and all forms of police misconduct is demonstrably incorrect.[4] We hold only that, on these facts, the challenged conduct falls short

---

4. Among its other failings, the dissent declines to follow *Oregon v. Elstad*, a decision that categorically forecloses Justice Stevens' major premise—that *Miranda* requires the police to inform a suspect of any and all information that would be useful to a decision whether to remain silent or speak with the police. The dissent also launches a novel "agency" theory of the Fifth Amendment under which any perceived deception of a lawyer is automatically treated as deception of his or her client. This argument entirely disregards the elemental and established proposition that the privilege against compulsory self-incrimination is, by hypothesis, a personal one that can only be invoked by the individual whose testimony is being compelled.

Most importantly, the dissent's misreading of *Miranda* itself is breathtaking in its scope. For example, it reads *Miranda* as creating an undifferentiated right to the presence of an attorney that is triggered automatically by the initiation of the interrogation itself. Yet, as both *Miranda* and subsequent decisions construing *Miranda* make clear beyond refute, " 'the interrogation must cease until an attorney is present' *only* '[i]f the individual states that he wants an attorney.' " *Michigan v. Mosley* (emphasis added). The dissent condemns us for embracing "incommunicado questioning [as] a societal goal of the highest order that justifies police deception of the shabbiest kind." We, of course, do nothing of the kind. As any reading of *Miranda* reveals, the decision, rather than proceeding from the premise that the rights and needs of the defendant are paramount to all others, embodies a carefully crafted balance designed to fully protect *both* the defendant's and society's interests. The dissent may not share our view of the kind of misbehavior that so shocks the sensibilities of civilized society as to warrant a federal intrusion into the criminal processes of the States. * * *

JUSTICE STEVENS, with whom JUSTICE BRENNAN and JUSTICE MARSHALL join, dissenting.

This case poses fundamental questions about our system of justice. As this Court has long recognized, * * * "ours is an accusatorial and not an inquisitorial system." The Court's opinion today represents a startling departure from that basic insight.

[The] Court's holding focuses on the period after a suspect has been taken into custody and before he has been charged with an offense. The core of the Court's holding is that police interference with an attorney's access to her client during that period is not unconstitutional. The Court reasons that a State has a compelling interest, not simply in custodial interrogation, but in lawyer-free, incommunicado custodial interrogation. Such incommunicado interrogation is so important that a lawyer may be given false information that prevents her presence and representation; it is so important that police may refuse to inform a suspect of his attorney's communications and immediate availability.[8] This conclusion flies in the face of this Court's repeated expressions of deep concern about incommunicado questioning.[a] Until today, incommunicado questioning has been viewed with the strictest scrutiny by this Court; today, incommunicado questioning is embraced as a societal goal of the highest order that justifies police deception of the shabbiest kind. * * *

Police interference with communications between an attorney and his client is a recurrent problem. The factual variations in the many state court opinions condemning this interference as a violation of the federal Constitution suggest the variety of contexts in which the problem emerges. In Oklahoma, police led a lawyer to several different locations while they interrogated the suspect; in Oregon, police moved a suspect to a new location when they learned that his lawyer was on his way; in Illinois, authorities failed to tell a suspect that his lawyer had arrived at the jail and asked to see him; in Massachusetts, police did not tell suspects that their lawyers were at or near the police station. In all

that the Fifth Amendment rights of the defendant are amply protected by application of *Miranda as written*. But the dissent is "simply wrong" in suggesting that exclusion of Burbine's three confessions follows perfunctorily from *Miranda's* mandate. Y. Kamisar, *Police Interrogation and Confessions* 217–218, n. 94 (1980).

Quite understandably, the dissent is outraged by the very idea of police deception of a lawyer. Significantly less understandable is its willingness to misconstrue this Court's constitutional holdings in order to implement its subjective notions of sound policy.

**8.** This kind of police-maintained incommunicado questioning becomes, in the Court's rendition, "an essential part of the investigatory process." Police interference in communications between a lawyer and her client are justified because "[a]dmissions of guilt [are] essential to society's compelling interest in finding, convicting, and punishing those who violate the law." It is this overriding interest in obtaining self-incriminatory statements in the lawyer-free privacy of the police interroga-

tion room that motivates the Court's willingness to swallow its admitted "distaste for the deliberate misleading of an officer of the court."

**a.** [Justice Stevens refers to, and quotes from, numerous cases and then adds:]

To be sure, in many of these cases, the evidence showed that the suspect had requested, and was denied access to, a lawyer. Until today, however, the Court has never viewed "incommunicado" as applying only to the denial of the suspect's efforts to reach the attorney, and not to the attorney's efforts to reach the suspect. * * * It is also true that many of these cases involved incommunicado interrogations for very long periods of time; not one of those cases suggested that incommunicado interrogations for shorter periods, maintained by misinforming attorney and client of each other's actions, was supported by a compelling societal interest that justified police deception and misinformation about attorney communications.

these cases, the police not only failed to inform the suspect, but also misled the attorneys. The scenarios vary, but the core problem of police interference remains.

[The] near-consensus of state courts and the legal profession's Standards about this recurrent problem lends powerful support to the conclusion that police may not interfere with communications between an attorney and the client whom they are questioning. Indeed, at least two opinions from this Court seemed to express precisely that view.[20] The Court today flatly rejects that widely held view and responds to this recurrent problem by adopting the most restrictive interpretation of the federal constitutional restraints on police deception, misinformation, and interference in attorney-client communications.

\* \* \*

[A]lthough there are a number of ambiguities in the record, the state court findings established (1) that Attorney Munson made her call at about 8:15 p.m.; (2) that she was given false information; (3) that Burbine was not told of her call; and (4) that he was thereafter given the *Miranda* warnings, waived his rights, and signed three incriminating statements without receiving any advice from an attorney. The remainder of the record underscores two points. The first is the context of the call—a context in which two police departments were on the verge of resolving a highly publicized, hauntingly brutal homicide and in which, as Lieutenant Gannon testified, the police were aware that counsel's advice to remain silent might be an obstacle to obtaining a confession. The second is the extent of the uncertainty about the events that motivated Burbine's decision to waive his rights. The lawyer-free privacy of the interrogation room, so exalted by the majority, provides great difficulties in determining what actually transpired. It is not simply the ambiguity that is troublesome; if so, the problem would be not unlike other difficult evidentiary problems. Rather, the particularly troublesome aspect is that the ambiguity arises in the very situation—incommunicado interrogation—for which this Court has developed strict presumptions and for which this Court has, in the past, imposed the heaviest burden of justification on the government. It is in this context, and the larger context of our accusatorial system, that the deceptive conduct of the police must be evaluated.

Well-settled principles of law lead inexorably to the conclusion that the failure to inform Burbine of the call from his attorney makes the subsequent waiver of his constitutional rights invalid. Analysis should begin with an acknowledgment that the burden of proving the validity of a waiver of constitutional rights is always on the *government*. When such a waiver occurs in a custodial setting, that burden is an especially heavy one because custodial interrogation is inherently coercive, because disinterested witnesses are seldom available to describe what actually happened, and because history has taught us that the danger of overreaching during incommunicado interrogation is so real.

In applying this heavy presumption against the validity of waivers, this Court has sometimes relied on a case-by-case totality of the circumstances analysis. We have found, however, that some custodial interrogation situations require strict presumptions against the validity of a waiver. *Miranda* estab-

**20.** See *Miranda* n. 35 (in *Escobedo*, "[t]he police also prevented the attorney from consulting with his client. Independent of any other constitutional proscription, this action constitutes a violation of the Sixth Amendment right to the assistance of counsel and excludes any statement obtained in its wake");

*Escobedo* ("[I]t 'would be highly incongruous if our system of justice permitted the district attorney, the lawyer representing the State, to extract a confession from the accused while his own lawyer, seeking to speak with him, was kept from him by the police' ").

lished that a waiver is not valid in the absence of certain warnings. *Edwards* similarly established that a waiver is not valid if police initiate questioning after the defendant has invoked his right to counsel. In these circumstances, the waiver is invalid as a matter of law even if the evidence overwhelmingly establishes, as a matter of fact, that "a suspect's decision not to rely on his rights was uncoerced, that he at all times knew that he could stand mute and request a lawyer, and that he was aware of the state's intention to use his statement to secure a conviction." In light of our decision in *Edwards,* the Court is simply wrong in stating that "the analysis is complete and the waiver is valid as a matter of law" when these facts have been established. Like the failure to give warnings and like police initiation of interrogation after a request for counsel, police deception of a suspect through omission of information regarding attorney communications greatly exacerbates the inherent problems of incommunicado interrogation and requires a clear principle to safeguard the presumption against the waiver of constitutional rights. As in those situations, the police deception should render a subsequent waiver invalid.

Indeed, as *Miranda* itself makes clear, proof that the required warnings have been given is a necessary, but by no means sufficient, condition for establishing a valid waiver. As the Court plainly stated in *Miranda,* "any evidence that the accused was threatened, tricked, or cajoled into a waiver will, of course, show that the defendant did not voluntarily waive his privilege. The requirement of warnings and waiver of rights is a fundamental with respect to the Fifth Amendment privilege and not simply a preliminary ritual to existing methods of interrogation."

In this case it would be perfectly clear that Burbine's waiver was invalid if, for example, Detective Ferranti had "threatened, tricked, or cajoled" Burbine in their private pre-confession meeting—perhaps by misdescribing the statements obtained from DiOrio and Sparks—even though, under the Court's truncated analysis of the issue, Burbine fully understood his rights. For *Miranda* clearly condemns threats or trickery that cause a suspect to make an unwise waiver of his rights even though he fully understands those rights. In my opinion there can be no constitutional distinction—as the Court appears to draw—between a deceptive misstatement and the concealment by the police of the critical fact that an attorney retained by the accused or his family has offered assistance, either by telephone or in person.[38]

Thus, the Court's truncated analysis, which relies in part on a distinction between deception accomplished by means of an omission of a critically important fact and deception by means of a misleading statement, is simply untenable. If, as the Court asserts, "the analysis is at an end" as soon as the suspect is provided with enough information to have the *capacity* to understand and exercise his rights, I see no reason why the police should not be permitted to make the same kind of misstatements to the suspect that they are apparently allowed to make to his lawyer. *Miranda,* however, clearly establishes that both kinds of deception vitiate the suspect's waiver of his right to counsel.[39]

**38.** The Court cites *Johnson v. Zerbst,* a case involving a claim that a defendant had waived his right to trial counsel. I find it inconceivable that, in such a situation, an otherwise sufficient series of questions and answers can support a valid waiver if the government misinforms an attorney about the defendant's trial date, and if the government fails to tell the defendant of the attorney's communications. Yet that would be the con-sequence of the Court's "what the suspect doesn't know can't hurt him" approach to this case.

**39.** It is thus clear that the majority's comparison of a suspect in Burbine's position with "the same defendant [had] a lawyer not tele-phoned the police station" sets up a false comparison. For *Miranda's* condemnation of trickery and cajolery requires that an assess-

As the Court notes, the question is whether the deceptive police conduct "deprives a defendant of knowledge essential to his ability to understand the nature of his rights and the consequences of abandoning them." This question has been resoundingly answered time and time again by the state courts that, with rare exceptions, have correctly understood the meaning of [*Miranda*]. Particularly in an opinion that relies on a desire to avoid "a federal intrusion into the criminal processes of the States," one would expect at least some indication why, in the majority's view, so many state courts have been so profoundly wrong on this precise issue. Unlike the majority, the state courts have realized that attorney communication to the police about the client is an event that has a direct "bearing" on the knowing and intelligent waiver of constitutional rights. As the Oregon Supreme Court has explained: "To pass up an abstract offer to call some unknown lawyer is very different from refusing to talk with an identified attorney actually available to provide at least initial assistance and advice, whatever might be arranged in the long run. A suspect indifferent to the first offer may well react quite differently to the second." *State v. Haynes,* 602 P.2d 272, 278 (Ore.1979).[42]

In short, settled principles about construing waivers of constitutional rights and about the need for strict presumptions in custodial interrogations, as well as a plain reading of the *Miranda* opinion itself, overwhelmingly support the conclusion reached by almost every state court that has considered the matter— a suspect's waiver of his right to counsel is invalid if police refuse to inform the suspect of his counsel's communications.

The Court makes the alternative argument that requiring police to inform a suspect of his attorney's communications to and about him is not required because it would upset the careful "balance" of *Miranda.* Despite its earlier notion that the attorney's call is an "outside event" that has "no bearing" on a knowing and intelligent waiver, the majority does acknowledge that information of attorney Munson's call "would have been useful to respondent" and "might have affected his decision to confess." Thus, a rule requiring the police to inform a suspect of an attorney's call would have two predictable effects. It would serve "*Miranda's* goal of dispelling the compulsion inherent in custodial interrogation" and it would disserve the goal of custodial interrogation because it would result in fewer confessions. By a process of balancing these two concerns, the Court finds the benefit to the individual outweighed by the "substantial cost to society's legitimate and substantial interest in securing admissions of guilt."

The Court's balancing approach is profoundly misguided. The cost of suppressing evidence of guilt will always make the value of a procedural safeguard appear "minimal," "marginal," or "incremental." Indeed, the value

ment of police conduct figure importantly in the assessment of a suspect's decision to waive his fundamental constitutional rights. In the majority's comparison, however, the police conduct is irrelevant. In contrast, the appropriate comparison is between a suspect in Burbine's position and a suspect who is otherwise tricked and deceived into a waiver of his rights. *Miranda* itself, as well as the long-established presumption against the waiver of constitutional rights, requires that both kinds of waiver be held invalid.

**42.** * * * The majority mischaracterizes this dissent by stating that its "major premise" is that "*Miranda* requires the police to inform a suspect of any and all information that would be useful to a decision whether to remain silent or speak with police." The majority's response ignores the fact that the police action here is not simply a failure to provide "useful" information; rather, it is affirmative police interference in a communication between an attorney and a suspect. Moreover, the "information" intercepted by the police bears directly on the right to counsel that police are asking the suspect to waive. The "information" at issue is thus far different from information about "the nature and quality of the evidence," or about a grand jury witness's possible target status.

of any trial at all seems like a "procedural technicality" when balanced against the interest in administering prompt justice to a murderer or a rapist caught redhanded. The individual interest in procedural safeguards that minimize the risk of error is easily discounted when the fact of guilt appears certain beyond doubt.

What is the cost of requiring the police to inform a suspect of his attorney's call? It would decrease the likelihood that custodial interrogation will enable the police to obtain a confession. This is certainly a real cost, but it is the same cost that this Court has repeatedly found necessary to preserve the character of our free society and our rejection of an inquisitorial system. * * *

Just as the "cost" does not justify taking a suspect into custody or interrogating him without giving him warnings simply because police desire to question him, so too the "cost" does not justify permitting police to withhold from a suspect knowledge of an attorney's communication, even though that communication would have an unquestionable effect on the suspect's exercise of his rights. The "cost" that concerns the Court amounts to nothing more than an acknowledgment that the law enforcement interest in obtaining convictions suffers whenever a suspect exercises the rights that are afforded by our system of criminal justice. In other words, it is the fear that an individual may exercise his rights that tips the scales of justice for the Court today. The principle that ours is an accusatorial, not an inquisitorial, system, however, has repeatedly led the Court to reject that fear as a valid reason for inhibiting the invocation of rights.

If the Court's cost benefit analysis were sound, it would justify a repudiation of the right to a warning about counsel itself. There is only a difference in degree between a presumption that advice about the immediate availability of a lawyer would not affect the voluntariness of a decision to confess, and a presumption that every citizen knows that he has a right to remain silent and therefore no warnings of any kind are needed. In either case, the withholding of information serves precisely the same law enforcement interests. And in both cases, the cost can be described as nothing more than an incremental increase in the risk that an individual will make an unintelligent waiver of his rights.

[The] Court also argues that a rule requiring the police to inform a suspect of an attorney's efforts to reach him would have an additional cost: it would undermine the "clarity" of the rule of the *Miranda* case. This argument is not supported by any reference to the experience in the States that have adopted such a rule. The Court merely professes concern about its ability to answer three quite simple questions.[46]

Moreover, the Court's evaluation of the interest in "clarity" is rather one-sided. For a police officer with a printed card containing the exact text he is supposed to recite, perhaps the rule is clear. But the interest in clarity that the *Miranda* decision was intended to serve is not merely for the benefit of the

---

**46.** Thus, the Court asks itself:

(1) "To what extent should the police be held accountable for knowing that the accused has counsel?" The simple answer is that police should be held accountable to the extent that the attorney or the suspect informs the police of the representation.

(2) "Is it enough that someone in the station house knows, or must the interrogating officer himself know of counsel's efforts to contact the suspect?" Obviously, police should be held responsible for getting a message of this importance from one officer to another.

(3) "Do counsel's efforts to talk to the suspect concerning one criminal investigation trigger the obligation to inform the defendant before interrogation may proceed on a wholly separate matter?" As the facts of this case forcefully demonstrate, the answer is "yes."

police. Rather, the decision was also, and primarily, intended to provide adequate guidance to the person in custody who is being asked to waive the protections afforded by the Constitution. Inevitably, the *Miranda* decision also serves the judicial interest in clarifying the inquiry into what actually transpired during a custodial interrogation.[48] Under the Court's conception of the interest in clarity, however, the police would presumably prevail whenever they could convince the trier of fact that a required ritual was performed before the confession was obtained.

At the time attorney Munson made her call to the Cranston Police Station, she was acting as Burbine's attorney. Under ordinary principles of agency law the deliberate deception of Munson was tantamount to deliberate deception of her client. If an attorney makes a mistake in the course of her representation of her client, the client must accept the consequences of that mistake. It is equally clear that when an attorney makes an inquiry on behalf of her client, the client is entitled to a truthful answer. Surely the client must have the same remedy for a false representation to his lawyer that he would have if he were acting *pro se* and had propounded the question himself.

The majority brushes aside the police deception involved in the misinformation of attorney Munson. It is irrelevant to the Fifth Amendment analysis, concludes the majority, because that right is personal; it is irrelevant to the Sixth Amendment analysis, continues the majority, because the Sixth Amendment does not apply until formal adversary proceedings have begun.

In my view, as a matter of law, the police deception of Munson was tantamount to deception of Burbine himself. It constituted a violation of Burbine's right to have an attorney present during the questioning that began shortly thereafter. The existence of that right is undisputed. Whether the source of that right is the Sixth Amendment, the Fifth Amendment, or a combination of the two is of no special importance, for I do not understand the Court to deny the existence of the right.

The pertinent question is whether police deception of the attorney is utterly irrelevant to that right. In my judgment, it blinks at reality to suggest that misinformation which prevented the presence of an attorney has no bearing on the protection and effectuation of the right to counsel in custodial interrogation. The majority parses the role of attorney and suspect so narrowly that the deception of the attorney is of no constitutional significance. [The] character of the attorney-client relationship requires rejection of the Court's notion that the attorney is some entirely distinct, completely severable entity and that deception of the attorney is irrelevant to the right of counsel in custodial interrogation.[53]

The possible reach of the Court's opinion is stunning. For the majority seems to suggest that police may deny counsel all access to a client who is being held. At least since *Escobedo,* it has been widely accepted that police may not

---

**48.** Indeed, in contrast to the majority's remarks about clarity, the operation of the principle expressed by almost all the state courts would be far clearer than the operation of the Court's contrary principle. For it is surely easier to administer a rule that applies to an external event, such as an attorney's telephone call or a visit to the police station, than a rule that requires an evaluation of the state of mind of a person undergoing custodial interrogation.

**53.** Prevailing norms of legal practice prevent a lawyer from communicating with a party, rather than a lawyer. See Disciplinary Rule 7–104(A)(1), ABA Code of Professional Responsibility ("During the course of his representation of a client a lawyer shall not: Communicate or cause another to communicate on the subject of the representation with a party he knows to be represented by a lawyer in that matter unless he has the prior consent of the lawyer representing such other party or is authorized by law to do so").

\* \* \*

simply deny attorneys access to their clients who are in custody. This view has survived the recasting of *Escobedo* from a Sixth Amendment to a Fifth Amendment case that the majority finds so critically important. That this prevailing view is shared *by the police* can be seen in the state court opinions detailing various forms of police deception of attorneys. For, if there were no obligation to give attorneys access, there would be no need to take elaborate steps to avoid access, such as shuttling the suspect to a different location, or taking the lawyer to different locations; police could simply refuse to allow the attorneys to see the suspects. But the law enforcement profession has apparently believed, quite rightly in my view, that denying lawyers access to their clients is impermissible. The Court today seems to assume that this view was error—that, from the federal constitutional perspective, the lawyer's access is, as a question from the Court put it in oral argument, merely "a matter of prosecutorial grace." Certainly, nothing in the Court's Fifth and Sixth Amendments analysis acknowledges that there is *any* federal constitutional bar to an absolute denial of lawyer access to a suspect who is in police custody.

In sharp contrast to the majority, I firmly believe that the right to counsel at custodial interrogation is infringed by police treatment of an attorney that prevents or impedes the attorney's representation of the suspect at that interrogation.

The Court devotes precisely five sentences to its conclusion that the police interference in the attorney's representation of Burbine did not violate the Due Process Clause. In the majority's view, the due process analysis is a simple "shock the conscience" test. Finding its conscience troubled, but not shocked, the majority rejects the due process challenge.

In a variety of circumstances, however, the Court has given a more thoughtful consideration to the requirements of due process. For instance, we have concluded that use of a suspect's post-*Miranda* warnings silence against him violates the due process requirement of fundamental fairness because such use breaches an implicit promise that "silence will carry no penalty." * * * What emerges from these cases is, not the majority's simple "shock the conscience" test, but the principle that due process requires fairness, integrity, and honor in the operation of the criminal justice system, and in its treatment of the citizen's cardinal constitutional protections.

In my judgment, police interference in the attorney-client relationship is the type of governmental misconduct on a matter of central importance to the administration of justice that the Due Process Clause prohibits. Just as the police cannot impliedly promise a suspect that his silence will not be used against him and then proceed to break that promise, so too police cannot tell a suspect's attorney that they will not question the suspect and then proceed to question him. Just as the government cannot conceal from a suspect material and exculpatory evidence, so too the government cannot conceal from a suspect the material fact of his attorney's communication.

Police interference with communications between an attorney and his client violates the due process requirement of fundamental fairness. Burbine's attorney was given completely false information about the lack of questioning; moreover, she was not told that her client would be questioned regarding a murder charge about which she was unaware. Burbine, in turn, was not told that his attorney had phoned and that she had been informed that he would not be questioned. Quite simply, the Rhode Island police effectively drove a wedge between an attorney and a suspect through misinformation and omissions.

The majority does not "question that on facts more egregious than those presented here police deception might rise to the level of a due process violation." In my view, the police deception disclosed by this record plainly does rise to that level.

This case turns on a proper appraisal of the role of the lawyer in our society. If a lawyer is seen as a nettlesome obstacle to the pursuit of wrongdoers—as in an inquisitorial society—then the Court's decision today makes a good deal of sense. If a lawyer is seen as an aid to the understanding and protection of constitutional rights—as in an accusatorial society—then today's decision makes no sense at all. *  *  *

# SECTION 5.  *MASSIAH* REVISITED: *MASSIAH* AND *MIRANDA* COMPARED AND CONTRASTED

Until the Court handed down the first case in this section, *Brewer v. Williams,* often called the "Christian burial speech" case, lasting fame had eluded *Massiah v. United States* [§ 2 supra]. Many thought that *Massiah* had been only a steppingstone to *Escobedo,* decided a scant five weeks later, and that both cases had been largely displaced by *Miranda.* But *Williams* made plain that despite the Court's shift from a "right to counsel" base in *Escobedo* to a "compelled self-incrimination base" in *Miranda,* the *Massiah* doctrine was still alive and well. Indeed, although few, if any, would have predicted it in the early 1970's, the *Massiah* doctrine has emerged as a much more potent force than it had ever been in the Warren Court era.

In the process of revivifying *Massiah,* however, the *Williams* Court blurred the *Massiah* and *Miranda* rationales. Although this is not clear from the *Williams* opinion, application of *Massiah* turns on neither "custody" nor "interrogation," the key *Miranda* concepts. Rather, the *Massiah* doctrine represents a pure right to counsel approach.

Once adversary proceedings have commenced against an individual (e.g., he has been indicted or arraigned) he is entitled to the assistance of counsel and the government may not "deliberately elicit" incriminating statements from him, neither openly by uniformed police officers nor surreptitiously by "secret agents." This prohibition applies regardless of whether the individual is in "custody" or being subjected to "interrogation" in the *Miranda* sense. There need not be any compelling influences at work, inherent, informal or otherwise. (There certainly were not any in the *Massiah* case itself.)

Nevertheless, perhaps because the lower courts had treated *Williams* as a *Miranda* case, a majority of the *Williams* Court thought it important, if not crucial, to establish that the "Christian burial speech" delivered by Captain Leaming did constitute "interrogation"—and all four dissenters insisted it was not. Considering the Court's subsequent discussion of "interrogation" in *Rhode Island v. Innis* [§ 4 supra], the captain's "speech" does appear to have been a form of "*Miranda* interrogation," but *it did not have to be,* in order for the *Massiah* doctrine to have protected Williams.

*United States v. Henry,* 447 U.S. 264 (1980), not only reaffirmed the *Massiah–Williams* doctrine, but expanded it by applying it to a situation where the FBI had instructed its paid government informant, ostensibly defendant's "cellmate," not to question defendant about the crime, and there was no showing that he had. Nevertheless, the Court, per Burger, C.J., rejected the government's argument that the incriminating statements were not the result of any "affirmative conduct" on the part of government agents to elicit evidence. The informant "was not a passive listener; rather he had 'some conversations with Mr. Henry' while he was in jail and Henry's incriminatory statements were 'the product of this conversation.' "

Moreover, and more generally, observed the Court: Even if the FBI agent's statement is accepted that "he did not intend that [the informant] would take affirmative steps to secure incriminating information, he must have known that such propinquity likely would lead to that result. * * * By intentionally creating a situation likely to induce Henry to make incriminating statements without the assistance of counsel [after Henry had been indicted and counsel had been appointed for him], the government violated Henry's Sixth Amendment right to counsel."

This broad—some would say, loose—language would seem to prohibit the government from "planting" even a completely "passive" secret agent in a person's cell once adversary proceedings have commenced against him. But the *Henry* Court cautioned that it was not "called upon to pass on the situation where an informant is placed in [close] proximity [to a prisoner] but makes no effort to stimulate conversations about the crime charged." Moreover, concurring Justice Powell made it plain that he could not join the majority opinion if it held that "the mere presence or incidental conversation of an informant in a jail cell would violate *Massiah*." The *Massiah* doctrine, emphasized Powell, "does not prohibit the introduction of spontaneous conversations that are not elicited by governmental action."

May the government employ a "passive informant" without violating the *Massiah* doctrine? Must the informant be—is it possible for him to be—completely "passive"? These questions are addressed in the second case in this section, *Kuhlmann v. Wilson,* the most recent "jail plant" case. As is graphically illustrated by *Kuhlmann,* the line between "active" and "passive" secret agents—between "*stimulating*" conversations with a defendant in order to "elicit" incriminating statements from him and taking no action "beyond *merely listening*"—is an exceedingly difficult one to draw.

### BREWER v. WILLIAMS (WILLIAMS I)
430 U.S. 387, 97 S.Ct. 1232, 51 L.Ed.2d 424 (1977).

JUSTICE STEWART delivered the opinion of the Court. * * *

On the afternoon of December 24, 1968, a 10–year–old girl named Pamela Powers went with her family to the YMCA in Des Moines, Iowa. [When] she failed to return from a trip to the washroom, a search for her began. The search was unsuccessful.

Robert Williams, who had recently escaped from a mental hospital, was a resident of the YMCA. Soon after the girl's disappearance Williams was seen in the YMCA lobby carrying some clothing and a large bundle wrapped in a blanket. He obtained help from a 14–year–old boy in opening the street door of the YMCA and the door to his automobile parked outside. When Williams placed the bundle in the front seat of his car the boy "saw two legs in it and they were skinny and white." Before anyone could see what was in the bundle Williams drove away. His abandoned car was found the following day in Davenport, Iowa, roughly 160 miles east of Des Moines. A warrant was then issued in Des Moines for his arrest on a charge of abduction.

On the morning of December 26, a Des Moines lawyer named Henry McKnight went to the Des Moines police station and informed the officers present that he had just received a long distance call from Williams, and that he had advised Williams to turn himself in to the Davenport police. Williams did surrender that morning to the police in Davenport, and they booked him on the charge specified in the arrest warrant and gave him the [*Miranda* warnings]. The Davenport police then telephoned their counterparts in Des Moines to inform them that Williams had surrendered. McKnight, the lawyer, was still at the Des Moines police headquarters, and Williams conversed with McKnight on the telephone. In the presence of the Des Moines Chief of Police and a Police Detective named Leaming [a captain and 20–year veteran of the Des Moines police department], McKnight advised Williams that Des Moines police officers would be driving to Davenport to pick him up, that the officers would not interrogate him or mistreat him, and that Williams was not to talk to the officers about Pamela Powers until after consulting with McKnight upon his return to Des Moines. As a result of these conversations, it was agreed between McKnight and the Des Moines police officials that Detective Leaming and a fellow officer would drive to Davenport to pick up Williams, that they would bring him directly back to Des Moines, and that they would not question him during the trip.

In the meantime Williams was arraigned before a judge in Davenport on the outstanding arrest warrant. The judge advised him of his *Miranda* rights and committed him to jail. Before leaving the courtroom, Williams conferred with a lawyer named Kelly, who advised him not to make any statements until consulting with McKnight back in Des Moines.

Detective Leaming and his fellow officer arrived in Davenport about noon to pick up Williams and return him to Des Moines. Soon after their arrival they met with Williams and Kelly, who, they understood, was acting as Williams' lawyer. Detective Leaming repeated the *Miranda* warnings, and told Williams:

> "∗  ∗  ∗ we both know that you're being represented here by Mr. Kelly and you're being represented by Mr. McKnight in Des Moines, and ∗  ∗  ∗ I want you to remember this because we'll be visiting between here and Des Moines."

Williams then conferred again with Kelly alone, and after this conference Kelly reiterated to Detective Leaming that Williams was not to be questioned about the disappearance of Pamela Powers until after he had consulted with McKnight back in Des Moines. When Leaming expressed some reservations, Kelly firmly stated that the agreement with McKnight was to be carried out—that there was to be no interrogation of Williams during the automobile journey to Des Moines. Kelly was denied permission to ride in the police car back to Des Moines with Williams and the two officers.

The two Detectives, with Williams in their charge, then set out on the 160–mile drive. At no time during the trip did Williams express a willingness to be interrogated in the absence of an attorney. Instead, he stated several times that "[w]hen I get to Des Moines and see Mr. McKnight, I am going to tell you the whole story." Detective Leaming knew that Williams was a former mental patient, and knew also that he was deeply religious.

The Detective and his prisoner soon embarked on a wide-ranging conversation covering a variety of topics, including the subject of religion. Then, not long after leaving Davenport and reaching the interstate highway, Detective Leaming delivered what has been referred to [as] the "Christian burial speech." Addressing Williams as "Reverend," the Detective said:

> "I want to give you something to think about while we're traveling down the road. ∗  ∗  ∗ Number one, I want you to observe the weather conditions,

it's raining, it's sleeting, it's freezing, driving is very treacherous, visibility is poor, it's going to be dark early this evening. They are predicting several inches of snow for tonight, and I feel that you yourself are the only person that knows where this little girl's body is, that you yourself have only been there once, and if you get a snow on top of it you yourself may be unable to find it. And, since we will be going right past the area on the way into Des Moines, I feel that we could stop and locate the body, that the parents of this little girl should be entitled to a Christian burial for the little girl who was snatched away from them on Christmas Eve and murdered. And I feel we should stop and locate it on the way in rather than waiting until morning and trying to come back out after a snow storm and possibly not being able to find it at all."

Williams asked Detective Leaming why he thought their route to Des Moines would be taking them past the girl's body, and Leaming responded that he knew the body was in the area of Mitchellville—a town they would be passing on the way to Des Moines.[1] Leaming then stated: "I do not want you to answer me. I don't want to discuss it further. Just think about it as we're riding down the road."

As the car approached Grinell, a town approximately 100 miles west of Davenport, Williams asked whether the police had found the victim's shoes. When Detective Leaming replied that he was unsure, Williams directed the officers to a service station where he said he had left the shoes; a search for them proved unsuccessful. As they continued towards Des Moines, Williams asked whether the police had found the blanket, and directed the officers to a rest area where he said he had disposed of the blanket. Nothing was found. The car continued towards Des Moines, and as it approached Mitchellville, Williams said that he would show the officers where the body was. He then directed the police to the body of Pamela Powers.

[The trial judge admitted all evidence relating to or resulting from statements Williams made in the car ride. He found that "an agreement" had been made between defense counsel and the police that Williams would not be questioned on the return trip to Des Moines, but ruled that Williams had waived his rights before giving such information.]

[On federal habeas corpus, the] District Court made findings of fact as summarized above, and concluded as a matter of law that the evidence in question had been wrongly admitted at Williams' trial. This conclusion was based on three alternative and independent grounds: (1) that Williams had been denied his constitutional right to the assistance of counsel; (2) that he had been denied [his *Miranda* rights]; and (3) that in any event, [his] statements [had] been involuntarily made.

[The] Court of Appeals appears to have affirmed the judgment on [the first two] grounds. We have concluded that only one of them need be considered here.

Specifically, there is no need to review the [*Miranda* doctrine] [or the] the ruling of the District Court that Williams' self-incriminating statements were, indeed, involuntarily made. For it is clear that the judgment before us must in any event be affirmed upon the ground that Williams was deprived of a different constitutional right—the right to the assistance of counsel.

---

**1.** The fact of the matter, of course, was that Detective Leaming possessed no such knowledge.

* * * Whatever else it may mean, the right to counsel * * * means at least that a person is entitled to the help of a lawyer at or after the time that judicial proceedings have been initiated against him—"whether by way of formal charge, preliminary hearing, indictment, information, or arraignment." *Kirby v. Illinois* [Ch. 7, § 2].

There can be no doubt in the present case that judicial proceedings had been initiated against Williams before the start of the automobile ride from Davenport to Des Moines. A warrant had been issued for his arrest, he had been arraigned on that warrant before a judge in a Davenport courtroom, and he had been committed by the court to confinement in jail. The State does not contend otherwise.

There can be no serious doubt, either, that Detective Leaming deliberately and designedly set out to elicit information from Williams just as surely as—and perhaps more effectively than—if he had formally interrogated him. Detective Leaming was fully aware before departing for Des Moines that Williams was being represented in Davenport by Kelly and in Des Moines by McKnight. Yet he purposely sought during Williams' isolation from his lawyers to obtain as much incriminating information as possible. Indeed, Detective Leaming conceded as much when he testified at Williams' trial:

"Q. In fact, Captain, whether he was a mental patient or not, you were trying to get all the information you could before he got to his lawyer, weren't you?

"A. I was sure hoping to find out where that little girl was, yes, sir.

* * *

"Q. Well, I'll put it this way: You [were] hoping to get all the information you could before Williams got back to McKnight, weren't you?

"A. Yes, sir." [6]

The state courts clearly proceeded upon the hypothesis that Detective Leaming's "Christian burial speech" had been tantamount to interrogation. Both courts recognized that Williams had been entitled to the assistance of counsel at the time he made the incriminating statements. Yet no such constitutional protection would have come into play if there had been no interrogation.

The circumstances of this case are thus constitutionally indistinguishable from those presented in *Massiah*. [That] the incriminating statements were elicited surreptitiously in [*Massiah*], and otherwise here, is constitutionally irrelevant. Rather, the clear rule of *Massiah* is that once adversary proceedings have commenced against an individual, he has a right to legal representation when the government interrogates him. It thus requires no wooden or technical application of the *Massiah* doctrine to conclude that Williams was entitled to the assistance of counsel guaranteed to him by the Sixth and Fourteenth Amendments.

The Iowa courts recognized that Williams had been denied the constitutional right to the assistance of counsel. They held, however, that he had waived that right during the course of the automobile trip from Davenport to Des Moines. The state trial court explained its determination of waiver as follows:

"The time element involved on the trip, the general circumstances of it, and more importantly the absence on the Defendant's part of any assertion of his right or desire not to give information absent the presence of his

6. Counsel for the State, in the course of oral argument in this Court, acknowledged that the "Christian burial speech" was tantamount to interrogation * * *.

attorney, are the main foundations for the Court's conclusion that he voluntarily waived such right."

[The] District Court and the Court of Appeals were correct in the view that the question of waiver was not a question of historical fact, but one [that], requires "application of constitutional principles to the facts as found."

The [lower federal courts] were also correct in their understanding of the proper standard to be applied in determining the question of waiver as a matter of federal constitutional law—that it was incumbent upon the State to prove "an intentional relinquishment or abandonment of a known right or privilege." *Johnson v. Zerbst.* [That] strict standard applies equally to an alleged waiver of the right to counsel whether at trial or at a critical stage of pretrial proceedings.

We conclude, finally that the Court of Appeals was correct in holding that, judged by these standards, the record in this case falls far short of sustaining the State's burden. It is true that Williams had been informed of and appeared to understand his right to counsel. But waiver requires not merely comprehension but relinquishment, and Williams' consistent reliance upon the advice of counsel in dealing with the authorities refutes any suggestion that he waived that right. * * * His statements while in the car that he would tell the whole story *after* seeing McKnight in Des Moines were the clearest expressions by Williams himself that he desired the presence of an attorney before any interrogation took place. But even before making these statements, Williams had effectively asserted his right to counsel by having secured attorneys at both ends of the automobile trip, both of whom, acting as his agents, had made clear to the police that no interrogation was to occur during the journey. Williams knew of that agreement and, particularly in view of his consistent reliance on counsel, there is no basis for concluding that he disavowed it.

Despite Williams' express and implicit assertions of his right to counsel, Detective Leaming proceeded to elicit incriminating statements from Williams. Leaming did not preface this effort by telling Williams that he had a right to the presence of a lawyer, and made no effort at all to ascertain whether Williams wished to relinquish that right. The circumstances of record in this case thus provide no reasonable basis for finding that Williams waived his right to the assistance of counsel.

The Court of Appeals did not hold, nor do we, that under the circumstances of this case Williams *could not,* without notice to counsel, have waived his rights under the Sixth and Fourteenth Amendments. It only held, as do we, that he did not.

* * * Although we do not lightly affirm the issuance of a writ of habeas corpus in this case, so clear a violation of the Sixth and Fourteenth Amendments as here occurred cannot be condoned. * * * The judgment of the Court of Appeals is affirmed.[12]

---

**12.** The District Court stated that its decision "does not touch upon the issue of what evidence, if any, beyond the incriminating statements themselves must be excluded as 'fruit of the poisonous tree.'" We too have no occasion to address this issue, and in the present posture of the case there is no basis for the view of our dissenting Brethren [that] any attempt to retry the respondent would probably be futile. While neither Williams' incriminating statements themselves nor any testimony describing his having led the police to the victim's body can constitutionally be ad-

mitted into evidence, evidence of where the body was found and of its condition might well be admissible on the theory that the body would have been discovered in any event, even had incriminating statements not been elicited from Williams. In the event that a retrial is instituted, it will be for the state courts in the first instance to determine whether particular items of evidence may be admitted.

[On retrial, the state court admitted evidence of the condition of the body of Pamela Powers and the results of post mortem tests on the

JUSTICE MARSHALL, concurring.

I concur wholeheartedly in my Brother Stewart's opinion for the Court, but add these words in light of the dissenting opinions filed today. The dissenters have, I believe, lost sight of the fundamental constitutional backbone of our criminal law. They seem to think that Detective Leaming's actions were perfectly proper, indeed laudable, examples of "good police work." In my view, good police work is something far different from catching the criminal at any price. It is equally important that the police, as guardians of the law, fulfill their responsibility to obey its commands scrupulously.

[In] this case, there can be no doubt that Detective Leaming consciously and knowingly set out to violate Williams' Sixth Amendment right to counsel and his Fifth Amendment privilege against self-incrimination, as Leaming himself understood those rights. * * * Leaming surely understood, because he had overheard McKnight tell Williams as much, that the location of the body would be revealed to police. Undoubtedly Leaming realized the way in which that information would be conveyed to the police: McKnight would learn it from his client and then he would lead police to the body. Williams would thereby be protected by the attorney-client privilege from incriminating himself by directly demonstrating his knowledge of the body's location, and the unfortunate Powers child could be given a "Christian burial."

Of course, this scenario would accomplish all that Leaming sought from his investigation except that it would not produce incriminating statements or actions from Williams. Accordingly, Leaming undertook his charade to pry such evidence from Williams. After invoking the no-passengers rule to prevent attorney Kelly from accompanying the prisoner, Leaming had Williams at his mercy: during the three- or four-hour trip he could do anything he wished to elicit a confession.

* * * If Williams is to go free—and given the ingenuity of Iowa prosecutors on retrial or in a civil commitment proceeding, I doubt very much that there is any chance a dangerous criminal will be loosed on the streets, the blood-curdling cries of the dissents notwithstanding—it will hardly be because he deserves it. It will be because Detective Leaming, knowing full well that he risked reversal of Williams' conviction, intentionally denied Williams the right of *every* American under the Sixth Amendment to have the protective shield of a lawyer between himself and the awesome power of the State.

     * * *

JUSTICE POWELL, concurring.  * * *

The critical factual issue is whether there had been a voluntary waiver, and this turns in large part upon whether there was interrogation. * * *

body because the body "would have been found in any event"—if Williams had not led the police to the victim the search would have been taken up again where it left off and the body would have been discovered within a short time in essentially the same condition as it was actually found. Williams was again convicted of murder. The case came to the U.S. Supreme Court a second time, *Nix v. Williams* (*Williams II*), 467 U.S. 431 (1984). The Court, per Burger, C.J., upheld the state court's use of the "inevitable discovery" exception, observing:

["Exclusion of physical evidence that would inevitably have been discovered adds nothing to either the integrity or fairness of a criminal trial. * * * [I]f the government can prove that the evidence would have been obtained inevitably and, therefore, would have been admitted regardless of any over-reaching by the police, there is no rational basis to keep that evidence from the jury in order to ensure the fairness of the trial proceedings. In that situation, the State has gained no advantage at trial and the defendant has suffered no prejudice. Indeed, suppression of the evidence would operate to undermine the adversary system by putting the State in a *worse* position than it would have occupied without any police misconduct."]

Prior to the automobile trip from Davenport to Des Moines, Williams had been arrested, booked, and carefully given *Miranda* warnings. It is settled constitutional doctrine that he then had the right to the assistance of counsel. His exercise of this right was evidenced uniquely in this case. * * * Significantly, the recognition by the police of the status of counsel was evidenced by the *express agreement* between McKnight and the appropriate police officials that the officers who would drive Williams to Des Moines would not interrogate him in the absence of counsel.

The incriminating statements were made by Williams during the long ride while in the custody of two police officers, and in the absence of his retained counsel. The dissent of the Chief Justice concludes that prior to these statements, Williams had "made a valid waiver" of his right to have counsel present. This view disregards the record evidence clearly indicating that the police engaged in interrogation of Williams.

[The] dissenting opinion of the Chief Justice states that the Court's holding today "conclusively presumes a suspect is legally incompetent to change his mind and tell the truth until an attorney is present." I find no justification for this view. On the contrary, the opinion of the Court is explicitly clear that the right to assistance of counsel may be waived, after it has attached, without notice to or consultation with counsel. We would have such a case here if [the State] had proved that the police officers refrained from coercion and interrogation, as they had agreed, and that Williams freely on his own initiative had confessed the crime. * * *[a]

Chief Justice Burger, dissenting.

The result in this case ought to be intolerable in any society which purports to call itself an organized society. It continues the Court—by the narrowest margin—on the much-criticized course of punishing the public for the mistakes and misdeeds of law enforcement officers, instead of punishing the officer directly, if in fact he is guilty of wrongdoing. It mechanically and blindly keeps reliable evidence from juries whether the claimed constitutional violation involves gross police misconduct or honest human error.

Williams is guilty of the savage murder of a small child; no member of the Court contends he is not. While in custody, and after no fewer than *five* warnings of his rights to silence and to counsel, he led police to the concealed body of his victim. The Court concedes Williams was not threatened or coerced and that he spoke and acted voluntarily and with full awareness of his constitutional rights. In the face of all this, the Court now holds that because Williams was prompted by the detective's statement—not interrogation but a statement—the jury must not be told how the police found the body. * * *

Under well-settled precedents which the Court freely acknowledges, it is very clear that Williams had made a valid waiver of his Fifth Amendment right to silence and his Sixth Amendment right to counsel when he led police to the child's body. Indeed, even under the Court's analysis I do not understand how a contrary conclusion is possible. * * *

The evidence is uncontradicted that Williams had abundant knowledge of his right to have counsel present and of his right to silence. Since the Court does not question his mental competence, it boggles the mind to suggest that

---

**a.** Stevens, J., joined the opinion of the Court, but also added a brief comment concluding: "If, in the long run, we are seriously concerned about the individual's effective representation by counsel, the State cannot be permitted to dishonor its promise to this lawyer."

Williams could not understand that leading police to the child's body would have other than the most serious consequences. * * *

One plausible but unarticulated basis for the result reached is that once a suspect has asserted his right not to talk without the presence of an attorney, it becomes legally impossible for him to waive that right until he has seen an attorney. But constitutional rights are *personal*, and an otherwise valid waiver should not be brushed aside by judges simply because an attorney was not present. * * *[2]

* * * Mr. Justice Powell suggests that the result in this case turns on whether Detective Leaming's remarks constituted "interrogation," as he views them, or whether they were "statements" intended to prick the conscience of the accused. I find it most remarkable that a murder case should turn on judicial interpretation that a statement becomes a question simply because it is followed by an incriminating disclosure from the suspect. The Court seems to be saying that since Williams said he would "tell the whole story" at Des Moines, the police should have been content and waited; of course, that would have been the wiser course, especially in light of the nuances of constitutional jurisprudence applied by the Court, but a murder case ought not turn on such tenuous strands.

In any case, the Court assures us, this is not at all what it intends, and that a valid waiver was *possible* in these circumstances, but was not quite made. Here of course Williams did not confess to the murder in so many words; it was his conduct in guiding police to the body, not his words, which incriminated him. And the record is replete with evidence that Williams knew precisely what he was doing when he guided police to the body. The human urge to confess wrongdoing is, of course, normal in all save hardened, professional criminals, as psychiatrists and analysts have demonstrated.

Even if there was no waiver, and assuming a technical violation occurred, the Court errs gravely in mechanically applying the exclusionary rule without considering whether that draconian judicial doctrine should be invoked in these circumstances, or indeed whether any of its conceivable goals will be furthered by its application here.

* * * Today's holding interrupts what has been a more rational perception of the constitutional and social utility of excluding reliable evidence from the truthseeking process. In its Fourth Amendment context, we have now recognized that the exclusionary rule is in no sense a *personal* constitutional right, but a judicially conceived remedial device designed to safeguard and effectuate guaranteed legal rights generally [referring to *Stone v. Powell*, 428 U.S. 465 (1976), holding the exclusionary rule inapplicable to habeas review, *United States v. Janis*, 428 U.S. 433 (1976), holding the exclusionary rule inapplicable in a civil tax proceeding, *United States v. Calandra*, holding the exclusionary rule inapplicable in a grand jury proceeding]. We have repeatedly emphasized that deterrence of unconstitutional or otherwise unlawful police conduct is the only valid justification for excluding reliable and probative evidence from the criminal factfinding process.

Accordingly, unlawfully obtained evidence is not automatically excluded from the factfinding process in all circumstances. In a variety of contexts we inquire whether application of the rule will promote its objectives sufficiently to justify the enormous cost it imposes on society. * * *

**2.** [A] paternalistic rule is particularly anomalous in the Sixth Amendment context, where this Court has only recently discovered an independent constitutional right of self-representation, allowing an accused the absolute right to proceed without a lawyer at trial, once he is aware of the consequences. *Faretta* [Ch. 17 infra].

Against this background, it is striking that the Court fails even to consider whether the benefits secured by application of the exclusionary rule in this case outweigh its obvious social costs. Perhaps the failure is due to the fact that this case arises not under the Fourth Amendment, but under *Miranda,* and the Sixth Amendment right to counsel. The Court apparently perceives the function of the exclusionary rule to be so different in these varying contexts that it must be mechanically and uncritically applied in all cases arising outside the Fourth Amendment.

[W]hether considered under *Miranda* or the Sixth Amendment, there is no more reason to exclude the evidence in this case than there was in *Stone* [and] in other Fourth Amendment cases suggesting a balancing approach toward utilization of the exclusionary sanction. Rather than adopting a formalistic analysis varying with the constitutional provision invoked, we should apply the exclusionary rule on the basis of its benefits and costs, at least in those cases where the police conduct at issue is far from being outrageous or egregious. * * *

JUSTICE WHITE, with whom JUSTICE BLACKMUN and JUSTICE REHNQUIST join, dissenting.

* * * The issue in this case is whether respondent—who was entitled not to make any statements to the police without consultation with and/or presence of counsel [1]—validly waived those rights. * * *

[I disagree with the majority's finding that no waiver was proved in this case.] That respondent knew of his right not to say anything to the officers without advice and presence of counsel is established on this record to a moral certainty. He was advised of the right by three officials of the State—telling at least one that he understood the right—and by two lawyers.[4] Finally, he further demonstrated his knowledge of the right by informing the police that he would tell them the story in the presence of McKnight when they arrived in Des Moines. The issue in this case, then, is whether respondent relinquished that right intentionally.

Respondent relinquished his right not to talk to the police about his crime when the car approached the place where he had hidden the victim's clothes. Men usually intend to do what they do and there is nothing in the record to support the proposition that respondent's decision to talk was anything but an exercise of his own free will. Apparently, without any prodding from the officers, respondent—who had earlier said that he would tell the whole story when he arrived in Des Moines—spontaneously changed his mind about the timing of his disclosures when the car approached the places where he had hidden the evidence. However, even if his statements were influenced by Detective Leaming's above-quoted statement, respondent's decision to talk in the absence of counsel can hardly be viewed as the product of an overborn will. The statement by Leaming was not coercive; it was accompanied by a request that respondent not respond to it; and it was delivered hours before respondent decided to make any statement. Respondent's waiver was thus knowing and intentional.

The majority's contrary conclusion seems to rest on the fact that respondent "asserted" his right to counsel by retaining and consulting with one lawyer and

---

**1.** It does not matter whether the right not to make statements in the absence of counsel stems from *Massiah* or *Miranda.* In either case the question is one of waiver. Waiver was not addressed in *Massiah* because there the statements were being made to an informant and the defendant had no way of knowing that he had a right not to talk to him without counsel.

**4.** Moreover, he in fact received advice of counsel on at least two occasions on the question whether he should talk to the police on the trip to Des Moines.

by consulting with another. How this supports the conclusion that respondent's later relinquishment of his right not to talk in the absence of counsel was unintentional is a mystery. The fact that respondent consulted with counsel on the question whether he should talk to the police in counsel's absence makes his later decision to talk in counsel's absence *better* informed and, if anything, more intelligent.

The majority recognizes that even after this "assertion" of his right to counsel, it would have found that respondent waived his right not to talk in counsel's absence if his waiver had been express—i.e., if the officers had asked him in the car whether he would be willing to answer questions in counsel's absence and if he had answered "yes." But waiver is not a formalistic concept. Waiver is shown whenever the facts establish that an accused knew of a right and intended to relinquish it. Such waiver, even if not express, was plainly shown here. The only other conceivable basis for the majority's holding is the implicit suggestion that the right involved in *Massiah,* as distinguished from the right involved in *Miranda,* is a right not to be *asked* any questions in counsel's absence rather than a right not to *answer* any questions in counsel's absence, and that the right not to be *asked* questions must be waived *before* the questions are asked. Such wafer thin distinctions cannot determine whether a guilty murderer should go free. The only conceivable purpose for the presence of counsel during questioning is to protect an accused from making incriminating *answers.* Questions, unanswered, have no significance at all. Absent coercion— no matter how the right involved is defined—an accused is amply protected by a rule requiring waiver before or simultaneously with the giving by him of an answer or the making by him of a statement.

\* \* \*

MR. JUSTICE BLACKMUN, with whom MR. JUSTICE WHITE and MR. JUSTICE REHNQUIST join, dissenting. \* \* \*

What the Court chooses to do here, and with which I disagree, is to hold that respondent Williams' situation was in the mold of *Massiah,* that is, that it was dominated by a denial to Williams of his Sixth Amendment right to counsel after criminal proceedings had been instituted against him. The Court rules that the Sixth Amendment was violated because Detective Leaming "purposely sought during Williams' isolation from his lawyers to obtain as much incriminating information as possible." I cannot regard that as unconstitutional *per se.*

First, the police did not deliberately seek to isolate Williams from his lawyers so as to deprive him of the assistance of counsel. Cf. *Escobedo.* The isolation in this case was a necessary incident of transporting Williams to the county where the crime was committed.

Second, Leaming's purpose was not solely to obtain incriminating evidence. The victim had been missing for only two days, and the police could not be certain that she was dead. Leaming, of course, and in accord with his duty, was "hoping to find out where that little girl was," but such motivation does not equate with an intention to evade the Sixth Amendment. \* \* \*

Third, not every attempt to elicit information should be regarded as "tantamount to interrogation." I am not persuaded that Leaming's observations and comments, made as the police car traversed the snowy and slippery miles between Davenport and Des Moines that winter afternoon, were an interrogation, direct or subtle, of Williams. Williams, after all, was counseled by lawyers, and warned by the arraigning judge in Davenport and by the police, and yet it was he who started the travel conversations and brought up the subject of the criminal investigation.

[In] summary, it seems to me that the Court is holding that *Massiah* is violated whenever police engage in any conduct, in the absence of counsel, with the subjective desire to obtain information from a suspect after arraignment. Such a rule is far too broad. Persons in custody frequently volunteer statements in response to stimuli other than interrogation.  \*  \*  \*

## KUHLMANN v. WILSON

### 477 U.S. 436, 106 S.Ct. 2616, 91 L.Ed.2d 364 (1986).

JUSTICE POWELL delivered the opinion of the Court.

[Respondent Wilson and two confederates robbed a garage and fatally shot the night dispatcher. Four days later, respondent turned himself in. He admitted that he had witnessed the robbery and murder, but denied any involvement in them, claiming that he had fled because he was afraid of being blamed for the crimes. He gave the police a description of the robbers, but denied knowing them.

[After his arraignment, Wilson was placed in a cell with a prisoner named Benny Lee. Unknown to Wilson, Lee had agreed to act as a police informant. Since the police had positive evidence of Wilson's involvement, the purpose of placing Lee in the cell was to determine the identities of the other perpetrators. According to his arrangement with Detective Cullen, Lee was not to ask Wilson any questions, but simply to "keep his ears open" for the names of Wilson's confederates. Wilson first spoke to Lee about the crimes after looking out the cellblock window at the garage, where the crime had occurred. He told Lee the same story he had given the police. Lee advised Wilson that his story "didn't sound too good" and that "things didn't look too good for him," but Wilson did not alter his story at that time. However, several days later, after a visit from his brother, who mentioned that members of the family were upset because they believed he had killed the dispatcher, Wilson changed his story. He admitted to Lee that he and two other men had planned and carried out the robbery and killed the dispatcher. Lee reported these incriminating statements to Detective Cullen.

[The trial court denied Wilson's motion to suppress the incriminating statements, finding that Lee had obeyed police instructions only to listen to Wilson for the purpose of identifying his confederates, but not to question him about the crime. The trial court also found that Wilson's statements were "spontaneous" and "unsolicited." After he was convicted of murder and the conviction was affirmed, Wilson sought federal habeas corpus relief. After considering *Massiah,* the district court denied relief, finding "no interrogation whatsoever" by Lee and "only spontaneous statements" from Wilson. A divided U.S. Court of Appeals affirmed.

[Following the decision in *Henry,* Wilson decided to relitigate his Sixth Amendment claim. After his motion to vacate his conviction was denied, Wilson again sought federal habeas corpus relief. The district court concluded that the trial court's findings were "fatal" to Wilson's claim under *Henry* since they showed that the informant made "no affirmative effort" of any kind to elicit information from him. A divided Court of Appeals reversed, finding the circumstances indistinguishable from the facts of *Henry.*]

    \*  \*  \*

In *United States v. Henry,* the Court applied the *Massiah* test to incriminating statements made to a jailhouse informant. The Court of Appeals in that case found a violation of *Massiah* because the informant had engaged the defendant in conversations and "had developed a relationship of trust and confidence with [the defendant] such that [the defendant] revealed incriminating information." This Court affirmed, holding that the Court of Appeals reasonably concluded that the government informant "deliberately used his position to secure incriminating information from [the defendant] when counsel was not present." Although the informant had not questioned the defendant, the informant had "stimulated" conversations with the defendant in order to "elicit" incriminating information. The Court emphasized that those facts, like the facts of *Massiah,* amounted to " 'indirect and surreptitious interrogatio[n]' " of the defendant.  ＊ ＊ ＊

[As] *Maine v. Moulton,* 474 U.S. 159 (1985),[a] makes clear, the primary concern of the *Massiah* line of decisions is secret interrogation by investigatory techniques that are the equivalent of direct police interrogation. Since "the Sixth Amendment is not violated whenever—by luck or happenstance—the State obtains incriminating statements from the accused after the right to counsel has attached," a defendant does not make out a violation of that right simply by showing that an informant, either through prior arrangement or voluntarily, reported his incriminating statements to the police. Rather, the defendant must demonstrate that the police and their informant took some action, beyond merely listening, that was designed deliberately to elicit incriminating remarks.

It is thus apparent that the Court of Appeals erred in concluding that respondent's right to counsel was violated under the circumstances of this case. [It failed] to accord to the state trial court's factual findings the presumption of correctness expressly required by 28 U.S.C. § 2254(d).

The state court found that Officer Cullen had instructed Lee only to listen to respondent for the purpose of determining the identities of the other participants in the robbery and murder. The police already had solid evidence of respondent's participation. The court further found that Lee followed those instructions, that he "at no time asked any questions" of respondent concerning the pending charges, and that he "only listened" to respondent's "spontaneous" and "unsolicited" statements. The only remark made by Lee that has any support in this record was his comment that respondent's initial version of his participation in the crimes "didn't sound too good." Without holding that any of the state court's findings were not entitled to the presumption of correctness under § 2254(d), the Court of Appeals focused on that one remark and gave a description of Lee's interaction with respondent that is completely at odds with the facts found by the trial court. In the Court of Appeals' view, "Subtly and slowly, but surely, Lee's ongoing verbal intercourse with [respondent] served to exacerbate [respondent's] already troubled state of mind." [24] After thus revising some of the

**a.** *Moulton* holds that the *Massiah* doctrine applies to a crime for which the defendant has already been indicted even though the government had other, legitimate reasons for intercepting defendant's conversations—to insure the safety of its secret agent and to gather information concerning a report that defendant was planning to kill a witness. The Court, per Brennan, J., agreed that it was "entirely proper" for the government to conduct an investigation of defendant's activities, even though he had already been indicted, and statements obtained from him would be admissible at a subsequent trial for crimes *apart* from those for which defendant had already been indicted. But statement pertain-

ing to *pending charges* had to be excluded at the trial of those charges despite the fact the government was also investigating other crimes. For to allow incriminating statements pertaining to pending charges to be used "whenever the police assert an alternative, legitimate reason for their surveillance invites abuse by law enforcement personnel in the form of fabricated investigations and risks the evisceration of the Sixth Amendment right recognized in *Massiah.*"

**24.** Curiously, the Court of Appeals expressed concern that respondent was placed in a cell that overlooked the scene of his crimes. For all the record shows, however, that fact trial court's findings, and ignoring other more relevant findings, the Court of Appeals concluded that the police "deliberately elicited" respondent's incriminating statements. This conclusion conflicts with the decision of every other state and federal judge who reviewed this record, and is clear error in light of the provisions and intent of § 2254(d).[b]

JUSTICE BRENNAN, with whom JUSTICE MARSHALL joins, dissenting. * * *

[The] Court concludes [that] the Court of Appeals failed to recognize that this case presents the question, reserved in *Henry,* whether the Sixth Amendment forbids the admission into evidence of an accused's statements to a jailhouse informant who was "placed in close proximity but [made] no effort to stimulate conversations about the crime charged." I disagree with the Court's characterization of the Court of Appeals' treatment of the state court's findings and, consequently, I disagree with the Court that the instant case presents the "listening post" question.

The state trial court simply found that Lee did not ask respondent any direct questions about the crime for which respondent was incarcerated. The trial court considered the significance of this fact only under State precedents, which the court interpreted to require affirmative "interrogation" by the informant as a prerequisite to a constitutional violation. The court did not indicate whether it referred to a Fifth Amendment or to a Sixth Amendment violation in identifying "interrogation" as a precondition to a violation. * * *

The Court of Appeals did not disregard the state court's finding that Lee asked respondent no direct questions regarding the crime. Rather, the Court of Appeals *expressly accepted* that finding, but concluded that, as a matter of law, the deliberate elicitation standard of *Henry* and *Massiah,* encompasses other, more subtle forms of stimulating incriminating admissions than overt questioning. The court suggested that the police deliberately placed respondent in a cell that overlooked the scene of the crime, hoping that the view would trigger an inculpatory comment to respondent's cellmate.[8] The court also observed that, while Lee asked respondent no questions, Lee nonetheless stimulated conversation concerning respondents' role in [the] robbery and murder by remarking that respondent's exculpatory story did not " 'sound too good' " and that he had better come up with a better one. Thus, the Court of Appeals concluded that the respondent's case did not present the situation reserved in *Henry,* [but was] virtually indistinguishable from *Henry.*

The Sixth Amendment guarantees an accused, at least after the initiation of formal charges, the right to rely on counsel as the "medium" between himself and the State. *Moulton.* Accordingly, the Sixth Amendment "imposes on the State an affirmative obligation to respect and preserve the accused's choice to seek [the assistance of counsel]," and therefore "[t]he determination whether particular action by state agents violates the accused's right to * * * counsel must be made in light of this obligation." To be sure, the Sixth Amendment is not violated whenever, "by luck or happenstance," the State obtains incriminating statements from the accused after the right to counsel has attached. It is violated, however, when "the State obtains incriminating statements by know-

was sheer coincidence. Nor do we perceive any reason to require police to isolate one charged with crime so that he cannot view the scene, whatever it may be, from his cell window.

**b.** Chief Justice Burger, the author of *Henry,* joined the opinion of the Court, but also wrote a brief concurring opinion noting "a

vast difference between placing an 'ear' in the suspect's cell and placing a voice in the cell to encourage conversation for the 'ear' to record."

**8.** The Court of Appeals noted that "[a]s soon as Wilson arrived and viewed the garage, he became upset and stated that 'someone's messing with me.' "

ingly circumventing the accused's right to have counsel present in a confrontation between the accused and a state agent." As we explained in *Henry*, where the accused has not waived his right to counsel, the government knowingly circumvents the defendant's right to counsel where it "deliberately elicit[s]" inculpatory admissions, that is, "intentionally creat[es] a situation likely to induce [the accused] to make incriminating statements without the assistance of counsel."

In *Henry*, [we] rejected the Government's argument that because Henry initiated the discussion of his crime, no Sixth Amendment violation had occurred. We pointed out that under *Massiah*, it is irrelevant whether the informant asks pointed questions about the crime or "merely engage[s] in general conversation about it." * * *

In the instant case, as in *Henry*, the accused was incarcerated and therefore was "susceptible to the ploys of undercover Government agents." Like Nichols, Lee was a secret informant, usually received consideration for the services he rendered the police, and therefore had an incentive to produce the information which he knew the police hoped to obtain. Just as Nichols had done, Lee obeyed instructions not to question respondent and to report to the police any statements made by the respondent in Lee's presence about the crime in question. And, like Nichols, Lee encouraged respondent to talk about his crime by conversing with him on the subject over the course of several days and by telling respondent that his exculpatory story would not convince anyone without more work. However, unlike the situation in *Henry*, a disturbing visit from respondent's brother, rather than a conversation with the informant, seems to have been the immediate catalyst for respondent's confession to Lee. While it might appear from this sequence of events that Lee's comment regarding respondent's story and his general willingness to converse with respondent about the crime were not the *immediate* causes of respondent's admission, I think that the deliberate elicitation standard requires consideration of the entire course of government behavior.

The State intentionally created a situation in which it was foreseeable that respondent would make incriminating statements without the assistance of counsel, *Henry*, it assigned respondent to a cell overlooking the scene of the crime and designated a secret informant to be respondent's cellmate. The informant, while avoiding direct questions, nonetheless developed a relationship of cellmate camaraderie with respondent and encouraged him to talk about his crime. While the *coup de grace* was delivered by respondent's brother, the groundwork for respondent's confession was laid by the State. Clearly the State's actions had a sufficient nexus with respondent's admission of guilt to constitute deliberate elicitation within the meaning of *Henry*.[c]

    c. Stevens, J., filed a separate dissent, agreeing with Justice Brennan's analysis of the merits of respondent's habeas petition.

# Chapter 7

## LINEUPS, SHOWUPS AND OTHER PRE-TRIAL IDENTIFICATION PROCEDURES

Although mistaken identification has probably been the single greatest cause of conviction of the innocent, the Supreme Court did not come to grips with this problem until surprisingly late in the day. When it finally did, in 1967, the Court seemed bent on making up for lost time. Although it might have undertaken a case-by-case analysis of various identification situations, as had been done in the confession area in the thirty years prior to *Escobedo* and *Miranda,* only throwing out convictions based on unreliable identifications, the Court leapfrogged the fairness stage and applied the right to counsel to pretrial identifications in one swoop.

As explained in *United States v. Wade,* the first case set forth in this chapter, the right to counsel in the lineup context is supportive of another right—in this instance, the right to confrontation—in much the same manner that the *Miranda* counsel requirement rests upon the privilege against self-incrimination. (But see *Kirby v. Illinois,* the second case in this chapter.) For various reasons spelled out in the *Wade* opinion, under past lineup practices the defense was often unable "meaningfully to attack the credibility of the witness' courtroom identification." Moreover, pointed out the Court, the need to learn what occurred at the lineup is great, the risk of improper suggestion is substantial, and once the witness has picked out the accused in a pretrial identification proceeding, she is unlikely to go back on her word in court.[a]

Absent circumstances that presented "substantial countervailing policy considerations * * * against the requirement of the presence of counsel" (the Court may have had in mind "alley confrontations," i.e., prompt confrontations

---

a. *Wade* and *Gilbert* also raised a self-incrimination issue. Relying on *Schmerber v. California,* 384 U.S. 757 (1966), a 5–4 majority ruled that requiring a person to appear in a lineup and to speak for identification (*Wade*) or to provide handwriting exemplars (*Gilbert*) did not violate the privilege. In *Schmerber,* which involved the taking of a blood sample, over his objection, from a person arrested for drunken driving, the Court rejected the contention that the defendant had been "compelled [to] be a witness against himself" in violation of the Fifth Amendment. The self-incrimination clause, observed the Court, "protects an accused only from * * * provid[ing] the State with evidence of a testimonial or communicative nature." See also *Pennsylvania v. Muniz,* ___ U.S. ___ (1990) (evidence of slurred speech and lack of muscular coordination exhibited by drunk-driving arrestee during administration of sobriety tests amounts to non-testimonial information that falls outside scope of self-incrimination clause).

with the victim or an eyewitness at the scene of the crime),[b] the 1967 cases seemed to require the presence of counsel at *all* pretrial identifications. The pretrial identifications in *Wade* and *Gilbert* did take place after the defendants had been indicted, and the Court did mention this fact. But such references seemed—and most lower courts considered them to be—merely descriptive of the facts before the Court in those cases, not meant to restrict the operation of the new rule. For nothing in the *Wade* Court's reasoning suggested that a lineup or showup held before formal judicial proceedings begin—which is usually the case—is less riddled with dangers or less difficult for a suspect to reconstruct then one occurring after that point.

Nevertheless, in *Kirby v. Illinois* (1972), the second case in this chapter, the Court did announce a "post-indictment" rule—over the dissent of Justice Brennan, author of the *Wade* and *Gilbert* opinions. Following *Kirby* it became the common practice of law enforcement agencies to avoid the applicability of the right to counsel by conducting identification proceedings before the filing of formal charges.

A year after *Kirby*, the Burger Court struck the *Wade–Gilbert* rule another blow. This time, however, the Court's ruling confirmed the great weight of lower court authority. Unmoved by the argument that the availability of the photographs at trial provides no protection against the suggestive manner in which they may have been originally displayed to the witness or the comments or gestures that may have accompanied the display, the Court ruled in *United States v. Ash* (1973) (discussed infra, in a footnote to *Kirby*) that photographic identification may take place without defense counsel's participation, whether conducted before or after the filing of formal charges, and even though the suspect could have appeared in person at a lineup. Throughout the expansion of the constitutional right to counsel to certain pretrial proceedings, observed the Court, "the function of the lawyer has remained essentially the same as his function at trial"—to assist the accused "in meeting his adversary." But at a photo-identification, unlike a lineup, there is no "trial-like confrontation" involving the "presence of the accused." Again the author of *Wade* and *Gilbert*, Justice Brennan, was among those who dissented.[c]

Although *Kirby* and *Ash* severely restricted the potential reach of the original lineup decisions, abuses in photographic displays and in preindictment lineups are not, in theory at least, thereby placed beyond the reach of the Constitution: a defendant may still convince a court that the circumstances surrounding his identification present so "substantial" a "likelihood of misidentification" as to violate due process. But as illustrated by the last case in the chapter, *Manson v. Brathwaite*, this is a difficult task. An "unnecessarily

**b.** Even prior to *Kirby v. Illinois*, which limited the 1967 cases to post-indictment identifications, the great majority of lower courts had exempted alley confrontations from the right to counsel requirement.

**c.** The Warren Court had carved out an exception to the *Wade–Gilbert* rule for pretrial photographic identifications, but apparently a narrow one. In concluding that there was no right to have counsel present at the photo-identification in *Simmons v. United States*, 390 U.S. 377 (1968) and, alternatively, that the procedures utilized in that case were not "impermissibly suggestive," the Court stressed, first, that at the time the witnesses viewed the photographs for identification pur-

poses "the perpetrators were still at large" and "it was essential for the FBI agents swiftly to determine whether they were on the right track"; and second, that the witnesses were shown the photographs "only a day [after the bank robbery] while their memories were still fresh."

In *Ash*, although the defendant had been indicted, had been appointed counsel, and had been in detention for more than two years prior to trial, a photo-identification was conducted in the absence of counsel a day before the trial began. It was a photo display that seemed designed more to prompt the witness than to secure an identification.

suggestive" identification is not enough—the "totality of the circumstances" may still allow identification evidence if, despite the unnecessary "suggestiveness," the out-of-court identification "possesses certain features of reliability."

# SECTION 1. *WADE* AND *GILBERT*: CONSTITUTIONAL CONCERN ABOUT THE DANGERS INVOLVED IN EYEWITNESS IDENTIFICATIONS

## UNITED STATES v. WADE

388 U.S. 218, 87 S.Ct. 1926, 18 L.Ed.2d 1149 (1967).

JUSTICE BRENNAN delivered the opinion of the Court.

The question here is whether courtroom identifications of an accused at trial are to be excluded from evidence because the accused was exhibited to the witnesses before trial at a post-indictment lineup conducted for identification purposes without notice to and in the absence of the accused's appointed counsel.

The federally insured bank in Eustace, Texas, was robbed on September 21, 1964. A man with a small strip of tape on each side of his face entered the bank, pointed a pistol at the female cashier and the vice president, the only persons in the bank at the time, and forced them to fill a pillowcase with the bank's money. The man then drove away with an accomplice who had been waiting in a stolen car outside the bank. On March 23, 1965, an indictment was returned against respondent, Wade, and two others for conspiring to rob the bank, and against Wade and the accomplice for the robbery itself. Wade was arrested on April 2, and counsel was appointed to represent him on April 26. Fifteen days later [after counsel was appointed] an FBI agent, without notice to Wade's lawyer, arranged to have the two bank employees observe a lineup made up of Wade and five or six other prisoners and conducted in a courtroom of the local county courthouse. Each person in the line wore strips of tape such as allegedly worn by the robber and upon direction each said something like "put the money in the bag," the words allegedly uttered by the robber. Both bank employees identified Wade in the lineup as the bank robber.

At trial the two employees, when asked on direct examination if the robber was in the courtroom, pointed to Wade. The prior lineup identification was then elicited from both employees on cross-examination. At the close of testimony, Wade's counsel moved [to] strike the bank officials' courtroom identifications on [self-incrimination and right to counsel grounds]. The motion was denied, and Wade was convicted. The Court of Appeals for the Fifth Circuit reversed the conviction and ordered a new trial at which the in-court identification evidence was to be excluded, holding that [conducting the lineup in the absence of Wade's appointed counsel violated his Sixth Amendment rights]. * * *

[T]he principle of *Powell v. Alabama* and succeeding cases requires that we scrutinize *any* pretrial confrontation of the accused to determine whether the presence of his counsel is necessary to preserve the defendant's basic right to a fair trial as affected by his right meaningfully to cross-examine the witnesses against him and to have effective assistance of counsel at the trial itself. It calls upon us to analyze whether potential substantial prejudice to defendant's rights inheres in the particular confrontation and the ability of counsel to help avoid that prejudice.

The Government characterizes the lineup as a mere preparatory step in the gathering of the prosecution's evidence, not different—for Sixth Amendment purposes—from various other preparatory steps, such as systematized or scientific analyzing of the accused's fingerprints, blood sample, clothing, hair, and the like. We think there are differences which preclude such stages being characterized as critical stages at which the accused has the right to the presence of his counsel. Knowledge of the techniques of science and technology is sufficiently available, and the variables in techniques few enough, that the accused has the opportunity for a meaningful confrontation of the Government's case at trial through the ordinary processes of cross-examination of the Government's expert witnesses and the presentation of the evidence of his own experts. The denial of a right to have his counsel present at such analyses does not therefore violate the Sixth Amendment; they are not critical stages since there is minimal risk that his counsel's absence at such stages might derogate from his right to a fair trial.[a]

But the confrontation compelled by the State between the accused and the victim or witnesses to a crime to elicit identification evidence is peculiarly riddled with innumerable dangers and variable factors which might seriously, even crucially, derogate from a fair trial. The vagaries of eyewitness identification are well-known; the annals of criminal law are rife with instances of mistaken identification. * * * A major factor contributing to the high incidence of miscarriage of justice from mistaken identification has been the degree of suggestion inherent in the manner in which the prosecution presents the suspect to witnesses for pretrial identification. A commentator has observed that "[t]he influence of improper suggestion upon identifying witnesses probably accounts for more miscarriages of justice than any other single factor—perhaps it is responsible for more such errors than all other factors combined." Wall, *Eye–Witness Identification in Criminal Cases* 26 [1965]. Suggestion can be created intentionally or unintentionally in many subtle ways. And the dangers for the suspect are particularly grave when the witness' opportunity for observation was insubstantial, and thus his susceptibility to suggestion the greatest.

Moreover, "[i]t is a matter of common experience that, once a witness has picked out the accused at the line-up, he is not likely to go back on his word later on, so that in practice the issue of identity may (in the absence of other relevant evidence) for all practical purposes be determined there and then, before the trial."

The pretrial confrontation for purpose of identification may take the form of a lineup, also known as an "identification parade" or "showup," as in the present case, or presentation of the suspect alone to the witness, as in *Stovall v. Denno*.[b] It is obvious that risks of suggestion attend either form of confrontation and increase the dangers inhering in eyewitness identification. But as is the case with secret interrogations, there is serious difficulty in depicting what transpires

**a.** Consider, too, the companion case of *Gilbert v. California*, where the Court held, 5–4 on this issue, that the taking of handwriting exemplars from petitioner "was not a 'critical' stage of the criminal proceedings entitling petitioner to the assistance of counsel" for "there is minimal risk that the absence of counsel might derogate from his right to a fair trial. [If,] for some reason, an unrepresentative exemplar is taken, this can be brought out and corrected through the adversary process at trial since the accused can make an unlimited number of additional exemplars for analysis and comparison by government and defense handwriting experts."

**b.** In *Stovall*, discussed in § 3 infra, the Court noted the practice of showing suspects singly to potential witnesses "has been widely condemned," but held that under the extraordinary circumstances of the case ("an immediate hospital confrontation was imperative" because it appeared that the sole eye witness was near death) the one-person showing was justified.

at lineups and other forms of identification confrontations. [For] the same reasons, the defense can seldom reconstruct the manner and mode of lineup identification for judge or jury at trial. [The] impediments to an objective observation are increased when the victim is the witness. Lineups are prevalent in rape and robbery prosecutions and present a particular hazard that a victim's understandable outrage may excite vengeful or spiteful motives. In any event, neither witnesses nor lineup participants are apt to be alert for conditions prejudicial to the suspect. And if they were, it would likely be of scant benefit to the suspect since neither witnesses nor lineup participants are likely to be schooled in the detection of suggestive influences.[13] Improper influences may go undetected by a suspect, guilty or not, who experiences the emotional tension which we might expect in one being confronted with potential accusers. Even when he does observe abuse, if he has a criminal record he may be reluctant to take the stand and open up the admission of prior convictions. Moreover any protestations by the suspect of the fairness of the lineup made at trial are likely to be in vain; the jury's choice is between the accused's unsupported version and that of the police officers present. In short, the accused's inability effectively to reconstruct at trial any unfairness that occurred at the lineup may deprive him of his only opportunity meaningfully to attack the credibility of the witness' courtroom identification. * * *

The potential for improper influence is illustrated by the circumstances, insofar as they appear, surrounding the prior identifications in the three cases we decide today. In the present case, the testimony of the identifying witnesses elicited on cross-examination revealed that those witnesses were taken to the courthouse and seated in the courtroom to await assembly of the lineup. The courtroom faced on a hallway observable to the witnesses through an open door. The cashier testified that she saw Wade "standing in the hall" within sight of an FBI agent. Five or six other prisoners later appeared in the hall. The vice president testified that he saw a person in the hall in the custody of the agent who "resembled the person that we identified as the one that had entered the bank."

The lineup in *Gilbert* was conducted in an auditorium in which some 100 witnesses to several alleged state and federal robberies charged to Gilbert made wholesale identifications of Gilbert as the robber in each other's presence, a procedure said to be fraught with dangers of suggestion. And the vice of suggestion created by the identification in *Stovall* was the presentation to the witness of the suspect alone handcuffed to police officers. It is hard to imagine a situation more clearly conveying the suggestion to the witness that the one presented is believed guilty by the police.

The few cases that have surfaced therefore reveal the existence of a process attended with hazards of serious unfairness to the criminal accused and strongly suggest the plight of the more numerous defendants who are unable to ferret out suggestive influences in the secrecy of the confrontation. We do not assume that these risks are the result of police procedures intentionally designed to prejudice an accused. Rather we assume they derive from the dangers inherent in eyewitness identification and the suggestibility inherent in the context of the pretrial identification. * * *

13. An additional impediment to the detection of such influences by participants, including the suspect, is the physical conditions often surrounding the conduct of the lineup. In many, lights shine on the stage in such a way that the suspect cannot see the witness. [In] some a one-way mirror is used and what is said on the witness' side cannot be heard. * * *

Insofar as the accused's conviction may rest on a courtroom identification in fact the fruit of a suspect pretrial identification which the accused is helpless to subject to effective scrutiny at trial, the accused is deprived of that right of cross-examination which is an essential safeguard to his right to confront the witnesses against him. And even though cross-examination is a precious safeguard to a fair trial, it cannot be viewed as an absolute assurance of accuracy and reliability. Thus in the present context, where so many variables and pitfalls exist, the first line of defense must be the prevention of unfairness and the lessening of the hazards of eyewitness identification at the lineup itself. The trial which might determine the accused's fate may well not be that in the courtroom but that at the pretrial confrontation, with the State aligned against the accused, the witness the sole jury, and the accused unprotected against the overreaching, intentional or unintentional, and with little or no effective appeal from the judgment there rendered by the witness—"that's the man."

Since it appears that there is grave potential for prejudice, intentional or not, in the pretrial lineup, which may not be capable of reconstruction at trial, and since presence of counsel itself can often avert prejudice and assure a meaningful confrontation at trial, there can be little doubt that for Wade the post-indictment lineup was a critical stage of the prosecution at which he was "as much entitled to such aid [of counsel as] at the trial itself." *Powell v. Alabama.* Thus both Wade and his counsel should have been notified of the impending lineup, and counsel's presence should have been a requisite to conduct of the lineup, absent an "intelligent waiver." No substantial countervailing policy considerations have been advanced against the requirement of the presence of counsel. Concern is expressed that the requirement will forestall prompt identifications and result in obstruction of the confrontations. As for the first, we note that in the two cases in which the right to counsel is today held to apply, counsel had already been appointed and no argument is made in either case that notice to counsel would have prejudicially delayed the confrontations. Moreover, we leave open the question whether the presence of substitute counsel might not suffice where notification and presence of the suspect's own counsel would result in prejudicial delay. And to refuse to recognize the right to counsel for fear that counsel will obstruct the course of justice is contrary to the basic assumptions upon which this Court has operated in Sixth Amendment cases. [In] our view counsel can hardly impede legitimate law enforcement; on the contrary, for the reasons expressed, law enforcement may be assisted by preventing the infiltration of taint in the prosecution's identification evidence. That result cannot help the guilty avoid conviction but can only help assure that the right many has been brought to justice.

Legislative or other regulations, such as those of local police departments, which eliminate the risks of abuse and unintentional suggestion at lineup proceedings and the impediments to meaningful confrontation at trial may also remove the basis for regarding the stage as "critical." But neither Congress nor the federal authorities have seen fit to provide a solution.[c]

We come now to the question whether the denial of Wade's motion to strike the courtroom identification by the bank witnesses at trial because of the absence of his counsel at the lineup required, as the Court of Appeals held, the

---

**c.** Nor, it seems, is a solution provided by 18 U.S.C. § 3502, a part of the Omnibus Crime Control and Safe Streets Act of 1968, which states that "the testimony of a witness that he saw the accused commit [the] crime" is admissible in a federal court. This appears to be an unconstitutional attempt to "repeal" *Wade.* According to several commentators, the lower federal courts have ignored this statute and it exists on the books more as an expression of legislative hope than as a binding rule.

grant of a new trial at which such evidence is to be excluded. We do not think this disposition can be justified without first giving the Government the opportunity to establish by clear and convincing evidence that the in-court identifications were based upon observations of the suspect other than the lineup identification. * * * Where, as here, the admissibility of evidence of the lineup identification itself is not involved, a *per se* rule of exclusion of courtroom identification would be unjustified.[d] [A] rule limited solely to the exclusion of testimony concerning identification at the lineup itself, without regard to admissibility of the courtroom identification, would render the right to counsel an empty one. The lineup is most often used, as in the present case, to crystallize the witnesses' identification of the defendant for future reference. We have already noted that the lineup identification will have that effect. The State may then rest upon the witnesses' unequivocal courtroom identification, and not mention the pretrial identification as part of the State's case at trial. Counsel is then in the predicament in which Wade's counsel found himself—realizing that possible unfairness at the lineup may be the sole means of attack upon the unequivocal courtroom identification, and having to probe in the dark in an attempt to discover and reveal unfairness, while bolstering the government witness' courtroom identification by bringing out and dwelling upon his prior identification. Since counsel's presence at the lineup would equip him to attack not only the lineup identification but the courtroom identification as well, limiting the impact of violation of the right to counsel to exclusion of evidence only of identification at the lineup itself disregards a critical element of that right.

We think it follows that the proper test to be applied in these situations is that quoted in *Wong Sun v. United States,* 371 U.S. 471 (1963), " '[W]hether, granting establishment of the primary illegality the evidence to which instant objection is made has been come at by exploitation of that illegality or instead by means sufficiently distinguishable to be purged of the primary taint.' " Application of this test in the present context requires consideration of various factors; for example, the prior opportunity to observe the alleged criminal act, the existence of any discrepancy between any pre-lineup description and the defendant's actual description, any identification prior to lineup of another person, the identification by picture of the defendant prior to the lineup, failure to identify the defendant on a prior occasion, and the lapse of time between the alleged act and the lineup identification. It is also relevant to consider those facts which, despite the absence of counsel, are disclosed concerning the conduct of the lineup. * * *

On the record now before us we cannot make the determination whether the in-court identifications had an independent origin. [T]he appropriate procedure to be followed is to vacate the conviction pending a hearing to determine whether the in-court identifications had an independent source, or whether, in any event, the introduction of the evidence was harmless error, *Chapman v. California,* 386 U.S. 18 (1967), and for the District Court to reinstate the conviction or order a new trial, as may be proper.[e] * * *

**d.** In *Gilbert,* however, the Court did apply a *per se* exclusionary rule to the testimony of various prosecution witnesses that they had also identified petitioner at a pretrial lineup. See note e infra.

**e.** Compare *Gilbert,* where various witnesses who identified petitioner in the courtroom also testified, on direct examination by the prosecution, that they had identified petition-

er at a prior lineup. "That [pretrial lineup] testimony," ruled the Court, "is the direct result of the illegal lineup 'come at by exploitation of [the primary] illegality.' *Wong Sun.* The State is therefore not entitled to an opportunity to show that that testimony had an independent source. Only a *per se* exclusionary rule as to such testimony can be an effective sanction to assure that law enforce-

Judgment of Court of Appeals vacated and case remanded with direction.[f]

JUSTICE WHITE whom JUSTICE HARLAN and JUSTICE STEWART join, dissenting in part and concurring in part.

The Court has again propounded a broad constitutional rule barring the use of a wide spectrum of relevant and probative evidence, solely because a step in its ascertainment or discovery occurs outside the presence of defense counsel.

[The] Court's opinion is far-reaching. It proceeds first by creating a new *per se* rule of constitutional law: a criminal suspect cannot be subjected to a pretrial identification process in the absence of his counsel without violating the Sixth Amendment. If he is, the State may not buttress a later courtroom identification of the witness by any reference to the previous identification. Furthermore, the courtroom identification is not admissible at all unless the State can establish by clear and convincing proof that the testimony is not the fruit of the earlier identification made in the absence of defendant's counsel—admittedly a heavy burden for the State and probably an impossible one. To all intents and purposes, courtroom identifications are barred if pretrial identifications have occurred without counsel being present.

The rule applies to any lineup, to any other techniques employed to produce an identification and *a fortiori* to a face-to-face encounter between the witness and the suspect alone, regardless of when the identification occurs, in time or place, and whether before or after indictment or information.[g]

[The] premise for the Court's rule is not the general unreliability of eyewitness identifications nor the difficulties inherent in observation, recall, and recognition. The Court assumes a narrower evil as the basis for its rule— improper police suggestion which contributes to erroneous identifications. The Court apparently believes that improper police procedures are so widespread that a broad prophylactic rule must be laid down, requiring the presence of counsel at all pretrial identifications, in order to detect recurring instances of police misconduct. I do not share this pervasive distrust of all official investigations. None of the materials the Court relies upon supports it. Certainly, I would bow to solid fact, but the Court quite obviously does not have before it any reliable, comprehensive survey of current police practices on which to base its new rule. Until it does, the Court should avoid excluding relevant evidence from state criminal trials.

[The] Court goes beyond assuming that a great majority of the country's police departments are following improper practices at pretrial identifications. To find the lineup a "critical" stage of the proceeding and to exclude identifications made in the absence of counsel the Court must also assume that police "suggestion," if it occurs at all, leads to erroneous rather than accurate identifications and that reprehensible police conduct will have an unavoidable and largely undiscoverable impact on the trial. This in turn assumes that there is now no adequate source from which defense counsel can learn about the circumstances of the pretrial identification in order to place before the jury all of the considerations which should enter into an appraisal of courtroom identifica-

ment authorities will respect the accused's constitutional right to the presence of his counsel at the critical lineup. [That] conclusion is buttressed by the consideration that the witness' testimony of his lineup identification will enhance the impact of his in-court identification on the jury and seriously aggravate whatever derogation exists of the accused's right to a fair trial. Therefore, unless the [state supreme court] is 'able to declare a belief that it was harmless beyond a reasonable doubt,' *Chapman*, Gilbert will be entitled on remand to a new trial * * *."

**f.** Justice Black's opinion, dissenting in part and concurring in part, is omitted.

**g.** But see *Kirby v. Illinois*, infra § 2.

tion evidence. But these are treacherous and unsupported assumptions[3] resting as they do on the notion that the defendant will not be aware, that the police and the witnesses will forget or prevaricate, that defense counsel will be unable to bring out the truth and that neither jury, judge, nor appellate court is a sufficient safeguard against unacceptable police conduct occurring at a pretrial identification procedure. I am unable to share the Court's view of the willingness of the police and the ordinary citizen-witness to dissemble, either with respect to the identification of the defendant or with respect to the circumstances surrounding a pretrial identification.

There are several striking aspects to the Court's holding. First, the rule does not bar courtroom identifications where there have been no previous identifications in the presence of the police, although when identified in the courtroom, the defendant is known to be in custody and charged with the commission of a crime.[h] Second, the Court seems to say that if suitable legislative standards were adopted for the conduct of pretrial identifications, thereby lessening the hazards in such confrontations, it would not insist on the presence of counsel. But if this is true, why does not the Court simply fashion what it deems to be constitutionally acceptable procedures for the authorities to follow? Certainly the Court is correct in suggesting that the new rule will be wholly inapplicable where police departments themselves have established suitable safeguards.

Third, courtroom identification may be barred, absent counsel at a prior identification, regardless of the extent of counsel's information concerning the circumstances of the previous confrontation between witness and defendant— apparently even if there were recordings or sound-movies of the events as they occurred. But if the rule is premised on the defendant's right to have his counsel know, there seems little basis for not accepting other means to inform. A disinterested observer, recordings, photographs—any one of them would seem adequate to furnish the basis for a meaningful cross-examination of the eyewitness who identifies the defendant in the courtroom. * * *

Finally, I think the Court's new rule is vulnerable in terms of its own unimpeachable purpose of increasing the reliability of identification testimony.

Law enforcement officers have the obligation to convict the guilty and to make sure they do not convict the innocent. They must be dedicated to making the criminal trial a procedure for the ascertainment of the true facts surrounding the commission of the crime. To this extent, our so-called adversary system is not adversary at all; nor should it be. But defense counsel has no comparable obligation to ascertain or present the truth. Our system assigns him a different mission. He must be and is interested in preventing the conviction of the innocent, but, absent a voluntary plea of guilty, we also insist that he defend his

**3.** The instant case and its companions, *Gilbert* and *Stovall* certainly lend no support to the Court's assumptions. The police conduct deemed improper by the Court in the three cases seems to have come to light at trial in the ordinary course of events. One can ask what more counsel would have learned at the pretrial identifications that would have been relevant for truth determination at trial. * * *

**h.** These identifications are, in effect, one-person showups, albeit in the courtroom. They probably give the witness even a stronger impression that the authorities are con-

vinced they have the right person than do pretrial one-person showups.

In *Moore v. Illinois*, 434 U.S. 220 (1977), where "a one-on-one confrontation" occurred at a preliminary hearing, the Court stated that if defendant had been represented by counsel at this hearing, counsel might have avoided the suggestive identification by asking that the defendant be seated in the audience before the identifying witness was called or by seeking to have the hearing postponed until a lineup was conducted. Although such requests are occasionally granted, trial judges, in their discretion, often deny them.

client whether he is innocent or guilty. The State has the obligation to present the evidence. Defense counsel need present nothing, even if he knows what the truth is. [If] he can confuse a witness, even a truthful one, or make him appear at a disadvantage, unsure or indecisive, that will be his normal course. * * *

I would not extend this system, at least as it presently operates, to police investigations and would not require counsel's presence at pretrial identification procedures. Counsel's interest is in not having his client placed at the scene of the crime, regardless of his whereabouts. Some counsel may advise their clients to refuse to make any movements or to speak any words in a lineup or even to appear in one.[j] [Others] will hover over witnesses and begin their cross-examination then, menacing truthful factfinding as thoroughly as the Court fears the police now do. Certainly there is an implicit invitation to counsel to suggest rules for the lineup and to manage and produce it as best he can.[k] I therefore doubt that the Court's new rule, at least absent some clearly defined limits on counsel's role, will measurably contribute to more reliable pretrial identifications. My fears are that it will have precisely the opposite result. [In] my view, the State is entitled to investigate and develop its case outside the presence of defense counsel. This includes the right to have private conversations with identification witnesses, just as defense counsel may have his own consultations with these and other witnesses without having the prosecutor present. * * *

# SECTION 2. THE COURT RETREATS: *KIRBY* AND *ASH*

## KIRBY v. ILLINOIS
406 U.S. 682, 92 S.Ct. 1877, 32 L.Ed.2d 411 (1972).

JUSTICE STEWART announced the judgment of the Court in an opinion in which THE CHIEF JUSTICE, JUSTICE BLACKMUN, and JUSTICE REHNQUIST join.

* * * In the present case we are asked to extend the *Wade–Gilbert* per se exclusionary rule to identification testimony based upon a police station show-up that took place *before* the defendant had been indicted or otherwise formally charged with any criminal offense.

On February 21, 1968, [one] Willie Shard reported to the Chicago police that the previous day two men had robbed him on a Chicago street of a wallet containing, among other things, travellers checks and a Social Security card. On February 22, two police officers [investigating an unrelated crime] stopped petitioner and a companion, [Bean], [on a Chicago street]. When asked for

j. Since requiring a person to appear in a lineup or to use his voice as an identifying physical characteristic or to provide handwriting exemplars is not prohibited by the privilege against self-incrimination, the prosecution may comment on the suspect's refusal to cooperate. On occasion, courts have utilized civil or criminal contempt to coerce or punish the suspect who refuses to comply with a court order to participate in some identification proceeding.

k. The cases and commentaries indicate that the prevailing practice has been for counsel to attend the lineup merely as an observer to assure against abuse and bad faith by law enforcement officers, and to provide the basis for any attack she might wish to make on the identification at trial. Any attempt to give counsel at identification a more active role is fraught with difficulties not only for the police but for counsel herself. If she is entitled to make objections at the lineup procedure, she would be held to have waived these objections if she does not make them at the procedure. If such a possibility of waiver exists, will counsel be under an obligation to raise every conceivable objection?

identification, the petitioner produced a wallet that contained three travellers checks and a Social Security card, all bearing the name of Willie Shard. * * *

Only after arriving at the police station, and checking the records there, did the arresting officers learn of the Shard robbery. [A police car] picked up Shard and brought him to the police station. Immediately upon entering the room [where petitioner and Bean were seated], Shard positively identified them as [his robbers].[a] No lawyer was present [and neither suspect had asked for] or been advised of any right to the presence of counsel. [At the trial Shard] described his identification of the two men at the police station [and] identified them again in the courtroom as the men who had robbed him.

[In] a line of constitutional cases in this Court stemming back to the Court's landmark opinion in *Powell v. Alabama,* it has been firmly established that a person's Sixth and Fourteenth Amendment right to counsel attaches only at or after the time that adversary judicial proceedings have been initiated against him.

This is not to say that a defendant in a criminal case has a constitutional right to counsel only at the trial itself. [But] the point is [that] *all* of [the right to counsel cases] have involved points of time at or after the initiation of adversary judicial criminal proceedings—whether by way of formal charge, preliminary hearing, indictment, information, or arraignment.

The only seeming deviation from this long line of constitutional decisions was *Escobedo* [which] is not apposite here for two distinct reasons. First, the Court in retrospect perceived that the "prime purpose" of *Escobedo* was not to vindicate the constitutional right to counsel as such, but, like *Miranda,* "to guarantee full effectuation of the privilege against self-incrimination. * * *" *Johnson v. New Jersey,* 384 U.S. 719 (1966). Secondly, and perhaps even more important for purely practical purposes, the Court has limited the holding of *Escobedo* to its own facts, and those facts are not remotely akin to the facts of the case before us.

The initiation of judicial criminal proceedings is far from a mere formalism. It is the starting point of our whole system of adversary criminal justice. For it is only then that the Government has committed itself to prosecute, and only then that the adverse positions of Government and defendant have solidified. It is then that a defendant finds himself faced with the prosecutorial forces of organized society, and immersed in the intricacies of substantive and procedural criminal law. It is this point, therefore, that marks the commencement of the "criminal prosecutions" to which alone the explicit guarantees of the Sixth Amendment are applicable.[b]

In this case we are asked to import into a routine police investigation an absolute constitutional guarantee historically and rationally applicable only after the onset of formal prosecutorial proceedings. We decline to do so. * * * We decline to [impose] a *per se* exclusionary rule upon testimony concerning an identification that took place long before the commencement of any prosecution whatever.

**a.** According to dissenting Justice Brennan, Shard testified that he identified petitioner and Bean only after the officers who brought him to the room asked him if they were the robbers.

**b.** Except for the language in this paragraph, *Kirby* does not explore what constitutes the "initiation" of adversary judicial criminal proceedings. But this language was subsequently relied upon in holding it sufficed that defendant appeared at a preliminary hearing to determine whether he should be bound over to the grand jury and to set bail. *Moore v. Illinois,* 434 U.S. 220 (1977). It is generally agreed that a warrantless arrest is not sufficient, but courts differ as to whether adversary proceedings are initiated by the issuance of an arrest warrant upon information and oath.

What has been said is not to suggest that there may not be occasions during the course of a criminal investigation when the police do abuse identification procedures. Such abuses are not beyond the reach of the Constitution. [The] Due Process Clause of the Fifth and Fourteenth Amendments forbids a lineup that is unnecessarily suggestive and conducive to irreparable mistaken identification.[8] When a person has not been formally charged with a criminal offense, *Stovall* strikes the appropriate constitutional balance between the right of a suspect to be protected from prejudicial procedures and the interest of society in the prompt and purposeful investigation of an unsolved crime.

The judgment is affirmed.[c]

JUSTICE BRENNAN, with whom JUSTICE DOUGLAS and JUSTICE MARSHALL join, dissenting. ＊ ＊ ＊

While it should go without saying, it appears necessary, in view of the plurality opinion today, to re-emphasize that *Wade* did not require the presence of counsel at pretrial confrontations for identification purposes simply on the basis of an abstract consideration of the words "criminal prosecutions" in the Sixth Amendment, [but] in order to safeguard the accused's constitutional rights to confrontation and the effective assistance of counsel at his trial.

In view of *Wade*, it is plain, and the plurality today does not attempt to dispute it, that there inhere in a confrontation for identification conducted after arrest the identical hazards to a fair trial that inhere in such a confrontation conducted "after the onset of formal prosecutorial proceedings." The plurality apparently considers an arrest, which for present purposes we must assume to be based upon probable cause, to be nothing more than part of "a routine police investigation," and thus not "the starting point of our whole system of adversary criminal justice." [The] plurality offers no reason, and I can think of none, for concluding that a post-arrest confrontation for identification, unlike a post-charge confrontation, is not among those "critical confrontations of the accused by the prosecution at pretrial proceedings where the results might well settle the accused's fate and reduce the trial itself to a mere formality."

The highly suggestive form of confrontation employed in this case underscores the point. This showup was particularly fraught with the peril of mistaken identification. In the setting of a police station squad room where all present except petitioner and Bean were police officers, the danger was quite real that Shard's understandable resentment might lead him too readily to agree with the police that the pair under arrest, and the only persons exhibited to him, were indeed the robbers. [On] direct examination, Shard identified petitioner and Bean not as the alleged robbers on trial in the courtroom, but as the pair he saw at the police station. ＊ ＊ ＊

*Wade* and *Gilbert*, of course, happened to involve post-indictment confrontations. Yet even a cursory perusal of the opinions in those cases reveals that nothing at all turned upon that particular circumstance. In short, it is fair to conclude that rather than "declin[ing] to depart from [the] rationale" of *Wade* and *Gilbert*, the plurality today, albeit purporting to be engaged in "principled

8. In view of our limited grant of certiorari, we do not consider whether there might have been a deprivation of due process in the particularized circumstances of this case. That question remains open for inquiry in a federal habeas corpus proceeding.

[Following the U.S. Supreme Court's decision, the denial of Kirby's petition for federal habeas corpus relief was affirmed by the Seventh Circuit in *United States ex rel. Kirby v. Sturges*, 510 F.2d 397 (1975).]

c. As he "would not extend the *Wade–Gilbert* exclusionary rule," Powell, J., concurred in the result.

constitutional adjudication," refuses even to recognize that "rationale." * * * Because Shard testified at trial about his identification of petitioner at the police station showup, the exclusionary rule of *Gilbert* requires reversal.

JUSTICE WHITE, dissenting.

*Wade* and *Gilbert* govern this case and compel reversal of the judgment below.[d]

**d.** A year later, in a decision the dissenters there maintained "mark[ed] simply another step towards the complete evisceration of the fundamental constitutional principles" established in the 1967 lineup cases, the Court held that a defendant has no right to have his counsel present while witnesses view pictures of him for identification purposes at a post-indictment photographic display. *United States v. Ash*, 413 U.S. 300 (1973). Shortly before trial, almost three years after the crime, and long after defendant had been incarcerated and appointed counsel, the prosecutor showed five color photographs to a number of witnesses who previously had tentatively identified the black-and-white photograph of defendant. Three witnesses selected defendant's photo. In holding that the right to counsel did not extend to post-indictment photo-identifications, the Court, per Blackmun, J., observed:

"[Although the right to counsel guarantee has been expanded beyond the formal trial itself], the function of the lawyer has remained essentially the same as his function at trial. In all cases considered by the Court, counsel has continued to act as a spokesman for, or advisor to, the accused. * * *

"The function of counsel in rendering 'assistance' continued at the lineup under consideration in *Wade* and its companion cases. Although the accused was not confronted there with legal questions, the lineup offered opportunities for prosecuting authorities to take advantage of the accused. * * *

"Even if we were willing to view the counsel guarantee in broad terms as a generalized protection of the adversary process, we would be unwilling to go so far as to extend the right to a portion of the prosecutor's trial-preparation interviews with witnesses. [The] traditional counterbalance in the American adversary system for these interviews arises from the equal ability of defense counsel to seek and interview witnesses himself.

"That adversary mechanism remains as effective for a photographic display as for other parts of pretrial interviews. No greater limitations are placed on defense counsel in constructing displays, seeking witnesses, and conducting photographic identifications than those applicable to the prosecution. * * *

"Pretrial [photo-identifications] are hardly unique in offering possibilities for the actions of the prosecutor unfairly to prejudice the accused. [In] many ways the prosecutor, by accident or by design, may improperly subvert the trial. The primary safeguard against abuses of this kind is the ethical responsibility of the prosecutor. * * * If that safeguard fails, review remains available under due process standards. These same safeguards apply to misuse of photographs.

"We are not persuaded that the risks inherent in the use of photographic displays are so pernicious that an extraordinary system of safeguards is required."

Dissenting Justice Brennan, joined by Douglas and Marshall, JJ., observed:

"[A]lthough retention of the photographs may mitigate the dangers of misidentification due to the suggestiveness of the photographs themselves, it cannot in any sense reveal to defense counsel the more subtle, and therefore more dangerous, suggestiveness that might derive from the manner in which the photographs were displayed or any accompanying comments or gestures.

"[Moreover] and unlike the lineup situation, the accused himself is not even present at the photographic identification, thereby reducing the likelihood that irregularities in the procedures will ever come to light. * * *

"[A]lthough apparently conceding that the right to counsel attached, not only at the trial itself, but at all 'critical stages' of the prosecution, the Court holds today that, in order to be deemed 'critical,' the particular 'stage of the prosecution' under consideration must, at the very least, involve the physical 'presence of the accused,' at a 'trial-like confrontation' with the Government, at which the accused requires the 'guiding hand of counsel.' A pretrial photographic identification does not, of course, meet these criteria. * * *

"[But the] fundamental premise underlying *all* of this Court's decisions holding the right to counsel applicable at 'critical' pretrial proceedings, is that a 'stage' of the prosecution must be deemed 'critical' for the purposes of the Sixth Amendment if it is one at which the presence of counsel is necessary 'to protect the fairness of *trial itself*.'

"[This] established conception of the Sixth Amendment guarantee is, of course, in no sense dependent upon the physical 'presence of the accused,' at a 'trial-like confrontation' with the Government, at which the accused requires the 'guiding hand of counsel.' * * *

"[C]ontrary to the suggestion of the Court, the conclusion in *Wade* that a pretrial lineup is a 'critical stage' of the prosecution did not

# SECTION 3. DUE PROCESS AND OTHER LIMITATIONS

As pointed out in *Stovall v. Denno,* 388 U.S. 293 (1967), one unable to make a *Wade–Gilbert* right to counsel argument may still establish that the identification procedure conducted in his case "was so unnecessarily suggestive and conducive to irreparable mistaken identification that he was denied due process of law." In *Stovall,* the stabbing victim (Mrs. Behrendt), was hospitalized for major surgery. Without affording petitioner time to retain counsel (an arraignment had been promptly held but then postponed until petitioner could retain counsel), the police, with the cooperation of the victim's surgeon, arranged a confrontation between petitioner and the victim in her hospital room. Petitioner was handcuffed to one of the seven law enforcement officials who brought him to the hospital room. He was the only black person in the room. After being asked by an officer whether petitioner "was the man," the victim identified him from her hospital bed. Both Mrs. Behrendt and the police then testified at the trial to her identification in the hospital. Despite the suggestiveness of the confrontation, the Court, per Brennan, J., affirmed the Second Circuit's denial of federal habeas corpus relief, observing that "a claimed violation of due process of law in the conduct of a confrontation depends on the totality of the circumstances surrounding it, and the record in the present case reveals that the showing of Stovall to Mrs. Behrendt in an immediate hospital confrontation was imperative." The Court then quoted with approval from the court below: "Here was the only person in the world who could possibly exonerate Stovall. * * * No one knew how long Mrs. Behrendt might live. [Under the circumstances] and with the knowledge that Mrs. Behrendt could not visit the jail, the police followed the only feasible procedure and took Stovall to the hospital."

*Stovall* may not be as easy a case as it appears to be at first blush.[a] But it is a good deal easier than *Manson v. Brathwaite,* below.

## MANSON v. BRATHWAITE
### 432 U.S. 98, 97 S.Ct. 2243, 53 L.Ed.2d 140 (1977).

JUSTICE BLACKMUN delivered the opinion of the Court. * * *

[Several minutes before sunset, Glover, a black undercover police officer, purchased heroin from a seller through the open doorway of an apartment while standing for two or three minutes within two feet of the seller in a hallway

in any sense turn on the fact that a lineup involves the physical 'presence of the accused' at a 'trial-like confrontation' with the Government. And that conclusion most certainly did not turn on the notion that presence of counsel was necessary so that counsel could offer legal advice or 'guidance' to the accused at the lineup. On the contrary, *Wade* envisioned counsel's function at the lineup to be primarily that of a trained observer, able to detect the existence of any suggestive influences and capable of understanding the legal implications of the events that transpire. Having witnessed the proceedings, counsel would then be in a position effectively to reconstruct at trial any unfairness that occurred at the lineup, thereby preserving the accused's fundamental right to a fair trial on the issue of identification."

**a.** According to the two judges who dissented below, Friendly, J., joined by Waterman, J., the argument that law enforcement officers were confronted with an emergency "ignores the huge amount of circumstantial identification the excellent police investigation had produced." Moreover, if law enforcement officials were really motivated by solicitude for defendant "the natural course would have been to ask [him] whether he wanted to go. The emergency argument fails both on the facts and on the law." The question was also raised as to whether, if a lineup were out of the question, a photographic display might not have been preferable to a one-person showup.

illuminated by natural light. A few minutes later, Glover described the seller to a back-up officer, D'Onofrio, as being "a colored man, approximately five feet eleven inches tall, dark complexion, black hair, short Afro style, and having high cheekbones, and of heavy build. He was wearing at the time blue pants and a plaid shirt."

[On the basis of the description, D'Onofrio thought that respondent might be the heroin seller. He obtained a single photograph of respondent from police files and left it at Glover's office. Two days later, while alone, Glover viewed the photograph and identified it as that of the seller. At respondent's trial, Glover testified that there was "no doubt whatsoever" that the person shown in the photograph was respondent. Glover also made a positive in-court identification. No explanation was offered by the prosecution for the failure to utilize a photographic array or to conduct a lineup.

[After the Connecticut Supreme Court affirmed respondent's conviction, he sought federal habeas corpus relief. The Second Circuit, per Friendly, J., held that because the showing of the single photograph was "suggestive" and concededly "unnecessarily so," evidence pertaining to it was subject to a *per se* rule of exclusion.]

*Neil v. Biggers*, 409 U.S. 188 (1972), concerned a respondent who had been convicted [of] rape, on evidence consisting in part of the victim's visual and voice identification of Biggers at a [one-person] station-house showup seven months after the crime. * * * The Court expressed concern about the lapse of seven months between the crime and the confrontation, [but pointed out that the] "central question" [was] "whether under the 'totality of the circumstances' the identification was reliable even though the confrontation procedure was suggestive." Applying that test, the Court found "no substantial likelihood of misidentification. The evidence was properly allowed to go to the jury." [a]

*Biggers* well might be seen to provide an unambiguous answer to the question before us: The admission of testimony concerning a suggestive and unnecessary identification procedure does not violate due process so long as the identification possesses sufficient aspects of reliability. In one passage, however, the Court observed that the challenged procedure occurred pre-*Stovall* and that a strict rule would make little sense with regard to a confrontation that preceded the Court's first indication that a suggestive procedure might lead to the exclusion of evidence. One perhaps might argue that, by implication, the Court suggested that a different rule could apply post-*Stovall*. The question before us, then, is simply whether the *Biggers* analysis applies to post-*Stovall* confrontations as well to those pre-*Stovall*. * * *

**a.** The *Biggers* Court, per Powell, J., observed:

"The victim spent a considerable period of time with her assailant, up to half an hour. She was with him under adequate artificial light in her house and under a full moon outdoors, and at least twice, once in the house and later in the woods, faced him directly and intimately. [Her] description to the police, which included the assailant's approximate age, height, weight, complexion, skin texture, build, and voice [was] more than ordinarily thorough. She had 'no doubt' that respondent was the person who raped her. [The] victim here, a practical nurse by profession, had an unusual opportunity to observe and identify her assailant. She testified at the habeas corpus hearing that there was something about his face 'I don't think I could ever forget.'

"There was, to be sure, a lapse of seven months between the rape and the confrontation. This would be a seriously negative factor in most cases. Here, however, the testimony is undisputed that the victim made no previous identification at any of the showups, lineups, or photographic showings. Her record for reliability was thus a good one, as she had previously resisted whatever suggestiveness inheres in a showup. Weighing all the factors, we find no substantial likelihood of misidentification."

Petitioner at the outset acknowledges that "the procedure in the instant case was suggestive [because only one photograph was used] and unnecessary" [because there was no emergency or exigent circumstance]. The respondent, in agreement with the Court of Appeals, proposes a *per se* rule of exclusion that he claims is dictated by the demands of the Fourteenth Amendment's guarantee of due process. He rightly observes that this is the first case in which this Court has had occasion to rule upon strictly post-*Stovall* out-of-court identification evidence of the challenged kind.

Since the decision in *Biggers,* the Courts of Appeals appear to have developed at least two approaches to such evidence. The first, or *per se* approach, employed by the Second Circuit in the present case, focuses on the procedures employed and requires exclusion of the out-of-court identification evidence, without regard to reliability, whenever it has been obtained through unnecessarily suggested confrontation procedures.[10] The justifications advanced are the elimination of evidence of uncertain reliability, deterrence of the police and prosecutors, and the stated "fair assurance against the awful risks of misidentification."

The second, or more lenient, approach is one that continues to rely on the totality of the circumstances. It permits the admission of the confrontation evidence if, despite the suggestive aspect, the out-of-court identification possesses certain features of reliability. This second approach, in contrast to the other, is ad hoc and serves to limit the societal costs imposed by a sanction that excludes relevant evidence from consideration and evaluation by the trier of fact.

\* \* \*

There are, of course, several interests to be considered and taken into account. The driving force behind [*Wade, Gilbert* and *Stovall*] was the Court's concern with the problems of eyewitness identification. Usually the witness must testify about an encounter with a total stranger under circumstances of emergency or emotional stress. The witness' recollection of the stranger can be distorted easily by the circumstances or by later actions of the police. Thus, *Wade* and its companion cases reflect the concern that the jury not hear eyewitness testimony unless that evidence has aspects of reliability. It must be observed that both approaches before us are responsive to this concern. The *per se* rule, however, goes too far since its application automatically and peremptorily, and without consideration of alleviating factors, keeps evidence from the jury that is reliable and relevant.

The second factor is deterrence. Although the *per se* approach has the more significant deterrent effect, the totality approach also has an influence on police behavior. The police will guard against unnecessarily suggestive procedures under the totality rule, as well as the *per se* one, for fear that their actions will lead to the exclusion of identifications as unreliable.

The third factor is the effect on the administration of justice. Here the *per se* approach suffers serious drawbacks. Since it denies the trier reliable evidence, it may result, on occasion, in the guilty going free. Also, because of its rigidity, the *per se* approach may make error by the trial judge more likely than the totality approach. And in those cases in which the admission of identification evidence is error under the *per se* approach but not under the totality

---

10. Although the *per se* approach demands the exclusion of testimony concerning unnecessarily suggestive identifications, it does permit the admission of testimony concerning a subsequent identification, including an in-court identification, if the subsequent identification is determined to be reliable. The totality approach, in contrast, is simpler: if the challenged identification is reliable, then testimony as to it and any identification in its wake is admissible.

approach—cases in which the identification is reliable despite an unnecessarily suggestive identification procedure—reversal is a Draconian sanction. Certainly, inflexible rules of exclusion that may frustrate rather than promote justice have not been viewed recently by this Court with unlimited enthusiasm.
\*   \*   \*

We therefore conclude that reliability is the linchpin in determining the admissibility of identification testimony for both pre- and post-*Stovall* confrontations. The factors to be considered are set out in *Biggers*. These include the opportunity of the witness to view the criminal at the time of the crime, the witness' degree of attention, the accuracy of his prior description of the criminal, the level of certainty demonstrated at the confrontation, and the time between the crime and the confrontation. Against these factors is to be weighed the corrupting effect of the suggestive identification itself.

We turn, then, to the facts of this case and apply the analysis:

1. The opportunity to view. Glover testified that for two to three minutes he stood at the apartment door, within two feet of the respondent. The door opened twice, and each time the man stood at the door. \*   \*   \* Natural light from outside entered the hallway through a window. There was natural light, as well, from inside the apartment.

2. The degree of attention. Glover was not a casual or passing observer, [but] a trained police officer on duty—and specialized and dangerous duty—when he [made the heroin purchase]. Glover himself was a Negro and unlikely to perceive only general features of [black males].

3. The accuracy of the description. Glover's description was given to D'Onofrio within minutes after the transaction. It included the vendor's race, his height, his build, the color and style of his hair, and the high cheekbone facial feature. It also included clothing the vendor wore. No claim has been made that respondent did not possess the physical characteristics so described.
\*   \*   \*

4. The witness' level of certainty. There is no dispute that the photograph in question was that of respondent. Glover, in response to a question whether the photograph was that of the person from whom he made the purchase, testified: "There is no question whatsoever." This positive assurance was repeated.

5. The time between the crime and the confrontation. Glover's description of his vendor was given to D'Onofrio within minutes of the crime. The photographic identification took place only two days later. We do not have here the passage of weeks or months between the crime and the viewing of the photograph.

These indicators of Glover's ability to make an accurate identification are hardly outweighed by the corrupting effect of the challenged identification itself. Although identifications arising from single-photograph displays may be viewed in general with suspicion, we find in the instant case little pressure on the witness to acquiesce in the suggestion that such a display entails. D'Onofrio had left the photograph at Glover's office and was not present when Glover first viewed it two days after the event. There thus was little urgency and Glover could view the photograph at his leisure. And since Glover examined the photograph alone, there was no coercive pressure to make an identification arising from the presence of another. The identification was made in circumstances allowing care and reflection. \*   \*   \*

Surely, we cannot say that under all the circumstances of this case there is "a very substantial likelihood of irreparable misidentification." Short of that point, such evidence is for the jury to weigh. * * *

We conclude that the criteria laid down in *Biggers* are to be applied in determining the admissibility of evidence offered by the prosecution concerning a post-*Stovall* identification, and that those criteria are satisfactorily met and complied with here.

[Reversed].[b]

JUSTICE MARSHALL, with whom JUSTICE BRENNAN joins, dissenting.

Today's decision can come as no surprise to those who have been watching the Court dismantle the protections against mistaken eyewitness testimony erected a decade ago in [*Wade, Gilbert* and *Stovall*]. But it is still distressing to see the Court virtually ignore the teaching of experience embodied in those decisions and blindly uphold the conviction of a defendant who may well be innocent.

[The] development of due process protections against mistaken identification evidence, begun in *Stovall*, was continued in *Simmons v. United States* (1968). There, the Court developed a different rule to deal with the admission of in-court identification testimony that the accused claimed had been fatally tainted by a previous suggestive confrontation. In *Simmons*, the exclusionary effect of *Stovall* had already been accomplished, since the prosecution made no use of the suggestive confrontation. *Simmons*, therefore, did not deal with the constitutionality of the pretrial identification procedure. The only question was the impact of the Due Process Clause on an in-court identification that was not itself unnecessarily suggestive. *Simmons* held that due process was violated by the later identification if the pretrial procedure had been "so impermissibly suggestive as to give rise to a very substantial likelihood of irreparable misidentification." This test focused, not on the necessity for the challenged pretrial procedure, but on the degree of suggestiveness that it entailed. In applying this test, the Court understandably considered the circumstances surrounding the witnesses' initial opportunity to view the crime. Finding that any suggestion in the pretrial confrontation had not affected the fairness of the in-court identification, *Simmons* rejected petitioner's due process attack on his conviction.

[Thus,] *Stovall* and *Simmons* established two different due process tests for two very different situations. Where the prosecution sought to use evidence of a questionable pretrial identification, *Stovall* required its exclusion, because due process had been violated by the confrontation, unless the necessity for the unduly suggestive procedure outweighed its potential for generating an irreparably mistaken identification. The *Simmons* test, on the other hand, was directed to ascertaining due process violations in the introduction of in-court identification testimony that the defendant claimed was tainted by pretrial procedures. In the latter situation, a court could consider the reliability of the identification under all the circumstances.

[The] Court inexplicably seemed to erase the distinction between *Stovall* and *Simmons* situations in *Biggers*, [dealing with] a pretrial confrontation that was clearly both suggestive and unnecessary. Evidence of this, together with an in-

---

**b.** Stevens, J., concurring, joined the Court's opinion, but emphasized that although "the arguments in favor of fashioning new rules to minimize the danger of convicting the innocent on the basis of unreliable eyewitness testimony carry substantial force [this] rulemaking function can be performed 'more effectively by the legislative process than by somewhat clumsy judicial fiat,' and that the Federal Constitution does not foreclose experimentation by the States in the development of such rules."

court identification, was admitted at trial. *Biggers* was, in short, a case plainly cast in the *Stovall* mold. Yet the Court, without explanation or apparent recognition of the distinction, applied the *Simmons* test. The Court stated: "[T]he primary evil to be avoided is 'a very substantial likelihood of irreparable misidentification.' *Simmons*. [It] is the likelihood of misidentification which violates a defendant's right to due process." While this statement accurately describes the lesson of *Simmons*, it plainly ignores the teaching of *Stovall* [that] an unnecessarily suggestive pretrial confrontation itself violates due process.

But the Court did not simply disregard the due process analysis of *Stovall*. It went on to take the *Simmons* standard for assessing the constitutionality of an in-court identification—"'a very substantial likelihood of irreparable misidentification'"—and transform it into the "standard for the admissibility of testimony concerning [an] out-of-court identification." It did so by deleting the word "irreparable" from the *Simmons* formulation. This metamorphosis could be accomplished, however, only by ignoring the fact that *Stovall* [had] established a test for precisely the same situation that focused on the need for the suggestive procedure. It is not surprising that commentators almost unanimously mourned the demise of *Stovall* in the *Biggers* decision.

* * * The Court weighs three factors in deciding that the totality approach, which is essentially the test used in *Biggers*, should be applied. In my view, the Court wrongly evaluates the impact of these factors.

First, the Court acknowledges that one of the factors, deterrence of police use of unnecessarily suggestive identification procedures, favors the *per se* rule. Indeed, it does so heavily, for such a rule would make it unquestionably clear to the police they must never use a suggestive procedure when a fairer alternative is available. I have no doubt that conduct would quickly conform to the rule.

Second, the Court gives passing consideration to the dangers of eyewitness identification recognized in the *Wade* trilogy. It concludes, however, that the grave risk of error does not justify adoption of the *per se* approach because that would too often result in exclusion of relevant evidence. In my view, this conclusion totally ignores the lessons of *Wade*. The dangers of mistaken identification are, as *Stovall* held, simply too great to permit unnecessarily suggestive identifications. Neither *Biggers* nor the Court's opinion today points to any contrary empirical evidence. * * *

Finally, the Court errs in its assessment of the relative impact of the two approaches on the administration of justice. * * * Relying on little more than a strong distaste for "inflexible rules of exclusion," the Court rejects the *per se* test. In so doing, the Court disregards two significant distinctions between the *per se* rule advocated in this case and the exclusionary remedies for certain other constitutional violations.

First, the *per se* rule here is not "inflexible." Where evidence is suppressed, for example, as the fruit of an unlawful search, it may well be forever lost to the prosecution. Identification evidence, however, can by its very nature be readily and effectively reproduced. The in-court identification, permitted under *Wade* and *Simmons* if it has a source independent of an uncounseled or suggestive procedure, is one example. Similarly, when a prosecuting attorney learns that there has been a suggestive confrontation, he can easily arrange another lineup conducted under scrupulously fair conditions. * * *

Second, other exclusionary rules have been criticized for preventing jury consideration of relevant and usually reliable evidence in order to serve interest unrelated to guilt or innocence, such as discouraging illegal searches or denial of counsel. Suggestively obtained eyewitness testimony is excluded, in contrast, precisely because of its unreliability and concomitant irrelevance. Its exclusion both protects the integrity of the truth-seeking function of the trial and discourages police use of needlessly inaccurate and ineffective investigatory methods.

[For] these reasons, I conclude that adoption of the *per se* rule would enhance, rather than detract from, the effective administration of justice. In my view, the Court's totality test will allow seriously unreliable and misleading evidence to be put before juries. * * *

Even more disturbing than the Court's reliance on the totality test, however, is the analysis it uses, which suggests a reinterpretation of the concept of due process of law in criminal cases. The decision suggests that due process violations in identification procedures may not be measured by whether the government employed procedures violating standards of fundamental fairness. By relying on the probable accuracy of a challenged identification, instead of the necessity for its use, the Court seems to be ascertaining whether the defendant was probably guilty. * * *

Despite my strong disagreement with the Court over the proper standards to be applied in this case, I am pleased that its application of the totality test does recognize the continuing vitality of *Stovall*. In assessing the reliability of the identification, the Court mandates weighing "the corrupting effect of the suggestive identification itself" against the "indicators of [a witness'] ability to make an accurate identification." The Court holds, as *Biggers* failed to, that a due process identification inquiry must take account of the suggestiveness of a confrontation and the likelihood that it led to mis-identification, as recognized in *Stovall* and *Wade*. Thus, even if a witness did have an otherwise adequate opportunity to view a criminal, the later use of a highly suggestive identification procedure can render his testimony inadmissible. Indeed, it is my view that, assuming applicability of the totality test enunciated by the Court, the facts of the present case require that result.

I consider first the opportunity that Officer Glover had to view the suspect. Careful review of the record shows that he could see the heroin seller only for the time it took to speak three sentences of four or five short words, to hand over some money, and later after the door reopened, to receive the drugs in return. The entire face-to-face transaction could have taken as little as 15 or 20 seconds. But during this time, Glover's attention was not focused exclusively on the seller's face. He observed that the door was opened 12 to 18 inches, that there was a window in the room behind the door, and, most importantly, that there was a woman standing behind the man. Glover was, of course, also concentrating on the details of the transaction—he must have looked away from the seller's face to hand him the money and receive the drugs. The observation during the conversation thus may have been as brief as 5 or 10 seconds.

As the Court notes, Glover was a police officer trained in and attentive to the need for making accurate identifications. [But] the mere fact that he has been so trained is no guarantee that he is correct in a specific case. * * * Moreover, "identifications made by policemen in highly competitive activities, such as undercover narcotic [work], should be scrutinized with special care." P. Wall, *Eye–Witness Identification in Criminal Cases* 14 (1965). Yet it is just such a searching inquiry that the Court fails to make here.

Another factor on which the Court relies—the witness' degree of certainty in making the identification—is worthless as an indicator that he is correct. Even if Glover had been unsure initially about his identification of respondent's picture, by the time he was called at trial to present a key piece of evidence for the State that paid his salary, it is impossible to imagine his responding negatively to such questions as "is there any doubt in your mind whatsoever" that the identification was correct.  *  *  *

Next, the Court finds that because the identification procedure took place two days after the crime, its reliability is enhanced. While such temporal proximity makes the identification more reliable than one occurring months later, the fact is that the greatest memory loss occurs within hours after an event. After that, the drop-off continues much more slowly.  *  *  *

Finally, the Court makes much of the fact that Glover gave a description of the seller to D'Onofrio shortly after the incident. [But the description] was actually no more than a general summary of the seller's appearance.  *  *  * Conspicuously absent is any indication that the seller was a native of the West Indies, certainly something which a member of the black community could immediately recognize from both appearance and accent.[12]

From all of this, I must conclude that the evidence of Glover's ability to make an accurate identification is far weaker than the Court finds it. In contrast, the procedure used to identify respondent was both extraordinarily suggestive and strongly conducive to error. [By] displaying a single photograph of respondent to the witness Glover under the circumstances in this record almost everything that could have been done wrong was done wrong.

[The] use of a single picture (or the display of a single live suspect, for that matter) is a grave error, of course, because it dramatically suggests to the witness that the person shown must be the culprit. Why else would the police choose the person? And it is deeply ingrained in human nature to agree with the expressed opinions of others—particularly others who should be more knowledgeable—when making a difficult decision. In this case, moreover, the pressure was not limited to that inherent in the display of a single photograph. Glover, the identifying witness, was a state police officer on special assignment. He knew that D'Onofrio, an [experienced] narcotics detective, presumably familiar with local drug operations, believed respondent to be the seller. There was at work, then, both loyalty to another police officer and deference to a better-informed colleague. Finally, of course, there was Glover's knowledge that without an identification and arrest, government funds used to buy heroin had been wasted.  *  *  *

I must conclude that this record presents compelling evidence that there was "a very substantial likelihood of misidentification" of respondent Brathwaite. The suggestive display of respondent's photograph to the witness Glover likely erased any independent memory that Glover had retained of the seller from his barely adequate opportunity to observe the criminal.  *  *  *

---

**12.** Brathwaite had come to the United States from his native Barbados as an adult. It is also noteworthy that the informant who witnessed the transaction and was described by Glover as "trustworthy," disagreed with Glover's recollection of the event. The informant testified that it was a woman in the apartment who took the money from Glover and gave him the drugs in return.

# Chapter 8

# INVESTIGATION BY SUBPOENA

## INTRODUCTION

To understand the criminal investigation conducted by subpoena, one must understand the grand jury.[a]  For the grand jury historically was the primary agency conducting investigations through the use of subpoenas, and the vast majority of investigations by subpoena today, though directed by prosecutors, continue to be conducted through the grand jury.

Few elements of our criminal justice process have more ancient roots than the grand jury, which was introduced into the English criminal process in the twelfth century.  By the time the United States Constitution was adopted, the grand jury was well established in this country as both a screening and investigatory body.  The grand jury performed its screening function in determining whether the government had developed sufficient evidence to bring criminal charges through an indictment.  Under the federal constitution's Fifth Amendment and similar provisions in state constitutions, felony charges could be brought only on a grand jury's decision to indict.  The grand jury performed its investigatory function through its own resources and its capacity to require potential witnesses to come before it and testify as to suspected crimes.  As a result of its dual functions, the grand jury came to be known as the "shield and sword" of the criminal justice process.  In its role as a screening agency, the grand jury provided a shield against mistaken or vindictive prosecution of the innocent by refusing to indict.  In its role as an investigative agency, it provided the state with a sword to combat crime that could not be reached through other investigative processes.

The shielding or screening function of the grand jury will be discussed in Chapter Eleven.  In this Chapter, we will look only at the investigative authority of the grand jury.  While the grand jury remains an important investigative agency, its significance in this regard is less than it once was.  With the development of professional police departments, the major share of the responsibility for investigation today falls on the police.  Compared to police investigations, grand jury investigations are expensive, time-consuming, and logistically cumbersome.  The grand jury is a group of lay persons (as large as 23, its traditional size, in some jurisdictions), who commonly are selected in much the same manner as the trial jury.  The jurors meet as a body, hearing witnesses and examining physical evidence.  While early grand juries, operating in small

a.  The organization and operation of the grand jury are briefly described in Chapter 1, particularly in the description of step 11 (grand jury review).

communities, often could bring to an investigation relevant information gathered through the jurors' own efforts, the grand jury today must rely primarily on the lead of the prosecutor, who serves as its legal advisor and sets the direction, scope, and pace of its investigation. It is the prosecutor who determines which witnesses will be presented before the grand jury, and the prosecutor who examines those witnesses, although the grand jury has the power to ask its own questions and to insist that the prosecutor present such additional witnesses as it specifies. Those rare grand juries that have made extensive use of such powers and have taken investigations in new directions (commonly assisted by special prosecutors, appointed by the court at the grand jury's request) have come to be known as "runaway grand juries."

The extra burdens of the grand jury investigation lead prosecutors today to turn to the grand jury process only where it offers a distinct investigative advantage over the police. That advantage is most likely to be present where investigators must unravel a complex criminal structure, deal with victims reluctant to cooperate, obtain information contained in extensive business records, or keep a continuing investigative effort from the public gaze. Criminal activities presenting such investigative problems include public corruption (e.g., bribery), misuse of economic power (e.g., price-fixing), and widespread distribution of illegal services and goods (e.g., gambling or narcotics distribution), and most grand jury investigations are directed at such activities. The grand jury's advantages in investigating this type of criminal activity stem primarily from its use of subpoena authority to compel the production of testimony and physical evidence, although certain other aspects of the grand jury investigation—most notably secrecy requirements [b] and lay participation [c]—may also contribute to its effectiveness.

The subpoena authority utilized in a grand jury investigation comes from the courts. Although described as an independent body, the grand jury exists as an arm of the court. The court calls the grand jury into being and grants to it the power of the court to compel persons to appear and testify or produce physical evidence. A subpoena is a court order directing a person to appear to testify (the subpoena "ad testificandum") or to present to it physical evidence (the subpoena "duces tecum"). Both forms of subpoena may present significant investigative advantages over procedures available to the police.

**b.** Grand jury secrecy requirements vary in scope from one jurisdiction to another, but all jurisdictions prohibit the prosecution's staff, the grand jurors, and court personnel from disclosing what occurred before the grand jury (absent a court order allowing such disclosure). In several jurisdictions the witness himself is also subject to a secrecy requirement (being allowed to discuss his testimony only with his lawyer), but most do not restrict disclosure by the witness. The end result is that the witness who wants his testimony to be kept secret knows that those who have heard his testimony have been sworn to secrecy; disclosure lies in his own hands—at least until charges are brought (when the witness' testimony will most likely be made public if he is to testify at trial).

**c.** Lay participation is said to add primarily two elements to the effectiveness of grand jury investigations. First, witnesses are said to feel a "moral compulsion to be honest and forthright" in their testimony before a group of peers, who have themselves accepted the inconvenience of becoming involved. Second, particularly where the subject under investigation has political overtones that might produce claims of prosecutorial political partisanship, the participation of the lay jurors is said to help maintain public confidence in the integrity of the investigatory process. Critics discount both of these contentions. They suggest that the psychological pressures felt by the witness are more likely to come from the fact that the witness knows that he "stands alone"—that he must "appear before an often hostile prosecutor and a group of strangers, with no judge present to guard his rights, no counsel present to counsel him, and sometimes no indication of why he is being questioned." As for public confidence, critics suggest that the public recognizes that the key figure in a grand jury investigation is an elected official, the prosecutor, not the grand jury.

The subpoena duces tecum offers various advantages over the primary device available to the police for obtaining physical evidence—the search pursuant to a warrant. Initially, as will be seen, the subpoena duces tecum can issue without the showing of probable cause required for a search warrant. In the grand jury setting the subpoena duces tecum usually seeks documents, and it also has the advantage of requiring the party subpoenaed to sort through what may be a vast quantity of records in order to find the document subpoenaed (a sorting task that might often be so burdensome for police to undertake that a search would be impracticable). Finally, where records are to be obtained from an uninvolved third party (e.g., a bank), a subpoena may be preferred because it will be far less disruptive than a police search of the files of that party.[d]

The subpoena to testify similarly offers several advantages over police questioning. Initially, as will be seen in section one, there is no need for a showing of probable cause or even reasonable suspicion to require a person to come before the grand jury and testify. Second, whereas a person may simply refuse to answer police questions (having no duty to cooperate), a subpoenaed person must give testimony as requested (absent the exercise of some valid privilege)—or be held in contempt by the court. Moreover, when that person does testify, a failure to tell the truth will subject him to criminal liability for perjury, for the testimony is given under oath. Lying to police officers generally is not a crime under state law (although the federal system makes it criminal as to federal officers).

The power of the subpoena to compel testimony commonly is supplemented by legislation authorizing the prosecutor to obtain a court order granting a form of "immunity" to the grand jury witness. The primary limit upon the witness' legal duty to testify, as well as be seen, is the privilege against self-incrimination. The witness' self-incrimination privilege may be supplanted, however, through the grant of immunity, as discussed in the *Kastigar* case (see § 2). The immunity grant gives the prosecution an opportunity to "break" a case by forcing critical testimony from a lower-level participant in a criminal enterprise who otherwise would rely on his self-incrimination privilege. Of course, the price for such testimony ordinarily will be foregoing the prosecution of that person, but that may be a worthwhile cost for gaining from the immunized witness evidence that will permit prosecution of the high-level participants. Also, immunity may be used for prospective witnesses who have only an incidental relationship to the enterprise which probably would not justify their prosecution but would allow them to refuse to testify on the basis of the privilege if not given immunity.

Desiring to keep the advantages of investigation by subpoena, but to eliminate the element of lay participation in the investigation, a small group of states have created investigative alternatives to the grand jury that can make similar use of the court's subpoena authority and the grant of immunity. Several of these states allow the prosecutor to seek a judicial inquiry into possible criminal activity. The judge so designated may then conduct an investigation (commonly assisted by the local prosecutor or a specially appointed prosecutor) through the use of the subpoena power. Such judicial investigations are known in different parts of the country as "one-man grand juries" or "John Doe" proceedings. Still other states authorize the prosecutor, acting alone, to conduct investigations upon application to the court for use of its subpoena power. This authority is commonly used for investigations less extensive than those submitted to the

**d.** But consider *Zurcher v. Stanford Daily*, Ch. 3, § 2.

grand jury. The witnesses in these prosecutorial "investigatory deposition" proceedings are subpoenaed to appear at the prosecutor's office (with counsel, if they so choose), where they will be required to testify under oath or to present documents as specified in a subpoena duces tecum. Finally, most jurisdictions have allowed the subpoena authority to be used by administrative agencies or other bodies that have the responsibility for investigating possible infractions of civil laws, including those that may overlap with criminal offenses. Thus, one of the main cases in section two, *Fisher v. United States*, involves an Internal Revenue Service summons that is basically a subpoena duces tecum.

The investigation by subpoena, whether conducted through a grand jury or an alternative agency, is not without constitutional limitations. The cases presented in this chapter deal with the most significant of those limitations.

# SECTION 1. FOURTH AMENDMENT LIMITATIONS

The first case in this section, *Boyd v. United States*, is a widely celebrated case, once described by Justice Brandeis as a case "that will be remembered as long as civil liberty lives in the United States." *Olmstead v. United States*, 277 U.S. 438 (1928) (dissent). Although *Boyd* involved an order to produce documents at trial, its reasoning clearly encompassed as well a subpoena issued in the course of an investigatory setting. While one could contend that *Boyd* today constitutes no more than a "historic relic," a false start in the application to subpoenas of both the Fourth Amendment and the Fifth Amendment's self-incrimination clause, the *Boyd* opinion continues to be cited by the Supreme Court and its analysis continues to be treated as at least demanding reexamination, if not application. The *Fisher* and *Doe* cases, contained in the next section, reexamine the self-incrimination aspects of the *Boyd* analysis. The *Dionisio* opinion in this section considers the scope of the Fourth Amendment's application to subpoenas in light of post-*Boyd* precedent.[a]

## BOYD v. UNITED STATES

116 U.S. 616, 6 S.Ct. 524, 29 L.Ed. 746 (1886).

[Customs officials seized 35 cases of glass, imported by the partnership of Boyd and Sons, and instituted a forfeiture proceeding. That proceeding was brought under a statute providing that any importer who defrauded the government and thereby avoided payment of customs revenue was subject to fine, incarceration, and forfeiture of the imported merchandise. Utilizing an 1874

**a.** *Boyd*, *Dionisio*, and cases discussed therein deal only with constitutional limits upon the scope of an investigation conducted by subpoena. It should be kept in mind, however, that both state and federal courts recognize certain additional limitations that are not constitutionally based. Those limitations vary with the particular jurisdiction and are commonly tied to the use of subpoena authority by investigative grand juries. Among the limitations commonly recognized in this context are the prohibitions against the use of the grand jury subpoena to obtain evidence primarily for the purpose of developing civil suits or preparing criminal cases that have already resulted in an indictment. Several courts have also recognized witness objections to the alleged use of grand jury subpoenas to assist police investigations (as opposed to the grand jury's own investigation), and a few courts also permit objections challenging the prosecution's good faith by alleging that it is seeking information not relevant to the subject of the grand jury's investigation. Since all of these objections are based on the misuse of the grand jury for purposes other than its traditional investigatory role, and since jurisdictions generally recognize a "presumption of regularity" in the prosecution's use of the grand jury, courts traditionally impose a heavy burden on the subpoenaed party raising such objections, and the objections are not readily sustained.

statute, the government's attorney obtained a court "notice" directing Boyd to produce an invoice covering 29 of the cases of glass. That statute authorized the trial judge, on motion of the prosecutor describing a particular document and indicating what it might prove, to issue a notice directing the importer to produce the document. The importer could refuse to produce without being held in contempt (which distinguished the notice from a subpoena) but the consequence of a failure to produce was that the allegation of the prosecution as to what the document stated was "taken as confessed."]

[The defendants produced the invoice in compliance with the notice, but objected to the validity of the court's action, and objected again when the invoice was offered as evidence. The jury subsequently found for the United States, and a judgment of forfeiture against the 35 cases was granted.]

JUSTICE BRADLEY delivered the opinion of the Court.

* * * [I]n regard to Fourth Amendment, it is contended that * * * [the Act of 1874], under which the order in the present case was made, is free from constitutional objection, because it does not authorize the search and seizure of books and papers, but only requires the defendant or claimant to produce them. That is so; but it declares that if he does not produce them, the allegations which it is affirmed they will prove shall be taken as confessed. This is tantamount to compelling their production; for the prosecuting attorney will always be sure to state the evidence expected to be derived from them as strongly as the case will admit of. It is true that certain aggravating incidents of actual search and seizure, such as forcible entry into a man's house and searching amongst his papers, are wanting, and to this extent the proceeding under the act of 1874 is a mitigation of that which was authorized by the former acts; but it accomplishes the substantial object of those acts in forcing from a party evidence against himself. It is our opinion, therefore, that a compulsory production of a man's private papers to establish a criminal charge against him, or to forfeit his property, is within the scope of the Fourth Amendment to the Constitution, in all cases in which a search and seizure would be; because it is a material ingredient, and effects the sole object and purpose of search and seizure.

The principal question, however, remains to be considered. Is a search and seizure, or, what is equivalent thereto, a compulsory production of a man's private papers, to be used in evidence against him in a proceeding to forfeit his property for alleged fraud against the revenue laws—is such a proceeding for such a purpose an "*unreasonable* search and seizure" within the meaning of the Fourth Amendment of the Constitution? or, is it a legitimate proceeding?
* * *

In order to ascertain the nature of the proceedings intended by the Fourth Amendment to the Constitution under the terms "unreasonable searches and seizures," it is only necessary to recall the contemporary or then recent history of the controversies on the subject, both in this country and in England. * * * Prominent and principal among these was the practice of issuing general warrants by the Secretary of State, for searching private houses for the discovery and seizure of books and papers that might be used to convict their owner of the charge of libel. * * * The case, * * * which will always be celebrated as being the occasion of Lord Camden's memorable discussion of the subject, was that of *Entick v. Carrington and Three Other King's Messengers* * * *. The action was trespass for entering the plaintiff's dwelling-house in November, 1762, and breaking open his desks, boxes, &c., and searching and examining his papers. The jury rendered a special verdict, and the case was twice solemnly argued at the bar. Lord Camden pronounced the judgment of the court in

Michaelmas Term, 1765, and the law as expounded by him has been regarded as settled from that time to this, and his great judgment on that occasion is considered as one of the landmarks of English liberty. It was welcomed and applauded by the lovers of liberty in the colonies as well as in the mother country. It is regarded as one of the permanent monuments of the British Constitution, and is quoted as such by the English authorities on that subject down to the present time. As every American statesmen, during our revolutionary and formative period as a nation, was undoubtedly familiar with this monument of English freedom, and considered it as the true and ultimate expression of constitutional law, it may be confidently asserted that its propositions were in the minds of those who framed the Fourth Amendment to the Constitution, and were considered as sufficiently explanatory of what was meant by unreasonable searches and seizures. * * *

After describing the power claimed by the Secretary of State for issuing general search warrants, and the manner in which they were executed, Lord Camden says [in *Entick* ]:

* * * Papers are the owner's goods and chattels; they are his dearest property; and are so far from enduring a seizure, that they will hardly bear an inspection; and though the eye cannot by the laws of England be guilty of a trespass, yet where private papers are removed and carried away the secret nature of those goods will be an aggravation of the trespass, and demand more considerable damages in that respect. Where is the written law that gives any magistrate such a power? I can safely answer, there is none; and therefore, it is too much for us, without such authority, to pronounce a practice legal which would be subversive of all the comforts of society. * * *

Lastly, it is urged as an argument of utility, that such a search is a means of detecting offenders by discovering evidence. I wish some cases had been shown, where the law forceth evidence out of the owner's custody by process. There is no process against papers in civil causes. It has been often tried, but never prevailed. Nay, where the adversary has by force or fraud got possession of your own proper evidence, there is no way to get it back but by action. In the criminal law such a proceeding was never heard of; and yet there are some crimes, such, for instance, as murder, rape, robbery, and house-breaking, to say nothing of forgery and perjury, that are more atrocious than libelling. But our law has provided no paper-search in these cases to help forward the conviction. Whether this proceedeth from the gentleness of the law towards criminals, or from a consideration that such a power would be more pernicious to the innocent than useful to the public, I will not say. It is very certain that the law obligeth no man to accuse himself; because the necessary means of compelling self-accusation, falling upon the innocent as well as the guilty, would be both cruel and unjust; and it would seem, that search for evidence is disallowed upon the same principle. Then, too, the innocent would be confounded with the guilty.

* * * The principles laid down in this opinion affect the very essence of constitutional liberty and security. They reach farther than the concrete form of the case then before the court, with its adventitious circumstances; they apply to all invasions on the part of the government and its employees of the sanctity of a man's home and the privacies of life. It is not the breaking of his doors, and the rummaging of his drawers, that constitutes the essence of the offence; but it is the invasion of his indefeasible right of personal security, personal liberty and

private property, where that right has never been forfeited by his conviction of some public offence,—it is the invasion of this sacred right which underlies and constitutes the essence of Lord Camden's judgment. Breaking into a house and opening boxes and drawers are circumstances of aggravation; but any forcible and compulsory extortion of a man's own testimony or of his private papers to be used as evidence to convict him of crime or to forfeit his goods, is within the condemnation of that judgment. In this regard the Fourth and Fifth Amendments run almost into each other. * * *

We have already noticed the intimate relation between the two amendments. They throw great light on each other. For the "unreasonable searches and seizures" condemned in the Fourth Amendment are almost always made for the purpose of compelling a man to give evidence against himself, which in criminal cases is condemned in the Fifth Amendment; and compelling a man "in a criminal case to be a witness against himself," which is condemned in the Fifth Amendment, throws light on the question as to what is an "unreasonable search and seizure" within the meaning of the Fourth Amendment. And we have been unable to perceive that the seizure of a man's private books and papers to be used in evidence against him is substantially different from compelling him to be a witness against himself. * * * We are also clearly of opinion that proceedings instituted for the purpose of declaring the forfeiture of a man's property by reason of offences committed by him, though they may be civil in form, are in their nature criminal. In this very case, the ground of forfeiture * * * consists of certain acts of fraud committed against the public revenue in relation to imported merchandise, which are made criminal by the statute * * *. As, therefore, suits for penalties and forfeitures incurred by the commission of offences against the law, are of this quasi-criminal nature, we think that they are within the reason of criminal proceedings for all the purposes of the Fourth Amendment of the Constitution, and of that portion of the Fifth Amendment which declares that no person shall be compelled in any criminal case to be a witness against himself; and we are further of opinion that a compulsory production of the private books and papers of the owner of goods sought to be forfeited in such a suit is compelling him to be a witness against himself, within the meaning of the Fifth Amendment to the Constitution, and is the equivalent of a search and seizure—and an unreasonable search and seizure—within the meaning of the Fourth Amendment.

Though the proceeding in question is divested of many of the aggravating incidents of actual search and seizure, yet, as before said, it contains their substance and essence, and effects their substantial purpose. It may be that it is the obnoxious thing in its mildest and least repulsive form; but illegitimate and unconstitutional practices get their first footing in that way, namely, by silent approaches and slight deviations from legal modes of procedure. This can only be obviated by adhering to the rule that constitutional provisions for the security of person and property should be liberally construed. A close and literal construction deprives them of half their efficacy, and leads to gradual depreciation of the right, as if it consisted more in sound than in substance. It is the duty of courts to be watchful for the constitutional rights of the citizen, and against any stealthy encroachments thereon. Their motto should be *obsta principiis.* * * *

JUSTICE MILLER, with whom was THE CHIEF JUSTICE concurring:

I concur in the judgment of the court * * * and in so much of the opinion of this court as holds the 5th section of the act of 1874 void as applicable to the present case. * * * The order of the court under the statute is in effect a subpoena duces tecum, and, though the penalty for the witness's failure to appear in court with the criminating papers is not fine and imprisonment, it is one which may be made more severe, namely, to have charges against him of a criminal nature, taken for confessed, and made the foundation of the judgment of the court. That this is within the protection which the Constitution intended against compelling a person to be a witness against himself, is, I think, quite clear.

But this being so, there is no reason why this court should assume that the action of the court below, in requiring a party to produce certain papers as evidence on the trial, authorizes an unreasonable search or seizure of the house, papers, or effects of that party. There is in fact no search and no seizure authorized by the statute. No order can be made by the court under it which requires or permits anything more than service of notice on a party to the suit. * * *

Nothing in the nature of a search is here hinted at. Nor is there any seizure, because the party is not required at any time to part with the custody of the papers. They are to be produced in court, and, when produced, the United States attorney is permitted, under the direction of the court, to make examination in presence of the claimant, and may offer in evidence such entries in the books, invoices, or papers as relate to the issue. The act is careful to say that "the owner of said books and papers, his agent or attorney, shall have, subject to the order of the court, the custody of them, except pending their examination in court as aforesaid." * * *

The things * * * forbidden [by the Fourth Amendment] are two—search and seizure. * * * But what search does this statute authorize? If the mere service of a notice to produce a paper to be used as evidence, which the party can obey or not as he chooses is a search, then a change has taken place in the meaning of words, which has not come within my reading, and which I think was unknown at the time the Constitution was made. The searches meant by the Constitution were such as led to seizure when the search was successful. But the statute in this case uses language carefully framed to forbid any seizure under it, as I have already pointed out. * * * [a]

**a.** Insofar as *Boyd* suggested that the Fourth Amendment prohibited searches for property the defendant was entitled to possess (i.e., property other than the fruits or instrumentalities of crime), that aspect of *Boyd* was flatly rejected in *Warden v. Hayden*, 387 U.S. 294 (1967). Insofar as *Boyd* read the Fourth Amendment as prohibiting a search for documents, that interpretation was overturned in *Andresen v. Maryland*, 427 U.S. 463 (1976) (see Ch. 3, § 2). But long before these rulings, the Court restructured *Boyd*'s view of the bearing of the Fourth Amendment upon a subpoena duces tecum. In *Hale v. Henkel*, 201 U.S. 43 (1906), the Court had before it a challenge to a subpoena directing the petitioner to produce before a grand jury (which was conducting an investigation into possible violations of the antitrust laws) various corporate documents. Petitioner's challenge was based on the combined impact of the Fourth and Fifth Amendments, but the Court initially separated those claims. Cases subsequent to *Boyd*, it noted, had "treated the Fourth and Fifth Amendments as quite distinct, having different histo-

ries, and performing separate functions." Turning first to the petitioner's self-incrimination claim, the Court found that claim clearly failed since the statute authorizing the subpoena granted petitioner immunity from prosecution and the corporation itself had no self-incrimination privilege (see § 2 infra). The petitioner's Fourth Amendment claim did have merit, but for reasons other than what might have been assumed from *Boyd*. A subpoena compelling the production of documents violated the Fourth Amendment only where it was "far too sweeping in its terms to be regarded as reasonable." That was true here as the subpoena required production of a vast range of documents, covering a lengthy period, making it even questionable how the corporation could continue to carry on its business "after it had been denuded of this mass of material." In *See v. City of Seattle*, 387 U.S. 541 (1967), the Fourth Amendment limitation set forth in *Hale* was described as "requir[ing] that the subpoena be sufficiently limited in scope, relevant in purpose, and specific

## UNITED STATES v. DIONISIO

410 U.S. 1, 93 S.Ct. 764, 35 L.Ed.2d 67 (1973).

JUSTICE STEWART delivered the opinion of the Court.

A special grand jury was convened  *  *  * to investigate possible violations of federal criminal statutes relating to gambling.  In the course of its investigation the grand jury received in evidence certain voice recordings that had been obtained pursuant to court orders.  The grand jury subpoenaed approximately 20 persons, including the respondent Dionisio, seeking to obtain from them voice exemplars for comparison with the recorded conversations that had been received in evidence.  Each witness was advised that he was a potential defendant in a criminal prosecution.  Each was asked to examine a transcript of an intercepted conversation, and to go to a nearby office of the United States Attorney to read the transcript into a recording device.  The witnesses were advised that they would be allowed to have their attorneys present when they read the transcripts.  Dionisio and other witnesses refused to furnish the voice exemplars, asserting that these disclosures would violate their rights under the Fourth and Fifth Amendments.  The Government then filed separate petitions in the District Court to compel Dionisio and the other witnesses to furnish the voice exemplars to the grand jury.  *  *  * Following a hearing, the district judge rejected the witnesses' constitutional arguments and ordered them to comply with the grand jury's request.  *  *  * When Dionisio persisted in his refusal to respond to the grand jury's directive, the District Court adjudged him in civil contempt and ordered him committed to custody.  *  *  *

The Court of Appeals for the Seventh Circuit reversed.  *  *  * The court found that the Fourth Amendment applied to the grand jury process  *  *  *. Equating the procedures followed by the grand jury in the present case to the fingerprint detentions in *Davis v. Mississippi* [Ch. 3, § 7], the Court of Appeals reasoned that "[t]he dragnet effect here, where approximately 30 persons were subpoenaed for purposes of identification, has the same invidious effect on fourth amendment rights as the practice condemned in *Davis*." The Court of Appeals held that the Fourth Amendment required a preliminary showing of reasonableness before a grand jury witness could be compelled to furnish a voice exemplar, and that in this case the proposed "seizures" of the voice exemplars would be unreasonable because of the large number of witnesses summoned by the grand jury and directed to produce such exemplars.  We disagree.  *  *  *

[T]he obtaining of physical evidence from a person involves a potential Fourth Amendment violation at two different levels—the "seizure" of the "person" necessary to bring him into contact with government agents, see *Davis v. Mississippi,* and the subsequent search for and seizure of the evidence.  *  *  * The constitutionality of the compulsory production of exemplars from a grand jury witness necessarily turns on the same dual inquiry—whether either the initial compulsion of the person to appear before the grand jury, or the subsequent directive to make a voice recording is an unreasonable "seizure" within the meaning of the Fourth Amendment.

It is clear that a subpoena to appear before a grand jury is not a "seizure" in the Fourth Amendment sense, even though that summons may be inconvenient or burdensome.  Last Term we again acknowledged what has long been recognized, that "[c]itizens generally are not constitutionally immune from grand jury

in directive so that compliance will not be
unreasonably burdened."

subpoenas. * * *" *Branzburg v. Hayes* [408 U.S. 665 (1972)].[a] * * * [*Branzburg* and other decisions] are recent reaffirmations of the historically grounded obligations of every person to appear and give his evidence before the grand jury. "The personal sacrifice involved is a part of the necessary contribution of the individual to the welfare of the public." *Blair v. United States*, 250 U.S. 273 (1919).

The compulsion exerted by a grand jury subpoena differs from the seizure effected by an arrest or even an investigative "stop" in more than civic obligation. For, as Judge Friendly wrote for the Court of Appeals for the Second Circuit:

"The latter is abrupt, is effected with force or the threat of it and often in demeaning circumstances, and, in the case of arrest, results in a record involving social stigma. A subpoena is served in the same manner as other legal process; it involves no stigma whatever; if the time for appearance is inconvenient, this can generally be altered; and it remains at all times under the control and supervision of a court."

Thus, the Court of Appeals for the Seventh Circuit correctly recognized in a case subsequent to the one now before us, that a "grand jury subpoena to testify is not that kind of governmental intrusion on privacy against which the Fourth Amendment affords protection, once the Fifth Amendment is satisfied."

This case is thus quite different from *Davis v. Mississippi*, on which the Court of Appeals primarily relied. For in *Davis* it was the initial seizure—the lawless dragnet detention—that violated the Fourth and Fourteenth Amendments—not the taking of the fingerprints. * * * *Davis* is plainly inapposite to a case where the initial restraint does not itself infringe the Fourth Amendment.

This is not to say that a grand jury subpoena is some talisman that dissolves all constitutional protections. The grand jury cannot require a witness to testify against himself. It cannot require the production by a person of private books and records that would incriminate him. See *Boyd v. United States*. The Fourth Amendment provides protection against a grand jury subpoena *duces tecum* too sweeping in its terms "to be regarded as reasonable." *Hale v. Henkel*. And last Term, in the context of a First Amendment claim, we indicated that the Constitution could not tolerate the transformation of the grand jury into an instrument of oppression: "Official harassment of the press undertaken not for purposes of law enforcement but to disrupt a reporter's relationship with his news sources would have no justification. Grand juries are subject to judicial control and subpoenas to motions to quash. We do not expect courts will forget that grand juries must operate within the limits of the First Amendment as well as the Fifth." *Branzburg v. Hayes*.

But we are here faced with no such constitutional infirmities in the subpoena to appear before the grand jury or in the order to make the voice recordings. There is * * * no valid Fifth Amendment claim. There was no order to produce private books and papers, and no sweeping subpoena *duces tecum*. And even if *Branzburg* be extended beyond its First Amendment moorings and tied to

**a.** The Court in *Branzburg* rejected a First Amendment claim raised by reporters who had been subpoenaed to testify before grand juries. The reporters had argued that they should not be compelled to reveal the identity of confidential sources or relevant facts obtained from those sources, at least absent an initial showing by the grand jury of a "compelling need" to obtain such information. The Court majority responded that it was "unclear" whether requiring the reporters to testify before the grand jury might have a negative impact on their future newsgathering capacity, but, in any event, that impact did not outweigh the interest of the public in the grand jury's unencumbered investigation of crime.

a more generalized due process concept, there is still no indication in this case of the kind of harassment that was of concern there.

The Court of Appeals found critical significance in the fact that the grand jury had summoned approximately 20 witnesses to furnish voice exemplars. We think that fact is basically irrelevant to the constitutional issues here. The grand jury may have been attempting to identify a number of voices on the tapes in evidence, or it might have summoned the 20 witnesses in an effort to identify one voice. But whatever the case, "[a] grand jury's investigation is not fully carried out until every available clue has been run down and all witnesses examined in every proper way to find if a crime has been committed." * * * The grand jury may well find it desirable to call numerous witnesses in the course of an investigation. It does not follow that each witness may resist a subpoena on the ground that too many witnesses have been called. Neither the order to Dionisio to appear, nor the order to make a voice recording was rendered unreasonable by the fact that many others were subjected to the same compulsion.

But the conclusion that Dionisio's compulsory appearance before the grand jury was not an unreasonable "seizure" is the answer to only the first part of the Fourth Amendment inquiry here. Dionisio argues that the grand jury's subsequent directive to make the voice recording was itself an infringement of his rights under the Fourth Amendment. We cannot accept that argument. In *Katz v. United States* [Ch. 3, § 1], we said that the Fourth Amendment provides no protection for what "a person knowingly exposes to the public, even in his home or office * * *." The physical characteristics of a person's voice, its tone and manner, as opposed to the content of a specific conversation, are constantly exposed to the public. Like a man's facial characteristics, or handwriting, his voice is repeatedly produced for others to hear. No person can have a reasonable expectation that others will not know the sound of his voice, any more than he can reasonably expect that his face will be a mystery to the world. * * *

Since neither the summons to appear before the grand jury, nor its directive to make a voice recording infringed upon any interest protected by the Fourth Amendment, there was no justification for requiring the grand jury to satisfy even the minimal requirement of "reasonableness" imposed by the Court of Appeals. A grand jury has broad investigative powers to determine whether a crime has been committed and who has committed it. The jurors may act on tips, rumors, evidence offered by the prosecutor, or their own personal knowledge. *Branzburg v. Hayes.* No grand jury witness is "entitled to set limits to the investigation that the grand jury may conduct." And a sufficient basis for an indictment may only emerge at the end of the investigation when all the evidence has been received. * * * Since Dionisio raised no valid Fourth Amendment claim, there is no more reason to require a preliminary showing of reasonableness here than there would be in the case of any witness who, despite the lack of any constitutional or statutory privilege, declined to answer a question or comply with a grand jury request. Neither the Constitution nor our prior cases justify any such interference with grand jury proceedings.[14]

14. Mr. Justice Marshall in dissent suggests that a preliminary showing of "reasonableness" is required where the grand jury subpoenas a witness to appear and produce handwriting or voice exemplars, but not when it subpoenas him to appear and testify. Such a distinction finds no support in the Constitution. The dissent argues that there is a potential Fourth Amendment violation in the case of a subpoenaed grand jury witness because of the asserted intrusiveness of the initial subpoena to appear—the possible stigma from a grand jury appearance and the inconvenience of the official restraint. But the initial directive to appear is as intrusive if the witness is called simply to testify as it is if he is summoned to produce physical evidence.

The Fifth Amendment guarantees that no civilian may be brought to trial for an infamous crime "unless on a presentment or indictment of a Grand Jury." This constitutional guarantee presupposes an investigative body "acting independently of either prosecuting attorney or judge," whose mission is to clear the innocent, no less than to bring to trial those who may be guilty. Any holding that would saddle a grand jury with minitrials and preliminary showing would assuredly impede its investigation and frustrate the public's interest in the fair and expeditious administration of the criminal laws. The grand jury may not always serve its historic role as a protective bulwark standing solidly between the ordinary citizen and an overzealous prosecutor, but if it is even to approach the proper performance of its constitutional mission, it must be free to pursue its investigations unhindered by external influence or supervision so long as it does not trench upon the legitimate rights of any witness called before it. * * *

JUSTICE MARSHALL, dissenting.[b]

* * * There can be no question that investigatory seizures effected by the police are subject to the constraints of the Fourth and Fourteenth Amendments. *Davis v. Mississippi.* * * * Like *Davis,* the present cases involve official investigatory seizures which interfere with personal liberty. The Court considers dispositive, however, the fact that the seizures were effected by the grand jury, rather than the police. I cannot agree. * * * [I]n *Hale v. Henkel,* the Court held that a subpoena *duces tecum* ordering "the production of books and papers [before a grand jury] may constitute an unreasonable search and seizure within the Fourth Amendment," and on the particular facts of the case, it concluded that the subpoena was "far too sweeping in its terms to be regarded as reasonable." Considered alone, *Hale* would certainly seem to carry a strong implication that a subpoena compelling an individual's personal appearance before a grand jury, like a subpoena ordering the production of private papers, is subject to the Fourth Amendment standard of reasonableness. The protection of the Fourth Amendment is not, after all, limited to personal "papers," but extends also to "persons," "houses," and "effects." It would seem a strange hierarchy of constitutional values that would afford papers more protection from arbitrary governmental intrusion than people.

The Court, however, offers two interrelated justifications for excepting grand jury subpoenas directed at "persons," rather than "papers," from the constraints of the Fourth Amendment. These are an "historically grounded obligation of every person to appear and give his evidence before the grand jury," and the relative unintrusiveness of the grand jury subpoena on an individual's liberty.

In my view, the Court makes more of history than is justified. The Court treats the "historically grounded obligation" which it now discerns as extending to all "evidence," whatever its character. Yet, so far as I am aware, the obligation "to appear and give evidence" has heretofore been applied by this Court only in the context of testimonial evidence, either oral or documentary. * * * In the present case, * * * it was not testimony that the grand jury sought from respondents, but physical evidence. * * *

The Court seems to reason that the exception to the Fourth Amendment for grand jury subpoenas directed at persons is justified by the relative unintrusiveness of the grand jury process on an individual's liberty. * * * It may be that service of a grand jury subpoena does not involve the same potential for momentary embarrassment as does an arrest or investigatory "stop." But this difference seems inconsequential in comparison to the substantial stigma

---

**b.** The separate dissents of Justices Douglas and Brennan are omitted.

which—contrary to the Court's assertion—may result from a grand jury appearance as well as from an arrest or investigatory seizure. Public knowledge that a man has been summoned by a federal grand jury investigating, for instance, organized criminal activity can mean loss of friends, irreparable injury to business, and tremendous pressures on one's family life. Whatever nice legal distinctions may be drawn between police and prosecutor, on the one hand, and the grand jury, on the other, the public often treats an appearance before a grand jury as tantamount to a visit to the station house. Indeed, the former is frequently more damaging than the latter, for a grand jury appearance has an air of far greater gravity than a brief visit "downtown" for a "talk." The Fourth Amendment was placed in our Bill of Rights to protect the individual citizen from such potentially disruptive governmental intrusion into his private life unless conducted reasonably and with sufficient cause.

Nor do I believe that the constitutional problems inherent in such governmental interference with an individual's person are substantially alleviated because one may seek to appear at a "convenient time." In *Davis v. Mississippi*, it was recognized that an investigatory detention effected by the police "need not come unexpectedly or at an inconvenient time." But this fact did not suggest to the Court that the Fourth Amendment was inapplicable * * *. No matter how considerate a grand jury may be in arranging for an individual's appearance, the basic fact remains that his liberty has been officially restrained for some period of time. In terms of its effect on the individual, this restraint does not differ meaningfully from the restraint imposed on a suspect compelled to visit the police station house. Thus, the nature of the intrusion on personal liberty caused by a grand jury subpoena cannot, without more, be considered sufficient basis for denying respondents the protection of the Fourth Amendment.

Of course, the Fourth Amendment does not bar all official seizures of the person, but only those that are unreasonable and are without sufficient cause. With this in mind, it is possible at least to explain, if not justify, the failure to apply the protection of the Fourth Amendment to grand jury subpoenas requiring individuals to appear and *testify*. Thus, while it is true that we have traditionally given the grand jury broad investigatory powers, particularly in terms of compelling the appearance of persons before it, it must be understood that we have done so in heavy reliance on certain essential assumptions.

Certainly the most celebrated function of the grand jury is to stand between the Government and the citizen and thus to protect the latter from harassment and unfounded prosecution. The grand jury does not shed those characteristics which give it insulating qualities when it acts in its investigative capacity. Properly functioning, the grand jury is to be the servant of neither the Government nor the courts, but of the people. As such, we assume that it comes to its task without bias or self-interest. Unlike the prosecutor or policeman, it has no election to win or executive appointment to keep. The anticipated neutrality of the grand jury, even when acting in its investigative capacity, may perhaps be relied upon to prevent unwarranted interference with the lives of private citizens and to ensure that the grand jury's subpoena powers over the person are exercised in only a reasonable fashion. Under such circumstances, it may be justifiable to give the grand jury broad personal subpoena powers that are outside the purview of the Fourth Amendment, for—in contrast to the police—it is not likely that it will abuse those powers.

Whatever the present day validity of the historical assumption of neutrality which underlies the grand jury process, it must at least be recognized that if a grand jury is deprived of the independence essential to the assumption of neutrality—if it effectively surrenders that independence to a prosecutor—the dangers of excessive and unreasonable official interference with personal liberty are exactly those which the Fourth Amendment was intended to prevent. So long as the grand jury carries on its investigatory activities only through the mechanism of testimonial inquiries, the danger of such official usurpation of the grand jury process may not be unreasonably great. Individuals called to testify before the grand jury will have available their Fifth Amendment privilege against self-incrimination. Thus, at least insofar as incriminating information is sought directly from a particular criminal suspect, the grand jury process would not appear to offer law enforcement officials a substantial advantage over ordinary investigative techniques.

But when we move beyond the realm of grand jury investigations limited to testimonial inquiries, as the Court does today, the danger increases that law enforcement officials may seek to usurp the grand jury process for the purpose of securing incriminating evidence from a particular suspect through the simple expedient of a subpoena. * * * Thus, if the grand jury may summon criminal suspects [to obtain handwriting and voice exemplars] without complying with the Fourth Amendment, it will obviously present an attractive investigative tool to prosecutor and police. For what law enforcement officers could not accomplish directly themselves after our decision in *Davis v. Mississippi*, they may now accomplish indirectly through the grand jury process.

Thus, the Court's decisions today can serve only to encourage prosecutorial exploitation of the grand jury process, at the expense of both individual liberty and the traditional neutrality of the grand jury. * * * [B]y holding that the grand jury's power to subpoena these respondents for the purpose of obtaining exemplars is completely outside the purview of the Fourth Amendment, the Court fails to appreciate the essential difference between real and testimonial evidence in the context of these cases, and thereby hastens the reduction of the grand jury into simply another investigative device of law enforcement officials. By contrast, the Court of Appeals, in proper recognition of these dangers, imposed narrow limitations on the subpoena power of the grand jury which are necessary to guard against unreasonable official interference with individual liberty but which would not impair significantly the traditional investigatory powers of that body. * * *

## SECTION 2. THE PRIVILEGE AGAINST SELF–INCRIMINATION

A person subpoenaed in connection with a grand jury or any other criminal investigation has available all of the evidentiary privileges available to witnesses in general (i.e., the right, at the witness' option, to refuse to provide information where the law designates that information as "privileged" and therefore free from compelled disclosure). In this context, clearly the most significant privilege is that guaranteed by the Fifth Amendment of the Constitution—the privilege against compulsory self-incrimination.[a] The Fifth Amendment states

**a.** The other privileges that witnesses may raise as a grounding for refusing to disclose information ordinarily flow from the law of the particular jurisdiction, and therefore will vary in scope from one state to another. These include such privileges as the marital privilege (protecting at least the confidential communications between spouses), the doctor/ patient privilege (protecting information passed between doctor and patient that is germane to treatment or consultation), and the lawyer/client privilege (protecting, with some exceptions, communications of clients to lawyers for the purpose of legal consultation). While all of these may arise in the grand jury context, none rivals the self-incrimination that no person "shall be compelled in any criminal case to be a witness against himself." The self-incrimination clause has an extensive common law background, and it was with respect to the interpretation of this clause that Justice Frankfurter once noted that "a page of history is worth a volume of logic." *Ullmann v. United States,* 350 U.S. 422 (1956) (concurring). Yet the Court also has frequently cited the important and diverse values underlying the privilege [b] and noted the need to give the privilege a construction "as broad as the mischief against which it seeks to guard." *Counselman v. Hitchcock,* 142 U.S. 547 (1892).[c]

The first two cases in this section deal with the relinquishment of the privilege against self-incrimination by a grand jury witness. The *Rogers* case treats the issue of waiver through partial disclosure. *Mandujano* raises, but does not resolve by a majority decision, the question of whether there can be a waiver without first advising the grand jury witness of his rights and offering access to counsel, where the witness is one who may be viewed as a "target" of the investigation. Following the *Mandujano* decision, the Justice Department issued an internal guideline on federal grand jury practice which requires prosecutors to give the following notification to all grand jury witnesses: (1) "that the witness may refuse to answer any question if a truthful answer to the question would tend to incriminate him," (2) "that anything that the witness does say may be used against him," and (3) "that the grand jury will permit the witness the reasonable opportunity to step outside the grand jury room to consult with counsel if he desires." Warnings relating to the self-incrimination privilege are commonly used in state grand jury proceedings as well. As to consulting with counsel, most states follow the federal practice, but a small number of states allow the witness to be assisted by counsel located within the grand jury room and several of these provide for appointment of counsel at the state's expense where the witness is indigent.

The *Kastigar* case treats the important practice of providing to the witness a grant of immunity that precludes reliance upon the privilege. Following that decision, many states moved from transactional immunity grants to the use/ derivative-use grant upheld in *Kastigar,* but a fair number of states still provide transactional immunity.

The last two cases in this section, *Fisher* and *Braswell,* return to the issue first raised in *Boyd*—the availability of the privilege in responding to a subpoena

privilege either as to the frequency with which it arises or its practical significance.

**b.** The most frequently cited statement of those values comes from Justice Goldberg's opinion for the Court in *Murphy v. Waterfront Commission,* 378 U.S. 52 (1964), a case discussed infra in the *Kastigar* opinion. That opinion stated: "The privilege against self-incrimination * * * reflects many of our fundamental values and most noble aspirations: our unwillingness to subject those suspected of crime to the cruel trilemma of self-accusation, perjury or contempt; our preference for an accusatorial rather than an inquisitorial system of criminal justice; our fear that self-incriminating statements will be elicited by inhumane treatment and abuses; our sense of fair play which dictates 'a fair state-individual balance by requiring the government to leave the individual alone until good cause is shown for disturbing him and by requiring the government in its contest with the individual to shoulder the entire load';

our respect for the inviolability of the human personality and the right of each individual 'to a private enclave where he may lead a private life'; our distrust of self-deprecatory statements; and our realization that the privilege, while sometimes 'a shelter to the guilty,' is often 'a protection to the innocent.'"

**c.** *Counselman* accordingly concluded that the privilege went beyond granting a defendant the right not to testify in his own criminal case. The Fifth Amendment prohibition against compelling testimony "in a criminal case," the Court noted, referred to the eventual use of the compelled testimony in a criminal case, not to the type of proceeding in which the testimony was first compelled. The Fifth Amendment privilege therefore was available to a witness in "any proceeding" who is being compelled to give testimony that might be used as incriminating evidence in a subsequent criminal case. *Counselman* itself involved a witness before a grand jury.

duces tecum requiring the production of documents. As noted in these cases, the Court had earlier held that the privilege was not available to a corporation or similar entity, such as a partnership. Thus, as the Court notes in *Fisher,* A.E. Boyd and Sons, a partnership, would not have the privilege available to it today to contest a subpoena requiring production of its records. The question presented in *Fisher* is the extent to which the privilege applies (and *Boyd* survives) as to a subpoena directing production of the papers of an individual. *Braswell* considers whether, in light of *Fisher*'s analysis, an agent of an entity may assert his personal privilege in response to a subpoena directing him personally to produce entity records.

## ROGERS v. UNITED STATES
### 340 U.S. 367, 71 S.Ct. 438, 95 L.Ed. 344 (1951).

CHIEF JUSTICE VINSON delivered the opinion of the Court.

This case arises out of an investigation by the regularly convened grand jury of the United States District Court for the District of Colorado. The books and records of the Communist Party of Denver were sought as necessary to that inquiry and were the subject of questioning by the grand jury. In September, 1948, petitioner, in response to a subpoena, appeared before the grand jury. She testified that she held the position of Treasurer of the Communist Party of Denver until January, 1948, and that, by virtue of her office, she had been in possession of membership lists and dues records of the Party. Petitioner denied having possession of the records and testified that she had turned them over to another. But she refused to identify the person to whom she had given the Party's books, stating to the court as her only reason: "I don't feel that I should subject a person or persons to the same thing that I'm going through." The court thereupon committed petitioner to the custody of the marshal until ten o'clock the next morning, expressly advising petitioner of her right to consult with counsel.

The next day, counsel for petitioner informed the court that he had read the transcript of the prior day's proceedings and that, upon his advice, petitioner would answer the questions to purge herself of contempt. However, upon reappearing before the grand jury, petitioner again refused to answer the question. The following day she was again brought into court. Called before the district judge immediately after he had heard oral argument concerning the privilege against self-incrimination in another case, petitioner repeated her refusal to answer the question, asserting this time the privilege against self-incrimination. After ruling that her refusal was not privileged, the district judge imposed a sentence of four months for contempt. The Court of Appeals for the Tenth Circuit affirmed, and we granted certiorari.

* * * [T]he decisions of this Court are explicit in holding that the privilege against self-incrimination "is solely for the benefit of the witness," and "is purely a personal privilege of the witness." Petitioner expressly placed her original declination to answer on an untenable ground, since a refusal to answer cannot be justified by a desire to protect others from punishment, much less to protect another from interrogation by a grand jury. Petitioner's claim of the privilege against self-incrimination was pure afterthought. Although the claim was made at the time of her second refusal to answer in the presence of the court, it came only after she had voluntarily testified to her status as an officer of the Communist Party of Denver. To uphold a claim of privilege in this case would open the way to distortion of facts by permitting a witness to select any stopping place in the testimony. * * *

In *Patricia Blau v. United States,* 340 U.S. 159 (1950), we held that questions as to connections with the Communist Party are subject to the privilege against self-incrimination as calling for disclosure of facts tending to criminate under the Smith Act.[a] But petitioner's conviction stands on an entirely different footing, for she had freely described her membership, activities and office in the Party. Since the privilege against self-incrimination presupposes a real danger of legal detriment arising from the disclosure, petitioner cannot invoke the privilege where response to the specific question in issue here would not further incriminate her. Disclosure of a fact waives the privilege as to details. As this Court stated in *Brown v. Walker,* 161 U.S. 591 (1896):

"Thus, if the witness himself elects to waive his privilege, as he may doubtless do, since the privilege is for his protection and not for that of other parties, and discloses his criminal connections, he is not permitted to stop, but must go on and make a full disclosure."

* * * Requiring full disclosure of details after a witness freely testifies as to a criminating fact does not rest upon a further "waiver" of the privilege against self-incrimination. Admittedly, petitioner had already "waived" her privilege of silence when she freely answered criminating questions relating to her connection with the Communist Party. But when petitioner was asked to furnish the name of the person to whom she turned over Party records, the court was required to determine, as it must whenever the privilege is claimed, whether the question presented a reasonable danger of further crimination in light of all the circumstances, including any previous disclosures. As to each question to which a claim of privilege is directed, the court must determine whether the answer to that particular question would subject the witness to a "real danger" of further crimination. After petitioner's admission that she held the office of Treasurer of the Communist Party of Denver, disclosure of acquaintance with her successor presents no more than a "mere imaginary possibility" of increasing the danger of prosecution. * * *

JUSTICE CLARK took no part in the consideration or decision of this case.

JUSTICE BLACK, with whom JUSTICE FRANKFURTER and JUSTICE DOUGLAS concur, dissenting.

Some people are hostile to the Fifth Amendment's provision unequivocally commanding that no United States official shall compel a person to be a witness against himself. They consider the provision as an outmoded relic of past fears generated by ancient inquisitorial practices that could not possibly happen here. For this reason the privilege to be silent is sometimes accepted as being more or less of a constitutional nuisance which the courts should abate whenever and however possible. Such an end could be achieved by two obvious judicial techniques: (1) narrow construction of the scope of the privilege; (2) broad construction of the doctrine of "waiver." Any attempt to use the first of these methods, however, runs afoul of approximately 150 years of precedent. This Court has almost always construed the Amendment broadly on the view that compelling a person to convict himself of crime is "contrary to the principles of a free government" and "abhorrent to the instincts of an American"; that while

---

**a.** The Smith Act made it a crime to advocate the overthrow of the government by force or violence or to become a member of a group which advocates such overthrow with knowledge of that purpose. The Court in *Blau* noted that it was "immaterial" whether a witness' admission of "employment by the Communist Party or intimate knowledge of its workings" would in itself support a criminal conviction; such admissions surely "would have furnished a link in the chain of evidence needed in a prosecution of petitioner for violation of (or conspiracy to violate) the Smith Act" and that was sufficient, under longstanding Fifth Amendment precedent, to "give a witness the privilege of remaining silent."

such a coercive practice "may suit the purposes of despotic power  *  *  * it cannot abide the pure atmosphere of political liberty and personal freedom." *Boyd v. United States.*

The doctrine of waiver seems to be a more palatable but equally effective device for whittling away the protection afforded by the privilege, although I think today's application of that doctrine cannot be supported by our past decisions.  *  *  * In the case of this petitioner, there is no evidence that she intended to give up her privilege of silence concerning the persons in possession of the Communist Party records. To the contrary, the record—as set out in the Court's opinion—shows she intended to avoid answering the question on whatever ground might be available and asserted the privilege against self-incrimination at the first moment she became aware of its existence. This fact and the cases which make it crucial are ignored in the decision today.

Apparently, the Court's holding is that at some uncertain point in petitioner's testimony, regardless of her intention, admission of associations with the Communist Party automatically effected a "waiver" of her constitutional protection as to all related questions. To adopt such a rule for the privilege against self-incrimination, when other constitutional safeguards must be knowingly waived, relegates the Fifth Amendment's privilege to a second-rate position. Moreover, today's holding creates this dilemma for witnesses: On the one hand, they risk imprisonment for contempt by asserting the privilege prematurely; on the other, they might lose the privilege if they answer a single question. The Court's view makes the protection depend on timing so refined that lawyers, let alone laymen, will have difficulty in knowing when to claim it. In this very case, it never occurred to the trial judge that petitioner waived anything. And even if voluntary testimony can under some circumstances work a waiver, it did not do so here because what petitioner stated to the grand jury "standing alone did not amount to an admission of guilt or furnish clear proof of crime  *  *  *." *Arndstein v. McCarthy,* 254 U.S. 71 (1923).

Furthermore, unlike the Court, I believe that the question which petitioner refused to answer did call for additional incriminating information. She was asked the names of the persons to whom she had turned over the Communist Party books and records. Her answer would not only have been relevant in any future prosecution of petitioner for violation of the Smith Act but also her conviction might depend on testimony of the witnesses she was thus asked to identify. For these reasons the question sought a disclosure which would have been incriminating to the highest degree. Certainly no one can say that the answer "[could not] possibly be used as a basis for, or in aid of, a criminal prosecution against the witness  *  *  *." *Brown v. Walker,* 161 U.S. 591 (1896).

*  *  *

## UNITED STATES v. MANDUJANO

425 U.S. 564, 96 S.Ct. 1768, 48 L.Ed.2d 212 (1976).

CHIEF JUSTICE BURGER announced the judgment of the Court in an opinion in which JUSTICE WHITE, JUSTICE POWELL, and JUSTICE REHNQUIST join.

This case presents the question whether the warnings called for by *Miranda v. Arizona* [Ch. 6, § 3], must be given to a grand jury witness who is called to testify about criminal activities in which he may have been personally involved; and, whether absent such warnings, false statements made to the grand jury must be suppressed in a prosecution for perjury based on those statements.

[In March 1973, an undercover agent received information that Mandujano was dealing in narcotics. Keeping his identity secret, the agent met Mandujano and arranged for the purchase of heroin. Mandujano received $650.00 for the purchase, but returned the same night without the heroin and refunded the money. After Mandujano failed to keep a subsequent appointment, the agent closed the investigative file and reported his contact with Mandujano to federal prosecutors. Six weeks later Mandujano was subpoenaed to testify before a special grand jury investigating the drug traffic in the local area. Before testifying, the prosecutor informed Mandujano of his general duty to answer, his right not to answer incriminatory questions, and of possible perjury liability for false answers. Mandujano was also told that he could have a lawyer outside the room with whom he could consult. When asked if he had a lawyer, Mandujano responded: "I don't have one. I don't have the money to get one."]

[During the grand jury questioning, Mandujano admitted that he had purchased heroin as recently as five months ago, but denied knowledge of the identity of any dealers, except for one street-corner source. He maintained this position notwithstanding the prosecutor's suggestion that "our information is that you can tell us more * * * than you have today." Mandujano "steadfastly denied either selling or attempting to sell heroin since the time of his conviction 15 years before." He "specifically disclaimed having discussed the sale of heroin with anyone during the preceding year and stated that he would not even try to purchase an ounce of heroin for $650.00."]

[Mandujano subsequently was indicted for attempting to distribute heroin and for willfully and knowingly making a false material declaration to the grand jury. The prosecution sought to introduce the grand jury testimony as the basis for the false declaration charge. Mandujano argued that his grand jury testimony should be suppressed since he was not given full *Miranda* warnings prior to his testimony. The District Court sustained the motion on the ground that a "putative" or "virtual" defendant was entitled to *Miranda* warnings. The Court of Appeals affirmed.]

* * * The very availability of the Fifth Amendment privilege to grand jury witnesses suggests that occasions will often arise when potentially incriminating questions will be asked in the ordinary course of the jury's investigation. * * * It is in keeping with the grand jury's historic function as a shield against arbitrary accusations to call before it persons suspected of criminal activity, so that the investigation can be complete. This is true whether the grand jury embarks upon an inquiry focused upon individuals suspected of wrongdoing, or is directed at persons suspected of no misconduct but who may be able to provide links in a chain of evidence relating to criminal conduct of others, or is centered upon broader problems of concern to society. It is entirely appropriate—indeed imperative—to summon individuals who may be able to illuminate the shadowy precincts of corruption and crime. Since the subject matter of the inquiry is crime, and often organized, systematic crime—as is true with drug traffic—it is unrealistic to assume that all of the witnesses capable of providing useful information will be pristine pillars of the community untainted by criminality. * * *

Accordingly, the witness, though possibly engaged in some criminal enterprise, can be required to answer before a grand jury, so long as there is no compulsion to answer questions that are self-incriminating * * *. The witness must invoke the privilege, however, as the "Constitution does not forbid the asking of criminative questions." *United States v. Monia*, 317 U.S., at 433 (1943) (Frankfurter, J., dissenting).

> "The [Fifth] Amendment speaks of compulsion. It does not preclude a witness from testifying voluntarily in matters which may incriminate him. If, therefore, he desires the protection of the privilege, he must claim it or he will not be considered to have been 'compelled' within the meaning of the Amendment." Id.

Absent a claim of the privilege, the duty to give testimony remains absolute.

The stage is therefore set when the question is asked. If the witness interposes his privilege, the grand jury has two choices. If the desired testimony is of marginal value, the grand jury can pursue other avenues of inquiry; if the testimony is thought sufficiently important, the grand jury can seek a judicial determination as to the bona fides of the witness' Fifth Amendment claim, in which case the witness must satisfy the presiding judge that the claim of privilege is not a subterfuge. If in fact "there is reasonable ground to apprehend danger to the witness from his being compelled to answer," the prosecutor must then determine whether the answer is of such overriding importance as to justify a grant of immunity to the witness. If immunity is sought by the prosecutor and granted by the presiding judge, the witness can then be compelled to answer, on pain of contempt, even though the testimony would implicate the witness in criminal activity.   *   *   *

In this constitutional process of securing a witness' testimony, perjury simply has no place whatever. Perjured testimony is an obvious and flagrant affront to the basic concepts of judicial proceedings. Effective restraints against this type of egregious offense are therefore imperative. The power of subpoena, broad as it is, and the power of contempt for refusing to answer, drastic as that is—and even the solemnity of the oath—cannot insure truthful answers. Hence, Congress has made the giving of false answers a criminal act punishable by severe penalties; in no other way can criminal conduct be flushed into the open where the law can deal with it.

Similarly, our cases have consistently—indeed without exception—allowed sanctions for false statements or perjury; they have done so even in instances where the perjurer complained that the Government exceeded its constitutional powers in making the inquiry. See, e.g., *Bryson v. United States,* 396 U.S. 64 (1969). In *Bryson,* a union officer was required by federal labor law to file an affidavit averring that he was not a Communist. The affidavit was false in material statements. In a collateral attack on his conviction, Bryson argued that since the statute required him either to incriminate himself or lie, he could not lawfully be imprisoned for failure to comply. This Court rejected the contention:

> "[I]t cannot be thought that as a general principle of our law a citizen has a privilege to answer fraudulently a question that the Government should not have asked. Our legal system provides methods for challenging the Government's right to ask questions—lying is not one of them."

*   *   * In this case, the Court of Appeals required the suppression of perjured testimony given by respondent, as a witness under oath, lawfully summoned before an investigative grand jury and questioned about matters directly related to the grand jury's inquiry. The court reached this result because the prosecutor failed to give *Miranda* warnings at the outset of Mandujano's interrogation. Those warnings were required, in the Court of Appeals' view, because Mandujano was a "virtual" or "putative" defendant— that is, the prosecutor had specific information concerning Mandujano's partici- pation in an attempted sale of heroin and the focus of the grand jury interroga-

tion, as evidenced by the prosecutor's questions, centered on Mandujano's involvement in narcotics traffic. * * *

The court's analysis, premised upon the prosecutor's failure to give *Miranda* warnings, erroneously applied the standards fashioned by this Court in *Miranda*. Those warnings were aimed at the evils seen by the Court as endemic to police interrogation of a person in custody. *Miranda* addressed extra-judicial confessions or admissions procured in a hostile, unfamiliar environment which lacked procedural safeguards. The decision expressly rested on the privilege against compulsory self-incrimination; the prescribed warnings sought to negate the "compulsion" thought to be inherent in police station interrogation. But the *Miranda* Court simply did not perceive judicial inquiries and custodial interrogation as equivalents: " * * * the compulsion to speak in the isolated setting of the police station may well be greater than in courts or other official investigations, where there are often impartial observers to guard against intimidation or trickery."

The Court thus recognized that many official investigations, such as grand jury questioning, take place in a setting wholly different from custodial police interrogation. Indeed, the Court's opinion in *Miranda* reveals a focus on what was seen by the Court as police "coercion" derived from "factual studies [relating to] police violence and the 'third degree' * * * physical brutality—beating, hanging, whipping—and to sustained and protracted questioning incommunicado in order to extort confessions. * * * " To extend these concepts to questioning before a grand jury inquiring into criminal activity under the guidance of a judge is an extravagant expansion never remotely contemplated by this Court in *Miranda*; the dynamics of constitutional interpretation do not compel constant extension of every doctrine announced by the Court. * * *

The warnings volunteered by the prosecutor to respondent in this case were more than sufficient to inform him of his rights—and his responsibilities—and particularly of the consequences of perjury.[a] To extend the concepts of *Miranda*, as contemplated by the Court of Appeals, would require that the witness be told that there was an absolute right to silence, and obviously any such warning would be incorrect, for there is no such right before a grand jury. Under *Miranda*, a person in police custody has, of course, an absolute right to decline to answer any question, incriminating or innocuous, whereas a grand jury witness, on the contrary, has an absolute duty to answer all questions, subject only to a valid Fifth Amendment claim. And even when the grand jury witness asserts the privilege, questioning need not cease, except as to the particular subject to which the privilege has been addressed. Other lines of inquiry may properly be pursued.

Respondent was also informed that if he desired he could have the assistance of counsel, but that counsel could not be inside the grand jury room. That statement was plainly a correct recital of the law. No criminal proceedings had been instituted against respondent, hence the Sixth Amendment right to counsel had not come into play. *Kirby v. Illinois* [Ch. 7, § 2].[6] A witness "before a

---

a. At a subsequent point in the opinion, Chief Justice Burger added in a footnote [note 7] the following: "The fact that warnings were provided in this case to advise respondent of his Fifth Amendment privilege makes it unnecessary to consider whether any warning is required, as the Government asks us to determine. In addition to the warning implicit in the oath, federal prosecutors apparently make it a practice to inform a witness of the privilege before questioning begins."

6. The right to counsel mandated by *Miranda* was fashioned to secure the suspect's Fifth Amendment privilege in a setting thought inherently coercive. The Sixth Amendment was not implicated.

grand jury cannot insist, as a matter of constitutional right, on being represented by his counsel * * *." *In re Groban,* 352 U.S. 330 (1957).[b] Under settled principles the witness may not insist upon the presence of his attorney in the grand jury room. Fed.Rule Crim.Proc. 6(d).

* * * Respondent was free at every stage to interpose his constitutional privilege against self-incrimination, but perjury was not a permissible option. * * * The judgment of the Court of Appeals is therefore reversed.

JUSTICE STEVENS took no part in the consideration or decision of this case.

JUSTICE BRENNAN, with whom JUSTICE MARSHALL joins, concurring in the judgment.

I concur in the result reached by the Court, for "even when the privilege against self-incrimination permits an individual to refuse to answer questions asked by the Government, if false answers are given the individual may be prosecuted for making false statements." *Mackey v. United States,* 401 U.S. 667 (1971) (Brennan, J., concurring). * * * "Our legal system provides methods for challenging the Government's right to ask questions—lying is not one of them." *Bryson v. United States.* Further, the record satisfies me that the respondent's false answers were not induced by governmental tactics or procedures so inherently unfair under all the circumstances as to constitute a prosecution for perjury a violation of the Due Process Clause of the Fifth Amendment.

However, two aspects of the plurality opinion for the Court suggests a denigration of the privilege against self-incrimination and the right to the assistance of counsel with which I do not agree.

The plurality opinion mechanically quotes *United States v. Monia,* for the proposition that

> "[t]he [Fifth] Amendment speaks of compulsion. It does not preclude a witness from testifying voluntarily in matters which may incriminate him. If, therefore, he desires the protection of the privilege, he must claim it or he will not be considered to have been 'compelled' within the meaning of the Amendment." * * *

In my view, the conception of the Fifth Amendment privilege expressed in the *Monia* dictum is explainable only by reference to the facts and circumstances of the only case cited in support by *Monia*—[a case, Justice Brennan explained, in which the potential for incrimination could not be evaluated without a claim by the witness because that potential was not readily apparent from the context of the question]. * * * It is only in a context where this "lack of notice on the part of the government" rationale has significance that we can possibly justify the *Monia* dictum that a witness testifying under judicial compulsion—that

---

**b.** In *Groban,* a witness was not allowed to have counsel present during his examination by a state fire marshall in a proceeding designed to determine the cause of a fire. In finding that the denial of counsel did not violate due process, the majority cited as analogous the grand jury proceeding, where "a witness [also] * * * cannot insist as a matter of constitutional right, on being represented by his counsel." The dissent, by Justice Black, argued that the fire marshall's investigation was not analogous, but agreed as to the lack of a constitutional right to counsel before the grand jury. The dissent noted: "They [the grand jurors] bring into the grand jury room the experience, knowledge and viewpoint of all sections of the community. They have no axes to grind and are not charged personally with the administration of the law. No one of them is a prosecuting attorney or law-enforcement officer ferreting out crime. It would be very difficult for officers of the state seriously to abuse or deceive a witness in the presence of the grand jury. Similarly the presence of the jurors offers a substantial safeguard against the officers' misrepresentation, unintentional or otherwise, of the witness' statements and conduct before the grand jury."

classic form of compulsion to which the Fifth Amendment is centrally addressed—must claim the privilege or else, without any further analysis, "he will not be considered to have been 'compelled' within the meaning of the Amendment." * * *

* * * Indeed, in the situation where a prior claim is excused and a knowing and completely voluntary waiver of the privilege is required—the situation of the *Miranda*-type custodial interrogation—the reason is that "the inquiring government is *acutely aware* of the potentially incriminating nature of the disclosures sought." *Garner v. United States*, 424 U.S. 648 (1978). * * * I submit that this more discriminating analysis is also required in the situation in which a putative or *de facto* defendant is called to testify under judicial compulsion before a grand jury; otherwise we countenance a serious erosion of fundamental guarantees of the Constitution.

* * * [T]he use by prosecutors of the tactic of calling a putative defendant before a grand jury and interrogating him regarding the transactions and events for which he is about to be indicted is, in the absence of an "intentional relinquishment or abandonment" of his "known" privilege against compulsory self-incrimination, a blatant subversion of the fundamental adversary principle—that the State "establish its case, not by interrogation of the accused even under judicial safeguards, but by evidence independently secured through skillful investigation." * * * Such tactics by prosecutors are exemplars of the very evils sought to be prevented by the enshrinement of the Fifth Amendment privilege in the Constitution. * * *

Thus, I would hold that, in the absence of an intentional and intelligent waiver by the individual of his known right to be free from compulsory self-incrimination, the Government may not call before a grand jury one whom it has probable cause—as measured by an objective standard—to suspect committed a crime, and by use of judicial compulsion compel him to testify with regard to that crime. In the absence of such a waiver, the Fifth Amendment requires that any testimony obtained in this fashion be unavailable to the Government for use at trial. Such a waiver could readily be demonstrated by proof that the individual was warned prior to questioning that he is currently subject to possible criminal prosecution for the commission of a stated crime,[c] that he has a constitutional right to refuse to answer any and all questions that may tend to incriminate him, and by record evidence that the individual understood the nature of his situation and privilege prior to giving testimony. * * *

A second and also disturbing facet of the plurality opinion today is its statement that "[n]o criminal proceedings had been instituted against respondent, hence, the Sixth Amendment right to counsel had not come into play." It will not do simply to cite, as does the plurality opinion, *Kirby v. Illinois*, for this proposition. *Kirby's* premise, so fundamental that it was "note[d] at the outset," was that "the constitutional privilege against compulsory self-incrimination is in no way implicated here." In sharp contrast, the privilege against compulsory self-incrimination is inextricably involved in this case since a putative defendant is called and interrogated before a grand jury. Clearly in such a case a

---

**c.** In *United States v. Washington*, 431 U.S. 181 (1977), the Court held that a witness need not be warned that he is a target of a grand jury investigation. The Court majority, per Burger, C.J., noted that "even in the presumed psychologically coercive atmosphere of police custodial interrogation, *Miranda* does not require that any additional warnings be given simply because the suspect is a potential defendant." Justice Brennan, joined by Justice Marshall, dissented, relying on Justice Brennan's opinion in *Mandujano*. See also note a to *New York v. Quarles*, Ch. 6, § 4.

defendant is "faced with the prosecutorial forces of organized society, and immersed in the intricacies of substantive and procedural criminal law."

It is true that dictum in *In re Groban* [fn. b supra] denied there is any constitutional right of a witness to be represented by counsel when testifying before a grand jury. But neither *Groban* nor any other case in this Court has squarely presented the question. Moreover, more recent decisions, e.g., *Miranda v. Arizona*, and *Escobedo v. Illinois*, recognizing the "substantive affinity" and therefore the "coextensive[ness]" in certain circumstances of the right to counsel and the privilege against compulsory self-incrimination, have led many to question the continuing vitality of such older dicta.

\* \* \* Given the inherent danger of subversion of the adversary system in the case of a putative defendant called to testify before a grand jury, and the peculiarly critical role of the Fifth Amendment privilege as the bulwark against such abuse, it is plainly obvious that some guidance by counsel is required. \* \* \* It may be that a putative defendant's Fifth Amendment privilege will be adequately preserved by a procedure whereby, in addition to warnings, he is told that he has a right to consult with an attorney prior to questioning, that if he cannot afford an attorney one will be appointed for him, that during the questioning he may have that attorney wait outside the grand jury room, and that he may at any and all times during questioning consult with the attorney prior to answering any question posed.[22] At least if such minimal protections were present, a putative defendant would be able to consult with counsel prior to answering any question that he might in any way suspect may incriminate him. \* \* \*

It is of course unnecessary in this case to define the exact dimensions of the right to counsel since the testimony obtained by the grand jury interrogation was not introduced as evidence at respondent's trial on the charge concerning which he was questioned. I write only to make plain my disagreement with the implication in the plurality opinion that constitutional rights to counsel are not involved in a grand jury proceeding, and my disagreement with the further implication that there is a right to have counsel present for consultation outside the grand jury room but that it is not constitutionally derived and therefore may be enjoyed only by those wealthy enough to hire a lawyer. I cannot accede to a return to the regime of "squalid discrimination," where the justice "a man gets depends on the amount of money he has." *Griffin v. Illinois* [Ch. 5, § 2]. \* \* \* If indeed there is, as the plurality opinion says, a right to have counsel present outside the door to the grand jury room, it is most assuredly in my view everyone's right, regardless of economic circumstance. \* \* \*

JUSTICE STEWART, with whom JUSTICE BLACKMUN joins, concurring in the judgment.

The Fifth Amendment privilege against compulsory self-incrimination provides no protection for the commission of perjury. \* \* \* *Bryson v. United States*. The respondent's grand jury testimony is relevant only to his prosecution for perjury and was not introduced in the prosecution for attempting to distribute heroin. Since this is not a case where it could plausibly be argued that the perjury prosecution must be barred because of prosecutorial conduct amounting to a denial of due process, I would reverse the judgment without

---

**22.** [Justice Brennan here noted that several commentators had argued that more was needed, "that the presence of counsel inside the grand jury room is required." He then added: "Certainly there is no viable argument that allowing counsel to be present in the grand jury room for purposes of consultation regarding testimonial privileges would subvert the nature or functioning of the grand jury proceeding. Such a procedure is sanctioned by statute in several states."]

reaching the other issues explored in The Chief Justice's opinion and by Mr. Justice Brennan in his separate opinion.

## KASTIGAR v. UNITED STATES

406 U.S. 441, 92 S.Ct. 1653, 32 L.Ed.2d 212 (1972).

JUSTICE POWELL delivered the opinion of the Court.

This case presents the question whether the United States Government may compel testimony from an unwilling witness, who invokes the Fifth Amendment privilege against compulsory self-incrimination, by conferring on the witness immunity from use of the compelled testimony in subsequent criminal proceedings, as well as immunity from use of evidence derived from the testimony.

Petitioners were subpoenaed to appear before a United States grand jury * * *. The Government believed that petitioners were likely to assert their Fifth Amendment privilege. Prior to the scheduled appearances, the Government applied to the District Court for an order directing petitioners to answer questions and produce evidence before the grand jury under a grant of immunity conferred pursuant to 18 U.S.C. §§ 6002–6003. Petitioners opposed issuance of the order, contending primarily that the scope of the immunity provided by the statute was not coextensive with the scope of the privilege against self-incrimination, and therefore was not sufficient to supplant the privilege and compel their testimony. The District Court rejected this contention, and ordered petitioners to appear before the grand jury and answer its questions under the grant of immunity. * * *

The power of government to compel persons to testify in court or before grand juries and other governmental agencies is firmly established in Anglo–American jurisprudence. * * * While it is not clear when grand juries first resorted to compulsory process to secure the attendance and testimony of witnesses, the general common-law principle that "the public has a right to every man's evidence" was considered an "indubitable certainty" that "cannot be denied" by 1742. * * * Mr. Justice White noted the importance of this essential power of government in his concurring opinion in *Murphy v. Waterfront Comm'n*, 378 U.S. 52 (1964):

> "Among the necessary and most important of the powers of the States as well as the Federal Government to assure the effective functioning of government in an ordered society is the broad power to compel residents to testify in court or before grand juries or agencies. * * * Such testimony constitutes one of the Government's primary sources of information."

But the power to compel testimony is not absolute. There are a number of exemptions from the testimonial duty, the most important of which is the Fifth Amendment privilege against compulsory self-incrimination. The privilege reflects a complex of our fundamental values and aspirations, *Murphy*, supra, and marks an important advance in the development of our liberty. * * * This Court has been zealous to safeguard the values that underlie the privilege.

Immunity statutes, which have historical roots deep in Anglo–American jurisprudence, are not incompatible with these values. Rather, they seek a rational accommodation between the imperatives of the privilege and the legitimate demands of government to compel citizens to testify. The existence of these statutes reflects the importance of testimony, and the fact that many offenses are of such a character that the only persons capable of giving useful testimony are those implicated in the crime. Indeed, their origins were in the context of such offenses, and their primary use has been to investigate such offenses. Congress included immunity statutes in many of the regulatory measures adopted in the first half of this century. Indeed, prior to the enactment of the statute under consideration in this case, there were in force over 50 federal immunity statutes. In addition, every State in the Union, as well as the District of Columbia and Puerto Rico, has one or more such statutes. The commentators, and this Court on several occasions, have characterized immunity statutes as essential to the effective enforcement of various criminal statutes. As Mr. Justice Frankfurter observed, speaking for the Court in *Ullmann v. United States*, 350 U.S. 422 (1956), such statutes have "become part of our constitutional fabric."

Petitioners contend, first, that the Fifth Amendment's privilege against compulsory self-incrimination, which is that "[n]o person * * * shall be compelled in any criminal case to be a witness against himself," deprives Congress of power to enact laws that compel self-incrimination, even if complete immunity from prosecution is granted prior to the compulsion of the incriminatory testimony. In other words, petitioners assert that no immunity statute, however drawn, can afford a lawful basis for compelling incriminatory testimony. They ask us to reconsider and overrule *Brown v. Walker*, 161 U.S. 591 (1896), and *Ullmann v. United States*, decisions that uphold the constitutionality of immunity statutes. We find no merit to this contention and reaffirm the decisions in *Brown* and *Ullmann*.[a]

Petitioners' second contention is that the scope of immunity provided by the federal witness immunity statute, 18 U.S.C. § 6002, is not coextensive with the scope of the Fifth Amendment privilege against compulsory self-incrimination, and therefore is not sufficient to supplant the privilege and compel testimony over a claim of the privilege. The statute provides that when a witness is compelled by district court order to testify over a claim of the privilege:

> "the witness may not refuse to comply with the order on the basis of his privilege against self-incrimination; but no testimony or other information compelled under the order (or any information directly or indirectly derived from such testimony or other information) may be used against the witness in any criminal case, except a prosecution for perjury, giving a false statement, or otherwise failing to comply with the order." 18 U.S.C. § 6002.

The constitutional inquiry, rooted in logic and history, as well as in the decisions of this Court, is whether the immunity granted under this statute is coextensive with the scope of the privilege. If so, petitioners' refusals to answer based on the privilege were unjustified, and the judgments of contempt were proper, for the grant of immunity has removed the dangers against which the privilege protects. *Brown v. Walker.* If, on the other hand, the immunity granted is not as comprehensive as the protection afforded by the privilege,

---

**a.** In *Brown*, the Court reasoned that the Fifth Amendment could not be "construed literally as authorizing the witness to refuse to disclose any fact which might tend to incriminate, disgrace, or expose him to unfavorable comments." The history of the privilege clearly indicated that its objective was solely to "secure the witness against criminal prosecution." Thus the privilege had been held inapplicable where the witness' compelled testimony would relate only to an offense for which he had received a pardon or would tend to "disgrace him or bring him into disrepute" but would furnish no information relating to a criminal offense. In *Ullmann*, a witness who had received complete immunity from prosecution argued that the rationale of *Brown* should not apply where the compelled testimony (relating to alleged spying activities by certain members of the Communist Party) could subject him to a wide range of disabilities, such as "loss of job, expulsion from labor union, state registration and investigation statutes, passport eligibility, and general public opprobrium." Rejecting that contention, the Court majority concluded that *Brown* had correctly defined the total purpose of the privilege, and that purpose was fully met by granting the witness immunity from prosecution.

petitioners were justified in refusing to answer, and the judgments of contempt must be vacated. *McCarthy v. Arndstein*, 266 U.S. 34 (1924).

Petitioners draw a distinction between statutes that provide transactional immunity and those that provide, as does the statute before us, immunity from use and derivative use. They contend that a statute must at a minimum grant full transactional immunity in order to be coextensive with the scope of the privilege. In support of this contention, they rely on *Counselman v. Hitchcock*, 142 U.S. 547 (1892), the first case in which this Court considered a constitutional challenge to an immunity statute. The statute, [there] * * * provided that no "evidence obtained from a party or witness by means of a judicial proceeding . . . shall be given in evidence, or in any manner used against him . . . in any court of the United States . . .." * * * [T]his Court construed the statute as affording a witness protection only against the use of the specific testimony compelled from him under the grant of immunity. This construction meant that the statute "could not, and would not, prevent the use of his testimony to search out other testimony to be used in evidence against him." Since the [statute] * * * would permit the use against the immunized witness of evidence derived from his compelled testimony, it did not protect the witness to the same extent that a claim of the privilege would protect him. Accordingly, under the principle that a grant of immunity cannot supplant the privilege, and is not sufficient to compel testimony over a claim of the privilege, unless the scope of the grant of immunity is coextensive with the scope of the privilege, the witness' refusal to testify was held proper. In the course of its opinion, the Court made the following statement, on which petitioners heavily rely:

> "We are clearly of opinion that no statute which leaves the party or witness subject to prosecution after he answers the criminating question put to him, can have the effect of supplanting the privilege conferred by the Constitution of the United States. [The immunity statute under consideration] does not supply a complete protection from all the perils against which the constitutional prohibition was designed to guard, and is not a full substitute for that prohibition. In view of the constitutional provision, a statutory enactment, to be valid, must afford absolute immunity against future prosecution for the offence to which the question relates."

Sixteen days after the *Counselman* decision, a new immunity bill * * * was drafted specifically to meet the broad language in *Counselman* set forth above. The new Act removed the privilege against self-incrimination in [specified] hearings * * * and provided that:

> "no person shall be prosecuted or subjected to any penalty or forfeiture for or on account of any transaction, matter or thing, concerning which he may testify, or produce evidence, documentary or otherwise * * *." Act of Feb. 11, 1893.

This transactional immunity statute became the basic form for the numerous federal immunity statutes until 1970, when, after re-examining applicable constitutional principles and the adequacy of existing law, Congress enacted the statute here under consideration. The new statute, which does not "afford [the] absolute immunity against future prosecution" referred to in *Counselman*, was drafted to meet what Congress judged to be the conceptual basis of *Counselman*, as elaborated in subsequent decisions of the Court, namely, that immunity from the use of compelled testimony and evidence derived therefrom is coextensive with the scope of the privilege.

The statute's explicit proscription of the use in any criminal case of "testimony or other information compelled under the order (or any information directly or indirectly derived from such testimony or other information)" is consonant with Fifth Amendment standards. We hold that such immunity from use and derivative use is coextensive with the scope of the privilege against self-incrimination, and therefore is sufficient to compel testimony over a claim of the privilege. While a grant of immunity must afford protection commensurate with that afforded by the privilege, it need not be broader. Transactional immunity, which accords full immunity from prosecution for the offense to which the compelled testimony relates, affords the witness considerably broader protection than does the Fifth Amendment privilege. The privilege has never been construed to mean that one who invokes it cannot subsequently be prosecuted. Its sole concern is to afford protection against being "forced to give testimony leading to the infliction of 'penalties affixed to * * * criminal acts.'" Immunity from the use of compelled testimony, as well as evidence derived directly and indirectly therefrom, affords this protection. It prohibits the prosecutorial authorities from using the compelled testimony in *any* respect, and it therefore insures that the testimony cannot lead to the infliction of criminal penalties on the witness.

Our holding is consistent with the conceptual basis of *Counselman*. The *Counselman* statute, as construed by the Court, was plainly deficient in its failure to prohibit the use against the immunized witness of evidence derived from his compelled testimony. The Court repeatedly emphasized this deficiency * * *. The broad language in *Counselman* relied upon by petitioners was unnecessary to the Court's decision, and cannot be considered binding authority.

In *Murphy v. Waterfront Comm'n*, 378 U.S. 52 (1964), the Court carefully considered immunity from use of compelled testimony and evidence derived therefrom. The *Murphy* petitioners were subpoenaed to testify at a hearing conducted by the Waterfront Commission of New York Harbor. After refusing to answer certain questions on the ground that the answers might tend to incriminate them, petitioners were granted immunity from prosecution under the laws of New Jersey and New York. They continued to refuse to testify, however, on the ground that their answers might tend to incriminate them under federal law, to which the immunity did not purport to extend. * * *

The issue before the Court in *Murphy* was whether New Jersey and New York could compel the witnesses, whom these States had immunized from prosecution under their laws, to give testimony that might then be used to convict them of a federal crime. Since New Jersey and New York had not purported to confer immunity from federal prosecution, the Court was faced with the question what limitations the Fifth Amendment privilege imposed on the prosecutorial powers of the Federal Government, a nonimmunizing sovereign. After undertaking an examination of the policies and purposes of the privilege, the Court overturned the rule that one jurisdiction within our federal structure may compel a witness to give testimony which could be used to convict him of a crime in another jurisdiction. The Court held that the privilege protects state witnesses against incrimination under federal as well as state law, and federal witnesses against incrimination under state as well as federal law. Applying this principle to the state immunity legislation before it, the Court held the constitutional rule to be that:

> "[A] state witness may not be compelled to give testimony which may be incriminating under federal law unless the compelled testimony and its fruits cannot be used in any manner by federal officials in connection with a criminal prosecution against him. We conclude, moreover, that in order to implement this constitutional rule and accommodate the interests of the

State and Federal Governments in investigating and prosecuting crime, the Federal Government must be prohibited from making any such use of compelled testimony and its fruits."

The Court emphasized that this rule left the state witness and the Federal Government, against which the witness had immunity only from the *use* of the compelled testimony and evidence derived therefrom, "in substantially the same position as if the witness had claimed his privilege in the absence of a state grant of immunity."

It is true that in *Murphy* the Court was not presented with the precise question presented by this case, whether a jurisdiction seeking to compel testimony may do so by granting only use and derivative-use immunity, for New Jersey and New York had granted petitioners transactional immunity. * * * But both the reasoning of the Court in *Murphy* and the result reached compel the conclusion that use and derivative-use immunity is constitutionally sufficient to compel testimony over a claim of the privilege. Since the privilege is fully applicable and its scope is the same whether invoked in a state or in a federal jurisdiction, the *Murphy* conclusion that a prohibition on use and derivative use secures a witness' Fifth Amendment privilege against infringement by the Federal Government demonstrates that immunity from use and derivative use is coextensive with the scope of the privilege. As the *Murphy* Court noted, immunity from use and derivative use "leaves the witness and the Federal Government in substantially the same position as if the witness had claimed his privilege" in the absence of a grant of immunity. * * *

Although an analysis of prior decisions and the purpose of the Fifth Amendment privilege indicates that use and derivative-use immunity is coextensive with the privilege, we must consider additional arguments advanced by petitioners against the sufficiency of such immunity. * * * Petitioners argue that use and derivative-use immunity will not adequately protect a witness from various possible incriminating uses of the compelled testimony: for example, the prosecutor or other law enforcement officials may obtain leads, names of witnesses, or other information not otherwise available that might result in a prosecution. It will be difficult and perhaps impossible, the argument goes, to identify, by testimony or cross-examination, the subtle ways in which the compelled testimony may disadvantage a witness, especially in the jurisdiction granting the immunity.

This argument presupposes that the statute's prohibition will prove impossible to enforce. The statute provides a sweeping proscription of any use, direct or indirect, of the compelled testimony and any information derived therefrom:

> "[N]o testimony or other information compelled under the order (or any information directly or indirectly derived from such testimony or other information) may be used against the witness in any criminal case * * *."
> 18 U.S.C. § 6002.

This total prohibition on use provides a comprehensive safeguard, barring the use of compelled testimony as an "investigatory lead," and also barring the use of any evidence obtained by focusing investigation on a witness as a result of his compelled disclosures.

A person accorded this immunity under 18 U.S.C. § 6002, and subsequently prosecuted, is not dependent for the preservation of his rights upon the integrity and good faith of the prosecuting authorities. As stated in *Murphy*:

> "Once a defendant demonstrates that he has testified, under a state grant of immunity, to matters related to the federal prosecution, the federal authori-

ties have the burden of showing that their evidence is not tainted by establishing that they had an independent, legitimate source for the disputed evidence."

This burden of proof, which we reaffirm as appropriate, is not limited to a negation of taint; rather, it imposes on the prosecution the affirmative duty to prove that the evidence it proposes to use is derived from a legitimate source wholly independent of the compelled testimony.

This is very substantial protection, commensurate with that resulting from invoking the privilege itself. The privilege assures that a citizen is not compelled to incriminate himself by his own testimony. It usually operates to allow a citizen to remain silent when asked a question requiring an incriminatory answer. This statute, which operates after a witness has given incriminatory testimony, affords the same protection by assuring that the compelled testimony can in no way lead to the infliction of criminal penalties. The statute, like the Fifth Amendment, grants neither pardon nor amnesty. Both the statute and the Fifth Amendment allow the government to prosecute using evidence from legitimate independent sources.

The statutory proscription is analogous to the Fifth Amendment requirement in cases of coerced confessions. A coerced confession, as revealing of leads as testimony given in exchange for immunity, is inadmissible in a criminal trial, but it does not bar prosecution. Moreover, a defendant against whom incriminating evidence has been obtained through a grant of immunity may be in a stronger position at trial than a defendant who asserts a Fifth Amendment coerced-confession claim. One raising a claim under this statute need only show that he testified under a grant of immunity in order to shift to the government the heavy burden of proving that all of the evidence it proposes to use was derived from legitimate independent sources. On the other hand, a defendant raising a coerced-confession claim under the Fifth Amendment must first prevail in a voluntariness hearing before his confession and evidence derived from it become inadmissible.

There can be no justification in reason or policy for holding that the Constitution requires an amnesty grant where, acting pursuant to statute and accompanying safeguards, testimony is compelled in exchange for immunity from use and derivative use when no such amnesty is required where the government, acting without colorable right, coerces a defendant into incriminating himself.

JUSTICE BRENNAN and JUSTICE REHNQUIST took no part in the consideration or decision of this case.

JUSTICE DOUGLAS, dissenting.

\* \* \* In *Counselman v. Hitchcock*, the Court adopted the transactional immunity test. \* \* \* This Court, however, apparently believes that *Counselman* and its progeny were overruled *sub silentio* in *Murphy v. Waterfront Com'n. Murphy* involved state witnesses, granted transactional immunity under state law, who refused to testify for fear of subsequent federal prosecution. We held that the testimony in question could be compelled, but that the Federal Government would be barred from using any of the testimony, or its fruits, in a subsequent federal prosecution. \* \* \*

\* \* \* *Counselman*, as the *Murphy* Court recognized, "said nothing about the problem of incrimination under the law of another sovereign." That problem is one of federalism, as to require transactional immunity between jurisdictions might "deprive a state of the right to prosecute a violation of its criminal law on the basis of another state's grant of immunity [a result which] would be gravely in derogation of its sovereignty and obstructive of its administration of justice." *United States ex rel. Catena v. Elias*, 449 F.2d 40, 44 (CA3 1971).

* * * If, as some have thought, the Bill of Rights contained only "counsels of moderation" from which courts and legislatures could deviate according to their conscience or discretion, then today's contraction of the Self–Incrimination Clause of the Fifth Amendment would be understandable. But that has not been true, starting with Chief Justice Marshall's opinion in *United States v. Burr*, 25 F.Cas. 30 (C.C.Va. 1807) where he ruled that the reach of the Fifth Amendment was so broad as to make the privilege applicable when there was a mere possibility of a criminal charge being made. * * *

The Court said in *Hale v. Henkel*, 201 U.S. 43 (1906), that "if the criminality has already been taken away, the Amendment ceases to apply." In other words, the immunity granted is adequate if it operates as a complete pardon for the offense. *Brown v. Walker*. That is the true measure of the Self–Incrimination Clause. * * *

JUSTICE MARSHALL, dissenting.

* * * The Court recognizes that an immunity statute must be tested by * * * whether it "leaves the witness and the prosecutorial authorities in substantially the same position as if the witness had claimed the Fifth Amendment privilege." I assume, moreover, that in theory that test would be met by a complete ban on the use of the compelled testimony, including all derivative use, however remote and indirect. But I cannot agree that a ban on use will in practice be total, if it remains open for the government to convict the witness on the basis of evidence derived from a legitimate independent source. The Court asserts that the witness is adequately protected by a rule imposing on the government a heavy burden of proof if it would establish the independent character of evidence to be used against the witness. But in light of the inevitable uncertainties of the factfinding process, a greater margin of protection is required in order to provide a reliable guarantee that the witness is in exactly the same position as if he had not testified. That margin can be provided only by immunity from prosecution for the offenses to which the testimony relates, i.e., transactional immunity.

I do not see how it can suffice merely to put the burden of proof on the government. First, contrary to the Court's assertion, the Court's rule does leave the witness "dependent for the preservation of his rights upon the integrity and good faith of the prosecuting authorities." For the information relevant to the question of taint is uniquely within the knowledge of the prosecuting authorities. They alone are in a position to trace the chains of information and investigation that lead to the evidence to be used in a criminal prosecution. A witness who suspects that his compelled testimony was used to develop a lead will be hard pressed indeed to ferret out the evidence necessary to prove it. And of course it is no answer to say he need not prove it, for though the Court puts the burden of proof on the government, the government will have no difficulty in meeting its burden by mere assertion if the witness produces no contrary evidence. The good faith of the prosecuting authorities is thus the sole safeguard of the witness' rights. Second, even their good faith is not a sufficient safeguard. For the paths of information through the investigative bureaucracy may well be long and winding, and even a prosecutor acting in the best of faith cannot be certain that somewhere in the depths of his investigative apparatus, often including hundreds of employees, there was not some prohibited use of the compelled testimony. * * * The Court today sets out a loose net to trap tainted evidence and prevent its use against the witness, but it accepts an intolerably great risk that tainted evidence will in fact slip through that net.

In my view the Court turns reason on its head when it compares a statutory grant of immunity to the "immunity" that is inadvertently conferred by an unconstitutional interrogation. The exclusionary rule of evidence that applies in that situation has nothing whatever to do with this case. Evidence obtained through a coercive interrogation, like evidence obtained through an illegal search, is excluded at trial because the Constitution prohibits such methods of gathering evidence. The exclusionary rules provide a partial and inadequate remedy to some victims of illegal police conduct, and a similarly partial and inadequate deterrent to police officers. An immunity statute, on the other hand, is much more ambitious than any exclusionary rule. It does not merely attempt to provide a remedy for past police misconduct, which never should have occurred. An immunity statute operates in advance of the event, and it authorizes—even encourages—interrogation that would otherwise be prohibited by the Fifth Amendment. An immunity statute thus differs from an exclusionary rule of evidence in at least two critical respects.

First, because an immunity statute gives constitutional approval to the resulting interrogation, the government is under an obligation here to remove the danger of incrimination completely and absolutely, whereas in the case of the exclusionary rules it may be sufficient to shield the witness from the fruits of the illegal search or interrogation in a partial and reasonably adequate manner. * * * The Constitution does not authorize police officers to coerce confessions or to invade privacy without cause, so long as no use is made of the evidence they obtain. But this Court has held that the Constitution does authorize the government to compel a witness to give potentially incriminating testimony, so long as no incriminating use is made of the resulting evidence. Before the government puts its seal of approval on such an interrogation, it must provide an absolutely reliable guarantee that it will not use the testimony in any way at all in aid of prosecution of the witness. The only way to provide that guarantee is to give the witness immunity from prosecution for crimes to which his testimony relates.

Second, because an immunity statute operates in advance of the interrogation, there is room to require a broad grant of transactional immunity without imperiling large numbers of otherwise valid convictions. An exclusionary rule comes into play after the interrogation or search has occurred; and the decision to question or to search is often made in haste, under pressure, by an officer who is not a lawyer. If an unconstitutional interrogation or search were held to create transactional immunity, that might well be regarded as an excessively high price to pay for the "constable's blunder." An immunity statute, on the other hand, creates a framework in which the prosecuting attorney can make a calm and reasoned decision whether to compel testimony and suffer the resulting ban on prosecution, or to forgo the testimony.

For both these reasons it is clear to me that an immunity statute must be tested by a standard far more demanding than that appropriate for an exclusionary rule fashioned to deal with past constitutional violations. Measured by that standard, the statute approved today by the Court fails miserably. I respectfully dissent.

## FISHER v. UNITED STATES

### 425 U.S. 391, 96 S.Ct. 1569, 48 L.Ed.2d 39 (1976).

JUSTICE WHITE delivered the opinion of the Court.

In these two cases we are called upon to decide whether a summons directing an attorney to produce documents delivered to him by his client in connection with the attorney-client relationship is enforceable over claims that the documents were constitutionally immune from summons in the hands of the client and retained that immunity in the hands of the attorney. In each case, an Internal Revenue agent visited the taxpayer or taxpayers and interviewed them in connection with an investigation of possible civil or criminal liability under the federal income tax laws. Shortly after the interviews * * *, the taxpayers obtained from their respective accountants certain documents relating to the preparation by the accountant of their tax returns. Shortly after obtaining the documents * * *, the taxpayers transferred the documents to their lawyers— each of whom was retained to assist the taxpayer in connection with the investigation. Upon learning of the whereabouts of the documents, the Internal Revenue Service served summonses on the attorneys directing them to produce documents listed therein. [Those documents were accountants' work sheets, retained copies of income tax returns, and the accountants' copies of correspondence between the accounting firm and the taxpayer]. * * * In each case, the lawyer declined to comply with the summons directing production of the documents, and enforcement actions were commenced by the Government. * * *

All of the parties in these cases and the Court of Appeals have concurred in the proposition that if the Fifth Amendment would have excused a *taxpayer* from turning over the accountant's papers had he possessed them, the *attorney* to whom they are delivered for the purpose of obtaining legal advice should also be immune from subpoena. Although we agree with this proposition for the reasons set forth infra, we are convinced that, under our decision in *Couch v. United States,* 409 U.S. 322 (1973), it is not the taxpayer's Fifth Amendment privilege that would excuse the *attorney* from production.

The relevant part of that Amendment provides:

"No person * * * shall be *compelled* in any criminal case to be a *witness against himself."* (Emphasis added.)

The taxpayer's privilege under this Amendment is not violated by enforcement of the summonses involved in these cases because enforcement against a taxpayer's lawyer would not "compel" the taxpayer to do anything—and certainly would not compel him to be a "witness" against himself. The Court has held repeatedly that the Fifth Amendment is limited to prohibiting the use of "physical or moral compulsion" exerted on the person asserting the privilege. In *Couch v. United States,* we recently ruled that the Fifth Amendment rights of a taxpayer were not violated by the enforcement of a documentary summons directed to her accountant and requiring production of the taxpayer's own records in the possession of the accountant. We did so on the ground that in such a case "the ingredient of personal compulsion against an accused is lacking." Here, the taxpayers are compelled to do no more than was the taxpayer in *Couch.* The taxpayers' Fifth Amendment privilege is therefore not violated by enforcement of the summonses directed toward their attorneys. This is true whether or not the Amendment would have barred a subpoena directing the taxpayer to produce the documents while they were in his hands.

The fact that the attorneys are agents of the taxpayers does not change this result. *Couch* held as much, since the accountant there was also the taxpayer's agent, and in this respect reflected a longstanding view. * * * "It is extortion of information from the accused which offends our sense of justice." *Couch v. United States.* Agent or no, the lawyer is not the taxpayer. The taxpayer is the "accused," and nothing is being extorted from him. Nor is this one of those situations, which *Couch* suggested might exist, where constructive possession is so clear or relinquishment of possession so temporary and insignificant as to leave the personal compulsion upon the taxpayer substantially intact. * * *

The Court of Appeals suggested that because legally and ethically the attorney was required to respect the confidences of his client, the latter had a reasonable expectation of privacy for the records in the hands of the attorney and therefore did not forfeit his Fifth Amendment privilege with respect to the records by transferring them in order to obtain legal advice. It is true that the Court has often stated that one of the several purposes served by the constitutional privilege against compelled testimonial self-incrimination is that of protecting personal privacy. See, e.g., *Murphy v. Waterfront Comm'n.* But the Court has never suggested that every invasion of privacy violates the privilege. Within the limits imposed by the language of the Fifth Amendment, which we necessarily observe, the privilege truly serves privacy interests; but the Court has never on any ground, personal privacy included, applied the Fifth Amendment to prevent the otherwise proper acquisition or use of evidence which, in the Court's view, did not involve compelled testimonial self-incrimination of some sort.

The proposition that the Fifth Amendment protects private information obtained without compelling self-incriminating testimony is contrary to the clear statements of this Court that under appropriate safeguards private incriminating statements of an accused may be overheard and used in evidence, if they are not compelled at the time they were uttered, *Katz v. United States* [Ch. 3, § 2], and that disclosure of private information may be compelled if immunity removes the risk of incrimination. *Kastigar v. United States.* If the Fifth Amendment protected generally against the obtaining of private information from a man's mouth or pen or house, its protections would presumably not be lifted by probable cause and a warrant or by immunity. * * * We cannot cut the Fifth Amendment completely loose from the moorings of its language, and make it serve as a general protector of privacy—a word not mentioned in its text and a concept directly addressed in the Fourth Amendment. We adhere to the view that the Fifth Amendment protects against "compelled self-incrimination, not [the disclosure of] private information." *United States v. Nobles,* 422 U.S. 225 (1975). * * *

* * * [While the] taxpayers have erroneously relied on the Fifth Amendment without urging the attorney-client privilege in so many words, they have nevertheless invoked the relevant body of law and policies that govern the attorney-client privilege. * * * This Court and the lower courts have * * * uniformly held that pre-existing documents which could have been obtained by court process from the client when he was in possession may also be obtained from the attorney by similar process following transfer by the client in order to obtain more informed legal advice. * * * It is otherwise if the documents are not obtainable by subpoena duces tecum or summons while in the exclusive possession of the client, for the client will then be reluctant to transfer possession to the lawyer unless the documents are also privileged in the latter's hands. Where the transfer is made for the purpose of obtaining legal advice, the

purposes of the attorney-client privilege would be defeated unless the privilege is applicable.  *  *  *

Since each taxpayer [here] transferred possession of the documents in question from himself to his attorney in order to obtain legal assistance in the tax investigations in question, the papers, if unobtainable by summons from the client, are unobtainable by summons directed to the attorney by reason of the attorney-client privilege.  We accordingly proceed to the question whether the documents could have been obtained by summons addressed to the taxpayer while the documents were in his possession.  The only bar to enforcement of such summons asserted by the parties or the courts below is the Fifth Amendment's privilege against self-incrimination.  *  *  *

The proposition that the Fifth Amendment prevents compelled production of documents over objection that such production might incriminate stems from *Boyd v. United States*  *  *  *.

Several of *Boyd's* express or implicit declarations have not stood the test of time.  The application of the Fourth Amendment to subpoenas was limited by *Hale v. Henkel,* and more recent cases.  Purely evidentiary (but "nontestimonial") materials, as well as contraband and fruits and instrumentalities of crime, may now be searched for and seized under proper circumstances, *Warden v. Hayden* [see fn. a following *Boyd*, § 1 supra].  Also, any notion that "testimonial" evidence may never be seized and used in evidence is inconsistent with [various cases] approving the seizure under appropriate circumstances of conversations of a person suspected of crime.  It is also clear that the Fifth Amendment does not independently proscribe the compelled production of every sort of incriminating evidence but applies only when the accused is compelled to make a *testimonial* communication that is incriminating.  *  *  * Furthermore, despite *Boyd,* neither a partnership nor the individual partners are shielded from compelled production of partnership records on self-incrimination grounds.  *Bellis v. United States,* 417 U.S. 85 (1974).  It would appear that under that case the precise claim sustained in *Boyd* would now be rejected for reasons not there considered.

The pronouncement in *Boyd* that a person may not be forced to produce his private papers has nonetheless often appeared as dictum in later opinions of this Court.  *  *  * To the extent, however, that the rule against compelling production of private papers rested on the proposition that seizures of or subpoenas for "mere evidence," including documents, violated the Fourth Amendment and therefore also transgressed the Fifth, the foundations for the rule have been washed away.  In consequence, the prohibition against forcing the production of private papers has long been a rule searching for a rationale consistent with the proscriptions of the Fifth Amendment against compelling a person to give "testimony" that incriminates him.  Accordingly, we turn to the question of what, if any, incriminating testimony within the Fifth Amendment's protection, is compelled by a documentary summons.

A subpoena served on a taxpayer requiring him to produce an accountant's workpapers in his possession without doubt involves substantial compulsion. But it does not compel oral testimony;  nor would it ordinarily compel the taxpayer to restate, repeat, or affirm the truth of the contents of the documents sought.  Therefore, the Fifth Amendment would not be violated by the fact alone that the papers on their face might incriminate the taxpayer, for the privilege protects a person only against being incriminated by his own compelled testimonial communications.  The accountant's workpapers are not the taxpayer's. They were not prepared by the taxpayer, and they contain no testimonial declarations by him. Furthermore, as far as this record demonstrates, the preparation of all of the papers sought in these cases was wholly voluntary, and they cannot be said to contain compelled testimonial evidence, either of the taxpayers or of anyone else. The taxpayer cannot avoid compliance with the subpoena merely by asserting that the item of evidence which he is required to produce contains incriminating writing, whether his own or that of someone else.

The act of producing evidence in response to a subpoena nevertheless has communicative aspects of its own, wholly aside from the contents of the papers produced. Compliance with the subpoena tacitly concedes the existence of the papers demanded and their possession or control by the taxpayer. It also would indicate the taxpayer's belief that the papers are those described in the subpoena. The elements of compulsion are clearly present, but the more difficult issues are whether the tacit averments of the taxpayer are both "testimonial" and "incriminating" for purposes of applying the Fifth Amendment. These questions perhaps do not lend themselves to categorical answers; their resolution may instead depend on the facts and circumstances of particular cases or classes thereof. In light of the records now before us, we are confident that however incriminating the contents of the accountant's workpapers might be, the act of producing them—the only thing which the taxpayer is compelled to do—would not itself involve testimonial self-incrimination.

It is doubtful that implicitly admitting the existence and possession of the papers rises to the level of testimony within the protection of the Fifth Amendment. The papers belong to the accountant, were prepared by him, and are the kind usually prepared by an accountant working on the tax returns of his client. Surely the Government is in no way relying on the "truthtelling" of the taxpayer to prove the existence of or his access to the documents. The existence and location of the papers are a foregone conclusion and the taxpayer adds little or nothing to the sum total of the Government's information by conceding that he in fact has the papers. Under these circumstances by enforcement of the summons "no constitutional rights are touched. The question is not one of testimony but of surrender."

When an accused is required to submit a handwriting exemplar he admits his ability to write and impliedly asserts that the exemplar is his writing. But in common experience, the first would be a near truism and the latter self-evident. In any event, although the exemplar may be incriminating to the accused and although he is compelled to furnish it, his Fifth Amendment privilege is not violated because nothing he has said or done is deemed to be sufficiently testimonial for purposes of the privilege. This Court has also time and again allowed subpoenas against the custodian of corporate documents or those belonging to other collective entities such as unions and partnerships and those of bankrupt businesses over claims that the documents will incriminate the custodian despite the fact that producing the documents tacitly admits their existence and their location in the hands of their possessor. The existence and possession or control of the subpoenaed documents being no more in issue here than in the above cases, the summons is equally enforceable.

Moreover, assuming that these aspects of producing the accountant's papers have some minimal testimonial significance, surely it is not illegal to seek accounting help in connection with one's tax returns or for the accountant to prepare workpapers and deliver them to the taxpayer. At this juncture, we are quite unprepared to hold that either the fact of existence of the papers or of their possession by the taxpayer poses any realistic threat of incrimination to the taxpayer.

As for the possibility that responding to the subpoena would authenticate the workpapers, production would express nothing more than the taxpayer's belief that the papers are those described in the subpoena. The taxpayer would be no more competent to authenticate the accountant's workpapers or reports by producing them than he would be to authenticate them if testifying orally. The taxpayer did not prepare the papers and could not vouch for their accuracy. The documents would not be admissible in evidence against the taxpayer without authenticating testimony. Without more, responding to the subpoena in the circumstances before us would not appear to represent a substantial threat of self-incrimination. * * *

Whether the Fifth Amendment would shield the taxpayer from producing his own tax records in his possession is a question not involved here; for the papers demanded here are not his "private papers," see *Boyd v. United States,* supra. We do hold that compliance with a summons directing the taxpayer to produce the accountant's documents involved in this case would involve no incriminating testimony within the protection of the Fifth Amendment.

JUSTICE STEVENS took no part in the consideration or disposition of these cases.

JUSTICE BRENNAN, concurring in the judgment.

Given the prior access by accountants retained by the taxpayers to the papers involved in these cases and the wholly business rather than personal nature of the papers, I agree that the privilege against compelled self-incrimination did not in either of these cases protect the papers from production in response to the summonses. I do not join the Court's opinion, however, because of the portent of much of what is said of a serious crippling of the protection secured by the privilege against compelled production of one's private books and papers. * * * [I]t is but another step in the denigration of privacy principles settled nearly 100 years ago in *Boyd v. United States.* * * *

Expressions are legion in opinions of this Court that the protection of personal privacy is a central purpose of the privilege against compelled self-incrimination. * * * The Court pays lip-service to this bedrock premise of privacy in the statement that "[w]ithin the limits imposed by the language of the Fifth Amendment, which we necessarily observe, the privilege truly serves privacy interests." But this only makes explicit what elsewhere highlights the opinion, namely, the view that protection of personal privacy is merely a byproduct and not, as our precedents and history teach, a factor controlling in part the determination of the scope of the privilege. This cart-before-the-horse approach is fundamentally at odds with the settled principle that the scope of the privilege is not constrained by the limits of the wording of the Fifth Amendment but has the reach necessary to protect the cherished value of privacy which it safeguards. * * * History and principle, not the mechanical application of its wording, have been the life of the amendment. * * *

History and principle teach that the privacy protected by the Fifth Amendment extends not just to the individual's immediate declarations, oral or written, but also to his testimonial materials in the form of books and papers. * * * An individual's books and papers are generally little more than an extension of his person. They reveal no less than he could reveal upon being questioned directly. Many of the matters within an individual's knowledge may as easily be retained within his head as set down on a scrap of paper. I perceive no principle which does not permit compelling one to disclose the contents of one's mind but does permit compelling the disclosure of the contents of that scrap of paper by compelling its production. Under a contrary view, the constitutional protection would turn on fortuity, and persons would, at their peril, record their thoughts and the events of their lives. The ability to think private thoughts, facilitated as it is by pen and paper, and the ability to preserve intimate memories would be curtailed through fear that those thoughts or the events of those memories would become the subjects of criminal sanctions however invalidly imposed. Indeed, it was the very reality of those fears that helped provide the historical impetus for the privilege. * * *

The Court's treatment of the privilege falls far short of giving it the scope required by history and our precedents. * * * [The Court's] analysis is patently incomplete: the threshold inquiry is whether the taxpayer is compelled to produce incriminating papers. That inquiry is not answered in favor of production merely because the subpoena requires neither oral testimony from nor affirmation of the papers' contents by the taxpayer. To be sure, the Court correctly observes that "[t]he taxpayer cannot avoid compliance with the subpoena *merely* by asserting that the item of evidence which he is required to produce contains incriminating writing, whether his own or that of someone else." For it is not enough that the production of a writing, or books and papers, is compelled. Unless those materials are such as to come within the zone of privacy recognized by the Amendment, the privilege against compulsory self-incrimination does not protect against their production.

We are not without guideposts for determining what books, papers, and writings come within the zone of privacy recognized by the Amendment. * * * *Couch v. United States* expressly held that the Fifth Amendment protected against the compelled production of testimonial evidence only if the individual resisting production had a reasonable expectation of privacy with respect to the evidence. * * * Under *Couch,* therefore, one criterion is whether or not the information sought to be produced has been disclosed to or was within the knowledge of a third party. That is to say, one relevant consideration is the degree to which the paper holder has sought to keep private the contents of the papers he desires not to produce. * * *

A precise cataloguing of private papers within the ambit of the privacy protected by the privilege is probably impossible. Some papers, however, do lend themselves to classification. Production of documentary materials created or authenticated by a State or the Federal Government, such as automobile registrations or property deeds, would seem ordinarily to fall outside the protection of the privilege. They hardly reflect an extension of the person. Economic and business records may present difficulty in particular cases. The records of business entities generally fall without the scope of the privilege. But, as noted, the Court has recognized that the privilege extends to the business records of the sole proprietor or practitioner. Such records are at least an extension of an aspect of a person's activities, though concededly not the more intimate aspects of one's life. Where the privilege would have protected one's mental notes of his business affairs in a less complicated day and age, it would seem that that protection should not fall away because the complexities of another time compel one to keep business records.

Nonbusiness economic records in the possession of an individual, such as canceled checks or tax records, would also seem to be protected. They may provide clear insights into a person's total lifestyle. They are, however, like business records and the papers involved in these cases, frequently, though not always, disclosed to other parties; and disclosure, in proper cases, may foreclose reliance upon the privilege. Personal letters constitute an integral aspect of a person's private enclave. And while letters, being necessarily interpersonal, are not wholly private, their peculiarly private nature and the generally narrow extent of their disclosure would seem to render them within the scope of the privilege. Papers in the nature of a personal diary are *a fortiori* protected under the privilege.

The Court's treatment in the instant cases of the question whether the evidence involved here is within the protection of the privilege is, with all respect, most inadequate. The gaping hole is in the omission of any reference to the taxpayer's privacy interests and to whether the subpoenas impermissibly invade those interests. * * * For the reasons I have stated at the outset, however, I do not believe that the evidence involved in these cases falls within the scope of privacy protected by the Fifth Amendment. * * *

JUSTICE MARSHALL, concurring in the judgment.

* * * I would have preferred it had the Court found some room in its theory for recognition of the import of the contents of the documents themselves. * * * Nonetheless, I am hopeful that the Court's new theory, properly understood and applied, will provide substantially the same protection as our prior focus on the contents of the documents. * * * Indeed, there would appear to be a precise inverse relationship between the private nature of the document and the permissibility of assuming its existence. Therefore, under the Court's theory, the admission through production that one's diary, letters, prior tax returns, personally maintained financial records, or canceled checks exist would ordinarily provide substantial testimony. The incriminating nature of such an admission is clear, for while it may not be criminal to keep a diary, or write letters or checks, the admission that one does and that those documents are still available may quickly—or simultaneously—lead to incriminating evidence. If there is a "real danger" of such a result, that is enough under our cases to make such testimony subject to the claim of privilege. Thus, in practice, the Court's approach should still focus upon the private nature of the papers subpoenaed and protect those about which *Boyd* and its progeny were most concerned. * * * For the reasons stated by Mr. Justice Brennan, I concur in the judgment of the Court.[d]

**d.** In *United States v. Doe*, 465 U.S. 605 (1984), the lower court had concluded that, notwithstanding *Fisher*, the reasoning of *Boyd* continued to hold privileged under the self-incrimination clause a sole proprietor's business records, so long as the content of those records was potentially incriminatory. Rejecting that ruling, the Supreme Court in *Doe* held that the rationale of *Fisher had* established that, where "the preparation of business records is voluntary," the "contents of those records are not privileged." A self-incrimination claim could be based only on the act of production, not the contents of the subpoenaed records. Justice O'Connor, wrote separately "to make explicit what is implicit in the analysis of [the Court's] opinion: that the Fifth Amendment provides absolutely no protection for the contents of private papers of any kind. The notion that the Fifth Amendment protects the privacy of papers originated in *Boyd v. United States*, but our decision in *Fisher v. United States*, sounded the death-knell for *Boyd*." Justice Marshall, joined by Justice Brennan, responded to Justice O'Connor, noting: "Contrary to what Justice O'Connor contends, I do not view the Court's opinion in this case as having reconsidered whether the Fifth Amendment provides protection for the contents of 'private papers of any kind.' * * * [T]he documents at stake here are business records which implicate a lesser degree of concern for privacy interests than, for example, personal diaries. * * * I continue to believe that under the Fifth Amendment 'there are certain documents no person ought to be compelled to produce at the Government's request.'"

As to the Court's treatment in *Doe* of the subpoenaed party's claim that his act of producing the subpoenaed documents involved compelled self-incrimination, see the discussion of *Doe* in *Braswell*, infra.

# BRASWELL v. UNITED STATES

—— U.S. ——, 108 S.Ct. 2284, 100 L.Ed.2d 30 (1988).

CHIEF JUSTICE REHNQUIST delivered the opinion of the Court.

This case presents the question whether the custodian of corporate records may resist a subpoena for such records on the ground that the act of production would incriminate him in violation of the Fifth Amendment. We conclude that he may not. * * *

[A federal grand jury issued a subpoena to petitioner Braswell, as the president of two corporations, requiring him to produce the books and records of the two corporations. Worldwide Machinery, Inc. and Worldwide Purchasing, Inc. Petitioner had funded Worldwide Purchasing with his 100 percent interest in Worldwide Machinery and was the sole shareholder of Worldwide Purchasing. While both corporations had three directors, petitioner, his wife, and his mother, only petitioner had authority over the business affairs of the corporations. The grand jury subpoena provided that petitioner could deliver the records to the grand jury agent serving the subpoena and did not require petitioner to testify. Petitioner moved to quash the subpoena, arguing that the act or producing the records would continue a violation of his Fifth Amendment privilege against self-incrimination. The district court denied the motion and the Fifth Circuit affirmed.]

There is no question but that the contents of the subpoenaed business records are not privileged. See *United States v. Doe,* 465 U.S. 605 (1984); *Fisher v. United States.* Similarly, petitioner asserts no self-incrimination claim on behalf of the corporations; it is well established that such artificial entities are not protected by the Fifth Amendment. *Bellis v. United States,* 417 U.S. 85 (1974). Petitioner instead relies solely upon the argument that his act of producing the documents has independent testimonial significance, which would incriminate him individually, and that the Fifth Amendment prohibits government compulsion of that act. The bases for this argument are extrapolated from the decisions of this Court in *Fisher* and *Doe.*

In *Fisher,* the Court was presented with the question whether an attorney may resist a subpoena demanding that he produce tax records which had been entrusted to him by his client. * * * In analyzing the Fifth Amendment claim forwarded by the attorney, the Court considered whether the client-taxpayer would have had a valid Fifth Amendment claim had he retained the records and the subpoena been issued to him. After explaining that the Fifth Amendment prohibits "compelling a person to give 'testimony' that incriminates him," the Court rejected the argument that the contents of the records were protected. The Court, however, went on to observe [that] "the act of producing evidence in response to a subpoena nevertheless has communicative aspects of its own, wholly aside from the contents of the papers produced. * * *" The Court concluded that under the "facts and circumstances" there presented, the act of producing the accountants' papers would not "involve testimonial self-incrimination."

Eight years later, in *United States v. Doe,* the Court revisited the question, this time in the context of a claim by a sole proprietor that the compelled production of business records would run afoul of the Fifth Amendment. After rejecting the contention that the contents of the records were themselves protected, the Court proceeded to address whether respondent's act of producing the records would constitute protected testimonial incrimination. The Court concluded that respondent had established a valid Fifth Amendment claim. It deferred to the lower courts, which had found that enforcing the subpoenas at issue would provide the Government valuable information: By producing the records, respondent would admit that the records existed, were in his possession, and were authentic. *Doe* at n. 11.ᵃ

Had petitioner conducted his business as a sole proprietorship, *Doe* would require that he be provided the opportunity to show that his act of production would entail testimonial self-incrimination. But petitioner has operated his business through the corporate form, and we have long recognized that for purposes of the Fifth Amendment, corporations and other collective entities are treated differently from individuals. This doctrine—known as the collective entity rule—has a lengthy and distinguished pedigree.

The rule was first articulated by the Court in the case of *Hale* v. *Henkel*, 201 U.S. 43 (1906). Hale, a corporate officer, had been served with a subpoena ordering him to produce corporate records and to testify concerning certain corporate transactions. Although Hale was protected by personal immunity, he sought to resist the demand for the records by interposing a Fifth Amendment privilege on behalf of the corporation. The Court rejected that argument: "[W]e are of the opinion that there is a clear distinction * * * between an individual and a corporation, and * * * the latter has no right to refuse to submit its books and papers for an examination at the suit of the State." The Court explained that the corporation "is a creature of the State," with powers limited by the State. As such, the State may, in the exercise of its right to oversee the corporation, demand the production of corporate records. * * *

Although *Hale* settled that a corporation has no Fifth Amendment privilege, the Court did not address whether a corporate officer could resist a subpoena for corporate records by invoking his personal privilege—Hale had been protected by immunity. In *Wilson* v. *United States*, 221 U.S. 361 (1911), the Court answered that question in the negative. There, a grand jury investigating Wilson had issued a subpoena to a corporation demanding the production of corporate letter press copy books, which Wilson, the corporation's president, possessed. Wilson refused to produce the books, arguing that the Fifth Amendment prohibited compulsory production of personally incriminating books that be held and controlled. The Court rejected this argument, observing first that the records sought were not private or personal, but rather belonged to the corporation. The Court continued:

"[Wilson] held the corporate books subject to the corporate duty. If the corporation were guilty of misconduct, he could not withhold its books to

---

**a.** Setting forth the reasoning of the two lower courts, the Supreme Court in *Doe* noted that the District Court had concluded that " 'enforcement of the subpoenas would compel [respondent] to admit that the records exist, that they are in his possession, and that they are authentic.' " The District Court had taken note of the government's contention that the " 'existence, possession, and authenticity of the documents can be proved without [respondent's] testimonial communication,' " but had responded that it was not satisfied " 'as to how that representation can be implemented.' " *Doe* at n. 11. The Court of Appeals had stated that the record failed to indicate that the government knew that "each of the myriad documents demanded * * * in fact is in the appellee's possession," and that the " 'most plausible inference to be drawn from the broad-sweeping subpoenas is that the Government, unable to prove that the subpoenaed documents exist—or that the appellee even is somehow connected to the business entities under investigation—is attempting to compensate for its lack of knowledge by requiring the appellant to become in effect the primary informant against himself.' " *Doe* at n. 12. The Supreme Court later noted that the Government was not foreclosed "from rebutting respondent's claim by producing evidence that possession, existence, and authentication were a 'foregone conclusion' [citing *Fisher*]," but "in this case * * * the Government failed to make such a showing."

save it; and if he were implicated in the violations of law, he could not withhold the books to protect himself from the effect of their disclosures. The [State's] reserved power of visitation would seriously be embarrassed, if not wholly defeated in its effective exercise, if guilty officers could refuse inspection of the records and papers of the corporation. No personal privilege to which they are entitled requires such a conclusion. * * *"

In a companion case, *Dreier* v. *United States*, 221 U.S. 394 (1911), the Court applied the holding in *Wilson* to a Fifth Amendment attack on a subpoena addressed to the corporate custodian. Although the subpoena in *Wilson* had been addressed to the corporation, the Court found the distinction irrelevant: "Dreier was not entitled to refuse the production of the corporate records. By virtue of the fact that they were the documents of the corporation in his custody, and not his private papers, he was under the obligation to produce them when called for by proper process."

The next significant step in the development of the collective entity rule occurred in *United State v. White*, 322 U.S. 694 (1944), in which the Court held that a labor union is a collective entity unprotected by the Fifth Amendment. * * * We [reasoned] * * * that the Fifth Amendment privilege applies only to natural individuals and protects only private papers. Representatives of a "collective group" act as agents "[a]nd the official records and documents of the organization that are held by them in a representative rather than in a personal capacity cannot be the subject of the personal privilege against self-incrimination, even though production of the papers might tend to incriminate them personally." With this principle in mind, the Court turned to whether a union is a collective group:

"The test * * * is whether one can fairly say under all the circumstances that a particular type of organization has a character so impersonal in the scope of its membership and activities that it cannot be said to embody or represent the purely private or personal interests of its constituents, but rather to embody their common or group interests only. If so, the privilege cannot be invoked on behalf of the organization or its representatives in their official capacity. Labor unions—national or local, incorporated or unincorporated—clearly meet that test."

In applying the collective entity rule to unincorporated associations such as unions, the Court jettisoned reliance on the visitatorial powers of the State over corporations owing their existence to the State—one of the bases for earlier decisions.

The frontiers of the collective entity rule were expanded even further in *Bellis* v. *United States*, 417 U.S. 85 (1974), in which the Court ruled that a partner in a small partnership could not properly refuse to produce partnership records. * * * After rehearsing prior precedent involving corporations and unincorporated associations, the Court examined the partnership form and observed that is had many of the incidents found relevant in prior collective entity decisions. The Court suggested that the test articulated in *White* for determining the applicability of the Fifth Amendment to organizations was "not particularly helpful in the broad range of cases." The Court rejected the notion that the "formulation in *White* can be reduced to a simple proposition based solely upon the size of the organization. It is well settled that no privilege can be claimed by the custodian of corporate records, regardless of how small the corporation may be." * * *

The plain mandate of these decisions is that without regard to whether the subpoena is addressed to the corporation, or as here, to the individual in his capacity as a custodian, see *Dreier*; *Bellis*, a corporate custodian such as petitioner may not resist a subpoena for corporate records on Fifth Amendment grounds. Petitioner argues, however, that this rule falls in the wake of *Fisher* and *Doe*. In essence, petitioner's argument is as follows: In response to *Boyd v. United States*, with its privacy rationale shielding personal books and records, the Court developed the collective entity rule, which declares simply that corporate records are not private and therefore are not protected by the Fifth Amendment. The collective entity decisions were concerned with the contents of the documents subpoenaed, however, and not with the act of production. In *Fisher* and *Doe*, the Court moved away from the privacy based collective entity rule, replacing it with a compelled testimony standard under which the contents of business documents are never privileged but the act of producing the documents may be. Under this new regime, the act of production privilege is available without regard to the entity whose records are being sought. * * *

To be sure, the holding in *Fisher*—later reaffirmed in *Doe*—embarked upon a new course of Fifth Amendment analysis. We cannot agree, however, that it rendered the collective entity rule obsolete. The agency rationale undergirding the collective entity decisions, in which custodians asserted that production of entity records would incriminate them personally, survives. From *Wilson* forward, the Court has consistently recognized that the custodian of corporate or entity records holds those documents in a representative rather than a personal capacity. Artificial entities such as corporations may act only through their agents, and, a custodian's assumption of his representative capacity leads to certain obligations, including the duty to produce corporate records on proper demand by the Government. Under those circumstances, the custodian's act of production is not deemed a personal act, but rather an act of the corporation. Any claim of Fifth Amendment privilege asserted by the agent would be tantamount to a claim of privilege by the corporation—which of course possesses no such privilege. * * *

Indeed, the opinion in *Fisher*—upon which petitioner places primary reliance—indicates that the custodian of corporate records may not interpose a Fifth Amendment objection to the compelled production of corporate records, even though the act of production may prove personally incriminating. The *Fisher* court cited the collective entity decisions with approval and offered those decisions to support the conclusion that the production of the accountant's workpapers would "not * * * involve testimonial self-incrimination." * * * In a footnote, the Court explained: "In these cases compliance with the subpoena is required even though the books have been kept by the person subpoenaed and his producing them would itself be sufficient authentication to permit their introduction against him." n. 14. The Court thus reaffirmed the obligation of a corporate custodian to comply with a subpoena addressed to him.

That point was reiterated by Justice Brennan in his concurrence in *Fisher*. Although Justice Brennan diagreed with the majority as to its use of the collective entity cases to support the proposition that the act of production is not testimonial, he nonetheless acknowledged that a custodian may not resist a subpoena on the ground that the act of production would be incriminating. * * * [For] "one in control of the records of an artificial organization undertakes an obligation with respect to those records foreclosing any exercise of his privilege." Thus, whether one concludes—as did the Court—that a custodian's production of corporate records is deemed not to constitute testimonial self-incrimination, or instead that a custodian waives the right to exercise the privilege, the lesson of *Fisher* is clear: A custodian may not resist a subpoena for corporate records on Fifth Amendment grounds.   *   *   *

We note further that recognizing a Fifth Amendment privilege on behalf of the records custodians of collective entities would have a detrimental impact on the Government's efforts to prosecute "white-collar crime," one of the most serious problems confronting law enforcement authorities. "The greater portion of evidence of wrongdoing by an organization or its representatives is usually found in the official records and documents of that organization. Were the cloak of the privilege to be thrown around these impersonal records and documents, effective enforcement of many federal and state laws would be impossible." *White.* If custodians could assert a privilege, authorities would by stymied not only in their enforcement efforts against those individuals but also in their prosecutions of organizations. In *Bellis,* the Court observed: "In view of the inescapable fact that an artificial entity can only act to produce its records through its individual offices or agents, recognition of the individual's claim of privilege with respect to the financial records of the organization would substantially undermine the unchallenged rule that the organization itself is not entitled to claim any Fifth Amendment privilege, and largely frustrate legitimate governmental regulation of such organizations."

Petitioner suggests, however, that these concerns can be minimized by the simple expedient of either granting the custodian statutory immunity as to the act of production, 18 U.S.C. §§ 6002–6003, or addressing the subpoena to the corporation and allowing it to chose an agent to produce the records who can do so without incriminating himself. We think neither proposal satisfactorily addresses these concerns. Taking the last first, it is no doubt true that if a subpoena is addressed to a corporation, the corporation "must find some means by which to comply because no Fifth Amendment defense is available to it." The means most commonly used to comply is the appointment of an alternate custodian. But petitioner insists he cannot be required to aid the appointed custodian in his search for the demanded records, for any statement to the surrogate would itself be testimonial and incriminating. If this is correct, then petitioner's "solution" is a chimera. In situations such as this—where the corporate custodian is likely the only person with knowledge about the demanded documents—the appointment of a surrogate will simply not ensure that the documents sought will ever reach the grand jury room; the appointed custodian will essentially be sent on an unguided search.

This problem is eliminated if the Government grants the subpoenaed custodian statutory immunity for the testimonial aspects of his act of production. But that "solution" also entails a significant drawback. All of the evidence obtained under a grant of immunity to the custodian may of course be used freely against the corporation, but if the Government has any thought of prosecuting the custodian, a grant of act of production immunity can have serious consequences. Testimony obtained pursuant to a grant of statutory use immunity may be used neither directly nor derivatively. 18 U.S.C. § 6002. And "[o]ne raising a claim under [the federal immunity] statute need only show that he testified under a grant of immunity in order to shift to the government the heavy burden of proving that all of the evidence it proposes to use was derived from legitimate independent sources." *Kastigar.* Even in cases where the Government does not employ the immunized testimony for any purpose—direct or derivative—against the witness, the Government's inability to meet the "heavy burden" it bears may result in the preclusion of crucial evidence that was obtained legitimately.[10]

Although a corporate custodian is not entitled to resist a subpoena on the ground that his act of production will be personally incriminating, we do think certain consequences flow from the fact that the custodian's act of production is one in his representative rather than personal capacity. Because the custodian acts as a representative, the act is deemed one of the corporation and not the individual. Therefore, the Government concedes, as it must, that it may make no evidentiary use of the "individual act" against the individual. For example, in a criminal prosecution against the custodian, the Government may not introduce into evidence before the jury the fact that the subpoena was served upon and the corporation's documents were delivered by one particular individual, the custodian. The Government has the right, however, to use the corporation's act of production against the custodian. The Government may offer testimony—for example, from the process server who delivered the subpoena and from the individual who received the records—establishing that the corporation produced the records subpoenaed. The jury may draw from the corporation's act of production the conclusion that the records in question are authentic corporate records, which the corporation possessed, and which it produced in response to the subpoena. And if the defendant held a prominent position within the corporation that produced the records, the jury may, just as it would had someone else produced the documents, reasonably infer that he had possession of the documents or knowledge of their contents. Because the jury is not told that the defendant produced the records, any nexus between the defendant and the documents results solely from the corporation's act of production and other evidence in the case.[11]

Consistent with our precedent, the United States Court of Appeals for the Fifth Circuit ruled that petitioner could not resist the subpoena for corporate documents on the ground that the act of production might tend to incriminate him. The judgment is therefore affirmed.

Justice Kennedy, with whom Justice Brennan, Justice Marshall, and Justice Scalia join, dissenting.

* * * The majority's apparent reasoning is that collective entities have no privilege and so their employees must have none either. The Court holds that a corporate agent must incriminate himself even when he is named in the subpoena and is a target of the investigation, and even when it is conceded that compliance requires compelled, personal, testimonial, incriminating assertions. I disagree with that conclusion; find no precedent for it; maintain that if there is a likelihood of personal self-incrimination the narrow use immunity permitted by statute can be granted without frustrating the investigation of collective entities; and submit that basic Fifth Amendment principles should not be avoided and manipulated, which is the necessary effect of this decision.

10. The dissent asserts that recognition of an act of production privilege on behalf of corporate custodians will not seriously undermine law enforcement efforts directed against those custodians because only the custodian's act of production need be immunized. But the burden of proving an independent source that a grant of immunity places on the Government could, in our view, have just such a deleterious effect on law enforcement efforts.

11. * * * We leave open the question whether the agency rationale supports compelling a custodian to produce corporate records when the custodian is able to establish, by showing for example that he is the sole employee and officer of the corporation, that the jury would inevitably conclude that he produced the records.

* * * The majority does not challenge the assumption that compliance with the subpoena here would require acts of testimonial self-incrimination from Braswell; indeed, the Government itself made this assumption in submitted its argument. The question presented, therefore, is whether an individual may be compelled, simply by virtue of his status as a corporate custodian, to perform a testimonial act which will incriminate him personally. The majority relies entirely on the collective entity rule in holding that such compulsion is constitutional.

The collective entity rule provides no support for the majority's holding. * * * In none of the collective entity cases cited by the majority, and in none that I have found, were we presented with a claim that the custodian would be incriminated by the act of production, in contrast to the contents of the documents.

The distinction is central. * * * Our decision in *Wilson,* and in later collective entity cases reflected, I believe, the Court's understandable unease with drawing too close a connection between an individual and an artificial entity. On a more practical level, the Court was also unwilling to draw too close a connection between the custodian and the contents of business documents over which he had temporary control but which belonged to his employer, often were prepared by others, and in all events were prepared voluntarily. This last factor became the focus of our analysis in *Fisher,* where we made clear that the applicability of the Fifth Amendment privilege depends on compulsion. *Fisher* put to rest the notion that a privilege may be claimed with respect to the contents of business records that were voluntarily prepared.

The act of producing documents stands on an altogether different footing. While a custodian has no necessary relation to the contents of documents within his control, the act of production is inescapably his own. Production is the precise act compelled by the subpoena, and obedience, in some cases, will require the custodian's own testimonial assertions. That was the basis of our recognition of the privilege in *United States v. Doe.*

The entity processing the documents in *Doe* was, as the majority points out, a sole proprietorship, not a corporation, partnership, or labor union. But the potential for self-incrimination inheres in the act demanded of the individual, and as a consequence the nature of the entity is irrelevant to determining whether there is ground for the privilege. * * *

Recognition of the privilege here would * * * avoid adoption of the majority's metaphysical progression, which, I respectfully submit, is flawed. Beginning from ordinary principles of agency, the majority proceeds to the conclusion that when a corporate employee, or an employee of a labor union or partnership, complies with a subpoena for production of documents, his act is necessarily and solely the act of the entity. * * * [However,] [t]he heart of the matter, as everyone knows, is that the Government does not see Braswell as a mere agent at all; and the majority's thoery is difficult to square with what will often be the Government's actual practice. The subpoena in this case was not directed to Worldwide Machinery Sales, Inc., or Worldwide Purchasing, Inc. It was directed to "Randy Braswell, President, Worldwide Machinery Sales, Inc., Worldwide Purchasing, Inc." and informed him that "[y]ou are hereby commanded" to provide the specified documents. The Government explained at oral argument that it often chooses to designate an individual recipient, rather than the corporation generally, when it serves a subpoena because "[we] want the right to make that individual comply with the subpoena." This is not the language of agency. By issuing a subpoena which the Government insists is "directed to petitioner personally," it has forfeited any claim that it is simply making a demand on a corporation that, in turn, will have to find a physical agent to perform its duty. What the Government seeks instead is the right to choose any corporate agent as a target of its subpoena and compel that individual to disclose certain information by his own actions.

The majority gives the corporate agent fiction a weight it simply cannot bear. In a peculiar attempt to mitigate the force of its own holdings, it impinges upon its own analysis by concluding that, while the Government may compel a named individual to produce records, in any later proceeding against the person it cannot divulge that he performed the act. But if that is so, it is because the Fifth Amendment protects the person without regard to his status as a corporate employee; and once this be admitted, the necessary support for the majority's case has collapsed. * * *

The majority's abiding concern is that if a corporate officer who is the target of a subpoena is allowed to assert the privilege, it will impede the Government's power to investigate corporations, unions, and partnerships, to uncover and prosecute white collar crimes, and otherwise to enforce its visitatorial powers. There are at least two answers to this. The first, and most fundamental, is that the text of the Fifth Amendment does not authorize exceptions premised on such rationales. Second, even if it were proper to invent such exceptions, the dangers prophesied by the majority are overstated.

Recognition of the right to assert a privilege does not mean it will exist in many cases. In many instances, the production of documents may implicate no testimonial assertions at all. In *Fisher,* for example, we held that the specific acts required by the subpoena before us "would not itself involve testimonial self-incrimination" because, in that case, "the existence and location of the papers [were] a foregone conclusion and the taxpayer adds little or nothing to the sum total of the Government's information by conceding that he in fact has the papers." Whether a particular act is testimonial and self-incriminating is largely a factual issue to be decided in each case. In the case before us, the Government has made its submission on the assumption that the subpoena would result in incriminating testimony. The existence of a privilege in future cases, however, is not an automatic result.

Further, to the extent testimonial assertions are being compelled, use immunity can be granted without impeding the investigation. Where the privilege is applicable, immunity will be needed for only one individual, and solely with respect to evidence derived from the act of production itself. The Government would not be denied access to the records it seeks, it would be free to use the contents of the records against everyone, and it would be free to use any testimonial act implicit in production against all but the custodian it selects. In appropriate cases the Government will be able to establish authenticity, possession, and control by means other than compelling assertions about them from a suspect.

In one sense the case before use may not be a particularly sympathetic one. Braswell was the sole stockholder of the corporation and ran it himself. Perhaps that is why the Court suggests he waived his Fifth Amendment self-incrimination rights by using the corporate form. One does not always, however, have the choice of his or her employer, much less the choice of the business enterprise through which the employer conducts its business. Though the Court here hints at a waiver, nothing in Fifth Amendment jurisprudence indicates that the acceptance of employment should be deemed a waiver of a specific protection that is as basic a part of our constitutional heritage as is the privilege against self-incrimination.

The law is not captive to its own fictions. Yet, in the matter before us the Court employs the fiction that personal incrimination of the employee is neither sought by the Government nor cognizable by the law. That is a regrettable holding, for the conclusion is factually unsound, unnecessary for legitimate regulation, and a violation of the Self-Incrimination Clause of the Fifth Amendment of the Constitution. For these reasons, I dissent.

# Chapter 9

# PRETRIAL RELEASE

Persons apprehended by the police in the expectation that they will be prosecuted are usually provided an opportunity for pretrial release by one of a variety of means, depending upon the circumstances. If the offense is a very minor one, then release will occur in the field or at the stationhouse upon acceptance of a citation from the officer. In the case of more serious misdemeanors, the arrestee can obtain his release once at the police station by posting cash as a security payment in an amount set in a bail schedule, which simply lists bail amounts for various offenses. Other arrestees must await their first appearance before a judicial officer, when the magistrate will determine the conditions under which the defendant can obtain his release from custody pending the final disposition of the case.

Though bail was once limited almost entirely to the posting of cash or a secured bond, purchased from a professional bondsman, many jurisdictions now permit the defendant to obtain his release by depositing cash amounting to 10% of the amount of bond set by the magistrate. Sometimes the judge will instead release the defendant on his unsecured promise to appear, or in addition impose such nonfinancial conditions as a curfew or reporting periodically to a designated agency. In the many cases in which the magistrate sets financial conditions upon release, he is subject to the Eighth Amendment command: "Excessive bail shall not be required." Just what this means is considered in the first case in this chapter, *Stack v. Boyle.*

The term "preventive detention" is usually used to describe the pretrial detention of a defendant to protect society from the risk of criminal conduct by him pending disposition of the outstanding charges. For many years this was accomplished sub rosa; the magistrate would set money bail purportedly for the purpose of ensuring defendant's appearance at trial, but the amount would be high enough to prevent defendant's release. But because of reform in bail laws contemporaneous with more direct attention to the question of whether such pretrial detention is justified, the process of preventive detention is today a much more open one. This is especially true in the federal criminal justice system; the Bail Reform Act of 1984 on the one hand provides that a judicial officer "may not impose a financial condition that results in the pretrial detention of the person," but on the other expressly authorizes judicially-ordered pretrial detention of defendants in some circumstances to ensure "the safety of any other person or the community." Whether such preventive detention can be squared with the Eighth Amendment provision quoted above is the issue addressed in the other case in this chapter, *United States v. Salerno.*

# STACK v. BOYLE

342 U.S. 1, 72 S.Ct. 1, 96 L.Ed. 3 (1951).

CHIEF JUSTICE VINSON delivered the opinion of the Court.

Indictments have been returned in the Southern District of California charging the twelve petitioners with conspiring to violate the Smith Act, [proscribing advocacy of the overthrow of the government by force or violence]. Upon their arrest, bail was fixed for each petitioner in the widely varying amounts of $2,500, $7,500, $75,000 and $100,000. On motion of petitioner Schneiderman following arrest in the Southern District of New York, his bail was reduced to $50,000 before his removal to California. On motion of the Government to increase bail in the case of other petitioners, and after several intermediate procedural steps not material to the issues presented here, bail was fixed in the District Court for the Southern District of California in the uniform amount of $50,000 for each petitioner.

Petitioners moved to reduce bail on the ground that bail as fixed was excessive under the Eighth Amendment. In support of their motion, petitioners submitted statements as to their financial resources, family relationships, health, prior criminal records, and other information. The only evidence offered by the Government was a certified record showing that four persons previously convicted under the Smith Act in the Southern District of New York had forfeited bail. No evidence was produced relating those four persons to the petitioners in this case. At a hearing on the motion, petitioners were examined by the District Judge and cross-examined by an attorney for the Government. Petitioners' factual statements stand uncontroverted.

After their motion to reduce bail was denied, petitioners filed applications for habeas corpus in the same District Court. Upon consideration of the record on the motion to reduce bail, the writs were denied. The Court of Appeals for the Ninth Circuit affirmed.

\* \* \* From the passage of the Judiciary Act of 1789 to the present Federal Rules of Criminal Procedure, Rule 46(a)(1), federal law has unequivocally provided that a person arrested for a non-capital offense *shall* be admitted to bail. This traditional right to freedom before conviction permits the unhampered preparation of a defense, and serves to prevent the infliction of punishment prior to conviction. Unless this right to bail before trial is preserved, the presumption of innocence, secured only after centuries of struggle, would lose its meaning.

The right to release before trial is conditioned upon the accused's giving adequate assurance that he will stand trial and submit to sentence if found guilty. Like the ancient practice of securing the oaths of responsible persons to stand as sureties for the accused, the modern practice of requiring a bail bond or the deposit of a sum of money subject to forfeiture serves as additional assurance of the presence of an accused. Bail set at a figure higher than an amount reasonably calculated to fulfill this purpose is "excessive" under the Eighth Amendment.

Since the function of bail is limited, the fixing of bail for any individual defendant must be based upon standards relevant to the purpose of assuring the presence of that defendant. The traditional standards as expressed in the Federal Rules of Criminal Procedure [3] are to be applied in each case to each

---

3. Rule 46(c). "AMOUNT. If the defendant is admitted to bail, the amount thereof shall be such as in the judgment of the commission- er or court or judge or justice will insure the presence of the defendant, having regard to the nature and circumstances of the offense

defendant. * * * Upon final judgment of conviction, petitioners face imprisonment of not more than five years and a fine of not more than $10,000. It is not denied that bail for each petitioner has been fixed in a sum much higher than that usually imposed for offenses with like penalties and yet there has been no factual showing to justify such action in this case. The Government asks the courts to depart from the norm by assuming, without the introduction of evidence, that each petitioner is a pawn in a conspiracy and will, in obedience to a superior, flee the jurisdiction. To infer from the fact of indictment alone a need for bail in an unusually high amount is an arbitrary act. Such conduct would inject into our own system of government the very principles of totalitarianism which Congress was seeking to guard against in passing the statute under which petitioners have been indicted.

If bail in an amount greater than that usually fixed for serious charges of crimes is required in the case of any of the petitioners, that is a matter to which evidence should be directed in a hearing so that the constitutional rights of each petitioner may be preserved. In the absence of such a showing, we are of the opinion that the fixing of bail before trial in these cases cannot be squared with the statutory and constitutional standards for admission to bail.

* * * Accordingly, [p]etitioners may move for reduction of bail in the criminal proceeding so that a hearing may be held for the purpose of fixing reasonable bail for each petitioner. * * *[a]

## UNITED STATES v. SALERNO

481 U.S. 739, 107 S.Ct. 2095, 95 L.Ed.2d 697 (1987).

CHIEF JUSTICE REHNQUIST delivered the opinion of the Court. * * *

### I

Responding to "the alarming problem of crimes committed by persons on release," Congress formulated the Bail Reform Act of 1984, 18 U.S.C. § 3141 et seq., as the solution to a bail crisis in the federal courts. The Act represents the National Legislature's considered response to numerous perceived deficiencies in the federal bail process. By providing for sweeping changes in both the way federal courts consider bail applications and the circumstances under which bail is granted, Congress hoped to "give the courts adequate authority to make release decisions that give appropriate recognition to the danger a person may pose to others if released."

To this end, § 3141(a) of the Act requires a judicial officer to determine whether an arrestee shall be detained. Section 3142(e) provides that "[i]f, after a hearing pursuant to the provisions of subsection (f), the judicial officer finds that no condition or combination of conditions will reasonably assure the appearance of the person as required and the safety of any other person and the community, he shall order the detention of the person prior to trial." Section 3142(f) provides the arrestee with a number of procedural safeguards. He may request the presence of counsel at the detention hearing, he may testify and present witnesses in his behalf, as well as proffer evidence, and he may cross-examine other witnesses appearing at the hearing. If the judicial officer finds that no conditions of pretrial release can reasonably assure the safety of other persons and the community, he must state his findings of fact in writing, and support his conclusion with "clear and convincing evidence."

charged, the weight of the evidence against him, the financial ability of the defendant to give bail and the character of the defendant."

a. The separate opinion of Justice Jackson, joined by Justice Frankfurter, is omitted. Justice Minton did not participate.

The judicial officer is not given unbridled discretion in making the detention determination. Congress has specified the considerations relevant to that decision. These factors include the nature and seriousness of the charges, the substantiality of the government's evidence against the arrestee, the arrestee's background and characteristics, and the nature and seriousness of the danger posed by the suspect's release. Should a judicial officer order detention, the detainee is entitled to expedited appellate review of the detention order.

Respondents Anthony Salerno and Vincent Cafaro were arrested on March 21, 1986, after being charged in a 29–count indictment alleging various Racketeer Influenced and Corrupt Organizations Act (RICO) violations, mail and wire fraud offenses, extortion, and various criminal gambling violations. The RICO counts alleged 35 acts of racketeering activity, including fraud, extortion, gambling, and conspiracy to commit murder. At respondents' arraignment, the Government moved to have Salerno and Cafaro detained pursuant to § 3142(e), on the ground that no condition of release would assure the safety of the community or any person. The District Court held a hearing at which the Government made a detailed proffer of evidence. The Government's case showed that Salerno was the "boss" of the Genovese Crime Family of La Cosa Nostra and that Cafaro was a "captain" in the Genovese Family. According to the Government's proffer, based in large part on conversations intercepted by a court-ordered wiretap, the two respondents had participated in wide-ranging conspiracies to aid their illegitimate enterprises through violent means. The Government also offered the testimony of two of its trial witnesses, who would assert that Salerno personally participated in two murder conspiracies. Salerno opposed the motion for detention, challenging the credibility of the Government's witnesses. He offered the testimony of several character witnesses as well as a letter from his doctor stating that he was suffering from a serious medical condition. Cafaro presented no evidence at the hearing, but instead characterized the wiretap conversations as merely "tough talk."

The District Court granted the Government's detention motion, concluding that the Government had established by clear and convincing evidence that no condition or combination of conditions of release would ensure the safety of the community or any person. *  *  *

Respondents appealed, contending that to the extent that the Bail Reform Act permits pretrial detention on the ground that the arrestee is likely to commit future crimes, it is unconstitutional on its face. Over a dissent, the United States Court of Appeals for the Second Circuit agreed. Although the court agreed that pretrial detention could be imposed if the defendants were likely to intimidate witnesses or otherwise jeopardize the trial process, it found "§ 3142(e)'s authorization of pretrial detention [on the ground of future dangerousness] repugnant to the concept of substantive due process, which we believe prohibits the total deprivation of liberty simply as a means of preventing future crimes." The court concluded that the Government could not, consistent with due process, detain persons who had not been accused of any crime merely because they were thought to present a danger to the community. It reasoned that our criminal law system holds persons accountable for past actions, not anticipated future actions. Although a court could detain an arrestee who threatened to flee before trial, such detention would be permissible because it would serve the basic objective of a criminal system—bringing the accused to trial. The court distinguished our decision in *Gerstein v. Pugh* [ch. 3, § 4], in which we upheld police detention pursuant to arrest. The court construed *Gerstein* as limiting such detention to the " 'administrative steps incident to arrest.'" The Court of Appeals also found our decision in *Schall v. Martin,* 467 U.S. 253 (1984), upholding postarrest pretrial detention of juveniles, inapposite because juveniles have a lesser interest in liberty than do adults.  *  *  *

## II

A facial challenge to a legislative Act is, of course, the most difficult challenge to mount successfully, since the challenger must establish that no set of circumstances exists under which the Act would be valid. The fact that the Bail Reform Act might operate unconstitutionally under some conceivable set of circumstances is insufficient to render it wholly invalid, since we have not recognized an "overbreadth" doctrine outside the limited context of the First Amendment. We think respondents have failed to shoulder their heavy burden to demonstrate that the Act is "facially" unconstitutional.[3]

Respondents present two grounds for invalidating the Bail Reform Act's provisions permitting pretrial detention on the basis of future dangerousness. First, they rely upon the Court of Appeals' conclusion that the Act exceeds the limitations placed upon the Federal Government by the Due Process Clause of the Fifth Amendment. Second, they contend that the Act contravenes the Eighth Amendment's proscription against excessive bail. We treat these contentions in turn.

## A

The Due Process Clause of the Fifth Amendment provides that "No person shall  *  *  * be deprived of life, liberty, or property, without due process of law  *  *  *." This Court has held that the Due Process Clause protects individuals against two types of government action. So-called "substantive due process" prevents the government from engaging in conduct that "shocks the conscience," or interferes with rights "implicit in the concept of ordered liberty." When government action depriving a person of life, liberty, or property survives substantive due process scrutiny, it must still be implemented in a fair manner. This requirement has traditionally been referred to as "procedural" due process.

Respondents first argue that the Act violates substantive due process because the pretrial detention it authorizes constitutes impermissible punishment before trial. The Government, however, has never argued that pretrial detention could be upheld if it were "punishment." The Court of Appeals assumed that pretrial detention under the Bail Reform Act is regulatory, not penal, and we agree that it is.

As an initial matter, the mere fact that a person is detained does not inexorably lead to the conclusion that the government has imposed punishment. To determine whether a restriction on liberty constitutes impermissible punishment or permissible regulation, we first look to legislative intent. Unless Congress expressly intended to impose punitive restrictions, the punitive/regulatory distinction turns on " 'whether an alternative purpose to which [the restriction] may rationally be connected is assignable for it, and whether it appears excessive in relation to the alternative purpose assigned [to it].' "

We conclude that the detention imposed by the Act falls on the regulatory side of the dichotomy. The legislative history of the Bail Reform Act clearly indicates that Congress did not formulate the pretrial detention provisions as punishment for dangerous individuals. Congress instead perceived pretrial

---

**3.** We intimate no view on the validity of any aspects of the Act that are not relevant to respondents' case. Nor have respondents claimed that the Act is unconstitutional because of the way it was applied to the particular facts of their case.

detention as a potential solution to a pressing societal problem. There is no doubt that preventing danger to the community is a legitimate regulatory goal.

Nor are the incidents of pretrial detention excessive in relation to the regulatory goal Congress sought to achieve. The Bail Reform Act carefully limits the circumstances under which detention may be sought to the most serious of crimes. See 18 U.S.C. § 3142(f) (detention hearings available if case involves crimes of violence, offenses for which the sentence is life imprisonment or death, serious drug offenses, or certain repeat offenders). The arrestee is entitled to a prompt detention hearing, and the maximum length of pretrial detention is limited by the stringent time limitations of the Speedy Trial Act.[4] Moreover, as in *Schall v. Martin*, the conditions of confinement envisioned by the Act "appear to reflect the regulatory purposes relied upon by the" government. As in *Schall*, the statute at issue here requires that detainees be housed in a "facility separate, to the extent practicable, from persons awaiting or serving sentences or being held in custody pending appeal." We conclude, therefore, that the pretrial detention contemplated by the Bail Reform Act is regulatory in nature, and does not constitute punishment before trial in violation of the Due Process Clause.

The Court of Appeals nevertheless concluded that "the Due Process Clause prohibits pretrial detention on the ground of danger to the community as a regulatory measure, without regard to the duration of the detention." Respondents characterize the Due Process Clause as erecting an impenetrable "wall" in this area that "no governmental interest—rational, important, compelling or otherwise—may surmount."

We do not think the Clause lays down any such categorical imperative. We have repeatedly held that the government's regulatory interest in community safety can, in appropriate circumstances, outweigh an individual's liberty interest. For example, in times of war or insurrection, when society's interest is at its peak, the government may detain individuals whom the government believes to be dangerous. Even outside the exigencies of war, we have found that sufficiently compelling governmental interests can justify detention of dangerous persons. Thus, we have found no absolute constitutional barrier to detention of potentially dangerous resident aliens pending deportation proceedings. We have also held that the government may detain mentally unstable individuals who present a danger to the public, and dangerous defendants who become incompetent to stand trial. We have approved of postarrest regulatory detention of juveniles when they present a continuing danger to the community. *Schall v. Martin*. Even competent adults may face substantial liberty restrictions as a result of the operation of our criminal justice system. If the police suspect an individual of a crime, they may arrest and hold him until a neutral magistrate determines whether probable cause exists. *Gerstein v. Pugh*. Finally, respondents concede and the Court of Appeals noted that an arrestee may be incarcerated until trial if he presents a risk of flight or a danger to witnesses.

Respondents characterize all of these cases as exceptions to the "general rule" of substantive due process that the government may not detain a person prior to a judgment of guilt in a criminal trial. Such a "general rule" may freely be conceded, but we think that these cases show a sufficient number of exceptions to the rule that the congressional action challenged here can hardly be characterized as totally novel. Given the well-established authority of the

---

**4.** We intimate no view as to the point at which detention in a particular case might become excessively prolonged, and therefore punitive, in relation to Congress' regulatory goal.

government, in special circumstances, to restrain individuals' liberty prior to or even without criminal trial and conviction, we think that the present statute providing for pretrial detention on the basis of dangerousness must be evaluated in precisely the same manner that we evaluated the laws in the cases discussed above.

The government's interest in preventing crime by arrestees is both legitimate and compelling. In *Schall,* we recognized the strength of the State's interest in preventing juvenile crime. This general concern with crime prevention is no less compelling when the suspects are adults. Indeed, "[t]he harm suffered by the victim of a crime is not dependent upon the age of the perpetrator." The Bail Reform Act of 1984 responds to an even more particularized governmental interest than the interest we sustained in *Schall.* The statute we upheld in *Schall* permitted pretrial detention of any juvenile arrested on any charge after a showing that the individual might commit some undefined further crimes. The Bail Reform Act, in contrast, narrowly focuses on a particularly acute problem in which the government interests are overwhelming. The Act operates only on individuals who have been arrested for a specific category of extremely serious offenses. Congress specifically found that these individuals are far more likely to be responsible for dangerous acts in the community after arrest. Nor is the Act by any means a scattershot attempt to incapacitate those who are merely suspected of these serious crimes. The government must first of all demonstrate probable cause to believe that the charged crime has been commited by the arrestee, but that is not enough. In a full-blown adversary hearing, the government must convince a neutral decisionmaker by clear and convincing evidence that no conditions of release can reasonably assure the safety of the community or any person. While the government's general interest in preventing crime is compelling, even this interest is heightened when the government musters convincing proof that the arrestee, already indicted or held to answer for a serious crime, presents a demonstrable danger to the community. Under these narrow circumstances, society's interest in crime prevention is at its greatest.

On the other side of the scale, of course, is the individual's strong interest in liberty. We do not minimize the importance and fundamental nature of this right. But, as our cases hold, this right may, in circumstances where the government's interest is sufficiently weighty, be subordinated to the greater needs of society. We think that Congress' careful delineation of the circumstances under which detention will be permitted satisfies this standard. When the government proves by clear and convincing evidence that an arrestee presents an identified and articulable threat to an individual or the community, we believe that, consistent with the Due Process Clause, a court may disable the arrestee from executing that threat. Under these circumstances, we cannot categorically state that pretrial detention "offends some principle of justice so rooted in the traditions and conscience of our people as to be ranked as fundamental."

Finally, we may dispose briefly of respondents' facial challenge to the procedures of the Bail Reform Act. To sustain them against such a challenge, we need only find them "adequate to authorize the pretrial detention of at least some [persons] charged with crimes," whether or not they might be insufficient in some particular circumstances. We think they pass that test. As we stated in *Schall,* "there is nothing inherently unattainable about a prediction of future criminal conduct."

Under the Bail Reform Act, the procedures by which a judicial officer evaluates the likelihood of future dangerousness are specifically designed to further the accuracy of that determination. Detainees have a right to counsel at the detention hearing. They may testify in their own behalf, present information by proffer or otherwise, and cross-examine witnesses who appear at the hearing. Ibid. The judicial officer charged with the responsibility of determining the appropriateness of detention is guided by statutorily enumerated factors, which include the nature and the circumstances of the charges, the weight of the evidence, the history and characteristics of the putative offender, and the danger to the community. The government must prove its case by clear and convincing evidence. Finally, the judicial officer must include written findings of fact and a written statement of reasons for a decision to detain. The Act's review provisions provide for immediate appellate review of the detention decision.

We think these extensive safeguards suffice to repel a facial challenge. The protections are more exacting than those we found sufficient in the juvenile context, see *Schall,* and they far exceed what we found necessary to effect limited postarrest detention in *Gerstein v. Pugh.* Given the legitimate and compelling regulatory purpose of the Act and the procedural protections it offers, we conclude that the Act is not facially invalid under the Due Process Clause of the Fifth Amendment.

### B

Respondents also contend that the Bail Reform Act violates the Excessive Bail Clause of the Eighth Amendment. * * *

The Eighth Amendment addresses pretrial release by providing merely that "Excessive bail shall not be required." This Clause, of course, says nothing about whether bail shall be available at all. Respondents nevertheless contend that this Clause grants them a right to bail calculated solely upon considerations of flight. They rely on *Stack v. Boyle* in which the Court stated that "Bail set at a figure higher than an amount reasonably calculated [to ensure the defendant's presence at trial] is 'excessive' under the Eighth Amendment." In respondents' view, since the Bail Reform Act allows a court essentially to set bail at an infinite amount for reasons not related to the risk of flight, it violates the Excessive Bail Clause. Respondents concede that the right to bail they have discovered in the Eighth Amendment is not absolute. A court may, for example, refuse bail in capital cases. And, as the Court of Appeals noted and respondents admit, a court may refuse bail when the defendant presents a threat to the judicial process by intimidating witnesses. Respondents characterize these exceptions as consistent with what they claim to be the sole purpose of bail—to ensure integrity of the judicial process.

While we agree that a primary function of bail is to safeguard the courts' role in adjudicating the guilt or innocence of defendants, we reject the proposition that the Eighth Amendment categorically prohibits the government from pursuing other admittedly compelling interests through regulation of pretrial release. The above-quoted *dicta* in *Stack v. Boyle* is far too slender a reed on which to rest this argument. The Court in *Stack* had no occasion to consider whether the Excessive Bail Clause requires courts to admit all defendants to bail, because the statute before the Court in that case in fact allowed the defendants to be bailed. * * *

The holding of *Stack* is illuminated by the Court's holding just four months later in *Carlson v. Landon,* 342 U.S. 524 (1952). In that case, remarkably similar to the present action, the detainees had been arrested and held without bail pending a determination of deportability. The Attorney General refused to release the individuals, "on the ground that there was reasonable cause to believe that [their] release would be prejudicial to the public interest and *would endanger the welfare and safety of the United States.*" (emphasis added). The detainees brought the same challenge that respondents bring to us today: the Eighth Amendment required them to be admitted to bail. The Court squarely rejected this proposition:

> "The bail clause was lifted with slight changes from the English Bill of Rights Act. In England that clause has never been thought to accord a right to bail in all cases, but merely to provide that bail shall not be excessive in those cases where it is proper to grant bail. When this clause was carried over into our Bill of Rights, nothing was said that indicated any different concept. The Eighth Amendment has not prevented Congress from defining the classes of cases in which bail shall be allowed in this country. Thus, in criminal cases bail is not compulsory where the punishment may be death. Indeed, the very language of the Amendment fails to say all arrests must be bailable."

*Carlson v. Landon* was a civil case, and we need not decide today whether the Excessive Bail Clause speaks at all to Congress' power to define the classes of criminal arrestees who shall be admitted to bail. For even if we were to conclude that the Eighth Amendment imposes some substantive limitations on the National Legislature's powers in this area, we would still hold that the Bail Reform Act is valid. Nothing in the text of the Bail Clause limits permissible government considerations solely to questions of flight. The only arguable substantive limitation of the Bail Clause is that the government's proposed conditions of release or detention not be "excessive" in light of the perceived evil. Of course, to determine whether the government's response is excessive, we must compare that response against the interest the government seeks to protect by means of that response. Thus, when the government has admitted that its only interest is in preventing flight, bail must be set by a court at a sum designed to ensure that goal, and no more. We believe that when Congress has mandated detention on the basis of a compelling interest other than prevention of flight, as it has here, the Eighth Amendment does not require release on bail.

### III

In our society liberty is the norm, and detention prior to trial or without trial is the carefully limited exception. We hold that the provisions for pretrial detention in the Bail Reform Act of 1984 fall within that carefully limited exception. * * * We are unwilling to say that this congressional determination, based as it is upon that primary concern of every government—a concern for the safety and indeed the lives of its citizens—on its face violates either the Due Process Clause of the Fifth Amendment or the Excessive Bail Clause of the Eighth Amendment.

JUSTICE MARSHALL, with whom JUSTICE BRENNAN joins, dissenting. * * *

### II

The majority approaches respondents' challenge to the Act by dividing the discussion into two sections, one concerned with the substantive guarantees implicit in the Due Process Clause, and the other concerned with the protection afforded by the Excessive Bail Clause of the Eighth Amendment. This is a sterile formalism, which divides a unitary argument into two independent parts and then professes to demonstrate that the parts are individually inadequate.

On the due process side of this false dichotomy appears an argument concerning the distinction between regulatory and punitive legislation. The majority concludes that the Act is a regulatory rather than a punitive measure. The ease with which the conclusion is reached suggests the worthlessness of the achievement. The major premise is that "[u]nless Congress expressly intended to impose punitive restrictions, the punitive/regulatory distinction turns on ' "whether an alternative purpose to which [the restriction] may rationally be connected is assignable for it, and whether it appears excessive in relation to the alternative purpose assigned [to it]." ' " The majority finds that "Congress did not formulate the pretrial detention provisions as punishment for dangerous individuals," but instead was pursuing the "legitimate regulatory goal" of "preventing danger to the community." Concluding that pretrial detention is not an excessive solution to the problem of preventing danger to the community, the majority thus finds that no substantive element of the guarantee of due process invalidates the statute.

This argument does not demonstrate the conclusion it purports to justify. Let us apply the majority's reasoning to a similar, hypothetical case. After investigation, Congress determines (not unrealistically) that a large proportion of violent crime is perpetrated by persons who are unemployed. It also determines, equally reasonably, that much violent crime is committed at night. From amongst the panoply of "potential solutions," Congress chooses a statute which permits, after judicial proceedings, the imposition of a dusk-to-dawn curfew on anyone who is unemployed. Since this is not a measure enacted for the purpose of punishing the unemployed, and since the majority finds that preventing danger to the community is a legitimate regulatory goal, the curfew statute would, according to the majority's analysis, be a mere "regulatory" detention statute, entirely compatible with the substantive components of the Due Process Clause.

The absurdity of this conclusion arises, of course, from the majority's cramped concept of substantive due process. The majority proceeds as though the only substantive right protected by the Due Process Clause is a right to be free from punishment before conviction. The majority's technique for infringing this right is simple: merely redefine any measure which is claimed to be punishment as "regulation," and, magically, the Constitution no longer prohibits its imposition. Because, as I discuss in Part III, infra, the Due Process Clause protects other substantive rights which are infringed by this legislation, the majority's argument is merely an exercise in obfuscation.

The logic of the majority's Eighth Amendment analysis is equally unsatisfactory. The Eighth Amendment, as the majority notes, states that "[e]xcessive bail shall not be required." The majority then declares, as if it were undeniable, that: "[t]his Clause, of course, says nothing about whether bail shall be available at all." If excessive bail is imposed the defendant stays in jail. The same result is achieved if bail is denied altogether. Whether the magistrate sets bail at $1 billion or refuses to set bail at all, the consequences are indistinguishable. It would be mere sophistry to suggest that the Eighth Amendment protects against the former decision, and not the latter. Indeed, such a result would lead to the conclusion that there was no need for Congress to pass a preventive detention measure of any kind; every federal magistrate and district judge could simply refuse, despite the absence of any evidence of risk of flight or danger to the community, to set bail. This would be entirely constitutional, since, according to the majority, the Eighth Amendment "says nothing about whether bail shall be available at all."

But perhaps, the majority says, this manifest absurdity can be avoided. Perhaps the Bail Clause is addressed only to the judiciary. "[W]e need not decide today," the majority says, "whether the Excessive Bail Clause speaks at all to Congress' power to define the classes of criminal arrestees who shall be admitted to bail." The majority is correct that this question need not be decided today; it was decided long ago. Federal and state statutes which purport to accomplish what the Eighth Amendment forbids, such as imposing cruel and unusual punishments, may not stand. The text of the Amendment, which provides simply that "[e]xcessive bail shall not be required, nor excessive fines imposed, nor cruel and unusual punishments inflicted," provides absolutely no support for the majority's speculation that both courts and Congress are forbidden to inflict cruel and unusual punishments, while only the courts are forbidden to require excessive bail.[5]

* * * The majority concedes, as it must, that "when the government has admitted that its only interest is in preventing flight, bail must be set by a court at a sum designed to ensure that goal, and no more." But, the majority says, "when Congress has mandated detention on the basis of a compelling interest other than prevention of flight, as it has here, the Eighth Amendment does not require release on bail." This conclusion follows only if the "compelling" interest upon which Congress acted is an interest which the Constitution permits Congress to further through the denial of bail. The majority does not ask, as a result of its disingenuous division of the analysis, if there are any substantive limits contained in both the Eighth Amendment and the Due Process Clause which render this system of preventive detention unconstitutional. The majority does not ask because the answer is apparent and, to the majority, inconvenient.

### III

The essence of this case may be found, ironically enough, in a provision of the Act to which the majority does not refer. Title 18 U.S.C. § 3142(j) provides that "[n]othing in this section shall be construed as modifying or limiting the presumption of innocence." But the very pith and purpose of this statute is an abhorrent limitation of the presumption of innocence. The majority's untenable conclusion that the present Act is constitutional arises from a specious denial of the role of the Bail Clause and the Due Process Clause in protecting the invaluable guarantee afforded by the presumption of innocence.

"The principle that there is a presumption of innocence in favor of the accused is the undoubted law, axiomatic and elementary, and its enforcement lies at the foundation of the administration of our criminal law." Our society's belief, reinforced over the centuries, that all are innocent until the state has proven them to be guilty, like the companion principle that guilt must be proved beyond a reasonable doubt, is "implicit in the concept of ordered liberty," and is established beyond legislative contravention in the Due Process Clause.

5. The majority refers to the statement in *Carlson v. Landon* that the Bail Clause was adopted by Congress from the English Bill of Rights Act of 1689, and that "[i]n England that clause has never been thought to accord a right to bail in all cases, but merely to provide that bail shall not be excessive in those cases where it is proper to grant bail." A sufficient answer to this meagre argument was made at the time by Justice Black:

"The Eighth Amendment is in the American Bill of Rights of 1789, not the English Bill of Rights of 1689." *Carlson v. Landon* (dissenting opinion). Our Bill of Rights is contained in a written Constitution one of whose purposes is to protect the rights of the people against infringement by the Legislature, and its provisions, whatever their origins, are interpreted in relation to those purposes.

The statute now before us declares that persons who have been indicted may be detained if a judicial officer finds clear and convincing evidence that they pose a danger to individuals or to the community. The statute does not authorize the government to imprison anyone it has evidence is dangerous; indictment is necessary. But let us suppose that a defendant is indicted and the government shows by clear and convincing evidence that he is dangerous and should be detained pending a trial, at which trial the defendant is acquitted. May the government continue to hold the defendant in detention based upon its showing that he is dangerous? The answer cannot be yes, for that would allow the government to imprison someone for uncommitted crimes based upon "proof" not beyond a reasonable doubt. The result must therefore be that once the indictment has failed, detention cannot continue. But our fundamental principles of justice declare that the defendant is as innocent on the day before his trial as he is on the morning after his acquittal. Under this statute an untried indictment somehow acts to permit a detention, based on other charges, which after an acquittal would be unconstitutional. The conclusion is inescapable that the indictment has been turned into evidence, if not that the defendant is guilty of the crime charged, then that left to his own devices he will soon be guilty of something else.

To be sure, an indictment is not without legal consequences. It establishes that there is probable cause to believe that an offense was committed, and that the defendant committed it. Upon probable cause a warrant for the defendant's arrest may issue; a period of administrative detention may occur before the evidence of probable cause is presented to a neutral magistrate. See *Gerstein v. Pugh.* Once a defendant has been committed for trial he may be detained in custody if the magistrate finds that no conditions of release will prevent him from becoming a fugitive. But in this connection the charging instrument is evidence of nothing more than the fact that there will be a trial, and

> "release before trial is conditioned upon the accused's giving adequate assurance that he will stand trial and submit to sentence if found guilty. Like the ancient practice of securing the oaths of responsible persons to stand as sureties for the accused, the modern practice of requiring a bail bond or the deposit of a sum of money subject to forfeiture serves as additional assurance of the presence of an accused." *Stack v. Boyle.*[6]

The finding of probable cause conveys power to try, and the power to try imports of necessity the power to assure that the processes of justice will not be evaded or obstructed. "Pretrial detention to prevent future crimes against society at large, however, is not justified by any concern for holding a trial on the charges for which a defendant has been arrested." The detention purportedly authorized by this statute bears no relation to the government's power to try charges supported by a finding of probable cause, and thus the interests it serves are outside the scope of interests which may be considered in weighing the excessiveness of bail under the Eighth Amendment. * * *

## IV

* * * Honoring the presumption of innocence is often difficult; sometimes we must pay substantial social costs as a result of our commitment to the values

---

**6.** The majority states that denial of bail in capital cases has traditionally been the rule rather than the exception. And this of course is so, for it has been the considered presumption of generations of judges that a defendant in danger of execution has an extremely strong incentive to flee. If in any particular case the presumed likelihood of flight should be made irrebuttable, it would in all probability violate the Due Process Clause. Thus what the majority perceives as an exception is nothing more than an example of the traditional operation of our system of bail.

we espouse.  But at the end of the day the presumption of innocence protects the innocent; the shortcuts we take with those whom we believe to be guilty injure only those wrongfully accused and, ultimately, ourselves.   *   *   *

I dissent.

JUSTICE STEVENS, dissenting.

There may be times when the government's interest in protecting the safety of the community will justify the brief detention of a person who has not committed any crime.   *   *   * [But] it is clear to me that a pending indictment may not be given any weight in evaluating an individual's risk to the community or the need for immediate detention.

If the evidence of imminent danger is strong enough to warrant emergency detention, it should support that preventive measure regardless of whether the person has been charged, convicted, or acquitted of some other offense.  In this case, for example, it is unrealistic to assume that the danger to the community that was present when respondents were at large did not justify their detention before they were indicted, but did require that measure the moment that the grand jury found probable cause to believe they had committed crimes in the past.  It is equally unrealistic to assume that the danger will vanish if a jury happens to acquit them.  Justice Marshall has demonstrated that the fact of indictment cannot, consistent with the presumption of innocence and the Eighth Amendment's Excessive Bail Clause, be used to create a special class the members of which are, alone, eligible for detention because of future dangerousness.

*   *   *

# Chapter 10

# THE DECISION WHETHER TO PROSECUTE

## SECTION 1. THE DECISION TO PROSECUTE

The charging decision, made by the prosecutor except in minor cases, involves a determination of whether a person should be formally accused of a crime and thus subjected to trial if he does not first plead guilty. Although the charging decision is not inevitably so complex, it often involves these determinations: (i) whether there is sufficient evidence to support a prosecution (which, as a practical matter, the prosecutor will determine by assessing whether the likelihood of conviction is sufficiently strong to justify use of his resources to that end); (ii) if so, whether there are nonetheless reasons for not subjecting the defendant to the criminal process; and (iii) if so, whether nonprosecution should be conditioned upon the defendant's participation in a pretrial diversion program (much like probation, but without an antecedent conviction).

The American prosecutor has traditionally exercised considerable discretion in deciding whether or not to prosecute, that is, in determining whether prosecution is called for in a given case as a matter of enforcement policy. The explanations for this phenomenon most often given are (a) because of legislative "overcriminalization," (b) because of limitations in available enforcement resources; and (c) because of a need to individualize justice beyond that possible under existing crime definitions and sentencing options. This discretion is largely uncontrolled; especially when the prosecutor elects in a particular case *not* to proceed with prosecution, there is seldom available any mechanism by which any dissatisfied person may challenge that decision. When the prosecutor instead decides *in favor* of prosecution, the defendant is obviously motivated to challenge this exercise of discretion and at least sometimes may have a potential legal basis for doing so—such as that his selection for prosecution is a denial of equal protection of the laws or constitutes an impermissible "chilling" of some constitutional right (e.g., freedom of speech). But, as *Wayte v. United States* teaches, it is very difficult for a defendant to prevail in such a challenge.

## WAYTE v. UNITED STATES
470 U.S. 598, 105 S.Ct. 1524, 84 L.Ed.2d 547 (1985).

JUSTICE POWELL delivered the opinion of the Court. * * *

[A July 1980 Presidential Proclamation directed certain young male citizens to register with the Selective Service System during a specified week. Petitioner

**445**

fell within the prescribed class but did not register. Instead, he wrote letters to Government officials, including the President, stating that he had not registered and did not intend to do so. These letters were added to a Selective Service file of young men who advised that they had failed to register or who were reported by others as having failed to register. Subsequently, Selective Service adopted a policy of passive enforcement under which it would investigate and prosecute only the nonregistration cases contained in this file. In furtherance of this policy, Selective Service in June 1981 sent a letter to each reported nonregistrant warning that a failure to register could result in criminal prosecution. Petitioner received such a letter but did not respond. Thereafter, Selective Service transmitted to the Department of Justice, for investigation and potential prosecution, the names of petitioner and others identified under the passive enforcement policy. The Department of Justice, after screening out those who appeared not to be required to register, referred the remaining names to the Federal Bureau of Investigation and appropriate United States Attorneys. Petitioner's name was one of those so referred. Then, pursuant to the Department of Justice's so-called "beg" policy, whereby United States Attorneys, assisted by the FBI, made an effort to persuade nonregistrants to change their minds, the United States Attorney for petitioner's district sent him a letter urging him to register or face possible prosecution. Again petitioner failed to respond. Nor did he register during an authorized grace period or after further urging by FBI agents to do so. Accordingly, he was indicted for knowingly and willfully failing to register in violation of the Military Selective Service Act.]

On November 15, 1982, the District Court dismissed the indictment on the ground that the Government had failed to rebut petitioner's prima facie case of selective prosecution. [T]he District Court found that in order to establish a prima facie case petitioner had to prove that (i) others similarly situated generally had not been prosecuted for conduct similar to petitioner's and (ii) the Government's discriminatory selection was based on impermissible grounds such as race, religion, or exercise of First Amendment rights. Petitioner satisfied the first requirement, the District Court held, because he had shown that all those prosecuted were "vocal" nonregistrants and because "[t]he inference is strong that the Government could have located non-vocal non-registrants, but chose not to." The District Court found the second requirement satisfied for three reasons. First, the passive enforcement program was " 'inherently suspect' " because " 'it focuse[d] upon the vocal offender *  *  * [and was] vulnerable to the charge that those chosen for prosecution [were] being punished for their expression of ideas, a constitutionally protected right.' " Second, the Government's awareness that a disproportionate number of vocal nonregistrants would be prosecuted under the passive enforcement system indicated that petitioner was prosecuted because of his exercise of First Amendment rights. Finally, the involvement of high Government officials in the prosecution decisions "strongly suggest[ed] impermissible selective prosecution." The District Court then held that the Government had failed to rebut the prima facie case.

The Court of Appeals reversed. Applying the same test, it found the first requirement satisfied but not the second. The first was satisfied by petitioner's showing that out of the estimated 674,000 nonregistrants the 13 indicted had all been vocal nonregistrants. As to the second requirement the Court of Appeals held that petitioner had to show that the Government focused its investigation on him *because of* his protest activities. Petitioner's evidence, however, showed only that the Government was aware that the passive enforcement system would result in prosecutions primarily of two types of men—religious and moral objectors and vocal objectors—and that the Government recognized that the latter type would probably make claims of selective prosecution.  Finding no evidence of impermissible governmental motivation, the court held that the District Court's finding of a prima facie case of selective prosecution was clearly erroneous.  The Court of Appeals also found two legitimate explanations for the Government's passive enforcement system: (i) the identities of nonreported nonregistrants were not known, and (ii) nonregistrants who expressed their refusal to register made clear their willful violation of the law. * * *

In our criminal justice system, the Government retains "broad discretion" as to whom to prosecute.  "[S]o long as the prosecutor has probable cause to believe that the accused committed an offense defined by statute, the decision whether or not to prosecute, and what charge to file or bring before a grand jury, generally rests entirely in his discretion."  This broad discretion rests largely on the recognition that the decision to prosecute is particularly ill-suited to judicial review.  Such factors as the strength of the case, the prosecution's general deterrence value, the Government's enforcement priorities, and the case's relationship to the Government's overall enforcement plan are not readily susceptible to the kind of analysis the courts are competent to undertake.  Judicial supervision in this area, moreover, entails systemic costs of particular concern.  Examining the basis of a prosecution delays the criminal proceeding, threatens to chill law enforcement by subjecting the prosecutor's motives and decisionmaking to outside inquiry, and may undermine prosecutorial effectiveness by revealing the Government's enforcement policy.  All these are substantial concerns that make the courts properly hesitant to examine the decision whether to prosecute.

As we have noted in a slightly different context, however, although prosecutorial discretion is broad, it is not " 'unfettered.'  Selectivity in the enforcement of criminal laws is * * * subject to constitutional constraints."  In particular, the decision to prosecute may not be " 'deliberately based upon an unjustifiable standard such as race, religion, or other arbitrary classification,' " including the exercise of protected statutory and constitutional rights.

It is appropriate to judge selective prosecution claims according to ordinary equal protection standards.[9]  Under our prior cases, these standards require petitioner to show both that the passive enforcement system had a discriminatory effect and that is was motivated by a discriminatory purpose.[10]  All petitioner has shown here is that those eventually prosecuted, along with many not

9. Although the Fifth Amendment, unlike the Fourteenth, does not contain an equal protection clause, it does contain an equal protection component.  "[Our] approach to Fifth Amendment equal protection claims has * * * been precisely the same as to equal protection claims under the Fourteenth Amendment."

10. A showing of discriminatory intent is not necessary when the equal protection claim is based on an overtly discriminatory classification.  No such claim is presented here, for petitioner cannot argue that the passive policy discriminated on its face.

The dissent argues that Wayte made a nonfrivolous showing of all three elements of a prima facie case as established in the context of grand jury selection.  Neither the parties nor the courts below, however, discussed the prima facie case in these terms.  Rather, they used the phrase to refer to whether Wayte

had made a showing, which, if unrebutted, would directly establish discriminatory effect and purpose.  Even applying standards from the grand jury selection context, however, we believe that Wayte has failed to establish a prima facie case.  For example, although the dissent describes the first element as merely whether the individual "is a member of a recognizable, distinct class," it is clear for reasons we discuss that Wayte has not established the first element as actually defined by [a prior case]: whether the individual is a member of an "identifiable group" that is "a recognizable, distinct class, *singled out for different treatment under the laws, as written or as applied*." (emphasis added).  For these same reasons, we believe Wayte has failed to establish the other elements, particularly the third.  Furthermore, even assuming that Wayte did make out this kind of prima facie case, the "beg" policy would rebut it. * * *

prosecuted, reported themselves as having violated the law. He has not shown that the enforcement policy selected nonregistrants for prosecution on the basis of their speech. Indeed, he could not have done so given the way the "beg" policy was carried out. The Government did not prosecute those who reported themselves but later registered. Nor did it prosecute those who protested registration but did not report themselves or were not reported by others. In fact, the Government did not even investigate those who wrote letters to Selective Service criticizing registration unless their letters stated affirmatively that they had refused to comply with the law. The Government, on the other hand, did prosecute people who reported themselves or were reported by others but who did not publicly protest. These facts demonstrate that the Government treated all reported nonregistrants similarly. It did not subject vocal nonregistrants to any special burden. Indeed, those prosecuted in effect selected themselves for prosecution by refusing to register after being reported and warned by the Government.

Even if the passive policy had a discriminatory effect, petitioner has not shown that the Government intended such a result. The evidence he presented demonstrated only that the Government was aware that the passive enforcement policy would result in prosecution of vocal objectors and that they would probably make selective prosecution claims. As we have noted, however, " '[d]iscriminatory purpose' * * * implies more than * * * intent as awareness of consequences. It implies that the decisionmaker * * * selected or reaffirmed a particular course of action at least in part 'because of,' not merely 'in spite of,' its adverse effects upon an identifiable group." In the present case, petitioner has not shown that the Government prosecuted him *because of* his protest activities. Absent such a showing, his claim of selective prosecution fails.

Petitioner also challenges the passive enforcement policy directly on First Amendment grounds. In particular, he claims that "[e]ven though the [Government's passive] enforcement policy did not overtly punish protected speech as such, it inevitably created a content-based regulatory system with a concomitantly disparate, content-based impact on nonregistrants." This Court has held that when, as here, " 'speech' and 'nonspeech' elements are combined in the same course of conduct, a sufficiently important governmental interest in regulating the nonspeech element can justify incidental limitations on First Amendment freedoms." Government regulation is justified

> "if it is within the constitutional power of the Government; if it furthers an important or substantial governmental interest; if the governmental interest is unrelated to the suppression of free expression; and if the incidental restriction on alleged First Amendment freedoms is no greater than is essential to the furtherance of that interest."

In the present case, neither the first nor third condition is disputed.

There can be no doubt that the passive enforcement policy meets the second condition. Few interests can be more compelling than a nation's need to ensure its own security. * * * With these principles in mind, the three reasons the Government offers in defense of this particular enforcement policy are sufficiently compelling to satisfy the second requirement—as to either those who reported themselves or those who were reported by others.

First, by relying on reports of nonregistration, the Government was able to identify and prosecute violators without further delay. Although it still was necessary to investigate those reported to make sure that they were required to register and had not, the Government did not have to search actively for the names of these likely violators. Such a search would have been difficult and costly at that time. Indeed, it would be a costly step in any "active" prosecution system involving thousands of nonregistrants. The passive enforcement program thus promoted prosecutorial efficiency. Second, the letters written to Selective Service provided strong, perhaps conclusive evidence of the nonregistrant's intent not to comply—one of the elements of the offense. Third, prosecuting visible nonregistrants was thought to be an effective way to promote general deterrence, especially since failing to proceed against publicly known offenders would encourage others to violate the law.

The passive enforcement policy also meets the final requirement of the [above] test, for it placed no more limitation on speech than was necessary to ensure registration for the national defense. Passive enforcement not only did not subject "vocal" nonregistrants to any special burden, but also was intended to be only an interim enforcement system. Although Selective Service was engaged in developing an active enforcement program when it investigated petitioner, it had by then found no practicable way of obtaining the names and current addresses of likely nonregistrants. Eventually, it obtained them by matching state driver's license records with Social Security files. It took some time, however, to obtain the necessary authorizations and to set up this system. Passive enforcement was the only effective interim solution available to carry out the Government's compelling interest.

We think it important to note as a final matter how far the implications of petitioner's First Amendment argument would extend. Strictly speaking, his argument does not concern passive enforcement but self-reporting. The concerns he identifies would apply to all nonregistrants who report themselves even if the Selective Service engaged only in active enforcement. For example, a nonregistrant who wrote a letter informing Selective Service of his failure to register could, when prosecuted under an active system, claim that the Selective Service was prosecuting him only because of his "protest." Just as in this case, he could have some justification for believing that his letter had focused inquiry upon him. Prosecution in either context would equally "burden" his exercise of First Amendment rights. Under the petitioner's view, then, the Government could not constitutionally prosecute a self-reporter—even in an active enforcement system—unless perhaps it could prove that it would have prosecuted him without his letter. On principle, such a view would allow any criminal to obtain immunity from prosecution simply by reporting himself and claiming that he did so in order to "protest" the law. The First Amendment confers no such immunity from prosecution.   *   *   *

JUSTICE MARSHALL, with whom JUSTICE BRENNAN joins, dissenting.

The Court decides today that petitioner "has not shown that the Government prosecuted him *because of* his protest activities," and it remands to permit his prosecution to go forward. However interesting the question decided by the Court may be, it is not necessary to the disposition of this case. Instead, the issue this Court must grapple with is far less momentous but no less deserving of thoughtful treatment. What it must decide is whether Wayte has earned the right to discover Government documents relevant to his claim of selective prosecution.

The District Court ordered such discovery, the Government refused to comply, and the District Court dismissed the indictment. The Court of Appeals reversed on the grounds that Wayte had failed to prevail on the merits of his selective prosecution claim, and that the discovery order was improper. If Wayte is entitled to obtain evidence currently in the Government's possession, the Court cannot dismiss his claim on the basis of only the evidence now in the record. To prevail here, then, all that Wayte needs to show is that the District Court applied the correct legal standard and did not abuse its discretion in determining that he had made a nonfrivolous showing of selective prosecution entitling him to discovery. * * *

The Courts of Appeals have adopted a standard under which a defendant establishes his right to discovery if he can show that he has a "colorable basis" for a selective prosecution claim. To make this showing, a defendant must allege sufficient facts in support of his selective prosecution claim "to take the question past the frivolous state." In general, a defendant must present "some evidence tending to show the existence of the essential elements of the defense."
* * *

To evaluate the merit of Wayte's claim, I consider the elements of a *prima facie* case of selective prosecution and ascertain whether Wayte has made a nonfrivolous showing as to the existence of these elements. It is important to bear in mind at this stage that Wayte need not have made out a full *prima facie* case in order to be entitled to discovery. A *prima facie* case, of course, is one that if unrebutted will lead to a finding of selective prosecution. It shifts to the Government the burden of rebutting the presumption of unconstitutional action. But a defendant need not meet this high burden just to get discovery; the standard for discovery is merely nonfrivolousness. * * *

To make out a *prima facie* case, Wayte must show first that he is a member of a recognizable, distinct class. Second, he must show that a disproportionate number of this class was selected for investigation and possible prosecution. Third, he must show that this selection procedure was subject to abuse or was otherwise not neutral. The inquiry then is whether Wayte has presented sufficient evidence as to each of the elements to show that the claim is not frivolous.

Wayte has clearly established the first element of a *prima facie* case. The record demonstrates unequivocally that Wayte is a member of a class of vocal opponents to the Government's draft registration program. All members of that class exercised a First Amendment right to speak freely and to petition the Government for a redress of grievances, and either reported themselves or were reported by others as having failed to register for the draft.

To establish the second element, Wayte must show that the "passive" enforcement policy identified for investigation and possible prosecution a disproportionate number of vocal opponents of draft registration. The record, as it stands given the Government's refusal to comply with the District Court's discovery order, does not contain a breakdown of how many of the approximately 300 young men referred by Selective Service to the Justice Department were "vocal." However, the record suggests that responsible officials in the Justice Department were aware that the vast majority of these individuals would be vocal opponents of draft registration. * * *

Perhaps, by itself, this evidence would not suffice to establish the second element of a *prima facie* case. However, it is more than adequate to make nonfrivolous the claim that the "passive" enforcement scheme identified for possible prosecution a disproportionate number of vocal opponents of draft registration.

As to the third element, the decision to implement the "passive" enforcement system was certainly a decision susceptible to abuse. "This is indeed an exceptional area of national life where conscientious opposition to government policy has been intertwined with violations of the laws which implement the policy." The correlation between vocal opposition and violations of the law makes it relatively easy to punish speech under the guise of enforcing the laws.

Here, the enforcement scheme was implemented with full knowledge that its effects would be particularly harsh on vocal opponents of the Government's policies. Such knowledge makes the scheme directly vulnerable to the charge that its purpose was to punish individuals for the exercise of their First Amendment rights. This Court has recognized that "[a]dherence to a particular policy or practice, 'with full knowledge of the predictable effects of such adherence * * * is one factor among others which may be considered by a court'" in determining whether a decision was based on an impermissible ground.

Thus, Wayte has established the first and third elements of a *prima facie* case, and has presented a colorable claim as to the second. As a result, there can thus be no doubt that the District Court did not abuse its discretion when it found that Wayte's equal protection claim was not frivolous.

* * * The Court's analysis is flawed in two respects. First, as I have shown, the Court ignores the simple fact that, if Wayte is entitled to discovery, his claim cannot be rejected on the merits for lack of evidence.

Second, and of equal importance, the Court errs in the manner in which it analyzes the merits of the equal protection claim. It simply focuses on the wrong problem when it states that "the Government treated all reported nonregistrants similarly" and that "those prosecuted in effect selected themselves for prosecution by refusing to register after being reported and warned by the Government." Those issues are irrelevant to the correct disposition of this case.

The claim here is not that the Justice Department discriminated among *known* violators of the draft registration law either in its administration of the "beg" policy, which gave such individuals the option of registering to avoid prosecution, or in prosecuting only some reported nonregistrants. Instead, the claim is that the system by which the Department defined the class of possible prosecutees—the "passive" enforcement system—was designed to discriminate against those who had exercised their First Amendment rights. Such Governmental action cannot stand if undertaken with discriminatory intent. As this Court has clearly stated, "for an agent of the State to pursue a course of action whose objective is to penalize a person's reliance on his legal rights is 'patently unconstitutional.'" If the Government intentionally discriminated in defining the pool of potential prosecutees, it cannot immunize itself from liability merely by showing that it used permissible methods in choosing whom to prosecute from this previously tainted pool. * * *

I do not suggest that all prosecutions undertaken pursuant to passive enforcement schemes warrant evidentiary hearings on the question of selective prosecution. But where violations of the law are so closely intertwined with political activity, where the speech at issue is so unpalatable to the Government, and where the discriminatory effect is conceded, the need for a hearing is significant and in no way opens the door to an onslaught of such hearings in less compelling contexts. * * *

## SECTION 2. SELECTION OF THE CHARGE

If the prosecutor has decided upon prosecution, there often remains the question of what the charge should be. Sometimes this is simply a matter of whether the charge should be of a greater or lesser crime—for example, felony burglary versus misdemeanor breaking and entering. On other occasions, the prosecutor must determine whether to charge the defendant with more than one offense, either because the defendant has committed a series of offenses (e.g., a number of burglaries) over time or because the defendant violated more than one statute during a single course of conduct. In this third situation, the defendant's challenge, as in *United States v. Batchelder,* may be grounded primarily in the contention that the applicable statutes improperly overlap. More generally, as in the second case in this section, *United States v. Goodwin,* a defendant might challenge the prosecutor's charge selection decision on the ground of actual or apparent vindictiveness.

## UNITED STATES v. BATCHELDER
442 U.S. 114, 99 S.Ct. 2198, 60 L.Ed.2d 755 (1979).

JUSTICE MARSHALL delivered the opinion of the Court.

At issue in this case are two overlapping provisions of the Omnibus Crime Control and Safe Streets Act of 1968 (the Omnibus Act). Both prohibit convicted felons from receiving firearms, but each authorizes different maximum penalties. We must determine whether a defendant convicted of the offense carrying the greater penalty may be sentenced only under the more lenient provision when his conduct violates both statutes.

Respondent, a previously convicted felon, was found guilty of receiving a firearm that had traveled in interstate commerce, in violation of 18 U.S.C. § 922(h).[2] The District Court sentenced him under 18 U.S.C. § 924(a) to five years' imprisonment, the maximum term authorized for violation of § 922(h).

The Court of Appeals affirmed the conviction but, by a divided vote, remanded for resentencing. The majority recognized that respondent had been indicted and convicted under § 922(h) and that § 924(a) permits five years' imprisonment for such violations. However, noting that the substantive elements of § 922(h) and 18 U.S.C.App. § 1202(a) are identical as applied to a convicted felon who unlawfully receives a firearm, the court interpreted the Omnibus Act to allow no more than the two-year maximum sentence provided by § 1202(a).[4]  *  *  *

**2.** In pertinent part, 18 U.S.C. § 922(h) provides:

"It shall be unlawful for any person—

"(1) who is under indictment for, or who has been convicted in any court of, a crime punishable by imprisonment for a term exceeding one year;

"(2) who is a fugitive from justice;

"(3) who is an unlawful user of or addicted to marihuana or any depressant or stimulant drug * * * or narcotic drug * * *; or

"(4) who has been adjudicated as a mental defective or who has been committed to any mental institution;

"to receive any firearm or ammunition which has been shipped or transported in interstate or foreign commerce."

**4.** Section 1202(a) states:

"Any person who—

"(1) has been convicted by a court of the United States or of a State or any political subdivision thereof of a felony, or

"(2) has been discharged from the Armed Forces under dishonorable conditions, or

"(3) has been adjudged by a court of the United States or of a State or any political subdivision thereof of being mentally incompetent, or

"(4) having been a citizen of the United States has renounced his citizenship, or

"(5) being an alien is illegally or unlawfully in the United States,

"and who receives, possesses, or transports in commerce or affecting commerce, after the date of enactment of this Act, any firearm shall be fined not more than $10,000 or imprisoned for not more than two years, or both." 18 U.S.C.App. § 1202(a).

This Court has previously noted the partial redundancy of §§ 922(h) and 1202(a), both as to the conduct they proscribe and the individuals they reach. However, we find nothing in the language structure or legislative history of the Omnibus Act to suggest that because of this overlap, a defendant convicted under § 922(h) may be imprisoned for no more than the maximum term specified in § 1202(a). As we read the Act, each substantive statute, in conjunction with its own sentencing provision, operates independently of the other.

\*   \*   \*

In resolving the statutory question, the majority below expressed "serious doubts about the constitutionality of two statutes that provide different penalties for identical conduct." Specifically, the court suggested that the statutes might (1) be void for vagueness, (2) implicate "due process and equal protection interest[s] in avoiding excessive prosecutorial discretion and in obtaining equal justice," and (3) constitute an impermissible delegation of congressional authority. We find no constitutional infirmities.

It is a fundamental tenet of due process that "[n]o one may be required at peril of life, liberty or property to speculate as to the meaning of penal statutes." A criminal statute is therefore invalid if it "fails to give a person of ordinary intelligence fair notice that his contemplated conduct is forbidden." So too, vague sentencing provisions may pose constitutional questions if they do not state with sufficient clarity the consequences of violating a given criminal statute.

The provisions in issue here, however, unambiguously specify the activity proscribed and the penalties available upon conviction. That this particular conduct may violate both Titles does not detract from the notice afforded by each. Although the statutes create uncertainty as to which crime may be charged and therefore what penalties may be imposed, they do so to no greater extent than would a single statute authorizing various alternative punishments. So long as overlapping criminal provisions clearly define the conduct prohibited and the punishment authorized, the notice requirements of the Due Process Clause are satisfied.

This Court has long recognized that when an act violates more than one criminal statute, the Government may prosecute under either so long as it does not discriminate against any class of defendants. Whether to prosecute and what charge to file or bring before a grand jury are decisions that generally rest in the prosecutor's discretion.

The Court of Appeals acknowledged this "settled rule" allowing prosecutorial choice. Nevertheless, the court distinguished overlapping statutes with identical standards of proof from provisions that vary in some particular. In the court's view, when two statutes prohibit "exactly the same conduct," the prosecutor's "selection of which of two penalties to apply" would be "unfettered." Because such prosecutorial discretion could produce "unequal justice," the court expressed doubt that this form of legislative redundancy was constitutional. We find this analysis factually and legally unsound.

Contrary to the Court of Appeals' assertions, a prosecutor's discretion to choose between §§ 922(h) and 1202(a) is not "unfettered." Selectivity in the enforcement of criminal laws is, of course, subject to constitutional constraints.[9] And a decision to proceed under § 922(h) does not empower the Government to predetermine ultimate criminal sanctions. Rather, it merely enables the sentencing judge to impose a

---

**9.** The Equal Protection Clause prohibits selective enforcement "based upon an unjustifiable standard such as race, religion, or other arbitrary classification." Respondent does not allege that his prosecution was motivated by improper considerations.

longer prison sentence than § 1202(a) would permit and precludes him from imposing the greater fine authorized by § 1202(a). More importantly, there is no appreciable difference between the discretion a prosecutor exercises when deciding whether to charge under one of two statutes with different elements and the discretion he exercises when choosing one of two statutes with identical elements. In the former situation, once he determines that the proof will support conviction under either statute, his decision is indistinguishable from the one he faces in the latter context. The prosecutor may be influenced by the penalties available upon conviction, but this fact standing alone does not give rise to a violation of the Equal Protection or Due Process Clauses. Just as a defendant has no constitutional right to elect which of two applicable federal statutes shall be the basis of his indictment and prosecution neither is he entitled to choose the penalty scheme under which he will be sentenced.

Approaching the problem of prosecutorial discretion from a slightly different perspective, the Court of Appeals postulated that the statutes might impermissibly delegate to the Executive Branch the legislature's responsibility to fix criminal penalties. We do not agree. The provisions at issue plainly demarcate the range of penalties that prosecutors and judges may seek and impose. In light of that specificity, the power that Congress has delegated to those officials is no broader than the authority they routinely exercise in enforcing the criminal laws. Having informed the courts, prosecutors and defendants of the permissible punishment alternatives available under each Title, Congress has fulfilled its duty.

Accordingly, the judgment of the Court of Appeals is reversed.

## UNITED STATES v. GOODWIN

457 U.S. 368, 102 S.Ct. 2485, 73 L.Ed.2d 74 (1982).

JUSTICE STEVENS delivered the opinion of the Court. * * *

Respondent Goodwin was stopped for speeding by a United States Park Policeman on the Baltimore–Washington Parkway. Goodwin emerged from his car to talk to the policeman. After a brief discussion, the officer noticed a clear plastic bag underneath the armrest next to the driver's seat of Goodwin's car. The officer asked Goodwin to return to his car and to raise the armrest. Respondent did so, but as he raised the armrest he placed the car into gear and accelerated rapidly. The car struck the officer, knocking him first onto the back of the car and then onto the highway. The policeman returned to his car, but Goodwin eluded him in a highspeed chase.

The following day, the officer filed a complaint in the District Court charging respondent with several misdemeanor and petty offenses, including assault. Goodwin was arrested and arraigned before a United States Magistrate. The Magistrate set a date for trial, but respondent fled the jurisdiction. Three years later Goodwin was found in custody in Virginia and was returned to Maryland.

Upon his return, respondent's case was assigned to an attorney from the Department of Justice, who was detailed temporarily to try petty crime and misdemeanor cases before the Magistrate. The attorney did not have authority to try felony cases or to seek indictments from the grand jury. Respondent initiated plea negotiations with the prosecutor, but later advised the Government that he did not wish to plead guilty and desired a trial by jury in the District Court.[1]

The case was transferred to the District Court and responsibility for the prosecution was assumed by an Assistant United States Attorney. Approximately six weeks later, after reviewing the case and discussing it with several parties, the prosecutor obtained a four-count indictment charging respondent with one felony count of forcibly assaulting a federal officer and three related counts arising from the same incident.[2] A jury convicted respondent on the felony count and on one misdemeanor count.

Respondent moved to set aside the verdict on the ground of prosecutorial vindictiveness, contending that the indictment on the felony charge gave rise to an impermissible appearance of retaliation. The District Court denied the motion, finding that "the prosecutor in this case has adequately dispelled any appearance of retaliatory intent."

Although the Court of Appeals readily concluded that "the prosecutor did not act with actual vindictiveness in seeking a felony indictment," it nevertheless reversed. Relying on our decisions in *North Carolina v. Pearce,* [395 U.S. 711 (1969) ], and *Blackledge v. Perry,* [417 U.S. 21 (1974) ], the court held that the Due Process Clause of the Fifth Amendment prohibits the Government from bringing more serious charges against a defendant after he has invoked his right to a jury trial, unless the prosecutor comes forward with objective evidence to show that the increased charges could not have been brought before the defendant exercised his rights. Because the court believed that the circumstances surrounding the felony indictment gave rise to a genuine risk of retaliation, it adopted a legal presumption designed to spare courts the "unseemly task" of probing the actual motives of the prosecutor. * * *

In *North Carolina v. Pearce,* the Court held that neither the Double Jeopardy Clause nor the Equal Protection Clause prohibits a trial judge from imposing a harsher sentence on retrial after a criminal defendant successfully attacks an initial conviction on appeal. The Court stated, however, that "[i]t can hardly be doubted that it would be a flagrant violation [of the Due Process Clause] of the Fourteenth Amendment for a state trial court to follow an announced practice of imposing a heavier sentence upon every reconvicted defendant for the explicit purpose of punishing the defendant for his having succeeded in getting his original conviction set aside." The Court continued:

> "Due process of law, then, requires that vindictiveness against a defendant for having successfully attacked his first conviction must play no part in the sentence he receives after a new trial. And since the fear of such vindictiveness may unconstitutionally deter a defendant's exercise of the right to appeal or collaterally attack his first conviction, due process also requires that a defendant be freed of apprehension of such a retaliatory motivation on the part of the sentencing judge."

In order to assure the absence of such a motivation, the Court concluded:

1. At that time, there was no statutory provision allowing a trial by jury before a magistrate.

2. By affidavit, the Assistant United States Attorney later set forth his reasons for this action:

(1) he considered respondent's conduct on the date in question to be a serious violation of law, (2) respondent had a lengthy history of violent crime, (3) the prosecutor consid-ered respondent's conduct to be related to major narcotics transactions, (4) the prosecutor believed that respondent had committed perjury at his preliminary hearing, and (5) respondent had failed to appear for trial as originally scheduled. The Government attorney stated that his decision to seek a felony indictment was not motivated in any way by Goodwin's request for a jury trial in District Court.

"[W]henever a judge imposes a more severe sentence upon a defendant after a new trial, the reasons for his doing so must affirmatively appear. Those reasons must be based upon objective information concerning identifiable conduct on the part of the defendant occurring after the time of the original sentencing proceeding. And the factual data upon which the increased sentence is based must be made part of the record, so that the constitutional legitimacy of the increased sentence may be fully reviewed on appeal."

In sum, the Court applied a presumption of vindictiveness, which may be overcome only by objective information in the record justifying the increased sentence.[a]

In *Blackledge v. Perry,* the Court confronted the problem of increased punishment upon retrial after appeal in a setting different from that considered in *Pearce.* Perry was convicted of assault in an inferior court having exclusive jurisdiction for the trial of misdemeanors. The court imposed a 6-month sentence. Under North Carolina law, Perry had an absolute right to a trial *de novo* in the Superior Court, which possessed felony jurisdiction. After Perry filed his notice of appeal, the prosecutor obtained a felony indictment charging him with assault with a deadly weapon. Perry pleaded guilty to the felony and was sentenced to a term of five to seven years in prison.

In reviewing Perry's felony conviction and increased sentence, this Court first stated the essence of the holdings in *Pearce* and the cases that had followed it:

"The lesson that emerges from *Pearce* is that the Due Process Clause is not offended by all possibilities of increased punishment upon retrial after appeal, but only by those that pose a realistic likelihood of 'vindictiveness.' "

The Court held that the opportunities for vindictiveness in the situation before it were such "as to impel the conclusion that due process of law requires a rule analogous to that of the *Pearce* case." It explained:

"A prosecutor clearly has a considerable stake in discouraging convicted misdemeanants from appealing and thus obtaining a trial *de novo* in the Superior Court, since such an appeal will clearly require increased expenditures of prosecutorial resources before the defendant's conviction becomes

**a.** Stating that "the reach of *Pearce* is best captured" by this sentence, the Court in *Texas v. McCullough,* 475 U.S. 134 (1986), said of the above quotation from *Pearce:* "This language, however, was never intended to describe exhaustively all of the possible circumstances in which a sentence increase could be justified. Restricting justifications for a sentence increase to *only* 'events that occurred subsequent to the original sentencing proceedings' could in some circumstances lead to absurd results. The Solicitor General provides the following hypothetical example:

'Suppose * * * that a defendant is convicted of burglary, a non-violent, and apparently first, offense. He is sentenced to a short prison term or perhaps placed on probation. Following a successful appeal and a conviction on retrial, it is learned that the defendant has been using an alias and in fact has a long criminal record that includes other burglaries, several armed robbery convictions, and a conviction for murder committed in the course of a burglary. None of

the reasons underlying *Pearce* in any way justifies the perverse result that the defendant receive no greater sentence in light of this information than he originally received when he was thought to be a first offender.'

We agree with the Solicitor General and find nothing in *Pearce* that would require such a bizarre conclusion."

Marshall, J., joined by Blackmun and Stevens, JJ., dissenting, objected: "There is neither any reason nor any need for us to believe that dishonest and unconstitutionally vindictive judges actually hold sway in American courtrooms * * *. The message of *Pearce* is that the fear of such vindictiveness is real enough. And a defendant plagued by such an apprehension is likely to take small comfort in any presumption of vindictiveness established for his benefit if the means of rebutting that presumption will always be within the easy reach of the judge who will sentence him should the challenge to his conviction prove unsuccessful."

final, and may even result in a formerly convicted defendant's going free. And, if the prosecutor has the means readily at hand to discourage such appeals—by 'upping the ante' through a felony indictment whenever a convicted misdemeanant pursues his statutory appellate remedy—the State can insure that only the most hardy defendants will brave the hazards of a *de novo* trial."

The Court emphasized in *Blackledge* that it did not matter that no evidence was present that the prosecutor had acted in bad faith or with malice in seeking the felony indictment. As in *Pearce,* the Court held that the likelihood of vindictiveness justified a presumption that would free defendants of apprehension of such a retaliatory motivation on the part of the prosecutor.[8] * * *

In *Bordenkircher v. Hayes* [Ch. 14, § 1], the Court for the first time considered an allegation of vindictiveness that arose in a pretrial setting. In that case the Court held that the Due Process Clause of the Fourteenth Amendment did not prohibit a prosecutor from carrying out a threat, made during plea negotiations, to bring additional charges against an accused who refused to plead guilty to the offense with which he was originally charged. * * *

The outcome in *Bordenkircher* was mandated by this Court's acceptance of plea negotiation as a legitimate process. In declining to apply a presumption of vindictiveness, the Court recognized that "additional" charges obtained by a prosecutor could not necessarily be characterized as an impermissible "penalty." Since charges brought in an original indictment may be abandoned by the prosecutor in the course of plea negotiation—in often what is clearly a "benefit" to the defendant—changes in the charging decision that occur in the context of plea negotiation are an inaccurate measure of improper prosecutorial "vindictiveness." An initial indictment—from which the prosecutor embarks on a course of plea negotiation—does not necessarily define the extent of the legitimate interest in prosecution. For just as a prosecutor may forgo legitimate charges already brought in an effort to save the time and expense of trial, a prosecutor may file additional charges if an initial expectation that a defendant would plead guilty to lesser charges proves unfounded.

This case, like *Bordenkircher,* arises from a pretrial decision to modify the charges against the defendant. Unlike *Bordenkircher,* however, there is no evidence in this case that could give rise to a claim of *actual* vindictiveness; the prosecutor never suggested that the charge was brought to influence the respondent's conduct. The conviction in this case may be reversed only if a *presumption* of vindictiveness—applicable in all cases—is warranted.

There is good reason to be cautious before adopting an inflexible presumption of prosecutorial vindictiveness in a pretrial setting. In the course of preparing a case for trial, the prosecutor may uncover additional information that suggests a basis for further prosecution or he simply may come to realize that information possessed by the State has a broader significance. At this stage of the proceedings, the prosecutor's assessment of the proper extent of prosecution may not have crystallized. In contrast, once a trial begins—and certainly by the time a conviction has been obtained—it is much more likely that the State has discovered and assessed all of the information against an accused and has made a determination, on the basis of that information, of the extent to which he should be prosecuted. Thus, a change in the charging decision made

**8.** The presumption again could be overcome by objective evidence justifying the prosecutor's action. The Court noted: "This would clearly be a different case if the State had shown that it was impossible to proceed on the more serious charge at the outset."

after an initial trial is completed is much more likely to be improperly motivated than is a pretrial decision.

In addition, a defendant before trial is expected to invoke procedural rights that inevitably impose some "burden" on the prosecutor. Defense counsel routinely file pretrial motions to suppress evidence; to challenge the sufficiency and form of an indictment; to plead an affirmative defense; to request psychiatric services; to obtain access to government files; to be tried by jury. It is unrealistic to assume that a prosecutor's probable response to such motions is to seek to penalize and to deter. The invocation of procedural rights is an integral part of the adversary process in which our criminal justice system operates.

Thus, the timing of the prosecutor's action in this case suggests that a presumption of vindictiveness is not warranted. A prosecutor should remain free before trial to exercise the broad discretion entrusted to him to determine the extent of the societal interest in prosecution. An initial decision should not freeze future conduct. As we made clear in *Bordenkircher,* the initial charges filed by a prosecutor may not reflect the extent to which an individual is legitimately subject to prosecution.

The nature of the right asserted by the respondent confirms that a presumption of vindictiveness is not warranted in this case. After initially expressing an interest in plea negotiation, respondent decided not to plead guilty and requested a trial by jury in District Court. In doing so, he forced the Government to bear the burdens and uncertainty of a trial. This Court in *Bordenkircher* made clear that the mere fact that a defendant refuses to plead guilty and forces the government to prove its case is insufficient to warrant a presumption that subsequent changes in the charging decision are unjustified. Respondent argues that such a presumption is warranted in this case, however, because he not only requested a trial—he requested a trial by jury.

We cannot agree. The distinction between a bench trial and a jury trial does not compel a special presumption of prosecutorial vindictiveness whenever additional charges are brought after a jury is demanded. To be sure, a jury trial is more burdensome than a bench trial. The defendant may challenge the selection of the venire; the jury itself must be impaneled; witnesses and arguments must be prepared more carefully to avoid the danger of a mistrial. These matters are much less significant, however, than the facts that before either a jury or a judge the State must present its full case against the accused and the defendant is entitled to offer a full defense. As compared to the complete trial *de novo* at issue in *Blackledge,* a jury trial—as opposed to a bench trial—does not require duplicative expenditures of prosecutorial resources before a final judgment may be obtained. Moreover, unlike the trial judge in *Pearce,* no party is asked "to do over what it thought it had already done correctly." A prosecutor has no "personal stake" in a bench trial and thus no reason to engage in "self-vindication" upon a defendant's request for a jury trial. Perhaps most importantly, the institutional bias against the retrial of a decided question that supported the decisions in *Pearce* and *Blackledge* simply has no counterpart in this case.

There is an opportunity for vindictiveness, [but] a mere opportunity for vindictiveness is insufficient to justify the imposition of a prophylactic rule. As *Blackledge* makes clear, "the Due Process Clause is not offended by all possibilities of increased punishment * * * but only by those that pose a realistic likelihood of 'vindictiveness.'" The possibility that a prosecutor would respond to a defendant's pretrial demand for a jury trial by bringing charges not in the public interest that could be explained only as a penalty imposed on the defendant is so *unlikely* that a presumption of vindictiveness certainly is not warranted.

In declining to apply a presumption of vindictiveness, we of course do not foreclose the possibility that a defendant in an appropriate case might prove objectively that the prosecutor's charging decision was motivated by a desire to punish him for doing something that the law plainly allowed him to do. * * *

JUSTICE BLACKMUN, concurring in the judgment.

* * * I find no support in our prior cases for any distinction between pretrial and post-trial vindictiveness. * * *

[T]he Due Process Clause does not deprive a prosecutor of the flexibility to add charges after a defendant has decided not to plead guilty and has elected a jury trial in District Court—so long as the adjustment is based on "objective information concerning identifiable conduct on the part of the defendant occurring after the time of the original" charging decision. In addition, I believe that the prosecutor adequately explains an increased charge by pointing to objective information that he could not reasonably have been aware of at the time charges were initially filed.

Because I find that the Assistant United States Attorney's explanation for seeking a felony indictment satisfies these standards, I conclude that the Government has dispelled the appearance of vindictiveness and, therefore, that the imposition of additional charges did not violate respondent's due process rights. Accordingly, I concur in the judgment.

JUSTICE BRENNAN, with whom JUSTICE MARSHALL joins, dissenting. * * *

The Court suggests that the distinction between a bench trial and a jury trial is unimportant in this context. Such a suggestion is demonstrably fallacious. Experienced criminal practitioners, for both prosecution and defense, know that a jury trial entails far more prosecutorial work than a bench trial. Defense challenges to the potential-juror array, *voir dire* examination of potential jurors, and suppression hearings all take up a prosecutor's time before a jury trial, adding to his scheduling difficulties and caseload. More care in the preparation of his requested instructions, of his witnesses, and of his own remarks is necessary in order to avoid mistrial or reversible error. And there is always the specter of the "irrational" acquittal by a jury that is unreviewable on appeal. Thus it is simply inconceivable that a criminal defendant's election to be tried by jury would be a matter of indifference to his prosecutor. On the contrary, the prosecutor would almost always prefer that the defendant waive such a "troublesome" right. And if the defendant refuses to do so, the prosecutor's subsequent elevation of the charges against the defendant manifestly poses a realistic likelihood of vindictiveness. * * *

# Chapter 11

# SCREENING THE PROSECUTOR'S DECISION TO CHARGE

An innocent individual subjected to a trial pays a substantial price even though acquitted. Being accused of a serious crime creates a blot on one's reputation that may not be fully erased by an acquittal. Even where the acquittal does provide full vindication, it does not remedy other burdens borne in the course of gaining that vindication. Once accused, a defendant must await trial, a process that brings with it a degree of anxiety and insecurity that often disrupts the flow of daily life. The trial itself is even more of an ordeal and carries with it a significant expense. In light of these burdens, it is not surprising that a criminal justice process concerned with the protection of the innocent will incorporate safeguards that go beyond ensuring against erroneous convictions and seek also to ensure that unfounded charges are not brought against the innocent. A major element of such protection comes from the requirement that the prosecution's decision to charge be reviewed by some neutral agency. That agency generally is either the grand jury that "screens" the prosecution's case in deciding whether to indict or the magistrate who must determine at a preliminary hearing whether a charge has sufficient support to be sent forward to the next step in the process.[a]

The Fifth Amendment provides that, except in certain military cases, "no person shall be held to answer for a capital, or otherwise infamous offense, unless on presentment or indictment of a Grand Jury." It thus guarantees to any potential defendant in a federal criminal case involving an "infamous offense" (held to encompass all felony offenses) that no charge will be brought against him without the concurrence of a group of his peers, as expressed in the decision of the grand jury to issue an indictment. (The alternative form of accusation, the presentment, which was issued at the grand jury's own initiative, is no longer used). In requiring prosecution by indictment, the Fifth Amendment interposes the grand jury between the prosecutor and the prospective defendant and casts upon it a "shielding" function. The classic description of that function is found in *Wood v. Georgia*, 370 U.S. 375 (1962):

> "Historically, this body [the grand jury] has been regarded as a primary security to the innocent against hasty, malicious and oppressive prosecution; it serves the invaluable function in our society of standing between the accuser and the accused, whether the latter be an individual, minority

---

**a.** These screening procedures are briefly described in Ch. 1, § 1 at steps 10 and 11. As noted there, they are utilized in most jurisdictions only for felony charges. Neither is required for misdemeanors.

460

group, or other, to determine whether a charge is founded upon reason or was dictated by an intimidating power or by malice and personal ill will."

At the time of the adoption of the Fifth Amendment, all of the states also required that felony prosecutions be brought by indictment. In the mid-1800's, however, several of the newer states shifted from prosecution by grand jury indictment to prosecution by an information (an accusation issued by the prosecutor, rather than the grand jury). To ensure independent screening, those states restricted use of the information to cases in which the magistrate made a finding of probable cause in support of the information at a preliminary hearing. In *Hurtado v. California*, 110 U.S. 516 (1884), that procedure was sustained against constitutional challenge. The Supreme Court there held that the guarantee of prosecution by grand jury indictment, though found in the Fifth Amendment, did not reflect a "fundamental principle of liberty and justice" and therefore was not applicable to the states under the due process clause of the Fourteenth Amendment. Although the Supreme Court, with the adoption in the 1960's of a different view of the Fourteenth Amendment generally overruled its earlier decisions that had refused to find in due process a right specified in the Bill of Rights (see Ch. 2, § 1), the *Hurtado* ruling provided the one major exception to that pattern. The Court has continued to hold that the states need not prosecute by indictment, and today only about twenty states still require grand jury review.[b] In the remaining states, the prosecution may proceed by indictment or information, and most prosecutors in those states proceed by information in most cases.

In the vast majority of the states allowing prosecution by information at the prosecutor's discretion, the information can be filed only if there has been a determination of probable cause by a magistrate at a preliminary hearing.[c] Defense counsel generally view this requirement as providing a more favorable screening process than the grand jury because the preliminary hearing is an adversary proceeding at which the defense may cross-examine the prosecution's witnesses and present its own evidence. This stands in contrast to the secret and non-adversary grand jury proceeding, in which only the prosecution participates, presenting its side of the case and serving as the legal advisor to the lay jurors. The preliminary hearing also may provide the defense with other procedural advantages, as noted in *Coleman v. Alabama*, infra.

In a few of the states allowing prosecution by information, the prosecution has available the option of direct filing of the information without a preliminary hearing. Because the practice upheld in *Hurtado* required a preliminary hearing, it was not clear from that case whether due process permitted a state to utilize an accusatory process in a felony case that dispensed with any form of screening procedure by a neutral agency. That issue was presented in *Lem*

**b.** These jurisdictions commonly allow for defense waiver of the indictment, so a felony prosecution can be brought by information in such states when the defendant makes a proper waiver of his right to grand jury review.

**c.** These jurisdictions also allow for defense waiver of the preliminary hearing, so a felony information can be filed without a magistrate's probable cause determination when there has been a waiver.

Jurisdictions requiring prosecution by indictment also provide for a preliminary hearing in felony cases within a specified period after arrest, but that hearing will not be held if an indictment is obtained prior to the scheduled date of hearing. The indictment establishes probable cause as found by the grand jury, and since the grand jury finding prevails over any determination to the contrary that the magistrate might make, there is no need for the preliminary hearing. In some indictment jurisdictions, it is common for prosecutors to "bypass" the preliminary hearing by first obtaining an indictment, while the practice in other indictment jurisdictions is to have a prompt preliminary hearing followed by the taking of the case to the grand jury. The latter practice was followed in *Coleman v. Alabama*, infra.

*Woon v. Oregon,* 229 U.S. 586 (1913), which presented a challenge to the direct filing of an information without "any examination, or commitment by a magistrate * * * or any verification other than [the prosecutor's] official oath." Relying on the fundamental fairness analysis of *Hurtado,* the Court in *Lem Woon* sustained the state's direct filing procedure. It noted:

> "[T]his court has * * * held [that] the 'due process of law' clause does not require the State to adopt the institution and procedure of a grand jury, [and] we are unable to see upon what theory it can be held that an examination or the opportunity for one, prior to the formal accusation by the district attorney, is obligatory upon the States."

Although the Supreme Court subsequently held in *Gerstein v. Pugh,* 420 U.S. 103 (1975), that the Fourth Amendment requires a magistrate's ex parte determination of probable cause (as in the issuance of an arrest warrant) where there is "extended restraint of liberty following arrest" (see fn. a to *Watson* in Ch. 4, § 4), the opinion there reaffirmed the holding in *Lem Woon* "that a judicial hearing is not a prerequisite to prosecution by information." The Constitution does not require the state to provide "judicial oversight or review [as in a preliminary hearing] of the decision to prosecute." *Gerstein.*

While states are not constitutionally required to provide for screening by either the grand jury or the preliminary hearing, once they do afford such screening, constitutional limitations may apply. The first two cases in this chapter, *Coleman v. Alabama* and *Vasquez v. Hillery,* treat the two major constitutional limitations applicable to the preliminary hearing (*Coleman*) and the grand jury (*Hillery*). Those cases also raise the question of whether a conviction should be reversed where there was constitutional error in the screening process but the defendant was then found guilty after a trial that complied in all respects with constitutional requirements.[d]

In federal prosecutions, of course, the Fifth Amendment requires prosecution by grand jury indictment. The third case in the chapter, *Costello v. United States,* raises the question of whether the Fifth Amendment requires that the grand jury's decision to indict be based on evidence that would be admissible at trial. Following *Costello,* the Supreme Court indicated in a series of cases that the rationale of *Costello* was also applicable to grand jury consideration of evidence that would be inadmissible at trial because obtained in violation of the federal constitution. In the latest of those Supreme Court rulings, *United States v. Calandra,* 414 U.S. 338 (1974), holding that a grand jury witness could not

---

**d.** The issue posed in this regard relates to applicability of the constitutional "harmless error" doctrine set forth in *Chapman v. California,* 386 U.S. 18 (1967). Prior to *Chapman,* it frequently had been assumed that all constitutional errors automatically required reversal of a conviction on appeal because such errors were "per se injurious." *Chapman* held, however, that constitutional errors were not exempted from the usual rule of appellate review that requires affirmance where the error in prior proceedings is deemed "harmless" (see Ch. 1, § 1, at step 17). The Court reasoned that this "harmless error" principle served a "very useful purpose insofar as * * * [it] block[s] setting aside convictions for small errors or defects that have little, if any likelihood of having changed the result of the trial." Accordingly, as to most constitutional errors, reversal of a conviction would not be required where the state could establish that that error was in fact harmless. This required the state to "prove beyond a reasonable doubt that the error * * * did not contribute to the verdict obtained." The Court added, however, that "there are some constitutional rights so basic to a fair trial that their infraction can never be treated as harmless error." Cited as illustrations of such errors (calling for automatic reversal) were the admission in evidence of a coerced confession (see Ch. 6, § 1), the states failure to provide appointed counsel at trial as required under the Sixth Amendment (see Ch. 5, § 1), and a due process violation resulting from the possible bias of a trial judge whose fees were derived from the fines he imposed (see *Tumey v. Ohio,* described in the *Hillery* opinion).

refuse to answer questions based on information obtained through an unconstitutional search, the Court noted:

> "The grand jury's sources of information are widely drawn and the validity of an indictment is not affected by the character of the evidence considered. Thus, an indictment valid on its face is not subject to challenge on the ground that the grand jury acted on the basis of inadequate or incompetent evidence, *Costello v. United States;* or even on the basis of information obtained in violation of a defendant's Fifth Amendment privilege against self-incrimination."

## COLEMAN v. ALABAMA
### 399 U.S. 1, 90 S.Ct. 1999, 26 L.Ed.2d 387 (1970).

JUSTICE BRENNAN announced the judgment of the Court and delivered the following opinion.

Petitioners were convicted in an Alabama Circuit Court of assault with intent to murder in the shooting of one Reynolds after he and his wife parked their car on an Alabama highway to change a flat tire. The Alabama Court of Appeals affirmed, and the Alabama Supreme Court denied review. We vacate and remand.

Petitioners * * * argue that the preliminary hearing prior to their indictment was a "critical stage" of the prosecution and that Alabama's failure to provide them with appointed counsel at the hearing therefore unconstitutionally denied them the assistance of counsel. * * *

### II [2]

This Court has held that a person accused of crime "requires the guiding hand of counsel at every step in the proceedings against him," *Powell v. Alabama* [Ch. 5, § 1], and that that constitutional principle is not limited to the presence of counsel at trial. "It is central to that principle that in addition to counsel's presence at trial, the accused is guaranteed that he need not stand alone against the State at any stage of the prosecution, formal or informal, in court or out, where counsel's absence might derogate from the accused's right to a fair trial." *United States v. Wade* [Ch. 7, § 1]. Accordingly, "the principle of *Powell v. Alabama* and succeeding cases requires that we scrutinize *any* pretrial confrontation of the accused to determine whether the presence of his counsel is necessary to preserve the defendant's basic right to a fair trial as affected by his right meaningfully to cross-examine the witnesses against him and to have effective assistance of counsel at the trial itself. It calls upon us to analyze whether potential substantial prejudice to defendant's rights inheres in the particular confrontation and the ability of counsel to help avoid that prejudice."

Applying this test, the Court has held that "critical stages" include the pretrial type of arraignment where certain rights may be sacrificed or lost, *Hamilton v. Alabama*, 368 U.S. 52 (1961), and the pretrial lineup, *United States v. Wade.* Cf. *Miranda v. Arizona*, where the Court held that the privilege against compulsory self-incrimination includes a right to counsel at a pretrial custodial interrogation.

The preliminary hearing is not a required step in an Alabama prosecution. The prosecutor may seek an indictment directly from the grand jury without a preliminary hearing. The opinion of the Alabama Court of Appeals in this case

---

**2.** Justice Douglas, Justice White, and Justice Marshall join this Part II.

instructs us that under Alabama law the sole purposes of a preliminary hearing are to determine whether there is sufficient evidence against the accused to warrant presenting his case to the grand jury, and if so to fix bail if the offense is bailable. See Code of Alabama, Tit. 15, §§ 139, 140, 151. The court continued:

"At the preliminary hearing * * * the accused is not required to advance any defenses, and failure to do so does not preclude him from availing himself of every defense he may have upon the trial of the case. Also *Pointer v. Texas,* 380 U.S. 400 (1965), bars the admission of testimony given at a pre-trial proceeding where the accused did not have the benefit of cross-examination by and through counsel. Thus, nothing occurring at the preliminary hearing in the absence of counsel can substantially prejudice the rights of the accused on trial."

This Court is of course bound by this construction of the governing Alabama law. However, from the fact that in cases where the accused has no lawyer at the hearing the Alabama courts prohibit the State's use at trial of anything that occurred at the hearing, it does not follow that the Alabama preliminary hearing is not a "critical stage" of the State's criminal process. The determination whether the hearing is a "critical stage" requiring the provision of counsel depends, as noted, upon an analysis "whether potential substantial prejudice to defendant's rights inheres in the * * * confrontation and the ability of counsel to help avoid that prejudice." *United States v. Wade.* Plainly the guiding hand of counsel at the preliminary hearing is essential to protect the indigent accused against an erroneous or improper prosecution. First, the lawyer's skilled examination and cross-examination of witnesses may expose fatal weaknesses in the State's case, that may lead the magistrate to refuse to bind the accused over. Second, in any event, the skilled interrogation of witnesses by an experienced lawyer can fashion a vital impeachment tool for use in cross-examination of the State's witnesses at the trial, or preserve testimony favorable to the accused of a witness who does not appear at the trial. Third, trained counsel can more effectively discover the case the State has against his client and make possible the preparation of a proper defense to meet that case at the trial. Fourth, counsel can also be influential at the preliminary hearing in making effective arguments for the accused on such matters as the necessity for an early psychiatric examination or bail. The inability of the indigent accused on his own to realize these advantages of a lawyer's assistance compels the conclusion that the Alabama preliminary hearing is a "critical stage" of the State's criminal process at which the accused is "as much entitled to such aid [of counsel] * * * as at the trial itself." *Powell v. Alabama.*

### III [4]

There remains, then, the question of the relief to which petitioners are entitled. The trial transcript indicates that the prohibition against use by the State at trial of anything that occurred at the preliminary hearing was scrupulously observed. But on the record it cannot be said whether or not petitioners were otherwise prejudiced by the absence of counsel at the preliminary hearing. That inquiry in the first instance should more properly be made by the Alabama courts. The test to be applied is whether the denial of counsel at the preliminary hearing was harmless error under *Chapman v. California* [fn. d of introduction]. We accordingly vacate the petitioners' convictions and remand the case to the Alabama courts for such proceedings not inconsistent with this opinion as they may deem appropriate to determine whether such denial of counsel was

4. Justice Black, Justice Douglas, Justice White, and Justice Marshall join this Part III.

harmless error, and therefore whether the convictions should be reinstated or a new trial ordered.

JUSTICE BLACK, concurring.

I wholeheartedly agree with the Court's holding in Part II of its opinion that an accused has a constitutional right to the assistance of counsel at the preliminary hearing which Alabama grants criminal defendants. * * * The preliminary hearing is * * * a definite part or stage of a criminal prosecution in Alabama, and the plain language of the Sixth Amendment requires that "[i]n all criminal prosecutions, the accused shall enjoy the right * * * to have the Assistance of Counsel for his defence." * * * I fear that the Court's opinion seems at times to proceed on the premise that the constitutional principle ultimately at stake here is not the defendant's right to counsel as guaranteed by the Sixth and Fourteenth Amendments but rather a right to a "fair trial" as conceived by judges. While that phrase is an appealing one, neither the Bill of Rights nor any other part of the Constitution contains it. * * *

JUSTICE DOUGLAS.

While I have joined Mr. Justice Brennan's opinion, I add a word as to why I think that a strict construction of the Constitution requires the result reached.

The critical words are "In all criminal prosecutions, the accused shall enjoy the right * * * to have the assistance of Counsel for his defence." As Mr. Justice Black states, a preliminary hearing is "a definite part or stage of a criminal prosecution in Alabama." A "criminal prosecution" certainly does not start only when the trial starts. If the commencement of the trial were the start of the "criminal prosecution" in the constitutional sense, then indigents would likely go to trial without effective representation by counsel. Lawyers for the defense need time to prepare a defense. The prosecution needs time for investigations and procedures to make that investigation timely and telling. As a shorthand expression we have used the words "critical stage" to describe whether the preliminary phase of a criminal trial was part of the "criminal prosecution" as used in the Sixth Amendment. But it is the Sixth Amendment that controls, not our own ideas as to what an efficient criminal code should provide. It did not take nearly 200 years of doubt to decide whether Alabama's preliminary hearing is a part of the "criminal prosecution" within the meaning of the Sixth Amendment. The question has never been reached prior to this case. * * * If we are to adhere to the mandate of the Constitution and not give it merely that meaning which appeals to the personal tastes of those who from time to time sit here, we should read its terms in light of the realities of what "criminal prosecutions" truly mean. * * *

JUSTICE WHITE, concurring.

I agree with Mr. Justice Harlan that recent cases furnish ample ground for holding the preliminary hearing a critical event in the progress of a criminal case. I therefore join the opinion of the Court, but with some hesitation since requiring the appointment of counsel may result in fewer preliminary hearings in jurisdictions where the prosecutor is free to avoid them by taking a case directly to a grand jury. Our ruling may also invite eliminating the preliminary hearing system entirely.

I would expect the application of the harmless-error standard on remand to produce results approximating those contemplated by Mr. Justice Harlan's separately stated views. Whether denying petitioner counsel at the preliminary hearing was harmless beyond a reasonable doubt depends upon an assessment of those factors which made the denial error. But that assessment cannot ignore the fact that petitioner has been tried and found guilty by a jury.

The possibility that counsel would have detected preclusive flaws in the State's probable cause showing is for all practical purposes mooted by the trial where the State produced evidence satisfying the jury of the petitioner's guilt beyond a reasonable doubt. Also, it would be wholly speculative in this case to assume either (1) that the State's witnesses at the trial testified inconsistently with what their testimony would have been if petitioner had had counsel to cross-examine them at the preliminary hearing, or (2) that counsel, had he been present at the hearing, would have known so much more about the State's case than he actually did when he went to trial that the result of the trial might have been different. So too it seems extremely unlikely that matters related to bail or early psychiatric examination would ever raise reasonable doubts about the integrity of the trial. There remains the possibility, as Mr. Justice Harlan suggests, that important testimony of witnesses unavailable at the trial could have been preserved had counsel been present to cross-examine opposing witnesses or to examine witnesses for the defense. If such was the case, petitioner would be entitled to a new trial.

JUSTICE HARLAN, concurring in part and dissenting in part.

If I felt free to consider this case upon a clean slate I would have voted to affirm these convictions. But in light of the lengths to which the right to appointed counsel has been carried in recent decisions of this Court, see *Miranda v. Arizona, Wade v. United States,* \* \* \*—I consider that course is not open to me with due regard for the way in which the adjudicatory process of this Court, as I conceive it, should work. \* \* \*

While, given the cases referred to, I cannot escape the conclusion that petitioners' constitutional rights must be held to have been violated by denying them appointed counsel at the preliminary hearing, I consider the scope of the Court's remand too broad and amorphous. I do not think that reversal of these convictions, for lack of counsel at the preliminary hearing, should follow unless petitioners are able to show on remand that they have been prejudiced in their defense at trial, in that favorable testimony that might otherwise have been preserved was irretrievably lost by virtue of not having counsel to help present an affirmative case at the preliminary hearing. \* \* \* In my opinion mere speculation that defense counsel might have been able to do better at trial had he been present at the preliminary hearing should not suffice to vitiate a conviction. The Court's remand under the *Chapman* harmless-error rule seems to me to leave the way open for that sort of speculation. \* \* \*

JUSTICE STEWART, with whom THE CHIEF JUSTICE joins, dissenting.

\* \* \* If at the trial the prosecution had used any incriminating statements made by the petitioners at the preliminary hearing, the convictions before us would quite properly have to be set aside. But that did not happen in this case. Or if the prosecution had used the statement of any other witness at the preliminary hearing against the petitioners at their trial, we would likewise quite properly have to set aside these convictions. But that did not happen in this case either. For as the Court today perforce concedes, "the prohibition against use by the State at trial of anything that occurred at the preliminary hearing was scrupulously observed." \* \* \*

But the Court holds today that the Constitution required Alabama to provide a lawyer for the petitioners at their preliminary hearing, not so much, it seems, to assure a fair trial as to assure a fair preliminary hearing. A lawyer at the preliminary hearing, the Court says, might have led the magistrate to "refuse to bind the accused over." Or a lawyer might have made "effective arguments for the accused on such matters as bail or the necessity for an early psychiatric examination." If *those* are the reasons a lawyer must be provided, then the most elementary logic requires that a new preliminary hearing must now be held, with counsel made available to the petitioners. In order to provide such relief, it would, of course, be necessary not only to set aside these convictions, but also to set aside the grand jury indictments, and the magistrate's orders fixing bail and binding over the petitioners. Since the petitioners have now been found by a jury in a constitutional trial to be guilty beyond a reasonable doubt, the Court understandably boggles at these logical consequences of its own reasoning. It refrains, in short, from now turning back the clock by ordering a new preliminary hearing to determine all over again whether there is sufficient evidence against the accused to present their case to a grand jury. Instead, the Court sets aside these convictions and remands the case for determination "whether the convictions should be reinstated or a new trial ordered," and this action seems to me even more quixotic. ＊ ＊ ＊

No record or transcript of any kind was made of the preliminary hearing. Therefore, if the burden on remand is on the petitioners to show that they were prejudiced, it is clear that that burden cannot be met, and the remand is a futile gesture. If, on the other hand, the burden is on the State to disprove beyond a reasonable doubt any and all speculative advantages that the petitioners might conceivably have enjoyed if counsel had been present at their preliminary hearing, then obviously that burden cannot be met either, and the Court should simply reverse these convictions. All I can say is that if the Alabama courts can figure out what they are supposed to do with this case now that it has been remanded to them, their perceptiveness will far exceed mine.

The record before us makes clear that no evidence of what occurred at the preliminary hearing was used against the petitioners at their now completed trial. I would hold, therefore, that the absence of counsel at the preliminary hearing deprived the petitioners of no constitutional rights. Accordingly, I would affirm these convictions.

CHIEF JUSTICE BURGER, [dissenting]

I agree that as a matter of *sound policy* counsel should be made available to all persons subjected to a preliminary hearing and that this should be provided either by statute or by the rulemaking process. However, I cannot accept the notion that the Constitution commands it because it is a "criminal prosecution." ＊ ＊ ＊ Certainly, as Mr. Justice Harlan and Mr. Justice White suggest, not a word in the Constitution itself either requires or contemplates the result reached; unlike them, however, I do not acquiesce in prior holdings which purportedly, but nonetheless erroneously, are based on the Constitution. That approach simply is an acknowledgment that the Court having previously amended the Sixth Amendment now feels bound by its action. While I do not rely solely on 183 years of contrary constitutional interpretation, it is indeed an odd business that it has taken this Court nearly two centuries to "discover" a constitutional mandate to have counsel at a preliminary hearing. Here there is not even the excuse that conditions have changed; the preliminary hearing is an ancient institution.

＊ ＊ ＊ If the Constitution provided that counsel be furnished for every "critical event in the progress of a criminal case," that would be another story, but it does not. In contrast to the variety of verbal combinations employed by the majority to justify today's disposition, the Sixth Amendment states with laudable precision that "In all *criminal prosecutions,* the accused shall * * * have the Assistance of Counsel." (Emphasis added.) The only relevant determination is whether a preliminary hearing is a "criminal prosecution," *not* whether it is a "*critical event* in the progress of a criminal case." By inventing its own verbal formula the Court simply seeks to reshape the Constitution in accordance with its own predilections of what is desirable. Constitutional interpretation is not an easy matter, but we should be especially cautious of substituting our own notions for those of the Framers. * * *

Under today's holding we * * * have something of an anomaly under the new "discovery" of the Court that counsel is *constitutionally* required at the preliminary hearing since counsel cannot attend a subsequent grand jury inquiry, even though witnesses, including the person eventually charged, may be interrogated in secret session. If the current mode of constitutional analysis subscribed to by this Court in recent cases requires that counsel be present at preliminary hearings, how can this be reconciled with the fact that the Constitution itself does not permit the assistance of counsel at the decidedly more "critical" grand jury inquiry.

Finally, as pointed out, the Court has already protected an accused from absence of counsel at the preliminary hearing by providing that statements of an uncounseled person are inadmissible at trial. The Court fails to explain why that salutary—indeed drastic—remedy is no longer sufficient protection for the preliminary hearing stage, unless what the Court is doing—surreptitiously—is to convert the preliminary hearing into a discovery device. * * *

## VASQUEZ v. HILLERY

474 U.S. 254, 106 S.Ct. 617, 88 L.Ed.2d 598 (1986).

JUSTICE MARSHALL delivered the opinion of the Court.

The Warden of San Quentin State Prison asks this Court to retire a doctrine of equal protection jurisprudence first announced in 1880. The time has come, he urges, for us to abandon the rule requiring reversal of the conviction of any defendant indicted by a grand jury from which members of his own race were systematically excluded.

In 1962, the grand jury of Kings County, California, indicted respondent, Booker T. Hillery, for a brutal murder. Before trial in Superior Court, respondent moved to quash the indictment on the ground that it had been issued by a grand jury from which blacks had been systematically excluded. A hearing on respondent's motion was held by Judge Meredith Wingrove, who was the sole Superior Court Judge in the county and had personally selected all grand juries, including the one that indicted respondent, for the previous seven years. Absolving himself of any discriminatory intent, Judge Wingrove refused to quash the indictment. Respondent was subsequently convicted of first-degree murder.

For the next 16 years, respondent pursued appeals and collateral relief in the state courts, raising at every opportunity his equal protection challenge to the grand jury that indicted him. Less than one month after the California Supreme Court foreclosed his final avenue of state relief in 1978, respondent filed a petition for a writ of habeas corpus in federal court, raising that same challenge. The District Court concluded that respondent had established discrimination in the grand jury, and granted the writ.[a] The Court of Appeals affirmed, and we granted certiorari.

**a.** In a portion of its opinion that has been deleted, the Court sustained the district court's consideration of a computer analysis that had not been submitted before the state

* * * [P]etitioner urges this Court to find that discrimination in the grand jury amounted to harmless error in this case, claiming that the evidence against respondent was overwhelming and that discrimination no longer infects the selection of grand juries in Kings County. Respondent's conviction after a fair trial, we are told, purged any taint attributable to the indictment process. Our acceptance of this theory would require abandonment of more than a century of consistent precedent.

In 1880, this Court reversed a state conviction on the ground that the indictment charging the offense had been issued by a grand jury from which blacks had been excluded. We reasoned that deliberate exclusion of blacks "is practically a brand upon them, affixed by the law, an assertion of their inferiority, and a stimulant to that race prejudice which is an impediment to securing to individuals of the race that equal justice which the law aims to secure to all others." *Strauder v. West Virginia*, 100 U.S. 303 (1880).

Thereafter, the Court has repeatedly rejected all arguments that a conviction may stand despite racial discrimination in the selection of the grand jury.[b] Only six years ago, the Court explicitly addressed the question whether this unbroken line of case law should be reconsidered in favor of a harmless-error standard, and determined that it should not. *Rose v. Mitchell*, 443 U.S. 545 (1979). We reaffirmed our conviction that discrimination on the basis of race in the selection of grand jurors "strikes at the fundamental values of our judicial system and our society as a whole," and that the criminal defendant's right to equal protection of the laws has been denied when he is indicted by a grand jury from which members of a racial group purposefully have been excluded.

Petitioner argues here that requiring a State to retry a defendant, sometimes years later, imposes on it an unduly harsh penalty for a constitutional defect bearing no relation to the fundamental fairness of the trial. Yet intentional discrimination in the selection of grand jurors is a grave constitutional trespass, possible only under color of state authority, and wholly within the power of the State to prevent. Thus, the remedy we have embraced for over a century—the only effective remedy for this violation [5]—is not disproportionate to the evil that it seeks to deter. If grand jury discrimination becomes a thing of the past, no conviction will ever again be lost on account of it.

Nor are we persuaded that discrimination in the grand jury has no effect on the fairness of the criminal trials that result from that grand jury's actions. The grand jury does not determine only that probable cause exists to believe that a

courts. That analysis assessed the "mathematical probability that chance or accident could have accounted for the exclusion of blacks from the Kings County grand jury over the years at issue." The district court "accepted the experts conclusion that had the grand jurors been selected by chance, the probability that no black would have been selected over the 17 year period of Judge Wingrove's tenure was 2 in 1,000.

**b.** The Court here cited 13 Supreme Court opinion, decided between 1881 and 1972, in which convictions had been reversed on direct appeal based on racial discrimination in the selection of the grand jury.

**5.** As we pointed out in *Rose v. Mitchell*, alternative remedies are ineffectual. Federal law provides a criminal prohibition against discrimination in the selection of grand jurors,

18 U.S.C. § 243, but according to statistics compiled by the Administrative Office of the United States Courts, that section has not been the basis for a single prosecution in the past nine years. With respect to prior years, for which precise information is not available, we have been unable to find evidence of any prosecution or conviction under the statute in the last century. The other putative remedy for grand jury discrimination is 42 U.S.C. § 1983, which, in theory, allows redress for blacks who have been excluded from grand jury service. These suits are also extremely rare, undoubtedly because the potential plaintiffs, eligible blacks not called for grand jury service, are often without knowledge of the discriminatory practices and without incentive to launch costly legal battles to stop them.

defendant committed a crime, or that it does not. In the hands of the grand jury lies the power to charge a greater offense or a lesser offense; numerous counts or a single count; and perhaps most significant of all, a capital offense or a noncapital offense—all on the basis of the same facts. Moreover, "[t]he grand jury is not bound to indict in every case where a conviction can be obtained." *United States v. Ciambrone*, 601 F.2d 616, 629 (CA2 1979) (Friendly, J., dissenting). Thus, even if a grand jury's determination of probable cause is confirmed in hindsight by a conviction on the indicted offense, that confirmation in no way suggests that the discrimination did not impermissibly infect the framing of the indictment and, consequently, the nature or very existence of the proceedings to come.

When constitutional error calls into question the objectivity of those charged with bringing a defendant to judgment, a reviewing court can neither indulge a presumption of regularity nor evaluate the resulting harm. Accordingly, when the trial judge is discovered to have had some basis for rendering a biased judgment, his actual motivations are hidden from review, and we must presume that the process was impaired. See *Tumey v. Ohio*, 273 U.S. 510, 535 (1927) (reversal required when judge has financial interest in conviction, despite lack of indication that bias influenced decisions). Similarly, when a petit jury has been selected upon improper criteria or has been exposed to prejudicial publicity, we have required reversal of the conviction because the effect of the violation cannot be ascertained. Like these fundamental flaws, which never have been thought harmless, discrimination in the grand jury undermines the structural integrity of the criminal tribunal itself, and is not amenable to harmless-error review.[6]

Just as a conviction is void under the Equal Protection Clause if the prosecutor deliberately charged the defendant on account of his race, see *United States v. Batchelder* [see Ch. 10, § 2], a conviction cannot be understood to cure the taint attributable to a charging body selected on the basis of race. Once having found discrimination in the selection of a grand jury, we simply cannot know that the need to indict would have been assessed in the same way by a grand jury properly constituted. The overriding imperative to eliminate this systemic flaw in the charging process, as well as the difficulty of assessing its effect on any given defendant, requires our continued adherence to a rule of mandatory reversal.

The opinion of the Court in *Mitchell* ably presented other justifications, based on the necessity for vindicating Fourteenth Amendment rights, supporting a policy of automatic reversal in cases of grand jury discrimination. That analysis persuasively demonstrated that the justifications retain their validity in modern times, for "114 years after the close of the War Between the States and nearly 100 years after *Strauder*, racial and other forms of discrimination still remain a fact of life, in the administration of justice as in our society as a whole." The six years since *Mitchell* have given us no reason to doubt the continuing truth of that observation.

The dissent propounds a theory, not advanced by any party, which would condition the grant of relief upon the passage of time between a conviction and the filing of a petition for federal habeas corpus, depending upon the ability of a State to obtain a second conviction. Sound jurisprudence counsels against our adoption of that approach to habeas corpus claims.

---

**6.** Justice White does not join in the foregoing paragraph.

The Habeas Corpus Rules permit a State to move for dismissal of a habeas petition when it "has been prejudiced in its ability to respond to the petition by delay in its filing." Indeed, petitioner filed such a motion in this case, and it was denied because the District Court found that no prejudicial delay had been caused by respondent. Congress has not seen fit, however, to provide the State with an additional defense to habeas corpus petitions based on the difficulties that it will face if forced to retry the defendant. * * *

Today's decision is supported, though not compelled, by the important doctrine of *stare decisis*, the means by which we ensure that the law will not merely change erratically, but will develop in a principled and intelligible fashion. That doctrine permits society to presume that bedrock principles are founded in the law rather than in the proclivities of individuals, and thereby contributes to the integrity of our constitutional system of government, both in appearance and in fact. While *stare decisis* is not an inexorable command, the careful observer will discern that any detours from the straight path of *stare decisis* in our past have occurred for articulable reasons, and only when the Court has felt obliged "to bring its opinions into agreement with experience and with facts newly ascertained." *Burnet v. Coronado Oil & Gas Co.*, 285 U.S. 393 (1932) (Brandeis, J., dissenting). * * * [E]very successful proponent of overruling precedent has borne the heavy burden of persuading the Court that changes in society or in the law dictate that the values served by *stare decisis* yield in favor of a greater objective. In the case of grand jury discrimination, we have been offered no reason to believe that any such metamorphosis has rendered the Court's long commitment to a rule of reversal outdated, ill-founded, unworkable, or otherwise legitimately vulnerable to serious reconsideration. On the contrary, the need for such a rule is as compelling today as it was at its inception.[c]

JUSTICE POWELL, with whom THE CHIEF JUSTICE and JUSTICE REHNQUIST join, dissenting.

Respondent, a black man, was indicted by a grand jury having no black members for the stabbing murder of a 15–year–old girl. A petit jury found respondent guilty of that charge beyond a reasonable doubt, in a trial the fairness of which is unchallenged here. Twenty-three years later, we are asked to grant respondent's petition for a writ of habeas corpus—and thereby require a new trial if that is still feasible—on the ground that blacks were purposefully excluded from the grand jury that indicted him. It is undisputed that race discrimination has long since disappeared from the grand jury selection process in Kings County, California. It is undisputed that a grand jury that perfectly represented Kings County's population at the time of respondent's indictment would have contained only one black member. Yet the Court holds that respondent's petition must be granted, and that respondent must be freed unless the State is able to reconvict, more than two decades after the murder that led to his incarceration.

It is difficult to reconcile this result with a rational system of justice. The Court nevertheless finds its decision compelled by a century of precedent and by

c. Justice O'Connor's opinion, concurring in the judgment, is omitted. Justice O'Connor noted that she shared the "view expressed by Justice Powell in *Rose* [that] a petitioner who has been afforded by the state courts a full and fair opportunity to litigate the claims that blacks were discriminatorily excluded from the grand jury * * * should be foreclosed from relitigating that claim on federal habeas." The district court here, however, had held that respondent Hillery "was not given a full and fair hearing on his discrimination claim in state court." Nor had a "sufficiently compelling case been made for reversing this Court's precedents with respect to the remedy applicable to properly cognizable claims of discriminatory exclusion of grand jurors."

the interests of respondent and of society in ending race discrimination in the selection of grand juries. I dissent for two reasons. First, in my view, any error in the selection of the grand jury that indicted respondent is constitutionally harmless. Second, even assuming that the harmless-error rule does not apply, reversal of respondent's conviction is an inappropriate remedy for the wrong that prompts this case.

The Court concludes that the harmless-error rule does not apply to claims of grand jury discrimination. This conclusion is said to follow from a line of cases going back over 100 years. In my view, it follows from a misapplication of the doctrine of *stare decisis*. Adhering to precedent "is usually the wise policy, because in most matters it is more important that the applicable rule of law be settled than that it be settled right." *Burnet v. Coronado Oil & Gas Co.*, 285 U.S. 393 (1932) (Brandeis, J., dissenting). Accordingly, "any departure from the doctrine of *stare decisis* demands special justification." Nevertheless, when governing decisions are badly reasoned, or conflict with other, more recent authority, the Court "has never felt constrained to follow precedent." Instead, particularly where constitutional issues are involved, "[t]his Court has shown a readiness to correct its errors even though of long standing." In this case, the Court misapplies *stare decisis* because it relies only on decisions concerning grand jury discrimination. There is other precedent, including important cases of more recent vintage than those cited by the Court, that should control this case. Those cases hold, or clearly imply, that a conviction should not be reversed for constitutional error where the error did not affect the outcome of the prosecution.

In *Chapman v. California*, 386 U.S. 18 (1967), the Court held that a trial judge's improper comment on the defendant's failure to testify—a clear violation of the Fifth and Fourteenth Amendments—was not a proper basis for reversal if harmless. Since *Chapman*, "the Court has consistently made clear that it is the duty of a reviewing court to consider the trial record as a whole and to ignore errors that are harmless, including most constitutional violations." This rule has been applied to a variety of constitutional violations. See *Harrington v. California*, 395 U.S. 250 (1969) (use of co-conspirator confession in violation of Confrontation Clause); *Coleman v. Alabama*, 399 U.S. 1 (1970) (denial of counsel at preliminary hearing); *Milton v. Wainwright*, 407 U.S. 371 (1972) (use of confession obtained in violation of right to counsel); *Gerstein v. Pugh*, 420 U.S. 103 (1975) (illegal arrest).  *  *  *

In *Rose v. Mitchell*, 443 U.S. 545 (1979), the Court contended that the principle of these cases is inapplicable to grand jury discrimination claims, because grand jury discrimination "destroys the appearance of justice and thereby casts doubt on the integrity of the judicial process." But *every* constitutional error may be said to raise questions as to the "appearance of justice" and the "integrity of the judicial process." Nevertheless, as the cases cited above show, the Court has required some showing of actual prejudice to the defendant as a prerequisite to reversal, even when the constitutional error directly affects the fairness of the defendant's trial. Compare *Strickland v. Washington* [Ch. 17, § 2] (requiring prejudice in ineffective assistance of counsel claims), with *Gideon v. Wainwright* [Ch. 5, § 1] (emphasizing importance of right to counsel to ensure fair trial). Grand jury discrimination is a serious violation of our constitutional order, but so also are the deprivations of rights guaranteed by the Fourth, Fifth, Sixth, and Fourteenth Amendments to which we have applied harmless-error analysis or an analogous prejudice requirement. Moreover, grand jury discrimination occurs *prior* to trial, while the asserted constitutional violations in most of the above-cited cases occurred *during* trial. The Court does not adequately explain why grand jury discrimination affects the "integrity of the judicial process" to a greater extent than the deprivation of equally vital constitutional rights, nor why it is exempt from a prejudice requirement while other constitutional errors are not. ＊ ＊ ＊

Even assuming that now-established harmless-error principles are inapplicable, this case unjustifiably extends the "century of precedent" on which the Court relies. ＊ ＊ ＊ No one questions that race discrimination in grand jury selection violates the Equal Protection Clause of the Fourteenth Amendment. The issue in this case is not whether the State erred, but what should be done about it. The question is whether reversal of respondent's conviction either is compelled by the Constitution or is an appropriate, but not constitutionally required, remedy for racial discrimination in the selection of grand jurors.

The Constitution does not compel the rule of automatic reversal that the Court applies today. In *Hobby v. United States,* 468 U.S. 339 (1984), we acknowledged that discriminatory selection of grand jury foremen violated the Constitution, but we concluded that reversing the petitioner's conviction was an inappropriate remedy for the violation since grand jury foremen play a minor part in federal prosecutions. See also *Oregon v. Elstad* [Ch. 6, § 4] (suppression of evidence obtained in violation of *Miranda v. Arizona,* is not constitutionally compelled); *United States v. Leon* [Ch. 3, § 1] (suppression of evidence obtained in violation of the Fourth Amendment is not constitutionally compelled). ＊ ＊ ＊ The rationale of *Hobby* cannot be squared with the claim that discriminatory selection of the body that charged the defendant *compels* reversal of the defendant's conviction. Rather, it is necessary to determine whether reversal of respondent's conviction is an "appropriate remedy" for the exclusion of blacks from grand juries in Kings County, California, in 1962. ＊ ＊ ＊ That determination depends on (i) the utility of the remedy in either correcting any injustice to respondent or deterring unconstitutional conduct by state officials, and (ii) the remedy's costs to society. *United States v. Leon.*

The scope of the remedy depends in part on the nature and degree of the harm caused by the wrong. The Court perceives two kinds of harm flowing from grand jury discrimination: harm to the respondent's interest in not being charged and convicted because of his race, and harm to society's interest in deterring racial discrimination. I consider in turn these asserted interests and the degree to which they are served in this case by the Court's automatic reversal rule.

The Court does not contend that the discriminatory selection of the grand jury that indicted respondent calls into question the correctness of the decision to indict. Such a contention could not withstand analysis. Following his indictment for murder, respondent was convicted of that charge in a trial and by a jury whose fairness is not now challenged. The conviction, affirmed on direct appeal in 1965, establishes that the grand jury's decision to indict was indisputably correct. ＊ ＊ ＊

The Court nevertheless decides that discrimination in the selection of the grand jury potentially harmed respondent, because the grand jury is vested with broad discretion in deciding whether to indict and in framing the charges, and because it is impossible to know whether this discretion would have been exercised differently by a properly selected grand jury. The point appears to be that an all-white grand jury from which blacks are systematically excluded might be influenced by race in determining whether to indict and for what charge. Since the State may not imprison respondent for a crime if one of its elements is his race, the argument goes, his conviction must be set aside.

This reasoning ignores established principles of equal protection jurisprudence. We have consistently declined to find a violation of the Equal Protection Clause absent a finding of intentional discrimination. There has been no showing in this case—indeed, respondent does not even allege—that the Kings County grand jury indicted respondent because of his race, or that the grand jury declined to indict white suspects in the face of similarly strong evidence. Nor is it sensible to assume that impermissible discrimination might have occurred simply because the grand jury had no black members. This Court has never suggested that the racial composition of a grand jury gives rise to the inference that indictments are racially motivated, any more than it has suggested that a suspect arrested by a policeman of a different race may challenge his subsequent conviction on that basis. * * *

Once the inference of racial bias in the decision to indict is placed to one side, as it must be under our precedents, it is impossible to conclude that the discriminatory selection of Kings County's grand jurors caused respondent to suffer any cognizable injury. There may be a theoretical possibility that a different grand jury might have decided not to indict or to indict for a less serious charge. The fact remains, however, that the grand jury's decision to indict was *correct as a matter of law,* given respondent's subsequent, unchallenged conviction. A defendant has no right to a grand jury that errs in his favor. * * *

As respondent suffered no prejudice from the grand jury discrimination that prompted his claim, the Court's remedy must stand or fall on its utility as a deterrent to government officials who seek to exclude particular groups from grand juries, weighed against the cost that the remedy imposes on society. The Court properly emphasizes that grand jury discrimination is "a grave constitutional trespass," but it leaps from that observation to the conclusion that *no matter when the claim is raised* the appropriate response is to reverse the conviction of one indicted by a discriminatorily selected body. That conclusion is not, as the Court erroneously suggests, compelled by precedent; equally important, it seriously disserves the public interest.

The cases on which the Court relies involved relatively brief lapses of time between the defendant's trial and the granting of relief. This fact is unsurprising, since the Court only recently determined that claims of grand jury discrimination may be raised in federal habeas corpus proceedings. See *Rose v. Mitchell.* * * * In all of * * * [prior] cases, the time between the defendant's indictment and this Court's decision was six years or less. * * * This case raises the open question whether relief should be denied where the discrimination claim is pressed many years after conviction, and where the State can show that the delay prejudiced its ability to retry the defendant. * * * It is now almost a quarter-century since respondent was tried for murder and since the discrimination occurred. The Court finds this time lapse irrelevant. In my view, it is critically important, because it both increases the societal cost of the Court's chosen remedy and lessens any deterrent force the remedy may otherwise have.

In *Rose v. Mitchell,* supra, the Court reasoned that the rule of automatic reversal imposes limited costs on society, since the State is able to retry successful petitioners, and since "the State remains free to use all the proof it introduced to obtain the conviction in the first trial." This is not the case when relief is granted many years after the original conviction. In those circumstances, the State may find itself severely handicapped in its ability to carry its heavy burden of proving guilt beyond a reasonable doubt.  *  *  * Witnesses die or move away; physical evidence is lost; memories fade.  *  *  *

Long delays also dilute the effectiveness of the reversal rule as a deterrent. This case is illustrative. The architect of the discriminatory selection system that led to respondent's claim, Judge Wingrove, died 19 years ago. Respondent does not allege that the discriminatory practices survived Judge Wingrove, nor is there any evidence in the record to support such an allegation. It is hard to believe that Judge Wingrove might have behaved differently had he known that a convicted defendant might be freed 19 years after his death. Yet that is exactly the proposition that must justify the remedy imposed in this case: that people in positions similar to Judge Wingrove's will change their behavior out of the fear of successful habeas petitions long after they have left office or otherwise passed from the scene.  *  *  *

Twenty-three years ago, respondent was fairly convicted of the most serious of crimes. Respondent's grand jury discrimination claim casts no doubt on the adequacy of the procedures used to convict him or on the sufficiency of the evidence of his guilt. For that reason alone, the Court should reverse the Court of Appeals' decision.[16] Even assuming the harmlessness of the error is irrelevant, however, reversal is still required. The Court inappropriately applies a deterrence rule in a context where it is unlikely to deter, and where its costs to society are likely to be especially high. These considerations should at least lead the Court to remand for a determination of whether the long lapse of time since respondent's conviction would prejudice the State's ability to retry respondent.

# COSTELLO v. UNITED STATES
### 350 U.S. 359, 76 S.Ct. 406, 100 L.Ed. 397 (1956).

Justice Black delivered the opinion of the Court.

We granted certiorari in this case to consider a single question: "May a defendant be required to stand trial and a conviction be sustained where only hearsay evidence was presented to the grand jury which indicted him?"

Petitioner, Frank Costello, was indicted for wilfully attempting to evade payment of income taxes due the United States for the years 1947, 1948 and 1949. The charge was that petitioner falsely and fraudulently reported less income than he and his wife actually received during the taxable years in question. Petitioner promptly filed a motion for inspection of the minutes of the grand jury and for a dismissal of the indictment. His motion was based on an affidavit stating that he was firmly convinced there could have been no legal or competent evidence before the grand jury which indicted him since he had reported all his income and paid all taxes due. The motion was denied. At the trial which followed the Government offered evidence designed to show increases in Costello's net worth in an attempt to prove that he had received more income during the years in question than he had reported. To establish its case the Government called and examined 144 witnesses and introduced 368 exhibits. All of the testimony and documents related to business transactions and expenditures by petitioner and his wife. The prosecution concluded its case by calling three government agents. Their investigations had produced the evidence used

---

**16.** Confidence in our system of justice is eroded when one found guilty of murder, in a trial conceded to be fair, is set free. It is important to remember that the criminal law's aim is twofold: "that guilt shall not escape or innocence suffer." The Court's deci-sion in this case plainly undermines the State's interest in punishing the guilty, without either protecting the innocent or ensuring the fundamental fairness of the procedures pursuant to which one such as respondent is tried and convicted.

against petitioner at the trial. They were allowed to summarize the vast amount of evidence already heard and to introduce computations showing, if correct, that petitioner and his wife had received far greater income than they had reported. We have held such summarizations admissible in a "net worth" case like this.

Counsel for petitioner asked each government witness at the trial whether he had appeared before the grand jury which returned the indictment. This cross-examination developed the fact that the three investigating officers had been the only witnesses before the grand jury. After the Government concluded its case, petitioner again moved to dismiss the indictment on the ground that the only evidence before the grand jury was "hearsay," since the three officers had no first-hand knowledge of the transactions upon which their computations were based. Nevertheless the trial court again refused to dismiss the indictment, and petitioner was convicted. The Court of Appeals affirmed. * * * Petitioner here urges: (1) that an indictment based solely on hearsay evidence violates that part of the Fifth Amendment providing that "No person shall be held to answer for a capital, or otherwise infamous crime, unless on a presentment or indictment of a Grand Jury * * *." and (2) that if the Fifth Amendment does not invalidate an indictment based solely on hearsay we should now lay down such a rule for the guidance of federal courts. * * * [N]either the Fifth Amendment nor any other constitutional provision prescribes the kind of evidence upon which grand juries must act. The grand jury is an English institution, brought to this country by the early colonists and incorporated in the Constitution by the Founders. There is every reason to believe that our constitutional grand jury was intended to operate substantially like its English progenitor. The basic purpose of the English grand jury was to provide a fair method for instituting criminal proceedings against persons believed to have committed crimes. Grand jurors were selected from the body of the people and their work was not hampered by rigid procedural or evidential rules. In fact, grand jurors could act on their own knowledge and were free to make their presentments or indictments on such information as they deemed satisfactory. Despite its broad power to institute criminal proceedings the grand jury grew in popular favor with the years. It acquired an independence in England free from control by the Crown or judges. Its adoption in our Constitution as the sole method for preferring charges in serious criminal cases shows the high place it held as an instrument of justice. And in this country as in England of old the grand jury has convened as a body of laymen, free from technical rules, acting in secret, pledged to indict no one because of prejudice and to free no one because of special favor. As late as 1927 an English historian could say that English grand juries were still free to act on their own knowledge if they pleased to do so. And in 1852 Mr. Justice Nelson on circuit could say "No case has been cited, nor have we been able to find any, furnishing an authority for looking into and revising the judgment of the grand jury upon the evidence, for the purpose of determining whether or not the finding was founded upon sufficient proof * * *." *United States v. Reed,* 27 Fed.Cas. 727, 738 (1852).

In *Holt v. United States,* 218 U.S. 245 (1910), this Court had to decide whether an indictment should be quashed because supported in part by incompetent evidence. Aside from the incompetent evidence "there was very little evidence against the accused." The Court refused to hold that such an indictment should be quashed, pointing out that "The abuses of criminal practice would be enhanced if indictments could be upset on such a ground." The same thing is true where as here all the evidence before the grand jury was in the nature of "hearsay." If indictments were to be held open to challenge on the ground that there was inadequate or incompetent evidence before the grand jury, the resulting delay would be great indeed. The result of such a rule would be that before trial on the merits a defendant could always insist on a kind of preliminary trial to determine the competency and adequacy of the evidence before the grand jury. This is not required by the Fifth Amendment. An indictment returned by a legally constituted and unbiased grand jury, like an information drawn by the prosecutor, if valid on its face, is enough to call for trial of the charge on the merits. The Fifth Amendment requires nothing more.

Petitioner urges that this Court should exercise its power to supervise the administration of justice in federal courts and establish a rule permitting defendants to challenge indictments on the ground that they are not supported by adequate or competent evidence. No persuasive reasons are advanced for establishing such a rule. It would run counter to the whole history of the grand jury institution, in which laymen conduct their inquiries unfettered by technical rules. Neither justice nor the concept of a fair trial requires such a change. In a trial on the merits, defendants are entitled to a strict observance of all the rules designed to bring about a fair verdict. Defendants are not entitled, however, to a rule which would result in interminable delay but add nothing to the assurance of a fair trial. Affirmed.

JUSTICE CLARK and JUSTICE HARLAN took no part in the consideration or decision of this case.

JUSTICE BURTON, concurring.

I agree with the denial of the motion to quash the indictment. In my view, however, this case does not justify the breadth of the declarations made by the Court. I assume that this Court would not preclude an examination of grand jury action to ascertain the existence of bias or prejudice in an indictment. Likewise, it seems to me that if it is shown that the grand jury had before it no substantial or rationally persuasive evidence upon which to base its indictment, that indictment should be quashed. To hold a person to answer to such an empty indictment for a capital or otherwise infamous federal crime robs the Fifth Amendment of much of its protective value to the private citizen. * * *

# Chapter 12

# SPEEDY TRIAL AND OTHER
# SPEEDY DISPOSITION

---

The matter of the time within which a trial must be commenced is often treated in statutes and court rules. Some of these provisions are rather general in nature, meaning courts have considerable discretion in determining how long a delay is excessive and what intervals in the pretrial stages are to be discounted in ascertaining what the period of delay has actually been. Some other provisions, as illustrated by the federal Speedy Trial Act of 1974, go into considerable detail by setting specific time limits and enumerating what events toll the running of the specified time.

But speedy trial is not simply a matter of local law. The Sixth Amendment declares: "In all criminal prosecutions, the accused shall enjoy the right to a speedy * * * trial." Just what this means is explored in the first case, *Barker v. Wingo*. Certain periods of delay (e.g., prior to arrest or charge) are not encompassed by the Sixth Amendment, so that a defendant's constitutional challenge to them will likely be grounded in the due process clause, as in *United States v. Lovasco*.

## BARKER v. WINGO
### 407 U.S. 514, 92 S.Ct. 2182, 33 L.Ed.2d 101 (1972).

JUSTICE POWELL delivered the opinion of the Court.

[A] speedy trial is guaranteed the accused by the Sixth Amendment to the Constitution. [T]he right to speedy trial is "fundamental" and is imposed by the Due Process Clause of the Fourteenth Amendment on the States. [I]n none of [our prior] cases have we attempted to set out the criteria by which the speedy trial right is to be judged. This case compels us to make such an attempt.

On July 20, 1958, in Christian County, Kentucky, an elderly couple was beaten to death by intruders wielding an iron tire tool. Two suspects, Silas Manning and Willie Barker, the petitioner, were arrested shortly thereafter. The grand jury indicted them on September 15. Counsel was appointed on September 17, and Barker's trial was set for October 21. The Commonwealth had a stronger case against Manning, and it believed that Barker could not be convicted unless Manning testified against him. Manning was naturally unwilling to incriminate himself. Accordingly, on October 23, the day Silas Manning was brought to trial, the Commonwealth sought and obtained the first of what was to be a series of 16 continuances of Barker's trial. Barker made no objection. By first convicting Manning, the Commonwealth would remove possible problems of self-incrimination and would be able to assure his testimony against Barker.

The Commonwealth encountered more than a few difficulties in its prosecution of Manning. The first trial ended in a hung jury. A second trial resulted in a conviction, but the Kentucky Court of Appeals reversed because of the admission of evidence obtained by an illegal search. At his third trial, Manning was again convicted, and the Court of Appeals again reversed because the trial court had not granted a change of venue. A fourth trial resulted in a hung jury. Finally, after five trials, Manning was convicted, in March 1962, of murdering one victim, and after a sixth trial, in December 1962, he was convicted of murdering the other.

The Christian County Circuit Court holds three terms each year—in February, June, and September. Barker's initial trial was to take place in the September term of 1958. The first continuance postponed it until the February 1959 term. The second continuance was granted for one month only. Every term thereafter for as long as the Manning prosecutions were in process, the Commonwealth routinely moved to continue Barker's case to the next term. When the case was continued from the June 1959 term until the following September, Barker, having spent 10 months in jail, obtained his release by posting a $5,000 bond. He thereafter remained free in the community until his trial. Barker made no objection, through his counsel, to the first 11 continuances.

When on February 12, 1962, the Commonwealth moved for the twelfth time to continue the case until the following term, Barker's counsel filed a motion to dismiss the indictment. The motion to dismiss was denied two weeks later, and the State's motion for a continuance was granted. The State was granted further continuances in June 1962 and September 1962, to which Barker did not object.

In February 1963, the first term of court following Manning's final conviction, the Commonwealth moved to set Barker's trial for March 19. But on the day scheduled for trial, it again moved for a continuance until the June term. It gave as its reason the illness of the ex-sheriff who was the chief investigating officer in the case. To this continuance, Barker objected unsuccessfully.

The witness was still unable to testify in June, and the trial, which had been set for June 19, was continued again until the September term over Barker's objection. This time the court announced that the case would be dismissed for lack of prosecution if it were not tried during the next term. The final trial date was set for October 9, 1963. On that date, Barker again moved to dismiss the indictment, and this time specified that his right to a speedy trial had been violated. The motion was denied; the trial commenced with Manning as the chief prosecution witness; Barker was convicted and given a life sentence.

\*   \*   \*

The right to a speedy trial is generically different from any of the other rights enshrined in the Constitution for the protection of the accused. In addition to the general concern that all accused persons be treated according to decent and fair procedures, there is a societal interest in providing a speedy trial which exists separate from and at times in opposition to the interests of the accused. The inability of courts to provide a prompt trial has contributed to a large backlog of cases in urban courts which, among other things, enables defendants to negotiate more effectively for pleas of guilty to lesser offenses and otherwise manipulate the system. In addition, persons released on bond for lengthy periods awaiting trial have an opportunity to commit other crimes. It must be of little comfort to the residents of Christian County, Kentucky, to know that Barker was at large on bail for over four years while accused of a vicious and brutal murder of which he was ultimately convicted.  Moreover, the longer an accused is free awaiting trial, the more tempting becomes his opportunity to jump bail and escape.  Finally, delay between arrest and punishment may have a detrimental effect on rehabilitation.

If an accused cannot make bail, he is generally confined, as was Barker for 10 months, in a local jail.  This contributes to the overcrowding and generally deplorable state of those institutions.  Lengthy exposure to these conditions "has a destructive effect on human character and makes the rehabilitation of the individual offender much more difficult."  At times the result may even be violent rioting.  Finally, lengthy pretrial detention is costly.  The cost of maintaining a prisoner in jail varies from $3 to $9 per day, and this amounts to millions across the Nation.  In addition, society loses wages which might have been earned, and it must often support families of incarcerated breadwinners.

A second difference between the right to speedy trial and the accused's other constitutional rights is that deprivation of the right may work to the accused's advantage.  Delay is not an uncommon defense tactic.  As the time between the commission of the crime and trial lengthens, witnesses may become unavailable or their memories may fade.  If the witnesses support the prosecution, its case will be weakened, sometimes seriously so.  And it is the prosecution which carries the burden of proof.  Thus, unlike the right to counsel or the right to be free from compelled self-incrimination, deprivation of the right to speedy trial does not *per se* prejudice the accused's ability to defend himself.

Finally, and perhaps most importantly, the right to speedy trial is a more vague concept than other procedural rights.  It is, for example, impossible to determine with precision when the right has been denied.  * * * There is nothing comparable to the point in the process when a defendant exercises or waives his right to counsel or his right to a jury trial.  * * *

The amorphous quality of the right also leads to the unsatisfactorily severe remedy of dismissal of the indictment when the right has been deprived.  This is indeed a serious consequence because it means that a defendant who may be guilty of a serious crime will go free, without having been tried.  Such a remedy is more serious than an exclusionary rule or a reversal for a new trial, but it is the only possible remedy.

Perhaps because the speedy trial right is so slippery, two rigid approaches are urged upon us as ways of eliminating some of the uncertainty which courts experience in protecting the right.  The first suggestion is that we hold that the Constitution requires a criminal defendant to be offered a trial within a specified time period.  The result of such a ruling would have the virtue of clarifying when the right is infringed and of simplifying courts' application of it.  Recognizing this, some legislatures have enacted laws, and some courts have adopted procedural rules which more narrowly define the right.  * * *

But such a result would require this Court to engage in legislative or rulemaking activity, rather than in the adjudicative process to which we should confine our efforts.  We do not establish procedural rules for the States, except when mandated by the Constitution.  We find no constitutional basis for holding that the speedy trial right can be quantified into a specified number of days or months.  The States, of course, are free to prescribe a reasonable period consistent with constitutional standards, but our approach must be less precise.

The second suggested alternative would restrict consideration of the right to those cases in which the accused has demanded a speedy trial. * * * Under this rigid approach, a prior demand is a necessary condition to the consideration of the speedy trial right. This essentially was the approach the Sixth Circuit took below.

Such an approach, by presuming waiver of a fundamental right from inaction, is inconsistent with this Court's pronouncements on waiver of constitutional rights. The Court has defined waiver as "an intentional relinquishment or abandonment of a known right or privilege." Courts should "indulge every reasonable presumption against waiver," and they should "not presume acquiescence in the loss of fundamental rights." * * *

In excepting the right to speedy trial from the rule of waiver we have applied to other fundamental rights, courts * * * have relied on the assumption that delay usually works for the benefit of the accused and on the absence of any readily ascertainable time in the criminal process for a defendant to be given the choice of exercising or waiving his right. But it is not necessarily true that delay benefits the defendant. There are cases in which delay appreciably harms the defendant's ability to defend himself. Moreover, a defendant confined to jail prior to trial is obviously disadvantaged by delay as is a defendant released on bail but unable to lead a normal life because of community suspicion and his own anxiety.

The nature of the speedy-trial right does make it impossible to pinpoint a precise time in the process when the right must be asserted or waived, but that fact does not argue for placing the burden of protecting the right solely on defendants. A defendant has no duty to bring himself to trial; the State has that duty as well as the duty of insuring that the trial is consistent with due process. Moreover, for the reasons earlier expressed, society has a particular interest in bringing swift prosecutions, and society's representatives are the ones who should protect that interest.

It is also noteworthy that such a rigid view of the demand rule places defense counsel in an awkward position. Unless he demands a trial early and often, he is in danger of frustrating his client's right. If counsel is willing to tolerate some delay because he finds it reasonable and helpful in preparing his own case, he may be unable to obtain a speedy trial for his client at the end of that time. * * *

We reject, therefore, the rule that a defendant who fails to demand a speedy trial forever waives his right. This does not mean, however, that the defendant has no responsibility to assert his right. We think the better rule is that the defendant's assertion of or failure to assert his right to a speedy trial is one of the factors to be considered in an inquiry into the deprivation of the right. Such a formulation * * * allows the trial court to exercise a judicial discretion based on the circumstances, including due consideration of any applicable formal procedural rule. It would permit, for example, a court to attach a different weight to a situation in which the defendant knowingly fails to object from a situation in which his attorney acquiesces in long delay without adequately informing his client or from a situation in which no counsel is appointed. It would also allow a court to weigh the frequency and force of the objections as opposed to attaching significant weight to a purely *pro forma* objection.

In ruling that a defendant has some responsibility to assert a speedy-trial claim, we do not depart from our holdings in other cases concerning the waiver of fundamental rights, in which we have placed the entire responsibility on the prosecution to show that the claimed waiver was knowingly and voluntarily made. Such cases have involved rights which must be exercised or waived at a specific time or under clearly identifiable circumstances, such as the rights to plead not guilty, to demand a jury trial, to exercise the privilege against self incrimination, and to have the assistance of counsel. We have shown above that the right to a speedy trial is unique in its uncertainty as to when and under what circumstances it must be asserted or may be deemed waived. But the rule we announce today, which comports with constitutional principles, places the primary burden on the courts and the prosecutors to assure that cases are brought to trial. We hardly need add that if delay is attributable to the defendant, then his waiver may be given effect under standard waiver doctrine, the demand rule aside.

* * * The approach we accept is a balancing test, in which the conduct of both the prosecution and the defendant are weighed.

A balancing test necessarily compels courts to approach speedy-trial cases on an *ad hoc* basis. We can do little more than identify some of the factors which courts should assess in determining whether a particular defendant has been deprived of his right. Though some might express them in different ways, we identify four such factors: Length of delay, the reason for the delay, the defendant's assertion of his right, and prejudice to the defendant.

The length of the delay is to some extent a triggering mechanism. Until there is some delay which is presumptively prejudicial, there is no necessity for inquiry into the other factors that go into the balance. Nevertheless, because of the imprecision of the right to speedy trial, the length of delay that will provoke such an inquiry is necessarily dependent upon the peculiar circumstances of the case. To take but one example, the delay that can be tolerated for an ordinary street crime is considerably less than for a serious, complex conspiracy charge.

Closely related to length of delay is the reason the government assigns to justify the delay. Here, too, different weights should be assigned to different reasons. A deliberate attempt to delay the trial in order to hamper the defense should be weighed heavily against the government. A more neutral reason such as negligence or overcrowded courts should be weighed less heavily but nevertheless should be considered since the ultimate responsibility for such circumstances must rest with the government rather than with the defendant. Finally, a valid reason, such as a missing witness, should serve to justify appropriate delay.

We have already discussed the third factor, the defendant's responsibility to assert his right. Whether and how a defendant asserts his right is closely related to the other factors we have mentioned. The strength of his efforts will be affected by the length of the delay, to some extent by the reason for the delay, and most particularly by the personal prejudice, which is not always readily identifiable, that he experiences. The more serious the deprivation, the more likely a defendant is to complain. The defendant's assertion of his speedy trial right, then, is entitled to strong evidentiary weight in determining whether the right is being deprived. We emphasize that failure to assert the right will make it difficult for a defendant to prove that he was denied a speedy trial.

A fourth factor is prejudice to the defendant. Prejudice, of course, should be assessed in the light of the interests of defendants which the speedy trial right was designed to protect. This Court has identified three such interests: (i) to prevent oppressive pretrial incarceration; (ii) to minimize anxiety and concern of the accused; and (iii) to limit the possibility that the defense will be impaired. Of these, the most serious is the last, because the inability of a defendant adequately to prepare his case skews the fairness of the entire system. If witnesses die or disappear during a delay, the prejudice is obvious. There is also prejudice if defense witnesses are unable to recall accurately events of the distant past. Loss of memory, however, is not always reflected in the record because what has been forgotten can rarely be shown.

We have discussed previously the societal disadvantages of lengthy pretrial incarceration, but obviously the disadvantages for the accused who cannot obtain his release are even more serious. The time spent in jail awaiting trial has a detrimental impact on the individual. It often means loss of a job; it disrupts family life; and it enforces idleness. Most jails offer little or no recreational or rehabilitative programs. The time spent in jail is simply dead time. Moreover, if a defendant is locked up, he is hindered in his ability to gather evidence, contact witnesses, or otherwise prepare his defense. Imposing those consequences on anyone who has not yet been convicted is serious. It is especially unfortunate to impose them on those persons who are ultimately found to be innocent. Finally, even if an accused is not incarcerated prior to trial, he is still disadvantaged by restraints on his liberty and by living under a cloud of anxiety, suspicion, and often hostility.

We regard none of the four factors identified above as either a necessary or sufficient condition to the finding of a deprivation of the right of speedy trial. Rather, they are related factors and must be considered together with such other circumstances as may be relevant. In sum, these factors have no talismanic qualities; courts must still engage in a difficult and sensitive balancing process. But, because we are dealing with a fundamental right of the accused, this process must be carried out with full recognition that the accused's interest in a speedy trial is specifically affirmed in the Constitution.

The difficulty of the task of balancing these factors is illustrated by this case, which we consider to be close. It is clear that the length of delay between arrest and trial—well over five years—was extraordinary. Only seven months of that period can be attributed to a strong excuse, the illness of the ex-sheriff who was in charge of the investigation. Perhaps some delay would have been permissible under ordinary circumstances, so that Manning could be utilized as a witness in Barker's trial, but more than four years was too long a period, particularly since a good part of that period was attributable to the Commonwealth's failure or inability to try Manning under circumstances that comported with due process.

Two counter-balancing factors, however, outweigh these deficiencies. The first is that prejudice was minimal. Of course, Barker was prejudiced to some extent by living for over four years under a cloud of suspicion and anxiety. Moreover, although he was released on bond for most of the period, he did spend 10 months in jail before trial. But there is no claim that any of Barker's witnesses died or otherwise became unavailable owing to the delay. The trial transcript indicates only two very minor lapses of memory—one on the part of a prosecution witness—which were in no way significant to the outcome.

More important than the absence of serious prejudice, is the fact that Barker did not want a speedy trial. Counsel was appointed for Barker immediately after his indictment and represented him throughout the period. No question is raised as to the competency of such counsel. Despite the fact that counsel had notice of the motions for continuances, the record shows no action whatever taken between October 21, 1958, and February 12, 1962, that could be construed as the assertion of the speedy-trial right. On the latter date, in response to another motion for continuance, Barker moved to dismiss the indictment. The record does not show on what ground this motion was based, although it is clear that no alternative motion was made for an immediate trial.

Instead the record strongly suggests that while he hoped to take advantage of the delay in which he had acquiesced, and thereby obtain a dismissal of the charges, he definitely did not want to be tried. Counsel conceded as much at oral argument:

> "Your honor, I would concede that Willie Mae Barker—probably—I don't know this for a fact—probably did not want to be tried. I don't think any man wants to be tried. And I don't consider this a liability on his behalf. I don't blame him."

The probable reason for Barker's attitude was that he was gambling on Manning's acquittal. The evidence was not terribly strong against Manning, as the reversals and hung juries suggest, and Barker undoubtedly thought that if Manning were acquitted, he would never be tried. Counsel also conceded this:

> "Now, it's true that the reason for this delay was the Commonwealth of Kentucky's desire to secure the testimony of the accomplice, Silas Manning. And it's true that if Silas Manning were never convicted, Willie Mae Barker would never have been convicted. We concede this."

That Barker was gambling on Manning's acquittal is also suggested by his failure, following the *pro forma* motion to dismiss filed in February 1962, to object to the Commonwealth's next two motions for continuances. Indeed, it was not until March 1963, after Manning's convictions were final, that Barker, having lost his gamble, began to object to further continuances. At that time, the Commonwealth's excuse was the illness of the ex-sheriff, which Barker has conceded justified the further delay.

We do not hold that there may never be a situation in which an indictment may be dismissed on speedy-trial grounds where the defendant has failed to object to continuances. There may be a situation in which the defendant was represented by incompetent counsel, was severely prejudiced, or even cases in which the continuances were granted *ex parte*. But barring extraordinary circumstances, we would be reluctant indeed to rule that a defendant was denied this constitutional right on a record that strongly indicates, as does this one, that the defendant did not want a speedy trial. We hold, therefore, that Barker was not deprived of his due process right to a speedy trial. * * *[a]

## UNITED STATES v. LOVASCO

431 U.S. 783, 97 S.Ct. 2044, 52 L.Ed.2d 752 (1977).

JUSTICE MARSHALL delivered the opinion of the Court. * * *

On March 6, 1975, respondent was indicted for possessing eight firearms stolen from the United States mail, and for dealing in firearms without a license. The offenses were alleged to have occurred between July 25 and August 31, 1973, more than 18 months before the indictment was filed. Respondent moved to dismiss the indictment due to the delay.

The District Court conducted a hearing on respondent's motion at which the respondent sought to prove that the delay was unnecessary and that it had prejudiced his defense. In an effort to establish the former proposition, respondent presented a Postal Inspector's report on his investigation that was prepared one month after the crimes were committed, and a stipulation concerning the post-report progress of the probe. The report stated, in brief, that within the first month of the investigation respondent had admitted to Government agents

---

a. The concurring opinion of Justice White, joined by Justice Brennan, is omitted.

that he had possessed and then sold five of the stolen guns, and that the agents had developed strong evidence linking respondent to the remaining three weapons. The report also stated, however, that the agents had been unable to confirm or refute respondent's claim that he had found the guns in his car when he returned to it after visiting his son, a mail handler, at work. The stipulation into which the Assistant United States Attorney entered indicated that little additional information concerning the crimes was uncovered in the 17 months following the preparation of the Inspector's report.

To establish prejudice to the defense, respondent testified that he had lost the testimony of two material witnesses due to the delay. The first witness, Tom Stewart, died more than a year after the alleged crimes occurred. At the hearing respondent claimed that Stewart had been his source for two or three of the guns. The second witness, respondent's brother, died in April 1974, nine months after the crimes were completed. Respondent testified that his brother was present when respondent called Stewart to secure the guns, and witnessed all of respondent's sales. Respondent did not state how the witnesses would have aided the defense had they been willing to testify.

The Government made no systematic effort in the District Court to explain its long delay. The Assistant United States Attorney did expressly disagree, however, with defense counsel's suggestion that the investigation had ended after the Postal Inspector's Report was prepared. The prosecutor also stated that it was the Government's theory that respondent's son, who had access to the mail at the railroad terminal from which the guns were "possibly stolen," was responsible for the thefts. Finally, the prosecutor elicited somewhat cryptic testimony from the Postal Inspector indicating that the case "as to these particular weapons involves other individuals"; that information had been presented to a grand jury "in regard to this case other than * * * [on] the day of the indictment itself"; and that he had spoken to the prosecutors about the case on four or five occasions.

Following the hearing, the District Court filed a brief opinion and order. The court found that by October 2, 1973, the date of the postal inspector's report, "The Government had all the information relating to defendant's alleged commission of the offense charged against him," and that the 17–month delay before the case was presented to the grand jury "had not been explained or justified" and was "unnecessary and unreasonable." The Court also found that "[a]s a result of the delay defendant has been prejudiced by reason of the death of Tom Stewart, a material witness on his behalf." Accordingly, the court dismissed the indictment.

The Government appealed to the United States Court of Appeals for the Eighth Circuit. In its brief the Government explained the months of inaction by stating:

> "[T]here was a legitimate Government interest in keeping the investigation open in the instant case. The defendant's son worked for the Terminal Railroad and had access to mail. It was the Government's position that the son was responsible for the theft and therefore further investigation to establish this fact was important.
>
>   "* * * Although the investigation did not continue on a full time basis, there was contact between the United States Attorney's office and the Postal Inspector's office throughout * * * and certain matters were brought before a Federal Grand Jury prior to the determination that the case should be presented for indictment * * *."

The Court of Appeals accepted the Government's representation as to the motivation for the delay, but a majority of the court nevertheless affirmed the District Court's finding that the Government's actions were "unjustified, unnecessary, and unreasonable." The majority also found that respondent had established that his defense had been impaired by the loss of Stewart's testimony because it understood respondent to contend that "were Stewart's testimony available it would support [respondent's] claim that he did not know that the guns were stolen from the United States mails." * * *

We granted certiorari, and now reverse.

In *United States v. Marion*, 404 U.S. 307 (1971), this Court considered the significance, for constitutional purposes, of a lengthy preindictment delay. We held that as far as the Speedy Trial Clause of the Sixth Amendment is concerned, such delay is wholly irrelevant, since our analysis of the language, history, and purposes of the Clause persuaded us that only "a formal indictment or information or else the actual restraints imposed by arrest and holding to answer a criminal charge * * * engage the particular protections" of that provision. We went on to note that statutes of limitations, which provide predictable, legislatively enacted limits on prosecutorial delay, provide "the primary guarantee, against bringing overly stale criminal charges." [a] But we did acknowledge that the "statute of limitations does not fully define [defendants'] rights with respect to the events occurring prior to indictment," and that the Due Process Clause has a limited role to play in protecting against oppressive delay.

Respondent seems to argue that due process bars prosecution whenever a defendant suffers prejudice as a result of preindictment delay. To support that proposition respondent relies on the concluding sentence of the Court's opinion in *Marion* where, in remanding the case, we stated that "[e]vents of the trial may demonstrate actual prejudice, but at the present time appellees' due process claims are speculative and premature." But the quoted sentence establishes only that proof of actual prejudice makes a due process claim concrete and ripe for adjudication, not that it makes the claim automatically valid. Indeed, two pages earlier in the opinion we expressly rejected the argument respondent advances here:

---

**a.** The statute of limitations, in contrast to the speedy trial time limitations, runs from the date the offense is committed (or, in a few states, from the date the offense is discovered) to the date prosecution is commenced (in some states this means the date an indictment or information is filed, in others the date a warrant of arrest is issued). The typical statute specifies situations in which time is not counted against the period of limitation, such as when the defendant is out of the state or is away from his usual residence for the purpose of avoiding prosecution. "There are several reasons for the imposition of time limitations: First, and foremost, is the desirability that prosecutions be based upon reasonably fresh evidence. With the passage of time memories fade, witnesses die or leave the area, and physical evidence becomes more difficult to obtain, identify, or preserve. In short, possibility of erroneous conviction is minimized when prosecution is prompt. Second, if the actor long refrains from further criminal activity, the likelihood increases that he has reformed, diminishing the necessity for imposition of the criminal sanction. If he has repeated his criminal behavior, he can be prosecuted for recent offenses committed within the period of limitation. Hence, the need for protecting society against the perpetrator of a particular offense becomes less compelling as the years pass. Third, after a protracted period the retributive impulse which may have existed in the community is likely to yield to a sense of compassion aroused by the prosecution for an offense long forgotten. Fourth, it is desirable to reduce the possibility of blackmail based on a threat to prosecute or to disclose evidence to enforcement officials. Finally, statutes of limitations 'promote repose by giving security and stability to human affairs.'" *Model Penal Code* § 1.06, Comment (1985).

"[W]e need not \* \* \* determine when and in what circumstances actual prejudice resulting from preaccusation delay requires the dismissal of the prosecution. Actual prejudice to the defense of a criminal case may result from the shortest and most necessary delay; and no one suggests that every delay-caused detriment to a defendant's case should abort a criminal prosecution."

Thus *Marion* makes clear that proof of prejudice is generally a necessary but not sufficient element of a due process claim, and that the due process inquiry must consider the reasons for the delay as well as the prejudice to the accused.

The Court of Appeals found that the sole reason for the delay here was "a hope on the part of the Government that others might be discovered who may have participated in the theft \* \* \*." It concluded that this hope did not justify the delay, and therefore affirmed the dismissal of the indictment. But the Due Process Clause does not permit courts to abort criminal prosecutions simply because they disagree with a prosecutor's judgment as to when to seek an indictment. Judges are not free, in defining "due process," to impose on law enforcement officials our "personal and private notions" of fairness and to "disregard the limits that bind judges in their judicial function." Our task is more circumscribed. We are to determine only whether the actions complained of—here, compelling respondent to stand trial after the Government delayed indictment to investigate further—violates those "fundamental conceptions of justice which lie at the base of our civil and political institutions," and which define "the community's sense of fair play and decency."

It requires no extended argument to establish that prosecutors do not deviate from "fundamental conceptions of justice" when they defer seeking indictments until they have probable cause to believe an accused is guilty; indeed it is unprofessional conduct for a prosecutor to recommend an indictment on less than probable cause. It should be equally obvious that prosecutors are under no duty to file charges as soon as probable cause exists but before they are satisfied they will be able to establish the suspect's guilt beyond a reasonable doubt. To impose such a duty "would have a deleterious effect both upon the rights of the accused and upon the ability of society to protect itself." From the perspective of potential defendants, requiring prosecutions to commence when probable cause is established is undesirable because it would increase the likelihood of unwarranted charges being filed, and would add to the time during which defendants stand accused but untried. \* \* \* From the perspective of law enforcement officials, a requirement of immediate prosecution upon probable cause is equally unacceptable because it could make obtaining proof of guilt beyond a reasonable doubt impossible by causing potentially fruitful sources of information to evaporate before they are fully exploited. And from the standpoint of the courts, such a requirement is unwise because it would cause scarce resources to be consumed on cases that prove to be insubstantial, or that involve only some of the responsible parties or some of the criminal acts.[12] Thus, no one's interests would be well served by compelling prosecutors to initiate prosecutions as soon as they are legally entitled to do so.

It might be argued that once the Government has assembled sufficient evidence to prove guilt beyond a reasonable doubt, it should be constitutionally required to file charges promptly, even if its investigation of the entire criminal transaction is not complete. Adopting such a rule, however, would have many of

12. Defendants also would be adversely affected by trials involving less than all of the criminal acts for which they are responsible, since they likely would be subjected to multiple trials growing out of the same transaction or occurrence.

the same consequences as adopting a rule requiring immediate prosecution upon probable cause.

First, compelling a prosecutor to file public charges as soon as the requisite proof has been developed against one participant on one charge would cause numerous problems in those cases in which a criminal transaction involves more than one person or more than one illegal act. In some instances, an immediate arrest or indictment would impair the prosecutor's ability to continue his investigation, thereby preventing society from bringing lawbreakers to justice. In other cases, the prosecutor would be able to obtain additional indictments despite an early prosecution, but the necessary result would be multiple trials involving a single set of facts. Such trials place needless burdens on defendants, law enforcement officials, and courts.

Second, insisting on immediate prosecution once sufficient evidence is developed to obtain a conviction would pressure prosecutors into resolving doubtful cases in favor of early—and possibly unwarranted—prosecutions. The determination of when the evidence available to the prosecution is sufficient to obtain a conviction is seldom clear-cut, and reasonable persons often will reach conflicting conclusions. In the instant case, for example, since respondent admitted possessing at least five of the firearms, the primary factual issue in dispute was whether respondent knew the guns were stolen as required by 18 U.S.C. § 1708. Not surprisingly, the Postal Inspector's report contained no direct evidence bearing on this issue. The decision whether to prosecute, therefore, required a necessarily subjective evaluation of the strength of the circumstantial evidence available and the credibility of respondent's denial. Even if a prosecutor concluded that the case was weak and further investigation appropriate, he would have no assurance that a reviewing court would agree. To avoid the risk that a subsequent indictment would be dismissed for preindictment delay, the prosecutor might feel constrained to file premature charges with all the disadvantages that entails.[14]

Finally, requiring the Government to make charging decisions immediately upon assembling evidence sufficient to establish guilt would preclude the Government from giving full consideration to the desirability of not prosecuting in particular cases. The decision to file criminal charges, with the awesome consequences it entails, requires consideration of a wide range of factors in addition to the strength of the Government's case, in order to determine whether prosecution would be in the public interest. Prosecutors often need more information than proof of a suspect's guilt, therefore, before deciding whether to seek an indictment. Again the instant case provides a useful illustration. Although proof of the identity of the mail thieves was not necessary to convict respondent of the possessory crimes with which he was charged, it might have been crucial in assessing respondent's culpability, as distinguished from his legal guilt. If, for example, further investigation were to show that respondent had no role in or advance knowledge of the theft and simply agreed, out of paternal loyalty, to help his son dispose of the guns once respondent discovered his son had stolen them, the United States Attorney might have decided not to prosecute, especially since at the time of the crime respondent was over 60 years old and had no prior criminal record. Requiring prosecution once the evidence of guilt is clear, however, could prevent a prosecutor from awaiting the information necessary for such a decision.

---

**14.** In addition, if courts were required to decide in every case when the prosecution should have commenced, it would be necessary for them to trace the day-by-day progress of each investigation. Maintaining daily records would impose an administrative burden on prosecutors, and reviewing them would place an even greater burden on the courts.

We would be most reluctant to adopt a rule which would have these consequences absent a clear constitutional command to do so. We can find no such command in the Due Process Clause of the Fifth Amendment. In our view, investigative delay is fundamentally unlike delay undertaken by the Government solely "to gain tactical advantage over the accused," precisely because investigative delay is not so one-sided.[17] Rather than deviating from elementary standards of "fair play and decency," a prosecutor abides by them if he refuses to seek indictments until he is completely satisfied that he should prosecute and will be able promptly to establish guilt beyond a reasonable doubt. Penalizing prosecutors who defer action for these reasons would subordinate the goal of "orderly expedition" to that of "mere speed." This the Due Process Clause does not require. We therefore hold that to prosecute a defendant following investigative delay does not deprive him of due process, even if his defense might have been somewhat prejudiced by the lapse of time.

In the present case, the Court of Appeals stated that the only reason the Government postponed action was to await the results of additional investigation. Although there is, unfortunately, no evidence concerning the reasons for the delay in the record, the court's "finding" is supported by the prosecutor's implicit representation to the District Court, and explicit representation to the Court of Appeals, that the investigation continued during the time that the Government deferred taking action against respondent. The finding is, moreover, buttressed by the Government's repeated assertions in their Petition for Certiorari, their Brief, and their oral argument in this Court, "that the delay was caused by the Government's efforts to identify persons in addition to respondent who may have participated in the offenses." We must assume that these statements by counsel have been made in good faith. In light of this explanation, it follows that compelling respondent to stand trial would not be fundamentally unfair. The Court of Appeals therefore erred in affirming the District Court's decision dismissing the indictment.[b]

---

**17.** In *Marion* we noted with approval that the Government conceded that a "tactical" delay would violate the Due Process Clause. The Government renews that concession here, and expands it somewhat by stating that "A due process violation might also be made out upon a showing of prosecutorial delay incurred in reckless disregard of circumstances, known to the prosecution, suggesting that there existed an appreciable risk that delay would impair the ability to mount an effective defense." As the Government notes, however, there is no evidence of recklessness here.

**b.** Stevens, J., dissenting, agreed with the foregoing principles, but concluded the majority had erred in not deciding the case on the record made in the district court, wherein the government's delay was unexplained.

# Chapter 13

# THE DUTY TO DISCLOSE

In order to make the criminal trial "less a game of blindman's bluff and more a fair contest with the basic issues and facts disclosed to the fullest practical extent," *United States v. Procter & Gamble Co.*, 356 U.S. 677 (1958), the state and federal criminal justice systems, over the last few decades, have expanded dramatically the obligations of both prosecution and defense to disclose to the other side before trial the evidence that each intends to use at trial. This movement toward liberal pretrial "discovery" initially emphasized prosecution disclosure to the defense. The permissible scope of defense discovery varied,[a] but one constant objection to expanding such discovery was the absence of "reciprocity" in disclosure obligations—the failure to make discovery a "two-way street." This, in turn, led to expansion of the defense obligation to disclose its evidence to the prosecution. Most jurisdictions, however, concerned about possible constitutional objections to imposing such an obligation on the defense, initially provided the prosecution with very limited discovery. One of the earliest measures providing for prosecution discovery was the reciprocal alibi-notice statute. The first case in this chapter, *Williams v. Florida*, treats the constitutionality of such a statute. The ruling in *Williams* was seen by many as giving the states leeway constitutionally to grant the prosecution a fairly expansive right of discovery. It led to a variety of broadened reciprocal discovery requirements (e.g., requiring defense disclosure of the names of all of its intended witnesses), none of which have subsequently reached the Court.

While pretrial discovery requirements are designed primarily to avoid surprise and thereby allow a party ample time to build a case responsive to its opponent, the due process doctrine explored in *United States v. Bagley* actually requires the prosecution to assist the defense in building its case. In *Brady v. Maryland*, 373 U.S. 83 (1963), the Supreme Court established a constitutional duty of the prosecution to disclose to the defense exculpatory evidence that is material to the issues of either guilt or punishment. *Bagley* explores the scope

---

**a.** Some jurisdictions basically give the defense access to all of the evidence that the prosecution intends to use at trial, including not only a list of the prosecution's intended witnesses, but also any written summaries of statements those witnesses have made to the police or prosecutor. In other jurisdictions, discovery requirements are more limited out of concern that the defendant, if he knew who would be testifying for the prosecution and what they would say, would either develop perjured testimony to rebut their testimony or seek to intimidate those witnesses. Here disclosure is likely to be limited to documents, the reports of experts, and any recorded statements of defendant himself (usually given in response to police interrogation) that the prosecution intends to use at trial. What the states provide in the way of defense discovery is basically a matter of state choice. The Supreme Court had noted on several occasions that "there is no general constitutional right to discovery in a criminal case." *Weatherford v. Bursey*, 429 U.S. 545 (1977).

of this "*Brady* rule." *Pennsylvania v. Ritchie* raises the question of whether the prosecution's obligation to assist the defense in preparing its case goes beyond the *Brady* rule as a result of the defendant's Sixth Amendment rights to confront opposing witnesses and to present witnesses in his favor. Other aspects of those rights are considered in Chapter Eighteen.

## WILLIAMS v. FLORIDA

399 U.S. 78, 90 S.Ct. 1893, 26 L.Ed.2d 446 (1970).

JUSTICE WHITE delivered the opinion of the Court.

Prior to his trial for robbery in the State of Florida, petitioner filed a "Motion for a Protective Order," seeking to be excused from the requirements of Rule 1.200 [now Rule 3.200] of the Florida Rules of Criminal Procedure. That rule requires a defendant, on written demand of the prosecuting attorney, to give notice in advance of trial if the defendant intends to claim an alibi, and to furnish the prosecuting attorney with information as to the place he claims to have been and with the names and addresses of the alibi witnesses he intends to use. In his motion petitioner openly declared his intent to claim an alibi, but objected to the further disclosure requirements on the ground that the Rule "compels the defendant in a criminal case to be a witness against himself" in violation of his Fifth and Fourteenth Amendment rights. The motion was denied. * * *

Florida's notice-of-alibi rule is in essence a requirement that a defendant submit to a limited form of pretrial discovery by the State whenever he intends to rely at trial on the defense of alibi. In exchange for the defendant's disclosure of the witnesses he proposes to use to establish that defense, the State in turn is required to notify the defendant of any witnesses it proposes to offer in rebuttal to that defense. Both sides are under a continuing duty promptly to disclose the names and addresses of additional witnesses bearing on the alibi as they become available. The threatened sanction for failure to comply is the exclusion at trial of the defendant's alibi evidence—except for his own testimony—or, in the case of the State, the exclusion of the State's evidence offered in rebuttal to the alibi.

In this case, following the denial of his Motion for a Protective Order, petitioner complied with the alibi rule and gave the State the name and address of one Mary Scotty. Mrs. Scotty was summoned to the office of the State Attorney on the morning of the trial, where she gave pretrial testimony. At the trial itself, Mrs. Scotty, petitioner and petitioner's wife all testified that the three of them had been in Mrs. Scotty's apartment during the time of the robbery. On two occasions during cross-examination of Mrs. Scotty, the prosecuting attorney confronted her with her earlier deposition in which she had given dates and times which in some respects did not correspond with the dates and times given at trial. Mrs. Scotty adhered to her trial story, insisting that she had been mistaken in her earlier testimony. The State also offered in rebuttal the testimony of one of the officers investigating the robbery who claimed that Mrs. Scotty had asked him for directions on the afternoon in question during the time when she claimed to have been in her apartment with petitioner and his wife.

We need not linger over the suggestion that the discovery permitted the State against petitioner in this case deprived him of "due process" or a "fair trial." Florida law provides for liberal discovery by the defendant against the State, and the notice-of-alibi rule is itself carefully hedged with reciprocal duties requiring state disclosure to the defendant.[a]  Given the ease with which an alibi can be fabricated, the State's interest in protecting itself against an eleventh hour defense is both obvious and legitimate.  Reflecting this interest, notice-of-alibi provisions, dating at least from 1927, are now in existence in a substantial number of States.  The adversary system of trial is hardly an end to itself; it is not yet a poker game in which players enjoy an absolute right always to conceal their cards until played.  We find ample room in that system, at least as far as "due process" is concerned, for the instant Florida rule, which is designed to enhance the search for truth in the criminal trial by insuring both the defendant and the State ample opportunity to investigate certain facts crucial to the determination of guilt or innocence.

Petitioner's major contention is that he was "compelled to be a witness against himself" contrary to the commands of the Fifth and Fourteenth Amendments because the notice-of-alibi rule required him to give the State the name and address of Mrs. Scotty in advance of trial and thus to furnish the State with information useful in convicting him.  No pretrial statement of petitioner was introduced at trial; but armed with Mrs. Scotty's name and address and the knowledge that she was to be petitioner's alibi witness, the State was able to take her deposition in advance of trial and to find rebuttal testimony.  Also, requiring him to reveal the elements of his defense is claimed to have interfered with his right to wait until after the State had presented its case to decide how to defend against it.  We conclude, however, as has apparently every other court which has considered the issue, that the privilege against self-incrimination is not violated by a requirement that the defendant give notice of an alibi defense and disclose his alibi witnesses.

The defendant in a criminal trial is frequently forced to testify himself and to call other witnesses in an effort to reduce the risk of conviction.  When he presents his witnesses, he must reveal their identity and submit them to cross-examination which in itself may prove incriminating or which may furnish the State with leads to incriminating rebuttal evidence.  That the defendant faces such a dilemma demanding a choice between complete silence and presenting a defense has never been thought an invasion of the privilege against compelled self-incrimination.  The pressures generated by the State's evidence may be severe but they do not vitiate the defendant's choice to present an alibi defense and witnesses to prove it, even though the attempted defense ends in catastrophe for the defendant.  However "testimonial" and "incriminating" the alibi defense proves to be, it cannot be considered "compelled" within the meaning of the Fifth and Fourteenth Amendments.

Very similar constraints operate on the defendant when the State requires pretrial notice of alibi and the naming of alibi witnesses.  Nothing in such a rule requires the defendant to rely on an alibi or prevents him from abandoning the defense; these matters are left to his unfettered choice.  That choice must be made, but the pressures which bear on his pretrial decision are of the same nature as those which would induce him to call alibi witnesses at the trial: the force of historical fact beyond both his and the State's control and the strength of the State's case built on these facts.  Response to that kind of pressure by

a.  The critical nature of this feature of the Florida alibi-discovery rule was later brought home in *Wardius v. Oregon,* 412 U.S. 470 (1973).  Distinguishing *Williams,* the Court there held that an alibi-discovery rule which failed to provide reciprocal defense discovery violated due process.  *Wardius* noted: "The State may not insist that trials be run as a 'search for the truth' so far as defense witnesses are concerned, while maintaining 'poker game secrecy' for its own witnesses."

offering evidence or testimony is not compelled self-incrimination transgressing the Fifth and Fourteenth Amendments.

In the case before us, the notice-of-alibi rule by itself in no way affected petitioner's crucial decision to call alibi witnesses or added to the legitimate pressures leading to that course of action. At most, the rule only compelled petitioner to accelerate the timing of his disclosure, forcing him to divulge at an earlier date information which the petitioner from the beginning planned to divulge at trial. Nothing in the Fifth Amendment privilege entitles a defendant as a matter of constitutional right to await the end of the State's case before announcing the nature of his defense, any more than it entitles him to await the jury's verdict on the State's case-in-chief before deciding whether or not to take the stand himself.

Petitioner concedes that absent the notice-of-alibi rule the Constitution would raise no bar to the court's granting the State a continuance at trial on the grounds of surprise as soon as the alibi witness is called. Nor would there be self-incrimination problems if, during that continuance, the State was permitted to do precisely what it did here prior to trial: to depose the witness and find rebuttal evidence. But if so utilizing a continuance is permissible under the Fifth and Fourteenth Amendments, then surely the same result may be accomplished through pretrial discovery, as it was here, avoiding the necessity of a disrupted trial.[17] We decline to hold that the privilege against compulsory self-incrimination guarantees the defendant the right to surprise the state with an alibi defense.

CHIEF JUSTICE BURGER, concurring.

I join fully in Mr. Justice White's opinion for the Court. I see an added benefit to the alibi notice rule in that it will serve important functions by way of disposing of cases without trial in appropriate circumstances—a matter of considerable importance when courts, prosecution offices and legal aid and defender agencies are vastly overworked. [The Chief Justice noted that a prosecutor receiving the names of alibi witnesses in advance of trial often would be able to determine whether an alibi defense was "reliable and unimpeachable" or "contrived and fabricated." The former determination "would very likely lead to dismissal of the charges," while the latter could lead to a defense decision to plead guilty. In either instance, the Chief Justice noted, "the ends of justice will have been served and the processes expedited."] * * *

JUSTICE BLACK, with whom JUSTICE DOUGLAS joins, dissenting.

* * * Although this case itself involves only a notice-of-alibi provision, it is clear that the decision means that a State can require a defendant to disclose in advance of trial any and all information he might possibly use to defend himself at trial. This decision, in my view, is a radical and dangerous departure from the historical and constitutionally guaranteed right of a defendant in a criminal case to remain completely silent, requiring the State to prove its case without any assistance of any kind from the defendant himself.

The core of the majority's decision is an assumption that compelling a defendant to give notice of an alibi defense before a trial is no different from requiring a defendant, after the State has produced the evidence against him at trial, to plead alibi before the jury retires to consider the case. * * * [But] when a defendant is required to indicate whether he might plead alibi in

---

17. It might also be argued that the "testimonial" disclosures protected by the Fifth Amendment include only statements relating to the historical facts of the crime, not statements relating solely to what a defendant proposes to do at trial.

advance of trial, he faces a vastly different decision than that faced by one who can wait until the State has presented the case against him before making up his mind. Before trial the defendant knows only what the State's case *might* be. Before trial there is no such thing as the "strength of the State's case," there is only a range of possible cases. At that time there is no certainty as to what kind of case the State will ultimately be able to prove at trial. Therefore any appraisal of the desirability of pleading alibi will be beset with guesswork and gambling far greater than that accompanying the decision at the trial itself. * * * Clearly the pressures on defendants to plead an alibi created by this procedure are not only quite different than the pressures operating at the trial itself, but are in fact significantly greater. Contrary to the majority's assertion, the pretrial decision cannot be analyzed as simply a matter of "timing," influenced by the same factors operating at the trial itself.

The Court apparently also assumes that a defendant who has given the required notice can abandon his alibi without hurting himself. Such an assumption is implicit in and necessary for the majority's argument that the pretrial decision is no different than that at the trial itself. I, however, cannot so lightly assume that pretrial notice will have no adverse effects on a defendant who later decides to forego such a defense. Necessarily the defendant will have given the prosecutor the names of persons who may have some knowledge about the defendant himself or his activities. Necessarily the prosecutor will have every incentive to question these persons fully, and in doing so he may discover new leads or evidence. Undoubtedly there will be situations in which the State will seek to use such information—information it would probably never have obtained but for the defendant's coerced cooperation.

It is unnecessary for me, however, to engage in any such intellectual gymnastics concerning the practical effects of the notice-of-alibi procedure, because the Fifth Amendment itself clearly provides that "[n]o person * * * shall be compelled in any criminal case to be a witness against himself." If words are to be given their plain and obvious meaning, that provision, in my opinion, states that a criminal defendant cannot be required to give evidence, testimony, or any other assistance to the State to aid it in convicting him of crime. The Florida notice-of-alibi rule in my opinion is a patent violation of that constitutional provision because it requires a defendant to disclose information to the State so that the State can use that information to destroy him. * * *

It is no answer to this argument to suggest that the Fifth Amendment as so interpreted would give the defendant an unfair element of surprise, turning a trial into a "poker game" or "sporting contest," for that tactical advantage to the defendant is inherent in the type of trial required by our Bill of Rights. The Framers were well aware of the awesome investigative and prosecutorial powers of government and it was in order to limit those powers that they spelled out in detail in the Constitution the procedure to be followed in criminal trials. * * * The defendant, under our Constitution, need not do anything at all to defend himself, and certainly he cannot be required to help convict himself. Rather he has an absolute, unqualified right to compel the State to investigate its own case, find its own witnesses, prove its own facts, and convince the jury through its own resources. Throughout the process the defendant has a fundamental right to remain silent, in effect challenging the State at every point to "Prove it!" * * *

This constitutional right to remain absolutely silent cannot be avoided by superficially attractive analogies to any so-called "compulsion" inherent in the trial itself which may lead a defendant to put on evidence in his own defense.

Obviously the Constitution contemplates that a defendant can be "compelled" to stand trial, and obviously there will be times when the trial process itself will require the defendant to do something in order to try to avoid a conviction. But nothing in the Constitution permits the State to add to the natural consequences of a trial and compel the defendant in advance of trial to participate in any way in the State's attempt to condemn him. * * *

On the surface this case involves only a notice-of-alibi provision, but in effect the decision opens the way for a profound change in one of the most important traditional safeguards of a criminal defendant. The rationale of today's decision is in no way limited to alibi defenses, or any other type or classification of evidence. The theory advanced goes at least so far as to permit the State to obtain under threat of sanction complete disclosure by the defendant in advance of trial of all evidence, testimony and tactics he plans to use at that trial. In each case the justification will be that the rule affects only the "timing" of the disclosure, and not the substantive decision itself. * * *[b]

# UNITED STATES v. BAGLEY

473 U.S. 667, 105 S.Ct. 3375, 87 L.Ed.2d 481 (1985).

JUSTICE BLACKMUN announced the judgment of the Court and delivered an opinion of the Court except as to Part III.

In *Brady v. Maryland*, 373 U.S. 83 (1963), this Court held that "the suppression by the prosecution of evidence favorable to an accused upon request

**b.** A footnote in the *Williams* opinion noted that the case there before the Court did not present the question of the "validity of the threatened sanction" (the exclusion of the testimony of unlisted witnesses) as "no such penalty was exacted here." In a later case, *Taylor v. Illinois,* 108 S.Ct. 646 (1988), the Court upheld the exclusion of the testimony of defense witness who had not been listed at discovery. In that case, as authorized by state law, the prosecution requested a pretrial listing of all defense witnesses after it had provided defense with a list of its witnesses. Defense counsel listed four witnesses, but during the midst of the trial, sought to add two additional witnesses. Counsel initially stated that he had just been informed about these persons and that they had probably seen the incident in question (a shooting). In response to the trial judge's inquiry, counsel then acknowledged that the defendant had previously told him about one of the witnesses, but counsel stated that he had been unable until now to locate that witness. The trial court then questioned that witness and learned both that the witness had not actually seen the incident (although he claimed to have information that would be relevant to defendant's explanation of the shooting) and that counsel had met with the witness a week before trial. The trial court concluded that counsel's failure to give earlier notice of his intent to call the witness constituted a "blatant" and "willful" violation of the discovery rules that would require precluding the witness from testifying.

Sustaining the application of the preclusion sanction, the Supreme Court majority initially rejected the contention that the Sixth Amendment's compulsory process clause creates an absolute bar to the preclusion of the testimony of a surprise witness. It noted that the "adversary process could not function effectively without rules of procedure that govern the orderly presentation of facts and arguments to provide each party with a fair opportunity to assemble and submit evidence to contradict or explain the opponent's case," and that those rules served "the same high purpose" in "full and truthful disclosure of critical facts" as the compulsory process clause and other rights protected by the Sixth Amendment. Defendant argued that alternative and more appropriate sanctions than preclusion were available, (e.g., allowing the state a continuance or disciplining the defense counsel), but the Court responded that, while "it may well be true that alternative sanctions are adequate and appropriate in most cases," a preclusion sanction could not be absolutely barred as it is "equally clear that [those alternative sanctions] would be less effective than the preclusion sanction and that there are instances in which they would perpetuate rather than limit the prejudice to the State and harm to the adversary process." As for the case before it, the Court concluded that circumstances clearly indicated that defense counsel was "deliberately seeking a tactical advantage," and "regardless of whether the prejudice to the prosecution could have been avoided," the case fit into "the category of willful misconduct in which the severest sanction is appropriate."

violates due process where the evidence is material either to guilt or punishment." The issue in the present case concerns the standard of materiality to be applied in determining whether a conviction should be reversed because the prosecutor failed to disclose requested evidence that could have been used to impeach Government witnesses.

I

[Respondent Bagley was indicted on 15 counts of violating federal narcotics and firearms statutes. The Government's two principal witnesses were O'Connor and Mitchell, private security guards who had assisted the Bureau of Alcohol, Tobacco and Firearms (ATF) in conducting an undercover investigation of respondent. Several weeks before trial, respondent filed a discovery motion that requested disclosure of a variety of matters, including "any deals, promises or inducements made to witnesses in exchange for their testimony." The Government's response to the discovery motion did not disclose that any "deals, promises or inducements" had been made to O'Connor or Mitchell. In apparent reply to another part of the discovery request, the Government produced a series of affidavits that O'Connor and Mitchell had signed while the undercover investigation was in progress. Those affidavits recounted in detail their undercover dealings with respondent. Each affidavit concluded with the statement, "I made this statement freely and voluntarily without any threats or rewards, or promises of reward having been made to me in return for it."]

[Respondent waived his right to a jury trial and was tried before the district court. At the trial, O'Connor and Mitchell testified about both the firearms and the narcotics charges. The court found respondent guilty on the narcotics charges, but not guilty on the firearms charges. Sometime later, respondent filed requests for information pursuant to the Freedom of Information Act. He received in response copies of ATF form contracts between ATF and O'Connor and Mitchell. The printed portion of the form stated that the informant would provide information to ATF and that "upon receipt of such information * * * and upon the accomplishment of the objective sought to be obtained by the use of such information to the satisfaction of (the ATF), the United States will pay to said vendor a sum commensurate with services and information rendered." The figure "$300.00" was handwritten in each form on a line entitled "Sum to Be Paid to Vendor." Because these contracts had not been disclosed in response to his pretrial discovery motion, respondent moved the district court to vacate his sentence. The Assistant United States Attorney who prosecuted respondent stated that he had not known that the contracts existed, and that he would have furnished them to respondent had he known of them, but the government also argued that there had been no constitutional error.]

[The motion came before the same district judge who had presided at respondent's bench trial. The district judge accepted the findings of a magistrate that the printed form contracts were blank when O'Connor and Mitchell signed them, that they were not signed by an ATF representative until after the trial, and that ATF made payments of $300 to both O'Connor and Mitchell at that time. Although the ATF case agent who dealt with O'Connor and Mitchell testified that the $300 payments simply reimbursed expenses, the district judge found that it was "probable" that O'Connor and Mitchell expected to receive compensation, in addition to their expenses. The judge concluded that "the United States did * * * withhold, during pretrial discovery, information as to any 'deals, promises or inducements' to these witnesses," but also found, beyond a reasonable doubt, that had the existence of the agreements been disclosed during trial, the disclosure would have had no effect upon his finding that the

Government had proved its case on the narcotics charges. The United States Court of Appeals for the Ninth Circuit reversed, reasoning that the failure to disclose automatically required reversal of the conviction.]

## II

The holding in *Brady v. Maryland,* 373 U.S. 83 (1963), requires disclosure only of evidence that is both favorable to the accused and "material either to guilt or punishment." The Court explained in *United States v. Agurs,* 427 U.S. 97 (1976): "A fair analysis of the holding in *Brady* indicates that implicit in the requirement of materiality is a concern that the suppressed evidence might have affected the outcome of the trial." The evidence suppressed in *Brady* would have been admissible only on the issue of punishment and not on the issue of guilt, and therefore could have affected only Brady's sentence and not his conviction. Accordingly, the Court affirmed the lower court's restriction of Brady's new trial to the issue of punishment.[a]

The *Brady* rule is based on the requirement of due process. Its purpose is not to displace the adversary system as the primary means by which truth is uncovered, but to ensure that a miscarriage of justice does not occur.[6] Thus, the prosecutor is not required to deliver his entire file to defense counsel,[7] but only to disclose evidence favorable to the accused that, if suppressed, would deprive the defendant of a fair trial. \* \* \* As *Agurs* noted: "For unless the omission deprived the defendant of a fair trial, there was no constitutional violation requiring that the verdict be set aside; and absent a constitutional violation, there was no breach of the prosecutor's constitutional duty to disclose. \* \* \* " *United States v. Agurs.*

In *Brady* \* \* \*, the prosecutor failed to disclose exculpatory evidence. In the present case, the prosecutor failed to disclose evidence that the defense might have used to impeach the Government's witnesses by showing bias or interest. Impeachment evidence, however, as well as exculpatory evidence, falls within the *Brady* rule. Such evidence is "evidence favorable to an accused,"

---

**a.** The defendant Brady and a companion, Boblit, had been found guilty of felony murder and sentenced to death. Prior to Brady's separate trial, his counsel had asked the prosecutor to allow him to examine all of the statements that Boblit had given to the police. Counsel was shown several of Boblit's statements, but for some unexplained reason failed to receive one statement in which Boblit admitted that he had done the actual killing. At trial, defendant admitted his participation in the crime, but claimed that he had not himself killed the victim. Defense counsel stressed this claim in his closing argument, asking the jury to show leniency and not impose the death penalty. Following defendant's conviction, defense counsel learned of the undisclosed statement and sought a new trial based on this newly discovered evidence. The Supreme Court affirmed a state court ruling granting a new trial as to the issue of punishment alone. Whether or not defendant himself killed the victim had no bearing on his liability for the homicide, and Boblit's statement therefore would not have been admissible in evidence on that issue. On the other hand, the statement could have been used to support defendant's plea for leniency as to punishment, and the prosecution's failure to disclose the statement had deprived Brady of a fair hearing on that issue.

**6.** By requiring the prosecutor to assist the defense in making its case, the *Brady* rule represents a limited departure from a pure adversary model. The Court has recognized, however, that the prosecutor's role transcends that of an adversary: he "is the representative not of an ordinary party to a controversy, but of a sovereignty \* \* \* whose interest \* \* \* in a criminal prosecution is not that it shall win a case, but that justice shall be done." *Berger v. United States,* 295 U.S. 78 (1935).

**7.** \* \* \* An interpretation of *Brady* to create a broad, constitutionally required right of discovery "would entirely alter the character and balance of our present systems of criminal justice." *Giles v. Maryland,* 386 U.S. 66 (1967) (dissenting opinion). Furthermore, a rule that the prosecutor commits error by any failure to disclose evidence favorable to the accused, no matter how insignificant, would impose an impossible burden on the prosecutor and would undermine the interest in the finality of judgments.

*Brady,* so that, if disclosed and used effectively, it may make the difference between conviction and acquittal.  Cf. *Napue v. Illinois* [fn. 8 infra] ("The jury's estimate of the truthfulness and reliability of a given witness may well be determinative of guilt or innocence, and it is upon such subtle factors as the possible interest of the witness in testifying falsely that a defendant's life or liberty may depend").  *  *  *

### III

It remains to determine the standard of materiality applicable to the nondisclosed evidence at issue in this case.  Our starting point is the framework for evaluating the materiality of *Brady* evidence established in *United States v. Agurs.*  The Court in *Agurs* distinguished three situations involving the discovery, after trial, of information favorable to the accused that had been known to the prosecution but unknown to the defense.  The first situation was the prosecutor's knowing use of perjured testimony or, equivalently, the prosecutor's knowing failure to disclose that testimony used to convict the defendant was false.  The Court noted the well-established rule that "a conviction obtained by the knowing use of perjured testimony is fundamentally unfair, and must be set aside if there is any reasonable likelihood that the false testimony could have affected the judgment of the jury."  427 U.S., at 103.[8]  Although this rule is stated in terms that treat the knowing use of perjured testimony as error subject to harmless-error review, it may as easily be stated as a materiality standard under which the fact that testimony is perjured is considered material unless failure to disclose it would be harmless beyond a reasonable doubt.  The Court in *Agurs* justified this standard of materiality on the ground that the knowing use of perjured testimony involves prosecutorial misconduct and, more importantly, involves "a corruption of the truth-seeking function of the trial process."

At the other extreme is the situation in *Agurs* itself, where the defendant does not make a *Brady* request and the prosecutor fails to disclose certain evidence favorable to the accused.  The Court rejected a harmless-error rule in that situation, because under that rule every nondisclosure is treated as error, thus imposing on the prosecutor a constitutional duty to deliver his entire file to defense counsel.  At the same time, the Court rejected a standard that would require the defendant to demonstrate that the evidence if disclosed probably would have resulted in acquittal.[b]  The Court reasoned: "If the standard applied

**8.**  In fact, the *Brady* rule has its roots in a series of cases dealing with convictions based on the prosecution's knowing use of perjured testimony.  In *Mooney v. Holohan,* 294 U.S. 103 (1935), the Court established the rule that the knowing use by a state prosecutor of perjured testimony to obtain a conviction and the deliberate suppression of evidence that would have impeached and refuted the testimony constitutes a denial of due process.  The Court reasoned that "a deliberate deception of court and jury by the presentation of testimony known to be perjured" is inconsistent with "the rudimentary demands of justice."  The Court reaffirmed this principle in broader terms in *Napue v. Illinois,* 360 U.S. 264 (1959).  In *Napue,* the principal witness for the prosecution falsely testified that he had been promised no consideration for his testimony.  The Court held that the knowing use of false testimony to obtain a conviction violates due process regardless of whether the prosecutor solicited the false testimony or merely allowed

it to go uncorrected when it appeared.  The Court explained that the principle that a State may not knowingly use false testimony to obtain a conviction—even false testimony that goes only to the credibility of the witness—is "implicit in any concept of ordered liberty."  Finally, the Court held that it was not bound by the state court's determination that the false testimony "could not in any reasonable likelihood have affected the judgment of the jury."  The Court conducted its own independent examination of the record and concluded that the false testimony "may have had an effect on the outcome of the trial."  Accordingly, the Court reversed the judgment of conviction.

**b.**  The reference here was to what *Agurs* described as the "Rule 33 Standard"—the test applied to a motion for a new trial based on evidence newly discovered by the defense.  That standard typically requires that the defense establish (1) that its failure to learn of to the usual motion for a new trial based on newly discovered evidence were the same when the evidence was in the State's possession as when it was found in a neutral source, there would be no special significance to the prosecutor's obligation to serve the cause of justice." The standard of materiality applicable in the absence of a specific *Brady* request is therefore stricter than the harmless-error standard but more lenient to the defense than the newly discovered evidence standard.

The third situation identified by the Court in *Agurs* is where the defense makes a specific request and the prosecutor fails to disclose responsive evidence. The Court did not define the standard of materiality applicable in this situation, but suggested that the standard might be more lenient to the defense than in the situation in which the defense makes no request or only a general request. The Court also noted: "When the prosecutor receives a specific and relevant request, the failure to make any response is seldom, if ever, excusable."

The Court has relied on and reformulated the *Agurs* standard for the materiality of undisclosed evidence in two subsequent cases arising outside the *Brady* context. In neither case did the Court's discussion of the *Agurs* standard distinguish among the three situations described in *Agurs*. In *United States v. Valenzuela–Bernal,* 458 U.S. 858 (1982), the Court held that due process is violated when testimony is made unavailable to the defense by Government deportation of witnesses "only if there is a reasonable likelihood that the testimony could have affected the judgment of the trier of fact." And in *Strickland v. Washington,* [Ch. 17, § 2], the Court held that a new trial must be granted when evidence is not introduced because of the incompetence of counsel only if "there is a reasonable probability that, but for counsel's unprofessional errors, the result of the proceeding would have been different." The *Strickland* Court defined a "reasonable probability" as "a probability sufficient to undermine confidence in the outcome."

We find the *Strickland* formulation of the *Agurs* test for materiality sufficiently flexible to cover the "no request," "general request," and "specific request" cases of prosecutorial failure to disclose evidence favorable to the accused: The evidence is material only if there is a reasonable probability that, had the evidence been disclosed to the defense, the result of the proceeding would have been different. A "reasonable probability" is a probability sufficient to undermine confidence in the outcome.

The Government suggests that a materiality standard more favorable to the defendant reasonably might be adopted in specific request cases. The Government notes that an incomplete response to a specific request not only deprives the defense of certain evidence, but has the effect of representing to the defense that the evidence does not exist. In reliance on this misleading representation, the defense might abandon lines of independent investigation, defenses, or trial strategies that it otherwise would have pursued.

We agree that the prosecutor's failure to respond fully to a *Brady* request may impair the adversary process in this manner. And the more specifically the defense requests certain evidence, thus putting the prosecutor on notice of its value, the more reasonable it is for the defense to assume from the nondisclosure that the evidence does not exist, and to make pretrial and trial decisions on the basis of this assumption. This possibility of impairment does not necessitate a different standard of materiality, however, for under the *Strickland* formulation

the evidence previously was due to no lack of diligence, (2) that the evidence is material, not merely "cumulative or impeaching," and (3) that the evidence "will probably produce an acquittal."

the reviewing court may consider directly any adverse effect that the prosecutor's failure to respond might have had on the preparation or presentation of the defendant's case. The reviewing court should assess the possibility that such effect might have occurred in light of the totality of the circumstances and with an awareness of the difficulty of reconstructing in a post-trial proceeding the course that the defense and the trial would have taken had the defense not been misled by the prosecutor's incomplete response.

In the present case, we think that there is a significant likelihood that the prosecutor's response to respondent's discovery motion misleadingly induced defense counsel to believe that O'Connor and Mitchell could not be impeached on the basis of bias or interest arising from inducements offered by the Government. Defense counsel asked the prosecutor to disclose any inducements that had been made to witnesses, and the prosecutor failed to disclose that the possibility of a reward had been held out to O'Connor and Mitchell if the information they supplied led to "the accomplishment of the objective sought to be obtained * * * to the satisfaction of [the Government]." This possibility of a reward gave O'Connor and Mitchell a direct, personal stake in respondent's conviction. The fact that the stake was not guaranteed through a promise or binding contract, but was expressly contingent on the Government's satisfaction with the end result, served only to strengthen any incentive to testify falsely in order to secure a conviction. Moreover, the prosecutor disclosed affidavits that stated that O'Connor and Mitchell received no promises of reward in return for providing information in the affidavits implicating respondent in criminal activity. In fact, O'Connor and Mitchell signed the last of these affidavits the very day after they signed the ATF contracts. While petitioner is technically correct that the blank contracts did not constitute a "promise of reward," the natural effect of these affidavits would be misleadingly to induce defense counsel to believe that O'Connor and Mitchell provided the information in the affidavits, and ultimately their testimony at trial recounting the same information, without any "inducements."

The District Court, nonetheless, found beyond a reasonable doubt that, had the information that the Government held out the possibility of reward to its witnesses been disclosed, the result of the criminal prosecution would not have been different. If this finding were sustained by the Court of Appeals, the information would be immaterial even under the standard of materiality applicable to the prosecutor's knowing use of perjured testimony. Although the express holding of the Court of Appeals was that the nondisclosure in this case required automatic reversal, the Court of Appeals also stated that it "disagreed" with the District Court's finding of harmless error. * * * Accordingly, we reverse the judgment of the Court of Appeals and remand the case to that court for a determination whether there is a reasonable probability that, had the inducement offered by the Government to O'Connor and Mitchell been disclosed to the defense, the result of the trial would have been different.

JUSTICE POWELL took no part in the decision of this case.

JUSTICE WHITE, with whom THE CHIEF JUSTICE and JUSTICE REHNQUIST join, concurring in part and concurring in the judgment.

I agree with the Court that respondent is not entitled to have his conviction overturned unless he can show that the evidence withheld by the Government was "material," and I therefore join Parts I and II of the Court's opinion. I also agree with Justice Blackmun that for purposes of this inquiry, "evidence is material only if there is a reasonable probability that, had the evidence been disclosed to the defense, the result of the proceeding would have been different."

As the Justice correctly observes, this standard is "sufficiently flexible" to cover all instances of prosecutorial failure to disclose evidence favorable to the accused. Given the flexibility of the standard and the inherently factbound nature of the cases to which it will be applied, however, I see no reason to attempt to elaborate on the relevance to the inquiry of the specificity of the defense's request for disclosure, either generally or with respect to this case. I would hold simply that the proper standard is one of reasonable probability and that the Court of Appeals' failure to apply this standard necessitates reversal. I therefore concur in the judgment.

JUSTICE MARSHALL, with whom JUSTICE BRENNAN joins, dissenting.

The Court today chooses to reverse and remand the case for application of its newly stated standard to the facts of this case. While I believe that the evidence at issue here, which remained undisclosed despite a particular request, undoubtedly was material under the Court's standard, I also have serious doubts whether the Court's definition of the constitutional right at issue adequately takes account of the interests this Court sought to protect in its decision in *Brady v. Maryland.*

I begin from the fundamental premise, which hardly bears repeating, that "[t]he purpose of a trial is as much the acquittal of an innocent person as it is the conviction of a guilty one." When evidence favorable to the defendant is known to exist, disclosure only enhances the quest for truth; it takes no direct toll on that inquiry. Moreover, the existence of any small piece of evidence favorable to the defense may, in a particular case, create just the doubt that prevents the jury from returning a verdict of guilty. The private whys and wherefores of jury deliberations pose an impenetrable barrier to our ability to know just which piece of information might make, or might have made, a difference.

\* \* \* We have long recognized that, within the limit of the State's ability to identify so-called exculpatory information, the State's concern for a fair verdict precludes it from withholding from the defense evidence favorable to the defendant's case in the prosecutor's files. \* \* \* This recognition no doubt stems in part from the frequently considerable imbalance in resources between most criminal defendants and most prosecutors' offices. Many, perhaps most, criminal defendants in the United States are represented by appointed counsel, who often are paid minimal wages and operate on shoestring budgets. In addition, unlike police, defense counsel generally is not present at the scene of the crime, or at the time of arrest, but instead comes into the case late. Moreover, unlike the Government, defense counsel is not in the position to make deals with witnesses to gain evidence. Thus, an inexperienced, unskilled, or unaggressive attorney often is unable to amass the factual support necessary to a reasonable defense. When favorable evidence is in the hands of the prosecutor but not disclosed, the result may well be that the defendant is deprived of a fair chance before the trier of fact, and the trier of fact is deprived of the ingredients necessary to a fair decision. This grim reality, of course, poses a direct challenge to the traditional model of the adversary criminal process, and perhaps because this reality so directly questions the fairness of our longstanding processes, change has been cautious and halting. Thus, the Court has not gone the full road and expressly required that the State provide to the defendant access to the prosecutor's complete files, or investigators who will assure that the defendant has an opportunity to discover every existing piece of helpful evidence. Instead, in acknowledgment of the fact that important interests are served when potentially favorable evidence is disclosed, the Court has fashioned a compromise, requiring that the prosecution identify and disclose to the defendant favorable material that it possesses. This requirement is but a small, albeit important; step toward equality of justice.

*Brady v. Maryland,* of course, established this requirement of disclosure as a fundamental element of a fair trial by holding that a defendant was denied due process if he was not given access to favorable evidence that is material either to guilt or punishment. Since *Brady* was decided, this Court has struggled, in a series of decisions, to define how best to effectuate the right recognized. To my mind, the *Brady* decision, the reasoning that underlay it, and the fundamental interest in a fair trial, combine to give the criminal defendant the right to receive from the prosecutor, and the prosecutor the affirmative duty to turn over to the defendant, *all* information known to the government that might reasonably be considered favorable to the defendant's case. Formulation of this right, and imposition of this duty, are "the essence of due process of law. It is the State that tries a man, and it is the State that must insure that the trial is fair." * * * If that right is denied, or if that duty is shirked, however, I believe a reviewing court should not automatically reverse but instead should apply the harmless error test the Court has developed for instances of error affecting constitutional rights. See *Chapman v. California,* 386 U.S. 18 (1967).[c]

My view is based in significant part on the reality of criminal practice and on the consequently inadequate protection to the defendant that a different rule would offer. * * * At the trial level, the duty of the state to effectuate *Brady* devolves into the duty of the prosecutor; the dual role that the prosecutor must play poses a serious obstacle to implementing *Brady.* The prosecutor is by trade, if not necessity, a zealous advocate. He is a trained attorney who must aggressively seek convictions in court on behalf of a victimized public. At the same time, as a representative of the State, he must place foremost in his hierarchy of interests the determination of truth. Thus, for purposes of *Brady,* the prosecutor must abandon his role as an advocate and pore through his files, as objectively as possible, to identify the material that could undermine his case. Given this obviously unharmonious role, it is not surprising that these advocates oftentimes overlook or downplay potentially favorable evidence, often in cases in which there is no doubt that the failure to disclose was a result of absolute good faith. Indeed, one need only think of the Fourth Amendment's requirement of a neutral intermediary, who tests the strength of the policeman-advocate's facts, to recognize the curious status *Brady* imposes on a prosecutor. * * *

The prosecutor surely greets the moment at which he must turn over *Brady* material with little enthusiasm. In perusing his files, he must make the often difficult decision as to whether evidence is favorable, and must decide on which side to err when faced with doubt. In his role as advocate, the answers are clear. In his role as representative of the State, the answers should be equally clear, and often to the contrary. Evidence that is of doubtful worth in the eyes of the prosecutor could be of inestimable value to the defense, and might make the difference to the trier of fact.

Once the prosecutor suspects that certain information might have favorable implications for the defense, either because it is potentially exculpatory or relevant to credibility, I see no reason why he should not be required to disclose it. After all, favorable evidence indisputably enhances the truth-seeking process at trial. And it is the job of the defense, not the prosecution, to decide whether

c. *Chapman* is discussed at footnote d of the introduction to Chapter 11 and in the *Coleman* and *Hillery* cases in Chapter 11.

and in what way to use arguably favorable evidence. In addition, to require disclosure of all evidence that might reasonably be considered favorable to the defendant would have the precautionary effect of assuring that no information of potential consequence is mistakenly overlooked. By requiring full disclosure of favorable evidence in this way, courts could begin to assure that a possibly dispositive piece of information is not withheld from the trier of fact by a prosecutor who is torn between the two roles he must play. A clear rule of this kind, coupled with a presumption in favor of disclosure, also would facilitate the prosecutor's admittedly difficult task by removing a substantial amount of unguided discretion. * * *

* * * The State's interest in nondisclosure at trial is minimal, and should therefore yield to the readily apparent benefit that full disclosure would convey to the search for truth. After trial, however, the benefits of disclosure may at times be tempered by the State's legitimate desire to avoid retrial when error has been harmless. However, in making the determination of harmlessness, I would apply our normal constitutional error test and reverse unless it is clear beyond a reasonable doubt that the withheld evidence would not have affected the outcome of the trial. See *Chapman v. California.*[6]

Any rule other than automatic reversal, of course, dilutes the *Brady* right to some extent and offers the prosecutor an incentive not to turn over all information. In practical effect, it might be argued, there is little difference between the rule I propose—that a prosecutor must disclose all favorable evidence in his files, subject to harmless error review—and the rule the Court adopts—that the prosecutor must disclose only the favorable information that might affect the outcome of the trial. According to this argument, if a constitutional right to all favorable evidence leads to reversal only when the withheld evidence might have affected the outcome of the trial, the result will be the same as with a constitutional right only to evidence that will affect the trial outcome. For several reasons, however, I disagree. First, I have faith that a prosecutor would treat a rule requiring disclosure of all information of a certain kind differently from a rule requiring disclosure only of some of that information. Second, persistent or egregious failure to comply with the constitutional duty could lead to disciplinary actions by the courts. Third, the standard of harmlessness I adopt is more protective of the defendant than that chosen by the Court, placing the burden on the prosecutor, rather than the defendant, to prove the harmlessness of his actions. It would be a foolish prosecutor who gambled too glibly with that standard of review. * * *[d]

6. In a case of deliberate prosecutorial misconduct, automatic reversal might well be proper. Certain kinds of constitutional error so infect the system of justice as to require reversal in all cases, such as discrimination in jury selection. A deliberate effort of the prosecutor to undermine the search for truth clearly is in the category of offenses anathema to our most basic vision of the role of the State in the criminal process.

d. Justice Stevens' dissent is omitted. Justice Stevens argued that where there was a specific request for the disclosure of relevant evidence that was exculpatory, the standard applied in the perjured testimony cases should control in determining whether the failure to disclose required a reversal of a conviction. A standard more lenient to the prosecution had been established for non-request cases in *Agurs* because, "where there had been no specific defense request for the later-discovered evidence, there was no notice to the prosecution that the defense did not already have that evidence or that it considered the evidence to be of particular value." As *Agurs* had noted, "where the prosecutor receives a specific and relevant request, the failure to make any response is seldom, if ever, excusable."

# PENNSYLVANIA v. RITCHIE

480 U.S. 39, 107 S.Ct. 989, 94 L.Ed.2d 40 (1987).

JUSTICE POWELL, announced the judgment of the Court and delivered the opinion of the Court with respect to Parts I, II, III–B, III–C, and IV, and an opinion with respect to Part III–A in which THE CHIEF JUSTICE, JUSTICE WHITE, and JUSTICE O'CONNOR join.

I

[Respondent Ritchie's 13 year-old daughter reported to the police that she had been sexually assaulted by Ritchie two or three times per week over the previous four years. The matter was referred to Children and Youth Services (CYS), a state protective service agency charged with investigating the suspected mistreatment or neglect of children. Ritchie subsequently was charged with rape, involuntary deviate sexual intercourse, incest, and corruption of a minor. During pretrial discovery, Ritchie served CYS with a subpoena, seeking access to all of its records relating to the immediate charges, as well as to certain earlier records compiled when CYS investigated a separate report that Ritchie's children were being abused. CYS refused to comply with the subpoena. It cited a Pennsylvania statute providing that all CYS records must be kept confidential, subject to specified exceptions, including one authorizing disclosure to a "court of competent jurisdiction pursuant to a court order." At an in-chambers hearing, respondent Ritchie argued that he was entitled to the CYS file because it might contain the names of favorable witnesses, as well as other, unspecified exculpatory evidence. Ritchie also claimed that the file contained a medical report prepared in conjunction with the earlier investigation, but CYS asserted that there was no such report in the record. The trial judge, without examining the entire file, refused to order disclosure. At the subsequent trial, which resulted in respondent's conviction, the main witness against him was his daughter. She was cross-examined at length by defense counsel, who questioned her on all aspects of the reported incidents, including her reasons for not reporting them sooner.]

[On appeal, the Pennsylvania Superior Court held that the failure to disclose the CYS file resulted in a constitutional violation insofar as it denied defendant the opportunity to cross-examine his daughter with respect to recorded statements she made to the CYS counselor. It ordered that a new trial be held unless the trial judge determined that the failure to disclose those statements had constituted harmless error. On appeal by the prosecution, the Pennsylvania Supreme Court agreed that the conviction should be vacated and the case remanded to determine if a new trial was necessary. However, it issued a broader ruling then the Superior Court. It directed that Ritchie, through his lawyer, be entitled to review the entire file to search for any useful evidence. This ruling was based on both the Confrontation and Compulsory Process clauses of the Sixth Amendment.]

II

[In part II of his opinion, Justice Powell concluded that the decision below constituted a "final judgment or decree," as required for United States Supreme Court review.[a] ]

---

    **a.**  Justice Stevens' separate dissent on this point is omitted.

### III

The Pennsylvania Supreme Court held that Ritchie, through his lawyer, has the right to examine the full contents of the CYS records. The court found that this right of access is required by both the Confrontation Clause and the Compulsory Process Clause. We discuss these constitutional provisions in turn.

### A

* * * Ritchie claims that by denying him access to the information necessary to prepare his defense, the trial court interfered with his right of cross-examination. Ritchie argues that he could not effectively question his daughter because, without the CYS material, he did not know which types of questions would best expose the weaknesses in her testimony. Had the files been disclosed, Ritchie argues that he might have been able to show that the daughter made statements to the CYS counselor that were inconsistent with her trial statements, or perhaps to reveal that the girl acted with an improper motive. * * * [R]itchie argues that the failure to disclose [such] information that might have made cross-examination more effective undermines the Confrontation Clause's purpose of increasing the accuracy of the truth-finding process at trial. The Pennsylvania Supreme Court accepted this argument, relying in part on our decision in *Davis v. Alaska* [Ch. 18, § 2]. * * * The Pennsylvania Supreme Court apparently interpreted our decision in *Davis* to mean that a statutory privilege cannot be maintained when a defendant asserts a need, prior to trial, for the protected information that might be used at trial to impeach or otherwise undermine a witness' testimony.

If we were to accept this broad interpretation of *Davis,* the effect would be to transform the Confrontation Clause into a constitutionally-compelled rule of pretrial discovery. Nothing in the case law supports such a view. The opinions of this Court show that the right of confrontation is a *trial* right, designed to prevent improper restrictions on the types of questions that defense counsel may ask during cross-examination. * * * The ability to question adverse witnesses, however, does not include the power to require the pretrial disclosure of any and all information that might be useful in contradicting unfavorable testimony.[9] Normally the right to confront one's accusers is satisfied if defense counsel receives wide latitude at trial to question witnesses. *Delaware v. Fensterer,* 474 U.S. 15 (1985). In short, the Confrontation Clause only guarantees "an *opportunity* for effective cross-examination, not cross-examination that is effective in whatever way, and to whatever extent, the defense might wish." Id. * * *

The lower court's reliance on *Davis v. Alaska* therefore is misplaced. There the state court had prohibited defense counsel from questioning the witness about his criminal record, even though that evidence might have affected the witness' credibility. The constitutional error in that case was *not* that Alaska made this information confidential; it was that the defendant was denied the right "to expose to the jury the facts from which jurors * * * could appropriately draw inferences relating to the reliability of the witness." Similarly, in this case the Confrontation Clause was not violated by the withholding of the CYS file; it only would have been impermissible for the judge to have prevented Ritchie's lawyer from cross-examining the daughter. Because defense counsel was able to cross-examine all of the trial witnesses fully, we find that the

---

**9.** This is not to suggest, of course, that there are no protections for pretrial discovery in criminal cases. See discussion in Part III(B), infra. We simply hold that with respect to this issue, the Confrontation Clause only protects a defendant's trial rights, and does not compel the pretrial production of information that might be useful in preparing for trial. * * *

Pennsylvania Supreme Court erred in holding that the failure to disclose the CYS file violated the Confrontation Clause.

## B

The Pennsylvania Supreme Court also suggested that the failure to disclose the CYS file violated the Sixth Amendment's guarantee of compulsory process. Ritchie asserts that the trial court's ruling prevented him from learning the names of the "witnesses in his favor," as well as other evidence that might be contained in the file. Although the basis for the Pennsylvania Supreme Court's ruling on this point is unclear, it apparently concluded that the right of compulsory process includes the right to have the State's assistance in uncovering arguably useful information, without regard to the existence of a state-created restriction—here, the confidentiality of the files. * * *

This Court has never squarely held that the Compulsory Process Clause guarantees the right to discover the *identity* of witnesses, or to require the Government to produce exculpatory evidence. * * * Instead, the Court traditionally has evaluated claims such as those raised by Ritchie under the broader protections of the Due Process Clause of the Fourteenth Amendment. See *United States v. Bagley.* Because the applicability of the Sixth Amendment to this type of case is unsettled, and because our Fourteenth Amendment precedents addressing the fundamental fairness of trials establish a clear framework for review, we adopt a due process analysis for purposes of this case. Although we conclude that compulsory process provides no *greater* protections in this area than those afforded by due process, we need not decide today whether and how the guarantees of the Compulsory Process Clause differ from those of the Fourteenth Amendment. It is enough to conclude that on these facts, Ritchie's claims more properly are considered by reference to due process.

It is well-settled that the Government has the obligation to turn over evidence in its possession that is both favorable to the accused and material to guilt or punishment. *Brady v. Maryland.* Although courts have used different terminologies to define "materiality," a majority of this Court has agreed, "[e]vidence is material only if there is a reasonable probability, that, had the evidence been disclosed to the defense, the result of the proceeding would have been different. A 'reasonable probability' is a probability sufficient to undermine confidence in the outcome." *United States v. Bagley,* supra (opinion of Blackmun, J.); see Id. (opinion of White, J.).

At this stage, of course, it is impossible to say whether any information in the CYS records may be relevant to Ritchie's claim of innocence, because neither the prosecution nor defense counsel has seen the information, and the trial judge acknowledged that he had not reviewed the full file. The Commonwealth, however, argues that no materiality inquiry is required, because a statute renders the contents of the file privileged. Requiring disclosure here, it is argued, would override the Commonwealth's compelling interest in confidentiality on the mere speculation that the file "might" have been useful to the defense.

Although we recognize that the public interest in protecting this type of sensitive information is strong, we do not agree that this interest necessarily prevents disclosure in all circumstances. This is not a case where a state statute grants CYS the absolute authority to shield its files from all eyes. Cf. 42 Pa. Cons.Stat. § 5945.1(b) (unqualified statutory privilege for communications between sexual assault counselors and victims).[14] Rather, the Pennsylvania law

---

14. We express no opinion on whether the result in this case would have been different if the statute had protected the CYS files from disclosure to *anyone,* including law-enforcement and judicial personnel.

provides that the information shall be disclosed in certain circumstances, including when CYS is directed to do so by court order. Given that the Pennsylvania Legislature contemplated *some* use of CYS records in judicial proceedings, we cannot conclude that the statute prevents all disclosure in criminal prosecutions. In the absence of any apparent state policy to the contrary, we therefore have no reason to believe that relevant information would not be disclosed when a court of competent jurisdiction determines that the information is "material" to the defense of the accused. * * * Ritchie is entitled to have the CYS file reviewed by the trial court to determine whether it contains information that probably would have changed the outcome of his trial. * * *

## C

This ruling does not end our analysis because the Pennsylvania Supreme Court did more than simply remand. It also held that defense counsel must be allowed to examine all of the confidential information, both relevant and irrelevant, and present arguments in favor of disclosure. The court apparently concluded that whenever a defendant alleges that protected evidence might be material, the appropriate method of assessing this claim is to grant full access to the disputed information, regardless of the State's interest in confidentiality. We cannot agree.

A defendant's right to discover exculpatory evidence does not include the unsupervised authority to search through the Commonwealth's files. Although the eye of an advocate may be helpful to a defendant in ferreting out information, this Court has never held—even in the absence of a statute restricting disclosure—that a defendant alone may make the determination as to the materiality of the information. Settled practice is to the contrary. * * *

We find that Ritchie's interest (as well as that of the Commonwealth) in ensuring a fair trial can be protected fully by requiring that the CYS files be submitted only to the trial court for *in camera* review. Although this rule denies Ritchie the benefits of an "advocate's eye," we note that the trial court's discretion is not unbounded. If a defendant is aware of specific information contained in the file (e.g., the medical report), he is free to request it directly from the court, and argue in favor of its materiality. * * *

To allow full disclosure to defense counsel in this type of case would sacrifice unnecessarily the Commonwealth's compelling interest in protecting its child abuse information. If the CYS records were made available to defendants, even through counsel, it could have a seriously adverse effect on Pennsylvania's efforts to uncover and treat abuse. Child abuse is one of the most difficult crimes to detect and prosecute, in large part because there often are no witnesses except the victim. A child's feelings of vulnerability and guilt, and his or her unwillingness to come forward are particularly acute when the abuser is a parent. It therefore is essential that the child have a state-designated person to whom he may turn, and to do so with the assurance of confidentiality. Relatives and neighbors who suspect abuse also will be more willing to come forward if they know that their identities will be protected. Recognizing this, the Commonwealth—like all other States—has made a commendable effort to assure victims and witnesses that they may speak to the CYS counselors without fear of general disclosure. The Commonwealth's purpose would be frustrated if this confidential material had to be disclosed upon demand to a defendant charged with criminal child abuse, simply because a trial court may not recognize exculpatory evidence. Neither precedent nor common sense requires such a result.

## IV

We agree that Ritchie is entitled to know whether the CYS file contains information that may have changed the outcome of his trial had it been disclosed. Thus we agree that a remand is necessary. We disagree with the decision of the Pennsylvania Supreme Court to the extent that it allows defense counsel access to the CYS file. An *in camera* review by the trial court will serve Ritchie's interest without destroying the Commonwealth's need to protect the confidentiality of those involved in child-abuse investigations. The decision of the Pennsylvania Supreme Court is affirmed in part, reversed in part, and remanded for further proceedings not inconsistent with this opinion.

JUSTICE BLACKMUN, concurring in part and concurring in the judgment.

I join Parts I, II, III–B, III–C, and IV of the Court's opinion. I write separately, however, because I do not accept the plurality's conclusion, as expressed in Part III–A of Justice Powell's opinion, that the Confrontation Clause protects only a defendant's trial rights and has no relevance to pretrial discovery. * * * The plurality believes that [the Confrontation Clause] is satisfied so long as defense counsel can *question* a witness on any proper subject of cross-examination. For the plurality, the existence of a confrontation violation turns on whether counsel has the opportunity to conduct such questioning; the Court in effect dismisses—or, at best, downplays—any inquiry into the effectiveness of the cross-examination. * * * If I were to accept the plurality's effort to divorce confrontation analysis from any examination into the effectiveness of cross-examination, I believe that in some situations the confrontation right would become an empty formality. * * *

The similarities between *Davis* and this case are much greater than are any differences that may exist. * * * It is true that, in a technical sense, the situations of Davis and Ritchie are different. Davis' counsel had access to the juvenile record of the witness and could have used it but for the Alaska prohibition. Thus, the infringement upon Davis' confrontation right occurred at the trial stage when his counsel was unable to pursue an available line of inquiry. Respondent's attorney could not cross-examine his client's daughter with the help of the possible evidence in the CYS file because of the Pennsylvania prohibition that affected his pretrial preparations. I do not believe, however, that a State can avoid Confrontation Clause problems simply by deciding to hinder the defendant's right to effective cross-examination, on the basis of a desire to protect the confidentiality interests of a particular class of individuals, at the pretrial, rather than at the trial, stage.

Despite my disagreement with the plurality's reading of the Confrontation Clause, I am able to concur in the Court's judgment because, in my view, the procedure the Court has set out for the lower court to follow on remand is adequate to address any confrontation problem. * * *

JUSTICE BRENNAN, with whom JUSTICE MARSHALL joins, dissenting.

* * * In this case, the trial court properly viewed Ritchie's vague speculations that the agency file might contain something useful as an insufficient basis for permitting general access to the file. However, in denying access to the prior statements of the victim the court deprived Ritchie of material crucial to any effort to impeach the victim at trial. I view this deprivation as a violation of the Confrontation Clause.

One way in which cross-examination may be restricted is through preclusion at trial itself of a line of inquiry that counsel seeks to pursue. The logic of our concern for restriction on the ability to engage in cross-examination does not suggest, however, that the Confrontation Clause prohibits *only* such limitation.

A crucial avenue of cross-examination also may be foreclosed by the denial of access to material that would serve as the basis for this examination. Where denial of access is complete, counsel is in no position to formulate a line of inquiry potentially grounded on the material sought. Thus, he or she cannot point to a specific subject of inquiry that has been foreclosed, as can a counsel whose interrogation at trial has been limited by the trial judge. Nonetheless, there occurs as effective preclusion of a topic of cross-examination as if the judge at trial had ruled an entire area of questioning off limits.

\* \* \* *Jencks v. United States*, 353 U.S. 657 (1957), held that the defendant was entitled to obtain the prior statements of persons to government agents when those persons testified against him at trial. \* \* \* As I later noted in *Palermo v. United States*, 360 U.S. 343 (1959), *Jencks* was based on our supervisory authority rather than the Constitution, "but it would be idle to say that the commands of the Constitution were not close to the surface of the decision." \* \* \*

The ability to obtain material information through reliance on a Due Process claim will not in all cases nullify the damage of the Court's overly restrictive reading of the Confrontation Clause. As the Court notes, evidence is regarded as material only if there is a reasonable probability that it might affect the outcome of the proceeding. Prior statements on their face may not appear to have such force, since their utility may lie in their more subtle potential for diminishing the credibility of a witness. The prospect that these statements will not be regarded as material is enhanced by the fact that due process analysis requires that information be evaluated by the trial judge, not defense counsel. By contrast, *Jencks,* informed by confrontation and cross-examination concerns, insisted that defense counsel, not the court, perform such an evaluation, "[b]ecause only the defense is adequately equipped to determine the effective use for the purpose of discrediting the Government's witness and thereby furthering the accused's defense." Therefore, while Confrontation Clause and due process analysis may in some cases be congruent, the Confrontation Clause has independent significance in protecting against infringements on the right to cross-examination.[b]

**b.** In *Arizona v. Youngblood*, 109 S.Ct. 333 (1988), the Court adopted a different due process standard for cases involving governmental loss or destruction of evidence of potential use to the defendant. The defendant there had been convicted of child molestation, sexual assault, and kidnapping. Prior to his arrest, state agents had collected semen samples from the 10-year-old victim's body and clothing, but they had then inadvertently failed to preserve those samples in a condition that would permit blood substance testing that could be matched against the accused's blood group. The state court held that since defendant had claimed mistaken identity, the state's loss of the possibly useful evidence precluded a conviction consistent with due process. Rejecting that ruling, the Supreme Court majority reasoned: "The Due Process Clause of the Fourteenth Amendment, as interpreted in *Brady v. Maryland*, makes the good or bad faith of the State irrelevant when the State fails to disclose to the defendant material exculpatory evidence. But we think the Due Process Clause requires a different result when we deal with the failure of the State to preserve evidentiary material of which no more can be said than that it could have been subjected to tests, the results of which might have exonerated the defendant. Part of the reason for the difference in treatment is found in the observation made by the Court in [an earlier case] that '[w]henever potentially exculpatory evidence is permanently lost, courts face the treacherous task of divining the import of materials whose contents are unknown and, very often, disputed.' Part of it stems from our unwillingness to read the 'fundamental fairness' requirement of the Due Process Clause as imposing on the police an undifferentiated and absolute duty to retain and to preserve all material that might be of conceivable evidentiary significance in a particular prosecution. We think that requiring a defendant to show bad faith on the part of the police both limits the extent of the police's obligation to preserve evidence to reasonable bounds and confines it to that class of cases where the interests of justice most clearly require it, i.e., those cases in which the police themselves by their conduct indicate that the evidence could form a basis for exonerating the defendant. We therefore hold that unless a criminal defendant can show bad faith on the part of the police, failure to preserve potentially useful evidence does not constitute a denial of due process of law."

# Chapter 14

# GUILTY PLEAS

## SECTION 1. PLEA BARGAINING

The great majority of criminal cases in the United States are disposed of by plea of guilty rather than by trial. The guilty plea is very often a negotiated plea, that is, a defendant's agreement to plead guilty to a criminal charge with the reasonable expectation of receiving some consideration from the government. Sometimes this plea is the result of nothing more than implicit plea bargaining; there is no actual bargaining between the defendant or his attorney and the prosecutor or judge, and the defendant enters his plea merely because it is generally known that this is the route to a lesser sentence. But more common is explicit bargaining in which the defendant enters a plea of guilty only after a commitment has been made that concessions will be granted (or at least sought) in his particular case.

One common form of plea negotiation consists of an arrangement whereby the defendant and prosecutor agree that the defendant should be permitted to plead guilty to a charge less serious than is supported by the evidence. A second form involves an agreement whereby the defendant pleads "on the nose," that is, to the original charge, in exchange for some kind of promise from the prosecutor concerning the sentence to be imposed (that he will recommend or not oppose a certain sentence, or even that he will ensure that the sentence will not exceed a certain amount). Still another kind of plea bargain—the one most likely to be illusory—is where the defendant pleads "on the nose" in exchange for the prosecutor's promise to drop or not file other charges.

Plea bargaining is a long time (though only recently highly visible) practice in the United States. There is considerable disagreement as to what caused this practice to develop and continue, though it seems likely a combination of factors is involved. One explanation is that plea bargaining is a response to crowded court dockets, but this is not inevitably the case, for negotiation practices have developed at times and places where there was no serious court congestion. Some have attributed plea bargaining to inadequate public defenders, the financial incentives of private attorneys, and the laziness of prosecutors, but this is hardly an entirely accurate or complete explanation either. Certainly there are at least some more favorable explanations, such as that there are today fewer genuine disputes of fact to be resolved by trials because of the increased professionalism of police and prosecutors and the enhanced role of defense attorneys at the pretrial stages.

But whether the institution of plea bargaining is viewed favorably or unfavorably, there is no denying that this process of negotiation for and granting of concessions can give rise to difficult and important legal issues. Just how much pressure may the prosecutor put on the defendant in an effort to induce him to go the guilty plea route? What are the defendant's rights if notwithstanding his plea he does not receive the contemplated concessions? How hard must the prosecutor try to obtain the concessions he promised to seek? If defendant has not yet entered his plea, may the prosecutor renege on the agreement? Those issues are explored in the four Supreme Court decisions in this section.

# BORDENKIRCHER v. HAYES

434 U.S. 357, 98 S.Ct. 663, 54 L.Ed.2d 604 (1978).

JUSTICE STEWART delivered the opinion of the Court. * * *

[Paul Hayes was indicted in Fayette County, Ky., on a charge of uttering a forged instrument in the amount of $88.30, punishable by two to 10 years in prison. Hayes and his retained counsel met with the prosecutor who offered to recommend a sentence of five years if Hayes would plead guilty and added that if Hayes did not plead guilty he would seek an indictment under the Kentucky Habitual Criminal Act, which would subject Hayes to a mandatory sentence of life imprisonment by reason of his two prior felony convictions. Hayes chose not to plead guilty, and the prosecutor did obtain such an indictment. A jury found Hayes guilty on the principal charge of uttering a forged instrument and, in a separate proceeding, further found that he had twice before been convicted of felonies. As required by the habitual offender statute, he was sentenced to a life term in the penitentiary. The Kentucky Court of Appeals rejected Hayes' constitutional objections to the enhanced sentence, and on Hayes' petition for a federal writ of habeas corpus the district court agreed that there had been no constitutional violation in the sentence or the indictment procedure. The Court of Appeals for the Sixth Circuit reversed on the ground that the prosecutor's conduct had violated the principles of *Blackledge v. Perry,* 417 U.S. 21 (1974), which "protect defendants from the vindictive exercise of a prosecutor's discretion."]

It may be helpful to clarify at the outset the nature of the issue in this case. While the prosecutor did not actually obtain the recidivist indictment until after the plea conferences had ended, his intention to do so was clearly put forth at the outset of the plea negotiations. Hayes was thus fully informed of the true terms of the offer when he made his decision to plead not guilty. This is not a situation, therefore, where the prosecutor without notice brought an additional and more serious charge after plea negotiations relating only to the original indictment had ended with the defendant's insistence on pleading not guilty. As a practical matter, in short, this case would be no different if the grand jury had indicted Hayes as a recidivist from the outset, and the prosecutor had offered to drop that charge as part of the plea bargain.

The Court of Appeals nonetheless drew a distinction between "concessions relating to prosecution under an existing indictment," and threats to bring more severe charges not contained in the original indictment—a line it thought necessary in order to establish a prophylactic rule to guard against the evil of prosecutorial vindictiveness. Quite apart from this chronological distinction, however, the Court of Appeals found that the prosecutor had acted vindictively in the present case since he had conceded that the indictment was influenced by his desire to induce a guilty plea. The ultimate conclusion of the Court of Appeals thus seems to have been that a prosecutor acts vindictively and in violation of due process of law whenever his charging decision is influenced by what he hopes to gain in the course of plea bargaining negotiations.

We have recently had occasion to observe that "[w]hatever might be the situation in an ideal world, the fact is that the guilty plea and the often concomitant plea bargain are important components of this country's criminal justice system. Properly administered, they can benefit all concerned." The open acknowledgment of this previously clandestine practice has led this Court to recognize the importance of counsel during plea negotiations, the need for a public record indicating that a plea was knowingly and voluntarily made, and the requirement that a prosecutor's plea bargaining promise must be kept. The decision of the Court of Appeals in the present case, however, did not deal with considerations such as these, but held that the substance of the plea offer itself violated the limitations imposed by the Due Process Clause of the Fourteenth Amendment. For the reasons that follow, we have concluded that the Court of Appeals was mistaken in so ruling.

This Court held in *North Carolina v. Pearce*, 395 U.S. 711 (1969), that the Due Process Clause of the Fourteenth Amendment "requires that vindictiveness against a defendant for having successfully attacked his first conviction must play no part in the sentence he receives after a new trial." The same principle was later applied to prohibit a prosecutor from reindicting a convicted misdemeanant on a felony charge after the defendant had invoked an appellate remedy, since in this situation there was also a "realistic likelihood of 'vindictiveness.'" *Blackledge v. Perry.*

In those cases the Court was dealing with the State's unilateral imposition of a penalty upon a defendant who had chosen to exercise a legal right to attack his original conviction—a situation "very different from the give-and-take negotiation common in plea bargaining between the prosecution and the defense, which arguably possess relatively equal bargaining power." The Court has emphasized that the due process violation in cases such as *Pearce* and *Perry* lay not in the possibility that a defendant might be deterred from the exercise of a legal right, but rather in the danger that the State might be retaliating against the accused for lawfully attacking his conviction.

To punish a person because he has done what the law plainly allows him to do is a due process violation of the most basic sort, and for an agent of the State to pursue a course of action whose objective is to penalize a person's reliance on his legal rights is "patently unconstitutional." But in the "give-and-take" of plea bargaining, there is no such element of punishment or retaliation so long as the accused is free to accept or reject the prosecution's offer.

Plea bargaining flows from "the mutuality of advantage" to defendants and prosecutors, each with his own reasons for wanting to avoid trial. *Brady v. United States*, 397 U.S. 742 (1970).[a] Defendants advised by competent counsel

---

**a.** Although *Brady* did not involve a plea bargaining situation, the Court analogized the plea involved there to a plea obtained through plea bargaining, and then commented generally on the validity of a plea produced by the "mutuality of advantage" that flows from a negotiated plea: "We decline to hold * * * that a guilty plea is compelled and invalid under the Fifth Amendment whenever motivated by the defendant's desire to accept the certainty or probability of a lesser penalty rather than face a wider range of possibilities extending from acquittal to conviction and a higher penalty authorized by law for the crime charged. * * * [B]oth the state and the defendant often find it advantageous to preclude the possibility of the maximum penalty authorized by law. For a defendant who sees slight possibility of acquittal, the advantages of pleading guilty and limiting the probable penalty are obvious—his exposure is reduced, the correctional processes can begin immediately, and the practical burdens of a trial are eliminated. For the State there are also advantages—the more promptly imposed punishment after an admission of guilty may and protected by other procedural safeguards are presumptively capable of intelligent choice in response to prosecutorial persuasion, and unlikely to be driven to false self-condemnation. Indeed, acceptance of the basic legitimacy of plea bargaining necessarily implies rejection of any notion that a guilty plea is involuntary in a constitutional sense simply because it is the end result of the bargaining process. By hypothesis, the plea may have been induced by promises of a recommendation of a lenient sentence or a reduction of charges, and thus by fear of the possibility of a greater penalty upon conviction after a trial.

While confronting a defendant with the risk of more severe punishment clearly may have a "discouraging effect on the defendant's assertion of his trial rights, the imposition of these difficult choices [is] an inevitable"—and permissible—"attribute of any legitimate system which tolerates and encourages the negotiation of pleas." It follows that, by tolerating and encouraging the negotiation of pleas, this Court has necessarily accepted as constitutionally legitimate the simple reality that the prosecutor's interest at the bargaining table is to persuade the defendant to forego his right to plead not guilty.

It is not disputed here that Hayes was properly chargeable under the recidivist statute, since he had in fact been convicted of two previous felonies. In our system, so long as the prosecutor has probable cause to believe that the accused committed an offense defined by statute, the decision whether or not to prosecute, and what charge to file or bring before a grand jury, generally rests entirely in his discretion.[8] Within the limits set by the legislature's constitutionally valid definition of chargeable offenses, "the conscious exercise of some selectivity in enforcement is not in itself a federal constitutional violation" so long as "the selection was [not] deliberately based upon an unjustifiable standard such as race, religion, or other arbitrary classification." To hold that the prosecutor's desire to induce a guilty plea is an "unjustifiable standard," which, like race or religion, may play no part in his charging decision, would contradict the very premises that underlie the concept of plea bargaining itself. Moreover, a rigid constitutional rule that would prohibit a prosecutor from acting forthrightly in his dealings with the defense could only invite unhealthy subterfuge that would drive the practice of plea bargaining back into the shadows from which it has so recently emerged.

There is no doubt that the breadth of discretion that our country's legal system vests in prosecuting attorneys carries with it the potential for both individual and institutional abuse. And broad though that discretion may be, there are undoubtedly constitutional limits upon its exercise. We hold only that the course of conduct engaged in by the prosecutor in this case, which no more than openly presented the defendant with the unpleasant alternatives of foregoing trial or facing charges on which he was plainly subject to prosecution, did not violate the Due Process Clause of the Fourteenth Amendment.

Accordingly, the judgment of the Court of Appeals is reversed.

more effectively attain the objectives of punishment; and with the avoidance of trial, scarce judicial and prosecutorial resources are conserved for those cases in which there is a substantial issue of the defendant's guilt or in which there is substantial doubt that the State can sustain its burden of proof. It is this mutuality of advantage which perhaps explains the fact that at present well over three-fourths of the criminal convictions in this country rest on pleas of guilty, a great many of them no doubt motivated at least in part by the hope or assurance of a lesser penalty than might be imposed if there were a guilty verdict after a trial to judge or jury."

8. This case does not involve the constitutional implications of a prosecutor's offer during plea bargaining of adverse or lenient treatment for some person *other* than the accused, which might pose a greater danger of inducing a false guilty plea by skewing the assessment of the risks a defendant must consider.

JUSTICE BLACKMUN, with whom JUSTICE BRENNAN and JUSTICE MARSHALL, join dissenting.

I feel that the Court, although purporting to rule narrowly (that is, on "the course of conduct engaged in by the prosecutor in this case"), is departing from, or at least restricting, the principles established in *North Carolina v. Pearce,* and in *Blackledge v. Perry.* * * *

In *Pearce,* as indeed the Court notes, it was held that "vindictiveness against a defendant for having successfully attacked his first conviction must play no part in the sentence he receives after a new trial." * * *

Then later, in *Perry,* the Court applied the same principle to prosecutorial conduct where there was a "realistic likelihood of 'vindictiveness.'" * * *

The Court now says, however, that this concern with vindictiveness is of no import in the present case, despite the difference between five years in prison and a life sentence, because we are here concerned with plea bargaining where there is give-and-take negotiation, and where, it is said, "there is no such element of punishment or retaliation so long as the accused is free to accept or reject the prosecution's offer." Yet in this case vindictiveness is present to the same extent as it was thought to be in *Pearce* and in *Perry:* the prosecutor here admitted that the sole reason for the new indictment was to discourage the respondent from exercising his right to a trial. Even had such an admission not been made, when plea negotiations, conducted in the face of the less serious charge under the first indictment, fail, charging by a second indictment a more serious crime for the same conduct creates "a strong inference" of vindictiveness. As then Judge McCree aptly observed, in writing for a unanimous panel of the Sixth Circuit, the prosecutor initially "makes a discretionary determination that the interests of the state are served by not seeking more serious charges." I therefore do not understand why, as in *Pearce,* due process does not require that the prosecution justify its action on some basis other than discouraging respondent from the exercise of his right to a trial.

Prosecutorial vindictiveness, it seems to me, in the present narrow context, is the fact against which the Due Process Clause ought to protect. I perceive little difference between vindictiveness after what the Court describes as the exercise of a "legal right to attack his original conviction," and vindictiveness in the "give-and-take negotiation common in plea bargaining." Prosecutorial vindictiveness in any context is still prosecutorial vindictiveness. The Due Process Clause should protect an accused against it, however it asserts itself. The Court of Appeals rightly so held, and I would affirm the judgment.

It might be argued that it really makes little difference how this case, now that it is here, is decided. The Court's holding gives plea bargaining full sway despite vindictiveness. A contrary result, however, merely would prompt the aggressive prosecutor to bring the greater charge initially in every case, and only thereafter to bargain. The consequences to the accused would still be adverse, for then he would bargain against a greater charge, face the likelihood of increased bail, and run the risk that the court would be less inclined to accept a bargain plea. Nonetheless, it is far preferable to hold the prosecution to the charge it was originally content to bring and to justify in the eyes of its public.[2]

2. That prosecutors, without saying so, may sometimes bring charges more serious than they think appropriate for the ultimate disposition of a case, in order to gain bargaining leverage with a defendant, does not add support to today's decision, for this Court, in its approval of the advantages to be gained from plea negotiations, has never openly sanctioned such deliberate overcharging or taken such a cynical view of the bargaining process. Normally, of course, it is impossible to show that this is what the prosecutor is doing, and the courts necessarily have deferred to the

JUSTICE POWELL, dissenting.

Although I agree with much of the Court's opinion, I am not satisfied that the result in this case is just or that the conduct of the plea bargaining met the requirements of due process. * * *

The prosecutor's initial assessment of respondent's case led him to forego an indictment under the habitual criminal statute. The circumstances of respondent's prior convictions are relevant to this assessment and to my view of the case. Respondent was 17 years old when he committed his first offense. He was charged with rape but pled guilty to the lesser included offense of "detaining a female." One of the other participants in the incident was sentenced to life imprisonment. Respondent was sent not to prison but to a reformatory where he served five years. Respondent's second offense was robbery. This time he was found guilty by a jury and was sentenced to five years in prison, but he was placed on probation and served no time. Although respondent's prior convictions brought him within the terms of the Habitual Criminal Act, the offenses themselves did not result in imprisonment; yet the addition of a conviction on a charge involving $88.30 subjected respondent to a mandatory sentence of imprisonment for life. Persons convicted of rape and murder often are not punished so severely. * * *

It seems to me that the question to be asked under the circumstances is whether the prosecutor reasonably might have charged respondent under the Habitual Criminal Act in the first place. The deference that courts properly accord the exercise of a prosecutor's discretion perhaps would foreclose judicial criticism if the prosecutor originally had sought an indictment under that act, as unreasonable as it would have seemed.[2] But here the prosecutor evidently made

prosecutor's exercise of discretion in initial charging decisions.

Even if overcharging is to be sanctioned, there are strong reasons of fairness why the charges should be presented at the beginning of the bargaining process, rather than as a filliped threat at the end. First, it means that a prosecutor is required to reach a charging decision without any knowledge of the particular defendant's willingness to plead guilty; hence the defendant who truly believes himself to be innocent, and wishes for that reason to go to trial, is not likely to be subject to quite such a devastating gamble since the prosecutor has fixed the incentives for the average case.

Second, it is healthful to keep charging practices visible to the general public, so that political bodies can judge whether the policy being followed is a fair one. Visibility is enhanced if the prosecutor is required to lay his cards on the table with an indictment of public record at the beginning of the bargaining process, rather than making use of unrecorded verbal warnings of more serious indictments yet to come.

Finally, I would question whether it is fair to pressure defendants to plead guilty by threat of reindictment on an enhanced charge for the same conduct when the defendant has no way of knowing whether the prosecutor would indeed be entitled to bring him to trial on the enhanced charge. Here, though there

is no dispute that respondent met the then current definition of a habitual offender under Kentucky law, it is conceivable that a properly instructed Kentucky grand jury, in response to the same considerations that ultimately moved the Kentucky Legislature to amend the habitual offender statute, would have refused to subject respondent to such an onerous penalty for his forgery charge. There is no indication in the record that, once the new indictment was obtained, respondent was given another chance to plead guilty to the forged check charge in exchange for a five year sentence.

2. The majority suggests that this case cannot be distinguished from the case where the prosecutor initially obtains an indictment under an enhancement statute and later agrees to drop the enhancement charge in exchange for a guilty plea. I would agree that these two situations would be alike *only if* it were assumed that the hypothetical prosecutor's decision to charge under the enhancement statute was occasioned not by consideration of the public interest but by a strategy to discourage the defendant from exercising his constitutional rights. In theory, I would condemn both practices. In practice, the hypothetical situation is largely unreviewable. The majority's view confuses the propriety of a particular exercise of prosecutorial discretion with its unreviewability. In the instant case, however, we have no problem of proof.

a reasonable, responsible judgment not to subject an individual to a mandatory life sentence when his only new offense had societal implications as limited as those accompanying the uttering of a single $88 forged check and when the circumstances of his prior convictions confirmed the inappropriateness of applying the habitual criminal statute. I think it may be inferred that the prosecutor himself deemed it unreasonable and not in the public interest to put this defendant in jeopardy of a sentence of life imprisonment.

There may be situations in which a prosecutor would be fully justified in seeking a fresh indictment for a more serious offense. The most plausible justification might be that it would have been reasonable and in the public interest initially to have charged the defendant with the greater offense. In most cases a court could not know why the harsher indictment was sought, and an inquiry into the prosecutor's motive would neither be indicated nor likely to be fruitful. In those cases, I would agree with the majority that the situation would not differ materially from one in which the higher charge was brought at the outset.

But this is not such a case. Here, any inquiry into the prosecutor's purpose is made unnecessary by his candid acknowledgement that he threatened to procure and in fact procured the habitual criminal indictment because of respondent's insistence on exercising his constitutional rights. [I]n *Brady v. United States*, we drew a distinction between the situation there approved and the "situation where the prosecutor or judge, or both, deliberately employ their charging and sentencing powers to induce a particular defendant to tender a plea of guilty."

The plea-bargaining process, as recognized by this Court, is essential to the functioning of the criminal-justice system. It normally affords genuine benefits to defendants as well as to society. And if the system is to work effectively, prosecutors must be accorded the widest discretion, within constitutional limits, in conducting bargaining. This is especially true when a defendant is represented by counsel and presumably is fully advised of his rights. Only in the most exceptional case should a court conclude that the scales of the bargaining are so unevenly balanced as to arouse suspicion. In this case, the prosecutor's actions denied respondent due process because their admitted purpose was to discourage and then to penalize with unique severity his exercise of constitutional rights. Implementation of a strategy calculated solely to deter the exercise of constitutional rights is not a constitutionally permissible exercise of discretion. I would affirm the opinion of the Court of Appeals on the facts of this case.

## SANTOBELLO v. NEW YORK
404 U.S. 257, 92 S.Ct. 495, 30 L.Ed.2d 427 (1971).

CHIEF JUSTICE BURGER delivered the opinion of the Court.

[After negotiations with the prosecutor, petitioner withdrew his previous not-guilty plea to two felony counts and pleaded guilty to a lesser-included offense, the prosecutor having agreed to make no recommendation as to sentence. At petitioner's appearance for sentencing many months later a new prosecutor recommended the maximum sentence, which the judge (who stated that he was uninfluenced by that recommendation) imposed. Petitioner attempted unsuccessfully to withdraw his guilty plea, and his conviction was affirmed on appeal.]

* * * The disposition of criminal charges by agreement between the prosecutor and the accused, sometimes loosely called "plea bargaining," is an

essential component of the administration of justice. Properly administered, it is to be encouraged. If every criminal charge were subjected to a full-scale trial, the States and the Federal Government would need to multiply by many times the number of judges and court facilities.

Disposition of charges after plea discussions is not only an essential part of the process but a highly desirable part for many reasons. It leads to prompt and largely final disposition of most criminal cases; it avoids much of the corrosive impact of enforced idleness during pretrial confinement for those who are denied release pending trial; it protects the public from those accused persons who are prone to continue criminal conduct even while on pretrial release; and, by shortening the time between charge and disposition, it enhances whatever may be the rehabilitative prospects of the guilty when they are ultimately imprisoned. * * *

This phase of the process of criminal justice, and the adjudicative element inherent in accepting a plea of guilty, must be attended by safeguards to insure the defendant what is reasonably due in the circumstances. Those circumstances will vary, but a constant factor is that when a plea rests in any significant degree on a promise or agreement of the prosecutor, so that it can be said to be part of the inducement or consideration, such promise must be fulfilled. * * *

We need not reach the question whether the sentencing judge would or would not have been influenced had he known all the details of the negotiations for the plea. He stated that the prosecutor's recommendation did not influence him and we have no reason to doubt that. Nevertheless, we conclude that the interests of justice and appropriate recognition of the duties of the prosecution in relation to promises made in the negotiation of pleas of guilty will be best served by remanding the case to the state courts for further consideration. The ultimate relief to which petitioner is entitled we leave to the discretion of the state court, which is in a better position to decide whether the circumstances of this case require only that there be specific performance of the agreement on the plea, in which case petitioner should be resentenced by a different judge, or whether, in the view of the state court, the circumstances require granting the relief sought by petitioner, i.e., the opportunity to withdraw his plea of guilty.[2] * * *

JUSTICE DOUGLAS, concurring. * * *

I join the opinion of the Court and favor a constitutional rule for this as well as for other pending or oncoming cases. Where the "plea bargain" is not kept by the prosecutor, the sentence must be vacated and the state court will decide in light of the circumstances of each case whether due process requires (a) that there be specific performance of the plea bargain or (b) that the defendant be given the option to go to trial on the original charges. One alternative may do justice in one case, and the other in a different case. In choosing a remedy, however, a court ought to accord a defendant's preference considerable, if not controlling, weight inasmuch as the fundamental rights flouted by a prosecutor's breach of a plea bargain are those of the defendant, not of the State.

JUSTICE MARSHALL, with whom JUSTICE BRENNAN and JUSTICE STEWART join, concurring in part and dissenting in part.

* * * When a prosecutor breaks the bargain, he undercuts the basis for the waiver of constitutional rights implicit in the plea. This, it seems to me,

2. If the state court decides to allow withdrawal of the plea, the petitioner will, of course, plead anew to the original charge on two felony counts.

provides the defendant ample justification for rescinding the plea. Where a promise is "unfulfilled," *Brady v. United States* specifically denies that the plea "must stand." Of course, where the prosecutor has broken the plea agreement, it may be appropriate to permit the defendant to enforce the plea bargain. But that is not the remedy sought here.* Rather, it seems to me that a breach of the plea bargain provides ample reason to permit the plea to be vacated.

It is worth noting that in the ordinary case where a motion to vacate is made prior to sentencing, the government has taken no action in reliance on the previously entered guilty plea and would suffer no harm from the plea's withdrawal. More pointedly, here the State claims no such harm beyond disappointed expectations about the plea itself. At least where the government itself has broken the plea bargain, this disappointment cannot bar petitioner from withdrawing his guilty plea and reclaiming his right to a trial.

I would remand the case with instructions that the plea be vacated and petitioner given an opportunity to replead to the original charges in the indictment.

## MABRY v. JOHNSON
467 U.S. 504, 104 S.Ct. 2543, 81 L.Ed.2d 437 (1984).

JUSTICE STEVENS delivered the opinion of the Court.

The question presented is whether a defendant's acceptance of a prosecutor's proposed plea bargain creates a constitutional right to have the bargain specifically enforced.

In the late evening of May 22, 1970, three members of a family returned home to find a burglary in progress. Shots were exchanged resulting in the daughter's death and the wounding of the father and respondent—one of the burglars. Respondent was tried and convicted on three charges: burglary, assault, and murder. The murder conviction was set aside by the Arkansas Supreme Court. Thereafter, plea negotiations ensued.

At the time of the negotiations respondent was serving his concurrent 21- and 12-year sentences on the burglary and assault convictions. On Friday, October 27, 1972, a deputy prosecutor proposed to respondent's attorney that in exchange for a plea of guilty to the charge of accessory after a felony murder, the prosecutor would recommend a sentence of 21 years to be served concurrently with the burglary and assault sentences. On the following day, counsel communicated the offer to respondent who agreed to accept it. On the next Monday the lawyer called the prosecutor "and communicated [respondent's] acceptance of the offer." The prosecutor then told counsel that a mistake had been made and withdrew the offer. He proposed instead that in exchange for a guilty plea he would recommend a sentence of 21 years to be served consecutively to respondent's other sentences.

Respondent rejected the new offer and elected to stand trial. On the second day of trial, the judge declared a mistrial and plea negotiations resumed, ultimately resulting in respondent's acceptance of the prosecutor's second offer. In accordance with the plea bargain, the state trial judge imposed a 21-year sentence to be served consecutively to the previous sentences.

* Justice Douglas, although joining the Court's opinion (apparently because he thinks the remedy should be chosen by the state court), concludes that the state court "ought to accord a defendant's preference considerable, if not controlling, weight." Thus, a majority of the Court appears to believe that in cases like these, when the defendant seeks to vacate the plea, that relief should generally be granted. [Ed. note: there were two vacancies on the Court at the time.]

* * * The [federal] Court of Appeals reversed [on habeas review]. The majority concluded that "fairness" precluded the prosecution's withdrawal of a plea proposal once accepted by respondent. We now reverse [that judgment]. * * *

It is well-settled that a voluntary and intelligent plea of guilty made by an accused person, who has been advised by competent counsel, may not be collaterally attacked. It is also well-settled that plea agreements are consistent with the requirements of voluntariness and intelligence—because each side may obtain advantages when a guilty plea is exchanged for sentencing concessions, the agreement is no less voluntary than any other bargained-for exchange. It is only when the consensual character of the plea is called into question that the validity of a guilty plea may be impaired. In *Brady v. United States*, we stated the applicable standard:

> "[A] plea of guilty entered by one fully aware of the direct consequences, including the actual value of any commitments made to him by the court, prosecutor, or his own counsel, must stand unless induced by threats (or promises to discontinue improper harassment), misrepresentation (including unfulfilled or unfulfillable promises), or perhaps by promises that are by their nature improper as having no proper relationship to the prosecutor's business (e.g., bribes)."

Thus, only when it develops that the defendant was not fairly apprised of its consequences can his plea be challenged under the Due Process Clause. *Santobello v. New York* illustrates the point.

*Santobello* demonstrates why respondent may not successfully attack his plea of guilty. Respondent's plea was in no sense induced by the prosecutor's withdrawn offer; unlike Santobello, who pleaded guilty thinking he had bargained for a specific prosecutorial sentencing recommendation which was not ultimately made, at the time respondent pleaded guilty he knew the prosecution would recommend a 21–year consecutive sentence. Respondent * * * pleaded guilty with the advice of competent counsel and with full awareness of the consequences—he knew that the prosecutor would recommend and that the judge could impose the sentence now under attack. Respondent's plea was thus in no sense the product of governmental deception; it rested on no "unfulfilled promise" and fully satisfied the test for voluntariness and intelligence.

Thus, because it did not impair the voluntariness or intelligence of his guilty plea, respondent's inability to enforce the prosecutor's offer is without constitutional significance.[11] Neither is the question whether the prosecutor was negligent or otherwise culpable in first making and then withdrawing his offer relevant. The Due Process Clause is not a code of ethics for prosecutors; its concern is with the manner in which persons are deprived of their liberty. Here respondent was not deprived of his liberty in any fundamentally unfair way. Respondent was fully aware of the likely consequences when he pleaded guilty; it is not unfair to expect him to live with those consequences now. * * *

11. Indeed, even if respondent's plea were invalid, *Santobello* expressly declined to hold that the Constitution compels specific performance of a broken prosecutorial promise as the remedy for such a plea; the Court made it clear that permitting Santobello to replead was within the range of constitutionally appropriate remedies. It follows that respondent's constitutional rights could not have been violated. Because he pleaded after the prosecution had breached its "promise" to him; he was in no worse position than Santobello would have been had he been permitted to replead.

# UNITED STATES v. BENCHIMOL

471 U.S. 453, 105 S.Ct. 2103, 85 L.Ed.2d 462 (1985).

PER CURIAM.

[Respondent pleaded guilty to an information charging him with one count of mail fraud pursuant to a plea bargain whereby the Government agreed to recommend probation on condition that restitution be made. The District Court disregarded the recommendation and sentenced respondent to six years of treatment and supervision under the Youth Corrections Act. He filed a motion to withdraw his guilty plea or, in the alternative, to have his sentence vacated and be resentenced to the time already served, claiming that the Government had failed to comply with its part of the plea bargain.]

The District Court that had received the guilty plea also heard respondent's application for collateral relief, and denied it. The Court of Appeals by a divided vote reversed that judgment. * * * The Court of Appeals had this view of the facts:

"Benchimol agreed to plead guilty. The government concedes that in exchange for the guilty plea it promised to recommend probation with restitution. However, at the sentencing hearing, the presentence report incorrectly stated that the government would stand silent. Benchimol's counsel informed the court that the government instead recommended probation with restitution. The Assistant United States Attorney then stated: 'That is an accurate representation.'"

The Court of Appeals concluded that the Government had breached its plea bargain because, although the Assistant United States Attorney concurred with defense counsel's statement that the Government recommended probation with restitution, it "made no effort to explain its reasons for agreeing to recommend a lenient sentence but rather left an impression with the court of less-than-enthusiastic support for leniency."

We think this holding misconceives the effect of the relevant rules and of the applicable case law. Federal Rule of Criminal Procedure 11(e) provides an elaborate formula for the negotiation of plea bargains, which allows the attorney for the Government to agree to move for dismissal of other charges and to agree that a specific sentence is the appropriate disposition of the case. It also authorizes the Government attorney to make a recommendation for a particular sentence, or agree not to oppose the defendant's request for such a sentence, with the understanding that such recommendation or request shall not be binding upon the court.

It may well be that the Government in a particular case might commit itself to "enthusiastically" make a particular recommendation to the Court, and it may be that the Government in a particular case might agree to explain to the Court the reasons for the Government's making a particular recommendation. But respondent does not contend, nor did the Court of Appeals find, that the Government had in fact undertaken to do either of these things here. The Court of Appeals simply held that as a matter of law such an undertaking was to be implied from the Government's agreement to recommend a particular sentence. But our view of Rule 11(e) is that it speaks in terms of what the parties in fact agree to, and does not suggest that such implied-in-law terms as were read into this agreement by the Court of Appeals have any place under the Rule.

The Court of Appeals relied on [certain] cases for the conclusion it reached with respect to the requirement of "enthusiasm," but it appears to us that in each of these cases the Government attorney appearing personally in court at the time of the plea bargain expressed personal reservations about the agreement to which the Government had committed itself. This is quite a different proposition than an appellate determination from a transcript of the record made many years earlier that the Government attorney had "left an impression with the court of less-than-enthusiastic support for leniency." When the Government agrees pursuant to Rule 11(e) to make a recommendation with respect to sentence, it must carry out its part of the bargain by making the promised recommendation; but even if Rule 11(e) allows bargaining about degrees of enthusiasm, there appears to have been none here.

Rule 11(e) may well contemplate agreement by the Government in a particular case to state to the court its reasons for making the recommendation which it agrees to make. The Government suggests that spreading on the record its reasons for agreement to a plea bargain in a particular case—for example, that it did not wish to devote scarce resources to a trial of this particular defendant, or that it wished to avoid calling the victim as a witness—would frequently harm, rather than help, the defendant's quest for leniency. These may well be reasons why the defendant would not wish to exact such a commitment from the Government, but for purposes of this case it is enough that no such agreement was made in fact. Since Rule 11(e) speaks generally of the plea bargains that the parties make, it was error for the Court of Appeals to imply as a matter of law a term which the parties themselves did not agree upon.

For these reasons, we conclude that there was simply no default on the part of the Government in this case * * *.

Reversed.

JUSTICE STEVENS, concurring in the judgment.

* * * If the Government erred in failing to recommend affirmatively the proper sentence, the time to object was at the sentencing hearing or on direct appeal. * * *

JUSTICE BRENNAN, with whom JUSTICE MARSHALL joins, dissenting.

The Court today continues its unsettling practice of summarily reversing decisions rendered in favor of criminal defendants, based not on broad principle but on idiosyncratic facts and without full briefing or oral argument. * * * Because I find this one-sided practice of summary error correction inappropriate, I would vote merely to deny this petition for certiorari. Accordingly, I respectfully dissent.

# SECTION 2. REQUISITES OF A VALID PLEA

At an earlier time, when the validity of plea bargaining was in doubt, the general practice was not to reveal in court at the time the guilty plea was received that a bargain had been struck. This is no longer the case. Moreover, there has been increased acceptance of the notion that the plea receiving process should be more cautious in other respects as well, so that today in most jurisdictions a court rule or statute imposes several responsibilities upon the judge in connection with receipt of defendant's guilty plea. Typical is Federal Rule of Criminal Procedure 11, which requires the judge to (i) inform the defendant and determine that he understands the nature of the charge and the possible penalty and various rights he is surrendering by pleading guilty; (ii) determine that the plea is voluntary; (iii) require disclosure of any plea agreement and accept or reject that agreement; and (iv) make sufficient inquiry to ensure there is a factual basis for the plea.

As the cases in this section illustrate, constitutional considerations lie close to the surface of such provisions. *Boykin v. Alabama* deals with the waiver-of-rights aspect of a guilty plea, *Henderson v. Morgan* with the necessity that defendant understand the charge against him, and *North Carolina v. Alford* with the special circumstances in which a factual basis for the plea is constitutionally mandated. The final case, *Blackledge v. Allison,* considers the important question of whether full compliance with procedures such as those in rule 11 forecloses subsequent efforts by a defendant to have his guilty plea invalidated.

## BOYKIN v. ALABAMA
395 U.S. 238, 89 S.Ct. 1709, 23 L.Ed.2d 274 (1969).

JUSTICE DOUGLAS delivered the opinion of the Court.

In the spring of 1966, within the period of a fortnight, a series of armed robberies occurred in Mobile, Alabama. The victims, in each case, were local shopkeepers open at night who were forced by a gunman to hand over money. While robbing one grocery store, the assailant fired his gun once, sending a bullet through a door into the ceiling. A few days earlier in a drugstore, the robber had allowed his gun to discharge in such a way that the bullet, on ricochet from the floor, struck a customer in the leg. Shortly thereafter, a local grand jury returned five indictments against petitioner, a 27–year–old Negro, for common-law robbery—an offense punishable in Alabama by death.

Before the matter came to trial, the court determined that petitioner was indigent and appointed counsel to represent him. Three days later, at his arraignment, petitioner pleaded guilty to all five indictments. So far as the record shows, the judge asked no questions of petitioner concerning his plea, and petitioner did not address the court.

Trial strategy may of course make a plea of guilty seem the desirable course. But the record is wholly silent on that point and throws no light on it.

Alabama provides that when a defendant pleads guilty, "the court must cause the punishment to be determined by a jury" (except where it is required to be fixed by the court) and may "cause witnesses to be examined, to ascertain the character of the offense." In the present case a trial of that dimension was held, the prosecution presenting its case largely through eyewitness testimony. Although counsel for petitioner engaged in cursory cross-examination, petitioner neither testified himself nor presented testimony concerning his character and background. There was nothing to indicate that he had a prior criminal record.

In instructing the jury, the judge stressed that petitioner had pleaded guilty in five cases of robbery, defined as "the felonious taking of money * * * from another against his will * * * by violence or by putting him in fear * * * [carrying] from ten years minimum in the penitentiary to the supreme penalty of death by electrocution." The jury, upon deliberation, found petitioner guilty and sentenced him severally to die on each of the five indictments. * * *

A plea of guilty is more than a confession which admits that the accused did various acts; it is itself a conviction; nothing remains but to give judgment and determine punishment. Admissibility of a confession must be based on a "reliable determination on the voluntariness issue which satisfies the constitutional rights of the defendant." The requirement that the prosecution spread on the record the prerequisites of a valid waiver is no constitutional innovation. In [dealing with a problem of waiver of the right to counsel we] held: "Presuming waiver from a silent record is impermissible. The record must show, or there must be an allegation and evidence which show, that an accused was offered counsel but intelligently and understandingly rejected the offer. Anything less is not waiver."

We think that the same standard must be applied to determining whether a guilty plea is voluntarily made. For, as we have said, a plea of guilty is more than an admission of conduct; it is a conviction. Ignorance, incomprehension, coercion, terror, inducements, subtle or blatant threats might be a perfect cover-up of unconstitutionality. The question of an effective waiver of a federal constitutional right in a proceeding is of course governed by federal standards.

Several federal constitutional rights are involved in a waiver that takes place when a plea of guilty is entered in a state criminal trial. First, is the privilege against compulsory self-incrimination guaranteed by the Fifth Amendment and applicable to the States by reason of the Fourteenth. Second, is the right to trial by jury. Third, is the right to confront one's accusers. We cannot presume a waiver of these three important federal rights from a silent record.

What is at stake for an accused facing death or imprisonment demands the utmost solicitude of which courts are capable in canvassing the matter with the accused to make sure he has a full understanding of what the plea connotes and of its consequence. When the judge discharges that function, he leaves a record adequate for any review that may be later sought and forestalls the spin-off of collateral proceedings that seek to probe murky memories.

The three dissenting justices in the Alabama Supreme Court stated the law accurately when they concluded that there was reversible error "because the record does not disclose that the defendant voluntarily and understandingly entered his pleas of guilty."

Reversed.

JUSTICE HARLAN, whom JUSTICE BLACK joins, dissenting. \* \* \*

[T]he Court's disposition is plainly out of keeping with \* \* \* *Halliday v. United States*, 394 U.S. 831 (1969), [where the Court] affirmed the conviction even though Halliday's guilty plea was accepted in 1954 without any explicit inquiry into whether it was knowingly and understandingly made \* \* \* In justification, the Court noted that two lower courts had found in collateral proceedings that the plea was voluntary. \* \* \*

It seems elementary that the Fifth Amendment due process to which petitioner Halliday was entitled must be at least as demanding as the Fourteenth Amendment process due petitioner Boykin. Yet petitioner Halliday's federal conviction has been affirmed as "constitutionally valid," despite the omission of any judicial inquiry of record at the time of his plea, because he initiated collateral proceedings which revealed that the plea was actually voluntary. Petitioner Boykin, on the other hand, today has his Alabama conviction reversed because of exactly the same omission, even though he too "may \* \* \* resort to appropriate post-conviction remedies to attack his plea's voluntariness" and thus "is not without a remedy to correct constitutional defects in his conviction." In short, I find it utterly impossible to square today's holding with what the Court has so recently done. \* \* \*

## HENDERSON v. MORGAN
### 426 U.S. 637, 96 S.Ct. 2253, 49 L.Ed.2d 108 (1976).

[Respondent was indicted for first-degree murder, but by agreement with the prosecution and on counsel's advice respondent pleaded guilty to second-degree murder and was sentenced. Subsequently, after exhausting his state remedies in an unsuccessful attempt to have his conviction vacated on the ground that his guilty plea was involuntary, respondent filed a habeas corpus petition in Federal District Court, alleging that his guilty plea was involuntary because, *inter alia,* he was not aware that intent to cause death was an element of second-degree murder. The District Court ultimately heard the testimony of several witnesses, including respondent and his defense counsel in the original prosecution; and the transcript of the relevant state-court proceedings and certain psychological evaluations of respondent, who was substantially below average intelligence, were made part of the record. On the basis of the evidence thus developed the District Court found that respondent had not been advised by counsel or the state court that an intent to cause death was an essential element of second-degree murder, and, based on this finding, held that the guilty plea was involuntary and had to be set aside. The Court of Appeals affirmed.]

    JUSTICE STEVENS delivered the opinion of the Court.   *   *   *

    Petitioner contends that the District Court applied an unrealistically rigid rule of law. Instead of testing the voluntariness of a plea by determining whether a ritualistic litany of the formal legal elements of an offense was read to the defendant, petitioner argues that the court should examine the totality of the circumstances and determine whether the substance of the charge, as opposed to its technical elements, was conveyed to the accused. We do not disagree with the thrust of petitioner's argument, but we are persuaded that even under the test which he espouses, this judgment finding respondent guilty of second-degree murder was defective.

    We assume, as petitioner argues, that the prosecutor had overwhelming evidence of guilt available. We also accept petitioner's characterization of the competence of respondent's counsel and of the wisdom of their advice to plead guilty to a charge of second-degree murder. Nevertheless, such a plea cannot support a judgment of guilt unless it was voluntary in a constitutional sense.[13] And clearly the plea could not be voluntary in the sense that it constituted an intelligent admission that he committed the offense unless the defendant received "real notice of the true nature of the charge against him, the first and most universally recognized requirement of due process."

    The charge of second-degree murder was never formally made. Had it been made, it necessarily would have included a charge that respondent's assault was "committed with a design to effect the death of the person killed." That element of the offense might have been proved by the objective evidence even if respondent's actual state of mind was consistent with innocence or manslaughter. But even if such a design to effect death would almost inevitably have been inferred from evidence that respondent repeatedly stabbed Mrs. Francisco, it is nevertheless also true that a jury would not have been required to draw that inference. The jury would have been entitled to accept defense counsel's appraisal of the incident as involving only manslaughter in the first degree. Therefore, an admission by respondent that he killed Mrs. Francisco does not necessarily also admit that he was guilty of second-degree murder.

    There is nothing in this record that can serve as a substitute for either a finding after trial, or a voluntary admission, that respondent had the requisite intent. Defense counsel did not purport to stipulate to that fact; they did not

---

**13.** A plea may be involuntary either because the accused does not understand the nature of the constitutional protections that he is waiving, or because he has such an incomplete understanding of the charge that his plea cannot stand as an intelligent admission of guilt. Without adequate notice of the nature of the charge against him, or proof that he in fact understood the charge, the plea cannot be voluntary in this latter sense.

explain to him that his plea would be an admission of that fact; and he made no factual statement or admission necessarily implying that he had such intent. In these circumstances it is impossible to conclude that his plea to the unexplained charge of second-degree murder was voluntary.

Petitioner argues that affirmance of the Court of Appeals will invite countless collateral attacks on judgments entered on pleas of guilty, since frequently the record will not contain a complete enumeration of the elements of the offense to which an accused person pleads guilty.[18] We think petitioner's fears are exaggerated.

Normally the record contains either an explanation of the charge by the trial judge, or at least a representation by defense counsel that the nature of the offense has been explained to the accused. Moreover, even without such an express representation, it may be appropriate to presume that in most cases defense counsel routinely explain the nature of the offense in sufficient detail to give the accused notice of what he is being asked to admit. This case is unique because the trial judge found as a fact that the element of intent was not explained to respondent. Moreover, respondent's unusually low mental capacity provides a reasonable explanation for counsel's oversight; it also forecloses the conclusion that the error was harmless beyond a reasonable doubt, for it lends at least a modicum of credibility to defense counsel's appraisal of the homicide as a manslaughter rather than a murder.

Since respondent did not receive adequate notice of the offense to which he pleaded guilty, his plea was involuntary and the judgment of conviction was entered without due process of law.

Affirmed.

JUSTICE WHITE, with whom JUSTICE STEWART, JUSTICE BLACKMUN, and JUSTICE POWELL join, concurring. * * *

The problem in this case is that the defendant's guilt has been established neither by a finding of guilt beyond a reasonable doubt after trial nor by the defendant's own admission that he is in fact guilty. The defendant did not expressly admit that he intended the victim's death (such intent being an element of the crime for which he stands convicted); and his plea of guilty cannot be construed as an implied admission that he intended her death because the District Court has found that he was not told and did not know that intent to kill was an element of the offense with which he was charged.[2] * * *

The dissent concedes that the conviction in this case was entered in violation of the United States Constitution. The dissent argues, however, that to set this defendant's conviction aside is to apply a new constitutional rule retroactively. The argument was not made by the petitioner in this case and is, in any event, untenable. * * * Either a new constitutional rule is being established in *this* case—in which event we will have to address at some future time the question

18. There is no need in this case to decide whether notice of the true nature, or substance, of a charge always requires a description of every element of the offense; we assume it does not. Nevertheless, intent is such a critical element of the offense of second-degree murder that notice of that element is required.

2. This case is unusual in that the offense to which the defendant pleaded was not charged in the indictment. The indictment charged first-degree murder. The defendant pleaded guilty to the included offense of second-degree murder, the elements of which were not set forth in any document which had been read to the defendant or to which he had access. In those cases in which the indictment is read to the defendant by the court at arraignment or at the time of his plea, his plea of guilty may well be deemed a factual admission that he did what he is charged with doing so that a judgment of conviction may validly be entered against him.

whether this rule is retroactive—or, as I believe to be true, this case rests on the long-accepted principle that a guilty plea must provide a trustworthy basis for believing that the defendant is in fact guilty. If so, then the principle will and should govern all similar cases presented to us in the future. In any event, the judgment of the court below should be affirmed, and I join the opinion of the Court.

JUSTICE REHNQUIST, with whom THE CHIEF JUSTICE joins, dissenting.

Since it seems clear * * * that respondent's plea was "voluntarily made," and since it is undisputed that it was made with full understanding of its consequences, the only remaining issue is whether he was "properly advised." This inquiry, in turn, depends upon the sort of advice reasonably competent counsel would have been expected to give him. * * *

Respondent was originally indicted for the crime of first-degree murder, and that indictment charged that in April 1965, he had "willfully, feloniously and of malice aforethought, stabbed and cut Ada Francisco with a dangerous knife * * * and that thereafter * * * the said Ada Francisco died of said wounds and injuries, said killing being inexcusable and unjustifiable." Respondent's attorney at the habeas hearing testified that respondent had stabbed his victim "many times" which suggests that experienced counsel would not consider the "design to effect death" issue to be in serious dispute. * * *

I do not see how this Court, or any court, could conclude on this state of the record that respondent was not "properly advised" at the time he entered his plea of guilty to the charge of second-degree murder.

His attorneys were motivated by the eminently reasonable tactical judgment on their part that he should plead guilty to second-degree murder in order to avoid the possibility of conviction for first-degree murder with its more serious attendant penalties. Since the Court concedes both the competence of respondent's counsel and the wisdom of their advice, that should be the end of the matter.

There are intimations in the Court's opinion that the vice which it finds in the guilty plea is not that respondent was not *informed* of all the elements of the offense, but that instead he did not *admit* to all of those elements. But it is quite clear under our decision in *North Carolina v. Alford* that the latter fact, standing alone, is not sufficient to invalidate a guilty plea. * * *

## NORTH CAROLINA v. ALFORD
### 400 U.S. 25, 91 S.Ct. 160, 27 L.Ed.2d 162 (1970).

JUSTICE WHITE delivered the opinion of the Court.

[Appellee was indicted for the capital crime of first-degree murder. At that time North Carolina law provided for the penalty of life imprisonment when a plea of guilty was accepted to a first-degree murder charge; for the death penalty following a jury verdict of guilty, unless the jury recommended life imprisonment; and for a penalty of from two to 30 years' imprisonment for second-degree murder. Appellee's attorney, in the face of strong evidence of guilt, recommended a guilty plea, but left the decision to appellee. The prosecutor agreed to accept a plea of guilty to second-degree murder. The trial court heard damaging evidence from certain witnesses before accepting a plea. Appellee pleaded guilty, although disclaiming guilt, because of the threat of the death penalty, and was sentenced to 30 years' imprisonment. The Court of Appeals, on an appeal from a denial of a writ of habeas corpus, found that appellee's guilty plea was involuntary because it was motivated principally by fear of the death penalty.]

We held in *Brady v. United States,* 397 U.S. 742 (1970), that a plea of guilty which would not have been entered except for the defendant's desire to avoid a possible death penalty and to limit the maximum penalty to life imprisonment or a term of years was not for that reason compelled within the meaning of the Fifth Amendment.  * * * The standard was and remains whether the plea represents a voluntary and intelligent choice among the alternative courses of action open to the defendant.  * * * That he would not have pleaded except for the opportunity to limit the possible penalty does not necessarily demonstrate that the plea of guilty was not the product of a free and rational choice, especially where the defendant was represented by competent counsel whose advice was that the plea would be to the defendant's advantage. The standard fashioned and applied by the Court of Appeals was therefore erroneous and we would, without more, vacate and remand the case for further proceedings with respect to any other claims of Alford which are properly before that court, if it were not for other circumstances appearing in the record which might seem to warrant an affirmance of the Court of Appeals.

As previously recounted after Alford's plea of guilty was offered and the State's case was placed before the judge, Alford denied that he had committed the murder but reaffirmed his desire to plead guilty to avoid a possible death sentence and to limit the penalty to the 30–year maximum provided for second-degree murder. Ordinarily, a judgment of conviction resting on a plea of guilty is justified by the defendant's admission that he committed the crime charged against him and his consent that judgment be entered without a trial of any kind. The plea usually subsumes both elements, and justifiably so, even though there is no separate, express admission by the defendant that he committed the particular acts claimed to constitute the crime charged in the indictment. Here Alford entered his plea but accompanied it with the statement that he had not shot the victim.

If Alford's statements were to be credited as sincere assertions of his innocence, there obviously existed a factual and legal dispute between him and the State. Without more, it might be argued that the conviction entered on his guilty plea was invalid, since his assertion of innocence negatived any admission of guilt, which, as we observed last Term in *Brady,* is normally "[c]entral to the plea and the foundation for entering judgment against the defendant * * *."

In addition to Alford's statement, however, the court had heard an account of the events on the night of the murder, including information from Alford's acquaintances that he had departed from his home with his gun stating his intention to kill and that he had later declared that he had carried out his intention. Nor had Alford wavered in his desire to have trial court determine his guilt without a jury trial. Although denying the charge against him, he nevertheless preferred the dispute between him and the State to be settled by the judge in the context of a guilty plea proceeding rather than by a formal trial. Thereupon, with the State's telling evidence and Alford's denial before it, the trial court proceeded to convict and sentence Alford for second-degree murder.

State and lower federal courts are divided upon whether a guilty plea can be accepted when it is accompanied by protestations of innocence and hence contains only a waiver of trial but no admission of guilt. Some courts, giving expression to the principle that "[o]ur law only authorizes a conviction where guilt is shown," require that trial judges reject such pleas. But others have concluded that they should not "force any defense on a defendant in a criminal

case," particularly when advancement of the defense might "end in disaster
* * *." They have argued that, since "guilt, or the degree of guilt, is at times
uncertain and elusive," "[a]n accused, though believing in or entertaining doubts
respecting his innocence, might reasonably conclude a jury would be convinced
of his guilt and that he would fare better in the sentence by pleading guilty
* * *." [7]

This Court has not confronted this precise issue, but prior decisions do yield
relevant principles. In *Lynch v. Overholser,* 369 U.S. 705 (1962), Lynch, who had
been charged in the Municipal Court of the District of Columbia with drawing
and negotiating bad checks, a misdemeanor punishable by a maximum of one
year in jail, sought to enter a plea of guilty, but the trial judge refused to accept
the plea since a psychiatric report in the judge's possession indicated that Lynch
had been suffering from "a manic depressive psychosis, at the time of the crime
charged," and hence might have been not guilty by reason of insanity. Although
at the subsequent trial Lynch did not rely on the insanity defense, he was found
not guilty by reason of insanity and committed for an indeterminate period to a
mental institution. On habeas corpus, the Court ordered his release, construing
the congressional legislation seemingly authorizing the commitment as not
reaching a case where the accused preferred a guilty plea to a plea of insanity.
The Court expressly refused to rule that Lynch had an absolute right to have his
guilty plea accepted, but implied that there would have been no constitutional
error had his plea been accepted even though evidence before the judge indicated
that there was a valid defense.

The issue in *Hudson v. United States,* 272 U.S. 451 (1926), was whether a
federal court has power to impose a prison sentence after accepting a plea of *nolo
contendere,* a plea by which a defendant does not expressly admit his guilt, but
nonetheless waives his right to a trial and authorizes the court for purposes of
the case to treat him as if he were guilty.[8] The Court held that a trial court does
have such power, and except for the cases which were rejected in *Hudson,* the
federal courts have uniformly followed this rule, even in cases involving moral
turpitude. Implicit in the *nolo contendere* cases is a recognition that the
Constitution does not bar imposition of a prison sentence upon an accused who is
unwilling expressly to admit his guilt but who, faced with grim alternatives, is
willing to waive his trial and accept the sentence.

These cases would be directly in point if Alford had simply insisted on his
plea but refused to admit the crime. The fact that his plea was denominated a
plea of guilty rather than a plea of *nolo contendere* is of no constitutional
significance with respect to the issue now before us, for the Constitution is
concerned with the practical consequences, not the formal categorizations, of
state law. Thus, while most pleas of guilty consist of both a waiver of trial and
an express admission of guilt, the latter element is not a constitutional requisite

---

**7.** A third approach has been to decline to
rule definitively that a trial judge must either
accept or reject an otherwise valid plea containing a protestation of innocence, but to
leave that decision to his sound discretion.

**8.** Courts have defined the plea of *nolo
contendere* in a variety of different ways,
describing it, on the one hand, as "in effect, a
plea of guilty," and on the other, as a query
directed to the court to determine the defendant's guilt. As a result, it is impossible to
state precisely what a defendant does admit
when he enters a *nolo* plea in a way that will
consistently fit all the cases. * * *

Throughout its history, that is, the plea of
*nolo contendere* has been viewed not as an
express admission of guilt but as a consent by
the defendant that he may be punished as if
he were guilty and a prayer for leniency.
Fed.Rule Crim.Proc. 11 preserves this distinction in its requirement that a court cannot
accept a guilty plea "unless it is satisfied that
there is a factual basis for the plea"; there is
no similar requirement for pleas of *nolo contendere,* since it was thought desirable to permit defendants to plead *nolo* without making
any inquiry into their actual guilt.

to the imposition of criminal penalty. An individual accused of crime may voluntarily, knowingly, and understandingly consent to the imposition of a prison sentence even if he is unwilling or unable to admit his participation in the acts constituting the crime.

Nor can we perceive any material difference between a plea that refuses to admit commission of the criminal act and a plea containing a protestation of innocence when, as in the instant case, a defendant intelligently concludes that his interests require entry of a guilty plea and the record before the judge contains strong evidence of actual guilt. Here the State had a strong case of first-degree murder against Alford. Whether he realized or disbelieved his guilt, he insisted on his plea because in his view he had absolutely nothing to gain by a trial and much to gain by pleading. Because of the overwhelming evidence against him, a trial was precisely what neither Alford nor his attorney desired. Confronted with the choice between a trial for first-degree murder, on the one hand, and a plea of guilty to second-degree murder, on the other, Alford quite reasonably chose the latter and thereby limited the maximum penalty to a 30–year term. When his plea is viewed in light of the evidence against him, which substantially negated his claim of innocence and which further provided a means by which the judge could test whether the plea was being intelligently entered, its validity cannot be seriously questioned. In view of the strong factual basis for the plea demonstrated by the State and Alford's clearly expressed desire to enter it despite his professed belief in his innocence, we hold that the trial judge did not commit constitutional error in accepting it.[11]   *   *   *

JUSTICE BLACK, * * * concurs in the judgment and in substantially all of the opinion in this case.

JUSTICE BRENNAN, with whom JUSTICE DOUGLAS and JUSTICE MARSHALL join, dissenting.

* * * [I]t is sufficient in my view to state that the facts set out in the majority opinion demonstrate that Alford was "so gripped by fear of the death penalty" that his decision to plead guilty was not voluntary but was "the product of duress as much so as choice reflecting physical constraint."

## BLACKLEDGE v. ALLISON
431 U.S. 63, 97 S.Ct. 1621, 52 L.Ed.2d 136 (1977).

JUSTICE STEWART delivered the opinion of the Court.

[At the arraignment of respondent, who had been indicted in North Carolina for various state criminal offenses, he entered a guilty plea to a single count of attempted safe robbery. In response to two of various form questions that under then-applicable procedures were put by the trial judge to those entering guilty pleas, respondent acknowledged that he understood that he could be imprisoned for a minimum of 10 years to a maximum of life and that no one had made promises or threats to influence him to plead guilty. Without further questioning, the judge accepted the plea on an "Adjudication" form, which recited that respondent had pleaded guilty to attempted safe robbery "freely, understandingly and voluntarily," with full awareness of the consequences, and "without

---

**11.** Our holding does not mean that a trial judge must accept every constitutionally valid guilty plea merely because a defendant wishes so to plead. A criminal defendant does not have an absolute right under the Constitution to have his guilty plea accepted by the court, although the States may by statute or other- wise confer such a right. Likewise, the States may bar their courts from accepting guilty pleas from any defendants who assert their innocence. Cf. Fed.Rule Crim.Proc. 11, which gives a trial judge discretion to "refuse to accept a plea of guilty * * *." We need not now delineate the scope of that discretion.

undue * * * compulsion * * * duress, [or] promise of leniency." At a sentencing hearing three days later respondent was sentenced to 17–21 years. Respondent sought a writ of habeas corpus in a Federal District Court, claiming that his guilty plea had been induced by the promise of his attorney, who presumably had consulted with the judge and Solicitor, that he would get only a 10–year sentence. He also stated that he was aware that he had been questioned by the judge before sentencing but thought that he was going to get only 10 years and had been instructed to answer the questions so that the court would accept the guilty plea. The District Court granted a motion to dismiss the petition, on the ground that the form conclusively showed that respondent had chosen to plead guilty knowingly, voluntarily, and with full awareness of the consequences. The Court of Appeals reversed, holding that respondent's allegation of a broken promise, as amplified by the explanation that his lawyer instructed him to deny the existence of any promises, was not foreclosed by his responses to the form questions and that he was entitled to an evidentiary hearing, at least in the absence of counter-affidavits conclusively proving the falsity of respondent's allegations.]

Whatever might be the situation in an ideal world, the fact is that the guilty plea and the often concomitant plea bargain are important components of this country's criminal justice system. Properly administered, they can benefit all concerned. The defendant avoids extended pretrial incarceration and the anxieties and uncertainties of a trial; he gains a speedy disposition of his case, the chance to acknowledge his guilt, and a prompt start in realizing whatever potential there may be for rehabilitation. Judges and prosecutors conserve vital and scarce resources. The public is protected from the risks posed by those charged with criminal offenses who are at large on bail while awaiting completion of criminal proceedings.

These advantages can be secured, however, only if dispositions by guilty plea are accorded a great measure of finality. To allow indiscriminate hearings in federal postconviction proceedings would eliminate the chief virtues of the plea system—speed, economy, and finality. And there is reason for concern about that prospect. More often than not a prisoner has everything to gain and nothing to lose from filing a collateral attack upon his guilty plea. If he succeeds in vacating the judgment of conviction, retrial may be difficult. If he convinces a court that his plea was induced by an advantageous plea agreement that was violated, he may obtain the benefit of its terms. A collateral attack may also be inspired by "a mere desire to be freed temporarily from the confines of the prison."

Yet arrayed against the interest in finality is the very purpose of the writ of habeas corpus—to safeguard a person's freedom from detention in violation of constitutional guarantees. * * * And a prisoner in custody after pleading guilty, no less than one tried and convicted by a jury, is entitled to avail himself of the writ in challenging the constitutionality of his custody.

In *Machibroda v. United States,* 368 U.S. 487 (1962), the defendant had pleaded guilty in federal court to bank robbery charges and been sentenced to 40 years in prison. He later filed a § 2255 motion alleging that his plea had been induced by an Assistant United States Attorney's promises that his sentence would not exceed 20 years, that the prosecutor had admonished him not to tell his lawyer about the agreement, and that the trial judge had wholly failed to inquire whether the guilty plea was made voluntarily before accepting it. This Court noted that the allegations, if proved, would entitle the defendant to relief, and that they raised an issue of fact that could not be resolved simply on the basis of an affidavit from the prosecutor denying the allegations. Because those allegations "related primarily to purported occurrences outside the courtroom and upon which the record could, therefore, cast no real light," and were not so "vague [or] conclusory," as to permit summary disposition, the Court ruled that the defendant was entitled to the opportunity to substantiate them at an evidentiary hearing.

The later case of *Fontaine v. United States,* 411 U.S. 213 (1973), followed the same approach. The defendant there, having waived counsel, had also pleaded guilty to federal bank robbery charges. Before accepting the plea, the District Judge addressed the defendant personally, and the defendant stated in substance "that his plea was given voluntarily and knowingly, that he understood the nature of the charge and the consequences of the plea, and that he was in fact guilty." The defendant later filed a § 2255 motion to vacate his sentence on the ground that his plea had been coerced "by a combination of fear, coercive police tactics, and illness, including mental illness." The motion included supporting factual allegations, as well as hospital records documenting some of the contentions.

Although noting that in collaterally attacking a plea of guilty a prisoner "may not ordinarily repudiate" statements made to the sentencing judge when the plea was entered, the Court observed that no procedural device for the taking of guilty pleas is so perfect in design and exercise as to warrant a *per se* rule rendering it "uniformly invulnerable to subsequent challenge." Because the record of the plea hearing did not, in view of the allegations made, " 'conclusively show that the prisoner [was] entitled to no relief,' " the Court ruled that the prisoner should be given an evidentiary hearing.

These cases do not in the least reduce the force of the original plea hearing. For the representations of the defendant, his lawyer, and the prosecutor at such a hearing, as well as any findings made by the judge accepting the plea, constitute a formidable barrier in any subsequent collateral proceedings. Solemn declarations in open court carry a strong presumption of verity. The subsequent presentation of conclusory allegations unsupported by specifics is subject to summary dismissal, as are contentions that in the face of the record are wholly incredible.

What *Machibroda* and *Fontaine* indisputably teach, however, is that the barrier of the plea or sentencing proceeding record, although imposing, is not invariably insurmountable. In administering the writ of habeas corpus and its § 2255 counterpart, the federal courts cannot fairly adopt a *per se* rule excluding all possibility that a defendant's representations at the time his guilty plea was accepted were so much the product of such factors as misunderstanding, duress, or misrepresentation by others as to make the guilty plea a constitutionally inadequate basis for imprisonment.

The allegations in this case were not in themselves so "vague [or] conclusory" as to warrant dismissal for that reason alone. Allison alleged as a ground for relief that his plea was induced by an unkept promise. But he did not stop there. He proceeded to elaborate upon this claim with specific factual allegations. The petition indicated exactly what the terms of the promise were; when, where, and by whom the promise had been made; and the identity of one witness to its communication. The critical question is whether these allegations, when viewed against the record of the plea hearing, were so "palpably incredible," so "patently frivolous or false" as to warrant summary dismissal. In the light of the nature of the record of the proceeding at which the guilty plea was accepted, and of the ambiguous status of the process of plea bargaining at the time the guilty plea was made, we conclude that Allison's petition should not have been summarily dismissed.

Only recently has plea bargaining become a visible practice accepted as a legitimate component in the administration of criminal justice. For decades it was a *sub rosa* process shrouded in secrecy and deliberately concealed by participating defendants, defense lawyers, prosecutors, and even judges. Indeed, it was not until our decision in *Santobello v. New York* that lingering doubts about the legitimacy of the practice were finally dispelled.

Allison was arraigned a mere 37 days after the *Santobello* decision was announced, under a North Carolina procedure that had not been modified in light of *Santobello* or earlier decisions of this Court recognizing the process of plea bargaining. That procedure itself reflected the atmosphere of secrecy which then characterized plea bargaining generally. No transcript of the proceeding was made. The only record was a standard printed form. There is no way of knowing whether the trial judge in any way deviated from or supplemented the text of the form. The record is silent as to what statements Allison, his lawyer, or the prosecutor might have made regarding promised sentencing concessions. And there is no record at all of the sentencing hearing three days later, at which one of the participants might well have made a statement shedding light upon the veracity of the allegations Allison later advanced.

The litany of form questions followed by the trial judge at arraignment nowhere indicated to Allison (or indeed to the lawyers involved) that plea bargaining was a legitimate practice that could be freely disclosed in open court. Neither lawyer was asked to disclose any agreement that had been reached, or sentencing recommendation that had been promised. The process thus did nothing to dispel a defendant's relief that any bargain struck must remain concealed—a belief here allegedly reinforced by the admonition of Allison's lawyer himself that disclosure could jeopardize the agreement. Rather than challenging respondent's counsel's contention at oral argument in this Court that "at that time in North Carolina plea bargains were never disclosed in response to such a question on such a form," counsel for the petitioners conceded at oral argument that "[t]hat form was a minimum inquiry."

Although "[l]ogically the general inquiry should elicit information about plea bargaining, * * * it seldom has in the past." Particularly if, as Allison alleged, he was advised by counsel to conceal any plea bargain, his denial that any promises had been made might have been a courtroom ritual more sham than real. We thus cannot conclude that the allegations in Allison's habeas corpus petition, when measured against the "record" of the arraignment, were so "patently false or frivolous" as to warrant summary dismissal.

North Carolina has recently undertaken major revisions of its plea-bargaining procedures in part to prevent the very kind of problem now before us. Plea bargaining is expressly legitimate. The judge is directed to advise the defendant that courts have approved plea bargaining and he may thus admit to any promises without fear of jeopardizing an advantageous agreement or prejudicing himself in the judge's eyes. Specific inquiry about whether a plea bargain has been struck is then made not only of the defendant, but also of his counsel and the prosecutor. Finally, the entire proceeding is to be transcribed verbatim.

Had these commendable procedures been followed in the present case, Allison's petition would have been cast in a very different light. The careful explication of the legitimacy of plea bargaining, the questioning of both lawyers, and the verbatim record of their answers at the guilty-plea proceedings would almost surely have shown whether any bargain did exist and, if so, insured that it was not ignored. But the salutary reforms recently implemented by North Carolina highlight even more sharply the deficiencies in the record before the District Court in the present case.

This is not to say that every set of allegations not on its face without merit entitles a habeas corpus petitioner to an evidentiary hearing. As in civil cases generally, there exists a procedure whose purpose is to test whether facially adequate allegations have sufficient basis in fact to warrant plenary presentation of evidence. That procedure is, of course, the motion for summary judgment. Upon remand the warden will be free to make such a notion, supporting it with whatever proof he wishes to attach. If he chooses to do so, Allison will then be required either to produce some contrary proof indicating that there is a genuine issue of fact to be resolved by the District Court or to explain his inability to provide such proof. * * *

The Chief Justice concurs in the judgment.

Justice Rehnquist took no part in the consideration or decision of this case.

Justice Powell, concurring.

I join the opinion of the Court, and write briefly only to emphasize the importance of finality to a system of justice. * * *

As the Court's opinion indicates, there is every reason to believe that if a procedure similar to that prescribed by the new North Carolina statute is followed, a contention such as that made by respondent will justify an evidentiary hearing "only in the most extraordinary circumstances." If all participants in the process at the plea stage are mindful of the importance of adhering carefully to prescribed procedures and of preserving a full record thereof, the causes of justice and finality both will be served.

# Chapter 15

# TRIAL BY JURY

## SECTION 1. RIGHT TO JURY TRIAL

The Sixth Amendment declares that in "all criminal prosecutions, the accused shall enjoy the right to a \* \* \* trial, by an impartial jury of the State and district wherein the crime shall have been committed." *Duncan v. Louisiana* discusses why jury trial is so important in the American system of criminal justice and why, consequently, this Sixth Amendment right is also applicable to the states. *Blanton v. City of North Las Vegas* examines when an offense is "petty" and thus is not covered by the jury trial right. Though the traditional criminal jury is one made up of 12 persons who must unanimously agree to the verdict, *Burch v. Louisiana* teaches that something less will suffice under the Sixth Amendment. The final case in this section, *Singer v. United States*, considers whether a defendant should have an unrestrained right to have his case tried by the judge alone.

### DUNCAN v. LOUISIANA
*[set forth in Ch. 2, § 2]*

### BLANTON v. CITY OF NORTH LAS VEGAS
___ U.S. ___, 109 S.Ct. 1289, 103 L.Ed.2d 550 (1989).

JUSTICE MARSHALL delivered the opinion of the Court.

The issue in this case is whether there is a constitutional right to a trial by jury for persons charged under Nevada law with driving under the influence of alcohol (DUI). We hold that there is not. \* \* \*

It has long been settled "that there is a category of petty crimes or offenses which is not subject to the Sixth Amendment jury trial provision." *Duncan v. Louisiana*. In determining whether a particular offense should be categorized as "petty," our early decisions focused on the nature of the offense and on whether it was triable by a jury at common law. In recent years, however, we have sought more "objective indications of the seriousness with which society regards the offense." "[W]e have found the most relevant such criteria in the severity of the maximum authorized penalty." *Baldwin v. New York*, 399 U.S. 66, 68, 90 S.Ct. 1886, 1887, 26 L.Ed.2d 437 (1970). In fixing the maximum penalty for a crime, a legislature "include[s] within the definition of the crime itself a judgment about the seriousness of the offense." The judiciary should not substitute its judgment as to seriousness for that of a legislature, which is "far better equipped to perform the task, and [is] likewise more responsive to changes in attitude and more amenable to the recognition and correction of their misperceptions in this respect."

In using the word "penalty," we do not refer solely to the maximum prison term authorized for a particular offense. A legislature's view of the seriousness of an offense also is reflected in the other penalties that it attaches to the offense. * * *[6] Primary emphasis, however, must be placed on the maximum authorized period of incarceration. Penalties such as probation or a fine may engender "a significant infringement of personal freedom," but they cannot approximate in severity the loss of liberty that a prison term entails. Indeed, because incarceration is an "intrinsically different" form of punishment, it is the most powerful indication of whether an offense is "serious."

Following this approach, our decision in *Baldwin* established that a defendant is entitled to a jury trial whenever the offense for which he is charged carries a maximum authorized prison term of greater than six months. * * * As for a prison term of six months or less, we recognized that it will seldom be viewed by the defendant as "trivial or 'petty.'" But we found that the disadvantages of such a sentence, "onerous though they may be, may be outweighed by the benefits that result from speedy and inexpensive nonjury adjudications."

Although we did not hold in *Baldwin* that an offense carrying a maximum prison term of six months or less automatically qualifies as a "petty" offense, and decline to do so today, we do find it appropriate to presume for purposes of the Sixth Amendment that society views such an offense as "petty." A defendant is entitled to jury trial in such circumstances only if he can demonstrate that any additional statutory penalties, viewed in conjunction with the maximum authorized period of incarceration, are so severe that they clearly reflect a legislative determination that the offense in question is a "serious" one. This standard, albeit somewhat imprecise, should ensure the availability of a jury trial in the rare situation where a legislature packs an offense it deems "serious" with onerous penalties that nonetheless "do not puncture the 6-month incarceration line."[8]

Applying these principles here, it is apparent that petitioners are not entitled to a jury trial. The maximum authorized prison sentence for first-time DUI offenders does not exceed six months. A presumption therefore exists that the Nevada legislature views DUI as a "petty" offense for purposes of the Sixth Amendment. Considering the additional statutory penalties as well, we do not believe that the Nevada Legislature has clearly indicated that DUI is a "serious" offense.

In the first place, it is immaterial that a first-time DUI offender may face a minimum term of imprisonment. In settling on six months' imprisonment as the constitutional demarcation point, we have assumed that a defendant convicted of the offense in question would receive the *maximum* authorized prison sentence. It is not constitutionally determinative, therefore, that a particular defendant may be required to serve some amount of jail time *less* than six months. Likewise, it is of little moment that a defendant may receive the maximum prison term because of the prohibitions on plea bargaining and probation. As for the 90-day license suspension, it, too, will be irrelevant if it

**6.** In criminal contempt prosecutions, "where no maximum penalty is authorized, the severity of the penalty actually imposed is the best indication of the seriousness of the particular offense."

**8.** In performing this analysis, only penalties resulting from state action, *e.g.*, those mandated by statute or regulation, should be considered. * * *

runs concurrently with the prison sentence, which we assume for present purposes to be the maximum of six months.[9]

We are also unpersuaded by the fact that, instead of a prison sentence, a DUI offender may be ordered to perform 48 hours of community service dressed in clothing identifying him as a DUI offender. Even assuming the outfit is the source of some embarrassment during the 48-hour period, such a penalty will be less embarrassing and less onerous than six months in jail. As for the possible $1,000 fine, it is well below the $5,000 level set by Congress in its most recent definition of a "petty" offense, 18 U.S.C. § 1, and petitioners do not suggest that this congressional figure is out of step with state practice for offenses carrying prison sentences of six months or less.[11]  *  *  *

## BURCH v. LOUISIANA

441 U.S. 130, 99 S.Ct. 1623, 60 L.Ed.2d 96 (1979).

JUSTICE REHNQUIST delivered the opinion of the Court.

The Louisiana Constitution and Code of Criminal Procedure provide that criminal cases in which the punishment imposed may be confinement for a period in excess of six months "shall be tried before a jury of six persons, five of whom must concur to render a verdict." We granted certiorari to decide whether conviction by a nonunanimous six-person jury in a state criminal trial for a nonpetty offense as contemplated by these provisions of Louisiana law violates the rights of an accused to trial by jury guaranteed by the Sixth and Fourteenth Amendments.

Petitioners, an individual and a Louisiana corporation, were jointly charged in two counts with the exhibition of two obscene motion pictures. Pursuant to Louisiana law, they were tried before a six-person jury, which found both petitioners guilty as charged. A poll of the jury after verdict indicated that the jury had voted unanimously to convict petitioner Wrestle, Inc., and had voted 5–1 to convict petitioner Burch. Burch was sentenced to two consecutive 7–month prison terms, which were suspended, and fined $1,000; Wrestle, Inc., was fined $600 on each count.

Petitioners appealed their convictions to the Supreme Court of Louisiana, where they argued that the provisions of Louisiana law permitting conviction by a nonunanimous six-member jury violated the rights of persons accused of nonpetty criminal offenses to trial by jury guaranteed by the Sixth and Fourteenth Amendments. Though acknowledging that the issue was "close," the court held that conviction by a nonunanimous six-person jury did not offend the Constitution. The court concluded that none of this Court's decisions precluded use of a nonunanimous six-person jury. " 'If 75 percent concurrence ($^9/_{12}$) was enough for a verdict as determined in *Johnson v. Louisiana*, 406 U.S. 356 (1972), then requiring 83 percent concurrence ($^5/_6$) ought to be within the permissible limits of *Johnson*.' " And our recent decision in *Ballew v. Georgia*, 435 U.S. 223 (1978), striking down a Georgia law allowing conviction by a unanimous five-person jury in nonpetty criminal cases, was distinguishable in the Louisiana Supreme Court's view:

**9.** It is unclear whether the license suspension and prison sentence in fact run concurrently. But even if they do not, we cannot say that a 90-day license suspension is that significant as a Sixth Amendment matter, particularly when a restricted license may be obtained after only 45 days. Furthermore, the requirement that an offender attend an alcohol abuse education course can only be described as *de minimis*.

**11.** *  *  * We decline petitioners' invitation to survey the statutory penalties for drunken driving in other States. The question is not whether other States consider drunken driving a "serious" offense, but whether Nevada does.

"[I]n *Williams* [*v. Florida,* 399 U.S. 78 (1970)] the court held that a six-person jury was of sufficient size to promote adequate group deliberation, to insulate members from outside intimidation, and to provide a representative cross-section of the community. These values, which *Ballew* held a five-person jury is inadequate to serve, are not necessarily defeated because the six-person jury's verdict may be rendered by five instead of by six persons."

Since the Louisiana Supreme Court believed that conviction by a nonunanimous six-person jury was not necessarily foreclosed by this Court's decisions, it stated that it preferred to "indulg[e] in the presumption of federal constitutionality which must be afforded to provisions of our state constitution."

We agree with the Louisiana Supreme Court that the question presented is a "close" one. Nonetheless, we believe that conviction by a nonunanimous six-member jury in a state criminal trial for a nonpetty offense deprives an accused of his constitutional right to trial by jury.

Only in relatively recent years has this Court had to consider the practices of the several States relating to jury size and unanimity. *Duncan v. Louisiana* marked the beginning of our involvement with such questions. *  *  *

Two Terms later in *Williams v. Florida,* the Court held that this constitutional guarantee of trial by jury did not require a State to provide an accused with a jury of 12 members and that Florida did not violate the jury trial rights of criminal defendants charged with nonpetty offenses by affording them jury panels comprised of only 6 persons. After canvassing the common-law development of the jury and the constitutional history of the jury trial right, the Court concluded that the 12–person requirement was "a historical accident" and that there was no indication that the Framers intended to preserve in the Constitution the features of the jury system as it existed at common law. Thus freed from strictly historical considerations, the Court turned to examine the function that this particular feature performs and its relation to the purposes of jury trial. The purpose of trial by jury, as noted in *Duncan,* is to prevent government oppression by providing a "safeguard against the corrupt or overzealous prosecutor and against the compliant, biased, or eccentric judge." Given this purpose, the *Williams* Court observed that the jury's essential feature lies in the "interposition between the accused and his accuser of the commonsense judgment of a group of laymen, and in the community participation and shared responsibility that results from that group's determination of guilt or innocence." These purposes could be fulfilled, the Court believed, so long as the jury was of a sufficient size to promote group deliberation, free from outside intimidation, and to provide a fair possibility that a cross section of the community would be represented on it. The Court concluded, however, that there is "little reason to think that these goals are in any meaningful sense less likely to be achieved when the jury numbers six, than when it numbers 12—*particularly if the requirement of unanimity is retained.*" (emphasis added).[7]

A similar analysis led us to conclude in 1972 that a jury's verdict need not be unanimous to satisfy constitutional requirements, even though unanimity had been the rule at common law. Thus, in *Apodaca v. Oregon,* 406 U.S. 404 (1972), we upheld a state statute providing that only 10 members of a 12–person jury need concur to render a verdict in certain noncapital cases. In terms of the role of the jury as a safeguard against oppression, the plurality opinion perceived no difference between those juries required to act unanimously and those permitted

---

7. The Court also believed that a jury of 12 was neither more reliable as a factfinder, more advantageous to the defendant, nor more representative of the variety of viewpoints in the community than a jury of 6.

to act by votes of 10 to 2. Nor was unanimity viewed by the plurality as contributing materially to the exercise of the jury's common-sense judgment or as a necessary precondition to effective application of the requirement that jury panels represent a fair cross section of the community.

Last Term, in *Ballew v. Georgia*, we considered whether a jury of less than six members passes constitutional scrutiny, a question that was explicitly reserved in *Williams v. Florida*. The Court, in separate opinions, held that conviction by a unanimous five-person jury in a trial for a nonpetty offense deprives an accused of his right to trial by jury. While readily admitting that the line between six members and five was not altogether easy to justify, at least five Members of the Court believed that reducing a jury to five persons in nonpetty cases raised sufficiently substantial doubts as to the fairness of the proceeding and proper functioning of the jury to warrant drawing the line at six.

We thus have held that the Constitution permits juries of less than 12 members, but that it requires at least 6. And we have approved the use of certain nonunanimous verdicts in cases involving 12–person juries. These principles are not questioned here. Rather, this case lies at the intersection of our decisions concerning jury size and unanimity. As in *Ballew*, we do not pretend the ability to discern *a priori* a bright line below which the number of jurors participating in the trial or in the verdict would not permit the jury to function in the manner required by our prior cases. But having already departed from the strictly historical requirements of jury trial, it is inevitable that lines must be drawn somewhere if the substance of the jury trial right is to be preserved. Even the State concedes as much.

This line-drawing process, "although essential, cannot be wholly satisfactory, for it requires attaching different consequences to events which, when they lie near the line, actually differ very little." However, much the same reasons that led us in *Ballew* to decide that use of a five-member jury threatened the fairness of the proceeding and the proper role of the jury, lead us to conclude now that conviction for a nonpetty offense by only five members of a six-person jury presents a similar threat to preservation of the substance of the jury trial guarantee and justifies our requiring verdicts rendered by six-person juries to be unanimous. We are buttressed in this view by the current jury practices of the several States. It appears that of those States that utilize six-member juries in trials of nonpetty offenses, only two, including Louisiana, also allow nonunanimous verdicts. We think that this near-uniform judgment of the Nation provides a useful guide in delimiting the line between those jury practices that are constitutionally permissible and those that are not.

The State seeks to justify its use of nonunanimous six-person juries on the basis of the "considerable time" savings that it claims results from trying cases in this manner. It asserts that under its system, juror deliberation time is shortened and the number of hung juries is reduced. Undoubtedly, the State has a substantial interest in reducing the time and expense associated with the administration of its system of criminal justice. But that interest cannot prevail here. First, on this record, any benefits that might accrue by allowing five members of a six-person jury to render a verdict, as compared with requiring unanimity of a six-member jury, are speculative, at best. More importantly, we think that when a State has reduced the size of its juries to the minimum number of jurors permitted by the Constitution, the additional authorization of nonunanimous verdicts by such juries sufficiently threatens the constitutional principles that led to the establishment of the size threshold that any counter-vailing interest of the State should yield. \* \* \*ᵃ

# SINGER v. UNITED STATES

380 U.S. 24, 85 S.Ct. 783, 13 L.Ed.2d 630 (1965).

CHIEF JUSTICE WARREN delivered the opinion of the Court.

Rule 23(a) of the Federal Rules of Criminal Procedure provides:

> "Cases required to be tried by jury shall be so tried unless the defendant waives a jury trial in writing with the approval of the court and the consent of the government."

Petitioner challenges the permissibility of this rule, arguing that the Constitution gives a defendant in a federal criminal case the right to waive a jury trial whenever he believes such action to be in his best interest, regardless of whether the prosecution and the court are willing to acquiesce in the waiver.

Petitioner was charged in a federal district court with 30 infractions of the mail fraud statute. \* \* \* On the opening day of trial petitioner offered in writing to waive a trial by jury "[f]or the purpose of shortening the trial." The trial court was willing to approve the waiver, but the Government refused to give its consent. Petitioner was subsequently convicted by a jury on 29 of the 30 counts.

Petitioner's argument is that a defendant in a federal criminal case has not only an unconditional constitutional right, guaranteed by Art. III, § 2, and the Sixth Amendment, to a trial by jury, but also a correlative right to have his case decided by a judge alone if he considers such a trial to be to his advantage. \* \* \*

We have examined petitioner's arguments and find them to be without merit. We can find no evidence that the common law recognized that defendants had the right to choose between court and jury trial. Although instances of waiver of jury trial can be found in certain of the colonies prior to the adoption of the Constitution, they were isolated instances occurring pursuant to colonial "constitutions" or statutes and were clear departures from the common law. There is no indication that the colonists considered the ability to waive a jury trial to be of equal importance to the right to demand one. Having found that the Constitution neither confers nor recognizes a right of criminal defendants to have their cases tried before a judge alone, we also conclude that Rule 23(a) sets forth a reasonable procedure governing attempted waivers of jury trials.

*English Common Law.* \* \* \* Not until 1827, long after the adoption of our Constitution, did England provide by statute for the trial of those who stood mute. Even this statute did not give the defendant the right to plead his case before a judge alone, but merely provided that he would be subject to jury trial without his formal consent.

Thus, as late as 1827 the English common law gave criminal defendants no option as to the mode of trial. \* \* \*

*The Colonial Experience.* \* \* \* The most that can be said for these examples [of jury waiver] is that they are evidence that the colonists believed it was possible to try criminal defendants without a jury. They in no way show

---

**a.** The concurring opinion of Justice Stevens, and the opinion of Justice Brennan (joined by Stewart and Marshall, JJ.), concur-ring as to the jury trial issue, but dissenting as to the constitutionality of the obscenity statute, are omitted.

that there was any general recognition of a defendant's right to be tried by the court instead of by a jury. Indeed, if there had been recognition of such a right, it would be difficult to understand why Article III and the Sixth Amendment were not drafted in terms which recognized an option.

*The Constitution and Its Judicial Interpretation.* The proceedings at the Constitutional Convention give little insight into what was meant by the direction in Art. III, § 2, that the "Trial of all Crimes * * * shall be by Jury." The clause was clearly intended to protect the accused from oppression by the Government, but, since the practice of permitting defendants a choice as to the mode of trial was not widespread, it is not surprising that some of the framers apparently believed that the Constitution designated trial by jury as the exclusive method of determining guilt. * * *

The issue whether a defendant could waive a jury trial in federal criminal cases was finally presented to this Court in *Patton v. United States,* 281 U.S. 276 (1930). * * * The Court examined Art. III, § 2, and the Sixth Amendment and concluded that a jury trial was a right which the accused might "forego at his election." The Court also spoke of jury trial as a "privilege," not an "imperative requirement," and remarked that jury trial was principally for the benefit of the accused. Nevertheless, the Court * * * concluded its opinion, with carefully chosen language that dispelled any notion that the defendant had an absolute right to demand trial before a judge sitting alone:

> "Not only must the right of the accused to a trial by a constitutional jury be jealously preserved, but the maintenance of the jury as a factfinding body in criminal cases is of such importance and has such a place in our traditions, that, before any waiver can become effective, the consent of government counsel and the sanction of the court must be had, in addition to the express and intelligent consent of the defendant. And the duty of the trial court in that regard is not to be discharged as a mere matter of rote, but with sound and advised discretion, with an eye to avoid unreasonable or undue departures from that mode of trial or from any of the essential elements thereof, and with a caution increasing in degree as the offenses dealt with increase in gravity."

> * * *

Thus, there is no federally recognized right to a criminal trial before a judge sitting alone, but a defendant can, as was held in *Patton,* in some instances waive his right to a trial by jury. The question remains whether the effectiveness of this waiver can be conditioned upon the consent of the prosecuting attorney and the trial judge.

The ability to waive a constitutional right does not ordinarily carry with it the right to insist upon the opposite of that right. For example, although a defendant can, under some circumstances, waive his constitutional right to a public trial, he has no absolute right to compel a private trial; although he can waive his right to be tried in the State and district where the crime was committed, he cannot in all cases compel transfer of the case to another district; and although he can waive his right to be confronted by the witnesses against him, it has never been seriously suggested that he can thereby compel the Government to try the case by stipulation. Moreover, it has long been accepted that the waiver of constitutional rights can be subjected to reasonable procedural regulations. * * *

Trial by jury has been established by the Constitution as the "normal and * * * preferable mode of disposing of issues of fact in criminal cases." As with any mode that might be devised to determine guilt, trial by jury has its weaknesses and the potential for misuse. However, the mode itself has been surrounded with safeguards to make it as fair as possible—for example, venue can be changed when there is a well-grounded fear of jury prejudice, and prospective jurors are subject to *voir dire* examination, to challenge for cause, and to peremptory challenge.

In light of the Constitution's emphasis on jury trial, we find it difficult to understand how the petitioner can submit the bald proposition that to compel a defendant in a criminal case to undergo a jury trial against his will is contrary to his right to a fair trial or to due process. A defendant's only constitutional right concerning the method of trial is to an impartial trial by jury. We find no constitutional impediment to conditioning a waiver of this right on the consent of the prosecuting attorney and the trial judge when, if either refuses to consent, the result is simply that the defendant is subject to an impartial trial by jury— the very thing that the Constitution guarantees him. The Constitution recognizes an adversary system as the proper method of determining guilt, and the Government, as a litigant, has a legitimate interest in seeing that cases in which it believes a conviction is warranted are tried before the tribunal which the Constitution regards as most likely to produce a fair result. * * *

We are aware that the States have adopted a variety of procedures relating to the waiver of jury trials in state criminal cases. Some have made waiver contingent on approval by the prosecutor. Others, while not giving the prosecutor a voice, have made court approval a prerequisite for waiver. Still others have provided that the question of waiver is a matter solely for the defendant's informed decision, however, the framers of the federal rules were aware of possible alternatives when they recommended the present rule to this Court; this Court promulgated the rule as recommended; and Congress can be deemed to have adopted it.

In upholding the validity of Rule 23(a), we reiterate that the government attorney in a criminal prosecution is not an ordinary party to a controversy, but a "servant of the law" with a "twofold aim * * * that guilt shall not escape or innocence suffer." It was in light of this concept of the role of prosecutor that Rule 23(a) was framed, and we are confident that it is in this light that it will continue to be invoked by government attorneys. Because of this confidence in the integrity of the federal prosecutor, Rule 23(a) does not require that the Government articulate its reasons for demanding a jury trial at the time it refuses to consent to a defendant's proffered waiver. Nor should we assume that federal prosecutors would demand a jury trial for an ignoble purpose. We need not determine in this case whether there might be some circumstances where a defendant's reasons for wanting to be tried by a judge alone are so compelling that the Government's insistence on trial by jury would result in the denial to a defendant of an impartial trial. Petitioner argues that there might arise situations where "passion, prejudice * * * public feeling" or some other factor may render impossible or unlikely an impartial trial by jury. However, since petitioner gave no reason for wanting to forgo jury trial other than to save time, this is not such a case, and petitioner does not claim that it is. * * *

## SECTION 2. JURY SELECTION

Although the procedures for selecting juries to serve in criminal cases are governed by statute in all jurisdictions, the operation of those procedures sometimes produces serious and difficult constitutional questions. In most states, lists of prospective jurors are prepared by random selection from those registered to vote. Certain other lists (e.g., city directories) are sometimes used in addition or instead, and in some jurisdictions "key men" (political and civic leaders) supply names of prospective jurors. Some of those initially selected are thereafter stricken from the list because they are deemed lacking in the intellectual or other qualifications for jury service. Others are excused on the assumption that they would find jury service especially burdensome. It is apparent that the manner in which these lists of prospective jurors are initially prepared and then reduced can have a significant effect upon the makeup of particular jury panels available for jury selection in particular cases. It is not surprising, therefore, that defendants sometimes challenge the above described procedures on constitutional grounds. The first two cases in this section, *Carter v. Jury Commission* and *Taylor v. Louisiana,* discuss two types of challenges: respectively, the objection that the selection constitutes a denial of defendant's Fourteenth Amendment right to equal protection; and the objection that the selection does not accord with the Sixth Amendment right to a jury drawn from a cross-section of the community.

A process called voir dire is used to select from the panel of prospective jurors those who will serve as jurors in a particular case. The prospective jurors are questioned by the attorneys or the judge in order to reveal facts relevant to the exercise of challenges for cause and peremptory challenges. Each side may challenge for cause any prospective juror for lack of impartiality, and in addition each side has a specified number of peremptory challenges, for which no reason ordinarily need be given. The last three cases in this section illustrate the kinds of problems of constitutional dimension which can arise from this voir dire process. *Turner v. Murray* concerns how far it is necessary to go to protect the defendant against biased jurors; *Lockhart v. McCree* involves, on the other hand, how much can be done to ensure against anti-prosecution bias without violating the defendant's rights; and *Batson v. Kentucky* teaches that even the prosecution's manner of using peremptory challenges can run afoul of the Constitution.

## CARTER v. JURY COMMISSION
396 U.S. 320, 90 S.Ct. 518, 24 L.Ed.2d 549 (1970).

JUSTICE STEWART delivered the opinion of the Court.

The appellants, Negro citizens of Greene County, Alabama, commenced this class action against officials charged with the administration of the State's jury-selection laws: the county jury commissioners and their clerk, the local circuit court judge, and the Governor of Alabama. The complaint alleged that the appellants were fully qualified to serve as jurors and desired to serve, but had never been summoned for jury service. It charged that the appellees had effected a discriminatory exclusion of Negroes from grand and petit juries in Greene County—the Governor in his selection of the county jury commission, and the commissioners and judge in their arbitrary exclusion of Negroes. The complaint sought (1) a declaration that qualified Negroes were systematically excluded from Greene County grand and petit juries, that the Alabama statutes governing jury selection were unconstitutional on their face and as applied, and that the jury commission was a deliberately segregated governmental agency; (2) a permanent injunction forbidding the systematic exclusion of Negroes from Greene County juries pursuant to the challenged statutes and requiring that all eligible Negroes be placed on the jury roll; and (3) an order vacating the appointments of the jury commissioners and compelling the Governor to select new members without racial discrimination.

Alabama's jury-selection procedure is governed by statute. The Governor appoints a three-member jury commission for each county. The commission employs a clerk, who is charged with the duty of obtaining the name of every citizen of the county over 21 and under 65 years of age, together with his occupation and places of residence and business. The clerk must "scan the registration lists, the lists returned to the tax assessor, any city directories, telephone directories and any and every other source of information from which he may obtain information ∗ ∗ ∗." He must also "visit every precinct at least once a year to enable the jury commission to properly perform the duties required of it ∗ ∗ ∗." Once the clerk submits his list of names, the commission is under a duty to prepare a jury roll and jury box containing the names of all qualified, nonexempt citizens in the county, who are "generally reputed to be honest and intelligent and are esteemed in the community for their integrity, good character and sound judgment ∗ ∗ ∗."

A three-judge District Court ∗ ∗ ∗ conducted an extensive evidentiary hearing on the appellants' complaint. The record fully supports the trial court's conclusion, set out in its detailed opinion, that the jury-selection process as it actually operated in Greene County at the outset of this litigation departed from the statutory mandate in several respects:

"The clerk does not obtain the names of all potentially eligible jurors as provided by § 18, in fact was not aware that the statute directed that this be done and knew of no way in which she could do it. The starting point each year is last year's roll. Everyone thereon is considered to be qualified and remains on the roll unless he dies or moves away (or, presumably, is convicted of a felony). New names are added to the old roll. Almost all of the work of the commission is devoted to securing names of persons suggested for consideration as new jurors. The clerk performs some duties directed toward securing such names. This is a part-time task, done without compensation, in spare time available from performance of her duties as clerk of the Circuit Court. She uses voter lists but not the tax assessor's lists. Telephone directories for some of the communities are referred to, city directories not at all since Greene County is largely rural.

"The clerk goes into each of the eleven beats or precincts annually, usually one time. Her trips out into the county for this purpose never consume a full day. At various places in the county she talks with persons she knows and secures suggested names. She is acquainted with a good many Negroes, but very few 'out in the county.' She does not know the reputation of most of the Negroes in the county. Because of her duties as clerk of the Circuit Court the names and reputations of Negroes most familiar to her are those who have been convicted of crime or have been 'in trouble.' She does not know any Negro ministers, does not seek names from any Negro or white churches or fraternal organizations. She obtains some names from the county's Negro deputy sheriff. ∗ ∗ ∗

"At the August, 1966 meeting one commissioner was new and submitted no names, white or Negro, and merely did clerical work at the meeting. Another had been ill and able to seek names little if at all. The third could remember one Negro name that he suggested. This commissioner brought the name, or names, he proposed on a trade bill he had received, and after so using it threw it away. All lists of suggested names were destroyed. As a result of that meeting the number of Negro names on the jury roll increased by 37. ∗ ∗ ∗ Approximately 32 of those names came from lists given the clerk or commissioners by others. The testimony is that at the one-day August meeting the entire voter list was scanned. It contained the names of around 2,000 Negroes.

"Thus in practice, through the August, 1966 meeting the system operated exactly in reverse from what the state statutes contemplate. It produced a small group of individually selected or recommended names for consideration. Those potentially qualified but whose names were never focused upon were given no consideration. Those who prepared the roll and administered the system were white and with limited means of contact with the Negro community. Though they recognized that the most pertinent information as to which Negoes do, and which do not, meet the statutory qualifications comes from Negroes there was no meaningful procedure by which Negro names were fed into the machinery for consideration or effectual means of communication by which the knowledge possessed by the Negro community was utilized. In practice most of the work of the commission has been devoted to the function of securing names to be considered. Once a name has come up for consideration it usually has been added to the rolls unless that person has been convicted of a felony. The function of applying the statutory criteria has been carried out only in part, or by accepting as conclusive the judgment of others, and for some criteria not at all."

The District Court's further findings demonstrated the impact of the selection process on the racial composition of Greene County juries. According to the 1960 census, Negroes composed three-fourths of the county's population. Yet from 1961 to 1963 the largest number of Negroes ever to appear on the jury list was about 7% of the total. The court noted that in 1964 a single-judge federal district court had entered a declaratory judgment setting forth the duties of the jury commissioners and their clerk under Alabama law, instructing them not to pursue a course of conduct operating to discriminate against Negroes, forbidding them to employ numerical or proportional limitations with respect to race, and directing an examination of the jury roll for compliance with the judgment. Thereafter, the situation had improved only marginally. In 1966 only 82 Negroes appeared among the 471 citizens listed on the jury roll; 50% of the white male population of the county found its way to the jury roll in that year, but only 4% of the Negro. In 1967, following a statutory amendment, the commission added women to the jury roll. Upon the expansion of the list, Negroes composed 388 of the 1,198 potential jurors—still only 32% of the total, even though the 1967 population of the county was estimated to be about 65% Negro.

The District Court found that "there is invalid exclusion of Negroes on a racially discriminatory basis." It enjoined the jury commissioners and their clerk from systematically excluding Negroes from the jury roll, and directed them "to take prompt action to compile a jury list * * * in accordance with the laws of Alabama and * * * constitutional principles"; to file a jury list so compiled within 60 days, showing the information required by Alabama law for each potential juror, together with his race and, if available, his age; and to submit a report setting forth the procedure by which the commission had compiled the list and applied the statutory qualifications and exclusions.

The court declined, however, * * * to enjoin the enforcement of the challenged Alabama statutory provisions[, so] the appellants took a direct appeal to this Court.

This is the first case to reach the Court in which an attack upon alleged racial discrimination in choosing juries has been made by plaintiffs seeking affirmative relief, rather than by defendants challenging judgments of criminal conviction on the ground of systematic exclusion of Negroes from the grand juries that indicted them, the trial juries that found them guilty, or both. The

District Court found no barrier to such a suit, and neither do we. Defendants in criminal proceedings do not have the only cognizable legal interest in nondiscriminatory jury selection. People excluded from juries because of their race are as much aggrieved as those indicted and tried by juries chosen under a system of racial exclusion. * * *

On the merits, the appellants argue that the District Court erred in refusing to invalidate the Alabama statute requiring the jury commissioners to select for jury service those persons who are "generally reputed to be honest and intelligent and * * * esteemed in the community for their integrity, good character and sound judgment * * *." The appellants say § 21 is unconstitutional on its face because, by leaving Alabama's jury officials at large in their selection of potential jurors, it provides them an opportunity to discriminate on the basis of race—an opportunity of which they have in fact taken advantage. * * *

While there is force in what the appellants say, we cannot agree that § 21 is irredeemably invalid on its face. It has long been accepted that the Constitution does not forbid the States to prescribe relevant qualifications for their jurors. The States remain free to confine the selection to citizens, to persons meeting specified qualifications of age and educational attainment, and to those possessing good intelligence, sound judgment, and fair character. "Our duty to protect the federal constitutional rights of all does not mean we must or should impose on states our conception of the proper source of jury lists, so long as the source reasonably reflects a cross-section of the population suitable in character and intelligence for that civic duty."

Statutory provisions such as those found in § 21 are not peculiar to Alabama, or to any particular region of the country. Nearly every State requires that its jurors be citizens of the United States, residents of the locality, of a specified minimum age, and able to understand English. Many of the States require that jurors be of "good character" or the like; some, that they be "intelligent" or "well informed."

* * * Despite the overwhelming proof the appellants have adduced in support of their claim that the jury clerk and commissioners have abused the discretion that Alabama law confers on them in the preparation of the jury roll, we cannot say that § 21 is necessarily and under all circumstances invalid. The provision is devoid of any mention of race. Its antecedents are of ancient vintage, and there is no suggestion that the law was originally adopted or subsequently carried forward for the purpose of fostering racial discrimination. The federal courts are not incompetent to fashion detailed and stringent injunctive relief that will remedy any discriminatory application of the statute at the hands of the officials empowered to administer it. In sum, we cannot conclude, even on so compelling a record as that before us, that the guarantees of the Constitution can be secured only by the total invalidation of the challenged provisions of § 21. * * *

## TAYLOR v. LOUISIANA

419 U.S. 522, 95 S.Ct. 692, 42 L.Ed.2d 690 (1975).

JUSTICE WHITE delivered the opinion of the Court.

When this case was tried, Art. VII, § 41, of the Louisiana Constitution, and Art. 402 of the Louisiana Code of Criminal Procedure provided that a woman should not be selected for jury service unless she had previously filed a written declaration of her desire to be subject to jury service. The constitutionality of these provisions is the issue in this case. * * *

The Louisiana jury selection system does not disqualify women from jury service, but in operation its conceded systematic impact is that only a very few women, grossly disproportionate to the number of eligible women in the community, are called for jury service.[a]  In this case, no women were on the venire from which the petit jury was drawn.  The issue we have, therefore, is whether a jury selection system which operates to exclude from jury service an identifiable class of citizens constituting 53% of eligible jurors in the community comports with the Sixth and Fourteenth Amendments.

The State first insists that Taylor, a male, has no standing to object to the exclusion of women from his jury.  But Taylor's claim is that he was constitutionally entitled to a jury drawn from a venire constituting a fair cross section of the community and that the jury that tried him was not such a jury by reason of the exclusion of women.  Taylor was not a member of the excluded class; but there is no rule that claims such as Taylor presents may be made only by those defendants who are members of the group excluded from jury service. * * * Taylor, in the case before us, was * * * entitled to tender and have adjudicated the claim that the exclusion of women from jury service deprived him of the kind of fact finder to which he was constitutionally entitled.

* * * Our inquiry is whether the presence of a fair cross section of the community on venires, panels or lists from which petit juries are drawn is essential to the fulfillment of the Sixth Amendment's guarantee of an impartial jury trial in criminal prosecutions. * * *

The unmistakable import of this Court's opinions, at least since 1941, and not repudiated by intervening decisions, is that the selection of a petit jury from a representative cross section of the community is an essential component of the Sixth Amendment right to a jury trial. * * *

We accept the fair cross section requirement as fundamental to the jury trial guaranteed by the Sixth Amendment and are convinced that the requirement has solid foundation.  The purpose of a jury is to guard against the exercise of arbitrary power—to make available the common-sense judgment of the community as a hedge against the overzealous or mistaken prosecutor and in preference to the professional or perhaps overconditioned or biased response of a judge.  This prophylactic vehicle is not provided if the jury pool is made up of only special segments of the populace or if large, distinctive groups are excluded from the pool.  Community participation in the administration of the criminal law, moreover, is not only consistent with our democratic heritage but is also critical to public confidence in the fairness of the criminal justice system.  Restricting jury service to only special groups or excluding identifiable segments playing major roles in the community cannot be squared with the constitutional concept of jury trial. * * *

We are also persuaded that the fair cross section requirement is violated by the systematic exclusion of women, who in the judicial district involved here amounted to 53% of the citizens eligible for jury service.  This conclusion necessarily entails the judgment that women are sufficiently numerous and distinct from men that if they are systematically eliminated from jury panels, the Sixth Amendment's fair cross section requirement cannot be satisfied.  This very matter was debated in *Ballard v. United States,* 329 U.S. 187 (1946).  Positing the fair cross-section rule—there said to be a statutory one—the Court concluded that the systematic exclusion of women was unacceptable.  The

---

a.  It was stipulated that no more than 10% of the persons on the jury wheel were women, that only 12 females were among the 1,800 persons drawn to fill petit jury venires, and that this discrepancy was the result of the operation of the challenged provisions.

dissenting view that an all-male panel drawn from various groups in the community would be as truly representative as if women were included, was firmly rejected:

> "The thought is that the factors which tend to influence the action of women are the same as those which influence the action of men—personality, background, economic status—and not sex. Yet it is not enough to say that women when sitting as jurors neither act nor tend to act as a class. Men likewise do not act as a class. But, if the shoe were on the other foot, who would claim that a jury was truly representative of the community if all men were intentionally and systematically excluded from the panel? The truth is that the two sexes are not fungible; a community made up exclusively of one is different from a community composed of both; the subtle interplay of influence one on the other is among the imponderables. To insulate the courtroom from either may not in a given case make an iota of difference. Yet a flavor, a distinct quality is lost if either sex is excluded. The exclusion of one may indeed make the jury less representative of the community than would be true if an economic or racial group were excluded."

In this respect, we agree with the Court in *Ballard:* If the fair cross-section rule is to govern the selection of juries, as we have concluded it must, women cannot be systematically excluded from jury panels from which petit juries are drawn. This conclusion is consistent with the current judgment of the country, now evidenced by legislative or constitutional provisions in every State and at the federal level qualifying women for jury service.

There remains the argument that women as a class serve a distinctive role in society and that jury service would so substantially interfere with that function that the State has ample justification for excluding women from service unless they volunteer, even though the result is that almost all jurors are men. It is true that *Hoyt v. Florida,* 368 U.S. 57 (1961), held that such a system did not deny due process of law or equal protection of the laws because there was a sufficiently rational basis for such an exemption. But *Hoyt* did not involve a defendant's Sixth Amendment right to a jury drawn from a fair cross section of the community and the prospect of depriving him of that right if women as a class are systematically excluded. The right to a proper jury cannot be overcome on merely rational grounds. There must be weightier reasons if a distinctive class representing 53% of the eligible jurors is for all practical purposes to be excluded from jury service. No such basis has been tendered here.

The States are free to grant exemptions from jury service to individuals in case of special hardship or incapacity and to those engaged in particular occupations the uninterrupted performance of which is critical to the community's welfare. It would not appear that such exemptions would pose substantial threats that the remaining pool of jurors would not be representative of the community. A system excluding all women, however, is a wholly different matter. It is untenable to suggest these days that it would be a special hardship for each and every woman to perform jury service or that society cannot spare *any* women from their present duties. This may be the case with many, and it may be burdensome to sort out those who should serve. But that task is performed in the case of men, and the administrative convenience in dealing with women as a class is insufficient justification for diluting the quality of community judgment represented by the jury in criminal trials. * * *

Our holding does not augur or authorize the fashioning of detailed jury selection codes by federal courts. The fair cross section principle must have much leeway in application. The States remain free to prescribe relevant qualifications for their jurors and to provide reasonable exemptions so long as it may be fairly said that the jury lists or panels are representative of the community. * * *

It should also be emphasized that in holding that petit juries must be drawn from a source fairly representative of the community we impose no requirement that petit juries actually chosen must mirror the community and reflect the various distinctive groups in the population. Defendants are not entitled to a jury of any particular composition; but the jury wheels, pools of names, panels or venires from which juries are drawn must not systematically exclude distinctive groups in the community and thereby fail to be reasonably representative thereof. * * *

Reversed and remanded.

CHIEF JUSTICE BURGER concurred in the result.

JUSTICE REHNQUIST, dissenting. * * *

I cannot conceive that today's decision is necessary to guard against oppressive or arbitrary law enforcement, or to prevent miscarriages of justice and to assure fair trials. Especially is this so when the criminal defendant involved makes no claims of prejudice or bias. The Court does accord some slight attention to justifying its ruling in terms of the basis on which the right to jury trial was read into the Fourteenth Amendment. It concludes that the jury is not effective, as a prophylaxis against arbitrary prosecutorial and judicial power, if the "jury pool is made up of only special segments of the populace or if large, distinctive groups are excluded from the pool." It fails, however, to provide any satisfactory explanation of the mechanism by which the Louisiana system undermines the prophylactic role of the jury, either in general or in this case. The best it can do is to posit "a flavor, a distinct quality," which allegedly is lost if either sex is excluded. However, this "flavor" is not of such importance that the Constitution is offended if any given petit jury is not so enriched. This smacks more of mysticism than of law. The Court does not even purport to practice its mysticism in a consistent fashion—presumably doctors, lawyers, and other groups, whose frequent exemption from jury service is endorsed by the majority, also offer qualities as distinct and important as those at issue here.

* * *

## TURNER v. MURRAY
476 U.S. 28, 106 S.Ct. 1683, 90 L.Ed.2d 27 (1986).

JUSTICE WHITE announced the judgment of the Court and delivered the opinion of the Court with respect to Parts I and III, and an opinion with respect to Parts II and IV, in which JUSTICE BLACKMUN, JUSTICE STEVENS, and JUSTICE O'CONNOR join.

[Petitioner, a black man, was indicted in Virginia on charges of capital murder for fatally shooting the white proprietor of a jewelry store in the course of a robbery. During *voir dire*, the state trial judge refused petitioner's request to question the prospective jurors on racial prejudice. The jury convicted petitioner, and, after a separate sentencing hearing, recommended that he be sentenced to death, a recommendation the trial judge accepted. The Virginia Supreme Court upheld the death sentence, rejecting petitioner's argument that the trial judge deprived him of a fair trial by refusing to question the prospective jurors on racial prejudice. Petitioner then sought habeas corpus relief in Federal District Court, which rejected the same argument and denied relief, and the Court of Appeals affirmed.]

## II

The Fourth Circuit's opinion correctly states the analytical framework for evaluating petitioner's argument: "The broad inquiry in each case must be whether under all of the circumstances presented there was a constitutionally significant likelihood that, absent questioning about racial prejudice, the jurors would not be indifferent as they stand unsworn." The Fourth Circuit was correct, too, in holding that under *Ristaino* the mere fact that petitioner is black and his victim white does not constitute a "special circumstance" of constitutional proportions.[a] What sets this case apart from *Ristaino,* however, is that in addition to petitioner's being accused of a crime against a white victim, the crime charged was a capital offense.

In a capital sentencing proceeding before a jury, the jury is called upon to make a "highly subjective, 'unique, individualized judgment regarding the punishment that a particular person deserves.'" The Virginia statute under which petitioner was sentenced is instructive of the kinds of judgments a capital sentencing jury must make. First, in order to consider the death penalty, a Virginia jury must find either that the defendant is likely to commit future violent crimes or that his crime was "outrageously or wantonly vile, horrible or inhuman in that it involved torture, depravity of mind or an aggravated battery to the victim." Second, the jury must consider any mitigating evidence offered by the defendant. Mitigating evidence may include, but is not limited to, facts tending to show that the defendant acted under the influence of extreme emotional or mental disturbance, or that at the time of the crime the defendant's capacity "to appreciate the criminality of his conduct or to conform his conduct to the requirements of law was significantly impaired." Finally, even if the jury has found an aggravating factor, and irrespective of whether mitigating evidence has been offered, the jury has discretion not to recommend the death sentence, in which case it may not be imposed.

Virginia's death-penalty statute gives the jury greater discretion than other systems which we have upheld against constitutional challenge. However, our cases establish that every capital sentencer must be free to weigh relevant mitigating evidence before deciding whether to impose the death penalty, and that in the end it is the jury that must make the difficult, individualized judgment as to whether the defendant deserves the sentence of death.

Because of the range of discretion entrusted to a jury in a capital sentencing hearing, there is a unique opportunity for racial prejudice to operate but remain

---

**a.** The reference is to *Ristaino v. Ross,* 424 U.S. 589 (1976), where the Court elaborated upon *Ham v. South Carolina,* 409 U.S. 524 (1973). As the Court explained in fn. 3 of the instant case:

"In *Ham,* a young black man known in his small South Carolina hometown as a civil rights activist was arrested and charged with possession of marihuana. We held that the trial judge committed reversible error in refusing to honor Ham's request to question prospective jurors on racial prejudice. In *Ristaino,* supra, we specified the factors which mandated an inquiry into racial prejudice in *Ham:*

"'Ham's defense was that he had been framed because of his civil rights activities. His prominence in the community as a civil rights activist, if not already known to veniremen, inevitably would have been revealed to the members of the jury in the course of his presentation of that defense. Racial issues therefore were inextricably bound up with the conduct of the trial. Further, Ham's reputation as a civil rights activist and the defense he interposed were likely to intensify any prejudice that individual members of the jury might harbor.'"

undetected. On the facts of this case, a juror who believes that blacks are violence-prone or morally inferior might well be influenced by that belief in deciding whether petitioner's crime involved the aggravating factors specified under Virginia law. Such a juror might also be less favorably inclined toward petitioner's evidence of mental disturbance as a mitigating circumstance. More subtle, less consciously held racial attitudes could also influence a juror's decision in this case. Fear of blacks, which could easily be stirred up by the violent facts of petitioner's crime, might incline a juror to favor the death penalty.[7]

The risk of racial prejudice infecting a capital sentencing proceeding is especially serious in light of the complete finality of the death sentence. "The Court, as well as the separate opinions of a majority of the individual Justices, has recognized that the qualitative difference of death from all other punishments requires a correspondingly greater degree of scrutiny of the capital sentencing determination." In the present case, we find the risk that racial prejudice may have infected petitioner's capital sentencing unacceptable in light of the ease with which that risk could have been minimized. By refusing to question prospective jurors on racial prejudice, the trial judge failed to adequately protect petitioner's constitutional right to an impartial jury.

### III

We hold that a capital defendant accused of an interracial crime is entitled to have prospective jurors informed of the race of the victim and questioned on the issue of racial bias. The rule we propose is minimally intrusive; as in other cases involving "special circumstances," the trial judge retains discretion as to the form and number of questions on the subject, including the decision whether to question the venire individually or collectively. Also, a defendant cannot complain of a judge's failure to question the venire on racial prejudice unless the defendant has specifically requested such an inquiry.

### IV

The inadequacy of *voir dire* in this case requires that petitioner's death sentence be vacated. It is not necessary, however, that he be retried on the issue of guilt. Our judgment in this case is that there was an unacceptable risk of racial prejudice infecting the *capital sentencing proceeding*. This judgment is based on a conjunction of three factors: the fact that the crime charged involved interracial violence, the broad discretion given the jury at the death-penalty hearing, and the special seriousness of the risk of improper sentencing in a capital case." At the guilt phase of petitioner's trial, the jury had no greater discretion than it would have had if the crime charged had been noncapital murder. Thus, with respect to the guilt phase of petitioner's trial, we find this case to be indistinguishable from *Ristaino,* to which we continue to adhere.

THE CHIEF JUSTICE concurs in the judgment.

JUSTICE BRENNAN, concurring in part and dissenting in part.    *    *    *

To sentence an individual to death on the basis of a proceeding tainted by racial bias would violate the most basic values of our criminal justice system.

---

**7.** In referring to the facts of petitioner's crime, we do not retreat from our holding in *Ristaino.* The fact of interracial violence alone is not a "special circumstance" entitling the defendant to have prospective jurors questioned about racial prejudice. It should be clear, though, that our holding in *Ristaino* was not based on a blind belief that the facts presented in that case could not evoke racial prejudice.    *    *    *    *Ristaino*    *    *    * simply leaves it to the trial judge's discretion to decide what measures to take in screening out racial prejudice, absent a showing of "significant likelihood that racial prejudice might infect [the] trial."

This the Court understands. But what it seems not to comprehend is that to permit an individual to be *convicted* by a prejudiced jury violates those same values in precisely the same way. The incongruity of the Court's split judgment is made apparent after it is appreciated that the opportunity for bias to poison decisionmaking operates at a guilt trial in the same way as it does at a sentencing hearing and after one returns to the context of the case before us. Implicit in the Court's judgment is the acknowledgment that there was a likelihood that the jury that pronounced the death sentence acted, in part, on the basis of racial prejudice. But the exact same jury convicted Turner. Does the Court really mean to suggest that the constitutional entitlement to an impartial jury attaches only at the sentencing phase? Does the Court really believe that racial biases are turned on and off in the course of one criminal prosecution? * * *

JUSTICE MARSHALL, with whom JUSTICE BRENNAN joins, concurring in the judgment in part and dissenting in part.

* * * I believe that a criminal defendant is entitled to inquire on *voir dire* about the potential racial bias of jurors whenever the case involves a violent interracial crime. As the Court concedes, "it is plain that there is some risk of racial prejudice influencing a jury whenever there is a crime involving interracial violence." To my mind that risk plainly outweighs the slight cost of allowing the defendant to choose whether to make an inquiry concerning such possible prejudice. This Court did not identify in *Ristaino v. Ross,* nor does it identify today, any additional burdens that would accompany such a rule. I therefore cannot agree with the Court's continuing rejection of the simple prophylactic rule proposed in *Ristaino.* * * *

JUSTICE POWELL, with whom JUSTICE REHNQUIST joins, dissenting.

* * * In *Ristaino,* the Court expressly declined to adopt a *per se* rule requiring *voir dire* inquiry into racial bias in every trial for an interracial crime. Neither the Constitution nor sound policy considerations supported such a *per se* approach. But today the Court decides that the Constitution does require a *per se* rule in capital cases because the capital jury exercises discretion at the sentencing phase. The Court's reasoning ignores the many procedural and substantive safeguards, similar to those governing the jury's decision on guilt or innocence, that circumscribe the capital jury's sentencing decision.

Under Virginia law, murder is a capital offense only if it is "willful, deliberate and premeditated" and is committed while the perpetrator is engaged in another crime or under specified aggravating circumstances. As in any criminal prosecution, of course, the State carries the burden of proving all elements of the capital offense beyond a reasonable doubt. Following a sentencing hearing, the death sentence may not be imposed unless the State proves beyond a reasonable doubt statutorily defined aggravating factors. Virginia law recognizes only two aggravating factors: whether, based on the defendant's criminal record, there is a probability that he would commit future crimes of violence, and whether the defendant's crime was "outrageously or wantonly vile, horrible or inhuman, in that it involved torture, depravity of mind or aggravated battery to the victim." The jury also is required to consider any relevant mitigating evidence offered by the defendant.

The existence of these significant limitations on the jury's exercise of sentencing discretion illustrates why the Court's *per se* rule is wholly unfounded. Just as the trial judge's charge at the guilt phase instructs the jurors that they may consider only the evidence in the case and that they must determine if the prosecution has established each element of the crime beyond a reasonable doubt, the charge at the penalty phase directs the jurors to focus solely on considerations relevant to determination of appropriate punishment and to decide if the prosecution has established beyond a reasonable doubt factors warranting imposition of death. Accordingly, just as there is no reason to presume racial bias on the part of jurors who determine the guilt of a defendant who has committed a violent crime against a person of another race, there is no reason to constitutionalize such a presumption with respect to the jurors who sit to recommend the penalty in a capital case. * * *

## LOCKHART v. McCREE

476 U.S. 162, 106 S.Ct. 1758, 90 L.Ed.2d 137 (1986).

JUSTICE REHNQUIST delivered the opinion of the Court.

In this case we address the question left open by our decision nearly 18 years ago in *Witherspoon v. Illinois,* 391 U.S. 510 (1968)[a]: Does the Constitution prohibit the removal for cause, prior to the guilt phase of a bifurcated capital trial, of prospective jurors whose opposition to the death penalty is so strong that it would prevent or substantially impair the performance of their duties as jurors at the sentencing phase of the trial? * * *

McCree was charged with capital felony murder. In accordance with Arkansas law, the trial judge at *voir dire* removed for cause, over McCree's objections, those prospective jurors who stated that they could not under any circumstances vote for the imposition of the death penalty. Eight prospective jurors were excluded for this reason. The jury convicted McCree of capital felony murder, but rejected the State's request for the death penalty, instead setting McCree's punishment at life imprisonment without parole. McCree's conviction was affirmed on direct appeal, and his petition for state post-conviction relief was denied.

McCree then filed a federal habeas corpus petition raising *inter alia* the claim that "death qualification," or the removal for cause of the so-called

---

**a.** In *Witherspoon* the Court held "that a sentence of death cannot be carried out if the jury that imposed or recommended it was chosen by excluding veniremen for cause simply because they voiced general objections to the death penalty or expressed conscientious or religious scruples against its infliction."

In *Gray v. Mississippi,* 481 U.S. 648 (1987), the Court declined to abandon the ruling in *Davis v. Georgia,* 429 U.S. 122 (1976), that even a single misapplication of *Witherspoon* invalidates a death sentence. One way of looking at the trial judge's granting of an invalid *Witherspoon* motion in the instant case was that it was intended to remedy an earlier erroneous denial of a *Witherspoon* motion regarding another prospective juror. As to this, the Court declined to "condone the 'correction' of one error by the commitment of another," especially where, as here, the first error was a violation of the prosecutor's statutory right and the second a violation of defendant's constitutional right. The Court next rejected the state court's reasoning "that a *Witherspoon* violation constitutes harmless error when the prosecutor has an unexercised peremptory challenge that he states he would have used to excuse the juror," stating:

"The practical result of adoption of this unexercised peremptory argument would be to insulate jury-selection error from meaningful appellate review. By simply stating during *voir dire* that the State is prepared to exercise a peremptory challenge if the court denies its motion for cause, a prosecutor would ensure that a reviewing court would consider any erroneous exclusion harmless. A prosecutor, as a routine matter, would likely append a statement to this effect to his motion for cause."

Finally, as to the state's argument that a single *Witherspoon* error should be deemed harmless because it did not have any prejudicial effect, the Court found it "equally unavailing." Because courts do not generally review a prosecutor's exercise of peremptory challenges, which are often used (and in this case were used) to remove prospective jurors who express hesitation against the death penalty, "a court cannot say with confidence that an erroneous exclusion for cause of a scrupled, yet eligible, venire member is an isolated incident in that particular case."

"*Witherspoon*-excludable" prospective jurors,[1] violated his right under the Sixth and Fourteenth Amendments to have his guilt or innocence determined by an impartial jury selected from a representative cross-section of the community. * * *

The District Court held a hearing on the "death qualification" issue in July 1981, receiving in evidence numerous social science studies concerning the attitudes and beliefs of "*Witherspoon*-excludables," along with the potential effects of excluding them from the jury prior to the guilt phase of a bifurcated capital trial. In August 1983, the court concluded, based on the social science evidence, that "death qualification" produced juries that "were more prone to convict" capital defendants than "non-death-qualified" juries. The court ruled that "death qualification" thus violated both the fair cross-section and impartiality requirements of the Sixth and Fourteenth Amendments, and granted McCree habeas relief.

The Eighth Circuit found "substantial evidentiary support" for the District Court's conclusion that the removal for cause of "*Witherspoon*-excludables" resulted in "conviction-prone" juries, and affirmed the grant of habeas relief on the ground that such removal for cause violated McCree's constitutional right to a jury selected from a fair cross-section of the community. * * *

Before turning to the legal issues in the case, we are constrained to point out what we believe to be several serious flaws in the evidence upon which the courts below reached the conclusion that "death qualification" produces "conviction-prone" juries. * * *

Of the six studies introduced by McCree that at least purported to deal with the central issue in this case, namely, the potential effects on the determination of guilt or innocence of excluding "*Witherspoon*-excludables" from the jury, three were also before this Court when it decided *Witherspoon*. * * * It goes almost without saying that if these studies were "too tentative and fragmentary" to make out a claim of constitutional error in 1968, the same studies, unchanged but for having aged some eighteen years, are still insufficient to make out such a claim in this case.

Nor do the three post-*Witherspoon* studies introduced by McCree on the "death qualification" issue provide substantial support for the "*per se* constitutional rule" McCree asks this Court to adopt. All three of the "new" studies based on the responses of individuals randomly selected from some segment population, but who were not actual jurors sworn under oath to apply the the facts of an actual case involving the fate of an actual capital nt. We have serious doubts about the value of these studies in predicting behavior of actual jurors. * * *

ing identified some of the more serious problems with McCree's studies, we will assume for purposes of this opinion that the studies are both logically valid and adequate to establish that "death qualification" in uces juries somewhat more "conviction-prone" than "non-death-qualies. We hold, nonetheless, that the Constitution does not prohibit the m "death qualifying" juries in capital cases.

| | |
|---|---|
| proper constitutional standard is her a prospective juror's views ent or substantially impair the of his duties as a juror in accoris instructions and his oath.'" m "*Witherspoon*-excludable" is | something of a misnomer. Nevertheless, because the parties and the courts below have used the term "*Witherspoon*-excludables" to identify the group of prospective jurors at issue in this case, we will use the same term in this opinion. |

The Eighth Circuit ruled that "death qualification" violated McCree's right under the Sixth Amendment, as applied to the States via incorporation through the Fourteenth Amendment, to a jury selected from a representative cross-section of the community. But we do not believe that the fair cross-section requirement can, or should, be applied as broadly as that court attempted to apply it. We have never invoked the fair cross-section principle to invalidate the use of either for-cause or peremptory challenges to prospective jurors, or to require petit juries, as opposed to jury panels or venires, to reflect the composition of the community at large. * * * The limited scope of the fair cross-section requirement is a direct and inevitable consequence of the practical impossibility of providing each criminal defendant with a truly "representative" petit jury. * * * We remain convinced that an extension of the fair cross-section requirement to petit juries would be unworkable and unsound, and we decline McCree's invitation to adopt such an extension.

But even if we were willing to extend the fair cross-section requirement to petit juries, we would still reject the Eighth Circuit's conclusion that "death qualification" violates that requirement. The essence of a "fair cross-section" claim is the systematic exclusion of "a 'distinctive' group in the community." In our view, groups defined solely in terms of shared attitudes that would prevent or substantially impair members of the group from performing one of their duties as jurors, such as the "*Witherspoon*-excludables" at issue here, are not "distinctive groups" for fair cross-section purposes.

We have never attempted to precisely define the term "distinctive group," and we do not undertake to do so today. But we think it obvious that the concept of "distinctiveness" must be linked to the purposes of the fair cross-section requirement. In *Taylor,* we identified those purposes as (1) "guard[ing] against the exercise of arbitrary power" and ensuring that the "commonsense judgment of the community" will act as "a hedge against the overzealous or mistaken prosecutor," (2) preserving "public confidence in the fairness of the criminal justice system," and (3) implementing our belief that "sharing in the administration of justice is a phase of civic responsibility."

Our prior jury-representativeness cases, whether based on the fair cross-section component of the Sixth Amendment or the Equal Protection Clause of the Fourteenth Amendment, have involved such groups as blacks, women, and Mexican-Americans. The wholesale exclusion of these large groups from jury service clearly contravened all three of the aforementioned purposes of the fair cross-section requirement. Because these groups were excluded for reasons completely unrelated to the ability of members of the group to serve as jurors in a particular case, the exclusion raised at least the possibility that the composition of juries would be arbitrarily skewed in such a way as to deny criminal defendants the benefit of the common-sense judgment of the community. In addition, the exclusion from jury service of large groups of individuals not on the basis of their inability to serve as jurors, but on the basis of some immutable characteristic such as race, gender, or ethnic background, undeniably gave rise to an "appearance of unfairness." Finally, such exclusion improperly deprived members of these often historically disadvantaged groups of their right as citizens to serve on juries in criminal cases.

The group of "*Witherspoon*-excludables" involved in the case at bar differs significantly from the groups we have previously recognized as "distinctive." "Death qualification," unlike the wholesale exclusion of blacks, women, or Mexican–Americans from jury service, is carefully designed to serve the State' concededly legitimate interest in obtaining a single jury that can properly an impartially apply the law to the facts of the case at both the guilt and sentencing phases of a capital trial. There is very little danger, therefore, and McCree does not even argue, that "death qualification" was instituted as a means for the State to arbitrarily skew the composition of capital-case juries.

Furthermore, unlike blacks, women, and Mexican–Americans, "*Witherspoon*-excludables" are singled out for exclusion in capital cases on the basis of an attribute that is within the individual's control. It is important to remember that not all who oppose the death penalty are subject to removal for cause in capital cases; those who firmly believe that the death penalty is unjust may nevertheless serve as jurors in capital cases so long as they state clearly that they are willing to temporarily set aside their own beliefs in deference to the rule of law. Because the group of "*Witherspoon*-excludables" includes only those who cannot and will not conscientiously obey the law with respect to one of the issues in a capital case, "death qualification" hardly can be said to create an "appearance of unfairness."

Finally, the removal for cause of "*Witherspoon*-excludables" in capital cases does not prevent them from serving as jurors in other criminal cases, and thus leads to no substantial deprivation of their basic rights of citizenship. They are treated no differently than any juror who expresses the view that he would be unable to follow the law in a particular case. * * *

McCree argues that, even if we reject the Eighth Circuit's fair cross-section holding, we should affirm the judgment below on the alternative ground, adopted by the District Court, that "death qualification" violated his constitutional right to an impartial jury. * * * McCree argues that his jury lacked impartiality because the absence of "*Witherspoon* -excludables" "slanted" the jury in favor of conviction.

We do not agree. McCree's "impartiality" argument apparently is based on the theory that, because all individual jurors are to some extent predisposed towards one result or another, a constitutionally impartial *jury* can be constructed only by "balancing" the various predispositions of the individual *jurors*. Thus, according to McCree, when the State "tips the scales" by excluding prospective jurors with a particular viewpoint, an impermissibly partial jury results. We have consistently rejected this view of jury impartiality, including as recently as last Term when we squarely held that an impartial *jury* consists of nothing more than "*jurors* who will conscientiously apply the law and find the facts."

McCree argues, however, that this Court's decisions in *Witherspoon, supra,* and *Adams v. Texas,* 448 U.S. 38 (1980), [applying *Witherspoon,*] stand for the proposition that a State violates the Constitution whenever it "slants" the jury by excluding a group of individuals more likely than the population at large to favor the criminal defendant. We think McCree overlooks two fundamental differences between *Witherspoon* and *Adams* and the instant case, and therefore misconceives the import and scope of those two decisions.

First, the Court in *Witherspoon* viewed the Illinois system as having been deliberately slanted for the purpose of making the imposition of the death penalty more likely. * * *

Here, on the other hand, the removal for cause of "*Witherspoon*-excludables" serves the State's entirely proper interest in obtaining a single jury that could impartially decide all of the issues in McCree's case. Arkansas by legislative enactment and judicial decision provides for the use of a unitary jury in capital cases. * * *

The Arkansas Supreme Court recently explained the State's legislative choice to require unitary juries in capital cases:

"It has always been the law in Arkansas, except when the punishment is mandatory, that the same jurors who have the responsibility for determining guilt or innocence must also shoulder the burden of fixing the punishment. That is as it should be, for the two questions are necessarily interwoven."

Another interest identified by the State in support of its system of unitary juries is the possibility that, in at least some capital cases, the defendant might benefit at the sentencing phase of the trial from the jury's "residual doubts" about the evidence presented at the guilt phase. * * * Finally, it seems obvious to us that in most, if not all, capital cases much of the evidence adduced at the guilt phase of the trial will also have a bearing on the penalty phase; if two different juries were to be required, such testimony would have to be presented twice, once to each jury. * * *

Second, and more importantly, both *Witherspoon* and *Adams* dealt with the special context of capital sentencing, where the range of jury discretion necessarily gave rise to far greater concern over the possible effects of an "imbalanced" jury. * * *

In the case at bar, by contrast, we deal not with capital sentencing, but with the jury's more traditional role of finding the facts and determining the guilt or innocence of a criminal defendant, where jury discretion is more channeled. We reject McCree's suggestion that *Witherspoon* and *Adams* have broad applicability outside the special context of capital sentencing, and conclude that those two decisions do not support the result reached by the Eighth Circuit here. * * *

JUSTICE BLACKMUN concurs in the result.

JUSTICE MARSHALL, with whom JUSTICE BRENNAN and JUSTICE STEVENS join, dissenting.

* * * The data strongly suggest that death qualification excludes a significantly large subset—at least 11% to 17%—of potential jurors who could be impartial during the guilt phase of trial. Among the members of this excludable class are a disproportionate number of blacks and women.

The perspectives on the criminal justice system of jurors who survive death qualification are systematically different from those of the excluded jurors. Death-qualified jurors are, for example, more likely to believe that a defendant's failure to testify is indicative of his guilt, more hostile to the insanity defense, more mistrustful of defense attorneys, and less concerned about the danger of erroneous convictions. This pro-prosecution bias is reflected in the greater readiness of death-qualified jurors to convict or to convict on more serious charges. And, finally, the very process of death qualification—which focuses attention on the death penalty before the trial has even begun—has been found to predispose the jurors that survive it to believe that the defendant is guilty.

The evidence thus confirms, and is itself corroborated by, the more intuitive judgments of scholars and of so many of the participants in capital trials—judges, defense attorneys, and prosecutors. * * *

Faced with the near unanimity of authority supporting respondent's claim that death qualification gives the prosecution a particular advantage in the guilt phase of capital trials, the majority here makes but a weak effort to contest that proposition. Instead, it merely assumes for the purposes of this opinion "that 'death-qualification' in fact produces juries somewhat more 'conviction-prone' than 'non-death-qualified' juries," and then holds that this result does not offend the Constitution. This disregard for the clear import of the evidence tragically misconstrues the settled constitutional principles that guarantee a defendant the right to a fair trial and an impartial jury whose composition is not biased toward the prosecution. * * *

As the *Witherspoon* Court recognized, "the State's interest in submitting the penalty issue to a jury capable of imposing capital punishment" may be accommodated without infringing a capital defendant's interest in a fair determination of his guilt if the State uses "one jury to decide guilt and another to fix punishment." Any exclusion of death-penalty opponents, the Court reasoned, could await the penalty phase of a trial. The question here is thus whether the State has *other* interests that require the use of a single jury and demand the subordination of a capital defendant's Sixth and Fourteenth Amendment rights.

The only two reasons that the Court invokes to justify the State's use of a single jury are efficient trial management and concern that a defendant at his sentencing proceedings may be able to profit from "residual doubts" troubling jurors who have sat through the guilt phase of his trial. The first of these purported justifications is merely unconvincing. The second is offensive. * * *

In a system using separate juries for guilt and penalty phases, time and resources would be saved every time a capital case did not require a penalty phase. The *voir dire* needed to identify nullifiers before the guilt phase is less extensive than the questioning that under the current scheme conducted before *every* capital trial. The State could, of course, choose to empanel a death-qualified jury at the start of every trial, to be used only if a penalty stage is required. However, if it opted for the cheaper alternative of empanelling a death-qualified jury only in the event that a defendant were convicted of capital charges, the State frequently would be able to avoid retrying the entire guilt phase for the benefit of the penalty jury. Stipulated summaries of prior evidence might, for example, save considerable time. Thus, it cannot fairly be said that the costs of accommodating a defendant's constitutional rights under these circumstances are prohibitive, or even significant.

Even less convincing is the Court's concern that a defendant be able to appeal at sentencing to the "residual doubts" of the jurors who found him guilty. Any suggestion that the current system of death qualification "may be in the defendant's best interests, seems specious unless the state is willing to grant the defendant the option to waive this paternalistic protection in exchange for better odds against conviction." Furthermore, this case will stand as one of the few times in which any legitimacy has been given to the power of a convicted capital defendant facing the possibility of a death sentence to argue as a mitigating factor the chance that he might be innocent. Where a defendant's sentence but not his conviction has been set aside on appeal, States have routinely empanelled juries whose only duty is to assess punishment, thereby depriving defendants of the chance to profit from the "residual doubts" that jurors who had already sat through a guilt phase might bring to the sentencing proceeding. * * *

But most importantly, it ill-behooves the majority to allude to a defendant's power to appeal to "residual doubts" at his sentencing when this Court has consistently refused to grant certiorari in state cases holding that these doubts cannot properly be considered during capital sentencing proceedings. * * *

## BATSON v. KENTUCKY

476 U.S. 79, 106 S.Ct. 1712, 90 L.Ed.2d 69 (1986).

JUSTICE POWELL delivered the opinion of the Court.

This case requires us to reexamine that portion of *Swain v. Alabama*, 380 U.S. 202 (1965), concerning the evidentiary burden placed on a criminal defendant who claims that he has been denied equal protection through the State's use of peremptory challenges to exclude members of his race from the petit jury.[1]

Petitioner, a black man, was indicted in Kentucky on charges of second-degree burglary and receipt of stolen goods. On the first day of trial in Jefferson Circuit Court, the judge conducted *voir dire* examination of the venire, excused certain jurors for cause, and permitted the parties to exercise peremptory challenges. The prosecutor used his peremptory challenges to strike all four black persons on the venire, and a jury composed only of white persons was selected. Defense counsel moved to discharge the jury before it was sworn on the ground that the prosecutor's removal of the black veniremen violated petitioner's rights under the Sixth and Fourteenth Amendments to a jury drawn from a cross-section of the community, and under the Fourteenth Amendment to equal protection of the laws. Counsel requested a hearing on his motion. Without expressly ruling on the request for a hearing, the trial judge observed that the parties were entitled to use their peremptory challenges to "strike anybody they want to." The judge then denied petitioner's motion, reasoning that the cross-section requirement applies only to selection of the venire and not to selection of the petit jury itself.

The jury convicted petitioner on both counts. On appeal to the Supreme Court of Kentucky, petitioner pressed, among other claims, the argument concerning the prosecutor's use of peremptory challenges. Conceding that *Swain v. Alabama* apparently foreclosed an equal protection claim based solely on the prosecutor's conduct in this case, petitioner urged the court to follow decisions of other states, and to hold that such conduct violated his rights under the Sixth Amendment and Section 11 of the Kentucky Constitution to a jury drawn from a cross-section of the community. Petitioner also contended that the facts showed that the prosecutor had engaged in a "pattern" of discriminatory challenges in this case and established an equal protection violation under *Swain*.

The Supreme Court of Kentucky affirmed. * * * We granted certiorari, and now reverse.

In *Swain v. Alabama,* this Court recognized that a "State's purposeful or deliberate denial to Negroes on account of race of participation as jurors in the administration of justice violates the Equal Protection Clause." This principle has been "consistently and repeatedly" reaffirmed, in numerous decisions of this Court both preceding and following *Swain*. We reaffirm the principle today.[4]

* * *

1. Following the lead of a number of state courts construing their state's constitution, two federal Courts of Appeals recently have accepted the view that peremptory challenges used to strike black jurors in a particular case may violate the Sixth Amendment. Other Courts of Appeals have rejected that position * * *.

4. In this Court, petitioner has argued that the prosecutor's conduct violated his rights under the Sixth and Fourteenth Amendments

to an impartial jury and to a jury drawn from a cross-section of the community. Petitioner has framed his argument in these terms in an apparent effort to avoid inviting the Court directly to reconsider one of its own precedents. On the other hand, the State has insisted that petitioner is claiming a denial of equal protection and that we must reconsider *Swain* to find a constitutional violation on this record. We agree with the State that resolution of petitioner's claim properly turns on

Accordingly, the component of the jury selection process at issue here, the State's privilege to strike individual jurors through peremptory challenges, is subject to the commands of the Equal Protection Clause.[12] Although a prosecutor ordinarily is entitled to exercise permitted peremptory challenges "for any reason at all, as long as that reason is related to his view concerning the outcome" of the case to be tried, the Equal Protection Clause forbids the prosecutor to challenge potential jurors solely on account of their race or on the assumption that black jurors as a group will be unable impartially to consider the State's case against a black defendant. ∗ ∗ ∗

*Swain* required the Court to decide, among other issues, whether a black defendant was denied equal protection by the State's exercise of peremptory challenges to exclude members of his race from the petit jury. The record in *Swain* showed that the prosecutor had used the State's peremptory challenges to strike the six black persons included on the petit jury venire. While rejecting the defendant's claim for failure to prove purposeful discrimination, the Court nonetheless indicated that the Equal Protection Clause placed some limits on the State's exercise of peremptory challenges.

The Court sought to accommodate the prosecutor's historical privilege of peremptory challenge free of judicial control, and the constitutional prohibition on exclusion of persons from jury service on account of race. While the Constitution does not confer a right to peremptory challenges, those challenges traditionally have been viewed as one means of assuring the selection of a qualified and unbiased jury.[15] To preserve the peremptory nature of the prosecutor's challenge, the Court in *Swain* declined to scrutinize his actions in a particular case by relying on a presumption that he properly exercised the State's challenges.

The Court went on to observe, however, that a state may not exercise its challenges in contravention of the Equal Protection Clause. It was impermissible for a prosecutor to use his challenges to exclude blacks from the jury "for reasons wholly unrelated to the outcome of the particular case on trial" or to deny to blacks "the same right and opportunity to participate in the administration of justice enjoyed by the white population." Accordingly, a black defendant could make out a prima facie case of purposeful discrimination on proof that the peremptory challenge system was "being perverted" in that manner. For example, an inference of purposeful discrimination would be raised on evidence that a prosecutor, "in case after case, whatever the circumstances, whatever the crime and whoever the defendant or the victim may be, is responsible for the removal of Negroes who have been selected as qualified jurors by the jury commissioners and who have survived challenges for cause, with the result that no Negroes ever serve on petit juries." Evidence offered by the defendant in *Swain* did not meet that standard. While the defendant showed that prosecu-

---

application of equal protection principles and express no view on the merits of any of petitioner's Sixth Amendment arguments.

[**Editors' note:** Later in *Holland v. Illinois*, ___ U.S. ___ (1990), the Court rejected, 5–4, "the thesis that a prosecutor's use of peremptory challenges to eliminate a distinctive group in the community deprives the defendant of a Sixth Amendment right to the 'fair possibility' of a representative jury. While statements in our prior cases have alluded to such a 'fair possibility' requirement, satisfying it has not been held to require anything be-

yond the inclusion of all cognizable groups in the venire, and the use of a jury numbering at least six persons."]

**12.** We express no views on whether the Constitution imposes any limit on the exercise of peremptory challenges by defense counsel. ∗ ∗ ∗

**15.** In *Swain*, the Court reviewed the "very old credentials" of the peremptory challenge system and noted the "long and widely held belief that peremptory challenge is a necessary part of trial by jury."

tors in the jurisdiction had exercised their strikes to exclude blacks from the jury, he offered no proof of the circumstances under which prosecutors were responsible for striking black jurors beyond the facts of his own case.

A number of lower courts following the teaching of *Swain* reasoned that proof of repeated striking of blacks over a number of cases was necessary to establish a violation of the Equal Protection Clause. Since this interpretation of *Swain* has placed on defendants a crippling burden of proof,[17] prosecutors' peremptory challenges are now largely immune from constitutional scrutiny. For reasons that follow, we reject this evidentiary formulation as inconsistent with standards that have been developed since *Swain* for assessing a prima facie case under the Equal Protection Clause.

[S]ince the decision in *Swain*, this Court has recognized that a defendant may make a prima facie showing of purposeful racial discrimination in selection of the venire by relying solely on the facts concerning its selection *in his case*. These decisions are in accordance with the proposition that "a consistent pattern of official racial discrimination" is not "a necessary predicate to a violation of the Equal Protection Clause. A single invidiously discriminatory governmental act" is not "immunized by the absence of such discrimination in the making of other comparable decisions." For evidentiary requirements to dictate that "several must suffer discrimination" before one could object, would be inconsistent with the promise of equal protection to all.

The standards for assessing a prima facie case in the context of discriminatory selection of the venire have been fully articulated since *Swain*. These principles support our conclusion that a defendant may establish a prima facie case of purposeful discrimination in selection of the petit jury solely on evidence concerning the prosecutor's exercise of peremptory challenges at the defendant's trial. To establish such a case, the defendant first must show that he is a member of a cognizable racial group, and that the prosecutor has exercised peremptory challenges to remove from the venire members of the defendant's race.[a] Second, the defendant is entitled to rely on the fact, as to which there can

---

**17.** The lower courts have noted the practical difficulties of proving that the State systematically has exercised peremptory challenges to exclude blacks from the jury on account of race. [T]he defendant would have to investigate, over a number of cases, the race of persons tried in the particular jurisdiction, the racial composition of the venire and petit jury, and the manner in which both parties exercised their peremptory challenges. * * * In jurisdictions where court records do not reflect the jurors' race and where *voir dire* proceedings are not transcribed, the burden would be insurmountable.

**a.** But in *Holland v. Illinois*, supra note 4, not itself a *Batson* equal protection case, five members of the Court (the four dissenters and Kennedy, J., concurring) expressed the view that a defendant's race is irrelevant to his standing to raise a *Batson* equal protection claim. Justice Kennedy explained:

"Many of the concerns expressed in *Batson*, a case where a black defendant objected to the exclusion of black jurors, support as well an equal protection claim by a defendant whose race or ethnicity is different from the dismissed juror's. To bar the claim whenever

the defendant's race is not the same as the juror's would be to concede that racial exclusion of citizens from the duty, and honor, of jury service will be tolerated, or even condoned. We cannot permit even the inference that this principle will be accepted, for it is inconsistent with the equal participation in civic life that the Fourteenth Amendment guarantees. I see no obvious reason to conclude that a defendant's race should deprive him of standing in his own trial to vindicate his own jurors' right to sit. * * * *Batson* is based in large part on the right to be tried by a jury whose members are selected by nondiscriminatory criteria and on the need to preserve public confidence in the jury system. These are not values shared only by those of a particular color; they are important to all criminal defendants."

The reference to defendant's race in *Batson*, Kennedy added, was "procedural" in nature, indicating there are "grounds for suspicion where the prosecutor uses his strikes to exclude jurors whose only connection with the defendant is the irrelevant factor of race. * * * Where this obvious ground for suspibe no dispute, that peremptory challenges constitute a jury selection practice that permits "those to discriminate who are of a mind to discriminate." Finally, the defendant must show that these facts and any other relevant circumstances raise an inference that the prosecutor used that practice to exclude the veniremen from the petit jury on account of their race. This combination of factors in the empanelling of the petit jury, as in the selection of the venire, raises the necessary inference of purposeful discrimination.

In deciding whether the defendant has made the requisite showing, the trial court should consider all relevant circumstances. For example, a "pattern" of strikes against black jurors included in the particular venire might give rise to an inference of discrimination. Similarly, the prosecutor's questions and statements during *voir dire* examination and in exercising his challenges may support or refute an inference of discriminatory purpose. These examples are merely illustrative. We have confidence that trial judges, experienced in supervising *voir dire,* will be able to decide if the circumstances concerning the prosecutor's use of peremptory challenges creates a prima facie case of discrimination against black jurors.

Once the defendant makes a prima facie showing, the burden shifts to the State to come forward with a neutral explanation for challenging black jurors. Though this requirement imposes a limitation in some cases on the full peremptory character of the historic challenge, we emphasize that the prosecutor's explanation need not rise to the level justifying exercise of a challenge for cause. But the prosecutor may not rebut the defendant's prima facie case of discrimination by stating merely that he challenged jurors of the defendant's race on the assumption—or his intuitive judgment—that they would be partial to the defendant because of their shared race. Just as the Equal Protection Clause forbids the States to exclude black persons from the venire on the assumption that blacks as a group are unqualified to serve as jurors, so it forbids the States to strike black veniremen on the assumption that they will be biased in a particular case simply because the defendant is black. The core guarantee of equal protection, ensuring citizens that their State will not discriminate on account of race, would be meaningless were we to approve the exclusion of jurors on the basis of such assumptions, which arise solely from the jurors' race. Nor may the prosecutor rebut the defendant's case merely by denying that he had a discriminatory motive or "affirming his good faith in individual selections." If these general assertions were accepted as rebutting a defendant's prima facie case, the Equal Protection Clause "would be but a vain and illusory requirement." The prosecutor therefore must articulate a neutral explanation related to the particular case to be tried. The trial court then will have the duty to determine if the defendant has established purposeful discrimination.

The State contends that our holding will eviscerate the fair trial values served by the peremptory challenge. Conceding that the Constitution does not guarantee a right to peremptory challenges and that *Swain* did state that their use ultimately is subject to the strictures of equal protection, the State argues that the privilege of unfettered exercise of the challenge is of vital importance to the criminal justice system.

While we recognize, of course, that the peremptory challenge occupies an important position in our trial procedures, we do not agree that our decision today will undermine the contribution the challenge generally makes to the administration of justice. The reality of practice, amply reflected in many state

cion is absent, different methods of proof may
be appropriate."

and federal court opinions, shows that the challenge may be, and unfortunately at times has been, used to discriminate against black jurors. By requiring trial courts to be sensitive to the racially discriminatory use of peremptory challenges, our decision enforces the mandate of equal protection and furthers the ends of justice.[22] In view of the heterogeneous population of our nation, public respect for our criminal justice system and the rule of law will be strengthened if we ensure that no citizen is disqualified from jury service because of his race.

Nor are we persuaded by the State's suggestion that our holding will create serious administrative difficulties. In those states applying a version of the evidentiary standard we recognize today, courts have not experienced serious administrative burdens, and the peremptory challenge system has survived. We decline, however, to formulate particular procedures to be followed upon a defendant's timely objection to a prosecutor's challenges.[24]

In this case, petitioner made a timely objection to the prosecutor's removal of all black persons on the venire. Because the trial court flatly rejected the objection without requiring the prosecutor to give an explanation for his action, we remand this case for further proceedings. If the trial court decides that the facts establish, prima facie, purposeful discrimination and the prosecutor does not come forward with a neutral explanation for his action, our precedents require that petitioner's conviction be reversed.

JUSTICE MARSHALL, concurring. * * *

I wholeheartedly concur in the Court's conclusion that use of the peremptory challenge to remove blacks from juries, on the basis of their race, violates the Equal Protection Clause. I would go further, however, in fashioning a remedy adequate to eliminate that discrimination. Merely allowing defendants the opportunity to challenge the racially discriminatory use of peremptory challenges in individual cases will not end the illegitimate use of the peremptory challenge.

Evidentiary analysis similar to that set out by the Court has been adopted as a matter of state law in States including Massachusetts and California. Cases from those jurisdictions illustrate the limitations of the approach. First, defendants cannot attack the discriminatory use of peremptory challenges at all unless the challenges are so flagrant as to establish a prima facie case. This means, in those States, that where only one or two black jurors survive the challenges for cause, the prosecutor need have no compunction about striking them from the jury because of their race. Prosecutors are left free to discrimi-

---

**22.** While we respect the views expressed in Justice Marshall's concurring opinion, concerning prosecutorial and judicial enforcement of our holding today, we do not share them. The standard we adopt under the federal Constitution is designed to ensure that a State does not use peremptory challenges to strike any black juror because of his race. We have no reason to believe that prosecutors will not fulfill their duty to exercise their challenges only for legitimate purposes. Certainly, this Court may assume that trial judges, in supervising *voir dire* in light of our decision today, will be alert to identify a prima facie case of purposeful discrimination. Nor do we think that this historic trial practice, which long has served the selection of an impartial jury, should be abolished because of an appre-

hension that prosecutors and trial judges will not perform conscientiously their respective duties under the Constitution.

**24.** In light of the variety of jury selection practices followed in our state and federal trial courts, we make no attempt to instruct these courts how best to implement our holding today. For the same reason, we express no view on whether it is more appropriate in a particular case, upon a finding of discrimination against black jurors, for the trial court to discharge the venire and select a new jury from a panel not previously associated with the case, or to disallow the discriminatory challenges and resume selection with the improperly challenged jurors reinstated on the venire.

nate against blacks in jury selection provided that they hold that discrimination to an "acceptable" level.

Second, when a defendant can establish a prima facie case, trial courts face the difficult burden of assessing prosecutors' motives. Any prosecutor can easily assert facially neutral reasons for striking a juror, and trial courts are ill-equipped to second-guess those reasons. How is the court to treat a prosecutor's statement that he struck a juror because the juror had a son about the same age as defendant, or seemed "uncommunicative," or "never cracked a smile" and, therefore "did not possess the sensitivities necessary to realistically look at the issues and decide the facts in this case." If such easily generated explanations are sufficient to discharge the prosecutor's obligation to justify his strikes on nonracial grounds, then the protection erected by the Court today may be illusory.

Nor is outright prevarication by prosecutors the only danger here. "[I]t is even possible that an attorney may lie to himself in an effort to convince himself that his motives are legal." A prosecutor's own conscious or unconscious racism may lead him easily to the conclusion that a prospective black juror is "sullen," or "distant," a characterization that would not have come to his mind if a white juror had acted identically. A judge's own conscious or unconscious racism may lead him to accept such an explanation as well supported. * * *

The inherent potential of peremptory challenges to distort the jury process by permitting the exclusion of jurors on racial grounds should ideally lead the Court to ban them entirely from the criminal justice system. * * *

Some authors have suggested that the courts should ban prosecutors' per-emptories entirely, but should zealously guard the defendant's peremptory as "essential to the fairness of trial by jury" and "one of the most important of the rights secured to the accused." I would not find that an acceptable solution. Our criminal justice system "requires not only freedom from any bias against the accused, but also from any prejudice against his prosecution. Between him and the state the scales are to be evenly held." We can maintain that balance, not by permitting both prosecutor and defendant to engage in racial discrimination in jury selection, but by banning the use of peremptory challenges by prosecutors and by allowing the States to eliminate the defendant's peremptory as well. * * *

Chief Justice Burger, joined by Justice Rehnquist, dissenting.

* * * The Court acknowledges, albeit in a footnote, the " 'very old credentials' " of the peremptory challenge and " 'the widely held belief that peremptory challenge is a necessary part of trial by jury.' " But proper resolution of this case requires more than a nodding reference to the purpose of the challenge. * * *

The Court's opinion, in addition to ignoring the teachings of history, also contrasts with *Swain* in its failure to even discuss the rationale of the peremptory challenge. *Swain* observed:

"The function of the challenge is not only to eliminate extremes of partiality on both sides, but to assure the parties that the jurors before whom they try the case will decide on the basis of the evidence placed for them, and not otherwise. In this way the peremptory satisfies the rule that 'to perform its high function in the best way, justice must satisfy the appearance of justice.' "

Permitting unexplained peremptories has long been regarded as a means to strengthen our jury system in other ways as well. One commentator has recognized:

> "The peremptory, made without giving any reason, avoids trafficking in the core of truth in most common stereotypes. * * * Common human experience, common sense, psychosociological studies, and public opinion polls tell us that it is likely that certain classes of people statistically have predispositions that would make them inappropriate jurors for particular kinds of cases. But to allow this knowledge to be expressed in the evaluative terms necessary for challenges for cause would undercut our desire for a society in which all people are judged as individuals and in which each is held reasonable and open to compromise. * * * [For example,] [a]lthough experience reveals that black males as a class can be biased against young alienated blacks who have not tried to join the middle class, to enunciate this in the concrete expression required of a challenge for cause is societally divisive. Instead we have evolved in the peremptory challenge a system that allows the covert expression of what we dare not say but know is true more often than not."

For reasons such as these, this Court concluded in *Swain* that "the [peremptory] challenge is 'one of the most important of the rights' " in our justice system. For close to a century, then, it has been settled that "[t]he denial or impairment of the right is reversible error without a showing of prejudice."

[T]he Court also invokes general equal protection principles in support of its holding. But peremptory challenges are often lodged, of necessity, for reasons "normally thought irrelevant to legal proceedings or official action, namely, the race, religion, nationality, occupation or affiliations of people summoned for jury duty." *Swain.* Moreover, in making peremptory challenges, both the prosecutor and defense attorney necessarily act on only limited information or hunch. The process can not be indicted on the sole basis that such decisions are made on the basis of "assumption" or "intuitive judgment." As a result, unadulterated equal protection analysis is simply inapplicable to peremptory challenges exercised in any particular case. A clause that requires a minimum "rationality" in government actions has no application to " 'an arbitrary and capricious right' "; a constitutional principle that may invalidate state action on the basis of "stereotypic notions" does not explain the breadth of a procedure exercised on the " 'sudden impressions and unaccountable prejudices we are apt to conceive upon the bare looks and gestures of another.' "

That the Court is not applying conventional equal protection analysis is shown by its limitation of its new rule to allegations of impermissible challenge *on the basis of race;* the Court's opinion clearly contains such a limitation. * * * But if conventional equal protection principles apply, then presumably defendants could object to exclusions on the basis of not only race, but also sex, age, religious or political affiliation, mental capacity, number of children, living arrangements, and employment in a particular industry or profession.[4]

In short, it is quite probable that every peremptory challenge could be objected to on the basis that, because it excluded a venireman who had some characteristic not shared by the remaining members of the venire, it constituted a "classification" subject to equal protection scrutiny. Compounding the difficulties, under conventional equal protection principles some uses of peremptories

4. While all these distinctions might support a claim under conventional equal protection principles, a defendant would also have to establish standing to raise them before obtaining any relief.

would be reviewed under "strict scrutiny and * * * sustained only if * * * suitably tailored to serve a compelling state interest," others would be reviewed to determine if they were "substantially related to a sufficiently important government interest," and still others would be reviewed to determine whether they were "a rational means to serve a legitimate end."

The Court never applies this conventional equal protection framework to the claims at hand, perhaps to avoid acknowledging that the state interest involved here has historically been regarded by this Court as substantial, if not compelling. * * *

The Court also purports to express "no views on whether the Constitution imposes any limit on the exercise of peremptory challenges by *defense* counsel." But the clear and inescapable import of this novel holding will inevitably be to limit the use of this valuable tool to both prosecutors and defense attorneys alike. Once the Court has held that *prosecutors* are limited in their use of peremptory challenges, could we rationally hold that defendants are not?[6] * * *

Confronted with the dilemma it created, the Court today attempts to decree a middle ground. To rebut a prima facie case, the Court requires a "neutral explanation" for the challenge, but is at pains to "emphasize" that the "explanation need not rise to the level justifying exercise of a challenge for cause." I am at a loss to discern the governing principles here. A "clear and reasonably specific" explanation of "legitimate reasons" for exercising the challenge will be difficult to distinguish from a challenge for cause. Anything short of a challenge for cause may well be seen as an "arbitrary and capricious" challenge, to use Blackstone's characterization of the peremptory. Apparently the Court envisions permissible challenges short of a challenge for cause that are just a little bit arbitrary—but not too much. While our trial judges are "experienced in supervising *voir dire,*" they have no experience in administering rules like this.

An example will quickly demonstrate how today's holding, while purporting to "further the ends of justice," will not have that effect. Assume an Asian defendant, on trial for the capital murder of a white victim, asks prospective jury members, most of whom are white, whether they harbor racial prejudice against Asians. The basis for such a question is to flush out any "juror who believes that [Asians] are violence-prone or morally inferior. * * * Assume further that all white jurors deny harboring racial prejudice but that the defendant, on trial for his life, remains unconvinced by these protestations. Instead, he continues to harbor a hunch, an "assumption" or "intuitive judgment," that these white jurors will be prejudiced against him, presumably based in part on race. The time honored rule before today was that peremptory challenges could be exercised on such a basis. * * * The effect of the Court's decision, however, will be to force the defendant to come forward and "articulate a neutral explanation," for his peremptory challenge, a burden he probably cannot meet. This example demonstrates that today's holding will produce juries that the parties do not believe are truly impartial. This will surely do more than "disconcert" litigants; it will diminish confidence in the jury system. * * *

Today we mark the return of racial differentiation as the Court accepts a positive evil for a perceived one. Prosecutors and defense attorneys alike will build records in support of their claims that peremptory challenges have been exercised in a racially discriminatory fashion by asking jurors to state their

---

**6.** "[E]very jurisdiction which has spoken to the matter, and prohibited prosecution case-specific peremptory challenges on the ba- sis of cognizable group affiliation, has held that the defense must likewise be so prohibited."

racial background and national origin for the record, despite the fact that "such questions may be offensive to some jurors and thus are not ordinarily asked on voir dire." This process is sure to tax even the most capable counsel and judges since determining whether a prima facie case has been established will "require a continued monitoring and recording of the 'group' composition of the panel present and prospective. ∗ ∗ ∗" ∗ ∗ ∗

JUSTICE REHNQUIST with whom THE CHIEF JUSTICE joins, dissenting. ∗ ∗ ∗

I cannot subscribe to the Court's unprecedented use of the Equal Protection Clause to restrict the historic scope of the peremptory challenge, which has been described as "a necessary part of trial by jury." In my view, there is simply nothing "unequal" about the State using its peremptory challenges to strike blacks from the jury in cases involving black defendants, so long as such challenges are also used to exclude whites in cases involving white defendants, Hispanics in cases involving Hispanic defendants, Asians in cases involving Asian defendants, and so on. This case-specific use of peremptory challenges by the State does not single out blacks, or members of any other race for that matter, for discriminatory treatment. Such use of peremptories is at best based upon seat-of-the-pants instincts, which are undoubtedly crudely stereotypical and may in many cases be hopelessly mistaken. But as long as they are applied across the board to jurors of all races and nationalities, I do not see—and the Court most certainly has not explained—how their use violates the Equal Protection Clause.

Nor does such use of peremptory challenges by the State infringe upon any other constitutional interests. The Court does not suggest that exclusion of blacks from the jury through the State's use of peremptory challenges results in a violation of either the fair cross-section or impartiality component of the Sixth Amendment. And because the case-specific use of peremptory challenges by the State does not deny blacks the right to serve as jurors in cases involving non-black defendants, it harms neither the excluded jurors nor the remainder of the community.

The use of group affiliations, such as age, race, or occupation, as a "proxy" for potential juror partiality, based on the assumption or belief that members of one group are more likely to favor defendants who belong to the same group, has long been accepted as a legitimate basis for the State's exercise of peremptory challenges. Indeed, given the need for reasonable limitations on the time devoted to *voir dire*, the use of such "proxies" by both the State and the defendant may be extremely useful in eliminating from the jury persons who might be biased in one way or another. ∗ ∗ ∗

# Chapter 16

# FAIR TRIAL/FREE PRESS

This chapter introduces a new participant in the criminal justice process—the media (or, if one prefers, the public that is the audience of the media). In many situations the interests of the media and the accused coincide; indeed, the accused's Sixth Amendment right to insist upon a public trial is premised on the significant value of public disclosure in ensuring that the trial is a fair one. *In re Oliver,* 333 U.S. 257 (1948).[a] But there are instances when potential conflicts arise between the media's right to report and the accused's right to a fair trial. In *Nebraska Press Association v. Stuart,* 427 U.S. 539 (1976), the Supreme Court reviewed what had long been its basic approach in responding to such conflicts.

The Court in *Nebraska Press* noted that "the authors of the Bill of Rights did not undertake to assign priorities as between First Amendment and Sixth Amendment rights [although] fully aware of the potential conflicts between them." This placed the Supreme Court in a similar position. It could not "rewrite the Constitution by undertaking what they [the framers] declined to do." Rather, it had sought to develop constitutional standards, responsive to the particular situation, that accommodated both the freedom of the press under the First Amendment and the constitutional rights of the accused. The cases in this chapter reflect several different aspects of the Court's efforts in this process of accommodation or "balancing."

Perhaps the most significant source of conflict between the media and the accused arises from the impact upon the jury selection process of extensive media coverage of a case prior to trial. That coverage often starts with the reporting on the commission of the crime and carries through to the eve of the trial, reporting not only matters of public record but also information developed by the media itself. It produces what the Court commonly describes as "pretrial publicity." Such publicity, often adverse to the accused and sometimes highly inflammatory, has the potential for influencing the attitudes of a large segment of the potential pool of jurors—both those who themselves read, saw, or listened to the coverage and others who have heard about it second-hand.

Fortunately, as the Court noted in *Nebraska Press,* in "the overwhelming majority of criminal trials, pretrial publicity presents few unmanageable

---

**a.** *Oliver* noted that the public trial serves the defendant's interest in a fair trial in several ways: (i) the knowledge that the trial is "subject to contemporaneous review in the form of public opinion" serves as "an effective restraint on possible abuse of judicial power"; (ii) the presence of interested spectators assures testimonial trustworthiness by inducing a fear in witnesses that false testimony will be detected; and (iii) public disclosure may call the proceedings to the attention of key witnesses who might be unknown to the defense and who might respond by coming forward with critical testimony.

threats" to the selection of an impartial jury. "But when the case is a 'sensational' one," the defendant's right to an impartial jury may be severely threatened. *Nebraska Press* held that the first line of response to that threat, under a Constitution that also recognizes the value to society of press coverage of matters of public concern, is to look to remedies that preserve the accused's right to an impartial jury without restricting the press.

Thus, in holding invalid a "gag order" which sought to bar the pretrial publication of certain information about the defendant (in particular, that he had confessed), *Nebraska Press* stressed the lack of any showing there that the defendant's right to an impartial jury could not have been preserved through the alternative measures traditionally used by the courts.[b] These included: "(a) change of trial venue to a place less exposed to the intense publicity * * *; (b) postponement of the trial to allow public attention to subside; [and] (c) searching questioning of prospective jurors [to] screen out those with fixed opinions as to guilt or innocence."

Of these three measures, the most significant is the juror screening process. A postponement raises a potential for conflict with the defendant's right to a speedy trial, and a change of venue will be of little value where the publicity extends throughout the state. Moreover, notwithstanding the *Rideau* case (discussed in *Murphy* infra), many courts will not grant a change of venue unless the screening process is tried and fails to produce a satisfactory jury. *Murphy,* the first case in this chapter, explores the question of when that process requires the exclusion of a prospective juror based upon the possible impact of pretrial publicity.

The fair trial right of the accused also can be threatened by media coverage at the trial itself. Here, the concern is that the jurors (and perhaps other participants, such as witnesses) will be influenced in carrying out their responsibilities by the actions of media representatives in covering the trial. Thus, in finding a denial of defendant's right to a fair trial, the *Sheppard* case (discussed in *Murphy*) dwelt on two factors exerting such an influence: (i) the disruptive activities of media representatives (both in the noise and confusion they created within the courtroom and in their behavior in photographing the witnesses and jurors as they left the courtroom), and (ii) the trial court's failure to insulate the jurors from the media coverage during the trial (that coverage having included considerable material never introduced at trial). The *Sheppard* Court also

b. The Court in *Nebraska Press* noted that orders restraining publication had always been viewed as the "most serious and least tolerable infringements on First Amendment rights" and would be allowed only upon an extraordinary showing of justification. In the context of protecting the defendant's right to an impartial jury, this would require consideration of: "(a) the nature and extent of pretrial news coverage; (b) whether other measures would be likely to mitigate the effects of the unrestrained pretrial publicity; and (c) how effectively a restraining order would operate to prevent a threatened danger." Upon consideration of these factors, an order restraining publication would only be justified where " 'the gravity of the evil [to be avoided], discounted by its improbability, justifies such invasion of free speech as is necessary to avoid the danger.' " A concurring opinion for three Justices argued that this burden of justification could never be met, considering the

"broad spectrum of [alternative] devices" judges have available for "ensuring that fundamental fairness is accorded the accused." Another concurring Justice agreed generally with that conclusion, leaving aside special situations (e.g., where the information to be published was obtained by illegal means or was patently false). Still another Justice expressed "grave doubt" that a restraining order could ever be justified, and yet another stressed the "unique burden" that would rest on a party who sought to establish the "necessity for a prior restraint on pretrial publicity." Thus, while the opinion for the Court noted that it was not "ruling out the possibility of [a defendant] showing the kind of threat to fair trial rights that would possess the requisite degree of certainty to justify restraint," the combination of opinions signaled, as a practical matter, a death knell for such restraining orders.

stressed, however, that these difficulties were not the inevitable consequences of substantial media coverage, but could have been avoided through various precautions that would not have interfered with the media's capacity to cover the trial (e.g., controlling the location and number of newspersons in the courtroom, and directing the jurors not to read papers or watch television, or even sequestering the jury during the trial).

Will such administrative controls suffice when criminal trials are televised? The second case in this chapter, *Chandler v. Florida,* speaks to this question. In an earlier case discussed in *Chandler, Estes v. Texas,* four Justices had suggested that the televising of trials was "inherently prejudicial" and therefore constitutionally precluded under whatever form it might take.

While *Nebraska Press* held that the press could not be banned from reporting on judicial proceedings open to the public, it left open the question of whether the First Amendment was implicated in the closing of a proceeding to the public (and thereby to the press). *Richmond Newspapers, Inc. v. Virginia,* 448 U.S. 555 (1980), marked the first time the Court was asked to decide "whether *a criminal trial itself* may be closed upon the unopposed request of a defendant, without any demonstration that closure is required to protect the defendant's superior right to a fair trial [or] some other overriding consideration." (Emphasis added.) No, answered the Court, holding that the right of the public and the press to attend criminal trials is implicit in the guarantees of the First Amendment. There was no opinion of the Court. In the lead opinion, Burger, C.J., joined by White and Stevens, JJ., observed that "the Bill of Rights was enacted against the backdrop of the long history of trials being presumptively open" and that "the First Amendment can be read as protecting the right of everyone to attend trials" "so as to give meaning" to the explicit guarantees of freedom of speech and press. Concurring Justice Brennan, joined by Marshall, J., emphasized that public access to trials is essential "to achieve the objective of maintaining public confidence in the administration of justice."

*Richmond Newspapers* left open the question whether the right of access to the criminal trial itself extended to *pretrial* proceedings. The Court suggested this possibility in *Press-Enterprise Co. v. Superior Court,* 464 U.S. 501 (1984) (*Press-Enterprise I*), when it held, without a dissent, that the First Amendment right of access applied to the *voir dire* examination of potential jurors. The Court emphasized the historical tradition of openness and the functional value of openness for the particular proceeding rather than any characterization of the jury selection process as a part of the trial itself. Two years later, in *Press-Enterprise II,* the last case in this chapter, the Court applied the public right of access to a proceeding that was clearly not part of the trial—the preliminary hearing.

## MURPHY v. FLORIDA
### 421 U.S. 794, 95 S.Ct. 2031, 44 L.Ed.2d 589 (1975).

JUSTICE MARSHALL delivered the opinion of the Court.

The question presented by this case is whether the petitioner was denied a fair trial because members of the jury had learned from news accounts about a prior felony conviction or certain facts about the crime with which he was charged. Under the circumstances of this case, we find that petitioner has not been denied due process, and we therefore affirm the judgment below.

Petitioner was convicted in the Dade County, Fla., Criminal Court in 1970 of breaking and entering a home, while armed, with intent to commit robbery, and of assault with intent to commit robbery. The charges stemmed from the January 1968 robbery of a Miami Beach home and petitioner's apprehension, with three others, while fleeing from the scene. The robbery and petitioner's arrest received extensive press coverage because petitioner had been much in the news before. He had first made himself notorious for his part in the 1964 theft of the Star of India sapphire from a museum in New York. His flamboyant lifestyle made him a continuing subject of press interest; he was generally referred to—at least in the media—as "Murph the Surf."

Before the date set for petitioner's trial on the instant charges, he was indicted on two counts of murder in [adjoining] Broward County * * * [and] for conspiring to transport stolen securities in interstate commerce [in the federal courts], * * * and was convicted on one count of murder in Broward County (March 1969) and pleaded guilty to one count of the federal indictment * * * (December 1969). * * *

The events of 1968 and 1969 drew extensive press coverage. Each new case against petitioner was considered newsworthy, not only in Dade County but elsewhere as well. The record in this case contains scores of articles reporting on petitioner's trials and tribulations during this period; many purportedly relate statements that petitioner or his attorney made to reporters.

Jury selection in the present case began in August 1970. Seventy-eight jurors were questioned. Of these, 30 were excused for miscellaneous personal reasons; 20 were excused peremptorily by the defense or prosecution; 20 were excused by the court as having prejudged petitioner; and the remaining eight served as the jury and two alternates. Petitioner's motions to dismiss the chosen jurors, on the ground that they were aware that he had previously been convicted of either the 1964 Star of India theft or the Broward County murder, were denied, as was his renewed motion for a change of venue based on allegedly prejudicial pretrial publicity.

At trial, petitioner did not testify or put in any evidence; assertedly in protest of the selected jury, he did not cross-examine any of the State's witnesses. He was convicted on both counts, and after an unsuccessful appeal he sought habeas corpus relief in the [federal district court]. * * *

Petitioner relies principally upon *Irvin v. Dowd*, 366 U.S. 717 (1961), *Rideau v. Louisiana*, 373 U.S. 723 (1963), *Estes v. Texas*, 381 U.S. 532 (1965), and *Sheppard v. Maxwell*, 384 U.S. 333 (1966). In each of these cases, this Court overturned a state-court conviction obtained in a trial atmosphere that had been utterly corrupted by press coverage.

In *Irvin v. Dowd* the rural community in which the trial was held had been subjected to a barrage of inflammatory publicity immediately prior to trial, including information on the defendant's prior convictions, his confession to 24 burglaries and six murders including the one for which he was tried, and his unaccepted offer to plead guilty in order to avoid the death sentence. As a result, eight of the 12 jurors had formed an opinion that the defendant was guilty before the trial began; some went "so far as to say that it would take evidence to overcome their belief" in his guilt. In these circumstances, the Court readily found actual prejudice against the petitioner to a degree that rendered a fair trial impossible.

Prejudice was presumed in the circumstances under which the trials in *Rideau, Estes,* and *Sheppard* were held. In those cases the influence of the news media, either in the community at large or in the courtroom itself, pervaded the proceedings. In *Rideau* the defendant had "confessed" under police interrogation to the murder of which he stood convicted. A 20–minute film of his confession was broadcast three times by a television station in the community where the crime and the trial took place. In reversing, the Court did not examine the *voir dire* for evidence of actual prejudice because it considered the trial under review "but a hollow formality"—the real trial had occurred when tens of thousands of people, in a community of 150,000, had seen and heard the defendant admit his guilt before the cameras.

The trial in *Estes* had been conducted in a circus atmosphere, due in large part to the intrusions of the press, which was allowed to sit within the bar of the court and to overrun it with television equipment. Similarly, *Sheppard* arose from a trial infected not only by a background of extremely inflammatory publicity but also by a courthouse given over to accommodate the public appetite for carnival. The proceedings in these cases were entirely lacking in the solemnity and sobriety to which a defendant is entitled in a system that subscribes to any notion of fairness and rejects the verdict of a mob. They cannot be made to stand for the proposition that juror exposure to information about a state defendant's prior convictions or to news accounts of the crime with which he is charged alone presumptively deprives the defendant of due process. To resolve this case, we must turn, therefore, to any indications in the totality of circumstances that petitioner's trial was not fundamentally fair.

The constitutional standard of fairness requires that a defendant have "a panel of impartial, 'indifferent' jurors." *Irvin v. Dowd.* Qualified jurors need not, however, be totally ignorant of the facts and issues involved.

> "To hold that the mere existence of any preconceived notion as to the guilt or innocence of an accused, without more, is sufficient to rebut the presumption of a prospective juror's impartiality would be to establish an impossible standard. It is sufficient if the juror can lay aside his impression or opinion and render a verdict based on the evidence presented in court." *Irvin v. Dowd.*

At the same time, the juror's assurances that he is equal to this task cannot be dispositive of the accused's rights, and it remains open to the defendant to demonstrate "the actual existence of such an opinion in the mind of the juror as will raise the presumption of partiality." *Ibid.*

The *voir dire* in this case indicates no such hostility to petitioner by the jurors who served in his trial as to suggest a partiality that could not be laid aside. Some of the jurors had a vague recollection of the robbery with which petitioner was charged and each had some knowledge of petitioner's past crimes,[3] but none betrayed any belief in the relevance of petitioner's past to the present case. Indeed, four of the six jurors volunteered their views of its irrelevance, and one suggested that people who have been in trouble before are too often singled out for suspicion of each new crime—a predisposition that could only operate in petitioner's favor.

In the entire *voir dire* transcript furnished to us, there is only one colloquy on which petitioner can base even a colorable claim of partiality by a juror. In response to a leading and hypothetical question, presupposing a two- or three-

---

**3.** One juror who did not know that petitioner had been previously convicted for the theft of the Star of India sapphire, one who did not know of the murder conviction, and one who had never heard about the securities case were informed about them by petitioner's counsel, who then asked whether that knowledge would not prejudice them against peti-

tioner. We will not readily discount the assurances of a juror insofar as his exposure to a defendant's past crimes comes from the defendant or counsel. We note also, and disapprove, counsel's habitual references to his client, at *voir dire,* as "Murph the Surf" rather than by his name.

week presentation of evidence against petitioner and his failure to put on any defense, one juror conceded that his prior impression of petitioner would dispose him to convict.[5]  We cannot attach great significance to this statement, however, in light of the leading nature of counsel's questions and the juror's other testimony indicating that he had no deep impression of petitioner at all.

The juror testified that he did not keep up with current events and, in fact, had never heard of petitioner until he arrived in the room for prospective jurors where some veniremen were discussing him.  He did not know that petitioner was "a convicted jewel thief" even then; it was petitioner's counsel who informed him of this fact.  And he volunteered that petitioner's murder conviction, of which he had just heard, would not be relevant to his guilt or innocence in the present case, since "[w]e are not trying him for murder."

Even these indicia of impartiality might be disregarded in a case where the general atmosphere in the community or courtroom is sufficiently inflammatory, but the circumstances surrounding petitioner's trial are not at all of that variety. Petitioner attempts to portray them as inflammatory by reference to the publicity to which the community was exposed.  The District Court found, however, that the news articles concerning petitioner had appeared almost entirely during the period between December 1967 and January 1969, the latter date being seven months before the jury in this case was selected.  They were, moreover, largely factual in nature.

The length to which the trial court must go in order to select jurors who appear to be impartial is another factor relevant in evaluating those jurors' assurances of impartiality.  In a community where most veniremen will admit to a disqualifying prejudice, the reliability of the others' protestations may be drawn into question; for it is then more probable that they are part of a community deeply hostile to the accused, and more likely that they may unwittingly have been influenced by it.  In *Irvin v. Dowd,* for example, the Court noted that 90% of those examined on the point were inclined to believe in the accused's guilt, and the court had excused for this cause 268 of the 430 veniremen.  In the present case, by contrast, 20 of the 78 persons questioned were excused because they indicated an opinion as to petitioner's guilt.  This may indeed be 20 more than would occur in the trial of a totally obscure person, but it by no means suggests a community with sentiment so poisoned against

---

5.  The entire exchange appears at App. 139:

"Q.  Now, when you go into that jury room and you decide upon Murphy's guilt or innocence, you are going to take into account that fact that he is a convicted murderer; aren't you?

"A.  Not if we are listening to the case, I wouldn't.

"Q.  But you know about it?

"A.  How can you not know about it?

"Q.  Fine, thank you.

"When you go into the jury room, the fact that he is a convicted murderer, that is going to influence your verdict; is it not?

"A.  We are not trying him for murder.

"Q.  The fact that he is a convicted murderer and jewel thief, that would influence your verdict?

"A.  I didn't know he was a convicted jewel thief.

"Q.  Oh, I see.

"I am sorry I put words in your mouth.

"Now, sir, after two or three weeks of being locked up in a downtown hotel, as the Court determines, and after hearing the State's case, and after hearing no case on behalf of Murphy, and hearing no testimony from Murphy saying, 'I am innocent, Mr. [juror's name],'—when you go into the jury room, sir, all these facts are going to influence your verdict?

"A.  I imagine it would be.

"Q.  And in fact, you are saying if Murphy didn't testify, and if he doesn't offer evidence, 'My experience of him is such that right now I would find him guilty.'

"A.  I believe so."

petitioner as to impeach the indifference of jurors who displayed no animus of their own.

In sum, we are unable to conclude, in the circumstances presented in this case, that petitioner did not receive a fair trial. Petitioner has failed to show that the setting of the trial was inherently prejudicial or that the jury-selection process of which he complains permits an inference of actual prejudice. * * *

CHIEF JUSTICE BURGER, concurring in the judgment.

I agree with Mr. Justice Brennan that the trial judge was woefully remiss in failing to insulate prospective jurors from the bizarre media coverage of this case and in not taking steps to prevent pretrial discussion of the case among them. Although I would not hesitate to reverse petitioner's conviction in the exercise of our supervisory powers, were this a federal case, I agree with the Court that the circumstances of petitioner's trial did not rise to the level of a violation of the Due Process Clause of the Fourteenth Amendment.

JUSTICE BRENNAN, dissenting.

I dissent. *Irvin v. Dowd,* requires reversal of this conviction. As in that case, petitioner here was denied a fair trial. The risk that taint of widespread publicity regarding his criminal background, known to all members of the jury, infected the jury's deliberations is apparent, the trial court made no attempt to prevent discussion of the case or petitioner's previous criminal exploits among the prospective jurors, and one juror freely admitted that he was predisposed to convict petitioner.

During *voir dire,* petitioner's counsel had the following colloquy with that juror [Justice Brennan here set forth the latter part of the *voir dire* exchange quoted in note 5 of the Court's opinion].

I cannot agree with the Court that the obvious bias of this juror may be overlooked simply because the juror's response was occasioned by a "leading and hypothetical question." Indeed, the hypothetical became reality when petitioner chose not to take the stand and offered no evidence. Thus petitioner was tried by a juror predisposed, because of his knowledge of petitioner's previous crimes, to find him guilty of this one.

Others who ultimately served as jurors revealed similar prejudice toward petitioner on *voir dire.* One juror conceded that it would be difficult, during deliberations, to put out of his mind that petitioner was a convicted criminal. He also admitted that he did not "hold a convicted felon in the same regard as another person who has never been convicted of a felony," and admitted further that he had termed petitioner a "menace."

A third juror testified that she knew from several sources that petitioner was a convicted murderer, and was aware that the community regarded petitioner as a criminal who "should be put away." She disclaimed having a fixed opinion about the result she would reach, but acknowledged that the fact that petitioner was a convicted criminal would probably influence her verdict. * * * Still another juror testified that the comments of venire members in discussing the case had made him "sick to [his] stomach." He testified that one venireman had said that petitioner was "thoroughly rotten," and that another had said: "Hang him, he's guilty."

Moreover, the Court ignores the crucial significance of the fact that at no time before or during this daily buildup of prejudice against Murphy did the trial judge instruct the prospective jurors not to discuss the case among themselves. Indeed the trial judge took no steps to insulate the jurors from media coverage of the case or from the many news articles that discussed petitioner's last criminal exploits.

It is of no moment that several jurors ultimately testified that they would try to exclude from their deliberations their knowledge of petitioner's past misdeeds and of his community reputation. *Irvin* held in like circumstances that little weight could be attached to such self-serving protestations. * * *

On the record of this *voir dire*, therefore, the conclusion is to me inescapable that the attitude of the entire venire toward Murphy reflected the "then current community pattern of thought as indicated by the popular news media," and was infected with the taint of the view that he was a "criminal" guilty of notorious offenses, including that for which he was on trial. It is a plain case, from a review of the entire *voir dire*, where "the extent and nature of the publicity has caused such a build up of prejudice that excluding the preconception of guilt from the deliberations would be too difficult for the jury to be honestly found impartial." In my view, the denial of a change of venue was therefore prejudicial error, and I would reverse the conviction.

## CHANDLER v. FLORIDA
449 U.S. 560, 101 S.Ct. 802, 66 L.Ed.2d 740 (1981).

CHIEF JUSTICE BURGER delivered the opinion of the Court.

The question presented on this appeal is whether, consistent with constitutional guarantees, a state may provide for radio, television, and still photographic coverage of a criminal trial for public broadcast, notwithstanding the objection of the accused.

*Background.* Over the past 50 years, some criminal cases characterized as "sensational" have been subjected to extensive coverage by news media, sometimes seriously interfering with the conduct of the proceedings and creating a setting wholly inappropriate for the administration of justice. Judges, lawyers, and others soon became concerned, and in 1937, after study, the American Bar Association House of Delegates adopted Judicial Canon 35, declaring that all photographic and broadcast coverage of courtroom proceedings should be prohibited. In 1952, the House of Delegates amended Canon 35 to proscribe television coverage as well. [A] majority of the states, including Florida, adopted the substance of the ABA provision and its amendments. In Florida, the rule was embodied in Canon 3A(7) of the Florida Code of Judicial Conduct.

In February 1978, the American Bar Association Committee on Fair Trial–Free Press proposed revised standards. These included a provision permitting courtroom coverage by the electronic media under conditions to be established by local rule and under the control of the trial judge, but only if such coverage was carried out unobtrusively and without affecting the conduct of the trial. The revision was endorsed by the ABA's Standing Committee on Standards for Criminal Justice, [but] rejected by the House of Delegates on February 12, 1979.

[In] January 1975, while these developments were unfolding, the Post–Newsweek Stations of Florida petitioned the Supreme Court of Florida urging a change in Florida's Canon 3A(7). [The] Florida Supreme Court [eventually established a] 1–year pilot program during which the electronic media were permitted to cover all judicial proceedings in Florida without reference to the consent of participants, subject to detailed standards with respect to technology and the conduct of operators. * * * When the pilot program ended, the Florida Supreme Court received and reviewed briefs, reports, letters of comment, and studies. It conducted its own survey of attorneys, witnesses, jurors, and court personnel through the Office of the State Court Coordinator. A separate survey was taken of judges by the Florida Conference of Circuit Judges. The court also studied the experience of 6 States that had, by 1979, adopted rules relating to electronic coverage of trials, as well as that of the 10 other States that, like Florida, were experimenting with such coverage.

Following its review of this material, the Florida Supreme Court concluded "that on balance there [was] more to be gained than lost by permitting electronic media coverage of judicial proceedings subject to standards for such coverage." The Florida court was of the view that because of the significant effect of the courts on the day-to-day lives of the citizenry, it was essential that the people have confidence in the process. It felt that broadcast coverage of trials would contribute to wider public acceptance and understanding of decisions. Consequently, after revising the 1977 guidelines to reflect its evaluation of the pilot program, the Florida Supreme Court promulgated a revised Canon 3A(7). The Canon provides:

> "Subject at all times to the authority of the presiding judge to (i) control the conduct of proceedings before the court, (ii) ensure decorum and prevent distractions, and (iii) ensure the fair administration of justice in the pending cause, electronic media and still photography coverage of public judicial proceedings in the appellate and trial courts of this state shall be allowed in accordance with standards of conduct and technology promulgated by the Supreme Court of Florida." Ibid.

The implementing guidelines specify in detail the kind of electronic equipment to be used and the manner of its use. For example, no more than one television camera and only one camera technician are allowed. Existing recording systems used by court reporters are used by broadcasters for audio pickup. Where more than one broadcast news organization seeks to cover a trial, the media must pool coverage. No artificial lighting is allowed. The equipment is positioned in a fixed location, and it may not be moved during trial. Videotaping equipment must be remote from the courtroom. Film, videotape, and lenses may not be changed while the court is in session. No audio recording of conferences between lawyers, between parties and counsel, or at the bench is permitted. The judge has sole and plenary discretion to exclude coverage of certain witnesses, and the jury may not be filmed. The judge has discretionary power to forbid coverage whenever satisfied that coverage may have a deleterious effect on the paramount right of the defendant to a fair trial. * * *

In July 1977, appellants were charged with conspiracy to commit burglary, grand larceny, and possession of burglary tools. The counts covered breaking and entering a well-known Miami Beach restaurant.

The details of the alleged criminal conduct are not relevant to the issue before us, but several aspects of the case distinguish it from a routine burglary. At the time of their arrest, appellants were Miami Beach policemen. The State's principal witness was John Sion, an amateur radio operator who, by sheer chance, had overheard and recorded conversations between the appellants over their police walkie-talkie radios during the burglary. Not surprisingly, these novel factors attracted the attention of the media.

By pretrial motion, counsel for the appellants sought to have experimental Canon 3A(7) declared unconstitutional on its face and as applied. The trial court denied relief * * *. After several additional fruitless attempts by the appellants to prevent electronic coverage of the trial, the jury was selected. At *voir dire,* the appellants' counsel asked each prospective juror whether he or she would be able to be "fair and impartial" despite the presence of a television camera during some, or all, of the trial.  Each juror selected responded that such coverage would not affect his or her consideration in any way.  A television camera recorded the *voir dire*.

A defense motion to sequester the jury because of the television coverage was denied by the trial judge.  However, the court instructed the jury not to watch or read anything about the case in the media and suggested that jurors "avoid the local news and watch only the national news on television."  Subsequently, defense counsel requested that the witnesses be instructed not to watch any television accounts of testimony presented at trial.  The trial court declined to give such an instruction, for "no witness' testimony was [being] reported or televised [on the evening news] in any way."

A television camera was in place for one entire afternoon, during which the State presented the testimony of Sion, its chief witness.  No camera was present for the presentation of any part of the case for the defense.  The camera returned to cover closing arguments.  Only 2 minutes and 55 seconds of the trial below were broadcast—and those depicted only the prosecution's side of the case.

The jury returned a guilty verdict on all counts.  Appellants moved for a new trial, claiming that because of the television coverage, they had been denied a fair and impartial trial.  No evidence of specific prejudice was tendered.

[At] the outset, it is important to note that in promulgating the revised Canon 3A(7), the Florida Supreme Court pointedly rejected any state or federal constitutional right of access on the part of photographers or the broadcast media to televise or electronically record and thereafter disseminate court proceedings.  [The] Florida court relied on our holding in *Nixon v. Warner Communications, Inc.,* 435 U.S. 589 (1978), where we said:

> "In the first place, [there] is no constitutional right to have [live witness] testimony recorded and broadcast.  Second, while the guarantee of a public trial, in the words of Mr. Justice Black, is 'a safeguard against any attempt to employ our courts as instruments of persecution,' it confers no special benefit on the press.  Nor does the Sixth Amendment require that the trial—or any part of it—be broadcast live or on tape to the public.  The requirement of a public trial is satisfied by the opportunity of members of the public and the press to attend the trial and to report what they have observed."

The Florida Supreme Court predicated the revised Canon 3A(7) upon its supervisory authority over the Florida courts, and not upon any constitutional imperative.  Hence, we have before us only the limited question of the Florida Supreme Court's authority to promulgate the Canon for the trial of cases in Florida courts.  * * *

Appellants rely chiefly on *Estes v. Texas,* 381 U.S. 532 (1965), and Chief Justice Warren's separate concurring opinion in that case.  They argue that the televising of criminal trials is inherently a denial of due process, and they read *Estes* as announcing a *per se* constitutional rule to that effect.  Chief Justice Warren's concurring opinion, in which he was joined by Justices Douglas and Goldberg, indeed provides some support for the appellants' position.  * *, * [However], [t]he six separate opinions in *Estes* must be examined carefully to evaluate the claim that it represents a *per se* constitutional rule forbidding all electronic coverage.[a]  Chief Justice Warren and Justices Douglas and Goldberg

---

**a.**  Justice Clark delivered an opinion in *Estes* that was described as the "opinion for the Court," although (as the *Chandler* opinion notes infra) Justice Harlan was listed as concurring only to the extent indicated in his separate opinion.  Justice Clark's opinion reasoned: "The State * * * says that the use of television in the instant case was 'without joined Justice Clark's opinion announcing the judgment, thereby creating only a plurality.  Justice Harlan provided the fifth vote necessary in support of the judgment.  In a separate opinion, he pointedly limited his concurrence:

> "I concur in the opinion of the Court, subject, however, to the reservations and only to the extent indicated in this opinion."

A careful analysis of Justice Harlan's opinion is therefore fundamental to an understanding of the ultimate holding of *Estes.*

Justice Harlan began by observing that the question of the constitutional permissibility of televised trials was one fraught with unusual difficulty:

> "Permitting television in the courtroom undeniably has mischievous potentialities for intruding upon the detached atmosphere which should always surround the judicial process.  Forbidding this innovation, however, would doubtless impinge upon one of the valued attributes of our federalism by preventing the states from pursing a novel course of procedural experimentation.  My conclusion is that there is no constitutional requirement that television be allowed in the courtroom, *and, at least as to a notorious criminal trial such as this one, the considerations against allowing television in the courtroom so far outweigh the countervailing factors advanced in its support as to require a holding that what was done in this case infringed the fundamental right to a fair trial* assured by the Due Process Clause of the Fourteenth Amendment."  (emphasis added).

He then proceeded to catalog what he perceived as the inherent dangers of televised trials.

> "In the context of a trial of intense public interest, there is certainly a strong possibility that the timid or reluctant witness, for whom a court appearance even at its traditional best is a harrowing affair, will become more timid or reluctant when he finds he will also be appearing before a 'hidden audience' of unknown but large dimensions.  There is certainly a strong possibility that the 'cocky' witness having a thirst for the limelight will become more 'cocky' under the influence of television.  And who can say that the juror who is gratified by having been chosen for a front-line

injustice to the person immediately concerned; basing its position on the fact that the petitioner has established no isolatable prejudice and that this must be shown in order to invalidate a conviction \* \* \*.  The State paints too broadly \* \* \*, for this Court itself has found instances in which a showing of actual prejudice is not a prerequisite to reversal.  This is such a case. [In *Rideau* and certain other cases, e.g., one in which two sheriffs deputies who were principle prosecution witnesses also had custody of the jurors], the Court did not stop to consider the actual effect of the practice, but struck down the conviction on the ground that prejudice was inherent. [T]he circumstances were held to be inherently suspect and therefore, such a showing [of actual prejudice] was not held to be a requisite to reversal.  Likewise in this case the application of this principle is especially appropriate.  Television in its present state and by its very nature, reaches into a variety of areas in which it may cause prejudice to an accused.  Still one cannot put his finger on its specific mischief and prove with particularity wherein he was prejudiced. \* \* \* Forty-eight of our

states and the Federal Rules have deemed the use of television improper in the courtroom.  This fact is most telling in buttressing our conclusion that any change in procedure which would permit its use would be inconsistent with our concepts of due process in this field."

Three members of the majority, speaking through Chief Justice Warren's concurring opinion stated that they "join[ed] the Court's opinion and agree[d] that televising of criminal trials is inherently a denial of due process," but wished to offer "additional views on why this is so."  The concurring opinion of the fifth member of the majority, Justice Harlan, is discussed infra.  In addition, there were three dissents (reflecting the views of four dissenters).  The dissents argued against the adoption of a "per se rule" rendering the televising of trials constitutionally unacceptable without a showing that the risks of disruption, distraction, and juror viewing of the broadcasts actually had materialized in the particular case.

case, an ambitious prosecutor, a publicity-minded defense attorney, and even a conscientious judge will not stray, albeit unconsciously, from doing what 'comes naturally' into pluming themselves for a satisfactory television 'performance'?"

Justice Harlan faced squarely the reality that these possibilities carry "grave potentialities for distorting the integrity of the judicial process," and that, although such distortions may produce no telltale signs, "their effects may be far more pervasive and deleterious than the physical disruptions which all would concede would vitiate a conviction." The "countervailing factors" alluded to by Justice Harlan were, as here, the educational and informational value to the public.

[I]t is fair to say that Justice Harlan viewed the holding as limited to the proposition that "*what was done in this case* infringed the fundamental right to a fair trial assured by the Due Process Clause of the Fourteenth Amendment" (emphasis added). * * * Justice Harlan's opinion, upon which analysis of the constitutional holding of *Estes* turns, must be read as defining the scope of that holding; we conclude that *Estes* is not to be read as announcing a constitutional rule barring still photographic, radio, and television coverage in all cases and under all circumstances. [Since] we are satisfied that *Estes* did not announce a constitutional rule that all photographic or broadcast coverage of criminal trials is inherently a denial of due process, we turn to consideration, as a matter of first impression, of the appellants' suggestion that we now promulgate such a *per se* rule.

Any criminal case that generates a great deal of publicity presents some risks that the publicity may compromise the right of the defendant to a fair trial. Trial courts must be especially vigilant to guard against any impairment of the defendant's right to a verdict based solely upon the evidence and the relevant law. Over the years, courts have developed a range of curative devices to prevent publicity about a trial from infecting jury deliberations. See, e.g., *Nebraska Press Assn. v. Stuart.*

An absolute constitutional ban on broadcast coverage of trials cannot be justified simply because there is a danger that, in some cases, prejudicial broadcast accounts of pretrial and trial events may impair the ability of jurors to decide the issue of guilt or innocence uninfluenced by extraneous matter. The risk of juror prejudice in some cases does not justify an absolute ban on news coverage of trials by the printed media; so also the risk of such prejudice does not warrant an absolute constitutional ban on all broadcast coverage. A case attracts a high level of public attention because of its intrinsic interest to the public and the manner of reporting the event. The risk of juror prejudice is present in any publication of a trial, but the appropriate safeguard against such prejudice is the defendant's right to demonstrate that the media's coverage of his case—be it printed or broadcast—compromised the ability of the particular jury that heard the case to adjudicate fairly.

[T]he concurring opinions in *Estes* expressed concern that the very presence of media cameras and recording devices at a trial inescapably gives rise to an adverse psychological impact on the participants in the trial. This kind of general psychological prejudice, allegedly present whenever there is broadcast coverage of a trial, is different from the more particularized problem of prejudicial impact discussed earlier. If it could be demonstrated that the mere presence of photographic and recording equipment and the knowledge that the event would be broadcast invariably and uniformly affected the conduct of participants so as to impair fundamental fairness, our task would be simple; prohibition of broadcast coverage of trials would be required.

In confronting the difficult and sensitive question of the potential psychological prejudice associated with broadcast coverage of trials, we have been aided by *amici* briefs submitted by various state officers involved in law enforcement, the Conference of Chief Justices, and the Attorneys General of 17 States in support of continuing experimentation such as that embarked upon by Florida, and by the American College of Trial Lawyers, and various members of the defense bar representing essentially the views expressed by the concurring Justices in *Estes.*

Not unimportant to the position asserted by Florida and other states is the change in television technology since 1962, when Estes was tried. It is urged, and some empirical data are presented, that many of the negative factors found in *Estes* —cumbersome equipment, cables, distracting lighting, numerous camera technicians—are less substantial factors today than they were at that time.

It is also significant that safeguards have been built into the experimental programs in state courts, and into the Florida program, to avoid some of the most egregious problems envisioned by the six opinions in the *Estes* case. Florida admonishes its courts to take special pains to protect certain witnesses— for example, children, victims of sex crimes, some informants, and even the very timid witness or party—from the glare of publicity and the tensions of being "on camera."

The Florida guidelines place on trial judges positive obligations to be on guard to protect the fundamental right of the accused to a fair trial. The Florida Canon, being one of the few permitting broadcast coverage of criminal trials over the objection of the accused, raises problems not present in the rules of other states. Inherent in electronic coverage of a trial is the risk that the very awareness by the accused of the coverage and the contemplated broadcast may adversely affect the conduct of the participants and the fairness of the trial, yet leave no evidence of how the conduct or the trial's fairness was affected. Given this danger, it is significant that Florida requires that objections of the accused to coverage be heard and considered on the record by the trial court. In addition to providing a record for appellate review, a pre-trial hearing enables a defendant to advance the basis of his objection to broadcast coverage and allows the trial court to define the steps necessary to minimize or eliminate the risks of prejudice to the accused. Experiments such as the one presented here may well increase the number of appeals by adding a new basis for claims to reverse, but this is a risk Florida has chosen to take after preliminary experimentation. Here, the record does not indicate that appellants requested an evidentiary hearing to show adverse impact or injury. Nor does the record reveal anything more than generalized allegations of prejudice.

Nonetheless, it is clear that the general issue of the psychological impact of broadcast coverage upon the participants in a trial, and particularly upon the defendant, is still a subject of sharp debate—as the *amici* briefs of the American College of Trial Lawyers and others of the trial bar in opposition to Florida's experiment demonstrate. These *amici* state the view that the concerns expressed by the concurring opinions in *Estes,* have been borne out by actual experience. [Yet], [c]omprehensive empirical data are still not available—at least on some aspects of the problem. * * * Whatever may be the "mischievous potentialities [of broadcast coverage] for intruding upon the detached atmosphere which should always surround the judicial process," *Estes v. Texas,* at present no one has been able to present empirical data sufficient to establish that the mere presence of the broadcast media inherently has an adverse effect on that process.   *   *   *

Where, as here, we cannot say that a denial of due process automatically results from activity authorized by a state, the admonition of Justice Brandeis, dissenting in *New State Ice Co. v. Liebmann*, 285 U.S. 262 (1932), is relevant:

> "To stay experimentation in things social and economic is a grave responsibility.  Denial of the right to experiment may be fraught with serious consequences to the Nation.  It is one of the happy incidents of the federal system that a single courageous State may, if its citizens choose, serve as a laboratory; and try novel social and economic experiments without risk to the rest of the country.  This Court has the power to prevent an experiment.  We may strike down the statute which embodies it on the ground that, in our opinion, the measure is arbitrary, capricious, or unreasonable.  [But] in the exercise of this high power, we must be ever on our guard, lest we erect our prejudices into legal principles.  If we would guide by the light of reason, we must let our minds be bold."  (Footnote omitted.)

This concept of federalism, echoed by the states favoring Florida's experiment, must guide our decision.

*Amici* members of the defense bar vigorously contend that displaying the accused on television is in itself a denial of due process.  This was a source of concern to Chief Justice Warren and Justice Harlan in *Estes:* that coverage of select cases "singles out certain defendants and subjects them to trials under prejudicial conditions not experienced by others."  Selection of which trials, or parts of trials, to broadcast will inevitably be made not by judges but by the media, and will be governed by such factors as the nature of the crime and the status and position of the accused—or of the victim; the effect may be to titillate rather than to educate and inform.  The unanswered question is whether electronic coverage will bring public humiliation upon the accused with such randomness that it will evoke due process concerns by being "unusual in the same way that being struck by lighting" is "unusual."  *Furman v. Georgia*, 408 U.S. 238 (1972) (Stewart, J., concurring).  Societies and political systems, that, from time to time, have put on "Yankee Stadium" "show trials" tell more about the power of the state than about its concern for the decent administration of justice—with every citizen receiving the same kind of justice.

The concurring opinion of Chief Justice Warren joined by Justices Douglas and Goldberg in *Estes* can fairly be read as viewing the very broadcast of some trials as potentially a form of punishment in itself—a punishment before guilt.  This concern is far from trivial.  But, whether coverage of a few trials will, in practice, be the equivalent of a "Yankee Stadium" setting—which Justice Harlan likened to the public pillory long abandoned as a barbaric perversion of decent justice—must also await the continuing experimentation.

To say that the appellants have not demonstrated that broadcast coverage is inherently a denial of due process is not to say that the appellants were in fact accorded all of the protections of due process in their trial.  As noted earlier, a defendant has the right on review to show that the media's coverage of his case—printed or broadcast—compromised the ability of the jury to judge him fairly.  Alternatively, a defendant might show that broadcast coverage of his particular case had an adverse impact on the trial participants sufficient to constitute a denial of due process.  Neither showing was made in this case.

To demonstrate prejudice in a specific case a defendant must show something more than juror awareness that the trial is such as to attract the attention of broadcasters. *Murphy v. Florida.* No doubt the very presence of a camera in the courtroom made the jurors aware that the trial was thought to be of sufficient interest to the public to warrant coverage. Jurors, forbidden to watch all broadcasts, would have had no way of knowing that only fleeting seconds of the proceeding would be reproduced. But the appellants have not attempted to show with any specificity that the presence of cameras impaired the ability of the jurors to decide the case on only the evidence before them or that their trial was affected adversely by the impact on any of the participants of the presence of cameras and the prospect of broadcast.

Although not essential to our holding, we note that at *voir dire,* the jurors were asked if the presence of the camera would in any way compromise their ability to consider the case. Each answered that the camera would not prevent him or her from considering the case solely on the merits. The trial court instructed the jurors not to watch television accounts of the trial, and the appellants do not contend that any juror violated this instruction. The appellants have offered no evidence that any participant in this case was affected by the presence of cameras. In short, there is no showing that the trial was compromised by television coverage, as was the case in *Estes.*

[In] this setting, because this Court has no supervisory authority over state courts, our review is confined to whether there is a constitutional violation. We hold that the Constitution does not prohibit a state from experimenting with the program authorized by revised Canon 3A(7).

JUSTICE STEVENS took no part in the decision of this case.

JUSTICE STEWART, concurring in the result.

Although concurring in the judgment, I cannot join the opinion of the Court because I do not think the convictions in this case can be affirmed without overruling *Estes v. Texas.* I believe now, as I believed in dissent then, that *Estes* announced a *per se* rule that the Fourteenth Amendment "prohibits all television cameras from a state courtroom whenever a criminal trial is in progress." Accordingly, rather than join what seems to me a wholly unsuccessful effort to distinguish that decision, I would now flatly overrule it. * * *

JUSTICE WHITE, concurring in the judgment.

* * * Whether the decision in *Estes* is read broadly or narrowly, I agree with Justice Stewart that it should be overruled. I was in dissent in that case, and I remain unwilling to assume or conclude without more proof than has been marshaled to date that televising criminal trials is inherently prejudicial even when carried out under properly controlled conditions. * * * Although the Court's opinion today contends that it is consistent with *Estes,* I believe that it effectively eviscerates *Estes.* The Florida rule has no exception for the sensational or widely publicized case. Absent a showing of specific prejudice, *any* kind of case may be televised as long as the rule is otherwise complied with. Thus, even if the present case is precisely the kind of case referred to in Justice Harlan's concurrence in *Estes,* the Florida rule overrides the defendant's objections. The majority opinion does not find it necessary to deal with appellants' contention that because their case attracted substantial publicity, specific prejudice need not be shown. By affirming the judgment below, which sustained the rule, the majority indicates that not even the narrower reading of *Estes* will any longer be authoritative. * * *

## PRESS–ENTERPRISE CO. v. SUPERIOR COURT
### [PRESS–ENTERPRISE II]

478 U.S. 1, 106 S.Ct. 2735, 92 L.Ed.2d 1 (1986).

CHIEF JUSTICE BURGER delivered the opinion of the Court.

We granted certiorari to decide whether petitioner has a First Amendment right of access to transcripts of a preliminary hearing growing out of a criminal prosecution.

On December 23, 1981, the State of California filed a complaint in the Riverside County Municipal Court, charging Robert Diaz with 12 counts of murder and seeking the death penalty. The complaint alleged that Diaz, a nurse, murdered 12 patients by administering massive doses of the heart drug lidocaine. The preliminary hearing on the complaint commenced on July 6, 1982. Diaz moved to exclude the public from the proceedings under California Penal Code § 868, which requires such proceedings to be open unless "exclusion of the public is necessary in order to protect the defendant's right to a fair and impartial trial." The Magistrate granted the unopposed motion, finding that closure was necessary because the case had attracted national publicity and "only one side may get reported in the media."

The preliminary hearing continued for 41 days. Most of the testimony and the evidence presented by the State was medical and scientific; the remainder consisted of testimony by personnel who worked with Diaz on the shifts when the 12 patients died. Diaz did not introduce any evidence, but his counsel subjected most of the witnesses to vigorous cross-examination. Diaz was held to answer on all charges. At the conclusion of the hearing, petitioner Press–Enterprise Company asked that the transcript of the proceedings be released. The Magistrate refused and sealed the record.

On January 21, 1983, the State moved in Superior Court to have the transcripts of the preliminary hearing released to the public; petitioner later joined in support of the motion. Diaz opposed the motion, contending that release of the transcripts would result in prejudicial pretrial publicity. The Superior Court found that the information in the transcript was "as factual as it could be," and that the facts were neither "inflammatory" nor "exciting" but there was, nonetheless, "a reasonable likelihood that release of all or any part of the transcript might prejudice defendant's right to a fair and impartial trial."

Petitioner then filed a peremptory writ of mandate [seeking appellate review]. Meanwhile, Diaz waived his right to a jury trial and the Superior Court released the transcript. [The] California Supreme Court thereafter denied petitioner's peremptory writ of mandate, holding that there is no general First Amendment right of access to preliminary hearings. * * *

It is important to identify precisely what the California Supreme Court decided:

> "[W]e conclude that the magistrate shall close the preliminary hearing upon finding a reasonable likelihood of substantial prejudice which would impinge upon the right to a fair trial. Penal code section 868 makes clear that the primary right is the right to a fair trial and that the public's right of access must give way when there is conflict."

It is difficult to disagree in the abstract with that court's analysis balancing the defendant's right to a fair trial against the public right of access. It is also important to remember that these interests are not necessarily inconsistent. Plainly the defendant has a right to a fair trial but, as we have repeatedly recognized, one of the important means of assuring a fair trial is that the process be open to neutral observers.

The right to an open public trial is a shared right of the accused and the public, the common concern being the assurance of fairness. Only recently, in *Waller v. Georgia,* 467 U.S. 39 (1984), for example, we considered whether the defendant's Sixth Amendment right to an open trial prevented the closure of a suppression hearing over the defendant's objection. We noted that the First Amendment right of access would in most instances attach to such proceedings and that "the explicit Sixth Amendment right of the accused is no less protective of a public trial than the implicit First Amendment right of the press and public." When the defendant objects to the closure of a suppression hearing, therefore, the hearing must be open unless the party seeking to close the hearing advances an overriding interest that is likely to be prejudiced.

Here, unlike *Waller,* the right asserted is not the defendant's Sixth Amendment right to a public trial since the defendant requested a *closed* preliminary hearing. Instead, the right asserted here is that of the public under the First Amendment. The California Supreme Court concluded that the First Amendment was not implicated because the proceeding was not a criminal trial, but a preliminary hearing. However, the First Amendment question cannot be resolved solely on the label we give the event, i.e., "trial" or otherwise, particularly where the preliminary hearing functions much like a full scale trial.

In cases dealing with the claim of a First Amendment right of access to criminal proceedings, our decisions have emphasized two complementary considerations. First, because a " 'tradition of accessibility implies the favorable judgment of experience,' " we have considered whether the place and process has historically been open to the press and general public. * * * Second, [the] Court has traditionally considered whether public access plays a significant positive role in the functioning of the particular process in question. Although many governmental processes operate best under public scrutiny, it takes little imagination to recognize that there are some kinds of government operations that would be totally frustrated if conducted openly. A classic example is that "the proper functioning of our grand jury system depends upon the secrecy of grand jury proceedings." Other proceedings plainly require public access. In *Press–Enterprise I,* we summarized the holdings of prior cases, noting that openness in criminal trials, including the selection of jurors, "enhances both the basic fairness of the criminal trial and the appearance of fairness so essential to public confidence in the system."

These considerations of experience and logic are, of course, related, for history and experience shape the functioning of governmental processes. If the particular proceeding in question passes these tests of experience and logic, a qualified First Amendment right of public access attaches. But even when a right of access attaches, it is not absolute. *Globe Newspapers Co. v. Superior Court* [infra note 2]. While open criminal proceedings give assurances of fairness to both the public and the accused, there are some limited circumstances in which the right of the accused to a fair trial might be undermined by publicity.[2] In such cases, the trial court must determine whether the situation is

---

**2.** Similarly, the interests of those other than the accused may be implicated. The protection of victims of sex crimes from the trauma and embarrassment of public scrutiny may justify closing certain aspects of a criminal proceeding. See *Globe Newspaper Co. v. Superior Court,* 457 U.S. 596 (1982). [In *Globe*

*Newspaper,* the Court struck down as overbroad a state statute that required the trial court, at rape and sex offense trials involving complainants under age 18, to exclude the press and general public. The Court agreed that a state interest in "safeguarding the physical and psychological well-being of a misuch that the rights of the accused override the qualified First Amendment right of access.  In *Press-Enterprise I* we stated:

> "the presumption may be overcome only by an overriding interest based on findings that closure is essential to preserve higher values and is narrowly tailored to serve that interest.  The interest is to be articulated along with findings specific enough that a reviewing court can determine whether the closure order was properly entered."

The considerations that led the Court to apply the First Amendment right of access to criminal trials in *Richmond Newspapers* [and] the selection of jurors in *Press-Enterprise I* lead us to conclude that the right of access applies to preliminary hearings as conducted in California.

First, there has been a tradition of accessibility to preliminary hearings of the type conducted in California.  Although grand jury proceedings have traditionally been closed to the public and the accused, preliminary hearings conducted before neutral and detached magistrates have been open to the public.  Long ago in the celebrated trial of Aaron Burr for treason, for example, with Chief Justice Marshall sitting as trial judge, the probable cause hearing was held in the Hall of the House of Delegates in Virginia, the court room being too small to accommodate the crush of interested citizens.  From *Burr* until the present day, the near uniform practice of state and federal courts has been to conduct preliminary hearings in open court.  *  *  * Open preliminary hearings, therefore, have been accorded " 'the favorable judgment of experience.' "

The second question is whether public access to preliminary hearings as they are conducted in California plays a particularly significant positive role in the actual functioning of the process.  We have already determined [that] public access to criminal trials and the selection of jurors is essential to the proper functioning of the criminal justice system.  California preliminary hearings are sufficiently like a trial to justify the same conclusion.  [The] accused has the right to personally appear at the hearing, to be represented by counsel, to cross-examine hostile witnesses, to present exculpatory evidence, and to exclude illegally obtained evidence.  If the magistrate determines that probable cause exists, the accused is bound over for trial;  such a finding leads to a guilty plea in the majority of cases.

It is true that unlike a criminal trial, the California preliminary hearing cannot result in the conviction of the accused and the adjudication is before a magistrate or other judicial officer without a jury.  But these features, standing alone, do not make public access any less essential to the proper functioning of the proceedings in the overall criminal justice process.  Because of its extensive scope, the preliminary hearing is often the final and most important step in the criminal proceeding.  As the California Supreme Court stated, the preliminary hearing in many cases provides "the sole occasion for public observation of the criminal justice system."

Similarly, the absence of a jury, long recognized as "an inestimable safeguard against the corrupt or overzealous prosecutor and against the complaint, biased, or eccentric judge," makes the importance of public access to a preliminary hearing even more significant.  "People in an open society do not demand infallability from their institutions, but it is difficult for them to accept what they are prohibited from observing."  *Richmond Newspapers.*

nor" was a "compelling" interest, but found that it "does not justify a *mandatory*-closure rule, for it is clear that the circumstances of the particular case may affect the significance of the interest."]

Denying the transcripts of a 41-day preliminary hearing would frustrate what we have characterized as the "community therapeutic value" of openness. Criminal acts, especially certain violent crimes, provoke public concern, outrage, and hostility. "When the public is aware that the law is being enforced and the criminal justice system is functioning, an outlet is provided for these understandable reactions and emotions." *Press–Enterprise I.* * * *

We therefore conclude that the qualified First Amendment right of access to criminal proceedings applies to preliminary hearings as they are conducted in California. Since [that right] attaches to preliminary hearings in California [the] proceedings cannot be closed unless specific, on the record findings are made demonstrating that "closure is essential to preserve higher values and is narrowly tailored to serve that interest." *Press-Enterprise I.* If the interest asserted is the right of the accused to a fair trial, the preliminary hearing shall be closed only if specific findings are made demonstrating that first, there is a substantial probability that the defendant's right to a fair trial will be prejudiced by publicity that closure would prevent and, second, reasonable alternatives to closure cannot adequately protect the defendant's free trial rights.

The California Supreme Court, interpreting its access statute, concluded "that the magistrate shall close the preliminary hearing upon finding a reasonable likelihood of substantial prejudice." As the court itself acknowledged, the "reasonable likelihood" test places a lesser burden on the defendant than the "substantial probability" test which we hold is called for by the First Amendment. Moreover, the court failed to consider whether alternatives short of complete closure would have protected the interests of the accused.

In *Gannett Co., Inc. v. DePasquale*, 443 U.S. 368 (1979) [involving the closure of a pretrial suppression hearing in which evidence was taken to determine the voluntariness of defendant's confession], we observed that:

> "Publicity concerning pretrial suppression hearings such as the one involved in the present case poses special risks of unfairness. The whole purpose of such hearings is to screen out unreliable or illegally obtained evidence and insure that this evidence does not become known to the jury. Publicity concerning the proceedings at a pretrial hearing, however, could influence public opinion against a defendant and inform potential jurors of inculpatory information wholly inadmissible at the actual trial."

But this risk of prejudice does not automatically justify refusing public access to hearings on every motion to suppress. Through *voir dire,* cumbersome as it is in some circumstances, a court can identify those jurors whose prior knowledge of the case would disable them from rendering an impartial verdict. And even if closure were justified for the hearings on a motion to suppress, closure of an entire 41-day proceeding would rarely be warranted. The First Amendment right of access cannot be overcome by the conclusory assertion that publicity might deprive the defendant of that right. And any limitation " 'must be narrowly tailored to serve that interest.' " *Press-Enterprise I.* * * *

JUSTICE STEVENS, with whom JUSTICE REHNQUIST joins as to Part II, dissenting.

The constitutional question presented by this case is whether members of the public have a First Amendment right to insist upon access to the transcript of a preliminary hearing during the period before the public trial, even though the accused, the prosecutor, and the trial judge have all agreed to the sealing of the transcript in order to assure a fair trial. * * *

## I

Although perhaps obvious, it bears emphasis that the First Amendment right asserted by petitioner is not a right to publish or otherwise communicate information lawfully or unlawfully acquired.  That right, which lies at the core of the First Amendment and which erased the legacy of restraints on publication against which the drafters of that Amendment rebelled, may be overcome only by a governmental objective of the highest order attainable in no less intrusive way.  The First Amendment right asserted by petitioner in this case, in contrast, is not the right to publicize information in its possession, but the right to acquire access thereto.

I have long believed that a proper construction of the First Amendment embraces a right of access to information about the conduct of public affairs. * * * Neither our elected nor our appointed representatives may abridge the free flow of information simply to protect their own activities from public scrutiny.  An official policy of secrecy must be supported by some legitimate justification that serves the interest of the public office. * * *

But it has always been apparent that the freedom to obtain information that the Government has a legitimate interest in not disclosing, is far narrower than the freedom to disseminate information, which is "virtually absolute" in most contexts, *Richmond Newspapers, Inc. v. Virginia* (Stevens, J., concurring).  In this case, the risk of prejudice to the defendant's right to a fair trial is perfectly obvious.  For me, that risk is far more significant than the countervailing interest in publishing the transcript of the preliminary hearing sooner rather than later.  [The] interest in prompt publication—in my view—is no greater than the interest in prompt publication of grand jury transcripts.  [W]e have always recognized the legitimacy of the governmental interest in the secrecy of grand jury proceedings, and I am unpersuaded that the difference between such proceedings and the rather elaborate procedure for determining probable cause that California has adopted strengthens the First Amendment claim to access asserted in this case.

## II

[The Court] reaches the opposite conclusion by applying the "two complementary considerations," of "experience and logic."  In my view neither the Court's reasoning nor the result it reaches is supported by our precedents.

The historical evidence proffered in this case is far less probative than the evidence adduced in prior cases granting public access to criminal proceedings. In those cases, a common law tradition of openness at the time the First Amendment was ratified suggested an intention and expectation on the part of the Framers and ratifiers that those proceedings would remain presumptively open.  [In] this case, however, it is uncontroverted that a common law right of access did not inhere in preliminary proceedings at the time the First Amendment was adopted, and that the Framers and ratifiers of that provision could not have intended such proceedings to remain open.

[In] the final analysis, the Court's lengthy historical disquisition demonstrates only that in many States preliminary proceedings are generally open to the public.  In other States, numbering California * * * among them, such proceedings have been closed.  [That California's] particular approach has been adopted in few other States does not render [its] choice unconstitutional." * * *

If the Court's historical evidence proves too little, the "value of openness," on which it relies proves too much, for this measure would open to public scrutiny far more than preliminary hearings "as they are conducted in California" (a comforting phrase invoked by the Court in one form or another more than 8 times in its opinion). In brief, the Court's rationale for opening the "California preliminary hearing" is that it "is often the final and most important step in the criminal proceeding"; that it provides "'the sole occasion for public observation of the criminal justice system'"; that it lacks the protective presence of a jury; and that closure denies an outlet for community catharsis. The obvious defect in the Court's approach is that its reasoning applies to the traditionally secret grand jury with as much force as it applies to California preliminary hearings. A grand jury indictment is just as likely to be the "final step" in a criminal proceeding and the "sole occasion" for public scrutiny as is a preliminary hearing. Moreover, many critics of the grand jury maintain that the grand jury protects the accused less well than does a legally-knowledgable judge who personally presides over a preliminary hearing. * * * Finally, closure of grand juries denies an outlet for community rage. When the Court's explanatory veneer is stripped away, what emerges is the reality that the California preliminary hearing is functionally identical to the traditional grand jury. [Yet] [t]his Court has previously described grand jury secrecy as "indispensable," and has remarked that "the proper functioning of our grand jury system depends upon the secrecy of grand jury proceedings."

In fact, the logic of the Court's access right extends even beyond the confines of the criminal justice system to encompass proceedings held on the civil side of the docket as well. * * * Despite the Court's valiant attempt to limit the logic of its holding, the *ratio decidendi* of today's decision knows no bounds. [The] presence of a legitimate reason for closure in this case requires an affirmance. The constitutionally-grounded fair trial interests of the accused if he is bound over for trial, and the reputational interests of the accused if he is not, provide a substantial reason for delaying access to the transcript for at least the short time before trial. * * *

# Chapter 17

# THE ROLE OF COUNSEL

Chapter Five looked at where and when the defendant has a constitutional right to the assistance of counsel. This chapter looks at the level and range of the assistance that counsel must provide to fulfill that constitutional right of defendant. The first case, *Strickland v. Washington,* is the seminal ruling on the standards to be applied in determining whether defendant did in fact receive the "effective assistance" of counsel guaranteed by the Sixth Amendment. *Nix v. Whiteside,* the next case, applies the *Strickland* standards in the context of an age-old problem facing defense counsel, the client who desires to present perjured testimony.

The competency standard set forth in *Strickland* hardly requires perfection, and situations will arise in which counsel met the *Strickland* standard but nonetheless failed, for one reason or another, to raise at trial or on appeal a legal objection that could well have changed the outcome of the case. The question is then presented as to whether counsel's omission should be binding on the client—that is, whether counsel failure to raise the issue should mean that defendant cannot present it in a later challenge to his conviction. *Murray v. Carrier,* the third case in this section, considers that issue. It presents the question of whether a constitutional objection that competent counsel failed to raise properly in state proceedings (and state courts therefore refused to consider) is nonetheless open to review on the state prisoner's application for a federal writ of habeas corpus.[a]

A brief review of the standards that otherwise apply to judicial consideration of legal claims not properly raised might be helpful in understanding *Murray.* On a direct appeal of a conviction, appellate courts ordinarily will not consider legal issues unless they were properly raised both at trial and on appeal. This raise-or-waive position is based on a variety of considerations, including the need for orderly procedure, the desirability of binding parties to their tactical decisions, the inappropriateness of considering issues not fully developed factually at the trial level, and the desirability of avoiding unnecessary retrials (by requiring the defense to raise its objections as early as possible in the process, so curative action can be taken either before the trial starts, or at least before it comes to an end). Appellate courts do, however, make an exception for "plain error," that is,

a. The federal writ ordinarily is available to state prisoners to collaterally attack a conviction on most, but not all, federal constitutional grounds. See Ch. 1 at § 2, at step 18. Most notably, even where properly raised at trial, a claim that a conviction is based on the admission of evidence in violation of the Fourth Amendment (see Ch. 3) is not cognizable on federal habeas corpus if the "State has provided for full and fair litigation of * * * [that] Fourth Amendment claim." *Stone v. Powell,* 428 U.S. 465 (1976).

588

error that is both apparent on the face of the trial record and that clearly had an adverse impact upon the substantial rights of the defendant. Many states also recognize another exception to the raise-or-waive rule in permitting a collateral challenge to a conviction (e.g., *via* writ of habeas corpus) when that challenge goes to the very power of the state to prosecute. Such a challenge will be recognized even though counsel had the opportunity, but failed to present the particular objection at trial or on appeal. This exception, however, applies to a very limited range of objections, such as the unconstitutionality of the statute under which the prosecution was brought or a double jeopardy bar to the prosecution.[b] *Murray* assesses the extent to which federal habeas corpus will provide a still broader avenue for raising collateral issues that otherwise would be lost under the raise-or-waive rule.

As the Court also noted in *Strickland*, the possibility that counsel acted under the burden of a "conflict of interest" complicates a post-trial determination as to whether counsel rendered effective representation. This naturally leads to the question as to whether a trial court, upon determining prior to trial that such a conflict may or does exist, can insist that defendant proceed with another counsel who clearly will not be so burdened. *Wheat v. United States* considers that issue in its most troublesome context, where the conflict is "potential," rather than currently operating (i.e., "actual"), and the defendant is willing to waive his right to conflict-free counsel in order to be represented by counsel of his choice.

The last case in the chapter, *Faretta v. California* raises the question of whether the defendant has a constitutional right to refuse the assistance of counsel and proceed *pro se* at trial (i.e., represent himself). Defendants not infrequently will waive counsel when they wish to enter a guilty plea, but requests to proceed *pro se* at trial are fairly rare. These requests tend to arise in two somewhat different situations. First, there are the requests of defendants who decide at the outset that they would prefer to represent themselves. That choice may be based on a variety of reasons, including a general distrust of attorneys, a belief that an attorney's assistance will not be worth the expense (where defendant is not indigent), or a belief that self-representation will provide a tactical advantage (as where a codefendant in a joint trial will be represented by counsel and defendant believes that self-representation will permit him to present himself in a more sympathetic light, while still gaining the advantage of the challenge to the prosecution's case presented by codefendant's counsel). Second, there are the requests of defendants who would prefer representation by

---

**b.** This exception commonly applies to convictions following a guilty plea as well as convictions following a trial. In general, "a voluntary and intelligent plea of guilty made by an accused person, who has been advised by competent counsel, may not be collaterally attacked" by reference to procedural errors that occurred prior to the entry of the plea. *Mabry v. Johnson,* 467 U.S. 504 (1984). This is true even though such errors were constitutional violations. See e.g., *McMann v. Richardson,* 397 U.S. 759 (1970) (plea could not be challenged on the basis of an underlying coerced confession). Where a defendant chooses to take "the benefit, if any, of a guilty plea," he or she "accepts the inherent risk that good-faith evaluations of a reasonably competent attorney will turn out to be mistaken either as to the facts or as to what a court's judgment

might be on given facts." However, a constitutional claim will be open to review, notwithstanding the guilty plea, where it rests on a "right not to be hailed into court at all" as to the offense to which defendant pleaded. *Blackledge v. Perry,* 417 U.S. 21 (1974) (plea did not bar collateral challenge where the prosecution acted vindictively in bringing the charge, see Ch. 10, § 2). While a voluntary guilty plea admits "factual guilt" and thereby "renders irrelevant those constitutional violations not logically inconsistent with the valid establishment of factual guilt," that is not the case for a claim that argues "that the State may not convict petitioner no matter how validly his factual guilt is established." *Menna v. New York,* 423 U.S. 61 (1975) (guilty plea did not preclude collateral challenge based on double jeopardy bar to the prosecution).

counsel but are dissatisfied with their current counsel. Very often these defendants are not in a position where they can obtain alternative counsel and they would prefer continuing *pro se* to continuing with their current counsel.[c]

# STRICKLAND v. WASHINGTON

466 U.S. 668, 104 S.Ct. 2052, 80 L.Ed.2d 674 (1984).

JUSTICE O'CONNOR delivered the opinion of the Court.

This case requires us to consider the proper standards for judging a criminal defendant's contention that the Constitution requires a conviction or death sentence to be set aside because counsel's assistance at the trial or sentencing was ineffective.

During a 10-day period in September 1976, respondent planned and committed three groups of crimes, which included three brutal stabbing murders, torture, kidnaping, severe assaults, attempted murders, attempted extortion, and theft. After his two accomplices were arrested, respondent surrendered to police and voluntarily gave a lengthy statement confessing to the third of the criminal episodes. The State of Florida indicted respondent for kidnaping and murder and appointed an experienced criminal lawyer to represent him.

Counsel actively pursued pretrial motions and discovery. He cut his efforts short, however, and he experienced a sense of hopelessness about the case, when he learned that, against his specific advice, respondent had also confessed to the first two murders. By the date set for trial, respondent was subject to indictment for three counts of first-degree murder and multiple counts of robbery, kidnaping for ransom, breaking and entering and assault, attempted murder, and conspiracy to commit robbery. Respondent waived his right to a jury trial, again acting against counsel's advice, and pleaded guilty to all charges, including the three capital murder charges.

In the plea colloquy, respondent told the trial judge that, although he had committed a string of burglaries, he had no significant prior criminal record and that at the time of his criminal spree he was under extreme stress caused by his inability to support his family. He also stated, however, that he accepted responsibility for the crimes. The trial judge told respondent that he had "a

c. Defendants with court appointed counsel will find it difficult to obtain alternative counsel because courts commonly will not replace appointed counsel unless defendant can establish a complete breakdown in communications with counsel or a failure of counsel to provide effective representation. The Supreme Court has noted in this regard that the Sixth Amendment guarantees only competent representation, not a relationship with counsel that defendant views as personally satisfactory. *Morris v. Slappy*, 461 U.S. 1 (1983) (where original public defender was hospitalized, substitute announced that he was prepared to go to trial, and state trial court then refused to grant a continuance until the original defender could return, federal habeas court erred in reversing defendant's conviction; it could not be maintained that defendant was entitled to "a meaningful attorney-client relationship" rather than simply the effective assistance of counsel).

Where counsel is retained, defendant has more leeway in replacing current counsel with another attorney more to his liking, but he may face difficulties where such action would require a delay in the trial. The trial court in such a situation must balance the defendant's interest in having counsel of his choice against the public's interest in prompt and efficient administration of justice. As the Supreme Court has noted: "There are no mechanical tests for deciding when a denial of a continuance is so arbitrary as to violate * * * [defendant's constitutional right to counsel]. The answer must be found in the circumstances present in every case." *Ungar v. Sarafite*, 376 U.S. 575 (1964) (rejecting a constitutional challenge to a continuance denial that resulted in the withdrawal of defense counsel and self-representation by defendant, who was a lawyer, and citing such factors as defendant's delay in seeking the continuance, ample time for counsel's preparation in light of the evidence and clearly identified issues, and the need to give deference to the trial judge's judgment). Consider also *Wheat v. United States*, infra.

great deal of respect for people who are willing to step forward and admit their responsibility" but that he was making no statement at all about his likely sentencing decision.

Counsel advised respondent to invoke his right under Florida law to an advisory jury at his capital sentencing hearing. Respondent rejected the advice and waived the right. He chose instead to be sentenced by the trial judge without a jury recommendation.

In preparing for the sentencing hearing, counsel spoke with respondent about his background. He also spoke on the telephone with respondent's wife and mother, though he did not follow up on the one unsuccessful effort to meet with them. He did not otherwise seek out character witnesses for respondent. Nor did he request a psychiatric examination, since his conversations with his client gave no indication that respondent had psychological problems.

Counsel decided not to present and hence not to look further for evidence concerning respondent's character and emotional state. That decision reflected trial counsel's sense of hopelessness about overcoming the evidentiary effect of respondent's confessions to the gruesome crimes. It also reflected the judgment that it was advisable to rely on the plea colloquy for evidence about respondent's background and about his claim of emotional stress: the plea colloquy communicated sufficient information about these subjects, and by forgoing the opportunity to present new evidence on these subjects, counsel prevented the State from cross-examining respondent on his claim and from putting on psychiatric evidence of its own.

Counsel also excluded from the sentencing hearing other evidence he thought was potentially damaging. He successfully moved to exclude respondent's "rap sheet." Because he judged that a presentence report might prove more detrimental than helpful, as it would have included respondent's criminal history and thereby would have undermined the claim of no significant history of criminal activity, he did not request that one be prepared.

At the sentencing hearing, counsel's strategy was based primarily on the trial judge's remarks at the plea colloquy as well as on his reputation as a sentencing judge who thought it important for a convicted defendant to own up to his crime. Counsel argued that respondent's remorse and acceptance of responsibility justified sparing him from the death penalty. Counsel also argued that respondent had no history of criminal activity and that respondent committed the crimes under extreme mental or emotional disturbance, thus coming within the statutory list of mitigating circumstances. He further argued that respondent should be spared death because he had surrendered, confessed, and offered to testify against a codefendant and because respondent was fundamentally a good person who had briefly gone badly wrong in extremely stressful circumstances. The State put on evidence and witnesses largely for the purpose of describing the details of the crimes. Counsel did not cross-examine the medical experts who testified about the manner of death of respondent's victims.

\*　\*　\*

[T]he trial judge found numerous aggravating circumstances and no (or a single comparatively insignificant) mitigating circumstance. With respect to each of the three convictions for capital murder, the trial judge concluded: "A careful consideration of all matters presented to the court impels the conclusion that there are insufficient mitigating circumstances \*　\*　\* to outweigh the aggravating circumstances." He therefore sentenced respondent to death on each of the three counts of murder and to prison terms for the other crimes.

The Florida Supreme Court upheld the convictions and sentences on direct appeal.

Respondent subsequently sought collateral relief in state court on numerous grounds, among them that counsel had rendered ineffective assistance at the sentencing proceeding. Respondent challenged counsel's assistance in six respects. He asserted that counsel was ineffective because he failed to move for a continuance to prepare for sentencing, to request a psychiatric report, to investigate and present character witnesses, to seek a presentence investigation report, to present meaningful arguments to the sentencing judge, and to investigate the medical examiner's reports or cross-examine the medical experts. In support of the claim, respondent submitted 14 affidavits from friends, neighbors, and relatives stating that they would have testified if asked to do so. He also submitted one psychiatric report and one psychological report stating that respondent, though not under the influence of extreme mental or emotional disturbance, was "chronically frustrated and depressed because of his economic dilemma" at the time of his crimes.

The trial court denied relief without an evidentiary hearing, finding that the record evidence conclusively showed that the ineffectiveness claim was meritless. * * * Applying the standard for ineffectiveness claims articulated by the Florida Supreme Court * * *, the trial court concluded that respondent had not shown that counsel's assistance reflected any substantial and serious deficiency measurably below that of competent counsel that was likely to have affected the outcome of the sentencing proceeding. * * *

Respondent next filed a petition for a writ of habeas corpus in the United States District Court * * *. [After an evidentiary hearing,] the District Court disputed none of the state court factual findings concerning trial counsel's assistance and made findings of its own that are consistent with the state court findings. * * * [T]he District Court concluded that, although trial counsel made errors in judgment in failing to investigate nonstatutory mitigating evidence further than he did, no prejudice to respondent's sentence resulted from any such error in judgment. On appeal, * * * the Court of Appeals developed its own framework for analyzing ineffective assistance claims and reversed the judgment of the District Court and remanded the case for new factfinding under the newly announced standard. * * *

[P]utting guilty-plea cases to one side, [the Court of Appeals] attempted to classify cases presenting issues concerning the scope of the duty to investigate before proceeding to trial. If there is only one plausible line of defense, the court concluded, counsel must conduct a "reasonably substantial investigation" into that line of defense, since there can be no strategic choice that renders such an investigation unnecessary. * * * If there is more than one plausible line of defense, the court held, counsel should ideally investigate each line substantially before making a strategic choice about which lines to rely on at trial. * * * If counsel does not conduct a substantial investigation into each of several plausible lines of defense, assistance may nonetheless be effective. Counsel may not exclude certain lines of defense for other than strategic reasons. Limitations of time and money, however, may force early strategic choices, often based solely on conversations with the defendant and a review of the prosecution's evidence. * * * Among the factors relevant to deciding whether particular strategic choices are reasonable are the experience of the attorney, the inconsistency of unpursued and pursued lines of defense, and the potential for prejudice from taking an unpursued line of defense. * * * Petitioners, who are officials of the

State of Florida, filed a petition for a writ of certiorari seeking review of the decision of the Court of Appeals. * * *

Because of the vital importance of counsel's assistance, this Court has held that, with certain exceptions, a person accused of a federal or state crime has the right to have counsel appointed if retained counsel cannot be obtained. See *Argersinger v. Hamlin* [Ch. 5, § 1]; *Gideon v. Wainwright* [Ch. 5, § 1]. That a person who happens to be a lawyer is present at trial alongside the accused, however, is not enough to satisfy the constitutional command. The Sixth Amendment recognizes the right to the assistance of counsel because it envisions counsel's playing a role that is critical to the ability of the adversarial system to produce just results. An accused is entitled to be assisted by an attorney, whether retained or appointed, who plays the role necessary to ensure that the trial is fair.

For that reason, the Court has recognized that "the right to counsel is the right to the effective assistance of counsel." *McMann v. Richardson*, 397 U.S. 759 (1970). Government violates the right to effective assistance when it interferes in certain ways with the ability of counsel to make independent decisions about how to conduct the defense. See, e.g., *Geders v. United States*, 425 U.S. 80 (1976) (bar on attorney-client consultation during overnight recess); *Herring v. New York*, 422 U.S. 853 (1975) (bar on summation at bench trial); *Brooks v. Tennessee*, 406 U.S. 605 (1972) (requirement that defendant be first defense witness); *Ferguson v. Georgia*, 365 U.S. 570 (1961) (bar on direct examination of defendant). Counsel, however, can also deprive a defendant of the right to effective assistance, simply by failing to render "adequate legal assistance," *Cuyler v. Sullivan*, 446 U.S. 335 (1980) (actual conflict of interest adversely affecting lawyer's performance renders assistance ineffective).

The Court has not elaborated on the meaning of the constitutional requirement of effective assistance in the latter class of cases—that is, those presenting claims of "actual ineffectiveness." In giving meaning to the requirement, however, we must take its purpose—to ensure a fair trial—as the guide. The benchmark for judging any claim of ineffectiveness must be whether counsel's conduct so undermined the proper functioning of the adversarial process that the trial cannot be relied on as having produced a just result.

The same principle applies to a capital sentencing proceeding such as that provided by Florida law. We need not consider the role of counsel in an ordinary sentencing, which may involve informal proceedings and standardless discretion in the sentencer, and hence may require a different approach to the definition of constitutionally effective assistance. A capital sentencing proceeding like the one involved in this case, however, is sufficiently like a trial in its adversarial format and in the existence of standards for decision, that counsel's role in the proceeding is comparable to counsel's role at trial—to ensure that the adversarial testing process works to produce a just result under the standards governing decision. For purposes of describing counsel's duties, therefore, Florida's capital sentencing proceeding need not be distinguished from an ordinary trial.

A convicted defendant's claim that counsel's assistance was so defective as to require reversal of a conviction or death sentence has two components. First, the defendant must show that counsel's performance was deficient. This requires showing that counsel made errors so serious that counsel was not functioning as the "counsel" guaranteed the defendant by the Sixth Amendment. Second, the defendant must show that the deficient performance prejudiced the defense. This requires showing that counsel's errors were so serious as to deprive the defendant of a fair trial, a trial whose result is reliable. Unless a defendant makes both showings, it cannot be said that the conviction or death sentence resulted from a breakdown in the adversary process that renders the result unreliable.

As all the Federal Courts of Appeals have now held, the proper standard for attorney performance is that of reasonably effective assistance. The Court indirectly recognized as much when it stated in *McMann v. Richardson* that a guilty plea cannot be attacked as based on inadequate legal advice unless counsel was not "a reasonably competent attorney" and the advice was not "within the range of competence demanded of attorneys in criminal cases." When a convicted defendant complains of the ineffectiveness of counsel's assistance, the defendant must show that counsel's representation fell below an objective standard of reasonableness.

More specific guidelines are not appropriate. The Sixth Amendment refers simply to "counsel," not specifying particular requirements of effective assistance. It relies instead on the legal profession's maintenance of standards sufficient to justify the law's presumption that counsel will fulfill the role in the adversary process that the Amendment envisions. The proper measure of attorney performance remains simply reasonableness under prevailing professional norms.

Representation of a criminal defendant entails certain basic duties. Counsel's function is to assist the defendant, and hence counsel owes the client a duty of loyalty, a duty to avoid conflicts of interest. From counsel's function as assistant to the defendant derive the overarching duty to advocate the defendant's cause and the more particular duties to consult with the defendant on important decisions and to keep the defendant informed of important developments in the course of the prosecution. Counsel also has a duty to bring to bear such skill and knowledge as will render the trial a reliable adversarial testing process.

These basic duties neither exhaustively define the obligations of counsel nor form a checklist for judicial evaluation of attorney performance. In any case presenting an ineffectiveness claim, the performance inquiry must be whether counsel's assistance was reasonable considering all the circumstances. Prevailing norms of practice as reflected in American Bar Association standards and the like are guides to determining what is reasonable, but they are only guides. No particular set of detailed rules for counsel's conduct can satisfactorily take account of the variety of circumstances faced by defense counsel or the range of legitimate decisions regarding how best to represent a criminal defendant. Any such set of rules would interfere with the constitutionally protected independence of counsel and restrict the wide latitude counsel must have in making tactical decisions. Indeed, the existence of detailed guidelines for representation could distract counsel from the overriding mission of vigorous advocacy of the defendant's cause. Moreover, the purpose of the effective assistance guarantee of the Sixth Amendment is not to improve the quality of legal representation, although that is a goal of considerable importance to the legal system. The purpose is simply to ensure that criminal defendants receive a fair trial.

Judicial scrutiny of counsel's performance must be highly deferential. It is all too tempting for a defendant to second-guess counsel's assistance after conviction or adverse sentence, and it is all too easy for a court, examining counsel's defense after it has proved unsuccessful, to conclude that a particular act or omission of counsel was unreasonable. A fair assessment of attorney performance requires that every effort be made to eliminate the distorting effects of hindsight, to reconstruct the circumstances of counsel's challenged conduct, and to evaluate the conduct from counsel's perspective at the time. Because of the difficulties inherent in making the evaluation, a court must indulge a strong presumption that counsel's conduct falls within the wide range of reasonable professional assistance; that is, the defendant must overcome the presumption that, under the circumstances, the challenged action "might be considered sound trial strategy." There are countless ways to provide effective assistance in any given case. Even the best criminal defense attorneys would not defend a particular client in the same way.

The availability of intrusive post-trial inquiry into attorney performance or of detailed guidelines for its evaluation would encourage the proliferation of ineffectiveness challenges. Criminal trials resolved unfavorably to the defendant would increasingly come to be followed by a second trial, this one of counsel's unsuccessful defense. Counsel's performance and even willingness to serve could be adversely affected. Intensive scrutiny of counsel and rigid requirements for acceptable assistance could dampen the ardor and impair the independence of defense counsel, discourage the acceptance of assigned cases, and undermine the trust between attorney and client.

Thus, a court deciding an actual ineffectiveness claim must judge the reasonableness of counsel's challenged conduct on the facts of the particular case, viewed as of the time of counsel's conduct. A convicted defendant making a claim of ineffective assistance must identify the acts or omissions of counsel that are alleged not to have been the result of reasonable professional judgment. The court must then determine whether, in light of all the circumstances, the identified acts or omissions were outside the wide range of professionally competent assistance. In making that determination, the court should keep in mind that counsel's function, as elaborated in prevailing professional norms, is to make the adversarial testing process work in the particular case. At the same time, the court should recognize that counsel is strongly presumed to have rendered adequate assistance and made all significant decisions in the exercise of reasonable professional judgment.

These standards require no special amplification in order to define counsel's duty to investigate, the duty at issue in this case. As the Court of Appeals concluded, strategic choices made after thorough investigation of law and facts relevant to plausible options are virtually unchallengeable; and strategic choices made after less than complete investigation are reasonable precisely to the extent that reasonable professional judgments support the limitations on investigation. In other words, counsel has a duty to make reasonable investigations or to make a reasonable decision that makes particular investigations unnecessary. In any ineffectiveness case, a particular decision not to investigate must be directly assessed for reasonableness in all the circumstances, applying a heavy measure of deference to counsel's judgments.

The reasonableness of counsel's actions may be determined or substantially influenced by the defendant's own statements or actions. Counsel's actions are usually based, quite properly, on informed strategic choices made by the defendant and on information supplied by the defendant. In particular, what investigation decisions are reasonable depends critically on such information. For example, when the facts that support a certain potential line of defense are generally known to counsel because of what the defendant has said, the need for further investigation may be considerably diminished or eliminated altogether. And when a defendant has given counsel reason to believe that pursuing certain investigations would be fruitless or even harmful, counsel's failure to pursue those investigations may not later be challenged as unreasonable. In short, inquiry into counsel's conversations with the defendant may be critical to a proper assessment of counsel's investigation decisions, just as it may be critical to a proper assessment of counsel's other litigation decisions.

An error by counsel, even if professionally unreasonable, does not warrant setting aside the judgment of a criminal proceeding if the error had no effect on the judgment. The purpose of the Sixth Amendment guarantee of counsel is to ensure that a defendant has the assistance necessary to justify reliance on the outcome of the proceeding. Accordingly, any deficiencies in counsel's performance must be prejudicial to the defense in order to constitute ineffective assistance under the Constitution.

In certain Sixth Amendment contexts, prejudice is presumed. Actual or constructive denial of the assistance of counsel altogether is legally presumed to result in prejudice. So are various kinds of state interference with counsel's assistance. See *United States v. Cronic*, 466 U.S. 648 (1984).[a] Prejudice in these circumstances is so likely that case-by-case inquiry into prejudice is not worth the cost. Moreover, such circumstances involve impairments of the Sixth Amendment right that are easy to identify and, for that reason and because the prosecution is directly responsible, easy for the government to prevent.

One type of actual ineffectiveness claim warrants a similar, though more limited, presumption of prejudice. In *Cuyler v. Sullivan*, 446 U.S. 335 (1980), the Court held that prejudice is presumed when counsel is burdened by an actual conflict of interest. In those circumstances, counsel breaches the duty of loyalty, perhaps the most basic of counsel's duties. Moreover, it is difficult to measure the precise effect on the defense of representation corrupted by conflicting interests. Given the obligation of counsel to avoid conflicts of interest and the ability of trial courts to make early inquiry in certain situations likely to give rise to conflicts, see, e.g., Fed.Rule Crim.Proc. 44(c), it is reasonable for the criminal justice system to maintain a fairly rigid rule of presumed prejudice for

---

**a.** The reference here is to a discussion in *Cronic* of the *Geders, Herring, Brooks,* and *Ferguson* cases, also described previously in Justice O'Connor's opinion. *Cronic* characterized these cases as involving situations in which counsel was "prevented from assisting the accused during a critical stage of the proceeding" and therefore "no specific showing of prejudice was required." *Cronic* rejected a defense contention that a similar approach should be taken in an alleged "defective" appointment of counsel case. The lower court in *Cronic*, without referring to any specific error or inadequacy in counsel's performance, had found that counsel could not have been able to "discharge his duties" in light of five factors: "(1) [T]he [limited] time afforded for investigation and preparation; (2) the [in]experience of counsel; (3) the gravity of the charge; (4) the complexity of possible defenses; and (5) the [limited] accessibility of witnesses to counsel." The *Cronic* majority acknowledged that these five factors were "relevant to an evaluation of a lawyer's ineffectiveness in a particular case," but concluded that "neither separately nor in combination [did] they provide a basis for concluding that competent counsel was not able to provide * * * the guiding hand that the Constitution guarantees." The Court held

that a determination of competency in this case must rest on an examination of the actual performance of counsel in light of the circumstances of the case.

The *Cronic* Court did note, however, that there could be extreme circumstances in which the appointment process was so deficient as to be treated as an automatic violation of the Sixth Amendment in much the same fashion as a denial of counsel or a state interference at a critical stage. There may be "occasions when, although counsel is available to assist the accused during trial, the likelihood that any lawyer, even a fully competent one, could provide effective assistance is so small that a presumption of prejudice is appropriate without inquiry into the actual conduct of the trial." Offered as an illustration of such a case was *Powell v. Alabama*, 287 U.S. 45 (1932) [see Ch. 5, § 1]. The trial court there had utilized such a haphazard process of appointment—ordering admittedly unprepared outstate counsel to proceed with whatever help the local bar, appointed en masse, might provide—that there was no need to look at the actual performance of counsel in determining that defendant's constitutional rights had been violated.

conflicts of interest. Even so, the rule is not quite the *per se* rule of prejudice that exists for the Sixth Amendment claims mentioned above. Prejudice is presumed only if the defendant demonstrates that counsel "actively represented conflicting interests" and that "an actual conflict of interest adversely affected his lawyer's performance." 446 U.S. 335 *Cuyler v. Sullivan.*[b]

Conflict of interest claims aside, actual ineffectiveness claims alleging a deficiency in attorney performance are subject to a general requirement that the defendant affirmatively prove prejudice. The government is not responsible for, and hence not able to prevent, attorney errors that will result in reversal of a conviction or sentence. Attorney errors come in an infinite variety and are as likely to be utterly harmless in a particular case as they are to be prejudicial. They cannot be classified according to likelihood of causing prejudice. Nor can they be defined with sufficient precision to inform defense attorneys correctly just what conduct to avoid. Representation is an art, and an act or omission that is unprofessional in one case may be sound or even brilliant in another. Even if a defendant shows that particular errors of counsel were unreasonable, therefore, the defendant must show that they actually had an adverse effect on the defense.   *   *   *

[T]he appropriate test for prejudice finds its roots in the test for materiality of exculpatory information not disclosed to the defense by the prosecution, *United States v. Agurs,* 427 U.S. 97 (1976) and in the test for materiality of testimony made unavailable to the defense by Government deportation of a witness, *United States v. Valenzuela–Bernal,* 458 U.S. 858 (1982).[c] The defendant must show that there is a reasonable probability that, but for counsel's unprofessional errors, the result of the proceeding would have been different. A reasonable probability is a probability sufficient to undermine confidence in the outcome.

In making the determination whether the specified errors resulted in the required prejudice, a court should presume, absent challenge to the judgment on grounds of evidentiary insufficiency, that the judge or jury acted according to law. An assessment of the likelihood of a result more favorable to the defendant must exclude the possibility of arbitrariness, whimsy, caprice, "nullification," and the like. A defendant has no entitlement to the luck of a lawless decisionmaker, even if a lawless decision cannot be reviewed. The assessment of prejudice should proceed on the assumption that the decisionmaker is reasonably, conscientiously, and impartially applying the standards that govern the decision. It should not depend on the idiosyncracies of the particular decisionmaker, such as unusual propensities toward harshness or leniency. Although these factors may actually have entered into counsel's selection of strategies and, to that limited extent, may thus affect the performance inquiry, they are irrelevant to the prejudice inquiry. Thus, evidence about the actual process of decision, if not part of the record of the proceeding under review, and evidence about, for example, a particular judge's sentencing practices, should not be considered in the prejudice determination.

The governing legal standard plays a critical role in defining the question to be asked in assessing the prejudice from counsel's errors. When a defendant challenges a conviction, the question is whether there is a reasonable probability that, absent the errors, the factfinder would have had a reasonable doubt respecting guilt. When a defendant challenges a death sentence such as the one

**b.** See also note a to *Wheat v. United States,* 108 S.Ct. 1692, infra.

**c.** The materiality standard applicable in these situations is further discussed in *Bagley,* 473 U.S. 667, Ch. 13 supra.

at issue in this case, the question is whether there is a reasonable probability that, absent the errors, the sentencer—including an appellate court, to the extent it independently reweighs the evidence—would have concluded that the balance of aggravating and mitigating circumstances did not warrant death.

In making this determination, a court hearing an ineffectiveness claim must consider the totality of the evidence before the judge or jury. Some of the factual findings will have been unaffected by the errors, and factual findings that were affected will have been affected in different ways. Some errors will have had a pervasive effect on the inferences to be drawn from the evidence, altering the entire evidentiary picture, and some will have had an isolated, trivial effect. Moreover, a verdict or conclusion only weakly supported by the record is more likely to have been affected by errors than one with overwhelming record support. Taking the unaffected findings as a given, and taking due account of the effect of the errors on the remaining findings, a court making the prejudice inquiry must ask if the defendant has met the burden of showing that the decision reached would reasonably likely have been different absent the errors.

A number of practical considerations are important for the application of the standards we have outlined. Most important, in adjudicating a claim of actual ineffectiveness of counsel, a court should keep in mind that the principles we have stated do not establish mechanical rules. Although those principles should guide the process of decision, the ultimate focus of inquiry must be on the fundamental fairness of the proceeding whose result is being challenged. In every case the court should be concerned with whether, despite the strong presumption of reliability, the result of the particular proceeding is unreliable because of a breakdown in the adversarial process that our system counts on to produce just results. * * *

Although we have discussed the performance component of an ineffectiveness claim prior to the prejudice component, there is no reason for a court deciding an ineffective assistance claim to approach the inquiry in the same order or even to address both components of the inquiry if the defendant makes an insufficient showing on one. In particular, a court need not determine whether counsel's performance was deficient before examining the prejudice suffered by the defendant as a result of the alleged deficiencies. The object of an ineffectiveness claim is not to grade counsel's performance. If it is easier to dispose of an ineffectiveness claim on the ground of lack of sufficient prejudice, which we expect will often be so, that course should be followed. Courts should strive to ensure that ineffectiveness claims not become so burdensome to defense counsel that the entire criminal justice system suffers as a result. * * *

Having articulated general standards for judging ineffectiveness claims, we think it useful to apply those standards to the facts of this case in order to illustrate the meaning of the general principles. * * * The facts as described above make clear that the conduct of respondent's counsel at and before respondent's sentencing proceeding cannot be found unreasonable. They also make clear that, even assuming the challenged conduct of counsel was unreasonable, respondent suffered insufficient prejudice to warrant setting aside his death sentence.

With respect to the performance component, the record shows that respondent's counsel made a strategic choice to argue for the extreme emotional distress mitigating circumstance and to rely as fully as possible on respondent's acceptance of responsibility for his crimes. Although counsel understandably felt hopeless about respondent's prospects, nothing in the record indicates

* * * that counsel's sense of hopelessness distorted his professional judgment. Counsel's strategy choice was well within the range of professionally reasonable judgments, and the decision not to seek more character or psychological evidence than was already in hand was likewise reasonable.

The trial judge's views on the importance of owning up to one's crimes were well known to counsel. The aggravating circumstances were utterly overwhelming. Trial counsel could reasonably surmise from his conversations with respondent that character and psychological evidence would be of little help. Respondent had already been able to mention at the plea colloquy the substance of what there was to know about his financial and emotional troubles. Restricting testimony on respondent's character to what had come in at the plea colloquy ensured that contrary character and psychological evidence and respondent's criminal history, which counsel had successfully moved to exclude, would not come in. On these facts, there can be little question, even without application of the presumption of adequate performance, that trial counsel's defense, though unsuccessful, was the result of reasonable professional judgment.

With respect to the prejudice component, the lack of merit of respondent's claim is even more stark. The evidence that respondent says his trial counsel should have offered at the sentencing hearing would barely have altered the sentencing profile presented to the sentencing judge. As the state courts and District Court found, at most this evidence shows that numerous people who knew respondent thought he was generally a good person and that a psychiatrist and a psychologist believed he was under considerable emotional stress that did not rise to the level of extreme disturbance. Given the overwhelming aggravating factors, there is no reasonable probability that the omitted evidence would have changed the conclusion that the aggravating circumstances outweighed the mitigating circumstances and, hence, the sentence imposed. Indeed, admission of the evidence respondent now offers might even have been harmful to his case: his "rap sheet" would probably have been admitted into evidence, and the psychological reports would have directly contradicted respondent's claim that the mitigating circumstance of extreme emotional disturbance applied to his case. * * *

Failure to make the required showing of either deficient performance or sufficient prejudice defeats the ineffectiveness claim. Here there is a double failure. More generally, respondent has made no showing that the justice of his sentence was rendered unreliable by a breakdown in the adversary process caused by deficiencies in counsel's assistance. Respondent's sentencing proceeding was not fundamentally unfair. We conclude, therefore, that the District Court properly declined to issue a writ of habeas corpus. The judgment of the Court of Appeals is accordingly reversed.[d]

JUSTICE BRENNAN, concurring in part and dissenting in part.

I join the Court's opinion but dissent from its judgment.[e] * * *

d. In a later case, *Hill v. Lockhart,* 474 U.S. 52 (1985), the Court held "that the two-part *Strickland v. Washington* test" also applies to "challenges to guilty pleas based on ineffective assistance of counsel." The Court noted: "In the context of guilty pleas, the first half of the *Strickland v. Washington* test is nothing more than a restatement of the standard of attorney competence already set forth in * * * *McMann v. Richardson* [discussed supra in *Strickland* ]. The second, or 'prejudice,' requirement, on the other hand,

focuses on whether counsel's constitutionally ineffective performance affected the outcome of the plea process. In other words, in order to satisfy the 'prejudice' requirement, the defendant must show that there is a reasonable probability that, but for counsel's errors, he would not have pleaded guilty and would have insisted on going to trial."

e. Adhering to his view that the death penalty is in all circumstances forbidden cruel and unusual punishment, Justice Brennan

I join the Court's opinion because I believe that the standards it sets out today will both provide helpful guidance to courts considering claims of actual ineffectiveness of counsel and also permit those courts to continue their efforts to achieve progressive development of this area of the law. * * *

[T]he standards announced today can and should be applied with concern for the special considerations that must attend review of counsel's performance in a capital sentencing proceeding. In contrast to a case in which a finding of ineffective assistance requires a new trial, a conclusion that counsel was ineffective with respect to only the penalty phase of a capital trial imposes on the state the far lesser burden of reconsideration of the sentence alone. On the other hand, the consequences to the defendant of incompetent assistance at a capital sentencing could not, of course, be greater. * * *

JUSTICE MARSHALL, dissenting. * * *

The opinion of the Court revolves around two holdings. First, the majority ties the constitutional minima of attorney performance to a simple "standard of reasonableness." Second, the majority holds that only an error of counsel that has sufficient impact on a trial to "undermine confidence in the outcome" is grounds for overturning a conviction. I disagree with both of these rulings.

My objection to the performance standard adopted by the Court is that it is so malleable that, in practice, it will either have no grip at all or will yield excessive variation in the manner in which the Sixth Amendment is interpreted and applied by different courts. To tell lawyers and the lower courts that counsel for a criminal defendant must behave "reasonably" and must act like "a reasonably competent attorney" is to tell them almost nothing. In essence, the majority has instructed judges called upon to assess claims of ineffective assistance of counsel to advert to their own intuitions regarding what constitutes "professional" representation, and has discouraged them from trying to develop more detailed standards governing the performance of defense counsel. In my view, the Court has thereby not only abdicated its own responsibility to interpret the Constitution, but also impaired the ability of the lower courts to exercise theirs.

The debilitating ambiguity of an "objective standard of reasonableness" in this context is illustrated by the majority's failure to address important issues concerning the quality of representation mandated by the Constitution. It is an unfortunate but undeniable fact that a person of means, by selecting a lawyer and paying him enough to ensure he prepares thoroughly, usually can obtain better representation than that available to an indigent defendant, who must rely on appointed counsel, who, in turn, has limited time and resources to devote to a given case. Is a "reasonably competent attorney" a reasonably competent adequately paid retained lawyer or a reasonably competent appointed attorney? It is also a fact that the quality of representation available to ordinary defendants in different parts of the country varies significantly. Should the standard of performance mandated by the Sixth Amendment vary by locale? The majority offers no clues as to the proper responses to these questions.

* * * I agree that counsel must be afforded "wide latitude" when making "tactical decisions" regarding trial strategy, but many aspects of the job of a criminal defense attorney are more amenable to judicial oversight [than the majority indicates]. For example, much of the work involved in preparing for a trial, applying for bail, conferring with one's client, making timely objections to

noted that he would vacate respondent's death
sentence on that ground.

significant, arguably erroneous rulings of the trial judge, and filing a notice of appeal if there are colorable grounds therefor could profitably be made the subject of uniform standards. * * *

I object to the prejudice standard adopted by the Court for two independent reasons. First, it is often very difficult to tell whether a defendant convicted after a trial in which he was ineffectively represented would have fared better if his lawyer had been competent. Seemingly impregnable cases can sometimes be dismantled by good defense counsel. On the basis of a cold record, it may be impossible for a reviewing court confidently to ascertain how the government's evidence and arguments would have stood up against rebuttal and cross-examination by a shrewd, well prepared lawyer. The difficulties of estimating prejudice after the fact are exacerbated by the possibility that evidence of injury to the defendant may be missing from the record precisely because of the incompetence of defense counsel. In view of all these impediments to a fair evaluation of the probability that the outcome of a trial was affected by ineffectiveness of counsel, it seems to me senseless to impose on a defendant whose lawyer has been shown to have been incompetent the burden of demonstrating prejudice.

Second and more fundamentally, the assumption on which the Court's holding rests is that the only purpose of the constitutional guarantee of effective assistance of counsel is to reduce the chance that innocent persons will be convicted. In my view, the guarantee also functions to ensure that convictions are obtained only through fundamentally fair procedures. The majority contends that the Sixth Amendment is not violated when a manifestly guilty defendant is convicted after a trial in which he was represented by a manifestly ineffective attorney. I cannot agree. Every defendant is entitled to a trial in which his interests are vigorously and conscientiously advocated by an able lawyer. A proceeding in which the defendant does not receive meaningful assistance in meeting the forces of the state does not, in my opinion, constitute due process. * * * I would thus hold that a showing that the performance of a defendant's lawyer departed from constitutionally prescribed standards requires a new trial regardless of whether the defendant suffered demonstrable prejudice thereby.

Even if I were inclined to join the majority's two central holdings, I could not abide the manner in which the majority elaborates upon its rulings. * * *

Experienced members of the death-penalty bar have long recognized the crucial importance of adducing evidence at a sentencing proceeding that establishes the defendant's social and familial connections. The State makes a colorable—though in my view not compelling—argument that defense counsel in this case might have made a reasonable "strategic" decision not to present such evidence at the sentencing hearing on the assumption that an unadorned acknowledgment of respondent's responsibility for his crimes would be more likely to appeal to the trial judge, who was reputed to respect persons who accepted responsibility for their actions. But however justifiable such a choice might have been after counsel had fairly assessed the potential strength of the mitigating evidence available to him, counsel's failure to make any significant effort to find out what evidence might be garnered from respondent's relatives and acquaintances surely cannot be described as "reasonable." Counsel's failure to investigate is particularly suspicious in light of his candid admission that respondent's confession and conduct in the course of the trial gave him a feeling of "hopelessness" regarding the possibility of saving respondent's life.

If counsel had investigated the availability of mitigating evidence, he might well have decided to present some such material at the hearing. If he had done so, there is a significant chance that respondent would have been given a life sentence. In my view, those possibilities, conjoined with the unreasonableness of counsel's failure to investigate, are more than sufficient to establish a violation of the Sixth Amendment and to entitle respondent to a new sentencing proceeding. * * *

# NIX v. WHITESIDE

### 475 U.S. 157, 106 S.Ct. 988, 89 L.Ed.2d 123 (1986).

[In preparing for his Iowa state-court trial for murder, respondent Whiteside consistently told his appointed counsel, Robinson, that, although he had not actually seen a gun in the hand of the person he had stabbed to death, he was convinced that the victim had a gun. When Robinson interviewed those who were present during the stabbing, they told him that they had not seen a gun during the incident. And no gun was found on the premises. Robinson told his client that the actual existence of a weapon was not necessary to establish a claim of self-defense, and that only a reasonable belief that the victim had a gun nearby would suffice.

[Shortly before trial, during preparation for direct examination, Whiteside for the first time told his lawyer that he had seen "something metallic" in the victim's hand. When asked about this, Whiteside responded: "If I don't say I saw a gun, I'm dead." Robinson told Whiteside that such testimony would be lying and repeated that it was unnecessary to prove that the victim actually had a gun. On Whiteside's insisting that he would testify that he saw "something metallic," Robinson told him, according to Robinson's testimony, that if Whiteside testified falsely, "it would be my duty to advise the Court of what he was doing and that I felt he was committing perjury; also, that I probably would be allowed to impeach that particular testimony." Robinson also indicated that he would seek to withdraw from the case if his client insisted on committing perjury.

[Whiteside ultimately testified as originally contemplated, stating that he believed that the victim was reaching for a gun, but admitting on cross-examination that he had not actually seen a weapon in the victim's hand. The jury found Whiteside guilty of second-degree murder.

[Whiteside then moved for a new trial, claiming he had been denied a fair trial by his lawyer's admonitions not to state that he saw a gun or "something metallic." The trial court denied the motion and the state supreme court affirmed. Whiteside then sought federal habeas corpus relief, maintaining that he had been denied effective assistance of counsel by his attorney's refusal to allow him to testify as he proposed. The district court denied relief, but the Court of Appeals for the Eighth Circuit reversed, concluding that counsel's threatened violation of his client's confidences violated the "effective representation" standards set forth in *Strickland.*]

CHIEF JUSTICE BURGER delivered the opinion of the Court.

In *Strickland v. Washington,* we held that to obtain relief by way of federal habeas corpus on a claim of a deprivation of effective assistance of counsel under the Sixth Amendment, the movant must establish both serious attorney error and prejudice. To show such error, it must be established that the assistance rendered by counsel was constitutionally deficient in that "counsel made errors so serious that counsel was not functioning as 'counsel' guaranteed the defendant by the Sixth Amendment." To show prejudice, it must be established that the claimed lapses in counsel's performance rendered the trial unfair so as to "undermine confidence in the outcome" of the trial. * * *

Under the *Strickland* standard, breach of an ethical standard does not necessarily make out a denial of the Sixth Amendment guarantee of assistance of counsel. When examining attorney conduct, a court must be careful not to narrow the wide range of conduct acceptable under the Sixth Amendment so restrictively as to constitutionalize particular standards of professional conduct and thereby intrude into the State's proper authority to define and apply the standards of professional conduct applicable to those it admits to practice in its courts. In some future case challenging attorney conduct in the course of a state court trial, we may need to define with greater precision the weight to be given to recognized canons of ethics, the standards established by the State in statutes or professional codes, and the Sixth Amendment, in defining the proper scope and limits on that conduct. Here we need not face that question, since virtually all of the sources speak with one voice.

We turn next to the question presented: the definition of the range of "reasonable professional" responses to a criminal defendant client who informs counsel that he will perjure himself on the stand. We must determine whether, in this setting, Robinson's conduct fell within the wide range of professional responses to threatened client perjury acceptable under the Sixth Amendment.

In *Strickland,* we recognized counsel's duty of loyalty and his "overarching duty to advocate the defendant's cause." Plainly, that duty is limited to legitimate, lawful conduct compatible with the very nature of a trial as a search for truth. Although counsel must take all reasonable lawful means to attain the objectives of the client, counsel is precluded from taking steps or in any way assisting the client in presenting false evidence or otherwise violating the law. This principle has consistently been recognized in most unequivocal terms by expositors of the norms of professional conduct since the first Canons of Professional Ethics were adopted by the American Bar Association in 1908. * * *

> "No client, corporate or individual, however powerful, nor any cause, civil or political, however important, is entitled to receive nor should any lawyer render any service or advice involving disloyalty to the law whose ministers we are, or disrespect of the judicial office, which we are bound to uphold, or corruption of any person or persons exercising a public office or private trust, or deception or betrayal of the public. . . . He must . . . observe and advise his client to observe the statute law. . . ." Canons of Professional Ethics, Canon 32.

[This principle has] been carried through to contemporary codifications [4] of an attorney's professional responsibility. Disciplinary Rule 7–102 of the Model Code of Professional Responsibility (1980), entitled "Representing a Client Within the Bounds of the Law," provides that

> "(A) In his representation of a client, a lawyer shall not: . . . (4) Knowingly use perjured testimony or false evidence; . . . (7) Counsel or assist his client in conduct that the lawyer knows to be illegal or fraudulent."

---

**4.** There currently exist two different codifications of uniform standards of professional conduct. The Model Code of Professional Responsibility was originally adopted by the American Bar Association in 1969, and was subsequently adopted (in many cases with modification) by nearly every state. The more recent Model Rules of Professional Conduct were adopted by the American Bar Association in 1983. Since their promulgation by the American Bar Association, the Model Rules have been adopted by 11 States * * *. Iowa is one of the States that adopted a form of the Model Code of Professional Responsibility, but has yet to adopt the Model Rules.

This provision has been adopted by Iowa, and is binding on all lawyers who appear in its courts. The more recent Model Rules of Professional Conduct (1983) similarly admonish attorneys to obey all laws in the course of representing a client:

"*RULE 1.2* Scope of Representation . . .

"(d) A lawyer shall not counsel a client to engage, or assist a client, in conduct that the lawyer knows is criminal or fraudulent . . .."

Both the Model Code of Professional Conduct and the Model Rules of Professional Conduct also adopt the specific exception from the attorney-client privilege for disclosure of perjury that his client intends to commit or has committed. Indeed, both the Model Code and the Model Rules do not merely *authorize* disclosure by counsel of client perjury; they *require* such disclosure. * * *

These standards confirm that the legal profession has accepted that an attorney's ethical duty to advance the interests of his client is limited by an equally solemn duty to comply with the law and standards of professional conduct; it specifically ensures that the client may not use false evidence. This special duty of an attorney to prevent and disclose frauds upon the court derives from the recognition that perjury is as much a crime as tampering with witnesses or jurors by way of promises and threats, and undermines the administration of justice. * * * The suggestion sometimes made that "a lawyer must believe his client not judge him" in no sense means a lawyer can honorably be a party to or in any way give aid to presenting known perjury.

Considering Robinson's representation of respondent in light of these accepted norms of professional conduct, we discern no failure to adhere to reasonable professional standards that would in any sense make out a deprivation of the Sixth Amendment right to counsel. Whether Robinson's conduct is seen as a successful attempt to dissuade his client from committing the crime of perjury, or whether seen as a "threat" to withdraw from representation and disclose the illegal scheme, Robinson's representation of Whiteside falls well within accepted standards of professional conduct and the range of reasonable professional conduct acceptable under *Strickland.* * * *

While purporting to follow the Iowa's highest court "on all questions of state law," the Court of Appeals reached its conclusions on the basis of federal constitutional due process and right to counsel. * * * [While accepting the conclusion of the Iowa trial court that Whiteside's proposed testimony would have been a criminal act, the Court of Appeals held that Robinson's efforts to persuade Whiteside not to commit that crime were improper, *first,* as forcing an impermissible choice between the right to counsel and the right to testify; and *second,* as compromising client confidences because of Robinson's threat to disclose the contemplated perjury.[7] * * *

Whatever the scope of a constitutional right to testify, it is elementary that such a right does not extend to testifying *falsely.* * * * Robinson's admonitions to his client can in no sense be said to have forced respondent into an *impermissible* choice between his right to counsel and his right to testify as he proposed for there was no *permissible* choice to testify falsely. For defense

---

**7.** The Court of Appeals also determined that Robinson's efforts to persuade Whiteside to testify truthfully constituted an impermissible threat to testify against his own client. We find no support for a threat to testify against Whiteside while he was acting as counsel. The record reflects testimony by Robinson that he had admonished Whiteside that if he withdrew he "probably would be allowed to attempt to impeach that particular testimony," if Whiteside testified falsely. The trial court accepted this version of the conversation as true.

counsel to take steps to persuade a criminal defendant to testify truthfully, or to withdraw, deprives the defendant of neither his right to counsel nor the right to testify truthfully. * * *

On this record, the accused enjoyed continued representation within the bounds of reasonable professional conduct and did in fact exercise his right to testify; at most he was denied the right to have the assistance of counsel in the presentation of false testimony. Similarly, we can discern no breach of professional duty in Robinson's admonition to respondent that he would disclose respondent's perjury to the court. The crime of perjury in this setting is indistinguishable in substance from the crime of threatening or tampering with a witness or a juror. A defendant who informed his counsel that he was arranging to bribe or threaten witnesses or members of the jury would have no "right" to insist on counsel's assistance or silence. Counsel would not be limited to advising against that conduct. An attorney's duty of confidentiality, which totally covers the client's admission of guilt, does not extend to a client's announced plans to engage in future criminal conduct. In short, the responsibility of an ethical lawyer, as an officer of the court and a key component of a system of justice, dedicated to a search for truth, is essentially the same whether the client announces an intention to bribe or threaten witnesses or jurors or to commit or procure perjury. No system of justice worthy of the name can tolerate a lesser standard.

The rule adopted by the Court of Appeals, which seemingly would require an attorney to remain silent while his client committed perjury, is wholly incompatible with the established standards of ethical conduct and the laws of Iowa and contrary to professional standards promulgated by that State. The position advocated by petitioner, on the contrary, is wholly consistent with the Iowa standards of professional conduct and law, with the overwhelming majority of courts, and with codes of professional ethics. Since there has been no breach of any recognized professional duty, it follows that there can be no deprivation of the right to assistance of counsel under the *Strickland* standard.

We hold that, as a matter of law, counsel's conduct complained of here cannot establish the prejudice required for relief under the second strand of the *Strickland* inquiry. Although a defendant need not establish that the attorney's deficient performance more likely than not altered the outcome in order to establish prejudice under *Strickland,* a defendant must show "that there is a reasonable probability that, but for counsel's unprofessional errors, the result of the proceeding would have been different." According to *Strickland,* "[a] reasonable probability is a probability sufficient to undermine confidence in the outcome." The *Strickland* Court noted that the "benchmark" of an ineffective assistance claim is the fairness of the adversary proceeding, and that in judging prejudice and the likelihood of a different outcome, "[a] defendant has no entitlement to the luck of a lawless decisionmaker."

Whether he was persuaded or compelled to desist from perjury, Whiteside has no valid claim that confidence in the result of his trial has been diminished by his desisting from the contemplated perjury. Even if we were to assume that the jury might have believed his perjury, it does not follow that Whiteside was prejudiced. * * *

Whiteside's attorney treated Whiteside's proposed perjury in accord with professional standards, and since Whiteside's truthful testimony could not have prejudiced the result of his trial, the Court of Appeals * * * must be reversed.

JUSTICE BLACKMUN, with whom JUSTICE BRENNAN, JUSTICE MARSHALL, and JUSTICE STEVENS join, concurring in the judgment.[a]

How a defense attorney ought to act when faced with a client who intends to commit perjury at trial has long been a controversial issue. But I do not believe that a federal habeas corpus case challenging a state criminal conviction is an appropriate vehicle for attempting to resolve this thorny problem. When a defendant argues that he was denied effective assistance of counsel because his lawyer dissuaded him from committing perjury, the only question properly presented to this Court is whether the lawyer's actions deprived the defendant of the fair trial which the Sixth Amendment is meant to guarantee. Since I believe that the respondent in this case suffered no injury justifying federal habeas relief, I concur in the Court's judgment. * * *

The touchstone of a claim of prejudice is an allegation that counsel's behavior did something "to deprive the defendant of a fair trial, a trial whose result is reliable." *Strickland*. The only effect Robinson's threat had on Whiteside's trial is that Whiteside did not testify, falsely, that he saw a gun in Love's hand.[4] Thus, this Court must ask whether its confidence in the outcome of Whiteside's trial is in any way undermined by the knowledge that he refrained from presenting false testimony.

* * * To the extent that Whiteside's claim rests on the assertion that he would have been acquitted had he been able to testify falsely, Whiteside claims a right the law simply does not recognize. * * * Since Whiteside was deprived of neither a fair trial nor any of the specific constitutional rights designed to guarantee a fair trial, he has suffered no prejudice. * * *

In light of respondent's failure to show any cognizable prejudice, I see no need to "grade counsel's performance." *Strickland*. The only federal issue in this case is whether Robinson's behavior deprived Whiteside of the effective assistance of counsel; it is not whether Robinson's behavior conformed to any particular code of legal ethics.

Whether an attorney's response to what he sees as a client's plan to commit perjury violates a defendant's Sixth Amendment rights may depend on many factors: how certain the attorney is that the proposed testimony is false, the stage of the proceedings at which the attorney discovers the plan, or the ways in which the attorney may be able to dissuade his client, to name just three. The complex interaction of factors, which is likely to vary from case to case, makes inappropriate a blanket rule that defense attorneys must reveal, or threaten to reveal, a client's anticipated perjury to the court. Except in the rarest of cases, attorneys who adopt "the role of the judge or jury to determine the facts," *Wilcox,* pose a danger of depriving their clients of the zealous and loyal advocacy required by the Sixth Amendment.[8]

a. Justice Brennan also wrote a separate opinion concurring in the judgment. He agreed that "respondent has failed to prove the kind of prejudice necessary to make out a claim under *Strickland,*" and wrote separately to emphasize that the "Court's essay regarding what constitutes the correct response to a criminal client's suggestion that he will perjure himself is pure discourse without force of law."

4. This is not to say that a lawyer's threat to reveal his client's confidences may never have other effects on a defendant's trial. Cf. *United States ex rel. Wilcox v. Johnson,* 555 F.2d 115 (3d Cir.1977) (finding a violation of Sixth Amendment when an attorney's threat to reveal client's purported perjury caused defendant not to take the stand at all).

8. A comparison of this case with *Wilcox* [note 4 supra] is illustrative. Here, Robinson testified in detail to the factors that led him to conclude that respondent's assertion he had seen a gun was false. The Iowa Supreme Court found "good cause" and "strong support" for Robinson's conclusion. Moreover, Robinson gave credence to those parts of Whiteside's account which, although he found them implausible and unsubstantiated, were

I therefore am troubled by the Court's implicit adoption of a set of standards of professional responsibility for attorneys in state criminal proceedings. The States, of course, do have a compelling interest in the integrity of their criminal trials that can justify regulating the length to which an attorney may go in seeking his client's acquittal. But the American Bar Association's implicit suggestion in its brief *amicus curiae* that the Court find that the Association's Model Rules of Professional Conduct should govern an attorney's responsibilities is addressed to the wrong audience. It is for the States to decide how attorneys should conduct themselves in state criminal proceedings, and this Court's responsibility extends only to ensuring that the restrictions a State enacts do not infringe a defendant's federal constitutional rights. Thus, I would follow the suggestion made in the joint brief *amici curiae* filed by 37 States at the certiorari stage that we allow the States to maintain their "differing approaches" to a complex ethical question. The signal merit of asking first whether a defendant has shown any adverse prejudicial effect before inquiring into his attorney's performance is that it avoids unnecessary federal interference in a State's regulation of its bar. Because I conclude that the respondent in this case failed to show such an effect, I join the Court's judgment that he is not entitled to federal habeas relief.

JUSTICE STEVENS, concurring in the judgment.   *   *   *

As we view this case, it appears perfectly clear that respondent intended to commit perjury, that his lawyer knew it, and that the lawyer had a duty—both to the court and to his client, for perjured testimony can ruin an otherwise meritorious case—to take extreme measures to prevent the perjury from occurring. The lawyer was successful and, from our unanimous and remote perspective, it is now pellucidly clear that the client suffered no "legally cognizable prejudice."

Nevertheless, beneath the surface of this case there are areas of uncertainty that cannot be resolved today. A lawyer's certainty that a change in his client's recollection is a harbinger of intended perjury—as well as judicial review of such apparent certainty—should be tempered by the realization that, after reflection, the most honest witness may recall (or sincerely believe he recalls) details that he previously overlooked. Similarly, the post-trial review of a lawyer's pre-trial threat to expose perjury that had not yet been committed—and, indeed, may have been prevented by the threat—is by no means the same as review of the way in which such a threat may actually have been carried out. Thus, one can be convinced—as I am—that this lawyer's actions were a proper way to provide his client with effective representation without confronting the much more difficult questions of what a lawyer must, should, or may do after his client has given testimony that the lawyer does not believe. The answer to such questions may well be colored by the particular circumstances attending the actual event and its aftermath.

Because Justice Blackmun has preserved such questions for another day, and because I do not understand him to imply any adverse criticism of this lawyer's representation of his client, I join his opinion concurring in the judgment.

---

not clearly false. By contrast, in *Wilcox,* where defense counsel actually informed the judge that she believed her client intended to lie and where her threat to withdraw in the middle of the trial led the defendant not to take the stand at all, the Court of Appeals found "no evidence on the record of this case indicating that Mr. Wilcox intended to perjure himself," and characterized counsel's beliefs as "private conjectures about the guilt or innocence of [her] client."

## MURRAY v. CARRIER
### 477 U.S. 478, 106 S.Ct. 2639, 91 L.Ed.2d 397 (1986).

JUSTICE O'CONNOR delivered the opinion of the Court.

We granted certiorari in this case to consider whether a federal habeas petitioner can show cause for a procedural default by establishing that competent defense counsel inadvertently failed to raise the substantive claim of error rather than deliberately withholding it for tactical reasons.

Respondent Clifford Carrier was convicted of rape and abduction by a Virginia jury in 1977. Before trial, respondent's court-appointed counsel moved for discovery of the victim's statements to police describing "her assailants, the vehicle the assailants were driving, and the location of where the alleged rape took place." The presiding judge denied the motion by letter to counsel after examining the statements *in camera* and determining that they contained no exculpatory evidence. Respondent's counsel made a second motion to discover the victim's statements immediately prior to trial, which the trial judge denied for the same reason after conducting his own *in camera* examination.

After respondent was convicted, his counsel filed a notice of appeal to the Virginia Supreme Court assigning seven errors, of which the fifth was: * * * "the trial judge err[ed] by not permitting defendant's counsel to examine the written statements of the victim prior to trial, and during the course of the trial." * * * Without consulting respondent, counsel subsequently submitted the required petition for appeal but failed to include this claim, notwithstanding that Virginia Supreme Court Rule 5:21 provides that "[o]nly errors assigned in the petition for appeal will be noticed by this Court and no error not so assigned will be admitted as a ground for reversal of a decision below." The Virginia Supreme Court refused the appeal and this Court denied certiorari.

A year later respondent, by this time proceeding *pro se,* filed a state habeas corpus petition claiming that he had been denied due process of law by the prosecution's withholding of the victim's statements. The State sought dismissal of his petition on the ground that respondent was barred from presenting his due process discovery claim on collateral review because he failed to raise that claim on appeal. The state habeas court dismissed the petition "for the reasons stated in the Motion to Dismiss," and the Virginia Supreme Court denied certiorari.

Respondent next filed a *pro se* habeas petition in the District Court for the Eastern District of Virginia, renewing his due process discovery claim as grounds for relief. The State filed a motion to dismiss asserting that respondent's failure to raise the issue on direct appeal was a procedural default barring federal habeas review under *Wainwright v. Sykes,* 433 U.S. 72 (1977). * * * The United States Magistrate to whom the case was referred recommended dismissal by virtue of the procedural default * * *. In reply to the Magistrate's report, respondent alleged that his procedural default was "due to ineffective assistance of counsel during the filing of his appeal." The District Court approved the Magistrate's report, holding the discovery claim barred by the procedural default and indicating that respondent should establish cause for that default in the state courts.

At oral argument on appeal to the Court of Appeals for the Fourth Circuit, respondent abandoned any claim of ineffective assistance of counsel but asserted that counsel had mistakenly omitted his discovery claim from the petition for appeal and that this error was cause for his default. A divided panel of the Court of Appeals reversed and remanded. The court construed respondent's objection to the denial of discovery as having rested throughout on a contention that *Brady v. Maryland* [see *Bagley,* Ch. 13, at note a] requires the prosecution to disclose any evidence that might be material to guilt whether or not it is exculpatory, and concluded that when respondent's counsel omitted this discovery claim from the petition for review "the issue was lost for purposes of direct and collateral review." The court framed the issue before it as whether "a single act or omission by counsel, insufficient by itself to contravene the sixth amendment, [can] satisfy the 'cause' prong of the exception to preclusive procedural default discussed in *Wainwright v. Sykes?"* In answering this question, the court drew a dispositive distinction between procedural defaults resulting from deliberate tactical decisions and those resulting from ignorance or inadvertence. The court determined that only in the latter category does an attorney's error constitute cause because, whereas a tactical decision implies that counsel has, at worst, "reasonably but incorrectly exercise[d] her judgment," ignorance or oversight implies that counsel "fail[ed] to exercise it at all, in dereliction of the duty to represent her client." Thus, in order to establish cause a federal habeas petitioner need only satisfy the district court "that the failure to object or to appeal his claim was the product of his attorney's ignorance or oversight, not a deliberate tactic." * * *

*Wainwright v. Sykes* held that a federal habeas petitioner who has failed to comply with a State's contemporaneous-objection rule at trial must show cause for the procedural default and prejudice attributable thereto in order to obtain review of his defaulted constitutional claim.[a] In so holding, the Court explicitly rejected the standard described in *Fay v. Noia,* 372 U.S. 391 (1963), under which a federal habeas court could refuse to review a defaulted claim only if "an applicant ha[d] deliberately by-passed the orderly procedure of the state courts," by personal waiver of the claim amounting to " 'an intentional relinquishment or abandonment of a known right or privilege.' " At a minimum, then, *Wainwright v. Sykes* plainly implied that default of a constitutional claim by counsel pursuant to a trial strategy or tactical decision would, absent extraordinary circumstances, bind the habeas petitioner even if he had not personally waived that claim. Beyond that, the Court left open "for resolution in future decisions the precise definition of the 'cause'-and-'prejudice' standard."

We revisited the cause and prejudice test in *Engle v. Isaac,* 456 U.S. 107 (1982). * * * In language that bears directly on the present case, we said:

"* * * Every trial presents a myriad of possible claims. Counsel might have overlooked or chosen to omit respondents' due process argument while pursuing other avenues of defense. We have long recognized, howev-

a. The federal habeas petitioner (Sykes) sought relief on the ground that the evidence introduced at his trial included a confession obtained without his full understanding of the *Miranda* warnings. The state's procedural rules required that an objection based on allegedly unconstitutional police action (such as a *Miranda* objection) be raised by pretrial motion, but also allowed, under special circumstances, an objection at the time the unconstitutionally obtained evidence was introduced at trial (i.e., a "contemporaneous objection"). Defense counsel, however, failed to raise the objection at even that later point, and the prosecution contended that the claim had therefore been lost under the state's raise-or-waive rule. The Supreme Court held that this state rule should preclude consideration of the merits of the defendant's claim on federal habeas corpus unless the defendant could show both "cause" for the failure to comply with the state's contemporaneous objection requirement and "actual prejudice" resulting from the loss of the alleged constitutional claim. The Court limited to its facts an earlier ruling, *Fay v. Noia* (discussed infra). *Fay* had directed federal courts on habeas review to consider constitutional claims, even though viewed as procedurally "forfeited" or "defaulted" under state law, unless the failure to properly raise the claim under state law reflected a deliberate defense decision to bypass the state procedures in the hope of gaining review initially before the federal courts on collateral attack.

er, that the Constitution guarantees criminal defendants only a fair trial and a competent attorney. It does not insure that defense counsel will recognize and raise every conceivable constitutional claim. Where the basis of a constitutional claim is available, and other defense counsel have perceived and litigated that claim, the demands of comity and finality counsel against labeling alleged unawareness of the objection as a cause for a procedural default."

The thrust of this part of our decision in *Engle* is unmistakable: the mere fact that counsel failed to recognize the factual or legal basis for a claim, or failed to raise the claim despite recognizing it, does not constitute cause for a procedural default. At least with respect to defaults that occur at trial, the Court of Appeals' holding that ignorant or inadvertent attorney error is cause for any resulting procedural default is plainly inconsistent with *Engle.* It is no less inconsistent with the purposes served by the cause and prejudice standard. That standard rests not only on the need to deter intentional defaults but on a judgment that the costs of federal habeas review "are particularly high when a trial default has barred a prisoner from obtaining adjudication of his constitutional claim in the state courts." *Engle.* Those costs, which include a reduction in the finality of litigation and the frustration of "both the States' sovereign power to punish offenders and their good-faith attempts to honor constitutional rights" are heightened in several respects when a trial default occurs: the default deprives the trial court of an opportunity to correct any error without retrial, detracts from the importance of the trial itself, gives state appellate courts no chance to review trial errors, and "exacts an extra charge by undercutting the State's ability to enforce its procedural rules." Clearly, these considerable costs do not disappear when the default stems from counsel's ignorance or inadvertence rather than from a deliberate decision, for whatever reason, to withhold a claim.

Indeed, the rule applied by the Court of Appeals would significantly increase the costs associated with a procedural default in many cases. In order to determine whether there was cause for a procedural default, federal habeas courts would routinely be required to hold evidentiary hearings to determine what prompted counsel's failure to raise the claim in question. While the federal habeas courts would no doubt strive to minimize the burdens to all concerned through the use of affidavits or other simplifying procedures, we are not prepared to assume that these costs would be negligible, particularly since, as we observed in *Strickland v. Washington,* "[i]ntensive scrutiny of counsel * * * could dampen the ardor and impair the independence of defense counsel, discourage the acceptance of assigned cases, and undermine the trust between attorney and client." Nor will it always be easy to classify counsel's behavior in accordance with the deceptively simple categories propounded by the Court of Appeals. Does counsel act out of "ignorance," for example, by failing to raise a claim for tactical reasons after mistakenly assessing its strength on the basis of an incomplete acquaintance with the relevant precedent? The uncertain dimensions of any exception for "inadvertence" or "ignorance" furnish an additional reason for rejecting it.

We think, then, that the question of cause for a procedural default does not turn on whether counsel erred or on the kind of error counsel may have made. So long as a defendant is represented by counsel whose performance is not constitutionally ineffective under the standard established in *Strickland v. Washington,* we discern no inequity in requiring him to bear the risk of attorney error that results in a procedural default. Instead, we think that the existence of cause for a procedural default must ordinarily turn on whether the prisoner can show that some objective factor external to the defense impeded counsel's efforts to comply with the State's procedural rule. Without attempting an exhaustive catalog of such objective impediments to compliance with a procedural rule, we note that a showing that the factual or legal basis for a claim was not reasonably available to counsel, see *Reed v. Ross,* 468 U.S. 1 (1984),[b] or that "some interference by officials," *Brown v. Allen,* 344 U.S. 443, 486 (1953), made compliance impracticable, would constitute cause under this standard.[c] Similarly, if the procedural default is the result of ineffective assistance of counsel, the Sixth Amendment itself requires that responsibility for the default be imputed to the State, which may not "conduc[t] trials at which persons who face incarceration must defend themselves without adequate legal assistance." *Cuyler v. Sullivan,* 446 U.S. 335 (1980). Ineffective assistance of counsel, then, is cause for a procedural default. * * *

It is clear that respondent failed to show or even allege cause for his procedural default under this standard for cause, which *Engle* squarely supports. Respondent argues nevertheless that his case is not controlled by *Engle* because it involves a procedural default on appeal rather than at trial. * * * [R]espondent asks us to affirm the Court of Appeals' judgment on the narrow ground that even if counsel's ignorance or inadvertence does not constitute cause for a procedural default at trial, it does constitute cause for a procedural default on appeal. In support of this distinction, respondent asserts that the concerns that underlie the cause and prejudice test are not present in the case of defaults on appeal. A default on appeal, he maintains, does not detract from the significance of the trial or from the development of a full trial record, or deprive the trial court of an opportunity to correct error without the need for retrial. Moreover, unlike the rapid pace of trial, in which it is a matter of necessity that counsel's decisions bind the defendant, "the appellate process affords the attorney time for reflection, research, and full consultation with his client." Finally, respondent suggests that there is no likelihood that an attorney will preserve an objection at trial yet choose to withhold it on appeal in order to "sandbag" the prosecution by raising the claim on federal habeas if relief is denied by the state courts.

These arguments are unpersuasive. A State's procedural rules serve vital purposes at trial, on appeal, and on state collateral attack. The important role of appellate procedural rules is aptly captured by the Court's description in *Reed v. Ross* of the purposes served by the procedural rule at issue there, which required the defendant initially to raise his legal claims on appeal rather than on postconviction review:

> "It affords the state courts the opportunity to resolve the issue shortly after trial, while evidence is still available both to assess the defendant's claim

**b.** *Reed v. Ross* held that "cause" existed where the claim that counsel failed to raise was "so novel that its legal basis [was] not reasonably available" to counsel. The constitutional claim in *Reed* was deemed to fit this "novel issue" characterization in part because the theoretical grounding for the claim was first recognized in a Supreme Court ruling rendered several years after defendant's trial. The Court in *Engle v. Isaac* had refused to similarly characterize a claim which was grounded on a Supreme Court decision rendered prior to the habeas petitioner's state proceedings, although that claim required a considerable extension of the analysis of that Supreme Court precedent. The *Engle* Court noted also that numerous lower courts had suggested the possibility of extending that precedent prior to petitioner's state proceedings and various state defendants had raised analogous constitutional claims. The *Reed* majority concluded that neither of these bases for raising the claim had been available to petitioner's counsel in that case.

**c.** The cited discussion in *Brown v. Allen* referred to a case in which a warden had suppressed petitioner's timely appeal papers.

and to retry the defendant effectively if he prevails in his appeal.  *  *  *
This type of rule promotes not only the accuracy and efficiency of judicial
decisions, but also the finality of those decisions, by forcing the defendant to
litigate all of his claims together, as quickly after trial as the docket will
allow, and while the attention of the appellate court is focused on his case."

These legitimate state interests, which are manifestly furthered by the comparable procedural rule at issue in this case, warrant our adherence to the conclusion
to which they led the Court in *Reed v. Ross*—that the cause and prejudice test
applies to defaults on appeal as to those at trial.  *  *  *

Concurring in the judgment, Justice Stevens contends that our decision
today erects an unwarranted procedural barrier to the correction through
federal habeas corpus of violations of fundamental constitutional rights that
have resulted in a miscarriage of justice.  The cause and prejudice test, in his
view, "must be considered within an overall inquiry into justice," which requires
consideration in every case of the character of the constitutional claim.  If the
federal right asserted is of "fundamental importance," or if a violation of that
right "calls into question the accuracy of the determination of  *  *  * guilt,"
Justice Stevens would then balance "the nature and strength of the constitutional claim" and "the nature and strength of the state procedural rule that has not
been observed."  *  *  *

The effect of such a reworking of the cause and prejudice test would
essentially be to dispense with the requirement that the petitioner show cause
and instead to focus exclusively on whether there has been a "manifest injustice" or a denial of "fundamental fairness."  We are not told whether this
inquiry would require the same showing of actual prejudice that is required by
the cause and prejudice test as interpreted in *Engle* *  *  *, but the thrust of
the concurrence leaves little doubt that this is so.  The showing of prejudice
required under *Wainwright v. Sykes* is significantly greater than that necessary
under "the more vague inquiry suggested by the words 'plain error.' " *Engle.*
The habeas petitioner must show "not merely that the errors at . . . trial
created a *possibility* of prejudice, but that they worked to his *actual* and
substantial disadvantage, infecting his entire trial with error of constitutional
dimensions."  Such a showing of pervasive actual prejudice can hardly be
thought to constitute anything other than a showing that the prisoner was
denied "fundamental fairness" at trial.  Since, for Justice Stevens, a "constitutional claim that implicates 'fundamental fairness' *  *  * compels review
regardless of possible procedural defaults," it follows that a showing of prejudice
would invariably make a showing of cause unnecessary.

As the concurrence acknowledges, *Engle* expressly rejected this contention
that a showing of actual prejudice "should permit relief even in the absence of
cause."  *  *  * [A]t least three decisions of this Court—*Francis, Sykes,* and
*Engle*—are unambiguously contrary to the approach taken in the concurrence.
We are unprepared, in the face of this weight of authority and in view of the
principles of comity and finality these decisions reflect, to reduce the cause
requirement to the vestigial role Justice Stevens envisions for it.  *  *  *

However, as we also noted in *Engle,* "[i]n appropriate cases" the principles of
comity and finality that inform the concepts of cause and prejudice "must yield
to the imperative of correcting a fundamentally unjust incarceration."  We
remain confident that, for the most part, "victims of a fundamental miscarriage
of justice will meet the cause-and-prejudice standard."  But we do not pretend
that this will always be true.  Accordingly, we think that in an extraordinary
case, where a constitutional violation has probably resulted in the conviction of

one who is actually innocent, a federal habeas court may grant the writ even in the absence of a showing of cause for the procedural default.

There is an additional safeguard against miscarriages of justice in criminal cases * * *. That safeguard is the right to effective assistance of counsel, which, as this Court has indicated, may in a particular case be violated by even an isolated error of counsel if that error is sufficiently egregious and prejudicial. The presence of such a safeguard may properly inform this Court's judgment in determining "[w]hat standards should govern the exercise of the habeas court's equitable discretion" with respect to procedurally defaulted claims, *Reed v. Ross*. The ability to raise ineffective assistance claims based in whole or in part on counsel's procedural defaults substantially undercuts any predictions of unremedied manifest injustices. We therefore remain of the view that adherence to the cause and prejudice test "in the conjunctive," *Engle*, will not prevent federal habeas courts from ensuring the "fundamental fairness [that] is the central concern of the writ of habeas corpus." *Strickland v. Washington* * * *.

Respondent has never alleged any external impediment that might have prevented counsel from raising his discovery claim in his petition for review, and has disavowed any claim that counsel's performance on appeal was so deficient as to make out an ineffective assistance claim. * * * Respondent's petition for federal habeas review of his procedurally defaulted discovery claim must therefore be dismissed for failure to establish cause for the default, unless it is determined on remand that the victim's statements contain material that would establish respondent's actual innocence. * * * The judgment of the Court of Appeals is reversed, and the case is remanded for further proceedings consistent with this opinion.

Justice Stevens, with whom Justice Blackmun joins, concurring in the judgment. * * *

The character of respondent's constitutional claim should be central to an evaluation of his habeas corpus petition. Before and during his trial on charges of rape and abduction, his counsel made timely motions for discovery of the statements made by the victim to the police. By denying those motions, the trial court significantly curtailed the defendant's ability to cross-examine the prosecution's most important witness, and may well have violated the defendant's right to review "evidence favorable to an accused upon request * * * where the evidence is material either to guilt or to punishment." *Brady v. Maryland*, 373 U.S. 83 (1963). That right is unquestionably protected by the Due Process Clause. Indeed, the Court has repeatedly emphasized the fundamental importance of that federal right.

The constitutional claim advanced by respondent calls into question the accuracy of the determination of his guilt. On the record before us, however, we cannot determine whether or not he is the victim of a miscarriage of justice. Respondent argues that the trial court's analysis was severely flawed. Even if the trial judge applied the correct standard, the conclusion that there was no "exculpatory" material in the victim's statements does not foreclose the possibility that inconsistencies between the statements and the direct testimony would have enabled an effective cross-examination to demonstrate that respondent is actually innocent. On the other hand, it is possible that other evidence of guilt in the record is so overwhelming that the trial judge's decision was clearly not prejudicial to the defendant. The important point is that we cannot evaluate the possibility that respondent may be the victim of a fundamental miscarriage of justice without any knowledge about the contents of the victim's statements.

\* \* \* In my opinion, the "cause and prejudice" formula that the Court explicates in such detail today is not dispositive when the fundamental fairness of a prisoner's conviction is at issue. That formula is of recent vintage, particularly in comparison to the writ for which it is invoked. It is, at most, part of a broader inquiry into the demands of justice. \* \* \* An inquiry into the requirements of justice requires a consideration, not only of the nature and strength of the constitutional claim, but also of the nature and strength of the state procedural rule that has not been observed. In its opinion today, the Court relies heavily on cases in which the defendant failed to make a contemporaneous objection to an error that occurred during a trial. Most of the reasons for finding a waiver in that setting simply do not apply to the appellate process. Of special importance is the fact that the state interest in enforcing its contemporaneous-objection rule is supported, not merely by the concern with finality that characterizes state appellate rules, but also by the concern with making the trial the "main event" in which the issue of guilt or innocence can be fairly resolved.

\* \* \*

Procedural default that is adequate to foreclose appellate review of a claim of constitutional error in a state criminal trial should ordinarily also bar collateral review of such a claim in a federal district court. But the history of the Court's jurisprudence interpreting the Acts of Congress authorizing the issuance of the writ of habeas corpus unambiguously requires that we carefully preserve the exception which enables the federal writ to grant relief in cases of manifest injustice. That exception cannot be adequately defined by a simply stated rule. The procedural default is always an important factor to be carefully reviewed; as Justice Frankfurter explained: "All that has gone before is not to be ignored as irrelevant." *Brown v. Allen.* But it is equally clear that the prisoner must always have some opportunity to reopen his case if he can make a sufficient showing that he is the victim of a fundamental miscarriage of justice. Whether the inquiry is channeled by the use of the terms "cause" and "prejudice"—or by the statutory duty to "dispose of the matter as law and justice require," 28 U.S.C. § 2243—it is clear to me that appellate procedural default should not foreclose habeas corpus review of a meritorious constitutional claim that may establish the prisoner's innocence. \* \* \*

JUSTICE BRENNAN, with whom JUSTICE MARSHALL joins, dissenting.

Like the Great Writ from which it draws its essence, see *Engle v. Isaac,* the root principle underlying 28 U.S.C. § 2254 [authorizing the federal writ on behalf of state prisoners] is that government in a civilized society must always be accountable for an individual's imprisonment; if the imprisonment does not conform to the fundamental requirements of law, the individual is entitled to his immediate release. \* \* \*

The competing interests implicated by a prisoner's petition to a federal court to review the merits of a procedurally defaulted constitutional claim are easily identified. On the one hand, "there is Congress' expressed interest in providing a federal forum for the vindication of the constitutional rights of state prisoners." *Reed v. Ross.* In enacting § 2254, "Congress sought to 'interpose the federal courts between the States and the people, as guardians of the people's federal rights—to protect the people from unconstitutional action.'" This interest is at its strongest where the state court has declined to consider the merits of a constitutional claim, for without habeas review no court will ever consider whether the petitioner's constitutional rights were violated.

These interests must be weighed against the State's interest in maintaining the integrity of its rules and proceedings, an interest that would be undermined if the federal courts were too free to ignore procedural forfeitures in state court. The criminal justice system in each State is structured both to determine the guilt or innocence of defendants and to resolve all questions incident to that determination, including the constitutionality of the procedures leading to the verdict. Each State's complement of procedural rules facilitates this process by "channeling, to the extent possible, the resolution of various types of questions to the stage of the judicial process at which they can be resolved most fairly and efficiently." Procedural default rules protect the integrity of this process by imposing a forfeiture sanction for failure to follow applicable state procedural rules, thereby deterring litigants from deviating from the State's scheme. Generally, the threat of losing the right to raise a claim in state proceedings will be sufficient to ensure compliance with the State's procedural rules * * *. Nonetheless, to the extent that federal habeas review of a procedurally defaulted claim is available, the broad deterrent effect of these procedural default rules is somewhat diminished.

The Court's view of how properly to balance these competing concerns has changed over time. In *Fay v. Noia,* we concluded that the State's interest "in an airtight system of forfeitures" was generally insufficient to require federal courts to refrain from exercising their habeas jurisdiction. We held that federal courts should refuse to exercise their jurisdiction only "[i]f a habeas applicant * * * understandingly and knowingly forewent the privilege of seeking to vindicate his federal claims in the state courts, whether for strategic, tactical, or any other reasons that can fairly be described as the deliberate by-passing of state procedures." This holding sensibly accommodated the competing interests described above: on the one hand, the State's interest in preventing litigants from ignoring its procedural rules is at its strongest where the decision not to raise a claim is made knowingly and deliberately; correspondingly, the prisoner's entitlement to a federal forum is at its weakest since it may well be only the deliberate failure to submit the claim to the state courts that has necessitated federal review. Under these circumstances, the affront to comity principles is at its greatest: by its indifference in entertaining the petition to the prisoner's trial strategy, the federal court in effect ratifies the deliberate circumvention of state procedural rules. If refusal to exercise federal habeas power to upset a state-court conviction is ever appropriate, it is under circumstances such as these.

The Court struck a somewhat different balance 14 years later when it revisited the question of withholding federal habeas jurisdiction of procedurally defaulted claims in *Wainwright v. Sykes.* * * * Specifically, the Court held that federal habeas review of a procedurally defaulted claim should ordinarily be withheld unless the petitioner shows "cause" for the procedural default and "prejudice" to his case from the underlying error. * * * I thought then that *Wainwright v. Sykes* was wrongly decided, and I continue to believe so * * *. But at least the Court in *Wainwright v. Sykes* was prudent enough to leave the task of defining "cause" and "prejudice" to subsequent cases. * * *

The particular question we must decide in this case is whether counsel's inadvertent failure to raise a substantive claim of error can constitute "cause" for the procedural default. *Wainwright v. Sykes* held that defense counsel's tactical decision to bypass a state procedure does not constitute cause. That result may arguably be defended on grounds similar to those which justified the result in *Fay v. Noia,* i.e., that the deterrent interests underlying the State's procedural default rule are at their apogee where counsel's decision to bypass a state procedure is deliberate. However, to say that the petitioner should be bound to his lawyer's tactical decisions is one thing; to say that he must also bear the burden of his lawyer's inadvertent mistakes is quite another. Where counsel is unaware of a claim or of the duty to raise it at a particular time, the procedural default rule cannot operate as a specific deterrent to noncompliance with the State's procedural rules. Consequently, the State's interest in ensuring that the federal court help prevent circumvention of the State's procedural rules by imposing the same forfeiture sanction is much less compelling. To be sure, applying procedural default rules even to inadvertent defaults furthers the State's deterrent interests in a general sense by encouraging lawyers to be more conscientious on the whole. However, as the Court has pointed out in another context, such general deterrent interests are weak where the failure to follow a rule is accidental rather than intentional. See *United States v. Leon* [Ch. 3, § 1].

I believe that this incremental state interest simply is not sufficient to overcome the heavy presumption against a federal court's refusing to exercise jurisdiction clearly granted by Congress. This is especially so where the petitioner has satisfied the prejudice prong of the *Wainwright v. Sykes* test. That is, where a petitioner's constitutional rights have been violated and that violation may have affected the verdict, a federal court should not decline to entertain a habeas petition solely out of deference to the State's weak interest in punishing lawyers' inadvertent failures to comply with state procedures. I would therefore hold that "cause" is established where a procedural default resulted from counsel's inadvertence * * *.

## WHEAT v. UNITED STATES
486 U.S. 153, 108 S.Ct. 1692, 100 L.Ed.2d 140 (1988).

[Petitioner, along with numerous codefendants, including Gomez-Barajas and Bravo, was charged with participating in a far-flung drug conspiracy. Both Gomez-Barajas and Bravo were represented by attorney Iredale. Gomez-Barajas was tried first and was acquitted on drug charges overlapping with those against petitioner. To avoid a second trial on still further charges, Gomez-Barajas offered to plead guilty to tax-evasion and illegal-importation offenses stemming from the conspiracy. However, at the commencement of petitioner's trial, that plea had not yet been accepted by the district court, so there remained the possibility that it could be rejected by the district court or withdrawn by Gomez-Barajas. Bravo pleaded guilty in a proceeding that occurred two days before defendant's scheduled trial.

[At the conclusion of Bravo's guilty plea proceeding, petitioner moved for the substitution of Iredale as his counsel. The government objected on the ground that Iredale's representation of the defendant as well as the two other codefendants created a multiple conflict of interest: (1) In the event that Gomez-Barajas's plea and negotiated sentencing arrangement were rejected by the court, or Gomez-Barajas withdrew his plea, petitioner was likely to be called as a witness for the prosecution at Gomez-Barajas's second trial, and Iredale would face a conflict in cross-examining him; (2) In the likely event that Bravo was called as a witness for the prosecution against petitioner, Iredale would face a conflict of interest in cross-examining Bravo. Iredale, in either situation, the government argued, would not be able to fully cross-examine the prosecution witness because of confidences received from previously representing him, and could not effectively represent the particular criminal defendant, petitioner or Gomez-Barajas, without having the capacity to fully cross-examine the witness.

[In response, to the government, petitioner emphasized his right to have counsel of his own choosing and his willingness, and the willingness of the other codefendants, to waive the right to conflict-free counsel. Moreover, maintained petitioner, the circumstances posited by the government that would create a conflict of interest were highly speculative and bore no connection to the true relationship among the co-conspirators. If called to testify against petitioner, Bravo would simply say that he did not know petitioner and had had no dealings with him. In the unlikely event that Gomez-Barajas went to trial, petitioner's lack of involvement in his alleged crimes made his appearance as a witness highly improbable. According to petitioner, the government was "manufacturing implausible conflicts" in an attempt to disqualify Iredale, who had already proved extremely effective in representing the other codefendants.

[The district court denied petitioner's request to substitute Iredale as his attorney, concluding, on the basis of the representation of the government, that it "really has no choice at this point other than to find that an irreconcilable conflict of interest exists." Petitioner proceeded to trial with his original counsel and was convicted of various drug offenses. The Court of Appeals for the Ninth Circuit affirmed.]

CHIEF JUSTICE REHNQUIST delivered the opinion of the Court.

* * * [W]hile the right to select and be represented by one's preferred attorney is comprehended by the Sixth Amendment, the essential aim of the Amendment is to guarantee an effective advocate for each criminal defendant rather than to ensure that a defendant will inexorably be represented by the lawyer whom he prefers.

The Sixth Amendment right to choose one's own counsel is circumscribed in several important respects. Regardless of his persuasive powers, an advocate who is not a member of the bar may not represent clients (other than himself) in court. Similarly, a defendant may not insist on representation by an attorney he cannot afford or who for other reasons declines to represent the defendant. Nor may a defendant insist on the counsel of an attorney who has a previous or ongoing relationship with an opposing party, even when the opposing party is the Government. The question raised in this case is the extent to which a criminal defendant's right under the Sixth Amendment to his chosen attorney is qualified by the fact that the attorney has represented other defendants charged in the same criminal conspiracy. * * *

Petitioner insists that the provision of waivers by all affected defendants cures any problems created by the multiple representation. But no such flat rule can be deduced from the Sixth Amendment presumption in favor of counsel of choice. Federal courts have an independent interest in ensuring that criminal trials are conducted within the ethical standards of the profession and that legal proceedings appear fair to all who observe them. Both the American Bar Association's Model Code of Professional Responsibility and its Model Rules of Professional Conduct, as well as the rules of the California Bar Association (which governed the attorneys in this case), impose limitations on multiple representation of clients. Not only the interest of a criminal defendant but the institutional interest in the rendition of just verdicts in criminal cases may be jeopardized by unregulated multiple representation.

For this reason, the Federal Rules of Criminal Procedure direct trial judges to investigate specially cases involving joint representation. In pertinent part, Rule 44(c) provides:

"[T]he court shall promptly inquire with respect to such joint representation and shall personally advise each defendant of his right to the effective assistance of counsel, including separate representation. Unless it appears that there is good cause to believe no conflict of interest is likely to arise, the court shall take such measures as may be appropriate to protect each defendant's right to counsel."

Although Rule 44(c) does not specify what particular measures may be taken by a district court, one option suggested by the Notes of the Advisory Committee is an order by the court that the defendants be separately represented in subsequent proceedings in the case. This suggestion comports with our instructions in *Holloway* and in *Glasser v. United States* that the trial courts, when alerted by objection from one of the parties, have an independent duty to ensure that criminal defendants receive a trial that is fair and does not contravene the Sixth Amendment.[a]

To be sure, this need to investigate potential conflicts arises in part from the legitimate wish of District Courts that their judgments remain intact on appeal. As the Court of Appeals accurately pointed out, trial courts confronted with multiple representations face the prospect of being "whip-sawed" by assertions of error no matter which way they rule. If a district court agrees to the multiple representation, and the advocacy of counsel is thereafter impaired as a result, the defendant may well claim that he did not receive effective assistance. On the other hand, a district court's refusal to accede to the multiple representation may result in a challenge such as petitioner's in this case. Nor does a waiver by the defendant necessarily solve the problem, for we note, without passing judgment on, the apparent willingness of Courts of Appeals to entertain ineffective assistance claims from defendants who have specifically waived the right to conflict-free counsel.

a. In *Glasser v. United States*, 315 U.S. 60 (1942), the Court held that the defendant was denied the effective assistance of counsel when the trial court placed his retained counsel in an actual conflict situation by appointing the attorney to also represent a codefendant whose strategic position differed from defendant. In *Holloway v. Arkansas*, 435 U.S. 475 (1978), the Court found constitutional error in a trial court's failure to make an inquiry, such as that prescribed under Rule 44(c), into counsel's multiple representation of defendants. *Holloway* involved a situation in which previously appointed counsel had asked the trial court to relieve him of the obligation of jointly representing three codefendants. Counsel had explained that he would not be able to cross-examine a testifying codefendant on behalf of the other codefendants because of "confidential information" he had received from each of the codefendants. The trial court, however, refused to relieve counsel without even exploring the possibility that such a conflict existed. That failure, in light of the warning from counsel, constituted a violation of the Sixth Amendment in itself; there was no need to determine after the fact whether an actual conflict had indeed existed (as it had in *Glasser*).

The *Holloway* opinion specifically left open the question of what the trial court's constitutional responsibilities were "where the trial counsel did nothing to advise the trial court as to the actuality or possibility of a conflict." *Cuyler v. Sullivan*, 446 U.S. 335 (1980), subsequently held that a considerably different standard applied to that situation. The Court there rejected the contention that a trial court had a constitutional duty to make some inquiry as to a possible conflict in all cases of multiple representation (as Federal Rule 44(c) requires of federal courts). Ordinarily, the Court noted, the trial judge could rely upon the absence of any objection by counsel, since counsel has "an ethical obligation to avoid conflicting representations and to advise the court promptly when a conflict arises during the course of the trial." Thus, as a matter of constitutional law, "absent special circumstances" indicating that the court "reasonably should know" that a particular conflict exists, where counsel has raised no objection, the trial court "may assume either that multiple representation entails no conflict or that the lawyer and his clients knowingly accept such a risk of conflict as may exist." In such cases, to establish incompetency, defendant must show not merely a failure of the court to conduct an inquiry (as in *Holloway*), but "an actual conflict of interest [that] adversely affected his lawyer's performance." See also *Strickland*, supra, in the paragraph ending with note b.

Thus, where a court justifiably finds an actual conflict of interest, there can be no doubt that it may decline a proffer of waiver, and insist that defendants be separately represented.

Unfortunately for all concerned, a district court must pass on the issue of whether or not to allow a waiver of a conflict of interest by a criminal defendant not with the wisdom of hindsight after the trial has taken place, but the murkier pretrial context when relationships between parties are seen through a glass, darkly. The likelihood and dimensions of nascent conflicts of interest are notoriously hard to predict, even for those thoroughly familiar with criminal trials. It is a rare attorney who will be fortunate enough to learn the entire truth from his own client, much less be fully apprised before trial of what each of the Government's witnesses will say on the stand. A few bits of unforeseen testimony or a single previously unknown or unnoticed document may significantly shift the relationship between multiple defendants. These imponderables are difficult enough for a lawyer to assess, and even more difficult to convey by way of explanation to a criminal defendant untutored in the niceties of legal ethics. Nor is it amiss to observe that the willingness of an attorney to obtain such waivers from his clients may bear an inverse relation to the care with which he conveys all the necessary information to them.

For these reasons we think the District Court must be allowed substantial latitude in refusing waivers of conflicts of interest not only in those rare cases where an actual conflict may be demonstrated before trial, but in the more common cases where a potential for conflict exists which may or may not burgeon into an actual conflict as the trial progresses. In the circumstances of this case, with the motion for substitution of counsel made so close to the time of trial, the District Court relied on instinct and judgment based on experience in making its decision. We do not think it can be said that the court exceeded the broad latitude which must be accorded it in making this decision. Petitioner of course rightly points out that the government may seek to "manufacture" a conflict in order to prevent a defendant from having a particularly able defense counsel at his side; but trial courts are undoubtedly aware of this possibility, and must take it into consideration along with all of the other factors which inform this sort of a decision.

Here the District Court was confronted not simply with an attorney who wished to represent two coequal defendants in a straightforward criminal prosecution; rather, Iredale proposed to defend three conspirators of varying stature in a complex drug distribution scheme. The Government intended to call Bravo as a witness for the prosecution at petitioner's trial.[4] The Government might readily have tied certain deliveries of marijuana by Bravo to petitioner, necessitating vigorous cross-examination of Bravo by petitioner's counsel. Iredale, because of his prior representation of Bravo, would have been unable ethically to provide that cross-examination.

Iredale had also represented Gomez-Barajas, one of the alleged kingpins of the distribution ring, and had succeeded in obtaining a verdict of acquittal for him. Gomez-Barajas had agreed with the Government to plead guilty to other charges, but the District Court had not yet accepted the plea arrangement. If the agreement were rejected, petitioner's probable testimony at the resulting trial of Gomez-Barajas would create an ethical dilemma for Iredale from which one or the other of his clients would likely suffer.

4. Bravo was in fact called as a witness at petitioner's trial. His testimony was elicited to demonstrate the transportation of drugs that the prosecution hoped to link to petitioner.

Viewing the situation as it did before trial, we hold that the District Court's refusal to permit the substitution of counsel in this case was within its discretion and did not violate petitioner's Sixth Amendment rights. Other district courts might have reached differing or opposite conclusions with equal justification, but that does not mean that one conclusion was "right" and the other "wrong." The District Court must recognize a presumption in favor of petitioner's counsel of choice, but that presumption may be overcome not only by a demonstration of actual conflict but by a showing of a serious potential for conflict. The evaluation of the facts and circumstances of each case under this standard must be left primarily to the informed judgment of the trial court. * * *

JUSTICE MARSHALL, with whom JUSTICE BRENNAN joins, dissenting.

* * * The right to counsel of choice, as the Court notes, is not absolute. When a defendant's selection of counsel, under the particular facts and circumstances of a case, gravely imperils the prospect of a fair trial, a trial court may justifiably refuse to accede to the choice. Thus, a trial court may in certain situations reject a defendant's choice of counsel on the ground of a potential conflict of interest, because a serious conflict may indeed destroy the integrity of the trial process. As the Court states, however, the trial court must recognize a presumption in favor of a defendant's counsel of choice. This presumption means that a trial court may not reject a defendant's chosen counsel on the ground of a potential conflict of interest absent a showing that both the likelihood and the dimensions of the feared conflict are substantial.[1] Unsupported or dubious speculation as to a conflict will not suffice. The Government must show a substantial potential for the kind of conflict that would undermine the fairness of the trial process. In these respects, I do not believe my position differs significantly, if at all, from that expressed in the opinion of the Court.

I do disagree, however, with the Court's suggestion that the trial court's decision as to whether a potential conflict justifies rejection of a defendant's chosen counsel is entitled to some kind of special deference on appeal. The Court grants trial courts "broad latitude" over the decision to accept or reject a defendant's choice of counsel; although never explicitly endorsing a standard of appellate review, the Court appears to limit such review to determining whether an abuse of discretion has occurred. This approach, which the Court supports solely by noting the difficulty of evaluating the likelihood and magnitude of a conflict, accords neither with the nature of the trial court's decision nor with the importance of the interest at stake.

The trial court's decision as to whether the circumstances of a given case constitute grounds for rejecting a defendant's chosen counsel—that is, as to whether these circumstances present a substantial potential for a serious conflict of interest—is a mixed determination of law and fact. The decision is properly described in this way because it requires and results from the application of a legal standard to the established facts of a case. Appellate courts traditionally do not defer to such determinations. * * *

The inappropriateness of deferring to this determination becomes even more apparent when its constitutional significance is taken into account. * * * [The] interest at stake in this kind of decision is nothing less than a criminal defendant's Sixth Amendment right to counsel of his choice. The trial court simply does not have "broad latitude" to vitiate this right. In my view, a trial

1. In stating this principle, I mean to address only cases in which all parties to the potential conflict have made a fully informed waiver of their right to conflict-free representation. It is undisputed in this case that petitioner, as well as Juvenal Gomez-Barajas and Javier Bravo, had agreed to waive this right.

court that rejects a criminal defendant's chosen counsel on the ground of a potential conflict should make findings on the record to facilitate review, and an appellate court should scrutinize closely the basis for the trial court's decision. Only in this way can a criminal defendant's right to counsel of his choice be appropriately protected.

The Court's resolution of the instant case flows from its deferential approach to the District Court's denial of petitioner's motion to add or substitute counsel; absent deference, a decision upholding the District Court's ruling would be inconceivable. * * * At the time of petitioner's trial, Iredale's representation of Gomez-Barajas was effectively completed. * * * The only possible conflict this Court can divine from Iredale's representation of both petitioner and Gomez-Barajas rests on the premise that the trial court would reject the negotiated plea agreement and that Gomez-Barajas then would decide to go to trial. In this event, the Court tells us, "petitioner's probable testimony at the resulting trial of Gomez-Barajas would create an ethical dilemma for Iredale."

This argument rests on speculation of the most dubious kind. The Court offers no reason to think that the trial court would have rejected Gomez-Barajas's plea agreement; neither did the Government posit any such reason in its argument or brief before this Court. The most likely occurrence at the time petitioner moved to retain Iredale as his defense counsel was that the trial court would accept Gomez-Barajas's plea agreement, as the court in fact later did. Moreover, even if Gomez-Barajas had gone to trial, petitioner probably would not have testified. * * * The only alleged connection between petitioner and Gomez-Barajas sprang from the conspiracy to distribute marijuana, and a jury already had acquitted Gomez-Barajas of that charge. It is therefore disingenuous to say that representation of both petitioner and Gomez-Barajas posed a serious potential for a conflict of interest.

Similarly, Iredale's prior representation of Bravo was not a cause for concern. * * * [The facts] belie the claim that Bravo's anticipated testimony created a serious potential for conflict. Contrary to the Court's inference, Bravo could not have testified about petitioner's involvement in the alleged marijuana distribution scheme. As all parties were aware at the time, Bravo did not know and could not identify petitioner; indeed, prior to the commencement of legal proceedings, the two men never had heard of each other. Bravo's eventual testimony at petitioner's trial related to a shipment of marijuana in which petitioner was not involved; the testimony contained not a single reference to petitioner. Petitioner's counsel did not cross-examine Bravo, and neither petitioner's counsel nor the prosecutor mentioned Bravo's testimony in closing argument. All of these developments were predictable when the District Court ruled on petitioner's request that Iredale serve as trial counsel. * * * The District Court therefore had no authority to deny petitioner's Sixth Amendment right to retain counsel of his choice. * * * [b]

# FARETTA v. CALIFORNIA

422 U.S. 806, 95 S.Ct. 2525, 45 L.Ed.2d 562 (1975).

JUSTICE STEWART delivered the opinion of the Court.

The Sixth and Fourteenth Amendments of our Constitution guarantee that a person brought to trial in any state or federal court must be afforded the right

b. In a separate dissent, Stevens, J., joined by Blackmun, J., noted agreement with "the Court's premise that district judges must be afforded wide latitude in passing on motions of this kind," but found it "abundantly clear" that the district judge here "abused his discretion."

to the assistance of counsel before he can be validly convicted and punished by imprisonment. This clear constitutional rule has emerged from a series of cases decided here over the last 50 years. The question before us now is whether a defendant in a state criminal trial has a constitutional right to proceed *without* counsel when he voluntarily and intelligently elects to do so. Stated another way, the question is whether a State may constitutionally hale a person into its criminal courts and there force a lawyer upon him, even when he insists that he wants to conduct his own defense. It is not an easy question, but we have concluded that a State may not constitutionally do so.

Anthony Faretta was charged with grand theft in * * * the Superior Court of Los Angeles County, Cal. At the arraignment, the Superior Court Judge assigned to preside at the trial appointed the public defender to represent Faretta. Well before the date of trial, however, Faretta requested that he be permitted to represent himself. Questioning by the judge revealed that Faretta had once represented himself in a criminal prosecution, that he had a high school education, and that he did not want to be represented by the public defender because he believed that that office was "very loaded down with * * * a heavy case load." The judge responded that he believed Faretta was "making a mistake" and emphasized that in further proceedings Faretta would receive no special favors. Nevertheless, * * * the judge, in a "preliminary ruling," accepted Faretta's waiver of the assistance of counsel. The judge indicated, however, that he might reverse this ruling if it later appeared that Faretta was unable adequately to represent himself.

Several weeks thereafter, but still prior to trial, the judge *sua sponte* held a hearing to inquire into Faretta's ability to conduct his own defense, and questioned him specifically about both the hearsay rule and the state law governing the challenge of potential jurors. After consideration of Faretta's answers, and observation of his demeanor, the judge ruled that Faretta had not made an intelligent and knowing waiver of his right to the assistance of counsel, and also ruled that Faretta had no constitutional right to conduct his own defense. The judge, accordingly, reversed his earlier ruling permitting self-representation and again appointed the public defender to represent Faretta. Faretta's subsequent request for leave to act as cocounsel was rejected, as were his efforts to make certain motions on his own behalf. Throughout the subsequent trial, the judge required that Faretta's defense be conducted only through the appointed lawyer from the public defender's office. At the conclusion of the trial, the jury found Faretta guilty as charged, and the judge sentenced him to prison.

The California Court of Appeal * * * affirmed the trial judge's ruling that Faretta had no federal or state constitutional right to represent himself, * * * and the California Supreme Court denied review.

In the federal courts, the right of self-representation has been protected by statute since the beginnings of our Nation. Section 35 of the Judiciary Act of 1789, 1 Stat. 73, 92, enacted by the First Congress and signed by President Washington one day before the Sixth Amendment was proposed, provided that "in all the courts of the United States, the parties may plead and manage their own causes personally or by the assistance of * * * counsel * * *." * * * With few exceptions, each of the several States also accords a defendant the right to represent himself in any criminal case. The Constitutions of 36 States explicitly confer that right. Moreover, many state courts have expressed the view that the right is also supported by the Constitution of the United States. This Court has more than once indicated the same view. * * * [And] the

United States Courts of Appeals have repeatedly held that the right of self-representation is protected by the Bill of Rights.

This Court's past recognition of the right of self-representation, the federal-court authority holding the right to be of constitutional dimension, and the state constitutions pointing to the right's fundamental nature form a consensus not easily ignored. "[T]he mere fact that a path is a beaten one," Mr. Justice Jackson once observed, "is a persuasive reason for following it." We confront here a nearly universal conviction, on the part of our people as well as our courts, that forcing a lawyer upon an unwilling defendant is contrary to his basic right to defend himself if he truly wants to do so. This consensus is soundly premised. The right of self-representation finds support in the structure of the Sixth Amendment, as well as in the English and colonial jurisprudence from which the Amendment emerged.

The Sixth Amendment includes a compact statement of the rights necessary to a full defense. * * * The rights to notice, confrontation, and compulsory process, when taken together, guarantee that a criminal charge may be answered in a manner now considered fundamental to the fair administration of American justice—through the calling and interrogation of favorable witnesses, the cross-examination of adverse witnesses, and the orderly introduction of evidence. In short, the Amendment constitutionalizes the right in an adversary criminal trial to make a defense as we know it.

The Sixth Amendment does not provide merely that a defense shall be made for the accused; it grants to the accused personally the right to make his defense. It is the accused, not counsel, who must be "informed of the nature and cause of the accusation," who must be "confronted with the witnesses against him," and who must be accorded "compulsory process for obtaining witnesses in his favor." Although not stated in the Amendment in so many words, the right to self-representation—to make one's own defense personally—is thus necessarily implied by the structure of the Amendment.[15] The right to defend is given directly to the accused; for it is he who suffers the consequences if the defense fails.

The counsel provision supplements this design. It speaks of the "assistance" of counsel, and an assistant, however expert, is still an assistant. The language and spirit of the Sixth Amendment contemplate that counsel, like the other defense tools guaranteed by the Amendment, shall be an aid to a willing defendant—not an organ of the State interposed between an unwilling defendant and his right to defend himself personally. To thrust counsel upon the accused, against his considered wish, thus violates the logic of the Amendment. In such a case, counsel is not an assistant, but a master; and the right to make a defense is stripped of the personal character upon which the Amendment insists. It is true

---

**15.** This Court has often recognized the constitutional stature of rights that, though not literally expressed in the document, are essential to due process of law in a fair adversary process. It is now accepted, for example, that an accused has a right to be present at all stages of the trial where his absence might frustrate the fairness of the proceedings, to testify on his own behalf, and to be convicted only if his guilt is proved beyond a reasonable doubt. * * *

The inference of rights is not, of course, a mechanical exercise. In *Singer v. United States,* 380 U.S. 24 (1965), the Court held that an accused has no right to a bench trial, despite his capacity to waive his right to a jury trial. In so holding, the Court stated that "[t]he ability to waive a constitutional right does not ordinarily carry with it the right to insist upon the opposite of that right." But that statement was made only *after* the Court had concluded that the Constitution does not affirmatively protect any right to be tried by a judge. * * * We follow the approach of *Singer* here. Our concern is with an *independent* right of self-representation. We do not suggest that this right arises mechanically from a defendant's power to waive the right to the assistance of counsel. * * *

that when a defendant chooses to have a lawyer manage and present his case, law and tradition may allocate to the counsel the power to make binding decisions of trial strategy in many areas.[a] This allocation can only be justified, however, by the defendant's consent, at the outset, to accept counsel as his representative. An unwanted counsel "represents" the defendant only through a tenuous and unacceptable legal fiction. Unless the accused has acquiesced in such representation, the defense presented is not the defense guaranteed him by the Constitution, for, in a very real sense, it is not *his* defense.

The Sixth Amendment, when naturally read, thus implies a right of self-representation. This reading is reinforced by the Amendment's roots in English legal history. In the long history of British criminal jurisprudence, there was only one tribunal that ever adopted a practice of forcing counsel upon an unwilling defendant in a criminal proceeding. The tribunal was the Star Chamber. That curious institution, which flourished in the late 16th and early 17th centuries, was of mixed executive and judicial character, and characteristically departed from common-law traditions. For those reasons, and because it specialized in trying "political" offenses, the Star Chamber has for centuries symbolized disregard of basic individual rights. * * *

In the American Colonies the insistence upon a right of self-representation was, if anything, more fervent than in England. The colonists brought with them an appreciation of the virtues of self-reliance and a traditional distrust of lawyers. When the Colonies were first settled, "the lawyer was synonymous with the cringing Attorneys–General and Solicitors–General of the Crown and the arbitrary Justices of the King's Court, all bent on the conviction of those who opposed the King's prerogatives, and twisting the law to secure convictions." This prejudice gained strength in the Colonies where "distrust of lawyers became an institution." * * *

This is not to say that the Colonies were slow to recognize the value of counsel in criminal cases. Colonial judges soon departed from ancient English practice and allowed accused felons the aid of counsel for their defense. At the same time, however, the basic right of self-representation was never questioned. We have found no instance where a colonial court required a defendant in a criminal case to accept as his representative an unwanted lawyer. Indeed, even where counsel was permitted, the general practice continued to be self-representation. * * * After the Declaration of Independence, the right of self-repre-

**a.** Prior to *Faretta*, a long line of lower court cases had held that defense counsel had the authority to make various defense decisions on his own initiative. Those decisions, commonly characterized as relating to matters of "strategy" or "tactics," were said to be within the "exclusive province" of the lawyer. To provide effective assistance as required under the Sixth Amendment, counsel did not have to consult with the defendant on such strategic decisions, and if there was consultation, did not have to follow the defendant's wishes. A post-*Faretta* ruling, *Jones v. Barnes*, 463 U.S. 745 (1983), reaffirmed this traditional viewpoint. The Court there held that appellate counsel did not have to present a nonfrivolous claim that his client wished to press if counsel believed that the better strategy was to limit the appellate argument to other issues. Counsel was free to follow the time tested advice of countless advocates that inclusion of "every colorable claim" will "di-

lute and weaken a good case and will not save a bad one." It was for counsel to decide which claims were strong enough to be presented consistent with this strategy.

As Chief Justice Burger noted in a concurring opinion in *Jones*, there are certain decisions that fall outside the range of control given to counsel in determining strategy. These decisions, because of their special significance or their involvement with the personal actions of defendant, are matters as to which defendant's choice prevails over a strategic preference of counsel. The Supreme Court has stated in dictum or holding that the following five decisions fall in this category: (1) pleading guilty or taking action tantamount to entering a guilty plea; (2) waiving the right to jury trial; (3) waiving the right to be present at the trial (4) defendant testifying on his own behalf; and (5) foregoing an appeal.

sentation, along with other rights basic to the making of a defense, entered the new state constitutions in wholesale fashion. The right to counsel was clearly thought to supplement the primary right of the accused to defend himself, utilizing his personal rights to notice, confrontation, and compulsory process. * * * At the time James Madison drafted the Sixth Amendment, some state constitutions guaranteed an accused the right to be heard "by himself" and by counsel; others provided that an accused was to be "allowed" counsel. The various state proposals for the Bill of Rights had similar variations in terminology. In each case, however, the counsel provision was embedded in a package of defense rights granted personally to the accused. There is no indication that the differences in phrasing about "counsel" reflected any differences of principle about self-representation. * * *

There can be no blinking the fact that the right of an accused to conduct his own defense seems to cut against the grain of this Court's decisions holding that the Constitution requires that no accused can be convicted and imprisoned unless he has been accorded the right to the assistance of counsel. See *Powell v. Alabama; Johnson v. Zerbst; Gideon v. Wainwright; Argersinger v. Hamlin* [all discussed in Ch. 5, § 1]. For it is surely true that the basic thesis of those decisions is that the help of a lawyer is essential to assure the defendant a fair trial. And a strong argument can surely be made that the whole thrust of those decisions must inevitably lead to the conclusion that a State may constitutionally impose a lawyer upon even an unwilling defendant.

But it is one thing to hold that every defendant, rich or poor, has the right to the assistance of counsel, and quite another to say that a State may compel a defendant to accept a lawyer he does not want. The value of state-appointed counsel was not unappreciated by the Founders, yet the notion of compulsory counsel was utterly foreign to them. And whatever else may be said of those who wrote the Bill of Rights, surely there can be no doubt that they understood the inestimable worth of free choice.

It is undeniable that in most criminal prosecutions defendants could better defend with counsel's guidance than by their own unskilled efforts. But where the defendant will not voluntarily accept representation by counsel, the potential advantage of a lawyer's training and experience can be realized, if at all, only imperfectly. To force a lawyer on a defendant can only lead him to believe that the law contrives against him. Moreover, it is not inconceivable that in some rare instances, the defendant might in fact present his case more effectively by conducting his own defense. Personal liberties are not rooted in the law of averages. The right to defend is personal. The defendant, and not his lawyer or the State, will bear the personal consequences of a conviction. It is the defendant, therefore, who must be free personally to decide whether in his particular case counsel is to his advantage. And although he may conduct his own defense ultimately to his own detriment, his choice must be honored out of "that respect for the individual which is the lifeblood of the law." [46]

**46.** We are told that many criminal defendants representing themselves may use the courtroom for deliberate disruption of their trials. But the right of self-representation has been recognized from our beginnings by federal law and by most of the States, and no such result has thereby occurred. Moreover, the trial judge may terminate self-representation by a defendant who deliberately engages in serious and obstructionist misconduct. See *Illinois v. Allen* [Ch. 18, § 1]. Of course, a State may—even over objection by the accused—appoint a "standby counsel" to aid the accused if and when the accused requests help, and to be available to represent the accused in the event that termination of the defendant's self-representation is necessary.

The right of self-representation is not a license to abuse the dignity of the courtroom. Neither is it a license not to comply with relevant rules of procedural and substantive

When an accused manages his own defense, he relinquishes, as a purely factual matter, many of the traditional benefits associated with the right to counsel. For this reason, in order to represent himself, the accused must "knowingly and intelligently" forgo those relinquished benefits. Although a defendant need not himself have the skill and experience of a lawyer in order competently and intelligently to choose self-representation, he should be made aware of the dangers and disadvantages of self-representation, so that the record will establish that "he knows what he is doing and his choice is made with eyes open."

Here, weeks before trial, Faretta clearly and unequivocally declared to the trial judge that he wanted to represent himself and did not want counsel. The record affirmatively shows that Faretta was literate, competent, and understanding, and that he was voluntarily exercising his informed free will. The trial judge had warned Faretta that he thought it was a mistake not to accept the assistance of counsel, and that Faretta would be required to follow all the "ground rules" of trial procedure. We need make no assessment of how well or poorly Faretta had mastered the intricacies of the hearsay rule and the California code provisions that govern challenges of potential jurors on *voir dire*. For his technical legal knowledge, as such, was not relevant to an assessment of his knowing exercise of the right to defend himself.

In forcing Faretta, under these circumstances, to accept against his will a state-appointed public defender, the California courts deprived him of his constitutional right to conduct his own defense. * * *

CHIEF JUSTICE BURGER, with whom JUSTICE BLACKMUN and JUSTICE REHNQUIST join, dissenting. * * *

The most striking feature of the Court's opinion is that it devotes so little discussion to the matter which it concedes is the core of the decision, that is, discerning an independent basis in the Constitution for the supposed right to represent oneself in a criminal trial. Its ultimate assertion that such a right is tucked between the lines of the Sixth Amendment is contradicted by the Amendment's language and its consistent judicial interpretation.

[T]he conclusion that the rights guaranteed by the Sixth Amendment are "personal" to an accused reflects nothing more than the obvious fact that it is he who is on trial and therefore has need of a defense.[3] But neither that nearly trivial proposition nor the language of the Amendment, which speaks in uniformly mandatory terms, leads to the further conclusion that the right to counsel is merely supplementary and may be dispensed with at the whim of the accused. Rather, this Court's decisions have consistently included the right to counsel as an integral part of the bundle making up the larger "right to a defense as we know it." * * * The reason for this hardly requires explanation. The fact of the matter is that in all but an extraordinarily small number of cases an accused will lose whatever defense he may have if he undertakes to conduct the trial himself. The Court's opinion in *Powell v. Alabama*, puts the

law. Thus, whatever else may or may not be open to him on appeal, a defendant who elects to represent himself cannot thereafter complain that the quality of his own defense amounted to a denial of "effective assistance of counsel."

3. The Court's attempt to derive support for its position from the fact that the Sixth Amendment speaks in terms of the "Assis-

tance of Counsel" requires little comment. It is most curious to suggest that an accused who exercises his right to "assistance" has thereby impliedly consented to subject himself to a "master." And counsel's responsibility to his client and role in the litigation do not vary depending upon whether the accused would have preferred to represent himself.

point eloquently [in describing the difficulties facing "even the intelligent and educated layman" in representing himself]. * * *

* * * Nor is it accurate to suggest, as the Court seems to later in its opinion, that the quality of his representation at trial is a matter with which only the accused is legitimately concerned. Although we have adopted an adversary system of criminal justice, the prosecution is more than an ordinary litigant, and the trial judge is not simply an automaton who insures that technical rules are adhered to. Both are charged with the duty of insuring that justice, in the broadest sense of that term, is achieved in every criminal trial. That goal is ill-served, and the integrity of and public confidence in the system are undermined, when an easy conviction is obtained due to the defendant's ill-advised decision to waive counsel. The damage thus inflicted is not mitigated by the lame explanation that the defendant simply availed himself of the "freedom" "to go to jail under his own banner * * *." The system of criminal justice should not be available as an instrument of self-destruction.

In short, both the "spirit and the logic" of the Sixth Amendment are that every person accused of crime shall receive the fullest possible defense; in the vast majority of cases this command can be honored only by means of the expressly guaranteed right to counsel, and the trial judge is in the best position to determine whether the accused is capable of conducting his defense. True freedom of choice and society's interest in seeing that justice is achieved can be vindicated only if the trial court retains discretion to reject any attempted waiver of counsel and insist that the accused be tried according to the Constitution. This discretion is as critical an element of basic fairness as a trial judge's discretion to decline to accept a plea of guilty. See *Santobello v. New York* [Ch. 14, § 1].

The Court's attempt to support its result by collecting dicta from prior decisions is no more persuasive than its analysis of the Sixth Amendment. Considered in context, the cases upon which the Court relies to "beat its path" either lead it nowhere or point in precisely the opposite direction. * * *

The Court of Appeals cases relied upon by the Court are likewise dubious authority for its views. Only one of those cases, even attempted a reasoned analysis of the issue * * *. In short, what the Court represents as a well-traveled road is in reality a constitutional trail which it is blazing for the first time today, one that has not even been hinted at in our previous decisions. Far from an interpretation of the Sixth Amendment, it is a perversion of the provision to which we gave full meaning in *Gideon v. Wainwright* and *Argersinger v. Hamlin.*

* * * [T]he Court * * * attempts to use history to take it where legal analysis cannot. Piecing together shreds of English legal history and early state constitutional and statutory provisions, without a full elaboration of the context in which they occurred or any evidence that they were relied upon by the drafters of our Federal Constitution, creates more questions than it answers and hardly provides the firm foundation upon which the creation of new constitutional rights should rest. We are well reminded that this Court once employed an exhaustive analysis of English and colonial practices regarding the right to counsel to justify the conclusion that it was fundamental to a fair trial and, less than 10 years later, used essentially the same material to conclude that it was not. Compare *Powell v. Alabama* with *Betts v. Brady* [Ch. 5, § 1].

As if to illustrate this point, the single historical fact cited by the Court which would appear truly relevant to ascertaining the meaning of the Sixth Amendment proves too much. As the Court points out, § 35 of the Judiciary Act of 1789 provided a statutory right to self-representation in federal criminal trials. The text of the Sixth Amendment, which expressly provides only for a right to counsel, was proposed the day after the Judiciary Act was signed. It can hardly be suggested that the Members of the Congress of 1789, then few in number, were unfamiliar with the Amendment's carefully structured language, which had been under discussion since the 1787 Constitutional Convention. And it would be most remarkable to suggest, had the right to conduct one's own defense been considered so critical as to require constitutional protection, that it would have been left to implication. Rather, under traditional canons of construction, *inclusion* of the right in the Judiciary Act and its *omission* from the constitutional amendment drafted at the same time by many of the same men, supports the conclusion that the omission was intentional. * * *

In this case, therefore, history ought to lead judges to conclude that the Constitution leaves to the judgment of legislatures, and the flexible process of statutory amendment, the question whether criminal defendants should be permitted to conduct their trials *pro se*. See *Betts v. Brady*. And the fact that we have not hinted at a contrary view for 185 years is surely entitled to some weight in the scales. * * *

Society has the right to expect that, when courts find new rights implied in the Constitution, their potential effect upon the resources of our criminal justice system will be considered. However, such considerations are conspicuously absent from the Court's opinion in this case. * * * [T]he Court blandly assumes that once an accused has elected to defend himself he will be bound by his choice and not be heard to complain of it later. n. 46. This assumption ignores the role of appellate review, for the reported cases are replete with instances of a convicted defendant being relieved of a deliberate decision even when made *with the advice of counsel*. It is totally unrealistic, therefore, to suggest that an accused will always be held to the consequences of a decision to conduct his own defense. Unless, as may be the case, most persons accused of crime have more wit than to insist upon the dubious benefit that the Court confers today, we can expect that many expensive and good-faith prosecutions will be nullified on appeal for reasons that trial courts are now deprived of the power to prevent.

JUSTICE BLACKMUN, with whom THE CHIEF JUSTICE and JUSTICE REHNQUIST join, dissenting.

* * * I fear that the right to self-representation constitutionalized today frequently will cause procedural confusion without advancing any significant strategic interest of the defendant. * * * I note briefly the procedural problems that, I suspect, today's decision will visit upon trial courts in the future. Although the Court indicates that a *pro se* defendant necessarily waives any claim he might otherwise make of ineffective assistance of counsel, n. 46, the opinion leaves open a host of other procedural questions. Must every defendant be advised of his right to proceed *pro se?* If so, when must that notice be given? Since the right to assistance of counsel and the right to self-representation are mutually exclusive, how is the waiver of each right to be measured? If a defendant has elected to exercise his right to proceed *pro se,* does he still have a constitutional right to assistance of standby counsel? How soon in the criminal proceeding must a defendant decide between proceeding by counsel or *pro se?* Must he be allowed to switch in midtrial? May a violation of the right to self-representation ever be harmless error? Must the trial court treat the *pro se* defendant differently than it would professional counsel? I assume that many of these questions will be answered with finality in due course. Many of them,

however, such as the standards of waiver and the treatment of the *pro se* defendant, will haunt the trial of every defendant who elects to exercise his right to self-representation. The procedural problems spawned by an absolute right to self-representation will far outweigh whatever tactical advantage the defendant may feel he has gained by electing to represent himself.

If there is any truth to the old proverb that "one who is his own lawyer has a fool for a client," the Court by its opinion today now bestows a *constitutional* right on one to make a fool of himself.[b]

**b.** *McKaskle v. Wiggins*, 465 U.S. 168 (1984), the leading post-*Faretta* ruling of the Supreme Court, spoke to some of the issues raised by Justice Blackmun, but most have been left to lower court rulings. *McKaskle* involved a defense challenge to the actions of a standby counsel appointed to assist the *pro se* defendant. The Court initially held that "a defendant's Sixth Amendment rights are not violated when a trial judge appoints standby counsel—even over the defendant's objection—to relieve the judge of the need to explain and enforce basic rules of courtroom protocol or to assist the defendant in overcoming routine obstacles that stand in way of defendant's achievement of his own clearly indicated goals." The counsel in *McKaskle*, however, had gone beyond "steer[ing] the defendant through the basic procedures of the trial"; he had engaged in arguably unsolicited participation on various substantive matters (although defendant conducted the major portion of the trial). The Court held that, under the circumstances of the case, the unsolicited participation that went beyond "routine clerical or procedural matters" would not be deemed to violate defendant's pro se right because (i) it did not interfere with defendant's own actions in such a way as to deprive him of "actual control over the case he chose to present to the jury" and (ii) it did not "destroy the jury's perception that the defendant [was] representing himself."

Commenting generally on the *pro se* right, *McKaskle* added that denial of the right could not be treated as a harmless error even though counsel subsequently gave defendant far better representation than he could have given himself. The Court noted: "Since the right of representation is a right that when exercised usually increases the likelihood of a trial outcome unfavorable to the defendant, its denial is not amenable to 'harmless error' analysis." Lower courts speaking to other issues cited by Justice Blackmun have generally held that (1) the defendant need not be advised of a right to proceed *pro se* unless he or she expresses an interest in doing so; (2) the trial court has broad discretion to deny a request to proceed *pro se* on administrative grounds if the request is first presented after the trial has started; (3) *Faretta* does not demand that the defendant be given a standby counsel and does not require the court to allow a "hybrid representation"; and (4) *pro se* defendants will be treated on appeal no differently than defendants with counsel as to objections that were not properly raised at trial, as the trial court has no special obligation to bend rules relating to the presentation of evidence or the raising of objections (and, in the usual instance, defendant could have relied upon the assistance of standby counsel on those matters).

# Chapter 18

# THE TRIAL

As was noted in Chapter One, the trial has traditionally been viewed as the capstone of the criminal justice, the "crown jewel" that reflects most of the basic elements of the process. It is not surprising, therefore, that many of the Bill of Rights guarantees relating to the criminal justice process refer specifically to the trial. Materials in previous chapters explore the Supreme Court's interpretation of several of those guarantees—the rights to a speedy trial (Ch. 12), to a trial by an impartial jury (Ch. 15), to a public trial (discussed at various points in Ch. 16 in comparing the public's right of access), and to the assistance of counsel (Chs. 5 and 17). The cases in this chapter deal with still other trial guarantees.

## SECTION 1: PRESENCE OF THE DEFENDANT

Cases defining the defendant's constitutional "right of presence" tend to focus on two different issues. First, the constitutional right of presence, although "rooted to large extent in the confrontation clause of the Sixth Amendment," also has due process component. *United States v. Gagnon,* 470 U.S. 522 (1985). Accordingly, the right is not restricted to those parts of the trial in which the defendant is "actually confronting witnesses or evidence against him," and the issue is presented as to what other aspects of the trial itself, or proceedings related to the trial, fall within the scope of the defendant's right. The critical question here is whether defendant's presence at the particular proceeding "has a relation, reasonably substantial to the fullness of his opportunity to defend against the charge." *Gagnon.* As to proceedings not directly a part of the trial, the Court tends to focus on the context of the particular case in answering that question. See e.g., *Kentucky v. Stincer,* 107 S.Ct. 2658 (1987) (judge's in-chambers examination of two young victims of alleged sex offense, to determine solely whether they were competent to testify, did not constitutionally require defendant's presence where defense counsel participated and further questions concerning competency could be raised at trial with defendant present).

A second major issue presented in defining the defendant's right of presence is what conditions permissibly can be attached to that right, so that a defense failure to comply with those conditions results in a loss of the right. *Illinois v. Allen,* the single case in section one, deals with this issue. Prior to *Allen,* in *Taylor v. United States,* 414 U.S. 17 (1973), the Court had held that a defendant cannot complain if he voluntarily absents himself during trial and the court continues the trial through to verdict. The Court has not had occasion to rule on the state's authority to proceed to trial in defendant's absence where the defendant was not even present at the commencement of the trial.

## SECTION 2: THE RIGHTS OF CONFRONTATION AND COMPULSORY PROCESS

The Supreme Court has characterized its cases dealing with the Sixth Amendment's confrontation clause as "fall[ing] into two broad, albeit not exclusive categories: 'cases involving the admission of out-of-court statements and cases involving restrictions imposed by law or by the trial court on the scope of cross-examination.'" *Kentucky v. Stincer,* 107 S.Ct. 2658 (1987). The first two cases in this section fall within the first grouping while the third case falls within the second grouping.[a]

The cases in the first grouping generally have involved the constitutionality of admitting into evidence "hearsay"—that is, a statement that was made out of court and is being offered in evidence to prove the truth of the facts asserted in that statement. Under the rules of evidence currently applied in the different states, as at common law, most hearsay testimony is not admissible in evidence, but there are exceptions. Certain types of out-of-court statements are classified as not truly hearsay (as measured by the primary functions of the hearsay ban) and others are viewed as within special exceptions to the ban that support their admissibility. Confrontation clause concerns obviously arise when a state, under one rationale or another, allows a prosecution witness to testify to a hearsay statement made by a third party; here only the witness is before the defendant and subject to cross-examination, not the third party (the hearsay declarant) whose statement is being used to prove the truth of its contents. However, the confrontation clause has never been read literally to exclude from evidence all out-of-court statements of non-witnesses. The clause has been interpreted, in light of its common law background and the functions served by confrontation, to allow the admission of certain types of out-of-court statements that local evidentiary rules also accept.

Clearly the most significant of these constitutionally acceptable out-of-court statements is the out-of-court statement of the defendant himself (as where a defendant's confession is presented in evidence by the police officer witness to whom it was made). *Bourjaily v. United States,* the first case in this section deals with a related group of acceptable out-of-court statements, also of great practical significance in the administration of the criminal law—the out-of-court

**a.** The confrontation clause is not limited in scope, however, to these concerns, as previously suggested by its role in establishing the constitutional right of presence. So too, in Coy v. Iowa, 108 S.Ct. 2798 (1988), the Court held that the right of confrontation extends beyond cross-examination and includes also the right to a "face-to-face meeting with the witnesses appearing before the trier of fact." Accordingly, the defendant's right of confrontation was infringed where a state trial court (acting pursuant to a state statute designed to protect youthful victims of sexual abuse) allowed two 15-year-old female complainants to testify from behind a screen which blocked defendant from their sight but did allow defendant to dimly perceive them and to hear them. The trial court there had justified dispensing with the element of face-to-face confrontation on the basis of no more than a "legislatively imposed presumption of trauma." In *Maryland v. Craig,* ___ U.S. ___ (1990), a divided Court distinguished *Coy* in upholding the use of one-way closed circuit television to provide the testimony of a child alleged to have been the victim of sexual abuse. The statute in question initially required that the trial court make a specific determination that the child's courtroom testimony in the presence of the defendant would result in the child "suffering serious emotional distress, such that the child cannot reasonably communicate." The Supreme Court held that the state interest in protecting the child from trauma caused by defendant's physical presence, "at least where such trauma would impair the child's ability to communicate," as supported by a case-specific finding of necessity, justified dispensing with element of face-to-face confrontation. It stressed that all other elements of confrontation—oath, cross-examination by counsel present in the room in which the child testified (with defendant in electronic communication with counsel), and observation of demeanor by the judge and jury (who remained in the courtroom)—would be preserved.

statements of coconspirators made during the course of, and in furtherance of, a conspiracy in which defendant participated. Indeed, a major advantage (from a prosecution viewpoint) of prosecuting a defendant for conspiring to commit a crime, rather than simply for the crime itself, is the admissibility against the defendant of such statements made by his coconspirators.

*Richardson v. Marsh,* the second case in this section, considers the bearing of the confrontation clause on a joint trial in which the prosecution seeks to use a confession of one of the jointly tried codefendants. The difficulty posed here is that such an out-of-court statement would be admissible against the declarant codefendant but not against the other codefendants, since it would not fit under the coconspirator rule of *Bourjaily* or the general standards for admissibility of hearsay set forth in *Bourjaily.* The issue presented in *Richardson* also is of great practical significance. Few jurisdictions grant a defendant the right to trial separate from his codefendants. A jointly tried codefendant may request a severance based upon potential prejudice (e.g., a conflicting defense or strategy, or a risk of guilt by association), but such requests are only infrequently granted.

*Davis v. Alaska,* the third case, falls in the second grouping of confrontation clause cases—those cases concerned with the restriction of cross-examination opportunity by law or by trial court ruling. *Davis* should be read in light of *Pennsylvania v. Ritchie,* previously included in Chapter Thirteen on the duty to disclose.

*Ritchie* not only discusses the scope of *Davis* but also speaks to the scope of the Sixth Amendment's guarantee of compulsory process. The Supreme Court has had very little to say about the Sixth Amendment's compulsory process clause. The leading case applying the clause, *Washington v. Texas,* 388 U.S. 14 (1967), struck down a state rule that the Court characterized as an "absurdity"— one that prohibited the defendant from introducing the testimony of an accomplice on his behalf but allowed the prosecution to put on the stand accomplices who would testify in its favor. Not surprisingly, *Chambers v. Mississippi,* the last case in this section, is viewed as a more significant case in defining the defendant's right to present evidence, although the Court's ruling there was based upon due process rather than the Sixth Amendment.

### SECTION 3: THE DEFENDANT'S RIGHT TO REMAIN SILENT—OR TO TESTIFY

The Fifth Amendment privilege against self-incrimination has been examined previously in the context of the investigatory process (see Chs. 6, 7, and 8) and pretrial disclosure (see Ch. 13). In its application to the defendant at trial, the privilege has special meaning, for it confers on defendant a right not simply to refuse to respond to questioning, but to refuse to be placed on the stand where he can be subjected to such questioning. This right not to be called to testify—commonly described as the defendant's "right of silence"—is a basic element of an accusatorial system of justice that requires the government to make its case through its own evidence and allows the accused "to remain inactive and secure, until the prosecution has taken up its burden and produced evidence and effected persuasion." *Taylor v. Kentucky,* 436 U.S. 478 (1978). *Griffin v. California,* the first case in this section, is the leading case on the reach of this right of silence. The Court there considers whether the Fifth Amendment requires that there be no adverse comment, by trial judge or prosecutor, on the defendant's exercise of that right.

The second case in this section, *Rock v. Arkansas,* marks the Court's recognition of a constitutional right of the defendant to take the stand and testify, a practice that was not allowed at the time of the adoption of the Constitution. *Rock* also considers the appropriate scope of state authority to impose evidentiary limitations that restrict the defendant's exercise of this right to testify.

## SECTION 4: DUE PROCESS REQUIREMENTS

The Supreme Court has long held that due process can be the source of trial rights not found in the more specific guarantees of the Sixth and Fifth Amendments. Due process, for example, imposes upon the state the obligation to establish guilt beyond a reasonable doubt. *In re Winship,* 397 U.S. 358 (1970). From that requirement flows a series of related constitutional prerequisites. *Taylor v. Kentucky* considers whether one of these is a jury instruction on the "presumption of innocence."

Constitutional challenges to alleged prosecutorial misconduct at trial also are raised under the "fundamental fairness" standard of due process. Building upon the prosecutor's role as a representative of the state "whose interest in criminal prosecution is not that it shall win the case, but that justice shall be done," *Berger v. United States,* 295 U.S. 78 (1935), the Court has recognized prosecutorial obligations to correct the material testimony of its witnesses known to be false and to disclose material exculpatory evidence within its control. See *United States v. Bagley,* Ch. 13. The second case in this section, *Darden v. Wainwright,* considers the application of the due process clause to the misconduct of the prosecutor in presenting the state's closing argument.

# SECTION 1. PRESENCE OF THE DEFENDANT

## ILLINOIS v. ALLEN

397 U.S. 337, 90 S.Ct. 1057, 25 L.Ed.2d 353 (1970).

JUSTICE BLACK delivered the opinion of the Court.

[Allen was convicted by an Illinois jury of armed robbery and was sentenced to a term of 10 to 30 years. Before trial, the judge acceded to Allen's wish to conduct his own defense, although court-appointed counsel would "sit in and protect the record." During the *voir dire* examination, Allen "started to argue with the judge in a most abusive and disrespectful manner" when the judge directed him to confine his questioning to matters relating to the prospective juror's qualifications. The judge then asked appointed counsel to proceed with the examination, upon which Allen continued to talk and concluded his remarks by saying to the judge, "When I go out for lunchtime, you're going to be a corpse here." The judge then warned Allen that he would be removed from the courtroom if there was another outbreak of that sort. Allen continued to talk back, saying, "There's not going to be no trial, either. I'm going to sit here and you're going to talk and you can bring your shackles out and straight jacket and put them on me and tape my mouth, but it will do no good because there's not going to be no trial." After more abusive remarks, the judge ordered the trial to proceed in Allen's absence. After a noon recess, the judge permitted Allen to return to the courtroom with the warning that he could remain only so long as he behaved himself. Shortly thereafter, Allen spoke out again, saying, "There is going to be no proceeding. I'm going to start talking all through the trial. There's not going to be no trial like this." The judge again ordered Allen removed, and he remained out of the courtroom during the presentation of the State's case-in-chief except when brought in for purposes of identification. Thereafter, Allen was permitted to return to the courtroom upon his promise to conduct himself properly, and he remained for the rest of the trial, principally his defense, which was conducted by his appointed counsel. Allen's conviction was affirmed by the Supreme Court of Illinois, and on federal habeas corpus the district court found no constitutional violation and declined to issue the writ. The court of appeals reversed.]

The Court of Appeals felt that the defendant's Sixth Amendment right to be present at his own trial was so "absolute" that, no matter how unruly or disruptive the defendant's conduct might be, he could never be held to have lost that right so long as he continued to insist upon it, as Allen clearly did. * * * We cannot agree that the Sixth Amendment, the cases upon which the Court of Appeals relied, or any other cases of this Court so handicap a trial judge in conducting a criminal trial. * * * We accept instead the statement of Justice Cardozo who, speaking for the Court in *Snyder v. Massachusetts,* 291 U.S. 97, 106 (1934), said: "No doubt the privilege [of personally confronting witnesses] may be lost by consent or at times even by misconduct." Although mindful that courts must indulge every reasonable presumption against the loss of constitutional rights, we explicitly hold today that a defendant can lose his right to be present at trial if, after he has been warned by the judge that he will be removed if he continues his disruptive behavior, he nevertheless insists on conducting himself in a manner so disorderly, disruptive, and disrespectful of the court that his trial cannot be carried on with him in the courtroom. Once lost, the right to be present can, of course, be reclaimed as soon as the defendant is willing to conduct himself consistently with the decorum and respect inherent in the concept of courts and judicial proceedings.

It is essential to the proper administration of criminal justice that dignity, order, and decorum be the hallmarks of all court proceedings in our country. The flagrant disregard in the courtroom of elementary standards of proper conduct should not and cannot be tolerated. We believe trial judges confronted with disruptive, contumacious, stubbornly defiant defendants must be given sufficient discretion to meet the circumstances of each case. No one formula for maintaining the appropriate courtroom atmosphere will be best in all situations. We think there are at least three constitutionally permissible ways for a trial judge to handle an obstreperous defendant like Allen: (1) bind and gag him, thereby keeping him present; (2) cite him for contempt; (3) take him out of the courtroom until he promises to conduct himself properly.

Trying a defendant for a crime while he sits bound and gagged before the judge and jury would to an extent comply with that part of the Sixth Amendment's purposes that accords the defendant an opportunity to confront the witnesses at the trial. But even to contemplate such a technique, much less see it, arouses a feeling that no person should be tried while shackled and gagged except as a last resort. Not only is it possible that the sight of shackles and gags might have a significant effect on the jury's feelings about the defendant, but the use of this technique is itself something of an affront to the very dignity and decorum of judicial proceedings that the judge is seeking to uphold. Moreover, one of the defendant's primary advantages of being present at the trial, his ability to communicate with his counsel, is greatly reduced when the defendant is in a condition of total physical restraint. It is in part because of these inherent disadvantages and limitations in this method of dealing with disorderly defendants that we decline to hold with the Court of Appeals that a defendant cannot under any possible circumstances be deprived of his right to be present at trial. However, in some situations which we need not attempt to foresee, binding and gagging might possibly be the fairest and most reasonable way to handle a defendant who acts as Allen did here.

In a footnote the Court of Appeals suggested the possible availability of contempt of court as a remedy to make Allen behave in his robbery trial, and it is true that citing or threatening to cite a contumacious defendant for criminal contempt might in itself be sufficient to make a defendant stop interrupting a trial. If so, the problem would be solved easily, and the defendant could remain in the courtroom. Of course, if the defendant is determined to prevent *any* trial, then a court in attempting to try the defendant for contempt is still confronted with the identical dilemma that the Illinois court faced in this case. And criminal contempt has obvious limitations as a sanction when the defendant is charged with a crime so serious that a very severe sentence such as death or life imprisonment is likely to be imposed. In such a case the defendant might not be affected by a mere contempt sentence when he ultimately faces a far more serious sanction. Nevertheless, the contempt remedy should be borne in mind by a judge in the circumstances of this case.

Another aspect of the contempt remedy is the judge's power, when exercised consistently with state and federal law, to imprison an unruly defendant such as Allen for civil contempt and discontinue the trial until such time as the defendant promises to behave himself. This procedure is consistent with the defendant's right to be present at trial, and yet it avoids the serious shortcomings of the use of shackles and gags. It must be recognized, however, that a defendant might conceivably, as a matter of calculated strategy, elect to spend a prolonged period in confinement for contempt in the hope that adverse witnesses might be unavailable after a lapse of time. A court must guard against allowing a defendant to profit from his own wrong in this way.

The trial court in this case decided under the circumstances to remove the defendant from the courtroom and to continue his trial in his absence until and unless he promised to conduct himself in a manner befitting an American courtroom. As we said earlier, we find nothing unconstitutional about this procedure. Allen's behavior was clearly of such an extreme and aggravated nature as to justify either his removal from the courtroom or his total physical restraint. Prior to his removal he was repeatedly warned by the trial judge that he would be removed from the courtroom if he persisted in his unruly conduct, and, as Judge Hastings [of the Court of Appeals] observed in his dissenting opinion, the record demonstrates that Allen would not have been at all dissuaded by the trial judge's use of his criminal contempt powers. Allen was constantly informed that he could return to the trial when he would agree to conduct himself in an orderly manner. Under these circumstances we hold that Allen lost his right guaranteed by the Sixth and Fourteenth Amendments to be present throughout his trial.   *   *   *

JUSTICE BRENNAN, concurring.   *   *   *

I would add only that when a defendant is excluded from his trial, the court should make reasonable efforts to enable him to communicate with his attorney and, if possible, to keep apprised of the progress of his trial. Once the court has removed the contumacious defendant, it is not weakness to mitigate the disadvantages of his expulsion as far as technologically possible in the circumstances.

JUSTICE DOUGLAS.   *   *   *

Our real problems of this type lie not with this case but with other kinds of trials. *First* are the political trials. They frequently recur in our history and insofar as they take place in federal courts we have broad supervisory powers over them.   *   *   * In Anglo–American law, great injustices have at times been done to unpopular minorities by judges, as well as by prosecutors. I refer to London in 1670 when William Penn, the gentle Quaker, was tried for causing a riot when all that he did was to preach a sermon on Grace Church Street * * *. The panel of judges who tried William Penn were sincere, law-and-order men of their day. Though Penn was acquitted by the jury, he was jailed by the court for his contemptuous conduct [which consisted of repeatedly seeking to determine from the court "by what law it is you prosecute me, and upon what law you ground my indictment"]. Would we tolerate removal of a defendant from the courtroom during a trial because he was insisting on his constitutional rights, albeit vociferously, no matter how obnoxious his philosophy might have been to the bench that tried him? * * *

*Second* are trials used by minorities to destroy the existing constitutional system and bring on repressive measures. Radicals on the left historically have used those tactics to incite the extreme right with the calculated design of fostering a regime of repression from which the radicals on the left hope to emerge as the ultimate victor. The left in that role is the provocateur. The Constitution was not designed as an instrument for that form of rough-and-tumble contest. The social compact has room for tolerance, patience, and restraint, but not for sabotage and violence. Trials involving that spectacle strike at the very heart of constitutional government.

I would not try to provide in this case the guidelines for those two strikingly different types of cases. The case presented here is the classical criminal case without any political or subversive overtones. * * *

## SECTION 2. THE RIGHTS OF CONFRONTATION AND COMPULSORY PROCESS

### BOURJAILY v. UNITED STATES

483 U.S. 171, 107 S.Ct. 2775, 97 L.Ed.2d 144 (1987).

CHIEF JUSTICE REHNQUIST delivered the opinion of the Court.

Federal Rule of Evidence 801(d)(2)(E) provides, "A statement is not hearsay if * * * [t]he statement is offered against a party and is * * * a statement by a coconspirator of a party during the course and in furtherance of the conspiracy." We granted certiorari to answer * * * questions regarding the admission of statements under Rule 801(d)(2)(E): * * * whether the court must determine by independent evidence that the conspiracy existed and that the defendant and the declarant were members of this conspiracy; * * * and whether a court must in each case examine the circumstances of such a statement to determine its reliability.

In May 1984, Clarence Greathouse, an informant working for the Federal Bureau of Investigation, arranged to sell a kilogram of cocaine to Angelo Lonardo. Lonardo agreed that he would find individuals to distribute the drug. When the sale became imminent, Lonardo stated in a tape-recorded telephone conversation that he had a "gentleman friend" who had some questions to ask about the cocaine. In a subsequent telephone call, Greathouse spoke to the "friend" about the quality of the drug and the price. Greathouse then spoke again with Lonardo, and the two arranged the details of the purchase. They agreed that the sale would take place in a designated hotel parking lot, and Lonardo would transfer the drug from Greathouse's car to the "friend," who would be waiting in the parking lot in his own car. Greathouse proceeded with the transaction as planned, and FBI agents arrested Lonardo and petitioner immediately after Lonardo placed a kilogram of cocaine into petitioner's car in the hotel parking lot. In petitioner's car, the agents found over $20,000 in cash.

Petitioner was charged with conspiring to distribute cocaine, in violation of 21 U.S.C. § 846, and possession of cocaine with intent to distribute, a violation of 21 U.S.C. § 841(a)(1). The Government introduced, over petitioner's objection, Angelo Lonardo's telephone statements regarding the participation of the "friend" in the transaction. The District Court found that, considering the events in the parking lot and Lonardo's statements over the telephone, the Government had established by a preponderance of the evidence that a conspiracy involving Lonardo and petitioner existed, and that Lonardo's statements over the telephone had been made in the course of and in furtherance of the conspiracy. Accordingly, the trial court held that Lonardo's out-of-court statements satisfied Rule 801(d)(2)(E) and were not hearsay. Petitioner was convicted on both counts and sentenced to 15 years. The United States Court of Appeals for the Sixth Circuit affirmed. The Court of Appeals agreed with the District Court's analysis and * * * rejected petitioner's contention that because he could not cross-examine Lonardo, the admission of [the] statements violated his constitutional right to confront the witnesses against him. We affirm.

Before admitting a co-conspirator's statement over an objection that it does not qualify under Rule 801(d)(2)(E), a court must be satisfied that the statement actually falls within the definition of the rule. There must be evidence that there was a conspiracy involving the declarant and the nonoffering party, and that the statement was made "in the course and in furtherance of the conspiracy." * * *

* * * Petitioner argues that in determining whether a conspiracy exists and whether the defendant was a member of it, the court must look only to independent evidence—that is, evidence other than the statements sought to be admitted. Petitioner relies on *Glasser v. United States,* 315 U.S. 60 (1942), in which this Court first mentioned the so-called "bootstrapping rule." * * * Read in the light most favorable to petitioner, *Glasser* could mean that a court should not consider hearsay statements at all in determining preliminary facts under Rule 801(d)(2)(E). * * * *Glasser,* however, could also mean that a court must have *some* proof *aliunde,* but may look at the hearsay statements themselves in light of this independent evidence to determine whether a conspiracy has been shown by a preponderance of the evidence. * * *

[Moreover, *Glasser* was] decided before Congress enacted the Federal Rules of Evidence in 1975. Rule 104(a) provides: "Preliminary questions concerning . . . the admissibility of evidence shall be determined by the court. . . . In making its determination it is not bound by the rules of evidence except those with respect to privileges." * * * [P]etitioner nevertheless argues that the bootstrapping [as interpreted by petitioner] survived this apparently unequivocal change in the law unscathed and that Rule 104, as applied to the admission of co-conspirator's statements, does not mean what it says. We disagree. * * * We think that the Rule is sufficiently clear that to the extent that it is inconsistent with petitioner's interpretation of *Glasser* * * * the Rule prevails. * * *[a]

Nor do we agree with petitioner that this construction of Rule 104(a) will allow courts to admit hearsay statements without any credible proof of the conspiracy, thus fundamentally changing the nature of the co-conspirator exception. * * * We think that there is little doubt that a co-conspirator's statements could themselves be probative of the existence of a conspiracy and the participation of both the defendant and the declarant in the conspiracy. Peti-

---

**a.** Justice Stevens wrote a separate concurring opinion on the consistency of Rule 104(a) with a proper reading of *Glasser.*

tioner's case presents a paradigm. The out-of-court statements of Lonardo indicated that Lonardo was involved in a conspiracy with a "friend." The statements indicated that the friend had agreed with Lonardo to buy a kilogram of cocaine and to distribute it. The statements also revealed that the friend would be at the hotel parking lot, in his car, and would accept the cocaine from Greathouse's car after Greathouse gave Lonardo the keys. Each one of Lonardo's statements may itself be unreliable, but taken as a whole, the entire conversation between Lonardo and Greathouse was corroborated by independent evidence. The friend, who turned out to be petitioner, showed up at the prearranged spot at the prearranged time. He picked up the cocaine, and a significant sum of money was found in his car. On these facts, the trial court concluded, in our view correctly, that the Government had established the existence of a conspiracy and petitioner's participation in it.

We need not decide in this case whether the courts below could have relied solely upon Lonardo's hearsay statements to determine that a conspiracy had been established * * *. The courts below properly considered the statements of Lonardo and the subsequent events in finding that the Government had established by a preponderance of the evidence that Lonardo was involved in a conspiracy with petitioner. We have no reason to believe that the District Court's factfinding of this point was clearly erroneous. We hold that Lonardo's out-of-court statements were properly admitted against petitioner.

We also reject any suggestion that admission of these statements against petitioner violated his rights under the Confrontation Clause of the Sixth Amendment. That Clause provides, "In all criminal prosecutions, the accused shall enjoy the right * * * to be confronted with the witnesses against him." At petitioner's trial, Lonardo exercised his right not to testify. Petitioner argued that Lonardo's unavailability rendered the admission of his out-of-court statements unconstitutional since petitioner had no opportunity to confront Lonardo as to these statements. The Court of Appeals held that the requirements for admission under Rule 801(d)(2)(E) are identical to the requirements of the Confrontation Clause, and since the statements were admissible under the Rule, there was no constitutional problem. We agree.

While a literal interpretation of the Confrontation Clause could bar the use of any out-of-court statements when the declarant is unavailable, this Court has rejected that view as "unintended and too extreme." *Ohio v. Roberts,* 448 U.S. 56 (1980). Rather, we have attempted to harmonize the goal of the Clause— placing limits on the kind of evidence that may be received against a defendant—with a societal interest in accurate factfinding, which may require consideration of out-of-court statements. To accommodate these competing interests, the Court has, as a general matter only, required the prosecution to demonstrate both the unavailability of the declarant and the "indicia of reliability" surrounding the out-of-court declaration. *Roberts.*[b] Last Term in *United States v. Inadi,*

**b.** The Court's reference is to the following passage in *Roberts:* "The Confrontation Clause operates in two separate ways to restrict the range of admissible hearsay. First, in conformance with the Framers' preference for face-to-face accusation, the Sixth Amendment establishes a rule of necessity. In the usual case * * *, the prosecution must either produce, or demonstrate the unavailability of, the declarant whose statement it wishes to use against the defendant. * * * The second aspect operates once a witness is shown to be unavailable. Reflecting its underlying purpose to augment accuracy in the factfinding process by ensuring the defendant an effective means to test adverse evidence, the Clause countenances only hearsay marked with such trustworthiness that 'there is no material departure from the reason of the general rule.' *Snyder v. Massachusetts.* * * * In sum, when a hearsay declarant is not present for cross-examination at trial, the Confrontation Clause normally requires a showing that he is unavailable. Even then, his statement is admissible only if it bears adequate 'indicia of reliability.' Reliability

475 U.S. 387 (1986), we held that the first of these two generalized inquiries, unavailability, was not required when the hearsay statement is the out-of-court declaration of a co-conspirator.[c] Today, we conclude that the second inquiry, independent indicia of reliability, is also not mandated by the Constitution.

The Court's decision in *Ohio v. Roberts* laid down only "a general approach to the problem" of reconciling hearsay exceptions with the Confrontation Clause. In fact, *Roberts* itself limits the requirement that a court make a separate inquiry into the reliability of an out-of-court statement. Because " 'hearsay rules and the Confrontation Clause are generally designed to protect similar values,' 'stem from the same roots,' " we concluded in *Roberts* that no independent inquiry into reliability is required when the evidence "falls within a firmly rooted hearsay exception." We think that the co-conspirator exception to the hearsay rule is firmly enough rooted in our jurisprudence that, under this Court's holding in *Roberts,* a court need not independently inquire into the reliability of such statements. Cf. *Dutton v. Evans,* 400 U.S. 74 (1970) (reliability inquiry required where evidentiary rule deviates from common-law approach, admitting co-conspirators' hearsay statements made after termination of conspiracy). The admissibility of co-conspirators' statements was first established in this Court over a century and a half ago in *United States v. Gooding,* 12 Wheat. 460 (1827) and the Court has repeatedly reaffirmed the exception as accepted practice. In fact, two of the most prominent approvals of the rule came in cases that petitioner maintains are still vital today, *Glasser v. United States,* 315 U.S. 60 (1942), and *United States v. Nixon,* 418 U.S. 683 (1974). To the extent that these cases have not been superseded by the Federal Rules of Evidence [as to the bootstrapping rule], they demonstrate that the co-conspirator exception to the hearsay rule is steeped in our jurisprudence. In *Delaney v. United States,* 263 U.S. 586 (1924), the Court rejected the very challenge petitioner brings today, holding that there can be no separate Confrontation Clause challenge to the admission of a co-conspirator's out-of-court statement. In so ruling, the Court relied on established precedent holding such statements competent evidence. We think that these cases demonstrate that co-conspirators' statements, when made in the course and in furtherance of the conspiracy, have a long tradition of

can be inferred without more in a case where the evidence falls within a firmly rooted hearsay exception. In other cases, the evidence must be excluded, at least absent a showing of particularized guarantees of trustworthiness."

c. The most common grounds for deeming a declarant to be unavailable are: (1) the party using his out-of-court statement has been unable to obtain his presence by legal process; (2) the person has died or is suffering from physical or mental difficulties that preclude his testifying at trial; or (3) the person refuses to testify on the basis of some legitimate claim of privilege (e.g., the Fifth Amendment self-incrimination privilege). *Inadi* held that the government did not have to establish the unavailability of a coconspirator to use against defendant a statement of the coconspirator that met the requirements of Rule 801(d)(2)(E). The Court noted that the unavailability requirement set forth in *Roberts* had developed "in cases involving former testimony" (in *Roberts* itself, the admissibility of the preliminary hearing testimony of an unavailable witness). Such testimony commonly is "only a weaker substitute for live testimony." Thus, where "the declarant is available and the same information can be presented to the trier of fact in the form of live testimony, with full cross-examination * * *, there is little justification for relying on the weaker version." The coconspirator's statement was admissible, however, because it had a value distinct from the testimony that the coconspirator would provide at trial. "Conspirators are likely to speak differently when talking to each other in furtherance of their illegal aims than when testifying on the witness stand." Also, "the relative positions of the parties will have changed substantially between the time of the statements and the trial." Accordingly, without regard to the availability of the coconspirator, "the admission of coconspirators' declarations * * * actually furthers the 'Confrontation Clause's very mission' which is to 'advance the accuracy of the truth-determining process in criminal trials." The Court added that had the coconspirator in question been available to testify, the defense, under an applicable court rule, could have subpoenaed the coconspirator and subjected him to cross-examination.

being outside the compass of the general hearsay exclusion. Accordingly, we hold that the Confrontation Clause does not require a court to embark on an independent inquiry into the reliability of statements that satisfy the requirements of Rule 801(d)(2)(E).[4]

JUSTICE BLACKMUN, with whom JUSTICE BRENNAN and JUSTICE MARSHALL join, dissenting.

I disagree with the Court in three respects: First, I do not believe that the Federal Rules of Evidence changed the long- and well-settled law to the effect that the preliminary questions of fact, relating to admissibility of a nontestifying co-conspirator's statement, must be established by evidence independent of that statement itself. Second, I disagree with the Court's conclusion that allowing the co-conspirator's statement to be considered in the resolution of these factual questions will remedy problems of the statement's unreliability. * * * Third, because the Court alters the traditional hearsay exemption—especially an aspect of it that contributes to the reliability of an admitted statement—I do not believe that the Court can rely on the "firmly rooted hearsay exception" rationale, see *Ohio v. Roberts,* 448 U.S. 56 (1980), to avoid a determination whether any "indicia of reliability" support the co-conspirator's statement, as the Confrontation Clause surely demands. * * *

In order to understand why the Federal Rules of Evidence adopted without change the common-law co-conspirator exemption from hearsay, and why this adoption signified the Advisory Committee's intent to retain the exemption's independent-evidence requirement, it is useful to review briefly the contours of this exemption as it stood before enactment of the Rules. By all accounts, the exemption was based upon agency principles, the underlying concept being that a conspiracy is a common undertaking where the conspirators are all agents of each other and where the acts and statements of one can be attributed to all. As Judge Learned Hand explained this in a frequently quoted remark,

> "When men enter into an agreement for an unlawful end, they become ad hoc agents for one another, and have made a 'partnership in crime.' What one does pursuant to their common purpose, all do, and, as declarations may be such acts, they are competent against all."

Each of the components of this common-law exemption, in turn, had an agency justification. To fall within the exemption, the co-conspirator's statement had to be made "in furtherance of" the conspiracy, a requirement that arose from the agency rationale that an agent's acts or words could be attributed to his principal only so long as the agent was acting within the scope of his employment. The statement also had to be made "during the course of" the conspiracy. This feature necessarily accompanies the "in furtherance of" requirement, for there must be an employment or business relationship in effect between the agent and principal, in accordance with which the agent is acting, for the principal to be bound by his agent's deeds or words. The final feature of the co-conspirator hearsay exemption, the independent-evidence requirement, directly corresponds to the agency concept that an agent's statement cannot be used alone to prove the existence of the agency relationship. * * *

**4.** We reject any suggestion that by abolishing the bootstrapping rule, the Federal Rules of Evidence have changed the co-conspirator hearsay exception such that it is no longer "firmly rooted" in our legal tradition. The bootstrapping rule relates only to the *method of proof* that the exception has been satisfied. It does not change any element of the co-conspirator exception, which has remained substantively unchanged since its adoption in this country.

Thus, unlike many common-law hearsay exceptions, the co-conspirator exemption from hearsay with its agency rationale was not based primarily upon any particular guarantees of reliability or trustworthiness that were intended to ensure the truthfulness of the admitted statement and to compensate for the fact that a party would not have the opportunity to test its veracity by cross-examining the declarant.   As such, this exemption was considered to be a "vicarious admission."  Although not an admission by a defendant himself, the vicarious admission was a statement imputed to the defendant from the co-conspirator on the basis of their agency relationship.   *   *   *   [I]t was thought that a party could not complain of the deprivation of the right to cross-examine himself (or another authorized to speak for him) or to advocate his own, or his agent's, untrustworthiness.   *   *   *   The co-conspirator "admission" exception was also justified on the ground that the need for this evidence, which was particularly valuable in prosecuting a conspiracy, permitted a somewhat reduced concern for the reliability of the statement.

Although, under common law, the reliability of the co-conspirator's statement was never the primary ground justifying its admissibility, there was some recognition that this exemption from the hearsay rule had certain guarantees of trustworthiness, albeit limited ones.  This justification for the exemption has been explained:

"Active conspirators are likely to know who the members of the conspiracy are and what they have done.  When speaking to advance the conspiracy, they are unlikely to describe non-members as conspirators, and they usually will have no incentive to misdescribe the actions of their fellow members."
Lempert & Saltzburg, A Modern Approach to Evidence.

*   *   *   [T]he requirement that a conspiracy be established by independent evidence also is seen to contribute to the reliability issue.  Yet that requirement goes not so much to the reliability of the statement itself, as to the reliability of the process of admitting it:  a statement cannot be introduced *until* independent evidence shows the defendant to be a member of an existing conspiracy.   *   *   *

*   *   *   [D]espite the recognized need by prosecutors for co-conspirator statements, these statements often have been considered to be somewhat unreliable.  It has long been understood that such statements in some cases may constitute, at best, nothing more than the "idle chatter" of a declarant or, at worst, malicious gossip.  Moreover, when confronted with such a statement, an innocent defendant would have a difficult time defending himself against it, for, if he were not in the conspiracy, he would have no idea why the conspirator made the statement.   *   *   *   Even an experienced trial judge might credit an incriminatory statement that a defendant could not explain, precisely because the defendant had no ready explanation for it.  Because of this actual "real world" experience with the possible unreliability of these statements, the Advisory Committee retained the agency rationale for this exemption in Rule 801(d)(2)(E), as well as the safeguards, albeit limited, against unreliability that this rationale provided the defendant.  The independent-evidence requirement was one such safeguard.  If this requirement is set aside, then one of the exemption's safeguards is lost.   *   *   *

The Court [also] answers today a question left open in *United States v. Inadi*, 475 U.S. 387 (1986).  The Court in *Inadi* did not have occasion to reach the issue of the reliability of [a nontestifying co-conspirator's] statements for Confrontation Clause purposes, and said so specifically.  Today, the Court concludes that the Constitution does not require any independent "indicia of reliability" for such statements.  Relying upon *Ohio v. Roberts,* the Court reasons that no such "indicia" are needed to satisfy Confrontation Clause concerns, because the admissibility of these statements " 'falls within a firmly rooted hearsay exception.' " In a footnote, the Court dismisses any suggestion that it is altering the co-conspirator hearsay exemption: in its view, the exemption essentially remains the same, and what has changed is merely a "method of proof." n. 4 (emphasis omitted).

In *Roberts* the Court did observe that, for Confrontation Clause purposes, "[r]eliability can be inferred without more in a case where the evidence falls within a firmly rooted hearsay exception." To understand the significance of this statement, however, it is important to remember why hearsay exceptions satisfy the reliability concern of that Clause. The Court in *Roberts* explained that "accuracy in the factfinding process" is a central concern of the Confrontation Clause that cross-examination normally serves. This concern is sometimes satisfied when evidence is admitted under a hearsay exception, even where no cross-examination of the declarant occurs at trial. This is because " 'hearsay rules and the Confrontation Clause are generally designed to protect similar values,' " and because, with respect to a particular hearsay exception, there are adequate "indicia of reliability" of the out-of-court statement. These indicia serve to guarantee the trustworthiness of the declarant's statement and thus promote the accuracy of the trial—a function otherwise fulfilled by cross-examination. Thus, to answer the Confrontation Clause's concern for reliability with respect to a particular hearsay exception, one must examine what, if any, "indicia of reliability" it possesses. In addition, one must also see how "firmly rooted" the exception is, which suggests that, through experience in its use, the exception has proved to promote the "accuracy of the factfinding process."

The weakness of the Court's assertion—that the Confrontation Clause concern about reliability vanishes because Rule 801(d)(2)(E)'s exemption of a co-conspirator's statement from the hearsay definition is a "firmly rooted hearsay exception"—thus becomes immediately apparent. First, as has been explained and as its inclusion under the admissions rubric would indicate, this exemption has never been justified primarily upon reliability or trustworthiness grounds and its reliability safeguards are not extensive. Thus, it is surprising that, without any hesitation, the Court in this case turns to the "firmly rooted hearsay exception" rationale, which is based upon a confidence in adequate "indicia of reliability."

Second, and more astounding, is the Court's reliance upon the "firmly rooted hearsay exception" rationale as it simultaneously removes from the exemption one of the few safeguards against unreliability that it possesses. The Court cannot at all escape from this contradiction by dismissing its alteration of the exception as simply a change in "method of proof." Because the "firmly rooted hearsay exception" is defined in terms of its "indicia of reliability" for Confrontation Clause purposes, a removal of one of these "indicia" significantly transforms the co-conspirator exemption in a relevant respect. In addition, this change takes away from the exemption any weight that experience with its use by courts may have given it, thus undermining its "firmly rooted" status. In sum, the Court cannot have it both ways: it cannot transform the exemption, as it admittedly does, *and* then avoid Confrontation Clause concerns by conjuring up the "firmly rooted hearsay exception" as some benign genie who will extricate the Court from its inconsistent analysis. * * * Intellectual honesty thus demands, at the very least, that, having changed this hearsay exemption, the Court remand the case to allow the lower courts to explore any "particularized guarantees of trustworthiness" the statement might have.[11]

## RICHARDSON v. MARSH

### 481 U.S. 200, 107 S.Ct. 1702, 95 L.Ed.2d 176 (1987).

JUSTICE SCALIA delivered the opinion of the Court.

In *Bruton v. United States,* 391 U.S. 123 (1968), we held that a defendant is deprived of his rights under the Confrontation Clause when his nontestifying codefendant's confession naming him as a participant in the crime is introduced at their joint trial, even if the jury is instructed to consider that confession only against the codefendant. Today we consider whether *Bruton* requires the same result when the codefendant's confession is redacted to omit any reference to the defendant, but the defendant is nonetheless linked to the confession by evidence properly admitted against him at trial.

Respondent Clarissa Marsh, Benjamin Williams, and Kareem Martin were charged with assaulting Cynthia Knighton and murdering her 4–year–old son, Koran, and her aunt, Ollie Scott. Respondent and Williams were tried jointly, over her objection. (Martin was a fugitive at the time of trial). At the trial, Knighton testified as follows: On the evening of October 29, 1978, she and her son were at Scott's home when respondent and her boyfriend Martin visited. After a brief conversation in the living room, respondent announced that she had come to "pick up something" from Scott and rose from the couch. Martin then pulled out a gun, pointed it at Scott and the Knightons, and said that "someone had gotten killed and [Scott] knew something about it." Respondent immediately walked to the front door and peered out the peephole. The doorbell rang, respondent opened the door, and Williams walked in, carrying a gun. As Williams passed respondent, he asked, "Where's the money?" Martin forced Scott upstairs, and Williams went into the kitchen, leaving respondent alone with the Knightons. Knighton and her son attempted to flee, but respondent grabbed Knighton and held her until Williams returned. Williams ordered the Knightons to lie on the floor and then went upstairs to assist Martin. Respondent, again left alone with the Knightons, stood by the front door and occasionally peered out the peephole. A few minutes later, Martin, Williams, and Scott came down the stairs, and Martin handed a paper grocery bag to respondent. Martin and Williams then forced Scott and the Knightons into the basement, where Martin shot them. Only Cynthia Knighton survived.

In addition to Knighton's testimony, the State introduced (over respondent's objection) a confession given by Williams to the police shortly after his arrest. The confession was redacted to omit all reference to respondent—indeed, to omit all indication that *anyone* other than Martin and Williams participated in the crime.[1] The confession largely corroborated Knighton's account of the activities

---

11. Petitioner argues that, were the co-conspirator exemption to remain unaltered with respect to the independent-evidence rule, the exemption would satisfy the Confrontation Clause's concern for adequate "indicia of reliability," except in special cases where the defendant could show that the co-conspirator's statement was unusually unreliable and was crucial to the prosecution's case. Given the fact that the reliability foundation of this exemption is not as strong as that for traditional hearsay exceptions, I am inclined to agree

that the Confrontation Clause might well demand a particularized reliability analysis in cases where a statement is a significant part of the prosecution's case, before such statements could be admitted over a defendant's objection. * * *

1. The redacted confession in its entirety read:

"On Sunday evening, October the 29th, 1978, at about 6:30 p.m., I was over to my girl friend's house at 237 Moss, Highland of persons other than respondent in the house. In addition, the confession described a conversation Williams had with Martin as they drove to the Scott home, during which, according to Williams, Martin said that he would have to kill the victims after the robbery. At the time the confession was admitted, the jury was admonished not to use it in any way against respondent. Williams did not testify.

After the State rested, respondent took the stand. She testified that on October 29, 1978, she had lost money that Martin intended to use to buy drugs. Martin was upset, and suggested to respondent that she borrow money from Scott, with whom she had worked in the past. Martin and respondent picked up Williams and drove to Scott's house. During the drive, respondent, who was sitting in the back seat, "knew that [Martin and Williams] were talking" but could not hear the conversation because "the radio was on and the speaker was right in [her] ear." Martin and respondent were admitted into the home, and respondent had a short conversation with Scott, during which she asked for a loan. Martin then pulled a gun, and respondent walked to the door to see where the car was. When she saw Williams, she opened the door for him. Respondent testified that during the robbery she did not feel free to leave and was too scared to flee. She said that she did not know why she prevented the Knightons from escaping. She admitted taking the bag from Martin, but said that after Martin and Williams took the victims into the basement, she left the house without the bag. Respondent insisted that she had possessed no prior knowledge that Martin and Williams were armed, had heard no conversation about anyone's being harmed, and had not intended to rob or kill anyone.

During his closing argument, the prosecutor admonished the jury not to use Williams' confession against respondent. Later in his argument, however, he linked respondent to the portion of Williams' confession describing his conversa-

Park, when I received a phone call from a friend of mine named Kareem Martin. He said he had been looking for me and James Coleman, who I call Tom. He asked me if I wanted to go on a robbery with him. I said okay. Then he said he'd be by and pick me up. About 15 or 20 minutes later Kareem came by in his black Monte Carlo car. I got in the car and Kareem told me he was going to stick up this crib, told me the place was a numbers house. Kareem said there would be over $5,000 or $10,000 in the place. Kareem said he would have to take them out after the robbery. Kareem had a big silver gun. He gave me a long barrelled [sic] .22 revolver. We then drove over to this house and parked the car across the big street near the house. The plan was that I would wait in the car in front of the house and then I would move the car down across the big street because he didn't want anybody to see the car. Okay, Kareem went up to the house and went inside. A couple of minutes later I moved the car and went up to the house. As I entered, Kareem and this older lady were in the dining room, a little boy and another younger woman were sitting on the couch in the front room. I pulled my pistol and told the younger woman and the little boy to lay on the floor.

Kareem took the older lady upstairs. He had a pistol, also. I stayed downstairs with the two people on the floor. After Kareem took the lady upstairs I went upstairs and the lady was laying on the bed in the room to the left as you get up the stairs. The lady had already given us two bags full of money before we ever got upstairs. Kareem had thought she had more money and that's why we had went upstairs. Me and Kareem started searching the rooms but I didn't find any money. I came downstairs and then Kareem came down with the lady. I said, 'Let's go, let's go.' Kareem said no. Kareem then took the two ladies and little boy down the basement and that's when I left to go to the car. I went to the car and got in the back seat. A couple of minutes later Kareem came to the car and said he thinks the girl was still living because she was still moving and he didn't have any more bullets. He asked me how come I didn't go down the basement and I said I wasn't doing no shit like that. He then dropped me back off at my girl's house in Highland Park and I was supposed to get together with him today, get my share of the robbery after he had counted the money. That's all."

tion with Martin in the car.[2] (Respondent's attorney did not object to this.) After closing arguments, the judge again instructed the jury that Williams' confession was not to be considered against respondent. The jury convicted respondent of two counts of felony murder in the perpetration of an armed robbery and one count of assault with intent to commit murder. The Michigan Court of Appeals affirmed in an unpublished opinion, and the Michigan Supreme Court denied leave to appeal.

Respondent then filed a petition for a writ of habeas corpus pursuant to 28 U.S.C. § 2254. She alleged that * * * introduction of Williams' confession at the joint trial had violated her rights under the Confrontation Clause. The District Court denied the petition. The United States Court of Appeals * * * reversed. The Court of Appeals held that in determining whether *Bruton* bars the admission of a nontestifying codefendant's confession, a court must assess the confession's "inculpatory value" by examining not only the face of the confession, but also all of the evidence introduced at trial. Here, Williams' account of the conversation in the car was the only *direct* evidence that respondent knew before entering Scott's house that the victims would be robbed and killed. Respondent's own testimony placed her in that car. In light of the "paucity" of other evidence of malice and the prosecutor's linkage of respondent and the statement in the car during closing argument, admission of Williams' confession "was powerfully incriminating to [respondent] with respect to the critical element of intent." Thus, the Court of Appeals concluded, the Confrontation Clause was violated. We granted certiorari. * * *

The Confrontation Clause of the Sixth Amendment, extended against the States by the Fourteenth Amendment, guarantees the right of a criminal defendant "to be confronted with the witnesses against him." The right of confrontation includes the right to cross-examine witnesses. Therefore, where two defendants are tried jointly, the pretrial confession of one cannot be admitted against the other unless the confessing defendant takes the stand.

Ordinarily, a witness whose testimony is introduced at a joint trial is not considered to be a witness "against" a defendant if the jury is instructed to consider that testimony only against a codefendant. This accords with the almost invariable assumption of the law that jurors follow their instructions, which we have applied in many varying contexts. For example, in *Harris v. New York*, 401 U.S. 222 (1971), we held that statements elicited from a defendant in violation of *Miranda v. Arizona* can be introduced to impeach that defendant's credibility, even though they are inadmissible as evidence of his guilt, so long as the jury is instructed accordingly. * * * In *Bruton*, however, we recognized a narrow exception to this principle: We held that a defendant is deprived of his Sixth Amendment right of confrontation when the facially incriminating confession of a nontestifying codefendant is introduced at their joint trial, even if the jury is instructed to consider the confession only against the codefendant. We said:

**2.** The prosecutor said: "It's important in light of [respondent's] testimony when she says Kareem drives over to Benjamin Williams' home and picks him up to go over. What's the thing that she says? 'Well, I'm sitting in the back seat of the car.' 'Did you hear any conversation that was going on in the front seat between Kareem and Mr. Williams?' 'No, couldn't hear any conversation. The radio was too loud.' I asked [*sic*] you whether that is reasonable. Why did she say that? Why did she say she couldn't hear any conversation? She said, 'I know they were having conversation but I couldn't hear it because of the radio.' Because if she admits that she heard the conversation and she admits to the plan, she's guilty of at least armed robbery. So she can't tell you that."

"[T]here are some contexts in which the risk that the jury will not, or cannot, follow instructions is so great, and the consequences of failure so vital to the defendant, that the practical and human limitations of the jury system cannot be ignored.    Such a context is presented here, where the powerfully incriminating extrajudicial statements of a codefendant, who stands accused side-by-side with the defendant, are deliberately spread before the jury in a joint trial  *  *  *."

There is an important distinction between this case and *Bruton*, which causes it to fall outside the narrow exception we have created.  In *Bruton*, the codefendant's confession "expressly implicat[ed]" the defendant as his accomplice.  Thus, at the time that confession was introduced there was not the slightest doubt that it would prove "powerfully incriminating."  By contrast, in this case the confession was not incriminating on its face, and became so only when linked with evidence introduced later at trial (the defendant's own testimony).

Where the necessity of such linkage is involved, it is a less valid generalization that the jury will not likely obey the instruction to disregard the evidence. Specific testimony that "the defendant helped me commit the crime" is more vivid than inferential incrimination, and hence more difficult to thrust out of mind.  Moreover, with regard to such an explicit statement the only issue is, plain and simply, whether the jury can possibly be expected to forget it in assessing the defendant's guilt; whereas with regard to inferential incrimination the judge's instruction may well be successful in dissuading the jury from entering onto the path of inference in the first place, so that there is no incrimination to forget.  In short, while it may not always be simple for the members of a jury to obey the instruction that they disregard an incriminating inference, there does not exist the overwhelming probability of their inability to do so that is the foundation of *Bruton's* exception to the general rule.

Even more significantly, evidence requiring linkage differs from evidence incriminating on its face in the practical effects which application of the *Bruton* exception would produce.  If limited to facially incriminating confessions, *Bruton* can be complied with by redaction—a possibility suggested in that opinion itself. If extended to confessions incriminating by connection, not only is that not possible, but it is not even possible to predict the admissibility of a confession in advance of trial.  The "contextual implication" doctrine articulated by the Court of Appeals would presumably require the trial judge to assess at the end of each trial whether, in light of all of the evidence, a nontestifying codefendant's confession has been so "powerfully incriminating" that a new, separate trial is required for the defendant.  This obviously lends itself to manipulation by the defense—and even without manipulation will result in numerous mistrials and appeals.  It might be suggested that those consequences could be reduced by conducting a pretrial hearing at which prosecution and defense would reveal the evidence they plan to introduce, enabling the court to assess compliance with *Bruton ex ante* rather than *ex post*.  If this approach is even feasible  *  *  *, it would be time consuming and obviously far from foolproof.

One might say, of course, that a certain way of assuring compliance would be to try defendants separately whenever an incriminating statement of one of them is sought to be used.  That is not as facile or as just a remedy as might seem.  Joint trials play a vital role in the criminal justice system, accounting for almost one third of federal criminal trials in the past five years.  Many joint trials—for example, those involving large conspiracies to import and distribute illegal drugs—involve a dozen or more codefendants.  Confessions by one or more of the defendants are commonplace—and indeed the probability of confession increases with the number of participants, since each has reduced assurance that he will be protected by his own silence. It would impair both the efficiency and the fairness of the criminal justice system to require, in all these cases of joint crimes where incriminating statements exist, that prosecutors bring separate proceedings, presenting the same evidence again and again, requiring victims and witnesses to repeat the inconvenience (and sometimes trauma) of testifying, and randomly favoring the last-tried defendants who have the advantage of knowing the prosecution's case beforehand. Joint trials generally serve the interests of justice by avoiding inconsistent verdicts and enabling more accurate assessment of relative culpability—advantages which sometimes operate to the defendant's benefit. Even apart from these tactical considerations, joint trials generally serve the interests of justice by avoiding the scandal and inequity of inconsistent verdicts.[4] The other way of assuring compliance with an expansive *Bruton* rule would be to forgo use of codefendant confessions. That price also is too high, since confessions "are more than merely 'desirable'; they are essential to society's compelling interest in finding, convicting, and punishing those who violate the law." *Moran v. Burbine,* 475 U.S. 412 (1986).

The rule that juries are presumed to follow their instructions is a pragmatic one, rooted less in the absolute certitude that the presumption is true than in the belief that it represents a reasonable practical accommodation of the interests of the state and the defendant in the criminal justice process. On the precise facts of *Bruton,* involving a facially incriminating confession, we found that accommodation inadequate. As our discussion above shows, the calculus changes when confessions that do not name the defendant are at issue. While we continue to apply *Bruton* where we have found that its rationale validly applies, we decline to extend it further. We hold that the Confrontation Clause is not violated by the admission of a nontestifying codefendant's confession with a proper limiting instruction when, as here, the confession is redacted to eliminate not only the defendant's name, but any reference to her existence.[5]

In the present case, however, the prosecutor sought to undo the effect of the limiting instruction by urging the jury to use Williams' confession in evaluating respondent's case. See n. 2. On remand, the court should consider whether, in light of respondent's failure to object to the prosecutor's comments, the error can serve as the basis for granting a writ of habeas corpus. See *Wainwright v. Sykes* [discussed in *Murray v. Carrier,* Ch. 17].

JUSTICE STEVENS, with whom JUSTICE BRENNAN and JUSTICE MARSHALL join, dissenting.

The rationale of our decision in *Bruton v. United States,* applies without exception to all inadmissible confessions that are "powerfully incriminating." Today, however, the Court draws a distinction of constitutional magnitude

**4.** The dissent notes that "all of the cases in this Court that involved joint trials conducted after *Bruton* was decided, in which compliance with the rule of that case was at issue, appear to have originated in a state court." It concludes from this that *"[f]ederal* prosecutors seem to have had little difficulty" in implementing *Bruton* as the dissent believes it must be implemented. Since the cases in question number only a handful, the fact that they happened to be state cases may signify nothing more than that there are many times more state prosecutions than federal. There is assuredly no basis to believe

that federal prosecutors have been applying the dissent's interpretation of *Bruton.* Indeed the contrary proposition—as well as the harmfulness of that interpretation to federal law enforcement efforts—is suggested by the fact that the Solicitor General has appeared here as *amicus* to urge reversal for substantially the reasons we have given.

**5.** We express no opinion on the admissibility of a confession in which the defendant's name has been replaced with a symbol or neutral pronoun.

between those confessions that directly identify the defendant and those that rely for their inculpatory effect on the factual and legal relationships of their contents to other evidence before the jury. Even if the jury's indirect inference of the defendant's guilt based on an inadmissible confession is much more devastating to the defendant's case than its inference from a direct reference in the codefendant's confession, the Court requires the exclusion of only the latter statement. This illogical result demeans the values protected by the Confrontation Clause. Moreover, neither reason nor experience supports the Court's argument that a consistent application of the rationale of the *Bruton* case would impose unacceptable burdens on the administration of justice. * * *

[T]he Court * * * draws a line between codefendant confessions that expressly name the defendant and those that do not. The Court relies on the presumption that in the latter category "it is a less valid generalization that the jury will not likely obey the instruction to disregard the evidence." I agree; but I do not read *Bruton* to require the exclusion of *all* codefendant confessions that do not mention the defendant. Some such confessions may not have any significant impact on the defendant's case. But others will. If we presume, as we must, that jurors give their full and vigorous attention to every witness and each item of evidence, the very acts of listening and seeing will sometimes lead them down "the path of inference." Indeed, the Court tacitly acknowledges this point; while the Court speculates that the judge's instruction may dissuade the jury from making inferences at all, it also concedes the probability of their occurrence, arguing that there is no overwhelming probability that jurors will be unable to "disregard an incriminating inference." *Bruton* has always required trial judges to answer the question whether a particular confession is or is not "powerfully incriminating" on a case-by-case basis; they should follow the same analysis whether or not the defendant is actually named by his or her codefendant.

Instructing the jury that it was to consider Benjamin Williams' confession only against him, and not against Clarissa Marsh, failed to guarantee the level of certainty required by the Confrontation Clause. The uncertainty arose because the prosecution's case made it clear at the time Williams' statement was introduced that the statement would prove "powerfully incriminating" of the *petitioner* as well as of Williams himself. There can be absolutely no doubt that spreading Williams' carefully edited confession before the jury intolerably interfered with the jury's solemn duty to treat the statement as nothing more than meaningless sounds in its consideration of Marsh's guilt or innocence. * * *

The facts that joint trials conserve prosecutorial resources, diminish inconvenience to witnesses, and avoid delays in the administration of criminal justice have been well-known for a long time. It is equally well-known that joint trials create special risks of prejudice to one of the defendants, and that such risks often make it necessary to grant severances. See *Bruton.* The Government argues that the costs of requiring the prosecution to choose between severance and not offering the codefendant's confession at a joint trial outweigh the benefits to the defendant. Brief for United States as *Amicus Curiae.* On the scales of justice, however, considerations of fairness normally outweigh administrative concerns.

In the *Bruton* case the United States argued that the normal "benefits of joint proceedings should not have to be sacrificed by requiring separate trials in order to use the confession against the declarant." The Court endorsed the answer to this argument that Judge Lehman of the New York Court of Appeals had previously made:

"We still adhere to the rule that an accused is entitled to confrontation of the witnesses against him and the right to cross-examine them. * * * We destroy the age-old rule which in the past has been regarded as a fundamental principle of our jurisprudence by a legalistic formula, required of the judge, that the jury may not consider any admissions against any party who did not join in them. We secure greater speed, economy and convenience in the administration of the law at the price of fundamental principles of constitutional liberty. That price is too high."

The concern about the cost of joint trials, even if valid, does not prevail over the interests of justice. Moreover, the Court's effort to revive this concern in a state criminal case rests on the use of irrelevant statistics. The Court makes the startling discovery that joint trials account for "almost one-third of federal criminal trials in the past five years." In the interest of greater precision, the Court might have stated that there were 10,904 federal criminal trials involving more than one defendant during that 5 year period. The Court might have added that the data base from which that figure was obtained does not contain any information at all to show the number of times that confessions were offered in evidence in those 10,904 federal cases. The relevance of this data is also difficult to discern because all of the cases in this Court that involved joint trials conducted after *Bruton* was decided, in which compliance with the rule of that case was at issue, appear to have originated in a state court. *Federal* prosecutors seem to have had little difficulty, in conducting the literally thousands of joint trials to which the Court points, in avoiding "the great harm to the criminal justice system" that the Court speculates will occur if *Bruton*'s reasoning is applied to this case. Presumably the options of granting immunity, making plea bargains, or simply waiting until after a confessing defendant has been tried separately before trying to use his admissions against an accomplice have enabled the Federal Government to enforce the criminal law without sacrificing the basic premise of the Confrontation Clause.

The Court also expresses concern that trial judges will be unable to determine whether a codefendant's confession that does not directly mention the defendant and is inadmissible against him will create a substantial risk of unfair prejudice. In most such cases the trial judge can comply with the dictates of *Bruton* by postponing his or her decision on the admissibility of the confession until the prosecution rests, at which time its potentially inculpatory effect can be evaluated in the light of the government's entire case. The Court expresses concern that such a rule would enable "manipulation by the defense," by which the Court presumably means the defense might tailor its evidence to make sure that a confession which does not directly mention the defendant is deemed powerfully incriminating when viewed in light of the prosecution's entire case. As a practical matter, I cannot believe that there are many defense lawyers who would deliberately pursue this high-risk strategy of "manipulating" their evidence in order to enhance the prejudicial impact of a codefendant's confession. Moreover, a great many experienced and competent trial judges throughout the Nation are fully capable of managing cases and supervising counsel in order to avoid the problems that seem insurmountable to appellate judges who are sometimes distracted by illogical distinctions and irrelevant statistics. I respectfully dissent.[8]

---

**8.** Except for Williams' confession, and the prosecutor's closing argument that will be separately considered on remand, there was a paucity of other evidence connecting respondent with the plan discussed in the car on the way to the victim's home. The Court of Appeals was thus unquestionably correct in concluding that the violation of the Confrontation Clause in this case was not harmless error.

## DAVIS v. ALASKA

415 U.S. 308, 94 S.Ct. 1105, 39 L.Ed.2d 340 (1974).

CHIEF JUSTICE BURGER delivered the opinion of the Court.

We granted certiorari in this case to consider whether the Confrontation Clause requires that a defendant in a criminal case be allowed to impeach the credibility of a prosecution witness by cross-examination directed at possible bias deriving from the witness' probationary status as a juvenile delinquent when such an impeachment would conflict with a State's asserted interest in preserving the confidentiality of juvenile adjudications of delinquency.

When the Polar Bar in Anchorage closed in the early morning hours of February 16, 1970, well over a thousand dollars in cash and checks was in the bar's Mosler safe. About midday, February 16, it was discovered that the bar had been broken into and the safe, about two feet square and weighing several hundred pounds, had been removed from the premises. Later that afternoon the Alaska State Troopers received word that a safe had been discovered about 26 miles outside Anchorage near the home of Jess Straight * * *. The safe, which was subsequently determined to be the one stolen from the Polar Bar, had been pried open and the contents removed. Richard Green, Jess Straight's stepson, told investigating troopers on the scene that at about noon on February 16 he had seen and spoken with two Negro men standing alongside a late-model metallic blue Chevrolet sedan near where the safe was later discovered. The next day * * * Green was given six photographs of adult Negro males. After examining the photographs for 30 seconds to a minute, Green identified the photograph of petitioner as that of one of the men he had encountered the day before * * *. Petitioner was arrested the next day, February 18. On February 19, Green picked petitioner out of a lineup of seven Negro males.

At trial, evidence was introduced to the effect that paint chips found in the trunk of petitioner's rented blue Chevrolet could have originated from the surface of the stolen safe. Further, the trunk of the car contained particles which were identified as safe insulation characteristic of that found in Mosler safes. * * *

Richard Green was a crucial witness for the prosecution. He testified at trial that while on an errand for his mother he confronted two men standing beside a late-model metallic blue Chevrolet, parked on a road near his family's house. The man standing at the rear of the car spoke to Green asking if Green lived nearby and if his father was home. Green offered the men help, but his offer was rejected. On his return from the errand Green again passed the two men and he saw the man with whom he had had the conversation standing at the rear of the car with "something like a crowbar" in his hands. Green identified petitioner at the trial as the man with the "crowbar." The safe was discovered later that afternoon at the point, according to Green, where the Chevrolet had been parked.

Before testimony was taken at the trial of petitioner, the prosecutor moved for a protective order to prevent any reference to Green's juvenile record by the defense in the course of cross-examination. At the time of the trial and at the time of the events Green testified to, Green was on probation by order of a juvenile court after having been adjudicated a delinquent for burglarizing two cabins. Green was 16 years of age at the time of the Polar Bar burglary, but had turned 17 prior to trial.

In opposing the protective order, petitioner's counsel made it clear that he would not introduce Green's juvenile adjudication as a general impeachment of Green's character as a truthful person but, rather, to show specifically that at the same time Green was assisting the police in identifying petitioner he was on probation for burglary. From this petitioner would seek to show—or at least argue—that Green acted out of fear or concern of possible jeopardy to his probation. Not only might Green have made a hasty and faulty identification of petitioner to shift suspicion away from himself as who robbed the Polar Bar, but Green might have been subject to undue pressure from the police and made his identifications under fear of possible probation revocation. Green's record would be revealed only as necessary to probe Green for bias and prejudice and not generally to call Green's good character into question.

The trial court granted the motion for a protective order, relying on Alaska Rule of Children's Procedure 23,[1] and Alaska Stat. § 47.10.080(g) (1971).[2]

Although prevented from revealing that Green had been on probation for the juvenile delinquency adjudication for burglary at the same time that he originally identified petitioner, counsel for petitioner did his best to expose Green's state of mind at the time Green discovered that a stolen safe had been discovered near his home. Green denied that he was upset or uncomfortable about the discovery of the safe. He claimed not to have been worried about any suspicions the police might have been expected to harbor against him, though Green did admit that it crossed his mind that the police might have thought he had something to do with the crime. \* \* \* [After the defense counsel asked Green if he had "ever been questioned like that before by any law enforcement officers" and Green answered "No," the trial court cut off further questioning along this line on the prosecution's objection that such questioning was "a carry-on with rehash of the same thing"].

Since defense counsel was prohibited from making inquiry as to the witness' being on probation under a juvenile court adjudication, Green's protestations of unconcern over possible police suspicion that he might have had a part in the Polar Bar burglary and his categorical denial of ever having been the subject of any similar law-enforcement interrogation went unchallenged. The tension between the right of confrontation and the State's policy of protecting the witness with a juvenile record is particularly evident in the final answer given by the witness. Since it is probable that Green underwent some questioning by police when he was arrested for the burglaries on which his juvenile adjudication of delinquency rested, the answer can be regarded as highly suspect at the very least. The witness was in effect asserting, under protection of the trial court's ruling, a right to give a questionably truthful answer to a cross-examiner pursuing a relevant line of inquiry; it is doubtful whether the bold "No" answer would have been given by Green absent a belief that he was shielded from traditional cross-examination. It would be difficult to conceive of a situation more clearly illustrating the need for cross-examination. The remainder of the cross-examination was devoted to an attempt to prove that Green was making his identification at trial on the basis of what he remembered from his earlier

---

**1.** Rule 23 provides: "No adjudication, order, or disposition of a juvenile case shall be admissible in a court not acting in the exercise of juvenile jurisdiction except for use in a presentencing procedure in a criminal case where the superior court, in its discretion, determines that such use is appropriate."

**2.** Section 47.10.080(g) provides in pertinent part: "The commitment and placement of a child and evidence given in the court are not admissible as evidence against the minor in a subsequent case or proceedings in any other court . . . .."

identifications at the photographic display and lineup, and not on the basis of his February 16 confrontation with the two men on the road.

The Alaska Supreme Court affirmed petitioner's conviction, concluding that it did not have to resolve the potential conflict in this case between a defendant's right to a meaningful confrontation with adverse witnesses and the State's interest in protecting the anonymity of a juvenile offender since "our reading of the trial transcript convinces us that counsel for the defendant was able adequately to question the youth in considerable detail concerning the possibility of bias or motive." Although the court admitted that Green's denials of any sense of anxiety or apprehension upon the safe's being found close to his home were possibly self-serving, "the suggestion was nonetheless brought to the attention of the jury, and that body was afforded the opportunity to observe the demeanor of the youth and pass on his credibility." The court concluded that, in light of the indirect references permitted, there was no error.

Since we granted certiorari limited to the question of whether petitioner was denied his right under the Confrontation Clause to adequately cross-examine Green, the essential question turns on the correctness of the Alaska court's evaluation of the "adequacy" of the scope of cross-examination permitted. We disagree with that court's interpretation of the Confrontation Clause and we reverse.

The Sixth Amendment to the Constitution guarantees the right of an accused in a criminal prosecution "to be confronted with the witnesses against him." * * * Confrontation means more than being allowed to confront the witness physically. "Our cases construing the [confrontation] clause hold that a primary interest secured by it is the right of cross-examination." *Douglas v. Alabama*, 380 U.S. 415 (1965). * * *

Cross-examination is the principal means by which the believability of a witness and the truth of his testimony are tested. Subject always to the broad discretion of a trial judge to preclude repetitive and unduly harassing interrogation, the cross-examiner is not only permitted to delve into the witness' story to test the witness' perceptions and memory, but the cross-examiner has traditionally been allowed to impeach, i.e., discredit, the witness. One way of discrediting the witness is to introduce evidence of a prior criminal conviction of that witness. By so doing the cross-examiner intends to afford the jury a basis to infer that the witness' character is such that he would be less likely than the average trustworthy citizen to be truthful in his testimony. The introduction of evidence of a prior crime is thus a general attack on the credibility of the witness. A more particular attack on the witness' credibility is effected by means of cross-examination directed toward revealing possible biases, prejudices, or ulterior motives of the witness as they may relate directly to issues or personalities in the case at hand. * * * We have recognized that the exposure of a witness' motivation in testifying is a proper and important function of the constitutionally protected right of cross-examination. *Greene v. McElroy*, 360 U.S. 474 (1959).

In the instant case, defense counsel sought to show the existence of possible bias and prejudice of Green, causing him to make a faulty initial identification of petitioner, which in turn could have affected his later in-court identification of petitioner. We cannot speculate as to whether the jury, as sole judge of the credibility of a witness, would have accepted this line of reasoning had counsel been permitted to fully present it. But we do conclude that the jurors were entitled to have the benefit of the defense theory before them so that they could make an informed judgment as to the weight to place on Green's testimony which provided "a crucial link in the proof * * * of petitioner's act." *Douglas v. Alabama.* The accuracy and truthfulness of Green's testimony were key elements in the State's case against petitioner. The claim of bias which the defense sought to develop was admissible to afford a basis for an inference of undue pressure because of Green's vulnerable status as a probationer, as well as of Green's possible concern that he might be a suspect in the investigation.

We cannot accept the Alaska Supreme Court's conclusion that the cross-examination that was permitted defense counsel was adequate to develop the issue of bias properly to the jury. While counsel was permitted to ask Green *whether* he was biased, counsel was unable to make a record from which to argue *why* Green might have been biased or otherwise lacked that degree of impartiality expected of a witness at trial. On the basis of the limited cross-examination that was permitted, the jury might well have thought that defense counsel was engaged in a speculative and baseless line of attack on the credibility of an apparently blameless witness or, as the prosecutor's objection put it, a "rehash" of prior cross-examination. On these facts it seems clear to us that to make any such inquiry effective, defense counsel should have been permitted to expose to the jury the facts from which jurors, as the sole triers of fact and credibility, could appropriately draw inferences relating to the reliability of the witness. Petitioner was thus denied the right of effective cross-examination which "would be constitutional error of the first magnitude and no amount of showing of want of prejudice would cure it." *Smith v. Illinois,* 390 U.S. 129 (1968).

The claim is made that the State has an important interest in protecting the anonymity of juvenile offenders and that this interest outweighs any competing interest this petitioner might have in cross-examining Green about his being on probation. The State argues that exposure of a juvenile's record of delinquency would likely cause impairment of rehabilitative goals of the juvenile correctional procedures. This exposure, it is argued, might encourage the juvenile offender to commit further acts of delinquency, or cause the juvenile offender to lose employment opportunities or otherwise suffer unnecessarily for his youthful transgression.

We do not and need not challenge the State's interest as a matter of its own policy in the administration of criminal justice to seek to preserve the anonymity of a juvenile offender. Here, however, petitioner sought to introduce evidence of Green's probation for the purpose of suggesting that Green was biased and, therefore, that his testimony was either not to be believed in his identification of petitioner or at least very carefully considered in that light. Serious damage to the strength of the State's case would have been a real possibility had petitioner been allowed to pursue this line of inquiry. In this setting we conclude that the right of confrontation is paramount to the State's policy of protecting a juvenile offender. Whatever temporary embarrassment might result to Green or his family by disclosure of his juvenile record—if the prosecution insisted on using him to make its case—is outweighed by petitioner's right to probe into the influence of possible bias in the testimony of a crucial identification witness.

* * *

The State's policy interest in protecting the confidentiality of a juvenile offender's record cannot require yielding of so vital a constitutional right as the effective cross-examination for bias of an adverse witness. The State could have protected Green from exposure of his juvenile adjudication in these circumstances by refraining from using him to make out its case; the State cannot, consistent with the right of confrontation, require the petitioner to bear the full burden of vindicating the State's interest in the secrecy of juvenile criminal records. The judgment affirming petitioner's convictions of burglary and grand larceny is reversed and the case is remanded for further proceedings not inconsistent with this opinion.

JUSTICE STEWART, concurring.

The Court holds that, in the circumstances of this case, the Sixth and Fourteenth Amendments conferred the right to cross-examine a particular prosecution witness about his delinquency adjudication for burglary and his status as a probationer. Such cross-examination was necessary in this case in order "to show the existence of possible bias and prejudice * * *." In joining the Court's opinion, I would emphasize that the Court neither holds nor suggests that the Constitution confers a right in every case to impeach the general credibility of a witness through cross-examination about his past delinquency adjudications or criminal convictions.

JUSTICE WHITE, with whom JUSTICE REHNQUIST joins, dissenting.

As I see it, there is no constitutional principle at stake here. This is nothing more than a typical instance of a trial court exercising its discretion to control or limit cross-examination, followed by a typical decision of a state appellate court refusing to disturb the judgment of the trial court and itself concluding that limiting cross-examination had done no substantial harm to the defense. Yet the Court insists on second-guessing the state courts and in effect inviting federal review of every ruling of a state trial judge who believes cross-examination has gone far enough. I would not undertake this task, if for no other reason than that I have little faith in our ability, in fact-bound cases and on a cold record, to improve on the judgment of trial judges and of the state appellate courts who agree with them. I would affirm the judgment.

## CHAMBERS v. MISSISSIPPI
410 U.S. 284, 93 S.Ct. 1038, 35 L.Ed.2d 297 (1973).

JUSTICE POWELL delivered the opinion of the Court.

Petitioner, Leon Chambers, was tried by a jury in a Mississippi trial court and convicted of murdering a policeman. The jury assessed punishment at life imprisonment, and the Mississippi Supreme Court affirmed, one justice dissenting. * * * [C]ertiorari was granted, to consider whether petitioner's trial was conducted in accord with principles of due process under the Fourth Amendment. We conclude that it was not.

The events that led to petitioner's prosecution for murder occurred in the small town of Woodville in southern Mississippi. On Saturday evening, June 14, 1969, two Woodville policemen, James Forman and Aaron "Sonny" Liberty, entered a local bar and pool hall to execute a warrant for the arrest of a youth named C.C. Jackson. * * * The officers' first attempt to handcuff Jackson was frustrated when 20 or 25 men in the crowd intervened and wrestled him free. Forman then radioed for assistance and Liberty removed his riot gun, a 12–gauge sawed-off shotgun, from the car. Three deputy sheriffs arrived shortly thereafter and the officers again attempted to make their arrest. Once more, the officers were attacked by the onlookers and during the commotion five or six pistol shots were fired. Forman was looking in a different direction when the shooting began, but immediately saw that Liberty had been shot several times in the back. Before Liberty died, he turned around and fired both barrels of his riot gun into an alley in the area from which the shots appeared to have come. The first shot was wild and high and scattered the crowd standing at the face of the alley. Liberty appeared, however, to take more deliberate aim before the second shot and hit one of the men in the crowd in the back of the head and neck as he ran down the alley. That man was Leon Chambers.

Officer Forman could not see from his vantage point who shot Liberty or whether Liberty's shots hit anyone. One of the deputy sheriffs testified at trial that he was standing several feet from Liberty and that he saw Chambers shoot him. Another deputy sheriff stated that, although he could not see whether Chambers had a gun in his hand, he did see Chambers "break his arm down" shortly before the shots were fired. The officers who saw Chambers fall testified that they thought he was dead but they made no effort at that time either to examine him or to search for the murder weapon. Instead, they attended to Liberty, who was placed in the police car and taken to a hospital where he was declared dead on arrival. A subsequent autopsy showed that he had been hit with four bullets from a .22–caliber revolver.

Shortly after the shooting, three of Chambers' friends discovered that he was not yet dead. James Williams, Berkley Turner, and Gable McDonald loaded him into a car and transported him to the same hospital. Later that night, when the county sheriff discovered that Chambers was still alive, a guard was placed outside his room. Chambers was subsequently charged with Liberty's murder. He pleaded not guilty and has asserted his innocence throughout.

The story of Leon Chambers is intertwined with the story of another man, Gable McDonald. McDonald * * * was in the crowd on the evening of Liberty's death. Sometime shortly after that day, he left his wife in Woodville and moved to Louisiana and found a job at a sugar mill. In November of that same year, he returned to Woodville when his wife informed him that an acquaintance of his, known as Reverend Stokes, wanted to see him. * * * After talking to Stokes, McDonald agreed to make a statement to Chambers' attorneys * * *. Two days later, he appeared at the attorneys' offices and gave a sworn confession that he shot Officer Liberty. He also stated that he had already told a friend of his, James Williams, that he shot Liberty. He said that he used his own pistol, a nine-shot .22–caliber revolver, which he had discarded shortly after the shooting. In response to questions from Chambers' attorneys, McDonald affirmed that his confession was voluntary and that no one had compelled him to come to them. Once the confession had been transcribed, signed, and witnessed, McDonald was turned over to the local police authorities and was placed in jail.

One month later, at a preliminary hearing, McDonald repudiated his prior sworn confession. He testified that Stokes had persuaded him to confess that he shot Liberty. He claimed that Stokes had promised that he would not go to jail and that he would share in the proceeds of a lawsuit that Chambers would bring against the town of Woodville. On examination by his own attorney and on cross-examination by the State, McDonald swore that he had not been at the scene when Liberty was shot but had been down the street drinking beer in a cafe with a friend, Berkley Turner. When he and Turner heard the shooting, he testified, they walked up the street and found Chambers lying in the alley. He, Turner, and Williams took Chambers to the hospital. McDonald further testified at the preliminary hearing that he did not know what had happened, that there was no discussion about the shooting either going to or coming back from the hospital, and that it was not until the next day that he learned that Chambers had been felled by a blast from Liberty's riot gun. In addition, McDonald stated that while he once owned a .22–caliber pistol he had lost it many months before the shooting and did not own or possess a weapon at that time. The local justice of the peace accepted McDonald's repudiation and released him from custody. The local authorities undertook no further investigation of his possible involvement.

Chambers' case came on for trial in October of the next year. At trial, he endeavored to develop two grounds of defense. He first attempted to show that he did not shoot Liberty. Only one officer testified that he actually saw Chambers fire the shots. Although three officers saw Liberty shoot Chambers and testified that they assumed he was shooting his attacker, none of them examined Chambers to see whether he was still alive or whether he possessed a gun. Indeed, no weapon was ever recovered from the scene and there was no proof that Chambers had ever owned a .22–caliber pistol. One witness testified that he was standing in the street near where Liberty was shot, that he was looking at Chambers when the shooting began, and that he was sure that Chambers did not fire the shots.

Petitioner's second defense was that Gable McDonald had shot Officer Liberty. He was only partially successful, however, in his efforts to bring before the jury the testimony supporting this defense. Sam Hardin, a lifelong friend of McDonald's, testified that he saw McDonald shoot Liberty. A second witness, one of Liberty's cousins, testified that he saw McDonald immediately after the shooting with a pistol in his hand. In addition to the testimony of these two witnesses, Chambers endeavored to show the jury that McDonald had repeatedly confessed to the crime. Chambers attempted to prove that McDonald had admitted responsibility for the murder on four separate occasions, once when he gave the sworn statement to Chambers' counsel and three other times prior to that occasion in private conversations with friends.

In large measure, he was thwarted in his attempt to present this portion of his defense by the strict application of certain Mississippi rules of evidence. Chambers asserts in this Court, as he did unsuccessfully in his motion for new trial and on appeal to the State Supreme Court, that the application of these evidentiary rules rendered his trial fundamentally unfair and deprived him of due process of law. It is necessary, therefore, to examine carefully the rulings made during the trial. * * * At trial, after the State failed to put McDonald on the stand, Chambers called McDonald, laid a predicate for the introduction of his sworn out-of-court confession, had it admitted into evidence, and read it to the jury. The State, upon cross-examination, elicited from McDonald the fact that he had repudiated his prior confession. McDonald further testified, as he had at the preliminary hearing, that he did not shoot Liberty, and that he confessed to the crime only on the promise of Reverend Stokes that he would not go to jail and would share in a sizable tort recovery from the town. He also retold his own story of his actions on the evening of the shooting, including his visit to the cafe down the street, his absence from the scene during the critical period, and his subsequent trip to the hospital with Chambers.

At the conclusion of the State's cross-examination, Chambers [moved] * * * to examine McDonald as an adverse witness. The trial court denied the motion * * *. On appeal, the State Supreme Court upheld the trial court's ruling, finding that "McDonald's testimony was not adverse to appellant" because "[n]owhere did he point the finger at Chambers."

Defeated in his attempt to challenge directly McDonald's renunciation of his prior confession, Chambers sought to introduce the testimony of the three witnesses to whom McDonald had admitted that he shot the officer. The first of these, Sam Hardin, would have testified that, on the night of the shooting, he spent the late evening hours with McDonald at a friend's house after their return from the hospital and that, while driving McDonald home later that night, McDonald stated that he shot Liberty. The State objected to the admission of this testimony on the ground that it was hearsay. The trial court sustained the objection.

Berkley Turner, the friend with whom McDonald said he was drinking beer when the shooting occurred, was then called to testify. In the jury's presence, and without objection, he testified that he had not been in the cafe that Saturday and had not had any beers with McDonald. The jury was then excused. In the absence of the jury, Turner recounted his conversations with McDonald while they were riding with James Williams to take Chambers to the hospital. When asked whether McDonald said anything regarding the shooting of Liberty, Turner testified that McDonald told him that he "shot him." Turner further stated that one week later, when he met McDonald at a friend's house, McDonald reminded him of their prior conversation and urged Turner not to "mess him up." Petitioner argued to the court that, especially where there was other proof in the case that was corroborative of these out-of-court statements, Turner's testimony as to McDonald's self-incriminating remarks should have been admitted as an exception to the hearsay rule. Again, the trial court sustained the State's objection.

The third witness, Albert Carter, was McDonald's neighbor. They had been friends for about 25 years. Although Carter had not been in Woodville on the evening of the shooting, he stated that he learned about it the next morning from McDonald. That same day, he and McDonald walked out to a well near McDonald's house and there McDonald told him that he was the one who shot Officer Liberty. Carter testified that McDonald also told him that he had disposed of the .22–caliber revolver later that night. He further testified that several weeks after the shooting, he accompanied McDonald to Natchez where McDonald purchased another .22 pistol to replace the one he had discarded. The jury was not allowed to hear Carter's testimony. Chambers urged that these statements were admissible, the State objected, and the court sustained the objection. On appeal, the State Supreme Court approved the lower court's exclusion of these witnesses' testimony on hearsay grounds.

In sum, then, this was Chambers' predicament. As a consequence of the combination of Mississippi's "party witness" or "voucher" rule and its hearsay rule, he was unable either to cross-examine McDonald or to present witnesses in his own behalf who would have discredited McDonald's repudiation and demonstrated his complicity. * * * Chambers' defense was far less persuasive than it might have been had he been given an opportunity to subject McDonald's statements to cross-examination or had the other confessions been admitted.

The right of an accused in a criminal trial to due process is, in essence, the right to a fair opportunity to defend against the State's accusations. The rights to confront and cross-examine witnesses and to call witnesses in one's own behalf have long been recognized as essential to due process. * * * Both of these elements of a fair trial are implicated in the present case.

A

Chambers was denied an opportunity to subject McDonald's damning repudiation and alibi to cross-examination. He was not allowed to test the witness' recollection, to probe into the details of his alibi, or to "sift" his conscience so that the jury might judge for itself whether McDonald's testimony was worthy of belief. * * * [His] request to cross-examine McDonald was denied on the basis of a Mississippi common-law rule that a party may not impeach his own witness. The rule rests on the presumption—without regard to the circumstances of the particular case—that a party who calls a witness "vouches for his credibility." Although the historical origins of the "voucher" rule are uncertain, it appears to be a remnant of primitive English trial practice in which "oath-takers" or "compurgators" were called to stand behind a particular party's position in any controversy. Their assertions were strictly partisan and, quite unlike witnesses in criminal trials today, their role bore little relation to the impartial ascertainment of the facts.

Whatever validity the "voucher" rule may have once enjoyed, and apart from whatever usefulness it retains today in the civil trial process, it bears little present relationship to the realities of the criminal process. * * * [I]n modern criminal trials, defendants are rarely able to select their witnesses: they must take them where they find them. * * * In this Court, Mississippi has not sought to defend the [voucher] rule or explain its underlying rationale. Nor has it contended that its rule should override the accused's right of confrontation. Instead, it argues that there is no incompatability between the rule and Chambers' rights because no right of confrontation exists unless the testifying witness is "adverse" to the accused. The State's brief asserts that the "right of confrontation applies to witnesses *'against'* an accused." Relying * * * on the State Supreme Court's holding that McDonald did not "point the finger at Chambers," the State contends that Chambers' constitutional right was not involved.

The argument that McDonald's testimony was not "adverse" to, or "against," Chambers is not convincing. The State's proof at trial excluded the theory that more than one person participated in the shooting of Liberty. To the extent that McDonald's sworn confession tended to incriminate him, it tended also to exculpate Chambers. * * * We reject the notion that a right of such substance in the criminal process may be governed by that technicality or by any narrow and unrealistic definition of the word "against." The "voucher" rule, as applied in this case, plainly interfered with Chambers' right to defend against the State's charges.

B

We need not decide, however, whether this error alone would occasion reversal since Chambers' claimed denial of due process rests on the ultimate impact of that error when viewed in conjunction with the trial court's refusal to permit him to call other witnesses. The trial court refused to allow him to introduce the testimony of Hardin, Turner, and Carter. Each would have testified to the statements purportedly made by McDonald, on three separate occasions shortly after the crime, naming himself as the murderer. The State Supreme Court approved the exclusion of this evidence on the ground that it was hearsay.

* * * A number of exceptions have developed over the years to allow admission of hearsay statements made under circumstances that tend to assure reliability and thereby compensate for the absence of the oath and opportunity for cross-examination. Among the most prevalent of these exceptions is the one applicable to declarations against interest—an exception founded on the assumption that a person is unlikely to fabricate a statement against his own interest at the time it is made. Mississippi recognizes this exception but applies it only to declarations against pecuniary interest. It recognizes no such exception for declarations, like McDonald's in this case, that are against the penal interest of the declarant. *Brown v. State*, 99 Miss. 719, 55 So. 961 (1911).

This materialistic limitation on the declaration-against-interest hearsay exception appears to be accepted by most States in their criminal trial processes, although a number of States have discarded it. * * *

The hearsay statements involved in this case were originally made and subsequently offered at trial under circumstances that provided considerable assurance of their reliability. First, each of McDonald's confessions was made spontaneously to a close acquaintance shortly after the murder had occurred. Second, each one was corroborated by some other evidence in the case— McDonald's sworn confession, the testimony of an eye-witness to the shooting, the testimony that McDonald was seen with a gun immediately after the shooting, and proof of his prior ownership of a .22-caliber revolver and subsequent purchase of a new weapon. The sheer number of independent confessions provided additional corroboration for each. Third, whatever may be the parameters of the penal-interest rationale, each confession here was in a very real sense self-incriminatory and unquestionably against interest. * * * Finally, if there was any question about the truthfulness of the extrajudicial statements, McDonald was present in the courtroom and was under oath. He could have been cross-examined by the State, and his demeanor and responses weighed by the jury.

Few rights are more fundamental than that of an accused to present witnesses in his own defense. In the exercise of this right, the accused, as is required of the State, must comply with established rules of procedure and evidence designed to assure both fairness and reliability in the ascertainment of guilt and innocence. Although perhaps no rule of evidence has been more respected or more frequently applied in jury trials than that applicable to the exclusion of hearsay, exceptions tailored to allow the introduction of evidence which in fact is likely to be trustworthy have long existed. The testimony rejected by the trial court here bore persuasive assurances of trustworthiness and thus was well within the basic rationale of the exception for declarations against interest. That testimony also was critical to Chambers' defense. In these circumstances, where constitutional rights directly affecting the ascertainment of guilt are implicated, the hearsay rule may not be applied mechanistically to defeat the ends of justice.

We conclude that the exclusion of this critical evidence, coupled with the State's refusal to permit Chambers to cross-examine McDonald, denied him a trial in accord with traditional and fundamental standards of due process. In reaching this judgment, we establish no new principles of constitutional law. Nor does our holding signal any diminution in the respect traditionally accorded to the States in the establishment and implementation of their own criminal trial rules and procedures. Rather, we hold quite simply that under the facts and circumstances of this case the rulings of the trial court deprived Chambers of a fair trial. * * *[a]

a. Two Justices wrote separate opinions dealing with the question of whether petitioner's constitutional objections had been properly presented in the state courts. Justice White, concurring, noted that he was "inclined, although *dubitante,* to conclude with the Court that we have jurisdiction," and that "as to the merits, I would join in the Court's opinion and judgment." Justice Rehnquist, dissenting, concluded that "petitioner failed to properly raise the constitutional issue" and the writ of certiorari therefore should be dismissed. He added: "Were I to reach the merits in this case, I would have considerable difficulty in subscribing to the Court's further constitutionalization of the intricacies of the common law of evidence."

# SECTION 3.  THE DEFENDANT'S RIGHT TO REMAIN SILENT—OR TO TESTIFY

## GRIFFIN v. CALIFORNIA

380 U.S. 609, 85 S.Ct. 1229, 14 L.Ed.2d 106 (1965).

JUSTICE DOUGLAS delivered the opinion of the Court.

Petitioner was convicted of murder in the first degree after a jury trial in the California court.  He did not testify at the trial on the issue of guilt, though he did testify at the separate trial on the issue of penalty.  The trial court instructed the jury on the issue of guilt, stating that a defendant has a constitutional right not to testify.  But it told the jury: [2]

> "As to any evidence or facts against him which the defendant can reasonably be expected to deny or explain because of facts within his knowledge, if he does not testify or if, though he does testify, he fails to deny or explain such evidence, the jury may take that failure into consideration as tending to indicate the truth of such evidence and as indicating that among the inferences that may be reasonably drawn therefrom those unfavorable to the defendant are the more probable."

It added, however, that no such inference could be drawn as to evidence respecting which he had no knowledge.  It stated that failure of a defendant to deny or explain the evidence of which he had knowledge does not create a presumption of guilt nor by itself warrant an inference of guilt nor relieve the prosecution of any of its burden of proof.

Petitioner had been seen with the deceased the evening of her death, the evidence placing him with her in the alley where her body was found.  The prosecutor made much of the failure of petitioner to testify:

> "The defendant certainly knows whether Essie Mae had this beat up appearance at the time he left her apartment and went down the alley with her.

> "What kind of a man is it that would want to have sex with a woman that beat up if she was beat up at the time he left?

> "He would know that.  He would know how she got down the alley.  He would know how the blood got on the bottom of the concrete steps.  He would know how long he was with her in that box.  He would know how her wig got off.  He would know whether he beat her or mistreated her.  He would know whether he walked away from that place cool as a cucumber when he saw Mr. Villasenor because he was conscious of his own guilt and wanted to get away from that damaged or injured woman.

> "These things he has not seen fit to take the stand and deny or explain.

> "And in the whole world, if anybody would know, this defendant would know.

> "Essie Mae is dead, she can't tell you her side of the story.  The defendant won't."

---

**2.**  Article I, § 13, of the California Constitution provides in part: " . . . in any criminal case, whether the defendant testifies or not, his failure to explain or to deny by his testimony any evidence or facts in the case against him may be commented upon by the court and by counsel, and may be considered by the court or the jury."

The death penalty was imposed and the California Supreme Court affirmed. The case is here on a petition for a writ of certiorari which we granted to consider the single question whether comment on the failure to testify violated the Self–Incrimination Clause of the Fifth Amendment which we made applicable to the States * * *.

If this were a federal trial, reversible error would have been committed. *Wilson v. United States,* 149 U.S. 60 (1893) so holds. It is said, however, that the *Wilson* decision rested not on the Fifth Amendment, but on an Act of Congress. 18 U.S.C. § 3481. That indeed is the fact, as the opinion of the Court in the *Wilson* case states. * * * But that is the beginning, not the end of our inquiry. The question remains whether, statute or not, the comment rule, approved by California, violates the Fifth Amendment.

We think it does. It is in substance a rule of evidence that allows the State the privilege of tendering to the jury for its consideration the failure of the accused to testify. No formal offer of proof is made as in other situations; but the prosecutor's comment and the court's acquiescence are the equivalent of an offer of evidence and its acceptance. The Court in the *Wilson* case stated:

> " * * * the Act was framed with a due regard also to those who might prefer to rely upon the presumption of innocence which the law gives to every one, and not wish to be witnesses. It is not every one who can safely venture on the witness stand, though entirely innocent of the charge against him. Excessive timidity, nervousness when facing others and attempting to explain transactions of a suspicious character, and offenses charged against him, will often confuse and embarrass him to such a degree as to increase rather than remove prejudices against him. It is not every one, however honest, who would therefore willingly be placed on the witness stand. The statute, in tenderness to the weakness of those who from the causes mentioned might refuse to ask to be witnesses, particularly when they may have been in some degree compromised by their association with others, declares that the failure of a defendant in a criminal action to request to be a witness shall not create any presumption against him."

If the words "Fifth Amendment" are substituted for "Act" and for "statute" the spirit of the Self–Incrimination Clause is reflected. For comment on the refusal to testify is a remnant of the "inquisitorial system of criminal justice" which the Fifth Amendment outlaws. It is a penalty imposed by courts for exercising a constitutional privilege. It cuts down on the privilege by making its assertion costly. It is said, however, that the inference of guilt for failure to testify as to facts peculiarly within the accused's knowledge is in any event natural and irresistible, and that comment on the failure does not magnify that inference into a penalty for asserting a constitutional privilege. What the jury may infer given no help from the court is one thing. What they may infer when the court solemnizes the silence of the accused into evidence against him is quite another. * * *

We * * * hold that the Fifth Amendment, in its direct application to the federal government and its bearing on the States by reason of the Fourteenth Amendment, forbids either comment by the prosecution on the accused's silence or instructions by the court that such silence is evidence of guilt.

Reversed.[a]

a. The Chief Justice took no part in the decision of the case. Harlan, J., concurred "with great reluctance."

JUSTICE STEWART, with whom JUSTICE WHITE joins, dissenting. * * *

We must determine whether the petitioner has been "compelled to be a witness against himself." Compulsion is the focus of the inquiry. Certainly, if any compulsion be detected in the California procedure, it is of a dramatically different and less palpable nature than that involved in the procedures which historically gave rise to the Fifth Amendment guarantee. When a suspect was brought before the Court of High Commission or the Star Chamber, he was commanded to answer whatever was asked of him, and subjected to a far-reaching and deeply probing inquiry in an effort to ferret out some unknown and frequently unsuspected crime. He declined to answer on pain of incarceration, banishment, or mutilation. And if he spoke falsely, he was subject to further punishment. Faced with this formidable array of alternatives, his decision to speak was unquestionably coerced.

Those were the lurid realities which lay behind enactment of the Fifth Amendment, a far cry from the subject matter of the case before us. I think that the Court in this case stretches the concept of compulsion beyond all reasonable bounds, and that whatever compulsion may exist derives from the defendant's choice not to testify, not from any comment by court or counsel. In support of its conclusion that the California procedure does compel the accused to testify, the Court has only this to say: "It is a penalty imposed by courts for exercising a constitutional privilege. It cuts down on the privilege by making its assertion costly." Exactly what the penalty imposed consists of is not clear. It is not, as I understand the problem, that the jury becomes aware that the defendant has chosen not to testify in his own defense, for the jury will, of course, realize this quite evident fact, even though the choice goes unmentioned. Since comment by counsel and the court does not compel testimony by creating such an awareness, the Court must be saying that the California constitutional provision places some other compulsion upon the defendant to incriminate himself, some compulsion which the Court does not describe and which I cannot readily perceive.

* * * No doubt the prosecution's argument will seek to encourage the drawing of inferences unfavorable to the defendant. However, the defendant's counsel equally has an opportunity to explain the various other reasons why a defendant may not wish to take the stand, and thus rebut the natural if uneducated assumption that it is because the defendant cannot truthfully deny the accusations made. * * *

The California rule allowing comment by counsel and instruction by the judge on the defendant's failure to take the stand is hardly an idiosyncratic aberration. The Model Code of Evidence, and Uniform Rules of Evidence both sanction the use of such procedures. The practice had been endorsed by resolution of the American Bar Association and the American Law Institute, and has the support of the weight of scholarly opinion. * * * [b]

---

**b.** *Carter v. Kentucky,* 450 U.S. 288 (1981), held that the accused had a constitutional right to a requested instruction informing the jury that the defendant had a constitutional right not to testify and that "the fact that he does not [testify] cannot be used as an inference of guilt and should not prejudice him in any way." The Court reasoned that, while "no judge can prevent jurors from speculating about why a defendant stands mute in the face of a criminal accusation, * * * a judge can, and must, if requested to do so, use the unique power of the jury instruction to reduce the speculation to

a minimum." In *Lakeside v. Oregon,* 435 U.S. 333 (1978), the Court held that the trial court could insist upon giving a protective instruction even over objection of the defendant. The Court reasoned that such an instruction would be constitutionally objectionable only if it operated to encourage the jury to draw an adverse inference, and to reach such a conclusion "would require indulgence in two very doubtful assumptions: First, that the jurors have not noticed that the defendant did not testify and will not, therefore, draw adverse inferences on their own; second, that the jurors will totally disregard the

## ROCK v. ARKANSAS

483 U.S. 44, 107 S.Ct. 2704, 97 L.Ed.2d 37 (1987).

JUSTICE BLACKMUN delivered the opinion of the Court.

The issue presented in this case is whether Arkansas' evidentiary rule prohibiting the admission of hypnotically refreshed testimony violated petitioner's constitutional right to testify on her own behalf as a defendant in a criminal case.

Petitioner Vickie Lorene Rock was charged with manslaughter in the death of her husband, Frank Rock, on July 2, 1983. A dispute had been simmering about Frank's wish to move from the couple's small apartment adjacent to Vickie's beauty parlor to a trailer she owned outside town. That night a fight erupted when Frank refused to let petitioner eat some pizza and prevented her from leaving the apartment to get something else to eat. When police arrived on the scene they found Frank on the floor with a bullet wound in his chest. Petitioner urged the officers to help her husband, and cried to a sergeant who took her in charge, "please save him" and "don't let him die." The police removed her from the building because she was upset and because she interfered with their investigation by her repeated attempts to use the telephone to call her husband's parents. According to the testimony of one of the investigating officers, petitioner told him that "she stood up to leave the room and [her husband] grabbed her by the throat and choked her and threw her against the wall and * * * at that time she walked over and picked up the weapon and pointed it toward the floor and he hit her again and she shot him."

Because petitioner could not remember the precise details of the shooting, her attorney suggested that she submit to hypnosis in order to refresh her memory. Petitioner was hypnotized twice by Doctor Betty Back, a licensed neuropsychologist with training in the field of hypnosis. Doctor Back interviewed petitioner for an hour prior to the first hypnosis session, taking notes on petitioner's general history and her recollections of the shooting. Both hypnosis sessions were recorded on tape. Petitioner did not relate any new information during either of the sessions, id., at 78, 83, but, after the hypnosis, she was able to remember that at the time of the incident she had her thumb on the hammer of the gun, but had not held her finger on the trigger. She also recalled that the gun had discharged when her husband grabbed her arm during the scuffle. As a result of the details that petitioner was able to remember about the shooting, her counsel arranged for a gun expert to examine the handgun, a single action Hawes .22 Deputy Marshal. That inspection revealed that the gun was defective and prone to fire, when hit or dropped, without the trigger's being pulled.

When the prosecutor learned of the hypnosis sessions, he filed a motion to exclude petitioner's testimony. The trial judge held a pretrial hearing on the motion and concluded that no hypnotically refreshed testimony would be admitted. The court issued an order limiting petitioner's testimony to "matters remembered and stated to the examiner prior to being placed under hypnosis." At trial, petitioner introduced testimony by the gun expert, but the court limited petitioner's own description of the events on the day of the shooting to a reiteration of the sketchy information in Doctor Back's notes. The jury convicted petitioner on the manslaughter charge and she was sentenced to 10 years imprisonment and a $10,000 fine.

instruction and affirmatively give weight to
what they had been told not to consider at
all."

On appeal, the Supreme Court of Arkansas rejected petitioner's claim that the limitations on her testimony violated her right to present her defense. The court concluded that "the dangers of admitting this kind of testimony outweigh whatever probative value it may have," and decided to follow the approach of States that have held hypnotically refreshed testimony of witnesses inadmissible *per se.* \* \* \* [I]t ruled that the exclusion of petitioner's testimony did not violate her constitutional rights. Any "prejudice or deprivation" she suffered "was minimal and resulted from her own actions and not by any erroneous ruling of the court."

Petitioner's claim that her testimony was impermissibly excluded is bottomed on her constitutional right to testify in her own defense. At this point in the development of our adversary system, it cannot be doubted that a defendant in a criminal case has the right to take the witness stand and to testify in his or her own defense. This, of course, is a change from the historic common-law view, which was that all parties to litigation, including criminal defendants, were disqualified from testifying because of their interest in the outcome of the trial. The principal rationale for this rule was the possible untrustworthiness of a party's testimony. Under the common law, the practice did develop of permitting criminal defendants to tell their side of the story, but they were limited to making an unsworn statement that could not be elicited through direct examination by counsel and was not subject to cross-examination.

This Court in *Ferguson v. Georgia,* 365 U.S. 570 (1961), detailed the history of the transition from a rule of a defendant's incompetency to a rule of competency. As the Court there recounted, it came to be recognized that permitting a defendant to testify advances both the " 'detection of guilt' " and " 'the protection of innocence,' " and by the end of the second half of the 19th century, all States except Georgia had enacted statutes that declared criminal defendants competent to testify. \* \* \*

The right to testify on one's own behalf at a criminal trial has sources in several provisions of the Constitution. It is one of the rights that "are essential to due process of law in a fair adversary process." *Faretta v. California.* [Ch. 17]. The necessary ingredients of the Fourteenth Amendment's guarantee that no one shall be deprived of liberty without due process of law include a right to be heard and to offer testimony. \* \* \*

The right to testify is also found in the Compulsory Process Clause of the Sixth Amendment, which grants a defendant the right to call "witnesses in his favor" \* \* \*. Logically included in the accused's right to call witnesses whose testimony is "material and favorable to his defense," *United States v. Valenzuela–Bernal,* 458 U.S. 858 (1982), is a right to testify himself, should he decide it is in his favor to do so. In fact, the most important witness for the defense in many criminal cases is the defendant himself. There is no justification today for a rule that denies an accused the opportunity to offer his own testimony. Like the truthfulness of other witnesses, the defendant's veracity, which was the concern behind the original common-law rule, can be tested adequately by cross-examination.

Moreover, in *Faretta v. California,* the Court recognized that the Sixth Amendment "grants to the accused *personally* the right to make his defense." \* \* \* Even more fundamental to a personal defense than the right of self-representation, which was found to be "necessarily implied by the structure of the Amendment," *Faretta,* is an accused's right to present his own version of events in his own words. A defendant's opportunity to conduct his own defense by calling witnesses is incomplete if he may not present himself as a witness.

The opportunity to testify is also a necessary corollary to the Fifth Amendment's guarantee against compelled testimony. In *Harris v. New York*, 401 U.S. 222 (1971), the Court stated: "Every criminal defendant is privileged to testify in his own defense, or to refuse to do so." Three of the dissenting Justices in that case agreed that the Fifth Amendment encompasses this right: "[The Fifth Amendment's privilege against self-incrimination] is fulfilled only when an accused is guaranteed the right "to remain silent unless he chooses to speak in the unfettered exercise of his own will.' * * * The choice of whether to testify in one's own defense * * * is an exercise of the constitutional privilege."

The question now before the Court is whether a criminal defendant's right to testify may be restricted by a state rule that excludes her post-hypnosis testimony. This is not the first time this Court has faced a constitutional challenge to a state rule, designed to ensure trustworthy evidence, that interfered with the ability of a defendant to offer testimony. In *Washington v. Texas*, 388 U.S. 14 (1967), the Court [struck down] * * * a state statute that prevented persons charged as principals, accomplices, or accessories in the same crime from being introduced as witnesses for one another. * * * By preventing the defendant from having the benefit of his accomplice's testimony, "the State *arbitrarily* denied him the right to put on the stand a witness who was physically and mentally capable of testifying to events that he had personally observed, and whose testimony would have been relevant and material to the defense." (Emphasis added.) * * * Just as a State may not apply an arbitrary rule of competence to exclude a material defense witness from taking the stand, it also may not apply a rule of evidence that permits a witness to take the stand, but arbitrarily excludes material portions of his testimony. In *Chambers v. Mississippi* [§ 2] the Court invalidated a State's hearsay rule on the ground that it abridged the defendant's right to "present witnesses in his own defense."

Of course, the right to present relevant testimony is not without limitation. The right "may, in appropriate cases, bow to accommodate other legitimate interests in the criminal trial process." *Chambers*. But restrictions of a defendant's right to testify may not be arbitrary or disproportionate to the purposes they are designed to serve. In applying its evidentiary rules a State must evaluate whether the interests served by a rule justify the limitation imposed on the defendant's constitutional right to testify.

The Arkansas rule enunciated by the state courts does not allow a trial court to consider whether posthypnosis testimony may be admissible in a particular case; it is a *per se* rule prohibiting the admission at trial of any defendant's hypnotically refreshed testimony on the ground that such testimony is always unreliable. Thus, in Arkansas, an accused's testimony is limited to matters that he or she can prove were remembered *before* hypnosis. This rule operates to the detriment of any defendant who undergoes hypnosis, without regard to the reasons for it, the circumstances under which it took place, or any independent verification of the information it produced.

In this case, the application of that rule had a significant adverse effect on petitioner's ability to testify. It virtually prevented her from describing any of the events that occurred on the day of the shooting, despite corroboration of many of those events by other witnesses. Even more importantly, under the court's rule petitioner was not permitted to describe the actual shooting except in the words contained in Doctor Back's notes. The expert's description of the gun's tendency to misfire would have taken on greater significance if the jury had heard petitioner testify that she did not have her finger on the trigger and that the gun went off when her husband hit her arm.

In establishing its *per se* rule, the Arkansas Supreme Court simply followed the approach taken by a number of States that have decided that hypnotically enhanced testimony should be excluded at trial on the ground that it tends to be unreliable. Other States that have adopted an exclusionary rule, however, have done so for the testimony of *witnesses,* not for the testimony of a *defendant.* The Arkansas Supreme Court failed to perform the constitutional analysis that is necessary when a defendant's right to testify is at stake.

Although the Arkansas court concluded that any testimony that cannot be proved to be the product of prehypnosis memory is unreliable, many courts have eschewed a *per se* rule and permit the admission of hypnotically refreshed testimony. Hypnosis by trained physicians or psychologists has been recognized as a valid therapeutic technique since 1958, although there is no generally accepted theory to explain the phenomenon, or even a consensus on a single definition of hypnosis. The use of hypnosis in criminal investigations, however, is controversial, and the current medical and legal view of its appropriate role is unsettled.

Responses of individuals to hypnosis vary greatly. The popular belief that hypnosis guarantees the accuracy of recall is as yet without established foundation and, in fact, hypnosis often has no effect at all on memory. The most common response to hypnosis, however, appears to be an increase in both correct and incorrect recollections. Three general characteristics of hypnosis may lead to the introduction of inaccurate memories: the subject becomes "suggestible" and may try to please the hypnotist with answers the subject thinks will be met with approval; the subject is likely to "confabulate," that is, to fill in details from the imagination in order to make an answer more coherent and complete; and, the subject experiences "memory hardening," which gives him great confidence in both true and false memories, making effective cross-examination more difficult. See generally M. Orne, et al., Hypnotically Induced Testimony * * *. Despite the unreliability that hypnosis concededly may introduce, however, the procedure has been credited as instrumental in obtaining investigative leads or identifications that were later confirmed by independent evidence.

The inaccuracies the process introduces can be reduced, although perhaps not eliminated, by the use of procedural safeguards. One set of suggested guidelines calls for hypnosis to be performed only by a psychologist or psychiatrist with special training in its use and who is independent of the investigation. See Orne, The Use and Misuse of Hypnosis in Court * * *. These procedures reduce the possibility that biases will be communicated to the hypersuggestive subject by the hypnotist. Suggestion will be less likely also if the hypnosis is conducted in a neutral setting with no one present but the hypnotist and the subject. Tape or video recording of all interrogations, before, during, and after hypnosis, can help reveal if leading questions were asked. Such guidelines do not guarantee the accuracy of the testimony, because they cannot control the subject's own motivations or any tendency to confabulate, but they do provide a means of controlling overt suggestions.

The more traditional means of assessing accuracy of testimony also remain applicable in the case of a previously hypnotized defendant. Certain information recalled as a result of hypnosis may be verified as highly accurate by corroborating evidence. Cross-examination, even in the face of a confident defendant, is an effective tool for revealing inconsistencies. Moreover, a jury can be educated to the risks of hypnosis through expert testimony and cautionary instructions. Indeed, it is probably to a defendant's advantage to establish carefully the extent of his memory prior to hypnosis, in order to minimize the decrease in credibility the procedure might introduce.

We are not now prepared to endorse without qualifications the use of hypnosis as an investigative tool; scientific understanding of the phenomenon and of the means to control the effects of hypnosis is still in its infancy. Arkansas, however, has not justified the exclusion of *all* of a defendant's testimony that the defendant is unable to prove to be the product of prehypnosis memory. A State's legitimate interest in barring unreliable evidence does not extend to *per se* exclusions that may be reliable in an individual case. Wholesale inadmissibility of a defendant's testimony is an arbitrary restriction on the right to testify in the absence of clear evidence by the State repudiating the validity of all posthypnosis recollections. The State would be well within its powers if it established guidelines to aid trial courts in the evaluation of posthypnosis testimony and it may be able to show that testimony in a particular case is so unreliable that exclusion is justified. But it has not shown that hypnotically enhanced testimony is always so untrustworthy and so immune to the traditional means of evaluating credibility that it should disable a defendant from presenting her version of the events for which she is on trial.

In this case, the defective condition of the gun corroborated the details petitioner remembered about the shooting. The tape recordings provided some means to evaluate the hypnosis and the trial judge concluded that Doctor Back did not suggest responses with leading questions. Those circumstances present an argument for admissibility of petitioner's testimony in this particular case, an argument that must be considered by the trial court. Arkansas' *per se* rule excluding all posthypnosis testimony infringes impermissibly on the right of a defendant to testify on his or her own behalf.[20]

The judgment of the Supreme Court of Arkansas is vacated and the case is remanded to that court for further proceedings not inconsistent with this opinion.

CHIEF JUSTICE REHNQUIST, with whom JUSTICE WHITE, JUSTICE O'CONNOR, and JUSTICE SCALIA join, dissenting.

In deciding that petitioner Rock's testimony was properly limited at her trial, the Arkansas Supreme Court cited several factors that undermine the reliability of hypnotically induced testimony. Like the Court today, the Arkansas Supreme Court observed that a hypnotized individual becomes subject to suggestion, is likely to confabulate, and experiences artificially increased confidence in both true and false memories following hypnosis. No known set of procedures, both courts agree, can insure against the inherently unreliable nature of such testimony. Having acceded to the factual premises of the Arkansas Supreme Court, the Court nevertheless concludes that a state trial court must attempt to make its own scientific assessment of reliability in each case it is confronted with a request for the admission of hypnotically induced testimony. I find no justification in the Constitution for such a ruling.

In the Court's words, the decision today is "bottomed" on recognition of Rock's "constitutional right to testify in her own defense." While it is true that this Court, in dictum, has recognized the existence of such a right, the principles

---

**20.** This disposition makes it unnecessary to consider petitioner's claims that the trial court's order restricting her testimony was unconstitutionally broad and that the trial court's application of the order resulted in a denial of due process of law. We also need not reach petitioner's argument that Arkansas' restriction on her testimony interferes with her Sixth Amendment right to counsel. Petitioner concedes that there is a "substantial question" whether she raised this federal question on appeal to the Arkansas Supreme Court. Reply Brief for Petitioner 2.

identified by the Court as underlying this right provide little support for invalidating the evidentiary rule applied by the Arkansas Supreme Court.

As a general matter, the Court first recites, a defendant's right to testify facilitates the truth-seeking function of a criminal trial by advancing both the " 'detection of guilt' " and " 'the protection of innocence.' " Quoting *Ferguson v. Georgia.* Such reasoning is hardly controlling here, where advancement of the truth-seeking function of Rock's trial was the sole motivation behind limiting her testimony. The Court also posits, however, that "a rule that denies an accused the opportunity to offer his own testimony" cannot be upheld because, "[l]ike the truthfulness of other witnesses, the defendant's veracity * * * can be tested adequately by cross-examination." But the Court candidly admits that the increased confidence inspired by hypnotism makes "cross-examination more difficult," thereby diminishing an adverse party's ability to test the truthfulness of defendants such as Rock. * * *

This Court has traditionally accorded the States "respect * * * in the establishment and implementation of their own criminal trial rules and procedures." *Chambers.* * * * One would think that this deference would be at its highest in an area such as this, where, as the Court concedes, "scientific understanding * * * is still in its infancy." * * * The Supreme Court of Arkansas' decision was an entirely permissible response to a novel and difficult question. M. Orne et al., Hypnotically Refreshed Testimony * * *. As an original proposition, the solution this Court imposes upon Arkansas may be equally sensible, though requiring the matter to be considered *res nova* by every single trial judge in every single case might seem to some to pose serious administrative difficulties. But until there is a much more general consensus on the use of hypnosis than there is now, the Constitution does not warrant this Court's mandating its own view of how to deal with the issue.

## SECTION 4.   DUE PROCESS REQUIREMENTS

### TAYLOR v. KENTUCKY

436 U.S. 478, 98 S.Ct. 1930, 56 L.Ed.2d 468 (1978).

JUSTICE POWELL delivered the opinion of the Court.

Only two Terms ago, this Court observed that the "presumption of innocence, although not articulated in the Constitution, is a basic component of a fair trial under our system of criminal justice." *Estelle v. Williams,* 425 U.S. 501 (1976). In this felony case, the trial court instructed the jury as to the prosecution's burden of proof beyond a reasonable doubt, but refused petitioner's timely request for instructions on the presumption of innocence and the indictment's lack of evidentiary value. We are asked to decide whether the Due Process Clause of the Fourteenth Amendment requires that either or both instructions be given upon timely defense motions.

Petitioner was tried for robbery in 1976, allegedly having forced his way into the home of James Maddox and stolen a house key and a billfold containing $10 to $15. During *voir dire* of the jury, defense counsel questioned the panel about their understanding of the presumption of innocence, the burden of proof beyond a reasonable doubt, and the fact that an indictment is not evidence. The prosecutor then read the indictment to the jury.

The Commonwealth's only witness was Maddox. He testified that he had known petitioner for several years and had entertained petitioner at his home on several occasions. According to Maddox, petitioner and a friend knocked on his door on the evening of February 16, 1976, asking to be admitted. Maddox refused, saying he had to go to bed. The two left, but returned 15 minutes later. They forced their way in, hit Maddox over the head, and fled with his billfold and house key, which were never recovered.

Petitioner then took the stand as the only witness for the defense. He admitted having been at Maddox's home on other occasions, but denied going there on February 16 or participating in the robbery. He stated that he had spent that night with two friends sitting in a parked car, watching a rainstorm and a power failure. Defense counsel requested the trial court to instruct the jury that "[t]he law presumes a defendant to be innocent of a crime," and that the indictment, previously read to the jury, was not evidence to be considered against the defendant. The court declined to give either instruction, and did not convey their substance in its charge to the jury. It did instruct the jury as to the Commonwealth's burden of proving petitioner's guilt beyond a reasonable doubt. Petitioner was found guilty and sentenced to five years of imprisonment. The Kentucky Court of Appeals affirmed * * *, the Supreme Court of Kentucky denied discretionary review, and we granted certiorari.

"The principle that there is a presumption of innocence in favor of the accused is the undoubted law, axiomatic and elementary, and its enforcement lies at the foundation of the administration of our criminal law." *Coffin v. United States,* 156 U.S. 432, 453 (1895). The *Coffin* Court traced the venerable history of the presumption from Deuteronomy through Roman law, English common law, and the common law of the United States. While *Coffin* held that the presumption of innocence and the equally fundamental principle that the prosecution bears the burden of proof beyond a reasonable doubt were logically separate and distinct, sharp scholarly criticism demonstrated the error of that view. Nevertheless, these same scholars advise against abandoning the instruction on the presumption of innocence, even when a complete explanation of the burden of proof beyond a reasonable doubt is provided. * * * This admonition derives from a perceived salutary effect upon lay jurors. While the legal scholar may understand that the presumption of innocence and the prosecution's burden of proof are logically similar, the ordinary citizen well may draw significant additional guidance from an instruction on the presumption of innocence. Wigmore described this effect as follows:

> "[I]n a criminal case the term [presumption of innocence] does convey a special and perhaps useful hint over and above the other form of the rule about the burden of proof, in that it cautions the jury to put away from their minds all the suspicion that arises from the arrest, the indictment, and the arraignment, and to reach their conclusion solely from the legal evidence adduced. In other words, the rule about burden of proof requires the prosecution by evidence to convince the jury of the accused's guilt; while the presumption of innocence, too, requires this, but conveys for the jury a special and additional caution (which is perhaps only an implied corollary to the other) to consider, in the material for their belief, *nothing but the evidence,* i.e., no surmises based on the present situation of the accused. This caution is indeed particularly needed in criminal cases."

This Court has declared that one accused of a crime is entitled to have his guilt or innocence determined solely on the basis of the evidence introduced at trial, and not on grounds of official suspicion, indictment, continued custody, or other circumstances not adduced as proof at trial. And it long has been recognized that an instruction on the presumption is one way of impressing upon the jury the importance of that right. * * *

Petitioner argues that in the circumstances of this case, the purging effect of an instruction on the presumption of innocence was essential to a fair trial. He points out that the trial court's instructions were themselves skeletal, placing little emphasis on the prosecution's duty to prove the case beyond a reasonable doubt and none at all on the jury's duty to judge petitioner only on the basis of the testimony heard at trial.

Against the background of the court's rather Spartan instructions, the prosecutor's closing argument ranged far and wide, asking the jury to draw inferences about petitioner's conduct from "facts" not in evidence, but propounded by the prosecutor. For example, he described the reasonable-doubt standard by declaring that petitioner, "*like every other defendant* who's ever been tried who's in the penitentiary or in the reformatory today, has this presumption of innocence until proved guilty beyond a reasonable doubt." (emphasis added). This statement linked petitioner to every defendant who turned out to be guilty and was sentenced to imprisonment. It could be viewed as an invitation to the jury to consider petitioner's status as a defendant as evidence tending to prove his guilt. Similarly, in responding to defense counsel's rhetorical query as to the whereabouts of the items stolen from Maddox, the prosecutor declared that "[o]ne of the first things *defendants do after they rip someone off*, they get rid of the evidence as fast and as quickly as they can." (emphasis added). This statement also implied that all defendants are guilty and invited the jury to consider that proposition in determining petitioner's guilt or innocence.[14]

Additionally, the prosecutor observed in his opening statement that Maddox "took out" a warrant against petitioner and that the grand jury had returned an indictment, which the prosecutor read to the jury. Thus, the jury not only was invited to consider the petitioner's status as a defendant, but also was permitted to draw inferences of guilt from the fact of arrest and indictment. The prosecutor's description of those events was not necessarily improper, but the combination of the skeletal instructions, the possible harmful inferences from the references to the indictment, and the repeated suggestions that petitioner's status as a defendant tended to establish his guilt created a genuine danger that the jury would convict petitioner on the basis of those extraneous considerations, rather than on the evidence introduced at trial. That risk was heightened because the trial essentially was a swearing contest between victim and accused.

Against the need for a presumption-of-innocence instruction, the Commonwealth argues first that such an instruction is not required where, as here, the jury is instructed as to the burden of proof beyond a reasonable doubt. The trial court's truncated discussion of reasonable doubt, however, was hardly a model of clarity. It defined reasonable doubt as "a substantial doubt, a real doubt." This definition, though perhaps not in itself reversible error, often has been criticized as confusing. See, e.g., *United States v. Muckenstrum*, 515 F.2d 568 (1975). And even if the instruction on reasonable doubt had been more clearly stated, the Commonwealth's argument ignores both the special purpose of a presumption-of-innocence instruction and the particular need for such an instruction in this case.

The Commonwealth also contends that no additional instructions were required, because defense counsel argued the presumption of innocence in both his opening and closing statements. But arguments of counsel cannot substitute

14. We do not suggest that such prosecutorial comments, standing alone, would rise to the level of reversible error, an issue not raised in this case. But they are relevant to the need for carefully framed instructions designed to assure that the accused be judged only on the evidence.

for instructions by the court. Petitioner's right to have the jury deliberate solely on the basis of the evidence cannot be permitted to hinge upon a hope that defense counsel will be a more effective advocate for that proposition than the prosecutor will be in implying that extraneous circumstances may be considered. It was the duty of the court to safeguard petitioner's rights, a duty only it could have performed reliably. * * *

We hold that on the facts of this case the trial court's refusal to give petitioner's requested instruction on the presumption of innocence resulted in a violation of his right to a fair trial as guaranteed by the Due Process Clause of the Fourteenth Amendment. The judgment of conviction is reversed, and the case is remanded for further proceedings not inconsistent with this opinion.

JUSTICE BRENNAN, concurring.

I join the Court's opinion because in reversing petitioner's conviction it reaffirms that "the 'presumption of innocence, although not articulated in the Constitution, is a basic component of a fair trial under our system of criminal justice.'" It follows from this proposition, as is clear from the Court's opinion, that trial judges should instruct the jury on a criminal defendant's entitlement to a presumption of innocence in all cases where such an instruction is requested.

JUSTICE STEVENS, with whom JUSTICE REHNQUIST joins, dissenting.

In a federal court it is reversible error to refuse a request for a proper instruction on the presumption of innocence. *Coffin v. United States.* That is not, however, a sufficient reason for holding that such an instruction is constitutionally required in every criminal trial.

The function of the instruction is to make it clear that the burden of persuasion rests entirely on the prosecutor. The same function is performed by the instruction requiring proof beyond a reasonable doubt. One standard instruction adds emphasis to the other. Neither should be omitted, but an "omission, or an incomplete instruction, is less likely to be prejudicial than a misstatement of the law." *Henderson v. Kibbe,* 431 U.S. 145 (1977). In some cases the omission may be fatal, but the Court wisely avoids a holding that this is always so.

In this case the omission did not violate a specific constitutional guarantee, such as the privilege against compulsory self-incrimination. Nor did it deny the defendant his fundamental right to a fair trial. An instruction on reasonable doubt, admittedly brief, was given. The *voir dire* had made clear to each juror the defendant's right to be presumed innocent despite his indictment. The prosecutor's closing argument did not precipitate any objection from defense counsel who listened to it; it may not, therefore, provide the basis for a reversal. Although the Court's appraisal is not unreasonable, for this was by no means a perfect trial, I do not believe that constitutional error was committed. Accordingly, I respectfully dissent.[a]

**a.** *Kentucky v. Whorton,* 441 U.S. 786 (1979), reversed on prosecution appeal a Kentucky Supreme Court ruling that read *Taylor* as requiring a presumption of innocence instruction "in all criminal trials." The Court stressed that the *Taylor* ruling "focused on the failure to give the instruction as it related to the overall fairness of the trial in its entirety" and that the *Taylor* majority specifically limited its holding to "the facts of this case." The Court remanded to the Kentucky Supreme Court for reconsideration in light of the "totality of the circumstances—including all instructions to the jury, the arguments of counsel, whether the weight of the evidence was overwhelming and other relevant factors." Three Justices dissented, arguing that an instruction on the presumption of innocence should be "constitutionally required in every case where a timely request has been made," although the failure to give the instruction

# DARDEN v. WAINWRIGHT

477 U.S. 168, 106 S.Ct. 2464, 91 L.Ed.2d 144 (1986).

JUSTICE POWELL delivered the opinion of the Court.

Petitioner was tried and found guilty of murder, robbery, and assault with intent to kill in the Circuit Court for Citrus County, Florida, in January 1974. Pursuant to Florida's capital sentencing statute, the same jury that convicted petitioner heard further testimony and argument in order to make a nonbinding recommendation as to whether a death sentence should be imposed. The jury recommended a death sentence, and the trial judge followed that recommendation. On direct appeal, the Florida Supreme Court affirmed the conviction and the sentence. Petitioner made several of the same arguments in that appeal that he makes here. With respect to the prosecutorial misconduct claim, the court disapproved of the closing argument, but reasoned that the law required a new trial "only in those cases in which it is reasonably evident that the remarks might have influenced the jury to reach a more severe verdict of guilt * * * or in which the comment is unfair." * * * It concluded that the comments had not rendered petitioner's trial unfair. * * *

Petitioner then sought federal habeas corpus relief, raising the same claims he raises here. * * * A divided panel of the Court of Appeals for the Eleventh Circuit affirmed. * * *

Because of the nature of petitioner's claims, the facts of this case will be stated in more detail than is normally necessary in this Court. On September 8, 1973, at about 5:30 p.m., a black adult male entered Carl's Furniture Store near Lakeland, Florida. The only other person in the store was the proprietor, Mrs. Turman, who lived with her husband in a house behind the store. Mr. Turman, who worked nights at a juvenile home, had awakened at about 5:00 p.m., had a cup of coffee at the store with his wife, and returned home to let their dogs out for a run. Mrs. Turman showed the man around the store. He stated that he was interested in purchasing about $600 worth of furniture for a rental unit, and asked to see several different items. He left the store briefly, stating that his wife would be back to look at some of the items.

The same man returned just a few minutes later asking to see some stoves, and inquiring about the price. When Mrs. Turman turned toward the adding machine, he grabbed her and pressed a gun to her back, saying "Do as I say and you won't get hurt." He took her to the rear of the store and told her to open the cash register. He took the money, then ordered her to the part of the store where some boxsprings and mattresses were stacked against the wall. At that time Mr. Turman appeared at the back door. Mrs. Turman screamed while the man reached across her right shoulder and shot Mr. Turman between the eyes. Mr. Turman fell backwards, with one foot partially in the building. Ordering Mrs. Turman not to move, the man tried to pull Mr. Turman into the building and close the door, but could not do so because one of Mr. Turman's feet was caught in the door. The man left Mr. Turman face-up in the rain, and told Mrs. Turman to get down on the floor approximately five feet from where her husband lay dying. While she begged to go to her husband, he told her to remove her false teeth. He unzipped his pants, unbuckled his belt, and demanded that Mrs. Turman perform oral sex on him. She began to cry "Lord, have mercy." He told her to get up and go towards the front of the store.

could constitute harmless error under the rule
of *Chapman v. California* (see Ch. 11, note d).

Meanwhile, a neighbor family, the Arnolds, became aware that something had happened to Mr. Turman. The mother sent her 16 year-old son Phillip, a part-time employee at the furniture store, to help. When Phillip reached the back door he saw Mr. Turman lying partially in the building. When Phillip opened the door to take Turman's body inside, Mrs. Turman shouted "Phillip, no, go back." Phillip did not know what she meant and asked the man to help get Turman inside. He replied, "Sure, buddy, I will help you." As Phillip looked up, the man was pointing a gun in his face. He pulled the trigger and the gun misfired; he pulled the trigger again and shot Phillip in the mouth. Phillip started to run away, and was shot in the neck. While he was still running, he was shot a third time in the side. Despite these wounds, Phillip managed to stumble to the home of a neighbor, Mrs. Edith Hill. She had her husband call an ambulance while she tried to stop Phillip's bleeding. While she was helping Phillip, she saw a late model green Chevrolet leave the store and head towards Tampa on state highway 92. Phillip survived the incident; Mr. Turman, who never regained consciousness, died later that night.

Minutes after the murder petitioner was driving towards Tampa on highway 92, just a few miles away from the furniture store. He was out on furlough from a Florida prison, and was driving a car borrowed from his girlfriend in Tampa. He was driving fast on a wet road. Petitioner testified that as he came up on a line of cars in his lane, he was unable to slow down. He attempted to pass, but was forced off the road to avoid a head-on collision with an oncoming car. Petitioner crashed into a telephone pole. The driver of the oncoming car, John Stone, stopped his car and went to petitioner to see if he could help. Stone testified that as he approached the car, petitioner was zipping up his pants and buckling his belt. Police at the crash site later identified petitioner's car as a 1969 Chevrolet Impala of greenish golden brown color. Petitioner paid a bystander to give him a ride to Tampa. Petitioner later returned with a wrecker, only to find that the car had been towed away by the police.

By the time the police arrived at the scene of the accident, petitioner had left. The fact that the car matched the description of the car leaving the scene of the murder, and that the accident had occurred within three and one-half miles of the furniture store and within minutes of the murder, led police to suspect that the car was driven by the murderer. They searched the area. An officer found a pistol—a revolver—about forty feet from the crash site. The arrangement of shells within the chambers exactly matched the pattern that should have been found in the murder weapon: one shot, one misfire, followed by three shots, with a live shell remaining in the next chamber to be fired. A specialist for the FBI examined the pistol and testified that it was a Smith & Wesson .38 special revolver. It had been manufactured as a standard .38; it later was sent to England to be rebored, making it a much rarer type of gun than the standard .38. An examination of the bullet that killed Mr. Turman revealed that it came from a .38 Smith & Wesson special.

On the day following the murder petitioner was arrested at his girlfriend's house in Tampa. A few days later Mrs. Turman identified him at a preliminary hearing as her husband's murderer. Phillip Arnold selected petitioner's picture out of a spread of six photographs as the man who had shot him.[1] * * *

1. There are some minor discrepancies in the eyewitness identification. Mrs. Turman first described her assailant immediately after the murder while her husband was being taken to the emergency room. She told the investigating officer that the attacker was a heavyset man. When asked if he was "neat in his appearance, clean-looking, clean-shaven," she responded "[a]s far as I can remember, yes, sir." Ibid. She also stated to the officer that she thought that the attacker was about her height, 5'6" tall, and that he was

Petitioner \* \* \* contends that the prosecution's closing argument at the guilt-innocence stage of the trial rendered his conviction fundamentally unfair \* \* \*. It is helpful as an initial matter to place these remarks in context. Closing argument came at the end of several days of trial. Because of a state procedural rule petitioner's counsel had the opportunity to present the initial summation as well as a rebuttal to the prosecutors' closing arguments. The prosecutors' comments must be evaluated in light of the defense argument that preceded it, which blamed the Polk County Sheriff's Office for a lack of evidence,[5] alluded to the death penalty,[6] characterized the perpetrator of the crimes as an "animal," [7] and contained counsel's personal opinion of the strength of the state's evidence.[8]

The prosecutors then made their closing argument. That argument deserves the condemnation it has received from every court to review it, although no court has held that the argument rendered the trial unfair. Several comments attempted to place some of the blame for the crime on the Division of Corrections, because Darden was on weekend furlough from a prison sentence when the crime occurred.[9] Some comments implied that the death penalty would be the only guarantee against a future similar act.[10] Others incorporated the defense's use of the word "animal." [11] Prosecutor McDaniel made several

wearing a pullover shirt with a stripe around the neck. The first time she saw petitioner after the attack was when she identified him at the preliminary hearing. She had not read any newspaper accounts of the crime, nor had she seen any picture of petitioner. When she was asked if petitioner was the man who had committed the crimes, she said yes. She also repeatedly identified him at trial.

Phillip Arnold first identified petitioner in a photo line-up while in the hospital. He could not speak at the time, and in response to the written question whether petitioner had a mustache, Phillip wrote back "I don't think so." Phillip also testified at trial that the attacker was a heavyset man wearing a dull, light color knit shirt with a ring around the neck. He testified that the man was almost his height, about 6'2" tall.

A motorist who stopped at the scene of the accident testified that petitioner was wearing a white or off-grey button-down shirt and that he had a slight mustache. In fact, the witness stated that he "didn't know it was that [the mustache] or the raindrops on him or not. I couldn't really tell that much to it, it was real thin, that's all." Petitioner is about 5'10" tall, and at the time of trial testified that he weighed about 175 pounds.

**5.** "The Judge is going to tell you to consider the evidence or the lack of evidence. We have a lack of evidence, almost criminally negligent on the part of the Polk County Sheriff's Office in this case. You could go on and on about it." Record 728.

**6.** "They took a coincidence and magnified that into a capital case. And they are asking you to kill a man on coincidence." Record 730.

**7.** "The first witness you saw was Mrs. Turman, who was a pathetic figure; who

worked and struggled all of her life to build what little she had, the little furniture store; and a woman who was robbed, sexually assaulted, and then had her husband slaughtered before her eyes, by what would have to be a vicious animal." Record 717. "And this murderer ran after him, aimed again, and this poor kid with half his brains blown away. . . . It's the work of an animal, there's no doubt about it." Record 731–732.

**8.** "So they come up here and ask Citrus County people to kill the man. You will be instructed on lesser included offenses. . . . The question is, do they have enough evidence to kill that man, enough evidence? And I honestly do not think they do." Record 736–737.

**9.** "As far as I am concerned, there should be another Defendant in this courtroom, one more, and that is the division of corrections, the prisons. . . . Can we expect him to stay in a prison when they go there? Can we expect them to stay locked up once they go there? Do we know that they're going to be out on the public with guns, drinking?" Record 749–750. "Yes, there is another Defendant, but I regret that I know of no charges to place upon him, except the public condemnation of them, condemn them." Record 750–751.

**10.** "I will ask you to advise the Court to give him death. That's the only way I know that he is not going to get out on the public. It's the only way I know. It's the only way I can be sure of it. It's the only way anybody can be sure of it now, because the people that turned him loose—" Record 753.

**11.** "As far as I am concerned, and as Mr. Maloney said as he identified this man as an animal, this animal was on the public for one reason." Record 749.

offensive comments reflecting an emotional reaction to the case.[12] These comments undoubtedly were improper. But as both the District Court and the original panel of the Court of Appeals (whose opinion on this issue still stands) recognized, it "is not enough that the prosecutors' remarks were undesirable or even universally condemned." The relevant question is whether the prosecutors' comments "so infected the trial with unfairness as to make the resulting conviction a denial of due process." *Donnelly v. DeChristoforo,* 416 U.S. 637 (1974). Moreover, the appropriate standard of review for such a claim on writ of habeas corpus is "the narrow one of due process, and not the broad exercise of supervisory power." *DeChristoforo.*

Under this standard of review, we agree with the reasoning of every court to consider these comments that they did not deprive petitioner of a fair trial. The prosecutors' argument did not manipulate or misstate the evidence, nor did it implicate other specific rights of the accused such as the right to counsel or the right to remain silent. Much of the objectionable content was invited by or was responsive to the opening summation of the defense. As we explained in *United States v. Young,* 470 U.S. 1 (1985), the idea of "invited response" is used not to excuse improper comments, but to determine their effect on the trial as a whole. The trial court instructed the jurors several times that their decision was to be made on the basis of the evidence alone, and that the arguments of counsel were not evidence. The weight of the evidence against petitioner was heavy; the "overwhelming eyewitness and circumstantial evidence to support a finding of guilt on all charges," 329 So.2d, at 291, reduced the likelihood that the jury's decision was influenced by argument. Finally, defense counsel made the tactical decision not to present any witness other than petitioner. This decision not only permitted them to give their summation prior to the prosecution's closing argument, but also gave them the opportunity to make a final rebuttal argument. Defense counsel were able to use the opportunity for rebuttal very effectively, turning much of the prosecutors' closing argument against them by placing many of the prosecutors' comments and actions in a light that was more likely to engender strong disapproval than result in inflamed passions against petitioner.[14] For these reasons, we agree with the District Court below that "Darden's trial was not perfect—few are—but neither was it fundamentally unfair." 513 F.Supp., at 958.

JUSTICE BLACKMUN, with whom JUSTICE BRENNAN, JUSTICE MARSHALL, and JUSTICE STEVENS join, dissenting. * * *

---

12. "He shouldn't be out of his cell unless he has a leash on him and a prison guard at the other end of that leash." Record 750. "I wish [Mr. Turman] had had a shotgun in his hand when he walked in the back door and blown his [Darden's] face off. I wish I could see him sitting here with no face, blown away by a shotgun." Record 758. "I wish someone had walked in the back door and blown his head off at that point." Record 759. "He fired in the boy's back, number five saving one. Didn't get a chance to use it. I wish he had used it on himself." Record 774. "I wish he had been killed in the accident, but he wasn't. Again, we are unlucky that time." Record 775. "Don't forget what he has done according to those witnesses, to make every attempt to change his appearance from September the 8th, 1973. The hair, the goatee, even the moustache and the weight. The only thing he hasn't done that I know of is cut his

throat." Record 779. After this, the last in a series of such comments, defense counsel objected for the first time.

14. "Mr. McDaniel made an impassioned plea . . . how many times did he repeat [it]? I wish you had been shot, I wish they had blown his face away. My God, I get the impression he would like to be the man that stands there and pulls the switch on him." Record 791.

One of Darden's counsel testified at the habeas corpus hearing that he made the tactical decision not to object to the improper comments. Based on his long experience with prosecutor McDaniel, he knew McDaniel would "get much more vehement in his remarks if you allowed him to go on." By not immediately objecting, he hoped to encourage the prosecution to commit reversible error. Supp.App. 46–47.

The Court's discussion of Darden's claim of prosecutorial misconduct is noteworthy for its omissions. Despite the fact that earlier this Term the Court relied heavily on standards governing the professional responsibility of defense counsel in ruling that an attorney's actions did not deprive his client of any constitutional right, see *Nix v. Whiteside* [Ch. 17], today it entirely ignores standards governing the professional responsibility of prosecutors in reaching the conclusion that the summations of Darden's prosecutors did not deprive him of a fair trial.

The prosecutors' remarks in this case reflect behavior as to which "virtually all the sources speak with one voice," *Nix v. Whiteside*, that is, a voice of strong condemnation. The following brief comparison of established standards of prosecutorial conduct with the prosecutors' behavior in this case merely illustrates, but hardly exhausts, the scope of the misconduct involved:

1. "A lawyer shall not . . . state a personal opinion as to . . . the credibility [of] a witness . . . or the guilt or innocence of an accused." Model Rules of Professional Conduct, Rule 3.4(e). * * * Yet one prosecutor, White, stated: "I am convinced, as convinced as I know I am standing before you today, that Willie Jasper Darden is a murderer, that he murdered Mr. Turman, that he robbed Mrs. Turman and that he shot to kill Phillip Arnold. I will be convinced of that the rest of my life." And the other prosecutor, McDaniel, stated, with respect to Darden's testimony: "Well, let me tell you something: If I am ever over in that chair over there, facing life or death, life imprisonment or death, I guarantee you I will lie until my teeth fall out."

2. "The prosecutor should refrain from argument which would divert the jury from its duty to decide the case on the evidence, by injecting issues broader than the guilt or innocence of the accused under the controlling law, or by making predictions of the consequences of the jury's verdict." ABA Standards, The Prosecution Function, § 3–5.8(d). * * * Yet McDaniel's argument was filled with references to Darden's status as a prisoner on furlough who "shouldn't be out of his cell unless he has a leash on him." Again and again, he sought to put on trial an absent "defendant," the State Department of Corrections that had furloughed Darden. He also implied that defense counsel would use improper tricks to deflect the jury from the real issue. Darden's status as a furloughed prisoner, the release policies of the Department of Corrections, and his counsel's anticipated tactics obviously had no legal relevance to the question the jury was being asked to decide: whether he had committed the robbery and murder at the Turmans' furniture store. Indeed, the State argued before this Court that McDaniel's remarks were harmless precisely *because* he "failed to discuss the issues, the weight of the evidence, or the credibility of the witnesses."

3. "The prosecutor should not use arguments calculated to inflame the passions or prejudices of the jury." ABA Standards, § 3–5.8(c). Yet McDaniel repeatedly expressed a wish "that I could see [Darden] sitting here with no face, blown away by a shotgun." Indeed, I do not think McDaniel's summation, taken as a whole, can accurately be described as anything but a relentless and single-minded attempt to inflame the jury. * * * Almost every page contains at least one offensive or improper statement; some pages contain little else. The misconduct here was not "slight or confined to a single instance, but . . . was pronounced and persistent, with a probable cumulative effect upon the jury which cannot be disregarded as inconsequential." *Berger v. United States*.

The Court presents what is, for me, an entirely unpersuasive one-page laundry list of reasons for ignoring this blatant misconduct. First, the Court says that the summations "did not manipulate or misstate the evidence [or]

. . . implicate other specific rights of the accused such as the right to counsel or the right to remain silent." With all respect, that observation is quite beside the point. The "solemn purpose of endeavoring to ascertain the truth . . . is the *sine qua non* of a fair trial," and the summations cut to the very heart of the Due Process Clause by diverting the jury's attention "from the ultimate question of guilt or innocence that should be the central concern in a criminal proceeding."

Second, the Court says that "[m]uch of the objectionable content was invited by or was responsive to the opening summation of the defense." The Court identifies four portions of the defense summation that it thinks somehow "invited" McDaniel's sustained barrage. The State, however, did not object to any of these statements, and, to my mind, none of them is so objectionable that it would have justified a tactical decision to interrupt the defense summation and perhaps irritate the jury.

The Court begins by stating that defense counsel "blamed" the sheriff's office for a lack of evidence. The Court does not identify which, if any, of McDaniel's remarks represented a response to this statement. I cannot believe that the Court is suggesting, for example, that defense counsel's one mention of the "almost crimina[l] negligen[ce] on the part of the Polk County Sheriff's Office," justified McDaniel's express and repeated wish that he could try the Department of Corrections for murder.

Next, the Court notes that defense counsel "alluded" to the death penalty. While this allusion might have justified McDaniel's statement that "you are merely to determine his innocence or guilt, nothing else," it could hardly justify, for example, McDaniel's expressions of his personal wish that Darden be "blown away by a shotgun."

Moreover, the Court says, defense counsel twice referred to the perpetrator as an "animal." It is entirely unclear to me why this characterization called for any response from the prosecutor at all. Taken in context, defense counsel's statements did nothing more than tell the jury that, although everyone agreed that a heinous crime had been committed, the issue on which it should focus was whether *Darden* had committed it.

Finally, the Court finds that Darden brought upon himself McDaniel's tirade because defense counsel gave his "personal opinion of the strength of the State's evidence." Again, the Court gives no explanation of how the statement it quotes—a single, mild expression of defense counsel's overall assessment of the evidence—justified the "response" that followed, which consisted, to the extent it represented a comment on the evidence at all, of accusations of perjury, and personal disparagements of opposing counsel. In sum, McDaniel went so far beyond "respond[ing] substantially in order to 'right the scale,' " *Young,* that the reasoning in *Young* provides no basis at all for the Court's holding today.

The third reason the Court gives for discounting the effects of the improper summations is the supposed curative effect of the trial judge's instructions: the judge had instructed the jury that it was to decide the case on the evidence and that the arguments of counsel were not evidence. But the trial court overruled Darden's objection to McDaniel's repeated expressions of his wish that Darden had been killed, thus perhaps leaving the jury with the impression that McDaniel's comments were somehow relevant to the question before them. The trial judge's instruction that the attorneys were "trained in the law," and thus that their "analysis of the issues" could be "extremely helpful," might also have suggested to the jury that the substance of McDaniel's tirade was pertinent to their deliberations.

Fourth, the Court suggests that because Darden enjoyed the tactical advantage of having the last summation, he was able to "tur[n] much of the prosecutors' closing argument against them." But the issue before the jury was whether Darden was guilty, not whether McDaniel's summation was proper. And the question before this Court is not whether we agree with defense counsel's criticism of the summation but whether the jury was affected by it. Since Darden was ultimately convicted, it is hard to see what basis the Court has for its naked assertion that "[d]efense counsel were able to use the opportunity for rebuttal very effectively." * * *

Fifth, the Court finds, in essence, that any error was harmless: "The weight of the evidence against petitioner was heavy; the 'overwhelming eyewitness and circumstantial evidence to support a finding of guilt on all charges' reduced the likelihood that the jury's decision was influenced by argument." * * * I simply do not believe the evidence in this case was so overwhelming that this Court can conclude, on the basis of the written record before it, that the jury's verdict was not the product of the prosecutors' misconduct. The three most damaging pieces of evidence—the identifications of Darden by Phillip Arnold and Helen Turman and the ballistics evidence—are all sufficiently problematic that they leave me unconvinced that a jury not exposed to McDaniel's egregious summation would necessarily have convicted Darden.

Arnold first identified Darden in a photo array shown to him in the hospital. The trial court suppressed that out-of-court identification following a long argument concerning the reliability and constitutionality of the procedures by which it was obtained.

Mrs. Turman's initial identification was made under even more suggestive circumstances. She testified at trial that she was taken to a preliminary hearing at which Darden appeared in order "[t]o identify him." Instead of being asked to view Darden in a lineup, Mrs. Turman was brought into the courtroom, where Darden apparently was the only black man present. Over defense counsel's objection, after the prosecutor asked her whether "this man sitting here" was "the man that shot your husband," she identified Darden. * * * While the question whether the various in- and out-of-court identifications ought to have been suppressed is not now before the Court, my confidence in their reliability is nonetheless undermined by the suggestiveness of the procedures by which they were obtained, particularly in light of Mrs. Turman's earlier difficulties in describing the criminal.

Finally, the ballistics evidence is hardly overwhelming. The purported murder weapon was tied conclusively neither to the crime nor to Darden. Special Agent Cunningham of the FBI's Firearms Identification Unit testified that the bullets recovered at the scene of the crime "could have been fired" from the gun, but he was unwilling to say that they in fact had come from that weapon. He also testified, contrary to the Court's assertion, that rebored Smith & Wessons were fairly common. Deputy Sheriff Weatherford testified that the gun was discovered in a roadside ditch adjacent to where Darden had wrecked his car on the evening of the crime. But the gun was discovered the next day, and the ditch was also next to a bar's parking lot.

Darden testified at trial on his own behalf and denied any involvement in the robbery and murder. His account of his actions on the day of the crime was contradicted only by Mrs. Turman's and Arnold's identifications. Indeed, a number of the State's witnesses corroborated parts of Darden's account. The trial judge who had seen and heard Darden testify found that he "emotionally and with what appeared on its face to be sincerity, proclaimed his innocence."

In setting sentence, he viewed the fact that Darden "repeatedly professed his complete innocence of the charges" as a mitigating factor.

Thus, at bottom, this case rests on the jury's determination of the credibility of three witnesses—Helen Turman and Phillip Arnold, on the one side, and Willie Darden, on the other. I cannot conclude that McDaniel's sustained assault on Darden's very humanity did not affect the jury's ability to judge the credibility question on the real evidence before it. Because I believe that he did not have a trial that was fair, I would reverse Darden's conviction; I would not allow him to go to his death until he has been convicted at a fair trial. * * *

# Chapter 19

# RETRIALS

Although it has some bearing on multiple punishments, the double jeopardy clause of the Fifth Amendment is concerned primarily with multiple trials. That concern extends to trials for both felonies and misdemeanors. The Court concluded, in its first major double jeopardy ruling, that the reference in the double jeopardy clause to "life and limb," when read against its common law background, was broad enough to encompass all criminal offenses without regard to the particular form of punishment that might be imposed. *Ex parte Lange,* 85 U.S. 163 (1873). The double jeopardy clause becomes applicable, however, only after the accused has been placed "in jeopardy", and that does not occur until (i) the jury is "empaneled and sworn" in a case involving a jury trial, or (ii) the first witness is sworn in a case involving a bench trial. *Crist v. Bretz,* 437 U.S. 28 (1978). Dismissals before jeopardy has attached, even where based on the ground that the prosecution's case is too weak to prevail, do not raise double jeopardy difficulties; since the defendant has not been placed in jeopardy at the point of dismissal, a reprosecution that results in a trial would not place him "twice" in jeopardy. Thus, double jeopardy does not bar returning a case to a grand jury after it has refused to indict, refiling charges and seeking a new preliminary hearing after the magistrate found a lack of probable cause at the first hearing, or refiling charges after a trial court dismissed the initial charges on some pretrial objection (e.g., an insufficiency of the pleading) that could be cured in a new indictment or information. So too, where a trial court dismisses charges before trial on grounds that would bar reprosecution (e.g., that the defendant had been denied his right to a speedy trial), no double jeopardy concerns are presented by allowing the state to appeal that dismissal and continue with the prosecution if it should win on appeal.

The principles described above are well established and fairly easy to apply. That is not true of all double jeopardy principles. Indeed, in *United States v. DiFrancesco,* 449 U.S. 117 (1980), Justice Blackmun's opinion for the Court, citing 21 double jeopardy cases decided by the Court over the previous decade, acknowledged that the application of the double jeopardy bar "has not proved to be facile or routine," as demonstrated by the various "changes in direction or in emphasis" found in the Court's rulings. The cases in this Chapter deal with the most significant of those double jeopardy principles that have proved troublesome in their definition or application.

## SECTION 1: THE "SAME OFFENSE" LIMITATION

The double jeopardy clause states that no person shall twice be put in jeopardy for the same "offence." Early English common law had established that the "same offense" for this purpose was not measured simply by reference to the title of the crime. Two prosecutions under the same statutory provision were not for the same offense if each dealt with a different incident or resulted in the victimization of a different person. Thus, in the first case in this section *Ashe v. Swenson,* the separate prosecutions of the defendants for the robberies of different persons at the same poker game would be for different offenses. On the other hand, separate prosecutions under distinct criminal provisions could be for the same offense when they dealt with the same incident and same victim. The critical test under the common law standard, as explained by the Supreme Court in *Brown v. Ohio,* 432 U.S. 161 (1977), was whether "each provision requires proof of a fact that the other does not." Where only one of the provisions required such an additional element of proof, as is usually true of provisions establishing different degrees of the same crime (e.g., first degree and second degree murder), the double jeopardy clause requires that prosecution under the two provisions be brought in the same trial. When defendant was placed in jeopardy for violating only one of the provisions, he cannot subsequently be prosecuted for violating the second provision, without regard to whether the first prosecution resulted in a conviction or acquittal.

*Ashe v. Swenson* and *Grady v. Corbin,* the first two cases in this section, deal with the question of whether the double jeopardy bar affords protection beyond that provided by the common law definition of the same offense. While the majority in each case answers that question in the affirmative, the *Grady* ruling has far greater practical significance. The "collateral estoppel" doctrine adopted in *Ashe* applies only where the defendant was acquitted at the first trial and that acquittal bears a special relationship to the prosecution for the second offense, as explained in *Ashe.* It should be kept in mind that state law may impose limitations beyond that mandated by the double jeopardy prohibition. Thus, several states require a single prosecution for all offenses arising from the same transaction, as urged by Justice Brennan in his concurring opinion in *Ashe.*

The third case in this section, *Heath v. Alabama,* deals with the possible application of the double jeopardy bar to multiple prosecutions by different sovereigns. The position taken by the Court here stands in contrast to the Court's interpretation of the Fifth Amendment's self-incrimination clause as extending to potential incrimination under the laws of a jurisdiction other than that compelling the witness to testify. See *Murphy v. Waterfront Commission* (discussed in the *Kastigar* opinion in Ch. 8). Multiple prosecutions for basically the same criminal activity by different jurisdictions (i.e., two states, or the federal government and a state) do occur, but are uncommon. The overlap of prosecutorial authority is most likely to arise between the federal government and a state, and here non-constitutional limitations restrict multiple prosecutions. The internal regulations of the Justice Department bar federal prosecution following a state prosecution "for substantially the same act" except upon the approval of an Assistant Attorney General, and many states have provisions that prohibit a state prosecution for any activity that has been the basis for a previous federal prosecution.

## SECTION 2: ABORTED PROCEEDINGS

The two cases in this section, *Arizona v. Washington* and *Oregon v. Kennedy,* set forth the basic double jeopardy standards applicable to reprosecutions following a mistrial. The mistrial should be distinguished from the mid-trial dismissal, which is discussed in the *Scott* case in the next section. In contrast to dismissals of the type involved in *Scott*, a court ordering a mistrial does not find some fatal flaw in the prosecution that would present an absolute bar to conviction on the offense charged. Rather, the trial court rules that it would be inappropriate or impossible to continue with the trial and orders its termination without ending the prosecution. The judge ordering a mistrial assumes that a reprosecution can be brought, but as *Washington* and *Kennedy* indicate, that is not always the case.[9]

## SECTION 3: REPROSECUTIONS FOLLOWING ACQUITTALS AND CONVICTIONS

The double jeopardy clause was derived in large part from the common law pleas of *autrefois acquit* (formerly acquitted) and *autrefois convict* (formerly convicted), and the two bedrock elements of the clause are the prohibitions against reprosecution for the same offense following an acquittal or a conviction. It is here, however, more so than in any other area of double jeopardy jurisprudence, that the Court has found the need to reevaluate applicable standards. In both of the cases in this section, *United States v. Scott* and *Burks v. United States*, the Court found it necessary to reassess the assumptions of earlier rulings.

*Scott* raises the basic question of what type of ruling should be viewed as an "acquittal." In particular, should a trial court dismissal that bars reprosecution be viewed as an acquittal without regard to the grounding of that ruling? The fact that the ending of the case in *Scott* (through dismissal) came from the judge rather than the jury was not critical; the Court had long held that the acquittal rule applied to acquittals by judges as well as by juries, a position reaffirmed in a case decided the same day as *Scott*, *Sanabria v. United States*, 437 U.S. 54 (1978).

*Burks* considers the proper scope of the "*Ball* exception" to the prohibition against reprosecution following a conviction. By allowing a reprosecution whenever a conviction was successfully overturned on a defense challenge, the *Ball* exception had basically limited that prohibition to the situation in which the defendant was willing to abide by his conviction (i.e. bring no challenge), but the state desired to prosecute again in the hopes of either raising the charge or obtaining a higher sentence. *Burks* recognizes an exception to the *Ball* exception, whereby the prohibition can have a bearing, under limited circumstances, even where the defendant successfully challenges the conviction.

# SECTION 1.   THE "SAME OFFENSE" LIMITATION

## ASHE v. SWENSON

397 U.S. 436, 90 S.Ct. 1189, 25 L.Ed.2d 469 (1970).

JUSTICE STEWART delivered the opinion of the Court.   *   *   *

Sometime in the early hours of the morning of January 10, 1960, six men were engaged in a poker game in the basement of the home of John Gladson at Lee's Summit, Missouri. Suddenly three or four masked men, armed with a shotgun and pistols, broke into the basement and robbed each of the poker players of money and various articles of personal property. The robbers—and it has never been clear whether there were three or four of them—then fled in a

---

9. Where the court grants during trial a motion to dismiss based on a legal defect that is curable (and therefore assumes reprosecution), the applicable standards are the same as used for mistrials. See *Lee v. United States*, 432 U.S. 23 (1977) (prosecution dismissed during trial on a defense motion citing a defect in the charging instrument; the double jeopardy standard for defense requested mistrials held to govern the state's authority to reprosecute).

car belonging to one of the victims of the robbery. Shortly thereafter the stolen car was discovered in a field, and later that morning three men were arrested by a state trooper while they were walking on a highway not far from where the abandoned car had been found. The petitioner was arrested by another officer some distance away.

The four were subsequently charged with seven separate offenses—the armed robbery of each of the six poker players and the theft of the car. In May 1960 the petitioner went to trial on the charge of robbing Donald Knight, one of the participants in the poker game. At the trial the State called Knight and three of his fellow poker players as prosecution witnesses. Each of them described the circumstances of the holdup and itemized his own individual losses. The proof that an armed robbery had occurred and that personal property had been taken from Knight as well as from each of the others was unassailable. The testimony of the four victims in this regard was consistent both internally and with that of the others. But the State's evidence that the petitioner had been one of the robbers was weak. Two of the witnesses thought that there had been only three robbers altogether, and could not identify the petitioner as one of them. Another of the victims, who was the petitioner's uncle by marriage, said that at the "patrol station" he had positively identified each of the other three men accused of the holdup, but could say only that the petitioner's voice "sounded very much like" that of one of the robbers. The fourth participant in the poker game did identify the petitioner, but only by his "size and height, and his actions."

The cross-examination of these witnesses was brief, and it was aimed primarily at exposing the weakness of their identification testimony. Defense counsel made no attempt to question their testimony regarding the holdup itself or their claims as to their losses. Knight testified without contradiction that the robbers had stolen from him his watch, $250 in cash, and about $500 in checks. His billfold, which had been found by the police in the possession of one of the three other men accused of the robbery, was admitted in evidence. The defense offered no testimony and waived final argument.

The trial judge instructed the jury that if it found that the petitioner was one of the participants in the armed robbery, the theft of "any money" from Knight would sustain a conviction. He also instructed the jury that if the petitioner was one of the robbers, he was guilty under the law even if he had not personally robbed Knight. The jury—though not instructed to elaborate upon its verdict—found the petitioner "not guilty due to insufficient evidence."

Six weeks later the petitioner was brought to trial again, this time for the robbery of another participant in the poker game, a man named Roberts. The petitioner filed a motion to dismiss, based on his previous acquittal. The motion was overruled, and the second trial began. The witnesses were for the most part the same, though this time their testimony was substantially stronger on the issue of the petitioner's identity. For example, two witnesses who at the first trial had been wholly unable to identify the petitioner as one of the robbers, now testified that his features, size, and mannerisms matched those of one of their assailants. Another witness who before had identified the petitioner only by his size and actions now also remembered him by the unusual sound of his voice. The State further refined its case at the second trial by declining to call one of the participants in the poker game whose identification testimony at the first trial had been conspicuously negative. The case went to the jury on instructions virtually identical to those given at the first trial. This time the jury found the petitioner guilty, and he was sentenced to a 35-year term in the state penitentia-ry. * * *

"Collateral estoppel" is an awkward phrase, but it stands for an extremely important principle in our adversary system of justice. It means simply that when an issue of ultimate fact has once been determined by a valid and final judgment, that issue cannot again be litigated between the same parties in any future lawsuit. Although first developed in civil litigation, collateral estoppel has been an established rule of federal criminal law at least since this Court's decision more than 50 years ago in *United States v. Oppenheimer*, 242 U.S. 85 (1916). As Mr. Justice Holmes put the matter in that case, "It cannot be that the safeguards of the person, so often and so rightly mentioned with solemn reverence, are less than those that protect from a liability in debt." As a rule of federal law, therefore, "[i]t is much too late to suggest that this principle is not fully applicable to a former judgment in a criminal case, either because of lack of 'mutuality' or because the judgment may reflect only a belief that the Government had not met the higher burden of proof exacted in such cases for the Government's evidence as a whole although not necessarily as to every link in the chain."

The federal decisions have made clear that the rule of collateral estoppel in criminal cases is not to be applied with the hypertechnical and archaic approach of a 19th century pleading book, but with realism and rationality. Where a previous judgment of acquittal was based upon a general verdict, as is usually the case, this approach requires a court to "examine the record of a prior proceeding, taking into account the pleadings, evidence, charge, and other relevant matter, and conclude whether a rational jury could have grounded its verdict upon an issue other than that which the defendant seeks to foreclose from consideration." The inquiry "must be set in a practical frame, and viewed with an eye to all the circumstances of the proceedings." *Sealfon v. United States*, 332 U.S. 575 (1948). Any test more technically restrictive would, of course, simply amount to a rejection of the rule of collateral estoppel in criminal proceedings, at least in every case where the first judgment was based upon a general verdict of acquittal.

Straightforward application of the federal rule to the present case can lead to but one conclusion. For the record is utterly devoid of any indication that the first jury could rationally have found that an armed robbery had not occurred, or that Knight had not been a victim of that robbery. The single rationally conceivable issue in dispute before the jury was whether the petitioner had been one of the robbers. And the jury by its verdict found that he had not. The federal rule of law, therefore, would make a second prosecution for the robbery of Roberts wholly impermissible.

The ultimate question to be determined, then * * * is whether this established rule of federal law is embodied in the Fifth Amendment guarantee against double jeopardy. We do not hesitate to hold that it is. For whatever else that constitutional guarantee may embrace, it surely protects a man who has been acquitted from having to "run the gantlet" a second time. *Green v. United States*, 355 U.S. 184 (1957).

The question is not whether Missouri could validly charge the petitioner with six separate offenses for the robbery of the six poker players. It is not whether he could have received a total of six punishments if he had been convicted in a single trial of robbing the six victims. It is simply whether, after a jury determined by its verdict that the petitioner was not one of the robbers, the State could constitutionally hale him before a new jury to litigate that issue again. * * *

In this case the State in its brief has frankly conceded that following the petitioner's acquittal, it treated the first trial as no more than a dry run for the second prosecution: "No doubt the prosecutor felt the state had a provable case on the first charge and, when he lost, he did what every good attorney would do—he refined his presentation in light of the turn of events at the first trial." But this is precisely what the constitutional guarantee forbids. * * *

Reversed and remanded.[a]

JUSTICE BRENNAN, whom JUSTICE DOUGLAS and JUSTICE MARSHALL join, concurring.

I agree that the Double Jeopardy Clause incorporates collateral estoppel as a constitutional requirement and therefore join the Court's opinion. However, even if the rule of collateral estoppel had been inapplicable to the facts of this case, it is my view that the Double Jeopardy Clause nevertheless bars the prosecution of petitioner a second time for armed robbery. The two prosecutions, the first for the robbery of Knight and the second for the robbery of Roberts, grew out of one criminal episode, and therefore I think it clear on the facts of this case that the Double Jeopardy Clause prohibited Missouri from prosecuting petitioner for each robbery at a different trial. * * *

The Double Jeopardy Clause is a guarantee "that the State with all its resources and power [shall] not be allowed to make repeated attempts to convict an individual for an alleged offense, thereby subjecting him to embarrassment, expense and ordeal and compelling him to live in a continuing state of anxiety and insecurity . . . ." *Green v. United States*, 355 U.S. 184 (1957). This guarantee is expressed as a prohibition against multiple prosecutions for the "same offence." Although the phrase "same offence" appeared in most of the early common-law articulations of the double-jeopardy principle, questions of its precise meaning rarely arose prior to the 18th century, and by the time the Bill of Rights was adopted it had not been authoritatively defined.

When the common law did finally attempt a definition, in *The King v. Vandercomb* (Crown 1796), it adopted the "same evidence" test, which provided little protection from multiple prosecution:

"[U]nless the first indictment were such as the prisoner might have been convicted upon by proof of the facts contained in the second indictment, an acquittal on the first indictment can be no bar to the second."

The "same evidence" test of "same offence" was soon followed by a majority of American jurisdictions, but its deficiencies are obvious. It does not enforce but virtually annuls the constitutional guarantee. For example, where a single criminal episode involves several victims, under the "same evidence" test a separate prosecution may be brought as to each. The "same evidence" test permits multiple prosecutions where a single transaction is divisible into chronologically discrete crimes. E.g., *Johnson v. Commonwealth*, 201 Ky. 314 (1923) (each of 75 poker hands a separate "offense"). Even a single criminal act may lead to multiple prosecutions if it is viewed from the perspectives of different statutes. Given the tendency of modern criminal legislation to divide the phases of a criminal transaction into numerous separate crimes, the opportunities for multiple prosecutions for an essentially unitary criminal episode are frightening. And given our tradition of virtually unreviewable prosecutorial discretion con-

a. Separate concurring opinions of Justices Harlan and Black are omitted.

cerning the initiation and scope of a criminal prosecution, the potentialities for abuse inherent in the "same evidence" test are simply intolerable.

The "same evidence" test is not constitutionally required. It was first expounded *after* the adoption of the Fifth Amendment * * *. The "same evidence" test may once have been defensible at English common law, which, for reasons peculiar to English criminal procedure, severely restricted the power of prosecutors to combine several charges in a single trial. In vivid contrast, American criminal procedure generally allows a prosecutor freedom, subject to judicial control, to prosecute a person at one trial for all the crimes arising out of a single criminal transaction.

In my view, the Double Jeopardy Clause requires the prosecution, except in most limited circumstances, to join at one trial all the charges against a defendant that grow out of a single criminal act, occurrence, episode, or transaction. This "same transaction" test of "same offence" not only enforces the ancient prohibition against vexatious multiple prosecutions embodied in the Double Jeopardy Clause, but responds as well to the increasingly widespread recognition that the consolidation in one lawsuit of all issues arising out of a single transaction or occurrence best promotes justice, economy, and convenience. * * *

CHIEF JUSTICE BURGER, dissenting.

The Fifth Amendment to the constitution of the United States provides in part: "nor shall any person be subject for the same offence to be twice put in jeopardy of life or limb * * *." Nothing in the language or gloss previously placed on this provision of the Fifth Amendment remotely justifies the treatment that the Court today accords to the collateral-estoppel doctrine. Nothing in the purpose of the authors of the Constitution commands or even justifies what the Court decides today; this is truly a case of expanding a sound basic principle beyond the bounds—or needs—of its rational and legitimate objectives to preclude harassment of an accused. * * *

The concept of double jeopardy and our firm constitutional commitment is against repeated trials "for the *same offence*." This Court, like most American jurisdictions, has expanded that part of the Constitution into a "same evidence" test. *Blockburger v. United States*, 284 U.S. 299 (1932) * * *. Clearly and beyond dispute the charge against Ashe in the second trial required proof of a fact—robbery of Roberts—which the charge involving Knight did not. The Court, therefore, has had to reach out far beyond the accepted offense-defining rule to reach its decision in this case. What it has done is to superimpose on the same-evidence test a new and novel collateral-estoppel gloss. * * *

The collateral-estoppel concept—originally a product only of civil litigation—is a strange mutant as it is transformed to control this criminal case. In civil cases the doctrine was justified as conserving judicial resources as well as those of the parties to the actions and additionally as providing the finality needed to plan for the future. It ordinarily applies to parties on each side of the litigation who have the same interest as or who are identical with the parties in the initial litigation. Here the complainant in the second trial is not the same as in the first even though the State is a party in both cases. Very properly, in criminal cases, finality and conservation of private, public, and judicial resources are lesser values than in civil litigation. * * *

Some commentators have concluded that the harassment inherent in standing trial a second time is a sufficient reason for use of collateral estoppel in criminal trials. If the Court is today relying on a harassment concept to superimpose a new brand of collateral-estoppel gloss on the "same evidence" test, there is a short answer; this case does not remotely suggest harassment of an accused who robbed six victims and the harassment aspect does not rise to constitutional levels.

The essence of Justice Brennan's concurrence is that this was all one transaction, one episode, or, if I may so characterize it, one frolic, and, hence, only one crime. His approach, like that taken by the Court, totally overlooks the significance of there being *six entirely separate charges of robbery* against six individuals.

This "single transaction" concept is not a novel notion; it has been urged in various courts including this Court. One of the theses underlying the "single transaction" notion is that the criminal episode is "indivisible." The short answer to that is that to the victims, the criminal conduct is readily divisible and intensely personal; each offense is an offense against *a person*. For me it demeans the dignity of the human personality and individuality to talk of "a single transaction" in the context of six separate assaults on six individuals.

No court that elevates the individual rights and human dignity of the accused to a high place—as we should—ought to be so casual as to treat the victims as a single homogenized lump of human clay. I would grant the dignity of individual status to the victims as much as to those accused, not more but surely no less.

If it be suggested that multiple crimes can be separately punished but must be collectively tried, one can point to the firm trend in the law to allow severance of defendants and offenses into separate trials so as to avoid possible prejudice of one criminal act or of the conduct of one defendant to "spill over" on another.

What the Court holds today must be related to its impact on crimes more serious than ordinary housebreaking, followed by physical assault on six men and robbery of all of them. To understand its full impact we must view the holding in the context of four men who break and enter, rob, and then kill six victims. The concurrence tells us that unless all the crimes are joined in one trial the alleged killers cannot be tried for more than one of the killings even if the evidence is that they personally killed two, three, or more of the victims. Or alter the crime to four men breaking into a college dormitory and assaulting six girls. What the Court is holding is, in effect, that the second and third and fourth criminal acts are "free," unless the accused is tried for the multiple crimes in a single trial—something defendants frantically use every legal device to avoid, and often succeed in avoiding. This is the reality of what the Court holds today; it does not make good sense and it cannot make good law.  *   *   *

## GRADY v. CORBIN

___ U.S. ___, 110 S.Ct. 2084, ___ L.Ed.2d ___ (1990).

JUSTICE BRENNAN delivered the opinion of the Court.

We have long held, see *Blockburger v. United States,* 284 U.S. 299 (1932), that the Double Jeopardy Clause of the Fifth Amendment prohibits successive prosecutions for the same criminal act or transaction under two criminal statutes whenever each statute does not "requir[e] proof of a fact which the other does not." In *Illinois v. Vitale,* 447 U.S. 410 (1980), we suggested that even if two successive prosecutions were not barred by the *Blockburger* test, the second prosecution would be barred if the prosecution sought to establish an essential element of the second crime by proving the conduct for which the defendant was convicted in the first prosecution. Today we adopt the suggestion set forth in *Vitale*. We hold that the Double Jeopardy Clause bars a subsequent prosecution if, to establish an essential element of an offense charged in that prosecution, the government will prove conduct that constitutes an offense for which the defendant has already been prosecuted.

For purposes of this proceeding, we take the following facts as true. At approximately 6:35 p.m. on October 3, 1987, respondent Thomas Corbin drove his automobile across the double yellow line of Route 55 in LaGrange, New York, striking two oncoming vehicles. Assistant District Attorney (ADA) Thomas Dolan was called to the scene, where he learned that both Brenda Dirago, who had been driving the second vehicle to be struck, and her husband Daniel had been seriously injured. Later that evening, ADA Dolan was informed that Brenda Dirago had died from injuries sustained in the accident. That same evening, while at the hospital being treated for his own injuries, respondent was served with two uniform traffic tickets directing him to appear at the LaGrange Town Justice Court on October 29, 1987 [later amended to October 27th]. One ticket charged him with the misdemeanor of driving while intoxicated in violation of N.Y.Veh. & Traf. Law § 1192(3); the other charged him with failing to keep right of the median in violation of § 1120(a). A blood test taken at the hospital that evening indicated a blood alcohol level of 0.19%, nearly twice the level at which it is *per se* illegal to operate a motor vehicle in New York.

Three days later, Assistant District Attorney Frank Chase began gathering evidence for a homicide prosecution in connection with the accident. "Despite his active involvement in building a homicide case against [Corbin], however, Chase did not attempt to ascertain the date [Corbin] was scheduled to appear in Town Justice Court on the traffic tickets, nor did he inform either the Town Justice Court or the Assistant District Attorney covering that court about his pending investigation." 74 N.Y.2d 279. Thus, Assistant District Attorney Mark Glick never mentioned Brenda Dirago's death in the statement of readiness for trial and other pretrial pleadings he submitted to respondent and the LaGrange Town Justice Court on October 14, 1987.

Accordingly, when respondent pleaded guilty to the two traffic tickets on October 27, 1987, a date on which no member of the District Attorney's office was present in court, the presiding judge was unaware of the fatality stemming from the accident. Corbin was never asked if any others had been injured on the night in question and did not voluntarily incriminate himself by providing such information.[4] The presiding judge accepted his guilty plea, but because the District Attorney's office had not submitted a sentencing recommendation, the judge postponed sentencing until November 17, 1987, when an Assistant District Attorney was scheduled to be present in court. The Assistant District Attorney present at sentencing on that date was unaware that there had been a fatality, was unable to locate the case file, and had not spoken to ADA Glick about the case. Nevertheless, she did not seek an adjournment so that she could ascertain the facts necessary to make an informed sentencing recommendation. Instead,

**4.** The New York Court of Appeals held that, although an attorney may not misrepresent facts, "a practitioner representing a client at a traffic violation prosecution should not be expected to *volunteer* information that is likely to be highly damaging to his client's position." 74 N.Y.2d 279, 288, and n. 6, 545 N.Y.S.2d 71, 74 and n. 6, 543 N.E.2d 714, 718, and n. 6 (1989) (emphasis in original). Be-cause the Court of Appeals refused to characterize as misconduct the behavior of either Corbin or his attorney, we need not decide whether our double jeopardy analysis would be any different if affirmative misrepresentations of fact by a defendant or his counsel were to mislead a court into accepting a guilty plea it would not otherwise accept.

she recommended a "minimum sentence," and the presiding judge sentenced Corbin to a $350 fine, a $10 surcharge, and a 6–month license revocation.

Two months later, a grand jury investigating the October 3, 1987, accident indicted Corbin, charging him with reckless manslaughter, second-degree vehicular manslaughter, and criminally negligent homicide for causing the death of Brenda Dirago; third-degree reckless assault for causing physical injury to Daniel Dirago; and driving while intoxicated. The prosecution filed a bill of particulars that identified the three reckless or negligent acts on which it would rely to prove the homicide and assult charges: (1) operating a motor vehicle on a public highway in an intoxicated condition, (2) failing to keep right of the median, and (3) driving approximately 45 to 50 miles per hour in heavy rain, "which was a speed too fast for the weather and road conditions then pending." Respondent moved to dismiss the indictment on statutory and constitutional double jeopardy grounds.   *   *   *

[The New York Court of Appeals subsequently granted a writ of prohibition barring prosecution on all counts.] The court prohibited prosecution of the driving while intoxicted counts pursuant to New York's statutory double jeopardy provision. The court further ruled that prosecution of the two vehicular manslaughter counts would violate the Double Jeopardy Clause of the Fifth Amendment pursuant to the *Blockburger* test because, as a matter of state law, driving while intoxicated "is unquestionably a lesser included offense of second degree vehicular manslaughter." Finally, relying on the "pointed dictum" in this Court's opinion in *Vitale*, the court barred prosecution of the remaining counts because the bill of particulars expressed an intention to "rely on the prior traffic offenses as the acts necessary to prove the homicide and assault charges."

*   *   *

The facts and contentions raised here mirror almost exactly those raised in this Court 10 years ago in *Illinois v. Vitale*. Like Thomas Corbin, John Vitale allegedly caused a fatal car accident. A police officer at the scene issued Vitale a traffic citation charging him with failure to reduce speed to avoid an accident in violation of § 11–601(a) of the Illinois Vehicle Code. Vitale was convicted of that offense and sentenced to pay a $15 fine. The day after his conviction, the State charged Vitale with two counts of involuntary manslaughter based on his reckless driving. Vitale argued that this subsequent prosecution was barred by the Double Jeopardy Clause.

This Court held that the second prosecution was not barred under the traditional *Blockburger* test because each offense "require[d] proof of a fact which the other [did] not." *Blockburger.* Although involuntary manslaughter required proof of a death, failure to reduce speed did not. Likewise, failure to slow was not a statutory element of involuntary manslaughter. Thus, the subsequent prosecution survived the *Blockburger* test.

But the Court did not stop at that point. Justice White, writing for the Court, added that, even though the two prosecutions did not violate the *Blockburger* test:

"[I]t may be that to sustain its manslaughter case the State may find it necessary to prove a failure to slow or to rely on conduct necessarily involving such failure; it may concede as much prior to trial. In that case, because Vitale has already been convicted for conduct that is a necessary element of the more serious crime for which he has been charged, his claim of double jeopardy would be substantial under *Brown* [*v. Ohio*, 432 U.S. 161 (1977)] and our later decision in *Harris v. Oklahoma*, 433 U.S. 682 (1977)."

We believe that this analysis is correct and governs this case.[7] To determine whether a subsequent prosecution is barred by the Double Jeopardy Clause, a court must first apply the traditional *Blockburger* test. If application of that test reveals that the offenses have identical statutory elements or that one is a lesser included offense of the other, then the inquiry must cease, and the subsequent prosecution is barred.

The State argues that this should be the last step in the inquiry and that the Double Jeopardy Clause permits successive prosecutions whenever the offenses charged satisfy the *Blockburger* test. We disagree. The Double Jeopardy Clause embodies three protections: "It protects against a second prosecution for the same offense after acquittal. It protects against a second prosecution for the same offense after conviction. And it protects against multiple punishments for the same offense." *North Carolina v. Pearce*, 395 U.S. 711 (1969). The *Blockburger* test was developed "in the context of multiple punishments imposed in a single prosecution." *Garrett v. United States*, 471 U.S. 773, 778 (1985). In that context, "the Double Jeopardy Clause does no more than prevent the sentencing court from prescribing greater punishment than the legislature intended." *Missouri v. Hunter*, 459 U.S. 359 (1983). The *Blockburger* test is simply a "rule of statutory construction," a guide to determining whether the legislature intended multiple punishments.[a] *Hunter*.[8]

Successive prosecutions, however, whether following acquittals or convictions, raise concerns that extend beyond merely the possibility of an enhanced sentence:

"The underlying idea, one that is deeply ingrained in at least the Anglo–American system of jurisprudence, is that the State with all its resources

7. We recognized in *Brown v. Ohio* that when application of our traditional double jeopardy analysis would bar a subsequent prosecution, "[a]n exception may exist where the State is unable to proceed on the more serious charge at the outset because the additional facts necessary to sustain that charge have not occurred or have not been discovered despite the exercise of due diligence)." Because ADA Dolan was informed of Brenda Dirago's death on the night of the accident, such an exception is inapplicable here.

a. At issue in *Blockburger* was whether a defendant convicted in the same trial of violating two separate provisions of the Narcotic Act could be separately punished for each violation where they involved a single sale of narcotics. One provision prohibited a sale of a narcotic drug except in or from the original stamped package and the other barred sale not in pursuance of a written prescription. Applying the traditional common law definition of the "same offense," the Court held that the two violations constituted separate offenses carrying separate penalties. In *Missouri v. Hunter*, the Court held that the double jeopardy prohibition against multiple punishments looked primarily to proscribing punishment beyond that legislatively authorized. Thus, the violation of two distinct provisions could constitute the same offense under the double jeopardy prohibition against separate trials, but still produce separate punishments if the legislature so provided. As a standard applicable to multiple punishments, the *Blockburger* test furnished only a guideline for presuming legislative intent in the absence of an express legislative authorization of separate penalties. Since the Missouri legislature clearly evidenced an intent to impose multiple punishments for the offenses of armed robbery and committing a felony while armed, even though the former was the predicate of the latter, the double jeopardy clause did not bar separate sentences where the defendant was convicted of the two violations in the same trial.

8. Justice Scalia's dissent contends that *Blockburger* is not just a guide to legislative intent, but rather an exclusive definition of the term "same offense" in the Double Jeopardy Clause. To support this contention, Justice Scalia asserts that "[w]e have applied the [*Blockburger* test] in virtually every case defining the 'same offense' decided since *Blockburger*." Every one of the * * * cases cited in support of that proposition, however, describes *Blockburger* as a test to determine the permissibility of cumulative punishments. * * * To further support its contention, Justice Scalia's dissent relies on a lengthy historical discussion. But this Court has not interpreted the Double Jeopardy Clause as Justice Scalia would interpret it since at least 1889. See *In re Nielsen* discussed infra. We have not previously found, and we do not today find, history to be dispositive of double jeopardy claims. * * *

and power should not be allowed to make repeated attempts to convict an individual for an alleged offense, thereby subjecting him to embarrassment, expense and ordeal and compelling him to live in a continuing state of anxiety and insecurity * * *" *Green v. United States,* 355 U.S. 184 (1957).

Multiple prosecutions also give the State an opportunity to rehearse its presentation of proof, thus increasing the risk of an erroneous conviction for one or more of the offenses charged. * * * Even when a State can bring multiple charges against an individual under *Blockburger,* a tremendous additional burden is placed on that defendant if he must face each of the charges in a separate proceeding.

Because of these independent concerns, we have not relied exclusively on the *Blockburger* test to vindicate the Double Jeopardy Clause's protection against multiple prosecutions. As we stated in *Brown v. Ohio:*

> "The *Blockburger* test is not the only standard for determining whether successive prosecutions impermissibly involve the same offense. Even if two offenses are sufficiently different to permit the imposition of consecutive sentences, successive prosecutions will be barred in some circumstances where the second prosecution requires the relitigation of factual issues already resolved by the first." *Brown* at n. 6.

Justice Powell, writing for the Court in *Brown,* provided two examples. In *Ashe v. Swenson,* the Court had held that the Double Jeopardy Clause barred a prosecution for robbing a participant in a poker game because the defendant's acquittal in a previous trial for robbing a different participant in the same poker game had conclusively established that he was not present at the robbery. In *In re Nielsen,* 131 U.S. 176 (1889), the Court had held that a conviction for cohabiting with two wives over a 2½–year period barred a subsequent prosecution for adultery with one of the wives on the day following the end of that period. Although application of the *Blockburger* test would have permitted the imposition of consecutive sentences in both cases, the Double Jeopardy Clause nonetheless barred these successive prosecutions.

Furthermore, in the same Term we decided *Brown,* we reiterated in *Harris v. Oklahoma,* that a strict application of the *Blockburger* test is not the exclusive means of determining whether a subsequent prosecution violates the Double Jeopardy Clause. In *Harris,* the defendant was first convicted of felony murder after his companion shot a grocery store clerk in the course of a robbery. The State then indicted and convicted him for robbery with a firearm. The two prosecutions were not for the "same offense" under *Blockburger* since, as a statutory matter, felony murder could be established by proof of any felony, not just robbery, and robbery with a firearm did not require proof of a death. Nevertheless, because the State admitted that " 'it was necessary for all the ingredients of the underlying felony of Robbery with Firearms to be proved' " in the felony-murder trial, the Court unanimously held that the subsequent prosecution was barred by the Double Jeopardy Clause. As we later described our reasoning, "we did not consider the crime generally described as felony murder as a separate offense distinct from its various elements. Rather, we treated a killing in the course of a robbery as itself a separate statutory offense, and the robbery as a species of lesser-included offense." *Vitale.*

These cases all recognized that technical comparison of the elements of the two offenses as required by *Blockburger* does not protect defendants sufficiently from the burdens of multiple trials. This case similarly demonstrates the limitations of the *Blockburger* analysis. If *Blockburger* constituted the entire double jeopardy inquiry in the context of successive prosecutions, the State could try Corbin in four consecutive trials: for failure to keep right of the median, for driving while intoxicated, for assault, and for homicide. The State could improve its presentation of proof with each trial, assessing which witnesses gave the most persuasive testimony, which documents had the greatest impact, which opening and closing arguments most persuaded the jurors. Corbin would be forced either to contest each of these trials or to plead guilty to avoid the harassment and expense.

Thus, a subsequent prosecution must do more than merely survive the *Blockburger* test. As we suggested in *Vitale*, the Double Jeopardy Clause bars any subsequent prosecution in which the government, to establish an essential element of an offense charged in that prosecution, will prove conduct that constitutes an offense for which the defendant has already been prosecuted. This is not an "actual evidence" or "same evidence" test.[12] The critical inquiry is what conduct the State will prove, not the evidence the State will use to prove that conduct. As we have held, the presentation of specific evidence in one trial does not forever prevent the government from introducing that same evidence in a subsequent proceeding. See *Dowling v. United States,* 493 U.S. ___ (1990). On the other hand, a State cannot avoid the dictates of the Double Jeopardy Clause merely by altering in successive prosecutions the evidence offered to prove the same conduct. For example, if two bystanders had witnessed Corbin's accident, it would make no difference to our double jeopardy analysis if the State called one witness to testify in the first trial that Corbin's vehicle crossed the median (or if nobody testified in the first trial because Corbin, as he did, pleaded guilty) and called the other witness to testify to the same conduct in the second trial.

Applying this analysis to the facts of this case is straightforward. Respondent concedes that *Blockburger* does not bar prosecution of the reckless manslaughter, criminally negligent homicide, and third-degree reckless assault offenses. The rest of our inquiry in this case is simplified by the bill of particulars filed by the State on January 25, 1988.[14] * * * By its own pleadings, the State has admitted that it will prove the entirety of the conduct for which Corbin was convicted—driving while intoxicated and failing to keep right of the median—to establish essential elements of the homicide and assault offenses. Therefore, the Double Jeopardy Clause bars this successive prosecution, and the New York Court of Appeals properly granted respondent's petition for a writ of prohibition. This holding would not bar a subsequent prosecution on the homicide and assault charges if the bill of particulars revealed that the State would not rely on proving the conduct for which Corbin had already been

---

**12.** Terminology in the double jeopardy area has been confused at best. Commentators and judges alike have referred to the *Blockburger* test as a "same evidence" test. This is a misnomer. The *Blockburger* test has nothing to do with the *evidence* presented at trial. It is concerned solely with the statutory elements of the offenses charged. A true "same evidence" or "actual evidence" test would prevent the government from introducing in a subsequent prosecution any evidence that was introduced in a preceding prosecution. It is in this sense that we discuss, and do not adopt, a "same evidence" or "actual evidence" test.

**14.** Application of the test we adopt today will not depend, as Justice Scalia's dissent

argues, on whether the indictment "happens to show that the same evidence is at issue" or whether the jurisdiction "happen[s] to require the prosecution to submit a bill of particulars that cannot be exceeded." The Courts of Appeals * * * have adopted an essential procedural mechanism for assessing double jeopardy claims prior to a second trial. [They] have held that "when a defendant puts double jeopardy in issue with a non-frivolous showing that an indictment charges him with an offense for which he was formerly placed in jeopardy, the burden shifts to the government to establish that there were in fact two separate offenses." This procedural mechanism will ensure that the test set forth today is in fact "implementable."

convicted (*i.e.*, if the State relied solely on Corbin's driving too fast in heavy rain to establish recklessness or negligence).[15] * * *

Drunk driving is a national tragedy. Prosecutors' offices are often overworked and may not always have the time to monitor seemingly minor cases as they wind through the judicial system. But these facts cannot excuse the need for scrupulous adherence to our constitutional principles. * * * With adequate preparation and foresight, the State could have prosecuted Corbin for the offenses charged in the traffic tickets and the subsequent indictment in a single proceeding, thereby avoiding this double jeopardy question. We have concluded that the Double Jeopardy Clause of the Fifth Amendment demands application of the standard announced today, but we are confident that with proper planning and attention prosecutors will be able to meet this standard and bring to justice those who make our Nation's roads unsafe. * * *

JUSTICE O'CONNOR, dissenting.

I agree with much of what Justice Scalia says in his dissenting opinion. I write separately, however, to note that my dissent is premised primarily on my view that the inconsistency between the Court's opinion today and *Dowling v. United States*, 493 U.S. ___ (1990), decided earlier this Term, indicates that the Court has strayed from a proper interpretation of the scope of the Double Jeopardy Clause.

In *Dowling*, we considered whether an eyewitness' testimony regarding a robbery for which Dowling had been acquitted was admissible at a second trial of Dowling for an unrelated robbery. The eyewitness had testified at the first trial that a man had entered her house "wearing a knitted mask with cutout eyes and carrying a small handgun" and that his mask had come off during a struggle, revealing his identity. Based on this evidence, Dowling had been charged with burglary, attempted robbery, assault, and weapons offenses, but was acquitted of all charges. At a second trial for an unrelated bank robbery, the government attempted to use the witness' testimony to prove Dowling's identity as a robber. We held that the Double Jeopardy Clause did not bar the introduction of the evidence: Because the prior acquittal did not necessarily represent a jury determination that Dowling was not the masked man who had entered the witness' home, the testimony was admissible in the second trial to prove identity.

The Court's ruling today effectively renders our holding in *Dowling* a nullity in many circumstances. If a situation identical to that in *Dowling* arose after today's decision, a conscientious judge attempting to apply the test enunciated by the Court would probably conclude that the witness' testimony was barred by the Double Jeopardy Clause. The record in *Dowling* indicated that the Government was offering the eyewitness testimony to establish the defendant's identity, "an essential element of an offense charged in [the subsequent] prosecution," and that the testimony would likely "prove conduct that constitutes an offense for which the defendant has already been prosecuted." Under the Court's reasoning, the Government's attempt to introduce the eyewitness testimony would bar the second prosecution of Dowling for bank robbery. As a practical matter, this

---

**15.** Adoption of a "same transaction" test would bar the homicide and assault prosecutions even if the State were able to establish the essential elements of those crimes without proving the conduct for which Corbin previously was convicted. The Court, however, has "steadfastly refused to adopt the 'single transaction' view of the Double Jeopardy Clause."

*Garrett v. United States*, 471 U.S. 773 (1985). But see *Jones v. Thomas*, 491 U.S. ___ (1989) (Brennan, J., joined by Marshall, J., dissenting) (maintaining that "the Double Jeopardy Clause requires, except in very limited circumstances, that all charges against a defendant growing out of a single criminal transaction be tried in one proceeding").

means that the same evidence ruled admissible in *Dowling* is barred by *Grady*.

* * *

JUSTICE SCALIA, with whom CHIEF JUSTICE REHNQUIST and JUSTICE KENNEDY join, dissenting.

The State of New York seeks to prosecute respondent a second time for the actions that he took at 6:35 p.m. on October 3, 1987. If the Double Jeopardy Clause guaranteed the right not to be twice put in jeopardy for the same conduct, it would bar this second prosecution. But that Clause guarantees only the right not to be twice put in jeopardy for the same *offense*, and has been interpreted since its inception, as was its common-law antecedent, to permit a prosecution based upon the same acts but for a different crime. The Court today holds otherwise, departing from clear text and clear precedent with no justification except the citation of dictum in a recent case (dictum that was similarly unsupported, and inconclusive to boot). The effects of this innovation upon our criminal-justice system are likely to be substantial. In practice, it will require prosecutors to observe a rule we have explicitly rejected in principle: that all charges arising out of a single occurrence must be joined in a single indictment.

* * *

*Blockburger* furnishes, we have observed, the "established test" for determining whether successive prosecutions arising out of the same events are for the "same offence." This test focuses on the statutory elements of the two crimes with which a defendant has been charged, not on the proof that is offered or relied upon to secure a conviction. * * * We have departed from *Blockburger*'s exclusive focus on the statutory elements of crimes in only two situations. One occurs where a statutory offense expressly incorporates another statutory offense without specifying the latter's elements. [See, e.g.,] *Harris v. Oklahoma.* * * * The other situation in which we have relaxed the *Blockburger* "elements" test occurs where a second prosecution would require relitigation of factual issues that were necessarily resolved in the defendant's favor in the first prosecution. See *Ashe v. Swenson.*[b]

Subject to the *Harris* and *Ashe* exceptions, I would adhere to the *Blockburger* rule that successive prosecutions under two different statutes do not constitute double jeopardy if each statutory crime contains an element that the other does not, regardless of the overlap between the proof required for each prosecution in the particular case. That rule best gives effect to the language of the Clause, which protects individuals from being twice put in jeopardy "for the same *offence*," not for the same *conduct* or *actions*. "Offence" was commonly understood in 1791 to mean "transgression," that is, "the Violation or Breaking of a

---

**b.** Justice Scalia later noted that the *Vitale* decision had not departed from *Blockburger* in its holding; it had only suggested in dictum that a claim of double jeopardy against a second prosecution that required proof of the conduct for which *Vitale* had already been convicted *"would be substantial"* (emphasis added). Moreover, "the contention that *Vitale* characterized as 'substantial' finds no support whatever in the two cases that *Vitale* thought gave it substance, Brown v. Ohio and Harris v. Oklahoma." *Brown* "involved nothing more than a straight forward application of *Blockburger*." The defendant was first convicted of joyriding, and then charged with theft of the same auto, under a theft provision "which required all of the elements of joyrid-

ing plus an intent permanently to deprive the owner of his car." *Harris* presented a situation in which the earlier prosecution for felony murder "by definition incorporated all of the elements of the underlying felony" charged in the second prosecution for armed robbery. The Court there gave "no indication that the second prosecution would have been barred if—not because of the statutory definition of the crimes but merely because of the circumstances of the case—guilt could not be established without proving the same conduct charged in the first prosecution." Justice Scalia further noted that the Court had applied the "*Blockburger* formulation in virtually every case defining the 'same offense' decided since *Blockburger*."

Law." Dictionarium Britannicum (Bailey ed. 1730). If the same conduct violates two (or more) laws, then each offense may be separately prosecuted. Of course, this is not to say that two criminal provisions create "distinct" offenses simply by appearing under separate statutory headings; but if each contains an element the other does not, *i.e.*, if it is possible to violate each one without violating the other, then they cannot constitute the "*same* offence."

Another textual element also supports the *Blockburger* test. Since the Double Jeopardy Clause protects the defendant from being "twice put in jeopardy," *i.e.*, made to stand trial, for the "same offence," it presupposes that sameness can be determined before the second trial. Otherwise, the Clause would have prohibited a second "conviction" or "sentence" for the same offense. A court can always determine, before trial, whether the second prosecution involves the "same offence" in the *Blockburger* sense, since the Constitution entitles the defendant "to be informed of the nature and cause of the accusation." But since the Constitution does not entitle the defendant to be informed of the *evidence* against him, the Court's "proof-of-same-conduct" test will be implementable before trial only if the indictment happens to show that the same evidence is at issue, or only if the jurisdiction's rules of criminal procedure happen to require the prosecution to submit a bill of particulars that cannot be exceeded. More often than not, in other words, the Court's test will not succeed in preventing the defendant from being tried twice.

Relying on text alone, therefore, one would conclude that the Double Jeopardy Clause meant what *Blockburger* said. But there is in addition a wealth of historical evidence to the same effect. The Clause was based on the English common-law plea of *auterfoits acquit* and *auterfoits convict*, which pleas were valid only "upon a prosecution for the same identical act and crime." 4 W. Blackstone, Commentaries 330 (1769) (emphasis added). * * * The English practice, as understood in 1791, did not recognize *auterfoits acquit* and *auterfoits convict* as good pleas against successive prosecutions for crimes whose elements were distinct, even though based on the same act. * * * [In] the famous case of *King v. Vandercomb*, 2 Leach 708 (1796), * * * the defendants were first charged with burglary by breaking and entering a house and stealing goods. The Crown abandoned the prosecution because it developed at trial that the defendants had not removed any property. In a second prosecution for burglary by breaking and entering with *intent* to steal, the plea of *auterfoits acquit* was held bad. * * * The court's statement in *Vandercomb* that the "evidence of one of them will not support an indictment for the other," is the precise equivalent of our statement in *Blockburger* that "each provision requires proof of a fact which the other does not." The early American cases adhere to the same rule. * * *

The Court seeks to shrink the apparent application of its novel principle by saying that repetitive proof violates the Double Jeopardy Clause only if it is introduced "to establish an essential element of an offense charged in [the second] prosecution." That is a meaningless limitation, of course. *All* evidence pertaining to guilt seeks "to establish an essential element of [the] offense," and should be excluded if it does not have that tendency.

The other half of the Court's new test does seem to import some limitation, though I am not sure precisely what it means and cannot imagine what principle justifies it. I refer to the requirement that the evidence introduced in the second prosecution must "prove conduct that constitutes an offense for which the defendant has already been prosecuted." This means, presumably, that prosecutors who wish to use facts sufficient to prove one crime in order to establish guilt of another crime must bring both prosecutions simultaneously; but that those who wish to use only *some* of the facts establishing one crime—not enough facts to "prove conduct that constitutes an offense"—can bring successive prosecutions. But, one may reasonably ask, what justification is there *even in reason alone* (having abandoned text and precedent) for limiting the Court's new rule in this fashion? The Court defends the rule on the ground that a successive prosecution based on the same proof exposes the defendant to the burden and embarrassment of resisting proof of the same facts in multiple proceedings, and enables the State to "rehearse its presentation of proof, thus increasing the risk of an erroneous conviction for one or more of the offenses charged." But that vice does not exist only when the second prosecution seeks to prove *all* the facts necessary to support the first prosecution; it exists as well when the second prosecution seeks to prove some, rather than all of them—*i.e.*, whenever two prosecutions each require proof of facts (or even a single fact) common to both. If the Court were correct that the Double Jeopardy Clause protects individuals against the necessity of twice proving (or refuting) the same *evidence*, as opposed to the necessity of twice defending against the same *charge*, then the second prosecution should be equally bad whether it contains all or merely some of the proof necessary for the first.

Apart from the lack of rational basis for this latter limitation, I am greatly perplexed (as will be the unfortunate trial-court judges who must apply today's rootless decision) as to what precisely it means. It is not at all apparent how a court is to go about deciding whether the evidence that has been introduced (or that will be introduced) at the second trial "proves conduct" that constitutes an offense for which the defendant has already been prosecuted. Is the judge in the second trial supposed to pretend that he is the judge in the first one, and to let the second trial proceed *only if* the evidence would not be enough to go to the jury on the earlier charge? Or (as the language of the Court's test more readily suggests) is the judge in the second trial supposed to decide on his own whether the evidence before him really "proves" the earlier charge (perhaps beyond a reasonable doubt)? Consider application of the Court's new rule in the unusually simple circumstances of the present case: Suppose that, in the trial upon remand, the prosecution's evidence shows, among other things, that when the vehicles came to rest after the collision they were located on what was, for the defendant's vehicle, the wrong side of the road. The prosecution also produces a witness who testifies that prior to the collision the defendant's vehicle was "weaving back and forth"—*without* saying, however, that it was weaving back and forth over the center line. Is this enough to meet today's requirement of "proving" the offense of operating a vehicle on the wrong side of the road? If not, suppose in addition that defense counsel asks the witness on cross-examination, "When you said the defendant's vehicle was 'weaving back and forth,' did you mean weaving back and forth across the center line?"—to which the witness replies yes. Will this self-inflicted wound count for purposes of determining what the prosecution has "proved"? If so, can the prosecution then seek to impeach its own witness by showing that his recollection of the vehicle's crossing the center line was inaccurate? Or can it at least introduce another witness to establish that fact? There are many questions here, and the answers to all of them are ridiculous. Whatever line is selected as the criterion of "proving" the prior offense—enough evidence to go to the jury, more likely than not, or beyond a reasonable doubt—the prosecutor in the second trial will presumably seek to introduce as much evidence as he can without crossing that line; and the defense attorney will presumably seek to provoke the prosecutor into (or assist him in) proving the defendant guilty of the earlier crime. This delicious role-reversal, discovered to have been mandated by the Double Jeopardy Clause lo these 200 years, makes for high comedy but inferior justice. Often, the performance will even have an encore. If the judge initially decides that the previously prosecuted offense "will not be proved" (whatever that means) he will have to decide at the conclusion of the trial whether it "has been proved" (whatever that means). Indeed, he may presumably be asked to make the latter determination periodically during the course of the trial, since the Double Jeopardy Clause assuredly entitles the defendant to have the proceedings terminated as soon as its violation is evident. Even if we had no constitutional text and no prior case-law to rely upon, rejection of today's opinion is adequately supported by the modest desire to protect our criminal legal system from ridicule.

A limitation that is so unsupported in reason and so absurd in application is unlikely to survive. Today's decision to extend the Double Jeopardy Clause to prosecutions that *prove* a previously prosecuted offense will lead predictably to extending it to prosecutions that *involve the same facts as* a previously prosecuted offense. We will thus have fully embraced Justice Brennan's "same transaction" theory, which has as little support in the text and history of the Double Jeopardy Clause, but at least has the merit of being rational and easy to apply. One can readily imagine the words of our first opinion effecting this extension: "When we said in *Grady* that the second prosecution is impermissible if it 'will prove conduct' that constitutes the prior offense, we did not mean that it will establish commission of that offense with the degree of completeness that would permit a jury to convict. It suffices if the evidence in the second prosecution 'proves' the previously prosecuted offense in the sense of tending to establish one or more of the elements of that offense." The Court that has done what it has today to 200 years of established double jeopardy jurisprudence should find this lesser transmogrification easy. It may, however, prove unnecessary, since prosecutors confronted with the inscrutability of today's opinion will be well advised to proceed on the assumption that the "same transaction" theory has already been adopted. It is hard to tell what else has.

## HEATH v. ALABAMA

474 U.S. 82, 106 S.Ct. 433, 88 L.Ed.2d 387 (1985).

JUSTICE O'CONNOR delivered the opinion of the Court.   *   *   *

In August 1981, petitioner, Larry Gene Heath, hired Charles Owens and Gregory Lumpkin to kill his wife, Rebecca Heath, who was then nine months pregnant, for a sum of $2,000. On the morning of August 31, 1981, petitioner left the Heath residence in Russell County, Alabama, to meet with Owens and Lumpkin in Georgia, just over the Alabama border from the Heath home. Petitioner led them back to the Heath residence, gave them the keys to the Heaths' car and house, and left the premises in his girlfriend's truck. Owens and Lumpkin then kidnaped Rebecca Heath from her home. The Heath car, with Rebecca Heath's body inside, was later found on the side of a road in Troup County, Georgia. The cause of death was a gunshot wound in the head. The estimated time of death and the distance from the Heath residence to the spot where Rebecca Heath's body was found are consistent with the theory that the murder took place in Georgia, and respondent does not contend otherwise.

Georgia and Alabama authorities pursued dual investigations in which they cooperated to some extent.   *   *   * In November 1981, the grand jury of Troup County, Georgia indicted petitioner for the offense of "malice" murder. Georgia then served petitioner with notice of its intention to seek the death penalty, citing as the aggravating circumstance the fact that the murder was "caused and directed" by petitioner. On February 10, 1982, petitioner pleaded guilty to the Georgia murder charge in exchange for a sentence of life imprisonment, which he understood could involve his serving as few as seven years in prison.

On May 5, 1982, the grand jury of Russell County, Alabama, returned an indictment against petitioner for the capital offense of murder during a kidnaping. Before trial on this indictment, petitioner entered pleas of *autrefois convict* and former jeopardy under the Alabama and United States Constitutions, arguing that his conviction and sentence in Georgia barred his prosecution in Alabama for the same conduct. After a hearing, the trial court rejected petitioner's double jeopardy claims. It assumed, *arguendo*, that the two prosecutions could not have been brought in succession by one State but held that double jeopardy did not bar successive prosecutions by two different States for the same act. * * *

On January 12, 1983, the Alabama jury convicted petitioner of murder during a kidnaping in the first degree. After a sentencing hearing, the jury recommended the death penalty. * * * The judge accepted the jury's recommendation, finding that the sole aggravating factor, that the capital offense was "committed while the defendant was engaged in the commission of a kidnaping," outweighed the sole mitigating factor, that the "defendant was convicted of the murder of Rebecca Heath in the Superior Court of Troup County, Georgia, * * * and received a sentence of life imprisonment in that court." [The state appellate courts affirmed the conviction and sentence.]

Petitioner sought a writ of certiorari from this Court, raising double jeopardy claims and claims based on Alabama's exercise of jurisdiction. No due process objections were asserted. We granted certiorari limited to the question of whether Alabama's conviction was barred by this Court's decision in *Brown v. Ohio*, and requested the parties to address the question of the applicability of the dual sovereignty doctrine to successive prosecutions by two States.

Successive prosecutions are barred by the Fifth Amendment only if the two offenses for which the defendant is prosecuted are the "same" for double jeopardy purposes. Respondent does not contravene petitioner's contention that the offenses of "murder during a kidnaping" and "malice murder," as construed by the courts of Alabama and Georgia respectively, may be considered greater and lesser offenses and, thus, the "same" offense under *Brown v. Ohio*, absent operation of the dual sovereignty principle. See *Illinois v. Vitale*. We, therefore, assume *arguendo* that, had these offenses arisen under the laws of one State and had petitioner been separately prosecuted for both offenses in that State, the second conviction would have been barred by the Double Jeopardy Clause.

The sole remaining question upon which we granted certiorari is whether the dual sovereignty doctrine permits successive prosecutions under the laws of different States which otherwise would be held to "subject [the defendant] for the same offence to be twice put in jeopardy." Although we have not previously so held, we believe the answer to this query is inescapable. The dual sovereignty doctrine, as originally articulated and consistently applied by this Court, compels the conclusion that successive prosecutions by two States for the same conduct are not barred by the Double Jeopardy Clause.

The dual sovereignty doctrine is founded on the common law conception of crime as an offense against the sovereignty of the government. When a defendant in a single act violates the "peace and dignity" of two sovereigns by breaking the laws of each, he has committed two distinct "offences." * * *

In applying the dual sovereignty doctrine, then, the crucial determination is whether the two entities that seek successively to prosecute a defendant for the same course of conduct can be termed separate sovereigns.  This determination turns on whether the two entities draw their authority to punish the offender from distinct sources of power.  Thus, the Court has uniformly held that the States are separate sovereigns with respect to the Federal Government because each State's power to prosecute is derived from its own "inherent sovereignty," not from the Federal Government.  See *Abbate v. United States*, 359 U.S. 187 (1959). * * * See also *Bartkus v. Illinois*, 359 U.S. 121 (1959).[a] * * *

The States are no less sovereign with respect to each other than they are with respect to the Federal Government.  Their powers to undertake criminal prosecutions derive from separate and independent sources of power and authority originally belonging to them before admission to the Union and preserved to them by the Tenth Amendment. * * *

In those instances where the Court has found the dual sovereignty doctrine inapplicable, it has done so because the two prosecuting entities did not derive their powers to prosecute from independent sources of authority.  Thus, the Court has held that successive prosecutions by federal and territorial courts are barred because such courts are "creations emanating from the same sovereignty."  Similarly, municipalities that derive their power to try a defendant from the same organic law that empowers the State to prosecute are not separate sovereigns with respect to the State.  These cases confirm that it is the presence of independent sovereign authority to prosecute, not the relation between States and the Federal Government in our federalist system, that constitutes the basis for the dual sovereignty doctrine. * * *

Petitioner invites us to restrict the applicability of the dual sovereignty principle to cases in which two governmental entities, having concurrent jurisdiction and pursuing quite different interests, can demonstrate that allowing only one entity to exercise jurisdiction over the defendant will interfere with the unvindicated interests of the second entity and that multiple prosecutions therefore are necessary for the satisfaction of the legitimate interests of both entities.  This balancing of interests approach, however, cannot be reconciled with the dual sovereignty principle.  This Court has plainly and repeatedly stated that two identical offenses are *not* the "same offence" within the meaning of the Double Jeopardy Clause if they are prosecuted by different sovereigns.  If the States are separate sovereigns, as they must be under the definition of sovereignty which the Court consistently has employed, the circumstances of the case are irrelevant.

Petitioner, then, is asking the Court to discard its sovereignty analysis and to substitute in its stead his difficult and uncertain balancing of interests approach.  The Court has refused a similar request on at least one previous occasion, see *Abbate v. United States*, and rightfully so.  The Court's express rationale for the dual sovereignty doctrine is not simply a fiction that can be disregarded in difficult cases.  It finds weighty support in the historical under-

**a.**  These two cases combined held constitutionally permissible separate federal and state prosecutions for the same basic criminal conduct.  *Bartkus* upheld a state conviction of defendant for bank robbery where the defendant had previously been tried and acquitted in federal court for the same robbery of the same bank (which was federally insured).  *Abbate* upheld a conviction of defendants in federal court for conspiring to destroy communications facilities which were "essential and integral parts of systems * * * of communications operated and controlled by the United States", where defendants previously had "pleaded guilty to a charge in state court of conspiracy to destroy another's property" (the same telephone company facilities).

standing and political realities of the States' role in the federal system and in the words of the Double Jeopardy Clause itself, "nor shall any person be subject for the same *offence* to be twice put in jeopardy of life or limb."   \*   \*   \*

JUSTICE MARSHALL, with whom JUSTICE BRENNAN joins, dissenting.   \*   \*   \*[b]

Under the constitutional scheme, the Federal Government has been given the exclusive power to vindicate certain of our Nation's sovereign interests, leaving the States to exercise complementary authority over matters of more local concern. The respective spheres of the Federal Government and the States may overlap at times, and even where they do not, different interests may be implicated by a single act. See, e.g., *Abbate v. United States* (conspiracy to dynamite telephone company facilities entails both destruction of property and disruption of federal communications network). Yet were a prosecution by a State, however zealously pursued, allowed to preclude further prosecution by the Federal Government for the same crime, an entire range of national interests could be frustrated. The importance of those federal interests has thus quite properly been permitted to trump a defendant's interest in avoiding successive prosecutions or multiple punishments for the same crime. Conversely, because the States under our federal system have the principal responsibility for defining and prosecuting crimes, it would be inappropriate—in the absence of a specific congressional intent to preempt state action pursuant to the Supremacy Clause—to allow a federal prosecution to preclude state authorities from vindicating the historic right and obligation of the States to maintain peace and order within their confines.   \*   \*   \*

Where two States seek to prosecute the same defendant for the same crime in two separate proceedings, the justifications found in the federal-state context for an exemption from double jeopardy constraints simply do not hold. Although the two States may have opted for different policies within their assigned territorial jurisdictions, the sovereign concerns with whose vindication each State has been charged are identical. Thus, in contrast to the federal-state context, barring the second prosecution would still permit one government to act upon the broad range of sovereign concerns that have been reserved to the States by the Constitution. The compelling need in the federal-state context to subordinate double jeopardy concerns is thus considerably diminished in cases involving successive prosecutions by different States. Moreover, from the defendant's perspective, the burden of successive prosecutions cannot be justified as the *quid pro quo* of dual citizenship.

To be sure, a refusal to extend the dual sovereignty rule to state-state prosecutions would preclude the State that has lost the "race to the courthouse" from vindicating legitimate policies distinct from those underlying its sister State's prosecution. But as yet, I am not persuaded that a State's desire to further a particular policy should be permitted to deprive a defendant of his constitutionally protected right not to be brought to bar more than once to answer essentially the same charges.   \*   \*   \*

    **b.** Justice Brennan's separate dissent is omitted.

# SECTION 2. ABORTED PROCEEDINGS

## ARIZONA v. WASHINGTON

434 U.S. 497, 98 S.Ct. 824, 54 L.Ed.2d 717 (1978).

JUSTICE STEVENS delivered the opinion of the Court.

In 1971 respondent was found guilty of murdering a hotel night clerk. In 1973, the Superior Court of Pima County, Ariz., ordered a new trial because the prosecutor had withheld exculpatory evidence from the defense. The Arizona Supreme Court affirmed the new trial order * * *.

Respondent's second trial began in January 1975. During the *voir dire* examination of prospective jurors, the prosecutor made reference to the fact that some of the witnesses whose testimony the jurors would hear had testified in proceedings four years earlier. Defense counsel told the prospective jurors "that there was evidence hidden from [respondent] at the last trial." In his opening statement, he made this point more forcefully:

"You will hear testimony that notwithstanding the fact that we had a trial in May of 1971 in this matter, that the prosecutor hid those statements and didn't give those to the lawyer for George saying the man was Spanish speaking, didn't give those statements at all, hid them.

"You will hear that that evidence was suppressed and hidden by the prosecutor in that case. You will hear that that evidence was purposely withheld. You will hear that because of the misconduct of the County Attorney at that time and because he withheld evidence, that the Supreme Court of Arizona granted a new trial in this case."

After opening statements were completed, the prosecutor moved for a mistrial. In colloquy during argument of the motion, the trial judge expressed the opinion that evidence concerning the reasons for the new trial, and specifically the ruling of the Arizona Supreme Court, was irrelevant to the issue of guilt or innocence and therefore inadmissible. Defense counsel asked for an opportunity "to find some law" that would support his belief that the Supreme Court opinion would be admissible. After further argument, the judge stated that he would withhold ruling on the admissibility of the evidence and denied the motion for mistrial. Two witnesses then testified.

The following morning the prosecutor renewed his mistrial motion. Fortified by an evening's research, he argued that there was no theory on which the basis for the new trial ruling could be brought to the attention of the jury, that the prejudice to the jury could not be repaired by any cautionary instructions, and that a mistrial was a "manifest necessity." Defense counsel * * * argued that his comment was invited by the prosecutor's reference to the witnesses' earlier testimony and that any prejudice could be avoided by curative instructions. * * * Ultimately the trial judge granted the motion, stating that his ruling was based upon defense counsel's remarks in his opening statement concerning the Arizona Supreme Court opinion. The trial judge did not expressly find that there was "manifest necessity" for a mistrial; nor did he expressly state that he had considered alternative solutions and concluded that none would be adequate. * * * [A federal district court, upon application for federal habeas corpus, granted the writ because of the absence in the record of such express findings. The Court of Appeals affirmed.]

\* \* \* The constitutional protection against double jeopardy unequivocally prohibits a second trial following an acquittal. The public interest in the finality of criminal judgments is so strong that an acquitted defendant may not be retried even though "the acquittal was based upon an egregiously erroneous foundation." If the innocence of the accused has been confirmed by a final judgment, the Constitution conclusively presumes that a second trial would be unfair.

Because jeopardy attaches before the judgment becomes final, the constitutional protection also embraces the defendant's "valued right to have his trial completed by a particular tribunal." The reasons why this "valued right" merits constitutional protection are worthy of repetition. Even if the first trial is not completed, a second prosecution may be grossly unfair. It increases the financial and emotional burden on the accused, prolongs the period in which he is stigmatized by an unresolved accusation of wrongdoing, and may even enhance the risk that an innocent defendant may be convicted. The danger of such unfairness to the defendant exists whenever a trial is aborted before it is completed. Consequently, as a general rule, the prosecutor is entitled to one, and only one, opportunity to require an accused to stand trial.

Unlike the situation in which the trial has ended in an acquittal or conviction, retrial is not automatically barred when a criminal proceeding is terminated without finally resolving the merits of the charges against the accused. Because of the variety of circumstances that may make it necessary to discharge a jury before a trial is concluded, and because those circumstances do not invariably create unfairness to the accused, his valued right to have the trial concluded by a particular tribunal is sometimes subordinate to the public interest in affording the prosecutor one full and fair opportunity to present his evidence to an impartial jury. Yet in view of the importance of the right, and the fact that it is frustrated by any mistrial, the prosecutor must shoulder the burden of justifying the mistrial if he is to avoid the double jeopardy bar. His burden is a heavy one. The prosecutor must demonstrate "manifest necessity" for any mistrial declared over the objection of the defendant.

The words "manifest necessity" appropriately characterize the magnitude of the prosecutor's burden. For that reason Mr. Justice Story's classic formulation of the test has been quoted over and over again to provide guidance in the decision of a wide variety of cases. Nevertheless, those words do not describe a standard that can be applied mechanically or without attention to the particular problem confronting the trial judge. Indeed, it is manifest that the key word "necessity" cannot be interpreted literally; instead, contrary to the teaching of Webster, we assume that there are degrees of necessity and we require a "high degree" before concluding that a mistrial is appropriate.

The question whether that "high degree" has been reached is answered more easily in some kinds of cases than in others. At one extreme are cases in which a prosecutor requests a mistrial in order to buttress weaknesses in his evidence. Although there was a time when English judges served the Stuart monarchs by exercising a power to discharge a jury whenever it appeared that the Crown's evidence would be insufficient to convict, the prohibition against double jeopardy as it evolved in this country was plainly intended to condemn this "abhorrent" practice. \* \* \* Thus, the strictest scrutiny is appropriate when the basis for the mistrial is the unavailability of critical prosecution evidence, or when there is reason to believe that the prosecutor is using the superior resources of the State to harass or to achieve a tactical advantage over the accused.

At the other extreme is the mistrial premised upon the trial judge's belief that the jury is unable to reach a verdict, long considered the classic basis for a proper mistrial. The argument that a jury's inability to agree establishes reasonable doubt as to the defendant's guilt, and therefore requires acquittal, has been uniformly rejected in this country. Instead, without exception, the courts have held that the trial judge may discharge a genuinely deadlocked jury and require the defendant to submit to a second trial. This rule accords recognition to society's interest in giving the prosecution one complete opportunity to convict those who have violated its laws.

Moreover, in this situation there are especially compelling reasons for allowing the trial judge to exercise broad discretion in deciding whether or not "manifest necessity" justifies a discharge of the jury. On the one hand, if he discharges the jury when further deliberations may produce a fair verdict, the defendant is deprived of his "valued right to have his trial completed by a particular tribunal." But if he fails to discharge a jury which is unable to reach a verdict after protracted and exhausting deliberations, there exists a significant risk that a verdict may result from pressures inherent in the situation rather than the considered judgment of all the jurors. If retrial of the defendant were barred whenever an appellate court views the "necessity" for a mistrial differently from the trial judge, there would be a danger that the latter, cognizant of the serious societal consequences of an erroneous ruling, would employ coercive means to break the apparent deadlock. Such a rule would frustrate the public interest in just judgments. The trial judge's decision to declare a mistrial when he considers the jury deadlocked is therefore accorded great deference by a reviewing court.

We are persuaded that, along the spectrum of trial problems which may warrant a mistrial and which vary in their amenability to appellate scrutiny, the difficulty which led to the mistrial in this case also falls in an area where the trial judge's determination is entitled to special respect.

In this case the trial judge ordered a mistrial because the defendant's lawyer made improper and prejudicial remarks during his opening statement to the jury. * * * We recognize that the extent of the possible bias cannot be measured, and that the [federal] District Court was quite correct in believing that some trial judges might have proceeded with the trial after giving the jury appropriate cautionary instructions. In a strict, literal sense, the mistrial was not "necessary." Nevertheless, the overriding interest in the evenhanded administration of justice requires that we accord the highest degree of respect to the trial judge's evaluation of the likelihood that the impartiality of one or more jurors may have been affected by the improper comment. * * * The consistent course of decision in this Court in cases involving possible juror bias supports this conclusion. * * *

An improper opening statement unquestionably tends to frustrate the public interest in having a just judgment reached by an impartial tribunal. * * * The trial judge, of course, may instruct the jury to disregard the improper comment. In extreme cases, he may discipline counsel, or even remove him from the trial as he did in *United States v. Dinitz*, 424 U.S. 600 (1976). Those actions, however, will not necessarily remove the risk of bias that may be created by improper argument. Unless unscrupulous defense counsel are to be allowed an unfair advantage, the trial judge must have the power to declare a mistrial in appropriate cases. The interest in orderly, impartial procedure would be impaired if he were deterred from exercising that power by a concern that any time a reviewing court disagreed with his assessment of the trial situation a retrial would automatically be barred. The adoption of a stringent standard of appellate review in this area, therefore, would seriously impede the trial judge in the proper performance of his "duty, in order to protect the integrity of the trial, to take prompt and affirmative action to stop * * * professional misconduct." *Dinitz.*

There are compelling institutional considerations militating in favor of appellate deference to the trial judge's evaluation of the significance of possible juror bias. He has seen and heard the jurors during their *voir dire* examination. He is the judge most familiar with the evidence and the background of the case on trial. He has listened to the tone of the argument as it was delivered and has observed the apparent reaction of the jurors. In short, he is far more "conversant with the factors relevant to the determination" than any reviewing court can possibly be.

Our conclusion that a trial judge's decision to declare a mistrial based on his assessment of the prejudicial impact of improper argument is entitled to great deference does not, of course, end the inquiry. As noted earlier, a constitutionally protected interest is inevitably affected by any mistrial decision. * * * In order to ensure that this interest is adequately protected, reviewing courts have an obligation to satisfy themselves that, in the words of Mr. Justice Story, the trial judge exercised "sound discretion" in declaring a mistrial. * * * [I]f a trial judge acts irrationally or irresponsibly, his action cannot be condoned. But our review of this record indicates that this was not such a case. * * *

One final matter requires consideration. The absence of an explicit finding of "manifest necessity" appears to have been determinative for the District Court and may have been so for the Court of Appeals. If those courts regarded that omission as critical, they required too much. Since the record provides sufficient justification for the state-court ruling, the failure to explain that ruling more completely does not render it constitutionally defective.

Review of any trial court decision is, of course, facilitated by findings and by an explanation of the reasons supporting the decision. No matter how desirable such procedural assistance may be, it is not constitutionally mandated in a case such as this. The basis for the trial judge's mistrial order is adequately disclosed by the record, which includes the extensive argument of counsel prior to the judge's ruling. The state trial judge's mistrial declaration is not subject to collateral attack in a federal court simply because he failed to find "manifest necessity" in those words or to articulate on the record all the factors which informed the deliberate exercise of his discretion. * * *

JUSTICE BLACKMUN concurs in the result.

JUSTICE WHITE, dissenting.

I cannot agree with the Court of Appeals that the failure of a state trial judge to express the legal standard under which he had declared a mistrial is, in itself and without further examination of the record, sufficient reason to infer constitutional error foreclosing a second trial. * * * I would not, however, undertake an examination of the record here in the first instance. Rather, I would vacate the judgment of the Court of Appeals and direct that court to remand the case to the District Court to make the initial judgment, under the correct legal standard, as to whether the writ should issue.

JUSTICE MARSHALL, with whom JUSTICE BRENNAN joins, dissenting.

My disagreement with the majority is a narrow one. * * * I agree that, where a mistrial is declared over a defendant's objections, a new trial is permissible only if the termination of the earlier trial was justified by a "manifest necessity" and that the prosecution must shoulder the "heavy" burden of demonstrating such a "high degree" of necessity. Nor do I quarrel with the proposition that reviewing courts must accord substantial deference to a trial judge's determination that the prejudicial impact of an improper opening statement is so great as to leave no alternative but a mistrial to secure the ends of public justice. * * * Where I part ways from the Court is in its assumption that an "assessment of the prejudicial impact of improper argument," sufficient to support the need for a mistrial, may be implied from this record. * * *

Defense counsel's improper remarks occupied only one page of a lengthy opening statement. Despite the fact that the prosecutor had vigorously interrupted the opening statement at numerous points to assert various objections, he made no objection to the remarks that formed the basis for the mistrial. If the argument of defense counsel had had a visibly obvious impact on the jurors when uttered, it is hard to believe that this prosecutor would have waited until after the opening statement was finished and the luncheon recess concluded before making his objection known.

Although from this distance and in the absence of express findings it is impossible to determine the precise extent to which defense counsel's remarks may have prejudiced the jury against the State, the circumstances set forth above suggest that any such prejudice may have been minimal and subject to cure through less drastic alternatives. For example, the jury could have been instructed to disregard any mention of prior legal rulings as irrelevant to the issues at hand, and to consider as evidence only the testimony and exhibits admitted through witnesses on the stand. Were there doubt whether such instructions alone would suffice to cure the taint, the jury could have been questioned about the extent of any prejudice. Given the anticipated length of the trial (almost two weeks), it is not unlikely that, had the jury been appropriately instructed when the court first found defense counsel to have erred in his opening statement, any prejudice would have dissipated before deliberations were to begin. For these reasons, it is impossible to conclude that a finding of necessity was implicit in the mere grant of the mistrial. * * *

I do not propose that the Constitution invariably requires a trial judge to make findings of necessity on the record to justify the declaration of a mistrial over a defendant's objections. * * * What the "manifest necessity" doctrine does require, in my view, is that the record make clear either that there were no meaningful and practical alternatives to a mistrial, or that the trial court scrupulously considered available alternatives and found all wanting but a termination of the proceedings. * * * The record here * * * does neither. * * *

Had the court here explored alternatives on the record, or made a finding of substantial and incurable prejudice or other "manifest necessity," this would be a different case and one in which I would agree with both the majority's reasoning and its result. On this ambiguous record, however, the absence of any such finding—and indeed of any express indication that the trial court applied the manifest-necessity doctrine—leaves open the substantial possibility that there was in fact no need to terminate the proceedings. * * *

## OREGON v. KENNEDY

456 U.S. 667, 102 S.Ct. 2083, 72 L.Ed.2d 416 (1982).

JUSTICE REHNQUIST delivered the opinion of the Court.

* * * Respondent was charged with the theft of an oriental rug. During his first trial, the State called an expert witness on the subject of Middle Eastern rugs to testify as to the value and the identity of the rug in question. On cross-examination, respondent's attorney apparently attempted to establish bias on the part of the expert witness by asking him whether he had filed a criminal complaint against respondent. The witness eventually acknowledged this fact, but explained that no action had been taken on his complaint. On redirect examination, the prosecutor sought to elicit the reasons why the witness had filed a complaint against respondent, but the trial court sustained a series of objections to this line of inquiry.[1] The following colloquy then ensued:

"Prosecutor: Have you ever done business with the Kennedys?

"Witness: No, I have not.

"Prosecutor: Is that because he is a crook?"

The trial court then granted respondent's motion for a mistrial.

When the State later sought to retry respondent, he moved to dismiss the charges because of double jeopardy. After a hearing at which the prosecutor testified, the trial court found as a fact that "it was not the intention of the prosecutor in this case to cause a mistrial." On the basis of this finding, the trial court held that double jeopardy principles did not bar retrial, and respondent was then tried and convicted.

Respondent then successfully appealed to the Oregon Court of Appeals, which sustained his double jeopardy claim. * * * The Court of Appeals accepted the trial court's finding that it was not the intent of the prosecutor to cause a mistrial. Nevertheless, the court held that retrial was barred because the prosecutor's conduct in this case constituted what it viewed as "overreaching." * * *

Where the trial is terminated over the objection of the defendant, the classical test for lifting the double jeopardy bar to a second trial is the "manifest necessity" standard first enunciated in Justice Story's opinion for the Court in *United States v. Perez [22 U.S. 579 (1824)]*. * * * The "manifest necessity" standard provides sufficient protection to the defendant's interests in having his case finally decided by the jury first selected while at the same time maintaining "the public's interest in fair trials designed to end in just judgments." But in the case of a mistrial declared at the behest of the defendant, quite different principles come into play. Here the defendant himself has elected to terminate the proceedings against him, and the "manifest necessity" standard has no place in the application of the Double Jeopardy Clause. *United States v. Dinitz,* [424 U.S. 600, (1976)]. * * *

Our cases, however, have indicated that even where the defendant moves for a mistrial, there is a narrow exception to the rule that the Double Jeopardy Clause is no bar to retrial. See, e.g., *United States v. Dinitz.* The circumstances under which respondent's first trial was terminated require us to delineate the bounds of that exception more fully than we have in previous cases.

---

1. The Court of Appeals later explained that respondent's "objections were not well taken, and the judge's rulings were probably wrong." 49 Or.App. 415, 417, 619 P.2d 948, 949 (1980).

Since one of the principal threads making up the protection embodied in the Double Jeopardy Clause is the right of the defendant to have his trial completed before the first jury empaneled to try him, it may be wondered as a matter of original inquiry why the defendant's election to terminate the first trial by his own motion should not be deemed a renunciation of that right for all purposes. We have recognized, however, that there would be great difficulty in applying such a rule where the prosecutor's actions giving rise to the motion for mistrial were done "in order to goad the [defendant] into requesting a mistrial." *United States v. Dinitz.* In such a case, the defendant's valued right to complete his trial before the first jury would be a hollow shell if the inevitable motion for mistrial were held to prevent a later invocation of the bar of double jeopardy in all circumstances. But the precise phrasing of the circumstances which *will* allow a defendant to interpose the defense of double jeopardy to a second prosecution where the first has terminated on his own motion for a mistrial have been stated with less than crystal clarity in our cases which deal with this area of the law. * * * The language [of *Dinitz* at points] would seem to broaden the test from one of *intent* to provoke a motion for a mistrial to a more generalized standard of "bad faith conduct" or "harassment" on the part of the judge or prosecutor. It was upon this language that the Oregon Court of Appeals apparently relied in concluding that the prosecutor's colloquy with the expert witness in this case amount to "overreaching."

The difficulty with the more general standards which would permit a broader exception than one merely based on intent is that they offer virtually no standards for their application. Every act on the part of a rational prosecutor during a trial is designed to "prejudice" the defendant by placing before the judge or jury evidence pleading to a finding of his guilt. Given the complexity of the rules of evidence, it will be a rare trial of any complexity in which some proffered evidence by the prosecutor or by the defendant's attorney will not be found objectionable by the trial court. Most such objections are undoubtedly curable by simply refusing to allow the proffered evidence to be admitted, or in the case of a particular line of inquiry taken by counsel with a witness, by an admonition to desist from a particular line of inquiry.

More serious infractions on the part of the prosecutor may provoke a motion for mistrial on the part of the defendant, and may in the view of the trial court warrant the granting of such a motion. The "overreaching" standard applied by the court below and urged today by Justice Stevens, however, would add another classification of prosecutorial error, one requiring dismissal of the indictment, but without supplying any standard by which to assess that error.[5]

By contrast, a standard that examines the intent of the prosecutor, though certainly not entirely free from practical difficulties, is a manageable standard to apply. It merely calls for the court to make a finding of fact. Inferring the existence or nonexistence of intent from objective facts and circumstances is a familiar process in our criminal justice system. When it is remembered that resolution of double jeopardy questions by state trial courts are reviewable not only within the state court system, but in the federal court system on habeas corpus as well, the desirability of an easily applied principle is apparent.

**5.** If the Court were to hold, as would Justice Stevens, that such a determination requires an assessment of the facts and circumstances but without explaining how such an assessment ought to proceed, the Court would offer little guidance to the federal and state courts that must apply our decisions. Justice Stevens disagrees with this decision below because his reaction to a cold record is different from that of the Oregon Court of Appeals. The Court of Appeals found "overreaching"; Justice Stevens finds none. Neither articulates a basis for reaching their respective conclusions which can be applied to other factual situations. We are loath to adopt such an essentially standardless rule.

Prosecutorial conduct that might be viewed as harassment or overreaching, even if sufficient to justify a mistrial on defendant's motion, therefore, does not bar retrial absent intent on the part of the prosecutor to subvert the protections afforded by the Double Jeopardy Clause. A defendant's motion for a mistrial constitutes "a deliberate election on his part to forgo his valued right to have his guilt or innocence determined before the first trier of fact." *United States v. Scott* [§ 3 infra]. Where prosecutorial error even of a degree sufficient to warrant a mistrial has occurred, "[t]he important consideration, for purposes of the Double Jeopardy Clause, is that the defendant retain primary control over the course to be followed in the event of such error." *United States v. Dinitz*. Only where the governmental conduct in question is intended to "goad" the defendant into moving for a mistrial may a defendant raise the bar of double jeopardy to a second trial after having succeeded in aborting the first on his own motion.

Were we to embrace the broad and somewhat amorphous standard adopted by the Oregon Court of Appeals, we are not sure that criminal defendants as a class would be aided. Knowing that the granting of the defendant's motion for mistrial would all but inevitably bring with it an attempt to bar a second trial on grounds of double jeopardy, the judge presiding over the first trial might well be more loath to grant a defendant's motion for mistrial. If a mistrial were in fact warranted under the applicable law, of course, the defendant could in many instances successfully appeal a judgment of conviction on the same grounds that he urged a mistrial, and the Double Jeopardy Clause would present no bar to retrial. But some of the advantages secured to him by the Double Jeopardy Clause—the freedom from extended anxiety, and the necessity to confront the government's case only once—would be to a large extent lost in the process of trial to verdict, reversal on appeal, and subsequent retrial.

* * * We do not by this opinion lay down a flat rule that where a defendant in a criminal trial successfully moves for a mistrial, he may not thereafter invoke the bar of double jeopardy against a second trial. But we do hold that the circumstances under which such a defendant may invoke the bar of double jeopardy in a second effort to try him are limited to those cases in which the conduct giving rise to the successful motion for a mistrial was intended to provoke the defendant into moving for a mistrial. Since the Oregon trial court found, and the Oregon Court of Appeals accepted, that the prosecutorial conduct culminating in the termination of the first trial in this case was not so intended by the prosecutor, that is the end of the matter for purposes of the Double Jeopardy Clause of the Fifth Amendment to the United States Constitution. * * *

JUSTICE BRENNAN, with whom JUSTICE MARSHALL joins, concurring in the judgment.

I concur in the judgment and join in the opinion of Justice Stevens. However, it should be noted that nothing in the holding of the Court today prevents the state courts, on remand, from concluding that respondent's retrial would violate the provision of the Oregon Constitution that prohibits double jeopardy * * *.

JUSTICE POWELL, concurring.

I join the Court's opinion holding that the *intention* of a prosecutor determines whether his conduct, viewed by the defendant and the court as justifying a mistrial, bars a retrial of the defendant under the Double Jeopardy Clause. Because "subjective" intent often may be unknowable, I emphasize that a court—in considering a double jeopardy motion—should rely primarily upon the objective facts and circumstances of the particular case.

\* \* \* [T]his would have been a close case for me if there had been substantial factual evidence of intent beyond the question itself. Here, however, other relevant facts and circumstances strongly support the view that prosecutorial intent to cause a mistrial was absent. First, there was no sequence of overreaching prior to the single prejudicial question. Moreover, it is evident from a colloquy between counsel and the court, out of the presence of the jury, that the prosecutor not only resisted, but also was surprised by, the defendant's motion for a mistrial. Finally, at the hearing on respondent's double jeopardy motion, the prosecutor testified—and the trial found as a fact and the appellate court agreed—that there was no " 'intention \* \* \* to cause a mistrial.' " In view of these circumstances, the Double Jeopardy Clause provides no bar to retrial.

JUSTICE STEVENS, with whom JUSTICE BRENNAN, JUSTICE MARSHALL and JUSTICE BLACKMUN join, concurring in the judgment.

\* \* \* The rationale for the exception to the general rule permitting retrial after a mistrial declared with the defendant's consent is illustrated by the situation in which the prosecutor commits prejudicial error with the intent to provoke a mistrial. \* \* \* But the Court reaches out to limit the exception to that one situation, rejecting the previous recognition that prosecutorial overreaching or harassment is also within the exception.[22]

Even if I agreed that the balance of competing interests tipped in favor of a bar to reprosecution only in the situation in which the prosecutor intended to provoke a mistrial, I would not subscribe to a standard that conditioned such a bar on the determination that the prosecutor harbored such intent when he committed prejudicial error. It is almost inconceivable that a defendant could prove that the prosecutor's deliberate misconduct was motivated by an intent to provoke a mistrial instead of an intent simply to prejudice the defendant. The defendant must shoulder a strong burden to establish a bar to reprosecution when he has consented to the mistrial, but the Court's subjective intent standard would eviscerate the exception.

A broader objection to the Court's limitation of the exception is that the rationale for the exception extends beyond the situation in which the prosecutor intends to provoke a mistrial. There are other situations in which the defendant's double jeopardy interests outweigh society's interest in obtaining a judgment on the merits even though the defendant has moved for a mistrial. For example, a prosecutor may be interested in putting the defendant through the

---

**22.** The Court offers two reasons for cutting back on the exception. First, the Court states that "[t]he difficulty with the more general standards which would permit a broader exception than one merely based on intent is that they offer virtually no standards for their application." As I indicate in the text, however, some generality in the formula is a virtue and, in any event, meaningful and principled standards can be developed on a case-by-case basis that will not inhibit legitimate prosecution practices. Moreover, the general standards could hardly be more difficult to apply than the Court's subjective intent standard. \* \* \*

Second, the Court is "not sure that criminal defendants as a class would be aided" by a broader exception. If a mistrial will more frequently constitute a bar to reprosecution, the Court supposes that trial judges will tend to refuse the defendant's mistrial motion and permit the error to be corrected on appeal of the conviction, in which event there would be no bar to reprosecution. This reasoning is premised on the assumption that an appellate court that concluded not only that the defendant's mistrial motion should have been granted but also that the prosecutor intended to provoke a mistrial would not be obligated to bar reprosecution as well as reverse the conviction. The assumption is "irrational." *Commonwealth v. Potter,* 478 Pa. 251, 386 A.2d 918 (1978) (Roberts, J.) (Pomeroy, J.).

embarrassment, expense, and ordeal of criminal proceedings even if he cannot obtain a conviction. In such a case, with the purpose of harassing the defendant the prosecutor may commit repeated prejudicial errors and be indifferent between a mistrial or mistrials and an unsustainable conviction or convictions. Another example is when the prosecutor seeks to inject enough unfair prejudice into the trial to ensure a conviction but not so much as to cause a reversal of that conviction. This kind of overreaching would not be covered by the Court's standard because, by hypothesis, the prosecutor's intent is to obtain a conviction, not to provoke a mistrial. Yet the defendant's choice—to continue the tainted proceeding or to abort it and begin anew—can be just as "hollow" in this situation as when the prosecutor intends to provoke a mistrial.

To invoke the exception for overreaching, a court need not divine the exact motivation for the prosecutorial error. It is sufficient that the court is persuaded that egregious prosecutorial misconduct has rendered unmeaningful the defendant's choice to continue or to abort the proceeding. It is unnecessary and unwise to attempt to identify all the factors that might inform the court's judgment, but several considerations follow from the rationale for recognizing the exception. First, because the exception is justified by the intolerance of intentional manipulation of the defendant's double jeopardy interests, a finding of deliberate misconduct normally would be a prerequisite to a reprosecution bar. Second, because the defendant's option to abort the proceeding after prosecutorial misconduct would retain real meaning for the defendant in any case in which the trial was going badly for him, normally a required finding would be that the prosecutorial error virtually eliminated, or at least substantially reduced, the probability of acquittal in a proceeding that was going badly for the government. It should be apparent from these observations that only in a rare and compelling case will a mistrial declared at the request of the defendant or with his consent bar a retrial.

No one case, of course, is a proper vehicle for identifying the limits of the exception. The Court repeatedly has shunned inflexible standards in applying the comparable "manifest necessity" exception to the general rule that a defendant is entitled to go to final judgment before the initial tribunal. The value of the overreaching standard, like "[t]he value of the [manifest necessity standard], thus lies in [its] capacity for informed application under widely different circumstances without injury to defendants or to the public interest." *Wade v. Hunter,* 336 U.S. 684 [(1949)]. The inexactitude of the standard used to protect defendants in the exceptional case surely should not concern the Court any more than the equally ill-defined formula used to protect prosecutors in the exceptional case. * * *

* * * The isolated prosecutorial error [here] occurred early in the trial, too early to determine whether the case was going badly for the prosecution. If anyone was being harassed at that time, it was the prosecutor who was frustrated by improper defense objections in her attempt to rehabilitate her witness. The gist of the comment that the respondent was a "crook" could fairly have been elicited from the witness, since defense counsel injected the respondent's past alleged improprieties into the trial by questioning the witness about his bias towards the defendant. The comment therefore could not have injected the kind of prejudice that would render unmeaningful the defendant's option to proceed with the trial. Because the present case quite clearly does not come within the recognized exception, I join the Court's judgment.

# SECTION 3.  REPROSECUTION FOLLOWING ACQUITTALS AND CONVICTIONS

## UNITED STATES v. SCOTT

437 U.S. 82, 98 S.Ct. 2187, 57 L.Ed.2d 65 (1978).

JUSTICE REHNQUIST delivered the opinion of the Court.

On March 5, 1975, respondent, a member of the police force in Muskegon, Mich., was charged * * * with distribution of various narcotics.  Both before his trial in the United States District Court and twice during the trial, respondent moved to dismiss the two counts of the indictment which concerned transactions that took place during the preceding September, on the ground that his defense had been prejudiced by preindictment delay.  At the close of all the evidence, the court granted respondent's motion.  * * *

The Government sought to appeal the dismissals of the first two counts to the United States Court of Appeals for the Sixth Circuit.  That court, relying on our opinion in *United States v. Jenkins,* 420 U.S. 358 (1975), concluded that any further prosecution of respondent was barred by the Double Jeopardy Clause of the Fifth Amendment, and therefore dismissed the appeal.  * * * We granted certiorari to give further consideration to the applicability of the Double Jeopardy Clause to Government appeals from orders granting defense motions to terminate a trial before verdict.  We now reverse.  * * *

A detailed canvass of the history of the double jeopardy principles in *United States v. Wilson,* 420 U.S. 332 (1975), led us to conclude that the Double Jeopardy Clause was primarily "directed at the threat of multiple prosecutions," and posed no bar to Government appeals "where those appeals would not require a new trial."  We accordingly held in *Jenkins,* that, whether or not a dismissal of an indictment after jeopardy had attached amounted to an acquittal on the merits, the Government had no right to appeal, because "further proceedings of some sort, devoted to the resolution of factual issues going to the elements of the offense charged, would have been required upon reversal and remand." [a]

If *Jenkins* is a correct statement of the law, the judgment of the Court of Appeals * * * would in all likelihood have to be affirmed.  Yet, though our assessment of the history and meaning of the Double Jeopardy Clause in *Wilson, Jenkins,* and *Serfass v. United States,* 420 U.S. 377 (1975), occurred only three Terms ago, our vastly increased exposure to the various facets of the Double Jeopardy Clause has now convinced us that *Jenkins* was wrongly decided.  It placed an unwarrantedly great emphasis on the defendant's right to have his guilt decided by the first jury empaneled to try him so as to include those cases where the defendant himself seeks to terminate the trial before verdict on grounds unrelated to factual guilt or innocence.  We have therefore decided to

**a.** In *Wilson,* after the jury returned a verdict of guilty, the trial court reconsidered an earlier motion and dismissed the indictment on due process grounds.  The Supreme Court concluded that no double jeopardy concerns were raised by an appeal of that ruling.  An appellate court reversal of the dismissal would not require a new trial since the appellate court could simply reinstate the jury's verdict.  In *Jenkins,* the dismissal was issued by the trial judge, sitting in a bench trial, before the judge reached a verdict.  The trial judge's dismissal order was based on his interpretation of the substantive law, but the judge had not indicated what result he would have reached as the finder of fact if a contrary interpretation had been adopted.  Thus, if the trial judge's order were reversed, further resolution of the facts relating to the elements of the offense would be required.  The *Jenkins* opinion stressed this consequence of appellates reversal rather than the grounding of the trial court's ruling as a possible "acquittal."

overrule *Jenkins,* and thus to reverse the judgment of the Court of Appeals in this case.

\* \* \* At the time the Fifth Amendment was adopted, its principles were easily applied, since most criminal prosecutions proceeded to final judgment, and neither the United States nor the defendant had any right to appeal an adverse verdict. The verdict in such a case was unquestionably final, and could be raised in bar against any further prosecution for the same offense.

\* \* \* It was not until 1889 that Congress permitted criminal defendants to seek a writ of error in this Court, and then only in capital cases. Only then did it become necessary for this Court to deal with the issues presented by the challenge of verdicts on appeal. And, in the very first case presenting the issues, *United States v. Ball,* 163 U.S. 662 (1896), the Court established principles that have been adhered to ever since. Three persons had been tried together for murder; two were convicted, the other acquitted. This Court reversed the convictions, finding the indictment fatally defective, whereupon all three defendants were tried again. This time all three were convicted and they again sought review here. This Court held that the Double Jeopardy Clause precluded further prosecution of the defendant who had been *acquitted* at the original trial but that it posed no such bar to the prosecution of those defendants who had been *convicted* in the earlier proceeding.

\* \* \* These then, at least, are two venerable principles of double jeopardy jurisprudence. The successful appeal of a judgment of conviction, on any ground other than the insufficiency of the evidence to support the verdict, *Burks v. United States* [§ 3, infra], poses no bar to further prosecution on the same charge. A judgment of acquittal, whether based on a jury verdict of not guilty or on a ruling by the court that the evidence is insufficient to convict, may not be appealed and terminates the prosecution when a second trial would be necessitated by a reversal. What may seem superficially to be a disparity in [these] rules governing a defendant's liability to be tried again is explainable by reference to the underlying purposes of the Double Jeopardy Clause. \* \* \* [T]he law attaches particular significance to an acquittal. To permit a second trial after an acquittal, however mistaken the acquittal may have been, would present an unacceptably high risk that the Government, with its vastly superior resources, might wear down the defendant so that "even though innocent, he may be found guilty." *Green v. United States,* 355 U.S. 184 (1957). On the other hand, to require a criminal defendant to stand trial again after he has successfully invoked a statutory right of appeal to upset his first conviction is not an act of governmental oppression of the sort against which the Double Jeopardy Clause was intended to protect. \* \* \*

Although the primary purpose of the Double Jeopardy Clause was to protect the integrity of a final judgment, this Court has also developed a body of law guarding the separate but related interest of a defendant in avoiding multiple prosecutions even where no final determination of guilt or innocence has been made. Such interests may be involved in two different situations: the first, in which the trial judge declares a mistrial; the second, in which the trial judge terminates the proceedings favorably to the defendant on a basis not related to factual guilt or innocence.

\* \* \* In passing on the propriety of a declaration of mistrial granted at the behest of the prosecutor or on the court's own motion, this Court has [applied the *Perez* standard of manifest necessity]. \* \* \* Where, on the other hand, a *defendant* successfully seeks to avoid his trial prior to its conclusion by a motion for mistrial, the Double Jeopardy Clause is not offended by a second prosecution.

* * * Such a motion by the defendant is deemed to be a deliberate election on his part to forego his valued right to have his guilt or innocence determined before the first trier of fact. *United States v. Dinitz* [discussed in *Kennedy*, § ·2 supra]. * * *

We turn now to the relationship between the Double Jeopardy Clause and reprosecution of a defendant who has successfully obtained not a mistrial, but a termination of the trial in his favor before any determination of factual guilt or innocence. Unlike the typical mistrial, the granting of a motion such as this obviously contemplates that the proceedings will terminate then and there in favor of the defendant. The prosecution, if it wishes to reinstate the proceedings in the face of such a ruling, ordinarily must seek reversal of the decision of the trial court. * * *

* * * It is quite true that the Government with all its resources and power should not be allowed to make repeated attempts to convict an individual for an alleged offense. This truth is expressed in the three common-law pleas of *autrefois acquit, autrefois convict,* and pardon, which lie at the core of the area protected by the Double Jeopardy Clause. As we have recognized in cases from *Ball* to *Sanabria v. United States,* 437 U.S. 54 (1978), a defendant once acquitted may not be again subjected to trial without violating the Double Jeopardy Clause.

But that situation is obviously a far cry from the present case, where the Government was quite willing to continue with its production of evidence to show the defendant guilty before the jury first empaneled to try him, but the defendant elected to seek termination of the trial on grounds unrelated to guilt or innocence. This is scarcely a picture of an all-powerful state relentlessly pursuing a defendant who had either been found not guilty or who had at least insisted on having the issue of guilt submitted to the first trier of fact. It is instead a picture of a defendant who chooses to avoid conviction and imprisonment, not because of his assertion that the Government has failed to make out a case against him, but because of a legal claim that the Government's case against him must fail even though it might satisfy the trier of fact that he was guilty beyond a reasonable doubt.

We have previously noted that "the trial judge's characterization of his own action cannot control the classification of the action." * * * [A] defendant is acquitted only when "the ruling of the judge, whatever its label, actually represents a resolution [in the defendant's favor], correct or not, of some or all of the factual elements of the offense charged." Where the court, before the jury returns a verdict, enters [an order entitled] a judgment of acquittal pursuant to Fed.Rule Crim.Proc. 29, appeal will be barred only when "it is plain that the District Court * * * evaluated the Government's evidence and determined that it was legally insufficient to support a conviction." *United States v. Martin Linen Supply Company,* 430 U.S. 564 (1977).

Our opinion in *Burks* [infra] necessarily holds that there has been a "failure of proof" requiring an acquittal when the Government does not submit sufficient evidence to rebut a defendant's essentially factual defense of insanity, though it may otherwise be entitled to have its case submitted to the jury. The defense of insanity, like the defense of entrapment, arises from "the notion that Congress could not have intended criminal punishment for a defendant who has committed all the elements of a proscribed offense," *United States v. Russell* [Ch. 4], where other facts established to the satisfaction of the trier of fact provide a legally adequate justification for otherwise criminal acts. Such a factual finding *does* "necessarily establish the criminal defendant's lack of criminal culpability," post, (Brennan, J., dissenting), under the existing law; the fact that "the acquittal may result from erroneous evidentiary rulings or erroneous interpretations of governing legal principles," ibid., affects the accuracy of that determination, but it does not alter its essential character. By contrast, the dismissal of an indictment for preindictment delay represents a legal judgment that a defendant, although criminally culpable, may not be punished because of a supposed constitutional violation. * * *

[I]n the present case, [defendant] successfully avoided a submission of [a part] * * * of the indictment [to the jury] by persuading the trial court to dismiss it on a basis which did not depend on guilt or innocence. He was thus neither acquitted nor convicted, because he himself successfully undertook to persuade the trial court not to submit the issue of guilt or innocence to the jury which had been empaneled to try him. * * * [Defendant] has not been "deprived" of his valued right to go to the first jury; only the public has been deprived of its valued right to "one complete opportunity to convict those who have violated its laws." *Arizona v. Washington.* No interest protected by the Double Jeopardy Clause is invaded when the Government is allowed to appeal and seek reversal of such a mid-trial termination of the proceedings in a manner favorable to the defendant. * * *

JUSTICE BRENNAN, with whom JUSTICE WHITE, JUSTICE MARSHALL, and JUSTICE STEVENS join, dissenting.

* * * While the Double Jeopardy Clause often has the effect of protecting the accused's interest in the finality of particular favorable determinations, this is not its objective. For the Clause often permits Government appeals from final judgments favorable to the accused. See *United States v. Wilson* (whether or not final judgment was an acquittal, Government may appeal if reversal would not necessitate a retrial). The purpose of the Clause, which the Court today fails sufficiently to appreciate, is to protect the accused against the agony and risks attendant upon undergoing more than one criminal trial for any single offense. * * * Society's "willingness to limit the Government to a single criminal proceeding to vindicate its very vital interest in enforcement of criminal laws" bespeaks society's recognition of the gross unfairness of requiring the accused to undergo the strain and agony of more than one trial for any single offense. *United States v. Jorn,* 400 U.S. 470 (1971). Accordingly, the policies of the Double Jeopardy Clause mandate that the Government be afforded but one complete opportunity to convict an accused and that when the first proceeding terminates in a final judgment favorable to the defendant any retrial be barred. The rule as to acquittals can only be understood as simply an application of this larger principle.

Judgments of acquittal normally result from jury or bench verdicts of not guilty. In such cases, the acquittal represents the factfinder's conclusion that, under the controlling legal principles, the evidence does not establish that the defendant can be convicted of the offense charged in the indictment. But the judgment does not necessarily establish the criminal defendant's lack of criminal culpability; the acquittal may result from erroneous evidentiary rulings or erroneous interpretations of governing legal principles induced by the defense. Yet the Double Jeopardy Clause bars a second trial. * * * The reason is not that the first trial established the defendant's factual innocence, but rather that the second trial would present all the untoward consequences the Clause was designed to prevent. Government would be allowed to seek to persuade a second trier of fact of the defendant's guilt, to strengthen any weaknesses in its first presentation, and to subject the defendant to the expense and anxiety of a second trial.

\* \* \* The whole premise for today's \* \* \* [decision] \* \* \* is the Court's new theory that a criminal defendant who seeks to avoid conviction on a "ground unrelated to factual innocence" somehow stands on a different constitutional footing than a defendant whose participation in his criminal trial creates a situation in which a judgment of acquittal has to be entered. This premise is simply untenable. \* \* \* [T]he reasons that bar a retrial following an acquittal are equally applicable to a final judgment entered on a ground "unrelated to factual innocence." The heavy personal strain of the second trial is the same in either case. So too is the risk that, though innocent, the defendant may be found guilty at a second trial. If the appeal is allowed in either situation, the Government will, following any reversal, not only obtain the benefit of the favorable appellate ruling but also be permitted to shore up any other weak points of its case and obtain all the other advantages at the second trial that the Double Jeopardy Clause was designed to forbid.

Moreover, the Government's interest in retrying a defendant simply cannot vary depending on the ground of the final termination in the accused's favor. I reject as plainly erroneous the Court's suggestion that final judgments not based on innocence deprive the public of "its valued right to 'one complete opportunity to convict those who have violated its laws,'" quoting *Arizona v. Washington,* and therefore differ from "true acquittals." The Government has the same "complete opportunity" in either situation by virtue of its participation as an adversary at the criminal trial.

Equally significant, the distinction between the two is at best purely formal. Many acquittals are the consequence of rulings of law made on the accused's motion that are not related to the question of his factual guilt or innocence: e.g., a ruling on the law respecting the scope of the offense or excluding reliable evidence. \* \* \*

\* \* \* A critical feature of today's holding appears to be the Court's definition of acquittal as "a resolution [in the defendant's favor], correct or not, of some or all of the factual elements of the offense charged," \* \* \*. The language quoted from *Martin Linen Supply Co.,* was tied to the particular issue in that case and was never intended to serve as an all encompassing definition of acquittal for all purposes. Rather, *Martin Linen Supply* referred generally to "acquittal" as "a legal determination on the basis of facts adduced at trial relating to the general issue of the case," and this is the accepted definition. This \* \* \* traditional definition of "acquittal" obviously is responsive to the values protected by the Double Jeopardy Clause. \* \* \*

## BURKS v. UNITED STATES
### 437 U.S. 1, 98 S.Ct. 2141, 57 L.Ed.2d 1 (1978).

CHIEF JUSTICE BURGER delivered the opinion of the Court.

We granted certiorari to resolve the question of whether an accused may be subjected to a second trial when conviction in a prior trial was reversed by an appellate court solely for lack of sufficient evidence to sustain the jury's verdict.

Petitioner Burks was tried in the United States District Court for the crime of robbing a federally insured bank by use of a dangerous weapon \* \* \*. Burks' principal defense was insanity. To prove this claim petitioner produced three expert witnesses who testified, albeit with differing diagnoses of his mental condition, that he suffered from a mental illness at the time of the robbery, which rendered him substantially incapable of conforming his conduct to the requirements of the law.  In rebuttal the Government offered the testimony of two experts, one of whom testified that although petitioner possessed a character disorder, he was not mentally ill.  The other prosecution witness acknowledged a character disorder in petitioner,˙but gave a rather ambiguous answer to the question of whether Burks had been capable of conforming his conduct to the law.  Lay witnesses also testified for the Government, expressing their opinion that petitioner appeared to be capable of normal functioning and was sane at the time of the alleged offense.

Before the case was submitted to the jury, the court denied a motion for a judgment of acquittal.  The jury found Burks guilty as charged.  *  *  * On appeal petitioner narrowed the issues by admitting the affirmative factual elements of the charge against him, leaving only his claim concerning criminal responsibility to be resolved.  With respect to this point, the Court of Appeals agreed with petitioner's claim that the evidence was insufficient to support the verdict and reversed his conviction.  *  *  * [It concluded that] the prosecution's evidence with respect to Burks' mental condition, even when viewed in the light most favorable to the Government, did not "effectively rebu[t]" petitioner's proof with respect to insanity and criminal responsibility.

At this point, the Court of Appeals, rather than terminating the case against petitioner, remanded to the District Court "for a determination of whether a directed verdict of acquittal should be entered or a new trial ordered."  *  *  * [It indicated] that the District Court should choose the appropriate course "from a balancing of the equities,"  *  *  *.  The Court of Appeals assumed it had the power to order this "balancing" remedy by virtue of the fact that Burks had explicitly requested a new trial.  As authority for this holding the court cited, *Bryan v. United States*, 338 U.S. 552 (1950).  *  *  *

Petitioner's argument is straightforward.  He contends that the Court of Appeals' holding was nothing more or less than a decision that the District Court had erred by not granting his motion for a judgment of acquittal.  By implication, he argues, the appellate reversal was the operative equivalent of a district court's judgment of acquittal, entered either before or after verdict.  Petitioner points out, however, that had the District Court found the evidence at the first trial inadequate, as the Court of Appeals said it should have done, a second trial would violate the Double Jeopardy Clause of the Fifth Amendment.  Therefore, he maintains, it makes no difference that the determination of evidentiary insufficiency was made by a *reviewing* court since the double jeopardy considerations are the same, regardless of which court decides that a judgment of acquittal is in order.

The position advanced by petitioner has not been embraced by our prior holdings.  Indeed, as the Court of Appeals here recognized, *Bryan v. United States*, would appear to be contrary.  *  *  * [The Court here discussed *Bryan* at length and noted that *Bryan* and similar rulings had as their "common ancestor, *United States v. Ball*, 163 U.S. 662 (1896).]

*  *  * *United States v. Ball*  *  *  * [therefore] provides a logical starting point for unraveling the conceptual confusion arising from *Bryan* and the cases which have followed in its wake.  This is especially true since *Ball* appears to represent the first instance in which this Court considered in any detail the double jeopardy implications of an appellate reversal.

*Ball* came before the Court twice, the first occasion being on writ of error from federal convictions for murder.  On this initial review, those defendants who had been found guilty obtained a reversal of their convictions due to a fatally defective indictment. On remand after appeal, the trial court dismissed the flawed indictment and proceeded to retry the defendants on a new indictment. They were again convicted and the defendants came once more to this Court, arguing that their second trial was barred because of former jeopardy. The Court rejected this plea in a brief statement:

> "[A] defendant, who procures a judgment against him upon an indictment to be set aside, may be tried anew upon the same indictment, or upon another indictment, for the same offence of which he had been convicted."

The reversal in *Ball* was therefore based not on insufficiency of evidence but rather on trial error, i.e., failure to dismiss a faulty indictment. Moreover, the cases cited as authority by *Ball* were ones involving trial errors.

We have no doubt that *Ball* was correct in allowing a new trial to rectify *trial error*:

> "The principle that [the Double Jeopardy Clause] does not preclude the Government's retrying a defendant whose conviction is set aside because of an *error in the proceedings* leading to conviction is a well-established part of our constitutional jurisprudence." *United States v. Tateo,* 377 U.S. 463 (1964) (emphasis supplied).

As we have seen \* \* \*, the cases which have arisen since *Ball* generally do not distinguish between reversals due to trial error and those resulting from evidentiary insufficiency. We believe, however, that the failure to make this distinction has contributed substantially to the present state of conceptual confusion existing in this area of the law. Consequently, it is important to consider carefully the respective roles of these two types of reversals in double jeopardy analysis.

Various rationales have been advanced to support the policy of allowing retrial to correct trial error, but in our view the most reasonable justification is that advanced by *Tateo*.

> "It would be a high price indeed for society to pay were every accused granted immunity from punishment because of any defect sufficient to constitute reversible error in the proceedings leading to conviction."

In short, reversal for trial error, as distinguished from evidentiary insufficiency, does not constitute a decision to the effect that the government has failed to prove its case. As such, it implies nothing with respect to the guilt or innocence of the defendant. Rather, it is a determination that a defendant has been convicted through a judicial process which is defective in some fundamental respect, e.g., incorrect receipt or rejection of evidence, incorrect instructions, or prosecutorial misconduct. When this occurs, the accused has a strong interest in obtaining a fair readjudication of his guilt free from error, just as society maintains a valid concern for insuring that the guilty are punished.

The same cannot be said when a defendant's conviction has been overturned due to a failure of proof at trial, in which case the prosecution cannot complain of prejudice, for it has been given one fair opportunity to offer whatever proof it could assemble.[10] Moreover, such an appellate reversal means that the government's case was so lacking that it should not have even been *submitted* to the jury. Since we necessarily afford absolute finality to a jury's *verdict* of acquittal—no matter how erroneous its decision—it is difficult to conceive how society has any greater interest in retrying a defendant when, on review, it is decided as

---

**10.** In holding the evidence insufficient to sustain guilt, an appellate court determines that the prosecution has failed to prove guilt beyond a reasonable doubt. See *American Tobacco Co. v. United States,* 328 U.S. 781 (1946).

a matter of law that the jury could not properly have returned a verdict of guilty.

The importance of a reversal on grounds of evidentiary insufficiency for purposes of inquiry under the Double Jeopardy Clause is underscored by the fact that a federal court's role in deciding whether a case should be considered by the jury is quite limited. Even the trial court, which has heard the testimony of witnesses firsthand, is not to weigh the evidence or assess the credibility of witnesses when it judges the merits of a motion for acquittal. The prevailing rule has long been that a district judge is to submit a case to the jury if the evidence and inferences therefrom most favorable to the prosecution would warrant the jury's finding the defendant guilty beyond a reasonable doubt. Obviously a federal appellate court applies no higher a standard; rather, it must sustain the verdict if there is substantial evidence, viewed in the light most favorable to the Government, to uphold the jury's decision. While this is not the appropriate occasion to re-examine in detail the standards for appellate reversal on grounds of insufficient evidence, it is apparent that such a decision will be confined to cases where the prosecution's failure is clear. Given the requirements for entry of a judgment of acquittal, the purposes of the Clause would be negated were we to afford the government an opportunity for the proverbial "second bite at the apple."

In our view it makes no difference that a defendant has sought a new trial as one of his remedies, or even as the sole remedy. It cannot be meaningfully said that a person "waives" his right to a judgment of acquittal by moving for a new trial. * * * Since we hold today that the Double Jeopardy Clause precludes a second trial once the reviewing court has found the evidence legally insufficient, the only "just" remedy available for that court is the direction of a judgment of acquittal. To the extent that our prior decisions suggest that by moving for a new trial, a defendant waives his right to a judgment of acquittal on the basis of evidentiary insufficiency, those cases are overruled. * * *

JUSTICE BLACKMUN took no part in the consideration or decision of this case.[a]

**a.** In Lockhart v. Nelson, 109 S.Ct. 285 (1988), the question presented was "whether the Double Jeopardy Clause allows retrial when a reviewing court determines that a defendant's conviction must be reversed because evidence was erroneously admitted against him, and also concludes that without the inadmissible evidence there was insufficient evidence to support a conviction." The Court concluded that the "logic of *Burks* requires the question to be answered in the negative." The Court reasoned that the situation presented here was "that * * * described in *Burks* as reversal for 'trial error'— the trial court erred in admitting a particular piece of evidence, and without it there was insufficient evidence to support a judgment of conviction. But clearly *with* that evidence, there was enough * * *. It is quite clear from our opinion in *Burks* that a reviewing court must consider all of the evidence admitted by the trial court in deciding whether retrial is permissible under the Double Jeopardy Clause * * *. The basis for the *Burks* exception to the general rule is that a reversal for insufficiency of the evidence should be treated no differently than a trial court's granting a judgment of acquittal at the close of all the evidence. A trial court in passing on such a motion considers all of the evidence it has admitted, and to make the analogy complete it must be this same quantum of evidence which is considered by the reviewing court."

# Chapter 20

# SENTENCING PROCEDURES

Sentencing procedures vary substantially from jurisdiction to jurisdiction. A state's sentencing procedures are determined in part by the structure of the state's sentencing system. That structure may vary both as to who has responsibility for sentencing and how much discretion is granted that sentencer. Apart from capital punishment (where jury sentencing is traditionally used), sentencing authority is usually vested in the judge. A small group of states, however, also employ jury sentencing for non-capital, felony sentencing. Such jury sentencing focuses largely on the nature of the crime. The jury imposes a sentence, within a maximum and minimum set by law, based on the evidence it has heard at trial. It does not have before it the information on the defendant's background that would be developed through the presentence report in a judicial sentencing system or through a sentencing hearing in a capital case. As with its decision on guilt, the jury announces its sentence without explaining its grounding. Moreover, in non-capital jury sentencing, ordinarily no attempt is made to guide the jury's exercise of discretion by offering illustrations of those factors that might justify the choice of one sentence or another within the range allowed by the legislature.

Judicial sentencing, like jury sentencing, starts with legislative direction as to the maximum and minimum sentences allowed. Under an indeterminate sentencing structure, where the sentence is to be incarceration, the legislature requires the court to impose a sentence consisting of both maximum and minimum periods of incarceration, with the parole board determining the actual length of the incarceration within those limits. In such jurisdictions, judges often are given no direction as to choice of sentence within the legislatively prescribed limits, except that there must be a certain gap between the maximum and minimum sentence (e.g., the minimum can be no more than half of the maximum). The judge need not set forth any reason for selecting any particular maximum and minimum nor, where probation is a legislatively allowable alternative, for choosing incarceration over probation.

In recent years, numerous states have moved away from indeterminate sentences, requiring judges choosing incarceration to select a specific term of years. In some of these states, the legislature sets a presumptive sentence that falls between the permissible high and low for the crime. The judge can move the sentence up or down from that presumptive sentence only upon finding that certain aggravating or mitigating circumstances exist. In other jurisdictions, administrative guidelines are used to guide the judge's choice of sentence within the range specified by the legislature. The guidelines take into consideration a variety of factors relating to both the crime and the offender. The judge must

719

first determine which of those factors are present in the particular case so that the case can be placed in its proper category under the guidelines. If the judge then selects a sentence within the guidelines, no further explanation is required. The judge retains discretion, however, to go outside the guidelines, but here the judge must state the reasons for doing so.

Judicial sentencing under a structure calling for indeterminate sentences traditionally carried with it only limited procedural safeguards. The defense had the opportunity to present information that it believed to be relevant to sentencing and the defendant had a right to speak personally to the sentence (a right of "allocution"). The defense did not necessarily know, however, what other information the judge was considering or what factual assessments were being made by the judge in setting the sentence. That additional information came from a presentence report prepared by the probation department, and the defendant was given limited access, if any, to that report. The judge did not have to indicate what factors had been influential in setting the sentence, as the range of relevant considerations was thought to be too broad to require a sentencing judge to pinpoint the importance of any one factor or group of factors.

In recent years, there has been a movement toward more extensive disclosure of the presentence report to the defense, particularly in jurisdictions with presumptive or guideline sentencing. Also, as noted above, judges are required under guideline and presumptive sentencing structures to set forth the grounding of the sentence at least where it differs from the norm. Even here, however, the court's determination that a particular grounding exists is not a product of traditional trial procedures (such as the right of confrontation), and is not governed by traditional trial standards of proof.

Apart from the special setting of capital sentencing, the Supreme Court has spoken on relatively few occasions as to what the Constitution mandates in sentencing procedures. The first case in this chapter, *United States v. Grayson,* is the leading case of recent vintage considering the application of due process standards to non-capital sentencing. The next two cases, *Gardner v. Florida* and *McCleskey v. Kemp,* both involve capital sentencing, but they discuss issues of relevance as well as to non-capital sentencing.

## UNITED STATES v. GRAYSON
438 U.S. 41, 98 S.Ct. 2610, 57 L.Ed.2d 582 (1978).

CHIEF JUSTICE BURGER delivered the opinion of the Court.

We granted certiorari to review a holding of the Court of Appeals that it was improper for a sentencing judge, in fixing the sentence within the statutory limits, to give consideration to the defendant's false testimony observed by the judge during the trial.

In August 1975, respondent Grayson was confined in a federal prison camp under a conviction for distributing a controlled substance. In October, he escaped but was apprehended two days later by FBI agents in New York City. He was indicted for prison escape in violation of 18 U.S.C. § 751(a).

During its case in chief, the United States proved the essential elements of the crime, including his lawful confinement and the unlawful escape. In addition, it presented the testimony of the arresting FBI agents that Grayson, upon being apprehended, denied his true identity.

Grayson testified in his own defense. He admitted leaving the camp but asserted that he did so out of fear: "I had just been threatened with a large stick with a nail protruding through it by an inmate that was serving time at

Allenwood, and I was scared, and I just ran." He testified that the threat was made in the presence of many inmates by prisoner Barnes who sought to enforce collection of a gambling debt and followed other threats and physical assaults made for the same purpose. Grayson called one inmate, who testified: "I heard [Barnes] talk to Grayson in a loud voice one day, but that's all. I never seen no harm, no hands or no shuffling whatsoever."

Grayson's version of the facts was contradicted by the Government's rebuttal evidence and by cross-examination on crucial aspects of his story. For example, Grayson stated that after crossing the prison fence he left his prison jacket by the side of the road. On recross, he stated that he also left his prison shirt but not his trousers. Government testimony showed that on the morning after the escape, a shirt marked with Grayson's number, a jacket, and a pair of prison trousers were found outside a hole in the prison fence.[1] Grayson also testified on cross-examination: "I do believe that I phrased the rhetorical question to Captain Kurd, who was in charge of [the prison], and I think I said something if an inmate was being threatened by somebody, what would * * * he do? First of all he said he would want to know who it was." On further cross-examination, however, Grayson modified his description of the conversation. Captain Kurd testified that Grayson had never mentioned in any fashion threats from other inmates. Finally, the alleged assailant, Barnes, by then no longer an inmate, testified that Grayson had never owed him any money and that he had never threatened or physically assaulted Grayson.

The jury returned a guilty verdict, whereupon the District Judge ordered the United States Probation Office to prepare a presentence report. At the sentencing hearing, the judge stated:

> "I'm going to give my reasons for sentencing in this case with clarity, because one of the reasons may well be considered by a Court of Appeals to be impermissible; and although I could come into this Court Room and sentence this Defendant to a five-year prison term without any explanation at all, I think it is fair that I give the reasons so that if the Court of Appeals feels that one of the reasons which I am about to enunciate is an improper consideration for a trial judge, then the Court will be in a position to reverse this Court and send the case back for re-sentencing.

> "In my view a prison sentence is indicated, and the sentence that the Court is going to impose is to deter you, Mr. Grayson, and others who are similarly situated. Secondly, *it is my view that your defense was a complete fabrication without the slightest merit whatsoever. I feel it is proper for me to consider that fact in the sentencing, and I will do so."* (Emphasis added.)

He then sentenced Grayson to a term of two years' imprisonment, consecutive to his unexpired sentence.

On appeal, a divided panel of the Court of Appeals for the Third Circuit directed that Grayson's sentence be vacated and that he be resentenced by the District Court without consideration of false testimony. * * * We reverse.

---

1. The testimony regarding the prison clothing was important for reasons in addition to the light it shed on quality of recollection. Grayson stated that after unpremeditatedly fleeing the prison with no possessions and crossing the fence, he hitchhiked to New York City—a difficult task for a man with no trousers. The United States suggested that by prearrangement Grayson met someone, possibly a woman friend, on the highway near the break in the fence and that this accomplice provided civilian clothes. It introduced evidence that the friend visited Grayson often at prison, including each of the three days immediately prior to his penultimate day in the camp.

In *Williams v. New York,* 337 U.S. 241 (1949), Mr. Justice Black observed that the "prevalent modern philosophy of penology [is] that the punishment should fit the offender and not merely the crime," and that, accordingly, sentences should be determined with an eye toward the "[r]eformation and rehabilitation of offenders." But it has not always been so. In the early days of the Republic, * * * the period of incarceration was generally prescribed with specificity by the legislature. Each crime had its defined punishment. * * *

Approximately a century ago, a reform movement asserting that the purpose of incarceration, and therefore the guiding consideration in sentencing, should be rehabilitation of the offender, dramatically altered the approach to sentencing. A fundamental proposal of this movement was a flexible sentencing system permitting judges and correctional personnel, particularly the latter, to set the release date of prisoners according to informed judgments concerning their potential for, or actual, rehabilitation and their likely recidivism. * * * Indeterminate sentencing under the rehabilitation model presented sentencing judges with a serious practical problem: how rationally to make the required predictions so as to avoid capricious and arbitrary sentences, which the newly conferred and broad discretion placed within the realm of possibility. An obvious, although only partial, solution was to provide the judge with as much information as reasonably practical concerning the defendant's "character and propensities[,] * * * his present purposes and tendencies," and, indeed, "every aspect of [his] life." *Williams v. New York.* Thus, most jurisdictions provided trained probation officers to conduct presentence investigations of the defendant's life and, on that basis, prepare a presentence report for the sentencing judge.

Constitutional challenges were leveled at judicial reliance on such information, however. In *Williams v. New York,* a jury convicted the defendant of murder but recommended a life sentence. The sentencing judge, partly on the basis of information not known to the jury but contained in a presentence report, imposed the death penalty. The defendant argued that this procedure deprived him of his federal constitutional right to confront and cross-examine those supplying information to the probation officer and, through him, to the sentencing judge. The Court rejected this argument. It noted that traditionally "a sentencing judge could exercise a wide discretion in the sources and types of evidence used to assist him in determining the kind and extent of punishment to be imposed within limits fixed by law." "And modern concepts individualizing punishment have made it all the more necessary that a sentencing judge not be denied an opportunity to obtain pertinent information," indeed, "[t]o deprive sentencing judges of this kind of information would undermine modern penological procedural policies that have been cautiously adopted throughout the nation after careful consideration and experimentation." Accordingly, the sentencing judge was held not to have acted unconstitutionally in considering either the defendant's participation in criminal conduct for which he had not been convicted or information secured by the probation investigator that the defendant was a "menace to society."

Of course, a sentencing judge is not limited to the often far-ranging material compiled in a presentence report. "[B]efore making [the sentencing] determination, a judge may appropriately conduct an inquiry broad in scope, largely unlimited either as to the kind of information he may consider, or the source from which it may come." *United States v. Tucker,* 404 U.S. 443 (1972). Congress recently reaffirmed this fundamental sentencing principle by enacting 18 U.S.C. § 3577:

"No limitation shall be placed on the information concerning the background, character, and conduct of a person convicted of an offense which a court of the United States may receive and consider for the purpose of imposing an appropriate sentence."

Thus, we have acknowledged that a sentencing authority may legitimately consider the evidence heard during trial, as well as the demeanor of the accused. *Chaffin v. Stynchcombe,* 412 U.S. 17 (1973). More to the point presented in this case, one serious study has concluded that the trial judge's "opportunity to observe the defendant, particularly if he chose to take the stand in his defense, can often provide useful insights into an appropriate disposition." ABA Sentencing Alternatives and Procedures § 5.1 (App.Draft 1968).

A defendant's truthfulness or mendacity while testifying on his own behalf, almost without exception, has been deemed probative of his attitudes toward society and prospects for rehabilitation and hence relevant to sentencing. Soon after *Williams* was decided, the Tenth Circuit concluded that "the attitude of a convicted defendant with respect to his willingness to commit a serious crime [perjury] * * * is a proper matter to consider in determining what sentence shall be imposed within the limitations fixed by statute." *Humes v. United States,* 186 F.2d 875 (1951). The Second, Fourth, Fifth, Sixth, Seventh, Eighth, and Ninth Circuits have since agreed. * * * Only one Circuit has directly rejected the probative value of the defendant's false testimony in his own defense. In *Scott v. United States,* 135 U.S.App.D.C. 377 (1969), the court argued that

"the peculiar pressures placed upon a defendant threatened with jail and the stigma of conviction make his willingness to deny the crime an unpromising test of his prospects for rehabilitation if guilty. It is indeed unlikely that many men who commit serious offenses would balk on principle from lying in their own defense. The guilty man may quite sincerely repent his crime but yet, driven by the urge to remain free, may protest his innocence in a court of law."

The *Scott* rationale rests not only on the realism of the psychological pressures on a defendant in the dock—which we can grant—but also on a deterministic view of human conduct that is inconsistent with the underlying precepts of our criminal justice system. A "universal and persistent" foundation stone in our system of law, and particularly in our approach to punishment, sentencing, and incarceration, is the "belief in freedom of the human will and a consequent ability and duty of the normal individual to choose between good and evil." Given that long-accepted view of the "ability and duty of the normal individual to choose," we must conclude that the defendant's readiness to lie under oath—especially when, as here, the trial court finds the lie to be flagrant—may be deemed probative of his prospects for rehabilitation.

Against this background we evaluate Grayson's constitutional argument that the District Court's sentence constitutes punishment for the crime of perjury for which he has not been indicted, tried, or convicted by due process. A second argument is that permitting consideration of perjury will "chill" defendants from exercising their right to testify on their own behalf.

In his due process argument, Grayson does not contend directly that the District Court had an impermissible purpose in considering his perjury and selecting the sentence. Rather, he argues that this Court, in order to preserve due process rights, not only must prohibit the impermissible sentencing practice of incarcerating for the purpose of saving the Government the burden of bringing a separate and subsequent perjury prosecution but also must prohibit the otherwise *permissible* practice of considering a defendant's untruthfulness for the purpose of illuminating his need for rehabilitation and society's need for protection. He presents two interrelated reasons. The effect of both permissible and impermissible sentencing practices may be the same: additional time in prison. Further, it is virtually impossible, he contends, to identify and establish the impermissible practice. We find these reasons insufficient justification for prohibiting what the Court and the Congress have declared appropriate judicial conduct.

First, the evolutionary history of sentencing, set out [above] * * *, demonstrates that it is proper—indeed, even necessary for the rational exercise of discretion—to consider the defendant's whole person and personality, as manifested by his conduct at trial and his testimony under oath, for whatever light those may shed on the sentencing decision. * * * Second, in our view, *Williams* fully supports consideration of such conduct in sentencing. There the Court permitted the sentencing judge to consider the offender's history of prior antisocial conduct, including burglaries for which he had not been duly convicted. * * * Third, the efficacy of Grayson's suggested "exclusionary rule" is open to serious doubt. No rule of law, even one garbed in constitutional terms, can prevent improper use of firsthand observations of perjury. The integrity of the judges, and their fidelity to their oaths of office, necessarily provide the only, and in our view adequate, assurance against that.

Grayson's argument that judicial consideration of his conduct at trial impermissibly "chills" a defendant's statutory right, 18 U.S.C. § 3481, and perhaps a constitutional right, to testify on his own behalf is without basis. The right guaranteed by law to a defendant is narrowly the right to testify truthfully in accordance with the oath—unless we are to say that the oath is mere ritual without meaning. This view of the right involved is confirmed by the unquestioned constitutionality of perjury statutes, which punish those who willfully give false testimony. Further support for this is found in an important limitation on a defendant's right to the assistance of counsel: Counsel ethically cannot assist his client in presenting what the attorney has reason to believe is false testimony. Assuming, *arguendo,* that the sentencing judge's consideration of defendant's untruthfulness in testifying has any chilling effect on a defendant's decision to testify falsely, that effect is entirely permissible. There is no protected right to commit perjury.

Grayson's further argument that the sentencing practice challenged here will inhibit exercise of the right to testify truthfully is entirely frivolous. That argument misapprehends the nature and scope of the practice we find permissible. Nothing we say today requires a sentencing judge to enhance, in some wooden or reflex fashion, the sentences of all defendants whose testimony is deemed false. Rather, we are reaffirming the authority of a sentencing judge to evaluate carefully a defendant's testimony on the stand, determine—with a consciousness of the frailty of human judgment—whether that testimony contained willful and material falsehoods, and, if so, assess in light of all the other knowledge gained about the defendant the meaning of that conduct with respect to his prospects for rehabilitation and restoration to a useful place in society. Awareness of such a process realistically cannot be deemed to affect the decision of an accused but unconvicted defendant to testify truthfully in his own behalf. * * *

JUSTICE STEWART, with whom JUSTICE BRENNAN and JUSTICE MARSHALL join, dissenting.

The Court begins its consideration of this case with the assumption that the respondent gave false testimony at his trial. But there has been no determination that his testimony was false. This respondent was given a greater sentence than he would otherwise have received—how much greater we have no way of knowing—solely because a single judge *thought* that he had not testified truthfully.[1] In essence, the Court holds today that *whenever* a defendant testifies in his own behalf and is found guilty, he opens himself to the possibility of an enhanced sentence. Such a sentence is nothing more or less than a penalty imposed on the defendant's exercise of his constitutional and statutory rights to plead not guilty and to testify in his own behalf.

It does not change matters to say that the enhanced sentence merely reflects the defendant's "prospects for rehabilitation" rather than an additional punishment for testifying falsely.[3] The fact remains that all defendants who choose to testify, and only those who do so, face the very real prospect of a greater sentence based upon the trial judge's unreviewable perception that the testimony was untruthful. The Court prescribes no limitations or safeguards to minimize a defendant's rational fear that his truthful testimony will be perceived as false. Indeed, encumbrance of the sentencing process with the collateral inquiries necessary to provide such assurance would be both pragmatically unworkable and theoretically inconsistent with the assumption that the trial judge is merely considering one more piece of information in his overall evaluation of the defendant's prospects for rehabilitation. But without such safeguards I fail to see how the Court can dismiss as "frivolous" the argument that this sentencing practice will "inhibit exercise of the right to testify truthfully." * * *

The minimal contribution that the defendant's possibly untruthful testimony might make to an overall assessment of his potential for rehabilitation, see n. 3, cannot justify imposing this additional burden on his right to testify in his own behalf. I do not believe that a sentencing judge's discretion to consider a wide range of information in arriving at an appropriate sentence, *Williams v. New York,* allows him to mete out additional punishment to the defendant simply because of his personal belief that the defendant did not testify truthfully at the trial. Accordingly, I would affirm the judgment of the Court of Appeals.

## GARDNER v. FLORIDA

430 U.S. 349, 97 S.Ct. 1197, 51 L.Ed.2d 393 (1977).

JUSTICE STEVENS announced the judgment of the Court and delivered an opinion, in which JUSTICE STEWART and JUSTICE POWELL joined.

Petitioner was convicted of first-degree murder and sentenced to death. When the trial judge imposed the death sentence he stated that he was relying

---

1. We know this only because of the trial judge's laudable explication of his reasons for imposing the sentence in this case. In many cases it would be impossible to discern whether a sentencing judge had been influenced by his belief that the defendant had not testified truthfully, since there is no requirement that reasons be given. But that fact does not argue against correcting an erroneous sentencing policy that is apparent on the face of the record. * * *

3. Indeed, without doubting the sincerity of trial judges one may doubt whether the single incident of a defendant's trial testimony could ever alter the assessment of rehabilita-

tive prospects so drastically as to justify a perceptibly greater sentence. A sentencing judge has before him a presentence report, compiled by trained personnel, that is designed to paint as complete a picture of the defendant's life and character as is possible. If the defendant's suspected perjury is consistent with the evaluation of the report, its impact on the rehabilitative assessment must be minimal. If, on the other hand, it suggests such a markedly different character that different sentencing treatment seems appropriate, the defendant is *effectively* being punished for perjury without even the barest rudiments of due process.

in part on information in a presentence investigation report. Portions of the report were not disclosed to counsel for the parties. Without reviewing the confidential portion of the presentence report, the Supreme Court of Florida, over the dissent of two justices, affirmed the death sentence. We conclude that this procedure does not satisfy the constitutional command that no person shall be deprived of life without due process of law.

On June 30, 1973, the petitioner assaulted his wife with a blunt instrument, causing her death. On January 10, 1974, after a trial in the Circuit Court of Citrus County, Fla., a jury found him guilty of first-degree murder. The separate sentencing hearing required by Florida law in capital cases was held later on the same day. The State merely introduced two photographs of the decedent, otherwise relying on the trial testimony. That testimony, if credited, was sufficient to support a finding of one of the statutory aggravating circumstances, that the felony committed by petitioner "was especially heinous, atrocious, or cruel." In mitigation petitioner testified that he had consumed a vast quantity of alcohol during a day-long drinking spree which preceded the crime, and professed to have almost no recollection of the assault itself. His testimony, if credited, was sufficient to support a finding of at least one of the statutory mitigating circumstances.

After the jury retired to deliberate, the judge announced that he was going to order a presentence investigation of petitioner. Twenty-five minutes later the jury returned its advisory verdict. It expressly found that the mitigating circumstances outweighed the aggravating circumstances and advised the court to impose a life sentence.

The presentence investigation report was completed by the Florida Parole and Probation Commission on January 28, 1974. On January 30, 1974, the trial judge entered findings of fact and a judgment sentencing petitioner to death. His ultimate finding was that the felony "was especially heinous, atrocious or cruel; and that such aggravating circumstances outweighs the mitigating circumstance, to-wit: none." As a preface to that ultimate finding, he recited that his conclusion was based on the evidence presented at both stages of the bifurcated proceeding, the arguments of counsel, and his review of "the factual information contained in said pre-sentence investigation."

There is no dispute about the fact that the presentence investigation report contained a confidential portion which was not disclosed to defense counsel. Although the judge noted in his findings of fact that the State and petitioner's counsel had been given "a copy of that portion [of the report] to which they are entitled," counsel made no request to examine the full report or to be apprised of the contents of the confidential portion. The trial judge did not comment on the contents of the confidential portion. His findings do not indicate that there was anything of special importance in the undisclosed portion, or that there was any reason other than customary practice for not disclosing the entire report to the parties. * * *

The State places its primary reliance on this Court's landmark decision in *Williams v. New York,* 337 U.S. 241 (1949). In that case, as in this, the trial judge rejected the jury's recommendation of mercy and imposed the death sentence in reliance, at least in part, on material contained in a report prepared by the court's probation department. * * * Mr. Justice Black's opinion for the Court [in *Williams*] persuasively reasons why material developed in a presentence investigation may be useful to a sentencing judge, and why it may not be unfair to a defendant to rely on such information even if it would not be admissible in a normal adversary proceeding in open court. We consider the relevance of that reasoning to this case [later in] this opinion. Preliminarily, however, we note two comments by Mr. Justice Black that make it clear that the *holding* of *Williams* is not directly applicable to this case.

It is first significant that in *Williams* the material facts concerning the defendant's background which were contained in the presentence report were described in detail by the trial judge in open court. Referring to this material, Mr. Justice Black noted:

> "The accuracy of the statements made by the judge as to appellant's background and past practices was not challenged by appellant or his counsel, nor was the judge asked to disregard any of them or to afford appellant a chance to refute or discredit any of them by cross-examination or otherwise."

In contrast, in the case before us, the trial judge did not state on the record the substance of any information in the confidential portion of the presentence report that he might have considered material. There was, accordingly, no similar opportunity for petitioner's counsel to challenge the accuracy or materiality of any such information.

It is also significant that Mr. Justice Black's opinion recognized that the passage of time justifies a re-examination of capital-sentencing procedures. As he pointed out:

> "This whole country has traveled far from the period in which the death sentence was an automatic and commonplace result of convictions—even for offenses today deemed trivial."

Since that sentence was written almost 30 years ago, this Court has acknowledged its obligation to re-examine capital-sentencing procedures against evolving standards of procedural fairness in a civilized society.

In 1949, when the *Williams* case was decided, no significant constitutional difference between the death penalty and lesser punishments for crime had been expressly recognized by this Court. At that time the Court assumed that after a defendant was convicted of a capital offense, like any other offense, a trial judge had complete discretion to impose any sentence within the limits prescribed by the legislature. As long as the judge stayed within those limits, his sentencing discretion was essentially unreviewable and the possibility of error was remote, if, indeed, it existed at all. In the intervening years there have been two constitutional developments which require us to scrutinize a State's capital-sentencing procedures more closely than was necessary in 1949.

First, five Members of the Court have now expressly recognized that death is a different kind of punishment from any other which may be imposed in this country. * * * From the point of view of the defendant, it is different in both its severity and its finality. From the point of view of society, the action of the sovereign in taking the life of one of its citizens also differs dramatically from any other legitimate state action. It is of vital importance to the defendant and to the community that any decision to impose the death sentence be, and appear to be, based on reason rather than caprice or emotion.

Second, it is now clear that the sentencing process, as well as the trial itself, must satisfy the requirements of the Due Process Clause. Even though the defendant has no substantive right to a particular sentence within the range authorized by statute, the sentencing is a critical stage of the criminal proceeding at which he is entitled to the effective assistance of counsel. *Mempa v. Rhay*, 389 U.S. 128 (1967). The defendant has a legitimate interest in the character of the procedure which leads to the imposition of sentence even if he may have no right to object to a particular result of the sentencing process.

In the light of these developments we consider the justifications offered by the State for a capital-sentencing procedure which permits a trial judge to impose the death sentence on the basis of confidential information which is not disclosed to the defendant or his counsel.

The State first argues that an assurance of confidentiality to potential sources of information is essential to enable investigators to obtain relevant but sensitive disclosures from persons unwilling to comment publicly about a defendant's background or character. The availability of such information, it is argued, provides the person who prepares the report with greater detail on which to base a sentencing recommendation and, in turn, provides the judge with a better basis for his sentencing decision. But consideration must be given to the quality, as well as the quantity, of the information on which the sentencing judge may rely. Assurances of secrecy are conducive to the transmission of confidences which may bear no closer relation to fact than the average rumor or item of gossip, and may imply a pledge not to attempt independent verification of the information received. The risk that some of the information accepted in confidence may be erroneous, or may be misinterpreted, by the investigator or by the sentencing judge, is manifest.

If, as the State argues, it is important to use such information in the sentencing process, we must assume that in some cases it will be decisive in the judge's choice between a life sentence and a death sentence. If it tends to tip the scales in favor of life, presumably the information would be favorable and there would be no reason why it should not be disclosed. On the other hand, if it is the basis for a death sentence, the interest in reliability plainly outweighs the State's interest in preserving the availability of comparable information in other cases.

The State also suggests that full disclosure of the presentence report will unnecessarily delay the proceeding. We think the likelihood of significant delay is overstated because we must presume that reports prepared by professional probation officers, as the Florida procedure requires, are generally reliable. In those cases in which the accuracy of a report is contested, the trial judge can avoid delay by disregarding the disputed material. Or if the disputed matter is of critical importance, the time invested in ascertaining the truth would surely be well spent if it makes the difference between life and death.

The State further urges that full disclosure of presentence reports, which often include psychiatric and psychological evaluations, will occasionally disrupt the process of rehabilitation. The argument, if valid, would hardly justify withholding the report from defense counsel. Moreover, whatever force that argument may have in noncapital cases, it has absolutely no merit in a case in which the judge has decided to sentence the defendant to death. Indeed, the extinction of all possibility of rehabilitation is one of the aspects of the death sentence that makes it different in kind from any other sentence a State may legitimately impose. * * *

Even if it were permissible to withhold a portion of the report from a defendant, and even from defense counsel, pursuant to an express finding of good cause for nondisclosure, it would nevertheless be necessary to make the full report a part of the record to be reviewed on appeal. Since the State must administer its capital-sentencing procedures with an even hand, it is important that the record on appeal disclose to the reviewing court the considerations which motivated the death sentence in every case in which it is imposed.

Without full disclosure of the basis for the death sentence, the Florida capital-sentencing procedure would be subject to the defects which resulted in the holding of unconstitutionality in *Furman v. Georgia.*[a] In this particular case, the only explanation for the lack of disclosure is the failure of defense counsel to request access to the full report. That failure cannot justify the submission of a less complete record to the reviewing court than the record on which the trial judge based his decision to sentence petitioner to death.

Nor do we regard this omission by counsel as an effective waiver of the constitutional error in the record. There are five reasons for this conclusion. First, the State does not urge that the objection has been waived. Second, the Florida Supreme Court has held that it has a duty to consider "the total record" when it reviews a death sentence. Third, since two members of that court expressly considered this point on the appeal in this case, we presume that the entire court passed on the question. Fourth, there is no basis for presuming that the defendant himself made a knowing and intelligent waiver, or that counsel could possibly have made a tactical decision not to examine the full report. Fifth, since the judge found, in disagreement with the jury, that the evidence did not establish any mitigating circumstance, and since the presentence report was the only item considered by the judge but not by the jury, the full review of the factual basis for the judge's rejection of the advisory verdict is plainly required. For if the jury, rather than the judge, correctly assessed the petitioner's veracity, the death sentence rests on an erroneous factual predicate.

We conclude that petitioner was denied due process of law when the death sentence was imposed, at least in part, on the basis of information which he had no opportunity to deny or explain. * * *

THE CHIEF JUSTICE concurs in the judgment.

JUSTICE WHITE, concurring in the judgment.

In *Woodson v. North Carolina,* 428 U.S. 280 (1976), the Court addressed the question whether the mandatory death penalty imposed under the statute involved in that case was consistent with the *Eighth Amendment's* prohibition against cruel and unusual punishments. The plurality opinion stated * * *:

> "[W]e believe that in *capital cases* the fundamental respect for humanity underlying the *Eighth Amendment,* requires consideration of the character and record of the individual offender and the circumstances of the particular offense as a constitutionally indispensable part of the *process* of inflicting the penalty of death. This conclusion rests squarely on the predicate that the penalty of death is qualitatively different from a sentence of imprisonment, however long. * * * Because of that qualitative difference, there is a corresponding difference *in the need for reliability in the determination that death is the appropriate punishment in a specific case.*" (Emphasis added.)
> * * *

Here the sentencing judge indicated that he selected petitioner Gardner for the death penalty in part because of information contained in a presentence report which information was not disclosed to petitioner or to his counsel and to which petitioner had no opportunity to respond. A procedure for selecting people for the death penalty which permits consideration of such secret information relevant to the "character and record of the individual offender," fails to meet the "need for reliability in the determination that death is the appropriate punishment" which the Court indicated was required in *Woodson.* This conclusion

---

**a.** *Furman* is discussed infra in *McCleskey v. Kemp.*

stems solely from the Eighth Amendment's ban on cruel and unusual punishments on which the *Woodson* decision expressly rested, and my conclusion is limited, as was *Woodson*, to cases in which the death penalty is imposed. I thus see no reason to address in this case the possible application to sentencing proceedings—in death or other cases—of the Due Process Clause, other than as the vehicle by which the strictures of the Eighth Amendment are triggered in this case. For these reasons, I do not join the plurality opinion but concur in the judgment.

JUSTICE BLACKMUN, concurring in the judgment.

Given the judgments of the Court in *Woodson v. North Carolina*, 428 U.S. 280 (1976), and in *Roberts v. Louisiana*, 428 U.S. 325 (1976), * * * I concur in the judgment the Court reaches in the present case.

JUSTICE BRENNAN.

I agree for the reasons stated in the plurality opinion that the Due Process Clause of the Fourteenth Amendment is violated when a defendant facing a death sentence is not informed of the contents of a presentence investigation report made to the sentencing judge. However, I adhere to my view that the death penalty is in all circumstances cruel and unusual punishment prohibited by the Eighth and Fourteenth Amendments. * * * I therefore would vacate the death sentence, and I dissent from the Court's judgment insofar as it remands for further proceedings that could lead to its imposition.

JUSTICE MARSHALL dissenting.

Last Term, this Court carefully scrutinized the Florida procedures for imposing the death penalty and concluded that there were sufficient safeguards to insure that the death sentence would not be "wantonly" and "freakishly" imposed. *Proffitt v. Florida*, 428 U.S. 242 (1976). This case, however, belies that hope. While I continue to believe that the death penalty is unconstitutional in all circumstances, and therefore would remand this case for resentencing to a term of life, nevertheless, now that Florida may legally take a life, we must insist that it be in accordance with the standards enunciated by this Court. In this case I am appalled at the extent to which Florida has deviated from the procedures upon which this Court expressly relied. It is not simply that the trial judge, in overriding the jury's recommendation of life imprisonment, relied on undisclosed portions of the presentence report. Nor is it merely that the Florida Supreme Court affirmed the sentence without discussing the omission and without concern that it did not even have the entire report before it. Obviously that alone is enough to deny due process and require that the death sentence be vacated as the Court now holds. But the blatant disregard exhibited by the courts below for the standards devised to regulate imposition of the death penalty calls into question the very basis for this Court's approval of that system in *Proffitt*. * * *

JUSTICE REHNQUIST, dissenting.

Had I joined the plurality opinion in last Term's *Woodson v. North Carolina*, I would join the concurring opinion of my Brother White in this case. But if capital punishment is not cruel and unusual under the Eighth and Fourteenth Amendments, as the Court held in that case, the use of particular sentencing procedures, never previously held unfair under the Due Process Clause, in a case where the death sentence is imposed cannot convert that sentence into a cruel and unusual punishment. The prohibition of the Eighth Amendment relates to the character of the punishment, and not to the process by which it is imposed. I would therefore affirm the judgment of the Supreme Court of Florida.

# McCLESKEY v. KEMP

481 U.S. 279, 107 S.Ct. 1756, 95 L.Ed.2d 262 (1987).

JUSTICE POWELL delivered the opinion of the Court.

This case presents the question whether a complex statistical study that indicates a risk that racial considerations enter into capital sentencing determinations proves that petitioner McCleskey's capital sentence is unconstitutional under the Eighth or Fourteenth Amendment.

McCleskey, a black man, was convicted of two counts of armed robbery and one count of murder in the Superior Court of Fulton County, Georgia, on October 12, 1978. McCleskey's convictions arose out of the robbery of a furniture store and the killing of a white police officer during the course of the robbery. The evidence at trial indicated that McCleskey and three accomplices planned and carried out the robbery. * * * During the course of the robbery, a police officer, answering a silent alarm, entered the store through the front door. As he was walking down the center aisle of the store, two shots were fired. Both struck the officer. One hit him in the face and killed him. * * * At trial, the State introduced evidence that at least one of the bullets that struck the officer was fired from a .38 caliber Rossi revolver. This description matched the description of the gun that McCleskey had carried during the robbery. The State also introduced the testimony of two witnesses who had heard McCleskey admit to the shooting.

The jury convicted McCleskey of murder. At the penalty hearing, the jury heard arguments as to the appropriate sentence. Under Georgia law, the jury could not consider imposing the death penalty unless it found beyond a reasonable doubt that the murder was accompanied by one of the statutory aggravating circumstances. The jury in this case found two aggravating circumstances to exist beyond a reasonable doubt: the murder was committed during the course of an armed robbery, and the murder was committed upon a peace officer engaged in the performance of his duties, * * * The jury recommended that he be sentenced to death on the murder charge and to consecutive life sentences on the armed robbery charges. The court followed the jury's recommendation and sentenced McCleskey to death.

On appeal, the Supreme Court of Georgia affirmed the convictions and the sentences. This Court denied a petition for a writ of certiorari. The Superior Court of Fulton County denied McCleskey's extraordinary motion for a new trial. McCleskey then filed a petition for a writ of habeas corpus in the Superior Court of Butts County. After holding an evidentiary hearing, the Superior Court denied relief. The Supreme Court of Georgia denied McCleskey's application for a certificate of probable cause to appeal * * * and this Court again denied certiorari.

McCleskey next filed a petition for a writ of habeas corpus in the federal District Court for the Northern District of Georgia. His petition raised 18 claims, one of which was that the Georgia capital sentencing process is administered in a racially discriminatory manner in violation of the Eighth and Fourteenth Amendments to the United States Constitution. In support of his claim, McCleskey proffered a statistical study performed by Professors David C. Baldus, George Woodworth, and Charles Pulaski (the Baldus study) that purports to show a disparity in the imposition of the death sentence in Georgia based on the race of the murder victim and, to a lesser extent, the race of the defendant. The Baldus study is actually two sophisticated statistical studies that examine over 2,000 murder cases that occurred in Georgia during the 1970s. The raw numbers collected by Professor Baldus indicate that defendants charged with killing white persons received the death penalty in 11% of the cases, but defendants charged with killing blacks received the death penalty in only 1% of the cases. The raw numbers also indicate a reverse racial disparity according to the race of the defendant: 4% of the black defendants received the death penalty, as opposed to 7% of the white defendants.

Baldus also divided the cases according to the combination of the race of the defendant and the race of the victim. He found that the death penalty was assessed in 22% of the cases involving black defendants and white victims; 8% of the cases involving white defendants and white victims; 1% of the cases involving black defendants and black victims; and 3% of the cases involving white defendants and black victims. Similarly, Baldus found that prosecutors sought the death penalty in 70% of the cases involving black defendants and white victims; 32% of the cases involving white defendants and white victims; 15% of the cases involving black defendants and black victims; and 19% of the cases involving white defendants and black victims.

Baldus subjected his data to an extensive analysis, taking account of 230 variables that could have explained the disparities on nonracial grounds. One of his models concludes that, even after taking account of 39 nonracial variables, defendants charged with killing white victims were 4.3 times as likely to receive a death sentence as defendants charged with killing blacks. According to this model, black defendants were 1.1 times as likely to receive a death sentence as other defendants. Thus, the Baldus study indicates that black defendants, such as McCleskey, who kill white victims have the greatest likelihood of receiving the death penalty.

The District Court held an extensive evidentiary hearing on McCleskey's petition. * * * [That] court found that the methodology of the Baldus study was flawed in several respects.[6] * * * It dismissed the petition. The Court of Appeals for the Eleventh Circuit, sitting en banc, * * * assumed the validity of the study itself and addressed the merits of McCleskey's Eighth and Fourteenth Amendment claims. That is, the court assumed that the study "showed that systematic and substantial disparities existed in the penalties imposed upon homicide defendants in Georgia based on race of the homicide victim, that the disparities existed at a less substantial rate in death sentencing based on race of

---

**6.** Baldus, among other experts, testified at the evidentiary hearing. The District Court "was impressed with the learning of all of the experts." Nevertheless, the District Court noted that in many respects the data were incomplete. In its view, the questionnaires used to obtain the data failed to capture the full degree of the aggravating or mitigating circumstances. The Court criticized the researcher's decisions regarding unknown variables. The researchers could not discover whether penalty trials were held in many of the cases, thus undercutting the value of the study's statistics as to prosecutorial decisions. In certain cases, the study lacked information on the race of the victim in cases involving multiple victims, on whether or not the prosecutor offered a plea bargain, and on credibility problems with witnesses. The court concluded that McCleskey had failed to establish by a preponderance of the evidence that the data was trustworthy. * * *

The District Court noted other problems with Baldus' methodology. First, the researchers assumed that all of the information available from the questionnaires was available to the juries and prosecutors when the case was tried. The court found this assumption "questionable." Second, the court noted the instability of the various models. Even with the 230-variable model, consideration of 20 further variables caused a significant drop in the statistical significance of race. In the court's view, this undermined the persuasiveness of the model that showed the greatest racial disparity, the 39-variable model. Third, the court found that the high correlation between race and many of the nonracial variables diminished the weight to which the study was entitled. * * * Finally, the District Court noted the inability of any of the models to predict the outcome of actual cases.

defendants, and that the factors of race of the victim and defendant were at work in Fulton County." Even assuming the study's validity, the Court of Appeals found the statistics "insufficient to demonstrate discriminatory intent or unconstitutional discrimination in the Fourteenth Amendment context, [and] insufficient to show irrationality, arbitrariness and capriciousness under any kind of Eighth Amendment analysis." * * *

McCleskey's first claim is that the Georgia capital punishment statute violates the Equal Protection Clause of the Fourteenth Amendment.[7] He argues that race has infected the administration of Georgia's statute in two ways: persons who murder whites are more likely to be sentenced to death than persons who murder blacks, and black murderers are more likely to be sentenced to death than white murderers.[8] As a black defendant who killed a white victim, McCleskey claims that the Baldus study demonstrates that he was discriminated against because of his race and because of the race of his victim. In its broadest form, McCleskey's claim of discrimination extends to every actor in the Georgia capital sentencing process, from the prosecutor who sought the death penalty and the jury that imposed the sentence, to the State itself that enacted the capital punishment statute and allows it to remain in effect despite its allegedly discriminatory application. We agree with the Court of Appeals, and every other court that has considered such a challenge, that this claim must fail.

* * * [T]o prevail under the Equal Protection Clause, McCleskey must prove that the decisionmakers in *his* case acted with discriminatory purpose. He offers no evidence specific to his own case that would support an inference that racial considerations played a part in his sentence. Instead, he relies solely on the Baldus study. McCleskey argues that the Baldus study compels an inference that his sentence rests on purposeful discrimination. McCleskey's claim that these statistics are sufficient proof of discrimination, without regard to the facts of a particular case, would extend to all capital cases in Georgia, at least where the victim was white and the defendant is black.

The Court has accepted statistics as proof of intent to discriminate in certain limited contexts. First, this Court has accepted statistical disparities as proof of an equal protection violation in the selection of the jury venire in a particular district. * * * Second, this Court has accepted statistics in the form of multiple regression analysis to prove statutory violations under Title VII [employment discrimination].

**7.** Although the District Court rejected the findings of the Baldus study as flawed, the Court of Appeals assumed that the study is valid and reached the constitutional issues. Accordingly, those issues are before us. As did the Court of Appeals, we assume the study is valid statistically without reviewing the factual findings of the District Court. * * *

**8.** Although McCleskey has standing to claim that he suffers discrimination because of his own race, the State argues that he has no standing to contend that he was discriminated against on the basis of his victim's race. While it is true that we are reluctant to recognize "standing to assert the rights of third persons," this does not appear to be the nature of McCleskey's claim. He does not seek to assert some right of his victim, or the rights

of black murder victims in general. Rather, McCleskey argues that application of the State's statute has created a classification that is "an irrational exercise of governmental power," because it is not "necessary to the accomplishment of some permissible state objective." *Loving v. Virginia*, 388 U.S. 1 (1967). See *McGowan v. Maryland*, 366 U.S. 420 (1961) (statutory classification cannot be "wholly irrelevant to the achievement of the State's objective"). It would violate the Equal Protection Clause for a State to base enforcement of its criminal laws on "an unjustifiable standard such as race, religion, or other arbitrary classification." *Oyler v. Boles*, 368 U.S. 448 (1962). Because McCleskey raises such a claim, he has standing.

But the nature of the capital sentencing decision, and the relationship of the statistics to that decision, are fundamentally different from the corresponding elements in the venire-selection or Title VII cases. Most importantly, each particular decision to impose the death penalty is made by a petit jury selected from a properly constituted venire. Each jury is unique in its composition, and the Constitution requires that its decision rest on consideration of innumerable factors that vary according to the characteristics of the individual defendant and the facts of the particular capital offense. Thus, the application of an inference drawn from the general statistics to a specific decision in a trial and sentencing simply is not comparable to the application of an inference drawn from general statistics to a specific venire-selection or Title VII case. In those cases, the statistics relate to fewer entities,[14] and fewer variables are relevant to the challenged decisions.[15]

Another important difference between the cases in which we have accepted statistics as proof of discriminatory intent and this case is that, in the venire-selection and Title VII contexts, the decisionmaker has an opportunity to explain the statistical disparity. Here, the State has no practical opportunity to rebut the Baldus study. "[C]ontrolling considerations of * * * public policy," dictate that jurors "cannot be called * * * to testify to the motives and influences that led to their verdict." Similarly, the policy considerations behind a prosecutor's traditionally "wide discretion" suggest the impropriety of our requiring prosecutors to defend their decisions to seek death penalties, "often years after they were made."[17] Moreover, absent far stronger proof, it is unnecessary to seek such a rebuttal, because a legitimate and unchallenged explanation for the decision is apparent from the record: McCleskey committed an act for which the United States Constitution and Georgia laws permit imposition of the death penalty.

**14.** We refer here not to the number of entities involved in any particular decision, but to the number of entities whose decisions necessarily are reflected in a statistical display such as the Baldus study. The decisions of a jury commission or of an employer over time are fairly attributable to the commission or the employer. Therefore, an unexplained statistical discrepancy can be said to indicate a consistent policy of the decisionmaker. The Baldus study seeks to deduce a state "policy" by studying the combined effects of the decisions of hundreds of juries that are unique in their composition. It is incomparably more difficult to deduce a consistent policy by studying the decisions of these many unique entities. It is also questionable whether any consistent policy can be derived by studying the decisions of prosecutors. The District Attorney is elected by the voters in a particular county. Since decisions whether to prosecute and what to charge necessarily are individualized and involve infinite factual variations, coordination among DA offices across a State would be relatively meaningless. Thus, any inference from state-wide statistics to a prosecutorial "policy" is of doubtful relevance. Moreover, the statistics in Fulton County alone represent the disposition of far fewer cases than the state-wide statistics. Even assuming the statistical validity of the Baldus study as a whole, the weight to be given the results gleaned from this small sample is limited.

**15.** In venire-selection cases, the factors that may be considered [i.e., the qualifications for jury service] are limited, usually by state statute. * * * These considerations are uniform for all potential jurors, and although some factors may be said to be subjective, they are limited and, to a great degree, objectively verifiable. While employment decisions may involve a number of relevant variables, these variables are to a great extent uniform for all employees because they must all have a reasonable relationship to the employee's qualifications to perform the particular job at issue. Identifiable qualifications for a single job provide a common standard by which to assess each employee. In contrast, a capital sentencing jury may consider *any* factor relevant to the defendant's background, character, and the offense. There is no common standard by which to evaluate all defendants who have or have not received the death penalty.

**17.** Requiring a prosecutor to rebut a study that analyzes the past conduct of scores of prosecutors is quite different from requiring a prosecutor to rebut a contemporaneous challenge to his own acts. See *Batson v. Kentucky* [Ch. 15, § 2].

Finally, McCleskey's statistical proffer must be viewed in the context of his challenge. McCleskey challenges decisions at the heart of the State's criminal justice system. "[O]ne of society's most basic tasks is that of protecting the lives of its citizens and one of the most basic ways in which it achieves the task is through criminal laws against murder." Implementation of these laws necessarily requires discretionary judgments. Because discretion is essential to the criminal justice process, we would demand exceptionally clear proof before we would infer that the discretion has been abused. The unique nature of the decisions at issue in this case also counsel against adopting such an inference from the disparities indicated by the Baldus study. Accordingly, we hold that the Baldus study is clearly insufficient to support an inference that any of the decisionmakers in McCleskey's case acted with discriminatory purpose.

McCleskey also suggests that the Baldus study proves that the State as a whole has acted with a discriminatory purpose. He appears to argue that the State has violated the Equal Protection Clause by adopting the capital punishment statute and allowing it to remain in force despite its allegedly discriminatory application. * * * For this claim to prevail, McCleskey would have to prove that the Georgia Legislature enacted or maintained the death penalty statute *because of* an anticipated racially discriminatory effect. In *Gregg v. Georgia,* 428 U.S. 153 (1976), this Court found that the Georgia capital sentencing system could operate in a fair and neutral manner. There was no evidence then, and there is none now, that the Georgia Legislature enacted the capital punishment statute to further a racially discriminatory purpose.[20]

Nor has McCleskey demonstrated that the legislature maintains the capital punishment statute because of the racially disproportionate impact suggested by the Baldus study. As legislatures necessarily have wide discretion in the choice of criminal laws and penalties, and as there were legitimate reasons for the Georgia Legislature to adopt and maintain capital punishment, see *Gregg v. Georgia,* we will not infer a discriminatory purpose on the part of the State of Georgia. Accordingly, we reject McCleskey's equal protection claims.

McCleskey also argues that the Baldus study demonstrates that the Georgia capital sentencing system violates the Eighth Amendment. We begin our analysis of this claim by reviewing the restrictions on death sentences established by our prior decisions under that Amendment. [The Court here described a series of earlier decisions, starting with *Furman v. Georgia,* 408 U.S. 238 (1972). *Furman* held unconstitutional a death penalty statute which prescribed no standards for the imposition of the penalty, simply leaving the choice of that penalty to the unfettered discretion of the jury. In so ruling, the Court in *Furman* had "concluded that the death penalty was so irrationally imposed that any particular death sentence could be presumed excessive." In *Gregg v. Georgia,* 428 U.S. 153 (1976), the Court rejected the contention that the death penalty violated the Eighth Amendment "under all circumstances" and upheld the current Georgia statute, enacted after *Furman,* as having "met the concerns articulated in *Furman.*" That statute bifurcated guilt and sentencing proceedings, narrowed the class of murders subject to the death penalty to "cases in which the jury finds at least one statutory aggravating circumstance beyond a

---

**20.** McCleskey relies on "historical evidence" to support his claim of purposeful discrimination by the State. This evidence focuses on Georgia laws in force during and just after the Civil War. Of course, the "historical background of the decision is one evidentiary source" for proof of intentional discrimination. *Arlington Heights v. Metropolitan Hous-*ing Dev. Corp., 429 U.S. 252 (1977). But unless historical evidence is reasonably contemporaneous with the challenged decision, it has little probative value. * * * Although the history of racial discrimination in this country is undeniable, we cannot accept official actions taken long ago as evidence of current intent.

reasonable doubt," allowed the defense to introduce "any relevant mitigating evidence," required a "particularized inquiry into the circumstances of the offense together with the character and propensities of the offender," and provided for appellate review of the death sentence by the Georgia Supreme Court. Decisions after *Gregg* "imposed a number of requirements on the capital sentencing process to ensure that capital sentencing decisions rest on the individualized inquiry contemplated in *Gregg*."] * * *

In sum, our decisions since *Furman* have identified a constitutionally permissible range of discretion in imposing the death penalty. First, there is a required threshold below which the death penalty cannot be imposed. In this context, the State must establish rational criteria that narrow the decisionmaker's judgment as to whether the circumstances of a particular defendant's case meet the threshold. * * * Second, States cannot limit the sentencer's consideration of any relevant circumstance that could cause it to decline to impose the penalty. In this respect, the State cannot channel the sentencer's discretion, but must allow it to consider any relevant information offered by the defendant.

In light of our precedents under the Eighth Amendment, McCleskey cannot argue successfully that his sentence is "disproportionate to the crime in the traditional sense." See *Pulley v. Harris,* 465 U.S. 37 (1984). He does not deny that he committed a murder in the course of a planned robbery, a crime for which this Court has determined that the death penalty constitutionally may be imposed. *Gregg v. Georgia.* His disproportionality claim "is of a different sort." McCleskey argues that the sentence in his case is disproportionate to the sentences in other murder cases.

On the one hand, he cannot base a constitutional claim on an argument that his case differs from other cases in which defendants *did* receive the death penalty. On automatic appeal, the Georgia Supreme Court found that McCleskey's death sentence was not disproportionate to other death sentences imposed in the State. * * * Moreover, where the statutory procedures adequately channel the sentencer's discretion, such proportionality review is not constitutionally required. *Pulley v. Harris.*

On the other hand, absent a showing that the Georgia capital punishment system operates in an arbitrary and capricious manner, McCleskey cannot prove a constitutional violation by demonstrating that other defendants who may be similarly situated did *not* receive the death penalty. In *Gregg,* the Court * * * [rejected] the argument that "the opportunities for discretionary action that are inherent in the processing of any murder case under Georgia law," specifically the opportunities for discretionary leniency, rendered the capital sentences imposed arbitrary and capricious. * * *

Although our decision in *Gregg* as to the facial validity of the Georgia capital punishment statute appears to foreclose McCleskey's disproportionality argument, he further contends that the Georgia capital punishment system is arbitrary and capricious in *application,* and therefore his sentence is excessive, because racial considerations may influence capital sentencing decisions in Georgia. We now address this claim.

To evaluate McCleskey's challenge, we must examine exactly what the Baldus study may show. Even Professor Baldus does not contend that his statistics *prove* that race enters into any capital sentencing decisions or that race was a factor in McCleskey's particular case. Statistics at most may show only a likelihood that a particular factor entered into some decisions. There is, of course, some risk of racial prejudice influencing a jury's decision in a criminal case. There are similar risks that other kinds of prejudice will influence other criminal trials. The question "is at what point that risk becomes constitutionally unacceptable," *Turner v. Murray* [Ch. 15, § 2]. McCleskey asks us to accept the likelihood allegedly shown by the Baldus study as the constitutional measure of an unacceptable risk of racial prejudice influencing capital sentencing decisions. This we decline to do.

Because of the risk that the factor of race may enter the criminal justice process, we have engaged in "unceasing efforts" to eradicate racial prejudice from our criminal justice system. *Batson v. Kentucky* [Ch. 15, § 2]. Our efforts have been guided by our recognition that "the inestimable privilege of trial by jury * * * is a vital principle, underlying the whole administration of criminal justice," *Ex parte Milligan*, 4 Wall. 2 (1866). Thus, it is the jury that is a criminal defendant's fundamental "protection of life and liberty against race or color prejudice." Specifically, a capital sentencing jury representative of a criminal defendant's community assures a " 'diffused impartiality,' " in the jury's task of "express[ing] the conscience of the community on the ultimate question of life or death."

Individual jurors bring to their deliberations "qualities of human nature and varieties of human experience, the range of which is unknown and perhaps unknowable." The capital sentencing decision requires the individual jurors to focus their collective judgment on the unique characteristics of a particular criminal defendant. It is not surprising that such collective judgments often are difficult to explain. But the inherent lack of predictability of jury decisions does not justify their condemnation. On the contrary, it is the jury's function to make the difficult and uniquely human judgments that defy codification and that "buil[d] discretion, equity, and flexibility into a legal system."

McCleskey's argument that the Constitution condemns the discretion allowed decisionmakers in the Georgia capital sentencing system is antithetical to the fundamental role of discretion in our criminal justice system. Discretion in the criminal justice system offers substantial benefits to the criminal defendant. Not only can a jury decline to impose the death sentence, it can decline to convict, or choose to convict of a lesser offense. Whereas decisions against a defendant's interest may be reversed by the trial judge or on appeal, these discretionary exercises of leniency are final and unreviewable. Similarly, the capacity of prosecutorial discretion to provide individualized justice is "firmly entrenched in American law." As we have noted, a prosecutor can decline to charge, offer a plea bargain, or decline to seek a death sentence in any particular case. Of course, "the power to be lenient [also] is the power to discriminate," but a capital-punishment system that did not allow for discretionary acts of leniency "would be totally alien to our notions of criminal justice." *Gregg v. Georgia.*

At most, the Baldus study indicates a discrepancy that appears to correlate with race. Apparent disparities in sentencing are an inevitable part of our criminal justice system. The discrepancy indicated by the Baldus study is "a far cry from the major systemic defects identified in *Furman*," *Pulley v. Harris*. As this Court has recognized, any mode for determining guilt or punishment "has its weaknesses and the potential for misuse." Specifically, "there can be 'no perfect procedure for deciding in which cases governmental authority should be used to impose death.' " Despite these imperfections, our consistent rule has been that constitutional guarantees are met when "the mode [for determining guilt or punishment] itself has been surrounded with safeguards to make it as fair as possible." *Singer v. United States*, 380 U.S. 24 (1965). Where the discretion that is fundamental to our criminal process is involved, we decline to assume that what is unexplained is invidious. In light of the safeguards designed to minimize racial bias in the process, the fundamental value of jury trial in our criminal justice system, and the benefits that discretion provides to criminal defendants, we hold that the Baldus study does not demonstrate a constitutionally significant risk of racial bias affecting the Georgia capital-sentencing process.[37]

Two additional concerns inform our decision in this case. First, McCleskey's claim, taken to its logical conclusion, throws into serious question the principles that underlie our entire criminal justice system. The Eighth Amendment is not limited in application to capital punishment, but applies to all penalties. Thus, if we accepted McCleskey's claim that racial bias has impermissibly tainted the capital sentencing decision, we could soon be faced with similar claims as to other types of penalty.[38] Moreover, the claim that his sentence rests on the irrelevant factor of race easily could be extended to apply to claims based on unexplained discrepancies that correlate to membership in other minority groups,[39] and even to gender. Similarly, since McCleskey's claim relates to the race of his victim, other claims could apply with equally logical force to statistical disparities that correlate with the race or sex of other actors in the criminal justice system, such as defense attorneys, or judges. Also, there is no logical reason that such a claim need be limited to racial or sexual bias. If arbitrary and capricious punishment is the touchstone under the Eighth Amendment, such a claim could—at least in theory—be based upon any arbitrary variable, such as the defendant's facial characteristics, or the physical attractiveness of the defendant or the victim, that some statistical study indicates may be influential in jury decisionmaking. As these examples illustrate, there is no

**37.** Justice Brennan's eloquent dissent of course reflects his often repeated opposition to the death sentence. His views, that also are shared by Justice Marshall, are principled and entitled to respect. Nevertheless, since *Gregg* was decided in 1976, seven members of this Court consistently have upheld sentences of death under *Gregg*-type statutes providing for meticulous review of each sentence in both state and federal courts. The ultimate thrust of Justice Brennan's dissent is that *Gregg* and its progeny should be overruled. He does not, however, expressly call for the overruling of any prior decision. Rather, relying on the Baldus study, Justice Brennan, * * * questions the very heart of our criminal justice system: the traditional discretion that prosecutors and juries necessarily must have.

We have held that discretion in a capital punishment system is necessary to satisfy the Constitution. Yet, the dissent now claims that the "discretion afforded prosecutors and jurors in the Georgia capital sentencing system" violates the Constitution by creating "opportunities for racial considerations to influence criminal proceedings." The dissent contends that in Georgia "[n]o guidelines govern prosecutorial decisions * * *." Prosecutorial decisions necessarily involve both judgmental and factual decisions that vary from case to case. Thus, it is difficult to imagine guidelines that would produce the predictability sought by the dissent without sacrificing

the discretion essential to a humane and fair system of criminal justice. Indeed, the dissent suggests no such guidelines for prosecutorial discretion. * * *

The dissent repeatedly emphasizes the need for "a uniquely high degree of rationality in imposing the death penalty." Again, no suggestion is made as to how greater "rationality" could be achieved under any type of statute that authorizes capital punishment. * * * Given the * * * safeguards already inherent in the imposition and review of capital sentences, the dissent's call for greater rationality is no less than a claim that a capital-punishment system cannot be administered in accord with the Constitution. As we reiterate, the requirement of heightened rationality in the imposition of capital punishment does not "plac[e] totally unrealistic conditions on its use." *Gregg.*

**38.** Studies already exist that allegedly demonstrate a racial disparity in the length of prison sentences. * * *

**39.** In *Regents of the University of California v. Bakke,* 438 U.S. 265, 295, 98 S.Ct. 2733, 2750, 57 L.Ed.2d 750 (1978) (opinion of Powell, J.), we recognized that the national "majority" "is composed of various minority groups, most of which can lay claim to a history of prior discrimination at the hands of the State and private individuals." * * *

limiting principle to the type of challenge brought by McCleskey.[45] The Constitution does not require that a State eliminate any demonstrable disparity that correlates with a potentially irrelevant factor in order to operate a criminal justice system that includes capital punishment. As we have stated specifically in the context of capital punishment, the Constitution does not "plac[e] totally unrealistic conditions on its use." *Gregg v. Georgia.*

Second, McCleskey's arguments are best presented to the legislative bodies. It is not the responsibility—or indeed even the right—of this Court to determine the appropriate punishment for particular crimes. It is the legislatures, the elected representatives of the people, that are "constituted to respond to the will and consequently the moral values of the people." *Furman v. Georgia* (Burger, C.J., dissenting). Legislatures also are better qualified to weigh and "evaluate the results of statistical studies in terms of their own local conditions and with a flexibility of approach that is not available to the courts," *Gregg v. Georgia.* Capital punishment is now the law in more than two thirds of our States. It is the ultimate duty of courts to determine on a case-by-case basis whether these laws are applied consistently with the Constitution. Despite McCleskey's wide ranging arguments that basically challenge the validity of capital punishment in our multi-racial society, the only question before us is whether in his case, the law of Georgia was properly applied. We agree with the District Court and the Court of Appeals for the Eleventh Circuit that this was carefully and correctly done in this case.

JUSTICE BRENNAN, with whom JUSTICE MARSHALL joins, and with whom JUSTICE BLACKMUN and JUSTICE STEVENS join in all but Part I, dissenting.

I. Adhering to my view that the death penalty is in all circumstances cruel and unusual punishment forbidden by the Eighth and Fourteenth Amendments, I would vacate the decision below insofar as it left undisturbed the death sentence imposed in this case. * * * Even if I did not hold this position, however, I would reverse [for] petitioner McCleskey has clearly demonstrated that his death sentence was imposed in violation of the Eighth and Fourteenth

---

**45.** Justice Stevens, who would not overrule *Gregg,* suggests in his dissent that the infirmities alleged by McCleskey could be remedied by narrowing the class of death-eligible defendants to categories identified by the Baldus study where "prosecutors consistently seek, and juries consistently impose, the death penalty without regard to the race of the victim or the race of the offender." This proposed solution is unconvincing. First, "consistently" is a relative term, and narrowing the category of death-eligible defendants would simply shift the borderline between those defendants who received the death penalty and those who did not. A borderline area would continue to exist and vary in its boundaries. Moreover, because the discrepancy between borderline cases would be difficult to explain, the system would likely remain open to challenge on the basis that the lack of explanation rendered the sentencing decisions unconstitutionally arbitrary.

Second, even assuming that a category with theoretically consistent results could be identified, it is difficult to imagine how Justice Stevens' proposal would or could operate on a case-by-case basis. Whenever a victim is white and the defendant is a member of a different race, what steps would a prosecutor be required to take—in addition to weighing the customary prosecutorial considerations—before concluding in the particular case that he lawfully could prosecute? In the absence of a current, Baldus-type study focused particularly on the community in which the crime was committed, where would he find a standard? Would the prosecutor have to review the prior decisions of community prosecutors and determine the types of cases in which juries in his jurisdiction "consistently" had imposed the death penalty when the victim was white and the defendant was of a different race? And must he rely solely on statistics? Even if such a study were feasible, would it be unlawful for the prosecutor, in making his final decision in a particular case, to consider the evidence of guilt and the presence of aggravating and mitigating factors? However conscientiously a prosecutor might attempt to identify death-eligible defendants under the dissent's suggestion, it would be a wholly speculative task at best, likely to result in less rather than more fairness and consistency in the imposition of the death penalty.

Amendments. While I join [the parts] of Justice Blackmun's dissenting opinion discussing petitioner's Fourteenth Amendment claim, I write separately to emphasize how conclusively McCleskey has also demonstrated precisely the type of risk of irrationality in sentencing that we have consistently condemned in our Eighth Amendment jurisprudence.

II. At some point in this case, Warren McCleskey doubtless asked his lawyer whether a jury was likely to sentence him to die. A candid reply to this question would have been disturbing. First, counsel would have to tell McCleskey that few of the details of the crime or of McCleskey's past criminal conduct were more important than the fact that his victim was white. Furthermore, counsel would feel bound to tell McCleskey that defendants charged with killing white victims in Georgia are 4.3 times as likely to be sentenced to death as defendants charged with killing blacks. In addition, frankness would compel the disclosure that it was more likely than not that the race of McCleskey's victim would determine whether he received a death sentence: 6 of every 11 defendants convicted of killing a white person would not have received the death penalty if their victims had been black, while, among defendants with aggravating and mitigating factors comparable to McCleskey, 20 of every 34 would not have been sentenced to die if their victims had been black. Finally, the assessment would not be complete without the information that cases involving black defendants and white victims are more likely to result in a death sentence than cases featuring any other racial combination of defendant and victim. The story could be told in a variety of ways, but McCleskey could not fail to grasp its essential narrative line: there was a significant chance that race would play a prominent role in determining if he lived or died.

The Court today holds that Warren McCleskey's sentence was constitutionally imposed. It finds no fault in a system in which lawyers must tell their clients that race casts a large shadow on the capital sentencing process. * * *

III. It is important to emphasize at the outset that the Court's observation that McCleskey cannot prove the influence of race on any particular sentencing decision is irrelevant in evaluating his Eighth Amendment claim. Since *Furman*, the Court has been concerned with the *risk* of the imposition of an arbitrary sentence, rather than the proven fact of one. * * * This emphasis on risk acknowledges the difficulty of divining the jury's motivation in an individual case. In addition, it reflects the fact that concern for arbitrariness focuses on the rationality of the system as a whole, and that a system that features a significant probability that sentencing decisions are influenced by impermissible considerations cannot be regarded as rational.[1] * * *

The statistical evidence in this case * * * relentlessly documents the risk that McCleskey's sentence was influenced by racial considerations. This evidence shows that there is a better than even chance in Georgia that race will influence the decision to impose the death penalty: a majority of defendants in white-victim crimes would not have been sentenced to die if their victims had been black. In determining whether this risk is acceptable, our judgment must be shaped by the awareness that "[t]he risk of racial prejudice infecting a capital sentencing proceeding is especially serious in light of the complete finality of the death sentence" [and] that "[i]t is of vital importance to the defendant and to the

1. Once we can identify a pattern of arbitrary sentencing outcomes, we can say that a defendant runs a risk of being sentenced arbitrarily. It is thus immaterial whether the operation of an impermissible influence such as race is intentional. While the Equal Protection Clause forbids racial discrimination, and intent may be critical in a successful claim under that provision, the Eighth Amendment has its own distinct focus: whether punishment comports with social standards of rationality and decency. * * *

community that any decision to impose the death sentence be, and appear to be, based on reason rather than caprice or emotion." In determining the guilt of a defendant, a state must prove its case beyond a reasonable doubt. That is, we refuse to convict if the chance of error is simply less likely than not. Surely, we should not be willing to take a person's life if the chance that his death sentence was irrationally imposed is *more* likely than not. In light of the gravity of the interest at stake, petitioner's statistics on their face are a powerful demonstration of the type of risk that our Eighth Amendment jurisprudence has consistently condemned.

Evaluation of McCleskey's evidence cannot rest solely on the numbers themselves. We must also ask whether the conclusion suggested by those numbers is consonant with our understanding of history and human experience. Georgia's legacy of a race-conscious criminal justice system, as well as this Court's own recognition of the persistent danger that racial attitudes may affect criminal proceedings, indicate that McCleskey's claim is not a fanciful product of mere statistical artifice. * * *

[The dissent here noted that Georgia, at the time of the Civil War, had a "dual system" of criminal justice (distinguishing between crimes "committed by and against blacks and whites"). It noted further that Gunnar Myrdal's study of race relations in the United States (published in 1944) "mirrored McCleskey's evidence," that "the specter of race discrimination was acknowledged by the Court in striking down the Georgia death penalty statute in *Furman,*" and that the Court in *Coker v. Georgia,* 433 U.S. 584 (1977), striking down the death penalty for rape, although "it did not explicitly mention race," had before it evidence "that black men who committed rape, particularly of white women, were considerably more likely to be sentenced to death."] * * * This historical review of Georgia criminal law is not intended as a bill of indictment calling the State to account for past transgressions. Citation of past practices does not justify the automatic condemnation of current ones. But it would be unrealistic to ignore the influence of history in assessing the plausible implications of McCleskey's evidence. * * *

* * * Our cases reflect a realization of the myriad of opportunities for racial considerations to influence criminal proceedings: in the exercise of peremptory challenges; in the selection of the grand jury; in the selection of the petit jury; in the exercise of prosecutorial discretion; in the conduct of argument; and in the conscious or unconscious bias of jurors. The discretion afforded prosecutors and jurors in the Georgia capital-sentencing system creates such opportunities. No guidelines govern prosecutorial decisions to seek the death penalty, and Georgia provides juries with no list of aggravating and mitigating factors, nor any standard for balancing them against one another. Once a jury identifies one aggravating factor, it has complete discretion in choosing life or death, and need not articulate its basis for selecting life imprisonment. The Georgia sentencing system therefore provides considerable opportunity for racial considerations, however subtle and unconscious, to influence charging and sentencing decisions.

IV. The Court cites four reasons for shrinking from the implications of McCleskey's evidence: the desirability of discretion for actors in the criminal-justice system, the existence of statutory safeguards against abuse of that discretion, the potential consequences for broader challenges to criminal sentencing, and an understanding of the contours of the judicial role. While these concerns underscore the need for sober deliberation, they do not justify rejecting evidence as convincing as McCleskey has presented.

The Court maintains that petitioner's claim "is antithetical to the fundamental role of discretion in our criminal justice system." It states that "[w]here the discretion that is fundamental to our criminal process is involved, we decline to assume that what is unexplained is invidious." Reliance on race in imposing capital punishment, however, is antithetical to the very rationale for granting sentencing discretion. Discretion is a means, not an end. * * *

The Court also declines to find McCleskey's evidence sufficient in view of "the safeguards designed to minimize racial bias in the [capital sentencing] process." * * * It is clear that *Gregg* bestowed no permanent approval on the Georgia system. It simply held that the State's statutory safeguards were assumed sufficient to channel discretion without evidence otherwise. * * *

The Court next states that its unwillingness to regard the petitioner's evidence as sufficient is based in part on the fear that recognition of McCleskey's claim would open the door to widespread challenges to all aspects of criminal sentencing. Taken on its face, such a statement seems to suggest a fear of too much justice. Yet surely the majority would acknowledge that if striking evidence indicated that other minority groups, or women, or even persons with blond hair, were disproportionately sentenced to death, such a state of affairs would be repugnant to deeply rooted conceptions of fairness. The prospect that there may be more widespread abuse than McCleskey documents may be dismaying, but it does not justify complete abdication of our judicial role. * * *

In fairness, the Court's fear that McCleskey's claim is an invitation to descend a slippery slope also rests on the realization that any humanly imposed system of penalties will exhibit some imperfection. Yet to reject McCleskey's powerful evidence on this basis is to ignore both the qualitatively different character of the death penalty and the particular repugnance of racial discrimination, considerations which may properly be taken into account in determining whether various punishments are "cruel and unusual." Furthermore, it fails to take account of the unprecedented refinement and strength of the Baldus study. * * *

The Court also maintains that accepting McCleskey's claim would pose a threat to all sentencing because of the prospect that a correlation might be demonstrated between sentencing outcomes and other personal characteristics. Again, such a view is indifferent to the considerations that enter into a determination of whether punishment is "cruel and unusual." Race is a consideration whose influence is expressly constitutionally proscribed. We have expressed a moral commitment, as embodied in our fundamental law, that this specific characteristic should not be the basis for allotting burdens and benefits. * * *

Certainly, a factor that we would regard as morally irrelevant, such as hair color, at least theoretically could be associated with sentencing results to such an extent that we would regard as arbitrary a system in which that factor played a significant role. [However,] the evaluation of evidence suggesting such a correlation must be informed not merely by statistics, but by history and experience. One could hardly contend that this nation has on the basis of hair color inflicted upon persons deprivation comparable to that imposed on the basis of race. Recognition of this fact would necessarily influence the evaluation of data suggesting the influence of hair color on sentencing, and would require evidence of statistical correlation even more powerful than that presented by the Baldus study. * * *

Finally, the Court justifies its rejection of McCleskey's claim by cautioning against usurpation of the legislatures' role in devising and monitoring criminal punishment. The Court is, of course, correct to emphasize the gravity of constitutional intervention and the importance that it be sparingly employed. The fact that "[c]apital punishment is now the law in more than two thirds of our States," however, does not diminish the fact that capital punishment is the most awesome act that a State can perform. The judiciary's role in this society counts for little if the use of governmental power to extinguish life does not elicit close scrutiny. [The Court] fulfills, rather than disrupts, the scheme of separation of powers by closely scrutinizing the imposition of the death penalty, for no decision of a society is more deserving of the "sober second thought."  *  *  *

The Court's decision today will not change what attorneys in Georgia tell other Warren McCleskeys about their chances of execution. Nothing will soften the harsh message they must convey, nor alter the prospect that race undoubtedly will continue to be a topic of discussion. McCleskey's evidence will not have obtained judicial acceptance, but that will not affect what is said on death row. However many criticisms of today's decision may be rendered, these painful conversations will serve as the most eloquent dissents of all.

JUSTICE BLACKMUN, with whom JUSTICE MARSHALL and JUSTICE STEVENS join and with whom JUSTICE BRENNAN joins in all but Part IV-B,[a] dissenting.  *  *  *

In analyzing an equal protection claim, a court must first determine the nature of the claim and the responsibilities of the state actors involved to determine what showing is required for the establishment of a prima facie case. The Court correctly points out: "In its broadest form, McCleskey's claim of discrimination extends to every actor in the Georgia capital sentencing process, from the prosecutor who sought the death penalty and the jury that imposed the sentence, to the State itself that enacted the capital punishment statute and allows it to remain in effect despite its allegedly discriminatory application." Having recognized the complexity of McCleskey's claim, however, the Court proceeds to ignore a significant element of that claim. The Court treats the case as if it is limited to challenges to the actions of two specific decisionmaking bodies—the petit jury and the state legislature. This self-imposed restriction enables the Court to distinguish this case from the venire-selection cases and Title VII cases in which it long has accepted statistical evidence and has provided an easily applicable framework for review.

Considering McCleskey's claim in its entirety, however, reveals that the claim fits easily within that same framework. A significant aspect of his claim is that racial factors impermissibly affected numerous steps in the Georgia capital-sentencing scheme between his indictment and the jury's vote to sentence him to death. The primary decisionmaker at each of the intervening steps of the process is the prosecutor, the quintessential state actor in a criminal proceeding.  *  *  * [M]y analysis in this dissenting opinion  *  *  * concentrate[s] on the decisions within the prosecutor's office through which the State decided to seek the death penalty and, in particular, the point at which the State proceeded to the penalty phase after conviction. This is a step at which the evidence of the effect of the racial factors was especially strong, but is ignored by the Court.

A criminal defendant alleging an equal protection violation must prove the existence of purposeful discrimination. He may establish a prima facie case of purposeful discrimination "by showing that the totality of the relevant facts

---

**a.** The reference here is to the last paragraph of Justice Blackmun's dissent.

gives rise to an inference of discriminatory purpose." *Batson v. Kentucky* [Ch. 15, § 2]. Once the defendant establishes a prima facie case, the burden shifts to the prosecution to rebut that case. * * *

Under *Batson v. Kentucky* and the framework established in [the jury selection cases], McCleskey must meet a three-factor standard. First, he must establish that he is a member of a group "that is a recognizable, distinct class, singled out for different treatment." Second, he must make a showing of a substantial degree of differential treatment. Third, he must establish that the allegedly discriminatory procedure is susceptible to abuse or is not racially neutral.

There can be no dispute that McCleskey has made the requisite showing under the first prong of the standard. The Baldus study demonstrates that black persons are a distinct group that are singled out for different treatment in the Georgia capital-sentencing system. The Court acknowledges, as it must, that the raw statistics included in the Baldus study and presented by petitioner indicate that it is much less likely that a death sentence will result from a murder of a black person than from a murder of a white person. * * * The raw figures also indicate that even within the group of defendants who are convicted of killing white persons and are thereby more likely to receive a death sentence, black defendants are more likely than white defendants to be sentenced to death.

With respect to the second prong, McCleskey must prove that there is a substantial likelihood that his death sentence is due to racial factors. * * * McCleskey demonstrated the degree to which his death sentence was affected by racial factors by introducing multiple-regression analyses that explain how much of the statistical distribution of the cases analyzed is attributable to the racial factors. * * * McCleskey produced evidence concerning the role of racial factors at the various steps in the decisionmaking process, focusing on the prosecutor's decision as to which cases merit the death sentence. McCleskey established that the race of the victim is an especially significant factor at the point where the defendant has been convicted of murder and the prosecutor must choose whether to proceed to the penalty phase of the trial and create the possibility that a death sentence may be imposed or to accept the imposition of a sentence of life imprisonment. McCleskey demonstrated this effect at both the statewide level, and in Fulton County where he was tried and sentenced. The statewide statistics indicated that black defendant/white victim cases advanced to the penalty trial at nearly five times the rate of the black defendant/black victim cases (70% vs. 15%), and over three times the rate of white defendant/black victim cases (70% vs. 19%). The multiple-regression analysis demonstrated that racial factors had a readily identifiable effect at a statistically significant level. The Fulton County statistics were consistent with this evidence although they involved fewer cases.

Individualized evidence relating to the disposition of the Fulton County cases that were most comparable to McCleskey's case was consistent with the evidence of the race-of-victim effect as well. Of the 17 defendants, including McCleskey, who were arrested and charged with homicide of a police officer in Fulton County during the 1973–1979 period, McCleskey, alone, was sentenced to death. The only other defendant whose case even proceeded to the penalty phase received a sentence of life imprisonment. That defendant had been convicted of killing a black police officer.

As to the final element of the prima facie case, McCleskey showed that the process by which the State decided to seek a death penalty in his case and to pursue that sentence throughout the prosecution was susceptible to abuse. Petitioner submitted the deposition of Lewis R. Slaton, who, as of the date of the deposition, had been the District Attorney for 18 years in the county in which McCleskey was tried and sentenced. As Mr. Slaton explained, the duties and responsibilities of that office are the prosecution of felony charges within the Atlanta Judicial Circuit that comprises Fulton County. He testified that during his years in the office, there were no guidelines informing the Assistant District Attorneys who handle the cases how they should proceed at any particular stage of the prosecution. There were no guidelines as to when they should seek an indictment for murder as opposed to lesser charges, when they should recommend acceptance of a guilty plea to murder, acceptance of a guilty plea to a lesser charge, reduction of charges, or dismissal of charges at the postindictment-preconviction stage, or when they should seek the death penalty. Slaton testified that these decisions were left to the discretion of the individual attorneys who then informed Slaton of their decisions as they saw fit.

Slaton's deposition proves that, at every stage of a prosecution, the Assistant District Attorney exercised much discretion. The only guidance given was "on-the-job training." * * * The sole effort to provide any consistency was Slaton's periodic pulling of files at random to check on the progress of cases. Slaton explained that as far as he knew, he was the only one aware of this checking. The files contained information only as to the evidence in the case, not any indication as to why an attorney made a particular decision. The attorneys were not required to record why they sought an indictment for murder as opposed to a lesser charge, or why they recommended a certain plea. The attorneys were not required to report to Slaton the cases in which they decided not to seek the death penalty, or the cases in which they did seek the death penalty * * *.

The above-described evidence, considered in conjunction with the other record evidence outlined by Justice Brennan, and discussed in opinions dissenting from the judgment of the Court of Appeals, gives rise to an inference of discriminatory purpose. * * * McCleskey's showing is of sufficient magnitude that, absent evidence to the contrary, one must conclude that racial factors entered into the decisionmaking process that yielded McCleskey's death sentence. The burden, therefore, shifts to the State to explain the racial selections. It must demonstrate that legitimate racially neutral criteria and procedures yielded this racially skewed result. * * *

The Court's explanations for its failure to apply this well-established equal protection analysis to this case are not persuasive. It first reasons that "each particular decision to impose the death penalty is made by a petit jury" and that the "application of an inference drawn from the general statistics to a specific decision in a trial and sentencing simply is not comparable to the application of an inference drawn from general statistics to a specific venire-selection or Title VII case." According to the Court, the statistical evidence is less relevant because, in the two latter situations, there are fewer variables relevant to the decision and the "statistics relate to fewer entities."

I disagree with the Court's assertion that there are fewer variables relevant to the decisions of jury commissioners or prosecutors in their selection of jurors, or to the decisions of employers in their selection, promotion, or discharge of employees. Such decisions involve a multitude of factors, some rational, some irrational. Second, I disagree with the comment that the venire-selection and employment decisions are "made by fewer entities." Certainly in the employment context, personnel decisions are often the product of several levels of decisionmaking within the business or government structure. The Court's statement that the decision to impose death is made by the petit jury also disregards the fact that the prosecutor screens the cases throughout the pretrial proceedings and decides to seek the death penalty and to pursue a capital case to the penalty phase where a death sentence can be imposed. McCleskey's claim in this regard lends itself to analysis under the framework we apply in assessing challenges to other prosecutorial actions. See *Batson v. Kentucky,* see also *Wayte v. United States* [Ch. 10, § 1].

The Court's other reason for treating this case differently from venire-selection and employment cases is that in these latter contexts, "the decisionmaker has an opportunity to explain the statistical disparity," but in the instant case the State had no practical opportunity to rebut the Baldus study. According to the Court, this is because jurors cannot be called to testify about their verdict and because policy considerations render it improper to require "prosecutors to defend their decisions to seek death penalties, 'often years after they were made.'"

I agree with the Court's observation as to the difficulty of examining the jury's decisionmaking process. \* \* \* The Court's refusal to require that the prosecutor provide an explanation for his actions, however, is completely inconsistent with this Court's longstanding precedents. \* \* \* Prosecutors undoubtedly need adequate discretion to allocate the resources of their offices and to fulfill their responsibilities to the public in deciding how best to enforce the law, but this does not place them beyond the constraints imposed on state action under the Fourteenth Amendment. Cf. *Ex Parte Virginia,* 100 U.S. 339 (1880) (upholding validity of conviction of state judge for discriminating on the basis of race in his selection of jurors).

The Court attempts to distinguish the present case from *Batson v. Kentucky,* in which we recently reaffirmed the fact that prosecutors' actions are not unreviewable. I agree with the Court's observation that this case is "quite different" from the *Batson* case. The irony is that McCleskey presented proof in this case that would have satisfied the more burdensome standard of *Swain v. Alabama,* 380 U.S. 202 (1965), a standard that was described in *Batson* as having placed on defendants a "crippling burden of proof." As discussed above, McCleskey presented evidence of numerous decisions impermissibly affected by racial factors over a significant number of cases. The exhaustive evidence presented in this case certainly demands an inquiry into the prosecutor's actions. \* \* \*

One of the final concerns discussed by the Court may be the most disturbing aspect of its opinion. Granting relief to McCleskey in this case, it is said, could lead to further constitutional challenges. That, of course, is no reason to deny *McCleskey* his rights under the Equal Protection Clause. If a grant of relief to him were to lead to a closer examination of the effects of racial considerations throughout the criminal-justice system, the system, and hence society, might benefit. Where no such factors come into play, the integrity of the system is enhanced. Where such considerations are shown to be significant, efforts can be made to eradicate their impermissible influence and to ensure an evenhanded application of criminal sanctions.

Like Justice Stevens, I do not believe acceptance of McCleskey's claim would eliminate capital punishment in Georgia. Justice Stevens points out that the evidence presented in this case indicates that in extremely aggravated murders the risk of discriminatory enforcement of the death penalty is minimized. I agree that narrowing the class of death-eligible defendants is not too high a price to pay for a death-penalty system that does not discriminate on the basis of race.[b]  Moreover, the establishment of guidelines for Assistant District Attorneys as to the appropriate basis for exercising their discretion at the various steps in the prosecution of a case would provide at least a measure of consistency.  The Court's emphasis on the procedural safeguards in the system ignores the fact that there are none whatsoever during the crucial process leading up to trial.  As Justice White stated for the plurality in *Turner v. Murray,* I find "the risk that racial prejudice may have infected petitioner's capital sentencing unacceptable in light of the ease with which that risk could have been minimized."  I dissent.

**b.**  In a third dissenting opinion, Justice Stevens, joined by Blackmun, J., described the majority's evident fear "that the acceptance of McCleskey's claim would sound the death knell for capital punishment in Georgia" as "unfounded": "One of the lessons of the Baldus study is that there exist certain categories of extremely serious crimes for which prosecutors consistently seek, and juries consistently impose, the death penalty without regard to the race of the victim or the race of the offender.  If Georgia were to narrow the class of death-eligible defendants to those categories, the danger of arbitrary and discriminatory imposition of the death penalty would be significantly decreased, if not eradicated."

Although Justice Stevens would reverse, he believed that further proceedings were needed to determine whether McCleskey's death sentence should be set aside: "First, the Court of Appeals must decide whether the Baldus study is valid.  I am persuaded that it is, but orderly procedure requires that the Court of Appeals address this issue before we actually decide the question.  Second, it is necessary for the District Court to determine whether the particular facts of McCleskey's crime and his background place this case within the range of cases that present an unacceptable risk that race played a decisive role in McCleskey's sentencing."

*

# Appendix A

# SELECTED PROVISIONS OF THE UNITED STATES CONSTITUTION

ARTICLE I

Section 9. * * *

[2] The privilege of the Writ of Habeas Corpus shall not be suspended, unless when in Cases of Rebellion or Invasion the public Safety may require it.

[3] No Bill of Attainder or ex post facto Law shall be passed.

ARTICLE III

Section 1. The judicial Power of the United States, shall be vested in one supreme Court, and in such inferior Courts as the Congress may from time to time ordain and establish. The Judges, both of the supreme and inferior Courts, shall hold their Offices during good Behaviour, and shall, at stated Times, receive for their Services a Compensation, which shall not be diminished during their Continuance in Office.

Section 2. [1] The judicial Power shall extend to all Cases, in Law and Equity, arising under this Constitution, the Laws of the United States, and Treaties made, or which shall be made, under their Authority;—to all Cases affecting Ambassadors, other public Ministers and Consuls;—to all Cases of admiralty and maritime Jurisdiction;—to Controversies to which the United States shall be a Party;—to Controversies between two or more States;—between a State and Citizens of another State;—between Citizens of different States;—between Citizens of the same State claiming Lands under the Grants of different States, and between a State, or the Citizens thereof, and foreign States, Citizens or Subjects.

* * *

[3] The trial of all Crimes, except in Cases of Impeachment, shall be by Jury; and such Trial shall be held in the State where the said Crimes shall have been committed; but when not committed within any State, the Trial shall be at such Place or Places as the Congress may by Law have directed.

Section 3. [1] Treason against the United States, shall consist only in levying War against them, or, in adhering to their Enemies, giving them Aid and Comfort. No Person shall be convicted of Treason unless on the Testimony of two Witnesses to the same overt Act, or on Confession in open Court.

[2] The Congress shall have Power to declare the Punishment of Treason, but no Attainder of Treason shall work Corruption of Blood, or Forfeiture except during the Life of the Person attainted.

[1]

## ARTICLE IV

Section 2. [1] The Citizens of each State shall be entitled to all Privileges and Immunities of Citizens in the several States.

[2] A Person charged in any State with Treason, Felony, or other Crime, who shall flee from Justice, and be found in another State, shall on demand of the executive Authority of the State from which he fled, be delivered up, to be removed to the State having Jurisdiction of the Crime.

## ARTICLE VI

[2] This Constitution, and the Laws of the United States which shall be made in Pursuance thereof; and all Treaties made, or which shall be made, under the Authority of the United States, shall be the supreme Law.

## AMENDMENT I [1791]

Congress shall make no law respecting an establishment of religion, or prohibiting the free exercise thereof; or abridging the freedom of speech, or of the press; or the right of the people peaceably to assemble, and to petition the Government for a redress of grievances.

## AMENDMENT II [1791]

A well regulated Militia, being necessary to the security of a free State, the right of the people to keep and bear Arms, shall not be infringed.

## AMENDMENT III [1791]

No Soldier shall, in time of peace be quartered in any house, without the consent of the Owner, nor in time of war, but in a manner to be prescribed by law.

## AMENDMENT IV [1791]

The right of the people to be secure in their persons, houses, papers, and effects, against unreasonable searches and seizures, shall not be violated, and no Warrants shall issue, but upon probable cause, supported by Oath or affirmation, and particularly describing the place to be searched, and the persons or things to be seized.

## AMENDMENT V [1791]

No person shall be held to answer for a capital, or otherwise infamous crime, unless on a presentment or indictment of a Grand Jury, except in cases arising in the land or naval forces, or in the Militia, when in actual service in time of War or public danger; nor shall any person be subject for the same offence to be twice put in jeopardy of life or limb; nor shall be compelled in any criminal case to be a witness against himself, nor be deprived of life, liberty, or property, without due process of law; nor shall private property be taken for public use, without just compensation.

## AMENDMENT VI [1791]

In all criminal prosecutions, the accused shall enjoy the right to a speedy and public trial, by an impartial jury of the State and district wherein the crime shall have been committed, which district shall have been previously ascertained by law, and to be informed of the nature and cause of the accusation; to be confronted with the witnesses against him; to have compulsory process for obtaining witnesses in his favor, and to have the Assistance of Counsel for his defence.

## AMENDMENT VII [1791]

In Suits at common law, where the value in controversy shall exceed twenty dollars, the right of trial by jury shall be preserved, and no fact tried by jury, shall be otherwise re-examined in any Court of the United States, than according to the rules of the common law.

## AMENDMENT VIII [1791]

Excessive bail shall not be required, nor excessive fines imposed, nor cruel and unusual punishments inflicted.

## AMENDMENT IX [1791]

The enumeration in the Constitution, of certain rights, shall not be construed to deny or disparage others retained by the people.

## AMENDMENT X [1791]

The powers not delegated to the United States by the Constitution, nor prohibited by it to the States, are reserved to the States respectively, or to the people.

## AMENDMENT XIII [1865]

Section 1.  Neither slavery nor involuntary servitude, except as a punishment for crime whereof the party shall have been duly convicted, shall exist within the United States, or any place subject to their jurisdiction.

Section 2.  Congress shall have power to enforce this article by appropriate legislation.

## AMENDMENT XIV [1868]

Section 1.  All persons born or naturalized in the United States, and subject to the jurisdiction thereof, are citizens of the United States and of the State wherein they reside.  No State shall make or enforce any law which shall abridge the privileges or immunities of citizens of the United States; nor shall any State deprive any person of life, liberty, or property, without due process of law;  nor deny to any person within its jurisdiction the equal protection of the laws.

Section 5.  The Congress shall have power to enforce, by appropriate legislation, the provisions of the article.

## AMENDMENT XV [1870]

Section 1.  The right of citizens of the United States to vote shall not be denied or abridged by the United States or by any State on account of race, color, or previous condition of servitude.

Section 2.  The Congress shall have power to enforce this article by appropriate legislation.

†